ALBANIAN-ENGLISH
DICTIONARY

w, butterfly notes found
in an Eng.-Serb. dict. (02)

1993

ALBANIAN-ENGLISH DICTIONARY

Ramazan Hysa

HIPPOCRENE BOOKS, INC.
New York

Originally published by Shtepia Botuese,
8 Nentori, Tirane

Hippocrene Books paperback edition, 1993.
Second printing, 1995.

ISBN 0-87052-077-6

For information, address:
Hippocrene Books, Inc.
171 Madison Avenue
New York, NY 10016

Printed in the United States of America.

[handwritten annotation:] 1996 ed. Botime EDFA Rr. K Manastirit, P. 46/7, Sh. 4, Ap Tirana

PARATHËNIE

Fjalori i vogël shqip-anglisht plotëson një boshllëk të ndieshëm në serinë e fjalorëve dygjuhësh. Si i pari fjalor shqip-anglisht i botuar pas Çlirimit, ai, duke shërbyer si mjet pune i vlefshëm për të gjithë ata që studiojnë dhe përdorin gjuhën angleze në punën e tyre, mbetet megjithatë një fjalor modest dhe nuk pretendon të zgjidhë detyrat që do t'i takonin një fjalori të tipit të mesëm, me rreth 40 mijë fjalë. Megjithëse i kufizuar në numrin e fjalëve (20.000), ky fjalor pasqyron në një nivel të kënaqshëm zhvillimin e vrullshëm e të shumanshëm që ka njohur gjuha shqipe në këto dekada. Në këtë aspekt ai ndryshon nga të gjithë fjalorët shqip- -anglisht të botuar para Çlirimit kryesisht nga studiues të huaj, duke përfshirë këtu edhe fjalorë që për nga numri i fjalëve hyjnë në radhën e fjalorëve të tipit të mesëm, siç është Fjalori shqip- -anglisht (An historical Albanian-English dictionary) i S. Manit (bot. 1938).

Ndër synimet kryesore të fjalorit është pasqyrimi në të i gjuhës shqipe të sotme të shkruar e të folur, gjë që është realizuar duke u dhënë jetë fjalëve nëpërmjet shembujve të shumtë, shprehjeve idiomatike e deri edhe proverbave, me pikësynimin që ato të kenë në masën dërrmuese karakter aktual. Për zgjedhjen e fjalëve shqipe që janë përfshirë në fjalor, jemi mbështetur në radhë të parë në Fjalorin e Gjuhës Shqipe (bot. 1954) dhe në Fjalorin Drejtshkrimor të Gjuhës Shqipe (bot. 1976), të botuar nga Instituti i Gjuhësisë dhe i Letërsisë i Akademisë së Shkencave të RPSSH. Një ndihmë në këtë drejtim na ka dhënë edhe Fjalori shqip-frengjisht i V. Kokonës (bot. 1977), në të cilin është bërë një punë e mirë nga autori dhe redaksia për

*pasurimin dhe saktësimin e fondit të shqipes, veçanërisht në kushtet
e mungesës së fjalorit të gjuhës shqipe të tipit të mesëm, botimi i të
cilit kohët e fundit nga Instituti i Gjuhësisë dhe i Letërsisë do të jetë
një mbështetje e fuqishme për hartimin e fjalorëve shqip-gjuhë e
huaj më të mëdhenj e me nivel më të lartë shkencor në të ardhmen.
Fjalori shqip-anglisht do t'u vlejë edhe të huajve që intere-
sohen të mësojnë gjuhën shqipe. Kjo gjë është patur parasysh dhe,
në përputhje me këtë synim, në fjalor janë shënuar thekset tonike
të fjalëve dhe janë dhënë shembuj që ndihmojnë për të përvetësuar
shqiptimin e tingujve të shqipes, veçanërisht të disa tingujve,
të cilët i mungojnë gjuhës angleze (c, gj, nj, q, x, y).
Shprehim besimin se lexuesit do ta mirëpresin botimin e
fjalorit me gjithë mangësitë e mundshme, evidentimi i të cilave
do të ndihmojë në botimin e një fjalori shqip-anglisht të tipit
të mesëm në të ardhmen.*

R. HYSA

MBI PËRDORIMIN E FJALORIT

1. Fjalët shqipe janë shtypur me germa të zeza dhe radhiten sipas rendit alfabetik. Çdo fjale i është vënë theksi tonik. Menjëherë pas fjalës shqipe shënohen karakteristikat e saj gramatikore.

2. Emrat janë vënë në trajtën e pashquar dhe pasohen nga një presje, pastaj nga një vizë dhe, në fund, nga mbaresa e trajtës së shquar. Për shembull: **punëtor,-i**, pra **punëtor-punëtori**. Menjëherë pas mbaresës së trajtës së shquar jepet gjinia: **punëtor,-i** *m.* (gjinia mashkullore) dhe, pas gjinisë, numri shumës, që shënohet me shkronjën *sh.* (shumës). Këtë shkronjë e pason një vizë dhe mbaresa e trajtës së shquar të shumësit. Për shembull: **punëtor,-i** *m.sh.* **-ë**, pra **punëtor-punëtori**, gjinia mashkullore, në shumës **punëtorë**; ose **fshat-,i** *m.sh.* **-ra** (fshat--fshati, gjinia mashkullore, në shumës fshatra). Në qoftë se pas shkronjës *sh.* jepet vetëm një vizë, kjo do të thotë se shumësi i asaj fjale është i njëllojtë me njëjësin. Për shembull: **mësues,-i** *m.sh.* -Kur shumësi nuk jepet fare, kjo do të thotë se emri përdoret vetëm në numrin njëjës. Për shembull: **përvojë,-a** *f.*

3. Emrat që pësojnë ndryshim kur shquhen, ndahen nga një vizë e pjerrët, që tregon se pas kësaj vize fjala pëson ndryshim në trajtën e shquar. Për shembull: **tok/ë-a**, pra **tokë-toka**. Kur emri pëson ndryshim të madh në shumës, atëherë jepet shumësi i plotë. Për shembull: **djalë,-i** *m.sh.* **djem.**

4. Mbiemrat janë vënë në gjininë mashkullore, të cilën e pason një presje dhe një vizë dhe, në fund, mbaresa që jep trajtën femërore. Për shembull: **besnik,-e**, pra **besnik-besnike.** Mbiemrat e nyjshëm, të cilët nuk pësojnë ndryshim në gjininë femërore, pasohen nga nyjet e përparme *i, e* në kllapa, që tre-

gojnë gjininë. Për shembull: **bukur (i,e): i bukur, e bukur.**
Mbiemrat që pësojnë ndryshim në gjininë femërore, ndahen
me një vizë të pjerrët në trupin e mbiemrit, për të treguar se pas
kësaj vize mbiemri ndërron si në shqiptim ashtu edhe në shkrim.
Këtë mbiemër e pason nyja e përparme e gjinisë mashkullore
e vendosur në kllapa, pastaj një vizë dhe pastaj me, që shënon
femëroren, e pasuar nga nyja e përparme e femërores e vendosur
në kllapa. Për shembull: **nyjsh/ëm (i), -me(e): i nyjshëm — e
nyjshme.**
Mbiemrat e panyjshëm, të prejardhur nga emrat, janë dhënë
si zëra më vete, zakonisht pas emrave përkatës. Po kështu
emrat e prejardhur nga mbiemrat e nyjshëm janë dhënë pas
mbiemrave përkatës dhe, zakonisht, vetëm në gjininë mashkullore. Gjinia femërore e tyre formohet duke u shtuar mbaresën
e në fund, dhe trajta e shquar e tyre formohet njëlloj si tek
emrat femërorë me këtë mbaresë. Për shembull: **afërm(i), —
e(e)** mb. .... dhe, nën të, **afërm(i), — i (i)**m.sh. **— (të)**, pra të **afërm.**
Në gjininë femërore ky emër i prejardhur bën e **afërm/e,-ja.**
Njëlloj, me mbaresën e, formohet edhe gjinia femërore e emrave nga të cilët rrjedhin mbiemrat e panyjshëm: p.sh., **besnik,-u**
m.sh. **-ë** dhe **besnik/e,-ja** f.sh. **-e.**

5. Pas karakteristikave të emrit ose të mbiemrit jepen
përkthimet e ndryshme, që ndahen me shifra arabe. Brendapërbrenda ndarjeve me këto shifra vihen presje për të treguar
kuptimet sinonimike ose të përafërta të fjalëve dhe pikëpresje
për të treguar fjalët me një kuptim më pak të përafërt. Përveç
kuptimit të drejtpërdrejtë të fjalës, jepen edhe shembuj e
kontekste të ndryshëm, për të kapur shtrirjen ose ngushtimin
e kuptimit të saj dhe me qëllim që përdoruesi, midis fjalëve
angleze që i korrespondojnë një fjale shqipe, të zgjedhë atë
që i përshtatet më shumë në rastin e dhënë. Për shembull:
ulje 1. descent (e aeroplanit etj.). **2.** reduction, fall (e çmimeve
etj.).

Shpesh, fjala shqipe e përkthyer në krye me fjalën e një-
vlefshme angleze, përkthehet ndryshe në një kontekst të dhënë.
Për shembull: **ushqehem** — to feed oneself; ushqehem me shpresa
— to cherish illusions. Për fjalët që përdoren dendur në gjuhën
e folur dhe të shkruar dhe hyjnë në lokucione të larmishme dhe

të bukura, janë dhënë, sa ka qenë e mundur dhe e arsyeshme, shprehje dhe lokucione të gjuhës angleze. Për shembull: **i var shpresat te dikush:** to pin one's hopes on someone.

6. Siç dihet, në leksikografinë shqipe është bërë traditë që si trajtë përfaqësuese e foljes të jepet veta e parë e kohës së tashme të mënyrës dëftore; kjo pasohet nga karakteristikat e saj *f.k.*, *f.jk.*, *f.jv.* (folje kalimtare, jokalimtare, joveprore) dhe, në kllapa, jepen shpesh e kryera e thjeshtë dhe pjesorja (jo për foljet e lakimit të parë, për të cilat ndërtimi i të kryerës së thjeshtë dhe i pjesores është i rregullt: *mësoj, mësova, mësuar*). Ashtu si tek emrat e mbiemrat, edhe kuptimet e foljeve ndahen me shifra arabe dhe, brendapërbrenda këtyre ndarjeve, vihen presje për të shënuar kuptimet e përafërta të foljeve dhe pikëpresje për të shënuar kuptimet më pak të përafërta. Kuptimet e ndryshme të foljes i pasojnë gjithashtu lokucionet. Veç shënimit për foljen kalimtare ose jokalimtare jepen edhe diatezat mesore, pësore dhe vetvetore të foljes, të përfshira të gjitha me shënimin *f. jv.* (folje joveprore). Për shembull: *shihem, mbytem, rritem, krihem*. Këto forma nuk figurojnë në rendin alfabetik, por jepen te folja kalimtare përkatëse, bashkë me kuptimet e tyre. Në mjaft raste jepen shënime sqaruese brenda kllapash, kryesisht në gjuhën shqipe.

Në fund të fjalorit janë dhënë disa tabela gramatikore, për ta ndihmuar përdoruesin e fjalorit.

Phonetic transcription

The Albanian alphabet has thirty six letters: seven vowels and twenty nine consonants of which seven letter combinations (dh, gj, nj, sh, th, xh, zh,). The pronunciation of such letters is rendered in terms of equivalent sounds in English as follows:

a as **a** in father
b » **b** in better
c » **ts** in Tsar
ç » **ch** in cherry
d » **d** in door
dh» **th** in these, that, this
e » **e** in set
ë » **e** in term
f » **f** in for
g » **g** in go
gj » **g** in legion
h » **h** in her, history
i » **i** in machine
j » **y** in year
k » **k** in kind
l » **l** in land
ll » **ll** in all
m » **m** in man
n » **n** in now
nj » **ni** in onion
o » **o** in long
p » **p** in plural
q » **ky** in stockyard
r » **r** in room
rr as **rr** in burrow
s » **s** in sea
sh » **sh** in she
t » **t** in two
th » **th** in three
u » **oo** in loom
v » **v** in value
x » **dz** in adz(e)
xh » **j** in jester
y » **u** in une (in French)
z » **z** in zone
zh » **si** in vision

11

SHKURTIME GRAMATIKORE TË PËRDORURA NË FJALOR

Grammatical abbreviations used in the dictionary

as.	asnjanës	neutre / neuter
f.	femërore	feminine
fj. plk.	fjalë e palakueshme	indeclinable word
f.jk.	folje jokalimtare	intransitive verb
f.jv.	folje joveprore	passive, reflexive verb (negative)
f.k.	folje kalimtare	transitive verb
gj.bis.	gjuhë bisede	spoken language
krah.	krahinore	provincial
kr. thj.	e kryer e thjeshtë	past tense (p.t.)
lidh.	lidhëz	conjunction
lok.	lokucion	locution
m.	mashkullore	masculine
mb.	mbiemër	adjective
ndajf.	ndajfolje	adverb
num. rresht.	numëror rreshtor	ordinal numeral
num. them.	numëror themelor	cardinal numeral
paraf.	parafjalë	preposition
pasth.	pasthirrmë	interjection
p. d.	përemër dëftor	demonstrative pronoun
p. l.	përemër lidhor	relative pronoun
p. pk.	përemër i pakufishëm	indefinite pronoun
p. p.	përemër pyetës	interrogative pronoun
p. pr.	përemër pronor	possessive pronoun
p. v.	përemër vetor	personal pronoun
pj.	pjesëz	particle
pjes.	pjesore	past participle (p.p.)
sh.	shumës	plural
vjet.	e vjetëruar	ancient

Shkurtime të tjera
Other abbreviations

amer.	amerikane (gjuhë)	American
anat.	anatomi	anatomy
arkit.	arkitekturë	architecture
astron.	astronomi	astronomy
biol.	biologji	biology
bot.	botanikë	botany
bujq.	bujqësi	agriculture
det.	detari	marine
dr.	drejtësi	law
ek.	ekonomi	economy
el.	elektricitet	electricity
fam.	familiare (gjuhë)	colloquial
fet.	fetare	religious
fig.	figurativ	figurative
filoz.	filozofi	philosophy
fin.	financë	finance
fiz.	fizikë	physics
gram.	gramatikë	grammar
gjeog.	gjeografi	geography
gjeol.	gjeologji	geology
gjeom.	gjeometri	geometry
kim.	kimi	chemistry
let.	letërsi	litterature
mat.	matematikë	mathematics
mek.	mekanikë	mechanics
mjek.	mjekësi	medicine
muz.	muzikë	music
polig.	poligrafi	polygraphy
polit.	politikë	politics
sport.	sport	sport
teat.	teatër	theater
tek.	teknikë	technique
treg.	tregti	commerce
usht.	ushtarake	military
zool.	zoologji	zoology

A

a,A (letter of the Albanian alphabet) a, A
a, pj. is it?, do you?, is there? a bie shi? is it raining? a më kuptoni? do you understand me? a mungon ndonjëri? is there anybody absent?
a *lidh.* or; pak a shumë: more or less; sot a nesër: today or tomorrow; një a dy: one or two.
abací,-a *f.sh.*- abbey.
abanóz,-i *m.* ebony.
abát,-i *m.sh.* -ë abbot.
abazhúr,-i *m.sh.* -ë lampshade.
abdikím,-i *m.sh.* -e abdication.
abdikój *f.jk.* to abdicate.
abetár/e,-ja *f.sh.* primer, spelling book.
abëcë.-ja *f.* ABC.
aboním,-i *m.sh.* -e subscription; abonim në një gazetë etj.: subscription to a newspaper, etc.
abonój *f.k.* to take out a subscription. — abonohem *f.jv.* to subscribe to; abonohem në një gazetë, revistë: to subscribe to a newspaper, magazine.
absolút,-e *mb.* absolute.
absolutísht *ndajf.* absolutely; utterly; është absolutisht e pamundur: it is absolutely impossible.

absolutíz/ëm,-mi *m.* absolutism.
abstením,-i *m.sh.* -e abstention
abstenój *f.jk.* to abstain; abstenoj në votime: to abstain from voting.
abstenúes,- i *m.sh.* - abstainer.
abstrákt-e *mb.* abstract; emër abstrakt: abstract noun.
absúrd,-e *mb.* absurd, preposterous, nonsensical; kërkesa juaj është absurde: your request is preposterous.
absurditét,-i *m.sh.* -e absurdity, nonsense; them absurditete: to talk nonsense.
abshís/ë,-a *f.sh.* -a *mat.* abscissa.
abuzím,-i *m.sh.* -e abuse, misuse; bëj abuzime në të pirë: to drink to excess.
abuzój *f.jk.* 1. to abuse, to misuse. 2. to overindulge (in something), to use to excess, to abuse (something); abuzoj në duhan: to overindulge in smoking.
acár,-i *m.* frost, freezing cold, biting cold.
acarím,-i *m.sh.* -e irritation, aggravation; acarim i një plage: irritation of a wound; acarim i marrëdhënieve: aggravation of relations.
acarój *f.k.* to irritate, to aggravate. — acarohem *f.jv.* to be irritated, to be aggravated.

acarúar (i.e) *mb.* irritated, aggravated; **marrëdhënie të acaruara:** aggravated relations.
acetík,-e *mb.* acetic.
acetilén,-i *m.* acetilene.
acetón,-i *m.* acetone
acíd,-i *m.sh.* -e acid; **acid acetik:** acetic acid; **acid klorhidrik:** chloric acid; **acid nitrik:** nitric acid; **acid sulfurik:** sulphuric acid.
acid.-e *mb.* acid.
acidím,-i *m.* acidification.
aciditét.-i *m.* acidity.
acidój *f.k.* to acidify. — **acidohet** *f.jv.* to acidify.
açík *ndajf.* clearly, plainly, evidently; in plain words, in plain English; openly; **i foli açik:** he spoke to him clearly (openly, in plain English).
adápt,-e *mb.* proper, fit.
adaptím,-i *m.* 1. *biol. bot.* adaptation. 2. *(i një vepre letrare etj.)* adaptation (of a literary work etc.)
adaptój *f.k.* 1.to adapt, to adjust. 2. to turn, to adapt (for use as); **adaptoj një shkollë për spital:** to adapt a school for use as a hospital. — **adaptohem** *f.jv.* to adapt oneself.
adaptúesh/ëm (i).-me(e) *mb.* adaptable, adjustable.
adaptueshmërí,-a *f.* adaptability.
adásh,-i *m.sh.* -ë namesake.
aderím,-i *m.* adhesion.
aderój *f.jk.* to adhere.
aderúes,-i *m.sh.*- adherent.
adét,-i *m.sh.* -e custom, habitude.
adjutánt,-i *m.sh.* -ë *usht.* adjutant.
administrát/ë,-a *f.sh.* -a 1. administration. 2. administration offices.
administratív,-e *mb.* administrative; **në rrugë administrative:** through administrative channels.
administrativísht *ndajf.* administratively.

administratór,-i *m.sh.* -ë administrator, manager; **administrator i një pasurie:** steward of an estate.
administrím,-i *m.* administration, management; **nën administrimin e shtetit:** under state administration.
administrój *f.k.* to administer, *amer.* to administrate, to manage, to run. — **administrohet** *f.jv.* to be administered, to be managed, to be run.
admirál,-i *m.sh.* -ë *usht.* admiral.
admiraliát,-i *m.sh.* -e admiralty.
admirím,-i *m.* admiration; **me admirim:** admiringly, with admiration.
admirój *f.k.* to admire. — **admirohem** *f.jv.* to be admired; **që vlen të admirohet:** worthy of admiration.
admirúes,-i *m.sh.* - admirer.
admirúes,-e *mb.* admirative
admirúesh/ëm (i),-me (e) *mb.* admirable.
adoptím,-i *m.sh.* -e adoption.
adoptív,-e *mb.* adoptive.
adoptój *f.k.* 1. to adopt, to take, to embrace (an idea, custom etc.) and use. 2. to adopt; **adoptoj një jetim:** to adopt an orphan. — **adoptohem** *f.jv.* to be adopted.
adoptúar (i,e) *mb.* adopted; **fëmijë e adoptuar:** adopted child.
adoptúes,-i *m.sh.* - adoptive father.
adrés/ë,-a *f.sh.* -a address; **ç' adresë ke?** what's your address?
adresím,-i *m.* addressing.
adresój *f.k.* to address, to direct. — **adresohem** *f.jv.* to turn, to go , to apply *(tek,* to).
adresúar (i),-i (i) *m.sh.* - **(të)** addressee.

adhurím,-i *m.* adoration, worship.

adhurój *f.k.* to adore, to worship. — adhurohem *f.jv.* to be adored, to be worshipped.

adhurúes,-i *m.sh.* — adorer, worshipper.

adhurúesh/ëm(i),-me(e) *mb.* adorable.

aerodróm,-i *m.sh.* -e aerodrome, *emer.* airdrome, airfield.

aeronáut,-i *m.sh.* -ë *astron.* aeronaut.

aeronautík/ë,-a *f.* aeronautics.

aeroplán,-i *m.sh.* -ë aircraft, plane, *emer.* airplane; **aeroplan bombardues**: bomber; **aeroplan reaktiv**: jet aircraft; **hipi në aeroplan**: to take a plane; **udhëtoj me aeroplan**: to travel by plane (by air).

aeroplanmbájtës/e,-ja *f.sh.* -e aircraft-carrier.

aeropórt,-i *m.sh.* -e airport.

aerostát,-i *m.sh.* -e aerostat.

afaríst,-i *m.sh.* -ë businessman; profiteer, speculator.

afát,-i *m.sh.* -e term, date of expiry, due date, term day, deadline; **me afat gjashtë muaj**: falling due in six months; **në afat, brenda afatit**: on expiry, when due; **shtytje afati**: postponement; adjournment; **shtyj afatin**: to postpone, to adjourn; **me afat të gjatë**: long-term, long-dated; **plan me afat të gjatë**: a long-term plan; **me afat të shkurtër**: short-term, short-dated; **hua me afat të shkurtër**: a short-dated loan; **para afatit**: before schedule, ahead of time; **që i mbaron afati më 31 dhjetor**: falling due on December 31.

afetár,-i *m.sh.* - ë non-believer, unbeliever, irreligionist.

afetár,-e *mb.* irreligious, unbeliving.

áfër *l. ndajf.* near (by), close (by), near at hand; **banojnë këtu afër**: they live nearby; **vij më afër**: to draw near, to move closer, to come closer, to approach; **fare afër**: close by, close at hand, within hand reach, a few paces off; **më afër**: closer, nearer; **nga afër**: at close quarters (range), from close up; **e njoh dikë nga afër**: to know someone well; **i rri afër dikujt (në një dhimbje etj.)**: to be near (close to, with) one (in one's sorrow, etc.); **kjo ngjyrë është më afër jeshiles se grisë**: this colour is more of a green than a gray, this colour is nearer to green than to gray. **ishte ora dhjetë ose aty afër**: it was ten o'clock or thereabout, *ll. paraf.* close to, near to; about; **afër shkatërrimit**: close to ruin; **afër fundit**: nearing the end; **jam afër të gjashtëdhjetave**: to be nearly sixty, to be nearing (verging on) sixty; **afër një vit**: about a year.

áfërm(i),-e(e) *mb.* 1. next, near (in time or place), adjacent; **në mbledhjen e afërme**: in the next session, in the next meeting; **në një të ardhme të afërme**: in the near future. 2. kin, relative, closely allied (by blood or friendship); **njerëz të afërm**: close relatives; **jemi të afërm**: we are kith and kin (close relatives).

afërm (i), -i (i) *m.sh.* - (të) kinsman; (blood) relation.

afërméndsh *ndajf.* reasonably, logically; **është afërmendsh**: It stands to reason, it goes without saying.

áfërmi (së) *ndajf.* 1. shortly; **së**

afërmi del në pension: he is shortly to retire. 2. soon.

afërsí,-a *f.* nearness, proximity, adjacency, vicinity; **në afërsi të:** near to, close to; **ishim në afërsi të kryeqytetit:** we were close to (in the vicinity of) the capital; **me afërsi:** approximately, nearly.

afërsísht *ndajf.* approximately, about, roughly, around; **ai është afërsisht tridhjetë vjeç:** he is about thirty years old.

áfërt (i,e) *mb.* shih **afërm (l,e).**

afinitét,-i *m.* affinity.

afión,-i *m.* opium.

afirmój *f.k.* to affirm. — **afirmohem** *f.jv.* 1. to be affirmed. 2. *(për persona)* to make a name (a reputation) for oneself; **afirmohem si shkrimtar:** to make a name for oneself as a writer.

afísh/e,-ja *f.sh.* -e placard, bill, poster; **ngjis afishe:** to bill, to stick up posters.

afishím,-i *m.sh.* -e bill-posting, posting up.

afishój *f.k.* to bill, to post up, to placard. — **afishohet** *f.jv.* to be billed (posted up, placarded).

afri, -a *f.* affinity.

afrikán,-i *m.sh.* -ë African.

afrikán,-e *mb.* African.

afrím,-i *m.sh.* -e 1. approach, approaching; **afrimi i pushimeve verore:** the approach of summer vacations. 2. resemblance.

áfro *ndajf.* about, roughly, around, approximately; **afro dyzet gram:** about forty grammes.

afroj *f.k.* to approach, to bring near. — **afrohem** *f.jv.* to approach, to draw near, to come up, to advance, to come near.

afrúesh/ëm (i),-me (e) *mb.* 1. approachable, accessible. 2. sociable.

afsh,-i *m.sh.* -e 1. ardour, passion; **me afsh:** ardently, passionately. 2. heat. 3. breath 4. smell, odour; **lëshoj afsh:** to exhale.

áftë (i,e) *mb.* 1. able, capable; i **aftë për punë:** able-bodied. 2. competent, qualified.

aftësí,-a *f.sh.* – capacity, aptitude, aptness, ability, çapability; **aftësi për të bërë një punë:** ability to do a work; **aftësi prodhuese:** productive capacity; **njeri me aftësi të mëdha:** a man of great abilities.

aftësím,-i *m.* qualification; **aftësim profesional:** professional qualification.

aftësój *f.k.* to train, to render able. — **aftësohem** *fjv.* to qualify, to obtain a qualification.

agím,-i *m.sh.* -e dawn, daybreak, break of day; **në agim:** at dawn, at daybreak.

agón *f.jk.* to dawn.

agoní,-a *f.* agony; **jam në agoni:** to be in the agony of death, to be at one's last death struggle.

agrár,-e *mb.* agrarian; **reforma agrare:** land reform.

agregát,-i *m.sh.* -e aggregate.

agresión,-i *m.sh.* -e aggression.

agresív,-e *mb.* aggressive.

agresór,-i *m.sh.* -ë aggressor.

agresór,-e *mb.* aggressive.

agronóm,-i *m.sh.* -ë agronomist.

agronomí,-a *f.* agronomy, agronomics.

agronomík,-e *mb.* agronomic, agronomical.

agrúme,-t *m.sh. bot.* 1. *(pemët)* citrus (es). 2. *(frutat)* citrus fruits; **kultivimi i agrumeve:** citrus cultivation .

agulíç/e,-ja *f.sh.* -e *bot.* primrose.

agullím,-i *m.* shih agim.
agurídh,-e *mb.* 1. unripe; pemë agurídhe: green fruits, unripe fruits. 2. *fig.* aguridh nga mendja: greenhorn.
agjencí,-a *f.sh.* — agency; agjenci shtypi: press agency; agjenci transporti: forwarding agency. agjént,-i *m.sh.* -ë agent; agjent i tshehtë: secret agent. agjentúr/ë,-a *f.sh.* -a 1. spy network. 2. *fig.* agency, spy agency; revizionizmi është agjenturë e imperializmit: revisionism is an agency of imperialism.
agjërím,-i *m. fet.* fast; ditë agjërimi: fast day, fasting day; prish agjërimin: to break one's fast. agjërój *f.jk. fet.* to fast. agjitación,-i *m.* agitation; bëj agjitacion: to agitate, to carry on agitation. agjitatór,-i *m.sh.* -ë agitator.
ahl *pasth.* ahl
ah,-u *m.sh.* -e *bot.* beech; dru ahu: beech, beechwood. ahén/g,-gu *m.sh.* — gje merrymaking, revel, revelry, spree; bëj aheng: to revel, to make merry.
ahísht/ë,-a *f.sh.* -a beech-wood. ahúr,-i *m.sh.* -e stable; ahur derrash: pigsty.
af I. *p.d.* that; i kujt është ai libër?: whose book is that? më pëlqen ai qytet: I like that town; po ai: the same, the very one; *pl.* ata: those; *f.* ajo: that. II. *p.v.* he; ai që: he who; ai është: he is; (genitive) i(e) atij: his, of him; (dative) atij: him, to him; (accusative) atë: him; *pl.* ata: they; *f.* ajo: she.
ajázm/ë,-a *f.* holy water; spërkat me ajazmë: to besprinkle with holy water.
áj/ër,-ri *m.* air; ajër i pastër:

pure air; ajër i rëndë (i prishur): foul air; në ajër të pastër: in the open air, outdoors; pushkë me ajër: airgun.
ájk/ë,-a *f.* 1. cream; heq ajkën: to skim, to take off the cream; qumësht pa ajkë: skim-milk; me ajkë: creamy. 2. *fig.* prime; ajka e shoqërisë: the prime of the society, thё pick of the society.
ajó I. *p.d.* that; cila është ajo vajzë? who is that girl? ajo është: that is; ajo që u bë nuk zhbëhet: what is done, cannot be undone; *pl.* ato: those. II. *p.v.* she; (genitive) i(e) asaj: hers, of her; (dative) asaj: her, to her; (accusative) atë: her; *pl.* ato: they.
ajrím,-i *m.* airing, ventilation, air changing. ajrór *fik.* to alerate. ajrór,-e *mb.* aerial, air; alarm ajror: air raid alarm; vijë ajrore: airline; forcat ushtarake ajrore: airforce. ajrós *f.k.* to air, to ventilate. — ajroset *f.jv.* to be aired, to be ventilated. ajsbérg,-u *m.sh.* -ë iceberg akácj/e,-a *f.sh.* -e *bot.* acacia. akademí,-a *f.sh.* academy. akademík,-e *mb.* academic. akëcíli *p.k.* a certain person. akóma *ndajf.* yet, more, still; a-koma sëmurë është? is he still sick?; akoma jo: not yet; prit edhe dy ditë akoma: wait another two days, wait two more days; akoma edhe pak: a little more, a little longer.. akórd,-i *m.sh.* -e *muz.* tune, chord. akordím,-i *m.* 1. accordance. 2. bestowment, grant, allowance. akordój *f.k.* 1. to allow, to grant, to bestow, to confer, to accord

2. *muz.* to tune, to string, to accord.
akreditím,-i *m.* accreditation.
akreditój *f.k.* to accredit. — **akreditohem** *f.jv.* to be accredited.
akrép,-i *m.sh.* - a *zool.* scorpion.
akrep,-i *m.sh.,*-a hand (of a clock); **akrepi'i;orëve**: hour hand; **akrepi i minutave**: minute hand.
akrobací,-a *f.sh.* – 1. acrobatics. 2. acrobatie exercise.
akrobát,-í *m.sh.* -ë acrobat, tumbler, equilibrist, rope dancer.
aksidént,-i *m.sh.* -e accident.
aksidentál,-e *mb.* accidental, fortuitous; **vdekje aksidentale**: accidental death.
aksidentalísht *ndajf.* accidentaly, by chance.
aksióm / ë,-a *f.sh.* -a axiom.
aksión,-i *m.sh.* -e 1. action. 2. *fin.* share; share-certificate.
aksioníst,-i *m.sh.* -ë 1. volunteer. 2. *fin.* share-holder, stockholder.
akt,-i *m.sh.* -e 1. act, action. 2. document, act; **akt lindjeje, martese, etj.**: birth, marriage etc. certificate. 3. *teat.*act; **pjesë dy akte**: play in two acts.
aktakúz/ë,-a *f.sh.* -a indictment.
aktshítj/e,-a *f.sh.* -e bill of sale.
aktív,-i *m.sh.* -e 1. *polit.* meeting of activists; **mblidhet aktivi i rinisë**: a meeting of the activists of youth organization is held. 2. *ekon.* assets *pl.*
aktív,-e *mb.* active.
aktivist-i *m.sh,*-ë activist;
aktivitét,-i *m.sh.* -e activity.
aktór,-i *m.sh.* -ë actor.
aktuál,-e *mb.* 1. actual, present, current; **gjendja aktuale**: the actual situation. 2. topical; **një çështje shumë aktuale**: a very topical problem.
akuadúkt,-i *m.sh.* -e aqueduct.
akuarél,-i *m.sh.* -e water colour.

akuarium;-i *m.sh,*-e aquarium.
áku/**II,-IIi** *m.sh.* -j ice; **mal akulli**: iceberg -*Lok.* **bëhem akull**: to be freezing.
akullnáj/ë,-a .*f.sh.* -a glacier.
akullór/e,-ja *f.sh.* -e ice-cream.
akulloreshitës,-i *m.sh.* — icecream man, ice-cream vendor.
ákullt (i,e) *mb.* 1. icy, glacial. 2. *fig.* icy, chilly, frigid.
akullthýes/e,-ja *f.sh.* -e ice-boat, ice-breaker.
akumulatór,-i *m.,sh.* -ë accumulator, storage battery.
akumulím,-i *m.* 1. accumulation. 2. *fin. (i kapitalit):* accumulation (of capital). 3. *fig.* **(energjish)** storage (of energy).
akumulój *f.k.* to accumulate.
akustík,-e *mb.* acoustic, acoustical.
akustík/ë,-a *f.* acoustics.
akúz/ë,-a *f.sh.* -a 1. accusation, charge. 2. *drejt.* indictment.
akuzój *f.k.* to accuse, to arraign, to bring a charge against (someone); **e akuzoj (dikë) për**: to accuse someone of, to charge with, to indict for, to impeach. -**akuzohem** *f.jv.* to be accused (*për,* of), to be charged (with) to be- indicted, to be impeached (for).
akuzúar (e) *mb.* accused.
akuzúar(i),-i (i) *m.sh.* -(të) *dre t.* the accused; defendant.
akuzúes,-i *m.sh.* – accuser, indicter.
akuzúes,-e *mb.* accusing, accusatory.
alárm,- i *m.sh.* -e alarm; **jap alarmin**: to give (to sound) the alarm.
alarmánt,-e *mb.* alarming.
alarmój *f.k.* to alarm. — **alarmohem** *f.jv.* to be alarmed.
albúm -i *m.sh.* -e album.
albumín/ë,-a *f.sh.* -a albumin.
aleánc/ë,-a *f.sh.* -a alliance.

aleát,-i *m.sh.* -ë ally.
alegorí,-a *f.* allegory.
alegorík,-e *mb.* allegorical; **në mënyrë alegorike:** allegorically.
alfabét,-i *m.sh.* -e alphabet; **alfabeti i shurdhmemecëve:** finger alphabet.
alfabetík,-e *mb.* alphabetical; **rend alfabetik:** alphabetical order.
alfabetikísht *ndajf.* alphabetically.
algjéb/ër,-ra *f.* algebra.
algjebrík,-e *mb.* algebric.
aliázh,-i *m.sh.* -e alloy; **aliazh i bakrit me zinkun:** pinchbeck.
alisív/ë,-a *f.* washing-water, lye.
aliván,-i *m.* faint, swoon; **më bie alivan:** to faint to swoon.
alivanósem *f.jv.* to faint, to swoon.
alivanósj/e,-a *f.sh.* -e fainting, swooning.
alkoól,-i *m.sh.* -e alcohol, spirit; **alkool i denatyruar:** denaturated alcohol; **alkool metilik:** methylated spirit; **llambë me alkool:** spirit lamp.
alkoolík,-e *mb.* alcoholical; **pije alkoolike:** spirits.
alkoolíst,-i *m.sh.* -ë alcoholic.
alkoolizój *f.k.* to alcoholize. — **alkoolizohem** *f.jv.* to become alcoholized.
álpe,-t *f.sh.* Alps.
alpiníst,-i *m.sh.* -ë alpinist, mountaineer, mountain-climber.
altár,-i *m.sh.* -e *fet.* altar; chancel.
alternatív,-e *mb.* 1. alternate. 2. *el.* alternating; **rrymë alternative:** alternating current.
alternatív/ë,-a *f.sh.* -a alternative.
alternatívísht *ndajf.* alternately.
altoparlánt,-i *m.sh.* -ë loudspeaker.
altruíst,-i *m.sh.* -ë altruist.
altruíz/ëm,-mi altruism.
alumín,-i *m. kim.* aluminium, *amer.* aluminum.

aluzión,-i *m.sh.* -e allusion, hint; **bëj aluzion:** to hint, to allude.
allçí,-a *f.* gypsum, plaster.
allishverísh,-i *m.sh.* -e *treg. vjet.* deal, bargain; **bëj një allishverish (me dikë):** to bargain (with someone).
amanét,-i *m.sh.* -e *vjet.* supreme will, last will.
amatór,-i *m.sh.* -ë 1. amateur. 2. lover, devotee, enthusiast, fan; **amator filmash:** filmfan, *amer.* movie-fan; **amator zogjsh** bird fancier.
amazón/ë,-a *f.sh.* -e horsewoman.
ambalázh,-i *m.sh.* -e package; **letër ambalazhi:** packing paper, brown paper; **arkë ambalazhi:** packing case; **ambalazhi nuk kthehet:** empties not returnable.
ambalazhím,-i *m.* packing, wrapping; **shpenzime ambalazhimi:** package, packing charges.
ambalazhój *f.k.* to pack up. — **ambalazhohet** *f.jv.* to be packed up.
ambasád/ë,-a *f.sh.* -a embassy.
ambasadór,-i *m.sh.* -ë 1. ambassador; **ambasador i jashtëzakonshëm :** ambassador extraordinary. 2. *fam.* messenger.
ambícj/e,-a *f.sh.* -e 1. ambition. 2. envy.
ambicióz,-i *m.sh.* -ë ambitious person,
ambicióz,-e *mb.* ambitious; aspiring.
ambiént,-i *m.sh.* -e environment, milieu.
ambientój *f.k.* to accustom, to acclimate. — **ambientohem** *f.jv.* to accustom oneself to, to be acclimated, to be acclimatized.
ambuláncë/ë,-a *f.sh.* -a 1. dispensary. 2. ambulance.

L + outpatient clinic

ambulánt,-e *mb.* ambulant, walking; **shitës ambulant:** peddler.
amél,-i *m. mjek.* purgative.
amerikán,-i *m.sh.* -ë American; Yankee.
amerikán,-e *mb.* American.
amësí,-a *f.* maternity, motherhood.
ám/ëz,-za *f.* after-taste.
amfíb,-i *m.sh.* -ë *zool.* amphibian.
amfiteát/ër,-ri *m.sh.* -ro amphitheater.
amidón,-i *m.* starch.
amín! *pasth.* amen!; so be it!
amnezí,-a *f. mjek.* amnesia.
amnistí,-a *f.* amnesty.
amoniák,-u *m. kim.* ammonia.
amortizím,-i *m.* amortization; **fond amortizimi:** sinking fund.
amortizój *f.k. fiz. (zhurmën)* to muffle, to stifle (the noise); *(lëkundjet)* to absorb, to deaden.
-amortizohet *f.jv.* to be muffled (stiffled); to be absorbed (deadened).
ampér,-i *m. fiz.* ampere.
ampermét/ër,-ri *m.sh.* -ra ammeter, amperemeter.
amshím,-i *m.* eternity.
amshój *f.jk.* to render eternal, to immortalize.
amshúesh/ëm (i),-me(e) *mb.* eternal, perpetual.
amtár,-e *mb.* maternal, motherly; **gjuhë amtare:** mother tongue.
ámull *mb. ndajf.* stagnant; **ujë amull:** stagnant water.
amullí-a *f.* stagnation, standstill
amvís/ë-a *f.sh.* -a housewife,· housekeeper.
ámz/ë,-a *f.sh.* -a *zool.* queenbee.
ámz/ë,-a *f.* official register; **shënoj në amzë:** to matriculate.
anakroníz/ëm,-mi *m.* anachronism.

analfabét,-i *m.sh.* -ë illiterate person.
analfabét,-e *mb.* illiterate.
analfabetíz/ëm-mi *m.* illiteracy.
analitík,-e *mb.* analytical.
analíz/ë,-a *f.sh.* -a analysis; **analizë e imët:** close analysis; **analizë spektrale:** spectrum analysis; **në analizë të fundit:** in the final analysis, when all is said and done.
analizój *f.k.* to analyse. — **analizohet** *f.jv.* to be analysed.
analogjí,-a *f.* analogy; **në analogji me:** by analogy with, on the analogy of.
analogjikísht *ndajf.* analogycally.
ananás,-i *m. bot.* pineapple.
anarkí,-a *f.* anarchy.
anarkíst,-i *m.sh.* -ë anarchist.
anarkíz/ëm,-mi *m.* anarchism.
anasjelltas *ndajf.* vice versa.
anasón,-i *m.* shih **glikanxo.**
ánash *ndajf.* sidelong, sideways, edgeways, laterally; **pamje anash** sideview.
anatomí,-a *f.* anatomy.
andáj *lidh.* therefore.
andéj I. *ndajf.* that way, that side; **që andej;** from there; from that way.
II. *paraf.* beyond, on the other side; **andej malit:** beyond the mountain.
andráll/ë,-a *f.sh.* -a trouble, care.
anekdót/ë,-a *f.sh.* -a anecdote.
anéks,-i *m.sh.* -e *(i një ndërtese)* annexe (of a building).
anéks,-e *mb.* annexed.
aneksím,-i *m.* annexation.
aneksój *f.k.* to annex. — **aneksohet** *f.jv.* to be annexed.
anembánë I. *ndajf.* through, from side to side, from end to end.
II. *paraf.* **anembanë vend it:** all

over the country, throughout the country.

anemí,-a *f. mjek.* anaemia.

anemík,-e *mb.* anaemic.

anestezí,-a *f. mjek.* anaesthesia.

án/ë,-a *f.sh.* -ë 1. side; **nga kjo anë:** on this side; **nga ana tjetër e:** on the other side of; **në njërën anë:** on the one side; **në të dy anët:** on both sides; **era fryn nga të katër anët:** the wind blows from all sides, the wind blows from all four quarters at once; **nga të gjitha anët:** from all sides: *fig.* **ana tjetër e medaljes:** the other side of the question; **ana e mbarë e një stofi;** the right side of a cloth: **ana e prapme e një stofi:** the wrong side (the back) of a cloth. 2. edge, brim; **anët e kapelës:** the brims of the hat; **anët e një tryeze:** the edges of a table; **anët e një vizoreje:** the edges of a ruler; **anët e fletës:** the margin of the page. — *Lok.* **nga të dyja anët:** on both sides; **nga njëra anë. ... nga ana tjetër:** on the one hand .... on the other hand; **marr anën e dikujt :** to side with, to take sides with, to make common cause with; **me anën e:** with the help of; by the agency of, by means of, by; **me anën e kësaj letre:** by this letter; **nga ana ime:** on my part, on my behalf; **nga ana tjetër:** besides, moreover.

anëdét,-i *m.* shih **bregdet.**

anëdétas,-i *m.sh.* — shih **bregdetas.**

ánës *ndajf., paraf.* along; **anës e anës:** indirectly, in a round about way; **anës detit:** along the seashore; **anës liqenit:** along the

lakeside; **anës lumit:** along the riverside, by the river.

anësí,-a *f.* partiality.

anësísht *ndajf.* partially.

anësór,-e *mb.* 1. lateral; **dalje anësore:** side-exit. 2. *(rol etj)* minor, secondary (role etc.)

anëshkrím,-i *m.sh.* -e marginal note.

anëtár,-i *m.sh.* -ë member; **anëtar partie:** party member; **anëtarët e familjes:** family members.

anëtarësí,-a *f.* membership; **kuotë anëtarësie:** membership dues.

angazhím,-i *m.sh.* -e engagement, pledge; **marr angazhim (për të bërë diçka):** to bind (to commit) oneself, to pledge ose's word (to do something).

angazhój *f.k. (dikë)* to engage, to involve, to implicate (someone).

— **angazhohem** *f.jv.* to engage in, to be involved in; to bind (to commit) oneself, to pledge one's word, to undertake (*të,* to).

angléz,-i *m.sh.* -ë Englishman.

anglísht *ndajf.* in English.

anglísht/e,-ja *f.* English, the English language.

angullímë,-a *f.sh.* -a yelp.

angullín *f.jk.* to yelp.

angjinár/e,-ja *f.sh.* -e *bot.* artichoke.

angjín/ë,-a *f.sh.* -a *mjek.* angina, quinsy, tonsilitis.

áni/e,-a *f.sh.* -e plank out of standard.

aníj/e,-a *f.sh.* -e ship, boat, vessel; **anije me vela:** sailing boat; **anije me avull:** steamboat, steamship, steamer; **anije cisternë:** tanker, tank-vessel; **anije lufte:** warship, battleship; **anije pasagjerësh:** passenger steamer; **anije peshkimi:** fishing boat; **anije tregtare:** merchantman, merchant ship, merchant vessel; ani-

e me tri ura (me tri kuverta): three-decker; bashi i anijes: bow (prow) of a ship; direku i anijes: mast of a ship; kantier anijesh: dock, shipyard; kapiten anijeje: captain (of a ship); kiçi i anijes: poop of a ship, stern of a ship; kuvertë (urë) anijeje: bridge (deck) of a ship; hambar i anijes: hold of a ship; mbytje e anijes: shipwreck; ndërtues anijesh: shipwright, shipbuilder; ngarkim i anijes: shipment; pronar anijesh: shipowner; timon anijeje: helm of a ship; mbi anije! on shipboard:I hipi në anije: to embark, to go on board of a ship; nis anijen: to set sail; zbres nga anija: to land, to disembark; lidh (me litar a me zinxhir) anijen: to moor a ship. anijetár,-i *m.sh.* -ë shih marinar.
anilín/ë,-a *f. kim.* aniline.
aním,-i *m.* bias, inclination.
ankánd,-i *m.* auction; shes në ankand: to sell by auction; shitje në ankand: auction-sale.
ankés/ë,-a *f.sh.* -a grievance, complaint; parashtroj (bëj) një ankesë: to lodge a complaint, to air a grievance; ankesë e pathemeltë: unfounded complaint.
ankét/ë,-a *f.sh.* -a questionnaire, questionary; anketë gjyqësore; judicial inquiry.
ankím,-i *m.sh.* -e grievance, complaint.
ankóhem *f.jv.* to complain (*për*, about, for, over); i ankohem dikujt për fatkeqësitë e mija: to tell someone all one's troubles.
ankorím,-i *m.* anchoring, mooring.
ankorój *f.k.* to anchor, to lay anchor, to cast anchor, to bring (a ship) to anchor.

ánkth,-i *m.sh.* -e anxiety, anguish; me ankth: anxiously; jam në ankth: to be anxious.
ankúes,-i *m.sh.* – complainant.
ankúes,-e *mb.* (*ton*) plaintive (tone).
anód/ë,-a *f.sh.* -a *el.* anode, positive plate.
anój I. *f.k.* to bias, to incline; anoj nga e majta: to incline to the left side; anoj pjatën; to tilt one's plate. II. *f.jk.* 1. (*peshorja*) to lean (the balance); (*anija*) to list (the ship) inclined. 2. *fig.* to incline, to be inclined (*nga,* to*)* anoj nga mendimi i dikujt: to incline to someone's point of view.–anohem *fj.v.*to be inclined.
anomalí,-a *f.sh.* – anomaly.
anoním,-e *mb. (letër, vepër)* anonymous, authorless (letter, work); (*person*) nameless, unnamed (person).
anonimí,-a *f.* anonymity.
anormál,-e *mb.* 1. abnormal; unnatural; unusual; irregular. 2. *mjek.* mentally deficient (person), mentally retarded (child).
ansámb/ël,-li *m.sh.* -e ensemble; ansambël vokal: vocal ensemble.
ánsh/ëm (i), -me(e) *mb.* partial, biased, one-sided; tregohem i anshëm: to be partial (*ndaj,* to).
antagoníst,-e *mb.* antagonistic; kontradikta antagoniste: antagonistic contradictions.
antagoníz/ëm,-mi *m.* antagonism.
antarktík,-e *mb. gjeog.* antarctic; kontinenti antarktik: the antarctic continent.
antén/ë,-a *f.sh.* -a 1. *rad.* aerial antenna; antenë e drejtuar:

directional aerial. 2. zool. antenna, feeler.

antiajrór,-e mb. shih **kundërajror**.

antialkoolík,-e mb. antialcoholic.

antibiotík,-u m.sh. -ë mjek. antibiotic.

antiekonomík,-e mb. non-economic.

antifashíst,-i m.sh. -ë anti-fascist.

antifashíst,-e mb. anti-fascist; **luftë antifashiste**: anti-fascist struggle; **rinia antifashiste**: anti-fascist youth.

antifetár,-e mb. anti-religious.

antihigjieník,-e mb. unhealthy, unsanitary; **banesë antihigjienike**: unhealthy lodging..

antiimperialíst,-e mb. anti-imperialist.

antík/ë,-a f.sh. -a relic, antique; sh. antiquities; **dyqan antikash**: old curiosity shop.

antikitét,-i m. antiquity.

antipatí,-a f.sh. – antipathy (për, against, to), aversion, dislike (for).

antipatík,-e mb. antipathetic, antipathic.

antipód,-i m.sh. -e 1. gjeog. antipode. 2. fig. exact opposite or contrary.

antipopullór,-e mb. anti-popular.

antiseptík,-u m.sh. -ë antiseptic.

antiseptík,-e mb. antiseptic.

antishoqërór,-e mb. anti-social.

antitánk,-e mb. usht. anti-tank.

antitéz/ë-a f.sh. -a antithesis.

antologjí,-a f.sh.. – anthology.

antoním,-i m.sh. -ë antonym.

antracít,-i m. anthracite.

antropológ,-u m.sh. -ë anthropologist.

antropologjí,-a f. anthropology.

anuár,-i m.sh. -e year-book.

anulím,-i m.sh. -e annulment, invalidation.

anulój f.k. to annul, to revoke, to abrogate, to rescind; **anuloj një prokurë**: to revoke a proxy (a procuration); **anuloj një ligj**: to abrogate a law; **anuloj një kontratë**: to rescind a contract, to annul a contract. – **anulohet** f.jv. to be annulled (revoked abrogated, rescinded).

aórt/ë,-a f.sh.-a anat. aorta.

aparát,-i m.sh. -e 1. tek. apparatus, implement; **aparat fotografik**: camera; **aparat telefonik**: telephone; **aparat kirurgjie**: surgical apparatus. 2. (i librit) apparatus (of a book). 3. mjek. **aparati tretës**: alimentary canal.

aparatúr/ë,-a f.sh. -a apparatus.

apartamént,-i m.sh. -e apartment, flat.

apatí,-a f. apathy.

apatík,-e mb. apathetic.

apél,-i m.sh. -e roll call; **bëj apelin**: to call the roll.

apelím,-i m.sh. -e drejt. appeal; **kërkoj apelimin (e çështjes)**: to make (to lodge) an appeal.

apelój f.jk. drejt. to lodge an appeal.

apendicít,-i m.sh. -e mjek. appendicitis.

aperitív,-i m.sh. -e appetiser.

ap/ë-a m.sh;-ë krah. father.

aplikím,-i m-sh. -e application

aplikój f.k. to apply. – **aplikohet** f.jv. to be applied.

apó lidh. or; **sonte apo nesër**; this evening or tomorrow; **apo më mirë**: or rather; **më thuaj të pëlqen apo jo**: tell me whether you like it or not. **ju jeni i vëllai, apo jo?** you are his brother aren't you?

apolitík,-e *mb.* non-political.
apolitíz/ëm,-mi *m.* non-political nature.
apologjí,-a *f.* apology.
apostafát *ndajf.* on purpose, purposely, intentionally; **e bëj apostafat:** to do something on purpose (deliberately).
apostróf,-i *m.sh.* -a *gram.* apostrophe.
apóstu/ll,-lli *m.sh.* -j apostle.
aprovím,-i *m.sh.* -e approbation, approval, assent.
aprovój *f.k.* to approve of, to assent to, to agree to; **e aprovoj dikë:** to agree with someone. — **aprovohet** *f.jv.* to be approved; **çështja u shqyrtua dhe u' aprovua:** the question was discussed and approved.
aq *ndajf.* 1. so, so much, as, as much; that much; **aq... sa** so.... that; **bën aq ftohtë sa:** it is so cold that; **aq më keq:** so much the worse; **aq më mirë:** so much the better, all the better; **aq më pak:** so much the less; **aq më shumë:** all the more, so much the more; **aq shumë:** so much; **aq më bën:** it is the same to me; **po aq sa:** as much as; **njëra ka po aq sa dhe tjetra:** this one has as much as that one; **aq mirë sa s'ka ku të vejë:** as good as it can't be; **jo aq i mirë sa ti;** not so good as you; **unë e njoh atë po aq mirë sa dhe ti:** I know him as well as you do; **jo aq i zellshëm sa ai:** not as industrious as he is; **aq dua:** that will do.
ar,-i *m.* gold; **prej ari:** golden; **lyer me ar:** gold plated, gilt, gilt over; **fletë ari:** gold leaf;

shufër ari: gold rod; **monedhë ari:** gold coin, gold piece, gold money; **zinxhir ari:** gold chain.
ar,-i *m. gjeom.* unit of surface containing 100 square meters.
aráb,-i *m.sh.* -ë Arabian, Arab.
aráb,-e *mb.* Arabic (language); Arab, Arabian (people).
arabá,-ja *f.sh.* — carriage.
arabísht *ndajf.* in Arabic.
arabísht/e,-ja *f.* Arabic.
aráp,-i *m.sh.* -ë negro.
aráp,-e *mb.* black, dark.
arapésh/ë,-a *f.sh.* -a negress.
arbít/ër-ri *m.sh.* -ra arbiter, arbitrator, referee.
arbitrár,-e *mb.* arbitrary.
arbitraritét,-i *m.sh.* -e arbitrariness.
arbitrázh,-i *m.* arbitrage.
arbitrój *f.k. sport.* to umpire, to referee. — **arbitrohet** *f.jv.* to be umpired (refereed).
árdhës,-i *m.sh.* — immigrant.
árdhj/e,-a *f.sh..* — coming, arrival; *(në fuqi)* advent (to power); **biletë vajtje-ardhje:** return ticket.
árdhm/e(e), -ja(e) *f.* future.
árdhsh/ëm (i),-me (e) *mb.* future; next; forthcoming; **vitin e ardhshëm:** next year; **brezat e ardhshëm:** the future (coming) generations; **dhëndri im i ardhshëm:** my future (would be) son-in-law.
árdhshm/e (e),-ja (e) *f. gram.* future; **në të ardhshmen:** in the future, hereafter
ardhur *pjes.* e vij.
árdhur (i,e) *mb.* 1. imported, 2 not native.
árdhur (e),-a (e) *f.* income, revenue; **e ardhura vjetore:** annual income, yearly income; **caktoj, jap një të ardhur vjetore:** to allow a yearly income; **e ardhur bruto:** gross inco-

me; **e ardhur neto**: clear income.
árdhur (i,)-i(i) *m.sh*.- **(të)** immigrant.
árdhura,-t (të) *f.sh*. income, revenue; **tatim mbi të ardhurat**: income tax; **të ardhurat dhe shpenzimet**: assets and liabilities; **të ardhura neto**: clear income; **rroj me të ardhurat e mia**: to live upon one's income.
arén/ë,-a *f.sh*. -a arena; **arenë e cirkut**: circus ring; **arena ndërkombëtare**: international arena; **në arenën ndërkombëtare**: in the world arena.
ár/ë,-a *f.sh*. -a piece of ground, field.
áröz,-a *f.sh*. -a *zool*. wasp, hornet.
argás *f.k*. 1. *(lëkurët)* to tan (hides). 2. *fig*. to harden, to make hard (harder). – **argasem** *f.jv*. 1. to harden, to become hard (harder). 2. to be tanned; **më është argasur lëkura**: I have grown tougher.
argásj/e,-a *f*. 1. *(lëkurësh)* tanning (of hides); **punishte për argasjen e lëkurëve**: tannery, tan-yard. 2. *fig*. hardening, hardness,
argásës,-i *m.sh*. – tanner.
argásur (i,e) *mb*. 1. tanned; **lëkurë e argasur**: tanned hide. 2. *fig*. hardened; **i argasur në tregti**: well-used to business.
argát,-i *m.sh*. -ë day labourer, journey-man.
argëtím,-i *m.sh*. -e amusement, entertainment.
argëtój *f.k*. to amuse. – **argëtohem** *f.jv*. to amuse oneself.
argëtúes,-e *mb*. amusing.
argumént,-i *m.sh*. -e 1. argument, reason, reasoning; **argumenti i tij më bindi**: his reasoning convinced me. 2. pretext.

argumentím,-i *m.sh*. -e argumentation.
argumentój *f.k*. to provide arguments, to argue, to reason.
argjénd,-i *m*. silver; **pjatë argjendı**: silver dish; silver plate; **laj me argjend**: to silver over, to plate with silver, to silver, to silver-plate.
argjendár,-i *m.sh*. -e silverer, silversmith.
argjendarí,-a *f*. silversmith's trade.
argjéndtë(i,e) *mb*. 1. silver; **enë të argjendta**: silverware. 2. silver, silvery; **flokë të argjendtë**: silver hair.
argjentínas,-i *m.sh*. – Argentinian, Argentine.
argjentínas,-e *mb*. Argentinian.
argjíl/ë,-a *f*. clay.
argjilór,-e *mb*. clayey, claish; **tokë argjilore**: clayey earth.
arí,-u *m.sh*. -nj *zool*. bear; **këlysh ariu**: cub (of bear); **ari i bardhë**: polar bear, white bear.
aristokrací,-a *f*. aristocracy.
aristokrát,-i *m.sh*. -ë aristocrat
aristokratík,-e *mb*. aristocratic; **sjellje aristokratike**: aristocratic manners.
aritmetík,-e *mb*. arithmetical.
aritmetík/ë,-a *f*. *mat*. arithmetic.
aríthı *ndajf*. like a bear; **ngrihet arithi** *(kali):* to prance (the horse).
arixhí,-u *m.sh*. -nj gypsy.
arkaík,-e *mb*. archaic.
arkaíz/ëm,-mi *m*. archaism.
arkeológ,-u *m.sh*. -ë archaeologist.
arkeologjí,-a *f*. archaeology.
arkeologjík,-e *mb*. archaeological; **zbulime arkeologjike**: archaeological discoveries.
árk/ë,-a *f.sh*. -a chest, case, coffer, box; cash-desk, cashier's window; **arkë të hollash**: money-

box, money-chest, cash box; **mbaj arkën**: to be in charge of the cash; **derdh në arkë**: to pay at the cash-desk; **arkë kursimi**: savings bank; **arka e shtetit**: public treasure; **libri i arkës**: day-book, cash-book; **zyra e arkës**: pay office.
arkëtár,-i *m.sh.* -ë cashier; *(në bankë)* teller.
arkëtím,-i *m.* cashing, encashment.
arkëtój *f.k.* to cash; **arkëtoj një shumë mjaft të madhe**: to cash a considerable sum.
arkipelág,-u *m.sh.* -ë *gjeog.* archipelago.
arkitékt,-i *m-sh.* -ë architect.
arkitektúr/ë,-a *f.* architecture.
arkív,-i *m.sh.* -a archive; **dokumentet e arkivit**: archives.
arkivíst,-i *m.sh.* -ë archivist.
arkivól,-i *m.sh.* -e coffin; bier (of a dead), *amer.* casket.
arktík,-e *mb. gjeog.* Arctic: **Deti arktik**: Arctic Ocean.
armát/ë,-a *f.sh.* -a army; **një armatë me njëzet mijë vetë**: an army of twenty thousand men.
armatím,-i *m.sh.* -e armament; **gara e armatimeve**: the armament race.
armatós *f.k.* to arm, to provide (to supply) with arms. – **armatosem** *f.jv.* 1. to arm oneself *(me,* with); **rrëmbej armët**: to take up arms. 2. *fig.* to arm oneself.
armatúr/ë,-a *f.sh.* -a 1. armory. 2. *ndërt.* framework.
armé,-ja *f.* prickle.
árm/ë,-a *f.sh.* -ë *usht.* arm, weapon; **armë e ftohtë**: cold weapon; **armë zjarri**: fire-arms. **armë bërthamore**: nuclear weapon; **rrok armët**: to take up arms; **dorëzoj, lëshoj armët**: to lay down arms; **thirrem nën**

armë: to call to arms; **shok armësh**: comrade in-arms. 2. arm, force, service; **në ç'armë ke qenë?** which service were you in? 3. *fig.* weapon, means; **kjo letër është një armë e rrezikshme në duart e tij**: this letter is a dangerous weapon in his hands.
armëpushím,-i *m.sh.* -e armistice; **armëpushim i përkohshëm**: truce
armëtár,-i *m.sh.* -ë gunsmith.
armí/k,-ku *m.sh.* -q enemy, foe; **armik i betuar**: sworn enemy; **armik numër një**: number one enemy.
armiqësí,-a *f.sh.* – enmity, feud, hostility; **jam në armiqësi me dikë**: to be hostile to someone. **armiqësísht** *ndajf.* hostilely, with hostility.
armiqësój *f.k.* to make hostile; to make an enemy of. – **armiqësohem** *f.jv. (me dikë)* to antagonize (someone).
armiqësór,-e *mb.* hostile, inimical; **veprime armiqësore**: hostilities; **veprimtari armiqësore**: subversive activity.
árn/ë,-a *f.sh.* -a patch; **qep një arnë**: to sew a patch.
arním,-i *m.sh.* -e patching, patchwork.
arnój *f.k.* to patch, to mend.
arnúar (i,e) *mb.* patched.
aromatík,-e *mb.* aromatic, fragrant.
aróm/ë,-a *f.* aroma, fragrance, flavour.
arsenál,-i *m.sh.* -e arsenal.
arsím,-i *m.* aducation; **arsim i detyrueshëm**: compulsory education: **arsim i mesëm**: secondary education; **arsim profesional**: vocational training.
arsimór,-e *mb.* educational.
arsimtár,-i *m.sh.* -ë teacher.

arsimtár/e- ja *f.sh.* **-e** woman teacher.

arsýe,-ja *f.sh.* – reason; sense, correct jugdement; argument, justification; **humbas arsyen:** to go out of one's mind: **arsyet që nxirrni janë pa bazë** (nuk qëndrojnë): your arguments are unfounded (groundless). 2. reason, cause, motive; **zemërohem pa arsye:** to be offended for no reason; **për arsye shëndetësore:** for reason of health; **për arsye të:** because of; **për këtë arsye:** for this reason.

arsýesh/ëm (i)**,-me** (e) *mb.* 1. reasonable, sensible, rational; **njeri i arsyeshëm:** sensible man, reasonable man; **po t'a shihni të arsyeshme:** if you think it proper; **propozime të arsyeshme:** sensible, reasonable proposals. 2. reasonable, fair; **çmime të arsyeshme:** fair prices.

arsyetím,-i *m.sh.* **-e** reasoning, argumentation.

arsyetój I. *f.jk.* to reason. II. *f.k.* to justify; **arsyetoj një mungesë:** to justify an absence.

art,-i *m.sh.* **-e** art; **vepër arti:** work of art; **me art:** skilfully, with skill; **arti ushtarak:** art of war; **artet e bukura:** the fine arts; **art për art:** art for art's sake.

artéri/e,-a *f.sh.* **-e** *anat.* artery.

ártë (i,e) *mb.* golden.

artificiál,-e *mb.* artificial.

artíku/ll,-lli *m.sh.* **-j** 1. article (of newspaper) news item. 2. *treg.* article; **artikuj të konsumit të gjerë:** consumer goods; **artikuj të nevojës së parë:** prime necessities; **artikuj ushqimorë:** alimentary articles, food wares; **artikuj të prodhuar në**

seri: mass produced articles; **artikuj veshmbathjeje:** articles of clothing; **artikuj sportivë:** sport goods; **artikuj shtëpijakë:** household commodities.

artilerí,-a *f.* artillery; gunnery; **artileri fushore:** field artillery.

artiljér,-i *m.sh.* **-ë** artilleryman, gunner.

artist,-i *m sh.* **-e** artist.

artistík,-e *mb.* artistic.

artizán,-i *m sh.* **-ë** artisan, craftsman.

artizanát,-i *m.* artisanship; handicraft, craftsmanship, craftwork.

artrít,-i *m. mjek.* arthritis.

arúsh/ë,-a *f.sh.* **-a** *zool.* 1. shebear. 2. *astron.* **Arusha e Madhe:** Great Bear; **Arusha e Vogël:** Little Bear.

arratí,-a *f.* escape; **marr arratinë:** to take to the bush, to go into hiding, to flee.

arratísem *f.jv.* to escape, to run away (from prison), to flee (the country).

arratísj/e,-a *f.sh.* **-e** escape, flight.

arratísur (i)**,-i** (i) *m.sh.-* **(të)** escapee, fugitive, runaway.

arrést,-i *m.* arrest; **mbajtje në arrest:** detention.

arrestím,-i *m.sh.* **-e** arrest, custody.

arrestój *f.k.* to arrest, to take into custody, to put under arrest. – **arrestohem** *f.jv.* to be arrested.

árr/ë,-a *f.sh.* **-a** *bot.* walnut; (*druri*) walnut tree; **arrë hindi:** nutmag; **arrë kokosi:** coconut.

arrëthýes/e,-ja *f.sh.* **-e** nut-cracker.

arríj *f.jk.* 1. to arrive *(në,* at, in) to come (to), to get, to reach; **arrij në shtëpi shëndoshë e mirë:** to come home safe and sound, to arrive home safe and sound; **treni arrin në orën tre:** the train gets in at three; **arrij herët (vonë):** to arrive (to come) early (late); **arrij në kohë:** to arrive on time. 2. to come up; **djali më arrin gjer te supi:** my son comes up to my shoulder. 3. to attain, to succeed; **ia arrij qëllimit:** to achieve one's aim. 4. *(dikë)* to rejoin, to overreach (someone). 5. to reach; **arrij tavanin:** to reach the ceiling. 6. *(në vend)* to reach at (one's destination) **arrin:** it is enough.

arrirë (i,e) *mb.* ripe, mellow (of a fruit); **pemë e arrirë:** ripe fruit.

arritj/e,-a *f.sh.* -e 1. arrival; **data e arritjes:** date of arrival. 2. attainment, achievement; **arritje të mira:** good results.

arritsh/ëm (i),-me (e) *mb.* accessible.

arrogánc/ë,-a *f.* arrogance, brutality.

arrogánt,-e *mb.* arrogant, brutal.

as,-i *m.sh.* -e ace (in playing cards).

as *lidh.* nor, neither, either; **as i bardhë as i zi:** neither white nor black; **as ftohtë as ngrohtë:** neither cold nor warm; **as njëri as tjetri:** neither of them; **as më shumë as më pak:** neither more nor less; **as unë as ti:** neither I nor you; **as unë nuk e di:** I don't know that either; **ty nuk të pëlqen?** - **—as mua.** you don't like it? nor do I, I don't either; **as fryn as bie:** it is neither windy nor rainy; **as që:** not even; **as që e kam parë:** I did not even see him; **as një çikë:** not a bit.

asáj *p.v.* her, to her (shih **ajo**); **thashë asaj:** I told her.

asamblé,-ja *f.sh.* -e assembly; **asambleja kushtetuese:** the Constituent Assembly; **asambleja ligjvënëse:** the Legislative Assembly.

asamblíst,-im.sh.-ë assembly man.

asbést,-i *m.* asbestos.

asfált,-i *m.* asphalt, asphaltum.

asfaltím,-i *m.* asphalting.

asfaltój *f.k.* to asphalt. – **asfaltohet** *f.jv.* to be asphalted.

asfaltúar (i,e) *mb.* asphalted; **rrugë e asfaltuar:** asphalted road.

asfiksí,-a *f.* asphyxia.

asfiksój *f.k.* to asphyxiate, to suffocate.

asgjë *p.pk.* 1. nothing; **asgjë s'e ndal:** nothing can stop him. 2. anything, nothing; **nuk bleva asgjë:** I didn't buy anything, I bought nothing; **asgjë të përbashkët:** nothing in common; **thuajse asgjë:** almost (next to) nothing; **nuk vien për asgjë:** it is good for nothing; **asgjë tjetër:** nothing else; **sikur s'kishte ndodhur asgjë:** as if nothing had happened; **nuk di asgjë prej gjëje:** I know nothing at all, I don't know a thing; **s'bëj dot asgjë:** I can't do anything about it, there is nothing I can do; **s'më kushton asgjë të kthehem:** it won't take me a minute to come back.

asgjëkúnd *ndajf.* nowhere, not anywhere.

asgjësénd *p.pk.* nothing, nought.

asgjësím,-i *m.* annihilation, extermination.

asgjësój *f.k.* to annihilate, to exterminate, to destroy thoroughly. – **asgjësohet** *f.jv.* to be destroyed thoroughly (completely).

asimilím,-i *m.* assimilation. ·

asimilój *f.k.* to assimilate. — **asimilohet** *f.jv.* to be assimilated,

asisój I. *ndajf.* of that sort; in that mamer.

II. *p.d.* of that kind; **asisoj njerë-zish**: that kind of people, people like that.
asisténc/ë,-a *f.* assitance, help, aid.
asistént,-i *m.sh.* -ë 1. assistant, helper. 2. assistant; **asistent re-gjizor**: assitant director.
asistój *f.jk.* 1. to assist, to lend help. 2. to attend, to be present at.
askét,-i *m.sh.* -ë ascetic.
asketík,-e *mb.* ascetical, ascetic.
asketíz/ëm,-mi *m.* asceticism.
askurrë *ndajf.* never.
askúsh *p.pk.* nobody, no one, none.
asnjánës,-e *mb.* 1. neutral; **rri asnjanës**: to remain neutral, to sit on the fence. 2. *gram.* neu-ter; **emër asnjanës**: neuter noun.
asnjanësí,-a *f.* neutrality.
asnjerí *p.pk.* nobody, no one, none, no man.
asnjë *p.pk.* no one, none, nobody; no, not any; **asnjë s'të beson**: no one believes you; **s'kam parë asnjë prej tyre**: I didn't see anyone of them, I saw no one of them; **ke ndonjë pyetje?** – **asnjë**: have you any question? – no, none; **asnjë tjetër**: no one else, nobody else; **asnjë njeri s'mund ta bënte**: no man could do it; **nuk pata as-një kënaqësi**: I got no (didn't get, have any) satisfaction.
asnjëhérë *ndajf.* never, at no time, not at any time.
asnjëri *p.pk.* shih: **asnjeri**.
asokóhe *ndajf.* at that time.
aspák *ndajf.* not at all.
aspirát/ë,-a *f.sh.* -a aspiration.
aspirín/ë,-a *f.sh.* -a aspirin.
astár,-i *m.sh.* -e lining; **vesh me astar**: to line (a cloth).
astmatík,-e *mb.* asthmatic.
ástm/ë,-a *f.* *mjek.* asthma.

astrológ,-u *m.sh.* -ë astrologer.
astrologjí,-a *f.* astrology.
astronóm,-i *m.sh.* -e astronomer.
astronomí,-a *f.* astronomy.
ashensór,-i *m.sh.* -ë lift, *amer.* ele-vator.
ashík,-u *m.sh.* -ë *vjet.* lover.
ashiqáre *ndajf.* evidently, obvious-ly, clearly, plainly, transparently, showy; **kjo duket ashiqare :** it is plain, it is transparent; **duket ashiqare se nuk e bën dot:** it is clear that you can't do it.
ásh/e,-ja *f.* *bot.* holly, holly-tree.
áshk/ël,-la *f.sh.* – **la** chip, splinter sliver; **heq ashkla:** to break spliters off, to chip.
ashkëlój *f.k.* to splinter, to sliver. — **ashkëlohet** *f.* *jv.* to splinter, to sliver, to chip.
áshpër *ndajf.* severely, sternly roughly, harshly, fiercely, rude-ly; **i flas ashpër (dikujt):** to speak harshly to someone.
áshpër (i,e) *mb.* harsh, stern, se-vere,rough, violent, coarse; **njeri i ashpër:** stern (severe, harsh) person; **duar të ashpra:** rough hands; **luftë e ashpër:** fierce struggle; **i ashpër në të prekur:** rough, harsh, not smooth, not refined (to the touch); **i ashpër në vesh:** harsh to the ear; **zë i ashpër:** harsh, rasping voice; **klimë e ashpër:** severe climate; **u tregove shumë i ashpër me të:** you were too hard on him; **qortim i ashpër:** harsh rebuke.
ashpërí,-a *f.* rudeness, fierceness, roughness; **ashpëri e lëkurës:** roughness of the skin.
ashpërím,-i *m.* roughness, coar-seness.
ashpërój *f.k.* 1. to render rough, to roughen. 2. *fig.* to aggravate. — **ashpërohem** *f.jv.* to become rude (rough).

ashpërsí,-a *f.* harshness, coarseness, roughness, fierceness, rudeness, asperity, severity; **me ashpërsi**: harshly, severely, rudely; **ashpërsia e luftës**: the rudeness of the fight.

ashpërsím,-i *n.* aggravation, embittering, embitterment, exacerbation; **ashpërsim i sëmundjes**: exacerbation of the illness; **ashpërsimi i luftës së klasave**: aggravation of the class struggle; **ashpërsim i marrëdhënieve ndërmjet dy vendeve**: worsening of relations between two countries.

ashpërsísht *ndajf.* harshly, roughly severely.

ashpërsój *f.k.* to embitter, to envenom, to aggravate, to roughen. − **ashpërsohem** *f.jv.* to become harsh (rough), to grow worse.

asht,-i *m.sh.* − **éshtra** *anat.* bone.

ashtëzím,-i *m.* ossification.

ashtú *ndajf.* so, like that, that way, in that way, in that manner, that; **ashtu tha**: that is what he said; **nuk është ashtu**: it is not so; **ashtu?** is that so?; **ashtu qoftël** so be itl; **po ashtu**: as well; **ajo doli, po ashtu bëra dhe unë**: she went out and so did I; **ashtu si**: just as; **ashtu si flet ashtu edhe shkruan**: he writes just as he speaks; **ashtu edhe**: also, as well as, too; **ashtu si, ashtu siç, ashtu sikurse**: as; **më pëlqen ashtu siç është**: I like it as it is.

ashtuqúajtur (i,e) *mb.* so called, self-styled.

at,-i *m.sh.*−**llarë** thoroughbred horse

atá I. *p.d.* those; **shoqëroi ata burra**: accompany those menl **ata që**: those who.
II. *p.v.* they; (genitive) *i (e) atyre:*: theirs, of them; (dative) **atyre** them, to them; (accusative) **ata**: them.

atashé,-u *m.sh.* − attaché; **atashe tregtar**: commercial attaché.

atdhé,-u *m.* fatherland, homeland; *fig.,* **jashtë atdheut**; abroad.

atdhedashurí,-a *f.* love for the fatherland.

atdhetár,-i *m.sh.* -ë patriot.

atdhetarí,-a *f.* patriotism.

ateíst,-i *m.sh.* -ë atheist.

ateíz/ëm,-m. *m.* atheism.

atelié,-ja *f.sh.*− studio, study; shop.

atentát,-i *m.sh.* -e attempt on someone's life; attempted attack; **i bëj atentat dikujt**: make an attempt on someone's life.

atentatór,-i *m.sh.* -ë assassin.

át/ë,-i *m.sh.* **étër** father; **im atë**: my father; **etërit tanë**: our fathers.

atë I. *p.d.* that; it; **unë e njoh atë vajzë**: I know that girl; **më sill atë libër**; bring me that book; **merrni atë rrugë**: take that way; **atë vit**:. that year; **atë mos e prek**: don't touch it.
II. *p.v.* him, her, it (shih **ai,** *rasa kallëzore*).

atëhére I. *ndajf.* then, at that time; **që atëhere**: from that time, since then, ever since
II. *lidh.* 1. then, in that case; **atëhere po të pres**: I'll wait for you, then. 2. well then, so; **atëhere u morëm vesh, apo jo?** well then, we're agreed, aren't we?

atëhérsh/ëm (i),-me(e) *mb.* of that time.

atërór,-a *mb.* paternal; **në mënyrë atërore**; fatherly paternally.

atësí,-a *f.* paternity, fatherhood.

atíj *p.v.* him, to him (shih **ai,** *rasa dhanore*).

atíllë (i,e) *mb.* such, like, of that kind.

atjé *ndajf.* there; **atje lart:** up there; **atje poshtë:** down there; **atje tej:** over there; beyond; **që atje:** from that place; **atje rrotull:** thereabout.

atjésh/ëm(i),-me(e) *mb.* of that place.

atlás,-i *m.sh.* -ë *gjeog. hist.* atlas.

atlét,-i *m.sh.* -ë athlete; **trup atleti:** athletic build.

atletík,-e *mb.* athletic; **gara atletike:** athletic events; **stërvitje atletike:** athletic training.

atletík/ë,-a *f.* athletics (pl.); **atletikë e lehtë:** track and field events;

atletíz/ëm,-mi *m.* athleticism.

atllás,-i *m.sh.* -e satin.

atmosfér/ë,-a *f.sh.* -a 1. *astron.* atmosphere. 2. *fiz.* atmosphere (a unit of pressure equal to 14.69 pounds per square inch). 3. *fig.* atmosphere, environment.

atmosferík,-e *mb.* atmospheric, atmospherical.

ató I. *p.d.* those; **shoqërojini ato gra:** accompany those women; **të kujt janë ato këpucë:** whose shoes are those? (shih **ata**).
II. *p.v.* they; (genitive) **i (e)atyre:** theirs, of them; (dative) **atyre:** them, to them; (accusative) **ato:** them (shih **ata**).

atóm,-i *m.sh.* -e *fiz.* atom.

atomík,-e *mb.* atomic; **bombë atomike:** atomic bomb; **peshë atomike:** atomic weight.

atrofí,-a *f. mjek.* atrophy.

atvrásës,-i *m.sh.* – parricide.

atý *ndajf.* there, to that place; **aty pak më parë:** recently, a short time ago; **aty këtu:** here and there; **aty për aty:** at once, then and there, right off,

right away, at the same instant, on the spot, immediately, instantly.

atýre *p.v.* them, to them (shih **ata, ato,** *m.f.sh. rasa dhanore).*

atýshëm(i), -me(e) *mb.* of that place.

áthët (i,e) *mb.* sour, tart, acidulous

athëtím,-i *m.* sourness, acidity, tartness.

audiénc/ë,-a *f.sh.* -a audience; **i caktoj dikujt audiencë;** to give an audience to.

auditór,-i *m.sh.* -e 1. hearers, listeners. 2. auditorium.

aullím/ë,-a *f.sh.* -a yelp, yell.

aullín *f.jk.* to yelp, to yell.

aureól/ë,-a *f.sh.* -a aureola.

australián,-i *m.sh.* -ë Australian.

australián,-e *mb.* Australian.

austriák,-u *m.sh.* -ë Austrian.

austriák,-e *mb.* Austrian.

autarkí,-a *f. polit.* autarky.

autarkík,-e *mb.* autarkic, autarkical.

autentík,-e *mb.* authentic.

autoambulánc/ë,-a *f.sh.* -a ambulance.

autobiografí,-a *f.sh.* – autobiography.

autobiografík,-e *mb.* autobiographic, autobiographical.

autoblínd/ë,-a *f.sh.* -a armoured car.

autobót,-i *m.sh.* -e tank truck.

autobús,-i *m.sh.* -ë bus.

autodidákt,-i *m.sh.* -ë autodidact.

autográf,-i *m.sh.* -e autograph.

autokrát,-i *m.sh.* -ë autocrat.

autokritík/ë,-a *f.* self-criticism; **bëj autokritikë:** to make self-criticism.

automat,-i *m.sh.* -ë automaton, self-acting machine, slotmachine, automatic machine.

automatík,-e *mb.* automatic self-

acting; **pushkë automatike:** automatic gun.
automatík,-u *m.sh.* -ë submachine gun; **amer.** machine carbine; tommy gun.
automatikísht *ndajf.* automatically
automjét,-i *m.sh.* -ë vehicle.
automobíl,-i *m.sh.* -a automobile; **ngas automobilin:** to drive a motor-car.
automobilistík,-e *mb.* automobilistic; **transport automobilistik:** motor-transport.
autonóm,-e *mb.* self-governing, autonomous.
autonomí,-a *f.* self-government, autonomy.
autopsí,-a *f.sh.* - *mjek.* autopsy.
autór,-i *m.sh.* -ë author; *(vepre letrare)* writer; *(vepre muzikore)* composer; **e drejtë e autorit:** copyright.
autór/e,-ja *f.sh.* -e authoress.
autoritár,-e *mb.* authoritative; **në mënyrë autoritare:** authoritatively.
autoritét,-i *m.* 1. authority, prestige; **fitoj autoritet:** to win authority (prestige); **kam autoritet:** to have authority (over). 2. *sh.* authorities.
autorizím,-i *m.sh.* -e autorization.
autoriój *f.k.* to authorize, to give authority to. – **autorizohem** *f.jv.* to act on the authority of (someone).
autorizúes,-i *m.sh.* – authorizer.
autostrád/ë,-a *f.sh.* -a motorway, *amer,* speedway, super highway.
avánc/ë,-a *f.* advance; **arrij me pesë minuta avancë:** to arrive five minutes before time.
avancím,-i *m.* advancing, putting forward, furtherance.
avancój *f.k.* to advance, to put forward; to make (something)

earlier. – **avancohet** *f.jv.* to be advanced.
avantázh,-i *m.sh.* -e advantage.
avarí,-a *f.sh.* – break-down; **pësoj avari:** to break down.
aváz,-i *m.sh.* -e *vjet.* 1. melody; refrain; **mbaj avazin:** to harp on the same refrain, to sing in chorus with. 2. *fig.* story, song; **vazhdoj avazin e parë:** to harp on the same string, to sing the same old song (tune); **vazhdon po ai avaz:** it's always the same old story. 3. trouble weariness, tediousness; **nxjerr** (hap) **avaze:** to cause trouble.
avdés,-i *m. fet.* ablution.
aventurésk,-e *mb.* adventurous, venturesome.
aventúr/ë,-a *f.sh.* -a adventure.
aventuriér;-i *m.sh.* -ë adventurer.
aviación,-i *m.* aviation; **fushë aviacioni:** airfield.
aviatór,-i *m.sh.* -ë aviator, airman, pilot.
avít *f.k.* to approach, to draw close. – **avitem** *f.jv.* to draw near, to come near; **avitu!** come up!
avítj/e,-a *f.* approach.
avlëménd,-i *m.sh.* -e loom.
avllí,-a *f.sh.* – 1. courtyard, yard (of a house), court (of a house). 2. garden wall.
avokát,-i *m.sh.* -ë advocate, barrister; *amer.* attorney at law; **bëhem avokat:** to become barrister; **mbrojtja e avokatit:** plea
ávu/ll,-lli *m.sh.* -j steam, vapour; **avull i gojës:** whiff, exhalation; **banjë me avull:** steambath; **anije me avull:** steamer, steamer-boat, steamship; **kazan me avull:** steam boiler; **makinë me avull:** steam engine.
avullím,-i *m.* evaporation; **aftësi avullimi:** volatillity.

avullój I. *f.k.* to evaporate, to convert into vapour; to volatilize. — **avullohet** *f.jv.* to be evaporated. II. *f.jk.* to vaporize. **avullór/e,-ja** *f.sh.* -e steamer, steam-ship.
ávullt (i,e) *mb.* vaporous, steamy.
avullúes,-i *m.sh.* vaporiser.
avullúesh/ëm (i),-me(e) *mb.* volatile, evaporative.
axhamí,-u *m.sh.* -nj child; **prej axhamiu:** childish.
áxh/ë,-a *m.sh.* -a paternal uncle.
axhustatór,-i *m.sh.* -ë adjuster.
azát *mb* uncontrollable, out of hand.

azgán,-e *mb.* 1. dasing (of a fellow). 2. frisky (of a horse)
aziatík,-u *m.sh.* -ë Asiatic.
aziatík,-e *mb.* Asiatic, Asian.
azíl,-i *m.sh.* -e asylum; **azil i pleqve:** alms house.
azót,-i *m.* azote, nitrogen.
azotik,-e *mb.* azotic.
azhurním,-i *m.* adjournment.
azhurnój *f.k.* 1. to postpone, to put off, to adjourn, to defer. 2. to settle; **azhurnoj një llogari:** to settle (to adjust) an account.

B

b, B (letter of the Albanian alphabet) b, B.
babá,-i *m.sh.* -allarë father; **pa baba:** fartherless; *gj. fol.* dad, daddy.
babagjýsh,-i *m.sh.* -ë grandfather.
babaxhán,-i *m.sh.* -ë good natured man.
babaxhán,-e *mb.* good natured (of a man).
báb/ë,-a *m.* shih **baba.**
babëlók,-u *m.sh.* -ë 1. dad. 2. good old chap.
babëzí,-a *f.* greediness.
babëzítur (i,e) *mb.* greedy.
bábo,-ja *f.sh.* — *vjet.* midwife; **shumë babo e mbysin foshnjën:** too many cooks spoil the broth.

babush,-i *m. fam.* grandpa.
bac/ë, -a *m.sh.* -a 1. father. 2. elder brother.
bacíl,-i *m.sh.* -e *mjek.* bacillus.
badihavá *ndajf.* very cheap; **e bleva badihava:** I got it for nothing,
baft,-i *m.* shih **fat.**
bagázh,-i *m.sh.* -e luggage, baggage.
bagëtí,-a *f.sh.-* — cattle; **bagëti e imët:** smaller livestock, sheep; **bagëti e trashë:** cattle; **kope bagëtish:** herd, flock.
bah I *pasth.* bah I
báhç/e,-ja *f.sh.* -e garden.
bahçeván,-i *m.sh.* -ë gardener.
baján/e,-ja *f.sh.* -e 1. *bot. (fruti)* almond; *(druri)* almond-tree. 2. *mjek.* tonsils, amygdales.

3 — 292

baját,-e *mb.* stale; trite; **bukë bajate:** stale bread.

bájg/ë,-a *f.sh.* -a dung, droppings; **bajga kali (lope):** dungs of horse (of cow).

bajlóz,-i *m.sh.* -ë *vjet.* emissary.

bajonét/ë,-a *f.sh.* -a bayonet.

bajrák,-u *m.sh.* -ë *vjet.* flag.

bajraktár,-i *m.sh.* -ë chieftain.

bajúk/ë,-a *f.sh.* -a *zool.* waterfowl.

bakaláro,-ja *f. zool.* kipper, dried cod fish.

bakáll,-i *m.sh.* -bakej grocer.

bakelít,-i *m.* bakelite.

bakëm,-i *m.sh.* -e *bot.* logwood, campeachy wood.

bák/ër,-ri *m.* copper; **prej bakri:** copper; **ngjyrë bakri:** coppercoloured; **enë prej bakri:** brassy ware, brazen ware; **sulfat bakri:** copper sulphate, blue stone; **tel bakri:** copper wire.

bakërpunúes,-i *m.sh.* — coppersmith.

bákërt (i,e) *mb.* copper, brassy, brazen.

bakllavá,-ja *f.sh..* — baklava.

bakshísh,-i *m.sh.* -e tip, gratuity; **i jap bakshish dikujt:** to tip someone.

baktér,-i *m.sh.* -e *mjek.* bacterium.

bakteriológ,-u *m.sh.* -ë bacteriologist.

bakteriologjí,-a *f.* bacteriology.

balád/ë,-a *f.sh.* -a ballad.

balánc/ë,-a *f.sh.*-a balance; scales; **vë në balancë dy gjëra:** to weigh one thing against the other.

balancím,-i *m.* equilibrium, equipoise.

balancój *f.k.* to balance, to keep in equilibrium. — **balancohet** *f.jv.* to be in equipoise.

balásh,-e *mb.* roan; **kalë balash:** roan horse.

baldós/ë,-a *f.sh.* -a *zool.* badger.

balén/ë,-a *f.sh.* -a *zool.* whale.

balerín/ë,-a *f.sh.* -a ballerina.

balést/ër,-ra *f.sh.* -ra spring.

balét,-i *m.sh.* -e ballet.

balón/ë,-a *f.sh.* -a balloon; kite

balsám,-i *m.sh.* -e balm.

balsamím,-i *m.sh.* -e embalment.

balsamój *f.k.* to embalm. — **balsamohet** *f.jv.* to be embalmed.

balsamúar (i,e) *mb.* embalmed.

bált/ë,-a *f.sh:* -ëra mire, mud, slush, sludge; **baltë poçerie:** clay, potter's earth; **heq baltën:** to brush off the mud; **ndyhem me baltë:** to be sputted with mud; **spërkat rrobat me baltë:** to spatter one's clothes with mud; **me baltë:** muddy, miry, slushy, sludgy.

baltovín/ë,-a *f.sh.* -a quagmire, slough, deep mudy place.

ballafaqím,-i *m.sh.* -e confrontation.

ballafaqój *f.k.* to confront. — **ballafaqohem** *f.jv.* to be confronted *(me,* with).

ballamár,-i *m.sh.* -e *det.* mooring rope, mooring line; **lidh me ballamar:** to moor (a ship).

báll/ë,-i *m.sh.* -ë 1. *anat.* forehead. 2. front, face; **ballë për ballë:** face to face; **në ballë:** to the front; **në ballë të:** in the van of; **balli i një ndërtese:** frontage, facade; **i ballit:** frontal.

ballëhápur *mb.,* *nda'f.* with head erect.

ballgám,-i *m.sh.* -e shih **gëlbazë.**

ballkón,-i *m.sh.* -e balcony.

bállo,-ja *f.sh.* — ball, dance; **ballo me maska:** masked-ball.

ballóm/ë,-a *f.sh.* -a patch, rag, tatter; **u hedh ballomë këpucëve:** to patch (to cobble) the shoes.

ballúke,-t *f.sh.* forelocks.
bamírës,-i *m.sh.* – benefactor.
bamírës,-e *mb.* charitable, beneficent.
bamirësí,-a *f.* beneficence, charity.
bámj/e,-a *f.sh.* -e *bot.* okra.
banák,-u *m.sh.* -ë bar, counter.
banakiér,-i *m.sh.* -ë counter-man.
banál,-e *mb.* banal.
banalitét,-i *m.sh.* -e banality.
banán/e,-ia *f.sh.* -e *bot.* banana.
banderól/ë,-a *f.sh.* -a streamer.
bánd/ë,-a *f.sh.* -a *muz.* 1, brassband, band; **bandë ushtarake:** military band. 2. band; **bandë kusarësh:** gang of thieves; **bandë terroristësh:** gang of terrorists.
bandíll,-i *m.sh.* -ë gallant
bandít,-i *m.sh.* -ë bandit, brigand, freebooter, *amer.* gunman.
banés/ë,-a *f.sh.* -a dwelling house, residence; **banesë e përkohshme:** lodging. + *apartment* set side by side. /\
baním,-i *m.sh.* -e dwelling, residence, inhabitation; **banim i përkohshëm:** sojourn; **me banim në:** residing in; **ndërrim banimi:** change of residence.
bankét,-i *m.sh.* -e banquet.
bánk/ë,-a *f.sh.* -a 1. bank; **Banka e Shtetit Shqiptar:** Albanian State Bank. 2. *(bankë shkolle)* bench; *(pune)* work-bench.
bankënót/ë,-a *f.sh.* -a bank-note.
bankiér,-i *m.sh.* -ë banker.
banój *f.jk.* to dwell, to inhabit, to reside; **banoj përkohësisht në një vend:** to sojourn.
banór,-i *m.sh.* -ë inhabitant, resident, dweller, resider.
banúes,-i *m.sh.* – inhabitant .dweller.
banuesh/ëm (i,)-me(e) *mb.* inhabitable.
bánj/ë,-a *f.sh.* -a bath; **banjë me avull:** steam-bath; **banjë deti:** sea bathing; **banjë dielli:** sun-

bath; **banjë popullore:** bath house, public baths; **sallë banje:** bath-room; **rroba banje:** bathing-suit, bathing-costume, bathing-dress; **bëj banjë:** to bathe, to take (to have) a bath.
bar,-i *m.sh.* -ëra *bot.* grass; herb, weed; **bar i njomë:** grass, herb; **bar i thatë:** hay; **bar i keq:** weed; **korr bar:** to mow grass; **mullar bari (të thatë):** haycock, hayrick, haystack; **ahur bari:** barn.
bar-i *m.sh.*-na *mjek.* remedy, cure; medicine, medicament.
bar,-i *m.sh.* -e bar (for drinking); **bar-bufe:** bar-buffet.
barabár *ndajf.* 1. equally. 2. *sport.* equal in points, neck and neck, all square.
barabártë (i,e) *mb.* equal; **në mënyrë të barabartë:** equally.
barabís *f.k. krah.* to compare, to set side by side.
barabítj/e,-a *f. krah.* comparison.
barabítsh/ëm (i),-me(e) *mb. krah.* comparable.
barabrinjës,-e *mb. gjeom.* equilateral.
barák/ë,-a *f.sh.* -a barrack.
báras *ndajf.* equal, equally; equal to, equivalent to; **2 × 2 baras me 4 :** 2 × 2 is equal to 4.
baraslargësí,-a *f.* equidistance.
barasvlérsh/ëm(i), -me(e) *mb* equivalent.
barazí,-a *f.* equality.
barazój *f.k.* to equalize, to make even (equal). – **barazohem** *f.jv.* to equalize; *sport.* to tie.
barazúesh/ëm (i),-me (e) *mb.* that can be equalled (to, with).
barbár,-i *m.sh.* -ë barbarian.
barbár,-e *mb.* barbarious, cruel, atrocious, inhuman, uncivilised.
barbarísht *ndajf.* cruelly, atrociously, in a barbarous manner.

barbaríz/ëm,-mi *m.sh.* -ma barbarism, cruelty, atrocity.
barbú/n,-i *m.sh.* -nj *zool.* flounder.
bar-bufé,-ja *f.sh.* – bar-buffet.
barbúnj/ë,-a *f.sh.* -a *bot.* kidneybean.
bardhák,-u *m.sh.* -ë glass, drinking-glass, cup.
bardhém/ë(i),-e(e) *mb.* whitish.
bárdhë (i,e) *mb.* 1. white. 2. happy; **ditë të bardha:** happy days.
bárdh/ë (e),-a(e) *f.sh.* -a (të)1. white; **vishem me të bardha:** to be dressed in white, to be in white. 2. *anat.* **e bardha e syrit:** the white of the eye.
bardhësí,-a *f.* whiteness.
bardhósh,-e *mb.* lily-white, snowwhite.
barél/ë,-a *f.sh.* -a stretcher.
barés *f.jk.* to walk.
barésh/ë,-a *f.sh.* -a shepherdess.
barí,-u *m.sh.* -nj shepherd, herdsman; **bari dhish:** goat¡herd; **bari lopësh:** cowherd.
barísht/e,-ja *f.sh.* -e greens, herbage.
baritón,-i *m.sh.* -ë *muz.* barytone.
baritór,-e *mb.* pastoral; **jetë baritore:** pastoral life.
bark,-u *m.sh.* **barqe** 1. *anat.* belly, abdomen; **zgavra e barkut:** abdomen; **vë bark:** to acquire a corporation; **dhimbje barku:** belly-ache. 2. *mjek.* diarrhea; **më heq barku:** to have the diarrhea; **dal bark:** to have frequent evacuations.
barkaléc,-i *m.sh.* -ë bellied man.
barkaléc,-e *mb.* bellied, pot-bellied, big-bellied.
bárkas *ndajf.* flat on one's belly; **bie barkas:** to lie flat on one's belly (on one's stomach).
bárk/ë,-a *f.sh.* -a shih varkë.
barkmádh,-e *mb.* big-bellied, pot-bellied.

barkór,-e *mb.* ventral.
barkór/e,-ja *f.sh.* -e girth,saddlegirth.
barkthátë *mb.* barren: **grua barkthatë:** barren woman.
barkúsh/e,-ja *f.sh.* -e *anat.* ventricle.
barnatór/e,-ja *f.sh.* -e pharmacy, dispensary, drug-store.
barngrënës,-i *m.sh.* – herbivore.
barngrënës,-e *mb.* herbivorous.
baromét/ër,-ri *m.sh.* -ra barometer, weather-glass; **barometri tregon shi:** the barometer points to rain.
bart *f.k..* to carry, to convey, to transport, to remove, to transfer (goods, etc. from one place to another); **bart plaçkat e shtëpisë:** to remove goods and chattels (homethings); **bart mallra:** to convey (to transport) goods. – **bartem** *f.jv.* to remove, to change residence, to move to some other place; **bartem me shtëpi:** to remove.
bártës,-i *m.sh..* – carrier, conveyer, transporter.
bártj/e,-a *f.sh.* -e carriage, conveyance, transport; **shpenzime të bartjes:** freight charges.
barút,-i *m.* powder.
bárr/ë,-a *f.sh.* -ë 1. burden, load. 2. duty, task. 3. pregnancy; **grua me barrë:** pregnant woman, expectant mother; **jam me barrë:** to be with child, to be in the family way, to be pregnant; **mbetem me barrë:** to become (to get) pregnant. – *Lok.* **nuk e vlen barra qiranë:** it is not worth the trouble.
barrikád/ë,-a *f.sh.* -a barricade.
bárrsë *mb.* big (with young); **lopë barrsë:** cow with calf; **pelë barrsë:** mare in foal.
bas,-i *m.sh.* -ë *muz.* bass,
basketbóll,-i *m.* basket-ball.

basketbollíst,-i *m.sh.* **-ë** basketball player.

básm/ë,-a *f.sh.* **-a** chintz, *amer.* calico.

bast,-i *m.sh.* **-e** bet, wager; **vë bast:** to bet, to lay a bet, to wager.

bastárd,-i *m.sh.* **-ë** bastard, mongrel.

bastárd,-e *mb.* not pure, mixed; **qen bastard:** mongrel, crossbred.

bastardím,-i *m.* bastardization, degeneration; **bastardim i një gjuhe:** bastardization of a language.

bastardój *f.k.* to bastardize. — **bastardohem** *f.jv.* to degenerate, to deteriorate.

bastís *f.k.* to raid. **bastísj/e,-a** *f.sh.* **-e** *drejt.* raid; **bëj një bastisje:** to make a raid on (into), to carry out a raid.

bastún,-i *m.sh.* **-ë** walking stick, cane; **qëlloj dikë me bastun:** to cane someone, to beat someone with a cane.

bash,-i *m.sh.* **-e** *det.* stem (of a ship).

bashibozúk,-u *m.sh.* **-ë** bashibazouk (a volunteer or irregular in the Turkish army).

bashkarísht *ndajf.* in common, together, conjointly, jointly.

bashkatdhetár,-i *m.sh.* **-ë** compatriot, fellow-countryman.

báshkë *ndajf.* jointly, together, collectively, in common; **të gjithë bashkë:** all together.

báshk/ë,-a *f.sh.* **-a** fleece, fleecewool.

bashkëbaním,-i *m.* cohabitation.

bashkëbanój *f.jk.* to cohabit.

bashkëbanúes,-i *m.sh.* — cohabitant.

bashkëbisedím,-i *m.sh.* **-e** conversation, colloquy.

bashkëbisedój *f.jk.* to converse, to confer with, to discourse' to talk with.

bashkëbisedúes,-i *m.sh.* — interlocutor.

bashkëfajësí,-a *f.* complicity.

bashkëfajtór,-i *m.sh.* **-ë** accomplice; **jam bashkëfajtor në një krim:** to be party to a crime.

bashkëfjalím,-i *m.sh.* **-e** shih **bashkëbisedim.**

bashkëfólës,-i *m.sh.* — shih **bashkëbisedues.**

bashkëfshatár,-i *m.sh.* **-ë** fellow-countryman.

bashkëjetés/ë,-a *f.* coexistence; **bashkëjetesë e paligjshme** *(ma një grua):* concubinage.

bashkëjetój *f.jk.* to coexist.

bashkëkóhës,-i *m.sh.* — coeval, contemporary.

bashkëlojtár,-i *m.sh.* **-ë** partner (in a game).

bashkëluftëtár,-i *m.sh.* **-ë** comrade in arms, companion of arms.

bashkëngjís *f.k.* to conjoin, to subjoin. — **bashkëngjitet** *f.jv.* to be conjoined.

bashkëngjítur *ndajf.* here included, here inclosed; **sendet (fletët) bashkëngjitur:** enclosures.

bashkënxënës,-i *m.sh.* — schoolmate, schoolfellow.

bashkëpjestár,-i *m.sh.* **-ë** jointpartaker, associate.

bashkëpronár,-i *m.sh.* **-ë** jointowner.

bashkëpronësí,-a *f.* jointownership.

bashkëpunëtór,-i *m.sh.* **-ë** collaborator, co-operator.

bashkëpuním,-i *m.* collaboration, co-operation.

bashkëpunój *f.jk.* to collaborate, to co-operate.

bashkëqéni/e,-a *f.* coexistence.

bashkëqytetár,-i *m.sh.* -ë fellow-citizen.
bashkërendís *f.k.* to co-ordinate. — bashkërenditet *f.jo.* to be co-ordinated.
bashkërendítj/e,-a *f.* co-ordination
bashkësí,-a *f.sh.* — community; bashkësi primitive: primitive community.
bashkëshórt,-i *m sh.* -ë husband, spouse.
bashkëshórt/e,-ja *f.sh.* -e wife, spouse.
bashkëshortór,-e *mb.* conjugal, matrimonial, connubial, marital; jetë bashkëshortore; married life; lidhje bashkëshortore: marriage ties.
bashkëtingëllór/e,-ja *f.sh.* -e *gram.* consonant; bashkëtingëllore dhëmbore: fricative consonant.
bashkëtrashëgimí,-a *f.* co-heirship, parcenary.
bashkëtrashëgimtar,-i *m.sh.* -ë co-heir, joint-heir, parcener.
bashkëthemelúes,-i *m.sh.* — cofounder.
bashkëveprím,-i *m.sh.* -e co-operation, joint act.
bashkëveprój *f.jk.* to co-operate, to act jointly.
bashkí,-a *f.sh.* — 1. town-hall, municipal buildings. 2 municipality.
bashkiák,-e *mb.* municipal; anëtar i këshillit bashkiak: alderman; sekretar i këshillit bashkiak: town-clerk.
bashkím,-i *m.sh.* -e 1. union; bashkimet profesionale: trade-union. 2. concord, harmony (of people). 3. *(i dy zogjve femër e mashkull)*: copulation (of birds); *(i dy gjymtyrëve)* articulation, joint, juncture (of bones). 4. *polit.* (*i dy a më shumë*

shteteve të pavarura): confederation: *(i shumë shteteve të vogla në një qeveri qendrore)* federation. 5. *fiz. (i dy trupave)* adherence, adhesion.
bashkój *f.k.* 1. to unite, to connect, to link, to associate, to join. 2. to rally, to assemble 3. to adhere. 4. *(një çift zogjsh)* to copulate. — bashkohem *f.jv.* to unite with; to join with; bashkohem me dikë: to join someone; bashkohem me mendimin e dikujt: to comply with, to agree with, to share the same opinion with.
báshku (së) *ndajf.* together, collectively; të marrë së bashku: taken together.
bashkúar (i,e) *mb.* 1. (familje) harmonious (family). 2. joined, united; me duar të bashkuara; with clasped hands.
bashkudhëtár,-i *m.sh.* -ë fellow traveller, co-traveller, companion of trip.
baták,-u *m.sh.* -e slough, mire, cesspool.
batakçí,-u *m.sh.* -nj swindler, defrauder, rogue, sharper, grafter.
batakçillë/k,-ku *m. sh.* -qe cheat, swindle, fraud, roguery; me batakçillëk: fraudulently; bëj batakçillëqe: to cheat, to swindle, to rook, to defraud.
batalión,-i *m.sh.* -e *usht.* battalion.
batáll,-e I. *mb.* useless, worthless. II *ndajf.* më lë batall *(një vegël etj.)*: to go out of use.
bata níj/e,-a *f.sh.* -e blanket, bedspread, bedcloth.
bataré,-ja *f.sh.* — volley (of gun shots).
baterí,-a *f.sh.* — 1. *usht.* battery. 2. *fiz.* electric battery.

batërdí,-a *f.* ruin catastrophe, destruction, devastion.
batërdís, *f.k.* to ruin, to destroy, to ravage, to devastate, to lay waste — batërdisem *f.jv.* to be ruined (destroyed, ravaged, devastated).
batíc/ë,-a *f.sh.* -a high tide; baticë dhe zbaticë: tide.
batís *f.k., f.jk.* shih shemb.
batísj/e,-a *f.sh.* -e shih shembje.
báth/ë,-a *f.sh.* -ë *bot.* bean.
baúl/e,-ja *f.sh.* -e travelling box, trunk
báxh/ë,-a *f.sh.* -a sky-light, dormer-window; dritare baxhe: gable window.
báxho,-ja *f.sh.* — cheese dairy.
bazamént,-i *m.sh.* -e basis, basement (of a building), the ground work.
báz/ë,-a *f.sh.* -a 1. lower part, foot base. 2. *usht.* base of operations; bazë ajrore; airbase; bazë detare: naval base. 3. *kim.* base. 4. basis, foundation; pa bazë: baseless, groundless, ungrounded, unfounded, without foundation; dyshime pa bazë: ungrounded suspicions. në bazë të nenit: in virtue of the article. 5. source, resource; bazë materiale: material resources.
bazój *f.k.* to base, to found, to ground. — bazohem *f.jv.* to base oneself on, to depend on, to rest (on); to rely on; bazohemi në forcat tona: we rely on our own forces.
be,-ja *f.sh.* — oath; bëj be: to swear, to take an oath.
beb/e, -ja *f.sh.* -e baby.
béb/e,-ja *f.sh.* -e pupil, apple (of the eye).
bébëz,-a *f.sh.* -a *anat.* iris; bebëza e syrit: the pupil (the apple, the ball) of the eye.

béfas *ndajf.* suddenly, on (all of) a sudden, by surprise, unexpectedly.
befasí,-a *f.* surprise, suddeness; zë në befasi: to take by surprise, to surprise, to catch unawares; zihem në befasi: to be caught napping.
befasísh/ëm,(i),-me(e) *mb.* unexpected, sudden.
befasísht *ndajf.* on a sudden, unawares, unexpectedly.
beft,-i *m.* watchfulness; rri me beft: to be on one's guard.
begatí,-a *f.sh.* — abundance, prosperity.
begátsh/ëm (i),-me(e) *mb.* abundant, prosperous, opulent; tokë e begatshme: fertile ground; vendi i begatshëm: prosperous country.
begenís *f.k.* to deign, to condescend; ajo kaloi edhe as që begenisi të më hidhte sytë (të më shihte): she passed by without deigning to look at me.
begóni/e,-a *f.sh.* -e *bot.* begonia.
beh(ia)*f.jk.* to arrive unexpectedly.
behár,-i *m.sh.* -e *vjet.* summer.
behárna,-t *f.sh.* spices, condiments.
be/j,-u *m.sh.* -jlerë bey (formerly a landlord, a landsman).
bejlé/g,-gu *m.sh.* -gje *vjet.* single combat, duel; thërras dikë në bejleg: to call someone out, to throw down the glove.
bekím,-i *m.sh.* -e blessing; jap bekimin: to give the blessing.
bekój *f.k.* to bless.
bekúar (i,e) *mb.* blessed.
bel,-i *m.sh.* -a spade; punoj me bel: to spade; to dig with a spade; punim me bel: spade work.
belá,-ja *f.sh.* — annoyance; shpëtoj nga një bela: to get out of a scrape.
belbacák,-u *m.sh.* -ë stammerer, stutterer.

belbëzím,-i *m.sh.* **-e** stammering, stuttering, lisping.
belbëzoj *f.jk.* to stammer, to stutter, to lisp, to falter.
belg,-u *m.sh.* -ë Belgian.
belg,-e *mb.* Belgian.
belhóllë *mb.* wasp-waisted.
belúshk/ë,-a *f,sh.* -a *zool.* red cohortleberry.
belvedér/e,-ja *f.sh.* belvedere; observation tower.
benevrékë,-t *m.sh.* underpants.
beng,-u *m.sh.* **bengje** *zool.* lory.
benzín/ë,-a *f.* benzine, amer. gazolene.
benzól,-i *m.* benzol.
beqár,-i *m.sh.* **-ë** bachelor; **jetë beqari:** celibacy life.
beqar,-e *mb.* unmarried, celibate; **burrë beqar:** unmarried (single) man.
beqári,-a *f.* bachelorhood, celibacy, single state.
berbér,-i *m.sh.* **-ë** barber, shaver. hair-dresser.
bereqét,-i *m.sh.* **-e** harvest; **mbledh bereqetin:** to get in (to gather in) the harvest, to harvest.
berihá,-ja *f.* *vjet.* alarm, alert.
berónj/ë,-a *f.sh.* -a 1. *bot.* hollytree. 2. barren woman.
berr,-i *m.sh.* -a *zool.* smaller livestock, lamb.
bés/ë,-a *f.* 1. faith, oath; **jap besën;** to pledge one's faith, to plight one's troth; **mbaj besën:** to keep one's faith; **shkel besën:** to break faith. 2. belief, confidence, trust; **i zë besë:** to believe, to trust, to take on trust, to give credit; **që zë besë lehtë:** credulous, easy of belief; **që nuk zë besë:** unbelieving, incredulos; **që nuk i zihet besë:** unreliable, treacherous. -*Lok.* ha **në besë:** not to keep faith with, to break one's word (promise),

to go back on one's word. **besëlídhës,-i** *m.sh.* - ally. **besëlídhj/e,-a** *f.sh.* **-e** 1. pledge, bond. 2. alliance.
besëpákë *mb.* incredulous, distrustful, unbelieving.
besím,-i *m.sh.* **-e** 1. confidence, faith, trust, belief; **njeri i besimit:** a man of confidence; **kam besim te dikush:** to have trust in, to believe in, to confide in someone; **besim në vetvete:** self-confidence, selfassurance; **besim i terpruar:** overconfidence; **i lë diçka dikujt në besim:** to entrust something to someone. 2. credit; **humbas besimin e dikujt:** to lose all credit.
besimtár.-i *m.sh.* **-ë** believer.
besimtár,-e *mb.* pious, devout.
besnik,-e *mb.* faithful, loyal, devoted, trustworthy; **shoku yt besnik;** your faithful friend.
besnikërí,-a *f.* faithfulness, loyalty, fidelity; **me besnikëri:** devoutly, with devotion; **besnikëri ndaj idealeve:** adherence to the ideals.
besnikërísht *ndajf.* faithfully, loyally.
besój *f.k.* 1. to trust, to entrust, to believe; **i besoj dikujt;** to trust in someone, to entrust someone; **i besoj dikujt një mision:** to entrust someone with a mission; **bëj dikë të besojë:** to make someone believe; **besoménil** believe me! 2. to think; **a besoni se...?** do you think that ...?; **besoj se po:** I think so; **nuk e besoj:** I don't think so. - **besohet** *f.jv.* **nuk më besohet:** I dont believe it.
bestytní,-a *f.sh.* - superstition.
besuesh/ëm **(i),-me(e)** *mb.* 1. credible. 2. reliable, trustworthy (person).

betéj/ë,-a f.sh. -a battle; nis be-
tejën me armikun: to give
battle to the enemy.
betím,-i m.sh. -e swear, oath, vow;
betim i rremë: false oath; bëj
betimin: to take an oath, to
swear; shkel betimin: to break
an oath, to forswear oneself.
betój f.k. to make swear. – betohem f.jv. to swear, to take
an oath: betohem solemnisht:
to vow solemnly; betohem në
të rremë: to swear falsely; të
betohem! I swear!
betón,-i m.sh. -e concrete, beton.
betonarmé,-ja f.sh. – reinforced
concrete, ferro-concrete.
betoniér/ë,-a f.sh. -a ndërt. con-
crete-mixer.
betoním,-i m. ndërt. concreting.
betonój f.k. to concrete.
betùar (i,e) mb. sworn; armik
betuar: sworn enemy.
bezdí,-a f. annoyance, discomfort,
disturbance.
bezdís f.k. to annoy, to distrub;
më falni që po ju bezdis:
excuse my disturbing you. –
bezdisem f.jv. to be troubled;
mos u bezdisni: please don't
move, don't trouble yourself.
bezdíssh/ëm(i),-me(e) mb. troublesome, tiresome, irksome, annoying; njeri i bezdisshëm:
tiresome person.
béz/e,-ja f.sh. -e lawn.
bézhë mb. beige. '
bëj f.k., f.jk. (p.t. bëra, p.p. bërë)
1. to do, to make; bëj një shërbim (detyrat, një ushtrim,
një përkthim): to do a service (the homework, en exercise, a translation); bëj një
gabim: to make a mistake;
furrtari bën bukë: the baker
makes bread; këpucari bën këpucë: the shoemaker makes
shoes. 2. bëj të ditur: to make

known; bëj një vizitë: to pay
a visit; bëj një kompliment: to
pay a compliment. 3. bëj luftë:
to make, (to wage) war; bëj
të mjerë: to render unhappy. –
Lok. bëj ç'është e mundur:
to do one's best; bën ftohtë:
it is cold; bën nxehtë: it is
hot; aq më bën: I don't care
a bit; nuk kam ç'ti bëj: there is
no help for him; there is nothing
I can do for him; bëj sipas kokës: to have (to get) one's
own way; bëj edhe me pak:
to make (to do) with little;
bëj edhe pa (diçka): not to be
in need of (something); bëj
për nga dera: to make for
the door; bëj gjoja, bëj sikur:
to make as if: çfarë bëni?
what are you doing?; çfarë të
bëj unë tani? what shall I
do now?: ka akoma shumë
për të bërë: there is much
work to be done; e bëra vetë
(me forcat e mia): I did it
by myself. – bëhem f.jv. to become, to grow; bëhem i fortë:
to grow (to become) strong;
përse bëhet fjalë? what is
the matter?, what is the question (the business in hand)?;
mirë t'i bëhet: it serves him
right; varrimi do të bëhet
nesër: the burial will take place
tomorrow; të bëhet ç'të bëhet!
come what may!; po bëhet
vonë: it is getting late; ç'u
bë me të? what became of
him?
bërë done, made (p.p. of the
verb bëj).
bërsí,-a f.sh. – marc (o grapes,
olives, etc.).
bërtás f.jk. 1. to shout, to cry,
to cry out; ai zu të bërtis-
te që të tërhiqte vëmendjen
e kalimtarëve: he started

shouting to attract the attention of the passers-by. 2. *(flas me zë të lartë)* to shout; **mos bërtit se nuk jam shurdh**: don't shout, I'm not deaf; **bërtas me sa mund**: to shout (to cry) at the top of one's voice.
bërtítur (e),-a (e) *.sh.. -a(të)* shout, cry.
bërthám/ë,-a *.sh. -a* kernel, fruit stone.
bërthamór,-e *mb. fiz.* nuclear; **energji bërthamore**: nuclear energy (power).
bërxóll/ë,-a *f.sh. -a* chop; **bërxollë derri (shqerre)**: porc (mutton) chop.
bërrýl,-i *m.sh. -a* 1. elbow; **mbështetem mbi bërryl**: to lean on one's elbow; **çik me bërryl**: to elbow; **çaj me bërryla**: a) to elbow one's way forward; b) *fig.* to elbow one's way ahead. 2. *(rruge, etj).* sharp bend, sharp turn; **bërryl lumi**: meander; **lumi bën një bërryl**: the river makes a sharp turn.
bësh/ëm (i),-me(e) *mb.* plump, corpulent, buxom.
bëzáj *f.k. krah.* : o speak, to call; **i bëzaj dikujt**: to call someone.
biberón,-i *m.sh. -ë* sucking-bottle, soother, feeding-bottle.
bíb/ë,-a *f.sh. -a* 1. *zool. (pate)* gosling; *(rose)* duckling. 2. *fig.* silly girl.
bibliofíl,-i *m.sh. -ë* bibliophile, lover of books.
bibliográf,-i *m.sh. -ë* bibliographer
bibliografí,-a *f.sh. -a* bibliography.
bibliotekár,-i *m.sh. -ë* librarian.
biblioték/ë,-a *f.sh. -a* 1. library; **biblioteka e qytetit**: town library. 2. bookcase, bookstand.
biçák,-u *m.sh. -ë* pocket-knife, penknife, jack-knife.
biçiklét/ë,-a *f.sh. -a* bicycle, bike;

biçikletë me motor: motorbicycle; **timon biçiklete**: handle-bar.
bidón,-i *m.sh. -ë* drum, tin, *amer.* can.
bíe *f.jk.* (p.t. **rashë**, p.p. **rënë**) 1. to fall, to tumble, to fall down, to come down, to drop; **bie përdhé**; to fall, to fall down, to tumble over; **pjata i ra nga dora**: the plate dropped from her hand. 2. *(shi, borë)* to fall, to come down (rain, snow); **binte një dëborë e dendur**: a thick snow was falling; **bie borë (dëborë)**: it snows; **bie shi**: it rains; **bie breshër**: it hails. 3. *(pakësohet, zbret)* to go down, to come down, to decrease, to drop, to fall; **temperatura ra nën zero**: the temperature dropped (fell) below zero. 4. **bie nata**: night is falling; **bie dielli**: the sun rises (peeps through). 5. **bie të fle**: to go to bed. 6. **bie në dashuri**: to fall in love. 7. **bie ora**: the clock strikes; **bie zilja**: the bell rings. 8. **bie në luftë**: to fall fighting. 9. **bie në gabim**: to fall into error. 10. **bie viktimë e dikujt**: to fall a prey to someone. 11. **bie erë të keqe**: it smells stink, it stinks. 12. **bie në dorë të armikut**: to fall into the hands of the enemy. 13. **i bie (dikujt, diçkaje)**: to strike, to hit, to beat, to knock (someone, something); **i bie daulles**: to beat the drum; **i bie derës**: to knock at the door; **i bie ziles**: to ring the bell. 14. **i bie një vegle muzikore**: to play a musical instrument. 15. **i bie dikujt prapa**: to pursue (to follow) someone. 16. **bie në sy të dikujt**: to attract someone's attention. 17.

bie keq (ngushtë): to be in a difficult situation, to be in a tight spot (corner), to get into a scrape

bie *f.k.* (p.t. **prura,** p.p. **prurë)** to bring; to carry, to bear; **bie lajme:** to bring news; **bie me vete:** to bring, to fetch; **i bie dikujt një dhuratë:** to bring someone a gift; **ia bie në majë të hundës dikujt:** to put (to get, to set) someone's back up.

biéll/ë.-a *f.sh.* -a *mjek* piston rod, connecting rod.

bifk/ë,-a *f.sh.* -a *bot.* spring, slip, offset, offshoot; **lëshon bifka:** to bud, to shoot, to sprout.

bifték,-u *m.sh.* -ë beefsteak.

bigamí,-a *f.* bigamy.

bíg/ë,-a *f.sh.* -a 1. prong, spike (of a fork). 2. **bigë lundruese:** floating crane.

bigëzím,-i *m.sh.* -e bifurcation, ramification, embranchement, fork.

bigëzój ⸱ *.k.* to cause to branch, to bifurcate. − **bigëzohet** *f.jv.* to fork, to bifurcate.

bigudí,-a *f.sh.* − curler, hair-roller.

bíj/ë,-a *f.sh.* -a daughter; **bijë e gjetur:** stepdaughter; **ime bijë:** my daughter.

bijór,-e *mb.* filial.

bilánc,-i *m.sh.* -e *fin.* balance-sheet; **bëj bilancin:** to draw up the balance-sheet.

bilárdo-ja *m.sh.* − 1. *(loja)* billiards; **luaj bilardo:** to play biliards; *stekë bilardoje;* billiard-cue. 2. billiard-table.

bilbíl,-i *m.sh.* -a 1. *zool.* nightingale. 2. whistle.

bilé *pj.* even, or rather, or better; in fact, indeed; **bile po vij andej:** or better, I'll drop by; **ajo e do, bile e adhuron:** she loves him, in fact she worships him; **ai pi duhan vazhdimisht, bile**

edhe në shtrat: he smokes continually, even in bed.

biletarí,-a *f.sh.* − ticket-window; booking-office.

bilét/ë.-a *f.sh.* -a ticket; **biletë treni:** railway (train) ticket; **biletë avioni:** air (plane) ticket; **biletë vajtje ardhje;** return ticket; **kontrollor biletash:** ticket-collector, gate man; **biletë banke njësterlinëshe:** 1 pound note; **pres (blej) biletë:** to take (to buy) a ticket.

bíl/ë,-a *f.sh.* -a billiard ball.

bím/ë,-a *f.sh.* -ë *bot.* plant; **bimë aromatike;** herb, aromatic plant; **bimë foragjere:** forage (fodder) plant; **bimë mjekësore;** medicinal plant; **bimë industriale:** industrial crops; **bimë zbukuruese:** ornamental plant; **bimë helmuese;** hemlock; **bimë pranverore:** spring crops.

bimësí,-a *f.* vegetation **bimësia e një vendi:** flora.

bimór,-e *mb.* vegetable; **bota bimore:** the vegetable kingdom.

biná,-ja *f.sh.* − building.

binár,-i *m.sh.* -ë 1. beam; joist, rafter; **binar hekurudhe:** railway-bed, rail, track; **del (treni) nga binarët:** to jump the metals; to be derailed. − *Lok.* **dal nga binarët:** to follow the wrong course, to go astray.

bind *f.k.* to convince, to persuade. − **bindem** *f.jv.* to be convinced; **i bindem (dikujt):** to yield, to submit; to obey (someone), to be obedient to (someone); **i bindem një urdhri:** to comply with an order.

bindës,-e *mb.* convincing, persuasive; **arsye bindëse:** convincing arguments.

bíndj/e,-a *f.sh.* -e 1. conviction, persuasion; **kam bindjen se:** am convinced that. 2. obedien-

ce; dutifulness, submission; **me bindje:** obediently, dutifully.
bíndur (i,e) *mb.* 1. convinced, persuaded; **jam i bindur se:** I am convinced (I feal sure) that. 2. obedient, docile, dutiful; submitted, yielded; **nxënës i bindur;** dutiful pupil.
binják,-u *m.sh.* **-ë** twin.
binják,-e *mb.* twin; **vëllezër binjakë:** twin brothers.
biografí,-a *f.sh.* – biography.
biografík,-e *mb.* biographic, biographical.
biologjí,-a *f.* biology.
bir,-i *m.sh.* **-bij** son; **bir i gjetur:** stepson; **bir i vetëm:** an only son.
bír/ë,-a *f.sh.* **-a** hole; **shpoj (hap) një birë:** to cut (to bore, to prick) a hole.
birój *f.k.* to hole, to make holes, to perforate.
birúc/ë,-a *f.sh.* **-a** cell.
birrarí,-a *f.sh.* – beer-house, beershop, ale-house.
bírr/ë,-a *f.* ale, beer; **fabrikë birre:** brewery; **birrë e zezë:** porter, dark ale.
bis! *pasth.* once more! again!, encore!, bis!
biséd/ë,-a *f.sh.* **-a** talk, conversation, discussion; **bisedë e përzemërt:** cordial talk, heart to heart talk; **bisedë intime:** private (confidential) conversation: **bisedë familjare;** family talk: **bisedë e shthurur:** smut talk, obscene talk; **bisedë e shkurtër;** small talk; **hap bisedë, zë bisedë, hyj në bisedë:** to engage (to enter) into conversation.
bisedím,-i *m.sh.* **-e** conversation; negotiation; **bisedime paraprake:** pourparlers; **zhvilloj bisedime:** to conduct negotia-

tions; **ndërpres (pres) bisedimet:** to break off negotiations.
bisedój *f.jk.* to talk, to converse, to dicourse with, to confer with, to hold a conversation. – **bisedohet** *f.jv.* to be talked about (of); **përse bisedohet?** what is the subject (the topic) of the conversation?, what are you talking about?
bisk,-u *m.sh.* **bisqe** *bot.* green shoot.
biskót/ë,-a *f.sh.* **-a** cookie, biscuit.
bístër *mb.* 1. sour; **kumbull bistër:** sour plum. 2. *fig.* sagacious, acute; **grua bistër:** sagacious woman.
bísh/ë,-a *f.sh.* **-a** wild beast, wild animal.
bísht,-i *m.sh.* **-a** 1. tail (of an animal); **bisht dhelpre:** tail of a fox. 2. handle; **bisht furçe (fshese, lopate etj.)** handle of a brush (of a broom, of a shovel, etc.); **i vë bisht lopatës:** to put a handle to the shovel. 3. **bisht pene:** penholder. 4. **bisht cigareje:** butt of cigarette. – *Lok.* **shoh me bishtin e syrit:** to look from the corner of the eye; **i bëj bisht punës:** to shirk one's job; **mbledh bishtin:** to turn the tail, to go away.
bishtáj/ë,-a *f.sh.* **-a** *bot.* 1. kidneybean, string bean, French-bean. 2. pod.
bishtaléc,-i *m.sh.* **-a** plait, braid.
bishtatúndës,-i *m.sh.* – *zool.* wagtail.
bishtór/e,-ja *f.sh.* **-e** long-tailed stewpan.
bishtúk,-u *m.sh.* **-ë** long-tailed oil lamp.
bitúm,-i *m.sh.* **-e** bitumen; **me bitum:** bituminous.
bixhóz,-i *m.* gambling; **luaj bi-**

xhoz: to gamble, to play cards.
bixhozçí,-u *m.sh.* -nj gambler.
bizéle,-ja *f.sh.* -e *bot. (bima)*
pea *(kokrrat)* grean peas.
bíz/ë,-a *f.sh.* -a awl.
bjéshk/ë,-a *f.sh.* -ë alpine land,
highlands.
bjond,-e *mb.* fair (of hairs); **djalë bjond:** fair-haired boy.
blegërím/ë,-a *f.sh.* -a bleating
(of sheep), bleat.
blegërín *f.jk.* to bleat.
blegtór,-i *m.sh.* -ë stock-breeder.
blegtorál,-e *mb.* pertaining to
stock-farming; **prodhime blegtorale:** animal products.
blegtorí,-a *f.* stock-breeding, animal husbandry.
blej *f.k. (p.t.* **bleva** *p.p.* **blerë)**
to buy, to purchase. — Lok.
ia blej mendjen: to fathom
someone's intentions, to read
someone's thoughts.
blérës,-i *m.sh.* — buyer, purchaser.
blérës,-e *mb.* purchasing; **fuqi
blerëse:** purchasing power.
blerím,-i *m.* evergreen, greenery,
verdure.
blérj/e,- *f.sh.* -e purchase.
blértë (i,e) *mb.* green, verdant; **që
vjen në të blertë:** greenish.
bletár,-i *m.sh.* -ë bee-keeper, api-
culturist, apiarist.
bletarí,-a *f.* bee-keeping.
blét/ë,a *f.sh.* -ë *zool.* bee, honey-
bee; **mbretëresha e bletëve:**
queen-bee; **bletë punëtore:**
working-bee; **zgjua bletësh:**
bee-hive; **luzmë bletësh:** swarm
cluster of bees; **mashkulli i
bletës:** drone.
blil imperative of the verb **blej.**
bli,-ri *m.sh.* -rë *bot.* linden-tree,
lime-tree; **lule bliri:** linden flower.
bli,-ni *m.sh.* -nj *zool.* sturgeon.
blof,-i *m.sh.* -e bluff.
blój/ë,-a *f.* shih **bluarje.**

blóz/ë,-a *f.sh.* -a soot; **e zëzë
blozë:** sooty.
blu *mb.* blue; **që vjen si në blu:**
bluish.
blúaj *f.k.* 1. to grind, to mill;
bluaj grurin: to grind wheat.
2. to crush; **bluaj me dhëmbë:**
to crush with one's teeth. 3.
fig. **bluaj diçka në kokë:** to
chew the cud, to ruminate;
**bluaj mendime të zymta në
kokë:** to be in the blues, to
be in low spirits.
blúarj/e,-a *f.* grinding.
bluáshk/ë,-a *f.sh.* -a chip, shaving.
blúz/ë,-a *f.sh.* -a blouse, shirt;
bluzë marinari: sailor's jacket; **bluzë punëtori;** surtout.
bllok,-u *m.sh.* -blloqe 1. block,
lump; **bllok betoni:** concrete
block. 2. **bllok shënimesh:**
memorandum block. writing-
pad. 3. *polit.* block, coalition
(of parties, states); **bllok ushtarak:** military block. 4. **bllok
banesash:** block of houses.
bllokád/ë,-a *f.sh.* -a blockade;
çaj bllokadën (ushtarake): to
run the blockade; **çaj bllokadën
(ekonomike):** to smash (to
break through) the economic
blockade.
bllokím,-i *m.* 1. blockage, obstruction; **bllokim i pagave:**
wage freeze. 2. congestion (of
traffic), traffic jam.
bllokój *f.k.* 1. *tek.* to lock, to
clamp (piece of machinery);
bllokoj rrotat: to lock the
wheels. 2. to block, to obstruct (a road, etc.); to blockade (a port). 3. *fin.* **bllokoj
pagat:** to freeze wages. — **bllo-
kohem** *f.jv.* to jam, to get jam-
med.
bóa *f.sh.* — *zool.* boa.
bobín/ë,-a *f.sh.* -a 1. *el.* coil;

bobinë induksioni; spark coil.
2. spool, roll (of film).
bóc/ë,-a *f.sh.* -**a** 1. bottle, flask.
2. *polig.* proof.
bóç/e,-ja *f.sh.* -**e** *bot.* cone; **boçe pambuku:** cotton cone.
bodéc,-i *m.sh.* -**ë** goad, prod; **shpoj me bodec:** to goad, to prick with a goad.
bodrúm,-i *m.sh.* -**e** cellar; **bodrum i një ndërtese:** basement, basement flat.
bojatís *f.k.* 1. to colour, to tinge. 2. to paint up; to cover (to coat) with paint. 3. to polish; **bojatis këpucët:** to black one's shoes. – **bojatisem** *f.jv.* to be coloured (tinged); to be covered (coated) with paint.
bojatísj/e,-a *f.sh.* -**e** 1. colouring. 2. painting.
bojaxhí,-u *m.sh.* -**nj** white-washer, house-painter.
bój/ë,-a *f.sh.* -**ëra** 1. colour, tint; **lyej me bojë:** to paint, to tinge; **bojë këpucësh:** shoe polish; **bojë kine:** indian ink; **bojë shtypi:** printer's ink; **bojë shkrimi:** ink; **bojra uji:** water colours; **bojra vaji:** oil-colours, oil-paints; **ruhuni nga bojaI** mind the paintI – *Lok.* **i doli boja:** he has been discredited, he has shown his face (colours), he is seen in his true colours. 2. colour; **bojë jargavani:** mauve colour; **bojë qielli:** sky-colour, azure; **bojë trëndafili:** pinky, rose colour; **bojë e kuqe e mbyllur:** dark red.
bojëgják,-e *mb.* crimson.
bojëkáfe *mb.* brown.
bojëlimón *mb.* lemon-coloured.
bojëmanusháqe *mb.* violet.
bojëportokáll *mb.* orange, orange coloured.
bojëtrëndafíl,-e *mb.* pinky.

bojëvíshnjë *mb.* cherry-coloured, murrey.
bojëvjóllcë *mb.* shih **bojëmanushaqe.**
bojkotím,-i *m.sh.* -**e** boycotting, boycott.
bojkotój *f.k.* to boycot. – **bojkotohem** *f.jv.* to be boycotted.
bojkotúar (i,e) *mb.* boycotted.
bojkotúes,-i *m.sh.* – boycotter.
bok/ël,-la *f.sh.* -**la** *bot.* corn-cob.
bokërím/ë,-a *f.sh.* -**a** reef.
boks,-i *m.* boxing.
boksiér,-i *m.sh.* -**ë** boxer.
boksít,-i *m.sh.* -**e** bauxite.
bolshevík,-u *m.sh.* -**ë** Bolshevik, Bolshevist.
bolshevíz/ëm,-mi *m.* bolshevism.
boll *ndajf.* enough.
bóll/ë,-a *f.sh.* -**a** *zool.* copperhead.
bollëk,-u *m.* abundance, plenty; **me bollëk:** profusely, abundantly, abounding (in).
bollgúr,-i *m.sh.* -**e** groats, grit (meal); **bollgur tërshëre:** oatmeal.
bóllsh/ëm,(i),-me (e) *mb.* plentiful.
bombardím,-i *m.sh.* -**e** bombardment.
bombardó *f.k.* to bombard, to bomb.
bombardúes,-i *m.sh.* – bomber.
bombardúes,-e *mb.* bombarding; **aeroplan bombardues:** bomber
bombastík,-e *mb.* bombastic, pompous.
bómb/ë,-a *f.sh.* -**a** bomb; **bombë aeroplani:** aerial bomb; **bombë me gaz lotues:** tear -gas bomb.
bonbóne,-ja *f.sh.* -**e** bon-bon.
bonifikím,-i *q.sh.* -**e** reclamation.
bonifikój *f.k.* to reclaim.
bóno,-ja *f.sh.* – 1. coupon, ticket. 2. bond.
bonják,-u *m.sh.* -**ë** orphan boy.
bonják,-e *mb.* orphan.

bonjakërí,-a *f.* orphanage.
bordero,-ja *f.sh.* – pay-roll, pay-sheet.
bordúr/ë,-a *f.sh.* -a border, edging, hem. edge; bordurë guri: curb stone.
bór/ë,-a *f.sh.* -ëra shih dëborë.
borgjéz,-i *m.sh.* -ë bourgeois, middle-class person.
borgjéz,-e *mb.* bourgeois, middle-class.
borgjezí,-a *f.* bourgeoisie, middle-classes; borgjezia e lartë (e madhe) : upper middle-classes; borgjezi e mesme; middle-classes. borgjezi e vogël: lower middle-classes.
borgjezój *f.k.* to render, to make (to turn into a) bourgeois. – borgjezohem *f.jv.* to become bourgeois (in one's ways and habits).
borí,-a *f.sh.* – 1. cornet, trumpet, clarion-horn; bori gjahu: bugle; i bie borisë: to toot a horn, 'to blare. 2. bori automobili: klaxon, horn push.
borí,-a *f.sh.* – chimney pot; bori sobe: chimney-pot.
boríg/ë,-a *f.sh.* -a *bot.* pine-tree.
borík,-e *mb. kim.* boracic; acid· borik: boracic acid.
borizán,-i *m.sh.* -ë trumpeter.
boroníc/ë,-a *f.sh.* -a *bot.* bilberry, wortle berry.
bóɩs/ë,-a *f.sh.* -a 1. foot-warmer. 2. handbag.
borxh,-i *m.sh.* -e 1. debt; marr (hyj) borxh: to incur a debt; futem në borxhe: to run (to go, to get) into debt; marr diçka borxh: to borrow something; shlyej (paguaj) një borxh: to settle (to pay off) a debt; jam mbytur në borxh: to be over head and ears in debt, to be up to one's ears in debt;

i kam një borxh dikujt: to be in debt to someone, to owe someone a sum, to be someone's debtor. 2. duty, obligation; kam borxh t'ju them: it is my duty to tell you, I feel it my duty (I feel duty-bound) to tell you.
borxhlí,-u *m.sh.* -nj debtor; të jam borxhli për jetë: I am indebted to you for life; i jam borxhli dikujt: to feel obliged (indebted) to someone.
borzilók,-u *m. bot.* basil, sweet basil.
bostán,-i *m.sh.* -e *vjet.* 1. *bot.* water-melon. 2. kitchen – garden.
bostanxhí,-u *m.sh.* -nj kitchen-gardener.
bosh *ndajf., mb.* (-e) 1. empty, void. 2. hollow. 3. *fig.* futile, trifling; frivolous, silly; fjalë boshe: empty words.
boshatís *f.k.* 1. (*një kupë, një enë*): to empty, to void (a cup, a pot). 2. (*një qytet, një vend*) to evacuate (a town, a place). – boshatiset *f.jv.* 1. to become empty. 2. to be evacuated.
boshatísj/e,-a *f.* 1. emptying (out). 2. evacuation (of a town, of a place).
boshllë/k,-ku *m.sh.* -qe 1. emptiness, void. 2. empty place, hollow, cavity. 3. void, space. 4. *fig.* gap, void; vdekja e tij na ka lënë një boshllëk të madh: his death has left a great void.
bosht,-i *m.sh.* -e 1. *tek.* axle-tree. axle. 2. *mat., fiz.* axis; boshti i Tokës: axis of the Earth. 3. *anat.* boshti kurrizor: back-bone. 4. (*për tjerrje leshi*) spindle.
botaník,-e *mb.* botanic, botanical; kopshti botanik: botanical garden.
botaník/ë,-a *f.* botany.

botanist,-i *m.sh.* -ë botanist.
bót/ë,-a *f.sh.* -ëra 1. world, universe. 2. world, life; **marr vesh nga bota**: to be wise in (to know) the ways of the world; **në këtë botë**: in this world; **kështu e ka kjo botë**: that's (such is) life. 3. kingdom; **bota bimore**: the vegetable kingdom; **bota shtazore**: the animal kingdom. 4. world, humanity, mankind; **teoria reaksionare e tri botëve**: the reactionary theory of «three worlds». 5. world; **bota artistike**: the artistic world. 6. people, the others; **mos dëgjo se ç'thonë bota**: don't pay attention to what the people say.
botëkuptím,-i *m.sh.* -e world-outlook.
botërísht *ndajf.* publicly, in public.
botërór,-e *mb.* world; world-wide; **Lufta e Parë Botërore**: the First World War; **ngjarje me rëndësi botërore**: event of world-wide importance.
bótës (i,e) *mb.* alien foreign, other people's.
botím,-i *m.sh.* -e 1. edition, publication; **botim i plotë**: complete (unabridged) edition: **botim i posaçëm**: special edition. 2. printing.
botój *f.k.* 1. to publish, to issue. 2. to print. – **botohet** *f.jv.* to be published (printed).
botór,-e *mb.* public.
botúes,-i *m.sh.* – editor, publisher.
botúes,-e *mb.* editorial, publishing; **shtëpi botuese**: publishing house.
botúesh/ëm(i),-me(e) *mb.* publishable.
bóz/ë,-a *f.* refreshing drink made of cornflower.
bozhúr/e,-ja *f.sh.* -e bot. peony flower.

braktís *f.k.* to abandon, to quit, to forsake, to reliquish, to desert. – **braktisem** *f.jv.* to be abandoned (forsaken).
braktísj/e,-a *f.* abandonment, desertion (of a land); defection.
bramc,-i *m.* slag, dross (of a metal).
brán/ë,-a *f.sh.* -a harrow.
braním,-i *m.sh.* -e harrowing.
bránoj *f.k.* to harrow.
bravár,-i *m.sh.* -ë herdsman.
bráv/ë-a *f.sh.* -a lock; **gjuhëz e bravës**: bolt, the bit of the lock; **vrimë e bravës**: keyhole.
brávo! *pasth.* bravo!, well done!
brázd/ë,-a *f.sh.* -a furrow.
brazilián,-i *m.sh.* -ë Brasilian.
bredh,-i *m.sh.* -a bot. fir, fir-tree; **dru bredhi**: fir-wood.
bredh *f.jk.* (p.t. **brodha,** p.p. **bredhur**) to wander, to saunter, to roam, to loiter, to ramble.
bredharák,-u *m.sh.* -ë wanderer, rambler, loiterer, roamer.
brédhj/,e-a *f.sh.* -e wandering, ramble.
breg,-u *m.sh.* **brigje** 1. hill. 2. shore, side, coast; **breg liqeni**: lakeside, lakefront; **breg lumi**: river-side; **breg deti**: sea-side, sea-coast, sea-shore, littoral.
bregalúmas,-i *m.sh.* – coast-dweller.
bregdét,-i *m.sh.* -e coast, seacoast, shore, sea-shore, seaside.
bregdetár,-e *mb.* littoral, coasting, coastal; **male bregdetare**; littoral mountains.
bregdétas,-i *m.sh.* – coast-dweller.
bregór/e,-ja *f.sh.* -e hillock, small hill, knoll, hummock.
brej *f.k.* 1. to nible, to gnaw. 2. to corrode (of a metal). 3. fig. to cause remorse.
bréjtës,-i *m.sh.* – zool. rodent.

bréjtës,-e *mb.* 1. gnawing. 2. corroding.

bréjtj/e,-a *f.sh.* -e 1. gnawing. 2. corrosion (of a metal). 3. *fig.* remorse; **brejtje e ndërgjegjes:** qualm of conscience, remorse.

brékë,-t *f.* drawers.

brekúshe,-t *f.sh.* — slacks, long and loose drawers.

brénda I. *ndajf.* in, inside; *(në shtëpi etj.)* indoors inside; **brenda është ngrohtë:** it is warm indoors; **nga brenda:** from inside, from within; **hyj brenda:** to go (to come) in. *Lok.* **jam brenda (në burg):** to be in prison; **fus (rras) brenda dikë:** to send someone to prison, të imprison someone, to throw (to cast) someone in prison. II. *paraf.* 1. *(për kohë)* in, within; **brenda një ore:** within an hour, in an hour, in an hour's time; **brenda së shtunës:** by Saturday. 2. *(për vend)* in, inside, within; **brenda mureve të shtëpisë:** inside the house, within the four walls of the house, within doors, indoors.

brendësí,-a *f.* inside, interior; **në brendësi të:** on the inside of inside; **jam në brendësi të çështjes:** to know the matter inside out, to have a thorrough knowledge of the question, to be well informed of the question, to know the question fully well.

brendí,-a *f.* contents; **brendia e një letre:** contents of a letter.

bréndsh/ëm (i),-me (e) *mb.* inner, internal, interior; **pjesa e brendshme:** the inner part; **motor me djegie të brendshme:** internal combustion engine; **det i brendshëm:** inland sea; **Ministria e Punëve të Brendshme:** Ministry of the Interior, Home Office, *amer.* Department of the Interior; **tregu i brendshëm:** the home market.

bréndshme,-t (të) *f.sh.* entrails (of animals), guts.

bréng/ë,-a *f.sh.*-a sorrow, sadness, grief, torment.

brengós *f.k.* to sadden, to distress, to grieve. — **brengosem** *f.jv.* to feel distressed, to grieve.

brengósur (i,e) *mb.* sorrowful, sad, grieved; **jam i brengosur:** to be in low spirits, to be downcast, to be depressed.

brerím/ë,-a *f.sh.* -a shower.

br erón *f.jv.* it showers.

bréshë/r,-ri *m.* hail; **breshër i imët** *(me shi)*: sleet; **kokërr-breshëri:** hailstone; **bie breshër:** it hails. — *Lok.* **bie nga shiu në breshër:** to jump out of the frying pan into the fire.

breshërí,-a *f.sh.* — volley, salvo; **një breshëri plumbash:** a volley of shots; **një breshëri duartrokitjesh:** a salvo (a round) of applauses.

bréshk/ë,-a *f.sh.* -a *zool.* tor toise; **breshkë uji:** turtle; *fig* **eci me hapin e breshkës:** to go at a snail's pace.

bréshkëz,-a *f. mjek.* scrofula.

bretkós/ë,-a *f.sh.* -a *zool.* frog, toad)

brez,-i *m.sh.* -a 1. sash, girdle, belt; **brez i leshtë:** woolen belt; **brez shpëtimi:** life belt. 2. *(zonë e territorit)* strip, belt. **brez ekuatorial:** equatorial belt (zone). 3. generation; **brezi i ardhshëm:** the coming generation. — *Lok.* **lëshoj brezin** *(për sherr)*: to provoke someone, to make up a quarrel.

bri *paraf.* aside, alongside, along the side of; **rruga shkon bri**

kodrinës: the road runs along the side of the hill.
bri,-ri *m.sh.* -**rë** horn; **prej briri:** horny; **me brirë:** horned; **pa brirë:** unhorned.
brigád/ë,-a *f.sh.* -**a** brigade; **brigadë sulmuese:** shock brigade; **komandant brigade:** brigadier.
brigadiér,-i *m.sh.* -**ë** brigade-leader.
brigím,-i *m.sh.* -**e** censure, blame, vituperation.
brigój *f.k.* to censure, to blame, to vituperate.
brilánt,-i *m.sh.* -**e** brilliant; **brilant i rremë:** false brilliant.
brilantín/ë,-a *f.* brilliantine.
brím/ë,-a *f.sh.* -**a** 1. hole. 2. aperture.
brimój *f.k.* 1. to pierce, to bore, to drill. 2. *fig.* to ferret, to search out.
brisk,-u *m.sh.* -**brisqe** 1. *(brisk rroje)* razor, safety-razor; **tek brisku:** blade. 2. *(brisk për prerje)* pocket-knife, penknife **Lok. e kam gjuhën brisk:** to have a voluble tongue; **është i ftohtë brisk (ujët)** to be very cold.
brishtë (i, e) *mb.* 1. brittle, fragile, frail. 2. leap, bissextile; **vit i brishtë:** leap year.
brishtësí,-a *f.* brittleness, fragility.
brítm/ë,-a *f.sh.* -**a** cry, shout, outcry, scream, bawl; clamour, squeal *(kafshësh)*; **britmë therëse:** shriek; **britmë e foshnjës:** wail; **britmë gëzimi:** cry of joy, exclamation; **britmë lufte:** war cry.
brohorás *f.k.* to cheer, to applause, to acclaim.
brohorítj/e,-a *f.sh.* -**e** cheer, applause, acclamation.
brók/ë,-a *f.sh.* -**a** water-jug.
brompl *pasth.* chin-chin.

bronkít,-i *m. mjek.* bronchitis.
bronz,-i *m.* bronze, brass.
broshúr/ë,-a *f.sh.* -**a** booklet.
brúmbu/ll,-lli *m.sh.* -**j** *zool.* humble-bee, *amer.* bug.
brúm/ë,-i *m.sh.* -**ëra** 1. dough, paste; **brumë i fryrë:** leavened dough, puffy dough; **prej brumi:** doughy, pasty; **zë brumë:** to knead. 2. *fig.* **s'është prej brumi të mirë:** he is a bad lot.
brumór,-e *mb.* doughy, pasty.
brumós *f.k.* 1. to knead. 2. *fig.* to mould, to shape (a person's character).
brumósj/e,-a *f.sh.* -**e** 1. kneading. 2. *fig.* moulding, shaping.
brumtór/e,-ja *f.sh.* -**e** kneading-machine.
brúsh/ë,-a *f.sh.* -**a** shih **furçë**
brutál,-e *mb.* brutal, rough (person).
brutalísht *ndajf.* brutally, roughly.
brutalitét,-i *m.* brutality, roughness
brúto *mb.* 1. raw, coarse, rough; **material bruto:** raw material. 2. *treg.* gross; **peshë bruto:** gross weight.
brýdhët (i,e) *mb.* soft.
brým/ë,-a *f.* rime, hoar, frost, hoar-frost; **me brymë:** rimy, frosty; **bie brymë:** to rime.
búa/ll,-lli *m.sh.* -**j** *zool.* buffalo; **lëkurë bualli:** buff.
buallíc/ë,-a *f.sh.* -**a** *zool.* buffalo-cow.
búb/ë,-a *f.sh.* -**a** *zool.* larva, silk-worm.
búbi *fj. plk. zool.* puppy, young dog.
bubrék,-u *m.sh.* -**ë** *anat.* kidney.
bubullím/ë,-a *f.sh.* -**a** thunder.
bubullín *f.jv.* to thunder.
buburréc,-i *m.sh.* -**a** *zool.* cockchafer, bug.
bucél/ë,-a *f.sh.* -**a** 1. cask, keg, water-keg.

2. *tek.* axle-bearing; **bucelë rrote:** hub.

buçás *f.jk.* (p.t. **buçita.** p.p. **buçitur)** to boom, to rumble, to roar, to make a loud voice, to utter with a loud voice.

buçítj/e,-a *f.sh.* -e rumble, rumbling (of thunder); roaring (of the storm); booming (of waves, of guns).

búçkë, búçko *mb.* podgy, dumpy, chubby.

budall/á,-ai *m.sh.* -enj fool, idiot, imbecile; **mos u bëj budalla:** don't be a fool, don't be stupid; **budalla me gjithë rroba:** a great fool, a regular fool.

budallallë/k,-ku *m.sh.* -qe foolery, idiocy, stupidity; *sh.* **budallallëqe:** fooleries; **flas budallallëqe:** to talk nonsense.

budallallós *f.k.* to make stupid, to dull, to daze, to stun. — **budallallosem** *f.jv.* to become stupid, to grow dull (dull-witted).

budalláq/e,-ja *f.sh.* -e stupid woman (girl).

buf,-i *m.sh.* -ë 1. *zool.* screech owl. 2. *fig.* numskull, dunce, dolt.

bufé,-ja *f.sh.* — 1. cupboard. sideboard, pantry. 2. buffet.

bufetiér,-i *m.sh.* -ë counter-man, barman.

búfk/ë,-a *f.sh.* -a pompon.

bufón,-i *m.sh.* -ë buffoon.

buís *f.jk.* to throng, to come in multitude; **buis (bleta) :** to throng (bees).

buj I. *f.k.* to lodge (someone).
II. *f.jk.* to lodge, to stay, to take lodging; **buj te dikush:** to stay at someone's house.

bujár,-i *m.sh.* -ë gentleman.

bujár,-e *mb.* 1. bountiful, bounteous, gentle. 2. generous, munificient, open-handed.

bujarí,-a *f.* 1. bounty, gentleness. 2. generosity, munificence.

bujarísht *ndajf.* bountifully, gallantly, generously.

búj/ë,-a *f.* sensation; **që bën bujë:** sensational; **pa bujë:** without sensation; **bëj bujë:** to cause sensation, to be a sensation.

bujk,-u *m.sh.* -bujq. farmer, peasant farmer, agriculturist, tiller.

bujkrób,-i *m.sh.* -ër serf.

bujkrobërí,-a *f.* serfdom.

bujqësí,-a *f.* agriculture, farming.

bujqësór,-e *mb.* agricultural, farm; **prodhime bujqësore:** agricultural products; **vegla bujqësore:** agricultural implements; **makinë bujqësore:** farm machine.

bújrëm *pasth.* come! **bujrëm të hamë!** come to eat with us!, help yourself!

bújsh/ëm(i),-me (e) *mb.* sensational; **lajm i bujshëm:** sensational news.

bujtár,-i *m.sh.* -ë shih **bujtës.**

bújtës,-i *m.sjh.* — lodger.

bujtinár,-i *m.sh.* -ë lodging-house keeper, tenant of a house, lodger, inn keeper.

bujtín/ë,-a *f.sh.* -a 1. hostel, hostelry, inn, lodging-house. 2. dormitory.

búk/ë,-a *f.sh.* -ë 1. bread; **bukë gruri:** wheat bread; **bukë misri:** corn bread; **bukë e zezë:** brown bread, wholemeal bread; **bukë taze:** fresh (new) bread; **bukë e ftohtë (bajate):** stale bread; **kore buke:** crust of bread; **thërrime buke:** crumbs of bread; **bukë me gjalpë:** bread and butter, buttered bread; **fetë buke:** slice of bread; **furrë buke:** bake-house; **gatuaj bukë:** to knead bread dough. 2. pulp; **arrë me bukë:** pulpy nut. — *Lok.* **fitoj (nxjerr) bukën e**

gojës: to earn one's living; **për një copë bukë**: for a crust of bread; **i heq bukën e gojës dikujt**: to take the bread out of someone's mouth.

bukëbërës,-i *m.sh.* — bread maker, kneader.

búk/ël,-la *f.sh.* -la 1. *zool.* weasel. 2. curl of hairs.

bukëpjé/kës,-i *m.sh.* — baker.

bukësheqér/e,-ja *f.sh.* -e sponge-cake.

búkur *ndajf.* prettily, finely, handsomely; well-done.

búkur (i,e) *mb.* 1. beautiful, handsome, pretty, nice, graceful; **vajzë e bukur**: beautiful girl. 2. fine; **mot i bukur**: fine weather.

bukurí,-a *f.sh.* — beauty, prettiness; **plot bukuri**: beautiful, graceful; **për pukuri**: admiringly; very well.

bukurósh,-i *m.sh.* -ë handsome man; playboy.

bukurósh,-e *mb.* charming, beautiful, pretty, handsome.

bukurshkrím,-i *m.* handwriting, calligraphy; **mësues bukurshkrimi**: writing-master.

bulçí,-a *f.sh.* — cheek.

buldozér,-i *m.sh.* -ë bulldozer.

buletín-i *m-sh.* -e bulletin

bulevárd,-i *m.sh.* -e boulevard.

búl/ë,-a *f.sh.* -a *anat.* lobe; **bulë e veshit**: earlap, lobe of the ear.

búlëz,-a *f.sh.* -a 1. *bot.* bud. 2. droplet (of water, etc.).

bulëzím,-i *m.* budding; **bulëzim i pemëve**: the budding of trees.

bulëzón *f.jk.* to bud (a tree).

bulkth,-i *m.sh.* -a *zool.* cricket.

bulmét,-i *m.sh.* -ra dairy-produce, milk products.

bulmetór/e,-ja *f.sh.* -e dairy shop.

bulón,-i *m.sh.* -a *mek.* bolt.

bullár,-i *m.sh.* -ë *zool.* grass-snake, harmless snake.

bullgár,-i *m.sh.* -ë Bullgarian Bulgar.

bullgár,-e *mb.* Bulgarian.

bunác/ë,-a *f.* 1. slack, calmness, dead calm. 2. darkness.

bunkér,-i *m.sh.* -ë 1. *usht.* bunker. 2. *tek* bunker.

buqét/ë,-a *f.sh.* -a nosegay, bunch; **buqetë me lule**: nosegay, a bunch of flowers.

burbúq/e,-ja *f.sh.* -e *bot.* bud **burbuqe trëndafili**: rose bud.

burg-,u *m.sh.* — **burgje** prison, jail, gaol; **birucë burgu**: cell, dungeon; **roje burgu**: jailler, warden.

burgím,-i *m.sh.* -e imprisonment, confinement; **burgim me punë të detyruar**: confinement with hard labour; **dënohem me një vit burgim**: to be sentenced to a year's imprisonment.

burgós *f.k.* to imprison, to jail, to confine, to put in prison. — **burgosem** *f.jv.* to be imprisoned, to be put in prison.

burgósj/e,-a *f.sh.* -e imprisoning, confinement.

burgósur(i),-i(i) *m.sh.* — (të) prisoner.

burgjí,-a *f.sh.* — 1. *mek.* screw. 2. gimlet. — *Lok.* **më janë liruar burgjitë**: to have a screw loose.

burí,-a *f.sh.* — shih **bori**.

burím,-i *m.sh.* -e 1. source, spring (of water), fountain; **ujë burimi**: spring water. 2. source, springhead, fountain-head (of a river). 3. *fig.* source, origin; **pija është burim i shumë të këqijave**: drinking is the source of much evil. 4. *fiz.* source; **burim nxehtësie**: source of heat; **burim drite**: light source.

búrm/ë,-a *f.sh.* -a screw.

buront;-i *m.* snuff; **heq burnot**: to take snuff.

burokrací,-a f bureaucracy, red-tape.

burokrát,-i *m.sh.* **-ë** bureaucrat.

burokratík,-e *mb.* bureaucratic.

burón *f.jk.* 1. to gush, to spring. 2. to derive, to emanate; **pushteti buron nga populli dhe i takon popullit**: the power emanates from the people, and belongs to the people.

búrs/ë,-a *f.sh.* **-a** 1. *(bursë studimi)* scholarship, stipend. 2. **bursë tregtare**: stock exchange, bourse, *amer.* stock market.

bursíst,-i *m.sh.* **-ë** scholarship holder.

burracák,-u *m.sh.* **-ë** coward, dastard, poltroon.

burracák,-e *mb.* coward, poltroon, slack, hubby.

búrr/ë,-i *m.sh.* **-a** 1. man; male; **burrë shteti**: statesman; **burrë i fjalës (i besës)**: man of his word; **burrë trim**: brave man; **burrë i mirë**: good (honest) man; **burrë i shquar**: distinguished (great) man; **burrash, për burra**: man's, men's; **s'është nga ata burra ai**: he is not the man to do it. 2. *(bashkëshort)* husband; **burrë e grua**: husband and wife.

burrërí,-a *f.* 1. manhood; virility. 2. valour, bravery, courage, prowess, pluck; **i bëj ballë diçkaje me burrëri**: to bear something like a man.

burrërísht *ndajf.* bravely, courageously, valiantly, valorously, like a man.

burrërój *f.k.* to make virile, to virilize, to make a man (of someone); **lufta e burrëroi shumë shpejt**: the war made a man of him very soon. − **burrërohem** *f.jv.* to become virile.

burrërór,-e *mb.* brave, valiant, valorous, courageous.

bust,-i *m.sh.* **-e** bust; **bust mermeri**: marble bust.

búsull,-a *f.sh.* **-a** compass.

bush,-i *m.sh.* **-e** *bot.* box-tree, box-wood.

bushllíz/ë,-a *f.sh.* **-a** *bot.* convolvulus.

búsht/ër,-ra *f.sh.* **-ra** *zool.* 1. bitch, she-dog. 2. *fig.* bitch.

but,-i *m.sh.* **-e** tun, large barrel, hogshead. 2. *anat.* buti i kresë: the top of the head, epicranium.

bútë *ndajf.* gently, nicely, softly, smoothly.

bútë (i,e) *mb.* 1. soft, smooth; mellow. 2. meek, lenient. benignant, mild (of a man). 2. tamed, domesticated (animal); cultivated (plant). 1. softness, smoothness. 2. meekness, mildness; **me butëtsi**: meekly, mildly.

butësír/ë-a *f.* warm and wet weather.

buxhák,-u *m.sh.* **-ë** *bot.* vetch (fodder for cattle).

buxhét,-i *m.* budget.

buzáç,-i *m.sh.* **-ë** blubber-lipped (tuck-lipped) man.

buzáç,-e *mb.* thick-lipped.

buzagáz *mb.* 1. smiling. 2. gay, joyful, cheerful, smilefaced.

búz/ë,-a *f.sh.* **-ë** 1. *anat.* lip; **buza e poshtme**: lower lip; **buza e sipërme**: upper lip; **buzë të kuqe**: cherry lips; **lye buzët me të kuq**: to put lipstick on, to paint (to make up) one's lips; **të kuq buzësh**: lipstick; **rrudh buzët**: to curl one's lips; **kafshoj buzët**: to bite one's lips. 2. edge, brim, brink; **buza e një gote**: the brim of a glass; **buzët e vizores:** the edge of a rule. 3. **buzë deti:** sea-shore; **buzë liqeni:** lakeside; **buzë lumi:** riverside. — *Lok.* var **buzët:** to pout; **jam në buzë të varrit:** to be on the brink of the grave.

búzë *paraf.* on the edge, on the brink; **buzë greminës:** on the edge of the abyss.

buzëplásur *mb.* rueful, mournful, woeful, disheartened, downcast. dejected.

buzëqésh *f.jk.* to smile.

buzëqéshj/e,-a *f.sh.* -e smile.

buzëqéshur *ndajf., mb.* smilingly.

buzëvárur *mb.* sulky, sullen; **njeri buzëvarur:** pouter.

buzëvíç *mb.* shih **buzaç.**

byc,-i *m.sh.* -e *mjek.* shih **elbth.**

byk,-u *m.* chaff.

byméj *f.k.* to dilate, to expand, — **bymehet** *f.jv.* to expand.

bymím,-i *m.* dilatation, expansion.

byrazér,-i *m.sh.* -ë *vjet.* shih **vëlla.**

býrd/e,-ja *f.sh.* -e horse-cloth, saddle-cloth.

byrék,-u *m.sh.* -ë pie.

byró,-ja *f.sh.* — bureau; **Byroja Politike e Komitetit Qendror të Partisë së Punës të Shqipërisë:** The Political Bureau of the Central Committee of th. Party of Labour of Albania.

býth/ë,-a *f.sh.* -ë 1. *anat.* bottom buttocks, behind. 2. stern, hinder part (of anything); **bytha e shishes:** the bottom of the bottle.

bythëpúle *f. mjek.* herpes, tetter.

byzylýk,-u *m.sh.* -ë bracelet, armlet

C

c, C (letter of the Albanian alphabet; is pronounced like *tz* in *hertz*) c, C.

ca *p.pk., ndajf.* some; a few; a little; **kam ca libra:** I have some books; **ka ca cigare në kuti:** there are some cigarettes in the box; **më jep ca duhan:** give me some tabacco; **më jep ca djathë:** give me some cheese (a little cheese); **ca nga ca:** little by little, by

and by, gradually, progressively by inches, by degrees.

cafullím,-i *m.* yelping (of dogs).

cafullón *f.jk.* to yelp (the dog).

cak,-u *m.sh.* caqe limit, boundary, border.

caktím,-i *m.* 1. fixation, fixing; **caktim i çmimeve:** fixing of prices. 2. assessment; **caktim i taksave:** assessment of taxes. 3. demarcation, delimitation; **caktimi i kufijve;** demarcation of bounds, delimitation of confines. 4. designation, affectation; **caktimi i fondeve (i kredive)**: allocation of funds (of credits), designation of funds. 5. designation, appointment, nomination (of an employee in a post).

caktój *f.k.* 1. to fix, to settle; **caktoj çmimin**: to fix the price; **caktoj datën**: to fix the date. 2. *(kufijtë)* to demarcate (to delimitate, to determine, to settle) the boundaries. 3. *(fonde)* to designate, to allocate (funds). 4. *(në një punë)*: to appoint, to to designate. 5. *(diçka për dikë)* to destine. – **caktohem** *f.jv.* to be appointed, to be designated.

caktúar (i,e) *mb.* 1. fixed, settled; **çmim i caktuar**: fixed price. 2. appointed, fixed, set; **dita e caktuar**: the appointed day; **për një shumë të caktuar**: for a fixed (determined) sum. 3. destined; **vend i caktuar për**: place destined for; **të holla të caktuara për**: money (cash) destined for. 4. definite; **pa ndonjë qëllim të caktuar**: without any definite object.

cáng /ë,-a *f.sh.* -a *bot.* green pear.

cáp /ë,-a *f.sh.* -a hoe.

car,-i *m.* tsar, tzar, czar.

caríst,-e *mb.* tsarist, czarist.

caríz /ëm,-mi *m.* tsarism, czarism.

cékët (i,e) *mb.* 1. shallow, shoal. 2. *fig.* superficial.

cektësí,-a *f.* 1. shoaliness, shallowness. 2. *fig.* superficiality.

cektín /ë,-a *f.sh.* -a shallow.

celfís *f.k.* to peel, to scale. – **celfisem** *f.jv.* to peel off.

celúl /ë,-a *f.sh.* -a cell.

celulóz /ë,-a *f.* cellulose.

cen,-i *m.sh.* -e defect, flaw (in-

herent defect); **me cen**: defective; **pa cen**: flawless.

cením,-i *m.* 1. intrusion, encroachment. 2. *fig.* lesion, injury.

cenój *f.k.* 1. to intrude, to encroach. 2. *fig.* to infringe (on), to grieve, to hurt. – **cenohem** *f.jv.* to be grieved (injured).

cenúesh /ëm (i),-me (e) *mb.* vulnerable.

censúr /ë,-a *f.sh.* -a censure.

censurím,-i *m.sh.* -e censuring.

censurój *f.k.* to censure.

centigrád /ë,-a *f.sh.* -ë centigrade.

centigrám,-i *m.sh.* -e centigram.

centilít /ër,-ri *m.sh.* -ra centiliter.

centimét /ër,-ri *m.sh.* -ra centimeter.

centrál,-i *m.sh.* -e central; **central elektrik**: power station; **central telefonik**: telephone exchange.

centrál,-e *mb.* central.

centralíst,-i *m.sh.* -ë telephonist.

centralíz /ëm,-mi *m.* centralism.

centralizím,-i *m.* centralization.

centralizój *f.k.* to centralize.

cep,-i *m.sh.* -a 1. extreme end, point, extremity. 2. corner; **cep më cep**: from end to end, everywhere; **në një cep të dhomës**: in a corner of the room; **një cep i tryezës**: a corner of the table.

ceremoní,-a *f.sh.* – 1. ceremony; **ceremoni fetare**: rite. 2. *sh.* ceremony; **e pres dikë pa shumë ceremoni**: to recieve someone without much ceremony.

cérg /ë,-a *f.sh.* -a 1. covert of rough wool. 2. rag, tatter.

cérm /ë,-a *f. mjek.* gout.

ciás *f.jk.* to squawk.

cicamí,-u *m.sh.* -nj. *zool.* warbler.

cicërím /ë,-a *f.sh.* -a warble, chirp, chirping, tweet.

cicërón *f.jk.* to warble, to chirp, to tweet.

cíf/ël,-la *f.sh.* -la splinter, spill, ship, sliver.
ciflós *f.k.* to scale. – **ciflosem** *f.jv.* to peal off.
cigán,-i *m.sh.* -ë Bohemian.
cigár/e,-ja *f.sh.* -a cigarette; **kuti cigaresh**: cigarette-case; **thith (pij) cigaren**: to smoke a cigarette, to puff at a cigarette; **cigare me filtër**: filter-tip (filter-tipped) cigarette; **cigare pa filtër**: non-filter (regular) cigarette.
cigarís *f.k.* to fry. – **cigarisem** *f.jv.* to be fried; **cigarisem me dhjamin tim**: to stew in one's own juice.
cigarísj/e,-a *f.* frying, toasting.
cigarísht/e,-ja *f.sh.* -e cigar holder.
cík/ël,-li *m.sh.* -le cycle; **cikël biologjik**: biological cycle; **cikël bisedash**: series of lectures; **cikël i një sëmundjeje**: course of an illness.
cikërrím/ë-a *f.sh.* -a odds end ends, fancy goods, trinkets, bits and pieces; **merrem me cikërrima**: to occupy oneself with trifles.
cikërrimtár,-i *m.sh.* -ë haberdasher, fancy goods merchant.
cikërrimtarí,-a *f.* 1. haberdashery. 2. fancy goods shop.
ciklón,-i *m.sh.* -e cyclone.
ciklóp,-i *m.sh.* -e cyclop.
cíkn/ë,-a *f.* frost.
ciknós *f.k.* *(gjellën)* to burn, to fry in excess (a meal) – **ciknoset** *f.jv.* to be burnt, to be fried in excess.
cíla *p-lidh.* who, what, which (shih **cili**); **cila është pikëpamja juaj?** what is your opinion? **cilën rrugë të marrim?** which road must we take? **cila?** (nga të dyja, nga disa) which one? **cíla (e)** *p.lidh.* shih **cili (i).**

ciladó *p.pk.* shih **cilido.**
cilatdó *p.pk.* shih **cilido.**
cílën *p.pk.* which (shih **cili).**
cilëndó *p.pk.* shih **cilido.**
cilësí,-a *f.sh.* – 1. quality; **me cilësi të lartë**: of first rate quality, of high quality. 2. *fig.* virtue.
cilësój *f.k.* to qualify.
cilësór,-e *mb. gram.* qualificative; **mbiemër cilësor**: qualificative, qualificative adjective.
cilësúar (i,e) *mb.* qualified.
cilëtdó *p.pk.* shih **cilido.**
cíli *p.pk.* (fem, **cíla** pl. **cílët,** fem. **cilat**) who, which; **cili është atje?** who is there? **cila po luan?** who is playing? **cili libër është juaji?** which book is yours? **cila fletore është juaja?** which copy-book is yours? **cila nga këto të dyja është juaja?** which of these two is yours? **cili është mendimi juaj?** what is your opinion? (dative) **cilit, cilës,** pl. **cilëve, cilave:** whom, to whom; **cilëve ua dhe?** to whom did you give it? whom did you give it to? (accusative): **cilin, cilën:** pl. **cilët, cilat** vhom, which; **cilin (cilën) kërkoni?** whom do you want? **cilin (cilën) preferoni (nga këto dy sende)?** which do you prefer? which do you like best (of these two things).
cíli (i) *p. lidh.* (fem. **e cíla;** pl. **të cilët, të cílat** 1. who, that, which (for things); **burri, i cili nuk shikon, është gjyshi im;** the man who cannot see is my grandfather; **gruaja, e cila ju thërret, është mësuese:** the woman who calls you is a teacher; (genitive) **i të cilit, i së cilës, i të cilëve, i të cilave;** whose (for persons), of which (for things); **Agimi, librin e të cilit ju dhashë:**

Agim whose book I gave you; **libri, kapaku i të cilit është kafe, është imi:** the book, the cover of which is brown, is mine; **vajza, motrën e së cilës e ftuam.. , ,** the girl, whose sister we invited. .. ; (dative) **të cilit, së cilës;** pl. **të cilëve, të cilave:** to whom; **ky është burri, të cilit i shita kalin:** this is the man to whom I sold the horse; **ajo është gruaja, së cilës i fola:** that is the woman to whom I spoke; **të cilin, të cilën,** pl. **të cilët, të cilat:** whom, **burri të cilin po e thërrisni, është i shurdhër:** the man whom you call is deaf; **vajza, të cilën e takuat dje, është nxënësja ime:** the girl whom you met yesterday is my pupil.

cilidó *p.p.k.* (fem. **ciladó,** pl. **cilëtdó, cilatdó**) whoever; anybody anyone, whichever; **cilido qoftë:** whoever may be; **cilido mund ta bëjë këtë:** anyone would do it; **cilido nga ju:** whichever of you; **cilëtdo qofshin ata:** whoever they may be; **cilado qoftë:** whoever she may be; **cilatdo qofshin:** whoever they may be.

cilínd/ër,-ri *m.sh.* **-ra** 1. *gjeom.* cylinder. 2. *tek* cylinder, roller.
cilindrík,-e *mb.* cylindric, cylindrical.
cimbís *f.k.* to pinch, to nip.
cíng/ël,-li *m.sh.* **-la** short wooden rod for children's play.
cingërím,-i *m.* shrill, yelping.
cingërím/ë,-a *f.sh.* **-a** frost.
cingërój *f.jk.* to freeze, to shudder (of cold), to have the cold shivers.
cingërój *f.jk.* to yelp, to shrill.
cingún,-i *m.sh.* **-ë** miser, niggard.

cingún,-e *mb.* miserly, close-fisted, stingy.
ciník,-e *mb.* cynical.
ciníz/ëm,-mi *m.* cynism.
cinkografí,-a *f.* zincography.
cín/xër,-ri *m.sh.* **-ra** *zool.* cicada.
cíp/ë,-a *f.sh.* **-a** membrane, layer; *fig.* njeri pa cipë: shameless person.
cipëplásur *mb.* impudent, shameless.
cirk,-ku *m.sh.* **-qe** 1. circus. 2. *gjeog.* ciraque.
cirkát/ë,-a *f.sh.* **-a** shih **shatërvan.**
cirónk/ë,-a *f.sh.* **-a** *zool.* bleak.
cir/úa,-oi *m.sh.* **-ni** *zool.* shih **cironkë.**
cistérn/ë,-a *f.sh.* **-a** tank, cistern.
citát,-i *m.sh.* **-e** quotation.
civíl,-i *m.sh.* **-ë** civilian.
civíl,-e *mb.* civil, civilian; **rroba civile:** civilian dress; **luftë civile:** civil war; **gjendje civile:** civil status; **vishem civil:** to be in plain clothes.
cjap,-i *m.sh.* **cjep.** *zool.* he-goat, billy-goat.
cof *f.jk.* shih **ngordh.**
cóh/ë,-a *f.sh.* **-ëra** serge, woolen cloth.
cóp/ë,-a *f.sh.* **-a** 1. bit, piece, fragment; **një copë mish:** a bit of meat; **një copë shkumës:** a piece of chalk; **copa metalesh:** scraps of metals; **një copë letër:** a piece (a fragment) of paper; **copë gjalpi:** a clot of butter; **një copë tokë:** a patch of ground; **copë plaçke, stofi:** a scrap of cloth; **një copë bukë:** a piece of bread; **bëj copa-copa:** to break into pieces, to smash to smithereens; **copë-copë:** ragged.
copëtím,-i *m.sh.* **-e** cutting up, parcelling out.
copëtój *f.k.* 1. to parcel out. 2.

to shred, to tear into small pieces, to break into pieces. – copëtohem *f./v.* 1. to be parcelled out; to be shred (broken) into pieces. 2. to wear out, to be tired to death.

cópëz,-a *f.sh.* -a small piece; copëz toke: a small parcel of ground.

cub,-i *m.sh.* -a highwayman, brigand, robber.

cubní,-a *f.* brigandage.

cúc/ë,-a *f.sh.* -a *krah.* lass.

cullúfe,-t *f.sh.* lock of hair, tuft of hair.

cung,-u *m.sh.* cungje 1. *bujq.* *(peme)* stump; *(hardhie)* stock. 2. *anat.* *(gjymtyre)* stump.

cungím,-i *m.sh.* -e amputation, cutting off.

cungój *f.k.* 1. *bujq.* *(degët)* to prune, to lop. 2. *mjek.* to amputate, to cut off. 3. *fig.* *(një tekst, etj).* to mangle. – cungohem *f./v.* 1. to be pruned, to be lopped. 2. *fig.* to be mangled.

curríl,-i *m.sh.* -a trickle.

Ç

ç, Ç (letter of the Albanian alphabet; is pronounced like ch in cherry).

ç' *p.p.* what, how (abbreviation of the word çfarë); ç'dëshlroni? what do you want? ç'po kërkoni? what are you seeking?, what are you searching for? ç'do të thotë kjo? what does it mean? ç' doni të thoni me këtë? what do you mean by this? ç'është, ç'ka ndodhur? what's up?, what has happened? ç'të reja kemi? what's the news? ç'kohë e bukur! what a fine weather!

çaçaník,-u *m.* *bot.* walnut-tree.

çáçk/ë,-a *f.sh.* -a cup (of the head).

çád/ër,-ra *f.sh.* -ra 1. *(çadër*

shiu) umbrella; *(çadër dielli)l* parasol. 2. *(çadër fushe)* tent; ngreh çadrën: to pitch (to put up) one's tent.

çáfk/ë,-a *f.sh.* -a *zool.* mew.

çáfk/ë,-a *f.sh.* -a cup (of tea).

çáfk/ë,-a *f.sh.* -a *anat.* top of the head.

çaír,-i *m.sh.* -e *vjet.* meadow, lea. – Lok, e hëngra çairin: I am already old, I've lived my life.

çaj,-i *bot.* tea; bima e çajit: tea-plant; çaj mali: mountain tea; kuti çaji: tea-caddy, teacanister; filxhan çaji: cup of tea; lugë çaji: tea-spoon; takëm çaji: tea service, teathings.

çaj I. *f.k.* (p.t. çava, p.p. çarë) 1. to cleave; çaj dru: to cleave

wood; **çaj më dysh:** to split
in two. 2. **më çajnë egërsirat:**
to be devoured by wild beasts.
3. *fig.* **çaj turmën:** to force
one's way through the crowd,
to elbow one's way through
the crowd. – *Lok.* **nuk e çaj
kokën fare:** not to care a bit,
not care a straw about, to care
nothing for; **i çaj veshët dikujt:** to split someone's ears.
II. *f.jk.* to go, to walk; **çaj përpara:** to step (to go) forward.
çajník,-u *m.sh.* -**ë** tea-kettle, tea-
pot.
çakáll,-i *m.sh.* -**çakej** *zool.* jackal.
çákëll,-i *m.* gew-gaw.
çakërdís *f.k.* to scatter. – **çakër-
disem** *f.jv.* to be scattered.
çakërr,-e *mb.* skew-eyed, squint-
eyed.
çakërrís *f.k.* to squint; **çakërris
sytë:** to squint.
çakërrqéjf *mb.* merry, mirthful;
bëhem çakërqejf: to be tipsy,
to develop a great glow.
çakmák,-u *m.sh.* -**ë** lighter (for
cigarettes).
çakordím,-i *m.* *muz.* discord; discordance.
çakordój *f.k.* to put out of tune,
to untune. – **çakordohet** *f.jv.*
to get out of tune.
çakordúar (**i,e**) *mb.* *muz.* out
of tune.
çalamán,-i *m.sh.* -**ë** lame person,
cripple.
çalamán,-e *mb.* lame, cripple, lim-
ping.
çálas *ndajf.* lamely.
çálë (**i,e**) *mb.* lame, cripple, lim-
ping.
çálë-çálë *ndajf.* limpingly; **eci
çalë-çalë:** to hobble along.
çalím,-i *m.sh.* -**e** lameness, lim-
ping.
çalój *f.k.*1 to limp, to hobble.

2. *fig.* **çalon diçka:** something
is going wrong.
çallëstís *f.jk.* to endeavor, to
make an effort (attempt), to
muddle through.
çallëstísj/e,-a *f.sh.* -**a** endeavour
exertion.
çallëstísur (**i,e**) *mb.* shifty, full
of expedient, resourceful.
çállm/ë,-a *f.sh.* -**a** turban.
çalltis *f.jk* shih **çallëstis.**
çamarrók,-e *mb.* naughty child.
çamçakëz-i *m.* chewing-gum.
çanák,-u *m.sh.* -**ë** bowl.
çanaklëpírës,-i *m.sh.* – shih **sahan-
lëpirës.**
çáng/ë,-a *f.sh.* -**a** gong; **i ble
çangës:** to strike the gong.
çánt/ë,-a *f.sh.* -**a** handbag, sac;
bag; **çantë grash:** handbag;
çantë pazari: market bag; **çantë shkolle:** satchel; **çantë
gjahtarësh:** pouch for hun-
ters; **çantë shpine:** knap/sack.
çap,-i *m.sh.* -**e** step; **çap i shpejtë:**
quick step; **çap pas çapi:**
step by step: **nuk bëj asnjë
çap prapa:** not to give way,
not to budge an inch.
çap *f.k.* 1. to chew. 2. *krah.* **çap i**
go!
çapaçúl,-i *m.sh.* -**ë** a nobody.
çapëlój *f.k.* to quarter, to tear
to pieces. – **çapëlohem** *f.jv.* tobe
quartered, to be torn to pieces,
çapís *f.k.* to step. – **çapitem** *f.jv.*
to take one's first steps.
çapítj/e,-a *f.sh.* -**e** stepping.
çapkën,-i *m.sh.* -**ë** urchin, imp.
çapkën,-e *mb.* minx, impish.
çapók,-u *m.sh.* -**ë** *anat.* 1 haunch.
2. hip. 3. tibia, shinbone.
çap/úa,-oi *m.sh.* -**onj** spur; **çapua
këndezi:** cock's spur.
çarçáf,-i *m.sh.* -**ë** sheet, bed-sheet.
çardhák,-u *m.sh.* -**ë** corridor, lobby.
çaré,-ja *f.* remedy.

çarë   60   çeliktë

çár/ë(e),-a(e) *f.sh.* -a(të) 1. gap, crevice, flaw, split, cranny, rift, cleft, fissure, chink, 2. *mjek.* incision.

çárj/e,-a *f.sh.* -e clearing, splitting çark,-u *m.sh.* çarqe 1. trap; çark minjsh: rat-trap, mouse-trap. 2. çark pushke: hammer. 3. *fig.* çark i prishur: chatterbox. çarmatím,-i *m.* disarmament (of a nation). çarmatós *f.k.* 1. to disarm (someone). 2. *usht.* to unload (a cannon). 3. *fig.* to disarm (someone). – çarmatosem *f.jv.* to be disarmed. çarmatósj/e,-a *f.* disarming (of someone). çarmatósur (i,e) *mb.* disarmed, armless. çart,-i *m. mjek* delirium. çart *f.k. krah.* to deprave, to destroy. çast,-i *m.sh.* -e instant, moment; çast kritik: critical moment, turning-point; bukuri e çastit: momentary beauty; fotografi e çastit: snapshot; këtë çast: just now, at this moment; për një çast: for a moment, for a while; në çastet e fundit: in his last moments; në çast: in a flash, in the twinkling of an eye. çatáll/ë,-ja *m.sh.* -e notch, indentation. çatáll,-e *mb.* dhëmb çatall: irregular tooth, fang. çatí,-a *f.sh.* – roof; çati prej kashte: thatch roof. çatmá,-ja *f.sh.* – partition-wall. çdo *p.pk.* 1. every, any; çdo ditë: every day; çdo dy ditë: every other day; një herë në çdo dy javë: once every fortnight; çdo gjë: everything; çdo njeri: everybody, everyone. 2. each;

çdo rregull ka përjashtim: each rule has its exception. çdokúsh *p.pk.* shih çdonjeri. çdonjëri *p.pk.* each, everyone. çdollójsh/ëm (i),-me(e) *mb.* of any kind, of any sort. çéhre,-ja *f.* mien, air; appearance, complexion (of the face); kam çehre të mirë: to look well kam çehre të vrarë: to look poorly; çehre e zbetë: paleness; kam çehre më të mirë: to look better. – *Lok.* ndërroj çehre: to change countenance. çek,-u *m.sh.* -çeqe *treg.* check, cheque; bllok çeqesh: checkbook. çek,-u *m.sh.* -ë Czech. çek,-e *mb.* Czech. çekán,-i *m.sh.* -ë hammer. çekíç,-i *m.sh.* -ë small hammer. çel I. *f.k.* 1. to open, to unlock. 2. *(pula zogj)* to hatch. – çelem *f.jv.* to cheer up, to enliven. II. *f.jk.* 1. to bloom, to blossom (flowers). 2. *(moti)* to clear up (the weather). çélës,-i *m.sh.* -a 1. key; mbyll me çelës: to lock. 2. *tek.* çelës anglez: crescent – type wrench, monkey-wrench, monkey-spanner. 3. *el.* switchkey 4. çelës për të kurdisur orën: watch-key. 5. *muz.* clef; çelës i solit: C clef, tuble clef. 6. *fig.* key (of the problem, etc.). çelësabërës,-i *m.sh.* – locksmith. çélët (i, e) *mb.* light (colour). çelí/k,-ku *m.sh.* -qe steel; uzinë për shkrirjen e çelikut: steel works. çelikós *f.k.* 1. to steel. 2. *fig.* to temper. – çelikosem *f.jv.* steel oneself. çelikósj/e,-a *f.* steeling, hardening. çelíktë (i, e) *mb.* 1. steely, steel.

2. *fig.* iron, steely; disiplinë e **çeliktë**: iron discipline.
çélj/e,-a *f.sh.* — 1. opening, aperture: 2. *(çelja e luleve)* blossoming, flowering, opening. 3. *(çelja e zogjve)* hatching.
çengél,-i *m.sh.* -a hook, crook; **çengel me shumë kanxha;** grapple.
çep,-i *m.sh.* -a nozzle; lip; spout; **çep çajniku:** nozzle of a teapot.
çepkát *f.k. (leshin)* to unravel (wool).
çérdh/e,-ja *f.sh.* -e 1. *(zogjsh)* nest. 2. *(çerdhe fëmijësh)* crèche; **çerdhe ditore:** *day-nursery;* **edukatore çerdheje:** nursery maid. 3. *usht.* nest; **çerdhe mitralozi:** machine-gun nest.
çerék,-u *m.sh.* -ë quarter; **një çerek ore:** a quarter of an hour; **ora është dy pa një çerek:** it is a quarter to two; **ora është dy e një çerek:** it is a quarter past two.
çerép,-i *m.sh.* -ë tray (shallow pot) for baking.
çerr,-i *m.sh.* -a *zool.* wren.
çét/ë,-a *f.sh.* -a fighting unit; **çetë partizane:** partisan fighting unit.
çézm/ë,-a *f.sh.* -a fountain.
çënjt *f.k. mjek.* to reduce the swelling of. — **çënjtem** *f.jv.* to become less swollen.
çënjtj/e,-a *f. mjek.* reducing (of an abscess).
çështj/e,-a *f.sh.* -e 1. matter, question, affair, problem; **si qëndron çështja?** what is the matter?; **kjo është çështja:** that is the question; **zgjidh një çështje:** to solve a problem, to settle a question; **ngre një çështje të re:** to raise a new point; **çështje e papërfunduar:** an open question; **i kthehem prapë një**

çështjeje: to come back to a question, to go back over a matter. 2. cause: **çështja e madhe e proletariatit:** the great cause of the proletariat; **çështja e socializmit:** the cause of socialism
çfárë *p.p.* what; **çfarë doni?** what do you want?; **çfarë thatë?** what did you say?; **për çfarë bisedohet?** what is the matter?, what is being discussed?
çfárë *p.pk.* 1. what, which: **ja në çfarë ka të drejtë ai:** that is precisely where he is right; **nuk e di se çfarë:** I don't know what. 2. whatever; **thuaj çfarë të duash:** say whatever you like.
çfarëdó *p.pk.* whatever, any; anything; **çfarëdo qoftë:** anything, whatsoever; **çfarëdo që të thoni:** whatever you say, say what you will; **çfarëdo që të ndodhë:** whatever may happen; **më jep një libër çfarëdo:** give me any book (no matter which); **në çfarëdo mënyrë:** in whatever manner.
çfarëdósh/ëm(i),-me(e) *mb.* any whatever, of any kind, of any sort; **gjatë një dite të çfarëdoshme:** in the course of any one day.
çibán,-i *m.sh.* -ë *mjek* furunculum, boil.
çibúk,-u *m.sh.* -ë smoking-pipe, cigar-holder.
çiflí/g,-gu *m.sh.* -gje estate, country estate.
çifligár,-i *m.sh.* -ë landlord, landsman, land-owner, squire.
çift,-i *m.sh.* -e l. couple; **një çift pëllumbash:** a couple of doves. 2. couple; **një çift i ri:** a newly married couple.
çift,-e *mb.* even; **numër çift:** even number.

çíft/ë,-ja *f.sh.* -e fowling gun, hunting gun, double-barrelled gun, fowling-piece.
çiftelí,-a *f.sh.* —a two stringed musical instrument.
çíft,-i *m.sh.* -ë Jew, Israelite, Hebrew.
çifút,-e *mb.* Jewish.
çik *f.k.* to graze, to touch lightly.
çík/ë,-a *f.sh.* -a 1. bit; një çikë bukë: a bit of bread; asnjë çikë: not a bit: 2. prit një çikë: wait a moment (a minute). 3. për një çikë: by a hair's breadth.
çík/ë,-a *f.sh.* -a *krah.* girl, lass.
çikërrim/ë; -a *f.sh* -á shih çikërrimë.
çíkj/e,-a *f.* grazing, touching.
çiklíst,-i *m.sh.* -ë cyclist.
çiklíz/ëm,-mi *m.* cycling.
çikór/e,-ja *f. bot.* chicory.
çikrík,-u *m.sh.* -ë 1. spinning wheel. 2. *fiz.* pulley; çikrik pusi: hand winch of well: çikrik për mbështjelljen e kabllit:capstan.
çilimí,-u *m.sh.* -nj kid, child; prej çilimiu: childish.
çilimillë/k,-ku *m.sh.* -qe adolescent pranks, tricks, mischie vousness.
çíltas *ndajf.* 1. openly, frankly, sincerely. 2. plainly, clearly.
çíltër (i,e) *mb.* open-hearted, candid, sincere.
çiltërí,-a *f.* sincerity, frankness, candor, openness.
çimentím,-i *m.sh.* -e 1. cementation, cementing. 2. *fig.* strengthening.
çiménto,-ja *f.sh.* — cement.
çimentój *f.k.* 1. to cement. 2. *fig.* to strengthen: çimentoj miqësinë: to strengthen the friendship. — çimentohet *f.jv.* 1. to be cemented. 2. *fig.* to be strengthened.
çímk/ë,-a *f.sh.* -a *zool.* bug, bed-bug.

çinár,-i *m.sh.* -ë *bot.* shih rrap.
çiní,-a *f.sh.* — porcelain plate.
çinteresím,-i *m.* disinterestedness.
çinteresúar (i,e) *mb.* 1. disinterested. 2. not interested. 3. indiferent, not caring.
çip,-i *m.sh.* -a 1. extremity, end. 2. corner; në çip të tryezës: at the corner of the table.
çirák,-u *m.sh.* -ë apprentice. — *Lok.* na nxore çirak: you have much obliged us (ironically).
çírrem *f.jv.* shih çjerr.
çitjáne,-t *f.sh.* puffy trousers.
çiví,-a *f.sh.* — hinge; çivi dere: hinge of a door.
çivít,-i *m.* dark blue.
çízm/e,-ja *f.sh.* -e boot; çizme lëkure: leather boots; çizme gome, llastiku: rubber boots, waders; vesh çizmet: to put on one's boots.
çjerr *f.k.* (p.t. çora, p.p. çjerrë) 1. to tear up, to lacerate. 2. to scratch, to claw. 3. *fig.* çjerr maskën: to unmask, to tear off the mask, to lay bare; i çjerr veshët dikujt: to split someone's ears. — çirrem *f.jv.* 1. to be torn, to be scratched. 2. çirrem së thirruri: to get hoarse of crying.
çjérrë (i,e) *mb.* zë i çjerrë: hoarse voice.
çjérrës,-e *mb.* piercing, jarring; zë çjerrës: piercing voice.
çjérrj/e,-a *f.* 1. (e një letre etj.) 1. tearing. 2. (çjerrje mbi lëkurë): scratch (on the skin).
çka *p.lidh.* what; çka mësohet shpejt, harrohet shpejt: what is quickly learned, is quickly forgotten.
çka *ndajf.* so-so; si ndjehesh? — çka: how do you feel? — so-so.
çlírët (i,e) *mb.* loose; xhaketë e çlirët; loose jacket.
çlirím,-i *m.* liberation, emancipa-

tion, freeing; release; **çlirim kombëtar:** national liberation; **çlirim shoqëror:** social emancipation.
çlirimtár,-i *m.sh.* -e liberator.
çlirimtár,-e *mb.* liberation; **luftë çlirimtare:** liberation war.
çlirój *f.k.* 1. to liberate; to deliver; to set free; to release, to free, to loose, to let off; **çliroj dikë nga robëria:** to free someone from bondage. 2. *fig.* to release, to set free, to exempt *(nga një premtim).* – **çlirohem** *f.jv.* to free oneself *(nga,* from), to make oneself free, to get free; **çlirohem nga zgjedha e huaj:** to shake off the foreign yoke; **çlirohem nga një siklet:** to be delivered from a care.
çlodh *f.k.* 1. to rest; **çlodh këmbët:** to rest one's legs. 2. to rest, to be restful to; **ngjyra që të çlodhin sytë:** colours that are restful to the eyes. – **çlodhem.** *f.jv.* to rest, to repose, to take (to have) a rest; to relax.
çlódhës,-e *mb.* restful, relaxing; **një pushim çlodhës:** a relaxing holiday.
çlodhj/e,-a *f.* 1. rest, repose; **vend çlodhjeje:** restingplace. 2. recreation, divertissement; **çlodhje e mendjes:** divertissement of the mind.
çmállem *f.jv.* to satisfy one's nostalgia.
çmbështjéll *f.k.* to uncoil, to unwrap; *(velat)* to unfurl (the sails). – **çmbështillet** *f.jv.* to be uncoiled (unwrapped).
çmbreh *f.k.* to unharness, to unyoke. – **çmbrehet** *f.jv.* to be unharnessed.
çmend *f.k.* to drive someone mad, to drive someone crazy; **sot më çmendën fëmijët:** the children have been driving me

mad today. – **çmendem** *f.jv.* 1. to go mad (crazy, insane), to lose one's wits; **mos u çmende?** are you mad?, are you crazy?; **të vjen të çmendesh:** it's enough to drive one mad. 2. **çmendem pas dikujt:** to be madly in love with someone.
çmendín/ë,-a *f.sh.* -a mentalhome, madhouse, lunatic asilum, mental hospital.
çméndj/e,-a *f.* going mad.
çméndur (i,e) *mb.* mad, crazy, insane, demented; cracked-brained; **njeri i çmendur;** madman.
çmendurí,-a *f.* craziness, insanity, dementia.
çmërs,-i *m.* incrustation.
çmësój *f.k.* to disaccustom, to make unused *(me,* to), to break (to get out) of a habit. – **çmësohem** *f.jv.* to lose (to get out of, to get rid of) a habit, to disaccustom oneself, to become unused; **çmësohem me diçka:** to lose the habit of doing something.
çmilitarizím,-i *m.* demilitarization.
çmilitarizój *f.k.* to demilitarize. – **çmilitarizohet** *f.jv.* to be demilitarized.
çmim,-i *m.sh.* -e 1. price; **çmim i caktuar:** fixed price; **çmim i prerë:** set price; **çmime tregu:** market prices; **rënie e çmimeve:** drop of prices; **ngritje e çmimeve:** rise of prices; **blej me çmim të ulët:** to buy cheap; **blej me çmim të lartë;** to buy at a high price, to buy dearly. 2. *(çmim konkursi)* prize, award; **i– jap një çmim dikujt:** to award a prize to someone; **fitoj çmim:** to win a prize. – *Lok.* **me çdo çmim:** at all costs, at any price.
çmobilizím,-i *m. usht.* demobilization.

çmobilizój *f.k. usht.* to demobilize. – çmobilizohem *f.jv.* to be demobilized.

çmoj *f.k.* 1. to estimate, to appraise, to evaluate, to value, to assess. 2. to appreciate, to esteem. – çmohem *f.jv.* to be esteemed (appreciated).

çmontím,-i *m.sh.* -e dismantling, taking to pieces.

çmontój *f.k.* to dismantle, to disassemble, to dismount.

çmos *p.pk.* anything; bëj çmos: to do one's best, to do all (everything), one can, to do the utmost, to try one's best.

çmpij *f.k. (këmbët)* to stretch (one's legs).

çmúar (i,e) *mb.* 1. precious; gur i çmuar: precious stone. 2. *fig.* precious, valued; këshilla të çmuara: valuable advice.

çmúarj/e,-a *f.* appreciation, estimation.

çmúes,-i *m.sh.* – estimator, appreciator.

çmúesh/ëm (i), -me(e) *mb.* precious; appreciable, estimable.

çnderím,- *m.sh.* -e 1. dishonour; *(i një vajze)* violation (of a girl).

çnderój *f.k.* 1. *(dikë)* to dishonour, to disgrace, to bring dishonour upon (someone). 2. *(një vajzë)* to rape, to violate (a girl). – çnderohem *f.jv.* 1. to be dishonoured. 2. to be violated (a girl).

çndérsh/ëm(i),-me(e) *mb.* dishonest, dishonorable.

çnderúes,-i *m.sh.* – violator (of a girl).

çnderúes,-e *mb.* dishonouring, discrediting.

çndryshk *f.k.* to rub the rust (of something), to unrust, – çndryshket *f.jv.* to be unrusted.

çngjyrós *f.k.* to decolourize, to

bleach, – çngjyroset *f.jv.* to be decolourized (decoloured).

çngjyrósës,-i *m.sh.* – decolorant.

çngjyrósës,-e *mb.* decolourizing, decolorant.

çnjerëzór,-e *mb.* inhuman; në mënyrë çnjerëzore; inhumanely.

çobán,-i *m.sh.* -ë herdsman, shepherd.

çobánk/ë,-a *f.sh.* -a herdgirl.

çoj *f.k.* 1. to send, to dispatch, to forward (a letter etc.). 2. to send, to dispatch; çoj një korier: to send a messenger. 3 to lead; kjo rrugë s'të çon në stacion: this road does not lead to the station. 4. *fig.* to lead, to drive; çoj në rrugë të shtrembër: to mislead, to lead on the wrong way; çoj në rrugë të drejtë: to lead on the right way. 5. to transmit; çoj të fala: to give (to transmit) regards (to). 6. to convey; çoj mallra: to carry (to convey) goods.

çoj I. *f.k.* 1. to wake up, to awaken; më çoj në orën tetë: wake me up at eight, call me at eight. 2. *(gjahun)* to drive out, to rouse. II. *f.jk.* (ia) 1. *(me shëndet)* si ia çon? how are you?, how are you doing? 2. to pass; ia çova mirë këtë të diel: I had a good time this Sunday. – çohem *f.jv.* 1. to get up, to stand up. 2. to wake up, to awaken; sot u çova vonë: I woke up late today; çohem nga shtrati: to get up; çohem më këmbë: to stand up; çohu! get up! stand up! ,up!; ai çohet gjithnjë herët: he always gets up early.

ço/k,-ku *m.sh.* -qe knocker, knob (of a door); çok dere: doorknob; çok kambane: clapper.

çokás I *f.jk.* to knock.

II. *f.k.* **çokas gotat**: to touch glasses (in drinking).

çók/ë,-a *f.sh.* -a fillip; **i jap një çokë**: to fillip.

çokollát/ë,-a *f.sh.* -a chocolate.

çománg/e,-ia *f.sh.* -e club, cudgel, bludgeon.

çomlёk,-u *m.* dish of meat, onions and garlics.

çoráp,-i *m.sh.* -e *(çorape burrash)* socks; *(çorape grash)* stockings; **çorape leshi**: woolen socks; **çorape mёndafshi**: silk stockings; **çorape pambuku**: cotton stockings; **mbath çorapet**: to put (to pull) on one's socks (stockings); **heq çorapet**: to put (to pull) off one's socks (stockings).

çórb/ë,-a *f.* porridge; *fig.* **çorbë derri**: hodgepodge.

çorganizím,-i *m.sh.* -e disorganization.

çorganizój *f.k.* to disorganize. – **çorganizohem** *f.jv.* to become disorganized.

çorientím,-i *m.* confusion, disorientation.

çorientój *f.k.* 1. to disorient. 2. *fig.* to confuse. – **çorientohem** *f.jv.* 1. to lose one's bearings 2. to get confused.

çorodís *f.k.* 1. to disconcert, to confuse, to embarrass. 2. to defile; to corrupt. – **çoroditem** *f.jv*: 1. to become confused. 2. *fig.* to be corrupted, to degenerate.

çoroditёs,-e *mb.* 1. disconcerting, embarrassing. 2. *fig.* degenerative.

çoroditj/e,-a *f.sh.* -e 1. confusion, embarrasment. 2. *fig.* degeneration, corruption.

çregjistrím,-i *m.sh.* -e 1. striking off (a list). 2. *tek. (i zёrit)* wiping, erasure.

çregjistrój *f.k.* 1. to strike off (a list). 2. *tek. (nga shiriti i*

magnetofonit) to wipe out, to erase. – **çregjistrohem** *f.jv.* 1. to be stricken off. 2. *tek.* to be wiped out, to be erased.

çrregullím,-i *m.sh.*-e 1. disorder, untideness, confusion, disarray, muddle, mess; **në dhomë ishte një çrregullim i madh**: the room was in a great mess. 2. *fig. (mendor)* mental confusion, muddle. 3. *sh.* disorders, disturbances.

çrregullój *f.k.* to disorder, to throw into disorder; to disarrange, to upset, to confuse, to mess up. – **çrregullohet** *f.jv.* to be untidy, to be disorderly, to be in disorder, to be in a muddle, to be in a mess.

çrregullt (i, e) *mb.* 1. untidy, messy; **nxёnёs i çrregullt**: untidy pupil. 2. wild, irregular; **bёj një jetё tё çrregullt**: to lead a wild life.

çrregullúes,-e *mb.* disturbing, troblesome.

çrrënjós *f.k.* 1. *(pemёt)* to uproot (tress). 2. *fig.* to eradicate, to root out, to extirpate.

- **çrrënjoset** *f.jv.* to be extirpated, to be eradicated.

çrrënjósj/e,-a *f.sh.*-e 1. uprooting. 2. *fig.* eradication, rooting out.

çudí,-a *f.sh.*- 1. wonder, amazement, astonishment. 2. marvel, miracle; **pёr çudi**: for a wonder, miraculously, surprisingly; **çuditë e natyrës**: the marvels of the nature; **populli bёn çudira**: the people work (do) wonders. 3. surprise. – *Lok.* **ёshtё çudi si nuk u shtypa**: it was a miracle (wonder) I wasn't run over; **çudi si nuk mё telefonoi**: it's odd that he hasn't called me.

çudibёrёs,-e *mb.* miraculous; **ilaç çudibёrёs**: miraculous drug.

çudís *f.k.* to surprise, to astonish,

to astound, to stupefy, to amaze, to marvel; **mos u çuditІ** (it is) no wonder that. — **çuditem** *f.jv.* to be astonished, to be surprised, to be amazed, to wonder, to marvel *(me,* at). **çuditërisht** *ndajf.* strangely, surprisingly. **çudítës,-e** *mb.* astonishing, surprising. **çudítsh/ëm (i),-me(e)** *mb.* strange, uncommon, peculiar; **njeri i çuditshëm:** a strange man. **çudítur (i, e)** *mb.* surprised, astonished, amazed. **çúk/ë,-a** *f.sh.*-a summit of a mount.

çukís *f.k.* to peck; **zogu çukit pemën:** the bird pecks the fruit-tree. **çukítj/e,-a** *f.sh.*-e pecking. **çun,-i** *m.sh.*-a boy, youngster; **çun i mirë:** good boy; **çun i prapë:** naughty boy. **çunák,-u** *m-sh.* -ë little boy; **prej çunaku:** boyish. **çúp/ë,-a** *f.sh.*-a girl, lass. **çupërí,-a** *f.* 1. maidenhood. 2. virginity. **çúrk/ë,-a** *f.sh.*-a trickling; **shkon çurkë:** to trickle. **çyrék,-u** *m.sh.* -ë loaf (of bread). **çyrýk** *mb.* vicious, defective, faulty

D

d, D (letter of the Albanian alphabet) d, D. **dac,-i** *m.sh.*-a tom-cat, cat, he-cat, male-cat. **dáck/ë,-a** *f.sh.*-a slap, smack; **i jap dikujt një dackë turinjve:** to slap someone on the face. **dádo,-ja** *f.sh.* - nurse. **dádo,-ja** *f.sh.* - *mek.* nut (of a screw). **dafín/ë,-a** *f.sh.* -a *bot.* laurel, laurel wood; **kurorë dafinash:** garland, wreath of laurels. — *Lok.* **fle mbi dafina:** to rest on laurels. **daják,-u** *m.sh.* -ë 1. rod, cudgel, bastinado. 2. cudgelling, bastinado; **i dha një dajak:** he gave him a good beating.

dáj/ë,-a *m.sh.* -a uncle (mother's brother). **dájr/e,-ja** *f.sh.* -e tambourine. **dakórd** *ndajf.* agreed, all right; **bie dakord:** to agree, to come to terms, to come to an agreement; **jam dakord:** to agree; **s'jam dakord:** to disagree; **dakord:** all right!, agreed, *fam.* right you areІ, O.K.; **siç ramë dakord:** as agreed. **daktilografí,-a** *f.* type-writing, typing. **daktilografím,-i** *m.sh.* -e type-writing, typing. **daktilografíst,-i** *m.sh.* -ë typist. **daktilografój** *f.k.* to type, to type-write. **dal** *f.jk.* 1. to go out, to leave; to come out, to get out; **a dalim**

ca? shall we go out for a while?; dal nga banja: to come out of the bathroom. 2. to leave, to break away (from), to withdraw; dal nga grupi: to withdraw from the group, to leave the group. 3. to appear; to spring; dal para gjyqit: to appear before the tribunal; dal befas: to appear suddenly (unexpectedly), to spring; dal në shesh: to come into sight, to come out in the open. 4. (dal mbi sipërfaqen e ujit): to emerge. 5. fig. to get out; dal nga një situatë e vështirë: to get out of a predicament. – Lok. dal të pres dikë: to go to meet someone; dal faqebardhë: to come out successful (with flying colours); dalçi faqebardhë! may you be successful! ia dal në krye një pune: to succeed in a business; të dalë ku të dalë! come what may! dal jashtë: a) to go out; b) to move (to evacuate) the bowels.

dála,-t (të) f.sh. 1. goings; të hyra e të dala: entries and goings, entries and outgoings. 2. fin. expenses.

dále pasth. wait; dale pak: wait a little.

dál/ë (e),-a (e) f.sh. -a (të) projection, jut, protrusion.

dálë,-t (të) as. 1. going; në të dalë të dimrit: towards the end of the winter. 2. të dalët jashtë: dejection, evacuation of excrements.

dáli/e,-a f. bot. dahlia.

dálj/e,-a f.sh. -e 1. going out, coming out; bëj daljen e parë pas një sëmundjeje: to go out for the first time after an illness. 2. way out, exit; dalje sigurimi: emergency exit. 3. appearance; dalje para gjyqit: appearance before a tribunal. 4. (dalje mbi ujë)

emergence, emerging 5. (e n/ë vepre letrare) publication (of a book).

dalngadálë ndajf. slowly; gradually.

dált/ë,-a f.sh. -a mek. chisel, graver.

dallaveraxhí,-u m.sh. -nj swindler.

dallavér/e,-ja f.sh. -e swindle; bëj dallavere: to swindle, to defraud, to practice fraud upon.

dalldí,-a f. 1. extasy. 2. infatuation.

dalldís f.jk. to fall in extasy; (pas diçkaje) to go daft, to go batty (over something). – dalldisem f.jv. to be infatuated (pas dikujt, with someone).

dalldísj/e,-a f. falling in extasy; going daft, going batty.

dalldísur (i, e) mb. 1. fallen in extasy. 2. foolhardy, reckless, daring, dare-devil, rash; njeri i dalldisur: reckless man.

dallëndýsh/e,-ja f.sh. -e zool. swallow

Prov. me një dallëndyshe nuk vjen pranvera: one swallow does not make a summer.

dállg/ë,-a f.sh. -ë wave; (dallgë e madhe) billow, surge; (dallgë e vogël) ripple; det me dallgë: wavy sea.

dállgë-dállgë ndajf. wavy.

dallgëzím,-i m.sh. -e waving, rippling, surging.

dallgëzúar (i, e) mb. wavy, waved.

dallím,-i m.sh. -e 1. distinction, discernement, differentiation; bëj dallim: to make a distinction, to differentiate. 2. discrimination; dallim racial: racial discrimination.

dallkaúk,-u m.sh. -ë yes-man, flatterer, likspittle.

dallkaukllë/k-u m.sh. -qe fawning.

dallój f.k. 1. to distinguish, to discern. 2. to differenciate. – da-

llohem *f.jv.* to be distinguished *(nga,* from).

dallúar (i, e) *mb.* prominent, noted, eminent, distinguished, remarkable.

dallúes,-e *mb.* distinctive.

dallúesh/ëm (i),-me(e) *mb.* discernible, visible; evident, perceptible; evident, obvious.

damalúg,-u *m.sh.* -e ploughshare.

damár,-i *m.sh.* -ë 1. *anat.* vein; **me damarë:** veinous, full of veins. 2. *(i drurit, i mermerit)* grain. 3. *(damar minerali)* lode. 4. *fig.* vein, humour, mood; **s'jam në damar të mirë:** to be in a bad mood.

damáz,-i *m.sh.* -ë *zool.* breeder, stud.

dám/ë,-a *f. (lojë)* draughts, *amer.* checker.

dám/ë,-a *f.sh.* -a lady.

damixhán/ë,-a *f.sh.* -a demijohn.

dámk/ë,-a *f.sh.* -a 1. earmark, stamp. 2. *fig.* stigma; **më vuri damkë:** he dishonoured me.

damkós *f.k.* 1. to stamp; **damkos me hekur të nxehtë:** to brand. 2. *fig.* to stigmatize, to brand.

damkósj/e,-a *f.sh.* -e 1. stamping. 2. stigmatization. stigmatizing.

damllá,-ja *f. mjek.* apoplexy, cerebral congestion.

damllósur (i,e) *mb.* attacked by apoplexy.

danéz,-i *m.sh.* -ë Dane.

danéz,-e *mb.* Danish.

dans,-i *m.* dance.

dansój *f.jk.* to dance.

dantéll/ë,-a *f.sh.* -a lace-work, point-lace, knotting lace.

dárdh/ë,-a *f.sh.* -a *bot.* pear; *(druri)* pear-tree.

dár/ë,-a *f.sh.* -e pinchers, nippers, pincers; **darë për gozhdë:** pinchers, pincers; **darë e vogël:** nippers;

dárk/ë,-a *f.sh.* -a 1. dinner, supper;

ha darkë: to dine, to have dinner, to sup, to have supper; **shkoj te dikush për darkë:** to go to dinner, to go for dinner; **pas darke:** after dinner, after supper; **dje isha për darkë tek ...** yesterday I had dinner at ..., yesterday I went to .... for dinner; **shtroj një darkë:** to give a dinner-party. 2. evening; **në darkë:** in the evening; **në orën tetë të darkës:** at eight o'clock in the evening, at eight at night.

darkëherë (më) *ndajf.* in the evening, at dusk.

darkój *f.k.* to give a dinner-party. – **darkohem** *f.jv.* to dine, to sup.

daróv/ë,-a *f.sh.* -a *krah.* gift; **darovë dasme:** wedding gift.

darovísht *ndajf.* gratis, gratuitously.

darovís *f.k.* to make a present of.

dásm/ë,-a *f.sh.* -a wedding; **gosti dasme:** wedding feast; **të hëngsha dasmën:** may I attend your wedding (a form of wish for young men).

dasmór,-i *m.sh.* -ë wedding host.

dasmór/e,-ja *f.sh.* -e bridesmaid.

dash,-i *m.sh.* -desh *zool.* ram; **mish dashi:** mutton; **dash i tredhur:** wether, castrated ram; **dashi bajloz:** leading ram.

dashakéq,-i *m.sh.* -ë malevolent (malignant) person.

dashaligësí,-a *f.* malevolence, ill-will.

dashamír,-i *m.sh.* -ë benevolent person, kind person.

dashamirësí,-a *f.* benevolence, goodwill; kindness, amability, affability; **me dashamirësi:** kindly; **kini dashamirësinë të:** have the kindness to, be willing to.

dáshj/e,-a *f.* will, willingness; **me dashje:** willingly, voluntarily; **pa dashje:** unwillingly, reluctantly, involuntarily; **me dashjen e të**

gjitha palëve: with one accordj me dashjen e vet: of h s own will: dashje pa dashje: willy- -nilly.
dáshtë! *pasth.* may!
dashnór,-i *m.sh.* -ë lover, sweet⌐ heart.
dásht/ër,-ra *f. bot.* accanthus.
dáshur (i, e) *mb.* dear, beloved; loving, lovable, amiable; fort i dashur: very dear, dearest, darling; i dashur mik: my dear friend.
dáshur (i),-i (i) *m.sh.* -(të) lover; i dashuri i saj: her lover, her sweetheart.
dashurí,-a *f.* 1. love, affection; kam (ndiej, ushqej) dashuri për dikë: to feel (to cherish) love for someone; dashuri fëmijësh: childish love; dashuri prindërore: paternal tenderness (affection); dashuri vëllazërore: fraternal love; letër dashurie: love letter; bëj dashuri: to flirt, to make love; bie në dashuri: to fall in love (with); i shfaq dashurinë dikujt: to declare one's love to someone; i djegur nga dashuria: love-sick; me dashuri: lovely, lovingly, dearly; tenderly, fondly, affectionately, with love. 2. love, enthusiasm; dashuria për artin: love for art, love of art.
dashurój *f.k.* to love, to be in love with; to be fond of, to like, to be keen on; dashuroj marrëzisht: to love passionately. – dashurohem *f.jv.* 1. to be loved. 2. to be in love; dashurohemi: to love one another.
dashurúar (i, e) *mb.* beloved, in love.
dát/ë,-a *f.sh.* -a date; sa është data sot? what day (of the month) is it today? në ç'datë? when? i datës së djeshme:

yesterday's, dated yesterday; datë përkujtimore: memorable date; datë e lindjes: date of birth.
dát/ë,-a *f.* dread, terror; i kall datën dikujt: to strike terror into, to scare stiff, to scare to death.
datëlindj/e,-a *f.sh.* -e birth-date, birthday.
daúlle,-ja *f.sh.* -e drum; i bie daulles: to beat the drum. – *Lok.* i hedh këmbët sipas daulles: to go with the tide, to go with the stream.
davá,-ja *f.sh.* - *vjet.* litigation, lawsuit; *fig.* kjo është dava e vjetër: this is an old tale.
davarís *f.k.* to scatter, to disperse, to dissipate; era davarit retë: the wind dissipates the clouds.
debát,-i *m.sh.* -e debate, discussion, controversy.
debí,-a *f. treg.* debit.
debitój *f.k.* to debit.
debitór,-i *m.sh.* -ë debtor.
debutój *f.k.* to make one's debut, to come out.
debutúes,-i *m.sh.* - 1. debutante, *fam.* deb. 2. beginner, novice.
decilít/ër,-ri *m.sh.* -ra deciliter.
decimét/ër,-ri *m.sh.* -ra decimeter.
dedikím,-i *m.sh.* -e dedication.
dedikój *f.k.* 1. *(një vepër letrare)* to dedicate. 2. *(kohën, punën)* to devote. – dedikohem(i) *f.jv.* to dedicate oneself; to devote oneself.
deficít,-i *m.sh.* -e deficit; dal deficit: to have a deficit, to show a deficit.
deficitár,-e *mb. ekon.* showing a deficit, having a debit-balance.
deformím,-i *m.sh.* -e deformation, disfiguration.
deformój *f.k.* to deform, to disfigure, to deface; to warp. – deformohet *f.jv.* to warp.
deftér,-i *m.sh.* -ë *vjet.* register.

degdis *f.k.* to send away, to deport.
– **degdisem** *f.jv.* 1. to be sent away (deported). 2. to turn one's steps towards . . .
dég/ë,-a *f.sh.* -ë 1. *bot.* limb bough, branch. 2. *gjeog. (degë lumi)* affluent. 3. **degë tregtare:** branch-establishment, agency. 4. *(e shkencës)* branch.
dégëz,-a *f.sh.* -a twig, little branch, spray.
degëzím,-i *m.sh.* -e ramification, bifurcation.
degëzój *f.k.* to ramify, to bifurcate.
– **degëzohet** *f.jv.* to branch out, to ramify; **degëzohen rrugët:** the roads branch out.
degradím,-i *m.sh.* -e degradation, retrogression.
degradój *f.k.* 1. to degrade, to retrograde. 2. *usht.* to demote, to degrade. – **degradohem** *f.jv.* 1. to degrade, to sink (to demean) oneself. 2. *usht.* to be demoted, to degrade, to be degraded.
degjenerím,-i *m.* degeneration.
degjenerój I. *f.k.* to cause (someone) to degenerate. – **degjenerohem** *f.jv.* to degenerate, to deteriorate. II. *f.jk.* to degenerate, to deteriorate.
deh *f.k.* 1. to inebriate, to intoxicate, to fuddle, to make drunk. 2. *fig.* to elate; to go to the head of. – **dehem** *f.jv.* 1. to fuddle, to get drunk, to become intoxicated, *fam.* to get tipsy, to get high stoned; **dehem e bëhem tapë:** to be boozed. 2. *fig.* to become intoxicated; **dehem nga sukseset:** to be elated by success.
déhës,-e *mb.* 1. intoxicating; heady; **pije dehëse:** intoxicating drink. 2. *fig.* intoxicating, stirring, heady.
déhj/e,-a *f.sh.* -e intoxication, inebriation, inebriety, drunkenness.

déhur (i, e) *mb.* drunk, drunken, intoxicated, *fam.* tipsy.
déhur (i),-i (i) *m.sh.*-(të)drunkard.
dekadénc/ë,-a *f.* decay, decline, downfall, decadence.
dekadént,-e *mb.* decadent.
dekád/ë,-a *f.sh.* decade.
dekán,-i *m.sh.* -ë dean (of a faculty).
dekanát,-i *m.sh.* -e dean's office; deanery.
deklamím,-i *m.sh.* -e declamation.
deklamój *f.k.* to declaim.
deklamúes,-e *mb.* declamatory.
deklarát/ë,-a *f.sh.* -a declaration, statement; **deklaratë e rreme:** mis-state, false-state; **bëj një deklaratë të rreme:** to mis-state; **bëj një deklaratë me gojë:** to make a declaration: *(me shkrim)*: to make a statement.
deklarój *f.k.* to speak out, to speak up, to declare, to state; **deklaroj botërisht:** to declare openly (publicly). – **deklarohem** *f.jv.* to be declared, to declare oneself, to proclaim oneself.
deklarúes,-e *mb.* declaratory.
deklasój *f.k.* to declass.
deklasúar (i, e) *mb.* declassed.
dekompozím,-i *m.* decomposition.
dekompozój *f.k.* to decompose.
dekór,-i *m.sh.* -e décor.
dekoración,-i *m.sh.* -e decoration, ornamentation.
dekorát/ë,-a *f.sh.* -a decoration; **i jap një dekoratë dikujt:** to confer a decoration on someone.
dekoratív,-e *mb.* decorative; **art dekorativ:** decorative art.
dekorím,-i *m.sh.* -e decorating, confering of a decoration.
dekorój *f.k.* to decorate, to confer a decoration.
dekorúar (i, e) *mb.* decorated.
dekorúar (i),-i (i) *m.sh.* -(të) holder of a decoration.

dekovíl,-i *m.sh.* -a railway carriage.
dekrét,-i *m.sh.* -e decree.
dekretím,-i *m.sh.* -e enacting, enactement, decreeing.
dekretój *f.k.* to decree, to enact.
del *f.jk.* shih **dal** (1st and 2nd person)
dél/e,-ja *f.sh.* -e *zool.* ewe, sheep.
delegación,-i *m.sh.* -e delegation.
delegát,-i *m.sh.* -ë delegate.
delegúar (i, e) *mb.* delegated, deputed.
delegúar(i),-i (i) *m.sh.* -(të) delegate.
delenxhí,-u *m.sh.* -nj rascal, knave.
delfín,-i *m.sh.* -ë *zool.* delphin.
delikát,-e *mb.* delicate; fragile; ticklish; **një çështje tepër delikate:** a very delicate (acute) question.
delikatés/ë,-a *f.* delicacy; **ha me delikatesë:** to eat daintily.
delíkt,-i *m.sh.* -e delict.
deltín/ë,-a *f.sh.* -e clay, potter's earth.
deluzión,-i *m.sh.* -e disillusion.
dell,-i *m.sh.* - deje *anat.* tendon, sinew; **gjeth delli:** plantain.
dem,-i *m.sh.* -a *zool.* bull, steer; **dem i vogël:** young bull; **luftim (ndeshje) me dema:** bull-fight.
demagóg,-u *m.sh.* -ë demagogue.
demagogjí,-a *f.* demagogy.
demagogjík,-e *mb.* demagogic, demagogical.
demarkación,-i *m.* demarcation.
demaskím,-i *m.* unmasking.
demaskój *f.k.* to unmask, to show up. – **demaskohem** *f.jv.* to be unmasked.
dembél,-i *m.sh.* -ë lazy-bones. – *Prov.* **dembeli zihet me veglat e punës:** a bad workman quarrels with his tools.
dembél,-e *mb.* lazy, idle; **djalë dembel:** a lazy boy.
dembelí,-a *f.* laziness, idleness; **me dembeli:** lazily, idly.

dembelíz/ëm,-mi *m.* shih **dembeli.**
dembelós *f.k.* to make (someone) lazy; **qëndrimi pa punë të dembelos:** inactivity makes one lazy. – **dembelosem** *f.jv.* to grow lazy, to grow heavy, to grow sluggish.
demiroxhák,-u *m.sh.* -ë fire-dog.
demodúar (i, e) *mb.* out of date, out of fashion.
demografí,-a *f.* demography.
demokrací,-a *f.* democracy.
demokrát,-i *m.sh.* -ë democrat.
demokratík,-e *mb.* democratic.
demokratizím,-i *m.* democratization.
demokratizój *f.k.* to democratize. – **demokratizohet** *f.jv.* to be democratized.
demón,-i *m.sh.* -ë demon.
demonstrát/ë,-a *f.sh.* -a demonstration; **marr pjesë në një demonstratë:** to take part in a demonstration; **demonstratë proteste:** protest demonstration.
demonstrúes,-i *m.* demonstrator.
demonstrúes,-e *mb.* demonstrative
demoralizím,-i *m.* demoraliza-. tion.
demoralizój *f.k.* to demoralize, to dishearten. – **demoralizohem** *f.jv.* to get demoralized, to become demoralized, to lose heart.
dend *f.k.* 1. to heap up. 2. to stuff, to cram; to puff up. – **dendem** *f.jv.* to stuff oneself, to cram oneself, to fill oneself up, to gorge; **dendem me ëmbëlsira:** to gorge on sweets.
dendësí, -a *f.* density; **dendësia e popullsisë:** population density.
dendësój *f.k.*1. to thicken, to make dense. 2. to make more frequent. – **dendësohet** *f.jv.* 1. to thicken, to grow thick. 2. to become more frequent.
déndur *ndajf.* frequently, often;

shkoj dendur: to go often, to frequent; **më dendur:** more often; **ata takohen dendur:** they see each other often.

déndur (i, e) *mb.* 1. dense, thick; **pyll i dendur:** thick wood; **flokë të dendura:** thick hair; **popullsi e dendur:** dense population. 2. frequent, repeated; numerous.

denduri,-a *f.* frequency.

den /g,-gu *m.sh.* -gje bale, bundle.

denoncím,-i *m.sh.* -e denunciation; **denoncim i një traktati:** denunciation of a treaty.

denoncój *f.k.* 1. to denounce, to report; to inform against. 2. *polit.* to denounce (a treaty). – **denoncohem** *f.jv.* to be denounced, to be exposed.

denoncúes,-i *m.sh.* - denunciator, denouncer.

dentíst,-i *m.sh,* -ë dentist.

dénjë(i, e) *mb.* worthy, deserving; **i denjë për t'i zënë besë:** trustworthy.

denjësí,-a *f.* worthiness.

denjësísht *ndajf.* worthily, deservedly.

denjój *f.k.* to deign, to condescend, to vouchsafe.

depërtím,-i *m.sh.* -e penetration, infiltration, permeation; *(depërtim me forcë)* irruption.

depërtój *f.k.* to penetrate, to infiltrate, to permeate, to pervade. – **depërtohet** *f.jv.* to be penetrated, to be permeated, to be infiltrated.

depërtúes,-e *mb.* 1. piercing, penetrating. 2. *fig.* discerning, penetrating, piercing.

depërtúesh/ëm (i),-me(e) *mb.* penetrable; **i depërtueshëm nga uji:** permeable.

depërtueshmërí,-a *f.* penetrability, permeability.

dépo,-ja *f,sh.* - store, store-house,

warehouse;depository; **depo ushtarake:** depôt, magazine for military stores.

deponím,-i *m.sh.* -e affidavit, deposition.

deponój *f.k. drejt.* to bear witness, to give sworn evidence; **deponoj në dobi të dikujt:** to testify on someone's behalf.

deponúes,-i *m.sh.* - deponent, witness.

depozít/ë,a *f.sh.* -a 1. deposit; **depozitë të hollash në bankë:** money on deposit. 2. depot, depository.

depozitím,-i *m.sh.* -e leaving; depositing, lodging (of money, etc.)

depozitój *f.k.* 1. to deposit, to lodge; **depozitoj të holla në një bankë** to deposit (to lodge) money in bank. 2. to store. – **depozitohet** *f.jv.* 1. *kim.* to deposit, to settle, to make a sediment. 2. *(paratë etj.)* to be deposited, to be lodged.

depozitúes,-i *m.sh.* - depositor.

deputét,-i *m.sh.* -ë deputy, *amer.* congressman.

derdh *f.k.* 1. to pour (out), to shed; to spill; **derdh gjakun për atdheun:** to shed blood for one's country; **derdh lotë:** to shed tears *(për diçka,* over something). 2. *(një shumë të hollash)*: to pay, to deposit, to bank, to pay in; **derdh këstin e parë:** to pay the first installment. 3. to mould (metals, etc.); **derdh një statujë** : to cast a statue. – **derdhet** *f.jv.* 1. to spill; to be spilled; **m'u derdh kafeja në kostum:** I have spilled some coffee on my suit. 2. to overflow, to flow, to pour, to brim, to spill over. 3. to pour, to stream; **populli u derdh në rrugë:** people poured into the streets. 4. to be moulded, to be casted.

dérdhj/e,-a *f.sh.* **-e** 1. pouring (out); shedding, spilling; **derdhje gjaku:** shedding of blood; bloodshed; **derdhje lotësh:** shedding of tears. 2. **(derdhje të hollash):** payment; depositing, paying in, banking. 3. **(derdhje metalesh etj)** moulding (of metals), casting (of a statue); **derdhje e një statuje:** casting of a statue.

dér/ë,-a *f.sh.* - **dyer** 1. door; **derë e jashtme** *(në rrugë):* gate, door-way, street-door, front-door. 2. family.

derëbárdhë *mb.* lucky, fortunate; **jo, or derëbardhë!** no, my old chap!

dérëz/i,-ezë *mb.* unfortunate, unlucky.

dérgjem *f.jv.* to languish, to droop, to be bedridden.

dérgji/e,-a *f.* languishness, drooping, gradual wasting away, consumption.

déri *paraf.* till, until, as far as, to; **deri kur?** how long?; **deri nesër:** till tomorrow; **deri tani:** till now, up to now; **deri në fund:** till the end; **nga fillimi deri në fund:** from the beginning to the end, from end to end, from top to end; **numëroj nga 1 deri në 10:** to count from one to ten; **deri ku?** how far?; **deri ku kini shkuar?** how far have you gone? **deri këtu:** hither to, up to here; **deri atëherë:** until then; **deri sa të jem gjallë:** as long as I live, so far as I live; **kam lexuar deri në faqen njëzet:** I have read up to page twenty (as far as page twenty).

deríçk/ë,-a *f.sh.* **-a** side-door, small door.

derisá *lidh.* until, till, as long as, so far as, inasmuch.

deritanísh/ëm(i),-me(e) *mb.* up to now.

derivát,-i *m.sh.* **-e** derivative.

dermán,-i *m.* remedy; **nuk i gjendet dermani:** there is no remedy for that; **nuk gjej derman:** to be helpless, **që s'ka derman:** irremediable, incurable.

dermatológ,-u *m.sh.* **-ë** *mjek.* dermatologist.

dermatologjí,-a *f.* *mjek.* dermatology.

dervísh,-i *m.sh.* **-ë** *fet.* dervish.

derr,-i *m.sh.* **-a** *zool.* 1. pig, hog, swine; **derr i egër:** boar, wild boar; **bari derrash:** swineherd; **stallë derrash:** pig-sty. 2. *(mish derri):* pork. 3. *fig.* pig.

derrár,-i *m.sh.* **-ë** swineherd.

derrkúc,-i *m.sh.* **-ë** sucking pig.

despót,-i *m.sh.* **-ë** despot, tyrant.

despotík,-e *mb.* despotic, despotical, tyrannical.

despotíz/ëm,-mi *m.* despotism.

destiním,-i *m.* destination.

destinój *f.k.* to destine. — **destinohet** *f.jv.* to be destined.

deshifrím,-i *m.sh.* **-e** deciphering.

deshifrój *f.k.* to decipher, to decode. – **deshifrohet** *f.jv.* to be deciphered, to be decoded.

deshifrúesh/ëm(i),-me(e) *mb.* decipherable.

det,-i *m.sh.* **-e** sea; **det i brendshëm:** inland sea; **Deti Mesdhe;** Mediterranean Sea; **det me dallgë:** wavy sea; **det me stuhi** heavy sea; **në det:** at sea; **në mes të detit:** on the high (open) sea; **sëmundja e detit:** sea sickness.

detáj,-i *m.sh.* **-e** 1. piece (of engine). 2. detail, particular.

detár,-i *m.sh.* **-ë** mariner, sailor, seaman, blue-jacket.

detár,-e *mb.* 1. maritime, sea-marine; **klimë detare:** maritime climate. 2. sea – , maritime; **hartë**

detare: nautical, chart. 3. naval, sea; **kantier detar:** shipyard; **luftë detare:** naval war.

detarí,-a *f.* seamanship.

detashmént,-i *m.sh.* -e detachment.

detektív,-i *m.sh.* -ë detective.

detýr/ë,-a *f.sh.* -a I. duty, task; **detyrë ndaj atdheut:** duty towards one's fatherland; **kryej detyrën:** to do one's duty, to fulfil one's duty; **e kam për detyrë (të):** it is my duty, I am duty-bound, it is incumbent upon me (to); **ndjenja e detyrës:** sense of duty; **e ndiej për detyrë (të bëj diçka):** I feel it my duty (to do something). 2. *(detyrë shkolle)*: task. 3. *(detyrë shtetërore)* charge, mission, function, post.

detyrím,-i *m.sh.* -e 1. obligation; **detyrime familiare:** family obligations; **detyrim moral:** moral obligation. 2. debt. 3. **detyrim ushtarak:** compulsory military service; *amer.* draft. 4. constraint, compulsion, coercion; **bëj një gjë me detyrim:** to do something under constraint (by coercion, under compulsion).

detyrimísht *ndajf.* forcibly, obligatorily, necessarily, compulsorily.

detyrój *f.k.* 1. to compel, to oblige, to force, to constrain. 2. to owe; **këtë la detyrojmë atij:** we owe this to him. – **detyrohem** *f.jv.* to be obliged, to be under obligation.

detyrúar (i, e) *mb.* obliged, indebted.

detyrúesh/ëm(i), -me(e) *mb.* obligatory, forcible, compulsory; **shërbim ushtarak i detyrueshëm:** compulsory military service.

devé,-ja *f.sh* – *zool.* camel.

devijím,-i *m.sh.* -e deviation, digression.

devijój *f.jk.* to deviate, to digress. – **devijohet** *f.jv.* to be deviated, to be digressed.

devíz/ë,-a *f.sh.* -a device, motto, slogan.

devoción,-i *m.* devotion.

devótsh/ëm(i),-me(e) *mb.* 1. pious. 2. devoted, dedicated; **i devotshëm në punë:** devoted to duty.

dezertím,-i *m.sh.* -e 1. *usht.* desertion. 2. *fig.* desertion, defection.

dezertój *f.jk.* 1. *usht.* to desert. 2. to desert, to leave.

dezertór,-i *m.sh.* -ë 1. *usht.* deserter. 2. *fig.* deserter, abandoner; defectioner.

dezinfektím,-i *m.sh.* -e disinfection.

dezinfektój *f.k.* to disinfect, to decontaminate. – **dezinfektohet** *f.jv.* to be disinfected.

dezinfektúes,-i *m.sh.* - detergent, disinfectant.

dezintegrím,-i *m. fiz., polit.* disintegration.

dezintegrój *f.k.* 1. to disintegrate. 2. *fiz.* to split *(the atom)*. – **dezintegrohet** *f.jv.* to disintegrate.

dëbím,-i *m.sh.* -e 1. *(dëbim nga vendi i vet)* expulsion, banishment, expatriation. 2. *(dëbim nga puna)* discharge from work, dismissal.

dëbój *f.k.* 1. *(dëboj nga vendlindja)* to expel, to expulse, to banish, to expatriate. 2. *(dëboj nga puna)* to discharge from work, to dismiss from work, to send away, to discard from service, to fire out, to cashier off. 3. *(dëboj armikun nga një vend)* to dislodge (the enemy). – **dëbohem** *f.jv.* to be expelled, to be discharged, to be dislodged.

dëbór/ë,-a *f.* snow; **dëborë e shkrirë:** slush; **top dëbore:** snowball; **flokë dëbore:** snowflakes; **stuhi dëbore:** snow-storm; **mbuluar me dëborë:** *(malet)*: snow-capped, snow-bound (mountains); **kohë dëbore:** snowy weather; **e bardhë dëborë:** white as snow, snowwhite; **bie dëborë:** it snows.
dëfréj *f.k.* to amuse, to entertain. – **dëfrehem** *f.jv.* to amuse oneself, to entertain oneself.
dëfrím,-i *m.sh.* -e amusement, entertainment.
dëfrýes,-e *mb.* amusing, entertaining.
dëftés/ë,-a *f.sh.* -a 1. receipt (for money, documents), written acknowledgement; **dëftesë për dorëzim bagazhi:** baggage-check (ticket); **lëshoj një dëftesë:** to deliver a receipt. 2. *(dëftesë shkolle)* report of marks, school report.
dëftéj, dëftój *f.k.* 1. to show, to indicate. 2. *(dëftoj me gisht)* to point (to, at). 3. *(dëftoj një përrallë)* to tell (a story). – **dëftehem, dëftohem** *f.jv.* 1. to confess. 2. **dëftehem me gisht:** to be pointed at. 3. to show oneself, to prove, to turn out; **dëftehem trim:** to exhibit (to display) bravery. ;
dëftór,-e *mb.* 1. *gram.* 1. **mënyra dëftore:** indicative mood. 2. **përemër dëftor:** demonstrative pronoun.
dëgjím,-i *m.* 1. hearing; **kam dëgjim të mirë, të mprehtë:** to be sharp of hearing. 2. *mjek.* *(dëgjim i të sëmurit me stetoskop)* auscultation.
dëgjój *f.k.* 1. to hear; **dëgjoj një këngë:** to hear (to listen to) a song. **dëgjo këtu l** listen l, hear l listen to me l look here l 2. *(mbaj*

vesh) to listen to; **dëgjoj gjer në fund:** to hear out. 3. *(bindem)* to listen to, to obey; **i dëgjoj prindërit:** to obey one's parents. 4. to heed, to pay attention to; **mos e dëgjo atë l** take no notice of what he says. – **dëgjohem** *f.jv.* 1. to be heard (a noise). 2. to be hearkened; **s'më dëgjohet fjala:** to preach to deaf ears. 3. to be obeyed
dëgjúar (i, e) *mb.* famous, renowned, illustrious.
dëgjúes,-i *m.sh.* - listener, auditor.
dëgjúesh/ëm(i),-me(e) *mb.* 1. obedient. 2. audible.
dëlírë (i, e) *mb.* chaste, candid, unfeigned, fair, plain-spoken, frank; clean; **zemër e dëlirë:** clean heart, open heart; **dashuri e dëlirë:** unfeigned love, fair love.
dëlirësí,-a *f.* chastity, candour, fairness, frankness, open-heartedness; **me dëlirësi:** frankly, openly.
dëllínj/ë,-a *f.* *bot.* juniper; *(kokrra e dëllinjës)* gin, juniper-berry; *(druri i dëllinjës)* juniper-tree; **raki dëllinje:** gin.
dëm,-i *m.sh.* -e 1. damage, harm, scathe; **shkaktoj dëm:** to cause damage. 2. loss; **shes me dëm:** to sell at loss. **vete dëm koha:** it is sheer waste of time. 3. detriment; **është në dëmin tuaj:** it is to your detriment.
dëmprúrës,-e *mb.* harmful, nocuous, injurous.
dëmsh/ëm(i), -me(e) noxious, pernicious, injurious, harmful, nocuous.
dëmshpërbléj *f.k.* to indemnify, to redress, to compensate. – **dëmshpërblehem** *f.jv.* to be indemnified, to be reimbursed.
dëmshpërblím,-i *m.sh.* -e 1. In-

(handwritten: dërgonjës,-i m.sh. —, sender)

demnity, redress, compensation, indemnification. 2. **dëmshpër-blime të luftës:** reparations.
dëmtím,-i *m.sh.* -e damage, injury.
dëmtój *f.k.* to damage, to impair, to harm, to hurt, to injure, to scathe, to deteriorate. - **dëmtohem** *f.jv.* to hurt oneself, to be injured, to suffer damage.
dëmtúes,-i *m.sh.* - damager.
dëmtúes,-e *mb.* noxious, nocuous, harmful.
dëmtúesh/ëm(i),-me(e) *mb.* perishable, vulnerable.
dënés/ë,-a *f.sh.* -a sob, sobbing; **qaj me dënesë:** to sob.
dëním,-i *m.sh.* -e 1. condemnation, punishment, sentence, chastisement, castigation; **dënim me vdekje:** capital punishment; **zbutje dënimi:** mitigation, commutation.
dënój *f.k.* to chastise, to condemn, to punish, to sentence; **dënoj me vdekje:** to condemn to death, to put to death. - **dënohem** *f.jv.* to be condemned, to be chastised, to be punished.
dënúes,-e *mb.* condemnatory.
dënúesh/ëm (i),-me (e) *mb.* blamable, punishable, condemnable; **veprim i dënueshëm:** condemnable act; **sjellje e dënueshme:** blamable behaviour.
dërdëllís *f.jk.* to twaddle, to tattle.
dërdëllítj/e,-a *f.sh.* -e twaddle, tittle-tattle, tattle.
dërgát/ë,-a *f.sh.* -a delegation.
dërgés/ë,-a *f.* dispatch, shipment.
dërgím,-i *m.* 1. sending, remitting, dispatch, forwarding, consignment; **dërgim me anije:** shipment; **dërgim mallrash:** conveyance of goods; **dërgim të hollash:** remittance.
dërgój *f.k.* 1. to send, to send off, to dispatch, to forward; **dërgoj të thërrasin:** to send for;

dërgoj të holla: to remit money; **dërgoj (mallra etj.):** to convey, to carry, to transport, to expedite, to mail, to post, to send by post; **dërgoj një letër:** to address (to send) a letter. 2. **dërgoj fjalë:** to send word; **dërgoj të fala:** to give (to transmit, to remit) loves (regards).
dërgúar (i),-i (i) *m.sh.* - (te) envoy, deputate, delegate; **i dërguar i posaçëm:** special envoy.
dërgúes,-i *m.sh.* - sender, dispatcher, conveyer.
dërhém,-i *m.sh.* - dram (the lowest unit of weight in use formerly in Albania, equivalent to 3 grammes); *fig.* **burrë katërqind dërhemësh:** wise and valiant man.
dërm/ë,-a *f.* precipice, gulf, abyss. - *Lok.* **i jap dërmën armikut.** to rout the enemy out, to put the enemy to rout.
dërsíj *f.jk.* to sweat, to perspire; *fig.* **dërsij në punë:** to toil, to labour, to work with pain and fatigue. - **dërsihem** *f.jv.* to be in sweat.
dërsítj/e,-a *f.* sweating, perspiration.
dërstíl/ë,-a *f.sh.* -a full-mill, water wheel, turbine for beating woollens; **punoj me dërstilë:** to full woollens.
dërrás/ë,-a *f.sh.* -a 1. plank, board; **shtrat me dërrasa:** plank bed; **dërrasë e zezë** *(shkolle):* blackboard; **dërrasë e gjatë:** lath; **dërrasë vizatimi:** trestle-board, **dërrasë bredhi:** plank of fir-tree; **shtroj me dërrasë:** to plank. 2. *mjek.* **dërrasë e krahërorit:** sternum, breastbone. - *Lok.* **kam një dërrasë mangut:** to have a tile missing.
dërrmím, -i *m.* 1. crushing. 2.exhaustion, weariness.

dërrmój *f.k.* 1. to crush, to squash, to break into small pieces; **dërrmoj gurë, bërthama pemësh etj.**: to crush stones, fruit-stones, etc. 2. to exhaust, to wear out. 3. *(armikun)* to crush, to defeat, to overwhelm (the enemy).—**dërrmohem** *f.jv.* 1. to get crushed. 2. to be crushed, to crush. 3. *(në punë)* to be overstrained (in work), to be worn out. 4. *usht.* to be crushed, to be defeated (the enemy).

dërrmúes,-e *mb.* crushing, overwhelming; **shumica dërrmuese:** the overwhelming majority.

dëshír/ë,-a *f.sh.* -a desire, wish; **dëshirë e madhe:** longing, hankering, craving, eagerness, passion, strong desire, earnest desire, yearning; **me dëshirë të madhe:** eagerly, passionately; **kam dëshirë të:** to have a fancy for; to long for; to be in the mood for; **me dëshirën e të dy palëve:** with one accord; **me dëshirën e vet:** of one's own free will, on one's own; **sipas dëshirës:** at will; **sipas dëshirës së tij:** according to his own desire, to his liking; **me gjithë dëshirën:** with pleasure, willingly; **pa dëshirë:** unwillingly, grudgingly, reluctantly; **kundër dëshirës:** against one's will; **dëshira e fundit:** supreme will; **kjo është dëshira e popullit:** that is the will of the people.

dëshirój *f.k.* to desire, to wish, to will, to want; **dëshiroj të kem një aparat fotografik:** I wish I had a camera; **dëshiroj të di:** I wonder, I am envious to know, I would like to know; **dëshiroj shumë:** to long, to desire eagerly (strongly); **dëshironi gjë tjetër?** do you want anything

else? **po të dëshironi:** if you please. — **dëshirohem** *f.jv.* to long for, to be desiring; **dëshirohem për diçka**: to long for something.

dëshirór/e,-ja *f. gram.* optative, desiderative.

dëshirúar (i, e) *mb.* desirous, anxious, eager; **jam i dëshiruar për një fëmijë:** to be longing to have a child; **lë shumë për të dëshiruar:** one finds fault with it, it leaves much to be desired.

dëshirúesh/ëm (i),-me (e) *mb.* desirable, to be wished for; **s'është e dëshirueshme:** it is undesirable.

dëshmí,-a *f.sh.* - 1. witness, testimony, evidence, affidavit; attestation; **dëshmi e rreme:** false evidence. 2. certificate, testimonial.

dëshmitár,-i *m.sh.* -e witness, attestor; **dëshmitar i akuzës:** witness for the prosecution; **dëshmitar që e ka parë me sytë e vet:** eye-witness; **bango e dëshmitarëve:** witness box; **dal dëshmitar:** to witness, to give testimony; **marr si dëshmitar:** to take to witness; **thërras për dëshmitar:** to call to witness; **jam dëshmitar për:** to be a witness to.

dëshmój *f.k.* to witness, to testify, to attest, to give evidence, to bear witness; **faktet dëshmojnë:** the facts bear witness to.

dëshmór,-i *m.sh.* -ë martyr; **bie dëshmor:** to fall on the field of honour, to die for the fatherland.

dëshmúes,-e *mb.* testimonial.

dëshpërím,-i *m.* despair, desperation, discouragement, despondency; **dëshpërim i madh:** blank despair, deep mental depression;

bie në dëshpërim: to sink into despair.
dëshpërój *f.k.* to despair, to dishearten, to dispirit, to discourage, to drive to desperation. –
dëshpërohem *f.jv.* to despond, to be despaired, to be dispirited, to be discouraged, to be disheartened, to become hopeless, to give up all hope, to lose hope, to lose heart, to be in the blues.
dështím,-i *m.sh.* -e 1. failure; miscarriage (of a plan). 2. *mjek.* abortion, miscarriage (of a child), premature parturition.
dështój *f.jk.* 1. to fail; to miscarry (a plan); **bëj të dështojë:** to frustrate, to thwart. 2. *mjek.* to abort, to miscarry.
dështúar (i, e) *mb.* 1, *mjek.* stillborn; **fëmijë e dështuar:** abortive child, stillborn child. 2. *fig.* abortive.
di *f.k.* 1. to know; **di një gjuhë:** to know a language; **e di:** I know it; **a e di?** do you know? **nuk e di:** I don't know; **me sa di unë:** for all I know, as I know, to my knowledge, as far as I know. 2. can; **unë di të notoj:** I can swim; **di të flas anglisht:** I can speak English. 3. to take for, to consider, to hold; **njerëzit e dinë për doktor:** people take him for a doctor. – *Lok.* **s'dua t'ia di:** I don't care a bit, I don't care a straw for it. –
dihet *f.jv.* to be known; **siç (sikundër) dihet:** as it is well known.
diabét,-i *m. mjek.* diabetes.
diadém/ë,-a *f.* diadem.
diafrágm/ë,-a *f.sh.* -a diaphragme.
diagnóz/ë,-a *f.sh.* -a *mjek.* diagnosis.
diagonál,-e *mb.* diagonal.
diagonál/e,-ja *f.sh.* -e diagonal.
diagrám,-i *m.sh.* -e diagram.

dialekt, – i *m. sh.* – e dialect.
dialóg,-u *m.sh.* -ë dialogue.
diamánt,-i *m.sh.* -e diamond.
diamét/ër,-ri *m.sh.* -ra diameter; **diametri i një cilindri:** calibre.
diametralísht *ndajf.* diametrically; **diametralisht i kundërt:** antipodal, diametrally opposite.
diapazón,-i *m.sh.* -e 1. *muz.* tuningfork, diapason. 2. diapazon, pitch.
diarré,-ja *f. mjek.* diarrhea, purging.
diçká I. *p.pk.* something.
II. *ndajf.* somewhat, a little; **diçka më mirë:** a little better.
diel (e),-a (e) *f.sh.* - **a(të)** Sunday; **të dielave:** on Sundays.
díe/ll,-i *m.sh.* -j sun; **ditë me diell:** sunny day; **dritë dielli:** sunshine; **rri në diell:** to stand (to sit) in the sunshine; **banjë dielli:** sun-bath; **dj¬gie nga dielli:** sunburn; **i djegur nga dielli:** sunburnt; **lindja e diellit:** sunrise; **perëndimi i diellit:** sunset; **pika e diellit:** sunstroke; **rreze dielli:** sun-beam; **çadër dielli:** sun shade, parasol. – *Lok.* **mbetem në diell:** to be turned out on the streets, to be reduced to poverty.
diellór,-e *mb.* sunny; solar; **vit diellor:** solar year; **orë diellore:** sundial.
diét/ë,-a *f.* 1. *mjek.* diet; **mbaj dietë:** to be on a diet (dieting). 2. **dietë udhëtimi:** travelling pay.
diéz,-i *m.sh.* -ë *muz.* sharp.
diferénc/ë,-a *f.sh.* -a difference.
diferenciál,-e *mb.* differential.
diferencím,-i *m.sh.* -e differentiation.
difterí,-a *f. mjek.* diphteria.
diftón/g,-gu *m.sh.* -gje *gram.* diphthong.
díg/ë,-a *f.sh.* -a dyke; dam, barrier (accross a watercourse), break-

water; bank, embankment (of a river).

dígjem *f.jv.* shih **djeg.**

dihás *f.jk.* to breath rapidly, to gasp, to pant.

dihátj /e,-a *f.* gasping, panting.

díj /e,-a *f.sh,* -e knowledge, learning

dijení,-a *f.sh,* - knowledge; **me dijeninë time**: with my full knowledge (of the facts); **pa dijeninë time**: without my knowledge; **me dijeni të plotë**: knowingly, willingly; **jam në dijeni të** *(diçkaje),* **kam dijeni për** *(diçka)* to be aware of (something); **vë në dijeni** *(dikë për diçka)*: to inform (someone of something,

dijetár,-i *m.sh.* -ë scholar, savant, erudite person.

díjsh /ëm (i),-me(e) *mb.* learned.

dikastér,-i *m.sh.* -e ministry.

dikë *p.pk.* somebody, someone (shih **dikush,** accusative).

diktatór,-i *m.sh.* -ë dictator.

diktatoriál,-e *mb.* dictatorial.

diktatúr /ë,-a *f.sh.* -a dictatorship; **diktatura e proletariatit**: dictatorship of the proletariat.

diktím,-i *m.sh.* -e dictation.

diktój *f.k.* 1. *(një tekst)* to dictate. 2. *fig. (kushte)* to dictate, to lay down.

diktój *f.k.* to disclose; to track down. — **diktohem** *f.jv.* to be disclosed, to be tracked down.

dikú *ndajf.* somewhere; **ka vajtur diku**: he has gone somewhere; **deri diku**: to a certain extent.

dikújt *ndajf.* to somebody; **dikujt i përket**: it belongs to somebody (shih **dikush)**

dikúr *ndajf.* 1. formerly, long ago, in olden days (times), in the past. 2. some day.

dikúrsh /ëm (i),-me(e) *mb.*ancient, bygone, old-time.

dikúsh *p.pk.* somebody, someone;

dikush më tha: somebody told me; (dative) **ia dhashë dikujt:** I gave it to someone; (accusative) **pashë dikë:** I saw someone.

dilém /ë,-a *f.sh.* -a dilemma.

diletánt,-i *m.sh.* -ë dilettante, amateur.

dím /ër,-ri *m.sh.* -ra winter; **dimër i madh**: severe winter;**në dimër:** in winter, in winter time; **në mes të dimrit**: in the depth of the winter; **më të dalë të dimrit**: towards the end of the winter

dimërák,-e *mb.* winterly.

dimërím,-i *m.* hibernage.

dimërój *f.jk.* to hibernate, to winter, to pass the winter.

dimërór,-e *mb.* wintry, hibernal.

dimí,-të *f.sh.* shih **çitjane.**

din,-i *m.* faith: **s'ka din e iman:** he is merciless (hard-hearted).

dinák,-e *mb.* cunning, sly, artful, crafty, foxy, wily; **njeri dinak:** cunning person.

dinakërí,-a *f.sh.* - craftiness, slyness, wiliness; **me dinakëri;** craftily, artfully, slyly, cunningly.

dinakërísht *ndajf.* craftily, artfully, slyly.

dinamík,.e *mb.* dynamic.

dinamít,-i *m.* dynamite.

dinamíz /ëm,-mi *m.* dynamism.

dinámo,-ja *f.sh.* - *el.* dynamo, *emer.* generator.

dinastí,-a *f.sh.* - dynasty.

dinjitét,-i *m.* dignity.

dioqéz /ë,-a *f.sh.* -a diocese.

diplomací,-a *f.* diplomacy.

diplomát,-i *m.sh.* -ë diplomat; *fig.* diplomat, diplomatist.

diplomatik-e *mb.* diplomatic.

diplóm /ë,-a *f.sh.* -a diploma.

diplomím,-i *m.* graduation (of a student).

diplomój *f.k.* to confer a diploma. — **diplomohem** *f.jv.* to be graduated, to be provided with a diploma.

diplomúar (i),-i *m.sh.* -(të) graduate.

dirék,-u *m.sh.* -ë mast (of a ship); **direku i përparmë i anijes:** foremast.

direktív/ë,-a *f.sh.* -a directive; instruction.

dirigjént,-i *m.sh.* -ë orchestra leader, conductor.

dirigjím,-i *m.sh.* -e conducting (of an orchestra).

dirigjój *f.k.* to conduct (an orchestra). – **dirigjohet** *f.jv.* to be conducted.

dirigjúes,-i *m.sh.* - shih **dirigjent.**

disá *p.pk.* some, several; **disa njerëz:** some people, some persons; **disa lapsa:** several pencils; **disa prej tyre:** some of them.

disfát/ë,-a *f.sh.* -a defeat; **pësoj disfatë:** to suffer defeat.

disfatíst,-i *m.sh.* -ë defeatist.

disfatíz/ëm,-mi *m.* defeatism.

disfavór,-i *m.* disfavour, unfavour.

disfavórsh/ëm (i),-me(e) *mb.* disfavorable, unfavorable.

disharmoní,-a *f.* disharmony, disagreement.

disí *ndajf.* somehow, somewhat; passably, fairly, rather well, middling.

disiplín/ë,-a *f.sh.* -a discipline.

disiplinój *f.k.* to discipline, to bring under control.

disiplinóhet *f.jv.* to be disciplined.

disiplinór,-e *mb.* disciplinary; **masa disiplinore:** disciplinary measures.

disk,-u *m.sh.* -qe 1. disc, disk. 2. *muz.* (disk gramofoni) record, disc. 3. *sport.* discus; **hedhje disku:** discus throwing.

diskreditím,-i *m.sh.* -e discredit.

diskreditój *f.k.* to ˙ discredit, to ruin the reputation of. – **diskreditohem** *f.jv.* to bring dis-

credit upon oneself, to fall into discredit, to be discredited.

diskreditúes,-e *mb.* discrediting.

diskriminím,-i *m.sh.* -e discrimination; **diskriminim racial:** apartheid, racial discrimination.

diskutím,-i *m.sh.* -e discussion, debate, argument; **shtroj për diskutim:** to moot; to raise, to bring (to put) forward for discussion. **është në diskutim (çështja):** to be under discussion, to be pending, to be at issue.

diskutój *f.k.* to discuss, to debate, to dispute; **diskutoj një çështje:** to talk a question over, to discuss over a question. – **diskutohet** *f.jv.* to be discussed, to be under discussion.

diskutúes,-i *m.sh.* - arguer, orator, speaker.

diskutúesh/ëm (i),-me(e) *mb.* debatable, contestable, disputable.

disnivél,-i *m.sh.* -e difference(of level).

dispanserí,-a *f.sh.* - mjek. dispensary.

dispécer,-i *m.sh.* -a dispatcher, despatcher.

dispéns/ë,-a *f.sh.* -a polygraphied lecture.

dispepsí,-a *f.* mjek. dyspepsia.

disponój *f.k.* to possess, to have, to owe.

dispozición,-i *m.* disposal, command; **në dispozicionin tim:** at my disposal.

dispozít/ë,-a *f.sh.* -a drejt. provision, clause.

distánc/ë,-a *f.sh.* -a distance.

distilatór,-i *m.sh.* -ë still (for liquids).

distilerí,-a *f.sh.* - distillery.

distilím,-i *m.sh.* -e distillation.

distilój *f.k.* to distil. – **distilohet** *f.jv.* to be distilled.

distilúes,-i *m.sh.* - distiller.

distinktív,-i *m.sh.* **-a** distinctive, badge.
distríkt,-i *m.sh.* **-e** district, region.
dishépu/ll,-i *m.sh.* **-j** disciple.
ditár,-i *m.sh.* **-ë** diary, journal; mbaj **ditar**: to keep a journal.
dít/ë,-a *f.sh.-a* 1. day, daytime;**ditë e bukur**: a fine day; **çdo ditë**: every day; **ditën**: by day; **ditë feste, ditë pushimi**: holiday; **ditë e rrogave**: pay-day; **ditë pune**: day-work, work-day; **në ditë**: in a day; **në ditët tona**: at present, in our days, in our times, nowadays; **një vit më parë, ditë më ditë**: one year ago to the very day; **tërë ditën**: all day long, all day; **në mes të ditës**: in midday; in broad daylight; **rroj me ditë**: to live from day to day, to live from hand to mouth; **ndonjë ditë**: some day, one day or another; **nga dita në ditë (dita-ditës)**: from day to day, day in day out, daily, day by day; **çështje e ditës**: topical matter; **do të ta them ndonjë ditë**: some day I'll tell you. 2. daylight; **bëhet ditë**: it is growing light.
díta-dítës *ndajf.* daily, day in day out, day to day.
ditëgjátë *mb.* long-lived.
ditëlíndj/e,-a *f.sh.* **-a** birthday; **urime për ditëlindjen!** many happy returns of the day!
ditë-pún/ë,-a *f.sh.* **-** working day.
ditëshkúrtër *mb.* short-lived.
ditëz/í,-ézë *mb.* unfortunate.
ditëzí,-u *m.sh.* **-nj** poor wretch.
ditór,-e *mb.* daily; **pagë ditore**: daily pay.
dítur (i,e) *mb.* learned, erudite, well-read, well-informed; **bëj të ditur**: to inform.
diturí,-a *f.sh.* **-** knowledge; **dituri e madhe**: erudition.
dív,-i *m.sh.* **-a** giant.

6 — 292

diván,-i *m.sh.* **-e** divan, couch.
diversánt,-i *m.sh.* **-ë** diversionist, wrecker.
diversión-i *m. usht.* subversive activity, diversion.
divizión,-i *m.sh.* **-e** *usht.* division.
divórc,-i *m.sh.* **-e** divorce; **bëj divorc**: to divorce.
divorcóhem *f.jk.* to be divorced.
dizenterí,-a *f. mjek.* dysentery.
dizenjatór,-i *m.sh.* **-ë** draughtsman, draftsman, designer.
djál/ë,-i *m.sh.* djem 1. boy, lad; fellow; **djalë i mirë**: a good boy, a good fellow; **djalë i ri**: lad, youngster, a young boy. 2. son, child; **djalë i vetëm**: an only son, an only child.
djalërí,-a *f.* boyhood, adolescence, youth.
djalósh,-i *m.sh.* djelmosha stripling, youth, youngman, adolescent, juvenile, chap.
djaloshár,-e *mb.* juvenile.
djall,-i *m.sh.* djaj devil, demon, deuce, fiend; **në djall të vesh!** go to hell! go to blazes! **djalli ta marrë!** by gosh! the devil take him! confound him! **ç'djall ke?** what the deuce? what the hell do you want?
djallëzí,-a *f.sh.* **-** devilry, malice; **me djallëzi**: maliciously, devilishly, diabolically.
djallëzísht *ndajf.* diabolically, devilishly, maliciously.
djallëzój *f.k.* to render malicious (mischievous). — **djallëzohem** *f.jv.* to grow malicious (mischievous).
djallëzór,-e *mb.* diabolic, devilish, fiendish, sinister.
djallëzúar (i,e) *mb.* malicious, mischievous.
djallúsh,-i *m.sh.* **-ë** imp.
djallós *f.k. (një punë)* to bungle (a work).

djáth/ë,-i *m.sh.* -ra cheese; **shitës djathi:** cheese-monger.
djáthtas *ndajf.* on the right, right-wards.
djáthtë (i, e) *mb.* right, right-side; **dora e djathtë:** the right hand; **ana e djathtë:** the right side.
dje *ndajf.* yesterday; **dje mbrëma:** last night.
djeg I. *f.k.* 1. to burn; **djeg dorën:** to burn the hand. 2. to scorch, to char; **djeg bukën (mishin):** to char the bread (the meat). 3. *(me ujë)* to scald. − **digjem** *f.jv.* 1. to burn, to be burning. 2. *(ushqimet)* to burn, to get scorched (foods). 3. *fig.* **digjem nga dëshira për:** to be eager to, to be impatient to, II. *f.jk.* 1. *(sytë)* to burn, to smart (eyes). 2. *fig.* to cut to the quick; **ato fjalë më dogjën:** those words cut me to the quick.
djégës,-e *mb.* 1. biting, stinging, acrid (to the taste). 2. incendiary, inflamatory; **bombë djegëse:** fire-bomb; **lëndë djegëse:** combustible, fuel.
djégi/e,-a *f.*1. burn, burning;**djegie nga dielli:** sunburn; **djegie e kufomave:** cremation. 2. *(nga uji)* scald. 3. *mjek. (e stomakut)* heartburn. 4. *tek.* combustion; **motor me djegie të brendshme:** internal combustion engine.
djegësír/ë,-a *f.* 1. acridity, tartness. 2. *mjek.* heartburn.
djégsh/ëm (i),-me(e) *mb.* combustible.
djégur (e),-a (e) *f.sh.* -a (të) burn, scald.
djem,-të *m.sh.* (plural of **djalë**) boys.
djemurí,-a *f.* youth, boysi n general.
djep,-i *m.sh.* -e cradle.
djérs/ë,-a *f.sh.* -ë sweat, perspiration.

djersís *f.k.* shih **dërsij.** − **djersitem** *f.jv.* shih **dërsihem.**
djersítj/e,-a *f.* shih **dërsitje.**
djerr,-e *mb.* uncultivated, waste; **e lë tokën djerr:** to leave the ground uncultivated.
djésh/ëm (i),-me(e) *mb.* of yesterday, yesterday's.
djéshm/e (e),-ja(e) *f.* 1. day before, night before. 2. *fig.* the past; past times.
do (third person singular of the present indicative of the verb **dua**) he wants.
do (particle used to form the future and the conditional of all verbs); **do të shkoj:** I shall go; **do ta bëj:** I shall do it; **do të shkoja, po të kisha kohë:** I should go if I had time.
dobësí,-a *f.sh.* - weakness, feebleness.
dobësím,-i *m.* 1. wasting away, losing of flesh. 2. *(i forcave)* weakening, growing weeker; *(i shikimit)* failing.
dobësój *f.k.* 1. to enfeeble, to make weak. 2. to make meager (lean, thin). 3. *mjek. (të sëmurin)* to lay low; *(shëndetin)* to impair, to debilitate. − **dobësohem** *f.jv.* 1. *(zhurma)* to grow dim; to grow weaker; *(njeriu)* to lose one's strength. 2. to grow thin, to lose flesh, *amer.* to reduce.
dóbët (i, e) *mb.* 1. weak, feeble; **pikë e dobët:** weak point, 2. meager, lean, thin, scanty. 3. mean, low, base. 4. not good not efficient (schoolboy); **i dobët në gramatikë:** weak in grammar.
dobí,-a *f.sh.* - 1. utility, vantage, advantage, avail, profit, gain, benefit, efficacy, use, good; **cila është dobia e saj?** what is the good of it?; **me dobi:** usefully; **pa dobi:** useless, of no avail,

bootless, without advantage, of no use; **në dobi të:** to the good of. **dobíç,-i** *m.sh.* -**ë** bastard, illegitimate child.
dobiprúrës,-e *mb.* utilitarian.
dobísh/ëm (i),-me(e) *mb.* useful, beneficial, profitable, advantageous, serviceable; **bëj të dobishëm:** to make (to render) useful.
docént,-i *m.sh.* -**ë** reader (in university).
doç,-i *m.sh.* -**e** shih **dobiç.**
doemós *ndajf.* necessarily, absolutely, without fail, certainly.
dogán/ë,-a *f.* 1. custom-duties; **taksë dogane:** custom duty; **pa doganë:** duty-free. 2. custom— house.
doganiér,-i *m.sh.* -**e** custom-house officer.
doganór,-e *mb.* *(tarifa, etj.)* customs.
dógm/ë,-a *f.sh.* -**a** dogma.
dója (past tense of the verb **dua**) I would; **doja të dija:** I should *+*like to know; **do të doja më mirë që:** I would rather, I would prefer that.
dok,-u *m.* ticking, duck.
dóke,-t *f.sh.* habits, morals, customs.
dók/ërr,-rra *f.sh.* -**rra** nonsense, poppycock, rubbish, moonshine; **them dokrra:** to speak drivels, to talk nonsense.
doktór,-i *m.sh.* -**ë** 1. doctor, physician. 2. holder of a doctorate.
doktorát/ë,-a *f.* doctorate; **marr doktoratën:** to take one's doctorate, to take one's doctor's degree.
doktrín/ë,-a *m.sh.* -**a** doctrine, tenet, dogma.
dokumént,-i *m.sh.* -**e** document, record; **dokumente zyrtare:** public documents.

dokumentación,-i *m.sh.* -**e** documentation, documents.
dokumentár,-i *m.sh.* -**ë** documentary film.
dokumentój *f.k.* to document, to support by documents. — **dokumentohet** *f.jv.* to be documented, to be supported by documents.
dóla *f.jk.* (past tense of the verb **dal**) I came out; I went out.
dóli *f.jk.* (third person singular of the past tense of the verb **dal**) he (she) came out; he(she) went out.
dollák,-u *m.sh.* -**ë** gaiter, leggings.
dolláp,-i *m.sh.* -**ë** 1. cup-board, side-board. 2. *(dollap në mur)* pantry wall. 3. **dollap për libra:** book-case. 4. **dollap buke:** dresser; **dollap rrobash:** wardrobe. 5. **dollap kafeje:** coffee--roaster.
dollár,-i *m.sh.* - ë dollar.
dollí,-a *f.sh.* - toast; **ngre një dolli:** to raise a toast, to toast; **ngre një dolli për:** to propose a toast to.
dollmá,-ja *f.sh.* - vine leaves stuffed with mincemeat.
domát/e,-ja *f.sh.* -**e** *bot.* tomato.
domethëné *lidh.* (abbreviation d.m.th.) that is to say, i.e.
domethëni/e,-a *f.* meaning, signification.
dominión,-i *m.sh.* -**e** dominion.
dominó,-ja *f.* *(lojë)* domino.
dominój *f.jk.* to dominate.
dominúes,-e *mb.* overbearing, dominant, prevalent.
domosdó *ndajf.* of course, naturally; **me domosdo:** forcibly, absolutely, certainly.
domosdósh/ëm (i),-me(e) *mb.* indispensable.
domosdoshmërí,-i *f.* absolute necessity, indispensability.
dóni *f.k.* (second person, plural,

of the verb **dua**) will you?; **çfarë doni?** what do you want?; **doni gjë tjetër?** do you want anything else?; **si të doni:** as you please! as you like! **po të doni:** if you please. **doráç,-i** *m.sh.* -**ë** one-handed (one--armed) person. **doráshk/ë,-a** *f.sh.* -**a** glove; **dorashka lëkure:** kidgloves. **dordoléc,-i** *m.sh.* -**ë** scarecrow. **doréz/ë,-a** *f.sh.* -**a** 1. handle; **dorezë dere:** handle of a door. 2. glove; **dorezë boksi:** boxingglove. **dór/ë,-a** *f.sh.* -**dúar** 1. hand; **dora e djathtë:** right hand; **pëllëmba e dorës:** the palm of the hand; **kurrizi i dorës:** the back of the hand; **kyçi i dorës:** wrist; **shkruar me dorë:** written by hand; **i bërë me dorë:** handmade; **I shtrëngoj (i jap) dorën dikujt:** to shake hands with someone; **dorë për dore:** hand in hand; **dorë më dorë:** hand to hand; **me dorën e vet:** by his own hand; **punë dore:** handy work; needle-work. 2. receipt; **lëshoj një dorë:** to remit a receipt. 3. quality; **i dorës së parë, së dytë:** a) of first hand (rate), of second hand (rate); b) of first importance, of second importance; **këso dore:** of this kind (quality). 4. (quantity) handful; **një dorë miell:** a handful of flour. – *Lok.* **dora vetë:** himself, herself; **paguaj me lekë në dorë:** to pay cash down; **nën dorë:** underhand; **heq dorë:** to give up, to renounce, to desist; **jap dorën e fundit:** to give the finishing stroke (touches), to put the finishing stroke (touches); **vë dorë mbi dikë:** to lay hands on someone; **vë dorën në zemër:** to have pity, to be

pitiful; **i nder (shtrij) dorën dikujt:** to hold out one's hand to someone; **e shtrëngoj dorën:** to become stingy; **lë pas dore:** to neglect; **më iku nga duart:** he slipped through my fingers; **më ra në dorë:** he fell into my hands; **letra juaj më ra në dorë:** I received your letter, your letter reached me; **kam dorë të lehtë:** to have a light hand; **në njërën dorë kazmën në tjetrën pushkën:** pick (pickage) in one hand, and rifle in the other; **me sa kam në dorë:** as much as in me lies, as much as I can, accor**ding to my possibilities; **kjo është në dorën tuaj:** it depends on you; **më vjen dore:** to be handy, skilful; **i vjen dore për çdo gjë:** he is expert in any thing; **i jap dorën dikujt:** to help someone, to give a hand to someone. **dorëhápur** *mb.* open-handed, free-handed, generous, munificent, unsparing, spendthrift. **dorëhéqj/e,-a** *f.sh.* -**e** resignation; **jap dorëheqjen:** to resign, **dorëléhtë** *mb.* light-handed. **dorëlëshúar** *mb.* spendthrift. **dorëmbárë** *mb.* fortunate, lucky; **jam dorëmbarë:** to be fortunate, to be lucky, to be in luck. **dorëprápë** *mb.* unlucky. **dorëprérë** *mb.* one-handed. **dorëshkrím,-i** *m.sh.* -**e** manuscript; handwriting. **dorëshpúar** *mb.* shih **dorëhapur, dorëlëshuar.** **dorështrëngúar** *mb.* miserly, covetous, stingy, niggard, tight--fisted, close-fisted. **dorëthárë** *mb.* unhandy, unskilful, clumsy, awkward. **dorëthátë** *mb.* with empty hands. **dórëz,-a** *f.sh.* -**a** handle, haft; **dorëz thike (vegle, etj.):** haft, handle

(of a knife, of a tool, etc.)
dorëz shpate: hilt; **dorëz havani:** pestle, pounder.
dorëzán /ë,-i *m.sh.* -ë voucher, guarantor; **bëhem dorëzanë (për
dikë):** to stand surety (for someone).
dorëzaní,-a *f.* bail, guaranteee,
suretyship.
dorëzím,-i *m.sh.* -e 1. delivery;
dorëzim malli: delivery of
goods; **dorëzim bagazhi** *(në
doganë etj. për ruajtje)*: consignment of baggages. 2. *(dorëzim
qyteti, fortese)* surrender (of a
town, of a fortress). 3. *(dorëzim i një ushtrie)* capitulation
(of an army).4. *(dorëzim i një
krimineli)* extradition (of a criminal).
dorëzój *f.k.* 1. to deliver; **dorëzoj
mallra:** to deliver goods. 2.
(dorëzoj për ruajtje) to consign.
3. *(dorëzoj një qytet, një fortesë)*
to surrender (a town, a fortress).
4. *(dorëzoj një kriminel)* to extra-
dite (a criminal). – **dorëzohem**
f.jv. to give up, to surrender.
dosár,-i *m.sh.* -ë shih **dosje.**
dós /ë,-a *f.sh.* -a *zool.* sow.
dosidó *ndajf.* somehow, anyway;
bëj një punë dosido: to bungle
a work.
dósj /e,-a *f.sh.* -e brief-case, brief-
bag, file (of papers).
dot *pj.* (adverb of negation meaning
inability) **nuk e bëj dot:** I cannot
do it.
dóz /ë,-a *f.sh.* -a dose.
drág /ë,-a *f.sh.* -a 1. avalanche. 2.
drag, dredge.
drag /úa,-oi *m.sh.* -onj 1. dragon.
2. *fig.* brave.
dramatík,-e *mb.* dramatic.
dramatúrg,-u *m.sh.* -ë dramatur-
gist.
drám /ë,-a *f.sh.* -a 1. drama, play.
2. *fig.* drama.

dráp /ër,-ri *m.sh.* -inj sickle, rea-
ping-hook.
dre,-ri *m.sh.* -rë *zool.* deer; *(mashkulli)* stag, buck; *(femra)* doe,
hind; **dre i veriut:** reindeer,
cariboo.
dredh *f.k.* 1. to twist, to twine;
dredh leshin: to twist the wool.
2. to roll; **dredh një cigare:**
to roll a cigarette. 3. to curl;
dredh flokët: to curl (to frizzle)
one's hair. 4. **dredh zërin:** to
vibrate (to quaver) the voice. –
dridhem *f.jv.* to shudder; **dridhem nga të ftohtit:** to shiver,
to quiver; **dridhem nga frika:**
to tremble.
dredharák,-e *mb.* sly, crafty, wily,
cunning.
drédh /ë,-a *f.sh.* -a curve, curving;
sinuosity; **dredhë e lumit:** winding (meander) of a river; **dredhë
e rrugës:** turn of a road.
drédhëz,-a *f.* *bot.* ivy.
dredhí,-a *f.sh.* - slyness, craftiness;
me dredhi: slyly, craftily.
dredhój *f.jk.* to shirk, to tergiversate.
drég /ë,-a *f.sh.* -a *anat.* slough,
scab.
drejt I. *paraf.* towards; **drejt majave më të larta:** towards
the highest summits.
II. *ndajf.* 1. straight, directly, right
through; **shko drejt:** go right
on (right ahead). 2. rightly;
veproj drejt: to act rightly.
3. directly, straight; **drejt e në
fytyrë:** flush (right) in the face.
4. straight; **rri drejt!** stand up
straight! **me kokën drejt:** with
one's head upright (erect).
dréjtë (i, e) *mb.* 1. right; **kënd i
drejtë:** right angle. 2. *(njeri i
drejtë)*: just, justeous, righteous,
upright; **veprim i drejtë:** a
rightful act; **dënim i drejtë:**
a deserved punishment.
dréjt /ë(e),-a (e) *f.sh.* -a (të) 1.

right; **kam të drejtë të:** to have the right to; **kam të drejtë:** to be right, to be in the right; **i mohoj të drejtat dikujt:** to deprive someone of his rights. 2. reason, right; **me ç'të drejtë?** by what right? for what reason? **nuk keni të drejtë të ankoheni:** you have no right to complain. 3. **e drejta e autorit:** copyright. 4. **e drejta civile:** the civil law; **e drejta ndërkombëtare:** the law of nations. 5. truth, verity; **ç'është e drejta:** to tell the truth, as a matter of fact, strictly speaking.

drejtësí,-a *f.* 1. justice, rightfulness, justness, equity; **veproj me drejtësi:** to act with impartiality (with equity, with justice, impartially, equitably, justly, rightfully, rightly). 2. justice; **Fakulteti i Drejtësisë:** Law Faculty; **Ministria e Drejtësisë:** Ministry of Justice; **studjoj për drejtësi:** to study Law.

drejtësísht *ndajf.* rightly, justly, equitably, uprightly, rightfully.

dréjtëz,-a *f.sh.* -a *gjeom.* straight line.

drejtím,-i *m.sh.* -e 1. direction, course; **mbaj drejtimin:** to keep the same course; **ndërroj drejtim:** to change direction. 2. *(drejtim i një ndërmarrjeje):* direction, managment (of an enterprise). 3. **drejtim i timonit:** steerage. 4. **drejtim i një letre:** address. 5. orientation.

drejtkëndësh,-i *m.sh.* -a *gjeom.* rectangle.

drejtój *f.k.* 1. to straighten; **drejtoj trupin (hekurin):** to straighten the body (the iron). 2. *(një ndërmarrje):* to run, to manage (an enterprise); *(punën, etj,)* to direct (the work etc.) 3.*(një anije, një automobil):* to steer, to drive

(a ship, an automobile). 4. *(një letër)* to address (a letter). — **drejtohem** *:.jv.* to go, to direct one's steps, to make one's way *(për, në,* towards), to head for; **u drejtuam për në fshat:** we made for the village. 2. to straighten, to become straight. 3. to turn, to go; **i drejtohem dikujt për ndihmë:** to ask (to turn to) someone for help; **i drejtohem avokatit:** to go to a lawyer. 4. *(letra etj.)* to be sent, to be addressed. 5. *(automobili)* to be driven.

drejtór,-i *m.sh.* -ë director; **drejtor i një ndërmarrjeje:** director of an enterprise; **drejtor shkolle:** school director; **drejtor i përgjithshëm:** chief director.

drejtorí,-a *f.sh.* - 1. directorate. 2. director's office.

drejtpeshím,-i *m.* equipoise, equilibrium.

drejtpeshój *f.k.* to equipoise, to balance.

drejtpërdréjt *ndajf.* directly.

drejtpërdréjtë (i, e) *mb.* direct.

drejtpërsëdréjti *ndajf.* directly.

drejtshkrím,-i *m.* orthography.

drejtshkrimór,-e *mb.* orthographical; **fjalori drejtshkrimor:** the orthographical dictionary.

drejtúes,-i *m.sh.* - 1. head; **drejtues orkestre:** conductor. 2. *polit.* leader.

drejtúesh/ëm (i),-me(e) *mb.* 1. steerable, dirigible. 2. that can be straightened.

drék/ë,-a *f.sh.* -a 1. dinner, lunch, luncheon; **ha drekë:** to dine, to lunch, to have lunch, to have dinner; **ftoj dikë për drekë:** to ask someone for lunch. 2. midday; **në drekë:** at dinner time, at midday, at noon; **para dreke:**

before noon; **pas dreke:** in the afternoon.

drekëhérë (më) *ndajf.* at midday, at noon.

drekój *f.jk.* to lunch, to dine. — **drekohem** *f.jv.* to lunch, to dine.

drekór/e,-ja *f.sh.* - eating-house, restaurant.

dremís *f.jk.* to doze, to drowse, to nap, to slumber, to snooze.

dremítj/e,-a *f.* doze, drowsiness, snooze.

drenúsh/ë,-a *f.sh.* -a *zool.* doe, hind.

dreq,-i *m.sh.* -ër shih **djall.**

drídhem *f.jv.* shih **dredh.**

drídhj/e,-a *f.sh.* -e **dridhje e zërit:** vibration (quaver) of the voice; **dridhje të motorit:** trepidations (vibrations) of a motor; **dridhje e muskulit:** jerk; **dridhjet e zemrës:** throbbing (palpitations) of the heart; **dridhje nga të ftohtit:** shivering, quivering; **dridhje nga frika:** shuddering (trembling) from fear.

drídhm/ë,-a *f.sh.* -a shih **dridhje.**

dritár/e,-ja *f.sh.* -a window; **dritare qilari:** air-hole, vent-hole; **dritare baxhe:** gable window; **kanatë dritareje:** window-shu tter; **dritarja shikon nga kopshti:** the window looks into the garden.

drít/ë,-a *f.sh.* -a 1. light; **dritë e diellit:** sunlight, sunshine; **dritë elektrike:** electric light; **dritë e hënës:** moonlight; **drita e syrit:** eyesight; **dritë e zbehtë:** gleam, glimmer, dim light; **rreze drite:** beam of lght; **dritë automobili:** headlight.

dritëdhënës,-e *mb.* light-giving.

dritëshkúrtër *mb.* myop, short-sighted, near-sighted.

dríth/ë,-i *m.sh.* -ëra *bot.* cereals, grains.

drithërój *f.jk.* to frighten, to scare.

— **drithërohem** *f.jv.* to tremble; **drithërohet për fëmijët:** she trembles for her children.

drithërúar (i, e) *mb.* trembling.

dríthm/ë,-a *f.sh.* -a shivering; trembling, shaking, quivering, shuddering; **më hyjnë drithmat:** a) to be trembling with fear; b) to shiver.

drithník,-u *m.sh.* -e granary.

dríz/ë,-a *f.sh.* -a *bot.* brier, thornbush.

drobís *f.k.* to overtire, to wear out. — **drobitem** *f.jv.* to wear out, to be worn out, to be overtired.

drobítj/e,-a *f.* lassitude.

drój/ë,-a *f.* shyness, timidity; **me drojë:** shyly, bashfully; **ha pa drojë!** eat free and easy!

dru,-ri *m.sh.* -rë wood; **dru zjarri:** fire-wood; **dru mogani (dru i kuq):** mahogany; **dru i krimbur:** wormeaten wood; **lëndë druri:** timber, lumber; **qymyr druri:** charcoal; **fushë drush:** woodyard; **gdhendje në dru:** wood-engraving; **prej druri:** wooden, woody.

drúaj *f.jk.* to be shy of, to fear; **mos u druaj!** make yourself at home. — **druhem** *f.jv.* to shy from, to have fear, to fear; **nuk druhem nga vështirësitë:** to be undaunted by difficulties.

drúajtj/e,-a *f.* shih **drojë.**

drúajtur (i, e) *mb.* timid, shy, coy, bashful.

drúg/ë,-a *f.sh.* -a handspindle.

drunór,-e *mb.* woody, ligneous.

drúnjtë (i, e) *mb.* wooden.

druprérës,-i *m.sh.* - wood-cutter, hewer.

druvár,-i *m.sh.* -ë woodman, hewer.

dry, -ni *m.sh.* -na lock, padlock; **mbyll me dry:** to lock, to padlock.

dúa *f.k.* (p.t. **desha,** p. p. **dashur)**

1. to like; **i dua shumë librat:** I like books very much. 2. to love; **i dua prindërit:** to love one's parents; **dua atdheun:** to love one's fatherland; **dua një vajzë:** to love a girl; **dua më shumë:** I like best. 3. to want, to need: **nuk dua gjë:** I want nothing; **dua diçka:** to want (to need) something; **dua të bëj diçka:** to want to do something; **dua të flas me të:** I want to speak to him (to her). 4. to mean, to be going to; **doja të të telefonoja:** I meant to phone you. 5. to want, to look for; **të do babai:** your father wants you. 6. to wish, to want; **kush të dojë le të ikë:** whoever wishes may go out. – *Lok.* **dua të them:** I mean; **si të duash:** just as you like; **bëj si të duash:** do as you please. – **duhem** *f.jv.* 1. to be necessary, to need, to want; **për një kostum duhen dy metra stof:** you need two meters of cloth for a suit; **duhet durim:** one must be patient. 2. to be loved; **duhemi:** to love each other.
dúaj,-t *m.sh.* sheaves.
duajídhës,-i *m.sh.*-sheaves binder.
dualíst,-i *m.sh.* -ë dualist.
dualiz/ëm,-mi *m.* dualism.
duarkrýq *ndajf.* **rri duarkryq:** to stay with one's arms crossed.
duarlídhur *ndajf.* shih **duarkryq.**
duarplót *ndajf.* with full hands.
dúar,-t (plural of **dorë**) hands.
duartrokás *f.jk.* to applaud, to clap one's hands.
duartrokítj/e,-a *f.sh.* -e applause.
duarthárë *mb.* clumsy, awkward.
duarthátë *ndajf.* empty-handed, with empty hands.
dublánt,-i *m.sh.* -ë understudy.
dublikát/ë,-a *f.sh.* -a duplicate.
duél,-i *m.sh.* -a duel, challenge;

bëj duel: to fight a duel; **ftoj në duel:** to challenge.
duf,-i *m.* passion; **shfrej dufin:** to wreak a passion.
duhán,i *m.sh.* -e tobacco; **kuti duhani:** tobacco box; **pi duhan:** to smoke; **sallë për pirje duhani:** smoking-room; **ndalohet duhani** no smoking! **pirës duhani:** smoker (of tabocco).
duhanshítës,-i *m.sh.* seller of tobacco, tobacco-seller.
duhantór/e,-ja *f.sh.* -e tobaccoshop.
dúhet *f.jv.* to be necessary, must, to have to; **(më) duhet të shkoj:** I must go, I have to go; **më duhej të shkoja në shkollë:** I had to go to school; **duhet të prisni deri sa të kthehet:** you must wait till he comes back (returns); **duhet të themi se:** it is necessary to say that, we must say that; **siç duhet:** as it should be, duly; **ty s'ka ç'të duhet:** none of your business, that is no business of yours.
dúhur (i, e) *mb.* due, required, requested, necessary, needed, owing, owed; **në kohën e duhur:** in due time; **shuma e duhur:** the due amount; **marr masat e duhura:** to take the necessary measures, to take due precautions; **me respektin e duhur:** with all proper regard.
dukát,-i *m.sh.* -e dukedom.
dúke *pj.* (particle used to form the gerund)**duke marrë parasysh...:** seeing that, having in regard...; **e gjeta duke shkruar:** I found him writting; **duke bërë:** doing; **duke vënë:** placing; **duke folur në mbledhje, ai tha:** speaking at the meeting he said.
dúkem *f.jv.* 1. to appear; **mos u duk më këtu!** don't let me set eyes on you again, never show your

face here I 2. to seem; **më duket se**: it seems to me that, I think that; **duket se** : it seems that, it appears that; **më duket se po**: I think so, I believe so. 3. to look,to seem; **duket më i ri se ç'është**: he looks younger, he is young for his age; **Afërdita donte të dukej elegante**: Aphrodite wanted to look smart; **do të dukesh I ndershëm**: you want to seem honest; **dukem si**: to look like, to show oneself like; **si ju duket kjo pikturë?** how do you like this picture? **duket se do të bjerë shi**: it looks like rain; **kërkoj të dukem**: to show off, to put oneself forward, to put on airs; **me sa duket, siç duket**: presumably, probably; **duket sheshit (ashiqare)**: it is (evident).

dúk/ë,-a *m.sh.* -ë duke.

dúkj/e,-a *f.* appearance, look; **në dukje**: outwardly, in appearance, seemingly; **vë në dukje diçka**: to bring something out, to point something out.

dúksh/ëm (i),-me(e) *mb.* visible, apparent, evident, conspicuous, ostensible, obvious; **shkak I dukshëm**: ostensible motive; **në mënyrë të dukshme**: visibly, obviously, evidently.

dukurí,-a *f.sh.* - *fiz.* phenomenon.

durím,-i *m.* 1. forbearance, endurance. 2. perseverance. 3. patience: **bëj durim**: to be patient; **s'kam durim**: to lack patience; **humbas durimin**: to lose patience, to lose one's temper; **la humbas durimin dikujt**: to exhaust (to try, to wear out) someone's patience.

duroj I. *f.jk.* to be patient.

II. *f.k.* to resist, to endure, to bear, to tolerate; **duroj të ftohtët**: to put up with the cold; **duroj një fyerje**: to pocket an insult, to bear an injury; **s'mund ta duroj dot**: I cannot put up with him; **nuk duroj dot më**: I can't bear to. − **durohet** *f.jv.*; **kjo s'durohet**: that is insupportable (unendurable, unbearable, intolerable).

duruesh/ëm (i),-me(e) *mb.* bearable, supportable, tolerable, endurable.

dush,-i *m.sh.* -e 1. shower; **bëj një dush**: to have, to take a shower. 2. *fam.* rebuke; **ha një dush**: to get told off, to give it hot to someone.

dush/k,-ku *m.sh.* -qe *bot.* oak.

dushkáj/ë,-a *f.sh.* -a oak-plantation.

dúshku/ll,-lli *m.sh.* -j *bot.* peanut--tree.

duvák,-u *m.sh.* -ë bride's veil.

duzín/ë,-a *f.sh.* -a dozen; **dymbëdhjetë duzina**: gross.

dy *num.them.* two; **të dy**: both; **të dy pjesët**: the two parts; **dy herë**: twice, two times; **dy herë katër**: two times four; **dy nga dy**: two and two, by twos, in pairs; **rreshtohemi për dy**: to stand in two; **nja dy gjëra**: a thing or two; **për ne të dy**: for us two, for us both; **për dy**: in twos, in pairs. *(line up by twos)*

dyanësór,-e *mb.* bilateral.

dyánësh,-e *mb.* double-sided.

dyánsh/ëm (i),-me(e) *mb.* bilateral; **marrëveshje e dyanshme**: bilateral agreement.

dybék,-u *m.sh.* -ë churn.

dybrinjënjëshëm *mb. gjeom.* isosceles.

dýer *f.sh.* (plural of **derë**); **me dyer të mbyllura**: behind closed doors.

dyfáqësh,-e *mb. gjeom.* dihedral, two-sided.

dyfék,-u *m.sh.* -ë *vjet.* shih **pushkë**.

dyfísh *ndajf.* doubly, twofold, twice as much; **kushton dyfish:** it costs twice as much.

dyfísh,-i *m.* double; **dyfishi i rrugës:** twice the distance.

dyfísh,-e *mb.* double, twofold.

dyfishím,-i *m.sh.* **-e** redoubling.

dyfishòj *f.k.* to double, to redouble. – **dyfishohet** *f.jv.* to double, to increase twofold.

dyfíshtë (i, e) *mb.* 1. double, twofold; **me fund të dyfishtë** *(valixhe):* double-bottomed. 2. *mat., fiz.* double. 3. *fig.* double; **me veprim të dyfishtë:** double acting; **bëj jetë të dyfishtë:** to lead a double life.

dygéç,-i *m.sh.* **-ë** pestle, pounder, flail.

dyjavór,-i *m.sh.* **-ë** fortnight, fourteen days, two weeks.

dyjavór,-e *mb.* fortnightly, biweekly, semi-monthly, of two weeks, two weeks; **periudhë dyjavore:** a two week period; **pagë dyjavore:** fortinght's wage.

dykátësh,-e *mb.* two-storied; **shtëpi dykatëshe:** a two-storied house.

dykrenóre *mb.* bicephalous; **shqiponja dykrenore:** bicephalous eagle.

dykrérësh,-e *mb.* bicephalous, with two heads.

dylbén,-i *m.sh.* **-e** kerchief.

dylbí,-a *f.sh.* **-** spy-glass, field-glass; **dylbi teatri:** opera-glasses.

dyluftím,-i *m.sh.* **-e** duel, single combat.

dýll/ë,-i *m.* wax; **dyllë bletësh:** beeswax; **dyllë i kuq:** sealing-wax; **prej dylli:** waxen.

dyllós *f.k.* to wax, to seal up; **dyllos një letër:** to wax a letter, to seal up a letter. – **dylloset** *f.jv.* to be waxed (sealed).

dyllósj/e,-a *f.* sealing.

dymbëdhjétë *num.them.* twelve.
dymbëdhjétë (i, e) *num.rresht.* twelfth (the).

dymujór,-e *mb.* two-month, of two months (period).

dynd *f.k.* to run over. – *dyndem f.jv.* to overrun.

dýndj/e,-a *f.sh.* **-e** overrun, invasion; **dyndjet e barbarëve:** influx of barbarian hords.

dyngjýrësh,-e *mb.* two-coloured, of two colours.

dynÿm,-i *m.sh.* **-ë** one tenth of a hectare.

dynjá,-ja *f. vjet.* shih **botë.**

dypálësh,-e *mb.* bilateral; **marrëveshje dypalëshe:** bilatera agreement.

dyqán-i *m.sh.* **-e** shop, store; **dyqan buke:** shop-bread; **dyqan ushqimesh:** grocery.

dyqanxhí,-u *m.sh.* **-nj** shop-keeper, store-keeper, tradesman.

dyqínd *num. them.* two hundred.

dyqindvjetór,-i *m.sh.* **-ë** bicentenary.

dyrrókësh,-e *mb.* bisyllabic.

dyst *mb.* 1. *(cohë)* plain (tissue), devoid of ornament. 2. *(rrugë)* even, flat (of a road).

dýstë (i, e) *mb.* shih **dyst.**

dystím-i *m.* flattening, making even; **dystimi i tokës:** flattening of the ground.

dystój *f.k.* to even, to flatten, to level.

dysh,-i *m.sh.* **-a** 1. two; *(në lojë letrash)* **dyshi karò:** the two of diamonds. 2. ancient coin; **jam pa një dysh:** not have a penny, to be penniless; **s'vlen një dysh:** it's not worth a rap, *amer.* it's not worth two cents.

dysh *ndajf.* in two parts; **pres më dysh:** to cut into two equal parts, to cut in halves; **ndaj më dysh:** to bisect.

dyshék,-u *m.sh.* **-ë** mattress; **dy-**

shek me kashtë: straw-mattress; këllëf dysheku: tick.
dyshemé,-ja *f.sh.* - floor; shtrim dyshemeje: laying of floors.
dyshím,-i *m.sh.* -e 1. doubt; pa dyshim: undoubtfully, without doubt, undoubtedly, no doubt, evidently, certainly; me dyshim: doubtfully, uncertainly; jam në dyshim: to be in doubt. 2. suspicion; kam dyshim për dikë: to have suspicion for someone, to suspect someone.
dyshímtë (i, e) *mb.* doubtful, suspect, suspected, suspicious; njeri i dyshimtë: a suspect person.
dyshkolónë *ndajf.* in two ranks.
dyshój *f.jk.* to doubt, to suspect.
— dyshohem *f.jv.* to be suspected.

dyshúes,-i *m.sh.*-distrustful person.
dyshúes,-e *mb.* distrustful, doubtful.
dýtë (i, e) *num.rresht.* second; së dyti : secondly.
dythundrák,-e *mb.* two-hoofed.
dythundrákë,-t *m.sh.* two-hoofed animals.
dyvjeçár,-e *mb.* two-year, of two years.
dyzanór,-i *m.sh.* -ë diphthong.
dyzét *num. them.* fourty.
dyzétë (i, e) *num. rresht.* fortieth.
dyzím,-i *m.sh.*-e 1. dividing (splitting, division) in two parts. 2. *fiz.* duplication.
dyzój *f.k.* to cut (to split, to divide) into two.

DH

dh, Dh (letter of the Albanian alphabet; is pronounced like th in *th*at).
dha *f.k.* (past tense of the verb jap, 3ᵈ person) he gave, she gave.
dháll/ë,-a *f.* butter-milk.
dhanór/e,-ja *f. gram.* dative; rasa dhanore: dative case.
dhaskál,-i *m.sh.* -ë *vjet.* shih mësues.
dhaskalíc/ë,-a *f.sh. vjet.* shih mësuese.
dháshë *f.k.* (past tense of the verb jap,1ˢᵗ person) I gave.

dhe *f.k.* (past tense of the verb jap, 2ᵈ person) you gave.
dhe,-u *m.sh.* -ra 1. earth, ground; shtie në dhe: to bury; nxjerr nga dheu: to unearth; gërmime dheu: earthwork; gërmoj dhe: to dig up earth; grumbull dheu: mound. 2. land; shkoj në dhe të huaj: to emigrate.
dhe *lidh.* and.
dhelparák,-e *mb.* foxy, sly, cunning, artful, astute, crafty, wily.
dhélp/ër,-ra *f.sh.* -ra 1. *zool.* fox 2. *fig.* dhelpër e vjetër: a sly old fox.

dhelpërí,-a *f.* slyness, cunning, craftiness.

dhelpërísht *ndajf.* slyly, craftily, artfully.

dhemb (më) *f.jk.* to ache, to pain; **më dhemb koka:** my head aches, I have a headache.

dhémbj/e,-a *f.sh.* -e ache, pain; dolour; **dhembje e fortë:** pang; **dhembje barku:** bellyache; **dhembje e fortë barku:** colic; **dhembje dhëmbi:** toothache; **dhembje koke:** headache; **dhembje e fortë koke:** splitting headache; **dhembje veshi:** earache; **dhembje gryke:** sore throat; **dhembjet e lindjes:** birth throes; **kam dhembje:** to have pains.

dhémbura,-t (të) *f.sh.* pains.

dhémbsh/ëm(i),-me(e) *mb.* 1. compassionate. 2. painful.

dhémbshur (i, e) *mb.* affectionate, tender, warm-hearted.

dhembshurí,-a *f.* affection, tenderness, fondness; **me dhembshurí:** affectionately.

dhen,-të *m.sh.* sheep; **vathë për dhen:** sheepfold.

dhéntë (i, e) *mb.* sheepy.

dhéra,-t *m.sh.* plural of **dhe.**

dhespót,-i *m.sh.* -ë bishop.

dhëmb,-i *m.sh.* -ë 1. tooth; **dhëmb çatall:** fang, tusk; **dhëmb që luan:** loose tooth; **dhëmbët e përparmë:** incisve teeth; **dhëmbët e sipërm:** upper teeth; **dhëmbët e poshtëm:** lower teeth; **dhëmbi i pjekurisë:** wisdom tooth; **dhëmb i prishur:** rotten tooth; **dhëmbët e qumështit:** milk-teeth; **dhëmbi i syrit (i qenit):** eye-tooth, canine tooth; **dhëmb i vënë:** false tooth; **dhëmbë të vëna:** set of teeth; **dhëmbë elefanti:** tusks of an elephant; **furçë dhëmbësh:** tooth-brush; **dhembje**

dhëmbi: toothache; **heqje dhëmbi:** pulling of a tooth; **mbushje dhëmbi:** filling (stopping) of a tooth; **mishi i dhëmbëve:** gum of the teeth. 2. *tek. (ingranazhi)* cog, notch; *(sharre)* tooth. – *Lok.* **dhëmb për dhëmb:** tooth for tooth; **them (diçka) nëpër dhëmbë:** to grumble; **i tregoj dhëmbët dikujt:** to show one's teeth; **zbardh dhëmbët:** to snicker.

dhëmbáll/ë,-a *f.sh.* -ë molar-tooth, jaw-tooth, molar.

dhëmbërënë *mb.* toothless.

dhëmbës,-i *m.* rake.

dhëmbëz,-a *f.sh.* -a cog, dent, notch; **dhëmbëzat e ingranazhit:** cogs (dents, teeth) of a wheel; **dhëmbëz e ngrënë:** indentation; **dhëmbëza-dhëmbëza:** jagged; serrate, dentate.

dhëmbëzój *f.k.* to cog, to jag, to tooth, to indent. – **dhëmbëzohet** *f.jv.* to be cogged (jagged).

dhëmbëzúar (i, e) *mb.* cogged, notched, jaggy, jagged; serrate, dentate; **rrotë e dhëmbëzuar:** cogged wheel.

dhëmbór,-e *mb.* dental.

dhëmbór/e,-ja *f.sh.* -e *gram.* dental.

dhënd/ër,-ri *m.sh.* -urë 1. bridegroom. 2. *(karshi vjehërrit)* son-in-law.

dhën/ë (e),-a (e) *f.sh.* - a(të) l. datum; **të dhëna:** data; **të dhëna ekonomike:** economic data. 2. indication, information; **kemi të dhëna se:** we have information that.

dhënë (i, e) *mb.* 1. generous; **njeri i dhënë:** a generous man. 2. fond of, impassioned; **i dhënë pas muzikës:** fond of music.

dhënë *f.k.* (past participle of the verb **jap**) given; **kam dhënë:** I have given.

dhënës,-i *m.sh.* giver, donor.
dhëni/e,-a *f.* 1. giving, bestowal. 2. confering; **dhënie titulli, diplome, etj.**: confering of a title, a diploma etc.; **dhënie llogarie**: rendering (giving) account.
dhëntël *f.k.* 1. shih **jap.** 2. mayl
dhi,-a *f.sh.* - *zool.* she-goat; **dhi e egër**: wild she-goat, wild goat; **bari dhish**: goat-herd; **vathë për dhi**: goat-fold.
dhiár,-i *m.sh.* -ë goat-herd.
dhiát/ë,-a *f. fet.* testament; **Dhiata e Re**: New testament; **Dhiata e Vjetër**: Ancient testament.
dhímbet (më) *f.jk.* to compassionate, to have, to feel pity for.
dhímbsh/ëm (i),-me(e) *mb.* compassionate.
dhiqél,-i *m.sh.* -e hoe.
dhírtë (i, e) *mb.* mohair; **gunë e dhirtë**: mohair cape.
dhis/k,-ku *m.sh.* -qe salver, tray; **dhisk çaji**: tea tray; **dhisk kafeje**: coffee tray.
dhjak,-u . *sh.* -ë *fet.* deacon.
dhjám/ë,-i *m.* fat, grease; **dhjamë lope**: cow grease; **dhjamë derri**: pig's fat; **dhjamë për qirinj**: tallow, candle-grease; **dhjamë i tretur**: tallow, melted fat; **me dhjamë**: greasy, fatty; **vë dhjamë**: to grow fat.
dhjámtë (i, e) *mb.* greasy, fatty.
dhjes *f.k., f.jk.* to discharge one's excrement, to evacuate, to move the bowels. − **dhitem** *f.jv.* to discharge one's excrement.
dhjétë (e),-a(e) *f.sh.* -a (të) tithe; **marr të dhjetën**: to collect the tithe.
dhjetár,-i *m.sh.* -e collector of the tithe.
dhjétë *num. them.* ten.
dhjétë (i,e) *num. rresht.* tenth.
dhjetëdítësh,-i *m.sh.* -a shih **dhjetëditor.**

dhjetëditór,-i *m.sh.* -ë ten days decade.
dhjetëfísh,-i *m.* the tenfold.
dhjetëfísh *ndajf.* tenfold, ten times as much.
dhjetëfishím,-i *m.* decupling, intensifying tenfold.
dhjetëfishój *f.k.* to decuple, to increase tenfold. − **dhjetëfishohet** *f.jv.* to increase tenfold.
dhjetëmúajsh,-e *mb.* of ten months, ten-month; **foshnjë dhjetëmuajshe**: a ten-month old baby.
dhjetërrókësh,-i *m.* decasyllable.
dhjetërrókësh,-e *mb.* decasyllabic.
dhjétësh,-i *m.sh.* -a *vjet.* (ancient small money) farthing; **nuk kam asnjë dhjetësh**: I have not a farthing.
dhjétësh/e,-ja *f.sh.* -e ten.
dhjetëvjeçár,-i *m.sh.* -e ten years, decade.
dhjetëvjeçár,-e *mb.* decennial, ten-year.
dhjetëvjetór,-i *m.sh.* -ë tenth anniversary.
dhjetój *f.k.* to decimate, to thin out; to deplete; **dhjetoj radhët e armikut**: to decimate the enemy, to take heavy toll of the enemy.
dhjetór,-i *m.* December.
dhjetór,-e *mb. mat.* decimal; **numër dhjetor**: decimal number.
dhóg/ë,-a *f.sh.* -a *krah.* shih **dërrasë.**
dhóm/ë,-a *f.sh.* -a 1. room, chamber; **dhomë gjumi**: bedroom; **dhomë buke**: dining-room; **dhomë pritjeje**: parlo(u)r. sitting-room; spare room; **dhomë e miqve**: guest room; **shok dhomë**: room-mate; **muzikë dhome**: chamber music. 2. *fiz. tek., anat.* chamber; **dhomë e djegies**: combustion chamber; **dhomë e errët**: camera obscura. 3. cham-

ber; **Dhoma e tregtisë:** Chamber of commerce.
dhrahmí,-a *f.sh.* - drachma (the standard Greek money).
dhún/ë,-a *f.* violence; **hyj me dhunë:** to break into, to enter by violence.
dhuním,-i *m.sh.* -e 1. violation; **dhunim banese:** house breaking, illegal entry (into a house or enclosed premises). 2. rape.
dhunój *f.k.* 1. to violate; to break into. 2. to rape, to ravish.
dhunúes,-i *m.sh.* - violator, rapist.
dhuntí,-a *f.sh.* - gift, talent, flair.

dhurát/ë,-a *f.sh.* -a 1. gift, present; **dhuratë martese:** wedding gift; **dhuratë kujtimi:** keepsake; **dhuratë e Vitit të Ri:** handsel, New Year's gift, New Year box; **dhuratë e natyrës:** nature's gift, talent.
dhurím,-i *m.* offering, bestowal, bestowment, donation; **dhurim gjaku:** offering of blood, donation of blood.
dhurój *f.k.* to bestow, to give, to present; to make a present of.
dhurúes,-i *m.sh.* - giver, donor; **dhurues gjaku:** blood donor.

E

e, E (letter of the Albanian alphabet) e, E.
e *n.p.* (article) 1. **vajzë e mirë:** good girl; **e mira dhe e liga:** the good and the bad; *sh.* **të; djem të mirë:** good boys; **vajza të mira:** good girls. 2. of; **pjesët e trupit:** the parts of the body; **Partia e Punës e Shqipërisë:** the Party of Labour of Albania; **djemtë e mi:** my boys; **vajzat e mia:** my girls. 3. (when placed before a noun of the feminine gender it acts as a possessive adjective): **e ëma** = his (her) mother; **e mbesa** = his (her) niece; **e motra** = his (her) sister; *shumës:* **të motrat:** (his,her) sisters; **të vëllezërit:** their (his, her) brothers.
e *p.vet.* (the short form of the third person singular of the personal pronoun in the accusative case) **e takoj** (= takoj atë): I meet him (her); **nuk e kuptoj** (= nuk kuptoj atë): I don't understand it; (it is used also together with a noun): **e takova shokun (tim):** I met my friend.
e *lidh.* and; **mirë e më mirë:** better and better; **unë e ti:** both of us, you and me.
ecejáke,-t *f.sh.* goings and comings.
éca *f.jk.* (past tense of the verb **eci**) I walked, I went.
éci *f.jk.* 1. to walk, to go, to step; **eci më këmbë:** to go on foot; **eci me ngadalë:** to go slowly; **eci me të shpejtë:** to go quickly, **eci lehtë:** to go lightly; **eci me hapa të mëdha:** to stride, to

stradle, to walk with long steps; **eci me hapa të shpejtë:** to walk with hasty strides (at a quick pace); **eci mbi majat e gishtave:** to go on tiptoe; **eci me mundim:** to plod, to trudge; **eci në gjurmët e:** to tread in the footsteps of; **eci përpara:** to go forward, to advance, to get along; **eci prapa:** to go backward; **eci verbërisht (symbyllas):** to grope: **eci rëndë:** to tramp: **eci duke u lëkundur:** to stagger; **ec përparа** : come on! 2. to proceed, to go; **punët ecin mirë:** things are going well. – *Lok.* **më ecën:** to be lucky, to be successful; **s'më ecën:** to be unsuccessful; **i eci mirë atij:** It has fared well with him, he has done well, he has been fortunate; **ec e mos e prano po deshe:** it is impossible not to admit it.

écj/e,-a *f.* gait, going, walk, walking, step; **ecje krenare:** proud step, strut; **ecje e çrregullt:** irrregular gait, shuffling.

écurit (të) *as.* walk, gait; **njoh dikë nga të ecurit:** to recognize someone from his walk.

edukát/ë,-a *f.* education, politeness good-breeding; **me edukatë:** well-bred; **pa edukatë:** ill-bred, low-bred.

edukatív,-e *mb.* educative.

edukatór,-i *m.sh.* -ë educator.

edukatór/e,-ja *f.sh.* -e nursemaid, nursery maid.

edukím,-i *m.* education, upbringing; **edukim fizik:** physical training (education); **mësues i edukimit fizik:** gym and games teacher; **edukimi i fëmijëve:** the education (the upbringing) of the children.

edukój *f.k.* to educate, to bring up. – **edukohem** *f.jv.* to be educated.

edukuar (i, e) *mb.* well-bred well-mannered, well-brought up, polite; **vajzë e edukuar:** a polite girl.

edukúes,-e *mb.* educative.

édhe *lidh.* 1. and; **djemtë dhe vajzat e fshatit:** the boys and the girls of the village. 2. also; **edhe unë:** I also, I too; **edhe ti edhe unë:** both of us. ᶜ**dhe** *ndajf.* yet, more, still; **edhe më:** yet; **edhe një herë:** once more; **edhe më i gjatë:** still longer. ∧

efékt,-i *m.sh.* -e effect; **me efekt:** effective, efficacious; **pa efekt:** ineffectual.

efektív,-i *m.sh.* -a effective.

efektív,-e *mb.* effective.

efektivísht *ndajf.* effectually, in effect.

efikás,-e *mb.* efficacious.

efikasitét,-i *m.* efficacy.

égër (i, e) *mb.* 1. wild, savage; **kafshë e egër:** wild beast; **derr i egër:** boar, wild boar; **dhi e egër:** wild goat; **mace e egër:** wild cat; **njeri i egër:** savage man. 2. fierce, ferocious; **njeri i egër** *(nga shpirti)*: brutal man, fierce man; **luftë e egër:** ferocious struggle; **vend i egër:** wild country.

egërsí,-a *f.* cruelty, atrocity, ferocity, savagery; **me egërsi:** ferociously, atrociously, fiercely, savagely.

egërsír/ë,-a *f.sh.* -a wild beast.

egërsísht *ndajf.* ferociously, atrociously, cruelly, fiercely, savagely.

egërsój *f.k.* to render savage (wild), to infuriate. – **egërsohem** *f.jv.* to grow wild, to be infuriated.

egoíst,-i *m.sh.* -ë egotist, selfish person.

egoíst,-e *mb.* selfish, egotistic.

egoíz/ëm,-mi, *m.* egotism, selfishness, self-interest.

égj/ër,-ri *m. bot.* tare.

egjiptián,-i *m.sh.* -ë Egyptian.

egjiptián,-e *mb.* Egyptian.

ejal *pasth.* comel, come onl, come upl

ekíp,-i *m.sh.* -e 1. group. 2. *sport.* team, side.

eklíps,-i *m.sh.* -e *astron.* eclipse; **eklips i Hënës:** eclipse of the moon, lunar eclipse.

ekonomát,-i *m.sh.* -ë provider, supplier, furnisher.

ekonomí,-a *f.* 1. economy; **ekonomia socialiste:** the socialist economy; **ekonomia politike:** political economy; **ekonomia shtëpiake:** housekeeping, household management. 2. saving, thriftiness, thrift; **për ekonomi:** for the sake of economy, in order to save.

ekonomík,-e *mb.* economic, economical.

ekonomikísht *ndajf.* economically.

ekonomist,-i *m.sh.* -ë economist.

ekrán,-i *m.sh.* -e screen; **ekran televizori:** television screen.

eksíq *ndajf.* shih **mangët.**

ekskavatór,-i *m.sh.* -ë excavator, digging-machine; **kovë ekskavatori:** scoop; **gërmoj me ekskavator:** to excavate.

eksursión,-i *m.sh.* -e excursion, trip, journey; **bëj një ekskursion:** to go on an excursion.

ekspansión,-i *m.* expansion.

ekspedít/ë,-a *f.sh.* -a expedition.

eksperiénc/ë,-a *f.* experience; **pa eksperiencë:** unexperienced.

eksperimént,-i *m.sh.* -e experiment; test, trial.

eksperimentál,-e *mb.* experimental.

eksperimentúes,-i *m.sh.* - trier (of experiments).

ekspért,-i *m.sh.* -ë expert; *drejt.* surveyor.

ekspért,-e *mb.* expert, skilful.

ekspertím,-i *m.sh.* -e *drejt.* surveying.

ekspertíz/ë,-a *f.sh.* -a *drejt.* survey.

ekspertój *f.k. drejt.* to survey.

eksploratór,-i *m.sh.* -e explorer.

eksplorím,-i *m.sh.* -e exploration.

eksplorój *f.k.* to explore. – **eksplorohet** *f.jv.* to be explored.

ekspórt,-i *m.sh.* -e export.

eksportím,-i *m.sh.* -e exportation.

eksportój *f.k.* to export.

eksportúes,-i *m.sh.* – exporter.

ekspozím,-i *m.* 1. exhibition, display. 2. exposure.

ekspozít/ë,-a *f.* exhibition, display, show; **ekspozitë bagëtish;** cattle-show; **ekspozitë lulesh;** flower-show.

ekspozój *f.k.* to expose; **ekspozoj mallin:** to display (to exhibit) goods. – **ekspozohem** *f.jv.* to expose oneself; **ekspozohem për hiç gjë (më kot):** to run uselessly into danger.

ekspozúes,-i *m.sh.* -ë expositor.

eksprés *mb.* express; **tren ekspres:** express train; **kafe ekspres:** espresso.

ékstra *mb.* extra.

ekstrém,-i *m.sh.* -e shih **skaj.**

ekstrém,-e *mb.* extreme; **masa ekstreme:** extreme measures.

ekstremíst,-i *m.sh.* -ë extremist.

ekuación,-i *m.sh.* -e *mat.* equation.

ekuatór,-i *m.sh.* -e equator.

ekuatoriál,-i *m.sh.* -e equatorial.

ekuilíb/ër,-ri *m.* equipoise, equilibrium, balance; **humbas ekuilibrin:** to lose one's balance.

ekuilibrím,-i *m.* equilibration.

ekuilibrój *f.k.* to equipoise, to equilibrate. — **ekuilibrohem** *f.jv.* to be equiposed, to be equilibrated.

ekuinóks,-i *m.sh.* -e equinox.
ekuipázh,-i *m.sh.* -e crew (of a ship, etc.).
ekuivalénc/ë,-a *f.* equivalence.
ekuivalént,-e *mb.* equivalent.
ekzagjerím,-i *m.sh.* -e exaggeration.
ekzagjerój *f.k.* to exaggerate.
ekzákt,-e *mb.* exact, correct, accurate, precise.
ekzaktërísht *ndajf.* exactly, precisely.
ekzaltím,-i *m.* exaltation.
ekzaltój *f.k.* to exalt. – ekzaltohem *f.jv.* to be exalted, to be elated.
ekzaminím,-i *m.* examination.
ekzaminój *f.k.* to examine, to test. – ekzaminohem *f.jv.* to be examined.
ekzekutím,-i *m.sh.* -e 1. *muz.* *(ekzekutim i një pjese muzikore)*: execution 2. putting to death, execution; urdhër ekzekutimi: death warrant.
ekzekutív,-e *mb.* executive; Komiteti Ekzekutiv: the Executive Committee.
ekzekutój *f.k.* 1. to execute, to put to death. 2. *muz.* to perform. – ekzekutohem *f.jv.* 1. to be executed. 2. *muz.* to be performed.
ekzém/ë,-a *f. mjek.* eczema.
ekzemplár,-i *m.sh.* -ë exemplary, copy.
ekzisténc/ë,-a *f.* existence, life.
ekzistój *f.jk.* to exist, to live.
ekzistúes,-e *mb.* existing.
elasticitét,-i *m.* elasticity, resilience.
elastík,-e *mb.* elastic, resilient.
elb,-i *m. bot.* barley; elb distik: couplet.
elbaróz/ë,-a *f. bot.* geranium.
elbazé,-ja *f.sh.* - fan; freskohem me elbaze : to fan.
elbth,-i *m. mjek.* sty.
elefánt,-i *m.sh.* -ë *zool.* elephant.
elegánc/ë,-a *f.* elegance; smart-

ness; me elegancë: elegantly, smartly.
elegánt,-e *mb.* elegant, fashionable, smart; vishem elegant: to dress smartly.
elektorál,-e *mb.* electoral; fushatë elektorale: election campaign; zonë elektorale: election district.
elektricist,-i *m.sh.* -ë electrician.
elektricitét,-i *m.* electricity.
elektrifikím,-i *m.* electrification.
elektrifikój *f.k.* to electrify.
elektrík,-u *m.* electric; elektrik xhepi: electric torch.
elektrík,-e *mb.* electric; dritë elektrike: electric light; rrymë elektrike: electric current.
elektrizím,-i *m.* electrification.
elektrizój *f.k.* 1. to electrize. 2. *fig.* to electrify.
elektród/ë,-a *f.sh.* -a electrode; solder; ngjis me elektrodë: to solder.
elektromotór,-i *m.sh.* -ë electric motor, electromotor.
elemént,-i *m.sh.* -e element.
elementár,-e *mb.* elementary.
elevatór,-i *m.sh.* -ë elevator, crampoon.
eliminím,-i *m.* elimination.
eliminój *f.k.* to eliminate.
elít/ë,-a *f.* elite, cream; elita e shoqërisë: the cream of the society.
elmáz,-i *m.sh.* -ë glass-cutter.
elokuénc/ë,-a *f.* eloquence.
elokuént,-e *mb.* eloquent.
emancipím,-i *m.* emancipation.
emblém/ë,-a *f.sh.* -a emblem.
embrión,-i *m.sh.* -e embryo; *fig.* në emrion: in embryo. një plan në embrion: a plan in embryo.
ém/ër,-ri *m.sh.* -ra 1. *gram.* noun; emër i përveçëm: proper noun; emër i përgjithshëm: common

noun; **emër foljor**: verbal noun.
2. name; **si e keni emrin? (si
quheni?)**: what is your name?
emër përkëdhelës: pet name.
3. *fig.* name, reputation; **kam
emër të mirë**: to have a good
name (reputation); **jam me emër
për kopraci**: to be reputed a
miser; **veproj në emër të**:
to act on behalf of; **në emër të
ligjit**: in the name of the law.
emërím,-i *m.sh.* **-e** appointment;
marr emërimin në një shkollë:
to obtain an appointment in a
school.
emërój *f.k.* to nominate, to designate, to appoint. — **emërohem**
f.jv. to be nominated, designated,
appointed; to obtain an appointment.
emërór,-e *mb.* nominal, nominative;
listë emërore: list of names, roll
of names; **rasa emërore**: nominative case.
emërór/e,-ja *f. gram.* nominative.
emërím,-i *m.* denomination, designation (of articles).
emërtój *f.k.* to denominate, to designate, to name (articles). –
emërtohet *f.jv.* to be denomi-
nated.
emërúes,-i *m.sh.* - *mat.* denominator; **emërues i përbashkët**:
common denominator.
emigránt,-i *m.sh.* **-ë** emigrant,
colonist.
emigrím,-i *m.sh.* **-e** emigration.
emigrój *f.jk.* to emigrate.
emisár,-i *m.sh.* **-ë** emissary.
emisión,-i *m.sh.* **-e** 1. program. 2.
emission (of bank notes), pu-
tting into circulation (of bank
notes).
emoción,-i *m.sh.* **-e** emotion.
emocionánt,-e *mb.* emotional.
emocionój *f.k.* to encite, to move,
to touch, to effect, – **emocio-
nohem** *f.jv.* to get excited, to be

moved, to be touched, to be
affected.
emocionúes,-e *mb.* exciting, stirring; moving, touching, affecting.
émt/ë(e),-a(e) *f. krah.* aunt; **e
emta**: his (her) aunt.
emulación,-i *m.* emulation.
enciklopedí,-a *f.sh.* - encyclopa-
edia, encyclopedia.
enciklopedík,-e *mb.* encyclopae-
dic, encyclopedic.
end,-i *m. bot.* pollen.
end *f.k.* to weave.
endacák,-u *m.sh.* **-ë** wanderer,
saunterer, rover, vagrant, tramp.
endacák,-e *mb.* wandering, roving,
errand; **fis endacak**: nomad
tribe.
ende *ndajf.* still; yet; **nuk jam ende
gati**: I'm not ready yet.
éndem *f.jv.* to wander, to saunter,
to ramble, to lounge, to rove, to
roam, to loiter.
éndës,-i *m.sh.* - weaver.
éndës,-e *mb.* weaving; **makinë
endëse**: weaving machine.
éndj/e,-a *f.* weaving.
éndj/e,-a *f.sh.* **-e** lounging, rambling, wandering, vagrancy.
éndur,-it (të) *as.* 1. weaving; **zeja
e të endurit**: weaving handi-
craft. 2. rambling.
energjí,-a *f.* energy; **me energji**:
energetically.
energjí/k,-e *mb.* energetic, active,
pushing, enterprising (person). 2.
energetic, forcible, vigorous,
strong; drastic; **masa energjike**:
drastic steps.
energjikìsht *ndajf.* energetically.
én/ë,-a *f.sh.* **-e** utensil, vessel,
receptacle; **enë kuzhine**: kitchen
utensils, culinary utensils; **enë
prej fajance, majolike**: crockery ware, earthenware; **enë
sheqeri**; sugar-basin; **enë qelqi**:

glass-ware; **laj enët:** to wash up dishes.
englëdísem *f.jv. gj.fol.* to amuse oneself.
éngjë/ll,-lli *m.sh.* -j angel.
engjëllór,-e *mb.* angelical.
engjerdhí,-a *f. kim., vjet.* shih **zhivë.**
enigmatík,-e *mb.* enigmatic.
enígm/e,-a *f.sh.* -a enigma.
énkas *ndajf.* purposely, intentionally, on purpose.
ent,-i *m.sh.* -e institution, establishment.
entuziáz/ëm,-mi *m.* enthusiasm.
entuziazmój *f.k.* to enthuse, to make enthusiastic. − **entuziazmohem** *f.jv.* to be enthused, to become enthusiastic.
entuziást,-e *mb.* enthusiastic.
énjte (e) *f.* Thursday.
épem *f.jv.* 1. to bend. 2. to be (to become) submissive.
épërm (i),-e(e) *mb.* upper, higher; superior, supreme.
epërsí,-a *f.* superiority, preponderance, upper hand; **epërsi numerike:** numeric superiority; **kam epërsi mbi kundërshtarin:** to be superior to the opponent.
epidemí,-a *f.sh.* - *mjek.* epidemic.
epidemík,-e *mb.* epidemic.
epidérm/ë,-a *f. anat.* epidermis.
epík,-e *mb.* epical, epic.
epík/ë,-a *f.* epic.
epilepsí,-a *f. mjek.* epilepsy; **krizë epilepsie:** epileptoid crises.
epileptík,-e *mb.* epileptic.
epiqénd/ër,-ra *f.sh.* -ra epicenter.
epitáf,-i *m.sh.* -e epitaph.
epók/ë,-a *f.sh.* -a epoch.
epopé,-ja *f.sh.* -e epopee.
eprór,-i *m.sh.* -ë superior.
eprór,-e *mb.* superior.
epruvét/ë,-a *f.sh.* -a test-tube.
epsh,-i *m.* lust, lascivity, voluptuousness, concupiscence.
épsh/ëm (i),-me(e) *mb.* 1. flexi-

ble, pliable, pliant, supple. 2. lustful, concupiscent, lescivious.
érdha *f.jk.* (past tense of the verb **vij**) I came.
eremít,-i *m.sh.* -ë hermit.
ér/ë,-a *f.* era; **para erës së re:** before new era.
ér/ë,-a *f.sh.* -era 1. wind; **erë e ftohtë (e akullt):** ice wind, frozen wind; **erë e lehtë (fllad):** breeze, zephyr; **erë e marrë:** squall, whirlwind, high wind, water spout, blast, gale; **erë e kundërt:** headwind; **kohë me erë:** windy weather; **fryn erë:** it blows, it is windy; **pushoi era (ra era):** the wind fell.
2. odour, scent, smelling, smell; **erë e mirë:** scent, fragrance; **me erë të mirë:** odoriferous, fragrant; sweet smelling; **erë e keqe:** stench, stink; **me erë të keqe:** stinking, fetid; **erë kërmë:** cadavering smell; **me erë:** odorous; **pa erë:** inodour; **i marr erë një luleje:** to smell a flower.−
Lok. **më ra era:** I got wind of; **planet e tij i mori era:** his plans fell to the ground.
éréza,-t *f.sh.* spices, condiments.
ermík,-u *m.* rice-farina.
erozión,-i *m.* erosion.
err *f.k.* i **err sytë:** to expire, to breath one's last. − **erret** *f.jv.* to get dark, to darken; **po erret:** it is getting dark, evening is closing in; **m'u errën sytë:** I was dazzled, my eyes grew dim.
errësím,-i *m.* darkening, dimming, glooming, black-out; **sinjal errësimi (qyteti në kohë lufte):** curfew.
errësír/ë,-a *f.* darkness, dimness, gloominess, obscurity, obscureness; **errësirë e plotë:** complete (pitch) darkness.
errësój *f.k.* to darken, to dim, to

obscure. – errësohet *f.jv.* to become obscure.

érrët (i, e) *mb.* 1. obscure, dark, hazy, dim, gloomy. 2. dark; deep; ngjyrë e errët: dark colour. 3. *fig.* vague, obscure, unclear, ambiguous; mendim i errët: obscure thought (opinion); pasazh i errët: an ambiguous passage.

es ênc/ë,-a *f.sh.* -a 1. *filoz.* essence; essential (main) point. 2. *kim.* essence.

e senciál,-e *mb.* essential, main.

e sencialisht *ndajf.* essentially, mainly.

ë sëll *ndajf.* on an empty stomach, before eating, before meals; ilaçe që pihen esëll: medicine to be taken on an empty stomach (before meals). – *Lok.* bëhem esëll: to sober up; jam esëll në matematikë: to know no mathematics at all.

esnáf,-i *m.sh.* -e craftsman.

estetík,-e *mb.* esthetic.

estetík/ë,-a *f.* esthetics.

estrád/ë,-a *f.* variety show.

esh,-i *m. zool.* shih iriq.

éshk/ë,-a *f.sh.* -a tinder, touchwood.

ésht/ë,-a *f.sh.* -a *anat.* fiber.

ésht/ër,-ra *f.sh.* -ra *anat.* bone.

eshtërím,-i *m.* ossification.

etáp/ë.-a *f.sh.* -a phase, stage.

etér,-i *m. kim.* ether.

eternít,-i *m.* asbestos lumber.

étër,-it *m.sh.* fathers (the plural of at).

etikét/ë,-a *f.sh.* -a 1. labbel, ticket; vë etiketë: to ticket. 2. etiquette.

etiketój *f.k.* to label, to affix a label to. – etiketohet *f.jv.* to be marked with a label.

etík/ë,-a *f.* ethics.

etimologjí,-a *f.* etymology.

etj. (abbreviation of e të tjera) etc.

étj/e,-a *f.* 1. thirst; kam etje: to be thirsty; shuaj etjen: to quench (to satisfy) one's thirst. 2. *fig.* thirst, longing, yearning, craving; kam etje për (diçka): to thirst (to long) for (something).

etnográf,-i *m.sh.* -ë ethnographer

etnografí,-a *f.* ethnography.

étsh/ëm (i),-me(e) *mb.* eager, greedy; ai ishte i etshëm të dinte: he was eager to know.

étur (i, e) *mb.* thirsty, eager; i etur për gjak: blood-thirsty.

éthe,-t *f.sh.* 1. fever; kam ethe: to be feverish, to be in fever. 2. ethet e kënetës: malaria; ethe tropikale: jungle fever; ethet e verdha: yellow fever. – *Lok.* jam si në ethe: to be feverish.

éthsh/ëm (i),-me(e) *mb.* feverish.

eventualisht *ndajf.* eventually.

eventualitét,-i *m.* eventuality.

evgjít,-i *m.sh.* -e gipsy, gypsy.

evidénc/ë,-a *f.sh.* -a evidence; në evidencë: in evidence.

evolución,-i *m.* evolution.

evropián,-i *m.sh.* -e European.

evropián,-e *mb.* European.

ezmér,-e *mb.* brunet, brown, of dark complexion; vajzë ezmere: brunet, brunette.

ezofág,-u *m.sh.* -e *anat.* esophagus.

Ë

ë, Ë (letter of the Albanian alphabet; is pronounced like **e** in her).

ëma (e) *f.* his (her) mother.

ëmbël *ndajf.* **1.** sottly, sweetly, mildly, gently; **këndoj ëmbël:** to sing melodiously.

ëmbël (i, e) *mb.* **1.** sweet; **ujë i ëmbël:** sweet water. **2.** *fig.* sweet, melodious; **zë i ëmbël;** sweet voice. **3.** *fig.* sweet, pleasant, agreeable; **kujtime të ëmbla:** sweet memories. **4.** *fig.* gentle, mild; **fllad i ëmbël:** a gentle breeze; **pjerrësi e ëmbël:** gentle slope, easy slope.

ëmbëlsí,-a *f.* sweetness; mildness, softness; **me ëmbëlsi:** sweetly; *muz.* melodiously.

ëmbëlsír/ë,-a *f.sh.* -a cake, sweetmeat.

ëmbëlsísht *ndajf.* gently, tenderly.

ëmbëlsój *f.k.* to sweeten, to make sweet. − **ëmbëlsohem** *f.jv.* to become sweet.

ëmbëltór/e,-ja *f.sh.* -e sweetshop, confectionary.

ënd/ë,-a *f.* pleasure, delight; si **ta ka ënda:** as you like it.

ënd/ërr,-rra *f.sh.* -rra **1.** dream; **ëndërr e llahtarshme:** nightmare. **2.** illusion; **rroj me ëndrra:** to live with (on) dreams, to daydream; **njeri që rron me ëndrra:** idle-dreamer; **ëndërr me sy hapur:** reverie, daydream.

ëndërrím,-i *m.sh.* -e reverie, musing, meditation, contemplation.

ëndërrój *f.k.* to dream, to muse, to meditate.

ëndërrúes,-i *m.sh.* - dreamer.

ëndërrúes,-e *mb.* dreamy; fanciful.

ënjt *f.k.* **1.** to swell, to bloat. **2.** **ënjt në dru dikë:** to beat someone black and blue, to give someone a sound beating. − **ënjtem** *f.jv.* to swell (up, out), to become swollen.

ënjtj/e,-a *f.* swelling.

ënjtur (i, e) *mb.* swollen.

është *f.jk.* (third pers. sing. of the verb **jam**) is; **ai (ajo) është:** he (she) is; **ky është një libër:** this is a book; **kush është atje?** Who is there?

F

f, F (letter of the Albanian alphabet) *f, F.*

fa,-ja *f. muz.* F, fa; **fa bemol maxhor:** F flat major.

fabrikánt,-i *m.sh.* **-e** manufacturer, factory owner.

fabrík/ë,-a *f.sh.* **-a** factory, manufactory, mill, plant. **fabrikë birre:** brewery; **fabrikë filature:** spinning mill; **fabrikë letre:** paper mill; **fabrikë mielli:** flour mill; **fabrikë tekstili:** textile mill; **fabrikë shegeri:** sugar plant.

fabrikím,-i *m.* production, manufacturing.

fabrikój *f.k.* 1. to produce, to manufacture. 2. *fig.* to make up, to concot, to fabricate, to hatch up, to cook up. – **fabrikohet** *f.jv.* 1. to be produced (manufactured). 2. *fig.* to be concoted, to be fabricated, to be hatched up. to be cooked up.

fábul,-a *f.sh.* **-a** fable.

faíz,-i *m.* shih **kamatë.**

faj,-i *m.sh.* **-e** *(faj i lehtë)* fault; **është faji i tij:** he is to blame, it is his own fault; **ngarkoj tjetrin me faj:** to impute the fault to another, to put the blame on another; **i vë faj vetes sime, ngarkoj veten me faj:** to blame oneself for; **bëj një faj:** to commit a fault; **e marr përsipër fajin:** I am to be blamed, the fault lies with me; **zë në faj e sipër:** to catch in the act;

(faj i rëndë) crime, guilt; **laj fajin:** to atone (for), to expiate a crime.

fajánc/ë,-a *f.* crockery, faience, majolica; **prodhime fajance:** crockery ware.

fajdexhí,-u *m.sh.* **-nj** pawnbroker money-lender, usurer.

fajësí,-a *f. drejt.* guiltiness.

fajësím,-i *m.* incrimination, crimination.

fajësój *f.k.* to declare guilty, to criminate, to incriminate, to accuse of a crime. – **fajësohem** *f.jv.* to be declared guilty.

fajk/úa,-oi *m.sh.* **-onj** *zool.* hawk, falcon.

fajtór,-i *m.sh.* **-ë** guilty man.

fajtór,-e *mb.* guilty; **fajtor për krim:** guilty of a crime; **pranoj se jam fajtor:** to plead guilty; **dy prej tyre u gjykuan dhe u gjetën fajtorë:** two of them were tried and found guilty.

fakír,-i *m.sh.* **-ë** 1. fakir. 2. *fam.* poor man.

fakt,-i *m.sh.* **-e** fact; **fakt i kryer:** accomplished fact, fait accompli. – *Lok.* **në fakt:** the fact is.

faktój *f.k.* to bring proofs, to prove, to document.

faktór,-i *m.sh.* **-e** 1. factor, element; **faktorë klimatikë:** climatic factors. 2. *mat.* factor; **zbërthej në faktorë:** to put into factors.

fakultatív-e *mb.* 1. facultative, optional; **lëndë fakultative** *(në shkollë):* optiona subject (at school). 2. permissive.

fakultét, -i *m.sh.* **-e** faculty, *amer.* college; **Fakulteti i Inxhinieri-së:** Faculty of Engineering.
fal *f.k.* 1. to give, to make e present of. 2. to pardon, to forgive, to excuse; **më falni:** I beg your pardon; **po ju fal:** I forgive you. 3. *drejt.* to acquit, to absolve; **fal dikë:** to acquit someone of; *polit.* to amnesty, to grant amnesty. − **falem** *f.jv.* 1. to pray, to say prayers; **i falem dikujt (diçkaje):** to worship, to prostrate someone (something). 2. to be forgiven. 3. *drejt.* to be acquitted of. 4. **i falem nderit dikujt:** to thank someone; **të falem nderit:** thank you!
fála,-t (të) *f.sh.* regards, love, greetings, salutations, remembrances; **të fala familjes tuaj :**give (send) my love (regards) your family; **të fala motrës suaj (vëllait tuaj):** give (send) my love (regards) to your sister (to your brother); **të fala të gjithëve:** give my love (regards) to all; **të falat e mia të përzemërta:** my kind regards, my best regards, my kind remembrance; **u jepni të falat e mia, u bëni të fala:** give my love (my greetings, my regards) to (them).
fálas *ndajf.* 1. gratis, gratuitously. 2. free of charge.
falemindérit *pasth.* thank you.
fálë *ndajf.* thanks to, owing to. **falë aftësive të veta:** thanks to his ability.
falëmeshëndét! *pasth.* salute!
falënderím,-i *m.sh.* **-e** thanks *pl.*; **pranoni falënderimet e mia më të sinqerta:** please accept my sincere thanks.
falënderój *f.k.* to thank. − **falënderohem** *f.jv.* to be thanked.
falimént,-i *m. treg.* bankrupt; **dha faliment;** he went bankrupt.

falimentím,-i *m.* bankruptcy.
falimentój *f.jk.* to go bankrupt; **e bëj që të falimentojë:** to bankrupt, to cause to become bankrupt.
fálj/e,-a *f.* 1. donation. 2. pardon, forgiveness; **i kërkoj falje dikujt:** to ask someone's forgiveness. 3. *polit.* amnesty.
fals,-e *mb.* false, untrue.
falsifikatór,-i *m.sh.* **-ë** counterfeiter, falsifier; fabricator.
falsifikím,-i *m.sh.* **-e** counterfeit, counterfeiting, forgery, falsification; **falsifikim parash:** counterfeiting of coins (banknotes).
falsifikój *f.k.* to counterfeit, to forge, to falsify; **falsifikoj dokumenta:** to falsify documents.
falsifikúes,-i *m.sh.* **-** shih **falsifikator.**
falsitét,-i *m.* falsehood, falsity.
fálsh/ëm (i),-me(e) *mb.* venial, forgivable, excusable.
faltór/e,-ja *f.sh.* **-e** *fet.* temple, sanctuary.
fálur (i,e) *mb.* 1. forgiven. 2. *drejt.* absolved. 3. bestowed, given; **gjë e falur:** gift.
fálur,-it (të) *as.* pardon; **lyp të falur:** to beg pardon.
fall,-i *m.sh.* **-e** fortune-telling, divination: **shtie në fall:** to tell fortune, to divine.
fallxhésh/ë,-a *f.sh.* **-a** soothsayer (woman), seer, fortune-teller.
fallxhí,-u *m.sh.* **-nj** soothsayer, fortune-teller.
fallxhór/e,-ja *f.sh.* **-e** shih **fall-xheshë.**
fám/ë,-a *f.* fame, celebrity, reputation, good name; **fitoj famë:** to get fame.
famëkéq,-e *mb.* bad-famed.
famëmádh,-e *mb.* famous, renowned.

familjár,-e *mb.* 1. family, of family; **jetë familjare:** family life; **njeri familjar;** family man. 2. familiar; **në mënyrë familjare:** in a familiar way. **familjarísht** *ndajf.* with all one's family. **familiaritét,-i** *m.* familiarity, intimacy; **kam familiaritet me dikë:** to be over-familiar with someone. **familjarizój** *f.k.* to familiarize. – **familjarizohem** *f.jv.* 1. to become friendly *(me,* with*).* 2. to make oneself familiar, to get to know, to familiarize oneself with. **familj/e,-a** *f.sh.* -a 1. family; **kryetar familjeje:** head of family. 2. family, house; **familje e dëgjuar:** distinguished family. 3. *zool. bot.* family. **fámsh/ëm (i),-me(e)** *mb.* famous, renowned, illustrious, distinguished, eminent. **famullí,-a** *f.sh.* - *fet.* parish; **libër famullie:** parish register. **famullitár,-i** *m.sh.* -ë parson. **fanár,-i** *m.sh.* -ë beacon; **fanar deti:** light-house. **fanatík,-u** *m.sh.* -ë fanatic. **fanatík,-e** *mb.* fanatic, fanatical. **fanatíz/ëm,-mi** *m.* fanaticism. **fanellát/ë,-a** *f.* flannel, flannelet. **fanéll/ë,-a** *f.sh.* -ë flannel, singlet; **fanellë mishi:** flannel shirt; **fanellë leshi:** woollen flannel, jersey; **fanellë pa mëngë:** bodice. **fant,-i** *m.sh.* -e jack. **fantastík,-e** *mb.* 1. fantastic, fantastical; **në mënyrë fantastike:** fantastically. 2. *fam.* fantastic, ncredible; **çmim fantastik:** incredibly high price; **fantazí,-a** *f.* 1. imagination; **ke fantazi të tepruar:** you have too much imagination, you are too

maginative. 2. reverie, day-dream, fancies. **fantázm/ë,-a** *f.sh.* -a phantasm, phantom, spectre. **fáq/e,-ja** *f.sh.* -e 1. cheek; **gropëza në faqe:** cheek pouch. 2. *(faqe libri)*: page (of a book). 3. *(faqe jastëku)*: pillowcase. 4. **faqe e tokës:** superficy, face of the earth; **mbi faqe të tokës:** on the face of the earth. – *Lok.* **njeri me dy faqe, si mësalla me dy faqe:** doublefaced person, hypocrite; **ky djalë ia nxin faqen familjes:** this boy is a disgrace to his family. **fáqe** *paraf.* in presence of; **faqe botës:** in presence of others. **faqebárdhë** *ndajf. mb.* successful; **dalçi faqebardhë!** may you be successful!, may success attend you! **faqegrópkë** *mb.* cheek-pouched. **faqekúq,-i** *m.sh.* -e *zool.* redbreast. **faqezí,-u** *m.sh.* -nj dishonest person, infamous person, miserable (despicable) person. **faqór/e,-ja** *f.sh.* -e flat flagon. **faqós** *f.k. tipog.* to make up into pages, to page up. – **faqoset** *f.jv.* to be paged up. **faqósj/e,-a** *f. tipog.* paging-up, paging. **far,-i** *m.sh.* -e beacon, sea-mark. **fáre** *ndajf.* 1. at all; **nuk e di fare këtë mësim:** I have not learnt this lesson at all. 2. quite; **është fare e natyrshme:** it is quite natyral. 3. very; **fare mirë:** very well. 4. entirely, wholly; **është fare e zezë:** it is entirely black. – *Lok.* **për fare:** for ever. **farefís,-i** *m.* kin, kinsfolk, akin, relative, kindred. **farefisní,-a** *f.* kinship. **fár/ë,-a** *f.sh.* -e 1. seed; **farë drithi (bimësh):** seed of cereals (plants); **farë liri:** linseed, seed of flax. 2. *(farë frutash)* pip (of fruits). 3. *(farë kosi etj.)* leaven (for yoghurt etc.) 4. *fam.* race, birth; **farë e keqe:** bad race. – – *Lok.* **një farë zoti A** : a certain mister A (in a contemptuous form); **një farë përmirësimi:** some improvement.

farisht/e,-ja *f.sh,* -e *bujq.* seedbed. nursery.

fárk/ë,-a *f.sh,* -a forge.

farkëtár,-i *m.sh.* -ë smith, blacksmith.

farkëtarí,-a *f.* smithery, smith's profession.

farkëtój *f.k.* 1. *tek.* to forge. 2. *fig.* to forge, to mould, to shape. – **farkëtohet** *f.jv.* 1. to be forged. 2. *fig.* to be forged.

farkëtúesh/ëm(i),-me(e) *mb.* forgeable.

farmaceutík,-e *mb.* pharmaceutic.

farmací,-a *f.sh.* – pharmacy, drugstore.

farmacíst,-i *m.sh.* -e pharmacist, chemist, druggist.

farmá/k,-ku *m.sh.* -qe shih **helm.**

farmakologjí,-a *f.* pharmacology.

farmakós *f.k.* shih **helmoj.**

farós *f.k.* to exterminate, to eradicate. – **farosem** *f.jv.* to be exterminated.

farósj/e,-a . extermination, eradication.

fasad/ë,-a *f.sh.* -a frontange, facade, face (of a building).

fasúl/e,-ja *f.sh.* -e *bot.* white bean, haricot.

fásh/ë,-a *f.sh.* -a band, bandage; swathing bends.

fashíku/ll,-lli *m.sh.* -j fascicle.

fashíst,-i *m.sh.* -e fascist.

fashíz/ëm,-mi *m.* fascism.

fashój *f.k.* to bandage, to dress; **fashoj një plagë:** to bandage a wound; *(fëmijën)* to swathe (a baby).

fat,-i *m.sh.* -e 1. fate, luck, fortune; **fat i mirë:** good luck; **fat i keq:** ill luck, ill fortune; **njeri me fat:** lucky man, fortunate person; **njeri pa fat:** unfortunate person, unlucky person; **më ecën fati, kam fat, jam me fat:** to be lucky, to have good luck; **s'kam fat, jam pa fat:** to be unlucky, to be unfortunate; **i eci fati, pati fat:** he was lucky (fortunate), he had good luck; **për fat:** by chance; **fat i papritur:** unexpected fortune; windfall; **ç'fat!** what a windfall!; **trill i fatit:** turn of tide. 2. destiny, fate; **lë dikë në mëshirën e fatit:** to abandon someone to his fate.

fatál,-e *mb.* fatal.

fatalíst,-i *m.sh.* -e fatalist.

fatalitét,-i *m.* fatality.

fatbárdhë *mb.* fortunate, lucky.

fatbardhësí,-a *f.* luck, happiness.

fatbardhësísht, *ndajf.* fortunately, luckily, happily.

fatí,-a *f.sh.* - fairy.

fatkéq,-e *mb.* ill-fated, unlucky, unhappy, unfortunate.

fatkeqësí,-a *f.sh.* - mischance, misfortune, adversity; **pësoj fatkeqësi:** to suffer misfortune; **fatkeqësi e madhe:** calamity, disaster; **fatkeqësi në punë:** casualty, mishap, accident.

fatkeqësísht *ndajf.* unfortunately

fatlúm,-e *mb.* shih **fatbardhë.**

fatlúmtur *mb.* shih **fatbardhë.**

fatmírë *mb.* shih **fatbardhë.**

fatós,-i *m.sh.* -e 1. brave, valiant. 2. kid, a child between six and nine years.

fatúr/ë,-a *f.sh.* -a *treg.* invoice.

faturój *f.k.* to invoice, to state (to insert) in an invoice.

fatz/í,-ezë *mb.* unlucky, unfortunate.

favór,-i *m.sh.* -e 1. favour; **në**

favor të: in favour of. 2. kindness, favour; **të lutem të më bësh një favor:** do me a favour please.
favorit,-i *m.sh.* -ë favorite.
favorite,-t *f.sh.* wiskers.
favorizím,-i *m.* (aiding and) abetting.
favorizój *f.k.* to favour; **e favorizuan rrethanat:** circumstances favoured him. → **favorizohem** *f.jv.* to be favoured.
favórsh/ëm(i),-me(e) *mb.* favourable; **përgjigje e favorshme:** favourable answer.
fazán,-i *m.sh.* -e *zool.* pheasant.
fáz/ë,-a *f.sh.* -a onase, phasis, stage.
fe,-ja *f.sh.* -të religion.
féçk/ë,-a *f.sh.* -a trunc (of an elephant).
federál,-e *mb.* federal.
federát/ë,-a *f.sh.* -a federation.
federatív,-e *mb.* federative.
fejés/ë,-a *f.sh.* -a betrothal, engagement.
fejój *f.k.* to betroth, to affiance, to engage; **fejova vajzën:** I have betrothed my daughter. – **fejohem** *f.jv.* to get engaged, to become engaged.
fejtón,-i *m.sh.* -e feuilleton.
fejúar (i),-i(i) *m.sh.* -të fiancé; **i fejuari im:** my fiance; **të fejuarit:** the engaged couple.
fejúar (i, e) *mb.* engaged, betrothed; **jam i fejuar:** to be engaged (betrothed).
fekále,-t *f.sh.* excrements.
feks *f.ik.* 1. to brighten, to shine; **kjo ngjyrë feks:** this colour shines. 2. to arise; **në verë dielli feks shpejt:** in summer the sun arises early.
fém/ër,-ra *f.sh.* -ra 1. female. 2. woman; **i vij rrotull një femre:** to court a girl, a woman.
fémër *mb.* female; cow-,she-,

hind-; **lepur femër:** female hare; **majmun femër:** a she-monkey.
femërór,-e *mb.* 1. female. 2. *gram.* feminine; **emër femëror:** feminine noun. 3. feminine, womanly; **s'është e bukur, po është shumë femërore:** she is not pretty, but she is very feminine.
fenér,-i *m.sh.* -e 1. lantern, safety-lamp. 2. **fener për ndriçimin e rrugëve:** gas-lamp; **shtyllë feneri:** lamp post.
fenomén,-i *m.sh.* -e phenomenon.
fenomenál,-e *mb.* phenomenal.
ferexhé,-ja *f.sh.* - jash-mak, yashmac.
farmán,-i *m.* firman.
fermentím,-i *m.* fermentation.
fermentój *f.jk.* to ferment. – **fermentohet** *f.jv.* to be fermented.
férm/ë,-a *f.sh.* -a farm, ranch; **fermë blegtorale:** ranch, cattle-farm; **fermë shtetërore:** state farm.
ferr,-i *m.* Hell.
ferrác,-i *m.sh.* -ë *zool.* wren.
férr/ë,-a *f.sh.* -a *bot.* brier, bramble-bush.
ferrísht/e,-ja *f.sh.* -e shrubby ground.
fést/e,-ja *f.sh.* -e fez.
fést/ë,-a *f.sh.* -a 1. feast; festival; **festë e madhe:** gala. 2. holiday; **ditë feste:** holiday; **festë kombëtare:** national holiday.
festím,-i *m.sh.* -e celebration.
festivál,-i *m.sh.* -e festival.
festój *f.k.* to celebrate. – **festohet** *f.jv.* to be celebrated.
fetár,-e *mb.* religious, pious; **ceremoni fetare:** rite.
fét/ë,-a *f.sh.* -a slice.
fetishíz/ëm,-mi *m.* fetichism, fetishism.
feudál,-i *m.sh.* -ë feudal.
fëllíq *f.k.* 1. to dirty, to daub, to soil, to sully, to foul, to smear,

to besmear, to pollute; **fälliq me baltë:** to splash, to bespatter. 2. *fig.* to disgrace. — **fëlliqem** *f.jv.* 1. to get dirty, to become dirty. 2. to fall into disgrace.

fëlliqësí,-a *f.* dirtiness, filthiness; **fëlliqësi morale:** moral pollution, defilement.

fëlliqur (i, e) *mb.* 1. dirtied, soiled, sullied; **ujë i fëlliqur:** putrid water. 2. *fig.* mean; disgraceful.

fëmíj/ë,-a *f.sh.* -ë child (pl. children); **fëmijë e adoptuar:** adopted child; **fëmijë e gjetur (nga prindër të panjohur):** foundling; **fëmijë gjiri:** suckling, nursling; **fëmijë e dështuar:** stillborn child; **fëmija e parë:** firstling, firstborn; **fëmijë e vetme:** only child; **më i madhi i fëmijëve:** the eldest; **më i vogli i fëmijëve:** the youngest; **lindje fëmije:** child-birth; **lojë fëmijësh:** child's play; **si fëmijë:** childlike.

fëmijërí,-a *f.* childhood; **shok fëmijërie:** playfellow.

fëmijërór,-e *mb,* childish, childlike.

fëmivrásës,-i *m.sh.* - infanticide, child murderer.

fëmivrásj/e,-a *f.* infanticide.

fëndýe/ll,-lli *m.sh.* -j awl.

fërfërím/ë,-a *f.sh.* -a rustle; **fërfërimë e gjetheve:** rustle of leaves.

fërgés/ë,-a *f.* fry, fried food.

fërgëllím/ë,-a *f.sh.* -a shivering, shudder.

fërgëllój *f.jk.* to shiver, to shudder, to quiver.

fërgój *f.k.* to fry. — **fërgohet** *f.jv.* to be fried.

fërgúar (i,e) *mb.* fried; **patate të fërguara:** fried potatoes; **vezë të fërguara:** fried eggs.

fërkím,-i *m.* 1- friction. 2. rubbing, massage.

fërkój *f.k. (trupin)* to rub (the body);

fërkoj fort me furçë: to scrub; *(për t'i dhënë lustër)* to polish. — **fërkohem** *f.jv.* to rub oneself.

fërkúes,-e *mb.* rubbing.

fërtéle,-t *f.sh.* rags, tatters.

fërshëllím/ë,-a *f.sh.* -a rustle, rustling.

fërfërít *f.jk.* to rustle.

fërfërítj/e,-a *f.* rustle, rustling (of silk, etc.).

fëshfësh/e,-ja *f.sh.* -e raincoat, mackingtosh.

fët *ndajf.* quick, quickly; **fët e fët:** then and there.

fíce *mb.* soft; **dardhë fice:** soft pear.

fiçór,-i *m.sh.* -ë pebble, coble.

fidán,-i *m.sh.* -ë bot. sapling.

fidanísht/e,-ja *f.sh.* -e bot. seedplot, nursery.

fídhe,-t *f.sh.* vermicelli.

fíer,-i *m. bot.* fern, brake.

figuránt,-i *m.sh.* -ë figurant.

figuratív,-e *mb.* figurative.

figúr/ë,-a *f.sh.* -a figure, image; *fig.* **bëj figurë të keqe:** to cut a poor figure (a sorry figure); **bëj figurë të mirë:** to cut a fine figure, to show up to advantage.

figurój *f.jk.* to figure.

fíj/e,-a *f.sh.* -a 1. yarn, thread; fibre; **fije leshi:** yarn, spun thread; **shkoj fijen e perit në gjilpërë:** to thread (to pass the thread) through the eye of the needle. 2. *(fije bari)* blade (of grass). 3. *(fije dëbore)* flake (of snow). 4. *(fije letre)* sheet (of paper). 5. *(fije shkrepse):* strip of match. 6. *(fije lecke)* lint, scraped linen used for dressing wounds. 7. pl. of *fill.* — Lok. **s'kam asnjë fije shprese:** I have not even a ray of hope; **pa fije vështirësie:** without the slightest difficulty; **asnjë**

fije: not a bit; **tregoj fije e për pe:** to tell in detail.
fijëzim,-i *m.* spinning.
fijëzój *f.k.* to spin. – **fijëzohet** *f.jv.* to be spun.
fik,-u *m.sh.* **fiq** *bot. (fruta)* fig; *(pema)* fig-tree.
fik *f.k.* to quench, to extinguish, to blow up; **fik dritën:** to switch off, to blow out the light; **fikeni dritën!** switch the light off!; **fik zjarrin:** to extinguish (to quench) the fire. – **fikem** *f.jv.* 1. to go out, to die out; **zjarri u fik vetë:** the fire died out. 2. *fig.* to be lost, to be ruined; **u fika:** I am lost. – *Lok.* **fikem gazit:** to burst out laughing.
fíkës,-i *m.sh.* - extinguisher.
fíkët,-it (të) *as.* swoon, fainting; **më bie të fikët:** to swoon away, to faint.
fíkj/e,-a *f.* quenching, extinction; **fikje e dritave në rast alarmi:** curfew.
fiks *ndajf.* 1. sharp, punctually, precise, exact; **në orën pesë fiks:** at five o'clock sharp. 2. regular, fixed; **pagë fikse:** regular salary.
fiksím,-i *m.* fixation, fastening.
fiksój *f.k.* to fix, to affix, to fasten. – **fiksohem** *f.jv.* to be fixed, to be affixed.
fiktív,-e *mb.* fictitious, fictive, imaginary, unreal.
fil,-i *m.sh.* -e *zool., krah.* shih **elefant.**
filán,-i *p.pk.* so and so: **filan fësteku:** mister so and so.
filantróp,-i *m.sh.* -ë philanthropist.
filantropí,-a *f.* philanthropy.
filantropík,-e *mb.* philanthropic.
filatúr/ë,-a *f.sh.* -a spinning mill.
fildísh,-i *m.* ivory.
fildishtë(i,e) *mb.* ivory.
filetím,-i *m.* threading.
figilrám,-i *m.sh.* -e filigree.

filíz,-i *m.sh.* -a 1. *bot.* tender shoot, offshoot, offset, spring; **nxjerr filiza:** to bud, to sprout. 2. *fig.* youth.
film,-i *m.sh.* -a 1. *(film aparati fotografik)* film. 2. *(film kinemaje)* picture motion; **film me zë:** sound film; **marr në film:** to film; **xhiroj një film:** to shoot a film.
filoksér/ë,-a *bujq.* phyloxera.
filológ,-u *m.sh.* -ë philologist.
filologjí,-a *f.* philology.
filozóf,-i *m.sh.* -ë philosopher.
filozofí,-a *f.* philosophy.
filozofík,-e *mb.* philosophic.
fílt/ër,-ri *m.sh.* -ra strainer, filter.
filtrím,-i *m.* filtering.
filtrój I *f.k.* to filter, to strain, to percolate. – **filtrohet** *f.jv.* to be filtered, to be strained. II. *f.jk.* to filter, to percolate.
filxhán,-i *m.sh.* -ë cup; **filxhan çaji:** tea-cup; **filxhan kafeje:** coffee-cup; **pjatë filxhani:** saucer; *fig.* **sy filxhan:** saucer eyes.
fill,-i *m.sh.* **fije** thread, yarn; **fill pambuku:** cotton thread; **fill leshi:** yarn, spin thread. -*Lok.* **për fill:** to a hair's breadth; **bëhem fill:** to get back in shape, to be oneself again; **jam fill i vetëm:** to be alone.
fillestár,-e *mb.* 1. elementary, rudimentary; **njohuri fillestare:** rudiments. 2. initial, incipient; **shpenzime fillestare:** initial expenditures.
fillestár,-i *m.sh.* -ë novice, beginner.
fillím,-i *m.sh.* -e beginning, opening, commencing, start, onset; **nga fillimi deri në fund:** from start to finish, from the beginnig to the end; **që në fillim, që nga fillimi:** from the very beginning, right from the start; **fillim i mbarë:** good beginning, **në fillim:** at first, firstly.

fillimisht *ndajf.* in the beginning, at the start, at first, firstly.
fillój I. *f.jk.* to begin, to start, to commence; **filloj të bëj diçka:** to begin to do something, to start to do something, to set about; **rruga fillon më tutje:** the road begins farther on. II. *f.jk.* to begin, to start, to commence; **filloj një punë:** to begin a work. – **fillohet** *f.jv.* to be begun, to be commenced, to be started.
fillór,-e *mb.* primary, elementary; **shkollë fillore:** elementary school. *(or: primary)*
fillrójtës,-i *m.sh./*- lineman, linesman.
finánc/ë-a *f.sh.* -a finances.
financiár,-e *mb.* financial; **krizë financiare:** financial crisis.
financiárisht *ndajf.* financially.
financím,-i *m.* financing.
financój *f.k.* to finance. – **financohet** *f.jv.* to be financed.
financúes,-i *m.sh.* - financier.
finés/ë,-a *f.* fineness, delicacy, finesse; refinement.
finlandéz,-i *m.sh.* -ë Finn, Finlander
finlandéz,-e *mb.* Finnish, Finnic.
finók,-e *mb.* crafty, wily, sharp.
fínj/ë,-a *f.* lye, washing water, alkaline solution.
fiq,-të *f.sh.* (the plural of **fik**) figs.
fír/ë,-a *i. treg.* loss of weight; *(e drithit)* spillage (of grain); *(e frutave)* spoliage (of fruits); **bën firë:** to lose weight.
fírm/ë,-a *f.sh.* -a 1. signature. 2. *treg.* **firmë tregtare:** firm, business house.
firmój *f.k.* to sign. – **firmohet** *f.jv.* to be signed.
fis,-i *m.sh.* -e 1. *(nga gjaku)* kin. 2. tribe, clan.
fisník,-e *mb.* noble.

fisník,-u *m.sh.* -ë nobleman, gentleman.
fisnikërí,-a *f.* nobleness; nobility.
fisnikërísht *ndajf.* nobly.
fisnikërój *f.k.* to ennoble. – **fisnikërohet** *f.jv.* to be ennobled.
fístul,-a *f.sh.* -a *mjek.* fistula.
fish,-i *m.* fold.
fishék,-u *m.sh.* -ë cartridge; **gjerdhan fishekësh:** cartridge. belt; **krëhër fishekësh:** cartridge clip. – *Lok.* **dal fishek:** to give up all one's property.
fishekzjárr,-i *m.sh.* -ë fireworks.
físh/ë,-a *f.sh.* -a 1. *tek.* plug. 2. index-card.
fishk *f.k.* to fade, to wither. – **fishkem** *f.jv.* to fade away, to shrivel; *(lulet)* to fade.
fishkëllím/ë,-a *f.sh.* -a shih **fërshëllimë**
fishkëllój *f.jk.* shih **fërshëllej.**
físhkj/e,-a *f.* fading.
fishnjár,-i *n.sh.* -ë *zool.* marten.
fitíl,-i *m.sh.* -a wick; **fitil llampe:** lamp wick; **fitil qiriri:** candle wick; **fitil dinamiti:** match (of a mine), fuse, – *Lok.* **fus fitila:** to blow the cools, to fan the flame; **i fus fitilat dikujt:** to stir up someone to quarrel.
fitím,-i *m.sh.* -e gain, profit; **nxjerr fitime nga diçka:** to make a good profit on something.
fitimprúrës, -e *mb.* remunerative, profitable, gainful.
fitimtár,-i *m.sh.* -ë victor.
fitimtár,-e *mb.* triumphant, victorious; **dal fitimtar në nië betejë:** to win(to be victorious) in a battle, to come off victorious
fitój *f.k.* I. to earn, to gain; **fitoj bukën e gojës:** to earn one's livelihood; to gain one's living; **fitoj para:** to earn money, to get money. 2. to get; **fitoj një çmim:** to get a prize; **fitoj përvojë:** to get (to gain, to acqui-

re) experience; **fitoj famë**: to get fame. 3. *(luftën)* to win (the war). 4. **fitoj kohë**: to gain time. — **fitohet** *f.jv.* to be earned, to be gained.

fitór/e,-ja *f.sh.* -e victory, triumph; **korr fitore**: to gain (to score, to win) a victory; **më buzëqeshi fitorja**: victory smiled on me. **fitúes,-i** *m.sh.* - 1. gainer; **fitues lotarie**: gainer of a lottery. 2. victor, winner; **fitues i një beteje**: winner of a battle. 3. successful one; **dal fitues në konkurs**: to be succesful in an examination, topass an examination; **dal fitues në një garë (ndeshje)**: to win contest.

fizarmoník/ë,-a *f.s.h* -a *muz.* accordion.

fizík,-u *m.* constitution (of the body).

fizík,-e *mb.* physical; **kulturë fizike**: physical culture.

fizikán,-i *m.sh.* -ë physicist.

fizík/ë,-a *f.* physics.

fizikísht, *ndajf.* physically.

fiziologjí,-a *f.* physiology.

fizionomí,-a *f.* physionomy.

fizkultúr/ë,-a *f.* physical exercices, gjymnastics, physical culture.

fjalamán,-i *m.sh.* -ë tattler, chatterer.

fjalamán,-e *mb.* loquacious, longwinded, talkative, verbose.

fjál/ë,-a *f.sh.* -ë 1. word; **fjalë të një rrënje**: cognate words; **fjalët e një gjuhe (të një fjalori)**: the words of a language (of a vocabulary); **fjalë boshe (pa kuptim)**: meaningless (senseless) words; **fjalë të mprehta**: sharp words; **fjalë e urtë**: saying, maxim, proverb; **fjalë me vend**: witty remark. 2. term; **fjalë shkencore**: scientific term. 3. news;

a ka ndonjë fjalë? what is the news, what news? 4. question, matter; **përse bëhet fjalë?** what is the question?, what is the matter? **përse bën fjalë libri?** what is the book about?; **bëhet fjalë për**: it is about, there is a talk for; **personi në fjalë**: the person in question. 5. speech; **liri e fjalës**: freedom of speech; **fjalë e hapjes (në një mbledhje)**: opening speech; **fjala e mbylljes**: closing speech; **marr fjalën** *(në një mbledhje)* to take the floor (at a meeting); **kush e do fjalën?** who wards the floor? 7. word, promise; **fjalë e nderit**: word of honour; **për fjalë të nderit**: upon my word of honour; **besoj në fjalën e**: to believe someone's word; **jap fjalën**: to pledge one's word; **e mbaj fjalën**: to keep one's word; **nuk e mbaj fjalën**: not to keep one's word (promise), to break one's word. — *Lok.* **bie fjala**: for example, for instance; **i çoj fjalë**: to send a word, to drop a line; **fjalë për fjalë**: word by word; **jam në një fjalë me**: to be in accord with, to agree with; **këmbej fjalë**: to bandy words, to have words, to quarrel; **kthej fjalë**: to talk back; **luaj me fjalë**: to play on words; **me fjalë të tjera**: in other words; **me një fjalë**: in a a word; **me që ra fjala**: by the bye, by the way; **e peshoj fjalën**: to weigh one's words; **pres fjalën**: to break in (to interrupt) a talk; **tërheq fjalën**: to retract (to take back) one's word; to go back on one's word; **zgjatje fjalësh**: prolixity, verbosity; **mos i përtyp(mos i ha) fjalët**: do not mince the words!

fjalëkrýq, i *m.sh.* -e cross word.

fjalëpákë *mb.* taciturn, untalkative.

fjalëshúmë *mb.* talcative, loquacious, garrulous.

fjálëz,-a *f.sh.* -a *gram.* particle.

fjalí,-a *f.sh.* - *gram.* sentence, clause

fjalím,-i *m.sh.* -e speech, discourse; **mbaj një fjalim:** to deliver a speech.

fjalór,-i *m.sh.* -ë 1. dictionary, glossary; lexicon; **fjalor xhepi:** pocket dictionary; **fjalor emrash gjeografikë:** gazetteer, dictionary of geographical names. 2. vocabulary; **kjo fjalë nuk bën pjesë në fjalorin tim:** I don't use this word.

fjalórth,-i *m.sh.* -e small (pocket) dictionary.

fjalósem *f.jv.* to speak, to talk, to chat, to converse.

fjéta (past tense of the verb **fle**) I slept.

fjétj/e,-a *f.* sleep; **koha e fjetjes:** bed-time.

fjetór/e,-ja *f.sh.* -e dormitory.

fjétur (i,e) *mb.* 1. stagnant, standing; **ujë i fjetur:** stagnant water, standing water. 2. *fig.* sluggish, slow, listless, slack.

fjóngo,-ja *f.sh.* - ribbon.

flagránc/ë,-a *f.* flagrance; **kap (zë) në flag ancë:** to catch in the act, to catch in the very act.

flagránt,-e *mb.* flagrant.

flak *f.k.* to throw, to cast, to fling, to hurl; **flak tutje:** to throw away, to cast to a distance; **flak me forcë:** to hurl, to launch **flak përdhe:** to fling (to cast) to the ground; **flak si të panevojshëm:** to reject, to throw away, to discard, to cast off (as useless).

flák/ë,-a *f.sh.* -ë flame, blaze, flash; *(e ndritshme)* flare; **flakë llambe (zjarri):** flame; **flakë që del nga pushka (nga topi):** blaze, flash; **shpërthim flake:** blaze;

në flakë: in flames. – *Lok.* **marr flakë:** to fire up.

flakërój *f.k.* 1. to throw away (as useless). 2. to flame, to inflame.

flakërúes,-e *mb.* flaming, blazing.

flákj/e,-a *f.* throwing, casting, launching.

fláktë (i,e) *mb.* 1. flaming, burning. 2. *fig.* fiery, ardent; fervent, earnest; **patriot i flaktë:** ardent patriot.

flám/ë,-a *f. mjek.* pestilence of animals (especially of fowls). – *Lok.* **të rëntë flama!** may you have the pestilence!

flamú/r,-ri *m.sh.* -j flag, banner, standard; **flamuri i një shteti:** the flag of a state; **flamur me gjysmë shtize:** half-hoisted flag; **flamur tranzitor:** challenge banner; **ngre flamurin:** to hoist the flag, to raise the flag; **mbaj lart flamurin:** to hold aloft the flag.

flamurtár,-i *m.sh.* -ë flag-bearer, standard bearer.

flas I. *f.jk.* to speak, to talk, to converse; **flas gjerë e gjatë:** to speak at large; **flas me orë të tëra:** to speak by the hour; **flas në hava, flas kuturu:** to speak at random (at all hazards); **flas keq për dikë:** to speak ill of someone; **flas mirë për dikë:** to speak well of someone; **flas nëpër dhëmbë:** to grumble, to murmur (disncontentedly); **flas përçart:** to speak in delirium; **flas prapa krahëve:** to backbite; **flas mbarë e prapë:** to speak right and wrong; **flas me zë të lartë:** to talk (to speak) loud; **flas me zë të ulët:** to speak low.

II. *f.k.* to speak, to tell, to narrate; **flas mirë dhe rrjedhshëm (një gjuhë):** to speak well and fluently (a language); **flas keq** një gjuhë: to speak badly (a language); flas gjepura: to talk rubbish (nonsense). – flitet *f.jv.* they say, it· s rumoured that. flashkësí,-a *f.* 1. softness, sluggishness. 2. humidity, moisture, damp. fláshkët (i,e) *mb.* 1. sluggish. 2. moist, humid. fláut,-i *m.sh.* -e *muz.* flute. flautíst,-i *m.sh.* -ë flutist. fle I. *f.jk.* to sleep; fle pa merak (fle rëndë): to sleep soundly, to sleep like a top; fle shumë; to oversleep; bie të fle: to fall asleep; shkoj të fle: to go to sleep, to go to bed; ai po fle: he is sleeping. II. *f.k.* — flihet *f.jv.* flihet mirë atje: one sleeps well there. e fle mendjen (për diçka): to feel assured. flég/ër-ra *f.sh.* -ra *anat.* nostril; flegrat e hundës: nostrils. flegmatík,-e *mb.* phlegmatic. flét/ë,-a *f.sh.* -ë 1. wing; rrok fletët: to flap (to beat) one's wings; trim me fletë: brave (valiant) person. 2. fletë peme: leaf; rënia e fletëve: falling of leaves; pemët zhvishen nga fletët: the trees drop their leaves. 3. *(fletët e një libri)* leaves (of a book). 4. *(fletë metali)* foil, sheet (of metal). 5. *(fletë peshku)* fin (of a fish). – *Lok.* e kthej fletën (ndërroj fletën): to be a turncoat. fletë-dálj/e,-a *f.sh.* -e exit-ticket. fletëhýrje,-a *f.sh.* -e entrance-ticket. fletëlavdërím,-i *m.sh.* -e commendation paper. fletërrufé,-ja *f.sh.* - wall-poster. fletór/e,-ja *f.sh.* -e copy-book exercise -book, writing-book; fletore shënimesh: note-book.

flil (imperative mood of the· verb fle) sleep! fli, – a *f.* immolation, vicitim: fli për atdhe: dead for the fatherland;· bëhem fli: to sacrifice one's life for, to lay down one's life for. flijím,-i *n·.sh.* -e sacrifice, flijój *f.k.* to sacrifice, to immolate. – flijohem *f.jv.* to be sacrified to sacrifice oneself. flirtój *f.jk.* to flirt. flit,-i *m.* fly-tox. flítet shih flas. flok,-u *m.sh.* -ë 1. hair; flokë të dendur: thick hair; flokë të rrallë: scanty hair, thin hair; flokë kaçurrela (të dredhur): curly hair, ringlet; kapëse flokësh : hair-pin; qime (fije) floku: hairs, rënia e flokëve: falling of hair; pres flokët: to cut one's hair; më bien flokët: my ha·r come off; kapemi për flokësh: to tear each other's hair, 2. flok-dëbore: snow-flake. flokëbárdhë *mb.* hoary, white-haired. flokëdrédhur *mb.* curly haired. flokëgështénjë *mb.* auburn haired flokëkúq,-e *mb.* red-haired. flokëthínjur *mb.* grey-haired, hoary, grizzeld. flokëvérdhë *mb.* blond, fair-haired flokëzézë *mb.* brunette, brunet. flokëzí *mb.* brown-haired, dark-haired. floktár,-i *m.sh.* -ë hair-dresser, barber; floktar permanenti: hair-curler. floktór/e,-ja *f.sh.* -e hair-dressing shop, barber's shop. flór/ë,-a *f.* flora. florí,-ri *m.sh.* -nj gold; prej floriri: gold, golden; jam krimbur në florinj (para): to be rolling in money. – *Prov.* nuk është

fiori gjithçka që ndrit: all that glitters is not gold.
florinjtë (i,e) *mb.* golden.
flót/ë,-a *f.sh.* -a fleet (of vessels): **flota ajrore:** air-fleet; **flota tregtare:** mercantile-fleet, mercant fleet; **flota ushtarake:** navy.
flúg/ër,-ra *f.sh.* -ra weathercock.
fluróm/ë,-a *f.* 1. whiff. 2. soupbuble.
flútur,-a *f.sh.* -a *zool.* butterfly.
fluturím,-i *m.sh.* -e flight.
fluturímthi *ndajf.* 1. in mid-air, on the volley. 2. *fig.* like a shot.
fluturòj *f.jk.* 1. to fly, to wing; **zogjtë fluturojnë:** the birds fly; **fluturon larg:** to fly off, to take wing; **fluturon lart:** to soar; **fluturoj andej-këtej:** to flutter. 2. *fig.* **fluturoj nga gazi:** to jump for joy.
fluturúes,-e *mb.* flying, floating.
fllad,-i *m.sh.* -e breeze, zephyr, gentle gala.
fiiadís *f.k.* to freshen. — **fiiaditem** *f.jv.* to freshen oneself.
fiiaditës,-e *mb.* refreshing.
fiiaditj/e,-a *f.* refreshment.
fiiúsk/ë,-a *f.sh.* -a 1. *mjek.* blister. vesicle. 2. bubble; **fiiuskë sapuni:** soap bubble; **fiiuskë uji (të valë):** bubble of water.
fodúll,-e *mb.* proud, haughty.
fodullëk,-u *m.* pride, haughtiness; **me fodullëk:** proudly, haughtily.
fók/ë,-a *f.sh.* -a 1. *zool.* seal; **gjueti e fokave:** seal-fishery. 2. *mjek.* erysipelas.
fokist,-i *m.sh.* -ë fireman, stoker.
fólël *f.jk.* (imperative mood of the verb **flas**) speak! **mos folë kaq shumë:** don't speak so much.
folé,-ja *f.sh.* - 1. nest; **fole snqiponje:** eagle nest; **ngre fole:**
to nest, to nestle; **fole merimange:** cob-web; **fole pëllumbash:** pigeon-house, pigeon-hole, dove-cot.
fólës,-i *m.sh.* - speaker.
fólës,-e *mb.* speaking.
fólj/e,-a *f.sh.* -e *gram.* verb; **folje e rregullt:** regular verb; **folje e parregullt:** irregular verb; **folje kalimtare:** transitive verb; **folje jokalimtare** : intransitive verb; **folje pavetore:** impersonal verb; **folje vetëvetore:**reflexive verb.
foljór,-e *mb. gram.* verbal; **emër foljor:** verbal noun; **mbiemër foljor:** verbal adjective.
folklór,-i *m.* folklore.
fólm/e(e),-ja(e) *f.sh.* -e (të) language, speech.
fólur (past tense of the verb **flas**) spoken.
fólur (i,e) *mb.* spoken; **gjuhë e folur:** spoken language.
fólurit (të) *as.* speech, discourse.
fond,-i *m.sh.* -e stock (of money), fund; **fond amortizimi:** sinking fund; **fonde investimi:** investment funds.
fonderí,-a *f.sh.* - foundry.
fonditór,-i *m.sh.* -ë founder, foundryman, smelter.
fonetík/ë,-a *f.* phonetics.
fonográf,-i *m.sh.* -ë shih **gramafon.**
foragjére,-t *f.sh.* fodder.
fórc/ë,-a *f.sh.* -a 1. force, strength, power, vigour; **punoj me të gjitha forcat:** to work with all one's forces. 2. *usht.* force; **forcat e armatosura:** armed forces. 3. *fig.* force; **forca e gravitetit:** gravity force. 4. *(detyrim, dhunë)* force, violence, constraint, extortion; **hyj me forcë:** to break into, to enter by violence (by force); **marr me forcë:** to take by force (by violence), to obtain by constraint; **forcë**

[handwritten marginal note: "for is trada of- read vehicle, ~suv"]

madhore: absolute necessity. 5. hand; **forcë pune:** labour power (hands). **forcím,-i** *m.* strengthening, consolidation; **forcim i miqësisë:** strengthening of the friendship; **forcimi i trupit:** hardening of the body. 2. consolidation; **forcim i pushtetit popullor:** consolidation of the people's power. **forcój** *f.k.* 1. to reinforce, to fortify. 2. to make strong, to strengthen, to consolidate; **forcoj pushtetin:** to consolidate the power. 3. to harden; **forcoj trupin:** to harden the body. 4. *fig.* **forcoj një mendim:** to confirm an opinion. – **forcohem** *f.jv.* to become stronger (harder), to gather strength. **forcúes,-e** *mb.* 1. *mjek.* tonic; **ilaç forcues:** tonic. 2. strengthening; hardening; consolidating.

formación,-i *m.sh.* -e formation. **formál,-e** *mb.* formal. **formalísht** *ndajf.* formally. **formalitét,-i** *m.sh.* -e formality. **fòrm/ë,-a** *f.sh.* -a 1. form, shape; **me formë:** shapely; **pa formë:** shapeless; **në formë:** in form; **jap formë:** to give shape, to shape, to frame. 2. form, shape, appearance. 3. form; **formë qeverimi:** form of government. 4. *fig.* form, shape; **jam në formë:** to be in (good) form (in good shape). 5. *tek.* mould.

formím,-i *m.* 1. forming, formation. 2. *fig.* moulding. **formój** *f.k.* 1. to form, to constitute, to shape, to make. 2. *fig.* to mould. – **formohem** *f.jv.* to form, to take shape. 2. to develop, to grow up. 3. *fig.* to be moulded.

formulár,-i *m.sh.* -ë formulary, *amer.* blank. **formúl/ë,-a** *f.sh.* -a formula.

formulím,-i *m.sh.* -e wording, formulation. **formulój** *f.k.* to formulate. – **formulohet** *f.jv.* to be formulated. **fort** *ndajf.* 1. hard, tightly; **shtrëngoj fort:** to fasten tightly, to tie tightly; to hold tightly. 2. very much, greatly, deeply; **të dua fort:** I love you much; **fort i inatosur:** very angry. **fortés/ë,-a** *f.sh.* -a fortress, fort, bastion, stronghold, citadel. **fórtë (i,e)** *mb.* 1. strong, robust, vigorous, sturdy, stalwart, powerful. 2. intense: **dritë e fortë:** bright (dazzling) light; **zë i fortë:** loud voice; **dimër i fortë:** bitter winter. 3. sound, convincing, valid, strong; **shkaqe të forta:** sound motives. 4. hard, heavy, mighty; **erë e fortë:** strong (raging) wind. 5. good; **jam i fortë në matematikë:** to be good at mathematics. **fortësí,-a** *f.* hardness, strongness, solidity. **fortifikát/ë,-a** *f.sh.* -a field works, fortification. **fortifikój** *f.k.* to fortify, to erect works of defence. **forúm,-i** *m.sh.* -e forum. **foshnjarák,-e** *mb.* childish. **fóshnj/ë,-a** *f.sh.* -a baby, infant, nursling, child; **foshnjë gjiri:** suckingchild, nursling. **foshnjëri,-a** *f.* childhood, infancy. **foshnjór,-e** *mb.* infantile, childish. **fotográf,-i** *m.sh.* -ë photographer. **fotografí,-a** *f.sh.* - photography; photograph, *fam.* picture; **fotografi e çastit:** snapshot, *fam.* snap. **fotografím,-i** *m.sh.* -e photographing. **fotografój** *f.k.* to photograph, to snap, to take a picture of, to shoot a picture. – **fotografohem** *f.jv.* to be photographed.

fotoreportér,-i *m.sh.* -ë photo-reporter.
fotozheník,-e *mb.* photogenic.
fqínj,-i *m.sh.* -ë neighbour.
fqínj/ë,-e *mb.* neighbouring; near-by, adjacent.
fqinjësí,-a *f.* neighbourhood; ma-rrëdhënie të mira fqinjësie: good neighbourhood relations.
fragmént.-i *m.sh.* -e fragment, excerption; nxjerr fragmente nga një libër; to excerpt (to select) from a book, to take out extracts from a book.
frak,-u *m.sh.* -ë dress-coat.
fraksion,-i *m.sh.* -ë fraction.
francéz/,-i *m.sh.* -ë Frenchman.
francez,-e *mb.* French.
franxhóll/ë,-a *f.sh.* -a loaf, roll of bread
frásh/ër,-ri *m.sh.* -ra *bot.* ash, ash-tree.
frat,-i *m.sh.* fretër friar.
frazeologji,-a *f.sh.* phraseology.
fráz/ë-a *f.sh.* -a phrase; frazë bombastike claptrap.
fre,-ri *m.sh.* -rë rein, bridle, curb lëshoj (liroj) frerin: to slacken, (to release.) the rein.
fréna,-t *f.sh.* (e *makinës*) brakes (of a car).
frekuentím,- *m.* frequentation, fre-quenting.
frekuentój *f.k.* to frequent, to visit often. − frekuentohet *f.jv.* to be frequented.
frekuentúes,-i *m.sh.* − frequenter.
frením,-i *m.* 1. stopping (of a car). 2. *fig.* restriction, restraint.
frenój *f.k.* 1. to curb, to bridle; to brake; frenoj kalin: to curb a horse; frenoj makinën: to brake a car, to put on the brakes. 2. *fig.* to stop, to check, to keep in. − frenohem *f.jv.* to restrain one-self, to stop oneself, to hold one-self back.
fresk,-u *m.* freshness, coolness;

bën fresk: it's cool; rri në fresk: to sit out in the cool. bëj fresk: to fan oneself.
frésk/ë,-a *f.sh.* -a fresco.
fréskët (i, e) *mb.* 1. fresh, cool, brisk; ajër i freskët: fresh air. 2. fresh; bukë e freskët: fresh bread. 3. *fig.* fresh, recent; shem-bull i freskët: fresh example; lajme të freskëta: recent news. 4. *fig.* fresh, refreshed; trupa të freskëta: fresh troops.
freskí,-a *f.* 1. freshness; coolness; freskia e ujit të burimit: the freshness of spring water. 2. *fig.* freshness.
freskím,-i *m.* freshening up.
freskój *f.k.* to freshen, to refresh, to cool. − freskohem *f.jv.* to ref-resh oneself, to freshen up.
freskór/e,-ja *f.sh.* -e fan.
freskues,-e *mb.* refreshing, cooling; pije freskuese: refreshing drink.
frezatór,-i *m.sh.* -ë milling-ma-chine operator, miller.
fréz/ë,-a *f.sh.* -a *tek.* milling cu-tter, mill, miller.
frezím,-i *m.* milling.
frezój *f.k.* to mill.
fréng-u *m.sh.* frengj Frenchman.
frëngjísht/e,-ja *f.* French.
frëngjísht *ndajf,* in French; flas frëngjisht: to speak French.
frëngjí,-a *f.sh.* - loop-hole.
frëngjýz/ë,-a *f. mjek.* syphilis.
frigorifér,-i *m.sh.* -ë refrigerator, cooler, cold-storage.
frikacák,-u *m.sh.* -ë dastard, co-ward, poltroon.
frikacák,-e *mb.* timorous, fearful, white-livered, fainthearted, das-tard.
frikamán shih frikacak.
frík/ë,-a *f.* fear, fright; mos ki frikë: have no fear! don't be afraid! kam frikë: I am afraid of, I have fear for, I feel fear of; përse keni frikë? what are you afraid

of? **kisha frikë se mos nuk vinte:** I was afraid that he would not come; **kall frikën:** to frighten; to scare the life out of, to strike fear into, to put in fear; **nga frika se mos:** for fear that lest.

frikësím,-i *m.sh.* -e intimidation, threatening, menace, frightening.

frikësój *f.k.* to frighten, to fright, to appal, to intimidate, to daunt. − **frikësohem** *f.jv.* to be afraid, to be frightened; **frikësohem së tepërmi:** to be terribly scared, to be frightened out of one's wits.

fríksh/ëm(i),-me(e) *mb.* dreadful, fearful, redoutable.

fron,-i *m.sh.* -a 1. chair, stool, footstool. 2. throne; **rrëzoj nga froni një mbret:** to dethrone a king.

frúshku/ll,-lli *m.sh.* -j shih **fshikull.**

frutdhënës,-e *mb.* 1. fruitful. 2. *fig.* fruitful useful, profitable, advantageous.

frút/ë,-a *f.sh.* -a *bot.* fruit; **frutë e rënë nga era:** windfall; **dyqan frutash:** greengrocer's, fruiterer's, *amer.* vegetable store.

frutiér/ë,-a *f.sh.* -a fruit-stand, fruit-holder, fruit dish.

frutór,-e *mb.* fruit-bearing, fructiferous; **dru frutor:** fruit-tree.

frutór/e,-ja *f.sh.* -e orchard, fruit-trees plantation.

fruth,-i *m. mjek.* measles; **fruthi i zi (i keq):** scarlet fever; **më zuri fruthi:** I have got the measles.

fryj I. *f.k.* 1. to bloat, to inflate; **fryj topin:** to bloat (to distend) the ball. 2. **fryj hundët:** to blow one's nose. 3. *fig.* **fryj dikë (e mërzis):** to bear someone stiff, to huff someone. − **fryhem** *f.jv.* to swell (up,out) to puff up. II. *f.jk.* 1. to blow; **era frynte fort:**

the wind was blowing hard. 2. *fam.* **fryj (iki):** to scamper, to run away, to make off, to fly. 3. to blow; **i fryj flautit:** to wind the flute; **i fryj zjarrit** to blow the fire.

frým/ë,-a *f.* 1. breath; **marr frymë:** to breathe, to draw breath, to take breath, to inhale, to respire; **nxjerr frymë:** to expire, to exhale, to breathe out from the lungs; **vegla fryme:** wind instruments; **jap frymën e fundit:** to breathe one's last; to expire, to die; **pa frymë:** breathless, out of breath; **m'u zu fryma:** I got stiffled; **me një frymë:** all in one breath, in one go, at a breath; **iki me një frymë:** to go at a stretch; **e pi me një frymë** *(ujin, verën, etj.):* to drain one's glass at a draught (at one gulp).

frymëmárrës,-e *mb.* respirating.

frymëmárrj/e,-a *f.* breathing, respiration; **frymëmarrje artificiale:** artificial respiration.

frymëzím,-i *m.* inspiration.

frymëzój *f.k.* to inspire. − **frymëzohem** *f.jv.* to be inspired *(nga, by).*

frymëzúes,-i *m.sh.* - inspirator.

frymëzúes,-e *mb.* inspiratory.

frymór,-e *mb.* respiratory; **vegla frymore:** wind instruments.

frýrë (i, e) *mb.* 1. swollen, inflated, bloated, distended; **fytyrë e fryrë:** swollen face; 2. *(i fryrë nga të ngrënit):* stuffed, overstuffed. 3. *fig.* **i fryrë nga të tjerë:** incited by others.

frýrj/e,-a *f.* 1. turgidness, turgidity, bloatness. 2. *mjek.* **fryrje e barkut:** flatulence.

frytëzím,-i *m.* fructification.

frytëzój *f.k.* to fructify.

frýtsh/ëm *(i),-me(e)* *mb.* fruitful.

fshat,-i *m.sh.* -ra 1. village; **fshat**

i vogël: hamlet; jetë fshati: country (rural) life; shtëpi fshati country house, 2. country; nga fshati im: in my country. fshatár,-i *m.sh.* -ë peasant, villager, countryman; fshatar i mesëm: middle peasant; fshatar i varfër: poor peasant. fshatarák,-u *m.sh.* -ë peasant. fshatarák,-e *mb.* rustic, rural. fshatárçe *ndajf.* rustically, in a peasant-like manner. fshataresí,-a *f.* peasantry, country people; aleanca e klasës punëtore me fshatarësinë: the alliance of the working class with the peasantry. fsheh *f.k.* to hide, to conceal, to dissimulate, to dissemble. – fshihem *f.jv.* to hide (oneself), to be hidden; këtu diçka fshihet : I smell a rat, there is something fishy about it. fsheharák,-u *m.sh.* -ë dissembler, dissimulator. fsheharák,-e *mb.* dissimulating, dissembling. fshéhj/e,-a *f.* hiding, concealment; dissimulation. fshéhtas *ndajf.* furtively, stealthily, secretly. fshéht/ë(e),-a(e) *f.sh.* – a (të) secret; nuk i mbaj të fshehta dikujt: to hold (to keep) no secrets from someone. fshéhtë (i,e) *mb.* 1. hidden, concealed; vend i fshehtë: hiding place; dëshira të fshehta: hidden desires. 2. secret, private; në mënyrë të fshehtë: in a conspirative manner; in confidence, in private. 3. karakter i fshehtë: dissimulated character. – *Lok.* e mbaj të fshehtë: to keep secret. fshehtësí,-a *f.* secrecy. fshéhur (i, e) *mb.* hidden, concealed.

fshéhurazi *ndajf.* shih fshehtas. fshesár,-i *m.sh.* -ë scavenger. fshés/ë,-a *f.sh.* -a broom; fshesë me bisht: broom-stick. fshij *f.k.* 1. *(fshij me fshesë)* to sweep (with a broom); fshij rrugët me fshesë: to scavenger. 2. *(fshij me furçë)* to brush. 3. *(fshij dërrasën e zezë)* to rub (to wipe) out (the black-board), 4. fshij djersën: to wipe the sweat. 5. fshij duart (fytyrën): to wipe one's hands (one's face). 6. fshij lotët: to dry the tears, to wipe the tears. 7. *(fshij me gomë)*: to erase, to rub, te efface. 8. fshij oxhakun: to sweep the chimney. 9. *fig.* fshij nga faqja e dheut: to sweep away, to wipe out. fshíjsh/ëm(i),-me(e) *mb.* effaceable. fshik *f.k.* to graze, to touch lightly. – fshikem *f.jv.* to have blisters of fever on lips. fshík/ë,-a *f.sh.* -a 1. *mjek.* blister, vesicle. 2. *anat.* gallbladder. 3. *zool.* cocoon. fshíkëz,-a *f.sh.* -a *anat.* bladder (of urine). fshíkëz,-a *f.sh.* -a *zool.* fshikëz mëndafshi: cocoon. fshíkull,-i *m.sh* fshikuj whip, switch. fshikullój *f.k.* to whip, to switch, to lash, to flagellate. fshírës,-i *m.sh.* - 1. eraser, rubber. 2. fshirës oxhakësh: chimney sweeper; fshirës rrugësh: scavenger. fshírës/e,-ja *f.sh.* -e dish-cloth; fshirëse pluhuri: duster. fshírj/e,-a *f.* 1. *(fshirje nga lista)* effacement (from the list). 2. *(fshirje oxhakësh)* sweeping (of chimneys). ftés/ë,-a *f.sh.* -a 1, invitation; ftesë gjyqi: summons; ftesë

për darkë: invitation to dinner.
2. invitation card, invitation.
ftoh *f.k.* to cool, to chill, to make
cool. – **ftohem** *f.jv.* 1. to catch
cold. 2. to grow cool.
ftóhës,-i *m.sh.* - refrigerant.
ftóhës,-e *mb.* refrigeratory.
ftóhj/e,-a *f.* 1. cooling, chilling,
2. *fig.* alienation; **ftohje e miqësisë:** estrangement of friendship.
ftóhtë *ndajf.* coolly, chilly; coldly;
pres ftohtë dikë: to receive
someone coldly, to give the cold
shoulder to someone.
ftóhtë (i, e) *mb.* 1. cold; chilly,
cool; **shumë i ftohtë:** freezy,
icy; *(për gjellë)* cold; **mish i
ftohtë:** cold meat. 2. *fig.* cold,
cool, chilly; **pritje e ftohtë:**
cool reception.
ftóhtë(të),-t(të) *as.* cold, coldness;
frigidity; **bën ftohtë:** it is cold;
kam ftohtë: to feel cold; **të
ftohtë i hidhur:** bitter cold;
mblidhem nga të ftohtit: to
shrivel from cold.
ftohtësí,-a *f.* coolness, coldness;
**e pres një propozim me ftoh-
tësi:** to receive a suggestion
coldly.
ftóhur(të),-it(të) *as.* cold, coldness; **kam marrë të ftohur:**
I have caught cold.
ftoj *f.k.* to invite. – **ftohem** *f.jv.*
to be invited.
ftúa, ftoi *m.sh.* -ftonj *bot. (fruta)*
quince; *(druri)* quince-tree.
ftúar (i),-i(i) *m.sh.* -të guest.
ftúar (i,e) *mb.* guest; **artist i ftuar:**
guest artist.
ftúes,-i *m.sh. drejt.* distributer of
summons.
ftuják,-u *m.sh.* -ë *zool.* he-goat
about one year old; ewe-lamb.
ftúj/ë,-a *f.sh.* -a *zool.* she-goat
about one year old.
fuçí,-a *f.sh.* - barrel; *(fuçi e madhe)*
hogshead; *(fuçi e vogël)* keg.

fúg/ë,-a *f.sh.* -a *zool.* garden warbler.
fúg/ë,-a *f.sh.* -a whirligig.
fugój *f.k.* to run.
fukar/á,-i *m.sh.* -enj poor man.
fukará *mb.* poor, needy.
fukarallëk,-u *m.* poverty.
fulták/ë,-a *f.sh.* -a swelling, blister.
fund,-i *m.sh.* -e 1. depth: **fundi i
pusit:** the depth of the well.
2. bottom; **fundi i shishes:** the
bottom of a bottle; **shishe pa
fund:** bottomless bottle; **i vë një
fund të ri një karrigeje:** to new-
seat a chair; **fundi i një faqeje:**
the bottom of a page. 3. end,
conclusion; **fundi i një ngja-
rjeje:** conclusion of an event;
fundi i një romani: end, epilogue of a novel. 4. end; **fundi i
një perandorie:** the end of an
empire; **nga fundi i vitit:** by
the end of the year, at the close of
the year, towards the end of the
year. – *Lok.* **në fund:** in the end;
më në fund: finally, at last;
pi me fund: to drink thoroughly
(a glass); **me fund!** bottoms up!;
nga fillimi deri në fund: from
beginning to end; **i jap fund (një
pune etj.);** to finish (a work,
etc.), to bring to an end, to put
an end (to); **merr fund:** it
ends; **çoj deri në fund:** to carry
through to the end.
fund,-i *m.sh.* -e skirt.
fundërrí,-a *f.sh.* - dregs, lees;
fundërri (pijesh, likeri etj.)
dregs of liquor (less); **fundërri
e shoqërisë:** the ragtag of the
society, riff-raff.
fúndit (i,e) *mb.* the last, the latter,
the utmost, the hindmost, the
hindermost; **stacioni i fundit:**
terminal; **kohët e fundit:** lately, recently.
fundós *f.k.* to sink. – **fundosem**

f.jv. to go downwards; to sink; **u fundos anija:** the ship submerged; **fundoset toka:** the earth subsides. **fundósj/e,-a** *f.* 1. *(fundosje e anijes):* submersion, sinking down (of a ship). 2. *(fundosje e tokës):* subsidence, falling down (of the earth). **funerál,-i** *m.sh.* **-e** funeral. **funksión,-i** *m.sh.* **-e** 1. *mat., biol.* function; **funksion tretës:** digestive function. 2. function, role. 3. duty, assignment. 4. purpose, function. **funksionár,-i** *m.sh.* **-ë** functionary, official. **funksioním,-i** *m.* functioning, operating, working, running, operation; **vë në funksionim:** to start, to switch on, to put in operation. **funksionój** *f.jk.* to function, to work (of a machine), to run, to be in operation, to operate. **fuqí,-a** *f.sh.* - 1. *(fuqi trupore)* force, vigour, strength, might, energy; **punoj me tërë fuqinë:** to work with all one's forces (with vigour). 2. power; **fuqi hidraulike:** water-power; **fuqi motorike:** motor power; **fuqi punëtore:** labour power. 3. capacity, power; **fuqi blerëse:** purchasing power. 4. *fig.* force: **fuqi ligjore:** legal force; **pa fuqi ligjore** of no legal force, null; **ligji hyn në fuqi menjëherë:** the law will have force at once, the law comes into force at once; **vë një ligj në fuqi:** to enforce a law, to put a law in force; **ligji është në fuqi:** the law is in force, in power. 5. *fiz.* **kalë fuqi:** horse power. 6. *mat.* exponent (of a number). 7. *polit.* **Fuqitë e Mëdha:** the great powers, the big powers. –

Lok. **marr fuqi (përsëri):** to regain one's strength. **fuqidhënës,-e** *mb.* *mjek.* tonic. **fuqimádh,-e** *mb.* allpowerful, omnipotent. **fuqimísht** *ndajf.* vigorously, powerfully. **fuqiplótë** *mb.* allpowerful; **minisë tër fuqiplotë:** minister plenipotentiary. **fuqísh/ëm(i),-me(e)** *mb.* powerful, mighty, sturty, strong, vigoë rous, hefty. **fuqizím,-i** *m.* strengthening, consolidation. **fuqizój** *f.k.* to strengthen, to consolidate. **fúrç/ë,-a** *f.sh.* **-a** brush; **furçë dhëmbësh:** teeth brush; **furçë flokësh:** hair brush; **furçë rroje:** shaving brush; **furçë rrobash:** clothes brush. **furçós** *f.k.* to brush. – **furçosem** *f.jv.* to brush oneself. **furçósj/e,-a** *f.* brushing. **furí,-a** *f.* fury, frenzy; **me furi:** furiously, frantically. **furísh/ëm** (i),-me(ë) *mb.* furious, frantic. **furíshëm** *ndajf.* frantically, frenzlë edly, in a frenzy. **furkáç/e,-ja** *f.sh.* **-e** prop. **fúrk/ë,-a** *f.sh.* **-a** 1. distaff. 2. twisting bobbin. **furnéll/ë,-a** *f.sh.* **-a** kitchener, stove, cooker; **furnellë me vajguri:** primus stove, oil-stove; **furnellë elektrike:** electric cooker. **furnitór,-i** *m.sh.* **-ë** supplier. **furnizím,-i** *m.sh.* **-e** supplying, providing, furnishing; supply, provision. **furnizój** *f.k.* 1. to supply, to provide with, to furnish; **furnizoj dikë me diçka:** to supply (to provide) to furnish) someone with something. 2. *treg.* to supply, to furnish, to purvey. – **furnizohem** *f.jv.* 1.

to provide (to supply) oneself with. 2. treg. to obtain supplies.

furnizúes,-i m.sh. - shih **furnitor.**

furqét/ë,-a f.sh. -a hairpin.

furtún/ë,-a f.sh. -a storm, tempest.

fúrr/ë,-a f.sh. -a bake-house, bakery; furnace; kiln; **furrë bukësh:** bake-house; **furrë gëlqereje:** lime kiln; **furrë tullash e tjegullash:** brick-kiln; **furrë për shkrirjen e metaleve:** blast furnace

furrí/k,-ku m.sh. -qe hen-roost, hen-house.

furrnált/ë,-a f.sh. -a blast furnace.

furrtár,-i m.sh. -ë baker.

furxhí,-u m.sh. -nj shih **furrtar.**

fus f.k. shih **fut.**

fustán,-i m.sh. -e dress.

fustanèll/ë,-a f.sh. -a kilt.

fúst/ë,-a f.sh. -a skirt.

fusharák,-u m.sh. -ë plainsman.

fushát/ë,-a f.sh. -a campaign; **fushatë zgjedhjesh:** election campaign; **fushatë mbjelljesh:** sowing campaign.

fúsh/ë,-a f.sh. -a 1. field, plain; **lule fushe:** wild flowers; **fushë aeroplanësh:** air base; **fushë drush:** wood yard; **fushë sporti:** sports ground; **fushë lufte:** battle field, battle-ground; **prodhime fushe:** country produce. 2. fig. field, branch; **ekspert në të gjitha fushat:** expert in all fields; **fushë veprimtarie:** field of activity. 3. **fushë pamjeje:** field of vision. 4. fiz. field; **fushë magnetike:** magnetic field. 5. muz. **fushë pentagrami:** interline. 6. **fushë sahati:** dial.

fushím,-i m.sh. -e usht. camp, encampment.

fushój f.k. to camp, to encamp.

fushór,-e mb. field; **artileri fu-**

shore: field artillery; **spital fushor:** field hospital.

fushqét/ë,-a f.sh. -a shih **fishekzjarr.**

fut f.k. 1. to put, to insert; to introduce; **fut kyçin në bravë:** to put the key in the keyhole. 2. to show, to usher, to let in; **e futi në zyrën e drejtorit:** he showed him into the director's office -**futem** f.jv. 1. to get in (into), to enter; **futem me forcë:** to break into, to intrude; **futem tinës:** to steal in; **i futem thellë një çështjeje:** to go deeply into a subject. 2. (një zakon, moda etj.) to be introduced, to become popular.

futbóll,-i m. football, fam. soccer; **ndeshje futbolli:** football match.

futbollíst,-i m.sh. -ë footballer, fam. soccer player.

fút/ë,-a f.sh. -a 1. apron. 2. black kerchief.

fútj/e,-a f. introduction; **futje me forcë:** intrusion.

fyej f.k. to injure, to insult, to offend, to vex. – **fyhem** f.jv. to be injured (insulted, offended, vexed); **fyej me dashje:** to insult designedly.

fýell,-i m.sh. **fyej.** 1. shepherd's pipe, flute, fife; **i bie fyellit:** to wind the pipe. 2. anat. **fyelli i këmbës:** shink of the leg.

fýerj/e,-a f.sh. -e injury, insult, offense.

fýes,-e mb. injurious, insulting, offending.

fyt,-i m. anat. throat. – Lok. **lag fytin:** to wet one's whistle.

fýtas ndajf. hand-to-hand; **luftoj fytas me dikë:** to engage in hand-to-hand fighting.

fytafýt ndajf. shih **fytas.**

fytýr/ë,-a f.sh. -a face; **fytyrë e zbehtë:** pale face. – Lok. **s'kam**

fytyrë të bëj diçka: not to have the cheek to do something; **ndërroj fytyrë, më ndërron fytyra:** to change expression, to go pale, to change colour; **ia them në fytyrë:** to say things openly, to say something to someone's face; **pati fytyrë ta mohonte:** he had the face to deny it; **me dy fytyra:** double-faced.

fytyrëçélur *mb.* smiling.
fytyrëhéqur *mb.* pale-faced.
fytyrëngrýsur *mb.* dark-faced.
fytyrëqéshur *mb.* shih **fytyrëçe-lur.**
fytyrëvrárë *mb.* shih **fytyrëngry-sur.**
fytyrëvrénjtur *mb.* shih **fytyrë-ngrysur.**

G

g, G (letter of the Albanian alphabet; is pronounced like **g** in group) g, G.
gabardín/ë,-a *f.sh.* -a 1. *(stofë)* gabardine. 2. (gabardine) overcoat.
gabél,-i *m.sh.* -ë gipsy, gypsy.
gabím,-i *m.sh.* -ë mistake, error; lapse; fault; **detyra është plot gabime:** the exercise is full of mistakes; **bëj një gabim:** to commit (to make) a mistake; **bie në gabim:** to fall into error; **ndreq një gabim:** to correct a mistake; **gabim trashanik:** a foolish mistake, blunder; **gabim shtypi:** misprint, erratum; **gabim drejtshkrimi:** misspelling; **gabim gjyqësor:** miscarriage of justice; **e kam gabim:** to be wrong, to be mistaken; **e keni gabim, më duket:** I think you are wrong.
gabimísht *ndajf.* wrongly, by error, erroneously, incorrectly.

gabój I. *f.jk.* to mistake, to err; **gaboj rrugë:** to stray, to mislay, to take the wrong way; **njeri që nuk gabon:** infallible person; **gaboj rëndë:** to blunder. II. *f.k.* *(gaboj dikë)* to cheat, to fraud, to swindle. — **gabohem** *f.jv.* to be mistaken.
gabúar (i,e) *mb.* wrong, false, mistaken, erroneous; **mendim i gabuar:** false opinion.
gabuésh/ëm (i),-me(e) *mb.* mistakable, wrongful, fallible.
gabzhérr,-i *m.sh.* -ë *anat.* windpipe, trachea.
gác/ë,-a *f.sh.* -a live-coal.
gadíshu/ll,-lli *m.sh.* -j peninsula.
gáf/ë,-a *f.sh.* -a gross fault, gaffe.
gafórr/e,-ja *f.sh.* -e *zool.* crab.
gagáç,-i *m.sh.* -ë stammerer, lisper.
gajás *f.jk.* to exhaust, to wear out by exertion. — **gajasem** *f.jv.* to be exhausted; **gajasem së qeshuri:** to burst (to split) with laughter; **gajasem së ecuri:** to get exce-

ssively tired of walking; **gaja-sem së qari**: to coy one's eyes (heart) out.
gajásj/e,-a *f.* exhaustion, extreme fatigue.
gájde,-ja *f.sh.* – *muz.* bag-pipe.
gajdexhí,-u *m.sh.* -nj player of a bag-pipe.
gájgë *mb.* soft-shelled; **arrë gajgë**: soft-shelled walnut.
gájle,-ja *f.* care, worry, trouble; **s'ka gajle**: no matter, it does not matter, never mind.
galér/ë,-a *f.sh.* -a galley.
galerí,-a *f.sh.* - 1. *ndërt.* gallery, tunnel. 2. *(në teatër)* balcony, circle; **galeria e arteve**; (arts) gallery.
galét/ë,-a *f.sh.* -a hardtack, ship's (sea) biscuit; biscuit.
gál/ë,-a *f.sh.* -a *zool.* jack-daw.
galíç *ndajf.* squat; **rri galíç**: to squat.
gallóf,-i *m.sh.* -ë 1. *zool.* white raven. 2. *fig.* silly person.
gallósh/e,-ja *f.sh.* -e galosh, galoshe.
gám/ë,-a *f.sh.* -a *muz.*scale, gamut.
gamíl/e,-ja *f.sh.* -e *zool.* camel.
gangrén/ë,-a *f. mjek.* gangrene.
garancí,-a *f.sh.* - guaranty, guarantee; **garanci për dy vjet**: two year's guarantee.
garánt,-i *m.sh.* -ë guarantor, voucher, sponsor, bail, surety, warrantor; **bëhem garant**: to vouch for, to be guarantee for.
garantój *f.k.* to guarantee, to give a guarantee, to vouch. – **garan-tohem** *f.jv.* to be guaranteed (secured).
garázh,-i *m.sh.* -e garage, car-house.
gardalín/ë,-a *f.sh.* -a *zool.* goldfinch.
gardh,-i *m.sh.* -e fence, hedge, stockade; **gardh me dërrasa:**

palissade, paling; **gardh me gjemba**: prikly hedge; **rrethim me gardh**: fencing; **rrethoj me gardh**: to fence, to hedge.
gár/ë,-a *f.sh.* -a 1. competition, contest; **marr pjesë në garë**; to compete in an event. 2. *sport.* contest; **gara vrapimi**: sprint race. 3. *fig.* competition; race; **gara socialiste**: socialist competitions; **gara e armatimeve**; armament race.
gargár/ë,-a *f. mjek.* gargle; **bëj gargarë**: to gargle.
gárgu/ll,-lli *m.sh.* -j *zool.* starling.
garnitúr/ë,-a *f.sh.* -a 1. garniture, embellishment. 2. vegetables served in a dish.
garnizón,-i *m.sh.* -e garrison.
garúzhd/ë,-a *f.sh.* -a laddle.
gárz/ë,-a *f.sh.* -a *farm.* gauze.
gastár/e,-ja *f.sh.* -e shih **qelq.**
gastarína,-t *f.sh.* - shih **qelqurina.**
gastrít,-i *m. mjek.* gastritis, inflammation of the stomach.
gásht/ë,-a *f.* touch-stone.
gát/ë,-a *f.sh.* -a *zool.* heron.
gáti *ndajf.* 1. ready; **jam gati**; to be ready; **bëhem gati**: to get ready; **bëhem gati për rrugë**: to pack up. 2. almost, nearly, about; **gati po nisej**: he was about to depart, he was on the point of departure.
gatím,-i *m.sh.* -e cookery, cooking; **gatim gjelle**: cooking of food.
gatís *f.k.* to prepare, to make ready; **gatis mishin**: to cook meat, to dress meat. – **gatitem** *f.jv.* to prepare oneself, to get ready.
gatishmërí,-a *f.* readiness.
gatítj/e,-a *f.sh.* -e preparation.
gátsh/ëm (i),-me(e) *mb.* 1. predisposed, willing; **jam i gatshëm t'ju ndihmoj**: I am well disposed to help you; I am willing to help you. 2. ready made; **rroba**

të gatshme: ready-made clothes; ushqim i gatshëm: ready-made food.
gatúaj *f.k. (bukë)* to knead; *(gjellë)* to cook. – gatuhet *f.jv.* to be cooked.
gatúar (i.e) *mb.* cooked; mish i gatuar: cooked meat.
gavét/ë,-a *f.sh.* -a tin bowl.
gaz,-i *m.sh.* -e *kim.* gas; gaz helmues: toxic gas; gaz kënete: marsh gas; gaz lotues: tear gas; gaz miniere: coal gas; gaz ndriçimi: light gas; tub gazi: gas-pipe; maskë kundër gazit: gas-helmet, antigas mask; furnellë me gaz: gas-cooker. – *Lok.* i jap gaz (makinës): to accelarate.
gaz,-i *m.* joy, merriment, merriness, mirth.
gazél/ë,-a *f.sh.* -a *zool.* gazelle.
gazetár,-i *m.sh.* -ë journalist, gazetteer, *amer.* newspaperman, newsman.
gazetarí,-a *f.* journalism.
gazetashítës,-i *m.sh.* - newsman, newsboy.
gazét/ë,-a *f.sh.* -a newspaper, journal; gazetë letrare: literary journal; gazetë muri: wallpaper; gazetë e përditshme: daily paper, journal; gazetë e përjavshme: weekly-journal, weekly-paper; gazetë zyrtare: gazette; qoshk për shitjen e gazetave: news stand; shpërndarës gazetash: news-boy, newsman.
gazménd,-i *m.* great joy.
gazmór,-e *mb.* joyful, mirthful, cheerful, jolly, joyous, gladsome; jovial, convivial.
gazóz/ë,-a *f.* fizzy drink, fizz, efervescent drink.
gáztë (i,e) *mb.* gaseous; në gjendje të gaztë: in a gaseous state.

gdhend *f.k.* 1. to sculpture, to sculpt, to carve; *(gurin)* to carve; *(metalin)* to chisel; gdhend me thikë: to whittle; gdhend emrin në një pemë: to carve one's name on the trunk of a tree. 2. *fig.* to polish, to refine. – gdhendem *f.jv.* to be refined.
gdhéndës,-i *m.sh.* - carver, engraver, sculptor; gdhendës druri: wood engraver; wood cutter; gdhendës guri: stone-cutter, stone-carver; gdhendës metali: metal-cutter.
gdhéndj/e,-a *f.* carving, engraving; gdhendje në dru: xylography, wood engraving; gdhendje në gur: stone-cutting, stone-carving; gdhendje metali: chiseling; gdhendje me mjete kimike: etching; gdhendje në bakër: engraving in copper.
gdhë,-ri *m.sh.* -nj knot, knur, sang; me gdhënj: knotty; *fig.* dunce; kokë gdhë: block-head, loggerhead.
gdhij *f.jk.* 1. to grow light, to dawn. 2. e gdhij: to stay all night sleepless. – gdhihem *f.jv.* 1. to pass all the night without sleep. 2. po gdhihet: it is growing light, day is breaking.
gdhírë,-t (të) *as.* dawn, daybreak; ndaj të gdhirë: by dawn. ger,-i *m.sh.* -ë *zool.* shih ketër.
gérm/ë,-a *f.sh.* -a letter, character; *fig.* germë për germë: literally, word for word.
géte,-t *f.sh.* gaiter.
gëlbáz/ë,-a *f.sh.* -a *anat.* expectoration, phlegm; pështyj gëlbazë: to expectorate, to spit (to send out) phlegm.
gëlón *f.jk.* to throng; to come in multitude.
gëlqér/e,-ja *f.* lime; gëlqere e pashuar: quick lime; gëlqere e shuar: slaked lime; furrë gëlqe-

reje: lime-kiln; gur gëlqereje: limestone; sherbet gëlqereje: white-wash, hidrate of lime, lime- -water.
gëlqerór,-e *mb.* calcareous; gur gëlqeror: limestone, calcareous stone.
gëlltís *f.k.* to swallow, to swallow up, to gulp, to gulp down. — gëlltitet *f.jv.* to be swallowed.
gëlltítj/e,-a *f.* swallow, gulp.
gëmúsh/ë,-a *f.sh.* -a *bot.* brush-wood.
gënjéj I. *f.jk.* to lie, to fib, to tell fibs, to bamboozle. II. *f.k.* to dupe, to cheat, to beguile, to trick, to frustate; gënjej dikë: to cheat someone. —gënjehem *f.jv.* to be mistaken; to be cheated.
gënjeshtár,-i *m.sh.* -e liar, fibber; gënjeshtar i madh: a big liar.
gënjésht/ër,-ra *f.* lie, fib, flam; them gënjeshtra: to tell lies.
gënjéshtërt (i,e) *mb.* lying, false, untrue.
gënjím-i *m.* beguilement, defraud.
gërbúl/ë,-a *f. mjek.* leprosy.
gërbúlët (i,e) *mb.* leprous.
gërdáll/ë,-a *f.sh.* -a jade, scrag horse, nag.
gërdhúshta,-t *f.sh.* siftings.
gërgás *f.k.* to tease.
gërgër/e,-ja *f.* whirligig.
gërhás *f.jk.* to snore, to wheeze, to sniff; *(macja)* to purn.
gërhítës,-e *mb.* snoring.
gërhítj/e,-a *f.sh.* -e snore, wheeze, sniff; *(gërhitje e maces)* purr (of a cat).
gërmádh/ë,-a *f.sh.* -a ruins of buildings; shtëpi gërmadhë: a dilapidated old house.
gërmím,-i *m.sh.* -e digging, excavation; gërmime arkeologjike: excavations; punëtor gërmimi: digger.

gërmís *f.k.* to gnaw.
gërmój *f.k. f.jk.* to dig, to grub, to dig up, to excavate.
gërmúq,-e *mb.* bent, crooked.
gërnét/ë,-a *f.sh.* -a *muz.* clarionet.
gërnjár,-e *mb.* querrelsome.
gërnj/ë,-a *f.sh.* -a brawe.
gërshét,-i *m.sh.* -a tress, braid, plait.
gërshetím,-i *m.sh.* -e interlacement, interweaving.
gërshetój *f.k.* 1. to tress, to braid, to plait. 2. to interlace, to intertwine. — gërshetohet *f.jv.* to be interlaced.
gërshër/ë,-t *f.sh.* 1. scissors; gërshërë të mëdha: shears. 2. gërshërë dhensh: clippers.
gërshërëz,-a *f.sh.* -a *zool.* rafter.
gërthás *f.jk.* to shout, to scream, to cry.
gërthítj/e,-a *f.* shout, scream, outcry, clamour.
gërvísht *f.k.* 1. to scratch, to claw. 2. *fig.* to strum; që të gërvisht veshin: strident. — gërvishtem *f.jv.* to be scratched, to scratch oneself.
gërvíshtj/e-a *f.sh.* -e scratch, scratching.
gërrýej *f.k.* 1. to scoop out; gërryej dheun: to dig (to drag, to dredge) earth (ground). 2. *kim.* to errode; gërryej metalet: to errode (to corrode) metals. — gërryhet *f.jv.* 1. to be dredged. 2. to be erroded, to be corroded (metals).
gërrýerj/e,-a *f.* 1. *(gërryerje e tokës)* erosion. 2. *(gërryerje e metaleve)* corrosion.
gërrýes,-e *mb.* 1. corroding, corrosive. 2. *kim.* caustic.
gështénj/ë,-a *f.sh.* -a *bot.* chestnut; druri i gështenjës: chestnut-tree; ngjyrë gështenjë: maroon; flokë gështenjë: auburn hair.

gëzím,-i *m.sh.* -e joy, enjoyment, mirth, gaiety, merriment, glee, gladness, cheer; **me gëzim:** merrily, mirfully, joyfully, cheerfully.

gëzóf,-i *m.sh.* -e fur, peltry; **gëzof kastori:** beaver-fur; e **veshur me gëzof** *(pallto):* lined with fur (of an overcoat).

gëzofpunúes,-i *m.sh.* - furrier.

gëzoftár,-i *m.sh.* -ë shih **gëzof-punues.**

gëzottór /e,-ja *f.sh.* -e furriery.

gëzój *f.k.* 1. to enjoy; **gëzoj shëndet të plotë:** to enjoy good health. 2. to gladden, to delight, to cheer. — **gëzohem** *f.jv.* to enjoy oneself, to be glad; **gëzohem që ju njoha:** I am glad to know you, I am pleased to know you; **gëzohem së tepërmi:** I am overjoyed.

gëzúar! *pasth.* to your health! (when drinking); **gëzuar Vitin e Ri!** A happy New Year!

gëzúar (i, e) *mb.* 1. joyful, cheerful mirthful, gleeful, joyous, merry, glad, gladsome, blithe, blithesome; **jam shumë i gëzuar që ju njoha:** I am too glad (I am overjoyed) to know you. 2. happy; **qofsh nënë e gëzuar!** may you be a happy mother!

gëzúesh/ëm (i),-me(e) *mb.* joyful, cheerful, mirthful, gleeful.

gëzhój/ë,-a *f.sh.* -a shell, cartridge case.

gëzhút/ë,-a *f.sh.* -a siftings.

gic,-i *m.sh.* -a *zool.* sucking-pig.

gijotín/ë,-a *f.sh.* -a guillotine.

gílc /ë,-a *f.sh.* -a *anat.* tendon.

gisht,-i *m.sh.*-a,-ërinj 1. finger; **gishti i madh i dorës:** thumb; **gishti tregues:** forefinger;**gishti i mesit:** middle finger; **gishti i unazës:** ring finger; **gishti i vogël:** little finger; **gishti i këmbës:** toe; **tregoj me gisht:**

to point, to indicate; **eci mbi majat e gishtërinjve;** to tiptoe, to walk on tiptoes. — *Lok.* **kam gisht në një komplot:** to have a hand (to be mingled) in a plot, to be accomplice in a plot; **e di në majë të gishtave diçka:** to have something at one's finger tips; **një gisht verë:** just a drop of wine; **nuk luaj as gishtin:** not to lift (to stir) a finger, not to do a thing; **vë gishtin në plagë:** to lay (to put) one's finger on.

gíshtës,-i *m.sh.* -a spoke (of a wheel).

gíshtëz,-a *f.sh.* -a thimble (of sewing).

gíz/ë,-a *f. metal.* cast-iron.

glás/ë,-a *f.sh.* -a fly-blow.

gléb/ë,-a *f. krah.* shih **sklepë.**

glicerín /ë,-a *f.* glycerine, glycerol.

glikánxo,-ja *f. bot.* aniseed.

glikó,-ja *f.* jam.

glíst/ër,-ra *f.sh.* -a *zool.* trichina.

glob,-i *m.sh.* -e globe.

globál,-e *mb.* global.

globalíz/ëm,-mi *m.* globalism.

gllabërím,-i *m.* swallow, swallowing (up) (edhe *fig.*).

gllabërój *f.k.* to swallow up.

gllavín/ë,-a *f.sh.* -a hub, nave of a wheel.

gllënjk/ë,-a *f.sh.* -a sip, draught, gulp; **një gllënjkë verë:** a drop of wine; **pi me një gllënjkë:** to drink at one gulp (in a single draught).

góc/ë,-a *f.sh.* -a 1. girl, lass. 2. *zool.* **gocë deti:** mollusc, mollusk, shellfish.

godás *f.k.* to strike, to hit, to smite, to knock; **godas me grusht:** to strike with one's fist; **godas me pëllëmbë:** to slap; **godas me një çokë, etj.:** to knock. — **goditem** *f.jv.* to be struck.

godín/ë,-a *f.sh.* -a building.

godítj/e,-a *f.sh.* -a stroke, hit, knock, blow, thrust; **goditje rrufeje:** thundering; **goditje me pushkë:** discharge, shooting with a fire-arm.

goditur (i, e) *mb.* 1. *mjek.* struck (by hemiplegia, etc.); **i goditur nga rrufeja:** struck by thunder. 2. well-done; **përkthim i goditur:** a well-done translation.

góg/ël,-la *f.sh.* -la acorn, oak-apple.

gogësíj *f.jk.* to yawn, to gape.

gogësím/ë,-a *f.sh.* -a yawn, gape.

gogól,-i *m.sh.* -ë scarecrow.

gojác,-i *m.sh.* -ë stutterer.

gója-gójës *ndajf.* from mouth-to-mouth.

gojarísht *ndajf.* orally, verbally, on viva voce, by word of mouth.

gojáshpër *mb.* sharp-tongued, snappish, snappy.

gój/ë,-a *f.sh.* -ë 1. mouth; **më mbahet goja:** to stutter; **provim me gojë:** (oral) examination; **mbaj nëpër gojë të tjerët:** to gossip; **mbylle gojën!** shut up!, hold your tongue!; **mësoj me gojë** *(një mësim, një vjershë)*: to learn by heart; **gojët e liga:** scandal mongers; **te goja:** at hand, very near.

gojëmbël *mb.* sweet-tongued.

gojëhápur *mb.* open-mouthed.

gojëlëshuar *mb.* slanderous, back-biting; loquacious.

gojëmbýllur *mb.* close-mouthed, close-lipped.

gojëmjáltë *mb.* shih **gojëmbël.**

gojëndýrë *mb.* foul-mouthed.

gojëpríshur *mb.* foul-mouthed.

gojështhúrur *mb.* shih **gojëlëshuar.**

gojëtár,-i *m.sh.* -ë orator.

gojëtarí,-a *f.* oratory.

gójëz,-a *f.sh.* -a muzzle; **i vë**

gojëz qenit: to muzzle (to put a muzzle on) the dog.

gojór,-e *mb.* oral.

gojós *f.k.* to gossip, to backbite, to slander, to speak ill of someone.

gojósj/e,-a *f.sh.* -e gossip.

gol,-i *m.sh.* -a *sport* goal; **bëj një gol:** to score a goal.

gollogúng/ë,-a *bot.* juniper-berry.

gollomésh *mb.* *ndejf.* naked.

gomár,-i *m.sh.* -ë 1. ass, donkey; **gomar i egër:** onager, wild ass. 2. *fig.* stupid person; **ai është gomar i tëri:** he is a downright ass.

gomaríc/ë,-a *f.sh.* -a *zool.* she-ass.

gomarllë/k,-ku *m.sh.* -qe silliness, stupidity.

góm/ë,-a *f.sh.* -a 1. *(gomë për të fshirë)* rubber, eraser 2. caoutchouc, india rubber. 3. *(gomë automobili, biçiklete)* tire; **gomë rezervë:** spare-tire.

goniomét/ër,-ri *m.sh.* -ra goniometer.

gónxh/e,-ja *f.sh.* -e *bot.* bud.

gorén,-i *m.* northern ice-wind.

goríc/ë,-a *f.sh.* -a wild pear.

goríll/ë,-a *f.sh.* -a *zool.* gorilla.

gostí,-a *f.sh.* - feast, dinner party; **gosti dasme:** wedding feast; **gosti e shfrenuar:** carousal, revel; **shtroj një gosti:** to hold (to give) a dinner party.

gostís *f.k.* to feast, to regale, to entertain, to treat. – **gostitem** *f.jv.* to regale oneself.

gostítj/e,-a *f.sh.* -e treat, entertainment.

gót/ë,-a *f.sh.* -a glass; **gotë birre:** beer-glass, bock-beer; **gotë vere:** wine-glass; **një gotë verë:** a glass of wine; **gotë laboratori:** beaker.

govát/ë,-a *f.sh.* -a trough, wash-

tub; **govatë për ushqimin e kafshëve:** manger.
goxhá *ndajf. krah.* rather; **goxha shtrenjtë:** rather dear, costly too expensive.
gózhd/ë,-a *f.sh.* -a nail; **gozhdë e vogël me kokë:** stud; **gozhdë e vogël (shajkë):** rivet; **gozhdë potkojsh:** hobnail; **ngul një gozhdë:** to nail, to drive in a nail.
gozhdój *f.k.* to nail. – **gozhdohem** *f.jv.* to be nailed.
grabís *f.k.* to rob, to steal, to pillage, to plunder. – **grabitem** *f.jv.* to be robbed.
grabítës,-i *m.sh.* - robber, plunderer, pillager.
grabítj/e,-a *f.sh.* -a robbery, rapine, plunder, pillage, abduction.
grabitqár/,-e *mb.* rapacious; **zog grabitqar:** bird of prey.
grabúj/ë,-a *f.sh.* -a rake; **grabujë bari:** hay-rake; **punoj me grabujë:** to rake.
gráck/ë,-a *f.sh.* -a trap, pitfall, snare; **bie në grackë:** to fall into a trap; **kap në grackë:** to trap, to snare, to enshare; **ngren një grackë:** to set a trap.
gradél/ë,-a *f.sh.* -a gridiron.
grád/ë,-a *f.sh.* -a 1. degree, level. 2. rank. 3. *mat, fiz.* degree; **termometri shënon tridhjetë gradë:** the thermometer reads thirty degrees; **gradë gjerësie gjeografike:** latitude degree. 4. **gradë shkencore:** degree.
gradím,-i *m.sh.* -e 1. promotion. 2. *(gradimi i një instrumenti)* graduation (of an instrument).
gradín/ë,-a *f.sh.* -a small garden (round a house), kitchen garden.
gradój *f.k.* 1. to promote. 2. *(instrumentin)* to graduate. – **gradohem** *f.jv.* 1. to be promoted. 2. to be graduated.

graduál,-e *mb.* gradual.
gradualísht *ndajf.* gradually, by degrees, by and by.
grafík,-u *m.sh.* -ë graphic.
grafík,-e *mb.* graphical.
grafít,-i *m.* black-lead, graphite.
gráhm/ë,-a *f.sh.* -a death-rattle.
gram,-i *m.sh.* -ë gramme.
gramafón,-i *m.sh.* -e gramophone, phonograph; **disk gramafoni:** record (of a gramophone); *fig.* **gramafon i prishur:** chatterbox.
gramatík/ë,-a *f.sh.* -a grammar.
gramatíkísht *ndajf.* gramatically.
gramatikór,-e *mb.* grammatical.
grám/ë,-a *f. vjet.* writing; **njeri me gramë:** a literate (a lettered) person, a learned person, literati.
granát/ë,-a *f.sh.* -a *usht.* grenade.
graníl,-i *m.* granulated stone.
granít,-i *m.sh.* -e granite.
grarí,-a *f.* womenfolk.
grarísht *ndajf.* in a womanly manner.
graríshte *mb.* womanly, woman like.
grasatím,-i *m.sh.* -e greasing.
grasatój *f.k.* to grease.
gráso,-ja *f. tek.* grease.
grashín/ë,-a *f.sh.* -a *bot.* vetch.
gravitación,-i *m.* gravitation; **ligji i gravitacionit:** gravitation law.
gravitét,-i *m.* gravity; **qendra e gravitetit:** center of gravity.
grazhd,-i *m.sh.* -e manger, rak for cattle, crib for cattle, horse box, stall.
grazhdár,-i *m.sh.* -ë stable-boy, groom (for horses).
grebásh,-i *m.sh.* -ë shih **grabujë.**
gréhull,-i *m.* shih **korie.**
grek,-u *m.sh.* -ë Greek.
grek,-e *mb.* Greek.
gremç,-i *m.sh.* -a boat-hook.
gremín/ë,-a *f.sh.* -a abyss, precipice; **buzë greminës:** on the

edge of the abyss; *fig.* **shkoj drejt greminës:** to run to one's destruction (to one's ruin), to go downhill.

gremis *f.k.* to tumble. — **gremisem** *f.jv.* to tumble, to fall down.

gremisj/e,-a *f.sh.* -a downfall, tumble, fall.

grénz/ë,-a *f.sh.* -a *zool.* wasp, hornet.

grep,-i *m.sh.* -a 1. hook; **grep peshkimi:** fish hook. 2. **grep për qendisje:** needle for lacework.

greqísht *ndajf.* in Greek.

greqísht/e,-ja *f.* Greek.

grér/ë,-a *f.sh.* -a shih **grenzë.**

grév/ë,-a *f.sh.* -a strike; **grevë e përgjithshme:** general strike; **grevë urie:** starvation strike; **bëj grevë:** to strike, to go on strike; **jam në grevë:** to be on strike; **shpall grevë:** to go on strike.

grevëthýes,-i *m.sh.* - strike breaker, scab, blackleg.

grevíst,-i *m.sh.* -ë striker.

gri *mb.* gray, grey.

grib/ë,-a *f.sh.* -a 1. comb. 2. currycomb. 3. rake. 4. net (for fishing).

grífsh/ë,-a *f.sh.* -a 1. *zool.* jay. 2. shrew.

gríh/ë,-a *f.sh.* -a grindstone, wetstone, grinding wheel.

grij *f.k.* to grate, to mince, to cut into pieces; **grij mishin:** to mince the meat. — *Lok.* **më griu uria:** I am dying of hunger, I am very hungry; **më griu barku nga dhimbja:** I have a bad belly-ache, my belly aches badly. **-grihem** *f.jv.* to quarrel (with someone).

gril/ë,-a *f.sh.* -a 1. grille, grating. 2. lattice, lattice-work, iron-work.

grímc/ë,-a *f.sh.* - a crumb, mote; particle.

grím/ë,-a *f.* bit, a small piece; **një**

grimë bukë: a bit of bread; **asnjë grimë:** not a bit.

gríndem *f.jv.* to have words with, to bicker, to quarrel.

grindavéc,-e *mb.* pettish, peevish, ill-tempered, fretful, quarrelsome; **grua grindavece:** virago.

grindj/e,-a *f.sh.* -a quarrel, broil, brawl, bickering.

grip,-i *m. mjek.* influenza, **grip,** grippe.

g,rírë (i, e) *mb.* minced; **mish i grirë:** mincemeat, minced meat.

grírës/e,-ja *f.sh.* -e cutter.

grírj/e,-a *f.* cutting; **makinë për grirjen e kashtës:** chaff-cutter; **makinë për grirjen e mishit:** meat-cutter.

gris *f.k.* 1. to tear; to rend; **gris një letër:** to tear a paper. 2. **gris rrobat (këpucët):** to wear, to impair clothes (shoes). — **grisem** *f.jv.* to be torn.

grísj/e,-a *f.sh.* -e tear, laceration.

grísur (i, e) *mb.* torn, rent.

grísh *f.k.* to invite.

grízh/ël,-la *f.sh.* -la *zool.* magpie.

grishlémz/ë,-a *f.sh.* -a *zool.* jay.

gromësíj *f.jk.* to belch.

gromësír/ë,-a *f.sh.* -a belching.

grópa-grópa *mb.* rugh, rugged (of a road).

gróp/ë,-a *f.sh.* -a 1. hole; **shtie në gropë:** to bury, to inter, to entomb; **gropë e thellë:** pit; **gropa e ujërave të zeza:** sewage's hole, cesspool; *(e syrit)* orbit, eyehole.

grópëz,-a *f.sh.* -a small hole; **gropëza e syrit:** eyehole.

grópk/ë-a *f.sh.* -a small hole; **gropkë në faqe (në mjekër):** dimple in the cheek (in the chin).

gropós *f.k.* 1. to inter, to bury, to entomb. 2. to ditch. — **groposem** *f.jv.* to entrench oneself.

gropósj/e,-a *f.* burial.

grosíst,-i *m.sh.* -e wholesale dealer.

grosh,-i *m.sh.* -ë stiver; **s'kam asnjë grosh**: I haven't a stiver.

grósh/ë,-a *f.sh.* -ë *bot.* kidneybean, white bean.

grúa,-ja *f.sh.* -gra 1. woman; **grua e mirë**: good woman; **grua grindavece**: vexatious woman, ill-tempered woman; **grua e ligë**: bad woman; **grua lozonjare**: coquette; **grua llafazane**: talkative woman; **grua me edukatë**: well-bred woman; **grua mëndjelehtë**: jilt, hare-brained woman; **grua shterpë**: barren woman; **grua e shthurur**: woman of bad morals; **prej gruaje**: womanly. 2. wife, spouse; **grua nikoqire**: good house-wife; **grua pa kurorë**: concubine.

grúmbu/ll,-lli *m.sh.* -j heap, pile, mass, amassment; **grumbull drush**: pile (heap) of wood; **grumbull hekurishtesh**: scrap-iron, heap; **grumbull njerëzish**: crowd, throng, multitude;

grumbullím,-i *m.sh.* -e accumulation, agglomeration, conglomeration, amassment, gathering; **grumbullim ari**: hoarding of gold; **grumbullim njerëzish**: agglomeration (gathering) of people; **grumbullim sendesh**: accumulation, amassment of things; **grumbullim sendesh të ndryshme**: conglomeration.

grumbullój *f.k.* to gather, to amass, to hoard; **grumbulloj të holla**: to treasure up, to hoard money; **grumbulloj mall**: to lay up stores, to accumulate (to amass) goods; **grumbulloj popull (forca pune)**: to muster people (forces), to gather people. − **grumbullohet** *f./v.* to be amassed (gathered, mustered) (of people)

grumbullúes,-i *m.sh.* - collector, hoarder.

grunár,-i *m.sh.* -ë granary.

grunjtë (i, e) *mb.* wheaten; **bukë e grunjtë**: wheaten bread.

grup,-i *m.sh.* -e group; **një grup ushtarësh**: a group of soldiers; **një grup njerëzish**: a group of people; **një grup fshikëzash mbi lëkurë**: a cluster of vesicles.

grupím,-i *m.sh.* -e grouping.

grupój *f.k.* to group, to arrange in groups. − **grupohem** *f.jv.* to be grouped.

grúr/ë,-i *m.* wheat. − *Lok.* **e kam grurë me dikë**: to be on very good terms with someone.

grusht,-i *m.sh.* -e 1. fist; **qëlloj me grusht**: to strike with fist, to fist. 2. *fig.* handful; **një grusht njerëzish**: a handful of people. 3. grusht shteti: coup d'etat.

grykáshk/ë,-a *f.sh.* -a bib.

grýk/ë,-a *f.sh.* -a 1. *anat.* throat; *mjek.* **gryka e bardhë**: diphteria; maisje e grykës: angina, inflamation of the tonsils; **dhembje gryke**: sore throat; **më dhemb gryka**: to have a sore throat. 2. *gjeog.* mouth; **grykë lumi**: outfall, mouth of a river. 3. **grykë mali**: gorge of a mount. 4. **grykë pusi**: throat, neck (of a well). 5. **grykë pushke (topi, etj.)**: muzzle (of a gun, etc.). 6. **grykë shisheje**: throat, neck (of a bottle).

grýkës,-i *m.sh.* - glutton, gormand.

grýkës,-e *mb.* gluttonous, greedy.

grýkës/e,-ja *f.sh.* -a bib.

grykór,-e *mb.* 1. guttural. 2. *gram.* tingull grykor: guttural sound.

gúa/ll,-lli *m.sh.* -j nutshell.

guásk/ë,-a *f.sh.* -a 1. shell; **guaskë arre**: nutshell, walnut shell; **guaskë veze**: shell of an egg. 2. **guaskë deti**: shell fish.

gudulis *f.k.* to tickle, to titillate. –
gudulisem *f.jv.* to feel titillation;
që guduliset shpejt: ticklish.
gudulisj/e,-a *f.* tickle, tickling, titillation.
guerilj/e,-a *f.sh.* -e guerilla.
gúf/ë,-a *f.sh.* -a grotto, cave.
gúf/ër,-ra *f.sh.* -ra crater.
gufím,-i *m.* spout; gufim uji: water-spout.
gufón *f.jk.* to spout, to spring, to gush, to spurt.
gugúç/e,-ja *f.sh.* -e *zool.* turtle-dove.
gugurím /ë,-a *f.sh.* -a coo (of a pigeon).
gugurón *f.jk.* to coo.
guhák,-e *mb.* gawk, simpleton.
guhák,-u *m.sh.* -ë 1. *zool.* woodpigeon, ring-dove. 2. *fig.* gawk person, simpleton.
gulç,-i *m.sh.* -e *mjek.* pant, gasp.
gulçím,-i *m.sh.* -e hard breathing, panting.
gulçój *f.k.* to gasp, to pant, to breathe quickly and hardly, to breathe rapidly.
gulçúes,-e *mb.* panting, gasping.
gumallák,-u *m.* shellac.
gúm/ë,-a *f.sh.* -a shelf (ledge) of rock, reef, submerged reef.
gumëzhím/ë,-a *f.sh.* -a hum, humming, buzz, buzzing, whiz, murmuring; gumëzhima e bletëve: the humming of the bees.
gumëzhíj *f.jk.* to buz, to hum, to whiz.
gumëzhítj/e,-a *f.sh.* -a shih gumëzhimë.
gún/ë,-a *f.sh.* -a woolen pelerine or cape worn by shepherds.
gungáç,-i *m.sh.* -ë humpbacked person.
gungáç,-e *mb.* humpbacked, hunchbacked, humped.
gúng/ë,-a *f.sh.* -a 1. hunch, hump; gungë në kurriz: hump, hunch. 2. *(gungë druri)* knur; arrë gun-

g ë: walnut with a hard shell
gur,-i *m.sh.* -ë 1. stone; gur çakmaku: flint; gur i çmuar: precious stone, gem; gur gëlqeror: limestone; gur kaldrëmi: paving-stone; gur kilometrazhi: milestone; gur i latuar: cameo; gur mulliri: millstone; gur themeli: foundation stone; gur varri:gravestone, tomb-stone; gur vatre: hearths-stone; gur zalli: grit, gritstone; gur zjarri: flint-stone; gur zmeril *(grihë)*: grindstone; gur mprehës: whetstone. 2.*fig.* gur prove; touchstone. 3. gur dominoje:domino; gur tavlle: dice; gur shahu: pawn. 4. gur sahati. ruby. 5. *mjek.* calculus, stone; gur në veshkë: calculus in the reins; gur në tëmth: calculus biliary. – *Lok.* vë gurin e themelit: to lay the foundation stone; nuk lë gurë pa luajtur: to leave no stone unturned; djalë që nuk lë dy gurë bashkë: naughty boy, wayward boy.
gurabíj/e,-a *f.sh.* -e crumpet.
gurgdhéndës,-i *m.sh.* - stonecutter, stone-graver.
gurgulé,-ja *f.* tumult, commotion, hubbud.
gurgullím/ë,-a *f.* gurgle; gurgullima e ujit: gurgling of water.
gurgullón *f.jk.* to gurgle.
guríçk/ë,-a *f.sh.* -a flint, pebble.
gurín/ë,-a *f.sh.* -a rocky (stony, pebbly) ground.
guríshte *mb.* pebbly, flinty; tokë gurishte: pebbly ground, stony field.
gurísht/ë,-a *f.sh.* -a shih gurinë.
gurkáli *m.* copper sulphate, blue stone.
gurmáz,-i *m.sh.* -ë *anat.* gullet, larynx, pharynx, esophagus.
gurór,-e *mb.* stony.

gurór/e,-ja *f.sh.* -e quarry, stone-quarry, stone-pit; **punëtor guroreje**: quarry man.

gúrtë (i,e) *mb.* stonelike, solid.

gústo,-ja *f.* taste, gusto; **secill sipas gustos**: each to his own taste; **vishem me gusto**: to dress in good taste.

gúsh/ë,-a *f. anat.* 1. goitre. 2. **gushë zogu**: crop (of a bird), bird's crop.

gushëbárdhë *mb.* white-necked.

gushëkúq,-i *m.sh.* -ë *zool.* robin.

gushís *f.k.* to gut; **gushis peshkun**: to gut a fish, to pull of the gills of a fish.

gushór/e,-ja *f.sh.* -e necklace.

gusht,-i *m.* August.

guvernatór,-i *m.sh.* -ë governor.

gúv/ë,-a *f.sh.* -a cave.

guxím,-i *m.* boldness, hardiness, daring, audacity, heart; *fig.* courage, pluck; **me guxim** : boldly, daringly, hardily; **guxim prej të marri**: fool-hardiness; **i mungoi guximi**: his heart failed; **marr guximin të**: to take the liberty to, to make bold to.

guxímsh/ëm (i),-me(e) *mb.* audacious, hardy, sturdy, courageous, valiant.

guximtár,-i *m.sh.* -ë hardy man, bold man, courageous man.

guximtár,-e *mb.* shih **i guximshëm**.

guxój *f.jk.* to dare, to have courage; **nuk guxoj të flas**: I dare not speak.

gyp,-i *m.sh.* -a tube, pipe.

GJ

gj, Gj (letter of the Albanian alphabet).

gjah,-u *m.* 1. hunt, hunting; **dal për gjah**: to go out hunting. 2. game; **kafshë gjahu**: game, wild animal.

gjahtár,-i *m.sh.* -ë hunter, huntsman.

gjak,-u *m.* 1. blood; **gjak i piksur**: gore, clot of blood; **derdhje gjaku**: shedding of blood; **dhënie gjaku**: blood transfusion; **enë gjaku**: blood vessel; **helmim gjaku**: blood poisoning; **rruazat e gjakut**: globules of blood; **tensioni i gjakut**: blood pressure; **derdh gjakun për atdhé**: to shed one's blood for the country (the homeland); **humbas gjak**: to lose blood; **lyej me gjak**: to stain (to smear) with blood; **lidhje gjaku**: blood relationship, consanguinity, kindred. − *Lok.* **me gjak të ngrirë**: with the heart throbbing; **i etur për gjak**: blood-thirsty.

gjakatár,-i *m.sh.* -ë sanguinary person.

gjakatár,-e *mb.* sanguinary, bloodthirsty, cruel.

gjakdérdhj/e,-a *f.* bloodshed.

gjakësí,-a *f.* murder, assassination, killing.

gjakësór,-i *m.sh.* -ë 1. murderer. 2, sanguinary man.

gjakësór,-e *mb.* sanguinary.

gjakftóhtë *mb.* cold-blooded, calm, placid, serene, self-contained.

gjakftohtësí,-a *f.* self-control,self-possession, calmness, placidity, serenity, presence of mind; **me gjakftohtësi:** in cold blood, placidly.

gjakmárrës,-i *m.sh.* - avenger.

gjakmárrj/e,-a *f.* vengeance, revenge.

gjaknxéhtë *mb.* hot-blooded, hot-brained, irascible, quick-tempered.

gjaknxehtësí,-a *f.* irascibility.

gjakós *f.k.* 1. to bloody, to cover (to stain) with blood. 2. *fig.* to drench in blood, to cover with blood. – **gjakosem** *f.jv.* to be covered with blood, to be drenched in blood.

gjakósj/e,-a *f.* bleading, bloodiness.

gjakósur (i,e) *mb.* blood-stained, blood-shot, gory, bloody, stained with blood, covered with blood.

gjakpírës,-i *m.sh.* - blood-sucker, vampire.

gjaktrazím,-i *m.* incest.

gjálm/ë,-a *f.* lace, turne, cordon, strong thread; **lidh me gjalmë:** to lace; **zgjidh gjalmën:** to unlace.

gjálp/ë,-i *m.* butter; **gjalpë i freskët:** fresh butter; **gjalpë i tretur:** melted butter.

gjállë *ndajf.* 1. in life, living; **jam gjallë:** to be in life, to be alive; **ai është akoma gjallë:** he is still living; **deri sa të jetë gjallë:** as long as he lives; **mbahem gjallë:** to subsist, to exist;

ai që mbetet gjallë: survivor; **që kur ishte gjallë (në të gjallë të tij):** in his lifetime, in his days. 2. **është gjallë i ati:** he is the spit of his father.

gjállë (i,e) *mb.* 1. alive, living; **gjë e gjallë:** a) living creature; b) cattle; **njeri i gjallë:** live person. 2. *(njeri)* lively, sprightly, nimble. 3. raw, crude, uncooked; **mish i gjallë:** raw meat.

gjáll/ë (i),-i(i) *m.sh.* -ë (të) living person.

gjallërí,-a *f.* 1. vivacity, vitality, alacrity, liveliness, briskness, sprightliness; **me gjallëri:** vivaciously, with vivacity, briskly, sprightly, expressively; **pa gjalleri:** inexpresive; **gjalleri e një qyteti:** animation of a city.

gjallërím,-i *m.* vivification, vivifying, animation, invigoration.

gjallërísht *ndajf.* vividly, briskly, sprightly, vitally, with vivacity, energetically.

gjallërój *f.k.* 1. to vivify, to enlive, to animate. 2. to revive. – **gjallërohem** *f.jv.* to be vivified, to become spry.

gjallërúes,-e *mb.* vivifying, invigorating, tonic, enlivening; *(ajër, klimë)* bracing.

gjárp/ër,-ri *m.sh.* -ërinj *zool.* snake, serpent; **gjarpër me syze:** cobra; **gjarpër me zile:** rattlesnake; **gjarpër uji:** grass-snake.

gjarpërím,-i *m.* sinuosity; winding; **gjarpërim i një lumi:** winding of a river.

gjarpërój *f.jk. (rruga)* to wind; *(lumi)* to meander, to take a winding course.

gjarpërúes,-e *mb.* twisting, winding.

gjás/ë,-a *f.* 1. probability, likelihood, verisimilitude; **mbas gjase:** probably, likely. 2. symptom, sign.

gjasím,-i *m*. 1. sameness, resemblance, likeness, similarity, affinity; **gjasim i madh:** close resemblance. 2. identity; **gjasim mendimesh:** identity of views.

gjássh/ëm (i),-me(e) *mb*. identical, similar.

gjáshtë *num. them*. six.

gjáshtë (i,e) *num. rresht*. sixth.

gjashtëdhjétë *num. them*. sixty.

gjashtëdhjétë (i,e) *num.rresht*. sixtieth.

gjashtëdhjetëvjeçár,-i *m.sh*. -ë sexagenarian.

gjashtëdhjetëvjeçár,-e *mb*. sexagenary.

gjashtëdhjetëvjetór,-i *m*. sixtieth anniversary.

gjashtëfísh *ndajf*. sixfold, sextuple.

gjashtëfísh,-i *m*. the sixfold.

gjashtëkëndësh,-i *m.sh*. -a *gjeom*. hexagon.

gjashtëkëndësh,-e *mb. gjeom*. hexagonal.

gjashtëmbëdhjétë *num.them*. sixteen.

gjashtëmbëdhjétë (i,e) *num. rresht*. sixteenth.

gjashtëmúajsh,-e *mb*. of half a year, halfyearly.

gjashtëmujór,-i *m.sh*. -ë six months, halfyear.

gjashtëmujór,-e *mb*. of half year, of six months, halfyearly.

gjashtëqínd *num.them*. six hundred.

gjatamán,-e *mb*. tall.

gjátas, gjátazi *ndajf*. in length, lengthly, lengthways.

gjátë I. *paraf*. 1. along; **gjatë lumit:** along the river; **gjatë rrugës:** along the way. 2. during, through, throughout, in the course of, in the progress of; **gjatë dimrit;** during the winter; **gjatë vitit:** during the year; **gjatë gjithë vitit:** all through the year; **gjatë shekujve:** throughout the centuries, in the course of the centuries; **gjatë mbledhjes:** during the meeting; **gjatë intervistës:** during the interview; **gjatë një udhëtimi:** in the course of a journey. ·

II. *ndajf*. 1. long, a long time: a long while; **sa më gjatë:** as long as possible; **nuk do t'i mbajë gjatë:** it won't take him long. 2. lengthwise; **bie sa gjatë gjerë:** to fall flat on one's back. 3. **nuk di më gjatë:** that's all I know.

gjátë (i,e) *mb*. 1. tall, high in stature; **burrë i gjatë:** a tall man; **i gjatë dhe i hollë:** lanky, tall and thin. 2. long; **flokë të gjata:** long hair; **dy metra i gjatë:** two metres long; **rrugë e gjatë:** a long way; **një kohë e gjatë:** a long time; **ka një kohë të gjatë që nuk e kam parë:** I have not seen him for a long time, I haven't seen him for ages. – *Lok*. **nuk e ka të gjatë:** he is nearing the end, he is going to his doom; **kam gjuhë të gjatë:** to be unable to hold one's tongue, to be long-tongued, to be loose-tongued.

gjatësí,-a *f*. 1. length. 2. *gjeog*. longitude.

gjatovínë *mb. krah*. tall, high in stature.

gjedh,-i *m.sh*. -e *zool*. cattle.

gjej *f.k*. 1. to find; to discover, to come accross; **nuk e gjej dot lapsin:** I can't find my pencil. 2. to fetch; **shko më gjej pak shkumës:** go and fetch some chalk. 3. *(gjej me hamendje)* to guess. 4. to find, to get, to obtain; **gjej një punë:** to find a job; **do të të gjej një vend:** I'll find you a seat. – **gjendem** *f.jv*. 1. to be; to be present; to find oneself; **bimë që gjendet**

kudo: a widely spread plant, a plant found everywhere, a plant which one comes across everywhere. 2. to be, to be found, to stand; **shtëpia gjendet te qoshja**: the house stands on the corner. 3. to be found; to be discovered; **përgjigja nuk I gjendet lehtë**: it is difficult to find an answer to it. 4. **I gjendem dikujt**: to help someone, to be willing to help someone, to come to the aid of.

gjel,-i *m.sh.* **-a** *zool.* cock, rooster; **gjel i egër**: heath cock.

gjélbër (i,e) *mb.* green; **që vjen në të gjelbër**: greenish.

gjelbërím,-i *m.* verdure, greeness, greenery.

gjelbërój *f.jk.* to green, to make green. – **gjelbërohet** *f.jv.* to become green.

gjelbërúar(i,e) *mb.* verdant.

gjeldéti *m. zool.* turkey-cock.

gjéll/ë,-a *f.sh.* **-ë** dish; **bëj gjellë**: to cook (a dish).

gjellëbërës,-i *m.sh.* - cook.

gjellëbërës/e,-ja *f.sh.* - woman cook.

gjellëtór/e,-ja *f.sh.*-e eating house, restaurant.

gjemb,-i *m.sh.* **-a** 1. *bot.* thorn, prickle; **gjemb gomari**: thistle; **gjemb trëndafili**: prickle; **tel me gjemba**: barbed wire; **me gjemba**: prickly .2. **gjemb peshku**: fish-bone. – *Lok.* **rri si mbi gjemba**: to be on pins and needles.

gjembáç-i *m.sh.* **-ë** *bot.* thistle.

gjemí,-a *f.sh.* - *vjet.* steam-boat.

gjéndj/e,-a *f.sh.* **-e** 1.state; **gjendje fizike**: physical condition; **gjendje shoqërore**: social state; **gjendje shpirtërore**: spiritual state, state of mind. 2. situation,

circumstance, condition; **në gjendje të mirë ekonomike**: well-to-do,well off, in easy, in good circumstances; **në gjendje të keqe ekonomike**: in distressed conditions, in straitened circumstances; **në gjendje të mjeruar**: in a sorry plight, in a lamentable state, in a sad plight; *fig.* **në gjendje të vështirë**: in an awkward situation. 3. **gjendje civile**: civil state. – *Lok.* **jam në gjendje (të bëj një gjë)** to be able, to be capable (to do something), to be capable (of doing something); **jam në gjendje të përballoj shpenzimet**: I am able to bear the expenses, I can bear (afford) the expenses.

gjenealogjí,-a *f.sh.* - genealogy.

gjenealogjík,-e *mb.* genealogical; **trungu gjenealogjik i një familjeje**: genealogical tree.

gjenerál,-i *m.sh.* **-ë** *usht.* general.

gjenerát/ë,-a *f.sh.* **-a** generation.

gjeneratór,-i *m.sh.* **-ë** *el.* generator.

gjenerík,-u *m.sh.* **-ë** generic.

gjení,-u *m.sh.* - genius.

gjeniál,-e *mb.* of genius; **Ide gjeniale**: brilliant idea; **vepër gjeniale**: work of genius.

gjenitál,-e *mb.* genital; **organe gjenitale**: genital organs.

gjeodezí,-a *f.* geodesy.

gjeográf,-i *m.sh.* **-ë** geographer.

gjeografí,-a *f.* geography.

gjeografík,-e *mb.* geographical.

gjeológ,-u *m.sh.* **-ë** geologist.

gjeologjí,-a *f.* geology.

gjeologjík,-e *mb.* geological.

gjeomét/ër,-ri *m.sh.* **-ra** geometer, land-surveyor.

gjeometrí,-a *f.* geometry.

gjeometrík,-e *mb.* geometric, geometrical.

gjépura,-t *f.sh.* nonsense, rubbish, trash, drivels, fiddle-faddle.

gjer,-i *m. zool.* dormouse.
gjer *paraf.* 1. till, until, up; **gjer ne-sër:** till tomorrow; **gjer më sot, gjer tani:** up today, until now; **gjer atëhere:** until then; **gjer në:** till, until. 2. to; **gjer në Tiranë:** to Tirana; **që këtu gjer në Tiranë:** from here to Tirana; **gjer këtu:** hitherto.
gjeraqín/ë,-a *f.sh.* -a *zool.* hawk, sparrow-hawk.
gjéras, gjérazi *ndajf.* in the width, widthly, breadthways, breadth-wise.
gjerdán,-i *m.sh.* -ë 1. necklace. 2. gjerdanfishekësh: cartridgebelt.
gjérë *ndajf.* roomily, spaciously; **jam gjerë me banim:** I am roomy with lodging; **flas gjerë e gjatë:** to speak broadly, to speak at length; **tregoj gjerë e gjatë:** to tell in detail.
gjérë (i,e) *mb.* 1. broad, wide; **rru-gë e gjerë:** wide avenue; **derë e gjerë:** wide door; **lumë i gjerë:** broad river. 2. loose, ample; **rrobë e gjerë:** loose gar-ment. 3. vast; **fushë e gjerë:** vast field. 4. roomy, spacious; **banesë e gjerë:** roomy lodging; **për së gjeri:** breadthways, breadthwise.
gjerësí:-af. 1. breadth, width, wide-ness. 2. *gjeog.* gjerësi gjeo-grafike: latitude.
gjerësísht *ndajf.* broadly, widely, extensively, at length.
gjergjéf,-i *m.sh.* -ë loom; **gjer-gjef për të endur:** weaving loom.
gjermán,-i *m.sh.* -ë German.
gjermán,-e *mb.* German.
gjermanísht *ndajf.* in German.
gjermanísht/e,-ja *f.* German.
gjersá *lidh.* until; **prit gjersa të vijë:** wait until he comes.
gjertanísh/ëm(i),-me(e) *mb.* so far, as yet, to date, up to now, up to the present, up to this time;

rezultatet e gjertanishme: the so far results.
gjest,-i *m.sh.* -e gesture.
gjésht/ër,-ra *f. bot.* shih **gjinesh-tër.**
gjetíu *ndajf.* elsewhere.
gjétkë *ndajf.* *krah.* shih **gjetiu.**
gjétur (i,e) *mb.* found; **fëmijë i gjetur:** foundling.
gjeth,-i *m.sh.* -e foliage, leafage; **gjeth për ushqimin e bagë-tive:** foliage (for animals); **del gjethi:** to sprout, to bud.
gjevrék,-u *m.sh.* -ë cracknel.
gjezáp,-i *m.* chloric acid.
gjezdís *f.jk.* to travel.
gjë,-ja *f.sh.* -ra 1. thing, object; **gjë e kotë:** vain thing, futility; **gjë e vogël:** trifle; **çdo gjë:** everything; **vini çdo gjë në vendin e vet:** put everything in its place; **doni gjë tjetër?** do you want anything else? **e bleva për hiç gjë:** I bought it for nothing; **gjë prej gjëje:** nothing whatsoever. 2. **gjë e gjallë:** a) living creature; b) catt-le, livestock. 3. article, line; **gjëra ushqimore:** food-stuff. — *Lok* s'ka gjë: no matter, don't men-tion it, nothing.
gjëegjëz/ë,-a *f.sh.* -a puzzle.
gjëkáfshë *p,pk.* something.
gjëkúndi *ndajf.* somewhere; any-where
gjëm/ë,-a *f.* calamity, fatality, dis-aster, catastrophe.
gjëmëmádh,-e *mb.* sinister, fatal.
gjëmím,-i *m.* 1. rumble, roar, roa-ring, boom; **gjëmim topi:** roar of a canon. 2. thunder; **gjëmim bubullime:** thundering.
gjëmón *f.jv.* 1. to rumble, to roar; **gjëmon topi:** the canon roars. 2. to thunder; **gjëmon qielli:** it thunders.
gjënd/ër,-ra *f.sh.* -ra *anat.* glan-dule, gland; **gjëndra të pësh-**

tymës: salivant glands; gjëndra tuberkulare: tubercular glands.

gjësénd₄gjësendi *p₊pk.* something, anything.

gjëz/ë,-a *f.sh.* -a riddle.

gji₁-ri *m.sh.* -nj 1. bosom, breast; shtrëngoj në gji: to bosom. 2. milk; rrit me gji një fëmijë: to suckle, to nurse a child at the breast; foshnjë gjiri: suckling; zvjerdh nga gjiri një fëmijë: to wean a child. 3. *fig.* bosom; nga gjiri i popullit: from the bosom of the people; në gjirin e familjes së tij: in the bosom of his family. 4. entrail; nga gjiri i tokës: from the entrails of the earth. 5. *gjeog.* gulf, bay.

gjigánt,-i *m.sh.* -ë giant.

gjigánt,-e *mb.* giant, huge, gigantic.

gjilpër/ë,-a *f.sh.* -a 1. needle; gjilpërë për të qepur: needle for stitching; vrima e gjilpërës: eyelet, eye of a needle; shkoj perin në vrimën e gjilpërës: to thread, to pass the thread through the eye of the needle; shpoj me gjilpërë: to prick with a needle; jastëçkë gjilpërash: pin cushion; gjilpërë dyshekësh: packing needle; gjilpërë me kokë: pin. 2. *tek.* gjilpërë e pushkës: hammer; *(e mitralozit)* firing-pin; gjilpërë sahati: spire; gjilpërë busulle: needle. 2. *mjek.* injection; bëj një gjilpërë: to make an injection. − *Lok.* asnjë majë gjilpëre: not a bit

gjilpërýer,-i *m.sh.* packing needle.

gjimnastík/ë,-a *f.* gjymnastics, physical exercises.

gjimnáz,-i *m.sh.* -e college, middle school, gjymnasium.

gjimnazíst,-i *m.sh.* -ë schoolboy, college student.

gjínd/e,-ja *f.* folk, people.

gjinekológ,-u *m.sh.* ₊-ë *mjek.* gynecologist.

gjinekologjí,-a *f. mjek.* gynecology.

gjinësht/ër,-ra *f.sh.* -ra *bot.* gorse, broom.

gjiní,-a *f.sh.* - 1. filiation, relationship, kindred. 2. *gram.* gender. 3. *biol.* genus.

gjinkáll/ë,-a *f.sh.* -a *zool.* cicada.

gjinór/e,-ja *f. gram.* genitive, genitive case, *possessive*

gjips,-i *m.* gypsum.

gjiráf/ë,-a *f.sh.* -a *zool.* giraffe.

gjiríz,-i *m.sh.* -e sewer, sink; ujë gjirizi: sewage.

gjitón,-i *m.sh.* -ë *krah.* neighbour.

gjithandéj *ndajf.* everywhere.

gjithánsh/ëm(i),-me(e) *mb.* encyclopedic, universal, all-round.

gjithashtú *lidh.* a!so, too; gjithashtu edhe unë: I too; gjithashtu edhe për ju: the same to you, all the same.

gjithçká *p.pk.* all, everything; anything; po të shkojë mirë gjithçka … : if everything goes well.

gjithë *p.pk.* all; whole; gjithë bota: all the world; gjithë ditën: all the day, the whole day; me gjithë familjen e tij: with his whole family.

gjithë (i,e) *p.pk.* sh.-(të) all, everything; të gjitha sukseset ia detyrojmë Partisë: we owe all our successes to the Party; i gjithë qyteti: all the town; të gjithë bashkë: all together; të gjithë për një, një për të gjithë: one for all and all for one; nga të gjitha anët: on all sides; from all sides; kjo është e gjitha: that's all; do të t'l them të gjitha: I'm going to tell you everything; ai ha nga të gjitha: he will eat anything; të gjithë ne: all of us; dilni

jashtë të gjithë! get out all
of you l
gjíthë *ndajf.* full; **ishte gjithë gaz:**
he was full of joy; **gjithë shën-
det:** full of life and vigor, in
good health, in the pine of condition.
gjithëfuqísh/ëm(i),-me(e) *mb.*
omnipotent.
gjithësí,-a *f.* universe.
gjithfárë *p.pk.* diverse, various;
all kinds of, all sorts of; **gjith-
farë kafshësh:** all kinds of animals.
gjithhérë *ndajf.* always.
gjithkáh *ndajf. krah.* everywhere.
gjithkúnd *ndajf.* everywhere.
gjithkúsh *p.pk.* each, everybody,
everyone.
gjithmònë *ndajf.* always.
gjithnjè *ndajf.* always.
gjíthsahérë *lidh.* every time.
gjithseclli *p.pk.* everybody, everyone.
gjithséj *ndajf.* in all, in whole, in
total, wholly, totally, utterly.
gjithsekúsh *p.pk.* shih **gjithsecili.**
gjithsesí *ndajf.* anyhow, in any case;
by all means.
gjíz/ë,-a *f.* curd.
gjób/ë,-a *f.sh.* -a fine, penalty.
gjobís *f.k.* to fine. to penalize. –
gjobitem *f.jv.* to be fined.
gjobítj/e,-a *f.* penalty.
gjója *pj.* allegedly; **bëj gjoja:** to
pretend; **gjoja se:** under the pretext that, on the pretence that.
gjoks,-i *m.sh.* -e *anat.* breast,
thorax, chest. – *Lok.* **rrah gjoksin:** to pride oneself on; **i vē
gjoksin punës:** to settle down
to work, to buckle to work.
gjoksgjérë *mb.* broadchested.
gjóksit (i,e) *mb.* pectoral.
gjórë (i,e) *mb.* unlucky, unfortunate; **i gjori:** the unfortunate,
the poor man.
gju,-ri *m.sh.* -nj *anat.* knee; **kupa**

e gjurit: kneecap; **ulem në
gjunjë:** to sit on one's knees;
bie në gjunjë: to kneel. – *Lok.*
i bie në gjunjë dikujt: to kneel
down to someone.
gjúaj *f.k.* 1. to hunt; **gjuaj kafshë të egra:** to hunt game
(wild animals). 2. to shoot, to
hit, to aim; **gjuaj me pushkë:**
to shoot with a gun. 3. **gjuaj
me gurë:** to throw a stone (to
someone). 4. *(topin)* to shoot.
gjúajtës,-i *m.sh.* - 1. shooter,
marksman. 2. *av.* fighter, aircraft,
fighter plane, fighter.
gjúajtj/e,-a *f.sh.* -e 1. shooting
2. *sport. (në bilardo)* stroke,
shot; *(në futboll)* kick.
gjuetár,-i *m.sh.* -ë hunter; **gjue-
tar shpezësh:** fowler.
gjuetí,-a *f.* hunting; **gjueti pa
leje:** poaching; **gjueti drerësh,
lepujsh, dhelprash, derrash:**
deer-stalking, rabbit-shooting (ra-
bbiting), fox-hunting, pig-stick-
ing.
gjúhc/ë,-a *f.sh.* -a *zool.* small
hering.
gjúh/ë,-a *f.* 1. *anat.* tongue; **nxjerr
gjuhën:** to put one's tongue
out; **nxire gjuhën!** show your
tongue! 2. tongue, language;
gjuhë amtare: mother-tongue;
gjuhë e huaj: foreign language.
– *Lok.* **e kam gjuhën të
gjatë:** to be long-tongued; **e
ka gjuhën të shkurtër:** he
is tongue-tied.
gjuhësí,-a *f.* linguistics.
gjuhësór,-e *mb.* linguistic.
gjuhëtár,-i *m.sh.* -ë linguist.
gjúhëz,-a *f.sh.* -a 1. *gjeog. (toke)*
tongue, promontory. 2. claper,
tongue (of a bell, etc.).
gjumásh,-i *m.sh.* -ë sound (heavy)
sleeper.
gjumásh,-e *mb.* sleepful, sleepish.
gjúm/ë,-i *m.* sleep; **gjumë i**

shkurtër: slumber; gjumë i rëndë: sound sleep; gjumë: sleepless; jam nëpër gjumë: to be sleepy (drowsy, slumbery); bëj gjumë të rëndë: to sleep like a log; marr një sy gjumë: to take a nap, to nap, to doze; që të jep gjumë: somniferous.

gjúnjazi ndajf. on one's knees.

gjunjëzím,-i m. 1. kneeling, genuflection, genuflexion. 2. fig. submission.

gjunjëzój f.k. 1. (dikë) to bring (someone) to his knees. 2. fig. to submit, to subdue. – gjunjëzohem f.jv. 1. to kneel, to kneel down, to fall upon one's knees. 2. fig. to bend, to prostrate, to be submitted.

gjurmáshk/ë,-a f.sh. -a light shoe, sock.

gjúrm/ë,-a f.sh. -a 1. footprint, footstep, print track, track, trace; gjurmë kafshe të egër: spoor (of a wild animal). 2. (gjurmë rrote) rut (of a wheel). 3. gjurmë arkeologjike: vestige. – Lok. shkoj pas gjurmëve të dikujt: to follow someone's trail (tracks); ndjek gjurmët e : to follow in the footsteps of; i bie në gjurmët: to pick up the scent (the trail), to scent.

gjurmím,-i m. investigation, search.

gjurmój f.k. to spy upon, to track, to pursue; gjurmoj dikë: to spy someone, to hunt someone out. – gjurmohem f.jv. to be spied (pursued), to be chased.

gjurulídi,-a f. effervescence, mutiny.

gjykát/ë,-a f.sh. -a tribunal, lawcourt; gjykatë për çështje civile: civil tribunal; gjykata penale: policecourt; gjykata e lartë: Supreme Court; gjykatë ushtarake: martial court.

gjykátës,-i m.sh. - judge, magistrate.

gjykatór/e,-ja f.sh. -e hall of justice, court room.

gjykím,-i m. 1. drejt. trial 2. judgment, reasoning.

gjykój l. f.k. 1. to judge; to try; gjykoj dikë për vjedhje: to try someone for theft. 2. sport. to umpire, to referee. II. f.jk. to consider, to think about, to look into the matter.

gjykúar (i,e) mb. judged; i gjykuar në mungesë: judged in absence.

gjykúes,-e mb. drejt. trupi gjykues: the court, the judges.

gjykúesh/ëm(i),-me(e) mb. reasonable, rational.

gjýl/e,-ja f.sh. -e 1. cannon ball, cannon shot, bomb shell. 2. sport. shot; hedh gjylen: to put the shot.

gjym,-i m.sh. -a copper-jug.

gjýmtë (i, e) mb. crippled.

gjymtí,-a f. infirmity, invalidity.

gjymtím,-i m.sh. -e mutilation, maiming.

gjymtój f.k. to mutilate, to maim, to limb. – gjymtohem f.jv. to be mutilated.

gjymtýr/ë,-a f.sh. -ë 1. anat. limb. 2. mat. side (of an equation).

gjynáh,-u m.sh. -e sin; laj gjynahet: to atone, to expiate a sin; sa gjynah! what a pity.

gjynahqár,-i m.sh. -ë sinner.

gjyp,-i m.sh. -a zool. vulture.

gjyq,-i m.sh. -e 1. trial, judicial examination; gjyq me dyer të mbyllura: trial behind closed doors; dal në gjyq: to appear before a court; hedh në gjyq: to sue, to bring suit, to bring to court. 2. gjyq ushtarak: martial court; kryetar gjyqi: chief judge; thirrje në gjyq: summons; shpenzime gjyqi: law

costs; **humbas një gjyq:** to lose a lawsuit.
gjyqësór,-e *mb.* judiciary, judicial.
gjyqtár,-i *m.sh.* -**ë** 1. judge, magistrate. 2. *sport.* umpire, referee.
gjyrýk,-u *m.sh.* -**e** bellows (of a smith).
gjysmák,-e *mb. (njeri)* half-witted (man); **masa gjysmake:** halfway measures, partial measures; **bëj punë gjysmake:** to do things by halves.
gjýsm/ë,-a *f.sh.* -**a** 1. half; **gjysmë leku:** half-penny; **gjysmë ore;** half an hour; **ora është një e gjysmë:** it is half past one; **e lë punën në gjysmë:** to leave something half-way; **gjysma e së keqes:** small harm; **gjysmë i dehur:** half drunk; **me gjysmë çmimi:** at half price; **gjysmë filxhani:** half a cup; **e ndajmë (diçka, një shumë) gjysmë për gjysmë:** to go shares, to go half and half, to go fifty-fifty (in something), to share equally; **ndaj për gjysmë:** to cut in halves; **ndalem në gjysmë të rrugës:** to stop halfway; **gjysmë i vdekur:** half-dead; **gjysmë**

i egër: half wild; **gjysmë i fjetur:** half asleep; **gjysmë njeriu:** weak, feeble; **flas me gjysmë zëri:** to speak in a subdued voice (in an undertone, under one's breath). 2.sole; **këpucë me gjysma gome:** rubber-soled shoes; **u vë (u hedh) gjysma këpucëve:** to sole one's shoes.
gjysmëbósht,-i *m.sh.* -**e** semiaxis.
gjysmëerrësír/ë,-a semidarkness.
gjysmëfinále,-ja semi-final.
gjysmëlargësí,-a *f. sport.* half-length.
gjysmëzyrtár,-e *mb.* semi-official.
gjysmërr/éth,-ethi *m.sh.* -**athë** halfcircle.
gjysmësfér/ë,-a *f.sh.*-**a** half a sphere.
gjysmój *f.k.* to halve. – **gjysmohet** *f.jv.* to be halved.
gjysh,-i *m.sh.* -**ër** grandfather, granddad.
gjýsh/e,-ja *f.sh.* -**e** grandmother, granny.
gjyvéç,-i *m.* stew.
gjyzlýkë,-t *m.sh.* glasses, eye-glass, spectacles; **gjyzlykë dielli:** sunglasses.

H

h, H (letter of the Albanian alphabet; it is combined with the consonants d, s, t, x and z giving five letter combinations as follows: dh, sh, th, xh, zh) h, H.
ha I. *f.k.* (p.t. **hëngra,** p.p. **ngrënë**)

1. to eat; **ha bukë:** to take a repast (a meal), to eat; **ha darkë:** to dine, to lunch; **ha mëngjes:** to breakfast, to take the breakfast; **ha me tamaqarllëk:** to eat greedily; **ulem të ha:** to sit

down to table. 2. *(ndryshku)* to gnaw, to nibble, to corrode. 3. *(qeni)* to bite. 4. *fig.* **ha grushta:** to take (to receive) blows. II. *f.jk.* **më ha (trupi):** my body is itching; **më ha shpina:** my back is itching. – *Lok.* **i ha paratë dikujt:** to consume someone's fortune, to spend someone's money wastefully; **ha të shara:** to be scolded, to be chidden, to be offended, to bear offenses; **ha fjalën:** to eat (to go back on) one's words; **ha fjalët:** to mince the words; **më ha meraku:** to worry oneself; **i ha hakën dikujt:** to be iniquitous towards someone. – **hahem** *f.jv.* 1. *(hahem me një kundërshtar)* to vie, to rival, to strive (with a rival), to compete, to contend; **hahem me fjalë:** to bandy words; **hahem në pazar:** to bargain about the price (of an article). 2. to be eaten; **kjo gjellë nuk hahet:** this dish is uneatable; **më hahet:** to be hungry. 3. *(rroba, këpucë)* to wear, to wear away.

ha *fj.plk.* (abbreviation of **hektar,** shih).

habér,-i *m.sh.* -e *gj.fol.* 1. news; **haber i mirë:** good news. 2. knowledge; **s'kam haber nga shkenca:** not to have the slightest idea of science, to be absolutely ignorant of science.

habí,-a *f.* surprise, astonishment, amazement; **me habi:** with astonishment.

habís *f.k.* to astonish, to astound, to amaze, to perplex. – **habitem** *f.jv.* to be astonished, to be astounded, to be amazed.

habítj/e,-a *f.* amazement, astonishment, wonder.

habitór/e,-ja *f. gram.* admirative.

habítsh/ëm(i),-me(e) *mb.* astonishing.

háir,-i *m.* profit, gain, utility; **me hair qoftë!** may it be profitable!; **bëfsh hair!** may you have good luck!

haját,-i *m.sh.* -e porch, lobby.

hájde! *pasth.* come! come on!

hajdút,-i *m.sh.* -ë thief, robber, stealer, burglar; **hajdut dyqanesh:** burglar, shop-lifter; **hajdut xhepash:** pickpocket.

hajmalí,-a *f.sh.* - amulet, talisman.

hajván,-i *m.sh.* -ë 1. animal, beast. 2. *fig.* beast, brute, stupid.

hak,-u *m.sh.* **haqe** *gj.fol.* 1. remuneration. 2. due (what is owed or required by an obligation); **i jap hakun (dikujt):** to give his due to someone. 3. reason; **kam hak:** to be right, to be in the right. 4. vengeance, revenge; **marr hakun:** to have (get) revenge (for): to take vengeance on.

hakërrím,-i *m.* threatening (menacing) tone.

hakërróhem (i) *(dikujt)* *f.jv.* to threaten, to menace (someone).

hakmárrës,-i *m.sh.* - avenger, revenger.

hakmárrës,-e *mb.* revengeful, vindicative.

hakmárrj/e,-a *f.* revenge, vengeance.

hakmérrem *f.jv.* to revenge oneself, to have one's revenge.

halé,-ja *f.sh.- gj.fol.* shih **nevojtore.**

hál/ë,-a *f.sh.* -a 1. *(halë kalliri)* chaf. 2. *(halë-peshku)* fish-bone. 3. *(halë në sy):* mote (in the eye). – *Lok.* **më ka halë në sy:** he hates me, he has a grudge against me.

halíç,-i *m.sh.* -ë pebble.

halór,-e *mb. bot.* coniferous.

halórë,-t *m.sh. bot.* conifers.

hall,-i *m.sh.* -e scrape, trouble; **bie në hall:** to get into a scrape; **jam në hall:** to be in a trouble, to be into scrape, to be in na-

rrow circumstances; **plot halle:** full of troubles, mint of troubles.— *Lok.* **e bëra nga halli:** I did it out of necessity.
hallakás *f.k.* to scatter, to disperse here and there. — **hallakatem** *f.jv.* 1. to be dispersed. 2. *fig.* to get about, to get abroad, to get out.
hallakátj/e,-a *f.* dispersion; **hallakatje e mendimeve:** incoherence of opinions.
halláll *ndajf.* **e ka hallall;** he well deserves it; **bëj hallall:** to give with all one's heart.
hallát,-i *m.sh.* **-e** tool, instrument.
hallavítem *f.jv.* to dawdle, to loiter, to lose one's time.
hallexhí,-u *m.sh.* **nj** needy person.
háll/ë,-a *f.sh.* **-a** aunt (father's sister).
hállk/ë,-a *f.sh.* **-a** 1. link. 2. handcuff; **i hodh hallkën një të burgosuri:** to handcuff a prisoner. 3. *fig.* link; **hallkë e dobët:** weak link.
hállv/ë,-a *f.* halvah.
ha náll,-i *m.sh.* **hamej** coolie, porter; **hamall porti:** docker, stevedore, lighterman.
hamám,-i *m.sh.* **-e** steam-bath, Turkish-bath.
hambár,-i *m.sh.* **-e** 1. granary, bin. 2. *det. (i anijes)* hold.
haméndj/e,-a *f.* guesswork, supposition, presumption, conjecture; **gjej me hamendje:** to guess.
hámës,-i *m.sh.* - glutton, gormandiser.
hamshór,-i *m.sh.* **-ë** *zool.* stallion.
hamullór/e,-ja *f.* stubble.
han,-i *m.sh.* **-e** inn, roadhouse, pothouse; **u bë han shtëpia:** the house has become a low pub.
hangár,-i *m.sh.* **-ë** hangar.
hánko,-ja *f. vjet.* lady.

hanxhár,-i *m.sh.* **-ë** butcher's knife chopping-knife.
hanxhí,-u *m.sh.* **-nj** inn-keeper.
hap,-i *m.sh.* **-a** 1. step; footstep, pace; **hap i madh:** stride, long step; **eci me hapa të mëdha:** to stride, to walk with long steps; **me hapa të shpejta:** with hasty steps, at a quick pace; **hap pas hapi:** step by step; **mbaj hapin me dikë:** to keep step with someone; **mbaj hapat:** to stop. 5. *fig.* progress; **keni bërë shumë hapa përpara:** you have made great progress.
hap,-i *m.sh.* **-e** *mjek.* pill.
hap I. *f.k.* 1. to open; **hap derën:** to open the door; **hap derën me kyç:** to unlock the door; *(shishen etj.)* to open, to uncork (a bottle). 2. **hap gojën:** to open the mouth; **hap sytë:** a) to open the eyes; b) *fig.* to look out, to watch. 3. *fig.* **hap veshët:** to prick the ears, to prick up one's ears. 4. *mjek.* **hap një kufomë:** to dissect a cadaver (a corpse); **hap një abces:** to open an abscess. 5. **hap rrugë:** to cut (to blast) a way (through); **i hap rrugën dikujt, diçkaje:** to pave the way for. 6. **hap tokë të re:** to break up new land. 7. **i hap vend dikujt:** to make room for someone. 8. **hap rubinetin:** tu turn on the tap. 9. **hap zjarr:** to fire, to discharge (firearms). 10. *fig.* **hap zemrën:** to open one's heart.
II. *f.jk.* **po hapin lulet:** the flowers bloom, (blow up).-**hapem** *f.jv.* 1. to open, to come open; **hapet me forcë:** to fly open. 2. *fig. (një epokë e re)* to open, to begin (a new era). 3. *fig.* to open one's heart; **i hapem dikujt:** to confide in someone, to tell one's private thought's to

someone. 4. *(koha)* to clear up; **po hapet koha**: the weather is clearing up. Lok. **hapuni!** stand off!

hápës,-i *m.sh.* -a key.

hapësír/ë,-a *f.sh.* -a space.

hápj/e,-a *f.sh.* -e 1. opening; **hapja e mbledhjes**: the opening of the meeting. 2. *bujq. (tokash të reja)* grubbing, opening up (of new land).

háptas *ndajf.* openly, fairly; **flas haptas**: to speak openly.

hápur (i,e) *mb.* open, overt; **pres me krahë hapur**: to receive cordially; **me zemër të hapur**: open-heartedly.

harabél,-i *m.sh.* -a *zool.* sparrow.

haráç,-i *m.* tribute.

harám *m.* ill-gotten goods.

harár,-i *m.sh.* -ë *krah.* sac.

harbí,-a *f.sh.* - gunrod (for loading a rifle).

harbój *f.jk.* to ramble; **hardhitë qenë harbuar mbi gardh**: the vines rambled over the fence.

harbúar (i, e) *mb.* enraged; **kalë i harbuar**: frisky horse.

harbút,-i *m.sh.* -ë ill-bred person, swinish person, rugged person, uncouth person, ill-mannered person, brutal person.

harbút,-e *mb.* uncouth, uncivil, ill-bred, rud, rough, bestial, boorish, cad, vulgar; brutal.

harbutëri,-a *f.* brutality, rudeness, roughness, uncivility; **me harbutëri**: brutally.

hardhí,-a *f.sh.* - *bot.* 1. vine plant; **rrënjë hardhie**: vinestock; **degë hardhie**: vine-branch; **sëmundje e hardhisë**: chlorosis.

hardhúc/ë,-a *f.sh.* -a *zool.* lizard.

haré,-ja *f.* joy, gaiety, merriment, gladness.

harém,-i *m.sh.* -e harem, haram, hareem.

haréng/ë,-a *f. zool.* herring; **harengë e tymósur**: red herring.

har/k,-ku *m.sh.* -qe 1. arch; **hark ure (qemer)**: arch of a bridge. 2. **hark violine**: bow (of a violin). 3. *el.* **hark elektrik**: electric arc. 4. *gjeom.* **hark rrethi**: arc (of a circle). 5. **hark shigjete**: bow; **shtie me hark**: to shoot (an arrow) with a bow.

harkëtár,-i *m.sh.* -ë bowman, archer.

harlís *f.k.* to make exuberant (plants). — **harliset** *f.jv.* to be exuberant (a plant).

harlísj/e,-a *f.* exuberance (of plants).

harmoní,-a *f.* harmony; **me harmoni**: harmoniously; **jetoj në harmoni me gruan**: to live in harmony with one's wife.

harmonísh/ëm(i),-me(e) *mb.* harmonious.

harmonizím,-i *m.* harmonization.

harmonizój *f.k.* to harmonize. — **harmonizohet** *f.jv.* to be harmonized.

hárp/ë,-a *f.sh.* -a *muz.* harp.

hárt/ë,-a *f.sh.* -a *gjeog.* map; **harta e botës**: the map of the world.

hartím,-i *m.sh.* -e composition; **shkruaj një hartim**: to write a composition.

hartój *f.k.* to compile, to compose. — **hartohet** *f.jv.* to be compiled.

hartúes,-i *m.sh.* - compiler, composer.

harxh,-i *m.sh.* -e shih **harxhim**.

harxhím,-i *m.sh.* -e 1. expenditure. 2. consummation.

harxhój *f.k.* 1. to spend, to expense. 2. to consume, to spend; **harxhoj kohën**: to spend the time. — **harxhohet** *f.jv.* 1. to be spent (expended). 2. to be consumed. — *Lok.* **harxhoj frymën kot**: to waste someone's breath (words).

harr *f.k.* to weed, to free from weeds.

harrés/ë,-a *f.* 1. oblivion, forgetfulness; mbetet në harresë: to fall into oblivion. 2. missing, omission.

hárrj/e,-a *f.* weeding.

harrój *f.k.* 1. to forget; mos harroni: don't forget. 2. to omit, to miss; harroj një fjalë: to omit a word. — harrohem *f.jv.* to be forgotten.

harrúar (i,e) *mb.* 1. oblivious, forgetful. 2. omitted.

has I. *f.k.* to come across, to meet, to encounter; has dikë: to meet someone.
II. *f.jk.* to be in presence, to face; has në një vështirësi: to face a difficulty. — hasem *f.jv.* to meet with, to fall in with.

hasét,-i *m.* envy, grudge; jealousy; e kam haset dikë: to have a grudge against someone, to bear someone a grudge; to be jealous of someone.

hasetç/i,-eshë *mb.* envious, covetous.

haséll,-i *m.sh.* -e *bot.* barley of pasture.

hásër,-ra *f.sh.* -ra mat, straw-mat.

hasm,-i *m.sh.* -ë enemy, foe.

hasmërí,-a *f.sh.* - enmity, feud.

hasmërój *f.k.* to make hostile. — hasmërohem *(me dikë) f.jv.* to become an enemy (of someone).

hásha *ndajf.* bëj hasha *(dikë, diçka)* to deny, to gainsay (someone, something).

hashásh,-i *m.* hashish; bima e hashashit: white popy.

hatá,-ja *f.sh.* disaster, catastrophe.

hatásh/ëm(i),-me(e) *mb.* 1. excellent, wonderful. 2. disastrous, catastrophic.

hatër,-i *m.sh.* -e favour, favouritism; mbaj me hatër dikë: to favour someone; për hatrin e: for

the sake of; për hatrin tim: for my sake.

hátulla,-t *f.sh.* loft (the space under the roof).

haúr,-i *m.sh.* -e shih ahur.

haúz,-i *m.sh.* -e basin, pond; hauz për shtimin e peshqve: fishpond.

havá,-ja *f. vjet.* climate; ndërroj havà: to change climate. — *Lok.* fjalë në havà: idle talk.

haván,-i *m.sh.* -ë mortar (for pounding); dorezë havani: pestle; shtyp në havan: to pound. — *Lok.* rrah ujë në havan: to flog a dead horse, to beat the air.

havjár,-i *m.* caviar.

haxhí,-u *m.sh.* -lerë pilgrim.

haxhillëk,-u *m.* pilgrimage.

hazdísem *f.jv.* 1. to go unrestrained, to run wild. 2. to have one's fling.

hazdísur (i, e) *mb.* unrestrained.

hazër *ndajf. gj.fol.* ready.

hedh *f.k.* (p.t. hodha, pp. hedhur) 1. to throw, to cast, to fling, to launch, to toss, to dash, to project, to hurl; hedh një gur: to throw a stone, to toss a stone, to launch a stone; hidhe poshtë: drop it! 2. hedh në erë një urë, një ndërtesë: to blow up. 3. hedh në erë drithin (grurin, elbin etj.) to fan corns, to winnow (wheat, etc.) 4. hedh shigjetën: to shoot an arrow. 5. hedh themelet e një ndërtese: to lay the foundations of a building. 6. hedh në gjyq: to sue, to bring a lawsuit against. 7. hedh armët: to lay down arms. 8. hedh poshtë kundërshtarin: to throw down a rival. 9. hedh poshtë një argument: to refute an argument. 10. hedh një sy: to cast an eye, to cast a glance. 11. hedh një gotë: to drink a glass. 12. hedh në dorë:

to take unlawful possession of.
13. **ia hedh fajin tjetrit:** to
impute a fault to another, to
shift the blame to another. 14.
hedh një fjalë: to hint (at), to
refer (to), to allude (to). 15. **ia
hedh dikujt:** to outwit; to cheat
someone. 16. **hedh valle:** to
dance in ring. — **hidhem** *f.jv.* to
fling, to throw oneself, to pimp,
to spring, to hop, to leap; **hidhem përpjetë:** to jump up;
i hidhem në grykë dikujt:
to fall upon a person's neck, to
attack someone.
hédhj/e,-a *f.* 1. throwing, casting.
2. *sport.* **hedhje e diskut:** discus throwing; **hedhje e drithit
në erë:** winnowing of wheat.
3. **hedhje poshtë e një argumenti:** refutation of an argument. 4. *(kërcim)* bound, jump,
leap, spring. 5. *(e fajit)* imputa-
tion. 6. **hedhje në short:** drawing of lots.
hédhur (i,e) *mb.* 1. enterprising,
frisky, lively, active, pushing,
energetic; **djalë i hedhur:** pushing fellow. 2. *(trup)* slim,
slender.
hedhurín/ë,-a *f.sh.* -a trash, refuse, rubbish.
hegjemoní,-a *f.* hegemony.
hegjemón,-e *mb.* hegemonic.
héjbe,-t *f.sh.* saddle-bag.
héjd/ë,-a *f. bot.* buckwheat.
hákës,-i *m. anat.* clavicle, collar-
bone.
hektár,-i *m.sh.* -ë hectare.
hektolít/ër,-ri *m.sh.* -ra hecto-
litre.
hékur,-i *m.sh.* -a 1. iron; **hekur-
beton:** concreted iron; **hekur i
skuqur:** brand iron, red-hot iron;
shufër hekuri: iron bar; **mineral hekuri:** ironstone; **punishte
hekuri:** ironworks. 2. *(për hekurosje)* flat-iron, smoothing —

iron; **u jap një hekur** *(rrobave)*:
to iron (the clothes). 3. *sh.*
handcuffs, manacles; **i hedh he-
kurat dikujt:** to handcuff someone. — *Lok.* **u bë për hekura:**
he has gone mad, he must be
shut in an asylum.
hekurína,-t *f.sh.* shih **hekurishte.**
hekuríshte,-t *f.sh.* scrap-iron, scrap
metal; **dyqan hekurishtesh:**
ironmongery.
hekurkthýes,-i *m.sh.* - iron-ben-
der.
hekurós *f.k.* to iron. — **hekurosem**
f.jv. to iron one's clothes.
hekurósj/e,-a *f.* ironing; **hekur për
hekurosje:** flat-iron, smoothing-
iron, iron.
hekurpunúes,-i *m.sh.* - ironworker.
hékurt (i,e) *mb.* 1. irony, of iron.
2. *fig.* iron; **disiplinë e hekurt:**
iron discipline.
hekurúdh/ë,-a *f.sh.* -a railway,
railroad; **binar hekurudhe:** rail,
railway bed.
hekurudhór,-e *mb.* railway.
helbeté *ndajf. vjet.* of course, naturally.
helík/ë,-a *f.sh.* -a propeller.
helikoptér,-i *m.sh.* -ë helicopter.
helioterapí,-a *f.* heliotherapy.
helm,-i *m.sh.* -e 1. poison, venom,
toxic, bane; **helm i fortë:**
virulent poison; **me helm:** venomous. 2. *fig.* **jam në helm:** to
be in mourning. 3. affliction; **jam
bërë helm:** to be grieved.
helmatís *f.k.* to poison. — **helma-
tisem** *f.jv.* to be poisoned.
helmatísj/e,-a *f.* poisoning, intoxication.
helmatúes,-e *mb.* venomous, poisonous, toxic.
helmét/ë,-a *f.sh.* -a helmet, casque.
helmím,-i *m.* poisoning, intoxication; **helmim gjaku:** blood
poisoning.
helmój *f.k.* 1. to poison. 2. *fig.* to

afflict. − **helmohem** *f.jv.* 1. to be poisoned. 2. *fig.* to be afflicted, to be grieved.

helmúar (i,e) *mb.* 1. poisoned. 2. *fig.* desolated, afflicted.

helmúes,-e *mb.* venomous, poisonous, deleterious; **lëndë helmuese:** deleterious matter.

hell,-i *m.sh.* hej spit, broach, skewer; **shkoj në hell:** to skewer, to spit; **pjek në hell:** to roast in a spit.

hematít,-i *m. min.* hematite, bloodstone.

hemisfér/ë,-a *f.sh.* **-a** *gjeog.* hemisphere.

hemorragjí,-a *f. mjek.* hemorrhage.

hemorroíde,-t *f.sh. mjek.* hemorrhoids, *fam.* (bleeding) piles.

hendé/k,-ku *m.sh.* **-qe** 1. ditch; **hendek rrethues (i një fortese):** moat, trench. 2. *fig.* gap, breach; **hendeku midis të pasurve dhe të varfërve në kapitalizëm:** the ˍgap between the rich and the poor in capitalism. − *Lok.* **e hedh hendekun:** to overcome a difficulty, to get out of trouble.

heq I. *f.k.* 1. to pull off, to pull out, to take off, to put off; **heq kapelën:** to take off one's hat; **heq këpucët:** to take off one's shoes; **heq çorapet:** to pull off one's stockings. 2. *(dhëmbin):* to extract, to have a tooth pulled, to have a tooth out. 3. **heq rrobat:** to put off clothes, to take off one's clothes, to undress. 4. *(heq një gozhdë):* to draw (a nail). 5. *(heq një njollë)* to wipe a stain. 6. *mat.* **heq një numër nga një tjetër:** to take; **heq pesë nga njëzeta:** to take five from twenty. 7. *gjeom.* **heq një vijë:** to draw a line; **heq një rreth:** to circumscribe a circle. 8. **heq zvarrë:** to drag, to trail. 9. **heq**

pjesë të panevojshme nga një libër: to expurgate 10. **heq cigaren:** to puff at a cigarette. 11. **heq shpirt:** to expire, to be dying, to breathe one's last breath. − *Lok.* **heq dorë:** to renounce; to give up; **heq dorë nga një besim:** to abjure, to forswear; **heq qafe:** to get rid of; **heq të zitë e ullirit:** to suffer extremely. − **hiqem** *f.jv.* 1. **hiqem zvarrë:** to crawl, to creep along. 2. **hiqem mënjanë:** to withdraw apart. 3. **hiqem si i ditur:** to assume the appearance of a learned man.

II. *f.jk.* *(heq oxhaku)* to draw out smoke (of a chimney).

héqj/e,-a *f.sh.* **-e** 1. abolition; **heqje e privilegjeve:** abolition of privileges; **heqje e zakoneve:** interdiction of customs. 2. **heqje e një llotarie:** drawing of a lottery. 3. **heqje e një dhëmbi:** extraction of a tooth, pulling out of a tooth. 4. **heqje e pjesëve të panevojshme nga një libër:** expurgation.

héqur (i,e) *mb.* emaciated; **fytyrë e hequr:** emaciated face.

herák,-e *mb.* early, early-rising.

hérdhe,-t *f.sh. anat.* testicles.

heretík,-u *m.sh.* **-ë** heretic.

herezí,-a *f.sh.* - heresy.

hér/ë,-a *f.* time; **një herë:** once, one time; **dy herë:** twice, two times; **një herë e mirë:** once and for all; **disa herë:** several times, sometimes; **shumë herë:** many times; **më se një herë:** many a time; **edhe një herë:** once more; **një herë në javë:** once a week; **herën e fundit:** last time; **herën tjetër:** next time; **herë pas here:** now and then, at intervals, from time to time, time by time; **sa herë që:** whenever; **një herë e një kohë:**

once upon a time; *mat.* **dy herë
katër bëjnë tetë**; two times
four is eight.

hérë-hérë *ndajf.* at times, sometimes; **herë-herë ai është se-
rioz**: sometimes he is serious

hérët *ndajf.* early; **ngrihem herët**;
to get up early; **vij herët**: to come betimes (early); **vij shumë
herët**: to arrive before time.

hermelin/ë,-a *f. zool.* ermine.

hérni/e,-a *f. anat.* hernia.

heró,-i *m.sh.* **-nj** hero.

heroík,-e *mb.* heroical, heroic.

heroikísht *ndajf.* heroically.

heroín/ë,-a *f.sh.* **-a** heroine.

heroíz/ëm,-mi *m.sh.* **-a** heroism.

hérsh/ëm(i),-me(e) *mb.* 1. old;
ancient. 2. *(frutë)* early; **fiq të
hershëm**: early figs.

hesáp,-i *m.sh.* **-e** count, reckoning;
bëj hesap: to reckon; **prish pa
hesap**: to spend lavishly; **vë
(zë, përfshij) në hesap**: to
count in. – *Lok.* **në hesap tim**:
to my account; **s'më dalin hesapet**: to be out in one's rec-
konings; **për hesap të dikujt**:
on someone's account (behalf);
për hesapin tim: as for me;
i bëj hesapet pa hanxhiun:
to reckon without one's host;
me hesap: cheap, at small cost;
**kam një hesap të vjetër për
të larë me dikë**: to have an
old score to settle with someone;
i kërkoj hesap dikujt: to call
(to bring) someone to account;
**i rregulloj hesapin (qejfin) di-
kujt**: to settle someone's hash;
është tjetër hesap: that. is
another pair of shoes, that is quite
a different kettle of fish.

hesht *f.jk.* to hold one's tongue,
to be silent, to keep silent,

heshti *.pasth.* hold your tongue!,
keep silent! keep quiet! mum!
keep mum!

hésht/ë,-a *f.sh.* **-a** spear.

héshtj/e,-a *f.* silence; **heshtje
varri**: death-like silence, dead-
calm. – *Lok.* **kaloj në heshtje
një çështje**: to slur over a
question.

héshtur (i,e) *mb.* silent; tacit,
taciturn.

hetím,-i *m.sh.* **-e** inquiry; **hetim
paraprak**: inquest; **bëj hetí-
me**: to hold (to conduct) an
inquiry, to inquire, to make in-
vestigations.

hetój *f.k.* to inquire, to inquest. –
hetohet *f.jv.* to be inquired.

hetúes,-i *m.sh.* - inquirer.

hetuesí,-a *f.* inquest.

hezitím,-i *m.* hesitation, hesitancy;
pa hezitim: unhesitatingly.

hezitój *f.k.* to hesitate.

hën/ë,-a *f.* moon; **hënë e re**:
new moon; **hënë e plotë**: full
moon; **dritë hëne**: moonlight;
rreze hëne: moon beam. –
Lok. **një herë në hënë**: once
in a blue moon.

hën/ë,(e)-a(e) *f.sh.* **-a(të)** Mon-
day.

hënór,-e *mb.* lunar.

hëpërhë *ndajf.* for the present,
for the time being.

hi,-ri *m.sh.* **-ra** ash; cinders; **bëj
shkrumb e hi**: to burn to ashes
(to cinders); **hirat e qymyrgurit
të djegur**: cinders; **kuti për
mbledhjen e hirave**: fender(of
a chimney); **bojë hiri**: grey,
ashen (ashy, cinereous) grey. –
Lok. **i hedh hi syve dikujt**: to
throw dust in someone's eyes.

hibríd,-i *m.sh.* **-e** hybrid, cross-
breed.

hibríd,-e *mb.* hybrid.

hiç *p.pk.* nothing; at all; **nuk di
gjë hiç**: I know nothing; **hiç
fare**: not at all.

hiç,-i *m.* nothing, nothingness, mere nothing, nought. — *Lok.* **u ngrit nga hiçi:** he sprang of a low condition; **filloj nga hiçi:** to start from scratch.

híd/e,-ja *f.sh.* -e *bot.* jujube.

hidrát,-i *m.sh.* -e hydrate.

hidraulík,-u *m.sh.* -ë plumber.

hidraulík,-e *mb.* hydraulic; **punime hidraulike:** water-works; **rrotë hidraulike:** water-wheel.

hidraulík/ë,-a *f.* hydraulics.

hidrocentrál,-i *m.sh.* -e hydropower station.

hidrofobí,-a *f.* hydrophobia.

hidrografí,-a *f.* hydrography.

hidrogjén,-i *m.* hydrogen.

hidropizí,-a *f.mjek.* common dropsy

hidroplán,-i *m.sh.* -ë hydroplane, water-plane.

hídhem *f.jv.* shih **hedh.**

hidhërím,-i *m.sh.* -e affliction, sorrow, sorriness, sadness, bitterness; **hidhërim i thellë:** deep affliction, heartache; **me hidhërim:** sorrily, sorrowfully; **me hidhërim të madh:** with deep affliction.

hidhërój *f.k.* 1. to afflict, to sadden, to grieve. 2. to embitter, to make bitter. — **hidhërohem** *f.jv.* to be afflicted.

hidhërúar (i,e) *mb.* 1. sad, afflicted, ful lof grief, sorrowful, painful; **jam i hidhëruar:** I feel sad. 2. bitter (of taste).

hídhët (i,e) *mb.* bitter (of taste), acrid.

hídhur (i,e) *mb.* 1. bitter, acrid. 2. *fig.* painful; **marr një lajm të hidhur:** to receive sad news.

higjién/ë,-a *f.* hygiene.

higjieník,-e *mb.* hygienic.

híj/e,-a *f.sh.* -e 1. shade, shadow, umbrage; **nën hijen e fikut:** under the shade of the fig-tree; **vend me hije:** shady (shaded, umbrageous) place. 2. apparition.

3. suitability; **kjo rrobë ju ka hije:** this cloth suits you; **nuk ju ka hije të silleni kështu:** it is not proper for you to behave so.

hijerëndë *mb.* imposing, grave.

hijeshí,-a *f.* grace, gracefulness, charm; **plot hijeshi:** charming; **me hijeshi:** handsomely; **pa hijeshi:** graceless.

híjsh/ëm (i),-me(e) *mb.* graceful, charming; **sjellje e hijshme:** becoming behaviour; **sjellje jo e hijshme:** unbecoming behaviour; **kjo nuk është e hijshme për ju:** that is not proper(suitable) for you.

hík/ërr,-rra *f.* 1. sour-milk. 2. *bot.* buckwheat.

híl/e,-ja *f.sh.* -e trick, trickery, fraud; **bëj hile:** to trick; **me hile:** trickily, fraudulently.

hileqár,-i *m.sh.* -e trickster, defrauder.

hileqár,-e *mb.* fraudulent.

híme,-t *f.sh.* bran.

himn,-i *m.sh.* -e hymn; **himni kombëtar:** the national anthem.

hingëllím/ë,-a *f.sh.* -a neigh (of a horse).

hingëllín *f.jk.* to neigh.

hínk/ë,-a *f.sh.* -a funnel (for liquids).

hípi I. *f.jk.* 1. to mount, to climb; **i hipi kalit:** to mount a horse. 2. *(hipi në pemë)* to climb up (a tree) 3. *(hipi në anije)* to go on board (of a ship), to embark. 4. *(hipi në mal)* to ascend (a mountain). 5. to rise; **në vendet kapitaliste dhe revizioniste çmimet hipin vazhdimisht:** the prices rise up constantly in the capitalist and revisionist countries. II. *f.k.* to rise up, to tower; **e hipi djalin në kalë:** he got his son on horseback.

hípj/e,-a *f.* 1. climb, ascent. 2. rise; **hipja e çmimeve:** rise of prices

hipodróm,-i *m.sh.* -e hippodrome.
hipokrit,-i *m.sh.* -ë hypocrite.
hipokrít,-e *mb.* hypocritical, false.
hipokrizí,-a *f.* hypocrisy.
hipoték/ë,-a *f. drejt.* mortgage.
hipotenúz/ë,-a *f.sh.* -a *gjeom.* hypotenuse.
hipotéz/ë,-a *f.sh.* -a hypothesis.
híqem *f.jv.* shih heq.
hír,-i *m.* 1. sake; për hir të tij: for his sake; për hir tim: for my sake. 2. will, willing, goodwill; me hir: with a good grace; me hir a me pahir: goodwill or badwill, willingly or unwillingly, willingly or reluctantly, willy-nilly.
hirësí,-a *f. fet.* 1. holiness. 2. worship, eminence.
hirplótë *mb.* shih hirshëm(i).
hírsh/ëm(i),-me(e) *mb.* graceful, attractive, charming.
hírtë(i,e) *mb.* greyish, grayish, cinerary.
hírr/ë,-a *f.* whey.
hís/e,-ja *f.sh.* -e share, part, portion.
histerí,-a *f.* hysteria.
histerík,-e *mb.* hysterical.
historí,-a *f.* 1. history; historia e Shqipërisë: history of Albania. 2. story; tregoj një histori për: to tell a story about.
historián,-i *m.sh.* -ë historian.
historík,-e *mb.* 1. historical; monumente historike: historical monuments. 2. historic, memorable; fjalim historik: historic speech.
historikísht *ndajf.* historically.
híth/ër,-ra *f.sh.* -ra *bot.* nettle.
hobé,-ja *f.sh.* - sling; gjuaj me hobe: to sling.
hój/e,-a *f.sh.* -e honey-comb.
hójëz,-a *f.sh.* -a alveolus.
holandéz,-i *m.sh.* -e Dutchman.
holandéz,-e *mb.* Dutch.
hólla,-t (të) *f.sh.* 1. money, fam. cash; me të holla në dorë.

in cash. 2. *(para të vogla, të shkoqura)* small change, small money.
hóllë *ndajf.* 1. lightly; vishem hollë: to dress lightly. 2. jam hollë *(me para)*: to be short of money. 3. bluar hollë: small ground.
hóllë (i,e) *mb.* 1. *(i hollë nga trupi)* thin, lean, slim (of body); i hollë dhe i gjatë: lanky. 2. *(zë)* keen, sharp. 3. libër i hollë: thin book. 4. shi i hollë (i imtë) drizzling rain. 5. delicate; shije e hollë: delicate taste.
hollësí,-a *f.sh.* - detail, minutiae, particularity; flas (shkruaj, tregoj) me hollësi: to speak in detail, to write in detail, to tell in detail, to expatiate; me hollësitë më të vogla: in the minutest details.
hollësísh/ëm(i),-me(e) *mb.* circumstantial.
hollësísht *ndajf.* in detail, minutely.
hóllët (të) *as.* shih fikët(të).
hollím,-i *m.* 1. slimming. 2. (hollim i një lëngu): dilution.
hollój *f.k.* 1. to thin. 2. *(mpreh)* to point; holloj majën e lapsit: to point the pencil. 3. *(holloj një lëng)*: to dilute. - hollohem *f.jv.* to grow thin.
homogjén-e *mb.* homogeneous.
homoním,-i *m.sh.* -e *gram.* homonym.
hon,-i *m.sh.* -e abyss, precipice.
honéps *f.k.* 1. to digest. 2. *fig.* to abide, to bear, to put up with; ai nuk e honeps atë: he cannot abide (bear) him.
hop,-i *m.sh.* -e 1. time; nuk vij dot këtë hop: I cannot come this time. 2. punoj me hope: to work by fits and starts.
hordhí,-a *f.sh.* - horde; hordhitë barbare: barbarian hordes.
horizónt,-i *m.sh.* -e 1. horizon,

sky-line. 2. *fig.* prospect (perspective).

horizontál,-e *mb.* horizontal.

horizontalísht *ndajf.* horizontally.

horoskóp,-i *m.sh.* -e horoscope.

horr,-i *m.sh.* -a blackguard, knave, rascal, scamp, scoundrel, rouge.

horllë/k,-ku *m.sh.* -qe blackguardism, roguery.

hostén,-i *m.sh.* -ë goad: **shpoj me hosten:** to goad.

hosháf,-i *m.* dried fruit: **hoshaf molle:** dried apples: **hoshaf kumbulle:** prune, dried plums.

hotél,-i *m.sh.* -e hotel: **hotel-restorant:** hotel-restaurant; **hotel-pension:** boarding-house; **hotel i kategorisë së parë:** a first-rate hotel.

hotelxhí,-u *m.sh.* -nj hotel-keeper.

hov,-i *m.sh.* -e a leap forward, vigour, impetuosity.

hovardá *mb.* generous.

hóvsh/ëm (i),-me(e) *mb.* impetuous.

hóxh/ë,-a *f.sh.* -allarë muezzin.

hu,-ri *m.sh.* -nj stake, peg, picket.

huá,-ja *f.sh.* - loan: **jap hua:** to lend money, to loan; **marr hua:** to borrow (money, etc.); **ai më ka hua (më detyrohet):** he owes me, he is in debt to me.

huadhënës,-i *m.sh.* - lender, creditor.

huadhëni/e,-a *f.* lending.

húaj *f.k.* to lend, to loan; **huaj lekë:** to lend money. — **huhet** *f.jv.* to be loaned.

húaj (i),-i(i) *m.sh.* -(të) foreigner.

húaj (i,e) *mb.* 1. foreign, extraneous, alien. 2. other people's; **mall i huaj:** other people's property.

húajtur (i,e) *mb.* lent.

huamárrës,-i *m.sh.* - borrower.

huamárrj/e,-a *f.* borrowing.

húdh/ër,-ra *f.sh.* -ra *bot.* garlic; **thelb hudhre:** garlic's clove.

hulumtím,-i *m.sh.* -e investigation; research.

hullí,-a *f.sh.* - furrow.

humaí,-a *f.* fine cambric.

humaníst,-i *m.sh.* -ë humanist.

humanitár,-e *mb.* humanitarian.

humaníz/ëm,-mi *m.* humanism.

humb *f.k.* shih **humbas**.

humbaméno,-ja *f.sh.* - good for nothing.

humbás I. *f.k.* 1. to lose: **humbas një send:** to lose a thing. 2. to lose, to miss, to wander from; **humbas rrugën:** to lose one's way. 3. **humbas mendjen:** to lose one's head; **humbas ndjenjat:** to faint, to lose consciousness; **humbas gjakftohtësinë:** to lose one's self-control; **humbas durimin;** to be out of patience, to lose one's patience. 4. to lose, to miss, to let slip; **humbas një rast:** to miss an opportunity; **humbas bastin:** to lose a bet. 5. *drejt.* **humbas një gjyq:** to lose a case; to fail in a suit. 6. **humbas trenin:** to miss the train. 7. **humbas dritën e syrit:** to lose one's sight. 8. **humbas babain:** to lose one's father. 9. **humbas kohën kot:** to lose one's time in vain, to waste one's time. — *Lok.* **s'kam ç'të humbas:** I have nothing to lose.

II. *f.jk.* 1. to stray, to astray; **humbas në pyll:** to stray, to go astray into a forest; 2. **humbas në ëndërrime:** to lose oneself in musing (in reverie).

húmbët (i,e) *mb. (hon)* deep, remote.

humbëtír/ë,-a *f.sh.* -a remote place, the back of beyond.

húmbj/e,-a *f.sh.* -e 1. *(e një sendi)* loss; **dal me njëmijë lekë humbje:** to be one thousand leks to the bad; **shes me humbje:** to sell at loss; **prodhoj me humbje:** to produce at loss. 2. *(e kohës)* waste (of time). 3. *(e forcave, e energjive)* waste, loss (of forces, energies). 4. **humbje e luftës:** loss of a war, defeat. 5. **humbje e të drejtave civile.** loss of civil rights. 6. *(humbje e një të afërmi)* loss (of a relative). **húmbur** *ndajf.* wastefully; **më veta mundimi humbur:** my efforts have run to waste. **húmbur (i,e)** *mb.* 1. *(send, kohë,) para)* lost. 2. deep, remote. 3. *fig.* forgetful, oblivious, forgetmuch, absent-minded, unminded; **njeri i humbur:** good for nothing. **humnér/ë,-a** *f.sh.* -a abyss, precipice. **humór,-i** *m.* humour, temper, spirits; **në humor të mirë:** in a good humor, in good spirits; **në humor të keq:** in a bad humour, out of trim, out of temper. **húmus,-i** *m.* humus. **húnd/ë,-a** *f.sh.* -ë 1. *anat.* nose; **hundë me majë:** pointed nose; **hundë e drejtë:** right nose; **hundë me samar (hundë shkabë):** crooked nose; **hundë e shtypur:** flat nose; **hundë të zëna:** stuffed up nose; **maja e hundës:** the tip of the nose; **flegrat e hundës:** nostrils; **flas me hundë:** to speak through one's nose; **shfryj hundët:** to blow the nose; **më shkon gjak nga hundët:** to bleed, to lose blood from the nose; **më kullojnë hundët:** my nose rims. 2. *gjeog.* **hundë toke (kep):** headland. – *Lok.* **më bie hunda:** to be put out (by); **fus hundët në:** to poke (to push, to thrust) one's nose into; **heq për hunde:** to lead by the nose; **qesh nën hundë:** to snicker, to laugh slyly.

hundëpërpjetë *mb.* overweening; conceited. **húndëshkábë** *mb.* hawk-nosed, aquiline-nosed. **hundështýpur** *mb.* flat-nosed. **hundór,-e** *mb.* nasal; **shkronjë hundore:** nasal letter; **tingull hundor:** nasal sound. **hundrój** *f.jk.* to snuffle, to speak through the nose. **hungaréz,-i** *m.sh.* -ë Hungarian. **hungaréz,-e** *mb.* Hungarian. **hungërím/ë,-a** *f.sh.* -a grunt, snarl, growl. **hungërón** *f jk.* to grunt, to snarl, to growl. **huq,-i** *m.sh.* -e vice. **huqlli** *mb.* vicious; **kalë huqlli:** vicious horse. **húrdh/ë,-a** *f.sh.* -a puddle, pond. **húrm/ë,-a** *f.sh.* -a *bot.* date; **druri i hurmës:** date-tree. **hutáq,-i** *m.sh.* -ë giddy (forgetful) person. **hutáq,-e** *mb.* giddy, forgetful. **hút/ë,-a** *f.sh.* -a *zool.* vulture. **hutím,-i** *m.* bewilderment, perplexity, absence of mind, infatuation. **hutín,-i** *m.sh.* -ë *zool.* owl. **hutój** *f.k.* to bewilder, to perplex, to confuse, to disconcert, to infatuate. – **hutohem** *f.jv.* to be disconcerted (bewildered). **hutúar (i,e)** *mb.* bewildered. **hyj** *f.jk.* 1. to enter, to come in, to get in, to go in; **hyj në dhomë:** to enter the room, to come into the room; *(hyj me forcë)* to intrude, to break in; **hyj me/ rrëmbim:** to burst in; *(hy. tinës)* to steal into. 2. to accede to join; **hyj në parti:** to becoa me a party member, to join party; **hyj në punë:** to be employed in work, to find work; to find a job. 3. **hyn në fuqi (një ligj):** to enter in force (a law). 4.

hyn në ujë (një plaçkë):
to shrink (a tissue). 5. hyj padrej-
tësisht në një vend të ndaluar: to trespass.
hyjnésh/ë,-a *f.sh.* -a goddess.
hyjní,-a *f.* divinity.
hyjnizím,-i *m.* deification, divinisa-
tion.
hyjnizój *f.k.* to deify; – hyjnizohem
f.jv. to be deified.
hyjnór,-e *mb.* divine.
hyra,-t (të) *f.sh.* entries; të hyra
dhe të dala: entries and goings.
hýrë,-t (të) *as.* entry; më të hyrë

të dimrit: at the approach of
winter.
hyrj/e,-a *f.sh.* -e 1. entry, entering,
entrance, ingress; hyrje e lirë:
free entrance; hyrje e ndaluar:
forbidden entrance. 2. hyrje kryesore e një ndërtese: entrance,
ingress of a house, portal. 3. *muz.*
prelude. 4. hyrje në një libër:
introduction.
hyzmeqár,-i *m.sh.* -ë shih shërbëtor.
hyzmeqár,-e *mb.* shih shërbëtor.
hyzmét-i *m.* shih shërbim.

I

I,I (letter of the Albanian alphabet)
i, I.
n.p. (former article of the masculine gender) 1. (it follows an
adjective of the masculine gender)
djalë i mirë: good fellow; *sh(të);*
djem të mirë: good boys; i parl,
i dyti etj.: the first, the second,
etc. 2. (it is placed before nouns
of both genders in the genitive,
when the noun preceding them is
masculine) of; libri i djalit tim:
the book of my son, my son's
book; Komiteti Qendror i
Partisë së Punës të Shqipërisë: The Central Committee of
the Party of Labour of Albania.
3. (it is placed before a noun of
the masculine gender and acts
as a possessive adjective) his;
i vëllai (vëllai i tij): his bro-

ther; *sh.* të; të vëllezërit: his
brothers.
I *p.vet.* (short form of the personal
pronoun): a) (third person singular, dative case): to him,
to her; i dhashë (atij, asaj):
I gave (him, her); i thashë
(atij, asaj): I said (to him, to
her; b) (third person plural, accusative case): them ; i pashë
(ata, ato): I saw them.
ia (short form of the personal pronoun; it derives from the union
of the short forms i and e, or
i and i): (it) to him, (it) to her,
(it) to them; ia dhashë librin
(librat): I gave him the book (the
books); ia thashë të vërtetën: I
told him the truth; ia thashë të
gjitha: I told him all; t'ia thuash
të gjitha: tell him (her) every-

thing; **la dola në krye: I** succeeded.
brét *ndajf. gj.bis (nga pamja)* hideous, ugly; **bëhem ibret:** to smear (to dirty) one's face, clothes, etc.
brík,-u *m.sh.* -**ë** ewer, kettle; **ibrik kafeje:** coffee-pot.
íde,-ja *f.sh.* - idea, notion, conception; **ide e ngulët:** fixed idea; **për të patur një ide:** to have an idea of; **nuk kam as më të voglën ide: I** have not the slightest idea; **më lindi ideja:** it occured to me, an idea crossed my mind.
I deál,-i *m.sh.* -**e** ideal.
deál,-e *mb.* ideal.
I dealíst,-i *m.sh.* -**ë** idealist.
idealíst,-e *mb.* idealistic.
idealíz/ëm,-mi *m.* idealism.
idealizím,-i *m.* idealization.
idealizój *f.k.* to idealize. – **idealizohet** *f.jv.* to be idealized.
Identifikím,-i *m.* identification.
i dentifikój *f.k.* to identify. – **identifikohet** *f.jv.* to be identified.
identík,-e *mb.* identical.
dentitét,-i *m.* identity.
Ideológ,-u *m.sh.* -**ë** ideologist.
Ideologjí,-a *f.sh.* -ideology.
i deologjík,-e *mb.* ideological.
i deologjikísht *ndajf.* ideologically.
deopolitík,-e *mb.* ideo-political.
I deór,-e *mb.* ideological, conceptual; **përmbajtje ideore** *(e një vepre letrare etj.)* idea content (of a litterary work etc.).
i dërsháh,-u *m. bot.* geranium.
Idióm/ë,-a *f.sh.* -**a** idiom.
idiót,-i *m.sh.* -**ë** idiot.
idiót,-e *mb.* idiotic, dolt, oaf.
Idhët (i,e) *mb.* bitter.
Idhnák,-e *mb.* peevish, fretful, snappish.
i dhním,-i *m.* anger, spite, fret.
Idhnój *f.k.* 1. to anger, to make angry. 2. to vex, to fret. 3. to afflict.

– **idhnohem** *f.jv.* 1. to get angry. 2. to be vexed. 3. to be afflicted.
idhnúar (i,e) *mb.* vexed, fretted; **jam i idhnuar:** to be offended; **u ndanë të idhnuar:** they left one another offended.
idhujtár,-i *m.sh.* -**ë** idolater.
idhujtarí,-a *f.* idolatry.
ídh/ull,-lli *m.sh.* -**j** idol.
igrasí,-a *f.* humidity, dampness.
íj/ë,-a *f.sh.* -**e** *anat.* flank; side. – *Lok.* **rri me duar në ijë:** to stand with one's arms crossed. **mbaj ijet nga të qeshurit:** to split one's sides with laughter.
íki *f.jk.* 1. to go away, to get away, to get off, to set off, to drive off, to depart; **iki tinëz:** to go away secretly, to steal away; **iki me vrap:** to run away; **duhet të iki: I** must be off, I must be going; **eja të ikim!** let us go! **ikël** go! go away! be gone! 2. *(nga burgu)* to escape. 3. *(i iki, rrezikut, ndjekjes)* to elude. 4. *(nga puna)* to leave (one's job). 5. **iki ushtar:** to join the army, to enlist in the army. 6. *(koha)* to elapse; **iku një shekull:** a century has gone by (elapsed). 7. **më ikën treni, etj.:** to miss (the train). 8. to vanish away; **më ikën frika:** to relieve oneself (of fright); **më ikën inati:** to calm down; *(dhimbja)* to quiten down, to be soothed. – *Lok.* **më ikën mendja:** to become bewildered.
íkj/e,-a *f.sh.* -**e** 1. flight, getaway going, departure. 2. *(e të burgosurit)* escape. 3. *(e kohës)* flight.
iláç,-i *m.sh.* -**e** 1. medicine, medicament, *amer.* drug. 2. *fig.* remedy; **s'ka ilaç për këtë, kësaj nuk i gjindet ilaçi:** it is irre-

mediable, it is past (beyond) remedy.

llegál,-i *m.sh.* -ë underground worker.

llegál,-e *mb.* illegal; clandestine.

llegalísht *ndajf.* illegally; clandestinely.

llegalitét,-i *m.* illegality; clandestinity.

llét,-i *m.sh.* -e *gj.fol.* epilepsy.

lll/k,-ku *m.sh.* -qe button-hole.

llís *f.k.* to hem.

llustrím,-i *m.sh.* -e illustration.

llustrój *f.k.* to illustrate. — **ilustrohet** *f.jv.* to be illustrated.

lluzión,-i *m.sh.* -e illusion; **ushqej iluzione:** to cherish illusions; **s'kam iluzione:** to have no illusions (about).

im *p.pr.* (possessive pronoun masc. sing. of the genitive case; it is placed always after the noun, excepting the cases when this noun represents a member of the family) my; **djali (biri) im, im bir:** my son; **babai im, im atë:** my father; **ungji im, im ungj:** my uncle; **vëllai im, im vëlla:** my brother; **libri im:** my book; (genitive) **libri i djalit tim:** my son's book; **çanta e djalit tim:** my son's satchel; (dative) **birit tim, tim biri:** to my son; **ia dhashë stilografin shokut tim:** I gave the fountainpen to my comrade; (accusative) **e uruan mësuesin tim:** they congratulated my teacher; (plural, nominative) **e (të) mi:** my; **djemtë e mi:** my sons; (genitive) **librat e djemve të mi:** my sons' books; (dative) **u dhanë medalje shokëve të mi:** they gave medals to my comrades; (accusative) **përgëzuan djemt e mi:** they praised my sons; (feminine sing.) **ime:** my; **bija ime, ime bijë:** my dau-

ghter; **motra ime, ime motër;** my sister; (genitive), **libri i bijës sime, i sime bije:** my daughter's book; **çanta e bijës sime:** my daughter's satchel; (dative) **bijës sime, sime bije:** to my daughter; **i shkrova nënës sime:** I wrote to my mother; (accusative) **e dekoruan nënën time:** they decorated my mother; (plural, nominative) **vajzat e mia:** my daughters; (genitive) **i, e vajzave të mia:** of my daughters; (dative) **vajzave të mia:** to my daughters; (accusative) **vajzat e mia:** my daughters.

imagjinár,-e *mb.* imaginary, unreal; **vijë imagjinare:** imaginary line.

imagjinát/ë,-a *f.* imagination, fancy.

imagjinój *f.k.* to imagine, to fancy. — **imagjinohet** *f.jv.* to be imagined, to be contrived; **që nuk mund të imagjinohet:** unthinkable, unimaginable.

imagjinúesh/ëm (i)-me (e) *mb.* ima ginable.

imán,-i *m. vjet., fet.* faith; **pa din e pa iman:** faithless and pitiless.

ime *p.pr.* shih **im.**

imediát,-e *mb.* immediate; urgent, pressing; **nevoja imediate:** urgent imediate needs (necessities); **detyra imediate:** urgent duties.

imët (i,e) *mb.* thin, subtile; **shi i imët:** fine rain.

imi *p.pr.* (possessive pronoun of the nominative case) mine; (nominative) **ky është imi:** it is mine;(dative) **timit(sahatit tim) i mungon agrepi i sekondave:** my watch has not the handle of seconds; (accusative) **timin (sahatin tim) e rregullova:** I have repaired my watch; **e kam timin:** he is a relative of mine; (plural, nominative) **të mitë:**

mine; (feminine sing. nominative) **imja**: mine; **kjo është imja**: it is mine; (dative) **times**: to mine; (accusative) **timen**: mine; (feminine plural, nominative) **të miat**: mine; (dative) **të miave**: to mine; (accusative) **të miat**: mine.
imigránt,-i *m.sh.* -ë immigrant.
imitím,-i *m.sh.* -e imitation.
imitój *f.k.* to imitate, to mimic, to ape. – **imitohet** *f.jv.* to be imitated.
imitúes,-i *m.sh.* - imitator.
imitúes,-e *mb.* imitative.
imorál,-e *mb.* amoral, immoral.
imperialíst,-i *m.sh.* -ë imperialist.
imperialíst,-e *mb.* imperialist; **shtetet imperialiste**: the imperialist states.
imperialíz/ëm,-mi *m.* imperialism.
impiánt,-i *m.sh.* -e *tek.* plant, equipment.
imponím,-i *m.* constraint, imposition.
imponój *f.k.* to constrain, to impose.
impórt,-i *m.* import.
importím,-i *m.* importation.
importój *f.k.* to import. – **importohet** *f.jv.* to be imported.
importúes,-i *m.sh.* - importer.
impozánt,-e *mb.* imposing.
improvizím,-i *m.* improvisation.
improvizój *f.k.* to improvise; **improvizoj një këngë etj.**: to improvise a song. – **improvizohet** *f.jv.* to be improvised.
improvizúar (i,e) *mb.* (fjalim) improvised (speech).
improvizúes,-i *m.sh.* - improviser, improvisator.
improvizúes,-e *mb.* improvisatorial, improvisatory.
impúls,-i *m.sh.* -e impulse.
imtësí,-a *f.sh.* - minuteness, detail; **me imtësi**: minutely.

imtësísht *ndajf.* minutely, circumstantially.
imunitót,-i *m.* immunity.
imzót,-i *m.* my lord.
inát,-i *m.sh.* -e wrath, ire, anger, spite; **inat i madh**: rage, fury; **jam me inat**: to be angry, to be out of humour, to be full of spite; **marr inat me dikë**: to get angry with someone; **mbaj inat**: to keep rancour; **shfryj inatin**: to wreak.
inatçí,-eshë,-e *mb.* rancorous, spiteful.
inatçí,-u *m.sh.* -nj spiteful (rancorous) person.
inatós *f.k.* to anger, to make angry. – **inatosem** *f.jv.* to get angry.
inatósur (i,e) *mb.* angry.
inaugurím,-i *m.sh.* -e inauguration.
inaugurój *f.k.* to inaugurate. – **inaugurohet** *f.jv.* to be inaugurated.
incidént,-i *m.sh.* -e incident.
incizím,-i *m.sh.* -e according, registering (of a sound).
incizój *f.k.* to register, to record.
ind,-i *m.sh.* -e 1. *anat.* tissue. 2. weaving thread (used in a loom for textures, for webs).
indéks,-i *m.sh.* -e index.
indián,-i *m.sh.* -ë Indian.
indián,-e *mb.* Indian.
indiferénc/ë,-a *f.* indifference.
indiferént,-e *mb.* indifferent.
indiferentíz/ëm,-mi *m.* indifferentism.
indigjén,-i *m.sh.* -ë indigene, native.
indinját/ë,-a *f.* indignation.
indinjój *f.k.* to rouse the indignation. – **indinjohem** *f.jv.* to be indignant.
indinjúes,-e *mb.* indignant.
indirékt,-e *mb.* indirect.
indirékt *ndajf.* indirectly.
indivíd,-i *m.sh.* -ë individual; *fam.* person, fellow.

Individuál,-e *mb.* individual.
Individualísht *ndajf.* individually.
Individualitét,-i *m.* individuality.
Individualíz/ëm,-mi *m.* individualism. ....
Induksión,-i *m.* induction.
Induktív,-e *mb.* inductive.
Industrí,-a *f.* industry; industria kimike: chemical industry.
industriál,-e *mb.* industrial.
Industrialíst,-i *m.sh.* -ë industrialist.
Industrializím,-i *m.* Industrialization.
Industrializój *f.k.* to industrialize. – industrializohet *f.jv.* to be industrialized.
Inercí,-a *f.* inertia.
Infárkt,-i *m.sh.* -e *mjek.* infarct.
infeksión,-i *m.sh.* -e infection.
Infektím,-i *m.* infection, infecting.
Infektój *f.k.* to infect, to taint. – infektohem *f.jv.* to be infected.
Infektúes,-e *mb.* infectious, catching (disease).
Inferiór,-e *mb.* inferior.
Inferioritét,-i *m.* inferiority.
Infermiér,-i *m.sh.* -ë *mjek.* male nurse; medical orderly.
Infermiér/e,-ja *f.sh.* -e nurse.
Infermiéri,-a *f.sh-* infirmary; *usht.* hospital, sick-ward.
Infiltrát,-i *m. mjek.* infiltration.
Infiltrím,-i *m.* infiltration.
Infiltrój *f.jk.* to infiltrate.
Inflación,-i *m.* inflation; inflacion monetar: monetary inflation.
inflamación,-i *m. mjek.* inflamation.
Influénc/ë,-a *f.* influence; njeri me influencë: influential person.
Influencój *f.k.* to influence. – influencohem *f.jv.* to be influenced.
Información,-i *m.* information; news items; marr informacion: to make inquiries.
Informát/ë,-a *f.sh.* -a inquiry; sipas informatave: on inquiry;

marr informata: to take n- quiries, to make inquiries.
In ormatív,-e *mb.* informative.
informatór,-i *m.sh.* -ë informant, informer.
informój *f.k.* to inform, to give information, to notify, to make known. – informohem *f.jv.* to be informed.
ingranázh,-i *m.sh.* -e *tek.* pinion, gear.
inisiatív/ë,-a *f.sh.* -a initiative.
inisiatór,-i *m.sh.* -e initiator, promotor.
Inkandeshént,-e *mb.* incandescent; llambë inkandeshente: incandescent lamp.
Inkasím,-i *m.* encasement.
inkasój *f.k.* to encase, to incase. – inkasohet *f.jv.* to be incased.
Inkludój *f.k.* to include.
Inkluzív,-e *mb.* inclusive.
inkluzívisht *ndajf.* inclusively.
inkuadrím,-i *m.* framing.
inkuadrój *f.k.* to frame, to enclose. – inkuadrohet *f.jv.* to be framed.
inkubatór,-i *m.sh.* -ë incubator.
inkurajím,-i *m.* encouragement, exhortation.
Inkurajój *f.k.* to encourage, to exhort. – inkurajohem *f.jv.* to be encouraged, to be exhorted.
inkurajúes,-e *mb.* encouraging.
inkursión,-i *m.sh.* -e incursion, raid.
inorganík,-e *mb.* inorganic.
insékt,-i *m.sh.* -e *zool.* insect.
Insistím,-i *m.* insistence, insistency.
insistój *f.jk.* to insist, to persist, to be persistent.
inspektím,-i *m.sh.* -e inspection.
inspektój *f.k.* to inspect. – inspektohet *f.jv.* to be inspected.
Inspektór,-i *m.sh.* -ë inspector.
Instalím,-i *m.* installation.
Instalój *f.k.* 1. to install. 2. to establish, to settle. – instalohem

f.jv. to be settled, to be installed, to be established.

Instínkt,-i *m.sh.* -e instinct.

Instinktivisht *nda'f.* ins Inctively.

Instituc'ón,-i *m.sh.* -e institution.

Institút,-i *m.sh.* -e institute.

Instruksión,-i *m.sh.* -e instruction, direction.

Instruktór,-i *m.sh.* -e Instructor.

Instrumént,-i *m.sh.* -e 1. *tek.* instrument, tool. 2. *fig.* tool. 3. *muz.* musical instrument; **instrument me tela**: stringed instrument.

Instrumentál,-e *mb.* instrumental.

Integrál,-e *mb.* Integral.

integritét,-i *m.* integrity.

Intelektuál,-i *m.sh.* -ë intellectual.

Intelektuál,-e *mb.* intellectual.

Inteligjénc/ë,-a *f.* intelligence, intellect.

Inteligjént,-e *mb.* clever, intelligent, quickwited.

Intendénc/ë,-a *f. usht.* supply services, commissariat.

Intendént,-i *m.sh.* -ë *usht.* supplier, commissary.

Interés,-i *m.sh.* -a 1. interest, advantage, profit; **udhëhiqem nga interesi**: to be guided by self-interest; **vë interesin e përgjithshëm mbi interesin personal**: to put the general interest above the personal interest; **është në interesin tënd**: it is in your interest (to). 2. *treg.* interest. 3. *fig.* interest; concern; **ngjall interes**: to arouse interest; **interesohem shumë për**: to take a great interest in.

Interesánt,-e *mb.* interesting; **li bër interesant**: interesting book; **aspak interesant**: not at all interesting.

Interesím,-i *m.* concernment; **tregoj interesim**: to take an in-

terest in, to show concern for·

Interesój *f.jk.* 1. to interest, to concern; **kjo më intereson**: that interests me, that concerns me; **ç'ju intereson?** what does it matter to you? 2. to interest, to win the interest of. — **Interesohem** *f.jv.* to be interested in, to have an interest *(për,* in); to concern oneself (with).

Internaciónal,-e *mb.* international.

Internát,-i *m.sh.*-e boarding school.

Interním,-i *m.sh.* -e *drejt.* internment, deportation:

internój *f.k.* to intern. — **Internohem** *f.jv.* to be interned.

interprét,-i *m.sh.* -ë interpreter.

interpretím,-i *m.sh.* -e 1. interpretation, explanation. 2. *muz*: *teat.* interpretation.

interpretój *f.k.* 1. to interpret. 2. *muz.teat.* to execute, to perform. — **interpretohet** *f.jv.* to be interpreted, to be executed, to be performed.

Intervál,-i *m.sh.* -e interval; **interval i shkurtër kohe**: spell; **me intervale**: at intervals, intermittently, off and on.

Intervíst/ë,-a *f.sh.* -a interview; **i marr një intervistë dikujt**: to interview someone.

intervistoj *f.k.* to interview.

intím,-e *mb.* intimate, confidential, private.

Intimitét,-i *m.* intimacy, familiarity; **në intimitet**: in private.

Intrigánt,-i *m.sh.* -ë intriguer, intrigant.

Intríg/ë,-a *f.sh.* -a intrigue.

Intrigój *f.k.* to intrigue, to scheme, to plot.

Intuít/ë,-a *f.* intuition.

Invadím,-i *m. usht.* invasion.

Invadój *f.k.* to invade; to occupy.

invadúes,-i *m.sh.* - *usht.* invader.

invalíd,-i *m.sh.* -e invalid; **invalid**

lufte: disabled soldier.
Inventár,-i *m.sh.* -e *treg.* inventary, stock-taking; bëj inventarin: to take stock.
inventarizój *f.k.* to inventory, to make an inventory of; to take stock of.
investím,-i *m.sh.* -e *fin.* investment (of capital).
investój *f.k. fin.* to fund, to invest (capital).
investúes,-i *m.sh.* - investor (of capital).
inxhí,-a *f.sh.* - pearl.
inxhiniér,-i *m.sh.* -ë engineer; inxhinier elektrik: electrical engineer.
inxhinierí,-a *f.* engineering.
injeksión,-i *m.sh.* -e *mjek.* injection.
injektój *f.k.* to inject. − injektohet *f.jv.* to be injected.
injektór,-i *m.sh.* -e injector.
injoránc/ë,-a *f.* ignorance; nga injoranca: out of ignorance.
injoránt,-i *m.sh.* -ë ignorant.
injoránt,-e *mb.* ignorant.
injorój *f.k.* to ignore, to disregard. − injorohem *f.jv.* to be ignored, to be disregarded.
ireál,-e *mb.* unreal, fictive.
iríq,-i *m.sh.* -ë *zool.* hedgehog; iriq deti: sea-urchin.
irlandéz,-i *m.sh.* -e Irishman.
irlandéz,-e *mb.* Irish.

ironí,-a *f.* irony.
ironikísht *ndajf.* ironically.
iso,-ja *f.* chime; i mbaj ison dikujt: to chime in with someone.
íst/ëm,-mi *m.sh.* -me *gjeog.* isthmus.
istikám,-i *m.sh.* -e *vjet. usht.* trench
ish ex.,-former; ish-ministër: ex--minister.
ísha *f.jk.* (past tense of the verb jam) I was.
íshu/ll,-lli *m.sh.* -j island; ishull i vogël: islet; banor ishulli: islander.
italián,-i *m.sh.* -e Italian.
Italián,-e *mb.* Italian.
italisht *ndajf.* in Italian.
italisht/e,-ja *f.* Italian, the Italian language.
itinerár,-i *m.sh.* -e itinerary.
ithtár,-i *m.sh.* -e follower.
izolánt,-i *m.sh.* -ë *el.* insulator.
izolatór,-i *m.sh.* -ë insulator.
izolím,-i *m.* 1. isolation. 2. *el.* insulation.
izolój *f.k.* 1. to isolate. 2. *el.* to insulate. − izolohem *f.jv.* 1. to become isolated, to cut oneself off. 2. *el.* to be insulated.
izolúes,-e *mb.* 1. isolating; shtresë izoluese: dampproof course. 2. *el.* insulating; lëndë izoluese: insulating matter.
izraelít,-i *m.sh.* -e Israelite, Israeli, Jew.
izraelít,-e *mb.* Israelite, Israeli, Jewish.

J

j, J (letter of the Albanian alphabet; is pronounced like y in year) j, J.
ja *pj.* 1. here, there, here is, there is, here are, there are; **ja ku (tek) jam:** here I am; **ja ku (tek) po vjen:** here he comes; **ku është libri im?** — ja (tek është): where is my book? — here it is, there it is; **ja ku (tek) jemi:** here we are; **ja ku (tek) po vijnë:** here they come; **ku janë librat e mi?** ja (tek janë): where are my books? here they are, there they are. 2. that's; **ja se ç'duhej të thoje!** that's what you should have said! **ja ç'do të thotë kur gënjen (të gënjesh):** that's what you get by (for) telling lies; **ja pse:** this is the reason why, this is why.
Ja....., ja *lidh.* or; **ja sot ja nesër:** today or tomorrow.
jabanxhí,-u *m.sh.* -**nj** *vjet.* outlander.
jahní,-a *f.* mish jahni: sauce meat.
ják/ë,-a *f.sh.* -**a** collar; **këmishë me jakë të hapur:** open-necked shirt; **zë (kap) dikë për jake:** to seize someone by the collar.
jakí,-a *f. mjek.* plaster.
jam *f.jk.* (p.t. isha, pp. qenë) 1. to be; **unë jam:** I am; **unë nuk jam:** I am not; **kush është atje?** who is there? **çfarë je duke bërë?** what are you doing? **është:** is; **ai është marangoz:** he is a carpenter; **dje ishte ftohtë:** it was cold yesterday; **qenë:** been (past participle); **a keni qenë ndonjëherë në Shqipëri?** have you ever been

in Albania? **qofsh:** may you be; **qofsh i lumtur!** may you be happy! 2. *gram.* (auxiliary, is used to form the compound tenses of the verbs in the passive voice and of reflexive verbs); **jam trembur:** I am frightened; **jam larë:** I am washed; **jam veshur:** I am dressed. — *Lok.* si **është puna?, ç'është?** what is the matter?, what's up?
janár,-i *m.* January.
jap *f.k.* 1. to give; **jap një libër:** to give a book; **jap një darkë:** to give a dinner party; **jap ndihmë:** to give assistance. 2. to offer; **jap një pritje:** to give a reception; **jap dorën (për martesë):** to offer the hand; **i jap dorën dikujt:** to bear (to lend) a hand to someone, to help someone. 3. to confer; **jap një titull (një gradë, një çmim):** to confer a title (a degree, a prize). 4. *drejt.* to pass; **jap një dënim:** to pass sentence. 5. to deal; **jap një goditje:** to deal a blow (at). 6. **jap hua:** to lend, to grant a loan. 7. **jap kredi:** to grant a credit. 8. **jap me qira:** to lease, to rent. 9. **jap një shembull:** to set an example. 10. **jap (bëj) një zë:** to call someone. 11. **i jap hakë dikujt:** to give someone his due. — *Lok.* **jap e marr:** to make every effort, to exert oneself; **ia jap gazit:** to burst out laughing; **jap e marr (me dikë):** to have dealings with (someone); **jap shpirt:** to breathe one's last; **i jap zemër dikujt:** to encourage someone,

to give encouragement to someone.
Japonéz,-i *m.sh.* -ë Japanese.
Japonéz,-e *mb.* Japanese.
Jarán,-i *m.sh.* -ë *vjet.* lover, beau.
Jard,-i *m.sh.* -e yard (0,914 m).
jargamán,-i *m.sh.* -e slobberer.
Jargaván,-i *m.sh.* -ë *bot.* lilac; **bojë jargavani:** lilac-coloured.
Járg/ë,-t *f.sh.* slobber, dribble; **lëshoj jargë:** to slobber; **spërkas me jargë:** to sputter.
Jargëzím,-i *m.* slobbering.
Jargëzój, jargos *f.k.* to slobber, to dribble. - **jargosem** *f.jv.* to be sprinkled with saliva.
Jasemín,-i *m. bot.* jasmine, jasmin.
Jastëk,-u *m.sh.* -ë *(për të fjetur)* pillow; *(për t'u mbështetur)* cushion; *(për të vënë gjilpërat)* pin-cushion; **këllëf jastëku:** pillow case.
Jáshtë I. *ndajf.* out, outside; **ha jashtë:** to dine out; **lë jashtë:** to leave out; **nxjerr jashtë me shkelma:** to boot out, to kick out; **jashtë (shtëpisë):** outside the house; **dal jashtë (shtetit):** to go abroad; **jashtë!** out!, be gone!, off!, away! **dil jashtë:** get out! **nxirrini jashtë:** take them away!
II. *paraf.* outside, out of; beyond; **jashtë qytetit:** out of town; **nxjerr jashtë ligjit:** to outlaw; **jashtë masës:** beyond measure; **jashtë përdorimit:** out of use; **jashtë çdo dyshimi:** beyond doubt; **jashtë rrezikut:** out of danger.
Jashtëlígjsh/ëm(i),-me(e)*mb.* unlawful.
Jásht/ëm(i),-me(e) *mb.* extern, external, outer, exterior; outside, outward; foreign; **pjesa e jashtme:** the outside part; **politikë e jashtme:** foreign policy; **tregti e jashtme:** foreign trade; **pamje**

e jashtme: outside (outward, external) appearance.
Jashtëzakonísht *ndajf.* extraordinarily, exceedingly, uncommonly, unthinkably; **jashtëzakonisht mirë:** exceedingly (uncommonly) well.
Jashtëzakónsh/ëm(i),-me(e) *mb.* extraordinary, exceptional, unusual, uncommon.
Jatagán-i *m.sh.* -ë yataghan, yatagan.
jaták,-u *m.sh.* -ë *vjet.* bed.
javásh *ndajf.* slowly.
Javásh/ëm(i),-me(e) *mb.* slow; **kalë i javashëm:** ambling horse.
Javashllëk,-u *m.* sloth, slowness.
jáv/ë,-a *f.sh.* -e week; **brenda një jave:** within a week; **para një jave:** a week ago; **pas (brenda) një jave:** in a week; **si sot një javë:** today week; **gjithë javën:** week in week out; **çdo javë, javë për javë:** weekly.
Javór,-e *mb.* weekly; **të ardhura javore:** weekly takings.
Jaz,-i *m.sh.* -e mill-race, sluice.
jehón *f.jv.* to resound.
jehón/ë,-a *f.* resound, echo.
jél/e,-ja *f.sh.* -e mane; **jele luani;** lion's mane.
jelék,-u *m.sh.* -ë waistcoat.
jeniçér,-i *m.sh.* -ë janissary, janizary.
Jépem *f.jv.* 1. to give up, to surrender. 2. to be given; **kjo nuk jepet:** that's not given away. 3. *(pas diçkaje)* to betake oneself (to), to give oneself up (to), to devote oneself (to), to take up, to go in (for); *(pas një vesi)* to indulge (in), to become addicted (to); **jepem me mish e me shpirt:** to give oneself up with all one's soul (to). 4. **s'më jepet (të bëj një gjë):** to be very clumsy (awkward) (to do something).

jeremí,-a *f.* hermit.
jerm,-i *m.* rave; **flas jerm:** to rave.
jeshíl,-e *mb.* green.
jeshilón *f.jk.* to be green, to look green. – **jeshilohet** *f.jv.* to become green.
jeshillëk,-u *m.* greenness, verdure.
jetés/ë,-a *f.* livelihood, living, existence; **mjete jetese:** means (resources) of living; **siguroj mjetet e jetesës:** to earn (to secure) a living; **mënyra e jetesës:** way (mode) of living; **nivel jetese:** standard of living; **jetesë e shtrenjtë:** dear living.
jét/ë,-a *f.* 1. life, existence; **pa jetë:** lifeless; **plot jetë:** full of life; **për jetë:** for life, forever; **për tërë jetën:** for the whole of my life. 2. life, way (mode) of living; **jetë bashkëshortore:** conjugal life; **jetë beqari:** celibacy life; **jetë familjare:** family life; **jetë shoqërore:** social life. 3. life, lifetime; **miq për jetë:** friends for life, life-long friends; **kurrë në jetën time:** never in my life; **një herë në jetë:** once in a life time. – *Lok.* **ndërroj jetë:** to pass away, to breathe one's last; **vë në jetë:** to put into effect; **kthej në jetë:** to bring back to life; **t'u zgjattë jeta l** may you live long! **ju uroj jetë të gjatë l** I wish you a long life l may you have a long life l **filloj një jetë të re:** to turn over a new leaf; **bëj jetë të lumtur:** to lead a happy life; **bëj jetë të mjeruar:** to lead a miserable life; **bëj jetë të shthurur:** to lead an intemperate life; **bëj jetë: to live** a fast (gay) life.
jetëdhënës,-e *mb.* bracing, invigorating, tonic; enlivening; **ajër jetëdhënës:** bracing air.

jetëgjátë *mb.* long-lived.
jetëgjatësí,-a *f.* longevity.
jetërsím,-i *m. drejt.* alienation, estrangement.
jetërsój *f.k. drejt.* to alienate, to estrange.
jetërsúesh/ëm(i),-me(e) *mb. drejt.* alienable.
jetësór,-e *mb.* vital.
jetëshkrím,-i *m.* biography.
jetëshkúrtër *mb.* 1. short-lived. 2. *fig.* ephemeral.
jetík,-e *mb.* 1. vital. 2. *fig.* vital, fundamental.
jetím,-i *m.sh.* -ë orphan.
jetimór/e,-ja *f.sh.* -e orphanage.
jetój *f.jk.* 1. to live; **ato dyzet vjet që jetoi:** the forty years of his life. 2. to live, to spend one's life; **jetoj mirë:** to live in comfort; **jetoj keq:** to live poorly; to live form hand to mouth; **jetoj në Tiranë:** to live in Tirana. 3. to live, to subsist, to exist; **jetoj me perime:** to live on vegetables; **punoj për të jetuar:** to work for a living. 4. to dwell, to reside, to inhabit; **jetoj në fshat:** to dwell in the village.
jevg,-u *m.sh.* jevgj gypsy, gipsy.
jezuít,-i *m.sh.* -ë 1. jesuit. 2. *fig.* hypocrite, Jesuit.
jo *ndajf.* no, not, nay.
jod,-i *m. kim.* iodine.
jóna *p.pr.* ours (feminine).
jónë *p.pr.* ours (masculine).
jónxh/ë,-a *f. bot.* lucerne.
jorgán,-i *m.sh.* -ë quilt, bedquilt.
jorganxhí,-u *m.sh.* -nj. quilt maker
josh *f.k.* to allure, to entice, to decoy, to attract, to tempt.
jósh/ë,-a *f.* lure, allurement, decoy, enticement.
jóshës,-e *mb.* alluring, decoying.
jótja *p.pr.* yours.
ju *p.vet.* (nominative case) you; **ju jeni një nxënës i mirë:**

joveprór, -e *mb, gram.* non-active [voice of verb]

you are a good pupil; (dative)
ju them juve: I say to you;
(accusative) **ju shoh ju: I see**
you.
júaj *p.pr.* a) (masculine nominative)
your; **libri juaj**: your book; (genitive) **i(e) mikut tuaj**: of your
friend; (dative) **djalit tuaj nuk
i thashë gjë**: I said nothing to
your son; **nuk e pashë filmin
tuaj**: I didn't see your film. b) (feminine nominative) **vajza juaj**:
your daughter; (genitive) **i(e)
vajzës suaj**: of your daughter;
(dative) **vajzës suaj**: to your
daughter; (accusative) **vajzën tuaj**: your daughter c) (plural, nominative) **nxënësit tuaj**: your
pupils; (genitive) **i(e) nxënësve
tuaj**: of your pupils; (dative)
nxënësve tuaj: to your pupils;
(accusative) **nxënësit tuaj**: your
pupils. ç) (plural, nominative,
feminine) **vajzat tuaja**: your
daughters.
jubilé,-u *m.sh.* - jubilee.
júd/ë,-a *f.* Judas; *fig.* treacherous
person.
jug,-u *m.* *gjeog.* south; **drejt
jugut**: southward.
júg/ë,-a *f.* south wind.

juglíndj/e,-a *f.* south-east.
juglindór,-e *mb.* of the south-east,
south-eastern.
jugór,-e *mb.* southern; **poli jugor:**
south pole.
jugosllláv,-i *m.sh.* -ë Yougslav,
Jugoslav.
jugosllláv,-e *mb.* Yougoslav, Jugoslav.
jugperëndím,-i *m.* south-west.
jugperëndimór,-e *mb.* of the
south-west, south-western.
júnt/ë,-a *f.* *usht.* junto; **juntë
ushtarake:** military junto.
jurí,-a *f.sh.* - jury; **anëtar jurie:**
juryman, juror.
juridík,-e *mb.* juridical.
juridikísht *ndajf.* juridically.
juridiksión,-i *m.* jurisdiction.
jurisprudénc/ë,-a *f.* jurisprudence.
juríst,-i *m.sh.* -ë jurist.
justifikím,-i *m.sh.* -e justification.
justifikój *f.k.* to justify. – **justifikohem** *f.jv.* to justify oneself.
justifikúes,-e *mb.* justifying.
justifikúesh/ëm(i),-me(e) *mb.* justifiable.
jush (prej) *p.vet.* from you; **me
nder jush:** saving your presence.
jút/ë,-a *f.* *bot.* jute.

K

k, K (letter of the Albanian alphabet) k, K
ka 1. (third person singular of the
verb **kam**) (he, she) has. 2. there is, there are; **në figurë**

ka një mace: there is a cat
in the picture; **mbi mur ka
një fotografi:** there is a picture on the wall; **në kuti ka
dhjetë lapsa:** there are ten

pencils in the box; **ka disa nje-rëz:** there are some people; **s'ka përse:** not at all; **s'ka gajle:** never mind.

ka,-u *m.sh.* **qe** *zool.* mish kau: beef.

kabá *mb.* 1. awkward, unwieldy 2. bulky.

kabá,-ja *f.sh.* - *muz.* a popular melody played on a clarinet.

kabaré,-ja *f.sh.* - cabaret.

kabinét,-i *m.sh.* **-e** 1. cabinet; **kabineti pedagogjik:** pedagogical cabinet. 2. cabinet.

kabín/ë,-a *f.sh.* -a booth; **kabinë telefonike:** telephone booth, call-box, telephone kiosk; **kabinë vapori:** cabin.

kábllo,-ja *f.sh.* - 1. *el.* cable; **kabllo telegrafike, telefonike:** telegraphic and telephonic cable. 2. *ndërt.* cable.

kabllográm,-i *m.sh.* **-e** cablegram.

kacabú,-ni *m.sh.* **-nj** *zool.* coleopter.

kacafýtem *f.jv.* to wrestle, to engage in hand-to-hand fighting, to come to grips with.

kacafýtj/e,-a *f.* scuffle, wrestle.

kacambýtem *f.jv.* shih **kacafytem.**

kacavárem *f.jv.* to scramble.

kacavárj/e,-a *f.* scramble.

kacavírrem *f.jv.* to scramble, to clamber, to creep.

kacavjérrës,-e *mb.* scrambling, creeping, climbing; **bimë kacavjerrëse:** creeper.

kacék,-u *m.sh.* **-ë** 1. *(bulmeti)* leather-bottle. 2. *(farkëtari)* bellows (of smith). 3. *(kacek gajdeje)* bellows of a bag-pipe. – *Lok.* **m'u bë barku kacek:** my stomach is puffed up.

kaci,-a *f.* scoop.

kacídh/e,-ja *f.sh.* **-e** stiver; penny, cent; **s'kam asnjë kacidhe:** not to have a penny to one's name, to be pennyless.

kaçák,-u *m.sh.* **-ë** 1. outlaw, runaway; **duhan kaçak:** contraband tobacco.

kaçamák,-u *m.* polenta of maize, hominy.

kaçavíd/ë,-a *f.sh.* **-a** screw-driver.

káç/e,-ja *f.sh.* **-e** *bit.* sweet-brier.

kaçíl/e,-ja *f.sh.* **-e** basket; *(kaçile e madhe)* hamper.

kaçirúb/ë,-a *f.sh.* **-e** *(flokësh)* tuft.

káçk/ë,-a *f.sh.* **-a** *bot.* walnut.

kaçúb/ë,-a *f.sh.* **-e** *bot.* brushwood, bush, shrut.

kaçúl,-i *m.sh.* **-a** crest, tuft (of a bird).

kaçúl/e,-ja *f.sh.* **-e** hood (of a cloak).

kaçurrél-e *mb.* curly; **flokë kaçurrela:** curly hair.

kaçurrél/ë,-a *f.sh.* **-a** curl, ringlet.

kadást/ër,-ra *f.* cadastre; land registry.

kád/e,-ja *f.sh.* **-e** vat, cask; *(kade e vogël për bulmet)* firkin; *(kade për shtypjen e rrushit)* wine-vat.

kadét,-i *m.sh.* **-ë** *usht.* cadet.

kadexhí,-u *m.sh.* **-nj** maker of barrels.

kadí,-u *m.sh.* **-lerë** cadi.

kadífe,-ja *f.* plush, velvet; **prej kadifeje:** plushy, velvety.

kafáz,-i *m.sh.* **-ë** cage, coop; *(kafaz i madh zogjsh)* aviary; **kafaz dritareje:** window blind.

káf/e,-ja *f.* 1. coffee; **druri i kafesë:** coffee-tree; **ibrik kafeje:** coffee-pot; **lugë kafeje:** coffee-spoon; **filxhan kafeje:** coffee-cup; **mulli kafeje:** coffee-mill; **dollap kafeje:** box for roasting coffee; **plantacion kafeje:** coffee-plantation; **bojë kafe:** brown 2. *(lokali)* coffee-house, café.

kafené,-ja *f.sh.* coffee-house, café.

kafe-restoránt,-i *m.sh.* **-e** café-restaurant.

kafexhí,-u *m.sh.* -nj coffee-house keeper.

káfk/ë,-a *f.sh.* -a *anat.* cranium, skull.

kafshát/ë,-a *f.sh.* -a mouthful .

káfsh/ë,-a *f.sh.* -ë 1. animal, beast; **kafshë e egër**: wild beast, wild animal; **kafshë pune**: beast of burden; **kafshë shtëpiake**: domestic animals. 2. *fig.* rude person, brute, beast.

kafshím,-i *m.sh.* -e bite.

kafshój *f.k.* to bite; *(gjarpri)* to stitch (snake); *(qeni)* to bite, to snap (dog).

ḳafshúes,-e *mb.* biting.

kah,-u *m.sh.* -e direction (of a motion, etc.).

kaík/e,-ja *f.* skiff, canoe.

kajmák,-u *m.* cream.

kajsí,-a *f.sh.* - *bot.* apricot; **drurí i kajsisë**: apricot-tree; **reçel kajsie**: apricot-jam.

kakáo,-ja *f.* cocoa; **druri i kakaos**: cocoa-tree.

kakarís *f.jk.* to cluck, to cackle.

kakarísj/e,-a *f.* cluck, cackle.

kakërdhí,-a *f.sh.* dropping (of sheep and goats).

kakofoní,-a *f.* cacophony.

káktus,-i *m.sh.* -e *bot.* cactus.

kalá,-ja *f.sh.* -a fort, fortress.

kalamá,-ni *m.sh.* -j child, kid; **mos u bëj kalama**: don't be so childish; **mendje kalamani**: childish mind.

kalamallë/k-ku *m.sh.* -qe childish behaviour.

kalapíç *ndajf.* shih **kaliboç**.

kalaqáfë *ndajf.* astride, astraddle.

kalb *f.k.* to decay, to rot, to putrefy. – **kalbem** *f.jv.* to be decayed, to get rotten, to be putrefied, to become putrid.

kalbësí,-a *f.* putridity, putrescence.

kálbët (i, e) *mb.* putrid, rotten.

kalbëzím,-i *m.* putrefaction, decay, rotteness, putridity, putridness, decomposition, desintegration.

kalbëzój *f.k.* to rot, to decay, to putrefy, to desintegrate. – **kalbëzohem** *f.jv.* to be rotten (decayed, putrefied).

kalcíúm,-i *m. kim.* calcium.

kaldáj/ë,-a *f.sh.* -a large boiler.

kalém,-i *m.sh.* -a 1. pencil. 2. *bujq. (kalem shartimi)* scion.

kalemxhí,-u *m.sh.* -nj scribbler, petty author.

kalendár,-i *m.sh.* -ë calendar; almanac; **kalendar muri**: wall calendar.

kál/ë,-a *m.sh.* kuaj *zool.* horse; **kalë azgan**: frisky horse; **kalë balash**: roan horse; **kalë bryms (qimegështenjë)**: chestnut-horse; **kalë dori (qimekuq)** sorrelhorse, bay-horse; **kalë karroce**: cart-horse, draught-horse, drayhorse, shaft-horse; **kalë race**: thoroughbred horse; **kalë gërdallë**: jad-horse, nag; **kalë samari ose ngarkese**: pack-horse; **kalë shale**: saddle-horse; **mizë kali**: horse-fly; **shetitje me kalë**: riding; **vrapim me kuaj**: horse-racing; **zbutës kuajsh**: horse-breaker; **ia hipi kalit, hipi në kalë**: to mount a horse; **mbi kuaj!** on horseback! – *Lok.* punoj si kalë: to work like a horse.

kalë-fuqí,-a *f.sh.* **kuaj-fuqi** *fiz. (shkurt k.f.)* horse-power.

kalíbe,-ja *f.sh.* -e hut, cot, cottage; **kalibe me kashtë**: thatched cottage; **kalibe qeni**: kennel.

kalíb/ër,-ri *m.sh.* -ra caliber, calibre; **të një kalibri**: of the same caliber (size).

kaliboç *ndajf.* leap-frog.

kaligrafí,-a *f.* penmanship, calligraphy.

kalím,-i *m.sh.* -e 1. passage; **vend kalimi**: pass, narrow passage. 2. **kalimi i një provimi**: passing

(of an examination). 3. **ndalim
kalimi**: forbidden entrance. 4.
kalim kohe: pastime, 5. **kalimi
i një lumi**: crossing of a river.
kalimtár,-i *m.sh.* -ë pedestrian,
passer-by.
kalimtár,-e *mb.* 1. transitory; **periudhë kalimtare**: transitory pe-
riod. 2. ephemeral, momentary.
3. *gram.* transitive; **folje kalimtare**: transitive verb.
kalímthi *ndajf.* hastily; in passing.
kalít *f.k.* 1. to temper, to forge;
kalit çelikun: to temper steel.
2. *fig.* to harden; **kalit trupin**:
to harden the body. — **kalitem**
f.jv. to harden, to become hard,
to steel oneself.
kalítës,-i *m.sh.* -e forger.
kalítj/e,-a *f.* 1. temper, tempering
(of a metal). 2. *fig.* hardening (of
the body); **kalitje fizike**: hardening, physical training.
kalítur (i,e) *mb.* hardened.
kálium,-i *m. kim.* potassium.
kalkulím,-i *m.* calculation. computation, reckoning.
kalkulój *f.k.* to calculate, to compute, to reckon.
kalmár,-i *m.sh.* -ë *zool.* sepia, cuttle-fish.
kalój I. *f.jk.* 1. to pass, to pass
away, to go by; **kaloj përmes
fushave**: to pass through the
fields; **kaloj pranë**: to pass by;
kaloj më tej: to pass on to;
kaloj tinës: to steal away, to
slip in (out) unperceived, to pass
by stealthily. 2. *(kaloj një sëmundje)* to pass (an illness).
3. *(kalon afati)* to expire. 4.
(kalon koha) to pass. 5. *(kaloj
në provime)* to pass (an examination). 6. to cease, to stop;
shiu kaloi: the rain stopped.
II. *f.k.* 1. *(kaloj lumin)* to cross, to
get over (a river). 2. *(kaloj dikë)*
to excel, to surpass (someone).

3. **kaloj kohën**: to pass the time,
to spend the time, to while away
the time; **kaloj mbrëmjen**: to
pass (to spend) the evening;
e kalofshi mirë I may you have
a good time I **i kalofshi mirë
pushimet I** may you have a good
holiday I
kalórës,-i *m.sh.* - 1. rider, horse-
man. 2. *(titull)* knight.
kalorësí,-a *f.* 1. knighthood. 2.
usht. cavalry; **ushtar i kalorësisë**:
chivalry soldier.
kalorsiák,-e *mb.* chivalrous.
kalorí,-a *f.sh.* - *fiz.* calory, *amer.*
calorie.
kalorifér,-i *m.sh.* -ë radiator.
kalorifík,-e *mb.* calorific.
kalorík,-e *mb.* caloric.
kalorimét/ër,-ri *m.sh.* -ra calori-
meter.
káltër (i,e) *mb.* azure, sky-blue.
kaltërósh,-e *mb.* blueish.
kalúar *ndajf.* on horseback.
kalúar (i,e) *mb.* 1. past, gone, bygone; **vitin e kaluar**: last year.
2. old; **i kaluar nga mosha**:
old, aged.
kalúar (e),-a(e) *f.* past time, bygone time.
kalúes,-e *mb.* passing; **notë kalu-
ese**: passing mark.
kalúesh/ëm(i),-me(e) *mb.* traversable, passable; **lumë i kalue-
shëm**: traversable river.
kall *f.k.* 1. to put in, to insert. **kall
në dhé**: to bury, to inter. 2.
fig. **kall tmerrin**: to strike terror
into.
kallaballëk,-u *m.* crowd, multitude.
kallái,-i *m.* tin; **minierë kallaji**:
stannary; **lidhje kallaji dhe
plumbi**: pewter; **me përmbajtje kallaji**: stannous; **prej kallaji**: stannic.
kallajís *f.k.* to tin. — **kallajiset**
f.jv. to be tinned.
kallajísj/e,-a *f.* tinning.

kallajxhí,-u *m.sh.* -nj tinner, tin-smith.

kallám,-i *m.sh.* -a cane, reed-cane, reed, rush; **kallam sheqeri:** sugar-cane; **kallam peshkimi:** fishing rod; *(känete)* rush, bul-rush.

kallamár,-i *m.sh.* -ë inkpot, ink-stand.

kallambóq,-i *m. krah.* maize, *amer.* corn.

kallamídh/e,-ja *f.sh.* -e carridge-case.

kallaúz,-i *m.sh.* -ë guide.

kállc/ë,-a *f.sh.* -a gaiter.

kalldrëm,-i *m.sh.* -e pavement; **shtroj me kalldrëm:** to pave, to cobble; **udhë me kalldrëm:** paved road, paved way.

kalldrëmxhí,-u *m.sh.* -nj paver.

kallëp,-i *m.sh.* -ë 1. form, mould; **derdh në kallëp (një metal)** to mould (metal); **derdhje në kallëp:** moulding. 2. piece; ear; **një kallëp sapun:** a piece of soap; **kallëp misri:** ear of maize. 3. **kallëp këpucësh:** last for shoes. 4. *fig.* sort; stamp; **të një kallëpi:** of a feather, tarred with the same brush, of the same des-cription.

kallëzím,-i *m.* 1. narration. 2. de-nunciation, denouncement.

kallëzimtár,-i *m.sh.* -ë 1. narrator; **kallëzimtar përrallash:** tale-teller. 2. denouncer.

kallëzimtár,-e *mb.* narrative.

kallëzój *f.k.* 1. to narrate, to tell. 2. to show. 3. to denounce, to report.

kallëzór,-e *mb. gram.* accusative; **rasa kallëzore:** accusative case.

kallëzúes,-i *m.sh.* - .1. *gram.* pre-dicate. 2. denouncer.

kállf/ë,-a *m.sh.* -ë *vjet.* appren-tice.

kallí,-ri *m.sh.* -nj spike, ear (of wheat, etc.); **mbledh kallinj:** to glean; **mbledhje kallinjsh:** gleaning.

kallkán *ndajf.* **bëhet kallkan (rru-ga):** to freeze over (the road).

kallm,-i *m. bot.* reed.

kallmísht/ë,-a *f.sh.*-a reedy ground.

kállo,-ja *f.sh.* - *mjek.* callus, corn; **me kallo:** callous; **kallo në këm-bë:** bunion, callosity of the foot.

kallogré,-ja *f. vjet. fet.* nun.

kallogjér,-i *m.sh.* -ë *vjet. fet.* monk.

kallp,-e *mb.* false, counterfeit; **para kallpe:** conterfeit money, false money.

kallúm/ë,-a *f.sh.* -a *det.* keel (of a vessel).

kam I. *f.k.* (p.t. **kisha,** p.p. **pasur**) 1. to have, to possess; **kam një libër:** I have a book. 2. to be, to feel; **kam ftohtë:** I feel cold; **kam vapë:** to be warm; **kam të drejtë:** I am right; e **kam gabim:** I am wrong; **kam frikë:** to be afraid. 3. e **kam mirë me dikë:** to be on good terms with some-one. 4. **nga të kemi?** where are you from? 5. **sa e ke orën?** what time is it?; **si i ke fëmijët?** how are your children? 6. **sot ka erë:** it is windy today. 7. **ki mendjen!** be aware!, look out!, take care! caution!. 8. e **kam inat dikë:** to have a grudge against someone. 9. e **lehtë sa s'ka, s'ka më e lehtë:** as easy as anything.

II. *folje ndihmëse* **kam lexuar:** I have read; **kam për të vajtur diku:** I have to go somewhere.

kamár/e,-ja *f.sh.* -e niche.

kamát/ë,-a *f. fin.* interest, usury.

kambaléc,-i *m.sh.* -a trestle.

kambán/ë,-a *f.sh.* -a church-bell; **kumbimi i kambanave:** chime, peal, tolling; **kambana e vdek-jes:** passing-bell, death-bell; **u bie kambanave:** to chime.

kambanór/e,-ja *f.sh.* -e steeple, belfry, belltower.
kambanór/e,-ja *f.sh.* -e *bot.* bellflower.
kambiál,-i *m.sh.* -e *treg.* bill of exchange, draft, bill; **xhiroj një kambial:** to endorse a bill; **afati i pagimit të një kambiali:** usance.
kambrík,-u *m.* cambric.
kameleón,-i *m.sh.* -ë *zool.* cameleon.
kamerdár/,l-ja *f.sh.* -e tire. **kamerdare rezervë:** spare tire.
kameriér,-i *m.sh.* -ë waiter.
kám/ë,-a *f.sh.* -a dagger.
kámës,-i *m.sh.* - rich man, moneyedman, man of means.
kámës,-e *mb.* rich, wealthy, wellto-do.
kámfur,-i *m. kim.* camphor.
kamilláf,-i *m.sh.* -ë miter, mitre.
kaminét/ë,-a *f.sh.* -a small portable stove; **kaminetë me alkool, me vajguri:** spirit-stove, oil-stove.
kamión,-i *m.sh.* -a truck, lorry; **kamion vetshkarkues:** tip-lorry.
kámj/e,-a *f.* wealth.
kamomíl,-i *m. bot.* camomile; **lëng kamomili:** carnomile tea.
kamósh,-i *m.* wash-leather, shammy.
kamp,-i *m.sh.* -e camp; **kamp pushimi:** rest home.
kampión,-i *m.sh.* -ë 1. specimen, sample. 2. *sport.* champion.
kampionát,-i *m.sh.* -e championship.
kamuflój *f.k.* to camouflage, to conceal. — **kamuflóhem** *f.jv.* to be concealed, to be camouflaged.
kamzhík,-u *m.sh.* -ë whip, whipcord, flog, horse-whip; **rrah me kamzhik:** to whip, to flog, to flagellate.
kanakár,-i *m.sh.* -ë favourite, pet.

kanál,-i *m.sh.* -e 1. canal, ditch; **kanal kryesor:** main canal; **kanal kullues:** drain; **kanal i ujrave të zeza:** sewer; **kanal ujitës, vaditës:** irrigation canal; **pastrues kanalesh:** ditch-cleaner. 2. *mjek.* canal, duct. 3. *el.* *(televiziv)* channel. 4. *fig.* medium, channel.
kanalizím,-i *m.sh.* -e *bujq.* canalization, drainage; **kanalizimi i ujrave të zeza:** sewerage.
kanalizój *f.k. bujq.* to drain; to canalize. — **kanalizohet** *f.jv.* to be drained; to be canalized.
kanapé,-ja *f.sh.* - sopha, couch.
kanarín/ë,-a *f.sh.* -a *zool.* canarybird.
kanát,-i *m.sh.* -a 1. shutter; **kanat dritareje:** window-shutter; **kanat dere:** leaf of a door, fold of a door; **portë me dy kanata:** folding-door.
kanaváç/ë,-a *f.* canvas.
kancelár,-i *m.sh.* -ë chancellor.
kancelarí,-a *f.* 1. chancellery. 2. stationer's shop; **artikuj kancelarie:** stationery.
káncer,-i *m. mjek.* cancer; **kancer në zorrë:** intestinal cancer.
kandár,-i *m.sh.* -ë spring-balance, steelyard. — *Lok.* **nuk ngre kandar:** to be unimportant, to be of no importance.
kandidát,-i *m.sh.* -ë candidate; nominee.
kandidatúr/ë,-a *f.* candidature, *amer.* candidacy; **vë kandidaturën** *(në zgjedhje)* to stand (for election).
kandíl,-i *m.sh.* -ë grease pot.
kandís *f.k.* to convince, to persuade. —**kandisem** *f.jv.* to convince oneself.
kanéll/ë,-a *f. bot.* cinnamon; canella.
kán/ë,-a *f.sh.* -a can, watter-jug, watter-bottle.

kángjella,-t *f.sh.* banisters, lattice.
kanibál,-i *m.sh.* -ë cannibal, man-eater.
kaníst/ër,-ra *f.sh.* -ra basket.
kanoniér/ë,-a *f.sh.* -a gunboat.
kanósem *f.jv.* to threaten, to menace; **i kanosem dikujt:** to menace someone.
kanósj/e,-a *f.sh.* -e threat, menace.
kanotiér/ë,-a *f.sh.* -a undervest, undershirt.
kantiér,-i *m.sh.* -e yard, timberyard, wood-yard, workshop in a timber-yard; **kantier detar:** shipyard; **kantier ndërtimi:** construction-site.
kanún,-i *m.* canon.
kánxh/ë,-a *f.sh.* -a hook; cramp.
kaolín,-i *m.* kaolin, porcelain clay.
káos,-i *m.* chaos, confusion.
kap *f.k.* 1. to catch, to seize, to entrap, to clutch, to grab, to grasp; **kap në befasi:** to take by surprise, to catch unawares, to catch offguard. 2. *(kap duke e ndjekur)* to overtake, to overreach, to catch by pursuit; **nuk e kapa dot trenin:** I missed the train. 3. **kap rob:** to capture, to seize as a prisoner. 4. *fig. (kap me mend diçka)* to perceive. – **kapem** *f.jv.* to be caught, to be seized; **kapem në grackë:** to be caught in a trap; **kapem pas diçkaje:** to fasten to anything, to take hold of, to cling to; **kapem në vendin e krimit:** to be caught red-handed.
kapacitét,-i *m.* 1. capacity. 2. output.
kapadaí,-u *m.sh.* -nj bully.
kapadaillëk,-u *m.* blustering, bragging.
kapák,-u *m.sh.* -ë 1. lid, cover; **kapak tenxhereje:** lid. 2. *(kapak libri)* cover, wrapper. 3. *anat.* **kapaku i syrit:** eyelid.

kapár,-i *m.* earnest-money.
kapardísem *f.jv.* to strut, to swagger
kapardísj/e,-a *f.* strut, swager.
kaparós *f.k.* to give earnest-money.
kapedán,-i *m.sh.* -ë chieftain; *fig.* brave (courageous) person.
kapelabërës,-i *m.sh.* hetter, milliner.
kapél/ë,-a *f.sh.* -a hat, cap; **kapelë me strehë:** hat; **kapelë republike:** bowler derby hat; **heq kapelën:** to take off one's hat; **vë kapelën:** to put on the hat.
kapërcéj *f.k.* 1. to jump, to jump across, to leap, to cross, to get over; **kapërcej lumin:** to cross the river; to get over a river. 2. **kapërcej murin:** to climb over the wall. 3. *fig. (kapërcej një vështirësi)* to surmount, to tide over, to get over, to overcome (a difficulty); **kapërcej të gjitha pengesat:** to overcome all obstacles. 4. **kapërcej ushqimin:** to let down (to swallow) the food. – **kapërcehem** *f.jv.* to be surpassed, overpassed.
kapërcím,-i *m.* 1. jump, crossing (of a river, etc.). 2. *fig.* overcoming, overpassing (of an obstacle, of a difficulty)
kapërcýesh/ëm(i),-me(e) *mb.* passable, traversable, surmountable.
kapërdíj *f.k.* to let down, to swallow.
kápës/e,-ja *f.sh.* -e clasp; **kapëse flokësh:** hair-pin; **kapëse perdesh:** hook for curtains; **kapëse rrobash:** clothes peg; **zë me kapëse:** to clasp, to fasten with a clasp.
kapíc/ë,-a *f.sh.* -a mass, heap.
kapistáll,-i *m.sh.* -e halter, bridle, rein.
kapíst/ër,-ra *f.sh.* -ra shih **kapistall.**

kapít *f.k.* to harass, to overtire, to overstrain. – **kapitem** *f.jv.* to be harassed (overstrained)

kapitál,-i *m.sh.* -e capital; **kapital i një shoqërie:** capital of a company; **kapital qarkullues:** floating (circulating) capital; *fig.* **njeriu është kapitali më i çmuar:** man is the most precious capital.

kapitál,-e *mb.* 1. capital; **dënim kapital:** capital punishment. 2. **gërmë kapitale:** capital letter.

kapitalíst,-i *m.sh.* -ë capitalist.

kapitalíst,-e *mb.* capitalist; **shtetet kapitaliste:** the capitalist states; **shfrytëzimi kapitalist:** capitalist exploitation; **rendi kapitalist:** the capitalist system.

kapitalíz/ëm,-mi *m.* capitalism.

kapitén,-i *m.sh.* -ë *usht.* captain; **kapiten anijeje:** captain of a ship.

kapítj/e,-a *f.* lassitude, weariness.

kapítu/ll,-lli *m.sh.* -j chapter.

kapitullím,-i *m.* capitulation.

kapitullój *f.jk.* to capitulate.

kapitullúes,-e *mb.* capitulating.

kápj/e,-a *f.* 1. catch, seizure, grasp, clutch. 2. *(kapje robërish lufte)* capture (of prisoners).

kapósh,-i *m.sh.* -ë *zool.* shih **këndez.**

kapót/ë,-a *f.sh.* -a capote.

kapríç,-i *m.sh.* -e whim, caprice, freak, fancy.

kapriçóz,-e *mb.* whimsical, capricious, freakish.

kapró/ll,-lli *m.sh.* -j *zool.* roebuck; **kaproll i vogël:** young roebuck; **femra e kaprollit:** roe.

kaps *ndajf. mjek.* constipated, costive.

kapsallít *f.k.* to wink, to twinkle; **kapsallit sytë:** to wink one's eyes.

kapsallítj/e,-a *f.* winking, twinkling (of eyes).

kapsllëk,-u *m. mjek.* costiveness, constipation.

kapsóll/ë,-a *f.sh.* -a capsule.

kaptín/ë,-a *f.sh.* -a 1. *krah.* noddle, head; **më dhemb kaptina:** my head aches. 2. *vjet.* chapter (of a book).

kaptój *f.k.* 1. to swallow. 2. to climb over.

kapúç,-i *m.sh.* -ë 1. capouch, cowl, hood; **kapuç murgu:** cowl, a monk's hood. 2. **kapuç oxhaku:** chimneypot, cowl of a chimney.

kaq *ndajf., p.pk.* so, in such a manner, so much, such; **kaq shpejt:** so soon; **kaq shumë:** so much; **mos u ngut kaq shumë!** don't be in such a hurry! **kaq mirë!** so good! **një mbrëmje kaq e këndshme!** such an enjoyable evening!

karabiná,-ja *f.sh.* - framework, carcass of a building.

karabín/ë,-a *f.sh.* -a carabine, carabine.

karabiniér,-i *m.sh.* -ë *usht.* carabineer, carabinier.

karabinierí,-a *f.* carabinieri.

karabój/ë,-a *f.* heel-ball.

karabúsh,-i *m.sh.* -ë 1. maize-cob; *amer.* corn-cob. 2. *fig.* stupid head, dolt.

karadyzén,-i *m.sh.* - *muz.* shih **çifteli.**

karafíl,-i *m.sh.* -a *bot.* 1. carnation, pink. 2. *fig.* light-minded person.

karagjóz,-i *m.sh.* -ë jester, buffoon.

karagjozllë/k,-ku *m.sh.* -qe buffoonery.

karakatín/ë,-a *m.sh.* -a hovel.

karakóll,-i *m.sh.* -ë *vjet.* sentry, sentinel.

karaktér,-i *m.sh.* -e character; **jam njeri me karakter:** to be a man of character; **njeri pa karakter:** a man of no character.

karakteristík,-e *mb.* characteristic; typical.

karakteristík/ë,-a *f.sh.* -a characteristic.

karakterizím,-i *m.* characterization.

karakterizój *f.k.* to characterize. – karakterizohem *f.jv.* to be characterized.

karamanjóll/ë,-a *f.* gallows.

karamból,-i *m.sh.* -e 1. collision. 2. *(bilardo)* carom, cannon.

karamél/e,-ja *f.sh.* -e caramel.

karantín/ë,-a *f. mjek.* quarantine; vë në karantinë *(një vapor, etj.)*: to place under quarantine, to put in quarantine, to quarantine.

karát,-i *m.sh.* -ë carat (of gold).

karavél/ë,-a *f.sh.* -a *det.* caravel, carvel.

karavídh/e,-ja *f.sh.* -e *zool.* lobster, shrimp.

karbít,-i *m. kim.* carbide.

karbón,-i *m. kim.* carbon; letër karboni: carbon-paper.

karbonát,-i *m. kim.* carbonate; karbonat plumbi *(për pikturë)* white lead.

karburánt,-i *m.sh.* -e fuel.

karburatór,-i *m.sh.* -ë carburettor.

kardiák,-e *mb. mjek.* cardiac.

kardinál,-i *m.sh.* -ë *fet.* cardinal.

kardinál,-e *mb.* 1. cardinal, fundamental, main. 2. *gjeog.* cardinal, main; pikat kardinale: cardinal points.

karrék/ëll,-lla *f.sh.* - lla *krah.* shih karrige.

karfíc/ë,-a *f.sh.*-a safety-pin, brooch, pin; karficë flokësh: hair-pin; karficë kravate: tic-pin.

karfos *f.k.* to fix, to fasten; to nail.– karfoset *f.jv.* to be fixed, to be fastened, to be nailed.

karfósj/e,-a *f.* fastening; nailing.

karikatór,-i *m.sh.* -ë cartridge clip.

karikatúr/ë,-a *f.sh.* -a cartoon, caricature.

karikaturíst,-i *m.sh.* -ë cartoonist, caricaturist.

karjóll/ë,-a *f.sh.* -a *krah.* bed.

karkaléc,-i *m.sh.* -ë *zool.* grasshopper; karkalec deti: prawn.

karkát *f.jk.* to croak (of a frog).

karkátj/e,-a *f.* croak (of a frog).

karnavál,-i *m.sh.* -e carnival.

karót/ë,-a *f.sh.* -a *bot.* carrot.

karpentiér,-i *m.sh.* -ë carpenter.

karpúz,-i *m.sh.* -ë *bot., krah.* shih shalqi.

karshí I. *ndajf.* opposite, in front; rrinë karshi: to sit vis-a-vis, to sit face to face; shtëpia karshi: the house opposite, the house over the way.

II. *paraf.* 1. opposite, facing; karshi njëri-tjetrit: facing each other; karshi shtëpisë sime: in front of my house; karshi një veprimi të tillë: in front of such an action. 2. towards, in regard to, in relation to; sjellja e tij karshi meje: his conduct towards me.

kartél,-i *m.sh.* -e *ekon.* cartel, trust.

kartél/ë,-a *f.sh.* -a filing-card, index-card.

kárt/ë,-a *f.sh.* -a *krah.* 1. paper. 2. letter. 3. *pol.* charter; Karta e Kombeve të Bashkuara: Charter of the United Nations.

kartëmonédh/ë,-a *f.sh.* -a banknote, paper money, currency.

kartëpostál/e,-ja *f.sh.*-e post-card.

kartolerí,-a *f.sh.* -a stationary.

kartolín/ë,-a *f.sh.* -a post-card.

kartón,-i *m.sh.* -a pasteboard, cardboard, card-paper.

kartoték/ë,-a *f.sh.* -a card-index box.

karthí,-a *f.sh.* - dry twigs.

karván,-i *m.sh.* -e 1. *(njerëzish. udhëtarësh)* caravan (of travellers). 2. *(anijesh)* convoy (of ships).

karrém,-i *m.sh.* -a bait, lure.

karriér/ë,-a *f.* career (of a person).
karrieríst,-i *m.sh.* -ë careerist.
karríg/e,-ja *f.sh.* -e chair; **shpinë e karriges:** back of a chair.
karrigepunúes,-i *m.sh.* - chairmaker.
kárro,-ja *f.sh.* - cart.
karrocabërës,-i karrocapunues,--i *m.sh.* wheel wright, cart, wright.
karrocerí,-a *f.sh.* body, coachwork, *amer.* pannel body.
karróc/ë,-a *f.sh.* -a carriage; **karrocë dore:** push cart, wheelbarrow, hand-cart; **karrocë fëmijësh:** perambulator, fram (for children); **karrocë me dy rrota:** two-wheeled cab; **karrocë me katër rrota:** four-wheeled carriage; *(karrocë dyvendëshe me katër rrota)* chariot; *(karrocë për transportimin e mallrave)* van, wagon, coach, cart; **karrocë poste:** stage-coach.
karrociér,-i *m.sh.* -ë coachman, cartman, carter, cabman.
karróqe,-ja *f.sh.* -e bushel for grains, containing 8-10 kg.
kasafórt/ë,-a *f.sh.* -a safe.
kasáp,-i *m.sh.* -ë butcher.
kasaphán/ë,-a *f.* 1. slaughterhouse, butchery, shambles. 2. slaughter, carnage, massacre, shambles.
kasát/ë,-a *f.sh.* -a kind of icecream cake.
kasavét,-i *m.* care, worry; **mos ki kasavet:** don't worry.
kás/ë,-a *f.sh.* -a 1. safe. 2. moneycase. 3. *(kasa e tytës së pushkës)* stock of a gun.
kaskád/ë,-a *f.sh.* -a cascade.
kaskét/ë,-a *f.sh.* -a cap.
kasnéc,-i *m.sh.* -ë herald.
kasóll/e,-ja *f.sh.* -e hut, cot, cottage *amer.* shack.

kastén *ndajf.* shih **kastile.**
kastíle *ndajf.* purposely, intentionally.
kastór,-i *m.sh.* -ë 1. *zool.* beaver. 2. *(gëzof kastori)* beaver.
kastravéc,-i *m.sh.* -a 1. *bot.* cucumber; **kastravec turshi:** gherkin. 2. *fig.* greenhorn.
kashaí,-a *f.sh.* -a scrubbing brush.
kashaís *f.k.* to scrub.
kásht/ë,-a *f.* straw, thatch; **çati me kashtë:** thatch roof; **dyshek me kashtë:** straw-mattress; **mullar kashte:** straw cock, straw stack; **ngjyrë kashte:** straw coloured; **mbuloj me kashtë:** to thatch.
kashtór/e,-ja *f.sh.* -e 1. carboy. 2. thatched cottage. 3. hayloft, barn for the storage of the straw.
kat,-i *m.sh.* -e story (storey), floor; **kati i parë:** first floor; **kati përdhes:** ground floor, downstairs; **kati i sipërm:** upstairs; **në katin e poshtëm:** downstairs; **në katin e katërt:** the fourth floor; **shtëpi me dy kate:** two-storied house.
katalepsí,-a *f. mjek.* catalepsy.
katalóg,-u *m.sh.* -ë catalogue.
kataná,-ja *f.sh.* - kite; **ngre një katana:** to fly a kite.
katandí,-a *f.* assets, means, resources; **jam pa shtëpi e pa katandi:** to be reduced to poverty, not to have a penny.
katandís *f.k.* to render in a bad state. − **katandisem** *f.jv.* to be reduced in a low state.
katapúlt/ë,-a *f.sh.* -a catapult.
katarákt,-i *m.sh.* -e cataract.
katarósh,-i *m.sh.* -e overtooth, irregular tooth.
katastróf/ë,-a *f.sh.* -a catastrophe, disaster.
katéd/ër,-ra *f.sh.* -ra chair.
katedrál/e,-ja *f.sh.* -e cathedral.
kategorí,-a *f.sh.* - category, class,

sort, type; të një kategorie: of
the same category (class); i kategorisë së parë: of first class.
kategorík,-e mb. categorical; refuzim kategorik: flat refusal.
kategorikísht ndajf. categorically,
flatly; refuzoj kategorikisht: to
refuse flatly.
kategorizím,-i m. categorization.
kategorizój f.k. to class by catego-
ries, to categorize. – kategorizo-
hem f.jv. to be categorized.
katëk,-u m. anat. gizzard (of a
fowl).
kátër num. them. four; ndaj në
katër pjesë: to divide in four
parts; katër stinët e vitit: the
four seasons of the year; katër
herë katër bëjnë gjashtëmbëdhjetë: four time four is sixteen; rreshtohemi për katër:
to stand in four; vrapoj me të
katra: to take to flight, to run
at full speed, to gallop away;
me katër këmbë: four-legged.
katërbrínjësh,-e mb. gjeom. qua-
drilateral.
katërcíptë (i,e) mb. quadrangular.
katërfísh ndajf. fourfold.
katërfísh,-i m. the fourfold.
katërfíshój f.k. to quadruple, to
increase four fold (four times).
– katërfishohet f.jv. to increase
four times.
katërfíshtë (i,e) mb. fourfold.
katërkëmbësh,-it m.sh. zool. qua-
druped.
katërkëmbësh,-e mb. quadrupe-
dal, four-footed.
katërkëndësh,-i m.sh. -a gjeom.
quadrangle; katërkëndësh kënd-
drejtë: rectangle.
katërkëndësh,-e mb. quadrangular.
katërmbëdhjétë num.them. fourteen.
katërmbëdhjétë (i,e) num.rresht.
fourteenth.
katërqínd num.them. four hundred.

kátërt (i,e) num.rresht. fourth.
kátërta (e) f.sh. - (të) quarter.
katërvjeçár,-e mb. quadrennial.
katíl,-i m.sh. -ë criminal, murderer.
katod/ë,-a f.sh. -a el. cathode,
negative plate.
katolicíz/ëm,-mi m. catholicism.
katolík,-u m.sh. -ë catholic.
katolík,-e mb. catholic.
katragjýsh,-i m.sh. -ë shih stër-
gjysh.
katrán,-i m. tar, pitch; katran
qymyri: coal tar; lyej me katran: to tar, to pitch, to smear
with pitch; i zi katran: pitch-
black.
katranós f.k. (një punë) to botch,
to bungle (a business, a work).
– katranoset f.jv. to be botched,
to be bungled.
katrór,-i m.sh. -ë square.
katrór,-e mb. quadrate, square; rrënjë katrore: square root; metër
katror: square meter; në formë
katrore: squarely, in a square
form.
katrúv/ë,-a f.sh. -a pitcher, earthen
pot.
kat/úa,-oi m.sh. -onj 1. cellar,
stall. 2. stable.
katúnd,-i m.sh. -e village.
katundár,-i m.sh. -ë peasant.
katundarí,-a f. vjet. peasantry.
kath,-i m. mjek. sty.
kauçúk,-u m. caoutchouc.
kaurdís f.k. to roast. – kaurdiset
f.jv. to be roasted.
kaúsh,-i m.sh. -ë paper bag; cornet;
kaush duhani: tabacco paper
bag; kaush akulloreje:: ice-
cream cone.
káuz/ë,-a f. cause; kauza e madhe
e proletariatit: the great cause
of the proletariat; kauza e popullit: people's cause.
kavalerí,-a f. usht. cavalry.
kavalét,-i m.sh. -e easel, trestle
board.

kaváll,-i *m.sh.* -ё fife; **është vrima e fundit e kavallit:** to be the last in rank.
kavanóz,-i *m.sh.* -a jar, pot.
kavérn/ё,-a *f. mjek.* cavern, cavity; **kavernë në mushkëri:** cavity in the lungs.
kávo,-ja *f.sh.* - cable; **kavo çeliku:** steel cable; **lidh me kavo një anije:** to moor a vessel.
kazán,-i *m.sh.* -ё boiler; **kazan avulli:** steam-boiler, **kazan rakie:** distiller.
kazanpunúes,-i *m.sh.* - coppersmith.
kazérm/ё,-a *f.sh.* -a *usht.* barracks, quarters.
kazíno,-ja *f.sh.* - casino.
kázm/ё,-a *f.sh.* -a pick, pickax, mattock; **ndërtojmë socializmin duke mbajtur në njёrёn dorё kazmёn, në tjetrёn pushkёn:** we build socialism holding pick in the one hand and rifle in the other.
ke (ti) *f.k.* have (you) (second pers. sing. of the verb **kam).**
kec,-i *m.sh.* -a *zool.* kid.
kedh,-i *m.sh.* -a *zool.* shih **kec.**
kek,-u *m.sh.* -ё cake.
kep,-i *m.sh.* -a *gjeog.* 1. cape. 2. peak.
keq *ndajf.* 1. bad, ill, amiss, wrongly; **sillem keq:** to behave badly, to misbehave, to misdemean oneself; **shkruaj keq:** to write badly; **flas keq për dikё:** to speak ill of someone; **e kam keq (shkoj keq) me dikё:** to be on bad terms with someone; **keq e mё keq:** from bad to worse; **mendoj keq për dikё:** to think ill of someone; **mё keq:** worse; **aq mё keq:** so much the worse; **bёj keq:** to do wrong; **e bёj keq njё punё:** to botch (to bungle) a work; **i bёj keq di-**

kujt: to do harm to someone; **s'e ke keq:** it's not a bad idea; **i bёj keq vetes:** to harm oneself; **mё vjen keq:** I am sorry; **mё vjen keq për:** to feel sorry for. 2. much, very, badly; **e dua keq:** I love him much; **i dua keq kafshёt:** I like the animals badly, very much; **i ha keq fiqtё:** I am passionately fond of figs; **jam vrarё keq:** I hurt myself gravely; **jam sёmurё keq:** I am badly ill.
keq (i),-e(e) *mb.* 1. bad, evil; **shkrim i keq:** bad hand-writing; **sjellje e keqe:** bad conduct, ill conduct, ill behaviour, misbehaviour. 2. wicked; **njeri i keq:** wicked person, malevolent, malicious person, ill-natured person; **mё i keq:** worse; **mё i keq nga tё gjithё:** the worst of all.
keqárdhj/e,-a *f.* 1. regret; **shpreh keqardhje:** to express regret; **me keqardhje:** with regret, regretfully.
kéqas *ndajf.* badly, gravely; **u plagos keqas:** he was badly wounded.
kaqbёrёs,-i *m.sh.* - evil-doer, malefactor, misdoer.
keqbёrёs,-e *mb.* hurtful, injurious, mischievious.
keqbёrj/e,-a *f.* maleficence, mischieviousness.
kéq/e (e),-ja(e) *f.* 1. evil, badness, illness, wickedness; **e mira dhe e keqja:** the good and the evil. 2. necessity; **e bёra nga e keqja:** I did it by necessity, I was driven by necessity to do it; **s'ka asnjё tё keqe:** there is nothing bad.
keqёsím,-i *m.* aggravation; **keqёsim i marrёdhёnieve:** aggravation of relations.
keqёsój *f.k.* to aggravate, to make worse. – **keqёsohem** *f.jv.* to be aggravated, to grow worse.

keqinterpretím,-i *m.* misinterpretation.
keqinterpretój *f.k.* to misinterpret, to misconstrue. – **keqinterpretohet** *f.jv.* to be misinterpreted, to be misconstrued.
keqkuptím,-i *m.sh.* -e misunderstanding.
keqkuptój *f.k.* to misunderstand, to mistake. – **keqkuptohem** *f.jv.* to be misunderstood.
keqpërdór *f.k.* 1. to ill-treat, to maltreat. 2. to misuse. – **keqpërdorohem** *f.jv.* to be maltreated, to be ill-treated; **keqpërdorohet**: to be misused.
keqpërdorím,-i *m.* 1. ill-treatment. 2. ill-usage, abuse.
keqpërdorój *f.k.* shih **keqpërdor**.
keqtingëllím,-i *m.* dissonance.
keqtrajtím,-i *m.* ill-treatment.
két/ër,-ri *m.sh.* -ra *zool.* squirrel.
kë *p.vet.* whom (for persons), which (for things); **kë kërkoni?** whom do you want? **kë patë?** whom did you see? **kë shikoni në dritare?** whom do you see at the window? **për kë po flisnit?** whom were you speaking of? **me kë do të shkoni?** whom will you go with? **kë preferoni?** which do you prefer?, which do you like better? **nuk di kë të zgjedh:** I don't know which one to choose; **merr kë të duash:** take what you like (what you please); **kë të doni:** no matter which.
këlbáz/ë,-a *f. anat.* expectoration, phleom.
këlthás *f.jk.* shih **bërtas**.
këlýsh,-i *m.sh.* -ë 1. cub, welp; **këlysh ariu:** bear's cub; **këlysh dhelpre:** fox's cub; **këlysh luani:** lion's cub; **këlysh qeni:** dogs cub, pup, puppy; **këlysh ujku:** wolf's cub, whelp; **këlysh dreri:** fawn, younger deer.
këllás *f.k.* shih **kall**.

këlléç,-i *m.sh.* -ë *vjet.* sword.
këlléf,-i *m.sh.* -ë 1. case; **këlléf jastëku:** pillow-case; **këlléf gjyslykësh:** case for spectacles. 2. **këlléf shpate:** sheath, scabbard. 3. **këlléf dysheku:** tick for mattress.
këllír/ë,-a *f.* dish water, dirty, water, slop, house-slops; **kovë këllirash:** slop-pail, slop-bucket.
këll/k,-u *m.sh.* -qe *anat.* haunch, hip, huckle.
këmbác,-e *mb.* palsied, paralytic.
këmba-këmbës *ndajf.* at someone's heels.
këmbaléc,-i *m.sh.* -a trestle.
këmbéj *f.k.* to change; to exchange; to barter; **këmbej të holla:** to change money, to convert money; **këmbej një plaçkë me një tjetër:** to barter, to exchange, to give in return for an equivalent, to give in exchange. – **këmbehem** *f.jv.* to be exhanged.
këmb/ë,-a *f.sh.* -ë . *anat.* foot; **gishtërinjtë e këmbës:** toes; **tabani (shputa) i këmbës:** sole of the foot, heel of the foot; **nyja (kyçi) e këmbës:** ankle of the foot; **më këmbë:** on foot; **më këmbë!** up!, stand up! **çohem më këmbë:** to stand up; **eci më këmbë:** to go on foot, to walk; **eci me këmbë e me duar:** to go on all fours; **eci mbi majat e këmbëve:** to go on tip-toe; **eci me këmbë hapur:** to straddle, to walk with the legs wide aparat; **më merren këmbët:** to walk unsteadily, to waddle; **heq këmbët zvarrë:** to shuffle along; **më shket këmba:** to stumble; *fig.* to fall in disgrace; **më dhëmb këmba:** to have a sore foot; **më merren këmbët:** to totter, to stagger, to toddle; **hidhem (kërcej) me një këmbë:** to

hop on one foot; *fig.* **ngul këmbё: te** insist to obstinate, to persevere, to persist, to stamp down one's foot. 2. leg; **kёrciri (fyelli) i kёmbёs:** shankbone, shin of the leg; **kёmbё prej druri**:wooden leg; *(kёmbёt e kafshёve)* foot (of animals), leg (of animals), paw (of some animals as the dog, the cat, etc.). 3. *(shkalle)* stair. 4. *(kёmbёt e njё tavoline, karrigeje)* leg(of a table, of a chair).

kёmbёcingthi *ndajf.* shih **tingthi.**
kёmbёgjátё *mb.* long-legged.
kёmbёkrýq *ndajf.* with one's legs crossed; **rri kёmbёkryq:** to sit cross-legged.
kёmbёkúq/e,-ja *f. zool.* grouse, partridge.
kёmbёmbárё *mb.* lucky.
kёmbёngúl *f.jk.* to insist, to persist.
kёmbёngúlёs,-e *mb.* insistent, persistent, persevering, tenacious.
kёmbёngúlj/e,-a *f.* insistence, persistence, perseverance, tenacity, obstination; **me kёmbёngulje:** with perseverance; **punoj me kёmbёngulje** to work perseveringly (with tenacity).
kёmbёprápё *mb.* unlucky, ill-luck (person).
kёmbёpúpthi *ndajf.* shih **tingthi.**
kёmbёsor,-i *m.sh.* -ё 1. pedestrian. 2. *usht.* infantryman, foot-soldier.
kёmbёsorí,-a *f. usht.* infantry.
kёmbёshkúrtёr *mb.* short-legged.
kёmbёshtrémbёr *mb.* club-footed; bandy-legged.
kёmbёtёrs *mb.* shih **kёmbёprapё.**
kёmbёz,-a *f.sh.* -a 1. *(kёmbёz pushke)* trigger (of a gun). 2. *(kёmbёz shkalle)* step (of a ladder).
kёmbёzbáthur *mb.* barefoot, footnaked.
kёmbím,-i *m.* 1. *(kёmbim tё ho-*

llash) change, conversion (of money). 2. *(kёmbim i njё sendi me njё tjetёr)* exchange; **kёmbim reciprok:** mutual exchange.
kёmbór/ё,-a *f.sh.* -ё cow-bell, sheep-bell.
kёmbýes,-i *m.sh.* - *(tё hollash)* money-changer.
kёmbýesh/ёm (i),-me(e) *mb.* changeable, mutable, convertible.
kёmisharí,-a *f.sh.* - shirt-shop.
kёmísh/ё,-a *f.sh.* -ё shirt; **kёmishё nate:** nightgown, nightshirt; **kёmishё grash:** chemise.
kёmishёqépёs,-i *m.sh.* - shirtmaker.
kёná,-ja *f.* kenna (cosmetic paste used by women to dye the hair etc.).
kёnáq *f.k.* to satisfy, to delight, to gratify, to please; **besoj se do tё kёnaqeni:** I think you will be pleased. – **kёnaqem** *f.jv.* to be satisfied, to delight in; to take pleasure, to enjoy (something), to be pleased.
kёnaqёsí,-a *f.* satisfaction; **me kёnaqёsi:** with pleasure.
kёnáqsh/ёm(i),-me(e) *mb.* pleasing, satisfactory.
kёnáqur (i,e) *mb.* satisfied, pleased, content; **jam i kёnaqur me ju:** I am pleased with you; **mbetem i kёnaqur:** to remain satisfied.
kёnd,-i *m.sh.* -e 1. *gjeom.* angle; **kёnd i drejtё:** right angle; **kёnd i gjerё:** obtuse angle; **kёnd jo i drejtё:** oblique angle; **kёnd i ngushtё:** narrow angle. 2. corner, place; **kёnd pranё zjarrit:** chimney-corner.
kёnddréjtё *mb.* rectangular, orthogonal; **katёrkёndsh kёnddrejtё:** rectangle.
kёndéj *ndajf.* this way; **andej-kёndej:** hither and thither; **kёn-**

dej e tutje: hereafter, henceforth.

këndéz,-i *m.sh.* -ë cock, rooster.

këndím,-i *m.* reading; libër këndimi: reading book.

këndój *f.k., f.jk.* 1. to sing 2. *(zogu)* to chirp. 3. *(këndoj një libër)* to read. — këndohet *f.jv.* to be sung; kjo këngë këndohet kudo: this song is sung everywhere.

këndsh/ëm(i),-me(e) *mb.* nice, agreable, pleasing, delightful.

kënét/ë,-a *f.sh.* -a bog; marsh, swamp; shpend kënete: fen fowl.

këng/ë,-a *f.sh.* -ë 1. song; këngë djepi: lullaby; këngë për fëmijë: ditty; këngë popullore: folk-song; këngë vajtimi: threnody dirge, funeral song. 2. kënga e këndezit: cock-crow. 3. kënga e zogjve: chirp (of birds).

këngëtár,-i *m.sh.* -ë singer, chanter; këngëtar shëtitës: minstrel.

këngëtár,-e *mb.* singing; zog këngëtar: singing bird.

këpucár,-i *m.sh.* -ë 1. shoemaker, bootmaker. 2. cobbler.

këpúc/ë,-a *f.sh.* -ë shoe, boot; këpucë të lehta pa takë: pumps; këpucë të lustruara: polished shoes; këpucë me qafë: boots; këpucë grash me qafë: lady's boots; kallëp këpucësh: shoe-tree; lidhëse këpucësh: shoe-string, shoe-lace; vesh (mbath) këpucët: to put on one's shoes; heq këpucët: to take off one's shoes.

këpucëbërës,-i *m.sh.* - shih këpucar. 1.

këpucëtár,-i *m.sh.*-ë shih këpucar.

këpucëtarí,-a *f.sh.* - 1. shoemaking. 2. shoemaker's shop.

këpúj/ë,-a *f.sh.* -a 1. *bot.* bay (of fruit). 2. *gram* copula.

këpúsh/ë,-a *f.sh.* -a *zool.* tick.

këpús *f.k.* 1. *(këpus një lule, një pemë)*: to pick, to cull, to pluck (a flower, a fruit). 2. *(këpus zinxhirin)* to break (a chain); *(litarin)* to break (a rope). 3. *fig.* *(marrëdhëniet)* to break off (relations). — *Lok.* këput qafën! away with you! — këputem *f.jv.* këputem së punuari': to overwork oneself; këputem së qeshuri: to burst out laughing.

këpútj/e,-a *f.* 1. *(këputje e luleve, e pemëve)* gathering, picking up (of flowers, fruits). 2. *(këputje e zinxhirëve)* breaking (of chains). 3. *(këputje e marrëdhënieve)* rupture (of relations).

këqýr *f.k.* to examine, to look carefully, to observe, to scrutinize. — këqyrem *f.jv.* to be watched; këqyrem në pasqyrë: to look at the mirror.

këqýrj/e,-a *f.* observation, examination.

kërbáç,-i *m.sh.* -ë cudgel, club.

kërbísht,-i *m.sh.* -a *anat.* loins.

kërbishtórë-t *m.sh. zool.* vertebrata.

kërcás I. *f.k.* 1. to crack, to craunch; kërcas diçka me dhëmbë: to craunch, to crunch; kërcas dhëmbët: to grate one's teeth. 2. kërcas gishtërinjtë: to snap one's fingers.

II. *f.jk.* 1. *(zjarri)* to crackle. 2. *(dëbora nën këmbë etj.)* to crunch. 3. *(karrigia)* to creak, to squeak; karrigia kërciti nën peshën e tij: the chair creaked under his weight.

kërcéj *f.jk.* 1. to leap, to jump, to spring, to skip, to hop, to caper; kërcej nga gazi: to jump from joy; shiko mirë para se të kërcesh! look before you leap! 2. to dance. — *Lok.* më kërcen

damari: to get angry, to be fu-
furious, my blood is up.
kërcé/ll,-lli *m.sh.* **-j** *bot.* stalk.
kërc/ë,-a *f.sh.* -a cartillage, gristle;
me kërcë: cartillaginous, gristly.
kërcëllij *f.k.* to grind, to gnash;
kërcëllij dhëmbët: to grind
one's teeth, to gnash one's
teeth; *fig.* to show one's teeth.
kërcëllím,-i *m.* grinding, gnashing;
kërcëllimi i dhëmbëve: grinding of teeth.
kërcëllím/ë,-a *f.* **kërcëllima e**
pushkëve: discharge of rifles.
kërcëním,-i *m.sh.* **-e** threatening,
menace.
kërcënój *f.k.* to threaten. to menace. – **kërcënohem** *f.jv.* to be
threatened.
kërcënúes,-e *mb.* menacing, threatening.
kërcí,-ri *m.sh.* **-rë** *anat.* shin,
shank; **kërciri i këmbës:** shin
of the leg, shank-bone.
kërcím,-i *m.sh.* **-e** 1. leap, jumping,
jump, skip, spring, hop, 2. dance,
dancing.
kërcímtár,-i *m.sh.* **-ë** dancer.
kërcítj/e,-a *f.sh.* **-e** crack, crash;
kërcitje e derës: cracking of
the door; **kërcitje e dhëmbëve:**
chattering, gnashing of teeth;
kërcitje e gishtërinjve: snapping of the fingers; **kërcitje e**
gjuhës: clack of the tongue;
kërcitje e tapës: pop of a
cork; **kërcitje e druve kur ndi-**
zen: cracking of fire wood.
kërcór,-e *mb.* cartillaginous, gristly.
kërcú,-ri,- *m.sh.* **-nj** chunk, chump,
log; **shkul kërcunj:** to pull
logs.
kërdí,-a *f.* **mass** extermination,
slaughter, havoc; **bëj kërdinë:**
to play havoc.
kërkés/ë,-a *f.sh.* -a request, require-
ment, demand; **bëj një kër-**
kesë për: to make a request for;

plotësoj një kërkesë: to grant
a request, to satisfy a demand.
kërkím,-i *m.sh.* **-e** 1. research; **kër-**
kime shkencore: scientific re-
searches; **kërkime arkeologji-**
ke: archaelogical excavations;
kërkime gjeologjike: prospect.
2. search.
kërkój *f.k.* 1. *(diçka apo dikë që ka*
humbur) to look for, to search
for. 2. to seek, to try to find, to
be after; **kërkoj punë:** to seek
work, to look for work. 3. **kër-**
koj dikë: to seek someone.
4. **kërkoj një të drejtë:** to claim a right; **kërkoj të falur:** to
ask for pardon; **kërkoj audiencë:**
to solicit audience. – **kërkohem**
f.jv. to be in request; to be sought;
kërkohem nga policia: to be
wanted by the police.
kërkúes,-i *m.sh.* - 1. searcher, see-
ker; **kërkues ari:** gold-prospec-
tor, gold-digger. 2. *(në shkencë)*
researcher.
kërkúes,-e *mb.* 1. exigent, exac-
ting.
kërm/ë,-a *f.sh.* -a carrion.
kërmí/ll,-lli *m.sh.* **-j** snail; **me ha-**
pin e kërmillit: at a snail's
pace.
kërp,-i *m bot.* hemp; **farë kërpi:**
hemp-seed; **fije kërpi:** hemp-
fiber; **pëlhurë kërpi:** sackcloth.
kërpác,-i *m.sh.* **-ë** bungler.
kërpúdh/ë,-a *f.sh.* -a *bot.* mush-
room; **kërpudhë e helmët:** toad-
stool.
kërshëndélla,-t *f.sh.* - Christmas.
kërshërí,-a *f.* curiosity; lively interest, thirst for knowledge.
kërthí,-ri *m.sh.* **-nj** newborn babe.
kërthíng/ël,-la *f.* *zool.* lap-wing.
kërthíz/ë,-a *f.sh.* **-a** *anat.* 1. navel.
2. *fig.* middle; **në kërthizë të**
Shqipërisë: in the middle of
Albania.
kërráb/ë,-a *f.sh.* -a 1. crook; **kë-**

rrabë bariu; shepherd's crook, stoff.

kërríç,-i *m.sh.* -ë 1. *zool.* foal (of ass). 2. *fig.* urchin.

kërrús *f.k.* to bend, to curve, to hunch. — kërrusem *f.jv.* to be-came curved (crooked).

kësáj *p.d.* (dative case) this, to this one; para kësaj gjendjeje: in front of this situation; para kësaj kohe: before this time; jepja kësaj vajzës këtu: give it to this girl.

kësisój *ndajf.* so, thus, in this manner.

kësísh *p.pk.* such, this kind.

kësmét,-i *m.* luck.

kësodóre *ndajf.* in this way.

këst,-i *m.sh.* -e instalment; me këste: by instalments.

kësúl/ë,-a *f.sh.* -a cap, headdress; kësulë nate: nightcap.

këshíll,-i *m.sh.* -a council, board; Këshilli i Ministrave: Council of Ministers; Këshillat Nacionalçlirimtare: the National Liberation councils; këshillat popullore: the peoples councils.

këshíll/ë,-a *f.sh.* -a advice; veproj sipas këshillave të: to act on someone's advice.

këshillím,-i *m.* admonition.

këshillój *f.k.* to advigë. — këshillohem *f.jv.* to confer with, to consult with, to lay (to put) heads together, to advigë with.

këshilltár,-i *m.sh.* -ë adviser, counselor; këshilltar ushtarak: military adviser.

këshillúesh/ëm(i),-me(e) *mb.* advisable.

kështjáll/ë,-a *f.sh.* -a citadel, fortress, castle; kështjella në erë: castles in the air.

kështú *ndajf.* so, thus: pse kështu? why so? e kështu me rradhë: and so on.

kështú që *lidh.* so that.

këtá *p.d.* (pl.masc.) these; unë i njoh këta burra: I know these men (shih ky).

këtë *p.d.* (sing. masc. and fem., accusative) this; kush e bëri këtë? who has done this? merre këtë libër: take this book; këtë vit: this year (shih ky).

këtéj *ndajf.* this way, this side; andej-këtej: hither and thither; këtej e tutje: hereafter, henceforth; kaloni këtej: go this way.

këtéjm/ë (i),-me (e) *mb.* of this place, of this side.

këtéjsh/ëm(i),-me(e) *mb.* shih i këtejmë.

këtíj *p.d.* (dative case) to this one; i thashë këtij shokut: I said to this comrade (shih ky.)

këtíllë(i,e) *mb.* such; të këtillë njerëz: such people.

këtó *p.d.* (pl.fem.) these; merri këto fletore: take these copybooks.

këtú *ndajf.* here; këtu afër: nearby; këtu ngjitur: jointly; këtu rrotull: here about; këtu poshtë: down here; këtu sipër: up here; deri këtu: up to here, so far; që këtu: from here.

këtúesh/ëm(i),-me(e) *mb.* from here, from these parts.

këtýre *p.d.* to these ones (dative case, plural fem. and masc.) (shih ky).

kiamét,-i *m.* doomsday, disater, calamity, catastrophe, cataclysm.

kiç,-i *m.sh.* -e *det.* poop; kiçi i anijes: poop-deck, stern (of a ship).

kikirík,-u *m. bot.* peanut.

kilográm,-i *m.sh.* -ë kilogramme.

kilomét/ër,-ri *m.sh.* -ra kilometer.

kilóta,-t *f.sh.* breeches.

kilovát,-i *m.sh.* -ë *el.* kilowatt.

kilovat-ór/ë,-a *f.sh.* -ë *el.* kilowatt hour.

kímë,-a *f.* salmagundi.

kimí,-a *f.* chemistry.
kimík,-e *mb.* chemical; **prodhime kimike:** chemicals.
kimíst,-i *m.sh.* -ë chemist.
kinemá,-ja *f.sh.* - 1. *(ndërtesa)* cinema, picture-house, *amer.* movie-theater; **shkoj në kinema:** to go to the cinema (to the movies). 2. *(arti)* the cinema, *amer.* movies.
kinematografí,-a *f.* cinematography.
kinéz,-i *m.sh.* -ë Chinese.
kinéz,-e *mb.* Chinese.
kinín/ë,-a *f.sh.* -a quinine.
kinkaléri.-a *f.sh.* 1. fancy-goods shop. 2. trinkets, knickkuacks, fancy goods.
kinostúdio,-ja *f.sh.* - film studio.
kínse *lidh.* shih **gjoja.**
kirúrg,-u *m.sh.* -ë surgeon.
kirurgjí,-a *f.* surgery.
kirurgjík,-e *mb.* surgical.
kísha (past tense of the verb **kam**) I had.
kísh/ë,-a *f.sh.* -a church; **kishë e vogël fshati:** chapel; **kishë e madhe:** cathedral; **kisha katolike:** the catholic church.
kishtár,-i *m.sh.* - ë clergyman, churchman.
kishtár,-e *mb.* ecclesiastic, sacerdotal.
kitár/ë,-a *f.sh.* -a *muz.* guitar.
kíz/ë,-a *f.sh.* -a grafting knife.
kjasón *f.jk.* to ooze; **kjason muri:** the wall oozes.
kjo *p.d.* (sing. feminine, nominative case) this; **ç'është kjo?** what is this? **kjo është një vizore:** this is a ruler; **më pëlqen kjo vajzë:** I like this girl; **nga kjo del se:** hence, in consequence of this (shih **ky**).
klarinét/ë,-a *f.sh.* -a *muz.* clarinet.
klás/ë,-a *f.sh.* -a 1. class; **klasa**

punëtore: the working class; **klasat e pasura:** the rich classes; **klasat e larta:** the upper classes, the higher classes; **klasat e ulëta:** the lower classes; **lufta e klasave:** class struggle; **ndërgjegje e klasës:** class consciousness. 2. *(nxënësit)* class. 3. *(dhoma)* class-room. 4. *(klasë udhëtimi me tren e vapor)* class; **udhëtoj në klasë të parë, të dytë:** to travel in the first class, in the second class. 5. class , rank; **i klasës së parë:** first-class, first-rate, top-raking, high-class.
klasifíkím,-i *m.sh.* -e classification.
klasifikój *f.k.* to classify, to class. – **klasifikohem** *f.jv.* to be classified.
klasík,-e *mb.* classic, classical.
klasór,-e *mb.* (of) class; **kontradikta klasore:** class contradictions; **luftë klasore:** class struggle.
klauzól/ë,-a *f.sh.* -a clause, stipulation.
kléçk/ë,-a *f.sh.* -a small stick; **kleçkë dhëmbësh:** tooth-pick. *fig.* **gjej kleçka:** to find fault with.
kler,-i *m.* clergy, priesthood.
klerík,-u *m.sh.* -ë clergyman.
klerikál,-e *mb.* clerical.
kliént,-i *m.sh.* -ë client; purchaser, customer; *(në hotel)* guest.
klientál/ë,-a *f.sh.* -a clientele.
klík/ë,-a *f.sh.* -a *pol.* clique.
klimaterík,-e *mb.* climatic; **vend klimaterik:** climatic place, resort, health resort.
klimatizím,-i *m.* acclimation, acclimatization.
klimatizój *f.k.* to acclimatize, to acclimate. – **klimatizohem** *f.jv.* to be acclimatized.
klím/ë,-a *f.* climate; **klimë e butë:** mild climate.

kliník/ë,-a *f.sh.* -a clinic; **klinikë psikiatrike:** mental house.
klishé,-ja *f.sh. polig.* 1. block, cliché. 2. cliché (an expression that has become trite).
klithm/ë,-a *f.sh.* -a shih **britmë.**
klor,-i *m. kim.* chlorine.
kloroform,-i *m. kim.* chloroform.
klub,-i *m.sh.* -e club, society, circle; **klubi i gjuetarëve:** hunter's club.
kllaník,-u *m.* shıh **gllanik.**
klláp/ë,-a *f.sh.* -a 1. parenthesis; **vë në kllapa:** to put into parantheses. 2. door bolt.
kllapí,-a *f.* delirium, frenzy.
kllapodán,-i *m.sh.* -e brocade; **punuar me kllapodan:** brocaded.
kllóçk/ë,-a *f.sh.* -a *(pulë)* brooding-hen, brood-hen, sitting-hen; **zo-gjtë e klloçkës:** brood, hatch.
koalición,-i *m.sh.*-e *usht.* coalition; **hyj në një koalicion:** to enter a coalition;**formoj një koalicion:** to form a coalition.
kobált,-i *m.* **kim.** cobalt.
kobásh,-e *mb.* larcenous; **njeri kobash:** pilferer.
kób/ë,-a *f.* pilferage, larceny.
kobís *f.k.* to pilfer.
kobítj/e,-a *f.* pilfering.
kóbsh/ëm (i),-me(e) *mb.* fatal, sinister, disastrous.
kobúr/e,-ja *f.sh.* -e *vjet.* revolver, pistol.
kobz/í,-ezë *mb.* fatal, sinister, disastrous.
kóc/ë,-a *f.sh.* -a *zool.* skate.
kockamán,-e *mb.* bony, scraggy, raw-boned, skiny, *amer.* scranny.
kóck/ë,-a *f.sh.* -a bone; **mish me shumë kockë:** bony meat; **koc-ka e këmbës (kërciri):** shin-bone, shank-bone; **kocka e kof-shës:** thigh-bone; **kocka e no-fullës:** jaw-bone; **kocka e supit;** clavicle; **kocka e krahut:** heome-

rous; **kockë e lëkurë:** raw-boned, scraggy, skiny, *amer.* scrawny.
koçán,-i *m.sh.* -ë 1. cob; **koçan misri:** corn-cob. 2. **koçan lakre:** cabbage stalk, cabbage stump.
koçimár/e,-ja *f. bot.* strawberry tree.
kóçkull,-a *f.sh. bot.* vetch.
kod,-i *m.sh.* -e 1. *drejt.* code; **kodi i punës:** labour-code. 2. *(shi-fër)* code.
kód/ër,-ra *f.sh.* -ra hill. − *Lok.* **flas kodra pas bregu:** to talk nonsense.
kodósh,-i *m.sh.* -ë pander.
kodrín/ë,-a *f.sh.* -a hillock, knoll, small hill, hummock; **kodrinë rërë:** sandy hillock.
kodrinór,-e *mb.* hilly; **vend kodri-nor:** hilly region.
koeficiént,-i *m.sh.* -ë coefficient.
kófsh/ë,-a *f.sh.* -ë *anat.* thigh, hip; **kofshë dashi:** a leg of mutton.
kohezión,-i *m. fiz.* cohesion.
kóh/ë,-a *f.* 1. time; **kohë e gjatë:** long time, a long while; **kohë e humbur:** lost time; **kaloj ko-hën:** to pass the time; to while away one's time; **kaloi koha!:** time is up! **kohë pushimi** *(gjatë punës)* break; **kohë të vësh-tira:** hard times; **në kohën e duhur:** at the proper time, in good time, at the right moment; **arrij me kohë:** to come early; **arrij në kohën e duhur:** to come just in time; **jo në kohën e duhur:** untimely; **para kohe:** ahead of time, untimely; **me kali-min e kohës:** in the course of time; **në atë kohë:** at that time; **në çdo kohë:** at any time; **në të njëjtën kohë:** at the same time; **në këtë kohë:** at this time (mo-ment); **në kohët e para, shumë kohë më parë:** a long time ago, in past times; **një herë e një**

kohë: a long time ago; **kohë pas kohe:** from time to time; **prej kohësh:** of old, far away; **prej kohësh që nuk mbahen mend:** from time immemorial; **në kohë të ndryshme:** at different times; **brenda një kohe të shkurtër:** in a short time; **para pak kohe:** some time ago, recently. 2. weather; **parashikimi i kohës:** weather forecast; **kohë e bukur:** fine weather, splendid weather; **kohë e keqe:** bad weather, nasty weather, naughty weather, wretched weather, foul weather; **kohë me erë:** windy weather; **kohë me shi:** rainy weather, showery weather; **kohë e vrenjtur:** cloudy weather, nebulous weather; **si është koha?** how is the weather? **koha është e bukur:** it is fine. 3. while, moment; **për pak kohë:** for a while, for a moment. 4. time, times, day, days, age, era, epoch; **në kohën tonë:** in our days, nowadays, at the present time; **koha e lashtë:** antiquity; **në kohën e Skënderbeut:** in Scanderbeg times; **sot është koha e revolucionit:** this is the epoch of revolution. 5. period; **brenda një kohe prej:** within a period of. 6. occasion; **në një kohë të volitshme (të përshtatshme):** at the opportune time, at the convenient time (occasion). 7. *muz.* **mbaj kohën:** to keep time. 8. *gram.* tense; **koha e tashme:** present tense; **koha e kryer:** past tense; **koha e ardhshme:** future tense. — *Prov.* **koha është flori:** time is money; **koha e humbur nuk kthehet më:** lost time is never found again; **koha shëron plagët:** time is a great healer.
kohërrëfyes/,-i *m.sh.* - weathercock.

kohëshënúes,-i *m.sh.* time keeper
koincidím,-i *m.* coincidence.
koincidón *f.jk.* to coincide.
kok,-u koks,-i *m. kim.* coke.
kokaín/ë,-a *f.* cocaine.
kokáll/ë,-a *f.sh.* -a bone.
kokár/e,-ja *f.sh.* - *bot.* bulb of onions.
kók/ë,-a *f.sh.* -ë 1. head; **buti I kokës:** the top of the head, epicranium; **kafka e kokës:** skull, cranium; **laj kokën:** to shampoo, to wash the head; **var kokën:** to hang down one's head; **ngrije kokën!** raise your head!, hold up your head!; **më dhemb koka:** I have an headache, my headaches; **dhembje koke:** headache. 2. *(gozhde, gjilpëre)* head (of a nail, a pin). — *Lok.* **bëj sipas kokës:** to have one's own way; **bisedë kokë më kokë:** face to face (tête à tête) conversation, private conversation; **al nuk e çan kokën fare:** he does not care a rap, he does not care a bit; **ai e ka kokën bosh:** he is empty-headed; **nga koka te këmbët:** from head to foot; **për kokën time!** upon my life!; **kokë e madhe:** genius.
kokëçárj/e,-a *f.* care, tediousness.
kokëdrú *mb.* blockhead, loggerhead, dolt, numskull.
kokëfýell *mb.* rattlebrained.
kokëfórtë *mb.* headstrong, stubborn, recalcitrant, self-willed, wilful, stiff-necked.
kokëfortësí,-a *f.* wilfulness; pigheadedness, stubborness.
kokëgdhë *mb.* shih **kokëdru.**
kokëkrísur *mb.* madcap, fool-hardy, cracked-brained.
kokëkúngull *mb.* blockhead.
kók/ël,-la *f.sh.* -la lump; **kokël sheqeri:** lump of sugar.
kokëmádh-e *mb.* big-headed.
kokëndézur *mb.* rash.

kokëngjéshur *mb.* shih **kokëfortë.**
kokëpóshtë *ndajf.* with the heels over one's head; **kërcim kokëposhtë:** somersault.
kokërdhók,-u *m.sh.* -ë *anat. (i syrit);* eyeball.
kók/ërr,-rra *f.sh.* -rra grain; **kokërr gruri, elbi etj.:** grain of wheat, barley etc.
kokërrzím,-i *m.* granulation.
kokëshkëmb *mb.* shih **kokëdru.**
kokëshkrépur *mb.* shih **kokëkrisur**
kokëshkrétë *mb.* shih **kokëkrisur.**
kokëtráshë *mb.* thickheaded, thickwitted, block-headed.
koklavít *f.k.* **1.** to tangle, to knot, to entangle. **2.** to complicate. – **koklavitet** *f.jv.* **1.** to be entangled. **2.** to become complicated.
koklavítj/e,-a *f.* **1.** entanglement, knotting. **2.** complication.
kokón/ë,-a *f.sh.* -a nice girl (woman).
kokoròsh,-i *m.sh.* -ë sturdy man, stout man; **plak kokorosh :**a stout old man.
kokór/e,-ja *f.sh.* -e flapped hat.
kokrríz/ë,-a *f.sh.* -a granule; **me kokrriza:** granulated, granular.
koks,-i *m.* shih **kok.**
kokúlur *mb.* modest, humble.
ko|ég,-u *m.sh.* -ë colleague.
kolégj,-i *m.sh.* -e college.
koleksión,-i *m.sh.* -e collection; **koleksion pullash poste:** collection of postage stamps.
koleksioníst,-i *m.sh.* -ë collector (of postage stamps).
koleksionój *f.k.* to collect.
kolektív,-i *m.sh.* -a collective.
kolektív,-e *mb.* collective.
kolektivísht *ndajf.* collectively.
kolektivitét,-i *m.* collectivity.
kolektivizím,-i *m.* collectivization; **kolektivizimi i bujqësisë:** the collectivization of the agriculture.
kolektór,-i *m.sh.* -ë *tek.* collector.
kolér/ë,-a *f. mjek.* cholera.

kolí,-a *f.sh.* – postal package.
kolíb/e,-ja *f.sh.* -e hut, cot.
kolkóz,-i *m.sh.* -e kolkhoz (kolhoz, kolkhos).
kolkozián,-i *m.sh.* -ë member of a kolkhoz.
kolipóst/ë,-a *f.sh.* -a postal package.
kolofón,-i *m.* colophony.
kolokiúm,-i *m.sh.* -e colloquy.
kolonél,-i *m.sh.* -ë colonel.
kolón/ë,-a *f.sh.* -a 1. *(kolonë e një libri)* column. 2. *ndërt. (kolonë e një ndërtese, e një ure)* pillar, column. 3. *anat.* **kolona vertebrale:** back-bone, spinal column, vertebral column.
koloní,-a *f.sh.* – colony.
koloniál,-e *mb.* colonial; **trupa koloniale:** colonial troops.
kolonialíst,-i *m.sh.* -ë colonialist.
kolonialíz/ëm,-mi *m.* colonialism.
koloníst,-i *m.sh.* -ë colonist.
kolonizátor,-i *m.sh.* -ë coloniser.
kolonizím,-i *m.* colonisation.
kolonizój *f.k.* to colonize. – **kolonizohet** *f.jv.* to be colonized.
kolónj/ë,-a *f.* eau de Cologne.
kolopúç,-i *m.sh.* -ë healthy, young child.
kolós,-i *m.sh.* -ë colossus, giant.
kolosál,-e *mb.* colossal, giantlike, gigantic.
kolovájz/ë,-a *f.* 1. seesaw; **luaj me kolovajzë:** to play at seesaw.
kolovít *f.k.* to swing. – **kolovitem** *f.jv.* to seesaw.
kolovítj/e,-a *f.* swinging.
koll,-i *m.* starch; **hekuros me koll:** to iron with starch
kolláj *ndajf.* easily.
kollájsh/ëm(i),-me(e) *mb.* easy, facile.
kollán,-i *m.sh.* -e belt; **kollan shpate:** sword-belt.
kollarís *f.k.* to iron with starch.
kollár/e,-ja *f.sh.* -e neck-tie, cravat.

kóllem *f.jv.* to cough.
kóll/ë,-a *f.* cough; **kollë e mirë,
kollë e bardhë:** whooping cough, hooping cough; **kollë e thatë:** pleuresy.
kollítem *f.jv.* shih **kollem.**
kollítj/e,-a *f.* coughing.
kollodók,-u *m.sh.* -ë *mek.* crankshaft.
kollofís *f.k.* to gulp down, to swallow at once.
kollotúmba *f.* somersault; **bëj kollotumba:** to make a somersault.
kolltú/k,-ku *m.sh.* -qe 1. armchair. 2. a seat (position) of authority.
komandánt,-i *m.sh.* -ë commander; **komandant i përgjithshëm:** commander in chief.
komandím,-i *m.* commandment.
komandój *f.k.* to command, to head, to lead. – **komandohem** *f.jv.* to be commanded.
komandúes,-e *mb.* commanding, imperious; **ton komandues:** imperious tone.
komb,-i *m.sh.* -e nation; **kombi shqiptar:** the Albanian nation.
këmbájn/ë,-a *f.sh.* -a *bujq.* combine.
kombësí,-a *f.* nationality.
kombëtár,-e *mb.* national.
kombëtarísht *ndajf.* nationally.
kombëtarizím,-i *m.* nationalization.
kombëtarizój *f.k.* to nationalize. – **kombëtarizohet** *f.jv.* to be nationalized.
kombinación,-i *m.sh.* -e combination.
kombinát,-i *m.sh.* -e combine.
kombinezón,-i *m.sh.* -e combinations, combs.
kombiním,-i *m.sh.* -e combination; **kombinim ngjyrash:** combination of colours.
kombinój *f.k.* to combine. – **kombinohet** *f.jv.* to be combined.

komblík,-u *m.* *anat.* pelvis.
komedí,-a *f.sh.* - comedy.
komént,-i *m.sh.* -e comment.
komentój *f.k.* to comment. – **komentohet** *f.jv.* to be commented.
komentúes,-i *m.sh.* - commentator.
komét/ë,-a *f.sh.* -a *astron.* comet.
komík,-u *m.sh.* -ë comic.
komík,-e *mb.* comic, comical, droll.
kominóshe,-t *f.sh.* overalls.
komisár,-i *m.sh.* -ë commissar.
komisariát,-i *m.sh.* -e commissariat.
komisión,-i *m.sh.* -e commission, board; **komision i provimeve:** examining board; **komision hetues:** inquiring commission.
komisionér,-i *m.sh.* -ë commissioner; **komisioner anijesh:** shipbroker; **komisioner shëtitës:** commercial agent, traveller commissioner.
komít,-i *m.sh.* -ë outlaw, outcast.
komitét,-i *m.sh.* -e committee; **komiteti ekzekutiv:** executive committee.
komó,-ja *f.sh.* - commode, *amer.* bureau, dresser.
komodín/ë,-a *f.sh.* -a bed-sidetable, night table, nightstand.
komoditét,-i *m.* commodity.
kompákt,-e *mb.* compact.
kompaktësí,-a *f.* compactness.
kompaní,-a *f.sh.* - company.
kompás,-i *m.sh.* -e *gjeom.* compasses.
kompensát/ë,-a *f.* veneer; **vesh me kompensatë:** to veneer.
kompensím,-i *m.* compensation.
kompensój *f.k.* to compensate. – **kompensohet** *f.jv.* to be compensated.
kompetént,-e *mb.* competent.
kompeténc/ë,-a *f.* competence,
kompléks,-i *m.* 1. whole, group mass, collection, system; unit

combine,. complex. 2. *muz.* singing group.

kompletím,-i *m.* completion.

kompletój *f.k.* to complete. – **kompletohet** *f.jv.* to be completed.

komplimént,-i *m.sh.* -e compliment.

komplót,-i *m.sh.* -e plot, conspiracy.

komplotíst,-i *m.sh.* -e plotter, conspirator.

komplotój *f.jk.* to plot, to conspire.

komplotúes,-e *mb.* conspirative.

kompósto,-ja *f.* compote; stewed fruits; **komposto mollësh**: stewed apples.

kompozím,-i *m.sh.* -e *muz.* composition.

kompozitór,-i *m.sh.* -ë *muz.* composer.

kompozój *f.k. muz.* to compose.

kompozój *f.k. muz.* to compose.

komprés/ë,-a *f.sh.* -a *mjek.* compress.

komprometím,-i *m.* compromising.

komprometój *f.k.* to compromise. – **komprometohem** *f.jv.* to be compromised, to expose oneself.

komprometúes,- e *mb.* compromising.

kompromís,-i *m.sh.* -e compromise.

komshí,-u *m.sh.* -nj neighbour.

komunál,-e *mb.* communal; **shërbime komunale**: public services; **punime komunale**: public works.

komún/ë,-a *f.sh.* -a 1. district. 2. *polit.* **Komuna e Parisit** : Paris commune.

komunikación,-i *m.* communication.

komunikát/ë,-a *f.sh.* -a communiquè, buletin; **komunikatë në shtyp**: press release.

komunikím,-i *m.* communication.

komunikój I. *f.k.* to communicate, to impart. – **komunikohet** *f.jv.* to be communicated, to be imparted.

II. *f.jk.* to communicate.

komunikúes,-e *mb.* communicative, communicating.

komuníst,-i *m.sh.* -ë communist.

komuníst,-e *mb.* communist.

komunitét,-i *m.sh.* -e community; **komunitet fetar**: congregation.

komuníz/ëm,-mi *m.* communism.

kon,-i *m.sh.* -e *gjeom.* cone.

konák,-u *m.sh.* -ë lodging-house.

koncentrík,-e *mb.* concentric.

koncentrím,-i *m.* concentration.

koncentrój *f.k.* to concentrate. – **koncentrohet** *f.jv.* to be concentrated; **acid i koncentruar**: concentrated acid.

koncépt,-i *m.sh.* -e concept.

koncért,-i *m.sh.* -e concert.

koncesión,-i *m.sh.* -e concession; **i bëj konçesione (dikujt)**: to make concessions to (someone).

kondák,-u *m.sh.* -ë butt.

kondensatór,-i *m.sh.* -ë *el.* condenser.

kondensím,-i *m.* condensation.

kondensój *f.k.* to condense. – **kondensohet** *f.jv.* to be condensed; **qumësht i kondensuar**: condensed milk.

kondicionalísht *ndajf.* conditionally.

kondicionój *f.k.* to condition. – **kondicionohet** *f.jv.* to be conditioned.

kondít/ë,-a *f.sh.* -a condition; **i plotësoj konditat**: to have the required conditions; **me ç'kondita?** on what conditions? **me konditë që**: on condition that; **në këto kondita**: under the existing conditions.

kón/e,-ja *f.sh.* -e *zool.* doggie, pup, puppy.

konfederát/ë,-a *f.sh.* -a confederation.
konferénc/ë,-a *f.sh.* -a 1. conference. 2. lecture.
konferenciér,-i *m.sh.* -ë lecturer
konfirmím,-i *m.* confirmation.
konfirmój *f.k.* to confirm. — **konfirmohet** *f.jv.* to be confirmed
konfiskím,-i *m.* confiscation.
konfiskój *f.k.* to confiscate. — **konfiskohet** *f.jv.* to be confiscated; **mall i konfiskuar:** forfeit.
konfiskúes,-i *m.sh.* - confiscator.
konflíkt,-i *m.sh.* -e conflict.
konformíst,-i *m.sh.* -ë conformist.
konfuzión,-i *m.* 1. confusion, disorder. 2. abashment.
kongrés,-i *m.sh.* -e congress.
kongresíst,-i *m.sh.* -ë congressman.
koník,-e *mb.* conic, conical.
konízm/ë,-a *f.sh.* -a *fet.* i con.
konkáv,-e *mb.* concave.
konkluzión,-i *m.sh.* -e conclusion.
konkrét,-e *mb.* concrete; **rast konkret:** case in point.
konkretísht *ndajf.* concretely.
konkúrs,-i *m.sh.* -e competition, competitive examination.
konkurrénc/ë,-a *f.* competition, rivalry.
konkurrént,-i *m.sh.* -ë competitor.
konkurrím,-i *m.* competition.
konkurrój *f.jk.* to compete.
konóp,-i *m.sh.* -ë cord, rope.
konsekuénc/ë,-a *f.sh.* -a consequence.
konsekuént,-e *mb.* consequent, consistent.
konservatór,-i *m.sh.* -ë conservative.
konservatór,-e *mb.* conservative.
konsérv/ë,-a *f.sh.* -a preserve; **konservë mishi:** tinned meat, *amer.* canned meat; **fabrikë konservash:** cannery.

konservím,-i *m.* conservation, preservation.
konservój *f.k.* to conserve, to preserve. — **konservohet** *f.jv.* to be conserved, to be preserved; **ushqime të konservuara:** canned foods.
konsiderát/ë,-a *t.sh.* -a 1. consideration; **kam konsideratë për dikë:** to think highly of someone.
konsiderój *f.k.* to consider. — **konsiderohem** *f.jv.* to be considered.
konsiderúesh/ëm(i),-me(e) *mb.* considerable; **në mënyrë të konsiderueshme:** considerably.
konsistón *f.jk.* to consist.
konsolidím,-i *m.* consolidation.
konsolidój *f.k.* to consolidate.
konspékt,-i conspectus.
konspiratív,-e *mb.* conspirative, secret; **në mënyrë konspirative:** secretly.
konspiratór,-i *m.sh.* -ë conspirator, plotter.
konspirím,-i *m.* conspiracy, plot.
konspirój *f.jk.* to conspire, to plot.
konstánt,-e *mb.* constant.
konstatím,-i *m.sh.* -e ascertainment; observation.
konstatój *f.k.* 1. to ascertain. 2. to notice, to observe.
konstruksión,-i *m.sh.* -e building, construction.
konstruktív,-e *mb.* constructive.
konsultatív,-e *mb.* consultative.
konsúlt/ë,-a *f.sh.* -a *mjek.* consultation, counsel.
konsultím,-i *m.* consultation.
konsultój *f.k.* to consult, to deliberate. — **konsultohem** *f.ʲv.* to be consulted with, to consult one another, to take counsel (with others).
konsultór/e,-ja *f.sh.* -e child consultation; maternity consultation.
kónsu/ll,-lli *m.sh.* -j consul.
konsullát/ë,-a *f.sh.* -a consulate.
konsullór,-e *mb.* consular.

konsum,-i *m.* consumption; **artikuj të konsumit të gjerë:** (mass) consumer's goods, consumption goods.

konsumatór,-i *m.sh.* -ë consumer.

konsumím,-i *m.* 1. consumption. 2. *(i materialeve) usht.* expenditure.

konsumój *f.k.* to consume. – **konsumohem** *f.jv.* to be consumed; **mall që konsumohet:** consumable commodity.

kont,-i *m.sh.* -ë count, earl.

kontákt,-i *m.sh.* -e 1. contact, touch; **mbaj kontakt:** to keep in touch; **bie në kontakt:** to come (to get) into touch with. 2. *el.* switch, contact.

kontatór,-i *m. (uji, gazi, ı dritës elektrike)* counter.

kontékst,-i *m.* context.

kontestím,-i *m.* contestation.

kontestój *f.k.* to contest, to dispute. – **kontestohet** *f.jv* contested (disputed).

kontestúesh /ëm(i),-me(e) *mb.* contestable.

kontinént,-i *m.sh.* -e continent; mainland.

kontinentál,-e *mb.* continental; **klimë kontinentale:** continental climate.

kontingjént,-i *m.sh.* -e contingent.

kontrabánd /ë,-a *f.* contraband, smuggling; **mallra kontrabandë:** smuggled goods; **bëj kontrabandë:** to smuggle.

kontrabandíst,-i *m.sh.* -ë contrabandist, smuggler.

kontradíkt /ë,-a *f.sh.* -a contradiction.

kontradiktór,-e *mb.* contradictory.

kontraktím,-i *m.sh.* -e contraction.

kontraktój *f.k.* to make a contract. – **kontraktohet** *f.jv.* to be contracted.

kontraktúes,-i *m.sh.* - contractor.

kontraktúes,-e *mb.* contractual.

kontrást,-i *m.sh.* -e contrast.

kontrát /ë,-a *f.sh.* -a contract; **kontratë qiraje:** lease; **kontratë sigurimi:** contract of insurance; **anulloj një kontratë:** to rescind a contract; **përsëris një kontratë:** to renew a contract; **nënshkrues kontrate:** underwriter.

kontribuój *f.jk.* to contribute.

kontribút,-i *m.* contribution.

kontróll,-i *m.* control; **urdhër kontrolli:** searchwarrant.

kontrollím,-i *m.* controlling, verification.

kontrollój *f.k.* to control; to check, to verify-. – **kontrollohem** *f.jv.* to be controlled.

kontrollór,-i *m.sh.* -ë controller; **kontrollor biletash (treni):** ticket collector.

kontúr,-i *m.sh.* -e contour, outline.

konvaleshénc /ë,-a *f.* convalescence.

konvejér,-i *m.sh.* -ë conveyer.

konvéks,-e *mb.* convex.

konvención,-i *m.sh.* -e convention.

konvencionál,-e *mb.* conventional; **shenja konvencionale:** conventional marks.

konvént /ë,-a *f.* convention.

konvíkt,-i *m.sh.* -e boarding-school

konviktór,-i *m.sh.* -ë boarder.

konvulsión,-i *m.sh.* -e convulsion.

konják,-u *m.* cognac.

kooperatív /ë,-a *f.sh.* -a cooperative; **kooperativë bujqësore:** agricultural cooperative.

kooperativíst,-i *m.sh.* -ë cooperative member, cooperativist.

koordinát /ë,-a *f.sh.* -a *mat.* co-ordinate.

koordiním,-i *m.* coordination.

koordinój *f.k.* to coordinate.

kopáce,-ja *f.sh.* -e bludgeon, cudgel.

kopán,-i *m.sh.* -ë swingle, beetle (for betaing linen), beater; *(ko-*

pan për të rrahur grurin) flail (for threshing wheat.).

kopanís *f.k.* 1. to swingle, to beetle, to beat the linen with a beetle. 2. to belabour, to beat someone soundly (severely).

kopé,-ja *f.sh.* - herd, flock; **një kope dhensh:** a flock of sheep.

kóp/ër,-ra *f. bot.* fennel, dill.

kopíl,-i *,m.sh.* -ë brat.

kopíl/e,-ja *f.sh.* -e 1. bastard girl. 2. *krah* maid, chamber maid, servant girl.

kopíst,-i *m.sh.* -ë copyist.

kopjatív,-e *mb.* indelible; **laps kopjativ:** indelible pencil.

kópj/e,-a *f.sh.* -e copy; **kopje e pastër:** fair copy; **kopje me korrigjime:** rough copy.

kopjím,-i *m.* copying, transcription; **aparat kopjimi:** duplicator.

kopjój *f.k.* to copy, to transcribe, to reproduce. – **kopjohem** *f.jv.* to be copied.

koprác,-i *m.sh.* -ë niggard, miser, skinflint, pinchpenny.

koprác,-e *mb.* avaricious, miserly, niggardly, tight-fisted, parsimonious, grasping, stingy.

koprací,-a *f.* avarice, niggardliness, stinginess, parsimony.

kóps/ë,-a *f.sh.* -a button; **vrimë kopse:** button-hole; **m'u këput kopsa:** my button came off.

kopsít *f.k.* to button. – **kopsitem** *f.jv.* to button oneself.

kopsítj/e,-a *f.* buttoning.

kopsht,-i *m.sh.* -e 1. garden; **kopshti botanik:** botanical garden; **kopsht me lule:** flower-garden; **kopsht pemësh:** orchard; **kopsht perimesh:** kitchengarden. 2. **kopsht fëmijësh:** kindergarten. 3. **kopsht zoologjik:** zoo.

kopshtár,-i *m.sh.* -ë gardener, horticulturist.

kopshtarí,-a *f.* gardening, horticul-

ture; **vegla kopshtarie:** gardentools, pruning implements.

kopshtór/e,-ja *f.sh.* -e kindergarten.

kopúk,-u *m.sh.* -ë shih **horr.**

kóq/e,-ja *f.sh.* -e 1. grain. 2. *anat.* testicle.

kor,-i *m.sh.* -e *muz.* chorus.

koracát/ë,-a *f.sh.* -a ironclad (armourclad) battleship.

korác/ë,-a *f.sh.* -a cuirass; **vesh me koracë:** to arm with a cuirass.

koracúar (i,e) *mb.* armoured, steelclad.

korál,-e *mb.* choral.

korán,-i *m.sh.* -ë *zool.* speckled trout.

korb,-i *m.sh.* -a *zool.* crow, raven; **korb i zi:** as black as a raven.

kórb/ë,-a *f.sh.* -a unfortunate woman; **korba unë!** poor me! oh dear!

kordél/e,-ja *f.sh.* -e band, ribbon, tape; **kordele kapeleje:** hatband

kórd/ë,-a *f.sh.* -a *gjeom.* chord.

kordón,-i *m.sh.* -ë cordon, string.

kórdh/ë,-a *f.sh.* -a *vjet.* sword, saber.

kordhëtár,-i *m.sh.* -ë *vjet.* swordman.

kór/e,-ja *f.sh.* -e 1. crust; **kore buke:** crust of bread. 2. *gjeog.* **kore e tokës:** earth's crust. 3. *mjek.* **(kore e plagës)** crust. scab; **zë kore:** to become encrusted, to be covered with crust.

korént,-i *m.* current; **korent ajri:** draft of air, current of air; **mos rri në korent, se ftohesh:** don't sit in the draught or you'll catch cold; **korent elektrik:** electric current. – *Lok.* **e vë dikë në korent të një gjëja:** to keep someone informed of something.

koreografí,-a *f.* choreography.

kór/ë,-a *f.sh.* **-a** icon.
koríçk/ë,-a *f.sh.* **-a** crust.
koríj/e,-a *f.sh.* **-e** coppice, boscage, grove, bosket, thicket; **vend me korije:** braky land.
koríst,-i *m.sh.* **-ë** *muz.* chorister.
korís *f.k. krah.* to dishonour. – **koritem** *f.jv.* to be dishonoured, to be disgraced.
korít/ë,-a *f.sh.* **-a** trough; **koritë mulliri:** mill-pond.
korítj/e,-a *f. krah.* dishonour, disgrace.
korníz/ë,-a *f.sh.* **-a** 1. frame; **kornizë për fotografi, për tablo:** picture-frame; **vë në kornizë:** to frame. 2. *ndërt.* cornice. 3. **kornizë për perde:** curtainpole. 4. **kornizë dritareje:** window-sash, sash.
korón/ë,-a *f.sh.* **-a** 1. crown (silver money). 2. *mek.* coil.
korparmát/ë,-a *f.sh.* **-a** army corps.
korporát/ë,-a *f.sh.* **-a** corporation.
kórpus,-i *m.sh.* **-e** 1. body, central (main) part: *(i një ndërtese)* main body. 2. *usht.* armycorps.
korsé.-ja *f.sh.* – corset, stays, bodice
kortézh,-i *m.sh.* **-e** cortage, procession.
kortín/ë,-a *f.sh.* **-a** curtain.
korr *f.k.* 1. to reap, to crop. 2. *fig.* to attain, to obtain, to achieve, to win, to reach; **korr fitore:** to win, to gain victory; **korr sukses:** to achieve success. – **korret** *f.jv.* to be reaped (cropped).
kórra,-t (të) *f.sh.* harvest, crop; **marr të korra të mira:** to get good harvest.
korrékt,-e *mb.* 1. correct; **përgjigje korrekte:** a correct answer. 2. proper; **sjellje korrekte:** correct conduct.
korrektësí,-a *f.* 1. correctness 2. rectitude, uprightness.
korrektím,-i *m.* correction; **shtëpi**

korrektimi: penitentiary, reformatory, approved school.
korrektój *f.k.* to correct, to rectify; **korrektoj boca:** to read proofs. – **korrektohem** *f.jv.* to be corrected.
korrektòr,-i *m.sh.* **-ë** *polig.* reader; **korrektor shtypshkronje (bocash):** proof-reader.
korrektúr/ë,-a *f.sh.* **-a** *polig.* correction, reading; **korrekturë e fundit:** author's proof, pressproof.
korrespondénc/ë,-a *f.* correspondence.
korrespondént,-i *m.sh.* **-ë** correspondent; **korrespondent i një gazete:** reporter of a newspaper, *amer.* correspondent of a journal.
korrespondój *f.jk.* to correspond *(me,* with, to), to agree, to tally, to square (with); **shifrat korrespondojnë:** the figures tally (agree)
kórrës,-i *m.sh.* - reaper, harvester.
kórrës,-e *mb.* reaping; **makinë korrëse:** reaping-machine.
korridór,-i *m.sh.* **-e** 1. lobby, corridor. 2. *fig.* passage.
korriér,-i *m.sh.* **-ë** courier.
korrigjím,-i *m.sh.* **-e** correction▪ rectification, amendment; **korrigjim i një dorëshkrimi:** the correction of a manuscript.
korrigjój *f.k.* to correct, to rectify, to amend; **korrigjoni këto fjalë!** correct these words! – **korrigjohem** *f.jv.* to break oneself, to get rid of (bad habits); to mend one's ways, to reform; **përpiqu të korrigjohesh, përndryshe do të përfundosh keq:** try to mend your ways or you'll come to a bad end.
korrík,-u *m.* july.
kórrj/e,-a *f.sh.* **-e** harvesting, mowing, reaping; **koha e korrjeve:** harvest time.

korroz/í,-ezë *mb.* brown, swart, swarthy having dark hair.
korrupción,-i *m.* corruption, corruptness; *(me para)* bribery.
korruptím,-i *m.* corruption, corrupting.
korruptój *f.k.* to corrupt. – **korruptohem** *f.jv.* to become corrupted.
korruptúar (i,e) *mb.* corrupt, bribed; **nëpunës të korruptuar:** corrupt officials.
korruptúesh/ëm(i),-me(e) *mb.* corruptible, bribable.
kos,-i *m.* yogurt.
kosár,-i *m.sh.* -ë shih **kositës.**
kós/ë,-a *f.sh.* -a scythe.
kosís *f.k.* 1. to scythe, to mow. 2. *fig.* to mow (to cut) down. – **kositem** *f.jv.* 1. to be mowed, scythed. 2. *fig.* to be mown (cut) down; **ushtarët u kositën nga një breshëri mitralozi:** the soldiers were mown down by a machine-gun burst.
kosítj/e,·a *f.* scything, mowing; **kositje bari:** scything, (mowing) of grass.
kosór/e,-ja *f.sh.* -e small scythe.
kósto,-ja *f.* cost; **shes me çmimin e kostos:** to sell at cost price; **shes nën kosto:** to undersell; **ul koston e prodhimit:** to cut the cost of production.
kostúm,-i *m.sh.* -e 1. costume, dress , suit; **kostum (i bërë) me porosi:** suit made to order (made to measure). 2. **kostum banje:** bathing (swimming) costume, bathing suit; *(për burra)* swimming costume, trunks.
kosh,-i *m.sh.* -e 1. basket, large basket; **kosh me kapakë:** hamper, wicker-hamper; crate. 2. *(kosh për hedhjen e plehrave)* dustbin; **kosh letrash:** wastepaper basket. 3. *sport.* **kosh bas-**

ketbolli: basket; **kosh motoçiklete:** side-car.
koshér/e,-ja *f.sh.* -e *(koshere bletësh)* hive, bee-house, apiary.
koshiénc/ë,-a *f.* conscience.
koshiént,-e *mb.* 1. conscious. 2. conscientious.
koshtár,-i *m.sh.* -ë hamper maker, basket maker.
kot *ndajf.* uselessly, to no purpose, vainly; **më kot:** in vain; for nothing; **flas kot:** to speak in vain; **shkon kot së koti:** to go (run) waste; **kot që ngul këmbë:** it's no use insisting (on).
kotéc,-i *m.sh.* -ë hen roost, hen house.
kotél/e,-ja *f.sh.* -e *zool.* puss.
kótem *f.jv.* to doze, to drowse, to nap.
kótë (i,e) *mb.* vain, useless; **punë e kotë:** useless, fruitless work, bootless work.
kotësí,-a *f.* vanity; inanity; futility.
kótk/ë,-a *f.sh.* -a knot, hitch.
kotolét/ë,-a *f.sh.* -a cutlet.
kotórr,-i *m.sh.* -ë *zool.* young buffalo.
kotrúv/e,-ja *f.sh.* -e jar, jur, pitcher, cruse, earthen pot.
kotullím,-i *m.* drowsiness, drowse, doze.
kotullóhem *f.jv.* to doze, to drowse.
kothér/e,-je *f.sh.* -e crust; **një kothere bukë:** a crust of bread.
kováç,-i *m.sh.* -ë smith, forger, blacksmith.
kovaçán/ë,-a *f.sh.* -a smithy, forge.
kóv/ë,-a *f.sh.* -a 1. bucket, pail, scoop; **kovë uji:** water pail. 2. bucketful, bucket, pailful, pail. 3. *tek.* **kovë ekskavatori:** scoop of a digger (excavator).
kozmetík,-e *mb.* cosmetic.
kozmík,-e *mb.* cosmic.
kozmografí,-a *f.* cosmography.
kozmonáut,-i *m.sh.* -ë cosmonaut.

kozmopolít,-i *m.sh.* -ë cosmopolite, cosmopolitan.
kozmopolít,-e *mb.* cosmopolitan.
krah,-u *m.sh.* -ë 1. *anat.* arm; **punë krahu:** manual work. 2. *(krah zogu)* wing; **me krahë:** winged. 3: armful; **një krah dru, shkarpa:** an armful of wood, of twigs. 4. **krah pune:** labour power, hand. – *Lok.* **i dal krah dikujt:** to stand by someone; **me krahë hapur:** with open arms; **jam krahu i djathtë i dikujt:** to be the right hand of someone; to be the chief support of someone; **nga krahu i djahtë:** on the right side; **krah për krah:** side by side, shoulder to shoulder.
kráhas *ndajf.* parallelly, in parallel.
krahasím,-i *m.sh.* -e comparison; **në krahasim me:** in comparison with.
krahasój *f.k.* to compare. – **krahasohem** *f.jv.* to be compared.
krahasór,-e *mb. gram.* comparative; **shkalla krahasore:** the comparative.
krahasúesh/ëm(i),-me(e) *mb.* comparable.
krahasueshmërí,-a *f.* comparability.
krahëgjátë *mb.* long-armed.
krahëhápur *ndajf. mb.* open-armed, with open arms.
kraharór,-i *m.sh.* -e *anat.* breast, chest; **kafazi i kraharorit:** sternum, breat-bone, thorax.
krahín/ë,-a *f.sh.* -a 1. region, province. 2. provinces, country.
krahinór,-e *mb.* regional, provincial.
kral,-i *m.sh.* -ë *vjet.* shih **mbret.**
krap,-i *m.sh.* -ë *zool.* carp.
krasít *f.k.* to trim, to cut twigs, to lop, to prune. – **krasitet** *f.jv.* to be trimmed.
krasítës,-i *m.sh.* - trimmer.

krasítj/e,-a *f.* trim, lop, pruning (of trees); **gërshërë krasitjeje:** pruning shears; **vegla krasitjeje:** pruning implements.
kratér,-i *m.sh.* -e *gjeog.* crater.
kravát/ë,-a *f.sh.* -a neck-tie, cravat, tie; **karficë kravate:** breastpin, scarf-pin.
kreu shih **krye.**
kredenciál,-e *mb.* credential; **letra kredenciale:** credentials.
kredí,-a *f.sh.* - credit, trust; **me kredi:**on credit; **shitje me kredi:** sale on credit; **blej e shes me kredi:** to buy and sell on credit; **jap me kredi:** to give on credit; **kredi e hapur:** open credit.
kredít,-i *m.* credit; **bankë krediti:** credit bank.
kreditój *f.k.* to credit.
kreditór,-i *m.sh.* -ë creditor.
kredh *f.k.* to plunge, to dive. – **kridhem** *f.jv.* 1. to plunge, to submerge; to dive; **kridhem në lumë:** to dive into the river. 2. *(nëndetsja)* to dive, to submerge. 3. *fig.* to be immersed, to immerse oneself (in); **kridhem në punë:** to be absorbed in one's work.
krédhj/e,-a *f.* immersion, dipping, diving, plunging.
kreh *f.k.* to comb. – **krihem** *f.jv.* to comb one's hair.
kréh/ër,-ri *m.sh.* -ra 1. comb; **krehër flokësh:** comb. 2. **krehër leshi:** comb; **krehër lini, kërpi:** hackle. 3. **krehër fishekësh:** cartridge clip.
kréhj/e,-a *f.* combing.
krejt *ndajf.* all, entirely.
krejtësísht *ndajf.* thoroughly, completely, utterly, entirely, wholly.
kréko *ndajf.* smartly.
krekóhem, krekósem *f.jv.* to boast, to swagger, to strut and pose, to show off.

krekósj/e,-a *f.* boasting, swaggering.

kréla,-t *f.sh.* shih **kaçurela.**

krem,-i *m.sh.* -**ëra** cream; **krem karamele:** custard.

kremastár,-i *m.sh.* -**ë** suspensor, hanger.

krematórium,-i *m.sh.* -**e** crematórium.

krémt/e(e),-ja(e) *f.sh.* -**e (të)** holiday.

kremtím,-i *m.sh.* -**e** celebration.

kremtój *f.k.* to celebrate. – **kremtohet** *f.jv.* to be celebrated.

krenár,-e *mb.* proud.

krenarí,-a *f.* pride; **me krenari:** proudly.

krenarísht *ndajf.* proudly.

krenóhem *f.jv.* to boast, to become proud of, to pride oneself; **krenohem për:** to pride oneself on.

krérë,-t (pl. of **kokë**) heads; **njëzet krerë bagëti:** twenty heads of cattle.

krés/ë,-a *f.sh.* -**a** curry-comb; **kresë kali:** horse-comb, curry-comb; **kresë lope:** ox-comb.

kréshm/ë,-a *f.* fast.

kreshník,-u *m.sh.* -**ë** brave man, valiant man.

kreshník,-e *mb.* brave, valiant.

krésht/ë,-a *f.sh.* -**a** 1. *anat. (kreshtë kali)* mane, horse's mane. 2. *(kreshtë këndezi)* cock's comb. 3. *gjeog. (kreshtë mali)*ridge, crest (of a mountain).

kréshtë (i,e) *mb.* rough, shaggy, **flokë të kreshta:** shaggy hair; bristle.

krevát,-i *m.sh.* -**e** bed, **krevat fëmijësh:** child's bed, baby's crib; **krevat me sustë:** spring-bed; **krevat portativ:** cot; **anë e krevatit:** bedside.

krif/ë,-a *f.sh.* -**a** *anat. (kali, luani)* mane, crest.

krijés/ë,-a *f.sh.* -**a** creature.

krijím,-i *m.* 1. creation. 2. founda-

tion, establishment, formation. 3. *(vepër artistike)* creation; **krijimi i veprave artistike:** the creation of works of art.

krijimtarí,-a *f.* creation.

krijój *f.k.* to create. – **krijohem** *f.jv.* to be created.

krijúes,-i *m.sh.* - 1. creator. 2. founder. 3. artist, author.

krik,-u *m.sh.* -**ë** lifting jack, handscrew.

krík/ëll,-lla *f.sh.* -**lla** beer glass.

krim,-i *m.sh.* -**e** crime; **kryej një krim:** to commit a crime, to perpetrate a crime.

krimb,-i *m.sh.* -**a** *zool.* worm; **krimb mëndafshi:** silk-worm; **krimb toke:** earth-worm; **krimb zorrësh:**parasite;**në trajtë krimbi:** worm-like, worm-shaped.– **krimbem** *f.jv.* to become (to get) wormeaten.

krímbur (i,e) *mb.* 1. wormy, worm-eaten; **mollë e krimbur: a** wormy apple. 2. *mjek.* rotten; **dhëmb i krimbur:** rotten tooth.

kriminál,-e *mb.* criminal.

kriminalitét,-i *m.* criminality.

kriminél,-i *m.sh.* -**ë** criminal, murderer.

krín/ë,-a *f.sh.* -**a** bee.

krip *f.k.* 1. to salt. 2. *(krip me miell etj.)* to sprinkle (with flour, etc.).

kripaník,-u *m.* salt-box, salt-cellar.

kríp/ë,-a *f.* 1. salt; **kripë guri:** rock salt; **mbajtësa kripe:** salt-cellar; **me kripë:** salty, briny; **pa kripë:** saltless; insipid. 2. *mjek.* saltpurgative. 3. *fig.* salt, pungent, wit; **shaka pa kripë:** nasty joke. – *Lok.* **kam mbetur kripë:** I am penniless, I have not a farthing (a stiver).

kripëzím,-i *m.* salting.

kripór/e,-ja *f.sh.* -**e** 1. salt-mine, salt-works. 2. salt-box; salt-cellar.

kriptográm,-i *m.sh.* -e crypto-gram.
kris *f.jk.* to crack; **krisi qelqi:** the glass cracked.
krís/ë,-a *f.sh.* -a crack, fissure; **merr krisë (qelqi):** to be crack-ed (glass).
krísj/e,-a *f.* 1. cracking; **krisje e xhamit, e qelqit:** cracking of the glass. 2. **krisje e gishtërinj-ve:** snapping of fingers.
krísm/ë,-a *f.sh.* -a crash, clattering noise; **krismë pushke:** gunshot sound; **krismë topi:** roar of a cannon; **krismë bubullime:** thundering.
kristál,-i *m.* crystal.
kristalizím,-i *m.* crystallization.
kristalizój *f.k.* to crystallize. **krista-lizohet** *f.jv.* to be crystallized, to become crystal.
kristáltë (i,e) *mb.* 1. crystalline. 2. crystal-clear.
krísur (i,e) *mb.* 1. cracked, split; **gotë e krisur:** cracked glass; **lëkurë e krisur:** chapped skin. 2. *fig.* rash, reckless, cracked-brained, madcap.
krishtérë (i,e) *mb.* christian.
krishtérë(i),-i(i) *m.sh.* **(të)** chris-tian.
krishterím,-i *m.* christianity.
krishtlíndj/e,-a *f.* Christmas; **dita e krishtlindjes:** Christmas day:
kritér,-i *m.sh.* -e criterion.
kritík,-u *m.sh.* -ë critic.
kritík,-e *mb.* critical; **çast kritik:** critical moment, conjuncture; **gjen-dje kritike:** emergency; diffi-cult situation.
kritík/ë,-a *f.sh.* -a 1. criticism; **bë-hem objekt kritikash:** to be criticized, to be the object of criticism; **kritikë e ashpër:** sla-shing criticism. 2. critics; **romani u prit mirë nga kritika:** the critics have spoken well of the novel.

kritikój *f.k.* to criticize. – **kritiko-hem** *f.jv.* to be criticized.
kritikuésh/ëm (i),-me(e) *mb.* cri-ticable.
kríz/ë,-a *f.sh.* -a 1. crisis; **krizë ekonomike:** economic crisis; **krizë financiare:** financial crisis. 2. *mjek.* access, fit, crisis, attack; **krizë zemre:** heartattack, attack of heart.
kródh/ë,-a *f.sh.* -a crust; **krodhë buke:** crust of bread.
krokát *f.jk.* shih **karkat.**
krokátj/e,-a *f.* shih **karkatje.**
krokodíl,-i *m.sh.* -ë *zool.* crocodile.
krom,-i *m. kim.* chromium.
kromatík,-e *mb.* chromatic.
króm/ë,-a *mjek.* scab, mange.
kroník,-e *mb.* chronic; **sëmundje kronike:** chronic malady, chro-nic disease.
kroník/ë,-a *f.* 1. chronicle. 2. his-tory, narrative. 3.*(rubrikë)*column; **kronikë sportive:** sports news; sports page.
kronologjí,-a *f.* chronology.
kronologjík,-e *mb.* chronologic, chronological; **sipas rendit kro-nologjik:** in chronological order.
kronomét/ër,-ri *m.sh.* -ra chrono-meter; **orë kronometër:** chro-nometer watch.
kros,-i *m.sh.* -e cross-country race.
krúa,-krói *m.sh.* **kroje** fountain, spring of water.
krúaj *f.k.* to scratch; **kruaj kokën:** to scratch one's head. – **kruhem** *f.jv.* to scratch oneself.
krúarj/e,-a *f.* 1. scratching. 2. it-ching, itch; **kruarje e trupit:** itching of the body.
krúes/e,-ja *f.sh.* -e scraper.
krúnde,-t *f.sh.* bran, husks of wheat.
krúp/ë,-a *f.* nausea, disgust, loa-

thing; **kall krupën:** to cause nausea.
krúspull *ndajf.* **mblidhem krus-
pull:** to shrivel, to become contracted. − **kruspullohem** *f.jv.* to
shrivel, to become contracted.
kruspullósj/e,-a *f.* shrivelling.
krush/k,-ku *m.sh.* -q 1. allied (by
marriage). 2. wedding guest.
krushqí,-a *f.* alliance (by marriage);
lidh, bëj krushqi: to ally oneself by marriage, to intermarry.
krýe,-t *as.* head (shih **kokë).**
krýe, kreú *m.* 1. head; **në krye:**
at the head; **eci në krye të:**
to go at the head of (at the front
of), to lead the way; **në krye
të faqes:** at the head of the
page. 2. *(kreu i një libri)* chapter
(of a book). − *Lok.* **ngre krye:**
to revolt, to rebel; **ia dal në krye
një pune:** to succeed in a work,
to be successful in a work.
kryeártëzë,-a *f.sh.* -a *zool.* goldfinch.
kryeartíku/II,-IIi *m.sh.* -j editorial,
leading article.
kryefamiljár,-i *m.sh.* -ë head of
the household, pater familias.
kryefjál/ë,-a *f.sh.* -ë *gram.* subject.
krýej *f.k.* 1. to perfom, to accomplish, to fulfil; **kryej një detyrë:**
to accomplish a task, to fulfil a
duty; **kryej një punë:** to perform a work, to accomplish a
work; **kryej një porosi:** to
execute an order, to fulfil an
order. 2. to commit; **kryej një
krim:** to commit a crime, to
perpetrate a crime. − **kryhet**
f.jv. to be performed (accomplished, fulfilled).
kryekëpút *ndajf.* shih **krejt.**
kryekomandánt,-i *m.sh.* -ë co-
mmander-in-chief
kryekónsu/II,-IIi *m.sh.* -i chief consul.
kryelártë *mb.* proud, haughty.

kryelartësí-a *f.* pride, haughtiness; **me kryelartësi:** proudly,
haughtily.
kryellogaritár,-i *m.sh.* -ë chief
accountant.
kryeminíst/ër,-ri *m.sh.* .ra primi-
er , prime-minister.
kryeministrí,-a *f.sh.* - council
of ministers.
kryemjék,-u *m.sh.* -ë first doctor.
kryemjésht/ër,-ri *m.sh.* -ra master workman.
kryenéç,-e *mb.* stubborn, obstinate,
headstrong.
kryeneçësí,-a *f.* stubborness, ob-
stinacy.
kryengrítës,-i *m.sh.* - rebel, insurgent, insurrectionist.
kryengrítës,-e *mb.* rebellious, revolting, insurgent.
kryengrítj/e,-a *f.sh.* -e revolt,
rebellion, insurrection: **shtyp një
kryengritje:** to repress (to put
down) a revolt.
kryepeshkóp,-i *m.sh.* -ë archbi-
shop.
kryepeshkopát/ë,-a *f.sh.* -a arch-
diocese.
kryeplák,-u *m.sh.* **kryepléq** (formerly) bourgmaster, village di-
gnitary.
kryeprokurór,-i *m.sh.* -ë attor-
ney-general.
kryepunëtór,-i *m.sh.* -ë foreman,
a man in charge of a department or group of workers in a
factory, mill etc.
kryeqénd/ër,-ra *f.sh.* -ra chief-to-
wn; metropolis.
kryeqytét,-i *m.sh.* -e capital.
kryeqytétas,-i *m.sh.* - habitant
of a capital.
krýer (p.p of the verb **kryej)** performed, accomplished, achived,
executed, done.
krýer (i,e) *mb.* accomplished; **fakt
i kryer:** accomplished fact.
krýer (e),-a(e) *f. gram.* past tense;

e kryer e thjeshtë: simple past tense; **e kryera**: present perfect or past indefinite; **e kryer e plotë**: past perfect.
kryerádh/**ë,-a** *f.sh.* -**ë** head-line.
kryeredaktór,-i *m.sh.* -**ë** chief editor.
krýerj/**e,-a** *f.* performance, accomplishment, fulfilment, execution.
kryerrésht,-i *m.sh.* -**a** shih **kryeradhë**.
kryesí,-a *f.sh.* - chairmanship; **zgjidhem në kryesi**: to take the chair.
kryesísht *ndajf.* chiefly, mainly, essentially, principally, mostly.
kryesój *f.k.* to preside; **kryesoj mbledhjen**: to preside over a meeting, to take the chair. — **kryesohet** *f.jv.* to be presided over (by).
kryesór,-e *mb.* chief, main, essential, fundamental.
kryetár,-i *m.sh.* -**ë** chairman, chief, head; **kryetar shteti**: head of state; **kryetar zyre**: chief of an office; **kryetar i delegacionit**: head of a delegation; **kryetar bande**: ringleader.
kryeúlët *mb.* modest, humble, unassuming
kryeultësí,-a *f.* modesty, humility, humbleness.
kryeultësísht *ndajf.* modestly, humbly.
kryeúr/**ë,-a** *f.sh.* -**a** bridgehead.
kryevép/**ër,-ra** *f.sh.* -**ra** masterpiece.
kryezót,-i *m.sh.* -**ë** overlord.
kryq,-i *m.sh.* -**e** cross; **rrimë me duar kryq**: to stay armcrossed, to dawdle, to loiter; **fjalë kryq**: cross-words.
krýqas *ndajf.* crosswise, transversely.
krýqe,-t *f.sh. anat.* sacrum.
kryqëzát/**ë,-a** *f.sh.* -**a** crusade.
kryqëzím,-i *m.* 1. *(racash)* cross-

breed. 2. *(udhësh)* crossroad, cross-way, cross-street; **kryqëzim i rrugës automobilistike me rrugën e trenit**: level crossing. 3. crucifixion.
kryqëzój *f.k.* 1.to crucify, to cross. 2. *(kryqëzoj dy raca)* to crossbreed. 3. *(kryqëzoj krahët)*: to fold up, to cross (one's arms). — **kryqëzohem** *f.jv.* 1. to be crucified. 2. to intersect; *(rrugët)* to cross each-other. 3. to crossbreed, to hybridize.
kryqëzór,-i *m.sh.* -**ë** cruiser.
kryqëzúar (i,e) *mb.* 1. crucified. 2. cross, cross-bred, crossed; **racë e kryqëzuar**: cross-breed.
kryqtár,-i *m.sh.* -**ë** crusader.
kthej *f.k.* 1. to turn; **kthej kokën**: to turn the head. 2. to turn, to bend; **kthej sytë nga dikush**: to turn one's eyes to someone, to bend one's gaze on someone. 3. **kthej diçka nga ana tjetër**: to turn; **kthej një kostum**: to have a costume turned. 4. to change, to convert; **kthej mendje**: to change one's mind; **kthej besim**: to convert, to change religion. 5. **kthej përgjigje**: to answer, to reply, to respond. 6. **i kthej një send të zotit**: to restitute, to remit, to render, to return, to send back (something); **kthej në jetë dikë**: to bring someone back to life. — **kthehem** *f.jv.* 1. to return, to go back, to come back; **kthehem në shtëpi**: to get home, to return home, to come back home, to get back home; **kthehem majtas, djathtas**: to turn to the left, to the right; **kthehem nga rruga**: to turn back; **kur do të ktheheni?** when shall you be back? **do të kthehem së shpejti**: I shall be back soon; **kur të kthehem nga**: when I am back from.

2. *(kthehem me tërë trupin, kthehem nga ana tjetër)* to turn round; **kthehem befas:** to turn short.

kthés/ë,-a *f.sh.* **-a** 1. *(kthesë udhe)* bend, curve, turn; *(lumi)* bend, curve; **kthesë majtas, nga e majta:** left-hand bend, bend to the left; **bëj kthesë, marr kthesë:** to turn; **kthesë e fortë:** sharp bend. 2. *fig.* change; **kthesë rrënjësore:** radical change; **bëj kthesë:** to take a change, to change conduct.

kthét/ër,-ra *f.sh.* **-ra** claw, fang (of an eagle, etc.).

kthim,-i *m.sh.* **-e** 1. return; **kthim në shtëpi:** return at home; **kthim në shkollë:** re-entrance in school. 2. *(kthim i një sendi, pasurie)* restitution (of a thing, of property); **kthim të hollash:** reinbursement.

kthín/ë,-a *f.sh.* **-a** alcove.

kthjéllët (i,e) *mb.* clear, serene; **kohë e kthjellët:** clear weather; **qiell i kthjellët:** serene sky, clear sky; **ujë i kthjellët:** clear (limpid) water.

kthjellím,-i *m. (i ujit, i verës)* clarification, clarifying.

kthjellój *f.k.* to make clearer, to clarify. – **kthjellohem** *f.jv.* 1. to becon1e clear, to clear. 2. *fig.* to settle in one's own mind; **gjendja u kthjellua:** the situation was cleared up.

kthjelltësí,-a *f.* clearness, clarity.

ku *ndajf.* where; **ku është libri?** where is the book? **ku po shkoni?** where are you going? **shtëpia ku banoj:** the house where I live; **dhoma ku hymë, ishte e madhe:** the room we went into was a big one.

kuaçís *f.jk.* to chuck, to cluck (of hens).

kuaçítj/e,-a *f.* chuck, cluck.

kuád/ër,-ri *m.sh.* **-ro** 1. painting, picture. 2. *fig.* framework, limit, scope, range; **në këtë kuadër:** in this occasion, in this framework. 3. cadre. 4. personnel.

kuadrát,-i *m.sh.* **-ë** quadrate, square; **me kuadrate:** checkered.

kúaj,-t *m.sh.* plural of «**kalë**».

kualifikím,-i *m.* qualification.

kualifikój *f.k.* to qualify. – **kualifikohem** *f.jv.* to be qualified.

kualitét,-i *m.* quality.

kuárc,-i *m. kim.* quartz.

kuartet,-i *m. muz.* quartet.

kub,-i *m.sh.* **-e** *gjeom.* cube.

kubatúr/ë,-a *f.* cubage.

kubé,-ja *f.sh.* - dome, cupola, vault, arch; **me kube:** vaulted; **dritare në formë kubeje:** camberwindow.

kubík,-u *m.sh.* **-ë** cube.

kubík,-e *mb.* cubic, cubical.

kuçéd/ër,-ra *f.sh.* **-ra** hydra, harpy.

kudó *ndajf.* everywhere, all over, throughout; **kudo që:** wherever; **kudo qoftë:** anywhere.

kúdh/ër,-ra *f.sh.* **-ra** anvil (of a smith).

kuestór,-i *m.sh.* **-ë** questor.

kuestúr/ë,-a *f.* police headquarters.

kufít/ë,-a *f.sh.* **-a** confetto.

kufí,-ri *m.sh.* **-nj** 1. border, boundary; *(midis shtetesh)* frontier, border; **kufijtë e Shqipërisë:** the Albanian borders; **vijë kufiri:** boundary line; **rojë kufiri:** border guard; **kaloj kufirin:** to cross the border; **pa kufi:** boundless; **brenda kufijve:** within the limits (bounds). 2. measure; **çdo gjë me kufi:** anything with frugality.

kufitár,-i *m.sh.* **-ë** border guard.

kufitár,-e *mb.* boundary, border; **brez kufitar, zonë kufitare:**

border-land; **postë kufitare**: boundary post.
kufizím,-i *m.sh.* **-e 1.** limitation. 2. restriction, stint.
kufizój *f.k.* 1. to limit, to delimit, to bound, to border; **kufizoj një tokë**: to delimit a land. 2. to restrict, to restrain, to stint; **kufizoj shpenzimet**: to restrain the expenses. — **kufizohem** *f.jv.* 1. to keep within bounds, to confine oneself. 2. to border; **livadhi kufizohet me një pyll**: the meadow borders on a wood.
kúfkë *mb.* hollow; **arrë kufkë**: hollow walnut.
kufóm/ë,-a *f.sh.* **-a** cadaver, corpse, dead body; **vendi ku ruhen kufomat**: morgue; **nxjerr një kufomë nga dheu**: to exhume (to disinter) a cadaver; **hap një kufomë**: to dissect a cadaver; **hapja e kufomës**: autopsy, dissection of a cadaver.
kuintál,-i *m.sh.* **-ë** quintal.
kuís *f.jk.* to yelp (of puppies, etc.).
kuísj/e,-a *f.* yelping.
kuitánc/ë, -a *f.sh.* **-a** *fin.* quittance, receipt.
kujdes,-i *m.* care, caution, heedfulness; attention, prudence; regard; **tregoj kujdes për dikë**: totake care of someone; **kujdes në punë**: diligence, assiduity at work; **me kujdes**: carefully, cautiously, warily; **pa kujdes**: carelessly, unwarily, negligently; **kujdes!** mind!, be careful; **kujdes nga boja!** mind the paint!
kujdésem *f.jv.* to care, to take care of, to look after, to see after, to heed; **kujdesem për diçka**: to take care of, to care for, to care about, to attend for; **nuk kujdesem për vete**: to neglect oneself; **ai kujdeset për ju**:

he is well disposed towards you
kujdesím,-i *m.* concernement.
kujdésj/e,-a *f.* care, concern, attendance.
kujdesóhem *f.jv.* shih **kujdesem.**
kujdéssh/ëm (i),-me(e) *mb.* careful, heedful, mindful, attentive, cautious, painstaking, diligent; **djalë i kujdesshëm**: diligent boy, assiduous boy, cautious boy; **tepër i kujdesshëm**: overcareful.
kujdestár,-i *m.sh.* **-ë** tutor, protector.
kujdestarí,-a *f.* protectorship, ward, tutelage.
kúj/ë,-a *f.* bewailing, lamentation, whine; **vë kujën**: to lament, to whine.
kujt *p.p.* to whom; **kujt i fole?** whom did you speak to? **kujt ia the?** whom did you say that? (shih **kush**).
kujt (i,e) *p.p.* whose; **e kujt është ajo kapelë?** whose cap is that? **i kujt është ky libër?** whose book is this? (shih **kush**).
kujtdó *p.pk.* whomsoever.
kujtés/ë,-a *f.* memory; **në kujtesën time**: in my memory; **humbje e kujtesës**: amnesia, loss of memory.
kujtím,-i *m.sh.* **-e 1.** memory, remembrance, recollection; **kujtimet e rinisë**: memories of one's youth; **ruaj një kujtim të mirë për dikë**: to have a pleasant recollection of someone. 2. souvenir; memento; keepsake; **jap si kujtim**: to give as a record, as a keepsake; **si kujtim të miqësisë sonë**: as a keepsake of our friendship. 3. *(shenjë)* mark, souvenir; **kjo shenjë është kujtim nga një aksident me makinë**: this scar is a souvenir of a car accident. 4.

sh. memoirs; **shkruaj një libër me kujtime:** to write a book of memoirs.
kujtój I. *f.k.* to remind, to recollect, to evoke; **kujtoj kohën e shkuar:** to evoke the past time; **kujtoj dikë, një ngjarje:** to call to memory, to recall to mind, to remember (someone, an event). **II.** *f.jk.* to think, to imagine, to figure. – **kujtohem** *f.jv.* to remember, to call to mind; **më kujtohet:** I remember.
kujunxhí,-u *m.sh.* -nj goldsmith, jeweller, silverer, silversmith.
kukafshéhtas, kukafshéhti *ndajf.* hide-and-seek; **luaj kukafshehtas:** to play hide-and-seek.
kukúdh,-i *m.sh.* -ë goblin.
kúkull,-a *f.sh.* -a doll, puppet; **teatri i kukullave:** puppet theater; puppet show; **qeveri kukull:** puppet government.
kukumjáçk/ë,-a *f. zool.* owl, barnowl; **britmë kukumjaçke:** hoot.
kukuréc-i *m.sh.* -ë sheep entrails roasted in a spit.
kukuvájk/ë,-a *f.sh.* -a shih **kukumjaçkë.**
kuláç,-i *m.sh.* **kuleçë** muffin, bun; **mblidhem kulaç:** to squat, to shrivel.
kulák,-u *m.sh.* -ë kulak.
kulár,-i *m.sh.* -ë yoke.
kulét/ë,-a *f.sh.* -a purse.
kulm,-i *m.sh.* -e 1. summit, top; **kulmi i çatisë:** the top of the roof. 2. *gjeom.* summit; **kulmi i një trekëndëshi:** the summit of a triangle. 3. *fig.* acme, height, peak, climax; **kulmi i lavdisë:** the acme of glory; **jam në kulm të dëshpërimit:** to be in the depths of despair; **në kulmin e lumturisë:** at the height of one's happiness; **gëzimi (hareja) arriti kulmin:** the merriment was at its height; **ky është kul-**

mi! that's the limit, that beats all!
kulmák,-u *m.sh.* -ë *bot.* twigs of wiliow.
kúlp/ër,-ra *f.sh.* -ra *bot.* clematis.
kult,-i *m.* cult; **kulti i individit:** personality cult.
kultivatór,-i *m.sh.* -ë cultivator.
kultivím,-i *m.* cultivation. – **kultivoj** *f.k.* to cultivate, to till; **kultivoj tokën:** to cultivate the land (soil); **kultivoj lule:** to cultivate flowers. – **kultivohet** *f.jv.* to be cultivated.
kultivùes,-i *m.sh.* - grower, cultivator.
kultúr/ë,-a *f.sh.* -a 1. culture; learning; **kulturë e përgjithshme:** general knowledge. 2. *bujq.* crops; **breshëri i ka dëmtuar kulturat bujqësore:** the hail has damaged the crops.
kulturór,-e *mb.* cultural.
kulturúar (i,e) *mb.* cultured.
kulth,-i *m. bot.* hop.
kullés/ë,-a *f.sh.* -a colander, strainer, filter, percolator.
kùll/ë,-a *f.sh.* -a 1. tower. 2. **kullë hidraulike:** hydraulic tower, water-tower; **kullë vrojtimi:** watchtower. 3. *(kullë bari ose sane)* hayloft.
kúllëz,-a *f.sh.* -a turret.
kullím,-i *m.* 1. straining, percolation, filtering; *(kullimi i lëngjeve vetvetiu)* decantation. 2. *bujq.* **kullimi i ujit nga toka:** drainage, draining.
kullój *f.k.* 1. to strain, to percolate, to filter, to purify, to clarify, to decant. 2. to drain. – *Lok.* **kulloj në lotë:** to melt (to dissolve) in tears.
kullój/ë,-a *f.sh.* -a shih **kullesë.**
kullósht/ër,-ra *f.* colostrum.
kullós I. *f.k.* to graze, to pasture. **II.** *f.jk.* to graze, to pasture, to browse
kullót/ë,-a *f.sh.* -a pasture, pastu-

rage; **kullotë për kuaj**: paddock; **kullota të pasura**: lush pastures.

kullótj/e,-a *f.* grazing, pasturage, pasture.

kullúar (i,e) *mb.* 1. clear, pure, limpid, lucid; **ujë i kulluar**: clear water. 2. *fig.* immaculate.

kullúes,-e *mb.* draining; **kanal kullues**: draining channel.

kullúes/e,-ja *f.sh.* -e shih **kullesë**.

kullufís *f.k.* to swallow at once.

kullumbrí,-a *f.sh.* - *bot.* goosberry, sloe; **druri i kullumbrisë**: gooseberry-tree, sloe-tree.

kullúr/e,-ja *f.sh.* -e muffin.

kum,-i *m.* sand; alluvium.

kumár,-i *m.* gambling; **luaj kumar**: to gamble; **shtëpi kumari**: gamble house.

kumarxhí,-u *m.sh.* -nj gambler.

kumbár,-i *m.sh.* -ë godfather, bridesman, sponsor.

kumbará,-ja *f.sh.* - saving-pot.

kumbarí,-a *f.* sponsorship.

kumbím,-i *m.* resonance, sound, peal; **kumbim i këmbanave**: chime.

kumbón *f.jk.* to resound.

kumbúes,-e *mb.* sounding, resonant.

kúmbull,-a *f.sh.* -a *bot.* plum; *(druri i kumbullës)* plum-tree; **kumbull e egër**: savage-plum, savage plum-tree; **kumbulla të thata**: prunes.

kúm/ë,-a *f.sh.* -a god-mother.

kumtés/ë,-a *f.sh.* -a 1. communication, information. 2. scientific paper.

kúmt/ ër, -ri *m. sh.* -ër shih **kumbar**.

kumtím,- i *m. sh.* -e shih **komunikim**.

kumtój *f.k.* to impart, to make known to inform.

kunádh/e,-ja *f.sh.* -e *zool.* marten.

kunát,-i *m.sh.* **kunetër** brother-in-law.

kunát/ë,-a *f.sh.* -a sister-in-law.

kunatóll,-i *m.sh.* -ë shih **kunat**.

kúndër *paraf.* 1. against; **kundër vullnetit tim**: against my will; **luftoj kundër armikut**: to fight against the enemy; **jap kundër dëshirës**: to give against one's will. 2. *(si drejtim)* against; **notoj kundër rrymës**: to swim upstream; **kundër dritës**: against the light.

kúndër (prefix) counter, anti.

kundërajrór,-e *mb.* anti-aircraft.

kundërhélm,-i *m. sh.* -e antidote, counter-poison.

kundërmas/ë, -a *f.sh.* -a countermeasure.

kundërmím,-i *m.* 1. fragrance. 2. stink, fetidness, odour (agreable or disagreable).

kundërmón *f.jk.* 1. to smell good. 2. to smell bad.

kundërmúes,-e *mb.* 1. odoriferous, fragrant. 2. stinking, badsmelling.

kundërofensív/ë,-a *f.sh.* -a counter-attack, counter-offensive.

kundërpagés/ë,-a *f.sh.* -a counter-payment; **me kundërpagesë**; cash on delivery.

kundërparúll/ë,-a *f.sh.* -a counter-parole.

kundërpésh/ë,-a *f.sh.* -a counter-weight, counter-poise, counter-balance.

kundërpërgjígj/e,-ja *f.sh.* -a counter-reply.

kundërrevolución,-i *m.sh.* -e counter-revolution.

kundërrevolucionár,-i *m.sh.* -ë counter-revolutionary.

kundërrevolucionár,-e *mb.* counter-revolutionary.

kundërsúlm,-i *m.sh.* -e counter-attack, counter-blow.

kundërshtár,-i *m.sh.* -ë opponent, antagonist, contestant, rival, ad-

versoary; **pala kundërshtare:**
the oppsite party, the contesting
party, the adverse party, opposi-
tionist.
kundërshtí,-a *f.* contrariety, opposi-
teness.
kundërshtím,-i *m.* 1. opposition;
në kundërshtim me: contrary
to, in opposite with, in opposition to; **në kundërshtim me
ligjin:** in opposition to the law.
2. objection: **nuk kam asnjë
kundërshtim:** I have no objec-
tions; **bie në kundërshtim me
vetveten:** to contradict oneself;
**që bien në kundërshtim me
njëra-tjetrën:** contradictory.
kundërshtór,-e *mb.* contradictory,
opposing.
kundërshtój *f.k.* to oppose, to contradict, to object, to run counter to.
kundërshtúesh/ëm(i),-me(e) *mb.*
opposable, contestable, protes-
table, disputable, debatable.
kúndërt (i,e) *mb.* opposite, contrary; **marr anën e kundërt:**
to take the opposite side; **inte-
resa të kundërta:** opposite
interests.
kúndërt (e),-a (e) *f.sh.* -a(të)
1. *(e një fjale)* the contrary (of a
word). 2. reverse; **krejt e kundërta:** quite the reverse.
kundërthëni/e,-a *f.sh.* -e contradiction.
kundërúrdhër,-i *m.sh.* - countermand, counter-order.
kundërvájtës,-i *m.sh.* - infringer,
delinquent, transgressor.
kundërvájtj/e,-a *f.sh.* -e infringement, infraction, contravention,
transgression.
kundërveprím,-i *m.sh.* -e reaction,
counteraction.
kundërveprój *f.jk.* to react, to
counteract.
kundërveprúes,-e *mb.* reactive,
counteracting.

kundërvë *f.jk.* to oppose (to), to
set against. - **kundërvihem**
f.jv. to oppose, to contrast; **këto
dy teori i kundërvihen njëra-
tjetrës:** the two theories clash.
kundraxhí,-u *m.sh.* -nj shih **këpucar.**
kundréjt *paraf.* 1. against, in
front of, opposite to; **kundrejt
dyqanit:** in front of the shop.
2. towards; **dashuria kundrejt
atdheut:** love towards the fatherland.
kundrínor-i *m.sh -ë gram.* object;
kundrinor i drejtë, i zhdrejtë:
direct, indirect object.
kundrój *f.k.* to observe. - **kun-
drohem** *f.jv.* to be observed.
kunél,-i *m.sh.* -ë *zool.* rabbit.
kungát/ë,-a *f. fet.* eucharist.
kungím,-i *m.sh.* -e *fet.* communion, sacrament.
kungój *f.k. fet.* to commune, to
give communion. - **kungohem**
f.jv. to take the sacrament (the
communion).
kúngu/ll,-lli *m.sh.* -j 1. *bot.* pumpkin, gourd, *amer.* squash. 2.
kungull uji: water-bottle, decanter. 3. *fig.* greenhorn, simpleton. *
kungulléshk/ë,-a *f.sh.* -a 1. small
and thin pumpkin. 2. small water-bottle.
kunúp,-i *m.sh.* -ë *zool.* mosquito,
midge.
kunupiér/ë,-a *f.sh.* -a midge voile.
kunj,-i *m.sh.* -a peg.
kuót/ë,-a *f.sh.* -a quota; **kuota
anëtarësie:** dues.
kuotización,-i *m.sh.* -e dues.
kúp/ë,-a *f.sh.* -a 1. glass, cup;
një kupë verë: a glass of wine.
2. earthen pot. 3. *anat.* **kupa
e gjurit:** knee-cap. 4. *mjek.
(kupat që shtihen në kurriz)*
cupping; **hedh(shtie) kupa:** to
cup. 5. *(kupë e peshores)* scale

(of a balance). 6. **kupa e qiellit:** firmament, vault (of the sky). – *Lok.* **u mbush kupa:** the cup is filled up.

kuplét,-i *m.sh.* -e couplet.

kupón,-i *m.sh.* -a coupon, counter-foil.

kuptím,-i *m.sh.* -e 1. meaning, signification, sense; **kuptimi i një fjale:** meaning of a word; **pa kuptim:** senseless, void of sense; **në kuptimin e gjerë të fjalës:** in the broad sense of the word; **me dy kuptime:** equivocal. 2. understanding, comprehension. 3. conception.

kuptimplótë *m.* significative, significant; meaningful.

kuptój *f.k.* to understand, to comprehend, to perceive. – **kuptohem** *f.jv.* to be understood; **kuptohemi në mes tonë:** to understand one another; **kuptohet vetiu:** it goes without saying.

kuptúesh/ëm(i),-me(e) *mb.* understandable, intelligible, comprehensible; **bëj të kuptueshëm (një tekst):** to make intelligible (a text).

kuptueshmërí, -a *f.* comprehensiveness.

kuq *f.k.* 1. to fry; **kuq mishin:** to fry the meat. 2. to redden, to make red; **kuq hekurin:** to redden the iron. 3. to colour with red. – **kuqem** *f.jv.* to become red; **kuqem nga turpi:** to blush, to redden, to flush.

kuq (i,e) *mb.* red; **faqe të kuqe:** red cheeks; **që vjen në të kuq:** reddish.

kúq/e(e),-ja(e) *f.* red colour; **e kuqe e çelur:** vermilion; **e kuqe e mbyllur (e errët):** purple, crimson, russet colour; **e kuqe e ndezur:** scarlet.

kuqalásh,-i *m.sh.* -ë rubicund man.

kuqërrém(i),-e(e) *mb.* rubicund· reddish, ruddy.

kúqj/e,-a *f.* 1. *(e hekurit etj.)* reddening. 2. frying; **kuqje e mishit:** frying of meat. 3. **kuqje e flokëve:** reddening of the hair.

kúqtë (të) *as.* 1. redness, ruddiness; **të kuqtë e faqeve:** redness of the cheeks. 2. **të kuqtë e buzëve:** lipstick.

kúqur (i,e) *mb.* 1. reddened. 2. fried; **mish i kuqur:** fried meat.

kur *lidh.* 1. when; **nxënësit gëzohen kur vijnë pushimet:** the boys are pleased when holidays come; **që ditën kur:** since the day when; **ditën kur:** the day when. 2. since, as; **kur nuk të pëlqen, mos shko:** if you don't like to go, don't go.

kur *ndajf.* when, at what time; **kur do të shkoni?** when shall you go? **që kur?** how long?

kuraj/ë,-a *f.* courage, heart, pluck; **me kurajë:** courageously, pluckily; **pa kurajë:** without courage; **plot kurajë:** full of courage; **humb kurajën:** to lose heart, to feel desponded; **jap kurajë:** to give heart, to encourage, to cheer up; **marr kurajë:** to take heart, to muster up courage, to pluck up courage; **atij i mungon kuraja:** he is lacking in courage; **kurajë!** courage! cheer up!

kurajóz,-e *mb.* courageous.

kurán,-i *m. fet.* koran.

kurbán,-i *m.sh.* -e burnt offering, holocaust.

kurbát,-i *m.sh.* -ë bohemian.

kurbét,-i *m.* emigration.

kurbetçí,-u *m.sh.* -nj emigrant.

kúrb/ë,-a *f.sh.* -a *gjeom.* curve.

kurdís *f.k.* 1. to wind: **kurdis orën:** to wind up the watch. 2. *(kurdis një vegël muzikore)* to tune, to string, to put in tune (a musical instrument). 3. *fig. (kurdis një intrigë, një komplot)* to plot, to concot, to fabricate, to cook up, to contrive. − **kurdisem** *f.jv.* to chatter, to jabber, to talk without interruption.

kurdó *ndajf.* whenever; **kurdo që të vish:** whenever you come; **kurdo qoftë:** at any time.

kurdohérë *ndajf.* always, at any time, at all times.

kureshtár,-e *mb.* inquisitive, curious; **njeri kureshtar:** curious person; **jam kureshtar të di:** I am curious to know.

kuréshtj/e,-a *f.* curiosity, inquisitiveness, **me kureshtje:** curiously; **kënaq kureshtjen:** to give (to allow) full play to curiosity.

kúr/ë,-a *f.sh.* -a treatment, cure; **kurë për t'u dobësuar:** slimming cure; **jap një kurë:** to prescribe a cure; **kurë me banja dielli:** heliotherapy.

kurim,-i *m.sh.* -e treatment, healing; **kurimi i një sëmundjeje:** treatment of a malady.

kuriozitét,-i *m.sh.* -e curiosity; **shikoj kuriozitetet e qytetit etj.:** to see the sights of a city.

kurmagják,-u *m.* pudding of meat and blood.

kurnác,-i *m.sh.* -ë miser, niggard.

kurnác,-e *mb.* miserly, greedy, avaricious, stingy.

kurój *f.k.*to cure, to treat.− **kurohem** *f.jv.* to be cured, to be treated.

kurór/ë,-a *f.sh.*-a 1.garland, wreath; **kurorë lulesh:** garland of flowers. 2. **kurorë drite:** halo, gloriole, circle of light. 3. *(kurorë mbretërore)* crown, royal head-dress. 4. **kurorë varrimi:** funeral wreath. 5. *vjet. (kurorë martese)* wedlock **vë kurorë:** to celebrate the marriage.

kurorëshkélës,-i *m.sh.* - adulterer, violator of matrimony.

kurorëzím,-i *m.sh.* -e 1. *(kurorëzimi i një mbreti)* crowning, coronation. 2. *(kurorëzim martese)* wedding, nuptial ceremony.

kurorëzój *f.k.* 1. to crown (a king). 2. to wed, to celebrate the marriage. 3. *fig.* **kurorëzoj me sukses (një punë):** to perform with success (a work, a business), to crown (a work) with success.

kurs,-i *m.sh.* -e 1. *(kurs leksionesh)* course; **kurs përgatitor:** preparatory course. 2. *(kursi i një monedhe etj.)* rate, rate (course) of exchange. 3. year; **student i kursit të parë:** first-year student.

kursánt,-i *m.sh.* -ë course attendant; **kursant i shkollës ushtarake:** cadet.

kúrse *lidh.* whereas, while; **kurse në të vërtetë:** while in fact.

kurséj *f.k.* 1. to save, to economize; **kursej të holla:** to save money, to put money aside; **të kursejmë sa më shumë:** we must economize more and more. 2. to spare: **kursej forcat:** to spare one's strength. − **kursehem** *f.jv.* to spare oneself; **nuk kursehem:** not to spare oneself.

kursím,-i *m.sh.* -e 1. saving, economy; **librezë kursimi :** bankbook; **arkë kursimi:** savingbank. 2. thriftiness, parsimony; **të punojmë me kursim kudo e kurdoherë:** we must work with thriftiness everywhere and always; **pa kursim:** profusely, lavishly.

kursimtár,-i *m.sh.* -ë thrifty, parsimonious man.

kursív,-e *mb.* italic; **shkronja kursive:** italic types (characters), italics.

Kurvë, -a f.sh. -a, whore [handwritten annotation]

kurth,-i *m.sh.* -e trap, snare; **bie në kurth:** to fall into a trap; **kap në kurth:** to trap, to snare; **ngreh kurth:** to lay a trap, to stretch a trap.

kúrrë *ndajf.* never; **kurrën e kurrës:** never, never in my life; **kurrë më:** never more.

kurrfárë *p.pk.* not any.

kurrgjë *p.pk.* nothing.

kurríll/ë,-a *f.sh.* -a *zool.* crane.

kurríz,-i *m.sh.* -e 1. *anat.* back, spine; **palca e kurrizit:** spinal cord; **peshku i kurrizit:** backbone; **me kurriz:** hunch-backed, crooked; **ul kurrizin:** to cringe (to crouch, to bend, to incline) the back; **mos e ul kurrizin:** don't bend your back! *fig.* **punoj sa më del kurrizi:** to work oneself to death; **flas prapa kurrizit:** to speak ill of someone behind his back, to back-bite. 2. **kurrizi i një karrigeje:** the back of a chair.

kurrizdálë *mb.* hunch-backed, crook-backed, humpbacked.

kurrízo *mb.* shih **kurrizdalë.**

kurrizór,-e *mb.* spinal; **shtylla kurrizore;** spinal column, vertebral column, backbone.

kurrkújt *p.pk.* shih **kurrkush.**

kurrkúnd *ndajf.* nowhere.

kurrkúsh *p.pk.* nobody, no one; **kurrkush nuk besonte:** nobody believed.

kurrsesí *ndajf.* nohow, not at all, by no means, in no way.

kusár,-i *m.sh.* -ë brigand, gunsman, high-wayman, robber; **kryetar i një bande kusarësh:** ringleader.

kusarì,-a *f.* brigandage, robbery.

kusí,-a *f.sh.* — saucepan, stewpan.

kusúr,-i *m.sh.* -e 1. rest, remainder, remnant. 2. defect; **ai s'ka asnjë kusur:** he has no one defect.

3. sin, guilt; **ç'kusur kam unë që ai s'erdhi?** am I to blame (is it my fault) that he didn't come? 4. change; **ma dhe kusurin gabim:** you have given me the wrong change.

kush *p.pk.* who; **kush është atje?** who is there? **kush e fitoi garën?** who won the race? **kush jeni ju?** who are you? **i kujt është ky libër?** whose book is that? **kujt ia dhe?** to whom did you give it? **kë ke parë dje?** whom did you see yesterday? **prej kujt ke frikë?** who are you afraid of? **kujt po i thual** that's not news to me!

kush *p.pk.* nobody; **atë s'e do kush:** nobody loves him.

kushdó *p.pk.* 1. whosoever, whomsoever, whoever; whichever; **kushdo qoftë:** whoever he may be. 2. anybody, anyone; **më mirë se kushdo tjetër:** better than anybody else.

kushedí *ndajf.* perhaps, possibly; **kushedi kur vjen:** who knows when will he come.

kushërí,-ri *m.sh.* -nj cousin; **kushëri i parë:** first cousin; **kushëri i dytë;** second cousin; **një kushëri i im:** a cousin of mine.

kushërír/ë,-a *f.sh.* -a cousin (fem.); **një kushërira ime:** a cousin of mine.

kushinét/ë,-a *f.sh.* -a *mek.* bearing; **kushinetë me sfera:** ball bearing.

kusht,-i *m.sh.* -e 1. condition; **me kushte:** conditionally; **pa kushte:** unconditionally; **dorëzim pa kushte i një ushtrie:** capitulation, unconditional surrender of an army. 2. **kushtet e një marrëveshjeje, një kontrate:** clauses, stipulations, terms (of a contract, or agreement); **kusht**

paraprak: premise. – *Lok.* **eja me çdo kusht:** come by all means (at any cost, at all costs); **me kusht që:** on condition that, under stipulation that, provided that; **kam kushtet e duhura:** to have the required conditions.

kushtetúes,-e *mb.* constitutional; **asambleja kushtetuesa:** the constituent assembly.

kushtetút/ë,-a *f. pol.* constitution.

kushtëzím,-i *m.* conditioning.

kushtëzój *f.k.* to condition, to subject to a condition. – **kushtëzohet** *f.jv.* to be made conditional, to be conditioned; **kushtëzohet nga ambienti:** to be conditioned by environment.

kushtëzúar (i,e) *mb.* conditioned; **në mënyrë të kushtëzuar:** conditionally.

kushtím,-i *m.* 1. consecration. 2. dedication.

kushtój *f.k.* 1. to consecrate; to dedicate, to devote; **i kushtoj shumë vëmendje :** to pay much attention, to pay much heed, to apply close attention. 2. *(kushtoj një vepër)* to dedicate (a work). – **kushtohem** *f.jv.* to apply oneself (to something or someone), to addict oneself to.

kushtón *f.jk.* to cost; **sa kushton ajo?** how much does it cost? **kushton shumë:** it costs much.

kushtór/e,-ja *f. gram.* conditional (mood).

kushtrím,-i *m.* clarion call; **jap (lëshoj) kushtrimin:** to sound the clarion call.

kushtúesh/ëm (i),-me(e) *mb.* costly, expensive.

kut,-i *m.sh.* -e ancient measure of length equivalent to 80 cm.

kutí,-a *f.sh.* – 1. box, case; **kuti cigaresh:** cigarette-case; **kuti**

shkrepsesh: match-box; **kuti duhani:** snuff box; **kuti prej teneqeje:** tin box; **kuti postare:** pillar-box, letter-box, letter-case; **kuti për punë dore:** box for needlework: **kuti votimesh:** ballot-box. 2. square; **copë me kutia:** chequered cloth.

kuturis *f.jk.* to venture.

kuturísj/e,-a *f.sh.* -e venture.

kuturú *ndajf.* at haphazard, at all hazards, at random; **ai flet kuturu:** he speaks thoughtlessly.

kuvénd,-i *m.sh.* -e assembly; **Kuvendi Popullor:** The People's Assembly.

kuvendím,-i *m.sh.* -e conversation, talk, colloquy.

kuvendój *f.k.* to converse, to talk.

kuvért/ë,-a *f.sh.* -a 1. *(kuvertë anijeje)* deck (of a ship). 2. *(kuvertë krevati)* cover-bed.

kuvlí,-a *f.sh.* – cage, coop.

kuzhín/ë,-a *f.sh.* -a kitchen, cookery; **enë kuzhine:** culinary utensils; **kuzhinë (stufë) ekonomike:** kitchen range, cooking-stove.

kuzhiniér,-i *m.sh.* -ë cook.

ky l. *p.d.* (sing. masc. nominative case) this, this one; that; **ç'është ky?** what is this? **është i,e këtij:** it belongs to this one; **jepja këtij:** give it to this one; **këtë e dua më shumë:** I love this one better; **ky qytet më pëlqen:** I like this town; *sh.* **këta:** these, those; **i,e këtyre njerëzve:** of these men; **këtyre:** to these ones; **këta:** these; *f.* this, this one, that; **i, e kësaj:** of this one; **kësaj:** to this one; **këtë:** this one; *sh.* **këto:** these; **e pashë me këta sy:** I saw it with my own (with these very) eyes; **këto ditë nuk e kam parë:** I haven't seen him in the last few days; **do të vij këto ditë:** I'll come one of these days; **do të kthehem këtë dimër:** I'll be back this winter; **këtë s'e kisha dëgjuar ndonjëherë:** this is new to me; **e bukur kjo!** that is a good one!

kyç,-i *m.sh.* **-e** 1. key; **mbyll me kyç:** to lock; **mbyllur me kyç:** locked. 2. *anat. (kyçi i dorës)* wrist. **kyç** *f.k.* to lock, to lock up, to padlock. − **kyçem** *f.jv.* to lock oneself in.

L

l, L (letter of the Albanian alphabet) l, L.

la (kr. thj. e foljes **lë**) left (shih **lë**); *fig.* **ai na la:** he is dead, he died.

la,-ja *f. muz.* la.

labirínt,-i *m.sh.* **-.e** labyrinth.

laboránt,-i *m.sh.* **-ë** laboratory technician.

laboratór,-i *m.sh.* **-e** laboratory.

labót,-i *m. bot.* dock;

láfsh/ë,-a *f.sh.* **-a** crest, comb; **lafshë këndezi:** cock's comb; crest of a cock.

lag *f.k.* 1. to wet, to moisten. 2. to water; **lag lulet:** to water the flowers. 3. *fig.* **lag gurmazin, lag gojën:** to wet one's whistle. − **lagem** *f.jv.* to get wet.

lagështí,-a *f.* humidity, dampness; **nxjerr lagështinë:** to ooze.

lágët (i,e), lagësht (i,e) *mb.* wet, moist, humid, damp.

lági/e,-a *f.* wetting, watering.

lágur (i,e) *mb.* wet, damp.

lágj/e,-ja *f.sh.* **-e** ward, quarter (of a town); **lagje e jashtme**

e një qyteti të madh; periphery, outskirts, suburb.

lahút/ë,-a *f.sh.* **-a** *muz.* lute.

laík,-e *mb.* laic.

laj *f.k.* 1. to wash; **laj fytyrën:** to wash one's face; **laj rrobat:** to wash one's clothes; **laj enët:** to wash up the dishes. 2. *fig.* to liquidate, to settle, to pay up; **laj borxhin:** to settle (to pay up) a debt; **laj gjynahet:** to atone for. − **lahem** *f.jv.* 1. to wash oneself. 2. *(lahem në det, në lumë, në liqen)* to bathe. 3. *fig. (me dikë)* to pay (someone) off, to square accounts with someone.

lájka,-t *f.sh.* flatteries; **i bëj lajka dikujt:** to flatter someone.

lajkatár,-i *m.sh.* **-ë** flatterer, lickspitle.

lajkatár,-e *mb.* wheedling; **fjalë lajkatare:** wheedling speech.

lajkatím,-i *m.* flattering.

lajkatój *f.k.* to flatter, to wheedle, to blarney, to coax, to cajole

lajm,-i *m.sh.* **-e** news, tidings, notice; message; **mbledh lajme:** to gather news; **nuk kemi**

lajme prej tij: we have had no news of him; **lajme të reja:** new tidings; **po na jep një lajm të mirë:** that's good news.
lajmërím,-i *m.sh.* **-e** anouncement. notice; **lajmërim në gazetë:** announcement, advertisement; **lajmërim vdekjeje:** obituary; **gjer në një lajmërim të ri:** until further notice.
lajmërój *f.k.* to notify, to give notice, to advertise, to announce, to send word, to let know; **lajmëroj dikë për një rrezik:** to warn someone of a danger; **më lajmëro kur të vish:** let me know when you arrive; **ardhja e lejlekut lajmëron pranverën:** the coming of the stork announces the spring.– **lajmërohem** *f.jv.* to be informed, to be warned.
lájmës,-i *m.sh.* – go-between.
lajmëtár,-i *m.sh.* -ë messenger, harbinger, informer, herald, announcer.
lajthí,-a *f.sh.* – *bot.* hazelnut, cobnut: **druri i lajthisë:** hazel, hazel-tree; **thyerëse lajthish:** nutcracker.
lajthisht/ë,-a *f.sh.* -a hazel grove.
lajthís *f.jk.* 1. to mistake, to err, to commit an error, a mistake. 2. to go out of one's wits.
lajthítj/e,-a *f.* mistake, error.
lak,-u *m.sh.* **leqe** 1. chain-trap for wild beast. 2. noose, lasso, slip knot; **lak me litar:** lasso; **zë me lak:** to noose, to catch with a lasso (with a noose). – *Lok.* **më dridhen leqet e këmbëve:** my legs are shaking.
lák/ër,-ra *f.sh.* -ra *bot.* 1. cabbage; **lakër e kuqe:** sprouts, Brussel's sprouts. 2. *fig.* **lakra** *pl.* wrong conceptions; **kam lakra në kokë:** to nourish erroneous ideas.
lakërarmé,-ja *f.* pickled cabbage.

lakím,-i *m.sh.* **-e** *gram.* inflexion, declension; **lakimi i emrave:** declension of nouns.
lakmi-a *f.* 1. covetousness, envy; **me lakmi:** covetously. 2. cupidity, greediness, avidity; **lakmia e panginjur e kapitalistëve për fitime:** the insatiable cupidity (greediness) of capitalists for gains.
lakmitár,-i *m.sh.* -ë coveter.
lakmitár,-e *mb.* covetous, envious.
lakmój *f.k.* to covet, to envy. – **lakmohem** *f.jv.* to be coveted (envied).
lakmúes,-e *mb.* *(për të ngrënë)* gluttonous.
lakmúesh/ëm (i),-me(e) *mb.* enviable.
lakój *f.k.* 1. to bend. 2. *gram.* to inflect, to decline. – **lakohet** *f.jv.* to be declined.
lakór/e,-ja *f.sh.* -e *gjeom.* curved line, curve.
lakrór,-i *m.sh.* -ë pie.
lakúesh/ëm(i),-me(e) *mb.* 1. flexible, pliable. 2. **gram.** declinable, inflective.
lakuríq,-i *m.sh.* -ë *zool.* bat.
lakuríq *ndajf.* bare. nude, naked, uncovered; *fig.* **e vërteta lakuriq:** the naked truth.
lakuriqësí,-a *f.* nakedness, nudity, nudeness.
lambík,-u *m.sh.* -ë 1. still. alembic. 2. water-warmer for washing linen.
lamtumír/ë,-a *f.* farewell, leavetaking; **lë lamtumirën:** to bid farewell, to say good-bye.
lamtumirë! *pasth.* goodbye! farewell!
lanét,-i *m.sh.* -ë 1. devil, demon; **e bëj lanet dikë:** to curse, to damn someone; **lanet qofsh!** curse you, a curse upon you! 2 rascal.

lang/úa,-oi *m.sh.* -onj *zool.* hound, grey-hound, harrier, beagle.
lapangjóz,-i *m.sh.* -ë rascal.
laparós *f.k.* to dirty. — laparosem *f.jv.* to get dirty, to dirty oneself.
lapërdhár,-i *m.sh.* -ë foul-mouthed man.
ˡapërdhí,-a *f.sh.* – foul words, foul language.
lapidár,-i *m.sh.* -ë monolith, obelisk.
laps,-i *m.sh.* -a pencil; laps kopjativ: indelible pencil; laps plumbi: lead pencil; kuti lapsash: pencil-case, pencil-box; mpreh lapsin: to sharpen the pencil, to point the pencil. – *Lok.* i bie lapsit: to calculate accurately, to work something out carefully.
laracój *f.k.* to mottle.
laradásh,-i *m.sh.* -a *zool.* pelican.
laragán,-e *mb.* motley, partly-coloured, pied, spotted, variagated.
lára-lára *mb.* shih laragan.
laramán,-e *mb.* shih laragan.
larásk/ë,-a *f.sh.* -a *zool.* magpie.
larásh,-e, larosh,-e *mb.* shih laragan.
lárë (i,e) *mb.* 1. washed, clean; ndërresa të lara: clean linen; duar të lara: clean hands. 2. *(i larë nga një borxh)* discharged (of a debt).
lárës,-e *mb.* washing, cleansing; makinë larëse: washing-machine.
lárës/e,-ja *f.sh.* -e washer; larëse rrobash: washing-machine; larëse pjatash: dishwasher, dishwashing machine.
larg *ndajf.* far, far off, far away, away, off, a long way off; banoj larg: to live a long way off; jo shumë larg: not very far away; sa larg banoni? how far do you live? ndihet një kilome-

tër larg: you can smell it a mile away; nga larg, për së largu: from far, afar; from a distance; ndjek dikë nga larg: to follow someone at a distance; sa larg është: how far is it? a është larg që këtu? is it far from here? është shumë larg më këmbë: it is too far to walk; më larg; farther; fshati ishte pesë kilometra larg qyteṭit: the village was five kilometers off the town; i rri larg dikujt: to keep clear of someone. – *Lok.* shoh larg: to be farsighted; larg mejel far from mel – *Prov.* larg syve, larg zemrës: out of sight, out of mind.
largësí,-a *f.sh.* distance; në një largësi prej: at a distance of: nga një largësi e madhe; from a long distance; nga një largësi e vogël: from a short distance.
lárgët (i,e) *mb.* 1. far-off, far-away, distant, remote; më i largët; farthest, furthermost, farthermost, most remote; në një të ardhme të largët: in a remote future. 2. *(për kushtërinjtë)* distant. 3. *fig.* vague, slight; një idⅇ të largët: a vague idea.
largím,-i *m.sh.* -e 1. removal, moving away. 2. *(largim nga një detyrë)* removal; expulsion.
largój *f.k.* 1. to remove, to send (to move, to take) away; largoj nga një vend: to remove; largoj nga vetja: to estrange, to keep at a distance; to keep something away from oneself; ka një sjellje që i largon njerëzit: he's got a way about him that alienates everybody; largoj nga udha e drejtë: to mislead, to misguide, to lead (someone) astray. 2. *(largoj dikë nga*

puna) to dismiss, to remove, to put away (from service). 3. *fig.* to avert, to banish, to remove; **largoj dyshimin:** to banish suspicion. − **largohem** *f.jv.* to get away; **largohem nga tema:** to digress from a subject; **largohem nga udha e drejtë:** to deviate from the right path; **largohu!** get off!

largpámës,-e *mb.* far-sighted, far-seeing, clear-sighted.

largpámj/e,-a *f.* far-sightedness, clear-sightedness.

larín/g,-gu *m.sh.* **-gje** *anat.* larynx.

lárj/e,-a *f.sh.* **-e** 1. washing, cleansing, cleaning; **larje e teshave:** washing of clothes; **larje e duarve:** washing of hands; **larje e enëve:** washing up of dishes.- 2. **larje në det etj.** bath, bathing. 3. *(larje borxhi)* payment (of a debt).

lármë (i,e) *mb.* motley, pied, spotted, variagated.

láro-ja *m.sh.* − rascal.

lart *ndajf.* above; high up, on high, aloft, up; **nga lart:** from above; **një urdhër nga lart:** an order from above; **lart e poshtë:** up and down; **mbaj flamurin lart:** to hold the flag aloft; **mbaj kokën lart:** to keep the head aloft; **me ballin lart:** with the chin up; **si më lart:** as above; **në katin lart:** upstairs; **duart lart!** hands up!

lártë (i,e) *mb.* 1. high; **mur dy metra i lartë:** a wall two metres high. 2. tall; **njeri me shtat të lartë:** a tall man. 3. *(për tinguj, zë)* high-pitched; **nota të larta:** high notes; **me zë të lartë:** loudly. 4. *fig.* high, considerable; **çmimi është tepër i lartë:** the price is very high; **komanda e lartë:** high command; **në sferat e larta:** in

the upper spheres; **tradhti e lartë:** high treason. 5. lofty; **ndjenja të larta:** lofty sentiments. 6. *(për rang)* high, high ranking; **është nëpunës i lartë:** he is a high-ranking official.

lartësí,-a *f.sh.* − 1. height; **lartësia e një mali:** height of a mountain. 2. *(trupore)* height, stature. 3. highness, loftiness. 4. *gjeog.* altitude. 5. *(mbi nivelin e detit)* altitude; **qyteti ndodhet në lartësinë treqind metra:** the town is a hundred metres high (in altitude); **lartësi e madhe:** great height, high altitude; **lartësi mbi nivelin e detit;** height (altitude) above sea-level.

lartësím,-i *m.* raising, elevation, lifting up; exaltation.

lartësój *f.k.* 1. to raise, to elevate, to lift up, to uplift. 2. to exalt, te extol, to glorify. − **lartësohem** *f.jv.* to ascend, to mount up, to arise.

lartpërméndur (i,e) *mb.* above-mentioned, afore-mentioned, afore-said.

larúsh,-e *mb.* motley.

lárv/ë,-a *f.sh.* **-a** *zool.* larva, maggot.

lastár,-i *m.sh.* **-ë** *bot.* spray, sprig, slip, scion, offshoot, tender-shoot.

láshë *f.k.* (p.t. of the verb **lë**) I left.

láshta,-t (të) *f.sh.* cereals, crops.

láshtë (i,e) *mb.* antique, ancient; **koha e lashtë:** antiquity; **bashkësi elashtë:** primitive community.

lashtësí,-a *f.* antiquity, ancientness.

lát/ë,-a *f. sh.* **-a** ticket, coupon.

lát/ë,-a *f.sh.* **-a** hatchet.

latój *f.k.* to carve, to grave on wood, to engrave; **latoj me thikë**: to whittle. − **latohet** *f.jv.* to be carved, to be engraved.

latór/e,-ja *f.sh.* **-e** hatchet, small axe.

laturís *f.k.* to dirty, to soil, to daub, to besmear. − **laturisem** *f.jv.* to get dirty.

laureát,-i *m.sh.* **-ë** laureate.

laurésh/ë,-a *f.sh* **-a** *zool.* lark, sky lark.

laurój *f.k.* to give the laureate. − **laurohem** *f.jv.* to get the laureate.

lavamán,-i *m.sh.* **-ë** wash-hand, wash-stand.

lavanderí,-a *f.sh..* - wash-house, laundry.

lavapját/ë,-a *f.sh.* **-a** sink.

lavd,-i *m.sh.* **-e** praise; **thurr lavde**: to sing the praises of someone.

lavdërím,-i *m.sh.* **-e** commendation, praise; **fletë lavdërimi**: commendation-paper; **bëj një lavdërim**: to bestow commendation upon, to commend someone.

lavdërój *f.k.* to laud, to praise. − **lavdërohem** *f.jv.* to be lauded (praised); to vaunt, to brag; **që meriton të lavdërohet**: praiseworthy.

lavdërúesh/ëm (i), -me(e) *mb.* laudable, commendable, praiseworthy.

lavdí,-a *f.* glory; **lavdi Partisë së Punës të Shqipërisë!** glory to the Party of Labour of Albania! **plot lavdi**: full of glory; **pa lavdi**: without glory.

lavdiplótë *mb.* full of glory, glorious.

lavdísh/ëm (i), -me (e) *mb.* glorious; **Partia jonë e lavdishme**: our glorious Party; **Ushtria jonë e lavdishme**: our glorious army.

láv/ë,-a *f.* lava.

lavír/e,-ja *f.sh.* **-e** prostitute.

lavjérrës,-i *m.sh.* **-a** pendulum.

le *pjesëz* (particle wich is used to form the imperative) let; **le të shkojmë!** let us go! **le të hyjë**: let him come in!

le *lidh.* **le që**: not only; **le që s'më dha gjë, por më dëboi**: not only he gave me nothing, but he sent me away.

lebetí,-a *f.* panic, terror.

lebetít *f.k.* to dismay, to terrify. − **lebetitem** *f.jv.* to be terrified (dismayed).

lebetítj/e,-a *f.* shih **lebeti**.

leckamán,-i *m.sh.* **-ë** ragamuffin.

leckamán,-e *mb.* ragged.

léck/ë,-a *f.sh.* **-a** 1. rag, tatter; **veshur me lecka**: clothed in tattered garments, dressed in rags. 2. cloth; **leckë për të larë enët**: dish cloth; **leckä për fshirjen e pluhurit;** duster cloth. 3. *fam.* one's belongings; **ngre leckat**: to dislodge secretly and unceremoniously.

leckós *f.k.* to tatter, to rend into rags. − **leckosem** *f.jv.* to become ragged.

leckósj/e,-a *f.* tattering.

leckósur (i,e) *mb.* tattered, ragged, shabby, all in rags and tatters.

ledh,-i *m.sh.* **-e** bank.

ledhatár,-i *m.sh.* **-ë** flatterer.

ledhatím,-i *m.sh.* **-e** caress.

ledhatój *f.k.* to caress; **i ledhatoj flokët**: to stroke someone's hair.

ledhatúes,-e *mb.* caressing.

legál,-e *mb.* legal, lawful.

legalísht *ndajf.* legally, lawfully.

legalitét,-i *m.* legality, lawfulness.

legalizím,-i *m.* legalization.

legalizój *f.k.* to legalize. − **legalizohem** *f.jv.* to be legalized.

legát/ë,-a *f.sh.* **-a** legation.

legén,-i *m.sh.* -ë 1. wash-basin, basin. 2. *anat.* pelvis.

lég/ë,-a *f.sh.* -a league, geographical mile.

legjendár,-e *mb.* legendary.

legjénd/ë,-a *f.sh.* -a 1- legend. 2. *gjeog. (harte)* legend.

legjión,-i *m.sh.* -e legion.

legjionár,-i *m.sh.* -ë legionary.

legjislación,-i *m.* legislation.

legjislatív,-e *mb.* legislative.

legjislatór,-i *m.sh.* -ë legislator.

legjislatùr/ë,-a *f.* legislature.

legjitím,-e *mb.* legitimate, lawful; fëmijë legjitim: legitimate child.

legjitimitét,-i *m.* legitimacy.

leh *f.jk.* to bark, to yap, to bay.

léhe,-ja *f.sh,* -e garden-plot; lehe lulesh: flowerbed.

léhj/e,-a *f.sh.* -e barking, yap, baying.

lehón/ë,-a *f.sh.* -a woman in childbed, mother after child-birth (after confinement).

lehoní,-a *f.* lie in.

léhtas *ndajf.* shih lehtë.

léhtë *ndajf.* 1. easily; kjo shpjegohet lehtë: it is easily explained. 2. lightly; veshur lehtë: lightly dressed. 3. slightly; plagosur lehtë: slightly wounded.

léhtë (i,e) *mb.* 1. easy, not dificult; problem e lehtë: easy problem; mësim e lehtë: easy lesson. 2. light, not heavy; peshë e lehtë: light weight. 3. i lehtë nga këmbët: light footed. 4. *fig.* i lehtë nga mendja: noodle, simpleton.

lehtësí,-a *f.* 1. ease, facility; me lehtësi: easily, facilely. 2. *(të qenët i lehtë)* lightness. 3. favour; më bëj një lehtësi: do me a favour.

lehtësím,-i *m.* 1. relief; lehtësimi i shpirtit: relief of soul. 2. solace; lehtësim i një dhembjeje: solace, alleviation of a pain, of

a suffering. 3. lehtësimi i dënimit: attenuation (mitigation) of a punishment. 4. lehtësim peshe: unloading of burden.

lehtësísht *ndajf.* easily, lightly.

lehtësój *f.k.* 1. *(një dënim)* to mitigate, (to assuage, to soften) a punishment. 2. *(një dhembje morale)* to alleviate, to solace (a moral pain, a grief). 3. *(një dhembje fizike)* to allay, to calm, to assuage (a physical pain). 4. *(një peshë, një ngarkesë)* to unload or to disburden partly, to render less heavy, to lighten. 5. *(një punë)* to make easier, to make less difficult, to facilitate. – lehtësohem *f.jv.* to relieve oneself, to ease one's mind, to disburden.

lehtësúes,-e *mb.* alleviating, mitigating; rrethana lehtësuese: *(për një të akuzuar):* mitigating circumstances. 2. *(për një ilaç)* lenitive, assuaging, amollient.

léhurit (të) *as.* barking.

léj/ë,-a *f.* 1. *(për të ndërtuar etj.)* allowance, authorization, permit, licence (to build etc.). 2. *(kalimi)* pass, *amer.* check-pass. 3. *(pushshimi)* : furlough, leave. 4. *(për të folur, për të marrë fjalën)* permission, liberty; marr lejen t'ju parashtroj sa vijon: I take the liberty to put forward (to expound) as follows.

lejëkalím,-i *m.sh.* -e pass, laissez-passer.

lejím,-i *m.* permission, authorization.

lejék,-u *m.sh.* -ë *zool.* stork.

lejój *f.k.* 1. to allow, to permit, to let, to authorize; nuk lejoj: to forbid. 2. to make possible, to allow. 3. to permit, to let, to tolerate. – lejohem *f.jv.* to be allowed, to be permitted.

lejúar (i,e) *mb.* permitted, allowed: **nuk ishte e lejuar:** it was not allowed.

lejúesh/ëm(i),-me(e) *mb.* 1. permissible, permissive, allowable. 2. tolerable.

lek,-u *m.sh.* -ë lek (standard money of Albania); **lekë të shkoqura:** small change; **s'kam asnjë lek në xhep:** I have not a farthing.

leksík,-u *m.* lexicon, vocabulary.

leksikográf,-i *m.sh.* -ë lexicographer, compiler of a dictionary.

leksión,-i *m.sh.* -e lecture; **jap një leksion:** to lecture, to give a lecture.

lektór,-i *m.sh.* -ë lecturer.

lemerí,-a *f.* panic, terror.

lemerís *f.k.* to dismay, to terrify. — **lemerisem** *f.jv.* to be dismayed (terrified).

lemerísh/ëm(i),-me(e) *mb.* terrible, dreadful.

lémz/ë,-a *f.* hiccough, hiccup.

lénd/e,-ja *f.sh.* -e *bot.* accorn, oak-apple, nut-gall.

leopárd,-i *m.sh.* -ë *zool.* leopard.

lépu/r,-ri *m.sh.* -j *zool. (lepur i egër)* hare, wild rabbit. *(lepur i butë)* rabbit, cony. — *Lok.* **më ka hyrë lepuri në bark:** to have taken fright.

lepurúsh,-i *m.sh.* -ë *zool.* young cony, rabbit; **lepurush i egër:** young hare, leveret.

leqendís *f.k. gj. bis.* 1. to weaken, to enfeeble. 2. to afflict. — **leqendisem** *f.jv.* 1. to become weak, to dwindle. 2. to be afflicted.

lér/ë,-a *f.* dirt, filth.

lerós *f.k.* to dirty, to soil. — **lerosem** *f.jv.* to dirty oneself, to get dirty.

lerth,-i *m. bot.* ivy.

lés/ë,-a *f.sh.* -a harrow.

lesím,-i *m.sh.* -e harrowing.

lésk/ër,-ra *f.sh.* -ra scale, shell.

leskërój *f.k.* to scale, to peel off. — **leskërohem** *f.jv.* to be scaled.

lesój *f.k.* to harrow. — **lesohet** *f.jv.* to be harrowed.

lesh,-i *m.* 1. wool; **lesh i palarë:** unbleached wool; **leshi, prej leshi:** wool, wollen; **fije leshi:** wollen yarn; **lesh deleje:** sheep's wool; **lesh i krehur:** wollen yarn; **deng me lesh:** woolpack; **thes me lesh:** woolsac; **krehër leshi:** wool-comber; **stof leshi;** woollen-cloth, woollen tissue. 2. **lesh xhami:** glasswool, fibre-glass. 3. *sh.* **leshra, leshi i trupit, i kokës:** hair. — *Lok.* **më ngrihen leshrat përpjetë:** it makes my hair stand on end; **lesh e li:** hotch-potch, pell-mell, topsy-turvy, higgledy-piggledy, upside-down.

leshaták,-e *mb.* hairy, shaggy.

leshdrédhur *mb.* curly-haired, curly-headed.

léshko *mb.* ninny, simpleton.

leshterík,-u *m.sh.* -ë *bot.* seaweed, kelp.

léshtë (i,e) *mb.* woolly, woollen; **pallto e leshtë;** wollen coat.

leshtór,-e *mb.* shih **leshatak.**

leshvérdhë *mb.* fair-haired.

letargjí,-a *f. mjek.* lethargy.

lét/ër,-ra *f.sh.* -ra 1. letter; **letër dashurie:** love letter; **letër e porositur:** registered letter; **letër e hapur:** circular, open letter. 2. paper. **letër zmerile:** abrasive paper; **letër fotografike:** photographic paper; **letër milimetrike:** graph paper; **letër katramat:** trapaulin; **letër ambalazhi:** packing-paper, brownpaper, wrapping paper; **letër higjienike:** toilet paper; **letër shkrimi:** writing paper; **letër**

vizatimi: drawing paper; **letër ngjitëse:** gummed paper, adhesive paper; **fabrikë letre:** paper mill; **fije letre:** sheet of paper; **kosh për letrat:** wastepaper basket; **letër cigareje:** flimsy paper; **letër karboni:** carbon paper. 3. **letra loje:** playing cards; **lojë me letra:** game of cards; **ndaj letrat:** to deal the cards. – *Lok.* **hedh në letër diçka:** to put something in writing, to commit something to paper; **kam një letër të mirë në dorë:** to hold a strong hand; **i hap letrat:** to lay one's cards on the table.

letërkëmbím,-i *m.* correspondence.
letërkredenciále,-t *f.sh.* credentials.
letërmárrës,-i *m.sh.* – addressee.
letërnjoftím,-i *m.sh.* **-e** passport, identity document, identity card.
letërprúrës,-i *m.sh.* – bearer of a letter.
letërsí,-a *f.* literature.
letërshpërndarës,-i *m.sh.* lettercarrier, postboy, postman.
letërthirrj/e,-a *f.sh.* – writ, calling letter.
letërthíthës/e,-ja *f.sh.* – **e** blotting paper.
letrár,-i *m.sh.* **-ë** literary man.
letrár,-e *mb.* literary, of literature; **vepra letrare:** literary works.
levénd,-e *mb.* brisk, frisky.
leverdí,-a *f.* profit, advantage, interest, gain; **kjo punë s'ka pikë (kurrëfarë) leverdie:** there is no profit in this deal; **s'ka leverdi, është pa leverdi:** it is of no advantage (profit).
leverdís *f.jk.* to be convenient, to be of advantage (profit), it answers my purpose; **nuk më leverdis me këtë çmim:** it is of no benefit (advantage) at such a price.

leverdísh/ëm(i),-me(e) *mb.* profitable, advantageous, favourable; **me kushte të leverdishme:** on favourable terms: **me çmim të leverdishëm:** at an advantageous price.
lëv/ë,-a *f.sh.* **-a** 1. *mek.* lever- 2. *fig.* lever, helper; **bashkimet profesionale janë levat e Partisë:** the trade unions are the lever of the Party.
lexím,-i *m.sh.* **-e** reading; **lexim me vëmendje:** perusal; **lexim gërmë për gërmë:** spelling out; **libër leximi:** reading book, reader; **sallë leximi:** reading room.
lexój *f.k.* to read; **lexoj me kujdes:** to peruse; **lexoj gërmë për gërmë:** to spell out; **lexoj me vështirësi:** to read with difficulty; **lexoj rrjedhshëm:** to read fluently; **lexoj me zë të lartë:** to read loudly (in a loud voice). – **lexohet** *f.jv.* to be read.
lexúes,-i *m.* reader.
lexúesh/ëm(i),-me(e) *mb.* readable, legible.
lez,-i *m.sh.* **-e** *mjek.* wart.
lezét,-i *m.* 1. handsomness, prettiness. 2. delicacy, tact; **them me lezet:** to say with delicacy (with tact). 3. suitability, becomingness; **kjo rrobe ju ka lezet:** this cloth suits you, that dress becomes you; **nuk ju ka lezet të silleni kështu:** such behaviour is not becoming to you.
lezétsh/ëm(i),-me(e) *mb.* nice, handsome, pretty, comely, agreable, pleasing to look; **vajzë e lezetshme:** a nice girl.
lë *f.k.* (p.t. **lashë**, p.p. **lënë**). 1. to leave; **ma lërë mua:** leave it to me; **lë rehat dikë:** to leave someone alone (in peace); **lëmë rehat!** leave me alone! **e lë në dorë të fatit:'** a) *(një*

punë) to leave it to chance;
b) *(dikë)* to leave someone to
his fate; **e lë një çështje për
më vonë:** to leave a matter
over; **lë trashëgim:** to leave
(to give) by will, to bequeath. 2. to put; **lë mënjanë:**
to put aside; **lë diçka mbi tavolinë:** to put something on
the table. 3. to permit; **lë dikë të
hyjë:** to let someone come, to
let someone in; **lëre të hyjë!**
let him come! **(lë dikë) të ikë:**
to let go; **lëre të ikë!** let him
go! 4. to release: **e lë të lirë
dikë:** to release someone, to
set someone free. 5. to omit,
to miss; **lë diçka pa bërë etj.**
to leave something undone, to
miss something. 6. to quit; **i
lë shëndenë dikujt:** to take
leave of someone, to bid someone farewell, **ai na la shëndenë:** he died, he left us forever;
lë vendlindjen: to quit one's
country, to emigrate; **ju lë me
shëndet:** good-bye. — *Lok.* **lë
shumë për të dëshëruar:** it
leaves much to be desired. —
lihem *f.jv.* to be left.
lëçís *f.k. vjet.* shih **lexoj.**
lëçítës,-i *m.sh.* - *vjet.* shih **lexues.**
lëfýt,-i *m.sh.* — 1. neck (of a bottle, etc.). 2. *anat.* throat, larynx.
lëkúnd *f.k.* to shake, to quake, to
rock; **era lëkund pemët:** the
wind shakes the trees; **tërmeti
lëkundi shtëpitë:** the earthquake shaked the houses. —
lëkundem *f.jv.* 1. to shake, to
vibrate, to jolt, to rock, to os-
cillate, to vacillate. 2. *fig.* to
hesitate, to waver, to be undetermined.
lëkúndj/e,-a *f.sh.* **-e** 1. shake,
swing, quake, oscillation, vacillation; **lëkundje tërmeti:** earthquake. 2. *fig.* hesitation.

lëkúndsh/ëm(i),-me(e) *mb.* vaci-
llating, hesitating, wavering; **njeri i lëkundshëm:** unsteady person, undetermined person.
lëkúr/ë,-a *f.sh.* **-a** 1. *anat.* **cipa
e lëkurës:** epidermis. 2. *(lëku-
rë kafshe)* hide, fell, pell, skin
of an animal; **lëkurë dhensh:**
sheepskin; **sëmundje e lëkurës:** cutaneous malady; **mjek
për sëmundjet e lëkurës:** dermatologist; **lëkurë e regjur:**
leather, tanned skin, tanned
hide; **lëkurë e paregjur:** raw
hide, pelt; **lëkurë kamoshi:**
wash-leather, deerskin; **punishte lëkurësh:** tannery, tanyard;
lëkurë artificiale: leatherette.
3. *(lëkurë e bimëve(e pemës)* rind
lëkurëkúq,-i *m.sh.* — Red Indian,
redskin.
lëkurëkúq,-e *mb.* redskinned.
lëkurëpunúes,-i *m.sh.* — currier,
leather dresser.
lëkurërégjës,-i *m.sh.* — tanner.
lëkurtë (i, e) *mb.* leathern, made
of leather.
lëm/ë,-i *m.sh.-enj* thrashing gro-
und, thrashing floor.
lëmim,-i *m.* polishing.
lëmoj *f.k.* to polish, to smooth. -
lëmohet *f.jv.* to be polished.
lëmosh/ë,-a *f.sh.-a* alms, charity,
pittance.
lëmsh,-i *m.sh.* **-e** 1. clew, pellet
(of thread); *fig.* **mblidhem
lëmsh:** to shrink. 2. *gjeog.* **lëm-
shi i dheut:** globe, terrestria l
globe.
lëmúar (i,e) *mb.* polished, glossy-
smooth, sleek; **mermer i lë-
muar:** polished marble.
lëmúesh/ëm(i),-me(e) *mb.* that
may be polished.
lëna,-t (të) *f.sh.* leftovers, leavings;
të lënat e gjellës: leavings
of meals, leftovers.
lënd/ë,-a *f.sh.* **-ë** 1. matter; **lëndë**

e parё; stuff, raw stuff, raw material; **lёndё ndihmёse:** auxiliary material. 2. *kim.* substance, chemical substance: **lёndё djegёse:** fuel, combustible; **lёndё ndezёse;** inflammable substance (as benzine etc.); **lёndё plasёse:** explosive matter; **lёndё druri:** timber, lumber; **lёndё ndёrtimi:** building material. 2. subject, theme, matter; **lёndё mёsimore:** subject; **tryeza e lёndёs (e njё libri):** contents (of a book)

lёndím,-i *m.* hurt, lesion.

lёndín/ё,-a *f.sh.* **-a** lawn, sward, green sward, grass-plot.

lёndój *j.k.* 1. to hurt, to injure; **lёndoj sedrёn:** to touch one's self-esteem, to hurt someone's self-respect; **lёndoj plagёn:** to hurt the wound; **lёndoj zemrёn:** to break the heart. – **lёnndohem** *f.jv.* to be injured (grieved).

lёndór,-e *mb.* material.

lёndúar(i,e) *mb.* hurt, grieved; **zemёr e lёnduar:** broken heart; **ai mё ka lёnduar:** he has injured me, he has touched me to the quick.

lёnё (i,e) *mb.* *(nga mendtё)* absent-minded.

lёng,-u *m.sh.* **lёngje** liquid; **lёng frutash:** juice; **lёng limoni:** lemon-juice; **me lёng:** juicy; **pemё (frutё) me lёng:** juicy fruit; **lёngu i drurit:** sap of wood; **lёng mishi:** gravy of meat; **lёngu gastrik:** gastric-juices. – *Lok.* **me lёshon goja lёng:** to make one's mouth water.

lёngát/ё,-a *f.* languor, languidness, languishment.

lёngёshtím,-i *m.* liquefaction.

lёngёshtój *f.k.* to liquefy. – **lёngёshtohet** *f.jv.* to be liquefied.

lёngёshtúesh/ёm(i),-me(e) *mb.* liquefiable.

lёngёt (i,e) *mb.* liquid; **gjendje e lёngёt:** liquid state.

lёngёtýr/ё,-a *f.* ungreasy meal.

lёngёzím,-i *m.* liquefaction.

lёngёzój *f.k.* to liquefy. – **lёngёzohet** *f.jv.* to be liquefied.

lёngím,-i *m.* long malady, languidness.

lёngój *f.jk.* to languish, to suffer for a long time (from a disease).

lёngsh/ёm(i), -me(e) *mb.* liquid, fluid.

lёni/e,-a *f.* abandonment.

lёpíj *f.k.* to lick, to lick up; *(lёpin qeni)* to lap; *fig.* **lёpij buzёt, gishtat:** to lick (to smack) one's lips. – **lёpihem** *f.jv.* to lick oneself.

lёpírёs,-i *m.sh.* – licker, bootlicker, lickspittle, hanger-on.

lёpjét/ё,-a *f.sh.* **-a** *bot.* sorrel.

lёpúsh/ё,-a *f.sh.* **-a** *bot.* coltsfoot.

lёrím,-i *m.sh.* **-e** tillage, ploughing, plowing.

lёrój *f.k.* to till, to plough, to plow. – **lёrohet** *f.jv.* to be tilled, to be ploughed, to be plowed.

lёrúesh/ёm (i),-me(e) *mb.* arable, fit for plowing; **tokё e lёrueshme:** arable land.

lёshím,-i *m.sh.* **-e** 1. release. 2. concession, tolerance; **bёj lёshime:** to make concessions, to give ground.

lёshój *f.k.* 1. *(lёshoj nga dora pёrdhé)* to let fall, to drop; *(lёshoj nga dora qё tё ikё)* to let go, to release, to set free; **lёshoj armёt:** to lay down arms. 2. to give, to deliver; **lёshoj njё dёftesё:** to deliver a receipt, to give a certificate; **lёshoj njё britmё:** to give a cry. 3. **lёshoj me qira:** to hire, to lease. 4. **lёshoj vaporin:** to launch a ship. 5. **i lëshoj vendin dikujt:** to leave the place to someone. – *Lok.* **lëshoj pé:** to yield, to give way, to make concessions, to give ground. – **lëshohem** *f.jv.* 1. to go down, to be set free, to be released. 2. to be launched. 3. *(mbi armikun)* to rush on, to dash on (the enemy).

lëtýr/ë,-a *f.sh.* **-a** dirty water, house-slops; *fig.* **gjellë lëtyrë:** slop dish.

lëvdát/ë,-a *f.sh.* **-a** 1. boasting. 2. praise.

lëvdój *f.k.* to praise; to commend; to glorify, to laud. – **lëvdohem** *f.jv.* to boast, to brag.

lëvér/e,-ja *f.sh.* **-e** *krah.* clothes; **laj lëvere:** to wash clothes.

lëvíz I. *f.jk.* to move, to budge, to change place, to stir, to move off, to get going; **Toka lëviz rrotull Diellit:** the Earth moves (turns) round the Sun.
II. *f.k.* 1. to move, to stir; **lëviz krahët:** to move one's arms. 2. to move, to drive; **ujët lëviz rrotën e mullirit:** the water moves (turns) the mill wheel. – **lëvizem** *f.jv.* to be moved, to be set in motion; **kjo tryezë nuk lëvizet nga vendi:** this table can't be moved. – *Lok.* **nuk lëviz as qishtin:** not to lift a finger.

lëvízës,-e *mb.* 1. moving, mobile; **shkallë lëvizëse:** moving staircase. 2. movable, mobile. 3. motive, driving, motor, propellent; **forcë lëvizëse:** motive power (force).

lëvízj/e,-a *f.sh.* **-a** 1. motion, movement; **jam në lëvizje:** to be in motion, to be moving. **vë në lëvizje:** to propel, to impel, to sat in motion, to set going, to stir, to promote, to put into motion; **vihem në lëvizje:** to get moving, to set out. 2.

(zhvendosje) transfer. 3. movement, move; **një lëvizje e krahëve:** a movement of the arms. 4. traffic, movement; **lëvizje trenash:** rail traffic. 5. *(artistike, politike etj.)* (artistic, political) movement; **Lëvizja Nacionalçlirimtare:** National Liberation Movement. 6. *ekon.* movement, circulation; **lëvizje e mallrave:** circulation of commodities.

lëvízsh/ëm(i),-me(e) *mb.* 1. mobile, movable. 2. variable.

lëvizshmërí,-a *f.* 1. mobility, movability. 2. variability; mutability.

lëvózhg/ë,-a *f.sh.* **-a** 1. *(arre)* shell. 2. *(bishtaje)* pod; *(gruri)* husk. 3. *(e druve)* bark (of trees). 4. *(pjepri):* cortex. 5. *(portokalli)* rind; *(molle)* rind; **heq lëvozhgën, qëroj lëvozhgën:** to rind, to peel, to strip the rind from.

lëvríj *f.k.* 1. to roll in the mire. 2. *(lëvrin gjaku)* to run, to circulate.

lëvrím,-i *m.* 1. *(i tokës)* tillage. 2. *(i gjuhës)* cultivation. 3. *(i leshit)* combing (of wool.)

lëvrój *f.k.* 1. *(një gjuhë)* to cultivate (a language). 2. *(lesh)* to comb wool, to card wool.

lëvrúes,-i *m.sh.* – *(i gjuhës)* promoter, fosterer.

li,-ri *m. bot.* flax; **bima e lirit;** flaxplant; **farë liri:** flax-seed, linseed; **artikuj prej liri:** flaxen articles; **vaj liri:** linseed oil.

li,-a *f. mjek.* small pox; **pucër lie:** pock; **lia e bagëtive (e dhenve):** varicella, chicken-pox; **i vrarë lie (nga lia):** pock-marked.

liberál,-i *m.sh.* **-ë** liberal.

liberál,-e *mb.* liberal.

liberalíz/ëm,-mi *m.* liberalism.

líb/ër,-ri *m.sh.* **-ra** 1. book; **libër leximi:** reader, reading book;

libër për fëmijë (i ilustruar):
picture-book; libër shkolle:
school book. 2. book, register;
libri i arkës: cash book (register); libër llogarie: account
book, ledger; libër gatimi:
cookerybook.
librallídhës,-i m.sh. – book binder.
llbrár,-i m.sh. -ë bookseller.
librarí,-a f.sh. – bookshop, book-
store.
librashítës,-i m.sh. – bookseller.
libréz/ë,-a f.sh. -a (kursimi)
bankbook.
licé,-u m.sh. – middle school;
lice artistik: art school.
lidh f.k. 1. to tie, to bind, to fasten; lidh me spango: to tie
with a·twine; lidh kravatën: to
tie the necktie; lidh fort: to
tie up strongly, to bind strongly.
2. lidh duart: to bind the arms;
lidh sytë: to bind the eyes, to
blindfold; lidh një plagë: to
bind up a wound; lidh një
libër: to bind a book. 3. to
link; lidh me zinxhir: to chain.
4. to fetter; ia lidh këmbët
një kali: to fetter a horse; ia
lidh duart dikujt: to tie someone's hands. 5. to lace; lidh
këpucët: to lace the shoes. 6.
lidh një kontratë: to contract
(for), to make (to enter into) a
contract (with someone). 7. fig.
to bind, to link, to unite, to join;
ata i lidh një miqësi e sinqertë: they are bound by a sincere
friendship. – lidhem f.jv. to
bind oneself, to tie oneself;
lidhem me krushqi: to ally
oneself by marriage.
lídhës,-e mb. connective; ind li-
dhës: connective tissue.
ídhës/e,-ja f₁sh. – lace (of shoes),

tie; lidhëse këpucësh: boot
lace, shoe-string.
lídhëz,-a f.sh. -a gram. conjuction·
lídhj/e,-a f.sh. -e 1. tying, binding·
fastening, bandage: lidhje plage: bandage, dressing of a
wound; lidhje libri: binding of
a book. 2. lidhje krushqie:
alliance by marriage, connection by marriage; lidhje ushtarake: coalition, alliance; lidhje martese: bonds of marriage: lidhje gjaku: consanguinity, blood relationship; lidhje
miqësie: bonds of friendship:
lidhje familiare: family ties; lidhje kimike: chemical bond.
3. link, connexion conection;
midis këtyre ngjarjeve s'ka
asnjë lidhje: there is no connexion between these events.
– Lok. mbaj lidhje: to keep in
touch with; në lidhje me let-
rën tuaj: in reference to your
letter.
lidhór,-e mb. gram. relative; përemër lidhor: relative pronoun;
mënyra lidhore (e një foljeje):
subjunctive mood.
lídhur (i,e) mb. bound, tied,
linked; libër i lidhur: bound
book; trup i lidhur: strong
body; mendime të lidhura:
coherent ideas (opinions); e
çuan lidhur: they conducted
him bound.
lídhur (me) paraf. in reference to,
in respect to, with· regard to.
lig (i),-ë(e) mb. 1. wicked, bad,
evil, malevolent; njeri i lig:
wicked man. 2. nasty; erë e
ligë: nasty smell, stench smell.
lig f.k. to make lean, thin. – ligem
f.jv. to grow lean.
ligáç,-i m.sh. -ë driveller.
ligavéc,-i m.sh. -ë zool.
shelless snail, slug.

líg/ë, a f. league, alliance.
líg/ë, (e),-a (e) f.sh. -a(të) the evil; e mira dhe e liga s'kanë fund: the good and the evil have no end.
ligësí,-a f. badness, wickedness, evilness, malice.
ligështí,-a f. faintness, debility, weakness, feebleness.
ligështím,-i m. weakening, fainting.
ligështój f.k. to weaken, to enfeeble.— **ligështohem** f.jv. to weaken
lígët (i,e) mb. emaciated, lean.
ligsht ndajf. badly; **më vjen ligsht:** a) I am sorry; b) I am uneasy, I feel myself uneasy.
ligj,-i m.sh. -e law; **nxjerr një ligj:** to pass an act; **miratoj një ligj:** to pass a bill; **sipas ligjit:** according to the law, in conformity with the law; **njeri i ligjit;** lawyer, legislator; **njeri i nxjerrë jashtë ligjit:** outlaw; **nxjerr jashtë ligjit:** to outlaw **në vendet kapitaliste sundon ligji i kërbaçit:** in the capitalist countries reigns the club-law; **me ligj:** by law. **shkel ligjin:** to infringe (to violate, to break) the law.
ligjërát/ë,-a f.sh. -a discourse, speech.
ligjërím,-i m. 1. (i zogjve) chirp, warble. 2. drejt. legalization.
ligjërísht ndajf. lawfully, legally.
ligjërój f.jk. 1. to discourse. 2. to legalize, to sanction by law.
ligjór,-e mb. 1. lawful, legal; **fuqi ligjore:** legal force; **dispozita ligjore:** legal dispositions; **pa fuqi ligjore:** null, of no legal force. 2. judicial, forensic; **mjekësi ligjore:** forensic medicine.
lígjsh/ëm(i),-me(e) mb. lawful, legitimate; **kërkesat e ligjshme të punëtorëve:** the legitimate

demands of the workers; **trashëgimtari i ligjshëm:** presumtive heir.
ligjshmërí,-a f. 1. lawfulness, legitimation. 2. legislation, laws.
ligjvënës,-i m.sh. — legislator, lawmaker.
ligjvënës,-e mb. legislative; **asambleja ligjvënëse:** the legislative assembly.
lijósur (i,e) mb. pock-marked.
likér,-i m.sh. -na liquor; **liker vishnjeje:** cherry brandy.
likuidatór,-i m.sh. -ë liquidator.
likuidím,-i m.sh. -e 1. liquidation, winding up. 2. paying off; **likuidim fature:** payment of an invoice.
likuidój f.k. 1. to liquidate, to wind up. 2. to pay off; **likuidoj një faturë:** to pay a bill; **likuidohet** f.jv. to be liquidated.
lilth,-i m.sh. -a anat. uvula.
limán,-i m.sh. -e bay, haven, bight.
lím/ë,-a f.sh. -a file; **ha me limë:** to file; **limë për thonj:** nail file.
limfatík,-e mb. mjek. lymphatic.
limój f.k. to file.
limón,-i m.sh. -a bot. lemon; **druri i limonit;** lemon-tree; **lëng limoni:** lemon juice.
limonát/ë,-a f.sh. -a lemonade.
limontí,-a f. idleness.
limontóz,-i m. tartaric acid.
lind I. f.jk. (p.t. **linda,** p.p. **lindur)** 1. to be born, to see the light; **kam lindur në Korçë:** I was born in Korça; **kam lindur më 1940:** I was born in 1940. 2. to rise; **dielli lind në orën pesë:** the sun arises at 5 o'clock; (dita) to break, to dawn.3.(filizat) to come, to spring up. 4. fig. to arise (from, out of), to be

due (to), to come about (through), to spring (from); **gjithë kjo lindi nga një keqkuptim:** the whole thing came from a misunderstanding. II. *f.k.* 1. to give birth to; to be delivered of; **ajo lindi djalë:** she gave birth to a boy. 2. *fig.* to produce.

llndj/e,-a *f.sh.* -e 1. birth, childbirth, delivery; **dhembjet e lindjes:** throes; **dita e lindjes:** birthday; **vendi i lindjes:** native land; **përqindja e lindjeve:** birthrate, natality. 2. *gjeog.* East; **nga lindja:** eastwards. 3. rise, rising; **lindje e diellit:** sunrise, rising of the sun; **çertifikatë lindjeje:** birth certificate; **që nga lindja:** from birth.

lindór,-e *mb.* 1. natal. 2. *gjeog.* eastern, oriental.

lindshmërí,-a *f.* natality.

líndur (i,e) *mb.* 1. born; **i lindur para kohe:** still-born, born before time. 2. *(që ka lindur i tillë)* inborn, innate; **është i lindur për muzikë:** he is a born musician.

lineár,-e *mb.* linear; **metër linear:** linear metre.

linguíst,-i *m.sh.* -e linguist.

linguistík,-e *mb.* linguistic.

linoléum,-i *m.* linoleum.

linotíp,-i, *m.sh.* linotype.

línj/ë,-a *f.sh.* -a 1. line; **linjë ajrore:** air-line. 2. shop, factory.

linjít,-i *m.* lignite, brown coal.

línjta,-t (të) *f.sh.* drawers, pants, underpants.

línjtë (i.e) *mb.* linen; **rroba të linjta:** linen, linen articles.

lípset *f./v.* 1. to be necessary; **kjo më lipset:** I need it. 2. **lipset:** must, it is necessary; **lispej:** ought to, should; **lipset të punojmë:** we should work;

lipsej të shkoja atje: I ought to go there, I should go there; **lipsu! lipsur gofsh!** go to devil! **liqén,-i** *m.sh.* -e lake; **buzë liqenit:** on the lakeside.

lír/ë,-a *f.sh.* -a muz. lyre.

lírë *ndajf.* cheaply; **e bleva lirë:** I bought it cheaply; **kushton lirë:** it is cheap.

lírë (i,e) *mb.* 1. 1. free; **njerëz të lirë:** free people; **hyrje e lirë:** free entry; **i kam duart të lira:** to have one's hands free; **e lë të lirë qenin:** to let the dog run free. 2. unoccupied, free; **kam mjaft kohë të lirë:** to have a lot of leisure; **jam i lirë:** to be free from work, to be unoccupied. 3. clear, open; **lë të lirë kalimin:** to keep the passageway clear 4. free, vacant, **i lirë është ky vend?** is this seat free? 5. *treg.* free; **treg i lirë:** free market. 6. cheap; **mall i lirë;** cheap commodity.

lirësí,-a *f.* cheapness.

lirí,-a *f.* freedom, liberty; **liri e fjalës:** freedom of speech; **liri e shtypit:** freedom of the press; **fitoj lirinë:** to win one's liberty (freedom); **liria fitohet me gjak:** freedom is won by shedding blood; **i jap liri veprimi dikujt:** to give someone a freehand; **luftëtar i lirisë:** freedom fighter.

liridáshës,-e *mb.* freedom-loving; **popull liridashës:** freedom-loving people.

lirím-i *m.* 1. freeing, release, setting free; **lirim (i një të burgosuri) para kohe:** early release. 2. *usht.* discharge; **oficer në lirim:** officer in allowance.

lirísht *ndajf.* 1. freely; **qarkulloj lirisht:** to circulate freely; **veproj lirisht:** to act freely. 2.

easily, fluently; **flas lirisht një gjuhë:** to speak fluently a language.

lirísht/ë,-a *f.sh.* **-a** glade (in a forest).

lirój *f.k.* 1. to free, to set at liberty, to set free, to release, to liberate; **liroj një të burgosur:** to release to set free a prisoner; **liroj me shpërblesë:** to redeem. 2. *(çliroj)* to release; **shkarkoj nga çdo detyrim:** to release from any obligation. 3. *(liroj nga ushtria)* to disband, to dismiss (from military service), to discharge. 4. **i liroj vendin dikujt për t'u ulur:** to make room; 5. *(ul çmimin)* to cheapen; **liroj një artikull:** to cheapen (to lower the price of) an article. 6. **liroj pantallonat etj.:** to loosen one's pants, etc.

lírshëm *ndajf.* 1. loosely, in a loose manner; **lidh lirshëm:** to tie loosely. 2. easily, fluently; **e flet lirshëm anglishten:** he speaks English fluently.

lírsh/ëm(i),-me(e) *mb.* loose; **fustan i lirshëm:** a loose dress.

lis,-i *m.sh.* **-a** *bot.* oak; **prej lisi:** oaken: **dru lisi:** oak wood.

lís/ën,-na *f. bot.* thyme.

lisnáj/ë,-a *f.sh.* **-a** oak wood, oak forest.

listél/ë,-a *f.sh.* **-a** *ndërt.* slab.

líst/ë,-a *f.sh.* **-a** list; **vë dikë (diçka) në listë:** to list someone (something); *(regjistër)* roll, register; **lista e zgjedhësve:** electoral roll, register of voters; **listë e kandidatëve:** list of candidates; **lista e çmimeve:** price-list; **lista e gjellëve:** menu, bill of fare; **listë e pagave:** pay-roll, pay-sheet; *fig.* **listë e zezë:** black-list; **vë dikë në listën e zezë:** to black-list someone.

listëpagésë,-a *f.sh.* **-a** pay-roll, pay-sheet.

litár,-i *m.sh.* **-e** 1. rope; **lidh me litar:** to rope; **litar kërpi:** hempen rope; **njeri i hurit dhe i litarit:** an evil doer, a malefactor. 2. the rope, hanging; **vdes në litar:** to die by the rope. 3. *sport. sh.* ropes; **e ngjesh kundërshtarin te litarët:** to pin one's opponent by the ropes.

literatúr/ë,-a *f.* literature.

lít/ër,-ri *m.sh.* **-ra** litre; **në litra:** in litres, by the litre.

livádh,-i *m.sh.* **-e** meadow.

livánd/ë,-a *f. bot.* lavender.

lóço-ja *f.sh.* – booby, ninny, simpleton.

lód/ër,-ra *f.sh.* **-ra** 1. toy, plaything, **dyqan lodrash:** toy-shop. 2. *muz.* drum. 3. game.

lodërtár,-i *m.sh.* **-e** 1. playful fellow, 2. drummer.

lodërtár,-e *mb.* playful

lodrój *f.jk.* to play, to frisk.

lodh *f.k.* to tire, to fatigue, to weary, to harass, to irk. – **lodhem** *f.jv.* to tire, to weary, to get weary, to get tired, to be tired; **lodhem sa këputem:** to be tired to death.

lódhët (i,e) *mb.* tiresome, irksome, fatiguing, harassing, wearisome.

lódhj/e,-a *f.* weariness, tiredness, fatigue, lassitude, harassment; **lodhje e madhe:** exhaustion, lassitude; **lodhje mendore:** brainfag; **jap shenja lodhjeje:** to show signs of fatigue.

lódhsh/ëm (i),-me(e) *mb.* tiresome, toilsome, irksome.

lódhur (i,e) *mb.* 1. tired, fatigued, weary; **jam i lodhur:** I am tired; **i lodhur jashtë masës:** dead tired. 2. tired, bored, fed up;

jam i lodhur nga: to be tired of.
logarít/ëm,-mi *m.sh.* -**me** *mat.* logarithm.
logaritmík,e *mb.* logarithmic.
logjík,-e *mb.* logical.
logjík/ë,-a *f.* logic.
logjikísht *ndajf.* logically.
logjíksh/ëm (i),-me(e) *mb.* logical, rational; **përfundim i logjikshëm:** logical conclusion.
lój/ë,-a *f.sh.* -**ra** 1. play, game, play-game; **lojë fëmijësh:** children's game; **lojë futbolli:** football match; **lojra atletike:** athletic events; **loje dame:** draughts, *amer.* checkers; **bëj një lojë domino:** to play a game of domino; **lojë fjalësh:** quibble, play on words; **lojë me letra:** card-game. 2. **lojë bixhozi:** gambling. 3. *fig.* joke, fun; **e bëj diçka për lojë:** to do something in fun. 4. trick, practical joke; **i bëj (i punoj) një lojë dikujt:** to play a nasty trick on someone, — *Lok.* **vë në lojë dikë:** to make a fool of someone, **to** make fun of someone; **bëj lojë të dyfishtë:** to run with the hare and hunt with the hounds, to double-cross; **hyj në lojë:** to come into play; **bëj lojën e dikujt:** to play someone's game; **nderi i tij vihet në lojë:** his honour is at stake.
lojtár,-i *m.sh.* -**ë** player; **lojtar shahu:** chess player.
lójtur (i,e) *mb.* crazy, insane.
lokál,-i *m.sh.* -**e** 1. room, premises. 2. restaurant; café; bar.
lokalitét,-i *m.sh.* -**e** locality.
lokalíz/ëm-mi *m.* localism.
lokalizój *f.k.* to localize. — **lokalizohet** *f.jv.* to be localized.
lokomotív/ë,-a *f.sh.* -**a** locomotive, engine.

lokución,-i *m.sh.* -**e** *gram.* phrase, locution; idiom, idiomatic expression.
lopár,-i *m.sh.* -**ë** cow-keeper, cowherd, cowboy.
lopát/ë,-a *f.sh.* -**a** shovel; **lopatë furrtari:** peel (of a baker); **lopatë varke:** oar, scull.
lopçár,-i *m.sh.* -**ë** shih **lopar.**
lóp/ë,-a *f.sh.* -**ë** *zool.* 1. cow; **lopë barsë:** cow with calf. 2. **lopë deti:** walrus.
lord,-i *m.sh.* -**ë** lord.
lot,-i *m.sh.* -**ë** tear, **derdh lot:** to shed tears, to pour tears; **pa derdhur një pikë loti:** without shedding a tear; **fshij lotët:** to dry up one's tears; **shkrihem në lot:** to melt (to dissolve) in tears; **me lot në sy:** in tears, with tears in one's eyes.
lotári,-a *f.sh.* — lottery, raffle; **heq lotari:** to draw lots; **heqje lotarie:** drawing of lots; **blej një lotari:** to buy a lottery ticket.
lotój *f.jk.* 1. to shed tears. 2. *bujq.* to weep (a vine plant).
lotsjéllës,-e *mb.* lachrymatory, tear; **gaz lotsjellës:** tear-gas; **bombë me gaz lotsjellës:** tear-shell, lachrymatory bomb.
lotúes,-e *mb.* tearful, lachrymose **gaz lotues;** tear gas.
lozonjár,-e *mb.* playful, waggish, skittish.
lózh/ë,-a *f.sh.* -**a** 1, *ndërt.* loggia. 2. *teat.* open gallery.
luádh,-i *m.sh.* -**e** meadow.
lúaj I. *f.k.* 1. to move; **luaj nga vendi një mobilje:** to move a furniture. 2. *teat.* *(një rol)* to play; **luaj rolin e mësuesit:** to play the role of a teacher. 3. *(një pjesë muzikore)* to play.
II. *f.jk.* 1. to move, to change place (position), to stir; **i sëmuri nuk ishte në gjendje të luante:**

the sick man was unable to move. 2. to make a move; **asnjeri nuk luajti vendit ta ndihmonte:** nobody made a move to help him.3.**luan dhëmbi:** to budge (a tooth). 4. to play; **luaj me top:** to play with a ball; **a di të luash me letra?** can you play cards? **luaj bixhoz:** to gamble; **luaj në bursë:** to speculate. 5. *sport.* to play; **luan «Besa» me «Vllazninë»:** «Besa» is playing with «Vllaznia». 6. *muz.* play; **luaj në piano:** të play the piano. 7. *fig.* **luaj me fjalë:** to play on words, to quible; **luaj me kokën:** to stake one's life. – **luhet** *f.jv.* 1. to be played (a music piece, etc.). 2. to be moved. – *Lok.* **luaj mendsh:** to go (to run) mad (crazy); **këtu luan diçka:** I smell a rat, there is a snake in the grass, it smells fishy.

lúajtur (i,e) *mb.* crazy, madcap.

luán,-i *m.sh.* -ë *zool.* lion; **këlysh luani:** lion's cub, lion's whelp.

luanésh/ë,-a *f.sh.* -a *zool.* lioness.

lubí,-a *f.sh.* – ogre.

lubrifikánt,-i *m.sh.* -ë lubricant; **vaj lubrifikant:** lubricant oil.

lubrifikatór,-i *m.sh.* -ë lubricator.

lubrifikím,-i *m.sh.* -e lubrication, greasing.

lubrifikój *f.k.* to lubricate. – **lubrifikohet** *f.jv.* to be lubricated.

luftaníj/e,-a *f.sh.* -e warship, battleship, man of war.

luftarák,-e *mb.* 1. combative, militant; **miqësi luftarake:** militant friendship; **shpirt luftarak:** combative (fighting) spirit. 2. war. military; **aeroplanë luftarakë:** military aircraft, *amer.* warplanes.

lúft/ë,-a *f.sh.* -ëra 1. war; **shpall luftë:** to declare war; **britmë**

lufte: war cry; **jam në luftë me:** to be at war with; **ndez luftën:** to unleash war; **luftë botërore:** world war; **luftë civile:** civil war; **shokë lufte:** companions of arms; **luftë partizane:** partisan war 2. battle; **fushë lufte:** battle-field; **luftë vendimtare:** decisive battle; **nis luftën:** to give battle. 3. conflict, struggle: **luftë klasash:** class struggle; **luftë interesash të kundërta:** conflict of interests.– *Lok.* **bie në luftë (vritem në luftë):** to fall in action (in battle).

luftëdáshës,-i *m.sh.* – warmonger.

luftënxítës,-i *m.sh.* – shih **luftëdashës.**

luftëtár,-i *m.sh.* -ë warrior, combatant, fighter.

luftím,-i *m.sh.* -e combat, fighting, strife, fight, battle; **luftim fyta- -fytas:** hand to hand fighting; **nxjerr jashtë luftimit:** to put of action.

luftój I. *f.jk.* to fight; **luftoj kundër armikut:** to fight (against) the enemy; *fig.* to fight, to struggle, to battle, to strive *(me, kundër,* with, against), to wage war (on); **luftoj për një ideal:** to fight for an ideal; **luftoj kundër sëmundjes:** to fight (against) disease, to wage war on disease;**luftoj shpërdorimet:** to combat abuses; **luftoj që t'ia arrij qëllimit:** to strive to attain one's aim; **luftoj kundër stuhisë:** to strive against the storm. II. *f.k.* to fight, to combat, to wage war on; **mjekët luftojnë epideminë e gripit:** the doctors are fighting the flu epidemic. – **luftohem** *f.jv.* to be combated, to be fought.

luftúes,-e *mb.* combative.

lug,-u *m.sh.* **lugje** trough.

lugár/e,-ja *f.sh.* -e laddle.

lugát,-i *m.sh.* lugetër ghost, spectre, bogeyman, bogyman.

lúg /ë,-a *f.sh.* -ë spoon; lugë çaji: teaspoon; lugë supe: table spoon; lugë e madhe (garuzhdë): laddle.

lúgët (i,e) *mb.* concave.

lugín /ë,-a *f.sh.* -a valley.

luhátj /e,-a *f.sh.* -a oscillation, vacillation.

lújtsh /ëm (i),-me(e) *mb.* movable; pasuri e lujtshme: personal estate.

luks,-i *m.* luxury, sumptousity, pomp; jetoj në luks: to live in luxury.

luksóz,-e *mb.* luxurious, sumptuous; në mënyrë luksoze: luxuriously; hotel luksoz: luxurious (luxury, de luxe) hotel.

lukth,-i *m. anat.* stomach.

lúl /e,-ja *f.sh.* -e *bot.* flower; mbajtëse lulesh: flowerstand; saksi lulesh: flower-pot; tufë me lule: bunch, bouquet of flowers; shitëse lulesh: flower-girl. — *Prov.* me një lule nuk vjen pranvera: one swallow does not make a summer.

luleballsám,-i *m bot.* balm flower.

lulebléte *f. bot.* honey-suckle, hoodbine.

lulebíri *f. bot.* linden flower.

lulebór /ë,-a *f. bot.* snowdrop, snow-ball flower.

luledél /e,-ja *f. bot.* daisy.

luledíelli *f. bot.* sunflower.

luledhénsh *f. ' bot.* daisy.

lulegrúri *f. bot.* corn-flower, bluebottle.

lulekáç /e,-ja *f. bot.* eglantine.

lulekumbón /ë,-a *f. bot.* blue-bell, bell-flower.

lulelák /ër,-ra *f. bot.* cauliflower.

lulelivánd /ë,-a *f. bot.* lavender.

lulembájtës /e,-ja *f.sh.* -e flowerstand.

lulemëllág /ë,-a *f. bot.* hollyhock, soft lilac.

lulemos-më-harró *f. bot.* forget-me-not.

lulemusták,-i *m. bot.* shih lulebletë.

lulepllátk /ë,-a *f. bot.* gilly-flower, wall-flower.

luleqýq /e,-ja *f. bot.* cuckoo-flower.

lulesapúni *f. bot.* soap-wort.

luleshebójë *f. bot.* shih lulepllatkë.

luleshëmítri *f. bot.* chrysanthemum.

luleshëngjérgji *f. bot.* lily-of-the Valley.

luleshítës,-i *m.* florist.

luleshítës /e,-ja *f.* flower girl.

luleshpát /ë,-a *f. bot.* iris (flower).

luleshqérr /ë,-a *f. bot.* daisy.

luleshtrýdh /e,-ja *f. bot.* strawberry.

luletáç /e,-ja *f. bot.* anemone.

lulevíl /e,-ja *f. bot.* shih lulepllatkë.

lulevízh /ë,-a *f. bot.* sundew.

lulevjéshte *f. bot.* shih luleshëmitri.

lulezhabìn /ë,-a *f. bot.* buttercup.

lulekúq /e,-ja *f. bot.* poppy flower.

lulëzìm,-i *m.* 1. blooming, blossoming, flowering; lulëzimi i pemëve, i bimëve: blooming of trees, of plants. 2. *fig.* florescence, prosperity; lulëzimi i një vendi: prosperity of a country.

lulëzój *f.jk.* 1. to bloom, to flower. 2. *fig.* to flourish, to prosper, to thrive. — lulëzohet *f.jv.* to prosper.

lulëzúar (i,e) *mb.* 1. flowering. 2. *fig.* flourishing, thriving.

lulishtár,-i *m.sh.* -ë flower-gardener.

lulísht /e,-ja *f.sh.* -e flower-garden, public garden.

lum *pj.* blessed; lum ti! how lucky you are! lucky you!

lúm/ë,-i *m.sh.* **-enj** river; **bërryl lumi:** meander; **grykë lumi:** outfall, mouth of a river; **degë lumi:** affluent, branch; **shtrat lumi:** river-bed. – *Lok.* **më mori lumi!** I am lost, I am ruined!

lumëmádh,-e *mb.* unhappy, unfortunate.

lumór;-e *mb.* fluvial: **port lumor:** river port.

lúmtë! (**më, të, i**) *pasth.* bravo! well done!.

lúmtur (**i,e**) *mb.* happy, lucky, fortunate, felicitous; **shumë i lumtur:** blissful; **njeri i lumtur:** happy man; **bëj të lumtur:** to make happy; **qofsh i lumtur!** may you be happy!

lumturí,-a *f.* happiness; **lumturi e madhe:** beatitude, bliss; **për lumturinë e popullit të vet:** for the happiness of his people.

lumturísht *ndajf.* happily, luckily, fortunately.

lúmthi *pj.* blessed.

lúnd/ër,-ra *f.sh.* **-ra** boat, riverboat; canoe; **lundër me motor:** ferry-boat, barge; **lundër peshkimi:** fishing boat: **lundër me rrema:** row-boat.

lundërtár,-i *m.sh.*-**ë** navigator, sailor, seaman, seafarer.

lúndërz,-a *f.sh.* **-a** *zool.* otter.

lundrím,-i *m.sh.* **-e** navigation, sailing; seavoyage; **nisem për lundrim:** to set sail: **agjenci lundrimi:** shipping office; **lundrim detar:** maritime navigation: **lundrim lumor:** river navigation, inland navigation; **lundrim me varkë:** rowing; **lundrim me vela:** sailing.

lundrój *f.jk.* to navigate, to sail; **lundroj me varkë sportive:** to paddle, to row in a boat; *fig.* **lundroj kundër rrymës:** to go against the stream.

lundrúes,-e *mb.* navigating.

lundrúesh/ëm (i),-me(e) *mb.* navigable.

lundrueshmërí,-a *f.* navigabillty.

lúng/ë,-a *f.sh.* **-a** *mjek* abscess, cyst.

luqérbull,-i *m.sh.* **-ë** *zool.* lynx.

lus *f.k.* (p.t. **lut,** p.p. **lutur**) 1. to pray, to beg, to ask, to request, to solicit; **e luta të më ndihmonte:** I asked him to help me; **mos prit të të lusin:** don't wait to be asked. – **lutem** *f.jv.* to beg; **të lutem:** I beg you; **të lutem m'u përgjigj shpejt:** please, reply soon; **ju lutem kini mirësinë të:** please have the kindness to..., please.

lúsp/ë,-a *f.* scale; **luspë peshku:** scale of fish; **i heq luspat peshkut:** to scale a fish.

lúst/ër,-ra *f.* shine, polish; gloss, glaze, luster. varnish; **i jap një lustër diçkaje:** to give something a shine; **lustër mobiljesh:** varnish; **lustër këpucësh:** polish, shine: **me lustër:** glossy, glazed.

lustraxhí,-u *m.sh.* **-nj** boot-black, shoe-black. *amer.* shoeshine.

lustrím,-i *m.* glazing; varnishing; polishing, shining; **lustrim këpucësh:** blacking (of boots), shoe-blacking.

lustrinë *mb.* glazing; **këpucë lustrina:** glazing boots.

lustrój *f.k.* to varnish, to polish; **lustroj mobiljet:** to polish the furniture; **lustroj këpucët:** to shine, to polish one's shoes. – **lustrohem** *f.jv.* to be glossy.

lustrósj/e,-a *f.* polishing, shining.

lútem *f.jv.* shih **lus.**

lútës,-i *m.sh.* – petitioner.

lútës,-e *mb.* suppliant, supplicating, begging, imploring; **zë lutës:** imploring voice.

lútj/e,-a *f.sh.* **-e** 1. prayer; **lutje**

e nxehtë: supplication. 2. demand, request, claim; bëj lutje: to make (to adress, to present), a request.
luvarí,-a f. bot. shih dafinë.
lúv/ër,-ra f. bot. shih kulth.
lúzm/ë,-a f.sh. -a swarm (of bees), cluster (of bees).
luzmón f.jk. (third person) to swarm (of bees.)
lýej f.k. (p.t. leva, p.p. lyer) 1. (me gëlqere) to whitewash; (me bojë këpucët) to black (shoes); (me bojë murin) to paint, to colour. 2. (me vaj makinën) to lubricate. 3. (bukën me gjalpë) to butter (a slice of bread); 4. (me zamk etj.) to smear, to overspread (with-glue). 5. (lehtë) to tint; (trashë) to daub. 6. (fytyrën) to paint one's face. – Lok. lyej qerren (jap ryshfet):

to oil the wheels, to bribe. – lyhem f.jv. to paint one's face.
lýerj/e,-a f.sh. -e 1. (me gëlqere) whitewashing. 2. (me bojë) painting, colouring.
lym,-i m. slime, silt.
lymór,-e mb. slimy.
lyp f.k. 1. to beg; lyp të falur: to beg pardon. 2. (një lëmoshë) to beg, to ask alms of someone. 3. (kohë etj.) to need.
lýpës,-i m.sh. -a beggar.
lypsár,-i m.sh. -ë shih lypës.
lýrdhëz,-a f.sh. -a mjek. wart.
lýr/ë,-a f. grease.
lyrós f.k. to grease. – lyroset f.jv. to get greasy.
lyrósj/e,-a f. greasing.
lýrsh/ëm(i), -me(e) mb. greasy.
lyth,-i m.sh. -a mjek. 1. wart. 2. callus.

Ll

ll, Ll (letter of the Albanian alphabet) l, L.
llaç,-i m. mortar; punëtor llaçi: mortar worker.
llaf,-i m.sh. -e gj. bis. shih fjalë
llafazán,-i m.sh. -e chatter-box, chatterer, tattler.
llafazán,-e mb. loquacious, garrulous, talkative, long-winded, tongue-pad, windback.
llafós f.k. gj. bis. shih fjalos.
llagáp,-i m.sh. -e 1. nickname, by-name. 2. surname.
llagëm,-i m.sh. -e 1. common sewer. 2. subterranean channel.

llahtár,-i m. llahtar/ë, -a f. terror, dismay.
llahtarí,-a f. shih llahtar.
llahtarís f.k. to scare, to terrify, to dismay. – llahtarisem f.jv. to be scared (terrified, dismayed).
llahtársh/ëm(i),-me(e) mb. terrible, dreadful, tremendous; në mënyrë të llahtarshme: terribly, tremendously.
llamarín/ë,-a f.sh. -a sheet-iron.
llampadar, -i m.sh. -ë llamp-port.
llambádh/e,-ja f.sh. -e thick waxtaper.

llámb/ë,-a *f.sh.* -a lamp; **llambë elektrike:** electric lamp; **llammbë me alkool:** spirit lamp; **llambë me vajguri:** petroleum lamp: **llambë minatorësh:** miner's lamp: **llambë neoni (me neon)** neon-lamp (tube).

llamburít *f.jk.* to shine brightly, to glare.

llamburítës,-e *mb.* flaming, blazing, shining, radiant, illuminant.

llamburítj/e,-a *f.* illumination, radiance.

llambúshk/ë,-a *f.sh.* -a small lamp.

llap *f.jk.* to blab, to prate, to tattle, to prattle.

llapá,-ja *f.* 1. pap for infants, soft food for infants. 2. *mjek.* cataplasm: **i vë llapa një të sëmuri:** to apply a poultice to the body of a sickman.

lláp/ë,-a *f.sh.* -a 1. *gj. bis.* tongue: **e ka llapën të gjatë:** he has the gift of the gab, he is long-tongued. 2. *anat.* **llapë e veshit;** the lap of the ear. *

llapúsh,-e *mb.* lap-eared.

llastík,-u *f.* 1. elastic band. 2. *(për të mbajtur çorapet)* garter. 3. *(për të vrarë zogj)* sling (for killing birds).

llastój *f.k.* to pamper, to cocker, to coddle. -: **llastohem** *f.jv.* to pamper oneself.

llastúar (i,e) *mb.* petted, cockered; **fëmijë i llastruar:** pampered child.

lláv/ë,-a *f.* a flock of wolves.

llër/ë,-a *f.sh.* -ë *anat.* fore-arm; **përvesh llërët:** to roll up the sleeves of the fore-arms.

llërëpërvéshur *mb.* having the sleaves, of the fore-arms turned up.

llíxh/ë,-a *f.sh.* -a spa.

llogáç/e,-ja *f.* watter.-puddle, puddle.

llogarí,-a *f.sh.* account, reckoning, calculation; *ekon.* account; **hap një llogari:** to open an account; *fig.* **i kërkoj llogari dikujt:** to call (to bring) someone to account; to demand an explanation of someone; **mbyllje e llogarive:** closing of accounts; **bëj llogaritë:** to draw up the accounts, to do the accounts; **llogari rrjedhëse:** account current, current account, *amer.* checking account; **zyra e llogarisë:** counting-office, counting-house; *fig.* **nuk i bëj mirë llogaritë:** to be out in one's reckoning, to be mistaken in one's calculations; **për llogari të:**to someone's account; **për llogari time:** to my account; **m'u kërkua llogari për qër.drimin tim:** I was asked to account for my conduct.

llogarís *f.k.* to account, to count (up), to compute, to calculate, to reckon (up); **jemi tetë vetë pa llogaritur fëmijët:** we are eight people, not counting the children. — **llogaritet** *f.jv.* to be accounted; **ajo nuk llogaritet fare:** she doesn't count for anything.

llogaritár,-i *m.sh.* -ë accountant, reckoner, book-keeper.

llogarítës,-e *mb.* calculative; **makinë llogaritëse:** calculating machine, calculator, computer.

llogarítj/e,-a *f.sh.* — computation, calculation, reckoning.

llogarítsh/ëm(i),-me(e) *mb.* computable, accountable, calculable, estimable.

llogór/e,-ja *f.sh.* -e entrenchment, trench, ditch; **hap llogore:** to dig up trenches.

llóh/ë,-a *f.* sleet.

lloj,-i *m.sh.* -e kind, species, sort; **të çdo lloji:** of any kind; **të**

këtij lloji: of this kind; of this nature; **çfarë lloji?** what sort of? **nga të gjitha llojet:** of all sorts: **një lloj zogu:** a kind of bird.

lloj-lloj *mb.* various.

llókm/ë,-a *f.sh.* -a a small piece of (meat etc.).

llokoçís *f.k.* 1. to plash, to swash. 2. to stir, to agitate a liquid. – **llokoçitet** *f.jv,* to be plashed, to plash, to swash.

llokoçítës,-e *mb.* swashing.

llokoçítj/e,-a *f.* 1. plash: **llokoçitje e valëve të detit:** rippling of waves. 2. stirring, agitation of liquids.

llokúm,-i *m.sh.* -e Turkish delight, Turkish paste.

llom,-i *m.* 1. mire, sludge, mud. 2. *fig.* filth; **bie në llom:** to fall down in the mud.

llomotís *f.jk.* to chat, to chatter, to tattle, to babble, to gabble, to maunder, to gibber, to blurt out.

llomotítj/e,-a *f.sh.* -e chattering, gab, gibberish.

lloz,-i *m.sh.* -e 1. bolt; **mbyll derën me lloz:** to bolt, to secure the door with a bolt. 2. lever, bar (of iron). 3. **llozi i pushkës:** breech of a gun.

llúc/ë,-a *f.* slush, thin mire, fen.

lluffs *f.k.* to swallow up, to glutton, to devour.

llufítj/e,-a *f.* swallowing up, ingulfing.

llukaník,-u *m.sh.* -ë sausage; **mish i grirë për llukanik:** sausage meat.

llulláq,-i *m.* blue dark colour.

llúll/ë,-a *f.sh.* -a pipe; **thith llullën:** to pull at a pipe.

llum,-i *m.sh.* -ëra 1. sediment, deposit; **llum vaji:** deposit of oil; **llum likeri:** lees, dregs of liquor; **llum lëngjesh:** sediment of liquids. 2. *fig.* **llumi i shoqërisë:** the ragtag of the society, riffraff, rabble. mob *Lok.* e **bëj llum një punë:** to bungle (to botch) a work. *dregs*

llup *f.jk.* 1. to swallow up, to gulp at once. 2. to eat greedily, to glutton.

llupásh,-i *m.sh.* -ë shih **llupës.**

llupásh,-e *mb.* shih **llupëse.**

llúpës,-i *m.sh.* – glutton, gormandiser.

llúpës,-e *mb.* gluttonous, voracious, greedy.

llúrb/ë,-a *f.* sediment; *fig.* **u bë llurbë puna:** the work became slop: **gjellë llurbë:** a poor (liquid) food.

M

m, M (letter of the Albanian alphabet) m, M.

ma (short form of the pers. pron. **më** and the particle **a,** singular, for both genders; it is used only in the dative case; **ma jep:** give it (to) me; **ma trego:** show it (to) me; tell it (to) me; (with the function of a direct object) **ma pe vajzën?** have you seen my daughter?

m'i (short form of the pers. pron. **më** and the particle **i,** plural for both genders) **m'i pruri librat, fletoret:** he brought me the books, the copy-books; (in the emphatical form) **m'i bëj të fala (shokut):** give my regards to (my friend).

m'u (short form of the pers. pron. **më** and the particle **u** which follows a reflexive verb in the simple past tense) **m'u errën sytë:** my eyes were darkened.

máce,-ja *f.sh.* **-e** *zool.* cat, she-cat; **mace e vogël:** kitten, puss; **mace e egër:** wild cat; **mace angora:** angora cat. — *Prov.* **kur s'është macja, minjtë hedhin valle:** when the cat's away the mice will play.

maçók,-u *m.sh.* **-ë** cat, male cat, tom-cat, he-cat.

madém,-i *m.sh.* **-e** 1. stone-pit. 2. *vjet.* mine. 3. mineral.

madh (i),-e (e) *mb.* 1. **big;** **kafshë e madhe:** big animal. 2. great; **fitore e madhe;** great victory. 3. large; **lumë i madh:** large river. 4. *fig.* great, illustrious; **njeri i madh:** great man; **shumë i madh:** vast, immense, immeasurable; **fushë shumë e madhe:** vast plain; **dëme shumë të mëdha:** enormous, immeasurable damages; **me rëndësi shumë të madhe;** of considerable importance 5. **i madhi i fëmijëve:** the eldest of the children. 6. *(i rritur, i bërë burrë)* adult, grown up. — *Lok.* **mbahem më të madh:** to give oneself (to put on) airs.

madhërí,-a *f.* majesty.

madhërísh/ëm(i),-me(e) *mb.* majestic, grandiose.

madhërísht *ndajf* majestically.

madhësí,-a *f.sh.* - 1. size; **rroba të çdo madhësie:** dresses of all sizes. 2. *mat.* quantity; **madhësi negative:** negative quantity; **madhësi numerike:** numerical quantity.

madhështí,-a *f.* magnificence, solemnity, pomposity; greatness; **me madhështi:** magnificently, pompously, with great pomp.

madhështór,-e *mb.* grandiose majestical, grand, sublime, splendid, magnificent, imposing; **pritje madhështore:** grand reception.

madhój *f.k.* to make bigger (taller), to enlarge, to make larger, to increase. — **madhohem** *f.jv.* to grow bigger (larger, greater, taller).

madhór,-e *mb.* 1, major, of full age; **moshë madhore:** majority, full legal age. 2. *usht.* **shtabi madhor:** general staff.

mafíshe,-ja *f.sh.* **-e** meringue.

magazín/ë,-a *f.sh.* **-a** storage-house, store-house, depot, warehouse, store-room; **magazinë**

e madhe: department store;
mbaj në magazinë: to store.
magaziniér,-i *m.sh.* -ë storekeeper, warehousekeeper, warehouseman.
magaziním,-i *m.* storage.
magazinój *f.k.* to store, to warehouse.
magnét,-i *m.sh.* -ë magnet, loadstone.
magnetík,-e *mb.* 1. magnetical; fushë magnetike: magnetical field. 2. *fig.* magnetic; fuqi magnetike: magnetic power.
magnetizím,-i *m.* magnetization.
magnetizój *f.k.* to magnetize. — magnetizohet *f.jv.* to become magnetized.
magnetizúes,-e *mb.* magnetizing.
magnetofón,-i *m.sh.* -ë magnetophone, tape-recorder.
mágje,-ja *f.sh.* -e kneading trough
magjéps *f.k.* to bewitch, to charm, to enchant. — magjepsem *f.jv.* to be bewitched (charmed, enchanted).
magjépsës,-e *mb.* bewitching, charming, fascinating, enchanting.
magjépsj/e,-a *f.* incantation, enchantment, fascination, charm.
magjépsur (i,e) *mb.* under spell.
magjí,-a *f.* magic, sorcery, witchcraft, spell.
magjík,-e *mb.* 1. magic, magical; shkopi magjik: magic wand. 2. *fig.* magic.
magjistár,-i *m.sh.* -ë magician, wizard, sorcerer witch.
mahís *f.k. mjek.* 1. to irritate. 2. *fig.* to make fun of, to make a laughing stock of, to laugh at.—
mahiset *f.jv.* 1. to be irritated. 2. *fig.* to be laughed at, to be embittered.
mahísj/e,-a *f.* 1. *mjek* irritation. 2. *fig.* envenoming.
mahmúr *ndajf.* half-waked; ështä

ngritur mahmur: he got out of bed on the wrong side.
mahnís *f.k.* to astonish, to amaze, to marvel. — mahnitem *f.jv.* to be astonished (amazed).
mahnítës,-e *mb.* astonishing, marvellous, amazing.
mahnítj/e,-a *f.* astonishment, marvel.
mahnítsh/ëm(i),-me(e) *mb.* wonderful, admirable.
maj,-i *m.* May; dita e 1 Majit: May day.
majá,-ja *f.* leaven, yeast; maja birre: barm, leaven, yeast.
majasëll,-i *m. mjek.* hemorroids.
majdanóz,-i *m. bot.* parsley.
máj/ë,-a *f.sh.* -a 1. peak, summit; maja e një mali: the peak (summit) of a mountain: drejt majave më të larta: towards the highest summits. 2. top; maja e çatisë: the crest of a roof, the top of a roof; në majë të pemës: at the top of a tree. 3. *(maja e hundës, e veshit, etj.)* tip, top (of the nose, of the ear, etc.). 4. *(e perit)* the end, the extremity (of a thread). 5. point; maja e gjilpërës: the point of a needle; laps me majë: a pointed pencil; majë pene: pen. 6. *(e gishtërinjve)* tip (of a finger, of a toe); eci mbi maat e gishtërinjve: to go on tiptoe. 7. brim; mbush gjer në majë: to fill to the brim; mbushur me majë: filled to the brim, completely filled, full up. 8. *fig.* the flower; maja e miellit: the flower of the flour.
majhósh,-e *mb.* sourish.
majm *f.k.* to fat, to grease, to make fat, to fatten. — majmem *f.jv.* to grow fat (greasy), to get fat, to become fat (greasy).
májm/ë,(i),-e(e) *mb.* 1. fatty, greasy; mish i majmë: fatty

meat. 2. *bujq.* rich; **tokë e majme:** rich land. 3. *fig.* fat, abundant, prosperous; **fitime të majme:** fat profits.

majmërí,-a *f.* fatting, fatness, greasiness; **kafshë për majmëri:** fatling.

majmún,-i *m.sh.* -**ë** 1. *zool.* monkey, ape; **bëj si majmuni :** to ape, to imitate like an ape. 2. *fig.* imitator, (contemptuous name).

majolík/ë,-a *f.* majolica.

majonéz/ë,-a *f.* mayonnaise.

majór,-i *m.sh.* -**e** *usht.* major; **gjeneral major:** major-general.

májtë (e),-a(e) *f.* 1. left. left-side **nga e majta:** to the left. 2. *sport.* left 3. *polit.* left wing.

májtas *ndajf.* on the left side.

májtë (i,e) *mb.* 1. left; **dora e majtë:** left hand; **mbaj krahun e majtë:** to drive on the left. 2. *polit.* left.

majúng,-u *m.sh.* -**ë** *mek.* blacksmith's hammer.

makará,-ja *f.sh.* — *mek.* crab, windlass.

makaróna,-t *f.sh.* macaroni; **makarona petë:** noodle.

makijázh,-i *m.* make up, painting of the face.

makijój *f.k.* to make up the face, to paint the face. — **makijohem** *f.jv.* to paint one's face, to make oneself up.

makinerí,-a *f.sh.* — machinery, engine; **reparti i makinerisë:** engine-room.

makín/ë,-a *f.* 1. automobile, car, motor-car, motor-cab, motor-carriage; **hipi në makinë:** to get into the car. 2. machine, engine; **makinë me avull:** steam-engine; **makinë elektrike:** electric machine. 3. *fig.* mechanism, machinery; **makina shtetërore:** the state machine. 4. *fig. (person)* robot, automaton, machine. 5. *(pajisje mekanike)*: machine; **makinë qepëse:** sewing machine, **makinë korrëse:** reaping machine: **makinë korrëse e lidhëse:** reaper and binder machine; **makinë larëse** *rrobash*: washing-machine; **makinë për lidhjen e duajve** *(të grurit, etj.)*: self-binder, binder-machine; **makinë mishi:** meat grinder; **makinë llogaritëse:** computer, calculator, calculating machine; book-keeping machine; **makinë mbjellëse:** sowing machine; **makinë për shtrimin e rrugëve:** roller-machine, roller; **makinë shirëse:** threshing-machine, thresher; **makinë shkrimi:** typewriter; **shkruaj në makinë:** to type: **makinë për përzierjen e brumit:** kneading machine; **makinë shtypi (librash etj.):** printing-machine; **makinë për thyerjen e gurëve etj.:** crushing machine: **makinë zjarrfikëse:** fire engine.

makiníst,-i *m.sh.* -**ë** machinist.

maksimál,-e *mb.* utmost, extreme; highest, top, peak; maximal, maximum; **shpejtësi maksimale:** top speed; **dënimi maksimal:** maximum penalty; **temperatura maksimale:** the highest temperature.

maksím/ë,-a *f.sh.* -**a** maxim.

maksimúm,-i *m.sh.* -**e** maximum, limit, top; **në maksimum:** at the maximum.

makth,-i *m. bot.* melilot (a species of sweetscended trefoil or clover).

makth,-i *m. enat.* placenta.

makth,-i *m.* leveret, young cony or rabbit.

makth,-i *m.* 1. nightmare. 2. vision.
makút,-i *m.sh.* -ë gormandiser, glutton.
makút,-e *mb.* gluttonous, voracious, greedy.
makutërí,-a *f.* gluttony, voracity, greediness.
mal,-i *m.sh.* -e 1. mountain; **varg malesh**: chain (range) of mountains. 2. *fig.* heap, pile; **një mal me libra**: a pile of books. — *Lok.* **rrofsh sa malet!** may you live as long as the mountains! **më bëhet zemra mal**: to be radiant with joy; to cheer (to delight, to gladden, to rejoice, the cockles of one's heart; **marr malet**: to take to the bush.
malári/e,-a *f. mjek.* malaria.
malarík,-e *mb.* malarial, malarious.
malcím,-i *m. mjek* inflamation, irritation.
malcój *f.k. mjek.* to irritate, to inflame. — **malcohet** *f.jv.* to become irritated.
malësí,-a *f.* highland, upland; **rroj në malësi**: to live in the mountainous region.
malësór,-i *m.sh.* -ë highlander, mountaineer.
malók,-u *m.sh.* -ë boor, rustic, coarse person, unpolished man, uncouth person, rude person, illmannered person.
malór,-e *mb.* mountainous; **vend malor**: mountainous country, highland.
mall,-i *m.sh.* -ra 1. merchandise, goods, ware, commodity *pl.* **mall i zgjedhur**: quality goods; **qarkullimi i mallrave**: circulation of goods; **mallra për eksport**: export goods, goods for export; **mallra importi**: imported goods; **tren mallrash**: freight train. 2. property, estate; **zot malli**: proprietor, owner; **zotërim malli**: ownership. 3.

fig. sort, kind of people; **s'është asi malli**: he is not of that kind of people: **po ai mall është: he** is tarred with the same brush.
mall,-i *m.* nostalgia, longing; **mall për dikë, për diçka**: longing for someone, for something; **mall për vendlindjen**: homesickness; **më merr malli (për diçka, dikë)**: to long, to yearn (for something), to miss (someone); **kam mall për**: I miss, I am longing for; **me mall**: with longing.
mallëngjéj *f.k.* to move, to compassionate, to emotionate. — **mallëngjehem** *f.jv.* to be moved (compassionated), to be emotionated.
mallëngjím,-i *m.* heartache, emotion.
mallëngjýes,-e *mb.* heartbreaking, emotive.
mallëngjýesh/ëm(i),-me(e) *mb.* emotional.
mallkím,-i *m.sh.* -e curse, malediction, imprecation, damnation; **lëshoj mallkime**: to call down curses upon someone.
mallkój *f.k.* to curse, to maledict, to imprecate, to damn; **mallkoj veten**: to blame oneself.
mallkúar (i,e) *mb.* damned, cursed; **mallkuar qoftë!** damn it all!
mamá,-ja *f.sh.* — mamma, mother, *amer.* mommy, ma; **mamaja dhe babai**: mother and father, mommy and daddy.
mamí,-a *f.sh.* — midwife— *Prov.* **shumë mami e mbytin foshnjën**: too many cooks spoil the broth.
mamic/ë,-a *f.sh.* -a *krah.* midwife.
mamúz,-i *m.sh.* -e spur; **shpoj kalin me mamuze**; to spur the horse, to prick the horse with spurs.

man,-i *m.sh.* -a *bot.* mulberry; druri· i manit: mulberrytree.

manaférr/ë,-a *f.sh.* -a *bot.* bramble, blackberry.

manár,-i *m.sh.* -ë pet (of a kid or of a lamb).

manastír,-i *m.sh.* -e monastery, abbey, cloister; manastir burrash: monastery, friary; manastir grash: nunery.

mandapóst/ë,-a *f.sh.* -a money-order.

mandarín/ë,-a *f.sh.* -a *bot.* tangerine, mandarin.

mandát,-i *m.sh.* -e 1. *fin.* order, mandate, order for payment. 2. *polit.* mandate.

mandat-arkëtím,-i *m.sh.* -e money (collection) order, cash warrant.

mandát/ë,-a *f.sh.* -a bad news; i jap mandatën dikujt: to break the (bad) news to someone.

mandatpagés/ë,-a *f.sh.* -a order for payment, cash order.

mandolín/ë,-a *f.sh.* -a *muz.* mandolin.

mandríno,-ja *f.sh.* – *tek.* mandrel, mandril.

manekín,-i *m.sh.* -ë manikin, mannequin.

mangáll,-i *m.sh.* -ë coal-burner, brazier.

manganéz,-i *m.* manganese.

mángët *ndajf.* not full, not complete.

mángët (i,e) *mb.* 1. deficient, incomplete, defective. 2. *fig.* half-witted.

maní,-a *f.sh.* – mania; obsession, fixation.

maniák,-u *m.sh.* -ë maniac.

maniák,-e *mb. (njeri)* obsessed (by), mad, crazy (about).

manifaktúr/ë,-a *f.sh.* -a manufacture.

manifést,-i *m.sh.* -e manifesto; public declaration; Manifesti i Partisë Komuniste: Manifesto of the Communist Party.

manifestím,-i *m.sh.* -e manifestation, demonstration.

manifestój *f.jk.* 1. to manifest, to demonstrate. 2. to take part in a demonstration. – manifestohet *f.jv.* to be demonstrated (manifested).

manifestúes,-i *m.sh.* – manifestant, demonstrator.

manikýr,-i *m.* manicure.

manipullm,-i *m.* manipulation.

manipulój *f.k.* to manipulate. – manipulohet *f.jv.* to be manipulated.

manivél/ë,-a *f.sh.* -a *mek.* cranch, wink.

manomét/ër,-ri *m.sh.* -ra manometer, pressure gauge, airgauge, steam-gauge.

manóv/ër,-ra *f.sh.* -ra 1. move, manoeuvre. 2. military drills *pl.*, manoeuvres *pl.*, bëj manovra: to perform manoeuvres (with troops or war vessels). 3. *fig.* move, manoeuvre.

manovrój I. *f.jk.* to manoeuvre, to steer.
II. *f.k.* to manoeuvre.– manovrohet *f.jv.* to be manoeuvred.

manovrúesh/ëm (i),-me(e) *mb.* manoeuvrable.

mansárd/ë,-a *f.sh.* -a mansard-roof, garret, loft; dormer, mansard window.

manshét/ë,-a *f.sh.* -a *(këmishe)* wrist band, cuff; *(pantallonash)* turn-up, *amer.* cuff.

mantél,-i *m.sh.* -ë mantle.

mánto,-ja *f.sh.* – cloak.

manuál,-i *m.sh.* -e handbook, pocket-book, manual.

manusháq/e,-ja *f.sh.* -e *bot.* violet.

(Magazinë Popullore)

mápo,-ja *f.sh.* – department store.

marangóz,-i *m.sh.* -ë joiner, carpenter; **punishte marangozi:** joinery.

maráq,-i *m. bot.* camomile.

maráz,-i *m.* anger, spite, irritation; **vdiq nga marazi:** he died of sadness; **e kam maraz dikë:** to detest someone.

maré,-ja *f.sh.* – *bot. (druri)* arbutus berry-tree; *(fruta)* arbutus berry.

marén/ë,-a *f. bot.* chaste tree.

mareshál,-i *m.sh.* -ë *usht.* marshal.

margarín/ë,-a *f.* margarine.

margaritár,-i *m.sh.* -ë pearl.

marifét,-i *m.sh.* -e ingeniosity; trick, trickery.

marifetçí,-u *m.sh.* -nj ingenious man; trickster, juggler.

marinár,-i *m.sh.* -ë sailor, seaman, sea-farer, blue-jacket, mariner; **rroba marinari:** sailor-suit; **not marinari:** sidestroke swimming.

marín/ë,-a *f.* navy; **marina tregtare:** merchant navy; **marina luftarake:** navy.

markéz,-i *m.sh.* -ë marquis.

márk/ë,-a *f.sh.* -a 1. *(fabrike)* trade-mark. 2. *(prodhim)* brand; **kjo është marka më e mirë e automobilëve:** this is the best brand of cars.

marksíst,-i *m.sh.* -ë Marxist.

marksíst,-e *mb.* Marxist.

marksíz/ëm,-mi *m.* Marxism.

marksíz/ëm,-leniniz/ëm *m.* Marxism-Leninism.

markúç,-i *m.* hose.

marmelát/ë,-a *f.* marmalade.

mars,-i *m.* March.

marsh,-i *m.sh.* -e 1. *(automobili)* gear, speed; **ndërrim marshesh:** changing (shifting)- of gears; **marshi i parë:** bottom (low) gear. 2. *muz.* march;

marsh funebër: funeral, march; **marsh ushtarak:** military march. 3. march, walking; **marsh!** onward!

marshím,-i *m.sh.* -e march, walking; **marshim i sforcuar (i shpejtë):** forced march.

marshój *f.jk.* to march, to walk; **Shqipëria socialiste marshon përpara:** socialist Albania marches forward.

martés/ë,-a *m.sh.* -a 1. marriage, wedlock, matrimony; **martesë me dashuri:** love match; **dhuratë martese:** wedding gift, wedding present; **unazë martese:** wedding ring. 2. married life; **pas dhjetë vjet martese:** after ten years of married life.

martesór,-e *mb.* nuptial, matrimonial.

márt/ä(e),-a(e) *f.sh.* -a(të) Tuesday.

martír,-i *m.sh.* -ë martyr.

martirizím,-i *m.* martyrdom.

martirizój *f.k.* to martir, to martirize. – **martirizohem** *f.jv.* to be martired, to be (to become) a martyr.

martój *f.k.* to marry off, to wed, to give in marriage, to espouse, to match. – **martohem** *f.jv.* to marry *(me dikë,* someone) to get married (to), to wed (someone); **u martuan para një viti:** they got married a year ago.

martúar (i.e) *mb.* married; **burrä i martuar:** married man.

marúl/e,-ja *f.sh.* -e *bot.* lettuce.

marr I. *f.k.* (p.t. mora, p.p. marrë) 1. to take; **marr një libër:** to take a book; **merre këtë libër:** take this book; **e marr mbrapsht:** to take it back. 2. *(marr me vete)* to take with oneself, to take; **e mora çadrën sepse bie shi:** I took my umbrella

because it's raining. 3. to collect, to fetch; **marr valixhet
në stacion**: to pick up the
suitcases at the station. 4. to
take, to set off; **marr rrugën
nga e djathta**: to set off to the
right. 5. *fig.* **marr parasysh**:
to take into account (into consideration); **marr një punë me
qejf**: to take a job heartedly
(to one's heart); **marr përsipër**: to take upon oneself,
to assume, to task oneself, to
bind oneself; **marr seriozisht**:
to take in earnest; **marr pjesë**:
to take part, to partake; **marr
shenjë**: to take aim; **marr zjarr**:
to take fire, to catch fire; to
fly into a passion. 6. to get;
to obtain; **marr me forcë**: to
obtain by violence; **marr nota të mira**: to get good marks;
marr hua diçka: to obtain a
thing on loan, to borrow something; **marr çmimin e parë**:
to get, to obtain the first prize;
marr prodhime të mira; to
get good crops. 7. to receive;
marr një letër: to receive,
(to get) a letter. 8. to pass;
marr provimin: to pass an
examination. 9. to catch; **marr
të ftohtë**: to catch cold. 10.
to contract; **marr vese, sëmundje**: to contract habits, an
illness. — *Lok.* **marr malet**: to
take to the bush, to run away;
marr me mend: to guess;
**marr për burrë (ose për
grua)**: to spouse; **i marr erë
një luleje**: to smell a flower;
la marr këngës: to sing a song;
marr djathtas: to turn right.
II. *f.jk. (merr zjarri)* to catch fire,
to (begin to) burn. — **merrem**
f.jv. to occupy oneself; **me se
merreni?** what are you doing?
merrem me punë: I am wor-

king; **merremi vesh**: to understand one another.
márrë (i,e) *mb.* mad, crazy; **guxim prej të marri**: foolhar-
diness.
marrëdhëni/e,-a *f.sh.* **-e** relations, terms *pl.*; **lidh marrëdhënie me dikë**: to establish
relations with someone; **mbaj
marrëdhënie me**: to keep relations with; **jam në marrëdhënie të mira me**: to be in
good terms with; **marrëdhënie
të fqinjësisë së mirë**: good
neighbourhood relations; **marrëdhënie reciproke**: mutual
(reciprocal) relations; **marrëdhënie midis vendeve**: relations between nations; **marrëdhënie familjare**; family relations; **marrëdhënie tregtare**:
commercial relations; **marrëdhënie pune**: work relations.
márrës,-i *m.sh.* — 1. receiver,
recipient; **marrësi i një letre**:
addressee, receiver of a letter.
2. *tek. (radiomarrës)* receiver,
receiving set.
marrëvéshj/e,-a *f.sh.* **-e** 1. agreement, arrangement; **bie në
marrëveshje**: to come to an
agreement; **jam në marrëveshje me**: to be in agreement with,
to be in accord with; **në marrëveshje me**: in accord with;
**me marrëveshjen e të dy
palëve**: by mutual agreement.
2. **marrëveshje diplomatike**:
diplomatic agreement; **marrëveshje e fshehtë**: collusion,
secret agreement; **marrëveshje tregtare**: commercial agreement, transaction; **lidh marrëveshje tregtare**: to conclude
(të, close) a commercial agreement; **prish një marrëveshje**:
to rescint an agreement.
marrëzí,-a *f.sh.* **-ra** foolishness,

folly, foolery; **bëj marrëzira:**
to fool, to act foolishly; **flas
marrëzira:** to talk foolishly, to
to talk nonsense.
marrëzisht *ndajf.* foolishly; **dua
marrëzisht:** to dote, to love
foolishly (passionately, frantically).
marrí,-a *f.* shih **marrëzi.**
márrj/e,-a *f.* 1. taking, getting;
marrje e pushtetit: taking
seizure of the power. 2. *(e një
letre)* reception (of a letter).
3. *(e një çmimi)* obtainment (of
a prize). 4. *(këmbësh)* stagger,
tottering; *(mendsh)* dizziness,
gidiness.
marrós *f.k.* to make foolish, to
drive furious, to render mad,
to frenzy; **u marrose?** are you
mad? are you crazy? — **marrosem**
f.jv. 1. to become furious, frantic. 2. *fig.* to dote upon; **marrosem pas një vajze:** to be madly
in love with a girl.
marrósj/e,-a *f.* fury, frenzy, mad-
ness.
marrtë **(i,e)** *mb.* opaque.
mas *f.k.* shih **mat.**
masák/ër,-ra *f.sh.* **-ra** massacre,
slaughter.
masakrój *f.k.* to massacre, to slaughter. — **masakrohem** *f.jv.* to be
massacred.
masát,-i *m.sh.* **-e** tender-box.
masázh,-i *m. mjek.* massage; **bëj
masazh:** to have a massage.
más/ë,-a *f.sh.* **-a** mass, people;
masat e gjera të popullit:
the broad masses of the people; **vrasje në masë:** mass extermination.
más/ë,-a *f.sh.* **-a** 1. measure,
standard; *(gjatësie, sipërfaqeje,
vël'imi, peshe)* measure (of
length, of surface, of volume,
of weight); **njësia e masës:**
unity of measure. 2. *(e një kos-*

tumi) measure (of a suit), **size;
i marr masën** *(dikujt për një
kostum):* to take someone's mea-
surements. 3. limit; **çdo gjë me
masë:** anything with measure
(with limit, with frugality, tem-
perately, moderately); **jashtë masës:** beyond measure, above
measure, out of bounds; **tejka-
kaloj masën:** to go beyond
measure (beyond the limit), to
exceed all limits (bounds); **të
dua pa masë:** I love you too
much (passionately, excessively);
deri në një farë mase: to
a certain degree, in some measure.
4. steps, measures; **marr masat
e duhura:** to take the necessary
steps (measures); **marr masa
të rrepta:** to take drastic measures (stringest measures); **masa
paraprake:** precautions; **marr
masa paraprake:** to take preventive measures, to take precautions; **marr masa kundër
të ftohtit:** to be provided against
the cold. 5. *(muzike)* measure,
musical time. — *Lok.* **bën masë**
(një aparaturë elektrike): to make
contact.
masív,-e *mb.* massive.
masivizój *f.k.* to give a mass
character.
maskar/á,-ai *m.sh.* **-enj** scoundrel,
rascal, hooligan.
maskarallë/k,-ku *m.sh.* **-qe** ras-
cality, villainy.
másk/ë,-a *m.sh.* **-a** 1. mask;
ballo me maska: masked ball,
fancydress ball; **maskë kundër
gazit:** gas-mask; **maskë për
të notuar nën ujë:** diving
(underwater mask). 2. *fig.* mask,
guise; **hedh maskën:** to throw
off (to drop) one's mask: **nën
maskën e:** under the guise
of.

maskím-i *m.* camouflage, disguise, masking.

maskój *f.k.* to mask (to put on) a mask, to camouflage, to disguise. — maskohem *f.jv.* to wear (to put on) a mask, to disguise oneself.

maskúar (i,e) *mb.* masked, disguised, hidden, concealed.

masón,-i *m.sh.* -e freemason.

mastík/ë,-a *f.* mastic, chewing gum.

masúr,-i *m.sh.* -e bobbin, small bobbin, spool.

másh/ë,-a *f.sh.* -a fire-irons, tongs poker.

máshk/ë,-a *f.sh.* -a *(flokësh)* curling tongs.

máshkull,-i *m.sh.* meshkuj 1. male; man. 2. *(për kafshët)* male. 3. *mek, (vidë mashkull)* male screw; *(mashkull i qerres)* shaft (of a cart).

mashkullór,-e *mb.* 1. male, masculine, man's: tipare mashkullore: man's features; *(për gratë)* mannish. 2. *gram.* gjinia mashkullore: masculine (gender).

mashtrím,-i *m.sh.* -e cheat, defraud, fraud, bluff, swindle, humbug, imposture.

mashtrój *f.k.* to cheat, to dupe, to beguile, to defraud, to trick, to bamboozle; mashtroj një vajzë: to seduce a girl. — mashtrohem *f.jv.* to be beguiled (defrauded, duped).

mashtrúes,-i *m.sh.* - swindler, defrauder, impostor, sharper.

mashúrka,-t *f.sh. bot.* kidney beans.

mat *f.k.* 1. to measure; i mat temperaturën dikujt: to take someone's temperature; *(vëllimin e një sendi)* to gauge, to measure the capacity of; *(tokën)* to survey (land); *(me hapa)* to pace. 2. *fig.* to measure, to weigh; i mat

fjalët: to weigh one's words. — matem *f.jv.* 1. to be measured. 2. *(bëj garë)* to try one's strength (against), to compete, to contend *(me,* with); mat forcat e mia: to try one's strength. 3. to be going to; matem të iki: to be going, to leave.

matánë I. *ndajf.* beyond, on the other side; kaloj matanë: to pass on the other side. II. *paraf.* beyond, on the other side of; matanë asaj kodre do të gjeni fshatin: you will find the village beyond that hill; matanë lumit: on the other side of the river, beyond the river.

matará,-ja *f.sh.* — flask.

matematikán,-i *m.sh.* -ë mathematician.

matematík/ë,-a *f.* mathematics.

matematikísht *ndajf.* mathematically.

materiál,-i *m.sh.* -e 1. material; stuff; materiale ndërtimi: building materials. 2. equipment, supplies, materials *pl.;* materiale shkollore: school equipment.

materiál,-e *mb.* material; të mira materiale: material blessings; dëme materiale: material damage.

materialísht *ndajf.* materially.

materialíz/ëm,-mi *m.* materialism.

matéri/e,-a *f. filoz.* matter; *kim.* substance.

maternitét,-i *m.sh.* -e maternity-hospital, maternity-home, lying-in hospital.

mátës,-i *m.sh.* — measurer, gauge; matës thellësie: depthometer.

mátj/e,-a *f.sh.* — measurement, measuring; *(tokash)* surveying; *tek. (me instrumente)* gauging.

matrapáz,-i *m.sh.* -ë speculator, dealer.

matríc/ë,-a *f.sh.* -a *anat.* the womb, matrix.

matríkull,-i *m.* shih **amzë.**

matúf,-i *m.sh.* -ë dotard.

matufllëk,-u *m.* dotage.

matufòs *f.k.* to render dotard. — **matufosem** *f.jv.* to become dotard.

matufósj/e,-a *f.* dotage.

matufósur (i,e) *mb.* dotty.

mátur (i,e) *mb.* prudent, circumspect, discreet.

maturánt,-i *m.sh.* -ë candidate (for school-leaving examinations).

matúr/ë,-a *f.* school living (final) examination.

maturí,-a *f.* prudence, circumspection, discretion; **me maturi:** prudently, discreetly.

maún/ë,-a *f.sh.* -a *det.* barge, lighter.

mauzolé,-u *m,sh,* — mauzoleum.

maví *mb.* blueish, livid; **bëhem mavi në fytyrë nga inati:** to become livid with rage.

mavijós *f.k.* to make bluish, to bruise (the flesh). — **mavijosem** *f.jv.* to grow bluish (livid).

maxhór,-e *mb. muz.* major; **do diez maxhor:** C sharp major.

mazgáll/ë,-a *f.sh.* -a embrasure.

mazí,-u *m. bot.* nut-gall.

mazút,-i *m. kim.* mazut, black oil.

mbaj I. *f.k.* (p.t. **mbajta,** p.p. **mbajtur)** 1. to hold, to hold up; **mbaj lart flamurin:** to hold aloft the banner. 2. *muz.* to keep; **mbaj kohën:** to keep time; **mbaj një sekret:** to keep a secret; **mbaj një fjalim:** to hold a speech, to deliver a speech; **mbaj fjalën:** to keep one's word; **mbaj llogaritë:** to keep the accounts. 3. to preserve; **mbaj gjakftohtësinë:** to keep cool, to control oneself.

4. **mbaj shtëpinë:** to support one's family. 5. to bear; **mbaj një peshë:** to bear a weight; **mbaj një libër në dorë:** to bear a book in one's hand. 6. to wear; **mbaj një kostum, një xhaketë:** to wear a dress, a jacket; **mbaj çorape, këpucë, etj.:** to wear socks, shoes etc. 7. to carry; **mbaj ujë, qymyr, etj.:** to carry water, coal, etc. 8. to retain; **mbaj një vend:** to retain, to reserve a seat; **mbaj dikë të mos iki:** to retain (to withhold, to restrain) someone; **mbaj dikë nën vërejtje:** to keep someone under surveillance. – *Lok.* **mbaj vesh:** to keep one's ears open, to give ear, to hearken, to lend an ear; **mbaj veten:** to control oneself; **mbaje!** take! keep! hold on! **mbaj mend:** to bear in mind; to remember; **i mbaj mërì dikujt:** not to be on speaking terms with someone; **mbaj një rekord:** to hold a record; **s'di nga t'ia mbaj:** not to know what to do,not to know which way to turn. II.*f.jk.*1.to last; **mësimi(mbledhja) mban një orë:** class (meeting) lasts one hour; **sa mban që këtu?** how far is it from here? 2 to contain; **kjo vazo mban dy litra:** this vase contains two littres. 3. *(reziston)* to hold, to stick; **zamka nuk mban:** the glue doesn't stick. 4. to hold, to grip; **spiranca nuk mban:** the anchor doesn't hold. 5. to be nutritious, to be nourishing; **ushqim që të mban:** nourishing food. — **mbahem** *f.jv.* to support oneself, to maintain oneself, to be sustained; **mbahem mirë me shëndet:** to be well-preserved, to look well (for one's age), to be in

good shape, to have good health, to stand good; **mbahem gjallë, më këmbë:** to subsist. — *Lok.* **më mbahet goja:** to stammer, to stutter.

mbájta *f.k.* past tense of the verb **mbaj.**

mbájtës,-i *m.sh.* — holder, bearer,

mbájtës/e,-ja *f.sh.* -e *(lulesh)* flower stand.

mbájtj/e,-a *f.* 1. holding; *(e një mbledhjeje)* holding of a meeting. 2. *(llogarish)* keeping (of accounts). 3. *(uji, etj.)* carrying (of water, etc.). 4. *(me ushqime e veshmbathje)* maintenance, support.

mbájtur (i,e) *mb.* 1. used; **kostum i mbajtur:** a used suit. 2. well-preserved; **grua e mbajtur:** well-preserved woman; **shtëpi e mbajtur mirë:** well-kept house. 3. made; **procesverbal i mbajtur më. . . . :** report made the . ..

mballomatár,-i *m.sh.* -ë cobbler.

mballóm/ë,-a *f.sh.* -a patch.

mballós *f.k.* to patch, to cobble, to mend shoes. — **mballoset** *f.jv.* to be patched.

mballósj/e,-a *f.* patch-work; patching.

mbánë *ndajf.* through. — *Lok.* **ia dal mbanë një pune:** to go through with a work.

mbarés/ë,-a *f.sh.* -a *gram.* ending.

mbár/ë *ndajf.* 1. on the good side; **kjo plaçkë është mbarë:** this tissue is on the good side (on the right side). 2. favourably, propitiously; **puna vete mbarë:** the work is going on well; **filloj mbarë një punë:** to make a good start; **ai flet mbarë e prapë:** he speaks right and wrong; **puna mbarë!** good work!

mbárë *mb.* all; **bota mbarë: al** the world.

mbárë (i,e) *mb.* 1. good; **djalë i mbarë:** good fellow; **prodhim i mbarë:** abundant crops. 2. happy; **kam këmbën e mbarë:** to bring good luck; **ju uroj një vit të mbarë:** I wish you a happy year.

mbarësí,-a *f.* good fortune, fortunateness, luckiness.

mbarështím,-i *m.* arrangement, management, setting in order.

mbarështój *f.k.* to arrange, to manage, to set in order. — **mbarështrohet** *f.jv.* to be arranged, to be managed.

mbarëvájtj/e,-a *f.* smooth-course, progress.

mbarím,-i *m.* end, ending; **mbarim i mirë:** good end; **pa mbarim:** endless, neverending, unending, boundless; **vidë pa mbarim:** worn screw; **fillim e mbarim:** from start to finish, from beginning to end.

mbarój I. *f.k.* to end, to finish, to conclude, to achieve, to terminate, to bring to an end; **mbaroj një punë:** to finish a work; **mbaroj studimet:** to conclude one's studies.

II.*f.jk.* 1. to be over:**lufta mbaroi:** the war is over; **shkolla mbaroi:** school is over (ended); **mësimi mbaroi:** class is over. 2. to end; **rruga mbaron këtu:** the road ends here. 3. to be finished (used up), to be (all) gone, to have run out; **gjalpi mbaroi:** the butter is finished (all gone). 4. to die; **ai mbaroi:** he is dead, he is no more; **mbarova! I** am dead! I am done up! **mbaroi puna e tij:** it is all up with him. — **mbarohet** *f.jv.* 1. to be finished (terminated,

ended). 2. *(harxhohet)* to be
finished, to be used up, to be
all gone, to have run out; **na u
mbarua qymyri:** the coal has
run out.
mbars *f.k.* to make pregnant. –
mbarsem *f.jv.* to grow pregnant.
mbársë *mb.* *(lopa)* with calf,
(pela) in foal.
mbársj/e,-a *f.* pregnancy.
mbársur (e) *mb.* pregnant, *fam.*
in the family way expecting.
mbársurit (të) *as.* fecundation.
mbart *f.k.* 1. to convey, to transport, to carry; **mbart mallra:**
to convey goods. 2. *mat.* to
carry forward; **mbart një shumë** *(në llogari)* to carry forward
(an amount). – **mbartem** *f.jv.*
to move, to change one's residence.
mbártës,-i *m.sh.* – 1. porter, bearer, coolie; **mbartës porti:** docker. 2. *fig.* *(pikëpamjesh)* bearer. 3. *mjek.* *(mikrobesh)* carrier.
mbártj/e,-a *f.* 1. conveyance,
transport, carrying. 2. *det.* *(nga
një anije në tjetrën)* transship-
ment. 3. *(e sendeve)* transfer,
move, removal; *(e njerëzve)* removal, move; **pas mbartjes në
qytetin N:** after our move to N.
mbártur (i,e) *mb.* 1. conveyed,
transported. 2. *mat.* carried,
brought; **shuma e mbartur:**
amount forward.
mbarúar (i,e) *mb.* 1. finished, performed. 2. *fig.* real, perfect;
ai është doktor i mbaruar:
he is a perfect doctor.
mbáse *ndajf.* perhaps, possibly,
may be.
mbási *lidh.* 1. as, for, because; **ai
hëngri drekë vetëm, mbasi
e shoqja nuk ishte në shtëpi:**
he dined alone as his wife was
away; **mbasi ishte dita e
fundit e vitit shkollor;** as it

was the last day of the school
year; **nuk e zgjidha dot pro-
blemin mbasi ishte i vështirë:**
I could not solve the problem
because it was difficult. 2. after,
when; **mbasi hëngri, ai u çua:**
when he had finished lunch
(after eating) he rose; **pak mbasi
u nis:** a short while after leaving.
mbath *f.k.* 1. *(çorapet, këpucët)* to
put on (one's stockings, shoes).
2. *(kalin)* to shoe (the horse).
– *Lok.* **ua mbath këmbëve:** to
take to one's heels, to run away,
to scuttle away, to make a
clean pair of heels. – **mbathem**
f.jv. 1. to put one's stockings
(shoes). 2. to be shoed.
mbáthës,-i *m.sh.* – *(kuajsh)* farrier, blacksmith.
mbáthj/e,-a *f.* 1. *(e kalit)* farriery,
shoeing (of a horse). 2. *(kë-
pucësh, çorapesh)* wearing, putting on.
mbáthura,-t (të) *f.sh.* drawers;
një palë të mbathura: a pair
of drawers; **vesh të mbathurat:**
to put on one's drawers.
mbés/ë,-a *f.sh.* -a 1. *(vajzë mot-
re ose vëllai)* niece. 2. *(vajzë e
vajzës ose e djalit)* granddaugh-
ter.
mbétem *f.jv.* (p.t. **mbeta,** p.p.
mbetur) 1. to remain; **mbetem
miku juaj i sinqertë:** I remain
your faithful friend, yours truly.
2. to run; **mbetem pa ujë:** to
have run out of water. 3. *mat.*
to leave, to be; **dhjetë pa
shtatë mbeten tre:** seven from
ten leaves (is) three. 4. to stay,
to remain, to be left; **kanë mbetur vetëm pleqtë:** only the
old people are left. 5. *(tepron)* to
be left (over), to remain; **s'ka
mbetur gjë për ne?** isn't there
anything left for us? **kanë mbetur vetëm disa ditë nga Viti**

i Ri: there are only a few days left until New Year's Day. 6. to be left. to remain; **s'më mbetet të bëj gjë tjetër:** there is nothing more (left) for me to do. 7. to become; **mbetem jetim:** to be left (to become) an orphan, to be orphaned; **mbeta i habitur:** I was surprised. – *Lok.* **mbetem me gojë hapur:** to be dumbfounded (astonished); **mbetet në fuqi:** to remain in effect; **mbetem pa mend, pa gojë:** to be flabbergasted (speechless); **më la pa mend:** to take one's breath away; **mbetem prapa:** to lag, to stay behind; **mbetem në provim:** to fail in an examination.

mbétj/e,-a *f.* remain, remainder, remnant; rest.

mbétura,-t (të) *f.sh.* remains; **të mbeturat e gjellës:** leavings.

mbeturín/ë,-a *f.sh.* -a 1. residue, refuse matter, trash, offscourings; *(e anijes)* wreck; **mbeturina hekuri:** scraps of iron. 2. *fig.* residue, vestige, remnant.

mbërthéj *f.k.* 1. *(me gozhda)* to nail, to fasten with nails. 2. *(rrobën me kopsa)* to button (the overcoat, etc.). 3. *(një tabelë)* to fix, to affix (a board). – **mbërthehem** *f.jv.* to button oneself.

mbërthím,-i *m.* fastening; *(me gozhda)* nailing; *(tabele)* fixation (of a board).

mbërríj I. *f.jk.* to come, to arrive, to reach: *(në një vend)* to come (të arrive, to reach) at destination.
II. *f.k.* to reach (someone).

mbërrítj/e,-a *f.* arrival, coming.

mbështét *f.k.* 1. to lean, to rest; **mbështes shkallën në mur:** to lean the ladder against the wall. 2. *(një mendim)* to uphold, to support, to back up, to second; **mbështes një propozim:** to second a proposal; *(një person)* to support, to back up. 3. *(bazoj)* to base, to ground. – **mbështetem** *f.jv.* 1. to lean; **mbështetem në krahun e dikujt:** to lean on someone's arm. 2. to rest, to stand *(mbi, on)*; **qemeri mbështetet mbi dy shtylla:** the arch rests on two pillars. 3. to rely (on), to lay one's trust (in); **të mbështetemi në forcat tona:** to rely upon our own forces.

mbështétës/e,-ja *f.sh.* -e 1. *tek.* prop, stay, support; *(e karriges, divanit etj.)* back; **mbështetëse e lëvizshme:** adjustable back.

mbështétj/e,-a *f.* 1. *tek.* support, brace, standard. 2. aid, help, support, stay, prop; **jam mbështetja e vetme e familjes:** to be the only support of one's family.

mbështjéll *f.k.* 1. *(perin)* to wind up, to roll up (thread). 2. *(një plaçkë me letër etj.)* to wrap (up). 3. *(litarin etj.)* to coil. 4. *(në qefin)* to shroud. 5. *(qilimin, një top pëlhure etj.)* to rroll up. – **mbështillem** *f.jv.* 1. to muffle oneself up, to wrap oneself up. 2. to be rolled up; **mbështillet rreth vetes:** to be rolled upon itself, to be convoluted, to cringe. 3. *(peri)* to twine. 4. *(gjarpëri)* to coil (itself).

mbështjéllë (i,e) *mb.* rolled up, wrapped.

mbështjellës/e,-ja *f.sh.* -e envelope, wrapper, covering.

mbështjéllj/e,-a *f.* 1. wrapping, envelopment, covering; **letër për mbështjellje:** wrapper, packing-paper, brown papper. 2. rolling up.

mbi *paraf.* 1. on, upon **mbi karrige:** on the chair. 2. over; above; **çatia është mbi tavanin:** the roof is above the ceiling; **një urë mbi lumë:** a bridge over the river; **mbi dallgët e detit:** over the waves. 3. over, above; **mbi të gjitha:** above all others; **sundon mbi gjithë vendin:** to reign ove, all the country. 4. on, on to, onto; **dritarja sheh mbi kopësht:** the window looks out onto the garden. 5. about, concerning, regarding; **flas mbi gjendjen ekonomike:** to speak (to argue) about the economic situation. 6. over, more than; older than, past; \ **mbi njëmijë lekë:** over one thousand leks; **jam mbi pesëdhjetë vjeç:** to be over (past) fifty.

mbiçmój *f.k.* to overvalue, to overestimate, to overrate. — **mbiçmohem** *f.jv.* to be overvalued, overestimated, overrated.

mbiém/ër,-ri *m.sh.* -ra 1. family name, surname, nickname, cognomen. 2. *gram.* adjective.

mbiemërój *f.k.* to surname. — **mbiemërohem** *f.jv.* to surname oneself. to be surnamed.

mbiemërúar (i,e) *mb.* surnamed.

mbikëqýr *f.k.* to oversee, to overlook, to supervise; to superintend, to watch. — **mbikëqyrem** *f.jv.* to be overseen, to be watched.

mbikëqýrj/e,-a *f.* supervision, overlooking; superintendence, watching.

mbill imperative of the verb **mbjell**

mbin *f.jk.* to sprout, to germinate; **në pranverë farat e bimëve fillojnë të mbijnë:** seeds begin to sprout (to germinate) in spring. — *Lok.* **nga na mbiu ky?** where did he spring from?

mbinatýrsh/ëm,(i),-me(e) *mb.* supernatural, **forcë e mbinatyrshme:** supernatural strength.

mbingarkés/ë,-a *f.* 1. overload, excessive (surplus) load; overweight. 2. *fig.* excessive burden.

mbingarkój *f.k.* to overburden, to overload, to overcharge. — **mbingarkohem** *f.jv.* to be overloaded (owercharged).

mbingarkúar (i,e) *mb.* 1. overloaded, overburdened. 2. *fig.* down; **jam i mbingarkuar me punë:** to be weighed down with (up- to one's ears in) work.

mbinjerëzór,-e *mb.* superhuman

mbiprodhím,-i *m.sh.* -e overproduction.

mbiqúaj *f.k.* to nickname. — **mbiquhem** *f.jv.* to be nicknamed.

mbiqúajtur (i,e) *mb.* nicknamed, alias, otherwise named, called, known as.

mbírj/e,-a *f.* germination, growth.

mbishkrím,-i *m.sh.* -e inscription; **mbishkrim mbi një libër:** inscription upon a book.

mbishpenzím,-i *m.sh.* -e overexpense, overexpenditure.

mbitáks/ë,-a *f.* overtax.

mbiujór,-e *mb.* floating, buoyant, aflot.

mbivlér/ë,-a *f.* surplus value; **teoria e mbivlerës:** doctrine of surplus value.

mbivlerësím,-i *m.sh.* -e overevaluation. overestimation.

mbivlerësój *f.k.* to overvalue, to overestimate, to overrate. — **mbivlerësohem** *f.jv.* to be overestimated.

mbizotërím,-i *m.* predominancy, predomination, prevalence, preponderance.

mbizotërój *f.k.* to predominate, to

prevail. – **mbizotërohem** *f.jv.* to be predominated (prevailed).

mbizotërúes,-e *mb.* predominant, preponderant, prevalent; **opinion mbizotërues:** prevailing opinion.

mbjell *f.k.* 1. *(grurë, etj.)* to sow (wheat); *(një bimë, një pemë)* to plant (a tree). 2. *fig.* to sow, to spread, to propagate (opinions etc.); **mbjell përçarje:** to sow (the seeds of) discord. **mbillet** *f.jv.* to be sowed.

mbjélla,-t (të) *f.sh.* sown crops.

mbjéllës,-i *m.sh.* – 1. *(farash)* seedsman, sower. 2. *(pemësh)* planter.

mbjéllj/e,-a *f.sh.* – 1. *(farash)* sowing. 2. *(bimësh, pemësh)* planting; **farë për mbjellje:** seed; **koha e mbjelljes:** seedtime, sowingseason; **fushata e mbjelljeve:** seedcampaign; **mbjelljet e pranverës:** spring sowing.

mbledh (p.t. **mblodha,** p.p. **mbledhur).** 1. to gather, to collect, to assemble, to get together. 2. *(grurin)* to gather, to harvest (wheat). 3. *(lule, fruta)* to pick, to pick up, to pluck, to gather (flowers, fruits); *(kallinj)* to glean. 4. *mat.* to add, to sum up. 5. *(grumbulloj)* to accumulate, to collect, to amass, to gather; *(ndihma)* to collect (subsidies, aids); *(nënshkrime)* to collect (signings, signatures); *(taksa)* to collect (taxes); *(ushqime)* to lay in (stocks, supplies). 6. *(popullin)* to muster, to gather, to assemble (the people); *(efektivin)* to muster, to assemble (troops); *(rekrutë)* to levy (recruits). 7. *(supet)* to shrug (one's shoulders). 8. *(të hollat e huajtura)* to recover (one's money). – **mblidhem** *f.jv.* 1. *(nga të ftohtët, nga frika)* to shrink, to shrivel (from cold, from fear) 2. *nga dhemb-*

ja) to wince. 3. to shrink, to contract; **kjo plaçkë mblidhet në ujë:** this tissue contracts (shrinks) in water. 4. *(njerëzit në një vend)* to muster, to get together, to rally. – *Lok.* **mbledh mendjen:** to resign oneself, to reconcile oneself to: **mbledh veten:** to master oneself, to get hold of oneself, to control oneself.

mblédhës,-i *m.sh.* – 1. *(taksash)* tax-collector. 2. *(pullash poste)* collector (of postage stamps).

mblédhës,-e *mb.* additive.

mblédhj/e,-a *f.sh.* -e 1. collecting, gathering; **mbledhje të hollash:** fund collecting (raising). 2. *bujq.* harvesting, picking; **mbledhja e ullinjve:** olive harvesting. 3. *(e borxheve të mbetura)* recovery (of debts, of cash). 4. *(ndihmash)* collecting (of aids, of subsidies.). 5. *(rekrutësh)* levy (of recruits); *(trupash ushtarake)* muster (of troops). 6. *(njerëzish)* meeting, gathering; **mbledhje e fshehtë:** secret meeting; **mbledhje e Kuvendit Popullor: sesi**on of the People's Assembly; **mbledhje e Këshillit të Ministrave:** meeting of the Council of Ministers. 7. *mat.* addition.

mbles,-i *m.sh.* -ë marriage broker, matchmaker.

mblés/ë,-a *f.* betrothal, betrothment.

mblesërí,-a *f.* matchmaking.

mbllaçít *f.k.* to chew, to masticate; **mbllaçis fort:** to munch; **mbllaçis duhan:** to chew tobacco. – **mbllaçitem** *f.jv.* 1. to chew. 2. *fig.* to hesitate upon.

mbllaçítj/e,-a *f.* chewing, mastication.

mbrám/ë (i),-e(e) *mb.* shih **i fundit.**

mbrápa l. *ndajf.* 1. behind, at the

back, in the rear, backward, backwards; **të tjerët rrinin mbrapa:** the others sat behind; *(në automobil)* in the back. 2. at the back, behind; **fustani varet ngá mbrapa:** the dress hangs down at the back; **lë mbrapa:** to leave behind; **pamje nga mbrapa e një ndërtese:** backward view of a building. 3. *(në kohë)* later on; **tash e mbrapa:** from now on.

II. *paraf.* behind, at the back of; **mbrapa perdes:** behind the curtain; **i shkoj mbrapa dikujt:** to follow someone; **mbrapa shpine:** behind someone's back.

mbráps *f.k.* to force back, to repel, to drive back. — **mbrapsem** *f.jv.* to draw back.

mbrapsht *ndajf.* 1. amiss; **i marr gjërat mbrapsht:** to take things amiss. 2. back, toward the back, backwards; **eci mbrapsht:** to walk backwards; **dy hapa mbrapsht:** two steps backwards; **e kthej shtëpinë mbrapsht:** to turn the house upside-down; **kthehem mbrapsht:** to turn back.

mbrápshtë (i,e) *mb.* wayward, froward, perverse; **fëmijë i mbrapshtë:** a wayward child.

mbrapshtí,-a *f.* perversity, waywardness, frowardness.

mbrej *f.k. (kalin)* to harness; **mbrej një pendë qe:** to yoke a pair of oxen.

mbrés/ë,-a *f.sh.* -a 1. scar; **e kam fytyrën tërë mbresa plagësh:** to have a scarred face. 2. *fig.* scar, mark; **fatkeqësia më ka lënë mbresë:** the misfortune has left its mark on me. 3. impression, feeling, emotion, upset; **lajmi i fitores la mbresa të thella te njerëzit:** the news

of the victory made strong impressions on the people.

mbret,-i *m.sh.* -ër king.

mbretërésh/ë,-a *f.sh.* -a 1. queen. 2. *(e bletëve)* queen bee.

mbretërí,- a *f.sh.* — 1. kingdom. 2. *fig.* kingdom, realm.

mbretërím,-i *m.* reign.

mbretërój *f.jk.* to reign.

mbretërór,-e *mb.* royal, regal; **oborri mbretëror:** royal court.

mbrëma *ndajf.* in the evening; **të shtunën mbrëma:** Saturday evening, **dje mbrëma:** last night.

mbrëmë *ndajf.* last night.

mbrëmj/e,-a *f.sh.* -e 1. evening; **në mbrëmje:** in the evening. 2. party, dinner party; **mbrëmje vallëzimi:** evening dance; **mbrëmje dëfrimi:** evening party.

mbroj *f.k.* 1. to defend; **mbroj atdheun:** to defend the fatherland. 2. to protect; **mbroj dikë nga një rrezik:** to protect someone from a danger. 3. *(dikë në gjyq)* to plead in justice. 4. *(një tezë)* to support a thesis. — **mbrohem** *f.jv.* to defend oneself, to protect oneself.

mbrójtës,-i *m.sh.* — defender, protector.

mbrójtës,-e *mb.* defensive, protective.

mbrójtj/e,-a *f.* 1. defence; **mbrojtje e atdheut:** defence of the fatherland. 2. *(nga një rrezik)* protection (against a danger). 3. *(e avokatit)* plea, pleading (of an advocate). 4. *(e një teze)* maintenance, sustenance (of a thesis); **nën mbrojtjen e :** under the protectorship of.

mbroth *ndajf.* well; **puna i vete mbroth:** he is doing well.

mbrothësí,-a *f.* weal, progress, prosperity.

mbruj *f.k.* 1. to knead. 2. *fig.* to

form, to mould, to give shape to.
mbrújtj/e,-a *f.* 1. kneading. 2.
fig. formation; **mbrujtje e ka-
rakterit:** formation of character.

mbrújtur (i,e) *mb.* 1. kneaded.
2. *fig.* formed; **i mbrujtur me
qëllime të mira:** full of good
intentions.

mbufás *f.k.* to dilate, to make turgid
(swollen). − **mbufatem** *f.jv.* to
grow turgid.

mbufátj/e,-a *f.* dilatation, turgidity.

mbulés/ë,-a *f.sh.* -a cover; **mbulesë krevati:** bed quilt, coverlet;
mbulesë tavoline: table-cloth.

mbulím,-i *m.* covering; **mbulim i
çatisë:** covering of a roof.

mbulój *f.k.* 1. to cover; **mbuloj çatinë me tjegulla:** to tile the
roof; *(çatinë me plloça)* to
stale (the roof). 2. *(fëmijën)* to
cover up, to draw the bedclo-
thes over. 3. *(retë, hënën, die-
llin)* to cover, to conceal, to
hide, to screen. 4. *usht. (tër-
heqjen)* to cover (the withdrawal). 5. *(në dhe)* to bury. 6.
fig. to cover up, to hide, to
conceal; **donte t'ia mbulonte
të metat:** she tried to cover
up his faults.

mbulúar (i,e) *mb.* 1. covered;
mal i mbuluar me dëborë:
snow-clad mountain, snow cap-
ped mountain, mountain covered with snow; **i mbuluar me
lavdi:** covered with glory; **fushë e mbuluar me lule:** a
field strewn with flowers. 2.
(e mbuluar me çati) roofed-over.
3. *(qielli me re)* overcast,
cloudy. 4. covered, hidden, concealed; **ballin e kishte të
mbuluar nga flokët:** her
forehead was under her hair.

mburój/ë,-a *f.sh.* -a 1. breast-plate,
shield, buckler. 2. *fig.* shield,

screen; **mburojë termike:** ther-
mal shield.

mburr *f.k.* to vaunt, to praise, to
extol. − **mburrem** *f.jv.* to boast,
to brag, to pride oneself, to
flatter oneself.

mburracák,-u *m.sh.* -e boaster,
braggart.

mburracák,-e *mb.* boastful, vain-
glorious.

mburravéc,-i *m.sh.* -ë shih **mbu-
rracak.**

mbúrrj/e,-a *f.sh.* -e boasting, brag,
bragging, vanity, self-praise, self-
conceit, pride; **plot mburrje:**
boastfully, full of praise.

mbush *f.k.* 1. to fill, to fill up;
mbush një gotë me ujë: to
fill a glass with water. 2. to
fill, to cram, to stuff; **mbush
valixhen:** to fill a suitcase;
mbush dyshekun me kashtë:
to stuff a matress with straw.
3. *mjek. (dhëmbin)* to fill, to stop.
(a tooth). 4. to fill in; **mbush një
formular:** to fill in a form.
5. *fig.* to fill; **fjalët e tua më
mbushin me shpresë:** your
words fill me with hopes; **mbush
plëndësin:** to eat one's fill; **i
mbush mendjen dikujt:** to
convince, to persuade someone;
mbush moshën: to reach full
age; to be of age. − **mbushem**
f.jv. 1. to fill; **sytë iu mbushën
me lotë:** her eyes filled with
tears. 2. *(rrugët me njerëz)* to
become crowded with. 3. *(me
ajër)* to be distended (with air).
− *Lok.* **më mbushet mendja:**
to be convinced (persuaded);
mbushu! get out!

mbúshj/e,-a *f.* 1. *(me kashtë)*
stuffing (with straw); *(me mish)*
stuffing (with mincemeat); *(me
pambuk)* padding. 2. *(dhëmbi)*
stopping, filling (of a tooth).

mbúshur (i,e) *mb.* 1. filled (with),

full (of); **i mbushur plot, me
majë:** filled to the brim, brim-
med, completely filled. 2. stuffed; **speca të mbushura:** stuffed peppers. 3. *mjek. (dhëmbi)*
filled, stopped (tooth).
mbyll *f.k.* 1. *(derën)* to shut (the
door); *(dritaren)* to shut (the
window). 2. *(me kyç)* to lock,
to lock up. 3. *(me lloz)* to bolt.
4. *(brenda)* to lock in.
5. *(në, kuti)* to case, to enclose
(in a case). 6. *(dritën)* to switch
off. 7. *(rubinetin e ujit)* to turn
off (the tap). 8. *(një letër në
zarf)* to close up, to seal up
(an envelope, a letter.) 9. *(një
libër)* to close (a book). 10 *fig.*
mbyllni gojën! shut up your
mouth! 11. *(një vrimë)* to stop
up, to stuff (a hole). 12. *(shkollat)* to close. 13. *(përkohësisht)*
to shut down, to close down.
14. *(diskutimet)* to close, to
bring to an end, to wind up. —
— **mbyllem** *f.jv.* 1. to seclude
oneself, to shut oneself up
(away). 2. to close, to shut; **dera
mbyllet vetë:** the door shuts
automatically. 3. *(plaga)* to heal
up, to close up (a wound).
mbýllës/e,-ja *f.sh.* **-e** clasp, shutter.
mbýllët (i,e) *mb. (ngjyrë)* dark;
e kuqe e mbyllët: dark red.
mbýllj/e,-a *f.* 1. closing, shutting.
2. *(e një mbledhjeje)* ending,
closing (of a meeting). 3. *(e
diskutimeve)* ending, closing,
conclusion, winding up; **mbyllja
e vitit shkollor:** the end of the
school year. 4. fastening; **mbyllje automatike:** self-closing,
self-locking; **mbyllje hermeti-
ke:** hermetic seal; **mbyllje e
llogarive:** closing of accounts.
mbys *f.k.* 1. *(me duar)* to strangle,
to throttle, to choke. 2. *(duke i*

zënë frymën) to smother, to
suffocate, to stifle. 3. *(me gaz)*
to asphyxiate. 4. *(në ujë)* to
drown. 5. *(një anije)* to submerge (a ship). — **mbytem** *f.jv.*
1. *(në ujë)* to drown. 2. *(anija)* to
sink, to be submerged, to be
wrecked, to wreck (of a ship).
mbýtës,-i *m.sh.* — suffocator, cho-
ker.
mbýtës,-e *mb.* suffocating, stifling; **atmosferë mbytëse:** suffocating atmosphere.
mbýtj/e,-a *f.* 1. *(me duar)* stran-
gulation. 2. *(me zënien e frymës)* suffocation, stifling, smother. 3. *(nga mungesa e oksigje-
nit)*: asphyxia. 4. *(në ujë)* dro-
wning. 5. *(e anijes)* wreck, wrec-
kage, shipwrek.
mbýtur *ndajf.* vaguely.
mbýtur (i.e) *mb.* 1. *(me duar)*
strangulated, throttled. 2. *(me
zënie të frymës)* suffocated, cho-
ked, stifled, smothered. 3. *(me
gaz)* asphyxied. 4. *(në ujë)*
drowned. 5. *(anije)* wrecked
(ship). 6. *fig. (i mbytur në
borxhe)* (to be) over head and
ears (in debt); **jam i mbytur
me punë:** to be overwhelmed
in work, to be up to the ears
in work.

me *paraf.* 1. with, by; **eja me ne:**
come with us; **pres me thikë:**
to cut with a knife.2. *(për veshje)*
with, with (something) on, wearing; **doli me kapelë:** he went
out with his hat on. 3. *(bashkë
me)* with; **banon me të vëllanë:**
he lives with his brother. 4. to,
towards, with; **u soll keq me
mua:** he behaved badly towards me. 5. *(kundër)* against;
luftoj me armiqtë: to fight
(against) the enemies. 6. *(mjet)*
with, by; **marr diçka me forcë:**
to get something by force; *(mjet*

transporti) by; **udhëtoj me makinë:** to travel by car. 7. *(prej)* from, with, out of; **bëj një zar me dyllë:** to make a dice from (out of) wax. 8. *(mënyrë)* with, in; **me durim:** with patience, patiently; **flas me inat:** to speak in an angry tone. 9. with, because of; **me këtë vapë:** with this heat. — *Lok.* **iku që me natë:** he went early in the morning; **me disa kushte:** under certain conditions; **me ta parë:** as soon as he saw him; **me të thënë me të bërë:** no sooner said than done; **me të mbaruar lufta:** no sooner was the war over.

medalj/e,,-a *f.sh.*-e medal; **medalje argjendi:** silver medal; *fig.* **ana tjetër e medaljes:** the reverse (the other side) of the medal.

medalión,-i *m.sh.* -e medallion.

medoemós *ndajf.* necessarily, without fail.

megafón,-i *m.sh.* -ë megaphone.

megjithatë *lidh.* nevertheless, notwithstanding, in spite of that, yet, with all, for all that.

megjíthë *lidh.* in spite of.

megjíthëqë, megjithëse *lidh.* though, although.

mejdán,-i *m.sh.* -e *gj. bis.* arena; **dal në mejdan:** to appear, to make one's appearence.

mejhán/e,-ja *f.sh.* -e pot-house, tavern.

mejhanexhí,-u *m.sh.* -nj tavern-keeper.

mekaník,-u *m.sh.* -ë mechanician, mechanic.

mekaník,-e *mb.* mechanical (edhe, *fig.*); **forcë mekanike:** mechanical force.

mekaník/ë,-a *f.* mechanics; **mekanika qiellore:** celestial mechanics.

mekanikísht *ndajf.* mechanically.

mekaníz/ëm-mi *m.sh.* -ma 1. mechanism, device, gear; **mek a-nizmi i komandimit:** control. (driving) gear. 2. *fig.* mechanism.

mekanizím,-i *m.* mechanization.

mekanizój *f.k.* to mechanize. — **mekanizohet** *f.jv.* to be mechanized.

mékem *f.jv.* to swoon away; .**nekem së qari:** to sob.

mékj/e,-a *f.* swooning; **mekje nga të qarët:** sob, sobbing.

meksikán,-i *m.sh.* -e Mexican.

meksikán,-e *mb.* Mexican.

mel,-i *m. bot.* millet.

melankolí,-a *f.* melancholy.

melankolík,-e *mb.* melancholic.

melás/ë,-a *f.* molasses, treacle.

melhém,-i *m.sh.* -e *mjek.* ointment; **lyej me melhem:** to anoint.

melodí,-a *f.sh.*— *muz.* melody, tune, air; **luaj (ia marr) një melodi(e):** to play a tune.

melodík,-e *mb.* melodic, melodious; **shkalla melodike:** melodic scale.

melodikísht *ndajf.* melodically.

melodísh/ëm(i),-me(e) *mb.* melodious, toneful.

melodrám/ë,-a *f.sh.* -a melodrama.

mellán,-i *m. vjet.* ink.

membrán/ë,-a *f.sh.* -a membrane.

meméc,-i *m.sh.* -ë dumb person.

meméc,-e *mb.* mute, speechless, dumb.

memorandúm,-i *m.sh.* -e memorandum.

memóri/e,-a *f.* memory.

ménç/ëm(i),m-e(e)*mb.*wise, sagebrainy; clever; **njeri i merçëm:** wise man, brainy man; ny ënës i mençëm: clever boy.

mençurí,-a *f.* wisdom; rne mençuri: wisely.

mend *pj.* near to; rnend rashë: I nearly fell; **mend u mbyta:** I nearly got drowned; **mend vdi-**

qa nga frika: I nearly died of fear.
mend,-të *as.* 1. mind, reason; **djalë me mend:** brainy boy. 2. memory; **mbaj mend:** to keep in mind, to bear in mind; **sjel' ndër mend:** to call to mind, to evoke, to remind, to remember, to recollect. 3. imagination; **marr me mend:** to fancy, to imagine; **merret lehtë me mend gëzimi i tij;** you can easily imagine his joy. 4. intention; **kam ndërmend të:** I think to, I intend to, I have the intention of, it is my intention to, I have in mind to; **kam ndërmend të kaloj pushimet në malësi:** I intend to spend my holidays in the mountains. – *Lok.* **luaj mendsh:** to go mad (crazy), to lose one's wits; **me gjithë mend i sëmurë:** really ill; **afër mendsh:** (it is) self-understood; **mbetem pa mend:** to be astonished, to be struck dumb (speechless); **me mend në kokë:** with one's head screwed on the right way, with all one's wits about one: **marrje mendsh:** dizziness, giddiness; **lexoj me mend:** to read mentally; **pa mend:** unbrainy, senseless; **kjo është afër mendsh:** that goes without saying; **mend për tjetër herë:** let this be a lesson to you; **s'do mend:** this goes without saying; **më merren mendtë:** to feel dizzy (giddy), my head is spinning (going round).
ménd/ër,-ra *f. bot.* peppermint.
mendërisht *ndajf.* mentally.
mendësi,-a *f.* mentality.
mendim,-i *m.sh.* -e 1. thought; **mendime pa lidhje:** incongruous thoughts; **i zhytur në mendime:** absorbed in thought. 2. idea, notion, conception;

mendim i ngulët: a fixed idea; **mendim fantastik:** fantastic notion. 3. opinion; **mendim i paracaktuar;** prefixed opinion; **mendim i përgjithshëm:** prevailing opinion; **mendim i pjekur** well-matured opinion: **mbështes një mendim;** to uphold an opinion; **ndërroj mendim:** to change opinion; **shfaq mendim:** to express an opinion, to give one's opinion. 4. mind; **për mendimin tim:** to my mind, in my mind. 5. view; **përputhje mendimesh:** identity of views. – *Lok.* **bie në mendime:** to be lost in thought, to meditate, to muse; **këmbej mendime:** to exchange notes; **sipas mendimit tim:** in my opinion.
mendimtár,-i *m.sh.* -ë thinker.
méndj/e,-a *f.* mind, intellect, wit, head; -**Lok.** **humbas mendjen:** to lose one's head; **jam me dy mendje:** to be in two minds, to be hesitating; **kam diçka në mendje:** I have something in mind; **i kthej mendjen dikujt:** to talk someone out of, to dissuade someone; **më shkon në mendje të:** it occurs to me, it comes to my mind (to my head); **ia marr mendjen dikujt:** to befuddle, to stupefy; **i mbush mendjen dikujt:** to convince (to persuade) someone; **ndërroj mendje:** to change one's mind, to alter one's mind; **i pjell mendja:** he is ingenious; **që ta kap mendja:** perceivable; **i turbulloj mendjen dikujt:** to muddle someone's head; **vras mendjen:** to rack one's brain; **më thotë mendja:** I have a presentiment; **ki mendjen!** mind! look out! beware (of): **si ma pret, si ma merr mendja mua:** as I see it, to my mind; **e**

fle mendjen: to rest assured; me mendje të ngritur: upset, disturbed. *Prov.* mendje e shëndoshë në trup të shëndoshë: a sound mind in a sound body.

mendjefyçkë *mb.* shih mendjelehtë.

mendjehóllë *mb.* smart, snarp, witty, shrewd, sagacious, ingenious, intelligent.

mendjehollësí,-a *f.* ingeniosity, shrewdness, sagacity.

mendjeléhtë *mb.* light-minded, light-headed, hare-brained, scatter-brained, frivolous.

mendjelehtësí,-a *f.* light-mindedness, frivolity, levity.

mendjemádh *mb.* self-opinionated, haughty, self-conceited, overweening, presumptuous, puffed-up, *fam.* stuck-up.

mendjemadhësí,-a *f.* self-conceit, haughtiness, presumption, overconfidence.

mendjempréhtë *mb.* sharp-witted, witty, ingenious, sagacious.

mendjemprehtësí,-a *f.* ingeniosity, sagacity, sharpness.

mendjengúshtë *mb.* narrow-witted, half-witted, narrow-minded.

mendjengushtësí,-a *f.* narrow-mindedness.

mendjeshkúrtër *mb.* shih mendjengushtë.

mendój *f.jk.* to think, to judge, to meditate; të mendojmë, të punojmë, të jetojmë si revolucionarë: think, work and live as revolutionaries: mendoj për dikë, për diçka: to think of someone, of something; çfarë mendoni ju për këtë? what do you think of it? pasi u mendova mirë: on second thoughts.

mendór,-e *mb.* mental; lodhje mendore: mental depression;

sëmundje mendore: mental illness.

mendúar *ndajf.* pensively; rri menduar: to stay pensively.

mendúar (i,e) *mb.* thoughtful pensive, lost (wrapped) in thoughts.

mendúarit (të) *as.* reflection, thinking, meditation.

mendúeshëm *ndajf.* shih menduar.

mengené,-ja *f.sh.* mek. vice, vise.

me ngut *ndajf.* hastily.

meningjít,-i *m.* mjek. meningitis, brain fever.

méns/ë,-a *f.sh.* -a dining hall.

mentalitét,-i *m.sh.* -e mentality.

mént/e,-ja *f. bot.* mint.

mentésh/ë,-a *f.sh.* -a hinge (of a door, window).

menjëhérë *ndajf.* at once, imediately, on the instant, instantly, right away, on the spot, right off; bëjeni menjëherë: do it at once; duhej bërë menjëherë: it ought to be done at once; të gjithë menjëherë: all at once.

menjëhérsh/ëm(i),-me (e) *mb.* immediate, instantaneous; nevoja të menjëhershme: immediate necessities; shpërblim i menjëhershëm: immediate remuneration.

méqë *lidh.* as, since; meqë ra fjala: by the by, by the way.

meqénëse *lidh.* as, seeing that, because.

merák,-u *m.* care, anxiety; pa merak: careless, carefree, reckless; ç'bëhesh merak?, mos u bëj merak: don't worry (about it); s'bëhem merak fare: I don't care a bit.

merakós *f.k. gj. bis.* to trouble, — merakosem *f.jv.* to worry about, to be anxious.

mercenár,-i *m.sh.* -**ë** mercenary, hireling.

meremetím,-i *m.sh.* -**e** repair.

meremetój *f.k.* to repair, to fix, to mend; **meremetoj këpucët**: to mend one's shoes; **meremetoj një makinë**: to repair a machine. — **meremetohet** *f.jv.* to be repaired (mended, fixed).

merhúm,-i *m.sh.* -**ë** *vjet.* the deceased.

merídián,-i *m.sh.* -**e** *gjeog.* meridian.

merimáng/ë,-a *f.sh.* -**a** *zool.* spider; **pëlhurë merimange**: spider's web, cobweb.

merit/ë,-a *f.sh.* -**a** merit; **me meritë**: deservedly; **sipas meritave**: on one's merits, according to merits,

meritój *f.k.* to merit, to deserve; **ai e meritoi titullin e**: he deserved the title of; **siç e meritoni**: as you deserve it; **që meriton të lavdërohet**: worthy of praise.

meritúar(i,e) *mb.* deserved; **shpërblim i merituar**: a just reward; **artist i merituar**: honoured artist.

meritúesh/ëm(i),-me(e) *mb.* meritorious, worthy, deserving.

merlúc,-i *m.sh.* -**ë** *zool.* cod fish; **merluc i kripur**: stockfish.

mermér,-i *m.* marble; **punishte mermeri**: marble-works.

merxhán,-i *m.sh.* -**e** coral.

mérrem *f.jv.* shih **marr.**

mes,-i *m.* 1. middle, mid, midst; **në mes të rrugës**: in the middle of the way; **në mes të ditës**: in broad daylight; **mes për mes** : across, crosswise; **hyj në mes**: to come between, to intervene; **në mes të**: in the middle of, in the midst of, amidst; **mesi i ditës**: midday;

mesi i natës: midnight; **në mes të turmës**: in the midst of the crowd; **në mes tonë**: in our midst, between us; **në mes të detit**: in the open sea; **në mes të vapës**: in dog-days; **në mes të verës**; in midsummer; **mu në mes**: in the very midst, right (just) in the middle(midst). 2. affair, job, business, concern; **në këtë mes unë s'kam të bëj**: I have no hand here, it's not my business, it does not concern me.

mesatár,-e *mb.* 1, mean, medium, middle; **shtat mesatar**: medium height. 2. middling, fair, average; **me zgjuarësi mesatare**: of an average intelligence. 3. *mat.* *fiz.* mean, average; **temperaturë mesatare**: average temperature; **vlerë mesatare**: mean value.

mesatár/e,-ja *f.sh.* -**e** 1. average. 2. *mat.* mean; **mesatare aritmetike**: arithmetical mean; **mesatare vjetore**: annual average; **mbi mesataren**: above average.

mesatarísht *ndajf.* on the average.

mesázh,-i *m.sh.* -**e** message.

mesdít/ë,-a *f.* midday, noon, noonday; **në mesditë**: at midday, at noon.

mesdhetár,-e *mb.* mediterranean; **klimë mesdhetare**: mediterranean climate. *† medium, avera*

més/ëm(i),-me(e) *mb.* middle; **fshatar i mesëm**: middle peasant. *(avg.)*

mesës,-i *m.sh.* — go-between, middleman.

meshóllë *mb.* thin-waisted, wasp-waisted.

mesít,-i *m.sh.* .-**ë** broker.

mesjetár,-e *mb.* mediaeval.

mesjét/ë,-a *f.* the Middle Ages.

mesëpútur *mb.* thin-waisted, wasp-waisted.

mesnát/ë,-a *f.* midnight; **në mesnatë**: at midnight.

mesobúrr/ë,-i *m.sh.* -a middleaged man.

mesór/e,-ja *m.sh.* -e *gjeom.* median.

mesogr/úa-ja *f.sh.* -a middleaged woman.

mespërmés *ndajf.* through, across, crosswise.

meshár,-i *m.sh.* -ë *fet.* missal.

mésh/ë,-a *f. fet.* 1. mass (in a church); **mesha e madhe**; High-Mass. 2. wafer, the consacrated bread.

meshín,-i *m.* leather.

meshój *f.jk.* to officiate.

meshtár,-i *m.sh.* -ë *fet.* minister.

metafizík,-e *mb. filoz.* metaphysical.

metafizík/ë,-a *f. filoz.* metaphysics.

metafór/ë,-a *f.sh.* -a *gram.* metaphor.

metaforík,-e *mb. gram.* metaphorical, metaphoric.

metál,-i *m.sh.* -e metal; **derdhje metali**: moulding; **përzierje metalesh**: metal alloy; **prej metali**: metallic, metal; **fletë metali**: sheet metal.

metalík,-e *mb.* 1. metallic, metal; **enë metalike**: metal recipient. 2. *fig.* metallic; **zë metalik**: metallic voice.

metaloíd,-i *m.sh.* -e *kim.* metalloid.

metalurgjí,-a *f.* metallurgy; **metalurgji e zezë**: iron industry.

metalurgjík,-e *mb.* metallurgic; **uzinë metalurgjike**: metallurgical works.

metamorfóz/ë,-a *f.* metamorphosis.

meteór,-i *m.sh.* -ë 1. *astron.* meteor. 2. *fig.* shooting star.

meteorologjí,-a *f.* meteorology.

meteorologjík,-e *mb.* meteorolo-

gic; **buletini meteorologjik**: meteorological bulletin; **stacion meteorologjik**: weather station.

métë *ndajf.* shih **mangut.**

mét/ë(e),-a(e) *f.sh.* -a (të) defect, fault, flaw, imperfection, vice; **e metë mendore**: mental defect; **e metë fizike**: defect, blemish; **njeri me shumë të meta**: vicious person; **pa asnjë të metë**: impeccable, flawless, faultless; **ky film ka vetëm një të metë**: there is only one thing wrong with this film.

métë (i,e) *mb.* 1. deficient, wanting, incomplete. 2. *(nga mendtë)* demented, foolish, insane.

mét/ër,-ri *m.sh.* -ra 1. metre; **metër katror**: square metre; **metër shirit**: tape measure; **metër metalik**: ruler. 2. *fig. (kriter)* yardstick; **nuk duhet t'i masësh të tjerët me metrin tënd**: you can't judge everyone by the same yardstick.

metíl,-i *m.* methyl.

metilén,-i *m. kim.* methylene.

metilík,-e *mb.* methylic; **alkool metilik**: methylical alcohol.

metód/ë,-a *f.sh.* -a method; **metodë e re pune**: innovation.

metodík,-e *mb.* teaching methods.

metodologjí,-a *f.* methodology.

metrázh,-i *m.sh.* -e unit of length (in metres); **film me metrazh të shkurtër (të gjatë)**: short film, feature film (full-length film).

metrík,-e *mb.* metric; **sistemi metrik**: metric system.

metró,-ja *f.sh..* — *amer.* subway, underground (railway), *fam.* tube.

mexhít/e,-ja *f.sh.* -e Turkish silver coin.

méz/e,-ja *f.sh.* -e appetiser.

mezí *ndajf.* hardly, barely, scarcely, with difficulty.

mézhd /ë,-a *f.sh.* -a small ditch round a piece of ground.

më(lm) my mother (abreviation of **mëmë**).

më I. *pf.* 1. the, on the; **më një mars:** on the first of March, on March the first. 2. from, to: **shkoj qytet më qytet:** to go from town to town; **lajmi shkoi gojë më gojë:** the news spread rapidly, the news passed from mouth to mouth. II. *ndajf.* 1. more (it is used to make the comparative and superlative form of the adjectives and adverbs); **më pak:** less; **më shumë:** more; **më i zgjuar se:** more clever than; **më keq:** worse; **më mirë:** better; **më i mirë se:** better than (comparative); **më i mirë nga të gjithë:** the best of all (superlative); **më i madh:** bigger, larger; **më i vogël:** smaller. 2. yet, still, more; **dua edhe më:** I want some more; **nëm edhe më:** give me more, once more; **më se një herë:** more than once, many a time. – *Lok.* **ai nuk është më:** he is no more. *Prov.* **më mirë vonë se kurrë:** better late than never. III. *p. vet.* (pers. pron. of the first person sing. for both genders) me, to me; **më thuaj një fjalë:** say a word to me; **më jep: give me; më fol për (folmë për):** talk me about; **mos më fol doñt** speak to me! **a më kuptoni?** do you understand me?, do you follow me?

IV. *paraf.* on; **më të djathtë:** on the right (side); **më të majtë:** on the left (side).

mëdítës,-i *m.sh.* – day-labourer.

mëdítj /e,-a *f. sh.* -e daily-pay;

punëtor me mëditje: journeyman, day-labourer.

mëdýzaj *ndajf.* hesitatingly.

mëgójz /ë,-a *f.sh.* -a bit (of a horse).

mëháll /ë,-a *f.sh.* -a *vjet.* ward, quarter (of a town).

mëkát,-i *m.sh.* -e sin; **bie në mëkat, bëj mëkat:** to sin, to commit a sin.

mëkatár,-i *ms.h* -ë sinner.

mëkátár,-e *mb.* sinful.

mëkatój *f.jk.* to sin.

mëkëmb *f.k.* to restore, to renew. – **mëkëmbem** *f.jv.* to recover oneself, to regain one's health.

mëkëmbës,-i *m.sh.* – viceroy, governor, lieutenant of a king.

mëkëmbj /e,-a *f.* restoration, renewal, renovation.

mëkój *f.k.* to feed (a child). – **mëkohem** *f.jv.* to be fed (of a child).

mëkúarit (të) *as.* feeding (of a child).

mëlçí,-a *f.sh.* – *anat.* liver; **mëlçia e zezë:** liver.

mëllág /ë,-a *f.sh.* -a *bot.* hollyhock.

mëllenj /ë,-a *f.sh.* -a *zool.* blackbird, ouzel (ousel).

mëm /ë,-a *f.sh.* -a mother.

mëmëdhé,-u *m.* fatherland, motherland, mother country, homeland.

mëmëlíg /ë,-a *f.* hominy, pap of maize.

mëmësí,-a *f.* shih **amësi.**

mënd *f.k.* to breast-feed, to suckle.

mëndáfsh,-i *m.sh.* -e silk; **mëndafsh artificial:** artificial silk; **mëndafsh i papërpunuar:** raw silk, floss silk; **krimbi i mëndafshit:** silk-worm.

mëndáfshtë (i,e) *mb.* silken, silky.

nëndésh /ë,-a *f.sh.* -a wet-nurse.

mëng /ë,-a *m.sh.* -ë 1. sleeve (of. a shirt, of a coat). 2. *gjeog.*

(*lumi*) prong (of a river). 3. *(deti)* armlet.

mёng/ёr,-ra *f.sh.* **-ra** squashing machine for olives, olive-press.

mёngój *f.jk.* to rise early, to get up early, at dawn. *Prov.* **kush mёngon bluan:** the early bird catches the warm.

mёngór/e,-ja *f.sh.* **-e** a kind of jacket with long sleeves, doublet (man's garment).

mёngjarásh,-e *mb.* left-handed.

mёngjés,-i *m.sh.* **-e** 1. morning; **sot nё mёngjes:** this morning; **nesёr nё mёngjes:** tomorrow morning, next morning; **nё mёngjes herёt:** early in the morning; **ngrihem nё mёngjes herёt:** to get up early in the morning. 2. breakfast; **ha mёngjes:** to breakfast, to have breakfast.

mёngjesór,-e *mb.* morning, matutinal.

mёngjesór/e,-ja *f.sh.* **-e** eating-house for breakfast. ⌒*luncheonette*

mёngjёr (i,e) *mb.* left; **dorё e mёngjёr;** left hand; **nё tё mёngjёr:** on the left side.

mёnój *f.jk. krah.* to be late.

mёnýr/ё,-a *f.sh.* **-a** 1. manner, way, fashion; **mёnyrё tё foluri:** way of speaking; **mёnyrё jetese:** way of living; **nё kёtё mёnyrё:** in this manner (way); **nё tё njёjtёn mёnyrё:** in the same manner (way); **nё çdo mёnyrё:** anyway, in any way (manner); **nё asnjё mёnyrё:** nohow, by no means, under no circumstances, in no manner; **nё njё farё mёnyrё:** somehow, in some way or other; **nё mёnyrё qё:** in order that, so that. 2. fashion, style, way. 3. *gram.* mood; **mёnyra dёftore:** indicative mood.

mёnjánё *ndajf.* aside, apart, aloof; **lё mёnjanё:** to leave aside;

vё mёnjanё: to put aside, to set aside, to set by; **rri mёnjanё:** to stand aside, to stand off; **hiqem mёnjanё:** to draw back.

mёnjaním,-i *m.* 1. *(nga njё rrezik)* shunning, avoidance. 2. *(i njё konkurrenti)* elimination.

mёnjanój *f.k.* 1. to shun, to avoid. 2. to eliminate. – **mёnjanohem** *f.jv.* 1. to make room for. 2. to be eliminated.

mёnjёzaj *ndajf.* in one fold.

mёpársh/ёm (i),-me(e) *mb.* anterior, precedent, former, previous, foregoing; **ditёn e mёparshme:** the day before, the other day, the preceding day; **ndodhi e mёparshme:** antecedent.

mёpastájsh/ёm(i),-me(e) *mb.* posterior, next.

mёrdhác,-e *mb.* chilly.

mёrdhíj, mёrdhas *f.jk.* (p.t. **mёrdhiva** ose **mardha;** p.p. **mёrdhirё** ose **mardhur)** to feel cold, to have cold.

mёrgím,-i *m.* 1. emigration; **shkoj nё mёrgim:** to emigrate, to go abroad. 2. exile; **nё mёrgim:** in exile.

mёrgimtár,-i *m.sh.* **-ё** emigrant.

mёrgój *f.k.* to emigrate. – **mergohem** *f.jv.* to emigrate.

mёrí,-a *f.* grudge, rancour, spite; **i mbaj mёri dikujt:** to nurse a grudge against someone, not to be on speaking terms with somebody.

mёrítur (i,e) *mb.* spitefull, rancorous, resentful.

mёrkúr/ё (e),-a(e) *f.sh.* **-a (tё)** Wednesday.

mёrmёrís *f.j.k.* to murmur, to grumble.

mёrmёrítj/e,-a *f.* murmur, grubling.

mёrqínj/ё,-a *f.sh.* **-a** *bot.* brier.

mёrsín/ё,-a *f.sh.* **-a** *bot.* myrtle.

mërsh/ë,-a *f. anat.* flesh (of the body).

mërshór,-e *mb.* fleshy, carnal.

mërzí,-a *f.* annoyance, boredom, **mërzi e madhe;** spleen **tërbohem nga mërzia:** to be bored stiff (to death).

mërzís *f.k.* to annoy, to worry, to botner, to bore; **ai më mërzit:** he bores me; **mos u mërzit:** don't worry! — **mërzitem** *f.jv.* to get bored, to mope, to feel dull.

mërzítj/e,-a *f.* boredom, ennui.

merzítsh/ëm(i),-me(e)q*b.* boring, tedious, tiresome, annoying; **njeri i mërzitshëm:** tiresome person.

mërzítur(i,e) *mb.* annoyed, bored; **jam i mërzitur:** to be out of humour (out of temper).

mësáll/ë,-a *f.sh.* -a 1. tablecloth. 2. apron; *fig.* **mësallë me dy faqe:** hypocrite, doubledealer, double-faced.

mësím-i *m.sh.* -e 1. teaching; **lidhja e mësimit me punën prodhuese:** the linking of teaching with the productive labour: **mësimet e Partisë sonë:** the teachings of our Party. 2. lesson; **jap mësim:** to teach, to give lessons; **marr mësim:** to take lessons; **nxë një mësim përmendsh:** to learn a lesson by heart; **libri ka njëqind mësime:** the book has one hundred lessons; *(në universitet)* lecture. 3. class, school; **mësimi mbaroi:** class is over; **mësimi i gjeografisë:** the geography class (lesson); **sot nuk kemi mësim:** there's no school today. 4. *fig.* lesson, example, paragon; **jeta e tij është një mësim i dashurisë për popullin:** his life is a paragon of love for the peoplv;

kjo do t'i bëhet **mësim:** let this be a lesson to him; **do t'i jap një mësim të mirë:** I will teach him a good lesson.

mësímdhënës,-i *m.sh.* — teacher, professor, preceptor, instructor.

mësimdhënës,-e *mb.* instructive.

mësimór,-e *mb.* teaching; **trupi mësimor;** teaching staff.

mësípërm (i),-e (e) *mb.* aforesaid, above-mentioned.

mësój *f.k., f.jk.* 1. to teach; **mësoj një nxënës:** to teach a pupil. 2. to learn; **mësoj një mësim:** to learn a lesson; **mësoj përmendsh:** to learn byheart. 3. *(një zanat)* to be apprenticed. — **mësohem** *f.jv.* to accustom oneself; to get accustomed.

mësonjëtór/e,-ja *f.sh.-e* *vjet.* school.

mësúar (i,e) *mb.* 1. learned, wellread, instructed. 2. accustomed; **i mësuar me punë:** accustomed to work.

mësúes,-i *m.sh.-* teacher, instructor; **mësues filloreje:** elementary school teacher.

mësýj *f.k.* to attack, to assail. — **mësyhem** *f.jv.* to be assailed.

mësýmj/e,-a *f.sh.* — attack, assault.

mësýsh *ndajf.* **marr mësysh dikë:** to bewitch, to cast (to put) a spell on someone.

mëshír/ë,-a *f.* 1. pity, compassion, mercy, clemency, forbearance; **ki mëshirë!** have pity on me; **kam mëshirë për dikë:** to pity someone, to take pity on, to feel pity for; **lë në mëshirën e fatit:** to leave to the mercy of hazard (fate).

mëshirój *f.jk., f.k.* to pity, to compassionate, to feel pity for, to forbear; **e mëshiroj:** I pity him. — **mëshirohem** *f.jv.* to be pitied, to be forborn.

mëshírsh/ëm(i),-me(e) *mb,* merciful, pitiful, clement, compassionate.

mëshój *f.jk., f.k.* to press upon.

mëshqérr/ë,-a *f.sh.* **-a** *zool.* heifer.

mështék/ën,-na *f.sh.* **-na** *bot.* birch, birch-tree.

mëtéjsh/ëm-(i),-me(e) *mb.* further, ulterior.

mëvónsh/ëm(i),-me(e) *mb.* posterior, subsequent.

mëz,-i *m.sh.* **-a** *zool.* colt.

mëzór/e,-ja *f.sh.* **-e** zool. heifer.

mi,-a *f. muz.* mi; **mi bemol maxhore:** E flat major.

mi(e),-mia(e) *p.pr.* my; **djemtë e mi:** my sons; **vajzat e mia:** my daughters (shih **im**).

mi,-u *m.sh.* **-nj** *zool.* mouse, rat; **mi fushe:** field mouse; **mi shtëpie:** house mouse; *fig.* **mi librash:** bookworm; **kapem si miu në çark:** to be caught like a rat in a trap.

micák,-u *m.sh.* **-ë** *zool.* warbler, wagtail.

midé,-ja *f* 1. *anat. vjet.* stomach. 2. appetite; **më është prishur mideja:** to have lost one's appetite.

midís,-i *m.* middle, midst, center; **mu në midis:** right in the middle.

midís *paraf.* 1. among, amongst, amid; **midis të tjerave:** among others. 2. between; **midis nesh:** between us; **midis orës tetë e nëntë:** between eight and nine. 3. among, in, in the middle of, in the midst of; **një fshat midis maleve:** a village in the midst of mountains. 4. of, among; **më i riu midis nesh:** the youngest of us.

mídh/e,-ja *f.sh.* **-e** *zool.* oyster, mollusk, crab, lobster.

míell,-i *m.* flour; **krip me miell:** to flour; **fabrikë mielli:** flour mill.

míellt (i,e) *mb.* floury, mealy.

mih *f.k.* to hoe; to dig.

míj/ë,-a *f.sh.* **-ë** thousand.

míjësh/e,-ja *f.sh.* **-e** banknote of one thousand (leks).

mijëvjeçár,-e *mb.* millenary, millennial. [Used also as n., per KT]

mik,-u *m.sh.* **miq** 1. friend; crony; **mik i ngushtë:** close (intimate) friend, bosom-friend. 2. guest, newcomer; **pres miqtë:** to receive the guests; **patëm miq për darkë:** we had guests for dinner.

mikésh/ë,-a *f.sh.*-a women friend.

mikprítës,-e *mb.* hospitable.

mikprítj/e,-a *f.* hospitality.

mikrób,-i *m.sh.* **-e** microbe, germ.

mikrobiologjí,-a *f.* microbiology.

mikroborgjéz,-i *m.sh.* **-ë** pettybourgeois.

mikrofón,-i *m.sh.* **-ë** microphone.

mikroskóp,-i *m.sh.*-ë microscope.

mikroskopík,-e *mb.* microscopic.

miliárd,-i *m.sh.* **-ë** num. them. milliard. (amer.) billion

milíc,-i *m.sh.* **-ë** militiaman.

milicí,-a *f.* militia.

milimét/ër,-ri *m.sh.* **-ra** millimeter, millimetre.

milingón/ë,-a *f.sh.* **-a** *zool.* ant; **fole milingonash:** ant-hill.

milión,-i *m.sh.* **-a** *num. them.* million; **miliona njerëz:** millions of people.

milionér,-i *m.sh.* **-ë** millionaire,

militánt,-i *m.sh.* **-ë** militant.

militaríst,-i *m.sh.* **-ë** militarist.

militaríz/ëm,-mi *m.* militarism.

mílj/e,-a *f.sh.* **-e** mile; **milje detare:** nautical (sea) mile; **milje tokësore:** statute mile.

milór,-i *m.sh.* **-ë** *zool.* young ram.

mill,-i *m.sh.* **-e** 1. sheath; **nxjerr shpatën nga milli:** to pull the sword off the sheath; **shtie (fut) në mill:** to sheathe, to put into a sheath. 2. handle of a knife, etc.

mimík/ë,-a *f.* mimicry.

minár/e,-ja *f.sh.* -e minaret.

minatór,-i *m.sh.* -ë miner, collier, pitman; *(qymyrguri)* coal-mine worker, collier, coal miner.

mindér,-i *m.sh.* -ë settee, sofa.

minerál,-i *m.sh.* -e mineral, ore; **mineral hekuri:** iron ore; **mineral i varfër:** lean (lowgrade) ore.

minerál,-e *mb.* mineral; **pasuri minerale:** mineral resources; **ujë mineral:** mineral water.

mín/ë,-a *f.sh.* -a mine; **minë e nenujshme;** submarine (torpedo) mine.

minier/ë,-a *f.sh.* -a mine; **minierë ari:** gold mine; **minierë qymyrguri:** coal-mine, colliery; **industria e minierave:** mining industry.

minimum,-i *m.sh.* -e minimum.

minist/ër,-ri *m.sh.* -ra minister, *amer.* secretary of state; **ministri i bujqësisë:** minister of agriculture and forestry, *amer.* secretary of agriculture.

ministrí,-a *f.sh.* – ministry, office, board, *amer.* department; **Ministria e Punëve të Jashtme:** Foreign Office, Ministry of Foreign Affairs, *amer.* State Department; **Ministria e Tregtisë:** Ministry of Trade; **Ministria e Arsimit dhe e Kulturës:** Ministry of Education and Culture, *amer.* Department of Health, Education, and Welfare.

minój *f.k.* 1. *usht.* to mine. 2. *fig.* to undermine, to sap.

minór,-e *mb.* 1. *muz.* minor. 2. under age, minor. 3. *fig.* minor; **figurë minore:** minor personality.

minoritár,-i *m.sh.* -ë one who belongs to a national minority.

minoritár,-e *mb.* pertaining to a minority.

minoritét,-i *m.sh.* -e minority.

mínus,-i *m.sh.* -e 1. *mat.* minus. 2. *fig.* disadvantage.

minút/ë,-a *f.sh.* -a 1. minute. 2. moment; **prit një minutë:** wait a minute (a moment, a little while) l

mióp,-i *m.sh.* -ë myope, near-sighted person.

mióp,-e *mb.* myopic, short-sighted, near-sighted (edhe *fig.*).

miopí,-a *f.* myopia, short-sightedness; **miopi politike:** political short-sightedness.

miqësí,-a *f.* friendship, amity; **miqësi e ngushtë:** close (intimate) friendship; **në shenjë miqësie:** as a token of friendship; **miqësi e pathyeshme:** unbreakable friendship; **lidh miqësi me dikë:** to strike up a friendship (to make friends) with someone; **për miqësi:** out of friendship; **prish miqësinë:** to break off (a friendship).

miqësím,-i *m.* making friends (with someone).

miqësísht *ndajf.* friendly, amicably, in a friendly way.

miqësój *f.k.* to befriend, to make a friend of, to link by amity. – **miqësohem** *f.jv.* to make (to become) friend (*me,* with).

miqësór,-e *mb.* amicable, friendly; **pritje miqësore:** friendly reception; **marrëdhënie miqësore:** friendly relations.

miratím,-i *m.* approbation, approval.

miratój *f.k.* to approbate, to approve, to express one's approval. – **miratohet** *f.jv.* to be approbated (approved).

miratúes,-e *mb.* approbatory, approbative.

mírë *ndajf.* good, well, right, aright,

all right; **jam mirë me shën-det**: to be well, to enjoy good health; **nuk jam mirë me shën-det**: to be unwell; **dukeni mirë nga fytyra**: you look well; **jam (bëhem) më mirë**: to get better; **më mirë**: better; **më së miri**: at best; **mjaft mirë**: pretty well; **fort (fare) mirë**: very well, quite well; **jam fare mirë**: I am very well; **shumë mirë (në rregull)**: all right; **shumë më mirë**: much better; **ai ështč mirë e bukur tani**: he is all right now; **mirë t'i bëhet**: it serves him right; **aq më mirë**: so much the better; **mirë e më mirë**: better and better. − Lok. **ju bëftë mirë!** good appetite!; **për të mirë**: to your health!; **ai është mirë në anglisht**: he is well up in English; **shkoj (e kam) mirë me dikë**: to be in good terms with someone; **e mbaj mirë me dikë**: to keep on friendly terms with somoene; **deri këtu mirë shkoi!** so far so good! − Prov. **më mirë vonë se kurrë**: rather late than never.

mírë (i,e) mb. 1. good, kind, gentle, amiable, nice; **djalë i mirë**: good boy 2. fine; **kohë e mirë**: fine weather. 3. (i aftë) good, able, skilful, capable; **aktor i mirë**: good (fine) actor. 4. (erë, shije) good, tasty, delicious; **sa e mirë kjo gjellë!** how tasty this dish is! 5. (mendim) good, fit, suitable. − Lok. **natën e mirë**: good night; **të prita dy orë të mira**: I have waited a full (whole) two hours for you.

mír/ë(e),-a(e) f.sh. -a (të) 1. favour; **më bëj një të mirë**: do me a favour. 2. goodness, good; **e mirë e përgjithshme**: common weal; **për të mirën e**

popullit: for the good of the people, for the benefit of the people; **ç'të mirë ka kjo?**: what is the good of it? **për të mirën e tij**: for his own good; **(të uroj) gjithë të mirat!** I wish you all the best! 3. advantage, benefit.

mirëbesím,-i m. good faith, confidence; **lë në mirëbesim**: to trust someone with something.

mirëbërës,-i m. benefactor, beneficent, philanthropist.

mirëbërësí,-a f. goodness, benefaction, beneficence.

mirëdáshës,-e mb. bountiful, benevolent, kind.

mirëdáshj/e,-a f. benevolence, goodwill.

mirëdíta! pasth. good day! (when arriving).

mirëfílli ndajf. from the very start.

mirëfílltë (i,e) mb. authentic, genuine; direct.

mirëkuptím,-i m. understanding.

mirëmbáj f.k. to maintain, to hold in good state. − **mirëmbahet** f.jv. to be maintained.

mirëmbájtj/e,-a f. maintenance.

mirëmbrëma! pasth. good evening!

mirëmëngjés! pasth. good morning!

mirënjóhës,-e mb. grateful, thankful; **jam mirënjohës**: to be grateful, to feel obliged; **ju jam shumë mirënjohës**: I am much obliged to you.

mirënjóhj/e,-a f. gratitude, thankfulness.

mirënjóhur (i,e) mb. renowned, famous, well-known.

mirëpó lidh. but.

mirëprés f.k. to welcome, to receive with hospitality. − **mirëpritem** f.jv. to be welcomed, to be received kindly.

mirëprítj/e,-a *f.* welcome, hospitality.

mirëqéni/e,-a *f.* well-being, welfare.

mirërrítj/e,-a *f.* well-breeding, good-breeding.

mirëseárdhj/e,-a *f.* welcome; **uroj mirëseardhjen:** to bid welcome.

mirë se érdhët! *pasth.* welcome!, you are welcome!

mirë se víni! *pasth.* welcome!, you are welcome!

mirë se vjén! *pasth.* welcome!

mirësí,-a *f.* goodness, kindness, benevolence, amability, goodwill; **lutem, kini mirësinë:** please, be so kind as to.

mirësjéllj/e,-a *f.* good behaviour, courtesy, civility, politeness, good manner.

mirós *f.k. fet.* to anoint.

mirupáfshim! *pasth.* good bye!, bye-bye!, so long!

mís/ër,-ri *m.sh.* **-ra** *bot.* maize, Indian corn, *amer.* corn.

misërísht/e,-ja *f.sh.* **-e** ear of indian corn, corn-cob.

misërník/e,-ja *f.* bread of maize.

misërók,-u *m.sh.* **-ë** *zool.* turkeycock.

misión,-i *m.sh.* **-e** mission; **mision sekret:** secret mision.

misionár,-i *m.sh.* **-ë** missionary.

mísk/ë,-a *f.sh.* **-a** *zool.* turkey-hen.

mistér,-i *m.sh.* **-e** mystery.

misterióz,-e *mb.* mysterious.

mistréc,-i *m.sh.* **-ë** mischief.

mistrí,-a *f.sh.* — trowel.

misúr,-i *m.sh.* **-ë** bowl (half-spherical vase).

mish,-i *m.* 1. meat; *(dashi)* mutton; *(lope, kau)* beef; *(viçi)* veal; *(derri)* pork; *(pule)* chicken; *(gjahu)* venison; *(qëngji)* lamb meat; **mish i grirë:** mincemeat, ground meat; **mish kutie:** tinned meat, *amer.* canned meat; **mish**

i pjekur: roast beef, roasted meat. 2. *anat.* flesh; **vë mish:** to put on weight. 3. *anat.* **mishi i dhëmbëve:** gum. 4. *fig.* **mish për top:** cannon fodder; **as mish as peshk:** neither fish nor fowl.

mishërím,-i *m.* incarnacion, embodiment.

mishërój *f.k.* to incarnate, to embody. — **mishërohem** *f. jv.* to be incarnated.

mishërúes,-i *m.* personifier.

mishmásh *ndajf.* pell-mell;

mishngrënës,-i *m.sh.* — cannibal, flesh-eater, carnivore.

mishngrënës,-e *mb.* carnivorous, flesh-eating.

mishshítës,-i *m.sh.* — butcher, meat-seller.

mishtór,-e *mb.* fleshy, meaty.

mit,-i *m.sh.* **-e** myth.

mítë(të) *p.v.* mine (shih **im**).

mít/ë,-a *f.* graft, bribe.

mít/ër,-ra *f. anat.* womb, uterus.

mitín/g,-gu *m.sh.* **-gje** meeting; **marr pjesë në miting:** to attend (to be present at) a meeting.

mitologjí,-a *f.* mythology.

mitralím,-i *m.* machine-gunning, machine-gun fire.

mitraljér,-i *m.sh.* **-ë** machine-gunner.

mitralój *f.k.* to machine-gun.

mitralóz,-i *m.sh.* **-a** machine-gun; **gjerdhan mitralozi:** cartridgebelt.

mitropolí,-a *f.sh.* — metropolis.

mítur (i,e) *mb.* infant, underaged.

miturí,-a *f.* infancy, babyhood.

miúsh,-i *m.sh.* **-ë** small mouse.

mizantróp,-i *m.sh.* **-ë** misanthrope, man hater.

míz/ë,-a *f.sh.* **-a** *zool.* fly, housefly; **mizë dheu:** ant, emmet; **mizë gruri:** chinch bug; **mizë kali:** horse-fly; **kapëse mizash:** fly-trap, fly-catcher; **letër mizash:** flypaper.

mizëri,-a *f.* multitude, throng, crowd *(njerëzish)* bevy, crowd, multitude (of persons); *(mushkonjash)* throng (of mosquitoes).

mizërón *f.jk.* to throng, to come in multitude.

mizór,-e *mb.* cruel, barbarous, atrocious.

mizorí,-a *f.* cruelty, barbarism, atrocity.

mizorísht *ndajf.* cruelly, atrociously.

mjaft *ndajf.* 1. enough; **kam mjaft:** I have enough. 2. pretty; rather; **mjaft mirë:** pretty well; **mjaft i madh:** rather big; **mjaft mël** enough!, that will do!

mjáftë (i,e) *mb.* sufficient, adequate.

mjaftój *f.jk.* 1. to suffice; to be enough, to be sufficient; **më mjaftoi një vështrim për të kuptuar gjithçka:** a glance sufficed for me to understand everything. 2. to last; **këto para na mjaftojnë për të gjithë muajin:** this money will last us for a month. — **mjaftohem** *f.jv.* to be satisfied; **mjaftohem me një dënim të lehtë:** to be satisfied with a light punishment.

mjaftúesh/ëm(i),-me(e) *mb.* sufficient, adequate; **plotësisht e mjaftueshme:** fully sufficient.

mjált/ë,-i *m.* honey; fig. **muaji i mjaltit:** honeymoon.

mjaullím/ë,-a *f.sh.* -a mew.

mjaullín *f.jk.* to mew (the cat).

mjedís,-i *m.sh.* -e surroundings, environment, background; **temperatura e mjedisit:** room (ambient) temperature.

mjédh/ër,-ra *f.sh.* -ra *bot.* rasp-

berry; **kaçubë mjedhre:** raspberry-bush.

mjégull,-a *f.* fog. mist; *(e dendur)* haze; **kohë me mjegull:** hazy time.

mjegullín/ë,-a *f.* hazy-time.

mjégullt(i,e) *mb.* hazy, foggy.

mjek,-u *m.sh.* -ë doctor, physician; *(kirurg)* surgeon; *(patolog)*: pathologist; *(për nervat)* neurologist; *(për sytë)* oculist; *(për sëmundjet e lëkurës)* dermatologist; **mjek ushtarak:** medical officer.

mjék/ër,-ra *f.sh.* -ra 1. *anat.* chin. 2. beard; **me mjekër:** bearded.

mjekërósh,-e *mb.* bearded.

mjekërbárdhë *mb.* greybearded.

mjekësí,-a *f.* medicine; **student në mjekësi:** medical student; **mjekësi ligjore:** legal medicine.

mjekësór,-e *mb.* medical; **shërbim mjekësor:** health service; **shkollë mjekësore:** med cal school; **ndihmë mjekësore:** medical aid.

mjekím,-i *m.sh.* -e 1. medicament, medicine. 2. treatment, cure; **mjeku i dha një mjekim me kalcium:** the doctor prescribed calcium treatment.

mjekój *f.k.* to medicate, to treat; **mjekoj një plagë me jod:** to treat a wound with iodine. — **mjekohem** *f.jv.* to medicate oneself, to doctor oneself.

mjel *f.k.* to milk.

mjélës,-i *m.sh.* -milkman.

mjélës/e,-ja *f.sh.* -e milkwoman, milk-maid.

mjélj/e,-a *f.* milking.

mjéllm/ë,-a *f.sh.* -a *zool.* swam.

mjérë *pasth.* mishap to!, woe!, woe to!; **mjerë unë!** poor me! woe to me!, woe betide me!

mjérë(i,e) *mb.* miserable, woeful,

unhappy, unlucky, unfortunate; **l mjeril** the poor wretch!

mjerím,-i *m.sh.* -e misfortune, distress, grief, woe; **bie në mjerim:** to fall into distress, to come to qrief.

mjerísht *ndajf.* woefully, unfortunately.

mjerój *f.k.* to desolate, to make forlorn. — **mjerohem** *f.jv.* to be desolated.

mjerúar (i,e) *mb.* unfortunate, wretched.

mjerúesh/ëm (i,)-me(e) *mb.* lamentable, deplorable.

mjésht/ër,-ri *m.sh.* -ra 1. *muz.,* *art,* master; **mjeshtrat e mëdhenj të Rilindjes:** the old masters of the Renaissance. 2. *(punëtor i specializuar)* master hand, master workman, master; **mjeshtër marangoz:**master carpenter. 3. *(zanatçi)* handicraft's master; **punë prej mjeshtri:** the work of a master hand.

mjeshtërí,-a *f.sh.* — 1. art, skill. 2. handicraft, workmanship. 3. profession.

mjét,-i *m. sh.* -e 1. *(pune)* implement, tool. 2. means; **mjete transporti, komunikacioni:** means of transport; **mjet i rastit:** expedient. 3. material; **mjete shkollore:** school materials. 4. *fig.* means, ways; **përdor të gjitha mjetet:** to try all means; **me çdo mjet:** by all means; **mjete jetese:** subsistence, means of living (livelihood).

mlýsh,-i *m.sh.* -ë *zool.* jack (fish).

mobíli/e,-a *f.sh.* -e furniture; **pajis me mobilie:** to furnish; **mobilie zyre:** office furniture.

mobiliér,-i *m.sh.* -ë furniture manufacturer; furniture seller.

mobilierí,-a *f.sh.* — 1. workshop of furniture, furniture factory. 2 furniture shop.

mobilím,-i *m.* furnishing, providing with furniture.

mobilizím,-i *m.* mobilization; **mobilizim i popullsisë:** general mobilization.

mobilizój *f.k.* to mobilize. — **mobilizohem** *f.jv.* to be mobilized.

mobilój *f.k.* to supply with furniture, to furnish. — **mobilohet** *f.jv.* to be furnished.

mobilúar (i,e) *mb.* furnished, supplied with furniture; **dhomë e mobiluar:** furnished room; **apartament i mobiluar:** furnished apartment.

moçál,-i *m.sh.* -e swamp, morass, fen, marsh, bog, quag, quagmire.

moçalór,-e *mb.* swampy, marshy, boggy; **tokë moçalore:** marshy ground; **vend moçalor:** bogland.

móç/ëm(i),-me(e) *mb.* old, aged; ancient; olden, bygone.

modél,-i *m.sh.* -e 1, model, pattern. 2. *fig.* model, example; **punëtor model:** a model worker. 3. *(tip)* model, type.

modelím,-i *m.* modelling.

modelíst,-i *m.sh.* -ë modeller, pattern maker.

modelój *f.k.* to model, to shape, to fashion. — **modelohet** *f.jv.* to be modelled.

modelúes,-i *m.sh.* — modeller, pattern maker.

modérn,-e *mb.* modern, up-to-date.

modernizím,-i *m.* modernization.

modernizój *f.k.* to modernize — **modernizohet** *f.jv.* to be modernized.

modést,-e *mb.* modest, unassuming.

modestí,-a *f.* modesty.

mód/ë,-a *f.* fashion, style; **është në modë:** to be in fashion;

ndjek modën: to follow the fashion; **i dalë mode (nga moda)**: out-of-date, out of fashion, oldfashioned; **sipas modës së fundit**: in the latest style (fashion), in the new fashion; **me modën e vjetër**: in the old fashion; **njeri që ndjek modën**: man of fashion; **është i modës (në modë)**: it's fashionable.

modíst/e,-ja *f.sh.* -e milliner.

mohím,-i *m.sh.* -e disown, disavowal, denial, negation; **mohim i fesë**: apostasy (of faith), abjuration.

mohój *f.k.* to negate, to disown, to disavow, to deny; *(fenë)* to apostatyze; **mohoj veten**: to deny oneself. – **mohohet** *f.jv.* to be disowned (denied).

mohór,-e *mb.* negative; *gram.* **fjali mohore**: negative sentence.

mohúes,-i *m.sh.* – *(i një partie)* renegade; *(i fesë)* apostate.

mohúes,-e *mb.* negative; **përgjigje mohuese**: negative answer.

mók/ër,-ra *f.sh.* -ra millstone.

molekúl/ë,-a *f.sh.* -a molecule.

molép *f.k.* to infect, to contaminate, to taint, to pollute, to foul. – **molepsem** *f.jv.* to be infected (contaminated, polluted, tainted).

molépsës,-e *mb.* infective, infectious, pestiferous, pestilent.

molépsj/e,-a *f.* infection, contamination, pollution, pestilence; **molepsje e ajrit**: air pollution.

mól/ë,-a *f.sh.* -a *zool.* moth; **e ngrënë nga mola**: motheaten; **bar mole**: naphthalene.

molís *f.k.* to make weak, to enfeeble, to sap, to sap the strength of someone, to debilitate. – – **molisem** *f.jv.* to grow weak.

molísj/e,-a *f.* languor, weakness, debility.

mol,-i *m.sh.* -e pier, quay.

molláqe,-t *f.sh. anat.* buttocks.

móll/ë,-a *f.sh.* -ë *bot.* apple; **druri i mollës**: apple-tree; **byrek me mollë**: apple-pie; *fig.* **mollë sherri**: bone of discord (of contention).

mollëkúq/e,-ja *f.sh.* -e *zool.* ladybird (insect).

móllëz,-a *f.sh.* -a *anat.* **mollëzat e faqeve**: cheek-bones.

momént,-i *m.sh.* -e moment, instant.

monárk,-u *m.sh.* -ë monarch.

monarkí,-a *f.sh.* – monarchy.

monarkíst,-i *m.sh.* -ë monarchist.

monédh/ë,-a *f.sh.* -a 1. coin, piece; **monedhë ari**: gold coin; **monedhë false**: counterfeit coin. 2. currency; **nxjerr monedhë të re**: to mint (to coin, to emit) new money (coins); **monedhë e huaj**: foreign currency (money).

monetár,-e *mb.* monetary; **sistem monetar**: monetary system; **krizë monetare**: monetary crisis.

monológ,-u *m.sh.* -ë monologue.

monopát,-i *m.sh.* -e footway. .

monopól,-i *m.sh.* -e monopoly.

monopolíst,-i *m.sh.* -ë monopolist.

monopolizím,-i *m.* monopolization.

monopolizój *f.k.* to monopolize. – **monopolizohet** *f.jv.* to be monopolized.

monotón,-e *mb.* monotonous.

monotoní,-a *f.* monotony.

montatór,-i *m.sh.* -ë fitter.

montím,-i *m.sh.* -e fitting, mounting, assembling.

montój *f.k.* to assemble, to fit, to mount. – **montohet** *f.jv.* fo be fitted (assembled, mounted).

montúes,-i *m.sh.* – fitter.

monumént,-i *m.sh.* -e monument.
monumentál,-e *mb.* monumental.
móra (past tense of the verb marr)
morál,-i *m.* 1. moral, ethics; morali i fabulës: the moral of the fable. 2. morale; morali i ushtarëve ishte i lartë: the soldiers' morale was high; i ngre moralin dikujt: to boost someone's morale.
morál,-e *mb.* moral; edukatë morale: ethical education.
moralíst,-i *m.sh.* -ë moralist.
moralísht *ndajf.* morally; jam keq moralisht: to be in low spirits.
morfologjí,-a *f.* morphology
morfologjík,-e *mb.* morphological.
morí,-a *f.* multitude, host, throng, great number; *(njerëzish)* crowd, multitude, throng.
morníca,-t *f.sh.* shivering, shuddering; më shkojnë mornica: to shudder.
mort,-i *m.* death: s'ka mort *(një plaçkë):* it is everlasting (of a cloth).
mortáj/ë,-a *f.sh.* -a *usht.* mortar.
mórtj/e,-a *f.gj. bis.* death; e hëngërt mortja! may he be dead!
morr,-i *m.sh.* -a zool. louse (pl. lice); morri i bimëve: plantlouse, greenfly, green plantlouse.
morracák,-e *mb.* lousy.
morrís *f.k.* to kill lice.
mórs/ë,-a *f.sh.* -a shih mengene.
mos *ndajf.* 1. (it is used with a verb in the imperative mood) don't; mos vrapo: do not run; mos folë në klasë: do not talk in class; mos harroni: dot not forget. 2. (it is used alone, without verb, expressing prohibition) mos! don't make this! 3. (it is used in the interrogative sentences) do; mos e njihni atë? do you know him? 4. (with a verb expressing fear or doubt)

kam frikë se mos na shajë: I fear lest he scolds us. 5. (in elliptical expressions) si mos më keq: in a lamentable state.
mos *parashtesë* (it is equivalent to the English prefixes dis, im, in, mis, non, un, etc.)
mosaprovím,-i *m.* disapproval, disapprobation.
mosárdhje,-a *f.* absence.
mosbesím,-i *m.* mistrust, distrust, disbelief, incredulity.
mosbíndj/e,-a *f.* disobedience; mosbindje ndaj një urdhri: disobedience to an order.
mosdáshj/e,-a *f.* 1. unwillingness, reluctance. 2. dislike.
mosdëgjím,-i *m.* disobedience.
mosinteresím,-i *m.* unconcern, indifference.
moskokëçárj/e,-a *f.* indifference, carelessness, heedlessness, negligence, listlessness.
moskuptím,-i *m.* misunderstanding
moslejím,-i *m.* prohibition.
mosmarrëvéshj/e,-a *f.sh.* -e disagreement, divergence, variance; *(në mendime)* divergence (of opinions); jam në mosmarrëveshje me: to be at variance with.
mosmirënjóhës,-e *mb.* ungrateful, unthankful.
mosmirënjóhj/e,-a *f.* ungratefulness, ingratitude, unthankfulness.
mosndërhýrj/e,-a *f.* nonintervention; noninterference.
mosnjóhj/e,-a *f.* unknowingness, ignorance.
mospagím,-i *m.* non-payment.
mospajtím,-i *m.* 1. incompatibility. 2. irreconciliation.
mosparaqítj/e,-a *f.* non-forthcoming, non-appearance.
mospëlqim,-i *m.* unconsent, disapprobation.
mospërdorím,-i *m.* non-usage.

mospërfíllës,-e *mb.* contemptuous, irreverent, scornful, disdainful.

mospërfíllj/e,-a *f.* contempt, disdain, disregard, slight. scorn, irreverence; **me mospërfillje:** contemptuously, disdainfully.

mospërpúthj/e,-a *f.* non-conformity.

mosplotësím,-i *m.* unfulfillment, nonfulfillment, noncompletion.

mospraním,-i *m.* non-acceptance, rejection, refusal.

mospërgatítj/e,-a *f.* unpreparedness.

mosqéni/e,-a *f.* non-existence,

mosrealizím,-i *m.* non-fulfillment.

mosrespektim,-i *m.* 1. disrespect. 2. non-observance; **mosrespektimi i ligjit, i orarit:** non-observance of the law, of the time-table.

mossuksés,-i *m.sh.* -e nonsuccess.

mossulmím,-i *m.* non-aggression; **pakt mossulmimi:** nonaggression pact.

móst/ër,-ra *f.sh.* -ra sample, patern, specimen, model.

mostrétj/e,-a *f. mjek.* indigestion, dyspepsia.

mosveprím,-i *m.* inaction.

mosveprimtarí,-a *f.* inactivity, passivity.

moszbatím,-i *m.* non-performance, non-execution, non-completion.

móshatár,-i *m.sh.* -ë age-companion, *aqe-mate, coeval*

moshatár,-e *mb.* of the same age, contemporary (with).

mósh/ë,-a *f.sh.* -a age; **moshë madhore:** full legal age; **moshë e pjekurisë:** manhood; **moshë e thyer:** old age; **i thyer nga mosha:** elderly. – *Lok.* **në lulen e moshës:** in the prime of life; **rris moshën:** to grow in years; **ai tregon me moshë më të vogël nga ç'është:** he

is young for his years; **ç'moshë ke?** how old are you?

moshuar(i,e) *mb.* old, aged.

mot *ndajf.* next year.

mot,-i *m.sh.* -e 1. weather: **mot i bukur:** fine weather; **mot i keq:** bad weather. 2. year; **mot i mbarë:** good year. – *Lok.* **një herë në mot:** once in a blue moon.

moták,-e *mb.* yearling, of one year.

mót/ër,-ra *f.sh.* -ra sister; **motër prej babe, prej nëne:** half-sister, half-blood, step-sister.

motív,-i *m.sh.* -e 1. motive, cause, reason. 2. *muz.* motif, motive, theme, central theme.

motivación,-i *m.sh.* -e motivation.

motivój *f.k.* to motivate, to state reasons for.

móto,-ja *f.* motto, guiding principle.

motoçiklét/ë,-a *f.sh.* -a motorcycle; **kosh motoçiklete:** side car.

motoçiklíst, -i *m. sh.* -ë motor-. cyclist.

motór,-i *m.sh.* -ë 1. motor; **motor me djegie të brendshme:** combustion motor. 2. motorcycle.

motorík, -e *mb.* motor; **fuqi motorike:** motor power.

motoríst,-i *m.sh.* -ë motorman.

motoskáf,-i *m.sh.* -ë motor-boat, power-boat.

mozaík,-i *m.sh.* -ë 1. mosaic, 2. *fig.* mosaic, patchwork.

mozaík,-e *mb.* mosaic.

mpij *f.k.* 1. to numb, to benumb. 2. *mjek.* to mortify. – **mpihem** *f.jv.* to be numbed.

mpiks *f.k.* to clot, to coagulate; to curdle. – **mpikset** *f.jv.* to be clotted (coagulated), to curdle.

mpíksj/e,-a *f.* clot, coagulation, curdiness.

mpíksur (i,e) *mb.* clotted, coagulated; **gjak i mpiksur:** gore, clotted blood; **qumësht i mpik-sur:** curdled milk.

mpirë (i,e) *mb.* 1. numb. benumbed, torpid. 2. *mjek.* mortified, ankylosed, ankylotic. 3. fig. dull, heavy, sluggish, inactive.

mpirj/e,-a *f.* 1, numbness, torpidity. 2. *mjek.* mortification, ankylosis.

mpitë (i,e) *mb.* 1. *mjek.* stiff; **këmbë e mpitë:** stiff foot. 2. *fig.* **njeri i mpitë:** sluggish man.

mposht *f.k.* 1. *(një kryengritje)* to repress; (a revolt). 2. *(një kundërshtar)* to vanquish, to overpower, to bring down, to overthrow (a rival). 3. *fig. (një vështirësi)* to surmount, to overcome, to get over (a difficulty). 4. *(zemërimin)* to restrain someone's anger. – **mposhtem** *f.vj.* to be vanquished.

mpreh *f.k.* 1. *(thikën)* to whet, to sharpen, to grind (a knife); *(në gur)* to hone. 2. *(lapsin)* to point (the pencil). 3. *fig. (vigjilencën)* to sharpen (one's vigilance).

mpréhës,-i *m.sh.* – grinder; sharpener, hone.

mpréhës,-e *mb.* grinding.

mpréhës/e,-ja *f.sh.* -e *(lapsash)* pencil-sharpener.

mpréhj/e,-a *f.* sharpening, grinding, whetting.

mpréht/ë(i,e) *mb.* 1, sharp pointed. 2. *(tingull)* high-pitched, acute. 3. *(dhimbje)* acute, sharp, keen, piercing; **dhimbje e mprehtë:** keen pain. 4. *fig. (mendje)* acute, sharp, keen; *(njeri)* sharp-witted, shrewd, sagacious.

mprehtësí,-a *f.* 1. sharpness, acuteness. 2. *fig.* shrewdness, sagacity.

mrekullí,-a *f.sh.* – miracle, marvel, prodigy; **për mrekulli:** mira-culously; **bëj një mrekulli:** to work a miracle.

mrekullísht *ndajf.* 1. to a miracle, miraculously, marvelously, prodigiously. 2. admirably, wonderfully.

mrekullúesh/ëm(i),-me(e) *mb.* prodigious, miraculous, marvelous, wonderful.

mu *ndajf.* just, exactly; **mu në qendër:** just at the centre.

múa *p.v.* me, to me (the dative case and the accusative case of the pers. pron. **unë**); **na ftoi për darkë mua dhe tíme shoqe:** he invited my wife and me to dinner; **ma dha mua:** he gave it to me. – *Lok.* **sa për mua:** as for me.

múaj,-i *m.sh.* – month; **në muaj:** a month, per month; **të muajit në vazhdim, të këtij muaji:** of this month; **muaj për muaj:** from month to month, month by (after) month; **në fund të muajit:** by the end of the month; **tërë muajin:** all month, for the whole month.

mugëllón *f.jk.* to darken, to get dark.

múgët (të),-it(të) *as.* twilight; **ndaj të mugëtit:** at nightfall, at twilight.

mugëtír/ë,-a *f.* twilight, nightfall.

mugullón *f.jk. (pema)* to bud (a tree).

muhabét,-i *m.sh.* -e *vjet.* talk, conversation.

muhalebí,-a *f.* creammilk.

muhamedán,-i *m.sh.* -ë muham-medan, moslem.

muhaxhír,-i *m.sh.* -ë refugee.

mujór,-e *mb.* monthly; **revistë mujore:** monthly, monthly magazine, monthly periodical; **pagë mujore:** month's pay, month's wage.

mullár,-i *m.sh.* -ë stack, cock (of hay); *(bari)* haycock, hayrick, haystock; *(keshte)* straw-stack. **múllëz,-a** *f. anat.* maw (of animals). **mullí,-ri** *m.sh.* -nj 1. mill; *(me erë)* wind-mill; *(me ujë)* water-mill; *(drithi)* corn-mill; **gur mulliri** *(mokër):* millstone; **rrotë mulliri:** mill wheel. 2. *(kafeje):* coffe--mill. 3. *(revoleje)* cyiinder of a pistol. **mullibárdh/ë,-a** *f.sh.* -a *zool.* thrush. **mullís,-i** *m.sh.* -ë miller. **múmi/e,-a** *f.sh.* -e mummy. **mund** *f.jv.* (defective verb). 1. can, could, to be able to; **mund të të ndihmojmë:** we can help you; **nuk mund ta bëj këtë punë:** I wont be able to do this work; **nuk mund:** cannot, can't; **nuk munda:** I could not; **ai ˏnuk mund të vijë sepse bie shi:** he cannot come because it is raining. 2. can, may, could, be able, to be possible; **ai mund të vijë në çdo çast:** he may be here at any moment. 3. may, might; **mund të keni të drejtë:** you may be right; **mund edhe ta gjesh në shtëpi:** you may perhaps find him at home; **mund ta kem thënë këtë, por s'më kujtohet:** I may have said so, but I don't remember. 4. *(kam leje)* may, can, might, to be allowed (permitted); **mund të dal pak jashtë?** may I go out for a moment? 5. *(duhet, në fjali mohuese)* must, might, should; **roja nuk mund të largohet nga vendi:** the sentry must not leave his post. 6. **kush mund të jetë?** who can it be? — **mund** *f.k.* to vanquish, to defeat, to beat (the enemy). — **mundem**

f.jv. 1. can; **nuk mundem:** I cannot. 2. *(në luftë)* to be defeated (in a battle), to be vanquished. 3. *(mundem në lojë)* to be beaten (in a game). 4. *(mundem me dikë)* to wrestle (with someone). 5. **mundet** perhaps, may be, it's possible, could be; **mundet që nuk ma di emrin:** he may not know my name; **do të vish?** — **mundet:** will you come? — may be. **mund,-i** *m.* shih **mundim**. **múndës,-i** *m.sh.* — *sport.* wrestler. **mundësí,-a** *f.sh.* — 1. possibility; probability; **i jap mundësi dikujt të bëjë diçka:** to enable someone to do something. 2. means, power; **është brenda mundësive të mia:** it is within my power to. **mundësísht** *ndajf.* if possible. **mundím,-i** *m.sh.*-e fatigue, exertion, hardship, effort, pain; **me mundim:** hardly; **marr mundimin të bëj diçka:** to take the trouble of doing something; **nuk ia-vlen mundimi:** it isn't worth -while. **mundímsh/ëm(i),-me(e)** *mb.* tiring, laborous, trying. **múndj/e,-a** *f. sport.* wrestling. **mundój** *f.k.* 1. to harass, to tire out. 2. to torture, to torment. — **mundohem** *f.jv.* 1. *(në punë)* to toil, to sweat, to work hard. 2. *(të bëj diçka)* to strive, to attempt, to make efforts (to do something). **múndsh/ëm (i),-me(e)** *mb.* possible, probable. **múndur (i,e)** *mb.* 1. vanquished. 2. possible; **s'është e mundur:** it is not possible; **bëj ç'është e mundur:** to do one's utmost, to exert every effort, to try one's best; **sa më shpejt që** të jetë e mundur: as soon as possible, as quick as possible.

mungés/ë,-a *f.sh.*-a 1. want, lack; *(ushqimesh)* want, scarcity, lack, penury (of food); *(mallrash)* lack, want (of goods); për mungesë kohe: for lack of time. 2. *(ndërprerje)* failure, breakdown; mungesë korrenti: power failure. 3. absence; në mungesën time: in my absence; mungesë takti: tactlessness; mungesë edukate: ill-breeding. — ndiej mungesën e dikujt: to miss someone; i dënuar në mungesë: condemned in contumacy.

mungój *f.jk* 1. to be absent; to be away; kush mungon sot? who is absent today? asnjeri nuk mungon: nobody is absent. 2. to be lacking, to be wanting, to be short of; mungon folja: the verb is missing; asgjë nuk më mungon: to want for nothing; më mungon guximi (për të bërë diçka): to lack (not to have) the courage (to do something).

munición,-i *m.sh.* -e ammunition, munitions.

múnx/ë,-a *m.sh.* -a disparagement with the palm of the hand; jap munxat: to disparage with the palm of the hand.

mur,-i *m.sh.* -e wall; mur i ulët: parapet; mur i përbashkët: party-wall, middlewall; mbyllem brenda katër mureve: to shut oneself up; ngre një mur: to build a wall; rrethoj me mur: to enclose with a wall. — *Lok.* vë dikë me shpatulla në mur: to drive (to push) someone to the wall; nuk i bihet murit me kokë: one can't bash (run) one's head against a brick wall. — *Prov.*

edhe muret kanë veshë: walls have ears.

muratór,-i *m.sh.* -ë masón, bricklayer.

muratúr/ë,-a *f.* masonry, brickwork, stonework.

murg,-u *m.sh.* murgj monk, friar.

murgésh/ë,-a *f.sh.* -a nun.

múrm/ë(i),-e(e) *mb.* grey-dark, dun.

murmurít *f.jk.* to murmur, to mumble, to grumble.

murmurítj/e,-a *f.* murmur, grumble.

murój *f.k.* to wall (up).

murtáj/ë,-a *f. mjek.* pest, plague; murtaja e bagëtive: rinderpest, cattle plague.

murríz,-i *m.sh.* -a *bot.* whites thorn, hawthorn.

murlán,-i *m.* ice-wind; fryn murlani: it blows ice-wind, it blows frozen wind.

musánd/ër,-ra *f.sh.* -ra built-In cupboard, wall cupboard.

músku/l,-li *m.sh.* -j *anat.* muscle; muskul i krahut: biceps; me muskuj: muscled, brawny, muscular.

muskulatúr/ë,-a *f. anat.* musculature.

muskulór,-e *mb.* muscular; ind muskulor: muscular tissue.

muslúk,-u *m.sh.* -ë tinned vessel provided with a tap.

musták,-u *m.* 1. mustache, moustache. 2. *zool.* gudgeon.

mustáqe,-t *f.sh.* mustaches, moustaches; *(mustaqet e maces)* whiskers (of a cat).—*Lok.* zihem për mustaqet e Çelos: to quarrel for trifles.

mustárd/ë,-a *f.* mustard.

mushamá,-ja *f.* 1. *(shiu)* waterproof, raincoat. 2. oilcloth. 3. *(për mbulesën e makinave etj.)* tilt (for motor-car, etc); mbuloj me mushama një makinë:

to tilt a motor-car. 4. *(dysheme-je)* oilcloth, linoleum. 5. *(ta-voline)* mat, table mat.

mushíc/ë,-a *f.sh.* -a *zool.* shih **mushkonjë.**

mushk,-u *m.sh.* **mushq** *zool.* he-mule.

múshk/ë,-a *f.sh.* -a *zool.* mule.

mushkërí,-a *f.sh.* – *anat.* lung, lungs; **mbush mushkëritë me ajër:** to draw air into the lungs, to inhale.

mushkónj/ë,-a *f.sh.* -a *zool.* mos-quito.

mushllínz/ë,-a *f. bot.* convol-vulus.

mushmóll/ë,-a *f.sh.* -a *bot. (fruti)* medlar; *(pema)* medlar tree.

musht,-i *m.* must (of wine), new wine; *(molle)* cider.

mut,-i *m.* dreg, excrement.

muzé,-u *m.sh.* – museum.

múz/ë,-a *f.sh.* -a muse.

muz/g,-gu *m.sh.* – **gje** twilight, dusk, afterflow; **në muzg:** in the twilight, at dusk.

muzikánt,-i *m.sh.* -ë musician.

muzík/ë,-a *f.* 1. music; **notë muzike:** musical note. 2. *(goje)* harmonica, mouth organ.

muzikór,-e *mb.* musical: **vegël muzikore:** musical instrument.

myftí,-u *m.sh.* -j mufti.

myhýr,-l *m.sh.* -ë *vjet.* small seal with the initials of the name and surname.

myk,-u *m.sh.* **myqe** mold, mould.

mýkem *f.jv.* to go mouldy, to go musty; **u myk buka:** the bread has gone mouldy.

mýkur (i,e) *mb.* 1. mouldy, cove-red with mould, fusty, musty; **bukë e mykur:** musty bread. 2. *fig.* fusty, musty; **njeri me mendime të mykura:** a man with musty ideas.

mynxýr/ë,-a *f.sh.* -a calamity, di-saster.

mynxyrósur (i,e) *mb.* struck by a calamity.

mysafír,-i *m.sh.* -ë *vjet.* guest, host, visitor; **pres e përcjell mysa-firë:** to keep open house.

myslimán,-i *m.sh.* -ë Mussulman, Moslem.

myslimán,-e *mb.* islamic; **bota myslimane:** islamic world, islam world.

myslimaníz/ëm,-mi *m.* islamism·

mysh/k,-ku *m.sh.* -qe 1. moss· 2. musk, scent; **sapun myshku:** odoriferous soap, perfumed soap; **rrush myshk:** muscatel grapes.

myshterí,-u *m.sh.* -nj *vjet.* clien t, customer, purchaser.

N

n, N (letter of the Albanian alpha-bet) n, N.

na *p.v.* (pers. pron. of the first person plural) us, to us; **ai na**

foli: he spoke to us; **na thanë se:** they told us that.

na *pasth., pj.* takel **na këtë libër:** take this book.

nacionál,-e *mb.* national.
nacionalíst,-i *m.sh.* -ë nationalist
nacionalíst,-e *mb.* nationalist.
nacionalíz/ëm,-mi *m.* nationalism.
nacionalizój *f.k.* to nationalize. − nacionalizohet *f.jv.* to be nationalized.
nafór/ë,-a *f. fet.* consecrated bread.
naftalín/ë,-a naphtalene.
náft/ë,-a *f.* naphtha, oil; *(e papastruar)* crude oil; **pus nafte:** oil-well.
naftësjéllës,-i *m.sh.* -a pipeline.
nagáç/e,-ja *f.sh.* -e hatchet.
naív,-e *mb.* naive, ingenuous, artless.
naivitét,-i *m.* naivety, ingenuousness.
nakár,-i *m.* envy, grudge.
nakatós *f.k.* to mingle. − **nakatosem** *f.jv.* to be mingled; **nakatosem në punët e të tjerëve:** to meddle in the affairs of others.
nallán/e,-ja *f.sh.* -e wooden slippers, clog, sabot.
nallbán,-i *m.sh.* -ë farrier, blacksmith.
nam-i *m.* renown, fame, reputation, repute; **me nam të keq:** of ill reputation (repute); **me nam të mirë:** of good renown (reputation). − *Lok.* **më del nami:** to become famous; **jam me nam:** to have a good reputation, to be famous (renowned); **zhdukem pa nam e pa nishan:** to disappear without leaving a trace.
namatís *f.jk.* to conjure.
namatísj/e,-a *f.* Incantation.
namús,-i *m.* self-respect, dignity.
namuslí, namusqar,-e *mb.* dignified.

nanurís *f.jk* to lull, to lull to sleep.
náp/ë,-a *f.sh.* -a fine cambric.
napolón,-i *m.sh.* -a napoleon.
narcís,-i *m. bot.* narcissus.
nargjilé,-ja *f.sh.* -e narghile.
narkomán,-i *m.sh.* -ë dope-fiend, drug addict, toxicomaniac.
narkotík,-e *mb.* narcotic.
narkotík,-u *m.sh.* -ë narcotic.
narkóz/ë,-a *f. mjek.* narcosis.
nát/ë,-a *f.sh.* **netë** night; **çdo natë:** every night; **gjatë natës:** overnight, at night; **këtë natë:** tonight; **natë e ditë:** night and day; **këmishë nate:** night-gown; **punë nate:** night work; **shkollë nate:** night school; **roje nate:** night-watch; **që me natë:** early in the morning; **natën e mirë** good night; **natën vonë:** late at night; **tërë natën:** all night long.
nátën *ndajf.* at night, by night, nightly.
natyrál,-e *mb.* shih **natyror.**
natyralíst,-i *m.sh.* -ë naturalist.
natyralíz/ëm,-mi *m.* naturalism.
natýr/ë,-a *f.* 1, nature; **dukuri të natyrës:** natural phenomena; **histori natyre:** natural history; **prej natyre:** by nature; **kundër natyrës:** against nature; **të kësaj natyre:** of this nature, of this kind. 2. nature, character, disposition. 3. nature, type, kind; **kjo ka një natyrë krejt të ndryshme:** this is quite a dfiferent kind; **paguaj në natyrë:** to pay in kind.
natyrisht *ndajf.* of course, naturally.
natyrór,-e *mb.* natural; **pasuri natyrore:** natural resources.
natýrsh/ëm (i),-me(e) *mb.* natural; **është e natyrshme:** it is natural.
návllo,-ja *f. vjet.* fare, freight.
náze,-t *f.sh.* 1. fastidiousness.

particularity; pickiness; **mos bëj kaq naze**: don't be so particular. 2. coquetry.

nazeli,-e *mb*. fastidious, picky, choosy, hard to please; finicky, fussy; **fëmijë nazeli**: hard-to-please child; **është nazeli në të ngrënë**: he is very fussy about his food.

nazeqár,-e *mb*. shih **nazeli**.

ndaj *f.k*. 1. to part, to divide; to apportion; *(në shumë pjesë)* to divide into parts; **ndaj për gjysmë**: to divide into two equal parts, to halve; *(në pjesë të barabarta)* to apportion; **ndaj gëzimet dhe hidhërimet**: to share joys and sorrows. 2. to separate, to dissociate. 3. *(me forcë)* to sever, to sunder. 4. *(gruan, burrin)* to divorce (the wife, the husband). 5. *(ushqime)* to share; to distribute, to deal (meals), nutriments). 6. *(fitimet)* to allot, to share (profits). 7. *(letrat e lojës)* to deal the cards. 8. *fig*. to separate; **ndaj shapin nga sheqeri**: to separate the husk from the grain; to separate the sheep from the goats. – **ndahem** *f.jv*. 1. *(nga dikush)* to part, to depart, to take leave of. 2. *(nga gruaja, burri)* to divorce.

ndaj *paraf*. 1. by,at; **ndaj të gdhirë**: by the morning; **ndaj të ngrysur**: at dusk, at nightfall. 2. to; **me respekt ndaj**: with regard to. 3. towards; **dashuria ndaj prindërve**: the love towards the parents; **duhet të tregohemi të bindur ndaj prindërve**: we must show obedience towards our parents.

ndajfólj/e,-a *f.sh*. -e *gram*. adverb.

ndajfoljór,-e *mb*. adverbial; **shpre-**

hje ndajfoljore: adverbial phrase.

ndajnatëhérë *ndajf*. at nightfall.

ndajshtím,-i *m.sh*. -e *gram*. apposition.

ndal. *f.k*. 1. to stop; **ndal në vend**: to stop short; to halt, to bring to a halt (stop); **ndal kalin**: to pull up the horse. 2. to stop, to break off, to discontinue; **ndal lojën**: to stop playing. 3. to stop, to hold, to keep; **e ndal dikë për drekë**: to keep someone to dinner. 4. *(ndal një shumë nga rroga)* to stop the cost of something, to cut off someone with a sum of money. – **ndalem** *f.jv*. 1. to stop, to come to a stop, to halt; **u ndal përpara vitrinës**: he stopped in front of the shop-window. 2. *(makina etj.)* to pull up, to come to a stop, to stop, to come to rest; **treni ndalet dhjetë minuta**: the train stops ten minutes. 3. to stop, to pause; **fliste pa u ndalur**: he talked on and on and never stopped. 4. to stop oneself, to hold back.

ndalés/ë,-a *f.sh*. -a 1. stop, halt, stay; **bëjmë një ndalesë të shkurtër**: let's have a short stop; **pa ndalesë**: non-stop. 2. *(vend)* stop; **takohemi te ndalesa e autobuzit**: meet you at the bus-stop.

ndalím,-i *m*. 1. forbiddance, prohibition; **ndalim qarkullimi**: no thoroughfare. 2. cessation, ceasing.

ndalój *f.k*. 1. to forbid, to prohibit, to inhibit, to interdict. 2. to cease, to discontinue. 3. to retain, to withhold. 4. to hold back, to impede. 5. to rest, to pause. – **ndalohet'** *f.jv*. it is forbidden; **ndalohet hyrja l** for-

bidden entrance! **ndalohet du-hani** no smoking!
ndalúar (i,e) *mb.* forbidden; prohibited; **është e ndaluar të:** it is forbidden to.
ndalúes,-e *mb.* prohibitive; **masa ndaluese:** prohibitive measures.
ndánë *paraf.* aside, near, close to, by.
ndárë (i,e) *mb.* divided, separated; **grua e ndarë:** divorced woman.
ndár/ë(e),-a(e) *f.sh.* **-a (të)** *(në tren)* compartment; *(e një dollapi)* shelf.
ndárës,-i *m.sh.* – separator.
ndárës,-e *mb.* separatory.
ndárj/e,-a *f.* 1. divison; **ndarje e punës:** division of labour; **ndarje e punëve (midis punëtorëve etj.):** allotment of work, work distribution. 2. separation. 3. *(e gruas nga burri)* divorce, break. 4. *(e tokës)* division, allotment, apportionment (of the land). 5. *(e pasurisë)* separation, partition (of the property). 6. *(e fitimeve)* sharing (of profits). 7. *(çmimesh)* (prize–giving, awarding (of prizes). 8. *(e flokëve)* parting (of hair). 9. *(e letrave në lojë)* deal of cards. 10. *(e një dhome, e një dollapi)* compartment. 11. *(nga një shok etj.)* leave–taking, departure.
ndásh/ëm(i),-me(e) *mb.* divisible, separable.
ndej *f.k. (rrobat)* to hang (clothes).
ndénjës/e,-a *f.sh.* **-e** seat, chair, stool.
ndénjj/e,-a *f.* sitting; **dhoma e ndenjjes:** sitting-room.
ndénjur (i,e) *mb.* stagnant; **ujë i ndenjur:** stagnant water; **që rri zakonisht ndenjur:** sedentary; **rri ndenjur:** to sit, to be seated.
nder,-i *m.* 1. honour; **mbroj nderin:** to defend one's ho-

nour; **luhet me nderin e tij:** his honour is at stake; **anëtar nderi,** honorary member; **këshilltar nderi:** honorary counselor; **titull nderi:** honorary title; **kam nderin të:** to have the honour to: **fjalë e nderit:** word of honour. 2. favour; **më bëj një nder:** do me a favour. – *Lok.* **për nder:** upon my honour, upon my life; **për nder të:** in honour of; **me nder jush:** saving your presence.
ndérë (i,e) 1. stretched out, extended. 2. taut, tight; **litar i nderë:** taut rope. 3. *fig.* tense; **marrëdhënie të ndera:** tense relations.
nderím.-i *m.sh.* **-e** 1. honour, respect, homage, deference, reverence; **nderimet e mia:** my homages. my civilities; **me nderime** *(në fund të një letre)i* with respect.
nderój *f.k.* 1. *(dikë)* to honour, to hold in honour; **kjo nuk ju nderon:** it does not do you any credit. 2. to salute. – **nderohem** *f.jv.* to be honoured.
ndérsh/ëm (i), -me(e) *mb.* 1. honest; **njeri i ndershëm:** honest person. 2. upright, just; **gjykatës i ndershëm:** upright (just) judge.
ndershmërí,-a *f.* honour, honesty, probity, integrity, uprightness.
ndershmërísht *ndajf.* honourably.
ndértë (i,e) *mb.* honest, honourable, respectable.
nderúar (i,e) *mb.* honoured, respected; **njeri i nderuar:** honourable person; **shumë i nderuar:** right honourable.
ndesh *f.k.* 1. to encounter, to meet; **ndesh dikë:** to encounter, to meet someone. 2. **ndesh në një vështirësi:** to be faced with a difficulty, to be in presence of

a difficulty. – **ndeshem** *f.jv.* 1. to meet, to fall in, to run into, tc come across. 2. **ndeshem me dikë, me diçka:** to meet with, to run up against. 3. to fight. 4. to bump (to run) into each other. **ndéshj/e,-a** *f.sh.* -e 1. collision. 2. *sport.* match; competition; **ndeshje miqësore:** a friendly match. 3. *(ushtrish)* encounter. **ndez** *f.k.* (p.t.. **ndeza,** p.p. **ndezur)** 1. to light; **ndez zjarrin:** to light the fire, to ignite, to kindle the fire; **ndez një cigare:** to light a cigarette. 2. *(luftën)* to unleash. – **ndizem** *f.jv.* to take fire, to flare up, to fire up. **ndézës,-e** *mb.* incendiary. **ndézj/e,-a** *f.* ignition, kindling, inflamation; **me ndezje automatike:** self-winding. **ndézsh/ëm(i),-me(e)** *mb.* inflammable, ignitible. **ndézur(i,e)** *mb.* 1. alight, lighted burning. 2. *(llampë)* on, turned on, switched on; **radioja është e ndezur:** the radio is on. 3. on, running; **motor i ndezur:** engine running. 4. *(ngjyrë)* vivid, bright. **ndër** *paraf.* 1. among, amongst; **ndër të tjera:** among others. 2. in; **kam ndër mend të:** I have in mind to; **ndër ne:** in our country, in my hometown. **ndër** *parashtesë* (prefix corresponding in English to the word «inter» and «in»). **ndërgjégj/e,-ja** *f.* conscience; **me ndërgjegje të pastër:** with a clear conscience; **me ndërgjegje të plotë:** concientiously; **në ndërgjegjen e tij:** in his conscience; **njeri pa ndërgjegje:** man of no scruples; **brejtje e ndërgjegjes:** remorse, qualm.

ndërgjégjsh/ëm(i,)-me(e) conscientious. **ndërgjýqës,-i** *m.sh.* – pleader. **ndërhýj** *f.jk.* to intervene, to interfere, to intercede, to come between, to go between; *(për pajtim)* to mediate. **ndërhýrës,-i** *m.sh.* mediator, go-between, intercessor. **ndërhýrj/e,-a** *f.sh.* -e intervention, interference, intercession, interposition; *(për pajtim)* mediation. (kirurgjikale) surgiceli intervention. **ndërkáq** *ndajf.* meanwhile, meantime, in this time. **ndërkóhë** *ndajf.* upon this, thereupon, whereat, in this time, in the meanwhile. **ndërkombëtár,-e** *mb.* international. **ndërlídh** *f.k.* to contact, to establish connection. – **ndërlidhem** *f.jv.* to get in touch (with). **ndërlídhës,-i** *m.sh.* – communicator. **ndërlidhës,-e** *mb.* comunicative. **ndërlídhj/e,-a** *f.* communication, intercommunication. **ndërlikím,-i** *m.* complication. **ndërlikój** *f.k.* to complicate. – – **ndërlikohet** *f.jv.* to be complicated. **ndërluftúes,-e** *mb.* belligerent. **ndërmárr** *f.k.* to undertake. **ndërmárrj/e,-a** *f.sh.* -e enterprise, undertaking. **ndërmjét** *paraf.* 1. between; amid; among; **rrinte ndërmjet dy shokëve:** he was sitting between two friends. 2. of, among; **më i riu ndërmjet tyre:** the youngest of them; **ndërmjet të tjerash:** among other things. **ndërmjét/ëm(i),-me(e)** *mb.* intermediate, intermediary. **ndërmjétës,-i** *m.sh.* – mediator,

Intercessor, middleman, go-between.

ndërmjetësí,-a *f.* intermediation, mediation, interposition, intercession.

ndërmjetësój *f.jk.* to interpose, to mediate, to intercede.

ndërprérë (i,e) *mb.* intermitted, interrupted; **rrymë e ndërprerë:** intermittent current, dis-- continued current.

ndërprérës,-i *m.sh.* — interruptor.

ndërprérj/e,-a *f.sh.* -e 1, interruption, intermittence, intermission; **pa ndërprerje:** without interruption, uninterruptedly, continuing, in permanence; **punë pa ndërprerje:** uninterrupted work. 2. *gjeom.* intersection.

ndërprés *f.k.* 1. to interrupt, to intermit, to discontinue; **ndërpres mësimin:** to suspend the lesson. 2. *gjeom.* to intersect. — **ndërpritem** *f.jv.* to be interrupted.

ndërsá *lidh.* 1, while, whilst, as, when; **ndërsa ishin duke shkuar në shtëpi:** as they were going home, on their way home. 2. whereas, while, whilst; **ai është i kujdesshëm, ndërsa i vëllai është kokëkrisur:** he is cautious, while his brother is rash.

ndërséj *f.k.* 1. to instigate, to incite. 2. *(qenin)* to unleash (a dog). — **ndërsehem** *f.jv.* 1. to be incited. 2. *(qeni)* to be unleashed.

ndërtés/ë,-a *f.sh.* -a building.

ndërtím,-i *m.sh.* -e 1. building, construction; **ndërtimi i socializmit:** the building of socialism. 2. building; **ndërtime të reja:** new buildings.

ndërtimtár,-e *mb.* constructive.

ndërtój *f.k.* to build, to construct; **ndërtojmë socializmin:** to build socialism. — **ndërtohet** *f.jv.* to be built (constructed).

ndërtúes,-i *m.sh.* — *(ndërtesash)* builder; *(makinash)* constructor. (i keq) jerrybuilder

ndërzéj *f.k.* to pair off, to couple, to copulate (animals).

ndërzím,-i *m.* copulation, coupling (of animals).

ndërrésa-t *f.sh.* linen, underclothes, underwear, undergarments, underclothing; *(për fëmijë)* baby linen.

ndërrím,-i *m.* 1. change; **pjesë ndërrimi:** spare parts. 2. exchange, change (of money). 3. *(turni, roje)* shift (of work, of guard). 4. *(feje)* proselytism. 5. *(i qimes së kafshëve, i pendëve të zogjve)* molt, moult. 6. *(shtëpie)* removal, change (of residence).

ndërrój *f.k.* 1. to change; **ndërroj adresë:** to change one's address. 2. to change, to exchange; **ndërroj me diçka:** to exchange one thing for another, to change for something. 3. *(monedhë)* to change (money). 4. *(fenë)* to proselytize. 5. *(mendje)* to change one's mind, to alter one's mind. 6. *(shtëpi)* to remove, to move house. 7. *fig.* **ndërroj jetë:** to die. 8. *(qimet kafsha, pendët shpendi)* to molt, to moult, to cast the feathers (hair, skin). 9. (drejtim) — to veer Lok. **ujku qimen ndërron, huqin s'e harron:** can the leopard change his spots?. — **ndërrohem** *f.jv.* to dress in fresh clothes, to dress clean clothes, to change clothes or underclothes.

ndërrúesh/ëm(i),-me(e) *mb.* 1. variable; changeable; **kohë e ndërrueshme:** changeable weather. 2. convertible.

ndëshkím,-i *m.sh.* -e punishment, chastisement, castigation.

ndëshkimór,-e *mb.* 1. punitive; **ekspeditë ndëshkimore:** punitive expedition. 2. disciplinary: **masa ndëshkimore:** disciplinary measures.
ndëshkój *f.k.* 1. to punish, to chastise, to castigate. 2. *sport.* to penalize. 3. *drejt.* to condemn. — **ndëshkohem** *f.jv.* to be punished.
ndëshkúesh/ëm(i),-me(e) *mb.* punishable.
ndíej *f.k.* 1. to feel; **ndiej urrejtje:** to be filled with hate (hatred); **ndiej efektin e:** to feel the effect of. **ndihem më mirë:** to feel better. 2. to be heard; **nuk ndihem fare:** not to make the slightest noise; **pa u ndier:** noiselessly.
ndíhm/ë,-a *f.sh.* -a 1. help, aid, assistance; **thërres për ndihmë:** to call for help: **shkoj për ndihmë:** to go to someone's aid; **i vij në ndihmë dikujt:** to come to someone's assistance; **me ndihmën e:** with the help of; **me ndihmën tuaj:** with your help; **pa ndihmë:** helpless; **ndihmël** help! **i jap ndihmë dikujt:** to give assistance to someone: **kërkoj ndihmën e dikujt:** to ask someone for help. 2. subsidy; **mbledh ndihma:** to collect subsidies; **ndihmë në të holla:** pecuniary aid. 3. **ndihmë mjekësore:** medical attendance; **ndihmë e shpejtë:** first aid, emergency aid.
ndíhmës,-i *m.sh.* — assistant, helper, helpmate.
ndíhmës,-e *mb.* 1. auxiliary. 2. ancillary, accessory, subsidiary; **materiale ndihmëse:** auxiliary materials. 3. *gram.* **folje ndihmëse:** auxiliary verb.
ndihmësgjyqtár,-i *m.sh.* -ë deputy judge.

ndihmësmjék,-u *m.sh.* -ë assistant doctor.
ndihmësmuratór,-i *m.sh.* -ë assistant mason.
ndihmój *f.k.* to help, to aid; to assist; **të ndihmojmë shokushokun:** we must help one another; **nuk mund ta ndihmoj:** I cannot help him; **ndihmoj me të holla:** to help pecuniarily; **ndihmoj moralisht dikë:** to give someone moral support, to encourage someone.
ndijím,-i *m.sh.* -e sensation.
ndikím,-i *m.sh.* -e influence.
ndikój *f.k.* to influence, to exert influence on. — **ndikohem** *f.jv.* to be influenced.
ndikúes,-e *mb.* influential.
ndjej *f.k.* to forgive, to pardon; **më ndjel** pardon me!, excuse me!
ndjek *f.k.* (p.t. **ndoqa,** p.p. **ndjekur**) 1. to follow; **më ndiqni nga larg:** follow me at a distance. 2. to shadow, to follow; **e ndiqnin dy policë:** two policemen shadowed him. 3. *(një rrugë)* to follow, to proceed along 4. to follow, to keep to, to stick to; **ndjek këshillat e mjekut:** to follow the doctor's advice. 5. *(shkollën)* to attend (the school). 6. *fig. (situatën)* to keep up with (the situation). 7. **ndjek shembullin e dikujt:** to follow someone's example; **ndjek rrugën e drejtë:** to pursue the right course. — **ndiqem** *f.jv.* to be pursued, to be followed.
ndjékës,-i *m.sh.* — 1. pursuer. 2. follower 3. disciple.
ndjékj/e,-a *f.* 1. pursuit. 2. following. 3. *(ligjore)* prosecution.
ndjell *f.k.* (p.t. **ndolla,** p.p. **ndjellë**) 1. *(pula zogjtë)* to cluck, to chuck (of a hen). 2. *(qenin)*

to call (a dog), to whistle (to a dog). 3. *fig. (një fatkeqësi)* to forebode (a disaster).

ndjéllj/e,-a *f.* 1. *(e pulave)* cluck, chuck. 2. *(fatkeqësie)* foreboding (of a disaster).

ndjénj/ë,-a *f.sh.* -a feeling, passion, sentiment; **me ndjenja:** feelingly, with feeling; **pa ndjenja:** senseless, unfeelingly.

ndjérë (i,e) *mb.* late.

ndjés/ë,-a *f.* forgiveness, pardon, remission; **lyp, kërkoj ndjesë:** to beg pardon.

ndjesí,-a *f.sh.* – sensation, feeling.

ndjésh/ëm(i),-me(e) *mb.* sensible, sensitive, sentimental; **njeri i ndjeshëm:** sensible (susceptible) person.

ndjeshmërí,-a *f.* sensibility, sensitivity, sensitiveness, susceptibility.

ndodh *f.jk.* 1. to happen, to occur, to befall, to come to pass; **kur ndodhi kjo?** when did it happen? **kjo ndodhi:** it happened; **çfarë ndodhi në nëntor?** what happened in November? **që mund të ndodhë, që ka mundësi të ndodhë:** plausible; **sido që të ndodhë:** happen what may. 2. to be; **rastësisht ndodha atje:** I happened to be there. 3. to happen, to befall; **çfarë i ndodhi?** what befell him? **le të ndodhë ç'të ndodhë!** come what may! **kjo ndodhi për shkak se:** this happened because. – **ndodhem** *f.jv.* 1. to be present, to be; **atë kohë ndodhesha në Durrës:** at that time I was at Durrës. 2. to be, to be located, to be situated, to lie, to stand; **ku ndodhet shtëpia?** where is the house?

ndodhí,-a *f.sh.* – happening, occurence, incident.

ndófta *ndajf.* perhaps, possibly, maybe.

ndokújt *p. pk.* to somebody; **kjo i përket ndokujt:** it belongs to somebody (shih **ndokush**).

ndokúnd *ndajf.* somewhere, anywhere; **e ke parë ndokund?** have you seen him anywhere?

ndokúsh *p.pk.* somebody, anybody, anyone; **ka ndokush pyetje?** has anyone something to ask?

ndónëse *lidh.* though.

ndonjë *p.pk.* 1. any, some; **në ndonjë vend:** somewhere; **më huaj ndonjë libër:** lend me some book; **do të vij të të takoj ndonjë ditë:** I'll come and see you some day. 2. any; **ke ndonjë cigare?** have you any cigarettes? **a do ndonjë frutë?** do you want some fruit? 3. a; **a ka ndonjë mjek?** is there a doctor?

ndonjëhérë *ndajf.* 1. sometimes; **ndonjëherë s'e marr dot vesh:** sometimes I can't understand him. 2. never; **s'e kam parë ndonjëherë:** I' ve never seen him before.

ndonjëri *p.pk.* 1. anybody, anyone; **do të vijë ndonjëri me mua?** is anybody coming with me? **ndonjëri nga ata (prej tyre):** anyone of them. 2. somebody, someone; **po të pyeti ndonjëri, ç'do t'i thuash?** if somebody asks you, what are you going to say?

ndopák *ndajf.* a few, a little.

ndórmë (i,e) *mb.* unleavened; **bukë e ndormë:** unleavened bread.

ndóshta *ndajf.* shih **ndofta**.

ndot *f.k.* to dirty, to soil, to pollute, to foul, to grime, to make dirty; *(me baltë)* to splash, to bespatter. – **ndotem** *f.jv.* to get dirty.

ndot *ndajf.* disgust; **më vjen ndot:** I feel disgust (nausea).
ndótj/e,-a *f.* dirtiness, pollution
ndótë (i,e) *mb.* dirty, polluted, grimy; **ujëra të ndota:** polluted waters.
ndrag *f.k.* to dirty, to soil. — **ndragem** *f.jv.* to get dirty.
ndreq *f.k.* to mend, to repair, to adjust; *(një gabim)* to correct (a mistake); *(një aparat)* to repair (an apparatus); *(këpucët)* to mend, to repair (shoes). — **ndreqem** *f.jv.* 1. to correct oneself. 2. *(koha etj.)* to improve; **po ndreqet koha:** the weather is picking up.
ndréqj/e,-a *f.* repair, adjustment; *(gabimesh)* correction (of mistakes); *(këpucësh)* repairing, mending; *(rrobash)* arrangement (of clothes); *(makine)* adjustment (of a machine); *(e një ndërtese)* restoration (of a building).
ndriçím,-i *m.* 1. *(të ndriçuarit)* lighting, illumination. 2. *fig.* illumination.
ndriçój *f.k.* 1. to lighten, to illuminate. 2. *fig. (mendjen)* to enlighten, to illuminate. — **ndriçohem** *f.jv.* to be enlightened
ndricues,-e *mb.* luminous, illuminating, illuminative; **gaz ndricues:** illuminating gas.
ndríkull,-a *f.sh.* **-a** godmother.
ndrit *f.jk.* to shine, to brighten, to sparkle, to glitter, to gleam; **asaj i ndrisnin sytë:** her eyes were shining; *(yjtë)* to twinkle, to shine. — *Lok.* **e ndrite!** *(ironi)* well done! (ironically).
ndrítsh/ëm(i),-me(e) *mb.* bright shining, brilliant.
ndrítur (i,e) *mb.* bright; **sy të ndritur:** bright eyes.
ndrydh *f.k.* 1. to sprain; **ndrydh këmbën:** to sprain one's ankle.

2. *fig. (ndjenjat etj.)* to suppress, to subdue (one's feelings). — **ndrydhem** *f.jv.* to withdraw into oneself; to become restrained (repressed).
ndrýdhj/e,-a *f.* 1. *(e këmbës)* sprain (of an ankle). 2. *fig. (e ndjenjave)* suppression (of feelings).
ndryj *f.k.* to lock up, to keep under lock and key. — **ndryhem** *f.jv.* to shut oneself up.
ndrýmj/e,-a *f.* lock-up.
ndrys *f.k.* to massage.
ndrýshe *ndajf.* 1. otherwise, differently, in a different manner (way), in another manner; **unë do të isha sjellë ndryshe:** I should have behaved differently; **s'bëjmë dot ndryshe:** we cannot act otherwise; **ndryshe nga gjithë bota:** against the tide. 2. or else, otherwise; **nxito, ndryshe do të vonohesh:** hurry up or else you will be late.
ndrýsh/ëm(i),-me(e) *mb.* 1. different, distinct, dissimilar, diverse; **dy interpretime të ndryshme:** two different interpretations. 2. various, different, varied; **njerëz të moshave të ndryshme:** persons of various ages. 3. miscellaneous, sundry; **artikuj të ndryshëm:** sundry articles.
ndryshím,-i *m.sh.* **-e** change; alteration; difference; **bëj (sjell) një ndryshim:** to bring about a change, to make an alteration to make a change; **pësoj ndryshim:** to undergo a change; **ndryshim mendimesh:** divergence of opinions; *(ligji)* modification (of a law); *(i stinëve)* alteration (of seasons); **ndryshim i menjëhershëm:** sudden change; *(zëri)* inflection (of the

voice); *(radhe, vendi)* inversion;
(i kohës) change (in the weather,
of weather); *(i një funksioni
algjebrik)* variation (of an algebric function); *(i një qenie-
je të gjallë)* metamorphosis.
ndryshk,-u *m.* rust; **heq ndrysh-
kun:** to rub off the rust.
ndryshk *f.k.* 1. to rust, to make
rusty; **zë ndryshk:** to rust, to
go rusty. – **ndryshkem** *f.jv.*
to rust, to go (to become) rusty.
2. *fig.* to rust, to grow mouldy.
ndrýshkj/e,-a *f.* going rusty.
ndrýshkur (i,e) *mb.* rusty (edhe
fig.).
ndryshój I. *f.k.* 1. to change, to
alter; **ndryshoj mendim:** to
change one's mind. 2. to transform, to change; **këto flokë
të ndryshojnë fare:** this hair-
style changes you; **ndryshoj
drejtimin;** to change direction
**i ndryshoj pamjen një vendi
një qyteti:** to transform the
aspect of a country, of a city.
– **ndryshohem** *f.jv.* to change,
to undergo a change; to be
transformed.
II. *f.jk.* 1.to change; **qyteti ndryshon nga dita në ditë:** the
city is changing daily. 2. to be
different, do be unlike; **të dy
vëllezërit ndryshojnë shumë
nga njëri-tjetri:** the two brothers are very unlike.
ndryshúesh/ëm(i),-me(e) *mb.*
variable, changeable; unsteady,
unsettled; **kohë e ndryshuesh-
me:** changeable (unsettled) weather.
ndryshueshmërí,-a *f.* variability,
changeability.
nduk *f.k.* 1. to pull up (out), to
pluck. 2. to pinch, to nip.
ndyj *f.k.* to dirty, to soil, to pollute, to besmirch, to sully, to
besmear; *(me baltë)* to splash,

të bespatter, to daub. – *Lok.*
ndyj gojën: to say indecent
things, to use obscene (scurrilous)
language. – **ndyhem** *f.jv.* to
get dirty, to dirty oneself, to soil
oneself.
ndýrazi *ndajf.* meanly, foully.
ndýrë (i,e) *mb.* 1. dirty, filthy. 2.
fig. dirty, filthy, sordid, shabby;
kohë e ndyrë; nasty weather;
punë e ndyrë: dirty trick; **njeri
i ndyrë:** despicable person.
ndyrësí,-a *f.sh.* -ra 1. dirtiness,
filthiness. 2. *fig.* foul (sordid,
base) action, filth; **them ndy-
rësirë:** to talk filth.
ndyrësír/ë,-a *f.sh.* -a 1. excreta,
dregs of mankind. 2. *fig.* dirty-
ness.
ndyrësísht *ndajf.* meanly, filthily,
dirtily.
ndýtë (i,e) *mb.* shih I **ndyrë.**
ne *p.v* ' 1ominative case) we; **ne
jemi.** we are; (dative case)
neve; to us, us; **neve na thanë
se:** they told us that; (accusative) **ne:** us; **eja me ne:** come
with us; **nesh: ndërmjet nesh:**
among us.
nefés,-i *m. mjek., vjet.* asthma.
nefrít,-i *m.* 1. *mjek,* nephritis. 2.
min. jade, silicate of magne-
sium.
negatív,-i *m.sh.* -a *(i një fotografie)*
negative (of a photo).
negatív,-e *mb.* negative; **përgjigje
negative:** negative answer.
negativísht *ndajf.* negatively, in
the negative.
nég/ër,-ri *m.sh.* -ër negro.
néjse *pj. gj. bis* be it so.
nekrologjí,-a *f.sh.* – necrology.
nemítem. *fjv.* to become speechless.
nemítj/e,-a *f.* the rendering speechless, mutism.
nen,-i *m.sh.* -e *drejt.* article (of a
law), item (of a law).
nén/ë,-a *f.sh.* -a *bot.* amaranth,

nepërk/ë,-a *f.sh.* **-a** *zool.* adder, viper.

neps,-i *m.* greediness, voracity (edhe *fig.*).

nepsqár,-e *mb.* greedy, voracious.

neqéz,-i *m.sh.* **-ë** miser.

neqéz,-e *mb.* covetous, stingy.

nerënx/ë,-a *f.sh.* **-a** *bot.* grapefruit.

nergút *ndajf.* purposely.

nerv,-i *m.sh.* **-a** *anat.* nerve; **nervi shiatik**: sciatic nerve; **me nerva**: nervous; **njeri me nerva**: nervous man; **krizë nervash**: crisis of nerves. — *Lok.* **më hipin nervat, jam me nerva**: to be all nerves, to be irritable, to be on edge; **i ngre nervat dikujt**: to get on someone's nerves.

nervór,-e *mb. anat.* nervous; **sistem nervor**: nervous system.

nervóz,-e *mb.* nervous, irritable, edgy, excitable, *fam.* nervy; **ai më bën nervoz**: he gets on my nerves.

nervozitét,-i *m.* shih nervozizëm.

nervozíz/ëm,-mi *m.* *mjek.* irritability, nervousness, restlessness, edginess.

nésër *ndajf.* tomorrow; **nesër mbrëma**: tomorrow night; **nesër një javë**: tomorrow week.

nésërm(i,),-e(e) *mb.* tomorrow's, of tomorrow; **gazeta e nesërme**: tomorrow's paper.

nésërm/e(e),-ja(e) *f.* 1. the day after, the next day; **të nesërmen**: the day after. 2. the future, tomorrow; **kush e di ç'na sjell e nesërmja**: who knows what the future (tomorrow) holds in store for us.

neshtér,-i *m.sh.* **-ë** *mjek.* scalpel.

néto *mb. treg.* net; **peshë neto**: net weight; **të ardhura neto**: net income.

neurológ,-u *m.sh.* **-ë** *mjek.* neurologist.

neurologjí,-a *f. mjek.* neurology.

neutrál,-e *mb.* neutral.

neutralitét,-i *m.* neutrality.

neutralizím,-i *m.* neutralization.

neutralizój *f.k.* to neutralize. — **neutralizohet** *f.jv.* to be neutralized.

néve *p.v.* shih **ne**.

neverí,-a *f.* repugnance, repulsion, loathness, contempt, scorn, disdain, disgust, distaste.

neverít *f.k.* to disdain, to contempt, to repulse, to disgust, to scorn. — **neveritem** *f.jv.* to feel nausea.

neverítës,-e *mb.* repugnant, repulsive, nauseating, sickening.

neverítj/e,-a *f.* repugnance, repulsion, loathing; **ndiej neveritje** to loathe, to feel nausea.

neverítsh/ëm(i),-me(e) *mb.* contemptible, nauseating, sickening, despicable, repugnant.

nevój/ë,-a *f.* 1. need, want, necessity; **kam nevojë për**: I am in need of, I need, I want; **për çfarë kini nevojë?** what are you in need of? **nuk kam nevojë për gjë**: I need nothing; **nuk është nevoja të vini**: you need not come; **këto këpucë kanë nevojë për riparim**: these shoes want mending; **në rast nevoje**: in case of necessity; **është nevoja**: it is necessary; **nevojë e domosdoshme**: absolute necessity; **e bëra nga nevoja**: I did it by necessity; **artikuj të nevojës së parë**: necessaries of life; **nevojat e përditshme**: daily wants. 2. **bëj nevojën**: to relieve oneself, to empty the bowels.

nevojítem *f.jv.* to be necessary, to be useful; **nuk më nevojitet**: I don't need it.

nevójsh/ëm(i),-me(e) *mb.* needful, necessary, requisite; **shumë i nevojshëm**: indispensable, absolutely necessary: **më të nevojshmet**; the most necessary; **është e nevojshme të**: it is necessary to; **bëj ç'është e nevojshme**: to do what is necessary.

nevojtár,-i *m.sh.* -**ë** the needy, the poor, the have-nots.

nevojtár,-e *mb.* necessitous, needy, poor.

nevojtór/e,-ja *f.sh.* -**e** closet, water-closet. W.C.; **nevojtore publike**: privy, public W.C., necessary house.

nevralgjí,-a *f. mjek.* neuralgia, tic, tic-douloureux.

nevralgjík,-e *mb. mjek.* neuralgic.

nevrastení,-a *f. mjek.* neurasthenia.

nevrasteník,-e *mb.* neuropathic.

nevrík,-e *mb.* choleric, irate, quick-tempered.

nevrikós *f.k.* to get on the nerves of someone. − **nevrikosem** *f.jv.* to get angry, to fidget.

në I. *paraf.* in, to, into, at; **kam lindur në Elbasan në vitin 1960**: I was born in Elbasan in 1960; **banoj në Tiranë**: I live in Tirana; **në Shqipëri**: in Albania; **në mes të dhomës**: in the middle of the room; **shkoj në dhomë**: I go into the room; **ndërrohet në**: it changes into; **shkoj në shkollë**: I go to school; **ai shkon në fushën e sportit çdo ditë në orën 6**: he goes to the playground every day at six o'clock; **në qoshen e tryezës**: at the corner of the table; **në mesnatë**: at midnight; **tri herë në ditë**: three times a day; **në krye të rrugës**: at the head of the road; **në fund të luginës**: at the end of the valley; **në këtë fjali**: in this sentence; **në dimër**: in winter; **rri në shtëpi**: to stay at home.

II. *lidh.* if: **në qoftë se**: if; **në vjen, më shkruaj**: if you come, write me; **s'e di në është ende gjallë**: I don't know whether he is alive or not.

nëm/ë,-a *f.* curse, imprecation.

nën I. *paraf.* 1. under; beneath; **ai u fsheh nën shtrat**: he hid beneath the bed; **çlodhem nën hijen e një peme**: to rest under the shade of a tree; **nën regjimin e vjetër**: under the old regime; **ka dhjetë vetë nën urdhër**: he has ten men under him; **fëmijë nën gjashtëmbëdhjetë vjet**: children under sixteen; **nën rrezet e diellit**: in the sunshine; **thirrem nën armë**: to be called up to arms; **nën mbikëqyrjen e një doktori**: under the supervision of a doctor; **dyshemeja është nën këmbët tuaja**: the floor is under your feet; **ka një copë shkumës nën bankon**: there is a piece of chalk under the bench. 2. below, under, underneath; **termometri shënon dhjetë gradë nën zero**: the thermometer marks ten grades Celsius below zero; **nën nivelin e detit**: below sea − level. 3. *(për shkak)* under; **ai flet nën veprimin e alkoolit**: he talks under the influence of alchool.

II. *parashtesë* (prefix) under, sub.

nënbárkëz,-a *f.sh.* -**a** girth (of a horse).

nënbísht/e,-ja *f.sh.* -**e** crupper.

nënçmím,-i *m.* underestimation.

nënçmój *f.k.* to underestimate, to undervalue, to underrate. − **nënçmohem** *f.jv.* to be underestimated.

nëndétës/e,-ja *f.sh.* -**e** submarine.

nëndrejtór,-i *m.sh.* -ë vice-director, deputy (assistant) director.

nëndhésh/ëm(i),-me(e) *mb.* subterranean, underground.

nën/ë,-a *f.sh.* -a mother; pa nënë: motherless; pa nënë e pa babë: orphan; gjuha e nënës: mother tongue.

nënëmádh/e,-ja *f.* grandmother, granny.

nënfísh,-i *m.sh.* -a submultiple.

nënkolonél,-i *m.sh.* -ë subcolonel.

nënkónsu/ll,-lli *m.sh.* -j viceconsul.

nënkryetár,-i *m.sh.* -ë vice-chairman.

nënkuptím,-i *m.sh.* -e implication. allusion, hint.

nënkuptój *f.k.* to imply. – nënkuptohet *f.jv.* to be implied.

nënkuptúesh/ëm (i),-me (e) *mb.* implicit.

nënmbrét,-i *m.sh.* -ër viceroy.

nëndárj/e,-a *f.sh.* -e subdivision.

nënoficér,-i *m.sh.* -ë non-commissioned officer.

nënprefékt,-i *m.sh.* -ë subprefect.

nënpresidént,-i *m.* vice-president.

nënprodúkt.-i *m.sh.* -e by-product.

nënqésh *f.jk.* to smile

nënqéshj/e,-a *f.sh.* -e smile.

nënrendítës,-e *mb.* subordinate.

nënrendítj/e,-a *f.* subordination.

nënsekretár,-i *m.sh.* -ë undersecretary.

nënshkrím,-i *m.sh.* -e signature, signing.

nënshkrúaj *f.k.*, *f.jk.* to sign, to undersign; marrëveshja u nënshkrua nga: the agreement was signed by. – nënshkruhet *f.jv.* to be signed.

nënshkrúar(i),-i(i) *m.sh.* – (të) undersigned.

nënshkrúes,-i *m.sh.* – underwriter.

nënshtétas,-i *m.sh.* – citizen, subject.

nënshtetësí,-a *f.* nationality, citizenship.

nënshtrím,-i *m.* submission.

nënshtrój *f.k.* 1. to subdue, to put down. 2. *fig.* to subordinate. – nënshtrohem *f.jv.* to submit; to be subdued; i nënshtrohem fatit: to resign oneself to one's fate.

nëntë *num. them.* nine.

nëntë(i,e) *num rresht.* ninth.

nëntëdhjétë *num. them.* ninety.

nëntëdhjetëvjeçár,-i *m.sh.* -e nonagenarian.

nëntëmbëdhjétë *num. them.* nineteen.

nëntëmbëdhjétë (i,e) *num. rresht.* nineteenth.

nëntëqind *num. them.* nine hundred.

nëntítu/ll,-lli *m.sh.* -j subtitle.

nëntogér,-i *m.sh.* -ë sublieutenant.

nëntók/ë,-a *f,* subsoil, underground

nëntokësór,-e *mb.* subterranean.

nëntór,-i *m.* November.

nënvizím,-i *m.sh.* -e underline.

nënvizój *f.k.* to underline. – nënvizohet *f.jv.* to be underlined.

nënvleftësím,-i *m.* undervaluation, underestimation.

nënvleftësoj *f.k.* to undervalue, to underestimate, to underrate. – nënvleftësohem *f.jv.* to be undervaluated (underestimated, underrated).

nënvlerësím,-i *m.* shih nënvleftësim.

nënvlerësój *f.k.* shih nënvleftësoj.

nëpër *paraf.* through; nëpër botë: through the world; shikoj nëpër vrimëe çelësit:to look through the key-hole.

nëpërmés *ndajf., paraf.* accross; through.

nëpërmjét *paraf.* by, by the help of, through, by means of; **nëpërmjet jush:** through you.

nëpúnës,-i *m.sh.* – clerk, employee; **nëpunës i rangut të lartë:** functionary: **nëpunës i gjendjes civile:** registrar, city-recorder.

nëpunësí,-a *f.* employ, employment, place, post, office, public business.

në qóftë se *lidh.* if, supposing that. **nësé** *lidh.* if; whether.

nga *paraf.* 1. *(drejtim)* from, of, out of, out from; **nga i pari tek i fundit:** from first to last; **ai sapo erdhi nga shkolla:** he has just returned from school; **nga vini?** where do you come from? 2. *(veçim)* **ngushtica e La Manshit ndan Francën nga Anglia:** the English Channel separates France form England; **u ndava nga të afërmit:** I parted from my relatives. 3. *(prejardhje)* **shumë fjalë të gjuhës angleze vijnë nga latinishtja:** many English words are derived from Latin; **hekuri nxirret nga toka në gjendje të papastër:** iron is obtained from the ground in an impure state; **mora një letër nga djali juaj:** I have received a letter from your son; **djathi prodhohet nga qumështi:** cheese is made (obtained) from milk; **pikturoj nga natyra:** I paint from nature. 4. *(shkak)* from, of with; **e gjora kafshë ngordhi nga uria:** the poor animal died of hunger; **ata qanë nga gëzimi:** they wept from joy; **dridhem nga të ftohtit:** to tremble with cold. 5. *(distancë)* **njëzet kilometra nga Tirana:** twenty ki-

lometres from Tirana. 6. by; **ai u lavdërua nga mësuesi i tij:** he was praised by his teacher: **libri është shkruar nga Homeri:** the book is written by Homer. 7. at, toward, towards; **nga dreka:** at midday, towards midday; **nga mesnata:** at midnight, towards midnight; **nga fundi i vitit:** towards the end of the year. – *Lok.* **nga dita në ditë:** from day to day; **nga larg:** from far (away); **nga mbrapa:** from behind; **nga poshtë:** from beneath; **nga sipër:** from above; **nga ku:** hence, therefore, wherefrom, wherefore, consequently; **që nga kjo kohë:** from that time, thence, since; **kopjoj nga:** to copy from; **mbroj nga:** to protect from; **ruaj nga:** to guard from; **rrjedh nga:** to derive from; **vuaj nga:** to suffer from; **i ndryshëm nga:** different from; **i lirë nga:** free from: **i sigurt nga:** secure from.

ngacmím,-i *m.sh.* -e 1. teasing, nagging, bothering. 2. excitement, excitation, provocation.

ngacmój *f.k.* 1. to tease, to nag, to irritate, to bother. 2. to excite, to provoke. – **ngacmohem** *f.jv.* 1. to be teased (nagged, bothered). 2. to be excited (provoked).

ngacmúes,-i *m.sh.* – 1. teaser. 2. excitant, stimulant.

ngacmúes,-e *mb.* 1. annoying. 2. provoking, exciting.

ngadálë *ndajf.* slowly, gradually.

ngadalësí,-a *f.* slowness.

ngadalësím,-i *m.* retardation, deceleration.

ngadalësój *f.k.* to decelerate, to make slower, to slacken, to slack up, to retard. – **ngadalë-**

sohet *f.jv.* to become slower, to slacken.

ngadálsh/ëm,-(i),=me(e) *mb.* 1. slow, 2. dull, slow-witted.

ngadó *ndajf.* wherever; **ngado që shkoj;** wherever I go. – *Lok.* **ngado që ta kapësh (ta marrësh):** from any point of view.

ngadhënjéj *f.jk.* to triumph.

ngadhënjím,-i *m.* triumph, victory.

ngadhënjimtár,-i *m.sh.* -ë triumphator.

ngadhënjimtár,-e *mb.* triumphant.

ngadhënjýes,-i *m.sh.* – triumphant.

ngahérë *ndajf.* always, ever; **për ngaherë:** forever.

ngahérsh/ëm(i),-me(e) *mb,* perpetual, everlasting.

ngálët (i,e) *mb.* slow, sluggish, slack; **njeri i ngalët:** laggard, slow person.

ngandonjëhérë *ndajf.* sometimes, at times.

nganjëhérë *ndajf.* shih **ngandonjëherë.**

ngarkés/ë,-a *f.* load; *(e anijes)* cargo; **fletë ngarkese** *(e anijes):* bill of lading.

ngarkím,-i *m.* lading. loading. – *Lok.* **lë në ngarkim të dikujt:** to leave something (somebody) in the charge of someone.

ngarkím-shkarkím,-i *m.* leading and unlading.

ngarkój *f.k.* 1, *(karrocën etj.)* to load (the cart etc.). 2. *(dikë me një detyrë)* to charge someone to do something, to assign someone with a duty, to assign something to someone: *(me një faj)* to attribute (the fault) to someone. **-ngarkohem** *f.jv.* to take upon oneself, to take charge, to take over.

ngarkúar (i,e) *mb.* 1. laden, loaded. 2. charged; **i ngarkuar me mision:** charged with mission;

i ngarkuari me punë: charge d'affaires.

ngas *f.k.* (p.t. **ngava,** p.p. **ngarë**) 1. *(makinën)* to drive (a vehicle). 2. *(kalin)* to ride, to run (a horse). 3. *(varkën)* to steer, to pilot. 4. *(ngàcmoj)* to tease, to bother.

ngást/ër,-ra *f.sh.* -ra *(tokë)* parcel, plot.

ngashërím,-i *m.* sobbing; **qaj me ngashërim:** to sob.

ngashërój *f.k.* shih **mallëngjej.**

ngashnjéj *f.k.* to allure, to attract, to seduce.

ngashnjím,-i *m.* allurement, attraction, seduction.

ngashnjýes,-e *mb.* alluring, attractive, seductive.

ngatërrés/ë,-a *f.sh.* -a 1. confusion, huddle. 2. hindrance, obstruction. 3. intricacy, entanglement, complication. 4. quarrel.

ngatërrestár,-i *m.sh.* -ë intrigant, busybody, scandal-monger.

ngatërrój *f.k.* 1. to mistake. 2. to entangle, to intricate, to complicate. 3. to confuse, to muddle, 4. to embroil, to involve in contention.– **ngatërrohem** *f.jv.* 1. to be confounded, to be mistaken. 2. to entangle oneself, to be intricated (complicated). 3. to get confused. 4. to be involved in contention.

ngáthët (i,e) *mb.* clumsy, awkward, gawky, unhandy, unskilful, ungainly; **njeri i ngathët:** clumsy person; **djalë i ngathët:** clumsy fellow.

ngathtësí,-af. clumsiness, awkwardness, ungainliness.

ngazëllím,-i *m.* exultation, gladness.

ngazëllój *f.jk.* to exult. – **ngazëllohem** *f.jv.* to be exulted.

ngazëllúes,-e *mb.* exultant.

nge,-ja *f.* leisure, spare time; **më**

nge: at leisure. **kam nge**: to have leisure; **nuk kam nge të merrem me sport**: I have no leisure for sport; **me nge**: leisurely.

ngec *f.jk.* to stick; **më ka ngecur një kockë në grykë**: a bone has stuck in my throat; **ngec anija në cekëtirë**: the ship got aground

ngel *f.jk.* 1. to remain; **ngel vetëm**: to remain alone. 2. to fail; **ngel në një provim**: to fail in an examination.

ngësh/ëm (i),-me(e) *mb.* idle, unemployed, unoccupied; **njeri i ngeshëm**: idle person.

ngërç,-i *m. mjek.* cramp

ngërdhéshem *f.jv.* to make faces.

ngërdhéshje,-a *f.* grimace.

ngij *f.k.* to sate, to satiate, to glut. — **ngihem** *f.jv.* to satiate oneself; to get satiated; **ha, ngihul** eat your fill!

ngímj/e,-a *f.* satiety, glutting.

ngójc/ë,-a *f.sh.* **-a** curb-chain, bit of a bridle.

ngop *f.k.* shih **ngij.**

ngópj'/e,-a *f.* shih **ngimje.**

ngópur (i,e) *mb.* 1. satiated, sated; **ndihem i ngopur**: to feel satisfied, to have had enough. 2. *fig.* sated, satiated; fed up. 3. *kim.* saturated. — *Lok.* u **ngopa me tël** I am tired of him!

ngordh I. *f.k.* to make die; **e ngordh në dru dikë**: to beat someone black and blue. to berat someone to death;
II. *f.jk. (për kafshët)* to die; *fam.* to peg out, to kick the bucket; **ngordh urie**: to starve.

ngordhësír/ë,-a *f.sh.* **-a** 1. scrag (animal), starveling. 2. *(person)* walking skeleton, skin and bones, *fam.* wreck.

ngórdhj/e,-a *f. (urie)* starvation, starving; *(e kafshëve)* death.

ngórdhur (i,e) *mb. (kafshë)* dead; *(nga uria)* starved.

ngrátë (i,e) *mb.* unfortunate, poor.

ngre *f.k.* (p.t. **ngrita**, p.p. **ngritur)** 1. *(diçka nga toka)* to pick up, to rise from the ground. 2. *(kokën)* to hold up, to raise (the head). 3. *(flamurin)* to hoist (the flag). 4. *(trupin)* to straighten (the body). 5. *(supet)* to shrug one's shoulders. 6. *(sytë)* to look up, to raise the eyes. 7. *(zërin)* to raise one's voice, to lift up one's voice. 8. *(veshët)* to prick the ears. 9. *(një shtëpi)* to build up (a house, an edifice). 10. *(përmendore dikujt)* to put up, to erect a monument to someone. 11. *(një peshë, një barrë)* to raise, to lift up (a weight, a burden) 12. *(krye kundër)* to rise, to rebel, to revolt (against). 13. *(moralin)* to boost (the morale). 14. *(pantallonat, etj).* to tuck up (one's trousers). 15. *mat. (në fuqi të dytë, të tretë një numër)* to raise (to the second, to the third power a number, to the cube a number). 16. *(çmimet)* to raise (the prices). — **ngrihem** *f.jv.* 1. *(nga shtrati, zgjohem)* to rise, to wake up, to get up from bed. 2. *(më këmbë)* to stand up. 3. *(ngrihem në detyrë)* to be promoted. 4. *(ngrihet në ajër zogu)* to soar, to fly aloft; *(aeroplani etj.)* to ascend to take off. — *Lok.* **më ngrihet mendja**: to be alarmed; **ngrihem nga shtëpia**: to remove, to change residence; **ngre në qiell dikë**: to loud someone to the skies.

ngreh *f.k.* 1. *(një çadër)* to pitch (a tent). 2. *(çarkun e minjve)*

to set (the mouse-trap). 3. *(çarkun e pushkës)* to dress (the percussion-cap). 4. *(sahatin)* to wind up (the watch).
ngrehín/ë,-a *f.sh.* -a building; *(industriale)* industrial building, establishment.
ngrëni/e,-a *f.* eating, feeding; **ora e ngrënies;** mealtime; **dhoma e ngrënies:** dining-room.
ngrënsh/ëm(i),-me(e) *mb.* eatable, edible.
ngríc/ë,-a *f.sh.* -a frost, freeze; **bën ngricë e madhe:** it is freezing hard.
ngrij *f.k.* to feel cold, to chill, to ice, to congeal; **ngrin uji:** the water freezes.
ngrírë(i,e) *mb.* 1. congealed, frozen, frosty. 2. *fig. (njeri)* numb, stiff, dull (person).
ngrírj/e,-a *f.* freezing, congealing; **pika e ngrirjes:** freezing-point.
ngrísh/ëm(i),-me(e) *mb.* congealable.
ngríta *f.k.* shih **ngre.**
ngrítj/e,-a *f.sh.* -e 1. *(e çmimeve)* rise (of prices). 2. *(e pagave)* increase (of salaries). 3. *(shtëpie)* building (of a house). 4. *(e një peshe, e një barre)* lifting up, (of a weight, of a burden). 5. *(e flamurit)* hoist (of the flag). 6. *(e një përmendoreje)* putting up, setting up (of a monument). 7. (*e moralit)* boosting (of someone's morale).
ngroh *f.k.* 1. to warm, to heat moderately; **ngroh ujin:** to warm, to heat (the water); **ngroh duart:** to warm one's hands. 2. *(pula vezët)* to hatch (the eggs). 3. *fig. (zemrën e dikujt)* to warm the cockles of one's heart. − **ngrohem** *f.jv.* to warm oneself; **ngrohem në diell:** to bask.
ngróhj/e,-a *f.* warming.

ngróhtë *ndajf.* 1. warmly; **bën ngrohtë:** it is warm. 2. *fig.* warmly; **pres ngrohtë dikë:** to give someone a warm welcome.
ngróhtë (i,e) *mb.* 1. warm; *(shumë)* hot; **ujë i ngrohtë:** warm water 2. *fig.* warm; **pritje e ngrohtë:** warm welcome (reception).
ngróhtë,-t (të) *as.* warmth.
ngrohtësí,-a *f.* 1. warmth. 2. fervour, ardour; **ai u përgjigj me ngrohtësi:** he answered with warmth.
ngrohtësísht *ndajf.* warmly.
ngrys *f.k.* 1. to darken; **ngrys vetullat:** to frown one's brows, to knit one's brows. 2. to pass; **e ngrys jetën me:** to pass the life with. 3. **u ngrys:** it is getting dark. − **ngrysem** *f.jv.* 1. to be caught by the night; **si u ngryse?** have you passed a good day? 2. **ngryset:** to grow dark (dusk), to get dark; **po ngryset:** night is coming, it is getting dark, it is growing dark; **rri deri sa të ngryset:** stay until nightfall.
ngrýsj/e,-a *f.* gloaming, darkening.
ngrýsur (të),-it(të) *as.* nightfall; **ndaj të ngrysur:** at nightfall.
nguc *f.k.* to tighten, to squeeze. ze, − **ngucem** *f.jv.* to sit close, to squeeze oneself.
ngúcur *ndajf.* **rri ngucur:** to sit close.
ngul *f.k.* 1. to drive in; *(një gozhdë)* to drive a nail, to nail. 2. *(një hu në tokë)* to drive (a stake) into the ground. 3. *(thikën)* to thrust (the knife). 4. *(në hell)* to spit (in a rod). 5. *fig.* **ngul këmbë:** to insist, to persist, to persevere. 6. **ngul në kokë një mësim etj:** to inculcate (on), to get it into one's head. 7. **ngul sytë mbi:** to stare at, to fix

one's eyes on. – **ngulem** *f.jv.*
(në një vend) to establish oneself, to be lodged.
ngúlët *(i,e)* *mb.* fixed; **mendim i
ngulët:** a fixed idea.
ngulís *f.k.* *(një mendim etj.)* to
inculcate; **ngulis në kokë:** to
inculcate, to get it into one's
head. – **ngulitet** *f.jv.* to be
inculcated.
ngulítur(i,e) *mb.* deeply rooted.
ngúlj/e,-a *f.* fixation; *(gozhde)*
nailing.
ngulm,-i *m.* insistence, persistence,
perseverance; **me ngulm:** with
insistence.
ngulmój *f.jk.* to insist, to persist, to
persevere.
ngulmúes,-e *mb.* persistent, per-
severant; **punë ngulmuese:** per-
severant work.
ngurós *f.k.* to petrify. – **ngurosem**
f.jv. to be petrified.
ngurósj/e,-a *f.* petrifaction.
ngúrtë *(i,e)* *mb.* 1. rigid, stiff.
2. *fiz.* solid; **trup i ngurtë:**
solid body.
ngurtësí,-a *f.* 1. rigidity, stiffness.
2. *fig.* solidity.
ngurtësím,-i *m.* 1. solidification.
2. *mjek.* *(ngurtësim i një indi)*
induration.
ngurtësój *f.k.* to solidify. – **ngur-
tësohem** *f.jv.* to be solidified.
ngurrím,-i *m.sh.* -e hesitancy,
hesitation; **pa ngurrim:** without hesitation, unhesitatingly.
ngurrój *f.k.* to hesitate.
ngurrúes,-e *mb.* hesitating; di-
ffident.
ngushëllím,-i *m.sh.* -e condolence,
solace, consolation, confort; **nuk
gjej ngushëllim për dhembjen
time:** I can find no solace for
my grief.
ngushëllój *f.k.* to condole, to

console, to solace. – **ngushë-
llohem** *f.jv.* to be consoled.
ngushëllúes,-e *mb.* consolatory,
consoling.
ngúshtë *(i,e)* *mb.* 1. narrow;
**lumë i ngushtë, rrugë e ngu-
shtë:** narrow river, way. 2.
gjeom. **kënd i ngushtë:** narrow angle. 3. strait, tight: **xhaketë e ngushtë:** strait jacket;
pantallona të ngushta: tight
trousers. 4. *fig.* intimate; **shok i
ngushtë:** intimate (close) friend.
ngúshtë *ndajf.* 1. short; **jam
ngushtë me lekë:** I am short
of money. 2. **jam ngushtë me
shtëpi:** to be in strait of lodging. 3. tightly; **lidh ngushtë:**
to tie closely (tightly).
ngushtësí,-a *f.* 1. narrowness. 2.
straitness. 3. tightness.
ngushtësísht *ndajf.* closely, tightly.
ngushtíc/ë,-a *f.* 1. *gjeog.* strait,
channel; **ngushtica e La Man-
shit;** the English Channel. 2.
defile, narrow passage. 3. *(financiare)* pecuniary difficulty,
poverty.
ngushtím,-i *m.* 1. narrowing. 2.
(i një plaçke) shrinking (of a
cloth), contraction. 3. limitation;
**Partia e Punës e Shqipërisë
lufton për ngushtimin e
dallimeve midis fshatit dhe
qytetit:** the Party of Labour of
Albania fights to narrow down
the differences between town
and countryside.
ngushtój *f.k.* to narrow. – **ngush-
tohem** *f.jv.* 1. to grow narrower.
2. *(ngushtohet plaçka)* to shrink,
to be contracted (of a tissue).
ngut,-i *m.* haste, hurry; **me ngut:**
hastily, hurriedly.
ngut *f.k.* to hurry, to hasten. –
ngutem *f.jv.* to hurry, to hasten,
to be in a hurry; **mos u ngut:**

don't make haste, don't hurry, take your time.

ngutësí,-a *f.* hurry, hastening.

ngutësísht *ndajf.* hastily, hurriedly.

ngútj/e,-a *f.* hurry, haste.

ngútsh/ëm(i),-me(e) *mb.* urgent, pressing.

ngjaj *f.jk.* to resemble, to be like, to look like; **ata ngjajnë si dy pika uji:** they are as like as two peas; **ata i ngjajnë njëri- -tjetrit:** they resemble each other; **ai i ngjan krejt t'et:** he is the spitting image of his father.

ngjál/ë,-a *f.sh.* -a *zool.* eel.

ngjall *f.k.* 1. to bring to life, to give new life to, to revive. 2. *fig.* *(admirim)* to excite (admiration). 3. *krah.* to heal. — **ngjallem** *f.jv.* 1. to be recalled to life. 2. to grow fat. 3. to recover one's health.

ngjállur (i,e) *mb.* plump, stout, fatty, obese, fleshy fattish.

ngjan *f.jk.* to happen, to occur, to come to pass, to befall.

ngjárë,-t (të) *as.* probability; **ka të ngjarë:** it is probable.

ngjárj/e,-a *f.sh.* -e 1. event; **viti që shkoi ishte plot ngjarje:** the past year has been eventful. 2. episode. 3. incident, occurrence.

ngjas *f.jk.* shih **ngjaj.**

ngjasím,-i *m.* resemblance, likeness, semblance, similarity, sameness, likeness; **(i madh)** close resemblance.

ngjasój *f.jk.* shih **ngjaj.**

ngjásh/ëm(i),-me(e) *mb.* alike, same, similar, resembling; **të ngjashëm si dy pika uji:** as like as two peas.

ngjashmërí,-a *f.* sameness, likeness resemblance.

ngjatjetím,-i *m.* salutation.

ngjatjetój *f.k.* to salute. — **ngjatje-**

tohem *f.jv.* to be hailed, to hail, to greet.

ngjáu *f.jk.* shih **ngjan** (past tense), it happened.

ngjesh *f.k.* 1. *(pambukun etj.)* to compress *(cotton, etc.).* 2. *(token)* to ram down (the soil). 3. *(shpatën në brez)* to gird on the sword. — **ngjishem** *f.jv.* 1. *(së ngrëni)* to eat one's fill. 2. *(turma)* to crowd, to press together; *(pas dikujt)* to sit close.

ngjéshj/e,-a *f.* compression.

ngjéshur (i,e) *mb.* 1. compressed; **ajër \ i ngjeshur;** compressed air. 2. **tokë e ngjeshur:** rammed earth. 3. *fig.* **trup i ngjeshur (i lidhur):** strong body. 4. *fig.* **stil i ngjeshur:** concise style.

ngjet *f.jk.* shih **ngjan** .

ngjeth *f.k.* to make (to cause to) shiver. — **ngjethem** *f.jv.* 1. *(nga të ftohtit)* to shiver (with cold). 2. *fig.* të shudder, to shiver, to quake; **ngjethem nga tmerri:** to shudder with horror.

ngjéthës,-e *mb.* shivering, shuddering.

ngjéthje,-a *f.* shivering, shuddering, goose-flesh.

ngjéthura,-t (të) *f.sh.* shivers, shudders, shidderings.

ngjir *f.k.* to hoarsen. — **ngjirem** *f.jv.* to hoarsen; **ngjirem së thirruri:** to shout oneself hoarse.

ngjírur (i,e) *mb.* hoarse; **zë i ngjirur:** hoarse voice.

ngjis *f.k.* 1. to stick, to paste, to glue, to gum; *(një afishe në mur)* to put up, to stick up, to post up (a placard on the wall); *(një pullë poste)* to stick (a postage — stamp); *(me zamk)* to stick, to paste; *(me qiriç)* to gum; *(me tutkall)* to glue; *(me* *kallaj)* to solder; *(me oksigjen)* to weld (with oxyacetylene). 2. *(një sëmundje)* to transmit (a malady, a disease). 3. *fig. (një faj dikujt)* to attribute, to ascribe, to impute (the fault to someone). — **ngjitet** *f.jv.* 1. to be sticked (pasted); **ngjitet pas diçkaje**: to cling, to adhere. 2. to be put up, to be stuck up (posted up). 3. to be transmitted (a disease). 4. to be attributed, ascribed, imputed (a fault, etc.).

ngjis *f.k.* 1. *(shkallët)* to mount (the stairs). 2. *(malin, kodrën)* to climb (a mountain, a hill). — **ngjitem** *f.jv.* 1. to climb, to go up, to come up; **ngjitem në pemë**: to climb (up) a tree; **u ngjitem shkallëve**: to go up the stairs. 2. *(malit, etj.)* to climb up, to go up, to ascend; **i ngjitem malit**: to climb up a mountain.

ngjitës,-i *m.sh.* — glue, stick, hum paste.

ngjitës,-e *mb.* 1. glutinous, sticky. 2. *mjek (sëmundje)* catching, contagious, epidemic, transmissible (disease). 3. *muz.* **shkallë ngjitëse**: ascending scale.

ngjitj/e,-a *f.* 1. *(me zamk)* sticking; *(me tutkall)* gluing. 2. *(me kallaj)* soldering; *(me oksigjen)* welding. 3. *(e një mali)* climbing, ascension, ascent (of a mountain). 4. *(sëmundjeje)* contagion, transmission (of a disease).

ngjitur *ndajf.* close, near; **ngjitur me**: near, close to.

ngjitur (i,e) *mb.* 1. sticked. 2. welded, soldered.

ngjyej *f.k.* 1. *(leshin etj.)* to dye. 2. *(bukën në qumësht)* to soak (the bread into the milk); **ngjyej penën në bojë**: to soak the pen into the ink. 3. *(fytyrën)* to make oneself up. — **ngjyhet**

f.jv. 1. to be dyed. 2. to be soaked. 3. *(gruaja)* to paint one's face.

ngjýerj/e,-a *f.* dyeing.

ngjýra-ngjýra *mb.* iridescent.

ngjýr/ë,-a *f. sh.* -a paint, colour, dye, tint; **ngjyrë e çelur**: light colour; **pa ngjyrë**: colourless.

ngjyrím,-i *m.* dyeing, colouring, tincture.

ngjyrós *f.k.* to dye; to colour, to tinge — **ngjyroset** *f.jv.* to be dyed; to be coloured.

ngjyrósj/e,-a *f.* dyeing; **repart për ngjyrosje**: dye-works.

ngjyrúes,-e *mb.* colouring; **lëndë ngjyruese**: colouring matter, dye-stuff.

niét,-i *m.* intention, purpose; **kam niet të**: I intend to, I have in mind to, it is my intention to.

níkel,-i *m.* nickel.

nikelój *f.k.* to plate with nickel, to nickel.

nikoqír,-i *m.sh.* -ë economical (thrifty) person.

nikoqír,-e *mb.* thrifty, economical; **grua nikoqire**: house-wife.

nikoqír/e,-ja *f.sh.* -e housewife, hostess, mistress (of the house).

nikoqirllëk,-u *m.* thriftiness, economy; **përdor me nikoqirllëk**: to husband, to use with economy, to manage economically.

nímf/ë,-a *f.sh.* -a nymph.

nip,-i *m.sh.* -a 1. *(prej motrës ose prej vëllait)* nephew. 2. *(prej vajzës ose prej djalit)* grandchild, grandson.

nis *f.k.* 1. to begin, to commence; **nis një punë**: to begin a work; **nis të shkruaj**: to begin to write; **nis një bisedë**: to begin a conversation. 2. to send, to direct; **nis me postë**: to send by mail. — **nisem** *f.jv.* to start, to depart; *(me anije)* to embark (on a ship); **nisem për udhë**:

to set off, to set forth, to depart; **nisem për lundrim:** to set sail; **nisemil** let us go!; **nisul gol,** get ~~you gone?~~ *going!*

niseshté,-ja *f.* starch.

nísj/e,-a *f.* departure; **sinjali i nisjes:** starting signal.

nísm/ë,-a *f.sh.* **-a** initiative.

nishádër,-i *m. kim.* ammonium salt.

nishán,-i *m.sh.* **-e** *gj. bis. (shenjë)* aim, target; **marr nishan:** to aim, to take aim. 2. *(në trup)* birth-mark, mole. 3. *vjet.* mèdal. decoration, badge of honour. 4. *vjet.* gift of betrothal. – *Lok.* **nuk i mbeti as nam as nishan:** he was lost without leaving any trace; it went up in air.

nishanxhí,-u *m.sh.* **-nj.** sharp shooter.

nivél,-i *m.sh.* **-e** 1. level; **nivel i ujit:** water level; **mbi nivelin e detit:** above sea-level. 2. *fig.* level, standard; **nivel kulturor;** cultural level; **nivel jetese:** standard of life. 3. *tek.* water gauge.

nivelím.-i *m.* levelling, bringing to the same level.

nivelój *f.k.* to level. — **nivelohet** *f.jv.* to be levelled.

nivelúes,-i *m.sh.* – leveller.

nivelúes,-e *mb.* levelling.

nóçk/ë,-a *f.sh.* **-a** *anat.* 1. ankle (of the foot). 2. knuckle of the finger. 3. *zool.* trunk.

nófk/ë,-a *f.sh.* **-a** nickname.

nófull,-a *f.sh.* **-a** *anat.* jawbone, chap; **nofull e sipërme:** maxilla, the uper jawbone; **nofull e poshtme:** the lower jawbone; **e nofullës:** maxillary.

nójm/ë,-a *f.sh.* **-a** gesture; **bëj me nojmë:** to make a gesture.

nomenklatúr/ë,-a *f.sh.* **-a** nomenclature.

nominál,-e *mb.* nominal; **vleftë nominale:** nominal value.

noprán,-e *mb.* perverse, untractable.

normál,-e *mb.* 1. normal; **gjendje normale:** normal state. 2. sane, mentally sound; **njeri normal:** sane person, normal person.

normalísht *ndajf.* normally.

nórm/ë,-a *f.sh.* **-a** 1. rule, regulation. 2. norm; **plotësoj (tejkaloj) normën:** to fulfil (to overfulfil) the norm.

norvegjéz,-i *m.sh.* **-ë** Norwegian.

norvegjéz,-e *mb.* Norwegian.

not,-i *m.* swim; **i mësoj notin dikujt:** to teach someone how to swim; **kaloj liqenin me not:** to swim acrross a lake.

notár,-i *m.sh.* **-ë** swimmer.

notér,-i *m.sh.* **-ë** notary.

noteriál,-e *mb.* notarial.

nót/ë,-a *f.sh.* **-a** 1. *(muzike)* musical note; **gaboj një notë:** to play a wrong note; **gjysmë note:** half note; **çerek note;** quarter note; **notë tetëshe:** quaver; **notë gjashtëmbëdhjetëshe:** semi-quaver. 2. *(shkolla)* mark; **marr notën shumë mirë:** to get (to gain) a very good mark. 3. *(diplomatike)* diplomatic note.

notí,-a *f. krah.* hummidity.

notím,-i *m.* swimming.

notój *f.jk.* to swim; **notoj mbi sipërfaqe:** to float.

novación,-i *m.sh.* **-e** innovation.

novatór,-i *m.sh.* **-ë** innovator.

novél/ë,-a *f.sh.* **-a** a novel, tale.

novelíst,-i *m.sh.* novelist.

nozullím,-i *m.sh.* **-e** 1. supply, furnishing. 2. provisions.

nozullój *f.k.* to supply, to furnish.

nuánc/ë,-a *f.sh.* **-a** shade, nuance.

nugá,-ja *f.sh.* – almond cake.

nuhás *f.jk.* to smell, to scent, **to**

sniff; **nuhas burnot**: to snuff tobacco, to take snuff.
nuhátës,-e *mb. anat.* smelling, rous, smelly.
nuhátj/e,-a *f.* smelling, scent, sniff; **shqisa e nuhatjes**: olfactory.
nuk *pj.* 1. not; **nuk kam**: I have not, I haven't. 2. do not, don't: **nuk e di**: I don't know. 3. *(në fjali pyetëse)* **nuk më thua?** will you say me? **nuk vjen edhe ti?** aren't you coming too?
núll/ë,-a *f.sh.* a *anat.* gum of the teeth.
numerík,-e *mb.* numerical.
numerikísht *ndajf.* numerically.
núm/ër,-ri *m.sh.* -ra number; **numër çift (tek)**: even (odd) number; **numër dhjetor**: decimal number; **numër i plotë**: full number, whole number.
numerátór,-i *m.sh.* -ë numerator.
numërím,-i *m.* numeration, numbering, counting.
numërój *f.k.* to count, to number, to numerate; **të numërojmë prej 1-10**: let us count from one to ten. – **numërohem** *f.jv.* to be counted.
numërór,-e *mb.* numeral.
numërúes,.i *m.sh.* – *mat.* numerator.
nun,-i *m.sh.* -ë godfather, bridesman.
nún/ë,-a *f.sh.* -a godmother.
nur,-i *m.* charm, good looks.
nursëz,-e *mb.* shih **vrazhdë.**
núrsh/ëm(i),-me(e) *mb.* charming, good-looking; **vajzë e nurshme**: charming girl.
nús/e,-ja *f.sh.* – 1. bride. 2. *(e djalit)* daughter-in-law.
nuselál/e,-ja *f.sh.* -e *zool.* weasel.
nusërí,-a *f.* bridehood: **rroba nusërie**; bridal dresses.
nu sërój *f.jk.* 1. to stand still on foot (a bride) during the nuptial ceremony. 2. *fig.* to stay armcrossed.

nusërór,-e *mb.* bridal.
núsk/ë,-a *f.sh.* -a 1. doll. 2. fetish.
nxeh *f.k.* 1. to heat; **nxeh një metal**: to heat a metal; **nxeh jashtë masës**: to overheat; *(me fërkim)* to chafe. 2. *fig.* to excite, to irritate, to make angry. – **nxehem** *f.jv.* 1. *fig.* to get angry, to fly into a passion, to lose one's temper. 2. *(moti)* to get hot.
nxéhj/e,-a *f.* heating.
nxéhtë *ndajf.* hotly, warmly; **bën nxehtë**: it is hot.
nxéhtë (i,e) *mb.* hot, ardent, burning, fiery.
nxéht/ë (të),-it(të) *as.* 1. heat. 2. *mjek.* fever; **kam të nxehtë**: I have fever.
nxehtësí,-a *f.* warm, heat.
nxehtësísht *ndajf.* hotly, ardently, warmly; **pres nxehtësisht dikë**: to welcome someone, to receive someone warmly.
nxë *f.k.* 1. to hold, to contain; **kjo enë nxë një litër**: this vessel contains one litter. 2. to learn; **nxë përmendsh një mësim**: to learn a lesson by heart.
nxënës,-i *m.sh.* – 1. pupil, boy, school-boy; **nxënës i zellshëm**: diligent boy: **nxënës i shkëlqyer**: a bright pupil; **nxënës mesatar**: middling pupil. 2. *(për zanat)* novice. 3. disciple: **Stalini ka qenë nxënës besnik i Leninit**: Stalini has been a loyal disciple of Lenin.
nxënës/e,-ja *f.sh.* -e school-girl.
nxënie,-a *f.* learning, studying.
nxij *f.k.* 1. to blacken, to make black; **nxij këpucët me bojë**: to black one's shoes. 2. *(dielli lëkurën)* to tan. 3. *fig.* **i nxij jetën dikujt**: to lead someone a dog's life. – **nxihem** *f.jv.* 1. to blacken. 2. *(në diell)* to get suntaned.

nxír/ë (i,e) *mb.* blackened; **i nxirë nga dielli:** sunburnt.

nxírj/e,-a *f.* blackening, blackness.

nxis *f.k.* to stir up, to incite, to instigate, to stimulate; **nxis për një veprim të keq:** to abet. — **nxitem** *f.jv.* to be incited, to be encouraged.

nxítës,-i *m.sh.* — *(lufte)* warmonger; *(për kryengritje)* instigator; *(për krime)* abettor, abetter.

nxítës,-e *mb.* inciting, encouraging, stimulating, incentive.

nxitím,-i *m.* hurry, haste; **me nxitim;** hurriedly, hastily.

nxítj/e,-a *f.* incitement, egging, stimulant, impulsion; *(për trazira)* fomentation.

nxitoj *f.k.* to hurry, to hasten. — **nxitohem** *f.jv.* to hurry, to hasten, to be quick; **nxito!** hurry up! make haste!

nxitúar (i,e) *mb.* hurried, hasty; **punë e nxituar:** hasty work; **veprim i nxituar:** precipitate action.

nxítuar (i,e) *mb.* incited.

nxjerr *f.k.* (p.t. **nxora,** p.p. **nxjerrë**) 1. to pull off, to pull out, to take off, to take out; *(një dhëmb)* to have a tooth out, to have a tooth extracted, to have a tooth pulled out. 2. *(gjuhën)* to put out (the tongue). 3. *(jashtë, përzë)* to put out, to drive out, to expel. 4. **nxjerr jashtë përdorimit:** to put out of use. 5. *(lëng)* to secrete. 6. *(monedhë të re)* to emit (new money). 7. *(një përfundim)* to draw a conclusion, to conclude, to infer. 8. **nxjerr si pretekst, si shkak:** to give as pretext. 9.

nxjerr nga puna: to dismiss, të send away, to discharge (from work), to cashier. 10. *(një rënkim)* to heave (a sigh); *(një zë, një britmë)* to raise (to set up, to utter) (a cry). 11. *(sytë)* to tear off, (the eyes). 12. *(shpatën)* to draw (the sword). 13. *(një mall ne vitrinë)* to display, to exhibit (goods in the shop windows). 14. *(në pension)* to pension someone off. 15. *(nga varri)* to unearth, to exhume (from the grave), to dig out (of the ground). 16. *(zogj nga vezët)* to incubate, to hatch (eggs). 17. *(në shesh një sekret)* to bring out (to let out, to reveal) a secret. — **nxirrem** *f.jv.* 1. *(nga puna)* to be discharged (from work). 2. *(jashtë)* to be put out (of), to be driven out.

nxjérrj/e,-a *f.* 1. *(e dhëmbit)* extraction (of a tooth). 2. *(e një ligji, dekreti)* promulgation (of a law, of a decree). 3. *(zëri; monedhe, pullash poste)* emission (of a sound; of paper money, of postage stamps). 4. *(në pension)* superannuation. 5. *(lëngu)* secretion.

nýell,-i *m.sh.* neje 1. *(i këmbës)* ankle. 2. *(i gishtit)* knuckle. 3. *(e një druri)* knot; **dru me neje:** knotty wood.

nýj/ë,-a *f.sh.* **-e** 1. *gram.* article; **nyje e përparme:** former article; **nyje e mbrapme:** rear article; **nyje e shquar (e pashquar):** definite (indefinite) article. 2. *(komunikacioni)* center (of communication).

nýjsh/ëm (i),-me(e) *mb.* preceded by an article.

Nj

nj, Nj (letter of the Albanian alphabet).

nja *pj.* some, about; **janë nja dhjetë burra:** there are about ten men; **më jep nja dy fije letër:** give me some sheets of paper.

njehsím,-i *m.sh.* -e calculation, reckoning.

njehsój *f.k. mat.* to calculate, to reckon.

njélmët (i,e) *mb.* briny, saline, salty; **ujë i njelmët:** briny water.

njerëzí,-a *f.* 1. people; **flasin njerëzia:** the people say. 2. courtesy; politeness; **sillem me njerëzi:** to behave humanely.

njerëzím,-i *m.* mankind, humanity.

njerëzísh/ëm (i),-me(e) *mb.* human, kind, polite; **në mënyrë të njerëzishme;** humanly.

njerëzísht *ndajf.* humanly, courteously, politely, kindly, with kindness.

njerëzór,-e *mb.* human.

njerí,-u *m.sh.* **njerëz** man, human being; **s'kish njeri atje;** there was nobody there; **mos i thoni njeriu:** don't tell anybody; **njeri i mirë:** good man; **njeri i çuditshëm:** queer (strange) man; **njeri keqbërës;** malefactor, evil doer; **njerëzit e mi:** my folks, my people.

njeríth,-i *m. anat.* uvula.

njerk,-u *m.sh.* -ë stepfather.

njérk/ë,-a *f.sh.* -a stepmother.

një *num. them.* 1. one: **një ditë:** one day; **një mëngjes:** one morning; **një mijë, një milion:** one thousand, one million; **një nga një:** one by one; **një pas një:** successively. 2. *gram.* a, an; **një derë:** a door; **një album:** an album; **më jep një libër:** give me a book (no matter which). **një** *mb.* same; **jemi të një mendimi:** we are of the same opinion; **jemi të një moshe:** we are of the same age. **një** *ndajf.* **një të thënë, një të bërë:** no sooner said than done; **për mua është një:** it is all one to me, it is all the same to me, it makes no difference to me.

njëanësí,-a *f.* partiality.

njëánsh/ëm(i), me(e) *mb.* partial, biassed, one-sided.

njëanshmërí,-a *f.* partiality.

njëdítëzaj *ndajf.* the day before yesterday.

njëfárë *p.pk.* such-and-such.

njëfarësój *ndajf.* 1. somewhat. 2. middling; **jam njëfarësoj:** to be so so (middling).

njëfísh *ndajf.* onefold.

njëhérë *ndajf.* once, at one time; **na ishte njëherë:** once upon a time there was.

njëhérësh *ndajf.* 1. at a stretch, at a stroke; **pi njëherësh:** to drink at a draught. 2. at the same time, simultaneously.

njëjës,-i *m. gram.* singular.

njëjtë (i,e) *mb.* 1. identical, the same; **e njëjta gjë është:** it is all the same, it amounts to the same thing; **në të njëjtën kohë:** at the same time. 2. authentic, authentical; **është i**

njëjtë me origjinalin: it is authentic to the original.

njëkohësísht *ndajf.* simultaneously, at the same time.

njëkóhsh/ëm(i),-me (e) *mb.* instantaneous, simultaneous.

njëllój *ndajf.* alike, equally; the same; për mua është njëlloj: it is all the same to me.

njëllójsh/ëm(i),-me (e) *mb,* of a kind, of the same kind.

njëllójtë (i,e) *mb.* shih i njëllojshëm.

njëmbëdhjétë *num. them.* eleven.

njëmbëdhjetë (i,e) *num. rresht.* eleventh.

njëmijëvjeçár,-e *mb.* millenar.

njëmíjtë (i,e) *num. rresht.* thousandth.

njënátëzaj *ndajf.* the evening before yesterday.

njëngjýrësh,-e *mb.* plain, of one colour, monochromatic.

njënjësh/ëm (i),-me(e) *mb.* equal.

njëpasnjësh/ëm(i),-me(e) *mb.* successive, consecutive, repeated; urdhëra të njëpasnjëshëm: repeated orders.

njëqínd *num. them.* one hundred, a hundred; njëqind e një: a hundred and one.

njëqinqfísh *ndajf.* hundred fold.

njëqíndtë (i,e) *num. rresht.* hundredth.

njëqindvjeçár,-i *m.sh.* -ë centenarian.

njëqindvjeçár,-e *mb.* centenarian.

njëqindvjetór,-i *m.sh.* -ë centenary.

njëra *p,pk.* one (for feminine); njëra mbi tjetrën: one upon the other; njëra pas tjetrës: successively.

njëra-tjétra *p.pk.* one another (for feminine); ngjarjet ndjekinnjëra-tjerën: the events succeed one another.

njëri *p.pk.* one (for masc.); njëri prej tyre: one of them.

njëri-tjétri *p.pk.* each other, one another; duhet të ndihmojmë njëri-tjetrin: we must help one another.

njërrókësh,-e *mb.* monosyllabic, of one syllable; fjalë njërrokëshe: monosyllable.

njësí,-a *f.sh.* – unit; njësi matjeje: unit of measure; njësi monetare: monetary unit.

njësím,-i *m.sh.* -e unification; njësim i drejtshkrimit: unification of the orthography.

njësít,-i *m.sh.* -e *usht.* unit, detachment; njësiti gueril: guerilla detachment, guerilla unit.

njësój *ndajf.* identical, equal, identic, the same; është njësoj; it is the same; për mua njësoj është: it is all the same to me.

njësój *f.k.* to unify.

njësh,-i *m.sh.* -a the number one.

njëshkolónë *ndajf.* in file, in line; ecim njëshkolonë: to walk in file.

njëtrájtsh/ëm(i),-me(e) *mb. mat.* uniform.

njëthundrák,-ët *m.sh.* zool. perissodactyl.

njëthundrák,-e *mb.* zool. perissodactyl.

njëvetór,-e *mb. gram.* impersonal; folje njëvetore:impersonal verb.

njëvléfsh/ëm(i),-me(e) *mb.* equivalent, tantamount.

njëzét *num. them.* twenty.

njëzetenjëtë (i,e) *mb.* twentyfirst.

njëzétë (i,e) *num. resht.* twentieth.

njëzetfísh,-i *m.* twenty-fold.

njëzetfishój *f.k.* to multiply by twenty, to increase twenty-fold. – njëzetfishohet *f.jv.* to be multiplied by twenty.

njëzetkëndësh,-i *m.sh.* -a *gjeom.* icosahedron.

njëzetvjeçár,-i *m.sh.* -ë twenty-year-old man.

njëzetepesëvjetór,-i *m.sh.* -ë twenty fifth anniversary.

njëzëri *ndajf.* unanimously, with one voice, by acclamation; i pranuar njëzëri: carried by acclamation.

njoftím,-i *m.sh.* -e communication, notice, information; marr njoftim: to take notice.

njoftój *f.k.* to inform, to tell, to make known, to give notice; njoftoj dikë për diçka: to inform someone of something. – njoftohem *f.jv.* to be informed, to get information.

njoh *f.k.* 1. to know; duhet të njohim njëri-tjetrin: we must know each other. 2. to acknowledge, to recognize; *(gabimin)* to avow. – njihem *f.jv.* 1. to be known. 2. to be recognized (acknowlegded).

njóhës,-i *m.sh.* – connoisseur, expert.

njóhj/e,-a *f.* 1. acquaintance; njohje e rastit: casual acquaintance. 2. acknowledgment, recognition. 3. *(gabimi)* avowal. 4. *filoz.* cognition.

njóhur (i,e) *mb.* 1. known; i bëj të njohur dikujt: to make known to someone, to let so-

meone know. 2. recognized. 3. famous, renowned, reputable, noted, well-known.

njóhur(i),-i(i) *m.sh.* (të) acquaintance.

njohurí,-a *f.sh.* – 1. knowledge; njohuri të përcipta: smattering (superficial) knowledge; fitoj njohuri për diçka: to acquire knowledge of something.

njóll/ë,-a *f.sh.* -a blot, spot, speck, stain; njollë e madhe: blotch, me njollë: blotty, spotty; pa njolla: spotless, stainless.

njollós *f.k.* 1. to blot, to spot, to stain, to speck, to speckle. 2. *fig.* to blemish, to sully, to besmirch, to dishonour. – njollosem *f.jv.* 1. to get dirty, to stain oneself. 2. to have a stain on one's character, to blacken one's character.

njollósj/e,-a *f.* defilement pollution.

njom *f.k.* to wet, to soak, to moisten; njom bukën në qumësht: to soak the bread into the milk; njom gurmazin: to wet one's whistle. – njomen *f.jv.* to be soaked (through).

njómë (i,e) *mb.* 1. humid, wet, moist, soggy; këmishë të njoma: humid shirts. 2. fresh, new, tender; barishte të njoma: fresh vegetables.

njómj/e,-a *f.* soaking.

O

o, O (letter of the Albanian alphabet) o, O.

oáz/ë,-a *f.sh.* -a *gjeog.* oasis.

objékt,-i *m.sh.* -e ob;ect.

objektív,-i *m.sh.* -a 1. objective. 2. *fiz.* objective.

objektív,-e *mb.* objective.

objektivísht *ndajf.* objectively.

obligación,-i *m.sh.* -e. *fin.* bond, obligation.

obligím,-i *m.sh.* -e shih detyrim.

obórr,-i *m.sh.* -e 1. *(shtëpie)* yard, courtyard; oborr prapa shtëpisë: back-yard; oborr i shkollës: school yard. 2. *(mbretëror)* royal court.

oborrësí,-a *f.* courtesy.

oborrtár,-i *m.sh.* -ë courtier.

observatór,-i *m.sh.* -ë *astron.* observatory.

ód/e,-ja *f.sh.* -e *muz.* ode.

ód/ë,-a *f.sh.* -a shih dhomë.

ofendím,-i *m.sh.* -e shih fyerje.

ofendój *f.k.* shih fyej.

ofendúes,-e *mb.* shlh fyes.

ofensív/ë,-a *f.sh.* -a offensive.

ofért/ë,-a *f.sh.* -a offer.

oficér,-i *m.sh.* -ë *usht.* officer; officer rezervist: reserve officer; officer epror, i lartë: high ranking officer.

ofíq,-i *m.sh.* -e *vjet.* duty, function.

ofiqár ,-i *m.sh.* -ë official, officer; ofiqar i gjendjes civile: registrar, city recorder.

ofrój *f.k.* to offer, to bid.— ofrohem *f.jv.* to offer one's service.

ofsháj *f.jk.* to sigh.

ogíç,-i *m.sh.* -ë *zool.* head ram, leading ram.

ogúr,-i *m.sh.* -e omen.

ogurmírë *mb.* good-omened.

ogursëz,-i *m.sh.* -ë ill-omen person, ominous person.

ogurz/í,-ezë *mb.* ill-omened, ill-omen, ominous.

ók/ë,-a *f.sh.* -ë ancient unit of weight equivalent to 1408 gr.

okllaí,-a *f.sh.* – rolling-pin.

oksíd,-i *m.sh.* -e *kim.* oxide.

oksidím,-i *m.* oxidation.

oksidój *f.k.* to oxidize.— oksidohet *f.jv.* to be oxidized.

oksigjén,-i *m. kim.* oxygen.

oktáv/ë,-a *f.sh.* -a *muz.* octave.

okulíst,-i *m.sh.* -ë oculist.

okupación,-i *m.* occupation.

okupator,-i *m.sh.* -ë occupier.

okupím,-i *m.* occupation.

okupój *f.k.* to occupy. – okupohet *f.jv.* to be occupied.

oligarkí,-a *f.* oligarchy.

olimpiád/ë,-a *f.sh.* -a *sport.* olympiad.

olimpík,-e *mb.* olympic; lojëra olimpike: olympic games.

ombréll/ë,-a *f.sh.* -a umbrella; *(grash, për diell)* parasol, sunshade.

omëlét/ë,-a *f.* omelet, omelette.

ondulación,-i *m.* undulation (of hair).

operación,-i *m.sh.* -e 1. operation. 2. *mjek.* operation; bëhem operacion: to be operated on.

operatív,-e *mb.* operative.

operatór,-i *m.sh.* -ë 1. *(kinemaje)*
cameraman. 2. *(mjek.)* operator, operating surgeon.
óper/ë,-a *f.sh.* -a *muz.* 1. opera-
house. 2. opera.
operím,-i *m.sh.* -e *mjek.* operation.
operój *f.k. mjek.* to operate; **ope-
roj dikë nga apendiciti:** to
operate on someone for appendicitis.
operúar(i),-i(i) *m.sh.* -(të) *mjek.*
patient operated on.
opingár,-i *m.sh.* -ë cobbler.
opíng/ë,-a *f.sh.* -a moccasin.
opinión,-i *m.sh.* -e opinion;
opinioni publik: public opinion; **opinioni i përgjithshëm:**
general opinion, prevailing opinion; **kam opinion të mirë
për dikë:** to have good opinion
of someone.
opiúm,-i *m.* opium.
oportuníst,-i *m.sh.* -ë opportu-
nist.
oportunitét,-i *m.* opportunity.
oportuníz/ëm,-mi *m.* opportunism.
opozít/ë,-a *f.* opposition.
optík,-e *mb.* optical.
optík/ë,-a *f.* optics.
optimíst,-i *m.sh.* -ë optimist.
optimíst,-e *mb.* optimistic, buoyant.
optimíz/ëm, -mi *m.* optimism,
buoyancy.
oqeán,-i *m.sh.* -e ocean.
oráku/ll,-lli *m. sh.* -j oracle.
orár,-i *m.sh.* -e 1. timetable, schedule; **orari i trenave:** train timetable; **në orar:** on time, punctual, *fam.* on the dot; **nuk
mbërrij në orar (brenda orarit):** not to be on time, to be
behind time, *(treni)* to be over-
due (late). 2. hours, time, times;
orari i punës: office (working)
hours.
orár,-e *mb.* hourly, hour.
oratór,-i *m.sh.* -e orator, eloquent
speaker.

oratorí,-a *f.* oratory; declamation; **flas me oratori:** to orate,
to speak in a rhetorical style.
oratorík,-e *mb.* oratorical.
ordinánc/ë,-a *f.sh.* -a *usht.* orderly.
ordinát/ë,-a *f.sh.* -a *mat.* ordinate.
ordinér,-e *mb.* 1. common. 2.
vulgar, common.
oréks,-i *m.sh.* -e appetite; **oreks i
madh:** ravenous appetite; **mungesë oreksi:** inappetence; **që
çel oreksin:** appetizing, relishing; **kam oreks:** to have
an appetite; **gjëra për të çelur
oreksin:** appetizers; **oreksi
vjen duke ngrënë:** the appetite
comes with eating.
orendí,-të *f.sh.* furnitures.
ór/ë-a *f.sh.* -ë 1. hour; **një çerek
ore:** a quarter of an hour;
gjysmë ore: half an hour; **sa
është ora?** what time is it?;
ora është dy: it is two o'clock;
në orën tre: at three o'clock. 2.
(dore, xhepi) watch; **kurdis
orën:** to wind up the clock;
orë grash: lady's watch; **orë
muri:** wall clock; **orë me zile:**
alarm-clock; **orë dore:** wristwatch; **ora nuk më punon:**
my watch does not go; **ora
më shkon dhjetë minuta përpara:** my watch is ten minutes
fast; **ora ime është pesë minuta prapa:** my watch is five
minutes slow. 3. hour, hours,
time; **ora e mbylljes së tregut:**
closing time; **orë të lira për
çlodhje:** spare hours; **gjatë orë-
ve të punës;** during the working hours; **në orën e caktuar:**
at the appointed time; **shkoi
ora:** time is up. – *Lok.* **flas me
orë të tëra:** to speak for hours,
on end, to speak for hours and
hours; **jam në orë të mira:** to
be in good homour; **jam në orë**

të liga: to be in bad humour; (in ill humour).
orëndréqës,-i *m.sh.* – clock maker, watchmaker.
orgán,-i *m.sh.* -e 1. *anat., biol.* organ. 2. *fig.* body, organ; assembly. 3. *(i një partie politike)* organ.
organík,-e *mb.* 1. organic; **pleh organik**: manure. 2. *fig.* organic, organized.
organík/ë,-a *f.sh.* -a personnel, staff (of an establishment, of an institution).
organizát/ë,-a *f.sh.* -a organization; **organizata bazë e partisë**: basic party organization.
organizatór,-i *m.sh.* -ë organizer.
organíz/ëm,-mi *m.sh.* -ma organism (edhe *fig.*); **organizmi i njeriut**: human body.
organizím,-i *m.* organization; **s'ka organizim**: to lack organization.
organizój *f.k.* to organize.– **organizohem** *f.jv.* to organize, to get organized.
organizúar (i,e) *mb.* organized; **person i organizuar**: party member.
órgano,-ja *f.sh.* – *muz.* organ.
orgjí,-a *f.sh.* – orgy.
oriént,-i *m.* Orient, East.
orientál,-e *mb.* Oriental, Eastern.
orientím,-i *m.sh.* -e orientation; **pikë orientimi**: land mark.
orientój *f.k.* 1. to orientate. 2. *fig.* to direct, to steer.– **orientohem** *f.jv.* to take (to get) one's bearings, to orientate oneself, to see which way the land lies, to see which way the wind blows; **nuk orientohem dot në këtë punë**: I can't make head or tail in this matter, I am out of my bearings.

origjinál,-i *m.sh.* -e original.
origjinál,-e *mb.* original.
origjín/ë,-a *f.* origin; **fjalë me origjinë latine**: words of Latin origin; **jam me origjinë shqiptare**: to be of Albanian origin.
oríz,-i *m. bot.* rice; **oriz i qëruar (i paqëruar)**: polished (brown) rice.
orizór/e,-ja *f.sh.* -e rice-paddy, rice-field.
orkést/ër,-ra *f.sh.* -ra orchestra.
orták,-u *m.sh.* -ë associate, partner; **bëhem ortak me**: to enter into partnership with someone.
ortakërí,-a *f.* partnership, association.
orték,-u *m.sh.* -ë avalanche.
ortodóks,-e *mb.* orthodox.
ortodoksí,-a *f.* orthodoxy.
ortografí,-a *f.* orthography.
ortografík,-e *mb.* orthographic; **gagabim ortografik**: misspelling, misprint.
orvátem *f.jv.* to attempt, to strive, to try, to endeavour.
orvátj/e,-a *f.sh.* -e effort, endeavour, attempt, try; **bëj çdo orvajtje**: to make (to exert) every effort.
óse *lidh.* or, either; **ose njërin, ose tjetrin**: either one or the other.
osh *ndajf.* **heq osh**: to drag.
oshënár,-i *m.sh.* -ë eremite, hermit.
oshëtím/ë,-a *f.sh.* -a 1. echo, e-sound, resounding. 2. roar; **oshëtimë e detit**: the roar of the sea.
oshëtín *f.jk.* 1. to resound. 2. *(topi)* to roar.
oturák,-u *m.sh.* -ë chamber-pot.
oxhák,-u *m.sh.* -ë chimney; *(va-*

pori, uzine) funnel, chimney (of a steamship, of a steamengine); **qoshe oxhaku:** chimney – corner; **oxhak ajrimi:** smoke-vent, flue; **fshij oxhakun:** to sweep a chimney. **oxhakpastrúes,-i** *m.sh.* – chimney sweeper.

P

p,P (letter of the Albanian alphabet) **p, P.**
pa I. *paraf.* without, having no, bereft, void of; **pa kuptim:** senseless, void of sense; **njeri pa mend në kokë:** brainless man; **fëmijë pa prindër:** parentless child, child bereft of parents, orhpan; **pa e ditur:** unconsciously, unkowingly; **pa dyshim:** without doubt, undoubtedly, doubtless; **pa tjetër:** by all means; without fail; **mungesë pa arsye:** unjustifiable absence; **ai nxehet pa arsye:** he is offended (he gets angry) for no reason; **jam pa një dysh (pa një lek):** I am penniless, I have not a farthing. – *Prov.* **peshk pa hala s'ka:** there are no fish without bones.
II. *lidh.* before; **ai doli nga shtëpia pa gdhirë:** he went out of home before dawn.
III. *fjalëz* (particle of an imperative sentence) **pa më thuaj:** tell me; **shko një herë pa shohim e bëjmë:** go there, then we shall see what we have to do.
IV. *ndajf.* less, minus; to; then; **shtatë pa katër bëjnë tre (mbeten tre):** seven minus

three leaves three, four from seven remain three; **ora është dy pa dhjetë minuta:** it is ten minutes to two.
V. *parashtesë* (prefix equivalent to un, in, im, ir, dis) **i pafat:** unfortunate; **padrejtësi:** injustice; **e pamundur:** impossible; **i parregullt:** irregular; **pazotësi:** incapability.
VI. *f.k.* he saw, he found (past tense of the verb **shoh,** third person singular); **ai e pa me sytë e tij:** he saw it with his own eyes.
paafrúesh/ëm(i),-me(e) *mb.* 1. unapproachable. 2. *fig.* unsociable.
paáftë (i,e) *mb.* incapable, unable; inapt; **i paaftë për shërbimin ushtarak:** unfit for military service.
paaftësí,-a *f.* incapacity, inability; inaptitude.
paánë (i,e) *mb.* infinite, endless.
paanësi,-a *f.* 1. infinity. 2. impartiality.
paanësísht *ndajf.* impartially.
paangazhúar (i,e) *mb.* 1. disengaged. 2. non-aligned.
paánsh/ëm(i),-me(e) *mb.* impartial, just, equitable, unbiased

paanullúesh/ëm (i),- me (e) *mb.* irrevocable.

paaprovúar (i,e) *mb.* unapproved.

paargásur (i,e) *mb.* 1. *(lëkurë)* raw (skin). 2. *fig.* unexperienced; **njeri i paargasur:** unexperienced person.

paargumentúar (i,e) *mb.* unargued.

paarmatósur (i,e) *mb.* disarmed, unarmed.

paarsýesh/ëm(i),-me(e) *mb.* unreasonable, irrational.

paarrírë (i,e) *mb.* 1. unripe, green (of fruit); **pemë e paarrirë:** unripe fruit; 2. *fig.* immature; **vendim i paarrirë:** immature decision.

paarrítsh/ëm (i),-me(e) *mb.* inaccessible, unattainable, out of reach.

paautorizúar (i,e) *mb.* unauthorized, unwarranted.

pabanúar (i,e) *mb.* uninhabited.

pabanúesh/ëm(i),-me(e) *mb.* uninhabitable.

pabarabartë (i,e) *mb.* unequal, disproportionate.

pabarazí,-a *f.* inequality.

pabarazuesh/ëm(i),-me(e) *mb.* unequalled; incomparable.

pabazúar (i,e) *mb.* unfounded, unbased, groundless.

pabésë (i,e) *mb.* unfaithful, faithless, perfidious, unfair, disloyal, infidel; treacherous.

pabesí,-a *f.sh.* – unfaithfulness, perfidy, infidelity.

pabesísht *ndajf.* perfidiously.

pabesúesh/ëm(i),-me(e) *mb.* incredible, unbelievable.

pabërë (i,e) *mb.* 1. undone. 2. unripe; **rrush i pabërë:** unripe grapes.

pabíndur (i,e) *mb.* disobedient, indocile, recalcitrant; **kalë i pabindur:** restive horse.

pabotúar (i,e) *mb.* unpublished inedited.

paburrërí,-a *f.* cowardice, unmanliness.

pacaktûar (i,e) *mb.* indeterminate, indefinite, not precise, vague.

pacënúar (i,e) *mb.* intact.

pacënúesh/ëm (i),-me(e) *mb.* intangible, invulnerable.

pacilësúar (i,e) *mb.* unqualified.

pacilësûesh/ëm (i),-me(e) *mb.* unqualifiable.

pacípë (i,e) *mb.* insolent, impudent, shameless, saucy, unblushing

páça *f.k.* (optative mood of the verb **kam**) may I have! **paç dorën e mbarë!** may you have a hapy hand!

paçavúr/e,-ja *f.sh.* -e 1. rag, frippery; *(për larjen e enëve)* dishcloth. 2. trash.

páç/e,-ja *f.* a kind of broth.

paçmúar (i,e) *mb.* inestimable, invaluable, priceless.

paçmúesh/ëm(i),-me(e) *mb.* inapreciable, invaluable, inestimable, priceless.

padallúar (i,e) *mb.* indistinguished, indiscerned, indistinct.

padallúesh/ëm(i),-me(e) *mb.* indiscernible, indistinguishable.

padáshur *ndajf.* involuntarily, unintentionally.

padeklarúar (i,e) *mb.* undeclared; **luftë e padeklaruar:** undeclared war.

padénj/ë (i,e) *mb.* unworthy, undeserved; **vepër e padenjë:** unworthy act.

padenjësísht *ndajf.* unworthily, underservedly.

padepërtúesh/ëm(i),-me(e) *mb.* impenetrable, impermeable, tight; *(nga ajri)* air-tight; *(nga drita)* opaque; *(nga uji)* water-tight, impermeable.

padepërtueshmërí,-a *f.* impenetrability, impermeability, tightness.

padeshifrúesh/ëm(i),-me (e) *mb.* indecipherable.

padetyrúesh/ëm(i),-me (e) *mb.* facultative.

padëgjúar (i,e) *mb.* 1. unheard. 2. unheard-of, unprecedented. 3. disobedient.

padëgjúesh/ëm(i),- me (e) *mb.* 1. disobedient. 2. inaudible.

padëmsh/ëm(i),-me (e) *mb.* harmless, innoxious, innocuous.

padëmtúar (i,e) *mb.* intact, unimpaired.

padëshirúar (i,e) *mb.* unwished, unwelcome, unasked.

padëshirúesh/ëm (i),-me(e) *mb.* undesirable.

padí,-a *f.sh.* – *drejt.* accusation, charge, indictment; **ngre padi kundër dikujt:** to bring an action against someone, to charge (to accuse, to sue) someone.

padíj/e,-a *f.* ignorance.

padijení,-a *f.* lack of knowledge; **jam në padijeni të një çështjeje:** not to know about something, not to be informed of something, to be in the dark.

padíjsh/ëm(i),-me(e) *mb.* ignorant, illiterate, unlearned.

padiktúar (i,e) *mb.* undiscovered.

padiktúesh/ëm (i), -me (e) *mb.* unfindable, undiscernable.

padisiplinúar (i,e) *mb.* undisciplined.

padiskutúesh/ëm(i),-me (e) *mb.* indisputable, incontestable.

padís *f.k.* to charge, to accuse, to sue, to go to law against someone, to bring an action against someone, to have the law on someone.

padítës,-i *m.sh.* – *drejt.* suitor, prosecutor, litigant, plaintiff, accuser.

padítur (i),-i(i) *m.sh.* – **(të)** *drejt.* defendant, respondent.

padítur (i,e) *mb.* ignorant, unlearned, illiterate; **njeri i paditur:** ignoramus, ignorant person.

paditurí,-a *f.* ignorance.

padjallëzí,-a *f.* naivety, innocence.

padjallëzúar (i,e) *mb.* naive.

padjégsh/ëm(i),-me(e) *mb.* incombustible.

padobí,-a *f.* inutility, inefficacy.

padobísh/ëm (i),-me(e) *mb.* useless, unuseful, fruitless, unavailing, of no avail, without avail.

padréjtë (i,e) *mb.* unjust, inequitable, unfair, wrongful; **vendime të padrejta;** unjust decisions.

padrejtësí,-a *f.* injustice, inequity.

padrejtësísht *ndajf.* unjustly, inequitably, wrongfully.

padrójtur (i,e) *mb.* unbashful.

padrón,-i *m.sh.* -ë master, proprietor, owner.

padúksh/ëm(i),-me(e) *mb.* invisible.

padukshmërí,-a *f.* invisibility.

padurím,-i *m.* impatience; **me padurim:** impatiently, eagerly.

padurúar (i,e) *mb.* impatient (at), eager (for); **tregohem i paduruar me dikë:** to be impatient with someone.

padurúesh/ëm(i),-me(e) *mb.* 1. unbearable, intolerable, unquestionable. 2. unresisting, unendurable.

padyshímtë(i,e) *mb.* certain, undoubted, indubitable.

padhímbsh/ëm(i),-me(e) *mb.* 1. insensible. 2. unpainful.

padhunúesh/ëm(i),-me(e) *mb.* inviolable.

padhunueshmërí,- *af.* inviolability.

paedukátë (i,e) *mb.* uncivil, ill-bred, low-bred.

paedukúar (i,e) *mb.* ill-bred, ill--educated, low-bred.

paeféktsh/ëm(i),-me(e) *mb.* ineffective, inefficient, ineffectual.

paépur (i,e) *mb.* inflexible, rigid, stiff, implacable, inexorable, irreversible, unylieding, unrelenting.

paevitúesh/ëm (i,),-me (e) *mb.* unavoidable, inevitable.

pafáj(i,e) *mb.* innocent.

pafajësí,-a *f.* innocence.

pafájsh/ëm (i),-me(e) *mb.* innocent, guiltless.

pafálsh/ëm(i),-me(e) *mb.* unforgivable, unpardonable, inexcusable, irremissible; **gabim i pafalshëm;** unforgivable fault, irremissible fault.

pafát (i,e) *mb.* unfortunate, ill-fated.

pafé (i,e) *mb.* irreligious, impious.

pafëllíqur (i,e) *mb.* unsoiled, spotless, immaculate.

pafjálë(i,e) *mb.* wordless.

pafré (i,e) *mb.* unbridled.

pafrenúesh/ëm (i),-me(e) *mb.* irrepressible, irresistible, unrestrainable.

pafríksh/ëm(i),-me(e) *mb.* bold, unafraid, hardy, intrepid, unfearful, fearless.

pafrýtsh/ëm(i),-me(e) *mb.* fruitless, vain, useless; **përpjekje të pafrytshme:** fruitless efforts.

páft/ë,-a *f.sh.* -a plate.

paftúar (i,e) *mb.* uninvited, unwelcome.

pafúnd (i,e) *mb.* endless, infinite, interminable, never-ending.

pafundësí,-a *f.* infinity.

pafúndm/ë(i),-e(e) *mb.* shih **i pafund.**

pafuqí,-a *f.* weakness, feebleness, impotence.

pafuqí (i,e) *mb.* weak, feeble, impotent, powerless.

pafuqísh/ëm(i),-me(e) *mb.* shih **i pafuqi.**

pagabúesh/ëm(i),-me(e) *mb.* infallible, unerring.

pagabueshmërí,-a *f.* infallibility.

pagán,-i *m.sh.* -ë pagan.

paganíz/ëm,-mi *m.* paganism.

pagarantúar (i,e) *mb.* unwarranted.

pagdhéndur (i,e) *mb.* 1. coarse, rough, not carved; **dru i pagdhendur:** uncarved wood. 2. *fig.* uncouth, boorish, coarse, impolite; **njeri i pagdhendur:** clodhopper, uncouth person.

pagés/ë,-a *f.sh.* -a payment; **pagesë në natyrë:** payment in kind; *(e një borxhi)* reimbursement, payment (of a debt); **me pagesë:** against payment; **pa pagesë:** gratis, free of charge, without charge.

pág/ë,-a *f.sh.* -a pay, wage, salary; **pagë ditore:** daily pay; **bllokim i pagave :** wage-freeze; **ditë e pagave:** pay-day; **ulje e pagavë:** wage-reduction, wage-cut; **me gjysmë page:** on halfpay; **me pagë të plotë:** on full pay.

pagëzím,-i *m. fet.* baptism.

pagëzój *f.k.* 1. *fet.* to baptize. — **pagëzohem** *f.jv.* to be baptized.

pagím,-i *m.* payment; reimbursement.

pagójë(i,e)*mb.* mouthless, tongue--tied, dumb.

pagúaj *f.k.* to pay, *(një borxh)* to pay (a debt); *(një faturë)* to settle (an invoice); **paguaj peshin:** to pay in cash; **paguaj me kësto:** to pay in (by) installments; **paguaj më pak nga ç'vlen:** to underpay; **(më shumë nga ç'vlen)** to overpay; **paguaj para afatit:**to pay ahead of time; *fig.* **do të ma paguajë shtrenjtë:** he'll pay me dearly. — **paguhem** *f.jv.* to be paid.

pagúes,-i *m.sh.* – paymaster, payer.
pagúesh/ëm(i),-me(e) *mb.* payable.
pagúr,-i *m.sh.* -ё flask.
paguxímsh/ëm(i),-me(e) *mb.* undaring, uncourageous, pluckless.
pagjásë (i,e) *mb.* improbable, unlikely.
pagják (i,e) *mb. mjek.* anemic.
pagjúmë (i,e) *mb.* wakeful, sleepless.
pagjumësí,-a *f.* sleeplessness, insomnia; **vuaj nga pagjumësia:** to suffer from insomnia.
pagjykúesh/ëm(i),-me(e) *mb.* unreasonable.
pah,-u *m.* **vë në pah:** to point out.
paharrúar (i,e) *mb.* unforgotten
paharrúesh/ëm(i),-me(e) *mb.* unforgettable.
pahíjsh/ëm(i),-me(e) *mb.* improper, unbecoming, indecent, unpleasant, incongrous, disagreable, unseemly; **bisedë e pahíjshme:** indecent talk; **sjellje e pahijshme:** unbecoming behaviour; **në mënyrë të pahijshme:** indecently.
pahijeshí,-a *f.* impropriety, unseemliness, unbecomingness.
pahír *ndajf.* **me pahir:** unwillingly, against one's will, reluctantly;
pahonépssh/ëm (i),-me(e) *mb.* 1. indigestible. 2. *fig.* despicable, intolerable.
palmitúessh/ëm(i), -me (e) *mb.* inimitable.
painteresuar(i,e) *mb.* disinterested, unconcerned, indifferent.
pajetërsúesh/ëm(i),-me(e) *mb.* inalienable.
páj/ë,-a *f.* dowry, trousseau.
pajíme,-t *f.sh.* outfit, equipment, kit; *(ushtarake)* pack, kit; *(të kalit)* harness (of a horse); **i vë pajimet kalit:** to harness the

horse; **i heq pajimet kalit:** to unharness the horse;
pajís *f.k.* to provide with, to supply with, to equip with, to fit up; *(me armë etj. një ushtri)* to equip, to fit up an army with (ammunitions etc.); *(me njerëz)* to man, to staff. – **pajisem** *f.jv.* to provide oneself.
pajísj/e,-a *f.sh.* -e outfit, equipment; *(ushtrie)* kit, pack (of soldiers).
pajísur(i,e) *mb.* provided, equipped, fitted.
pajtím,-i *m.* 1. reconciliation. 2. *(në një gazetë, etj.)* subscription (to a newspaper etc.); *(në punë)* employment. – *Lok.* **në pajtim me:** according to, in accordance with, in conformity with.
pajtimtár,-i *m.sh.* -ë 1. *(në një gazetë etj.)* subscriber (to a newspaper). 2. conciliator.
pajtój *f.k.* 1. to reconcile, to conciliate. 2. *(në punë)* to employ, to give employment to someone. – **pajtohem** *f.jv.* 1. to be reconciled, to be conciliated; *(me mendimin e dikujt)* to agree (with someone's opinion), to fall in (with someone's opinion); **nuk pajtohem me mendimin e tjetrit:** to disagree with someone's opinion; **pajtohet me:** to correspond with, to comply with. 2. *(në gazetë)* to subscribe (to a newspaper).
pajtón,-i *m.sh.* -ë phaeton.
pajtúes,-i *m.sh.* – conciliator, peacemaker.
pajtúes,-e *mb.* conciliatory, reconcilatory: **fjalë pajtuese:** reconciliatory words.
pajtúesh/ëm (i),-me(e) *mb.* 1. concilable, reconcilable. 2. conformable, concordant, compatible.
pajtueshmërí,-a *f.* 1. compatibility. 2. conformity.

pajustifikúesh /ëm(i),-me(e) *mb.* unjustifiable, unwarrantable; **mungesë e pajustifikueshme**: unjustifiable absence, inexcusable absence.

pak *ndajf.* few, a few, some, a little, little, not much; **nëm pak duhan**: give me some tabacco; **nëm pak kripë**: give me a little salt; **pleqtë hanë shumë pak**: old people eat very little; **punova pak**: I worked a little; **nga pak**: by little, by inches; **pak nga pak**: little by little, by and by, gradually, by inches; **për pak u mbyt**: he nearly was drowned; **për pak rashë**: I nearly fell; **për pak kohë**: for a short time, for some time; **vetëm për pak javë**: only for a few weeks; **ai bëri pak për veten e tij**: he did little for himself; **pak më intereson**: it doesn't interest me much; **edhe pak**: a little more; **fare pak, shumë pak**: too little; **më pak**: less; **pas pak**: a little after, soon after; **sa më pak**: so much the less; **sado pak**: ever so little; **së paku**: at least; **pak si**: somewhat; **Toka vjen pak si e rrafshtë afër poleve**: the Earth is somewhat flat towards the poles.

pakalítur (i,e) *mb.* unhardened.
pakalúes,-e *mb.* *(nxënës)* failing; **notë pakaluese**: bad mark.
pakalúesh /ëm(i),-me(e) *mb.* impassable; **lumë i pakalueshëm**: impassable river.
pakallajísur (i,e) *mb.* untinned.
pakállur (i,e) *mb.* not interred.
pakapërcýesh /ëm (i),-me (e) *mb.* 1. impassable; **lumë i pakapërcyeshëm**: impassable river. 2. insuperable, unsurmountable; **vështirësi të pakapërcyeshme**: insuperable difficulties.

pakápsh /ëm(i),-me(e) *mb.* 1. unreachable. 2. *fig.* impercetible.
pakét /ë,-a *f.sh.* -a packet, small parcel; **paketë cigaresh**: packet of cigarettes; **hap paketën**: to unpack, to unbundle.
paketím,-i *m.* packing, encasement.
paketój *f.k.* to package, to pack. – **paketohet** *f.jv.* to be packaged.
paketúes,-i *m.sh.* – packer.
pákë (i,e) *mb.* scanty; week, feeble.
pakëmbýesh /ëm (i),-me(e) *mb.* unchangeable, inconvertible.
pakënáqësí,-a *f.* dissatisfaction.
pakënáqsh /ëm(i),-me(e) *mb.* unsatisfying, displeasing.
pakënáqur (i,e) *mb.* discontented, dissatisfied.
pakëndsh /ëm (i,)-me(e) *mb.* 1. disagreable, unpleasant. 2. unduly, unbecoming.
pakësím,-i *m.* lessening, reduction, diminution, decrement, abatement.
pakësój *f.k.* to lessen, to decrease, to diminish, to abate. – **pakësohet** *f.jv.* to be lessened (diminished, decreased).
pákët (i,e) *mb.* 1. few; **të pakët janë ata që**: few are those who. 2. scarce, scanty, poor, meagre; **të korra të pakëta**: poor harvest. 3. feeble; weak, poor; **dritë e pakët**: feeble light.
pákëz *ndajf.* little, not much, a little, a bit.
pakíc/ë,-a *f.* 1. small quantity; **me pakicë**: in small quantity; **tregti me pakicë**: retail business, retail trade. 2. minority.
páko,-ja *f.sh.* –pack, package, parcel, bundle; **hap pakon**: to unpack.
pakóhsh /ëm(i),-me(e) *mb.* out of time, untimely.

pakontrollúar (i,e) *mb.* uncontrolled.
pakontrollúesh/ëm(i),-me(e) *mb.* uncontrollable.
pakorrigjúar (i,e) *mb.* uncorrected.
pakorrigjúesh/ëm(i),-me(e) *mb.* incorrigible.
pakorruptúar (i,e) *mb.* incorruptible.
pakrahasúesh/ëm(i),-me (e) *mb.* incomparable, unparalleled, unequalled.
pakrasítur (i,e) *mb.* unpruned.
pakréhur (i,e) *mb.* uncombed.
pakritikúesh/ëm (i),-me (e) *mb.* uncriticizable.
pakrípur (i,e) *mb.* unsalted.
pakrýer (i,e) *mb.* 1. inaccomplished, unperformed, unfinished. 2. *gram.* koha e pakryer: imperfect tense.
paksá *ndajf.* too little; a little, a little bit.
paksëpáku *ndajf.* at least.
pakt,-i *m.sh.* -e pact; pakt mossulmimi: nonaggression pact.
pákët (i,e) *mb.* little, small, slight; me shpenzime të pakëta: with little expense.
páktën (të) I. *ndajf.* at least; nuk është fort i zgjuar, po të paktën studijon: he is not very clever, but at least he studies. II. *lidh.* at least; të paktën të punonte: if he would at least work.
páku (së) *ndajf.* at least.
pakthýesh/ëm(i),-me(e) *mb.* 1. irreversible. 2. irrevocable.
pakualifikúar (i,e) *mb.* unqualified.
pakufísh/ëm(i),-me(e) *mb.* 1. unlimited. 2. *gram.* indefinite; përemër i pakufishëm: indefinite pronoun.
pakufizím,-i *m.* illimitability.
pakufizúar (i,e) *mb.* unlimited;

fuqi e pakufizuar: unlimited authority, absolute authority.
pakujdesí,-a *f.* carelessness, neglect, negligence; inadvertence; për pakujdesi: for inadvertence.
pakujdéssh/ëm(i),-me(e) *mb.* careless, negligent; njeri i pakujdesshëm: careless person.
pakundërshtúesh/ëm (i) -me(e) *mb.* 1. incontestable, irrefutable, indisputable. 2. *drejt.* peremptory; vendim i pakundërshtueshëm: peremptory verdict.
pakuptím (i,e) *mb.* senseless, meaningless.
pakuptúesh/ëm(i),-me(e) *mb.* incomprehensible, abstruse, unintelligible.
pakuptueshmërí,-a *f.* incomprehensibility.
pakursýer (i,e) *mb.* unsparing; I pakursyer në lëvdata: unsparing of praise.
pakuptúesh/ëm (i),-me(e) *mb.* uncostly.
paláço,-ja *f.sh.* - clown, buffoon, jester.
palaçollë/k,-ku *m.sh.* -qe buffoonery, jesting.
palakúesh/ëm(i),-me (e) *mb. gram.* undeclinable.
palára,-t(të) *f.sh.* dirty linen; *fig.* nxjerr të palarat në shesh: to wash one's dirty linen in public.
palárë (i,e) *mb.* unclean, dirty; lesh i palarë: unbleached wool.
pálc/ë,-a *f.* 1. marrow; palca e kurrizit: spinal marrow; kockë me palcë: marrow-bone. 2. *(e drurit, e kërcellit)* pith.
palejúesh/ëm(i),-me(e) *mb.* inadmissible, illicit, unauthorized, unlicensed, prohibited.
palést/ër,-ra *f.sh.* -ra gymnasium, *fam.* gym.
paleverdí,-a *f.* disadvantage, unprofitableness.

paleverdísh/ëm(i),-me(e) *mb*. disadvantageous, unprofitable.
paleverdishmërí,-a *f.* disadvantage.
palexúesh/ëm(i),-me(e) *mb*. illegible.
palezétsh/ëm(i),-me(e) *mb*. unpleasant, disagreable; uncomely.
pál/ë,-a *f.sh.* -a 1. pair; **një palë këpucë:** a pair of shoes. 2. suit, costume; **një palë rroba grash:** an woman's suit, a costume. 3. pack, package; **një palë letra:** a pack of cards. 4. *drejt.* party; **pala e interesuar:** the interested party; **pala kundërshtare:** the opponent party.
pá/lë,-a *f.sh* -a *(e një plaçke)* crease, pleat, fold; **bëj me pala një plaçkë:** to pleat a tissue.
palëçítsh/ëm(i),-me (e) *mb. vjet.* illegible.
palëkúndsh/ëm (i),-me (e) *mb*. 1. unshakeable. 2. *fig.* firm, steady.
palëkundshmërí,-a *f.* 1. unshakeableness. 2. *fig.* firmness, steadiness.
palërúar (i,e) *mb*. untilled, uncultivated, unploughed; **fushë e palëruar:** unplowed field.
palërúesh/ëm(i),-me(e) *mb*. uncultivable, untillable.
palëvízsh/ëm(i),-me(e) *mb*. motionless, still; immovable.
palëvizshmërí,-a *f.* stillness, motionlessness, immobility.
palídhur(i,e) *mb*. 1. untied. 2. *fig.* incoherent; **stil i palidhur:** incoherent style.
palígjsh/ëm(i),-me(e). *mb*. unlawful, illegal, illegitimate.
paligjshmërí,-a *f.* unlawfulness, illegitimacy.
pálm/ë,-a *f.sh.* -a *bot.* palm-tree.
palódhsh/ëm(i),-me(e) *mb*. indefatigable, untiring.
palódhur (i,e) *mb*. tireless, restless, unweary, unremitting; **punë-**

tor i palodhur: a tireless worker.
palogjíksh/ëm(i),-me (e) *mb*. illogical.
palombár,-i *m.sh.* -ë *det.* diver.
palós *f.k.* to fold up, to roll up, to pleat; **palos një fletë letre:** to fold up a sheet of paper. – **paloset** *f.jv.* to be folded.
palósj/e,-a *f.* folding.
palmét/ë,-a *f. det.* cabia; berth (on a ship.
palúajtsh/ëm (i),-me (e) *mb*. immobile; **pasuri e paluajtshme:** real estate, immovables, immovable property.
palundrúesh/ëm(i),-me (e) *mb* unnavigable.
palýer (i,e) *mb*. not painted, not whitewashed.
pall *f.jk.* shih **pëllet**.
pallásk/ë,-a *f.sh.* -a *mek.* bucket; **rrotë me pallaska:** waterwheel.
pallát,-i *m.sh.* -e 1. palace. 2. building. 3. block of flats. *amer.* apartment building.
pallávra,-t *f.sh.* palavers, idle chatter.
palldëm,-i *m.sh.* -e harness.
páll/ë,-a *f.sh.* -a sword. – *Lok.* **bëj pallë:** to live in clover.
pállj/e,-a *f.* 1. *(e lopës)* low, moo (of a cow); *(e gomarit)* bray (of an ass).
pallogarítsh/ëm (i),-me(e) *mb*. incalculable.
pállto,-ja *f.sh.* – overcoat, greatcoat.
pall/úa,-oi *m.sh.*-onj *zool.*peacock.
pamartúar (i,e) *mb*. unmarried, bachelor.
pamásë (i,e) *mb*. immense, enormous, infinite.
památsh/ëm(i),-me(e) *mb*. immeasurable.
památur (i,e) *mb*. 1. unmeasured. 2. imprudent.

pambarúar (i,e) mb. 1. unfinished. 2. interminable, endless.

pambrójtur (i,e) mb. unprotected, undefended.

pambúk,-u m. cotton.

pambúktë (i,e) mb. cotton: veshje të pambukta: cotton clothes.

pamendúar (i,e) mb. unthoughtful, unthinking, thoughtless; fjalë të pamenduara: ill-considered words.

pameritúar (i,e) mb. undeserved; shpërblim i pamerituar: an undeserved reward.

pamëkátë (i,e) mb. sinless.

pamësúar (i,e) mb. 1. unlearned, illiterate. 2. unexperienced. 3. unaccustomed.

pamëshirsh/ëm(i), -me (e) mb. unmerciful, unpitiful, pitiless, merciless, ruthless, relentless.

pamiratúar (i,e) mb. unapproved.

pamjaftúesh/ëm (i),-me(e) mb. insufficient, inadequate.

pamjaftueshmërí,-a f. insufficiency.

pámj/e,-a f.sh. -e 1. view, sight, aspect; (e një qyteti) view of a city. 2. (e një shtëpie nga balli) frontage, front view (of a house). 3. (e fytyrës) look (of the face): pamje e jashtme: outward, external aspect, external appearance; nuk duhet gjykuar nga pamja e jashtme: one must not judge from the outside appearances, one must not judge by outward looks; në pamjen e parë: at first sight; marr një pamje serioze: to put on a serious face; pamja e përgjithshme: general aspect (view.)

pamobilúar(i,e) mb. unfurnished; dhomë e pamobiluar: unfurnished room.

pamohúesh/ëm(i),-me(e) mb. undeniable.

pamposhtur (i,e) mb. indomitable, invincible.

pampréhur (i,e) mb. blunt, unsharpened.

pamundësí,-a f. impossibility.

pamúndsh/ëm (i),-me(e) mb. 1. impossible. 2. invincible.

pamúndur (i,e) mb. 1, impossible; është e pamundur: it is impossible. 2. unwell, ill, indisposed; jam i pamundur: to be under the weather.

panafákë (i,e) mb. krah. shih i pafat.

panaír,-i m.sh. -e fair.

pandálsh/ëm(i),-me(e) mb. unceasing.

pandárë (i,e) mb. undivided, joint, unseparated; shokë të pandarë: inseparable friends.

pandásh/ëm (i),-me (e) mb. inseparable, indivisible.

pandashmërí,-a f. inseparability, indivisibility.

pandéh f.k., f.jk. to think, to imagine, to surmise, to supose, to presume; kush e pandehu kështu! who would ever have thought it!

pandéhj/e,-a f. surmise, presumption.

pandéhur (i,e) mb. drejt. accused; i pandehur për vjedhje: accused of theft.

pandéhur(i),-i(i) m.sh. -(të) drejt. the accused; fjala e të pandehurit: plea of the accused.

pandérsh/ëm(i),-me(e) mb. 1. dishonest, disreputable, discreditable, deceitful; përdor mjete të pandershme: to make use of dishonest means. 2. dishonorable, immoral, improper.

pandershmërí,-a f 1. dishonesty. 2. immorality, dishonourable behaviour.

pandershmërísht ndajf. dishonestly.

pandërgjégjsh/ëm(i),-me (e) mb. unconscious.
pandërgjegjshmërí,-a f. unconsiciousness.
pandërprérë (i,e) mb. uninterrupted, unintermitted, unceasing, continuous.
pandërrúar (i,e) mb. unchanged, the same.
pandërrúesh/ëm(i),-me (e) mb. 1. gram. invariable. 2. immutable, unchangeable.
pandëshkúar (i,e) mb. unpunished, uncondemned.
pandëshkúesh/ëm(i); -me(e)mb. unpunishable.
pandëshkueshmërí,-a f. impunity.
pandíer (i,e) mb. quiet, noiseless.
pandjesh/ëm(i),-me(e) mb. insensible, impassive, apathetic, unfeeling.
pandjeshmërí,-a f. insensibility, impassiveness, unfeelingness.
pandíhmë (i,e) mb. unaided, without support.
pandótur(i,e) mb. clean, undirty, unsullied, unsoiled.
pandréqsh/ëm(i),-me(e) mb. 1. irreclaimable, irreparable, irremediable, irretrievable; dëm i pandreqshëm: irreparable damage. 2. incorrigible; njeri i pandreqshëm: incorrigible person.
pandréqur (i,e) mb. unrepaired.
pandrýshksh/ëm(i),-me(e) mb. stainless; çelik i pandryshkshëm: stainless steel.
pandrýshkur (i,e) mb. inoxidized.
pandryshúesh/ëm(i),-me (e) mb. invariable, unchangeable, immutable, stable, constant.
pandryshueshmërí,-a f. invariability, immutability, stability.
panél,-i m.sh. -e panel; vesh me panele një mur: to panel a wall.
panevójsh/ëm(i),-me (e) mb. un-

necessary, useless, needless, of no use; send i panevojshëm: useless thing.
panënshtrúar (i,e) mb. unsubmitted, unsubdued.
pangínjur (i,e) mb. insatiated, greedy.
pangopësí,-a f. insatiability, cupidity, avidity, greediness; me pangopësi: greedily, voraciously.
pangópur (i,e) mb. greedy, voracious, gluttonous.
pangrënë (i,e) mb. unfed, uneating.
pangrënsh/ëm (i),-me(e) mb. uneatable.
pangushëllúesh/ëm(i),-me(e) mb. inconsolable.
pangjárë (i,e) mb. without precedent, unprecedented.
pangjásh/ëm(i),-me(e) mb. unlike, dissimilar.
pangjýrë (i,e) mb. colourless.
paník,-u m. panic.
panín/e,-ja f.sh. -e loaf, roll (of bread).
pankárt/ë,-a f.sh. -a placard.
pankreás,-i m.sh. -ë anat. pancreas.
panorám/ë,-a f.sh. -a panorama.
pantallóna,-t f.sh. trousers, pants; pantallona të shkurtëra: kneebreeches.
pantóf/ël,-la f.sh. -la slippers.
pantomím/ë,-a f.sh. -a pantomime.
panúmërt (i,e)—mb. numberless, countless.
panumërúesh/ëm(i),-me(e) mb. innumerable, incalculable, numberless.
panxhár,-i m.sh. -ë bot. beet, beetroot; panxhar sheqeri: sugar-beet.
pánxh/ë,-a f.sh. -a paw.
panýjsh/ëm(i),-me(e) mb. gram. having no article, with zero article.
panjerëzísh/ëm(i),-me(e) mb. in-

human; **në mënyrë të panjerë-zishme:** inhumanly.
pánj/ë,-a *f.sh.* **-a** *bot.* maple, maple-tree; **dru panje:** maple-wood.
panjóhsh/ëm (i),-me(e) *mb.* irre-cognizable, incognizable, un-knowable.
panjóhur (i,e) *mb.* unknown, in-cognito, unacquainted; **njeri i panjohur:** unknown person.
panjóllë (i,e) *mb.* stainless, spot-less, unspotted, unsullied, un-blemished, untarnished, unde-filed. immaculate; njeri i pa-njollë: unblemished person.
paorganizúar (i,e) *mb.* 1. disor-ganized. 2. non-member (of a party.)
papafíngo,-ja *f.sh.* — garret, attic.
papagá/ll,-i *m.sh.* **-j** *zool.* parrot.
papagúar (i,e) *mb.* unpaid.
papagúesh/ëm (i),-me (e) *mb.* unpayable.
papajísur (i,e) *mb.* unprovided.
papajtúesh/ëm (i), -me (e) *mb.* irreconcilable; incompatible.
papajtueshmërí,-a *f.* incompatibi-lity.
papandéhur *ndajf.* unexpectedly, suddenly, all of a sudden.
paparamendúar (i,e) *mb.* un-premeditated.
paparapárë (i,e) *mb.* unforeseen, unlooked for.
paparashikím,-i *m.sh.* **-e** inex-pectation, unanticipation, nonex-pectation.
paparashikúar (i,e) *mb.* unfore-seen.
papárë (i,e) *mb.* 1. unobserved, unnoticed. 2. unprecedented. 3. greedy.
papartí(i,e) *mb.* non-organized, non-party, non-partisan.
papástër (i,e) *mb.* unclean, im-pure, dirty; kopje e papastër: rough-copy; nxënës i papastër:

untidy boy; **ujë i papastër:** unclear water; **ajër i papastër:** impure air.
papastërtí,-a *f.* 1. dirtiness, un-cleanliness. 2. impurity.
papastrúar (i,e) *mb.* 1. uncleaned. 2. crude; **naftë e papastruar:** crude oil.
papát,-i *m.* papacy.
papengúar (i,e) *mb.* unobstructed.
papeshúar (i,e) *mb.* unthought of, unconsidered.
papëlqýer (i,e) *mb.* disagreable, unpleasant.
papëlqýesh/ëm(i),-me(e) *mb.* indecent; **sjellje e papëlqye-shme:** indecent behaviour.
papërballúesh/ëm (i),-me(e) *mb.* irresistible.
papërcaktúar (i,e) *mb.* undeter-mined, indefinite.
papërcaktúesh/ëm (i),-me(e) *mb.* undeterminable.
papërdórsh/ëm (i), -me(e) *mb.* unusable.
papërdórur (i,e) *mb.* unused.
papërfíllur (i,e) *mb.* neglected, unregarded, disdained, disregar-ded.
papërfundúar (i,e) *mb.* unfini-shed.
papërfytyrúesh/ëm(i),-me(e) *mb.* unimaginable.
papërgënjeshtrúar (i,e) *mb.* un-confuted.
papërgjégjsh/ëm (i),-me(e) *mb.* irresponsible, unanswerable.
papërkthýer (i,e) *mb.* untran-slated.
papërkthýesh/ëm (i),-me(e) *mb* untranslatable.
papërkúlsh/ëm(i),-me (e) *mb.* in-flexible, rigid, unpliant, stiff, un-bending.
papërkulshmërí,-a *f.* inflexibility, rigidity.
papërkúlur (i,e) *mb.* unbent.

papërlígjsh/ëm (i),-me (e) *mb.*
unjustifiable.
papërlýer (i,e) *mb.* 1, chaste. 2.
clean, undirty.
papërmbájtsh/ëm(i),-me(e) *mb.*
irresistible, unrestrained,
papërmbájtur (i,e) *mb.* unrestrained, intemperate, uncontained,
petulant.
papërmirësúar (i,e) *mb.* unimproved.
papërpunúar (i,e) *mb.* 1. raw,
crude; **lëkurë e papërpunuar:**
raw (undressed) skin; **material
i papërpunuar** raw material. 2.
fig. crude, unpolished.
papërsósur (i,e) *mb.* imperfect.
papërshkrúesh/ëm(i),-me(e) *mb.*
undescribable.
papërshkúesh/ëm(i),-me(e) *mb.*
impervious, impenetrable; **i papërshkueshëm nga ajri:** airtight; *(nga uji)* water-tight, damp-
-proof, impermeable; *(nga drita)*
opaque.
papërshkueshmërí,-a *f.* impenetrability; impermeability; opacity.
papërshtátsh/ëm(i),-me (e) *mb.*
unfit; unbecoming, unsuitable;
improper; undue; **fjalë e papërshtatshme:** improper term;
kohë e papërshtatshme: undue time; **sjellje e papërshtatshme:** unbecoming (unsuitable)
behaviour.
papërshtatshmërí,-a *f.* unfitness;
unsuitableness; impropriety.
papërtúar (i,e) *mb.* indefatigable,
industrious, unweary.
papërtúesh/ëm(i),-me(e) *mb.* indefatigable.
papërvójë (i,e) *mb.* unexperienced.
papërzíer (i,e) *mb.* 1. unmingled.
2. pure, unadulterated; **pije e papërzier:** pure drink, unadulterated drink.

papíjsh/ëm(i),-me(e) *mb.* undrinkable; **ujë i papijshëm:** undrinkable water.
papjékur (i,e) *mb.* 1. *(bukë)* unbaked (bread). 2. *(mish)* underdone (meat). 3. *(rrush, pemë)*
green, immature, unripe (fruit).
4. *fig.* inexperienced; **djalë i
papjekur:** greenhorn.
papjekurí,-a *f.* immaturity, greeness, childishness.
papjesëtúar (i,e) *mb.* undivided.
papjesëtúesh/ëm(i),-me (e) *mb.*
indivisible.
paplákur (i,e) *mb.* not old, relatively young.
paplásur (i,e) *mb.* unexploded.
paplótë (i,e) *mb.* incomplete.
paplotësúar (i,e) *mb.* unaccomplished, unfulfilled.
papraktikúar(i,e) *mb.* unexperienced, inexperienced.
papopullúar(i,e) *mb.* depopulated, unpopulated.
papranúesh/ëm(i),-me (e) *mb.*
inadmissible, inacceptable.
paprapsúesh/ëm(i),-me(e) *mb.*
irrevocable.
papërgatítur (i,e) *mb.* unprepared, improvised.
papréksh/ëm(i),-me (e) *mb.* 1.
intangible, impalpable. 2. invulnerable. 3. insensible.
paprekshmërí,-a *f.* 1. intangibility.
2. invulnerability.
paprékur (i,e) *mb.* intact.
paprérë *ndajf.* uninterruptedly, unceasingly.
papríshur (i,e) *mb.* 1. *(ushqim)*
undecayed, not rotten (food);
kufomë e paprishur: unputrefied corpse. 2. *(ndërtesë)* undestroyed (building).
paprítmas *ndajf.* suddenly, unexpectedly.
papritur (i,e) *mb.* unexpected;
vdekje e papritur: sudden
death.

paprítur(e),-a(e) *f.sh.* -a(të) surprise.

paprivilegjúar (i,e) *mb.* non-privileged.

paprovúar (i,e) *mb.* unproved.

paprovúesh/ëm(i),-me(e) *mb.* unprovable.

papúnë (i,e) *mb.* unemployed, jobless.

papún/ë(i),-i(i) *m.sh.* -(të) unemployed worker; **të papunët:** the unemployed.

papunësí,-a *f.* unemployment.

papunúar(i,e) *mb.* 1. *(tokë)* waste *(kopësht)* uncultivated. 2. raw; **mëndafsh i papunuar:** raw silk.

papushtúar (i,e) *mb.* unoccupied, uninvaded.

papushtúesh/ëm(i),-me(e) *mb.* impregnable, inexpugnable; **fortesë e papushtueshme:** impregnable fortress.

papyllëzúar(i,e) *mb.* unwooded.

paqártë (i,e) *mb.* inexplicit, vague, equivocal, ambiguous; **në mënyrë të paqartë:** vaguely.

paqartësí,-a *f.* vagueness, ambiguity.

páq/e,-ja *f.* peace; **vendosja e paqes:** the establishing of the peace; **paqe e qëndrueshme:** lasting peace; **luftë për paqe:** struggle for peace.

paqedáshës,-e *mb.* peace-loving.

paqénë(i,e) *mb.* unexisting, inexistant.

paqétë (i,e) *mb.* anxious, unquiet.

paqéthur (i,e) *mb.* unshorn.

paqëndrúesh/ëm(i),-me(e) *mb.* unstable, fickle, inconstant, inconsistant, versatile; variable; **kohë e paqëndrueshme:** changeable (variable) weather; **njeri i paqëndrueshëm :** inconstant, person.

paqëndrueshmërí,-a *f.* instability,

fickleness, inconstancy, versatility; variability.

paqërúar(i,e) *mb.* unpeeled; unshelled.

paqësím,-i *m.* pacification.

paqësísht *ndajf.* peacefully.

paqësój *f.k.* to pacify. — **paqësohem** *f.jv.* to be pacified.

paqësór,-e *mb.* 1. pacific; **Oqeani Paqësor:** Pacific Ocean. 2. peaceful: **njeri paqësor:** peaceful man.

páqm/ë(i),-me(e) *mb.* clean.

paqortúesh/ëm(i),-me(e) *mb.* irreproachable.

paqytetërúar (i,e) *mb.* uncivilized.

pará,-ja *f.sh.* — money, cash; pelf; *(të shkoqura)* small money, small change, ready change; *(metalike)* coin; *(prej letre);* paper-money; **para xhepi:** pocket-money; **sa para?** how much money? **s'kam para me vete:** I have not money with me; **jam pa para:** I have not a farthing, I am penniless; **pres para (nxjerr) në qarkullim,** to mint (to emit) money; **me para në dorë:** by cash, in cash. — *Lok.* **i bëj paratë rrush e kumbulla:** to throw one's money away, to spend money like water. — *Prov.* **nuk humbet paraja e ligë:** ill weeds grow apace.

pára I. *ndajf.* forward, ahead; **eci para:** to go forward, to go ahead; **ai iku para me hap të shpejtë:** he went forward at a rapid pace.

II. *paraf.* 1. before; in front of; **para jush:** in front of you; **ai rrinte para derës:** he stood before the door; **në anglisht mbiemri qëndron para emrit:** in English the adjective is placed before the noun. 2. in the presence of, in face of, before; **para rrezikut:** in face of danger

ger; **para këtyre fakteve:** in view of these facts. 3. *(për kohë)* **para kohës së re, para erës sonë:** before the new era; **para shumë kohësh:** long before; **ai erdhi para meje:** he came before me; **ai erdhi para kohe:** he came before time (in advance); **para një viti:** a year ago; **para disa ditësh:** some days ago; **para një jave:** a week ago.

pára *pj.* (particle expressing insufficiency after a negation) **nuk para shoh nga sytë:** I don't see well; **nuk para bën:** it is not so good.

pára! *pasth.* forward! onward! on!

pára(e) *f.* beginning, commencement; **nga e para:** from the beginning.

paraárdhës,-i *m.sh.* – predecessor, forerunner.

paraból/ë,-a *f.sh.* **-a** *gjeom.* parabola.

paraburgím,-i *m.* detention.

paracaktím,-i *m.* predetermination, foreshadowing; *(i fatit)* predestination.

paracaktój *f.k.* to predeterminate; to predestinate, to foreshadow.

paraçlirímit (i,e) *mb.* pre-liberation.

parád/ë,-a *f.sh.* **-a** parade, review.

paradréke *ndajf.* before noon.

paradrék/e,-ja *f.sh.* **-e** forenoon.

paradhëni/e,-a *f.* earnest-money, advance-money.

paradhóm/ë,-a *f.sh.* **-a** anteroom, antechamber.

parafángo,-ja *f.sh.* – fender (of automobile).

parafín/ë,-a *f.* paraffin.

parafjál/ë,-a *f.sh.* **-ë** *gram.* preposition.

parafólës,-i *m.sh.–* forespeaker.

parafráz/ë,-a *f.sh.* **-a** paraphrase.

parafúndit(i,e)*mb.* the last but one.

parafytyrím,-i *m.sh.* **-e** shih **përfytyrim.**

parafytyrój *f.k.* shih **përfytyroj.**

paragráf,-i *m.sh.* **-e** paragraph.

paragjykím,-i *m.sh.* **-e** prejudice, prepossession, preconceived notion; **kam paragjykime për:** to have a prejudice against.

parájs/ë,-a *f.* paradise.

parakalím-i *m.sh.* **-e** march, parade.

parakalój *f.jk.* to march, to parade.

parakóhsh/ëm(i),-me(e) *mb.* premature, precocious, before the time; **dimër i parakohshëm:** precocious winter; **falënderime të parakohshme:** anticipating thanks.

parakráh,-u *m.sh.-ë anat.* fore-arm.

paralajmërím,-i *m.sh.* **-e** premonition, admonition, warning.

paralajmërój *f.k.* to admonish, to warn, to forewarn.

paralajmërúes,-i *m.s.h.* – precursor, forerunner.

paralajmërúes,-e *mb.* premonitory, precursory.

paralél,-i *m.sh.* **-e** parallel.

paralél,-e *mb.* parallel.

paralelepipéd,-i *m.sh.* **-ë** *gjeom.* parallelepiped.

paralelísht *ndajf.* parallelly.

paralelíz/ëm,-mi *m.* parallelism.

paralelográm,-i *m.sh.* **-ë** parallelogram.

paralitík,-u *m.sh.* **-ë** *mjek.* paralytic.

paralíz/ë,-a *f. mjek.* paralysis, palsy.

paralizím,-i *m. mjek.* palsying.

paralizój *f.k.* to paralyze, to palsy.

paralúft/ë,-a *f.* pre-war.

paramendím,-i *m.sh.* **-e** premeditation; **me paramendim:** premeditately, with malice, with premeditation; **pa paramendim:** without premeditation, unpremeditately, uncalculatedly.

paramendój *f.k.* to premeditate.
paramendúar (i,e) *mb.* preconsidered, premeditated, prepense, aforethought.
parandalím,-i *m.* prevention.
parandalój *f.k.* to prevent, to forestal. – **parandalohet** *f.jv.* to be prevented.
parandalúes,-e *mb.* 1, preventive; **masa parandaluese:** preventive measures. 2. *mjek,* prophylactic.
parandiéj *f.k.* to forebode, to feel a presentiment of, to presage; **parandiej një fatkeqësi:** to forebode a disaster.
parandjénj/ë,-a *f.sh.* -a presentiment, foreboding; *(e keqe)* misgiving.
parantéz/ë,-a *f.sh.* -a parenthesis; **në parantezë:** in paranthesis.
parapagés/ë,-a *f.sh.* -a shih **parapagim.**
parapagím,-i *m.* prepayment.
parapagúaj *f.k.* to prepay. – **parapaguhet** *f.jv.* to be prepaid.
parapárë (i,e) *mb.* foreseen.
parapét,-i *m.sh.* -e parapet.
parapërgatítur (i,e) *mb.* prearranged.
paraprák,-e *mb.* preliminary, preparatory; introductory; **hetime paraprake:** preliminary inquiries; **bisedime paraprake:** preliminaries; **masa paraprake:** preparatory measures, precautions; **përgatitje paraprake:** preparations beforehand.
parapríj *f.k.* 1. to go before, to lead. 2. to precede. – **paraprí-het** *f.jv.* 1. to be led. 2. to be preceded.
paraqés *f.k.* 1. to present, to introduce. 2. *(një kërkesë)* to make, to present (a demand). 3. *(një mall në ekspozitë)* to exhibit, to show. 4. *(nderimet*

dikujt) to pay (homage to someone). – **paraqitem** *f.jv..* 1. to present oneself. 2. *(para gjyqit)* to appear (before a tribunal), to present oneself (for trial).
paraqítës,-i *m.sh..* – showman.
paraqítj/e,-a *f.* 1. representation; **paraqitje grafike:** graphic representation. 2. *(para gjyqit)* appearance (before a tribunal). 3. presentation. 4. *(mallrash në vitrinë)* exhibition (of wares).
paraqítsh/ëm(i),-me(e) *mb.* presentable.
pararéndës,-i *m.sh.* – forerunner, precursor.
pararój/ë,-a *f.* vanguard: **partla është pararoja e klasës punëtore:** the party is the vanguard of the working class.
parasýsh *ndajf.* in regard, into consideration, into account; **marr parasysh:** to take into consideration (into account); **kam parasysh:** to have in view, to bear in mind; **duke marrë parasysh se:** considering that, seeing that, having in regard that.
parashikím,-i *m.sh.* -e prediction, prevision, foresight; **parashikim i ngjarjeve:** foresight of events: **parashikim i kohës (i motit):** weather forecast; **jashtë çdo parashikimi:** beyond expectation.
parashikój *f.k.* to predict, to foretell, to foresee, to forecast; **parashikoj ngjarjet:** to foresee future events: *(kohën)* to forecast – **parashikohet** *f.jv.* to be forecasted, to be forecasted.
parashikúes,-i *m.sh.* – predictor, forecaster, foreteller, prognosticator, seer, foreseer,
parashikúes,-e *mb.* predictive, foretelling, forecasting; **njeri pa_**

rashíkues: prognosticator, prognosticative man.

parashkollór,-e *mb.* preschool, pre-elementary school.

parashkrím,-i *m. drejt.* prescription.

parashkrúaj *f.k. drejt.* to prescribe, to claim by prescription. — **parashkruhet** *f.jv.* to be prescribed (prescript).

parashkrúesh/ëm(i), -me *(e) mb.* prescriptible.

parashóh *f.k.* shih **parashíkoj.**

parashtés/ë,-a *f.s.h* -a *gram.* prefix.

parashtrím,-i *m.* presentation.

parashtrój *f.k.* to expound, to set forth, to put forward; **parashtroj një çështje:** to set forth a question. — **parashtrohet** *f.jv.* to be expounded.

parashút/ë,-a *f.sh.* -a parachute.

parashutíst,-i *m.sh.* -ë parachutist.

paratífo,-ja *f. mjek.* paratyphoid.

parathém *f.k.* to foretell, to predict, to forecast.

parathëni/e,-a *f.sh.* -e introduction, foreword, preface.

paraushtarák,-e *mb.* premilitary.

paravendós *f.k.* to predeterminate, to predecide, to pre-establish. — **paravendoset** *f.jv.* to be predecided (pre-established)

paravendós/je,-a *f.* predetermination, pre-establishment.

parazít,-i *m.sh.* -ë 1. parasite. 2. *fig.* parasite, sponger, vermin.

parazitár,-e *mb.* parasitic, parasitical.

parcél/ë,-a *f.sh.* -a *(toke)* plot (of ground).

pardjé *ndajf.* the day before yesterday.

pár/e,-ja *f.sh.* -e shih **parà.**

páre,-t *f.sh. (e peshkut)* scales (of fish).

parealizúar (i,e) *mb.* unrealized.

parealizúesh/ëm(i), -me(e) *mb.* unrealizable.

parégjur(i,e) *mb.* 1. *(lëkurë)* raw. 2. *fig.* unexperienced.

parehátsh/ëm(i),-me *(e) mb.* uncomfortable.

parespektúesh/ëm(i),-me(e) *mb.* disrespectful.

paréshtur *ndajf.* without interruption (intermission, reprive, respite, rest), uncessantly, unceasingly; **ra shi gjithë ditën pareshtur:** it rained all day long without interruption.

parét,-i *m.sh.* -e partition.

párë (më) *ndajf.* before, beforehand; previously; first; **më parë duhet ta këshillojmë:** first we must advise him; **kohë më parë:** long before, long ago; **vite më parë:** years ago; **një ditë më parë:** a day before; **që më parë:** in advance; **duke ju falënderuar që më parë :** thanking you in advance (beforehand); **sa më parë:** as soon as possible; **më parë se të:** prior to, previous to.

párë (p.p. of the verb **shoh**) seen; **kam parë:** I have seen.

párë (i,e) *num. rresht.* 1. first; **i pari i klasës:** the top boy; **dita e parë:** the first day; **kat i parë:** the first floor; **biletë e klasit të parë:** first-class ticket; **klasa e parë (e shkollës):** the first class (of a school); **më i pari:** the foremost. 2. *(njohuri etj.)* elementary, rudimentary, basic. 3. **lëndë e parë:** raw-material.

párë,-t (të) *as.* ancestors, forefathers.

parëndësísh/ëm,(i),-me *(e) mb.* unimportant, insignificant, unessential, trivial.

parësí,-a *f.* the nobility, the nobles.

parfúm,-i *m.sh.* **-e** perfume.
parfumerí,-a *f.sh.* — perfumery.
parfumój *f.k.* to perfume.
parí,-a *f.* shih **parësi.**
pári (së) *ndajf.* firstly, at first;
pikë së pari: first of all.
parím,-i *m.sh.* **-e** principle; **pa
parime:** unprincipled; **e kam
për parim të:** to make a point
of, to make it a matter of principle that.
parimísht *ndajf.* on principle, principally.
parímór,-e *mb.* principled: **politikë parimore:** principled policy; **Partía jonë ndjek një politikë parimore:** our Party
follows a principled policy.
paritét,i- *m.* parity.
par/k,-ku *m.sh.* **-qe** 1. park. 2.
car-repair shop.
parkét,-i *m.sh.* **-e** parquetry, wood
flooring; **shtroj me parket një
dhomë:** to parquet a room.
parlamént,-i *m.sh.* **-e** parliament;
godina e parlamentit: the
House of Parliament.
parlamentár,-e *mb.* parliamentary.
parlamentaríz/ëm,-mi *m.* par-
liamentarism.
parmák,-u *m.sh.* **-ë** banisters, rai-
ling, iron-railing, trellis, balus-
trade; *(shkalle)* hand rail.
parmbrëmë *ndajf.* the evening before yesterday.
parménd/ë,-a *f.sh.* **-a** wooden
plow (plough).
párm/ë(i),-e(e) *mb.* anterior; **këmbët e parme:** anterior legs
(of an animal).
parodí,-a *f.sh.* — parody.
partí,-a *f.sh.* — party; **Partía e
Punës e Shqipërisë:** The Party
of Labour of Albania; **anëtar
partie:** party member; **kuotë
partie:** party dues; **sekretar
partie:** party secretary; **teserë

partie: party card; **hyj në parti:**
to become a party member.
partishmërí,-a *f.* party-spirit.
partitúr/ë,-a *f.sh.* **-a** *muz.* score.
partizán,i- *m.sh.* **-ë** 1. *usht.* partisan. 2. partisan, follower, supporter (of a doctrine, etc.); **partizan i paqes:** peace — supporter,
partisan of peace.
partizán,-e *mb.* partisan; **luftë
partizane:** partisan warfare.
parúk/ë,-a *f.sh.* **-a** wig; periwig.
parúll/ë,-a *f.sh.* **-a** 1. slogan. 2.
usht. password.
parváz,-i *m.sh.* **-e** *(dere)* door-
case; *(dritareje)* window-case.
parvjét *ndajf.* two years ago.
parvjétsh/ëm(i),-me (e) *mb.* of
two years ago.
párz/ëm,-ma *f.sh.* **-a** breast.
parzmór/e,-ja *f.sh.* **-e** breast plate,
cuirass.
parrafshúar(i,e) *mb.* uneven, not
levelled, rugged, having an uneven surface.
parráhur (i,e) *mb.* 1. *(qumësht)*
unskimmed (milk). 2. *(rrugë)* by-
path, by-way. 3. *(qen)* unbeaten
(dog.) 4. *(njeri)* unexperienced
(man).
parregullsí,-a *f.* disorder, irregula-
rity.
parrégullt(i,e) *mb.* 1. *gram.* irregular; **folje e parregullt:** irregular verb. 2. *gjeom.* **trekëndësh
i parregullt:** scalene triangle.
3. untidy; **nxënës i parregullt:**
untidy boy; **në mënyrë të parregullt:** irregularly.
parrethúar(i,e) *mb.* unenclosed.
parrezíksh/ëm (i), -me (e) *mb.*
not dangerous.
parrúar(i,e) *mb.* unshaved.
pas *paraf., ndajf.* 1) *(tregon vend)*
behind; **nga pas:** from behind;
pas kujt është ulur ai? behind-
whom is he sitting? **ai është
ulur pas meje:** he is sitting

behind me; **fshihem pas derës:** I hide myself behind the door; **mbetem pas:** to lag behind. 2. *(tregon kohë)* after; **më pas:** afterwards, later on; **pas pranverës vjen vera:** after spring comes summer; **pas dy muajsh:** after two months; **pas kësaj:** after this; **ai erdhi pas meje:** he came after me; **brez pas brezi:** generation after generation: 3. *(afër)* by, near; against; **jam ulur pas zjarrit:** I am sitting by the fire (near the fire); **mbështetem pas murit:** to lean against the wall. 4. *(me anën e)* with, through; **i çova fjalë pas të vëllait:** I sent word to him with (through) his brother. 5. *(sipas)* according to, after; **pas autorit:** according to the author, after the author; **bëj diçka pas një modeli:** to do something after a model; **pas zakonít:** according to the custom; **pas rendit alfabetik:** after the alphabetic order. -*Lok.* **i bie pas një pune:** to attend to a work, to concern oneself with an affair; **ai e la pas dore këtë punë:** he has neglected this job; **ai e mori pas (me vete):** he took it with him; **pas kokës dhe festen:** as you make your bed so you must lie on it.

pasagjér,-i *m.sh.* -**ë** passenger.

pasákt/ë,-(i,e) *mb.* inexact, incorrect, inaccurate.

pasaktësí,-a *f.* inexactness, inexactitude, inaccuracy.

pasaktësísht *ndajf.* inexactedly.

pasaldúesh/ëm(i),-me (e) *mb.* unweldable.

pasaník,-u *m.sh.* -**ë** rich, man, wealthy man; **të pasurít:** the rich, the wealthy.

pasapórt/ë,-a *f. sh.* -**a** 1. passport. 2. identity cord.

pasaportizój *f.k.* to give (someone) permission for dwelling (in a town etc.). — **pasaportizohem** *f.jv.* to be given permission for dwelling.

pasárdhës,-i *m.sh.* — successor, descendant, offspring.

pasárdhës,-e *mb.* successive; **të muajit pasardhës:** of the successive month.

pasdárk/ë,-a *f.sh.* -**a** evening.

pasdárke *ndajf.* in the evening, after dinner.

pasdít/e,-ja *f.sh.* -**e** afternoon.

pasdíte *ndajf.* in the afternoon, after lunch.

pasdrék/e,-ja *f.sh.* -**e** afternoon.

pasdréke *ndajf.* in the afternoon, after lunch.

pási *lidh.* after; **pasi të kemi mbaruar punën:** after we have finished the work.

pasí,-a *f.* the first visit of the bride to her parents

pasigurí,-a *f.* uncertainty, insecurity.

pasígurt (i,e) *mb.* insecure, uncertain, doubtful.

pasigurúar (i,e) *mb.* 1. unsecured; **portë e pasiguruar:** unsecured door. 2. uninsured: **shtëpi e pasiguruar (nga zjarri etj.):** uninsured house.

pasinqértë (i,e) *mb.* unfair, insincere.

pasión,-i *m.sh.* -**e** passion.

pasionóhem *f.jv.* to be impassioned.

pasítur (i,e) *mb. (miell)* unsifted (flour).

pasív,-e *mb.* passive, inactive.

pasivitét,-i *m.* passivity, inactivity.

pásj/e,-a *f.* wealth.

pasjéllsh/ëm(i),-me (e) *mb.* ill-mannered, ill-behaved, impolite, uncivil, unkind.

paskajór/e,-ja *f. gram.* infinitive.
paskëtáj *ndajf.* hereafter, henceforth, in the future.
paslúft/ë,-a *f.* post-war.
paslúftës (i,e) *mb.* post-war.
pásm/ë (i), -e(e) *mb.* hind, back; **këmbët e pasme të një kafshe:** the hind legs of an animal.
pasnésër *ndajf.* the day after tomorrow.
pasnésërm/e (e),-ja(e) *f.* the day after the morrow (tomorrow).
pasój *f.k.* 1. to follow; **pasojnë njëra-tjetrën:** they succeed each other. 2. *sport.* to pass.
pasój/ë,-a *f.sh.* -a consequence, repercussion; **sí pasojë:** consequently.
pasósur (i,e) *mb.* interminable.
pasqýr/ë,-a *f.sh.* -a 1. mirror, looking-glass; **shikohem në pasqyrë:** to look oneself in the mirror. 2. *(e lëndës)* table (of contents). 3. *(shifrash)* table (of numbers).
pasqyrím,-i *m.sh.* -e reflection.
pasqyrój *f.k.* to reflect. — **pasqyrohem** *f.jv.* to be reflected.
pasqyrúes,-e *mb.* reflective.
pastáj *ndajf.* after, then, afterwards; **e pastaj?** what next? what then?
pastájm/ë (i),-e(e) *mb.* later, subsequent.
pást/ë,-a *f.sh.* -a 1. pastry. 2. *(dhëmbësh)* tooth-paste.
pástër *ndajf.* cleanly, purely.
pástër(i,e) *mb,* clean; **ujë i pastër:** clean water; **rroba të pastra:** clean dresses; **pjatë e pastër:** clean plate. 2. tidy; **nxënës i pastër:** tidy boy. 3. pure; **ajër i pastër:** pure air. 4. fair; **kopje e pastër:** fair copy; **hedh d1;ka në të pastër:** to write a fair copy of something. 5. clear: **ndërgjegje e pastër:** clear conscience.

pastërmá,-ja *f.* corned meat, preserved meat: *(kau)* corned beef; *(derri)* bacon.
pastërtí,-a *f.* 1. cleanliness, cleanness, neatness. 2. tidiness. 3. purity. 4. *(e shpirtit)* chastity, cleanness (of soul).
pastërvítur (i,e) *mb.* untrained.
pastiçér,-i *m,* -ë pastry-cook.
pastíceri,-a *f.sh.* — 1. pastry-making. confectionary. 2. confectioner's (shop).
pastréhë (i,e) *mb.* unsheltered, without lodging.
pastrím,-i *m.sh.* -e 1. cleaning, sweeping, cleansing; **pastrim i rrugëve;** sweeping (of streets). 2. *(oxhakësh)* sweeping (of chimneys). 3. *(i teshave)* cleaning, dry-cleaning (of clothes). 4. *(i enëve)* scrubbing, scouring (the dishes). 5. *(i kanalit)* clearing, dredging (of a canal). 6. *(i rrobave nga pluhuri)* brushing (of clothes). 7. *(i rrobave nga njollat)* cleaning (of clothes). 8. *(i gropave të ujërave të zeza)* clearing (of sewages). 9. *(i dhëmbëve)* brushing (of teeth). 10. *(i një lëngu)* clarification, purification (of liquids). 11. *fig. (i ndërgjegjes)* purging (of conscience).
pastrój *f.k.* 1. to clean, to cleanse; *(rrugët)* to scavenge, to sweep (the streets) 2. *(oxhakun)* to sweep (the chimney). 3. *(rrobat nga njollat)* to clean (the clothes). 4. *(rrobat nga pluhuri)* to brush, to wipe (clothes). 5. *(një plagë)* to deterge, to cleanse (a wound) 6. *(enët)* to scrub, to scour (the dishes). 7. *(nga dherat një vend)* to clear (a place). 8. *(gropat e ujërave të zeza)* to clear (sewages, cesspools). 9. *(fundërrinat e lumit)* to dredge, to clean out (the bottom of a river). 10 *(dhë-*

mbët) to brush (the teeth). 11.
(një lëng) to clarify, to purify
(a liquid). 12. *(tryezën e bukës)*
to clear (the table). 13. *fig.*
(ndërgjegjen) to purge (the conscience).

pastrùes,-e *mb.* purificative; clarifying, detergent.

pastrúes,i- *m.sh.* – *(rrugësh)* scavenger, streetcleaner; *(oxhakësh)*
chimney sweeper.

pastudjúar(i,e) *mb.* unstudied.

pasthëni/e,-a *f.sh.* -e after -word.

pasthírm/ë,-a *f.sh.* -a *gram.* in-
terjection.

pasúes,-i *m.sh.* – follower.

pasúes,-e *mb.* following, pur-
suing.

pasukséssh/ëm (i-),me (e) *mb.*
unsuccessful.

pásur(i,e) *mb.* 1. rich, wealthy,
well-to-do, well off, opulent;
njeri i pasur: wealthy man,
rich man; **njeri shumë i pasur:**
opulent person; **klasat e pasura:** the wealthy classes, the
propertied classes. 2. fertile; **tokë e pasur:** fertile soil.

pasurí,-a *f.sh.* – riches, wealth,
fortune, property; **pasuri e përbashkët:** common wealth; **pasuri e tundshme:** movables,
personal property; **pasuri e patundshme:** immovables, real
property; **ndarje pasurie:** division of property.

pasurím,-i *m.* enrichment.

pasúroj *f.k.* 1. to enrich, to make
rich, to render wealthy. 2.
(tokën me pleh) to fertilize, to
render fertile (the soil with manure). – **pasurohem** *f.jv.* to
get rich, to grow rich, to make a
fortune.

pash,-i *m.sh.* -ë span of the arms.

pashá,-i *m.sh.* -llarë pacha,
pasha.

pashémbsh/ëm(i),-me (e) *mb.*
undestructible.

pashémbullt(i,e) *mb.* unexam-
pled, unprecedented, unequalled.

pasheshúar (i,e) *mb.* unlevelled,
uneven.

pásh/ë,-a *m.* shih **pasha.**

páshë (past tense of the verb
shoh) I saw.

pásh/ëm(i),-me(e) *mb.* good-
looking, handsome; sightly, nice-
looking; **vajzë e pashme:** a
good-looking girl; **djalë i pa-
shëm:** a handsome boy.

pashëndét(i,e) *mb.* unhealthy,
weak, feeble.

pashërúesh/ëm (i),   – me(e)
mb. incurable; **sëmundje e pa-
shërueshme:** incurable disease.

pashfrytëzúar (i,e) *mb.* unexploited; **tokë e pashfrytëzuar:**
unexploited land.

pashfrytëzúesh/ëm (i),-me (e)
mb. unexploitable.

pashije(i,e) *mb.* insipid, tasteless,
unsavoury, without flavour.

pashíjsh/ëm(i),-me (e) *mb.* shih
i pashije.

pashkélur (i,e) *mb. (vend)* unex-
plored (land).

páshk/ë,-a *f.* Easter; **e pashkës:**
paschal; **dita e pashkës:** paschal day.

pashkëpútur (i,e) *mb.* continuous,
uninterrupted.

pashkóllë (i,e) *mb.* unlearned, un-
lettered, illiterate.

pashkoqítur (i,e) *mb.* unsolved;
unexplained.

pashkóqur (i,e) *mb.* unhulled, unhusked; **misër i pashkoqur:**
unhusked maize.

pashkréhsh/ëm(i),-me (e) *mb.*
inexplosive.

pashkrúar (i,e) *mb.* unwritten.

ligj i pashkruar: unwritten law.
pashkúesh/ëm (i),-me (e) mb. 1. unsociable. 2. impassable.
pashkúlsh/ëm(i),-me (e) mb. unextirpable.
pashlýer (i,e) mb. 1. uneffaced. 2. unpaid; faturë e pashlyer: unpaid (not liquidated) invoice.
pashlýesh/ëm(i),-me (e) mb. indelible; uneffaceable.
pashmángsh/ëm (i),-me(e) mb. unavoidable, inevitable.
pashóq (i), -e(e) mb. unmatched, unrivalled, unequalled, unparalleled.
pashoqërúar(i,e) mb. unsociable, dissociable.
pashoqërúesh/ëm(i),-me (e) mb. unsociable; njeri i pashoqërueshëm: unsociable man, misanthrope.
pashóshur (i,e) mb. unsifted; miell i pashoshur: unsifted flour.
pashoshítur (i,e) mb. unexamined; çështje e pashoshitur: an unexamined question.
pashpállur (i,e) mb. 1. undeclared. 2. (ligj) unpromulgated (law). 3. unpublished.
pashpërblýer (i,e) mb. unrewarded, irredeemed, unpaid,
pashpërblýesh/ëm (i), – me(e) mb. irredeemable, unpayable.
pashpërthýer(i,e) mb. unexploded.
pashpírt (i,e) mb. unmerciful, merciless, cruel, hard-hearted, stone-hearted, inexorable.
pashpjegúeshëm (i), -me (e) mb. inexplicable, unaccountable.
pashpréhsh/ëm(i),-me (e) mb. unspeakable, inexpressible, ineffable, unutterable.
pashprésë(i,e) mb. hopeless, forlorn, desperate.

pashpresúar (i,e) mb. unhoped, unexpected.
pashpronësúar(i,e) mb. not expropriated, propertied.
pashqiptúesh/ëm(i),-me (e) mb. unutterable.
pashqùar (i,e) mb. 1. indistinct. 2. gram. indefinite; trajta e pashquar: indefinite form.
pashqyrtúar(i,e) mb. unexamined; lutje e pashqyrtuar: unexamined request.
pashtérsh/ëm(i),-me (e) mb. inexhaustible.
pashtírur (i,e) mb. unfeigned.
pashtrúar (i,e) mb. 1. untoward, unruly, perverse; djalë i pashtruar: untoward boy, undisciplined boy. 2. unlaid; sofër e pashtruar: unlaid table.
pashtrúesh/ëm(i),-me (e) mb. indomitable, untamable, unmanageable, undisciplined.
pashtýpur (i,e) mb. 1. unoppressed, unrepressed; popull i pashtypur: unreppressed (unoppressed unsubdued) people. 2. not printed.
pashúar (i,e) mb. unquenched, inextinguished.
pashúesh/ëm (i),-me (e) mb. unquenchable, inextinguishable.
pat,-i m.sh. -e krah. floor. story.
páta (simple past tense of the verb kam) I had.
patát/e,-ja f.sh. -e bot. potato; patate të skuqura: fried potatoes; lule patate: dahlia (flower).
patejkalúesh/ëm(i), -me(e) mb. insuperable.
patejdúksh/ëm (i),-me (e) mb. opaque, intransparent.
patejdukshmërí,-a f. opacity.
pateklíf ndajf. unceremoniously.
patént/ë,-a f.sh. -a 1. (shpikjeje) patent (of an invention). 2. (shoferi) driving-licence.   3.

(zejtari etj.) licence, legal permit to exert a profession.

pateríc/ë,-a *f.sh.* -a clutch.

pát/ë,-a *f.sh.* -a *zool.* goose; pl. geese; **zog pate:** gosling.

patëllxhán,-i *m.sh.* -a *bot.* egg-plant.

patëmétë (i,e) *mb.* impeccable, irreproachable, flawless, faultless, perfect.

pátina,-t *f.sh.* skates; **patina me rrota:** roller-skates.

patinatór,-i *m.sh.* -ë skater.

patinázh,-i *m.* skating.

patjétër *ndajf.* without fail.

patllák/e,-ja *f.sh.* -e *vjet.* revolver.

patók,-u *m.sh.* -ë *zool.* gander.

patológ,-u *m.sh.* -ë pathologist.

patologjí,-a *f.* pathology.

patologjík,-e *mb.* pathological.

patós,-i *m.* pathos.

patrajtúesh/ëm (i),-me (e) *mb.* intractable.

patrazúar (i,e) *mb.* unmingled; intact.

patrédhur (i,e) *mb.* uncastrated

patregúesh/ëm (i),-me (e) *mb.* ineffable, inexpressible.

patrembur (i,e) *mb.* fearless, intrepid, dauntless, unafraid.

patretsh/ëm(i), -me (e)*mb.* indissoluble, indissolvable.

patrétur (i,e) *mb.* 1. unmelted; **gjalpë i patretur:** unmelted butter. 2. undigested; **ushqim i patretur:** undigested food. 2. undecayed; **kufomë e patretur:** undecayed corpse.

patrík,-u *m.sh.* -ë patriarch.

patriót,-i *m.sh.* -ë patriot.

patriót,-e *mb.* patriotic.

patriotík,-e *mb.* patriotic.

patriotízëm,-mi *m.* patriotism.

patronázh,-i *m.* patronage; **nën patronazhin e dikujt:** under the patronage of someone.

patrondítsh/ëm(i),-me (e) *mb.* imperturbable, unshakeable.

patrondítur (i,e) *mb.* undisturbed, undisconcerted.

patrúll/ë,-a *f.sh.* -a patrol.

patrullím,-i *m.* patrolling.

patrullój *f.jk.* to patrol.

patúndsh/ëm(i),-me(e) *mb.* unshakeable, immovable.

patúndur *mb.* immovable, unshaken; firm, staunch, still.

pátur, pásur (past participle of the v. **kam)** had.

paturbullúar (i,e) *mb.* imperturbable, undisturbed, indisconcerted, calm.

patúrp(i,e) *mb.* shameless, impudent, insolent, unblushing.

paturpësí,-a *f.* shamelessness, impudence, insolence, lewdness, effrontery.

paturpësisht *ndajf.* impudently, unshamefully.

patúrpshëm (i),-me(e) *mb.* shameless, unabashed, saucy, impudent.

patheksúar(i,e) *mb.* *gram.* unstressed.

patheméltë (i,e) *mb.* unfounded, groundless.

pathjeshtúesh/ëm(i),-me(e) *mb.* *mat.* irreducible; **thyesë e pathjeshtueshme:** irreducible fraction.

pathýesh/ëm (i),-me (e) *mb.* 1. unbreakable, infrangible. 2. invincible.

pathyeshmëri,-a *f.* 1. infrangibility. 2. invincibility.

paúdhë(i,e) *mb.* devilish.

paúdhësí,-a *f.sh.* – devilry.

paúdhi(i) *m.* the devil.

paujítur (i e) *mb.* unwatered.

paushqyer(i,e) *mb.* unfed.

páuz/ë,-a *f.sh.* -a pause.

pavadítur (i,e) *mb.* shih **i pauji-tur.**

pavarësí,-a *f.* independence.

pavarësisht *ndajf.* apart; **pa-**

varësísht nga: apart from; independent of.
pavárur (i,e) *mb.* independent.
pavdekësí,-a *f.* immortality.
pavdekësój *f.k.* to immortalize.
— **pavdekësohem** *f.jv.* to become immortal.
pavdéksh/ëm (i),-me(e) *mb.* immortal, deathless, never-dying, undying.
pavdekshmërí,-a *f.* immortality.
pavdírë (i,e) *mb.* imperishable.
pavénd (i,e) *mb.* 1. unjust; **vendim i pavend:** unjust resolution. 2. **pyetje e pavend:** irrelevent question. 3. inopportune, untimely. 4. preposterous. absurd.
pavendosmërí,-a *f.* irresolution, indecision.
pavendósur (i,e) 1. irresolute, undetermined, wavering, undecided. 2. unsettled.
pavetëdíj/ë,-a *f.* unconsciousness.
pavetëdíjsh/ëm(i),-me (e) *mb.* unconscious.
pavetór,-e *mb. gram.* impersonal; **folje pavetore:** impersonal verb.
pavënëré (i,e) *mb.* unobserved, unnoticed.
pavëméndsh/ëm (i), -me (e) *mb.* inattentive, inadvertent, listless, mindless.
pavërtetúar (i,e) *mb.* unverified, unproved, unconfirmed; **lajme të pavërtetuara:** unconfirmed news.
pavijón,-i *m.sh.* -e pavilion; outhouse; **pavijon spitali:** ward (of a hospital).
pavirtýtsh/ëm(i),-me (e) *mb.* profligate, vicious.
pavléfsh/ëm(i),-me(e) *mb.* useless, worthless, unavailing, priceless, invaluable, null, good-for-nothing.

pavlefshmërí,-a *f.* worthlessness, nullity, lack of valour.
pavolítsh/ëm(i),-me(e) *mb.* 1. unconvenient, unhandy, unwieldy; **vegël e pavolitshme:** unhandy tool. 2. inopportune, untimely, not in due time; **në kohë të pavolitshme:** at an inopportune time.
pavullnétsh/ëm(i),-me (e) *mb.* 1. unwilled; **njerì i pavullnetshëm:** unwilled person. 2. involuntary.
pazakónsh/ëm(i),-me(e) *mb.* uncommon.
pazár,-i *m.sh.* -e 1. market, marketplace; *(i frutave)* fruit-market; *(i peshkut)* fish market; *(i shpendëve)* poultry market; **dal në pazar:** to go to market; **bëj pazarin:** to go shopping, to go marketing. 2. price; **bëj pazar:** to bargain (with someone for something); **hahem në pazar:** to chaffer, to haggle, to higgle about the price. 3. *fig.* noise.
pazarákë,-t *m.sh. vjet.* villagers who came to the market for bying and selling.
pazarllë/k,-ku *m.sh.* -qe chaffering, bargaining; **bëj pazarllëk:** to chaffer, to higgle.
pazbatúar(i,e) *mb.* unapplied.
pazbatúesh/ëm(i),-me(e) *mb.* unapplicable; **rregull i pazbatueshëm:** unapplicable regulation.
pazbërthyer (i,e) *mb.* 1. *(problem)* unresolved (problem). 2. *(plan)* unresolved (plan).
pazbulúar (i,e) *mb. (vend)* undiscovered (land).
pazbútshëm(i),-me(e) *mb.* untameable.
pazësh/ëm(i),-me(e) *mb.* silent, voiceless.

pazëvendësúesh/ëm(í), -me(e) *mb.* irreplaceable.
pazgjédhur(l,e) *mb.* 1. unselected. 2. not elected.
pazgjídhshmërisht *ndajf.* inextricably.
pazgjídhsh/ëm (i),-me (e) *mb.* 1. inextricable. 2. *mat.* **problem i pazgjidhshëm**: unresolvable problem.
pazgjídhur(i,e) *mb.* unsolved, unsettled, unresolved; **problem i pazgjidhur**: unsolved problem.
pazíer (i,e) *mb.* uncooked, underdone, not boiled.
pazmbrápsh/ëm(i),-me(e) *mb.* unrepulsable.
pazónja (e) *mb.* shih i **pazoti.**
pazóti (i) *mb.* unable, incapable, disable, inapt.
pazotësí,-a *f.* inability, incapacity, disability.
pazvjérdhur (i,e) *mb,* unweaned.
pazvoglúesh/ëm(i),-me (e) *mb. mat.* irreducible.
pazhvillúar(i,e) *mb.* undeveloped.
pe,-ri *m.sh.* -nj thread, yarn. — *Lok* **lëshoj pé**: to yield, to give way.
péc/e,-ja *f.sh.* -e band (of cloth).
pecét/ë,-a *f.sh.* -a napkin.
péc/ë,-a *f,s.h.* -e patch of cloth.
péç/e,-ja *f.sh.* -e *vjet.* veil (used to cover the face); **heq peçen**: to unveil, to uncover the face.
pedál,-i *m.sh.* -e *mek.* pedal.
pedagóg,-u *m.sh.* -ë pedagogue.
pedagogjí,-a *f.* pedagogy.
pedagogjík,-e *mb.* pedagogic, pedagogical.
pediát/ër,-ri *m.sh.* -ër *mjek.* pediatrician.
pediatrí,-a *f. mjek.* pediatrics.
pehliván,-i *m.sh.* -ë acrobate, tumbler.
pehríz,-i *m. mjek.* diet; **mbaj peh-**

riz: to diet (oneself), to put oneself on a diet, to keep diet.
peizázh,-i *m.sh.* -e landscape.
péjz/ë,-a *f.sh.* -a *anat.* ligament, sinew.
pekméz,-i *m.* must.
pekúl,-i *m.sh.* -e; **rris me pekule**: to coddle, to pamper.
pelén/ë,-a *f.sh.* -a diaper, swaddling-clothes; **mbështjell me pelena**: to swaddle, to pat a diaper, to pat a diaper on (a baby).
pelerín/ë,-a *f.sh.* -a pelerine.
pél/ë,-a *f.sh.* -a *zool.* mare.
pelíç/e,-ja *f.sh.* -e fur-coat, pelisse.
pelín,-i *m. bot.* absinthium.
pélt/e,-ja *f.* jelly (of fruit).
pell/g,-gu *m.sh.* -gje 1. pond, pool; *(për shtimin e peshqve dekorativë)* fish-pond. 2. *gjeog.* basin.
pém/ë,-a *f.sh.* -ë *bot.* 1. tree; **pemë frutore**: fruit-tree. 2. fruit; **tregu i pemëve**: fruit-market; **kultivimi i pemëve**: arboriculture; **pemë të rëna nga era**: windfalls.
pemëshítës,-i *m.sh.* — fruiterer.
pemëtari,-a *f.* arboriculture.
pemísht/e,-ja *f.sh.* -e orchard.
penál,-e *mb. drejt.* penal; **ndjekje penale**: penal prosecution.
penallti,-a *sport.* penalty.
pendés/ë,-a *f.* penance, repentance.
pendestár,-i *m.sh.* -ë penitent.
pénd/ë,-a *f.sh.* -a 1. *(shpendi)* feather (of birds); *(e madhe që përdoret për të shkruar)* quill; **zog pa pendë**: unfledged young bird; **ndërrim i pendëve (të zogjve)**: moulting (of birds); **fshesë prej pendësh**: fe. therbroom. 2. *(lumi)* dike, dam, embankment. 3. pair; **një pendë**

qe: a pair of oxes. − *Lok.* **e lehtë pendë:** as light as a feather; **i ranë pendët:** he's come down a peg (or two).
pendím,-i *m.* repentance, contrition, remorse.
pendóhem *f.jv.* to rue, to repent, to regret.
pendúesh/ëm *ndajf.* grudgingly, reluctantly.
pendúar (i,e) *mb.* repentant, repented.
penél,-i *m.sh.* -a brush.
pén/ë,-a *f.sh.* -a pen-holder; **majë pene:** pen; **bisht pene:** pen-holder.
pen/g,-u *m.sh.* -gje 1. pawn, pledge; **plaçkë e lënë peng:** earnest; **lë peng një plaçkë:** to pawn, to pledge; **mbaj si peng një plaçkë:** to hold something as a pledge; **dyqan pengjesh:** pawnshop. 2. *(i një shtëpie)* mortgage; **lë peng shtëpínë** *(çdo gjë të patundshme):* to mortage. 3. *(i një njeriu)* hostage; **mbaj peng dikë:** to take someone hostage.
pengés/ë,-a *f.sh.* -a obstacle, obstruction, barrier, impediment, hindrance, handicap; barrier.
pengím,-i *m.* *(në një gur etj.)* stumbling.
pengój *f.k.* 1. to hinder, to obstruct, to impede. 2. *(rrugën)* to bar, to obstruct, to block up (the way). 3. *(me këmbë dikë)* to trip up (someone). 4. *(kalin duke ia lidhur këmbët)* to fetter (a horse). − **pengohem** *f.jv.* 1. to be impeded. to meet an obstacle. 2. to stumble, to trip up.
pengúes,-e *mb.* obstructive.
pensíon,-i *m.sh.* -e 1. superannuation, pension; **pension pleqërie:** superannuation, old-age pension; **e drejtë pensioni:** pension entitlement; **jap pension:** to grant a pension to: **dal në pension:** to be superannuated; **nxjerr në pension:** to superannuate, to pension off. 2. *(familjar me ngrënie e fjetje):* boarding-house.
pensionist,-i *m.sh.* -ë pensioner.
pentagrám,-i *m.sh.* -e *muz.* staff, stave; **fushë pentagrami:** space of a staff; **vijë pentagrami:** line of a staff.
penxhér/e,-ja *f.sh.* -e shih **drítare.**
pénjëz,-a *f.sh.* -a *anat.* fiber,
penjuár,-i *m.sh.* -e dressing-gown.
perandór,-i *m.sh.* -ë emperor.
perandorák,-e *mb.* imperial.
perandorésh/ë,-a *f.sh.* -a empress.
perandorí,-a *f.sh.* − empire; **rënia e një perandorie:** the fall of an empire.
pérç/e,-ja *f.sh.* -e 1. shock (of hair). 2. veil.
pérd/e,-ja *f.sh.* -e 1. curtain. 2. *anat.* leucoma.
perëndésh/ë,-a *f.sh.* -a goddess
perëndí,-a *f.sh.* − god.
perëndim,-i *m.sh.* -e 1. *gjeog.* west, occident. 2. *(i diellit)* sunset.
perëndimór,-e *mb.* western; **Evropa Perëndimore:** Western Europe.
perëndísh/ëm(i),-me(e) *mb.* divine, heavenly.
perëndój *f.jk. (dielli)* to set, to sink.
perfeksíon,-i *m.* perfection.
perfeksioním,-i *m.* perfecting.
perfeksionój *f.k.* 1. to perfect, to bring to perfection. 2. to make better, to improve. − **perfeksionohem** *f.jv.* to perfect oneself.
perfeksionúar (i,e) *mb.* perfect.
pergamén/ë,-a *f.sh.* -a parchment.
periferí,-a *f.sh.* − 1. periphery. 2. outskirts.
periferík,-e *mb.* peripheral.

períme,-t *f.sh.* greens, vegetables; *(të hershme)* first (early) greens of the season; **kultivues l perimeve**: vegetable – grower.

perimeshítës,-i *m.sh.* – greengrocer.

perimét/ër,-ri *m.sh.* **-ra** *gjeom.* perimeter.

perimór/e,-ja *f.sh.* **-e** kitchen-garden.

periód/ë,-a *f.sh.,* **-a** period.

periodicitét,-i *m.* periodicity.

períodík,-u *m.sh.* **-ë** periodical.

períodik,-e *mb.* periodical, recurrent; **botim periodik**: periodical publication.

periodikísht *ndajf.* periodically.

peripecí,-a *f.sh.* – peripety.

periskóp,-i *m.sh.* **-ë** periscope.

peritonít,-i *m. mjek.* peritonitis.

periúdh/ë,-a *f.sh.* **-a** period.

permanént,-e *mb.* 1. permanent, durable, lasting. 2. **flokë permanent**: curling hair.

permanganát,-i *m. kim.* permanganate.

perón/ë,-a *f.sh.* **-a** *krah.* nail.

persón,-i, *m.sh.* **-a** person.

personál,-e *mb.* personal.

personalísht *ndajf.* personally, in person.

personalitét,-i *m.sh.* **-e** 1. personality. 2. *(person)* personality, *fam.* big wig.

personázh,-i *m.sh.* **-e** 1. personage. 2. *teat.* character.

personél,-ı *m.* staff; **listë e personelit**: muster-roll.

personifikím,-i *m.* personification.

personifikoj *f.k.* to personify, to impersonate. – **personifikohet** *f.jv.* to be personified.

perspektív/ë,-a *f.sh.* **-a** perspective, outlook, prospect.

perustí,-a *f.sh.* – trivet.

pésë *num. them.* five.

pesëdítór,-i *m.sh.* **-ë** five-days.

pesëdítór,-e *mb.* five-day.

pesëdhjétë *num. them.* fifty.

pesëdhjétë (i,e) *num. rresht.* fiftieth.

pesëdhjetvjeçár,-e *mb.* fifty year sold.

pesëdhjetëvjetór,-i *m.sh.* **-e** the fiftieth anniversary.

pesëfísh,-i *m.* five fold, quintuple.

pesëmbëdhjétë *num. them.* fifteen.

pesëkëndësh,-i *m.sh.* **-a** *gjeom.* pentagon.

pesëqínd *num. them.* five hundred.

pesërrókësh,-e *mb.* pentasyllabic.

pésësh,-i *m.sh.* **-e** 1. five. 2. ancient monney of small value; *fig.* **s'kam asnjë pesësh:** I have not a farthing.

pesëvjeçár,-i *m.sh.* **-ë** five years.

pesëvjeçár,-e *mb.* quinquennial, five-year; **plani pesëvjeçar:** five-year plan.

pesëvjetór,-i *m.sh.* **-ë** fifth anniversary.

pesimíst,-i *m.sh.* **-ë** pessimist.

pesimíst,-e *mb.* pessimistic.

pesimíz/ëm,-mi *m.* pessimism.

pésh/ë,-a *f.sh.* **-a** weight: **peshë bruto:** gross weight; **peshë neto:** net weight; **peshë specifike:** specific weight; **me peshë të njëjtë:** equiponderant; **masat e peshës:** standards of weight; **forca e peshës:** gravity; **me peshë 10 kg:** weighing 10 kilograms; **i peshës së lehtë:** light weight class.

peshím,-i *m.sh.* **-e** weighing.

peshín *ndajf.* in ready money; **paguaj peshin:** to pay in (by) cash.

peshk,-u *m.sh.* **peshq** 1. *zool.* fish; **peshk i kripur:** salted fish; **peshk i tymosur:** smoke-dried fish; **shitës peshku:** fishmonger; **vezë peshku:** spawn; **pare peshku:** scales; **pastroj pesh-**

kun: to scale the fish; **tregu i
peshkut**: fish market; **zë peshk**:
to fish, to catch fish. 2. *anat.*
peshku i kurrizit: back-bone,
spinal column, vertebral column.
– *Prov.* **peshku në det, tigani
në zjarr**: first catch your hare
then cook him.
peshkaqén,-i *m.sh.* -ë *zool.* shark.
peshkatár,-i *m.sh.* -ë fisherman,
fisher.
peshkatarí,-a *f.* fishery.
peshkím,-i *m.* fishing, fishery; **kallam peshkimi**: fishing rod;
rrjetë peshkimi: fishing net,
trawl; **lundër peshkimi**: fishing
boat; **vend peshkími**: fishing
ground, fishery.
peshkój *f.k.* to fish, to catch fish;
peshkoj me grep: to angle.
peshkóp,-i *m.sh.* -ë bishop.
peshkopát/ë,-a *f.sh.* -a bishopric.
peshój *f.k.* 1. to weigh, to scale
(with a balance.) 2. *fig. (fjalët)*
to weigh the words; **e kam pe-
shuar mirë punën**: I've weighed it up. – **peshohem** *f.jv.* to
weigh in.
peshój/ë,-a *f.sh.* -a balance; *(për
pesha të rënda)* weighing-
machine.
peshór/e,-ja *f.sh.* -e weighing-ma-
chine.
peshqésh,-i *m.* -e gift.
peshqír,-i *m.sh.* -ë towel; **fshij
duart me peshqir**: to dry
one's hands with a towel.
peshtáf,-i *m.sh.* -ë jewel-box.
peshtamáll,-i *m.sh.* -ë large towel.
peshúes,-i *m.sh.* – balancer.
petáv/ër,-ra *f.sh.* -ra slat of wood.
pét/ë,-a *f.sh.* -ë 1. *(lakrori)* rolled dough; **hap petët për
lakror**: to turn over dough for
pie. 2. *(metali)* foil.
pét/ël,-la *f.sh.* -a *bot.* petal.
petëzím,-i *m. mek. (i metaleve)*
foliation, flattening (of metal);

makínë petëzimi metalesh:
rolling-mill.
petëzój *f.k.* to roll, to laminate (a
metal). – **petëzohet** *f.jv.* to
be laminated.
petk,-u *m.sh.* -a dress, clothes.
petkalárës/e,-ja *f.sh.* -e laundress,
washerwoman.
petrít,-i *m.sh.* -ë *zool.* hawk.
pétull,-a *f.sh.* -a pancake.
pezaul,-i *m.sh.* -ë trawl, fishing-net,
trammel; **peshkoj me pezaul**:
to trawl (to fish) with a trawl.
pezmatím,-i *m.* exasperation, irritation.
pezmatój *f.k.* 1. *(plagën)* to irritate (a wound). 2. *(dikë)* to
irritate, to exasperate (someone).
– **pezmatohem** *f.jv.* to be irritated, to be exasperated.
pezúl,-i *m.sh.* -e support, prop,
rest, shore; **pezul dritareje**:
window-sill.
pézull *ndajf.* hanging, pending;
çështje e lënë pezull: hanging
question.
pezullím,-i *m.* suspension; *(nga
puna)* suspension (from work).
pezullój *f.k.* 1. *(nga puna)* to
suspend (someone). 2. *(page-
sat)* to suspend (payment). 3.
(një vendim) to suspend the execution (of a sentence). – **pezullo-
hem** *f.jv.* to be suspended.
pezhíshk/ë,-a *f.sh.* -a *(merimange)* cobweb, spider's web.
pëgëj *f.k.* to pollute, to dirty.
pëlcás *f.jk.* 1. to burst, to blow up.
(pushka) to detonate (of a gun).
3. *(mina)* to explode. 4. *(lufta)*
to break out (the war).
pëlhúr/ë,-a *f.sh.* -a fabric, material;
cloth; **pëlhurë pambuku**: cotton
cloth; **pëlhurë kërpi**: sack cloth;
(dysheku): tickling; *(për perde)*
dimity; *(velash)* sail-cloth; *(liri)*
linen cloth.

pëlhuréndës/e,-ja *f.sh.* -e 1. weaver. 2. *(mekanike)* weaving machine.

pëlqéj *f.k.* 1. to like; to love, to relish; **po t'ju pëlqejë:** if you like; **më pëlqen shumë:** to be fond of; **më pëlqen shumë muzika:** I am fond of music; **nuk më pëlqen ai njeri:** I dislike that person. 2. *(miratoj)* to agree, to approve, to assent.

pëlqím,-i *m.* assent, consent, approbation, approval; *(i heshtur)* acquiescense, silent assent; **me pëlqimin e tij:** of his own accord; **me pëlqimin e të gjithëve:** with one accord; **jap pëlqimin:** to agree, to assent, to consent, to approbate; **nuk jap pëlqimin:** to disagree, to disapprove.

pëlqýer (i,e) *mb. (sjellje etj.)* polite, courtly, civil.

pëlqýesh/ëm(i),-me (e) *mb.* agreable, prepossessing.

pëllét *f.jk.* 1. *(lopa)* to bellow, to moo. 2. *(gomari)* to bray.

pëllëmb/ë,-a *f.sh.* -ë 1. palm (of the hand). 2. slap, buffet; **i jap një pëllëmbë fytyrës:** to slap, to smack, to buffet (someone) on the face. – *Lok.* **është një pëllëmbë njerì:** he is shrimp(a pygmy); **nuk luaj asnjë pëllëmbë:** I don't budge an inch.

pëllítj/e,-a *f.sh.* -e 1. *(e lopës)* bellow (of a cow); *(e gomarit)* bray (of an ass); *(e drerit)* bell (of a deer).

pëllúmb,-i *m.sh.* -a *zool.* dove, pigeon; **fole pëllumbash:** dove-cot, pigeon-hole, pigeon-house.

pëllumbésh/ë,-a *f.sh.* -a 1. she dove (female dove). 2. *fig.* good girl.

pëqf,-ri *m.sh.* -nj lap; **në pëqirin tim:** on my lap.

për *paraf.* 1. *(tregon qëllim)* for; **bojë për të shkruar:** ink for writing; **libër për fëmijë:** book for children; **misër për farë;** seed-corn; **vete për ujë:** I am going to fetch water; **punoj për nesër:** I'm working for tomorrow. 2. *(tregon dobi)* for; **ai punon për lulëzimin e vendit:** he works for the prosperity of his country. 3. *(pyetje)* **për ç'arsye?** what for? for what reason? **për se bëhet fjalë?** what is it about? **për se bën fjalë libri?** what is the book about? 4. *(shkak)* **për shkak të:** because of, on account of; **s'ka për se:** no matter, nothing. 5. *(kohë, afat)* for; in, within; **për të parën herë:** for the first time; **për pak kohë:** for a short time; **e mbaroj për tri javë:** I shall finish it within three weeks; **për herën tjetër:** for the next time; **vit për vit:** year after year, year in year out. 6. *(drejtim)* **nisem për në malësi:** to set out for the mountainous region; **për së gjati:** lengthwise; **për së gjerí:** breadth-wise. 7. *(vend)* **zë për veshi** (diikë): to catch someone by the ear. 8. *(shkëmbim)* **dhëmb për dhëmb:** blow for blow, tit for tat. 9. *(zëvendësim)* **për kryetarIn firmosi sekretari:** the secretary signed for the chairman. 10. *(çmim, sasi)* **pesë për qind:** five per cent: **prodhimi për hektar:** the yield për hectare. 11. *(mënyrë)* **për çudi:** to my (your, our, their) surprise; **për bukuri:** wonderfully, admirably; *(një plaçkë)* **për së mbari:** on the right side (of a cloth). 12. *(kufizim, krahasim)* as; for; **e njoh për burrë të mirë:** I know him as an honest person;

sa pёr mua: as for me; pёr
shembull: for example. 13. *(rast)*
to; pёr nder tё: in honour of.
14. *(betim)* upon; pёr nder!
upon my honour! pёr besёl
upon my faith! e kam pёr nder:
I take pride in. 15. *(urim)* pёr
tё mirё! *(kur pimё):* to your
health! pёr hatrin tim! for my
sake! 16. *(radhitje)* pёr dy e
pёr tre: by twos and by threes.
17. *(tregon pёrkatёsi)* kjo ёshtё
pёr mua: this is for me. 18.
(formon paskajoren) do tё vete
nё pazar pёr tё blerё perime:
I shall go to the market to buy
vegetables. 19. *(pёrdoret ndo-
njёherё nё fjalitё e kohёs sё
ardhshme)* kam pёr tё vajtur
nё shkollё: I have to go to
school. 20. *(shёrben pёr tё treguar domosdoshmёri)* in order to;
pёr tё mёsuar mirё njё gju-
hё tё huaj duhet punuar
shumё: to master a foreign language one must work hard.
pёrafёrsi,-a *f.* approximation; me
pёrafёrsi: approximatively.
pёrafёrsisht *ndajf.* approximatively.
pёrafёrt(i,e) *mb.* approximative.
pёrbállё I. *ndajf.* opposite; shtё-
pia pёrballё: the building opposite (to).
II. *paraf.* in front of, in face, before;
pёrballё kёsaj gjendjeje: in
(the) face of such a situation;
makina u ndal pёrballё shko-
llёs: the car stopped in front
of the shcool.
pёrballim,- i *m.* resistance, with-
standing.
pёrballój *f.k.* to brave, to face;
(provёn) to stand (the test);
(shpenzimet) to afford (the expenses); pёrballoj sulmet e
armikut: to stand up to the
enemy's attacks. – pёrballohet
f.jv. to be faced.

pёrbáshkёt (i,e) *mb.* 1. common;
dobi e pёrbashkёt: common
advantage; deklaratё e pёrbashkёt: joint declaration; ata
kanё shumё gjёra tё pёrbash-
kёta: they have much in common;
ata s'kanё asgjё tё pёrbashkёt: they have nothing in common. 2. collective, common;
pasuri e pёrbashkёt: common
property.
pёrbetím,-i *m.* oath-taking.
pёrbetóhem *f.jv.* to take an oath,
to vow.
pёrbёj *f.k.* to constitute, to form,
to make up. – pёrbёhet *f.jv.*
to consist, to be composed of,
to be made up; ky apartament
pёrbёhet nga tri dhoma: this
flat is made up of three rooms;
qё pёrbёhet: consisting of.
pёrbёrё (i,e) *mb.* 1. composite'
compound. 2. *gram.* compound;
kohёt e pёrbёra tё foljeve
compound tenses.
pёrbёrёs,-e *mb.* component, constituent, composing; pjesё pёr-
bёrёse: integral parts, component parts.
pёrbёrj/e,-a *f.* composition, constitution, make-up; pёrbёrja e
tokёs: the composition of the
soil.
pёrbíndёsh,-i *m.sh.* -a monster.
pёrbíndsh/ёm(i),-me (e) *mb.*
monstruous.
pёrbótsh/ёm(i),-me(e) *mb.* universal, world-wide.
pёrbrénda *ndajf.* in, inside, within
nga pёrbr enda: from inside
from within, from the inside.
pёrbréndёsa,-t *f.sh. anat.* entrails.
pёrbrí *ndajf., paraf.* next to, by,
beside; next-door, neighbouring; alongside: ata ecnín pёr-
bri njёri tjetrit: they walked
along side by side; apartamenti

përbrí: the next door flat; **shtepia përbrí shkollës:** the house by (next to) the school.

përbúz *f.k.* to contemn, to disdain, to despise, to disregard, to scorn, to hold in contempt. – **përbuzem** *f.jv.* to be contemned (disdained, scorned).

përbúzës,-e *mb.* contemptuous, disdainful, scornful.

përbúzj/e,-a *f.* contempt, disdain, despise, disregard, scorn; **tregoj përbuzje për:** to show contempt for; to look down upon; **me përbuzje:** contemptuously, disdainfully, scornfully.

përbúzsh/ëm(i),-me(e) *mb.* contemptible, despicable.

përbúzur (i,e) *mb.* contemned, disdained, despised, scorned; **njeri i përbuzur:** wretch, despicable (contemptible) person.

përcaktím,-i *m. sh.* **-e** determination; definition.

përcaktój *f.k.* to determine; *(kufijtë)* to fix, to settle (the bounds of); to define; *(kushtet e një kontrate etj.)* to settle (the clauses of a contract, of an agreement). – **përcaktohet** *f.jv.* to be determined, to be defined.

përcëllím/ë,-a *f.* parching, slight burn.

përcëllój *f.k.* to parch, to scorch, to singe, to burn slightly. – **përcëllohem** *f.jv.* to be parched (scorched, singed).

përcíptas *ndajf.* superficially.

përcíptë(i,e) *mb.* superficial; **njohje e përciptë:** superficial knowledge.

përcjéll *f.k.* 1. to accompany, to conduct, to escort; **pres e përcjell miq:** to keep open house. 2. to show out. 3. to swallow. – **përcillem** *f.jv.* 1. to be accompanied, to be escorted. 2. to swallow down.

përcjéllës, -i *m.sh.* - conductor.

përcjéllj/e,-a *f.* accompaniment.

përcjellór,-e *mb. gram.* gerund.

përçáj *f.k.* 1. to divide, to disunite; **përça e sundo – kjo është motoja e shfrytëzuesve:** the slogan of the exploiters is: divide and rule. 2. to separate. – **përçahem** *f.jv.* to be divided (disunited).

përçápj/e,-a *f.sh.*-e demarche,step.

përçárës,-i *m.sh.* – splitter.

përçárës,-e *mb.* splitting.

përçárj/e,-a *f.sh.* -e split, discord, disunion.

përçárt *ndajf.* deliriously; **flas përçart:** to speak in delirium, to rave.

përçártj/e,-a *f.* delirium, rave.

përçmím,-i *m.* disparagement, disdain, despise, scorn.

përçmój *f.k.* to disparage, to scorn, to disdain. – **përçmohem** *f.jv.* to be disparaged, to be disdained.

përçmúes,-e *mb.* disparaging, scornful.

përçój *f.k.* to transmit, to conduct, to pass on.

përçúes,-i *m.sh.* – transmitter, conductor.

përdálë(i,e) *mb.* immoral.

përderisá *lidh.* inasmuch as, as long as.

përdëlléj *f.k.* to compassionate, to commiserate. – **përdëllehem** *f.jv.* to pity, to be compassionate.

përdëllestár,-e *mb.* merciful, forgiving.

përdëllím,-i *m.* mercy, clemency.

përdítë *ndajf.* everyday, daily.

përdítsh/ëm(i),-me(e) *mb.* daily, everyday; **gazetë e përditshme:** daily paper; **nevojat e përditshme:** daily necessities; wants; **posta e përditshme:** daily mail.

përdór *f.k.* to use, to utilize, to employ, to make use of; **përdor dhunën:** to use violence; *(me* *shkathtësi)* to handle, to manipulate; **përdor me nikoqirllëk:** to use with economy, with dexterity, to manage with economy, to husband.

përdorím,-i *m.sh.* -e use, employment, usage, utilization; **artikuj të përdorimit të gjerë:** consumer goods; **për përdorim personal:** for one's personal use; **jashtë përdorimit:** out of use; out of order; **ashensori ka dalë jashtë përdorimit:** the lift is out of order; **koha e përdorimit:** utilization time; **mënyra e përdorimit:** mode of usage; **për përdorim të brendshëm (ilaç)** : to be taken internally; **vetëm për përdorim të jashtëm:** for external use only.

përdorój *f.k.* to use, to make use of, to utilize. — **përdorohem** *f.jv.* to be used, to be utilized.

përdórsh/ëm(i),-me (e) *mb.* usable, utilizable; manageable, fit for use,

përdorúes,-i *m.sh.* — user, utilizer.

përdórur (i,e) *mb.* used; **rrobë e përdorur:** used dress.

përdrédh *f.k.* 1. *(perin)* to twist (thread). 2. *(këmbën, krahun)* to sprain (the ankle, the leg, the arm). 3. *(trupin)* to twist, to contort (the body). — **përdridhem** *f.jv.* to wriggle, to twist, to writhe.

përdyjávsh/ëm(i),-me (e) *mb.* fortnightly, biweekly, semimonthly; **revistë e përdyjavshme:** biweekly, fortnightly review.

përdhé *ndajf.* down, on the ground.

përdhés,-e *mb.* ground, ground level, street level: **kati përdhes:** ground floor; **shtëpi përdhese:** single-story house.

përdhés/ë,-a *f. zool.* ant.

përdhós *f.k.* 1. to profane, to desecrate. 2. to corrupt, to depra-

ve, to vitiate, to degenerate. — **përdhosem** *f.jv.* to be corrupted (depraved, degenerated).

përdhósj/ej/-a *f.* 1. profanation, desecration, profanity, sacrilege. 2. pollution, corruption; depravity; degeneration.

përdhósur (i,e) *mb.* degenerate; perverse.

përdhún/ë,-a *f.* violence; **me përdhunë:** by violence.

përdhuním,-i *m.* violation.

përdhunisht *ndajf.* by violence.

përdhunój *f.k.* to violate. — **përdhunohem** *f.jv.* to be violated.

përdhunúes,-i *m.sh.* — violator.

përém/ër,-ri *m.sh.* -ra *gram.* pronoun.

përfaqësí,-a *f.sh.* — mission, embassy.

përfaqësím,-i *m.* representation.

përfaqësój *f.k.* to represent; **përfaqësoj një shtet:** to represent a state. — **përfaqësohem** *f.jv.* to be represented.

përfaqësúes,-i *m.sh.* — *(i një shteti)* representative (of a state).

përfaqësúes,-e *mb.* 1. representative; **organ përfaqësues:** representative organ. 2. *sport.* selected; **skuadër përfaqësuese:** selected team, national team.

përfaqësúes/e,-ja *f.sh.* -e *sport.* selected team; **përfaqësuesja e Shqipërisë në atletikë:** the Albanian track and field selected team.

përfíll *f.k.* to treat with regard, to consider, to regard with respect; **nuk përfill:** to disregard, to slight; **nuk e përfill fare dikë:** to put a slight on someone. — **përfillem** *f.jv.* to be considered, to be esteemed, to be regarded with respect.

përfillj/e,-a *f.* regard, respect.

përfitím,-i *m.sh.* -e vantage, advantage, benefit, profit.

përfitój *f.jk.* to profit by, to take advantage of, to benefit (by, from); **përfitoj nga rasti:** to take advantage of an opportunity, to avail oneself of an opportunity, to seize the occasion; **përfitoj nga përvoja e :** to profit by the experience of someone. ~ **përfitohet** *f.jv.* to be gained.

përflák *f.k.* to inflame. – **përflaket** *f.jv.* to be inflamed.

përfláksh/ëm(i),-me (e) *mb.* inflamable.

përflás *f.k.* to slander, to calumniate, to backbite, to speak ill of someone behind his back. – – **përflitem** *f.jv.* to be broiled with someone, to bandy words with someone.

përforcim,-i *m.sh.* -e 1. enforcement, reinforcement. 2. *usht.* *(përforcime ushtarake)* reinforcement.

përforcój *f.k.* to reinforce, to strengthen, to consolidate; *(një të vërtetë)* to confirm (a verity, a truth). – **përforcohem** *f.jv.* to be reinforced, to be strengthened, to be consolidated; to be confirmed.

përforcúes,-i *m.sh.* – 1. *mjek* tonic. 2. *fig.* *(zëri)* amplifier.

përforcúes,-e *mb.* 1. fortifying. 2. *fig.* amplificatory.

përfshíj *f.k.* to include, to embrace. – **përfshihet** *f./jv.* to be included; **që përfshihet:** inclusive; **duke u përfshirë këtu:** including.

përfshírj/e,-a *f.* inclusion.

përftím,-i *m.sh.* -e *kim.*, *fiz.* generation, begetting, procreation.

përftój *f.k. kim.*, *fiz.* to generate, to procreate.

përfundím,-i *m.sh.* -e 1. conclusion, inference, deduction; **nxjerr një përfundim:** to draw a con-clusion: **si përfundim:** in conclusion. 2. *(i një mbledhjeje)* the closing (of a meeting). 3. *(i një romani)* epilogue, end (of a novel). 4. *(i një fjalimi me rëndësi)* peroration.

përfundimísht *ndajf.* definitively, finally.

përfundimtár,-e *mb.* definitive; final; concluding, conclusive; **pjesa përfundimtare:** concluding part.

përfundój I. *f.k.* 1. to end; to terminate; *(një punë)* to end, to finish, to terminate (a work). 2. *(një marrëveshje tregtare)* to close (a bargain). II. *f.jk.* to conclude, to close, to finish, to end; **kështu përfundoi ajo çështje:** so ended that affair. – **përfundohet** *f.jv.* to be ended (finished).

përfýtem *f.jv.* to scuffle.

përfýtj/e,-a *f.* scuffle.

përfytyrím,-i *m.sh.* -e imagination, fancy.

përfytyrój *f.k.* to imagine, to fancy. – **përfytyrohem** *f.jv.* to be imagined.

përfytyrúesh/ëm(i),-me(e) *mb.* imaginable, conceivable.

përgatít *f.k.* to prepare, to make ready. – **përgatitem** *f.jv.* to prepare oneself, to be prepared, to get ready.

përgatítj/e,-a *f.sh.* -e preparation; **pa përgatitje:** off-hand, without previous preparation.

përgatitór,-e *mb.* preparatory.

përgënjeshtrím,-i *m.sh.* -e disproof, confutation.

përgënjeshtrój *f.k.* to disprove, to confute, to give the lie. – **përgënjeshtrohet** *f.jv.* to be disproved (confuted).

përgëzím,-i *m.sh.* -e congratulation, felicitation, compliment; për-

gёzimet e mia: my best compliments.
pёrgёzój *f.k.* 1. to congratulate, to felicitate. 2. to caress, to pet, to handle tenderly, to fondle; pёrgёzoj një kafshë: to pet an animal (a dog, a cat, etc). – pёrgёzohem *f.jv.* 1. to be congratulated. 2. to be caressed.
pёrgják *f.k.* to smear with blood. – pёrgjakem *f.jv.* to be stained with blood.
pёrgjáksh/ёm(i),-me(e) *mb.* bloody; luftё e pёrgjakshme: bloody war.
pёrgjákur(i,e) *mb.* blood-stained, blood-shot.
pёrgjégjёs,-i *m.sh.* – head, chief; pёrgjegjёs reparti: chief o a workshop.
pёrgjégjёs,-e *mb.* 1. accountable, answerable, responsible; pёr gjegjёs pёr: answerable, responsible for. 2. *mat.* correspondent; kёnd pёrgjegjёs: co-correspondent angle.
pёrgjegjёsi,-a *f.* responsibility; mbaj pёrgjegjёsi: to bear the responsibility.
pёrgjёrim,-i *m.* 1. longing. 2. tenderness, fondness; me pёrgjёrim: fondly, tenderly.
pёrgjёrój *f.k.* 1. to long. 2. to put in oath. – pёrgjёrohem *f.jv.* 1. to desire eagerly; pёrgjёrohem pёr: to long for; to love tenderly. 2. to vow, to swear, to take an oath.
pёrgjёrúar (i,e) *mb.* longing, fond of; jam i pёrgjёruar pёr: I am fond of.
pёrgj'gj/e,-ja *f.sh.* -e answer, reply, response; pa pёrgjigje: without reply; nё pёrgjigje tё letrёs suaj: in reply to your letter;

jap pёrgjigjen e duhur: to retort.
pёrgjigjem *f.jv.* 1. to answer, to reply; i pёrgjigjem një letre: to answer a letter. 2. to respond. 3. to correspond (with, to), to agree, to tally, to square (with).
pёrgjim,-i *m.* watchfulness.
pёrgjithёsi,-a *f.* generality; nё pёrgjithёsi: in general.
pёrgjithёsim,-i *m.sh.* -e generalization.
pёrgjithёsisht *ndajf.* generally, in general.
pёrgjithёsój *f.k.* to generalize. – pёrgjithёsohet *f.jv.* to be generalized.
pёrgjithmónё *ndajf.* forever, for good; një herё e pёrgjithmonё: once and for all, once and for good.
pёrgjithnjё *ndajf.* shih pёrgjithmonё.
pёrgjithsh/ёm(i),-me(e) *mb.* general, universal; rregull i pёrgjithshёm: general rule; grevё e pёrgjithshme: general strike.
pёrgjój *f.k.* 1. to watch. 2. to pry, to spy upon. 3. pёrgjoj nё pritё: to lurk. – pёrgjohem *f.jv.* to be watched; to be spied.
pёrgjúes,-i *m.sh.* – 1. watcher. 2. spy.
pёrgjúmur (i,e) *mb.* sleepy, drowsy.
pёrgjúnj *f.k.* to bring someone to his knees. – pёrgjunjem *f.jv.* to go down on one's knees, to kneel down.
pёrgjýsmё *ndajf.* half, by half, in half; ndaj pёrgjysmё: to divide in half; e zbraz shishen pёrgjysmё: to half empty the bottle: ndajmё pёrgjysmё midis nesh: to share equally, to go halves, to go fifty-fifty; i lё gjёrat pёrgjysmё: to do things by halves.

përgjysmój *f.k.* to half empty; to cut in half, to half. – **përgjys-mohet** *f.jv.* to be emptied in half, to be divided in half, to be halved.

përgjysmór/e,-ja *f.sh.* -e *gjeom.* bisector, bisecting line, bisectrix, mean line.

përháp *f.k.* 1. to spread, to propagate; **përhap kulturën**: to spread (to propagate, to diffuse) the culture. 2. *(një të fshehtë)* to divulge (a secret). 3. *(lajme)* to spread, to propagate (news). 4. *(një sëmundje)* to communicate (an illness). 5. *(shpërndaj)* to scatter, to pour out, to spread, to extend in all directions. – **përhapem** *f.jv,* 1. to be diffused. 2. to be propagated. 3. to be communicated. 4. to be spread. 5. to be scattered.

përhá pës,-i *m.sh.* – propagator, divulgator.

përhá pj/e,-a *f.* 1. *(e dritës, e zërit)* diffusion (of the sound, of the light). 2. *(e sëmundjes)* propagation (of an illness). 3. *(e kulturës)* propagation (of the culture). 4. *(e një sekreti)* divulgation (of a secret).

përhérë *ndajf.* always.

përhérsh/ëm(i),-me(e) *mb.* 1. permanent; **anëtar i përhershëm**: permanent member. 2. everlasting; standing; **paqe e përhershme**: everlasting peace: **ushtri e përhershme**: standing army.

përhím/ë(i), - me (e) *mb.* grey, dun.

përjáshta I. *ndajf.* out; outside; outwardly; **shfaqje përjashta**: open-air performance; **lojra sportive përjashta**: out-door games; **përjashta I** out! be gone !get out! II. *paraf.* **përjashta shtetit**: abroad; **përjashta shtëpisë**: outdoors.

përjashtím,-i *m.sh.* -e 1. *(nga një rregull)* exception (to a rule). 2. *(nga shërbimi ushtarak)* exemption; *(nga shkolla)* expulsion (from school). – *Lok.* **me përjashtim të**: except, save, with the exception of, except for; **bëj përjashtim**: to be (to constitute) an exception; **për ju po bëjmë përjashtim**: we will make an exception in your case.

përjashtój *f.k.* 1. *(nga shërbimi ushtarak)* to exempt (from military service; *(nga shkolla)* to expel (from school); *(nga puna)* to discharge, to dismiss (from a service, from a duty). 2. to except, to leave out, to exclude.

përjashtúar(i,e) *mb.* 1. exempted. 2. excluded.

përjávsh/ëm(i),-me(e) *mb.* weekly; **gazetë e përjavshme**: weekly paper.

përjétë *ndajf.* eternally, perpetually, forever.

përjetësí,-a *f.* eternity, perpetuity.

përjetësím,-i *m.* perpetuation.

përjetësísht *ndajf.* eternally, perpetually.

përjetësój *f.k.* to perpetuate, to render eternal. – **përjetëso-hem** *f.jv.* to be perpetuated, to become eternal.

përjétsh/ëm(i),-me(e) *mb.* eternal, perpetual, everlasting.

përkás I. *f.k.* (p.t. **përkita**, p.p **përkitur**) to touch.
II. *f.jk.* to belong, to appertain, to pertain to; **kjo më përket mua**: this belongs to me; **më përket mua të**: it belongs to me to; **për sa i përket**: as far as is concerned, concerning, regarding, in terms of, as regards, as for; **që i përket**: belonging pertaining, concerning, relative to.

përkátës,-e *mb.* respective; **në vendet përkatëse**: to the respective places; **në organet përkatëse:** to the competent organs.

përkatësí,-a *f.* appertaining, belonging, pertaining.

përkatësísht *ndajf.* respectively.

përkëdhél *f.k.* to caress, to fondle; to pamper; **i përkëdhel flokët:** to stroke someone's hair. − **përkëdhelem** *f.jv.* to pamper oneself.

përkëdhélës,-e *mb.* caressing.

përkëdhelí,-a *f.sh.* − caress.

përkëdhélur (i,e) *mb.* caressed; **fëmijë i përkëdhelur:** petted child.

përkëmb *f.k.* to recover, to return to health. − **përkëmbem** *f.jv.* to regain one's health, to get on feet again.

përkëmbj/e,-a *f.* recovery, pickup.

përkím,-i *m.sh.* -e coincidence.

përkohësísht *ndajf.* momentarily, temporarily, provisionally, for a time.

përkóhsh/ëm(i),-me(e) *mb.* 1. provisional, momentary, temporary; **qetësi e përkohshme:** temporary calm. 2. passing, fugitive; **bukuri e përkohshme:** fugitive beauty. 3. interim; **komitet i përkohshëm:** interim committee.

përkóhshm/e(e),-ja(e) *f.sh.* -e(të) periodical.

përkón *f.jk.* to coincide.

përkór/e,-ja *f.* frugality, temperance, sobriety.

përkórë (i,e) *mb.* frugal, temperate, sober.

përkorësí,-a *f.* sobriety, frugality.

përkráh *ndajf., paraf,* side by side; **ata ecnin përkrah njëritjetrit:** they walked along side by side.

përkráh *f.k. (dikë)* to protect, to support, to favour (someone); *(një keqbërës)* to abet, to encou-

rage (a malefactor); *(një mendim)* to uphold, to back up (an opinion) − **përkrahem** *f.jv.* to be protected (supported, favoured).

përkráhj/e,-a *f.* protection; stay, prop.

përkrenár/e,-ja *f.sh.* -e headpiece, helmet.

përkthéj *f.k. (me shkrim)* to translate; *(me gojë)* to interpret; **përktheni në shqip këtë tekst:** translate this text into Albanian. − **përkthehet** *f.jv.* to be translated.

përkthím,-i *m.sh.* -e translation.

përkthýes,-i *m.sh.* − *(i një teksti)* translator; *(i një bisede)* interpreter.

përkufizím,-i *m.sh.* -e definition.

përkufizój *f.k.* to define.− **përkufizohet** *f.jv.* to be defined.

përkujdésem *f.jv.* to take care of, to look after.

përkujdésj/e,-a *f.sh.* -e care; *(pranë një të sëmuri)* attendance.

përkujtím,-i *m.sh.* -e commemoration.

përkujtimór,-e *mb.* commemorative.

përkujtój *f.k.* to commemorate. − **përkujtohet** *f.j v.* to be commemorated.

përkúl *f.k.* 1. *(trupin)* to bend, to camber, to crouch (the body); **mos e përkulni kurrizin!** don't bend your back; *(gjurin)* to bend (the knee). 2. *(një shufër hekuri eti.)* to warp, to bend (an iron bar). − **përkulem** *f.jv.* 1. to bow; *(në shenjë nderimi)* to bow, to bend. 2. *fig. (jepem)* to give up, to yield, to submit.

përkúlj/e,-a *f.sh.* -e 1. *(e trupit)* bending; *(në shenjë nderimi)* bow. 2. *(e një shufre hekuri)* warping, bending.

përkúlsh/ëm(i),-me(e) *mb.* flexible, pliant, pliable.

përkulshmërí,-a *f.* flexibility, pliability.

përkúnd *f.k.* to shake; to rock; *(foshnjën)* to lull asleep, to cradle. − **përkundem** *f.jv.* to rock oneself.

përkúndër *paraf.* against; **përkundër dëshirës:** against the will.

përkúndrazi *ndajf.* on the contrary.

përkundréjt *ndajf.* vis-à-vis, face to face with.

përláj *f.k.* 1. to snatch, to clutch, to grip, to nab. 2. to devour, to guzzle. − **përlahet** *f.jv.* to be snatched, to be gripped; to be devoured.

përléshem *f.jv.* to wrestle, to fight hand to hand, to come to fisticuffs, to come to a hand to hand fight, to tussle.

përléshj/e,-a *f.sh.* -e wrestle, scrimmage, tussle, scuffle. clash; *(e vogël me armë)* skirmish.

përlígj *f.k.* to justify. − **përligjem** *f.jv.* to justify oneself.

përlígjij/e,-a *f.* justification.

përlótem *f.jv.* to weep, to have the eyes full of tears.

përlótj/e,-a *f.* tearfulness, weeping, crying, shedding of tears.

përlótur(i,e) *mb.* tearful; **sy të përlotur:** tearful eyes; **me sy të përlotur:** with tearful eyes.

përlýej *f.k.* to besmirch, to sully, to dishonour, to tarnish. − **përlyhem** *f.jv.* to be besmirched (sullied, dishonoured).

përlýer (i,e) *mb.* besmirched, sullied, dishonoured.

përlýerj/e,-a *f.* dishonour.

përllogarít *f.j.* to compute, to calculate. − **përllogaritet** *f.jv.* to be calculated (computed).

përllogarítj/e,-a *f.* computation, calculation.

përmallím,-i *m.* longing, emotion.

përmallój *f.k.* to move, to emotionate. − **përmallohem** *f.jv.* to be moved (touched, emotionated).

përmállsh/ëm(i),-me(e) *mb.* moving, touching, exciting.

përmás/ë,-a *f.sh.* -a dimension.

përmbáj *f.k.* 1. *(veten)* to control, to restrain, to contrain (oneself); **përmbaj inatin:** to restrain one's anger. 2. to contain; **kjo enë përmban një litër ujë:** this vessel contains one litter of water. − **përmbahem** *f.jv.* 1. to control oneself, to check oneself, to refrain; **nuk përmbahem dot:** to be unable to control oneself.

përmbájtj/e,-a *f.* 1. *(e lëndës, e një libri)* content. 2. *(e një ene)* contents of a vessel; *(e vetes)*: self-control, reticence, restraint.

përmbájtur (i,e) *mb.* composed, reticent, sedate, self-contained, self−collected, reserved, demure.

përmbarúes,-i *m.sh.* − *drejt.* bailiff, executor.

përmbí *paraf.* 1. over, above, upon, on: **ka shunë ura përmbi lumin Drin:** there are many bridges over the Drin river. 2. on, above; **flas përmbi një temë:** to speak on a subject.

përmblédh *f.k.* 1. *(një material, një roman)* to abridge, to recapitulate (a matter), to summarize *(a novel).* 2. *(forcat e mia)* to collect (one's forces). − **përmblidhem** *f.jv.* to collect oneself, to get hold (of oneself).

përmblédhës,-e *mb.* recapitulatory, summary, resumptive.

përmblédhj/e,-a *f.* 1. *(e një lënde etj)* recapitulation, summary, precis; abridgement, digest.

përmblédhtas *ndajf.* summarily, concisely.

përmblédhur (i,e) *mb.* concise, condensed.

përmbúsh *f.k.* to fulfil; *(dëshirën)* to realize (one's desire). — **përmbushet** *f.jv.* to be fulfilled.

përmbúshj/e,-a *f.* fulfilment, accomplishment.

përmbýs *ndajf.* upside-down.

përmbýs *f.k.* to upset, to upturn, to overturn, to overthrow, to topple, to throw down, to turn upside-down, to capsize. — **përmbysem** *f.jv.* to capsize, to be overturned, to fall down, to tumble down; **u përmbys anija:** the ship upset (capsized).

përmbýsj/e,-a *f.sh.* **-e** 1. *(e një anijeje)* capsize, upset, overturn (of a ship). 2. *(e një perandorie)* fall (of an empire). 3. *(e rendit shoqëror)* overthrow (of the social order).

përmbýsur (i,e) *mb.* overthrown, overturned.

përmbýt *f.k.* to inundate, to deluge, to flood, to overflow; *(anijen)* to submerge, to overwhelm (a ship). — **përmbytem** *f.jv.* to be inundated (overflowed, submerged.)

përmbýtj/e,-a *f.sh.* **-a** inundation, deluge, overflow, flood (*e madhe)* cataclysm.

përménd *f.k.* to mention; *(një shembull)* to give (an example). — **përmendem** *f.jv.* 1. to come to oneself, to recover consciousness. 2. to be called, to be reminded; to be named.

përmendór/e,-ja *f.sh.* **-e** monument.

përméndsh *ndajf.* by heart, by rote; **mësoj përmendsh:** to learn by heart (by rote).

përméndur (i,e) *mb.* 1. renowd, famous. 2. named, mentioned.

përmés *paraf.* through, across; **përmés lumit:** across the river; **një lumë i gjerë kalon për-**

mes qytetit: a broad river passes through the city.

përmirësím,-i *m.sh.* **-e** improvement, amendment, amelioration; *(i tokës)* improvement (of the land); **ka një farë përmirësimi:** there is some improvement; *(i një ligji)* amendment (of a law); *(i shëndetit)* improvement (of the health).

përmirësój *f.k.* to improve, to ameliorate, to better, to amend; *(tokën)* to improve (the land). — **përmirësohem** *f.jv.* 1. to improve oneself, to change (to alter) for the better. 2. to recover (to regain) one's heal·h.

përmjérr *f.jk.* to piss. — **përmirrm** *f.jv.* to piss.

përmórtsh/ëm(i),-me(e) *mb.* mournful.

përmótsh/ëm(i),-me(e) *mb.* annual, yearly.

përmuajsh/ëm(i),-me (e) *mb.* monthly.

përnátë *ndajf.* every night.

përndáj *f.k.* 1. to spread, to scatter, to disperse. 2. *(ushqime)* to distribute (food). — **përndahem** *f.jv.* to be dispersed.

përndárj/e,-a *f.* spread, dispersion, scattering; distribution.

përndrýshe *ndajf.* otherwise.

përngahérë *ndajf.* forever, always.

përngjáj *f.jk.* to resemble, to look-like; **i përngjajnë njëri-tjetrit:** they resemble each other.

përngjás *f.jk.* shih **përngjaj.**

përngjasím,-i *m.* resemblance, likeness.

përngjásh/ëm(i),-me(e) *mb.* similar, resembling.

përngjashmërí,-a *f.* similarity.

përngjítur (i,e) *mb. gram.* compound; **emër i përngjitur:** compound noun.

përnjëhérë *ndajf.* at a stretch, at

a stroke; **pi përnjëherë**: to drink at a draught (at a gulp).
përnjëhérësh *ndajf.* at once, instantly, immediately; **shfaqet përnjëherësh**: to start up.
përnjëmend *ndajf.* in earnest, verily.
përpára *paraf.* 1. before; **përpara derës**: before the door; **mbiemri vihet përpara emrit**: the adjective is placed before the noun; **rri përpara dikujt**: to stay before someone: *(në kohë)* before.
përpára (se) *lidh.* prior to, before; **trokisni përpara se të hyni**: knock before entering.
përpara *ndajf.* forward, forwards, onward, onwards, forth; ahead; **eci përpara**: to go ahead, to go forward; **ai ka shkuar përpara në mësime**: he has progressed in his studies; **shiko përpara!** look forward!; **më përpara**: formerly, first; **sill më përpara kalin**: bring the horse first; **aty përpara**: a short time ago; **që vjen përpara**: anterior, preceding, former; **që më përpara**: beforehand, previously; **e vë përpara armikun**: to put the enemy to flight: **ora ime shkon përpara**: my watch is fast. **përpara!** forward! onward! ahead!
përpárës/e,-ja *f.sh.* -e apron, pinafore; *(për fëmijë)* bib (for babies).
përparim,-i *m.sh.* -e progress, advancement, headway; **ai ka bërë përparime në mësime**: he has made progress in his studies; **bëj përparime të mëdha**: to make great strides.
përparimtár,-e *mb.* progressive.
përpárm/ë(i),-e(e) *mb.* 1. former. 2. fore; **këmba e përparme e një kafshe**: foreleg; **direku i përparmë i anijes**: foremast.

përparój *f.jk.* to advance, to progress, to get on.
përpársh/ëm(i,)-me(e) *mb.* anterior, former;**në kohët e përparshme**: in former (early) times.
përparshmërí,-a *f.* precedence, priority.
përparúar (i,e) *mb.* advanced: **industri, bujqësi e përparuar**: advanced industry, agriculture; **nxënës i përparuar**: advanced pupil.
përparúes,-e *mb.* progressive.
përpëlítem *f.jv.* to writhe, to wriggle.
përpëlítës,-e *mb.* wriggling, wriggly, writhing.
përpëlítj/e,-a *f.sh.* -e writhe, wriggle.
përpíj.*k.* to swallow up, to engulf, to devour; *fig.* **përpij me sy**: to gloat. − **përpihem** *f.jv.* to be engulfed (devoured); **përpihem nga dallgët**: to be engulfed by the waves.
përpikërí,-a *f.* preciseness, punctuality, exactness; accuracy, correctness; **me përpikëri**: precisely, exactly; punctually.
përpíktë (i,e) *mb.* 1. precise, exact, punctual, accurate; **jam i përpiktë në punë**: to be accurate in one's work. 2. strict; **zbatim i përpiktë i ligjeve**: strict application of the laws.
përpilím,-i *m.* compilation, compiling.
përpilój *f.k.* to compile. − **përpilohet** *f.jv.* to be compiled.
përpilúes,-i *m.sh.* − compiler.
përpíqem *f.jv.* shih **përpjek**.
përpírj/e,-a *f.* swallowing, engulfing.
përpjek *f.k.* (p.t. **përpoqa**, p.p. **përpjekur**) 1. to strike; **përpjek kokën**: to strike the head. 2. *(buzët)* to smack (the lips). 3. *(derën)* to slam, to bang, (the

door). 4. *(duart)* to clap (the hands). 5. *(gotat)* to touch glasses (in drinking). 6. *(këmbët)* to stamp (the feet). − − **përpiqem** *f.jv.* 1. to endeavour, to attempt, to try, to strive, to exert oneself, to make efforts (exertions); **u përpoqa të rendja përpara sa më shpejt që të mundja:** I endeavoured to run forward as fast as I could. 2. to hit upon, to run against; **përpiqemi njëri me tjetrin:** to strike one against another. **përpjékj/e,-a** *f.sh.* -e 1. endeavour, effort, exertion; **bëj çdo përpjekje:** to make every effort, to exert every effort, to try hard. 2. *(duarsh)* clapping (of hands); *(këmbësh)* stamp (of feet). 3. *(me armë)* clash, encounter; *(midis dy trupave)* collision, clash. **përpjesëtím,-i** *m.sh.* -e 1. proportion, ratio; **në përpjesëtim me:** in proportion to, proportionally; **në përpjesëtim të drejtë:** in just proportion. 2. apportionment; **ndaj në përpjesëtim të drejtë:** to apportion, to distribute in just proportions, to proportionate. **përpjesëtimísht** *ndajf.* proportionally, in proportion. **përpjesëtój** *f.k.* to proportionate, to apportion, to distribute in just proportions, to divide into equal parts. − **përpjesëtohet** *f.jv.* to be proportionated. **përpjéssh/ëm(i),-me (e)** *mb.* proportional, proportionate. **përpjétë** *ndajf.* upwards, up; **iu ngjit malit përpjetë:** he climbed up the mountain. **përpjét/ë(e),-a(e)** *f.sh.* -a (të) steep rise; **të përpjetat dhe të tatëpjetat:** the ups and downs. **përpjétë (i,e)** *mb.* ascending, mounting, upgoing, upward.

përplás *f.k.* 1. *(derën)* to bang, to slam (the door). 2. *(këmbët)* to stamp (the feet). 3.*(për tokë)* to dash down, to throw down; *fig.* **ia përplas në fytyrë:** to cast something in one's teeth. − **përplasem** *f.jv.* 1. *(dera)* to bang, to slam. 2. *(me diçka)* to bang (into, against something), to hit (something); **u përplas pas murit me makinë:** he banged his car into a wall. **përplásj/e,-a** *f.sh.* -e 1. *(makinash)* collision (of vehicles). 2. *(e derës)* bang, slam (of a door). 3. *(e këmbëve)* stamp (of feet). 4. *(për tokë)* throwing down. 5. *(duarsh)* clap, clapping of hands. **përpóqa** (past tense of the verb **përpjek).** **përpós** *paraf.* besides; **përpos kësaj:** besides this. **përpósh** *ndajf.* down, downward. **përpuním,-i** *m.* elaboration, working out; *(mineralesh)* processing, treatment (of minerals). **përpunój** *f.k.* to elaborate, to work out; *(minerale)* to process, to treat (minerals). − **përpunohet** *f.jv.* to be elaborated. **përpunúar (i,e)** *mb.* elaborate; wrought; **hekur i përpunuar:** wrought iron. **përpunúes,-e** *mb.* elaborative. **përpúth** *f.k.* 1. to fit, to adapt. 2. to agree, to be in accord. − **përputhem (me)** *f.jv.* to agree, to concur with; **përputhem në mendime:** to have the same opinions; **përputhet:** to correspond, to be in agreement with, to suit. **përpúthj/e,-a** *f.* agreement, accordance; **përputhje mendimesh:** concordance of opinions; **në përputhje me:** in conformity with (to), in compliance with.

përqafím,-i *m.sh.* -e embrace.

përqafój *f.k.* to embrace, to hug; – **përqafohem** *f.jv.* to embrace one another.

përqárk I. *paraf.* around; on all sides; **përqark shtëpisë:** around the house. II. *ndajf.* round about, round, from one side to another; **vij përqark:** to turn round and round.

përqëndrím,-i *m.* concentration; **kamp përqëndrimi:** concentration camp; *(i trupave)* concentration of troops.

përqëndrój *f.k.* to concentrate; *(vëmendjen)* to concentrate one's attention on, to focus one's attention on. – **përqëndrohem** *f.jv.* 1 to concentrate, to be attentive. 2. to be concentrated.

për qind *ndajf.* per cent; **sa për qind?** how much per cent? **përqíndj/e,-a** *f.sh.* -e percentage; **me një përqindje prej:** at the rate of.

përsé *ndajf.* why; **përse nuk erdhe?** why did you not come? **më thuaj arsyen përse nuk fole:** tell me the reason why you did not speak; **ja përse ai ngul këmbë:** that is why he insists.

përsërí *ndajf.* again, anew, over again; **ai erdhi përsëri:** he came back again; **e them përsëri :** I say it again; **sëmurem përsëri:** to relapse, to fall ill again; **provoj përsëri:** to try again.

përsërís *f.k.* 1. to repeat; *(një mësim)* to repeat (a lesson); *(atë që kam thënë ose shkruar)* to rehearse, to repeat (what has

been said or written). 2. *(klasën)* to be a repeater.– **përsëritet** *f.jv.* to be repeated; **që përsëritet herë pas here:** recurrent. **përsërítës,-i** *m.sh.* – 1. repeater. 2. *(krimi)* recidivist.

përsërítj/e,-a *f.* 1. *(e një mësimi)* repetition (of a lesson); *(e një fjale)* repetition (of a word). 2. *(e një sëmundjeje)* relapse (of a malady). 3. *(e një prove teatri)* rehearsal. 4. *drejt.* *(e një krimi)* recidivity. 5. *(kontrate)* renewal (of a contract); **në rast përsëritjeje** *(të një faji):* in case of relapse.

përsípër *ndajf., paraf.* above; upwards; on, upon; **çatia është përsipër tavanit:** the roof is above the ceiling; **marr përsipër:** to assume, to take upon oneself, to bind oneself, to task oneself.

përsós *f.k.* to perfect, to make perfect. – **përsosem** *f.jv.* to perfect oneself.

përsósj/e,-a *f.* prefection.

përsósur (i,e) *mb.* perfect; **në mënyrë të përsosur:** perfectly.

përsosurí,-a *f.* perfection.

përsosurísht *ndajf.* perfectly.

përshésh,-i *m.* pap.

përshésh *f.k.* to break; **përshesh hundën:** to break the nose.

përshëndés *f.k.* to greet, to hail, to salute; **përshëndes fitoren:** to hail a victory; **ata u përshëndetën me njëri-tjetrin:** they greeted one another. – **përshëndetem** *f.jv.* to be greeted (hailed, saluted).

përshëndétj/e,-a *f.sh.* -e 1. greetings; **përshëndetje drejtuar konferencës kombëtare:** greetings to the national conference. 2. hail, salute. 3. salutations, greetings; **përshëndetje revolucionare:** revolutionary greetings.

përshëndósh *f.k.* shih **përshëndes.**
përshëndóshj /e,-a *f.* shih **përshëndetje.**
përshkím,-i *m.* 1. penetration. 2. travel.
përshkój *f.k.* 1. to penetrate. 2. to traverse, to travel. – **përshkohet** *f.jv.* to be penetrated; to be traversed.
përshkrím,-i *m.sh.* -e description.
përshkrúaj *f.k.* 1. to describe. 2. *gjeom.* to circumscribe; **përshkruaj një rreth:** to circumscribe a circle. – **përshkruhet** *f.jv.* 1. to be described. 2. to be circumscribed.
përshkrúes,-i *m. sh.* – describer.
përshkrúes.-e *mb.* descriptive.
përshkúesh /ëm (i),-me (e) *mb.* describable.
përshkúeshëm(i),-me (e) *mb.* penetrable, traversable; *(nga drita)* translucent, transparent; *(nga uji)* permeable.
përshkueshmërí,-a penetrability; permeability.
përshpírtem (i) *f.jv.* *(dikujt)* to implore, to beseech, to supplicate (someone).
përshpírtj /e,-a *f.* requiem.
përshtás *f.k.* to adapt, to accomodate, – **përshtatem** *f.jv.* 1. to adapt oneself; **i përshtatet:** to suit; **kjo nuk i përshtatet:** it doesn't suit him.
përshtátj /e,-a *f.* 1. suitness, conformity; **në përshtatje me:** in conformity to (with). 2. adaptation.
përshtátsh /ëm(i),-me (e) *mb.* adapt, suitable, befitting, proper, appropriate; **masa të përshtatshme:** appropriate measures; **kohë e përshtatshme:** proper time; **sjellje e përshtatshme:** becoming behaviour; **ai nuk është i përshtatshëm për**

këtë punë: he is not fit for this work.
përshtatshmërí,-a *f.* adaptability, fitness.
përshtýpj /e,-a *f.sh.* -e impression; **lë përshtypje të mirë:** to make good impression (on someone).
përtác,-i *m.sh.* -ë lazy-bone, idler.
përtác,-e *mb.* lazy; **nxënës përtac:** a lazy pupil.
përtací,-a *f.* laziness.
përtéj I. *ndajf.* on the other side; **shko përtej:** get on the other side.
    II. *paraf.* beyond, over; **përtej maleve:** beyond the mounts; **përtej detit:** oversea; **vende përtej detit:** oversea countries; **fshatin do ta gjeni përtej asaj kodre:** you will find the village beyond that hill; **përtej masës** beyond measure.
përtéjm /ë(i),-e(e) *mb.* 1. of that side. 2. remote, distant.
përtés /ë,-a *f.* laziness.
përtëríj *f.k.* to renew, to renovate, to restore, to regenerate; *(nga shëndeti)* to rejuvenate, – **përtërihem** *f.jv.* to be rejuvenated, to grow young, to make oneself look younger, to refresh oneself, to gather new forces, to return to vigour.
përtërítj /e,-a *f.* renoval, renewal, renovation, restoration, regeneration.
përtím,-i *m.* laziness; **me përtim:** lazi ly.
përtój *f.jk.* to laze.
përtókë *ndajf.* down,on the ground.
përtýp *f.k.* 1. to chew, to masticate, to cud, to champ; *(duhan)* to chew (tobacco); *(duke përpjekur buzët)* to munch. 2. *fig.* **përtyp fjalët:** to chew the words. – **përtypem** *f.jv.* 1. to chew; *(lopa)* to ruminate.

2. *fig.* to chew the words, to hesitate.

përtýpj/e,-a *f.* chew, mastication.

përtháj *f.k. (plagën)* to cicatrize (a wound). — **përthahet** *f.jv.* to cicatrize.

përthárj/e,-a *f.* cicatrization; **shenja që mbetet mbas përtharjes së plagës:** cicatrix.

përthýej *f.k.* 1. *fiz.* to inflect (the light). 2. to fold up.

përthýerj/e,- a *f. fiz.* diffraction, refraction; **përthyerje e dritës:** light diffraction.

përthýes,-i *m.sh.* — *(i dritës)* refractor.

përthýes,-e *mb.* refracting.

përúl *f.k.* to humble, to abase; to humiliate, to mortify; *(fig.)* to lower. — **përulem** *f.jv.* to humble oneself, to abase oneself.

përúlës,-e *mb.* humiliating, mortifying.

përulësí,-a *f.* humility; **me përulësi:** humbly.

përulësísht *ndajf.* humbly.

përúlj/e,-a *f.* humiliation, abasement.

përúlur(i,e) *mb.* humble.

përvájsh/ëm(i),-me(e) *mb.* mournful, doleful, lamentable.

përvajtím,-i *m.* lamentation.

përvajtój *f.k.* to lament, to mourn.

përvajtúesh/ëm(i),-me(e) *mb.* lamentable, mournful.

përvéç *paraf.* besides, except, save, apart; **përveç kësaj:** besides this, in addition to this.

përvéçëm (i) *mb. gram.* **emër i përveçëm:** proper noun.

përvéçse *lidh.* except, unless.

përvésh *f.k. (mëngët)* to turn up, to roll up (the sleeves); *(pantallonat)* to turn up (one's trousers). — **përvishem** *f.jv.* to set to, to get down to; **i përvishem punës:** to set to work, to get down to work.

përvetësím,-i *m.,* 1. appropriation; peculation, embezzlement, *(i fronit mbretëror)* usurpation (of the royal throne). 2. *(i një mësimi)* assimilation (of a lesson).

përvetësój *f.k.* 1. to appropriate; *(të holla)* to peculate, to embezzle, to appropriate (money); *(një pasuri)* to arrogate (a property); *(fronin mbretëror)* to usurpate (the royal throne). 2. *(një mësim)* to assimilate (a lesson).

përvetím,-i *(pasurie)* arrogation (of property).

përvetój *f.k. (një pasuri)* to arrogate (a property) — **përvetohet** *f.jv.* to be arrogated, to be appropriated.

përvetúes,-i *m.sh* — *(të hollash)* peculator, embezzler.

përvëlój I. *f.k.* to scald. — **përvëlohem** *f.jv.* to burn oneself, to scald oneself.
II. *f.jk.* to be hot, to be burning, to be scorching; **dielli përvëlon:** the sun is burning (very hot).

përvëlúar (i,e) *mb.* scalded; **zemër e përvëluar:** a broken heart.

përvëlúes,-e *mb.* scalding (scorching, very hot); **diell përvëlues:** burning (scorching) sun.

përvítsh/ëm(i),-me(e) *mb.* annual, yearly.

përvjetór,-i *m.sh.* -ë anniversary.

përvój/ë,-a *f.* experience, practice; **me përvojë:** experienced; **pa përvojë:** inexpert, inexperienced, unexperienced.

përvúajtur (i,e) *mb.* 1. **suffering.** 2. humble.

përzemërsí,-a *f.* cordiality, heartiness, geniality.

përzemërsísht *ndajf.* cordially, heartily.

përzémërt(i,e) *mb.* cordial, hearty;

bisedim i përzemërt: cordial talk; pritje e përzemërt: hearty, cordial welcome.

përzë f.k. 1. (nga puna)to turn away; to dismiss, to discharge, to fire off, to cash (from work). 2. (nga dhoma, nga zyra dikë) to turn out (someone). 3. (nga atdheu) to expatriate.

përzíej f.k. 1. to mingle, to intermingle, to mix, to intermix, to blend; përziej dy lëngje: to blend, to mix, to mingle, to stir, to agitate (two liquids). 2. (supën) to stir, to agitate (the soup). 3. (letrat e lojës) to shuffle (the cards). 4. (një shishe me ilaç) to shake (a bottle of medicine). 5. (metalet) to alloy (metals). – përzihem f.jv. 1. to meddle, to intermeddle; përzihem në punët e të tjerëve: to interfere, to meddle in other people's affairs. 2. (në një komplot) to be involved, to be implicated (in a plot). 3. më përzihet: to have the nausea, to be ready to vomit.

përzíer (i,e) mb. 1. mixed; sallatë e përzier: mixed salad: 2. (në një komplot) implicated (in a plot). 3. hybrid; gjuhë e përzier: hybrid language: kafshë me gjak të përzier: hybrid animal.

përzíerës,-i m.sh. – mixer.

përzíerj/e,-a f. 1. (procesi) mixing. 2. (lëngjesh etj.) mixture. 3. (metalesh) alloy (of metals). 4. (në një komplot) implication. 5. (në punët e tjetrit) intermingling, interference.

përzísh/ëm(i),-me (e) mb. mournful; njeri i përzishëm: mourner; jam i përzishëm: to be in mourning.

përzhít f.k. to parch, to singe. –

përzhitem f.jv. to be parched (singed).

përzhítj/e,-a f. parching, singe.

përráll/ë,-a f.sh. -a 1. tale, fairytale, folk-tale, story; fig. përralla me mbret: cock and bull story, a fishy story. 2. lie, falsehood; këto janë përralla: these are tales.

përrallís f.jk. to speak falsely, to fib.

përrallór,-e mb. fabulous.

përréth I. ndajf. round, around; vështroj përreth: to look around. II. paraf. 1. round, around; përreth botës: round the world. 2. about, on, dealing with; përreth kësaj çështjeje: about this subject.

përr/úa,-oi m.sh. -enj 1. stream, torrent; shtrati i përroit: ravine; (mali) mountain torrent, mountain gorge.

pësím,-i m.sh. -e suffering.

pësój f.jk. to undergo, to incur; pësoj një disfatë: to undergo a defeat; pësoj humbje: to incur losses; mirë e pësoi: i served him right.

pësór,-e mb. gram. passive; trajta pësore e një foljeje: the passive voice of a verb.

pëshpërít f.k., f.jk. 1. to whisper, to murmur. 2. to rumour. – pëshpëritet f.jv. to be rumoured; pëshpëritet poshtë e lart se: it is rumoured about that.

pëshpërítës,-i m.sh. – whisperer

pëshpërítj/e,-a f.sh. – whisper, whispering, murmur; rumour.

pështírë (i,e) mb. loathsome, nauseating, sickening, disgusting.

pështírë(të),-t (të) as. nausea, disgust, loathing.

pështirós f.k. to disgust, to loath, to cause nausea. – pështirosem f.jv. to be disgusted.

pështirósj/e,-a *f.* disgust, nausea, loathing.
pështjéllë(të), -t (të) *as.* nausea, disgust, loathing; më vjen të pështjellët: to be overcome by nausea; që shkakton të pështjellët: nauseating.
pështjellím,-i *m.* confusion; disturbance, disorder, disarray.
pështjellój *f.k.* to confuse. − pështjellohem *f.jv.* to get confused.
pështýj *f.jk.* to spit, to sputter; lutemi mos pështyni mbi dysheme: don't spit on the floor, please!
pështým/ë,-a *f.* spit, spittle.
pështýrj/e,-a *f.* spitting; *(mize)* fly-blow.
pi *f.k.* 1. to drink; pi pije alkoolike: to tipple, to drink spirits; *(menjëherë)* to drink up, to drink off, to drink at a draught; pi me fund: to drink thoroughly (fully, completely); *(jashtä masës)* to guzzle, to booze, to boose, to drink immoderately; pi për shëndetin e: to drink to someone's health; to drink a person's health. 2. *(duhan)* to smoke. 3. *(ujë qeni, macja etj.)* to lap, to lick up. − pihem *f.jv.* 1. to get drunk. 2. to be drinkable (in the third person sing.); a pihet ky ujë? is this water drinkable?
pianíst,-i *m.sh.* -ë pianist.
piáno,-ja *f.sh.* − *muz.* piano.
pickím,-i *m.* 1. *(në lëkurë)* pinch, nip; *(i bletës)* sting.
pickój *f.k.* to pinch, to nip; *(bleta)* to sting (the bee).− pickohem *f.jv.* to be nipped.
piedestál,-i *m. sh.* -e piedestal.
pijanéc,-i *m.sh.* -ë drunkard, drinker, tippler, bibber, toper, *amer.* guzzler.
píj/e,-a *f.sh.* -e drink, beverage;

pije alkoolike: spirits, strong spirits, alcoholic beverages, tipple, strong liquors; pije freskuese: refreshing drink.
pijeshítës,-i *m. sh.* − drink-seller, barkeeper.
pijetór/e,-ja *f.s.h.* -e bar, pothouse, beer-house, wine-shop.
píjsh/ëm(i),-me(e) *mb.* drinkable, potable; ujë i pijshëm: drinkable (potable) water.
pikalósh,-e *mb.* freckled, specked.
pikás *f.k.* to nose out, to detect, to sniff (to smell) out. − pikasem *f.jv.* to be detected, to be sniffed out.
pikásj/e,-a *f.* detection.
pikatór/e,-ja *f.sh.* -e dropper, dropping tube; *(për ilaçe)* medicine dropper.
pikét/ë,-a *f.sh.* -a picket.
piketím,-i *m.* picketing.
piketój *f.jk.* to picket, to put landmarks, to stake out (off), to mark off with stakes. − piketohet *f.jv.* to be picketted.
pík/ë,-a *f.sh.* -a 1. *(uji)* drop (of water). 2. *mjek.* apoplexy; të rëntë një pikë! may you have a stroke of apoplexy! 3. *sport.* point. 4. *gram.* full stop; dy pika (:) colon. 5. *(në letër)* dot; vijë me pika: dotted line. 6. *gjeog.* pikat e orientimit: chief points, cardinal points. 7. *(njollë)* spot, speck, blot, stain. 8. *(e një programi)* item (of a program); pikat kryesore të një fjalimi: the main points (the chief points) of a speech. 9. *(e mëngjesit)* peep; që në pikë të mëngjezit: from the peep of the day. − *Lok.* vë pikat mbi i: to dot the i's and cross the t's; pikë për pikë: punctually, textually; mbi këtë pikë: on this subject (point); pa pikë turpi: impudently· kjo

ju shkon pikë: it fits you well.
pikëçudítj/e,-a *f.sh.* – -e *gram.*
exclamation mark.
pík/ël,-la *f.sh.* -la drop;
pikla uji: spray of water.
pikëllím,-i *m.* affliction, deep sorrow.
pikëllój *f.k.* to afflict. – pikëllohem *f.jv.* to be afflicted.
pikëliúar (i,e) *mb.* afflicted.
pikëllúes,-e *mb.* afflicting.
pikëmbështétj/e,-a *f.sh.* -e fulcrum.
pikënísj/e,-a *f.sh.* -e starting point.
pikëpámj/e,-a *f.sh.* -e 1. view, point of view, viewpoint; nga pikëpamja e: from the viewpoint of, regarding, concerning, from the point of view of; nga çdo pikëpamje: in all directions; nga kjo pikëpamje: from this point of view 2. opinion; cila është pikëpamja juaj? what is your opinion?
pikëpjékj/e,-a *f.sh.* -e appointment, date; lë një pikëpjekje me dikë: to make an appointment with someone.
pikëprésj/e,-a *f.sh.* -e *gram:* semicolon.
pikëpýetj/e,-a *f.sh.* -e *gram.* question mark.
pikërísht *ndajf.* precisely, just, right; pikërisht ashtu: precisely so; pikërisht atje: just there, right there.
pikësëpári *ndajf.* first of all, first, firstly, first and foremost.
pikësím,-i *m. gram.* punctuation; shenjat e pikësimit: punctuation marks; vë shenjat e pikësimit : to punctuate.
pikësyním,-i *m.sh.* -e objective, goal, aim, purpose.
pikësynój *f.jk.* to aim at.
píkëz,-a *f.sh.* -a small drop.
pikník,-u *m.sh.* -e picnic.

pikój I. *f.k.* 1. to pour drops. 2. to dirty, to soil. – pikohem *f.jv.* to dirty oneself. II. *f.jk.* to leak, to drop, to fall in drops; pikon çatia: the roof is leaking.
piks *f.k.* to clot, to coagulate, to thicken. – pikset *f.jv.* to be clotted (coagulated, thickened).
píksur-it (të) *as.* clotting, coagulation, thickening.
píksur, (i,e) *mb.* clotted, coagulated, thickened; qumësht i piksur: clotted milk; gjak i piksur: gore, clotted blood.
piktór,-i *m.sh.* -ë painter; piktor pejzazhesh: landscape painter, landscapist; piktor dekoresh *(teatri):* scene painter.
piktorésk,-e *mb.* picturesque.
piktúr/ë,-a *f.sh.* -a painting, picture; libër me piktura: picture-book.
pikturím,-i *m.* painting.
pikturój *f.k.* to picture, to paint; *(dikë)* to portray (someone).
pikturohem *f.jv.* to paint oneself.
piláf,-i *m.* risotto.
píl/ë,-a *f.sh.* -a *el.* pile.
pilivés/ë,-a *f.sh.* -a *zool.* dragonfly.
pilót,-i *m.sh.* -ë pilot, steersman, airman, flyer.
pilotím,-i *m.* pilotage, piloting.
pilotój *f.k.* to pilot. – pilotohet *f.jv.* to be piloted.
pínc/ë,-a *f.sh.* -a pinchers, pincers, nippers; *(për heqjen e dhëmbëve):* forceps; *(mekaniku)* pliers.
pinésk/ë,-a *f.sh.* -a drawing-pin, brad.
pingpóng,-u *m.* table tennis.
pingrím,-i *m.* chirping (of a bird).
pingrón *f.jk.* to chirp (of a bird).
pingúl *ndajf.* vertically, perpendicularly.

pingúl/e,-ja *f.sh.* -e perpendicular line.

pingúltë (í,e) *mb.* vertical, perpendicular; vijë e pingultë: perpendicular line.

pingúlthi *ndajf.* vertically, perpendicularly.

pinjóll,-i *m.sh.* -ë offspring.

pioniér,-i *m.sh.* -ë pioneer.

pipér,-i *m.* pepper; piper i kuq; red pepper; piper i zì: black pepper; kuti piperi: pepper box.

pipérk/ë,-a *f.sh.* -a *bot.* pepper.

pipét/ë,-a *f.sh.* -a *kim.* pipette, pipet.

píp/ë,-a *f.sh.* -a 1. pipe; heq pipën; to smoke a pipe. 2. *(për vegla fryme)* mouthpipe (of wind instruments).

pípëz,-a *f.sh.* -a thin cane; drinking straw.

pipirúq,-i *m.sh.* -ë coxcomb, dandy, fop.

pirát,-i *m.sh.* -ë sea-rover, pirate, corsair.

pírë(i,e) *mb.* drunk, intoxicated, tipsy; gjysmë i pirë *(bërë më qejf)* : half-tipsy.

pir/g,-gu *m.sh.* -gje 1. turret. 2. pile, heap.

pirografí,-a *f.* pyrography.

pir/ún,-ni *m.sh.* -nj fork.

pis,-e *mb.* dirty, filthy, grimy.

pís/ë,-a *f.* tar, pitch; i zi pisë: pitch-black.

pisk *ndajf.* e kam pisk punën: to be in a fix (tight) spot.

pisk,-u *m.* 1. knot. 2. në piskun e vapës: in the thick of summer.

pisllë/k,-ku *m.sh.* -qe dirtiness, filthiness, uncleanness.

pispillós *f.k.* to spruce oneself up. — pispillosem *f.jv.* to deck oneself out.

pisqóll/ë,-a *f.sh.* -a *vjet.* pistol.

pistón,-i *m.sh.* -a piston.

pish/ë,-a *f.sh.* -a *bot.* pine-wood, pine-tree; dru pishe: pine.

pishnáj/ë,-a *f.sh.* - pinery.

pishín/ë,-a *f.sh.* -a swimming--pool.

pishmán *ndajf.* bëhem pishman: to rue, to repent, to regret.

pishtár,-i *m.sh.* -ë torch; *fig.* pishtari i diturisë: the torch of learning.

pít/e,-ja *f.sh.* -e 1. pizza. 2. *(mjalti)* honey-comb.

pízg/ë,-a *f.* 1. stalkwhistle, 2. knot; lidh pizgë; to tie intricately.

pizháme,-t *f.sh.* pyjamas, pajamas.

pják/ë,-a *f.sh.* -a *vjet.* public square, piazza. – *Lok.* e ngre pjacën: to rise the price.

pjalm,-i *m.* *bot.* pollen.

pjatalárës,-i *m. sh.* – dish-washer.

pjatambájtës/e,-ja *f.sh.* -e pla--te-stand.

pjatánc/ë,-a *f.sh.* -a large plate.

pját/ë,-a *f.sh.* -a 1. dish, plate; *(e thellë supe)* soup-plate; *(filxhani)* saucer; laj pjatat: to wash the dishes, to wash up. 2. plate, plateful, dish; një pjatë me zarzavate: a plate of vegetables.

pjavíc/ë,-a *f.sh.* -a *zool.* blood--sucker, leech; *(e madhe)* horse-leech.

pjek *f.k.* (p.t. poqa, p.p. pjekur). 1. *(mishin)* to roast (meat); *(në skarë, mish, peshk)* to broil, to cook upon a gridiron (meat. fish). 2. *(bukën)* to bake (bread) 3. *(kafen)* to roast, to torrefy (coffee). – piqet *f.jv.* 1. *(mishi)* to be roasted. 2. *(buka)* to be baked 3. *(kafja)* to be roasted. 4. piqem në diell: to get sunburnt. 5. *(pema)* to become ripe.

pjek *f.k.* (p.t. poqa, p.p. pjekur) *(dikë)* to meet, to encounter (someone). – piqem *f.jv.* to meet with, to come across with.

pjékj/e,-a *f.sh.* -e 1. *(e bukës)* baking (of bread). 2. *(e mishit në hell)* roasting (of meat in a spit). 3. *(e mishit në skarë)* broiling (of meat upon a gridiron). 4. *(e kafes)* roasting (of coffee). 5. *(e frutave)* ripening (of fruits).

pjékur (i,e) *mb.* 1. roast, roasted; *(në furrë)* baked; i pjekur në skarë; grilled; i pjekur shumë: overdone; i pjekur pak: underdone. 2. *(pemë)* ripe; rrush i pjekur: ripe grapes. 3. *fig.* mature; gjykim i pjekur: mature judgement. 4. *(në moshë)* mature.

pjekurí,-a *f.* maturity; mosha e pjekurisë: age of maturity, years of discretion.

pjell *f.k.* (p.t. polla, p.p. pjellë); to procreate; *(lopa)* to calve; *(macja)* to kitten; *(pela)* to foal; *(delja)* to lamb; *(egërsirat)* to cub. − *Lok.* atij i pjell mendja: he is ingenious.

pjéll/ë,-a *f.sh.* -a progeny; outcome, product.

pjéllj/e,-a *f.* procreation.

pjellór,-e *mb.* 1. *(tokë)* fertile (soil). 2. *fig.* fertile, fruitful, inventive; mendje pjellore: fertile (inventive) mind.

pjellorí,-a *f.* fertility.

pjellshmërí,-a *f.* procreation

pjelltór,-e *mb.* procreant; pulë pjelltore: layer hen.

pjép/ër,-ri *m.sh.* -ra melon.

pjérgull,-a *f.sh.* -a *bot.* pergola vine.

pjerrës!,-a *f.* slant, slope, declivity, inclination.

pjérrët (i,e) *mb.* 1. slanting, leant, declivitous, inclined. 2. *gjeom.* oblique; vijë e pjerrët: oblique line.

pjérrj/e,-a *f.* inclination.

pjérrtas *ndajf.* slantingly, aslant, obliquely.

pjés/ë,-a *f.sh.* -ë 1. piece, part, portion; *(e vogël)* small part. 2. *(muzikë)* piece, fragment (of music); *(letrare)* piece. 3. part; pjesë e përparme: forepart; pjesë e pasme; hind part; bëj pjesë: to make part of; kam pjesë: to have a part; marr pjesë: to take part, to partake. 4. pjesë këmbimi: spare parts. 5. *(në një shoqëri me aksione)*: share. − *Lok.* në pjesën dërmuese: for the most part; pjesa më e madhe e tyre: most of them.

pjesëmárrës,-i *m.sh.* − participant, partaker, participator.

pjesëmarrj/e,-a *f.* participation(in); me pjesëmarrjen e: with the participation of.

pjésë-pjésë *ndajf.* piecemeal, part by part, piece by piece; paguaj pjesë-pjesë: to pay by instalments.

pjesérisht *ndajf.* partly, in part.

pjesétár,-i *m.sh.* -ë 1. *(i një shoqërie)* associate, partner. 2. *(i një familjeje)* member.

pjesëtím,-i *m.sh.* -e 1. *(pasurie etj.)* apportion, allotment, sharing. 2. *mat.* division.

pjesëtój *f.k.* 1. *(një pasuri etj)* to apportion, to allot, to share. 2. *mat.* *(një numër)* to divide (a number). − pjesëtohet *f.jv.* to be divided.

pjesëtúes,-i *m.sh.* − *mat.* divisor.

pjesëtúesh/ëm(i),-me(e) *mb.* *mat.* divisible.

pjesëtueshmërí,-a *f.* divisibility.

pjésëz,-a *f.sh.* -a 1. *gram.* particle. 2. *fiz.* particle.

pjesór,-e *mb.* partitive.

pjesór/e,-ja *f.* *gram.* participle.

pjéssh/ëm(i),-me(e) *mb.* partial.

pjéshk/ë,-a *f.sh.* -a *bot.* peach; *(druri)* peach-tree.

pláçk/ë;-a *f.sh.* -a 1. cloth, stuff,

tissue; **plaçkë e dobët;** poor stuff. 2. clothes *sh.; ***plaçka të përdorura:** used clothes. 3. belongings; **plaçkë lufte:** plunder, booty; – *fig.* **ai s'është plaçkë e mirë:** he is not a good sort.
plaçkís *f.k.* to pillage, to plunder, to sack, to ransack, to loot. – **plaçkitem** *f.jv.* to be spoiled.
plaçkítës,-i *m.sh.* – pillager, plunderer.
plaçkítj/e,-a *f.sh.* -e pillage, plundering, rapine.
plaçkurína,-t *f.sh.* old clothes, cast of clothes.
plág/ë,-a *f.sh.* -ë wound; *(e lehtë)* flesh wound; *(e thellë)* gash, deep wound; **lidh një plagë:** to bind up a wound; **djeg një plagë:** to cauterize a wound; **mjekoj një plagë:** to dress a wound; **marr një plagë:** to get wounded. – *Lok.* **e kam zemrën plagë:** my heart is breaking, my heart is wounded.
plagós *f.k.* 1. to wound. 2. *fig.* to hurt, to hurt the feelings of; *(zemrën)* to wound (the heart). – **plagosem** *f.jv.* to get wounded.
plagósj/e,-a *f.* wounding.
plagósur (i,e) *mb.* wounded.
plagósur (i),-i(i) *m.sh.*-(të) wounded; **gjithë të plagosurit ishin hequr:** all the wounded were evacuated.
plak,-u *m.sh.* **pleq** old man.
plak/,-ë *mb.* old, oldish, aged; **dua të dukem plak:** to make oneself look old; **ai nuk tregon shumë plak:** he is young for his years.
plak *f.k.* to make old; **hallet e plakin njeriun:** cares make a man old. – **plakem** *f.jv.* to get old, to grow old, to age.
plák/ë,-a *f.sh.* -a old woman.
plákj/e,-a *f,* ageing, growing old.
plákur (i,e) *mb.* aged.

plakúsh,-i *m.sh.* -ë old chap; **si je, plakush?** how are you my old chap?
plan,-i *m.sh.* -e 1, plan; **plani pesëvjeçar:** five-year plan; **hartimi i planit:** drawing (up) of the plan; **plan konspekt:** conspectus; **realizimi ;i planit:** fulfilment of the plan; **simbas planit:** according to the plan. 2. design, intention; **kam në plan të:** I intend to, I have planned to.
planét,-i *m.sh.* -ë *astr.* planet.
planifikím,-i *m.* planning.
planifikój *f.k.* to plan. – **planifikohet** *f.jv.* to be planed.
planifikúes,-i *m.sh.* -a planner.
planimetrí,-a *f.* planimetry.
plantación,-i *m.sh.* -e plantation; **pronar plantacioni:** planter, plantation-owner.
plas I. *f.k.* 1. to crack; **plas një gotë:** to crack a glass. 2. to burst, to break through. 3. *fig.* **ia plas shpirtin dikujt:** to bore someone to death, to bore out of one's life.
II *f.jk.* to burst; **plas nga mërzia:** to be bored stiff.
plasarít *f.k.* to crack, to chap. – **plasaritet** *f.jv.* to crack; **plasaritet qelqi:** the glass cracks; *(duart)* to chap.
plasarítj/e,-a *f.sh.* -e crack, chap; *(e enës)* crack, chink (of a vessel); *(e lëkurës)* chap (of the skin); *(e qelqit)* rift, fissure (of a glass); *(e murit)* crevice (of a wall).
plás/ë,-a *f.sh.* -a *(e tokës)* chasm; **zë plasat e një dere, të një dritareje:** to stuff the holes of a door, of a window.
plásj/e,-a *f.sh.* -e 1. exploision, outburst; *(e një bombe)* exploison (of a bomb); *fig.* **më vjen plasje:** to burst of anger.

plásj/e,-a *f. mjek. (e bagëtive)* anthrax (of the cattle).

plasticitét,-i *m.* plasticity.

plastík,e *mb.* plastic.

plastmás,-i *m.* plastic.

platé,-ja *f. (e një teatri, kinemaje)* pit (of a theater, of a cinema).

platfórm/ë,-a *f.sh.* -a 1. platform. 2. platform, political program.

platín,-i *m. kim.* platinum,

plázm/ë,-a *f. anat., fiz.* plasma.

plazh,-i *m.sh.* -e beach.

plebé,-u *m.sh.* -j plebeian.

plebishít,-i *m.sh.* -e plebiscite.

pleh,-u *m.sh.* -ra manure; *(kafshësh, ose pleh organik)* dung, muck; **pleh kimik;** fertilizer.

plehërím,-i *m.* manuring, fertilization.

plehërój *f.k.* to manure, to muck; *(me pleh organik):* to muck, to manure; *(me pleh kimik)* to fertilize. − **plehërohet** *f.jv.* to be manured (fertilized).

pléhra,-t *f.sh.* filths, garbages, sweepings; *(shtëpie)* household garbages; **kosh i plehrave:** dustbin.

pleks *f.k.* 1. to tress, to mat. 2. to knot, to involve, to entangle, to complicate. − **pleksem** *f.jv* to be mingled (intermingled).

pléksj/e,-a *f.* involution, entanglement, involvement.

plenár,-e *mb.* plenary; **mbledhje plenare:** plenary session.

plep,-i *m.sh.* -a *bot.* poplar.

pleqërí,-a *f.* old age, senility; **i pleqërisë:** senile; **sëmundje pleqërie:** senile malady.

pleqërísht *ndajf.* in the old folk's manner.

pleqërój *f.k.* 1. to sustain someone in his old age. 2. *fig. (një punë)* to discuss, to talk over (an affair).

pleqësí,-a *f.* (formerly) council of dignitaries of a village.

pleqësój *f.k.* shih **pleqëroj.**

plesht,-i *m.sh.* -a *zool.* flea; **pickim i pleshtit:** flea bite.

pléur/ë,-a *f.sh.* -a *anat.* pleura.

plevíc/ë,-a *f.sh.* -a hay-loft, barn.

plevít,-i *m. mjek* pleurisy.

plevitós *f.k.* to chill. − **plevitosem** *f.jv.* to catch cold, to be affected by pneumonia; to have a chill.

plëndës,-i *m.sh.* -a paunch (of a ruminant).

plëng,-u *m.* wealth, riches; **njeri pa plëng e pa shtëpi:** waif, homeless wanderer.

plëngpríshës,-i *m.sh.* − prodigal, spendthrift, waster, lavish person.

plëngpríshës,-e *mb.* prodigal, lavish, wasteful.

plëngpríshj/e,-a *f.* priodigality, lavishness, wastefulness.

plíko,-ja *f.sh.* − envelope.

plis,-i *m.sh.* -a sod; clod, lump; **me plisa:** lumpy, full of lumps.

plítk/ë,-a *f.sh.* a electric chafing -dish.

plithár,-i *m.sh.* -ë adobe, sun- -dried brick; **mur me plitharë:** mud-wall; **shtëpi me plitharë:** adobe (house).

plógësht(i,e) *mb.* shih **i plogët.**

plogështí,-a *f.* sloth, inactivity, indolence; **me plogështi:** slothly.

plógët (i,e) *mb.* slothful, indolent, sluggish, inactive; **njeri i plogët:** sluggard man.

plor,-i *m.sh.* -e plough-share, plow-share, plowblade.

plot *ndajf.* full, replete; **plot jetë:** full of life; **plot gabime:** full of mistakes; **një vit plot:** a whole year; **plot merak:** full of trouble; **plot e përplot:** replete, completely filled, chockfull, full-up; **me duart plot:** with the hands full; *fig.* **e kam xhepin plot:** to have money, to be rolling in money.

plótë (i,e) *mb.* full, whole, entire, complete; **numër i plotë:** full number; **hënë e plotë:** full moon. – *Lok.* **me vullnet të plotë:** of one's own free will.

plótës,-i *m.sh.* -a *gram.* adverbial modifier; **plotës rrethanor:** adverbial modifier of circumstances.

plotësím,-i *m.sh.* -e 1. fulfilment; **plotësimi i planit:** fulfilment of the plan. 2. *(i një detyre)* accomplishment, completion (of a duty); *(i një dëshire)* realization, satisfaction (of a wish).

plotësísht *ndajf.* completely, entirely, fully, wholly, thoroughly.

plotësój *f.k.* 1. to complete: **plotësoj një shumë:** to complete an amount. 2. *(nevojat e përditshme)* to provide oneself (with daily necessaries). 3. *(një dëshirë)* to satisfy, to realize (a wish). 4. *(detyrën)* to fulfil (ose's duty). – **plotësohet** *f.jv.* 1. *(një koleksion)* to be completed (a collection). 2. *(nevojat)* to be provided. 3. *(dëshira)* to be realized. 4. *(detyra)* to be fulfilled.

plotësúar (i,e) *mb.* *(dëshirë)* satisfied (desire).

plotës úes,-e *mb.* complementary, additional.

plotfuqísh/ëm (i),-me(e) *mb.* all--powerful, omnipotent.

plotfuqishmërí,-a *f.* omnipotence.

plotpjesëtúes,-i *m.sh.* – *mat.* full divider.

plotpjestúesh/ëm (i),-me(e) *mb.* fully divisible.

plug,-u *m.sh.* **plugje** plough.

plugím,-i *m.sh.* -e ploughing, plowing.

plugój *f.k.* to plough. – **plugohet** *f.jv.* to be (ploughed, plowed).

plúhur,-i *m.sh.* -a 1. dust; **rrugë me pluhur:** dusty road; **plu-**

hur qymyri: slack (of coal). 2. powder; **qumësht pluhur:** powdered milk; **sheqer pluhur:** powdered sugar, castor-sugar. – *Lok.* **bëj pluhur e hi:** to reduce to ashes, to reduce to dust.

pluhurós *f.k.* to cover with dust. – **pluhurosem** *f.jv.* to be covered with dust.

plumb,-i *m.sh.* -a *kim.* 1. lead; **laps plumbi:** lead pencil; **prej plumbi:** leaden; **ngjit me plumb:** to lead; **i rëndë plumb:** as heavy as lead. 2. *(pushke)* bullet (of a gun, of a revolver).

plumbç,-i *f.sh.* -a plumb, plummet; **plumbç muratori:** plumb of a mason.

plumbós *f.k.* to lead, to joint with lead.

plumbósj/e,-a *f.* lead-work. leading.

pluskím,-i *m.* floating.

pluskój *f.jk.* to float.

pluskúes,-i *m.sh.* – *tek.* float.

plláj/ë,-a *f.sh.* -a *gjeog.* plateau.

pllakáq/e,-ja *f.sh.* -e square-stone, flagstone, paving stone; **shtroj me pllakaqe:** to pave with squarestones.

pllakát,-i *m.sh.* -e placard.

pllák/ë,-a *f.sh.* -a 1. slab; *(guri, mermeri)* slab (of stone, of marble); **pllakë trotuari:** slab for foot-path. 2. **pllakë përkujtimore:** commemorative stone; **pllakë varri:** ledger. 3. *(gramafoni)* record. 4. *(për të shkruar)* tablet (for writing).

pllakós I. *f.jk.* to come unexpectedly, to supervene.
II. *f.k.* to overrun.

pllakósj/e,-a *f.* supervention; overrun, overrunning.

pllením,-i *m.* *bot.* fecundation, impregnation.

plloçák,-e *mb.* flat.

pllóç/ë,-a *f.sh.* -a slate; **plloça për**

mbullmin e çative: slates for roofing.
pllósk/ë,-a *f.sh.* -a *(vere)* small wooden bottle (to hold wine).
plluqurís I. *f.k.* to ripple. II. *f.jk.* to plash; to splash, to squelch.
plluqurítj/e,-a *f.* rippling; *(e va-lëve të detit)* lapping, swashing (of waves); *(e baltës)* squelch.
pnéumoní,-a *f. mjek.* pneumonia.
po I. *ndajf.* yes; **a do të vini me mua?** po, do të vij: will you come with me? yes, I will; **po ashtu:** all the same; likewise; **po ashtu mund të bëjmë edhe ne:** we may do like wise (follow suit); **po e njëjta gjë është:** it is all the same; **po në atë vend:** at the very place. II. *lidh* 1. if; **ma jep pak kriporen, po deshe:** pass me the salt-cellar if you please. 2. but; **jo unë, po ti:** not I, but you. III. *pjesëz.* (particle placed before a verb) **çfarë po bën?** po shkruaj: what are you doing? I am writing.
pocaqí,-a *f.sh..* – torment, suffering.
pocaqísem *f.jv.* to be tormented; *(në punë)* to toil, to work with pain and fatigue.
poçár,-i *m.sh.* -ë potter.
póç/e,-ja *f.sh.* -e 1. *(prej balte)* pipkin, earthen pot, cruse. 2. *(lulesh ose saksi)* flower pot. 3. *(elektriku)* electric lamp. 4. *(nate)* chamber – pot. 5. *(për shkrirje)* crucible, melting pot.
poçerí,-a *f.* 1. pottery; **artikuj ose enë poçerie:** pottery, earthenware. 2. pottery, potter's workshop.
podiúm,-i *m.sh.* -e scaffolding, podium, platform.
poém/ë,-a *f.sh.* -a poem.
poét,-i *m.sh.* -ë poet.
poetík,-e *mb.* poetical, poetic.

poezí,-a *f.sh.* – 1. *(arti)* poetry. 2. *(pjesë poetike)* poem.
pogáç/e,-ja *f.sh.* -e 1. loaf (of bread).
pohím,-i *m.sh.* -e avow, confession; acknowledgement.
pohimísht *ndajf.* affirmatively.
pohój *f.k.* 1. *(fajin)* to avow (a fault), to confess (one's fault); **pohoj se jam fajtor:** to plead guilty. – **pohohet** *f.jv.* to be confessed; to be affirmed.
pohóre *mb. gram.* affirmative.
pohúes,-e *mb.* positive; **përgjigje pohuese:** positive answer.
poják,-u *m.sh.* -ë watch-man.
póker,-i *m.* poker (game of cards).
pol,-i *m.sh.* -e 1. *gjeog.* pole; **poli i veriut:** the North Pole. 2. *fiz.* **poli magnetik:** magnetic pole.
polák,-u *m.sh.* -ë Pole.
polák,-e *mb.* Polish.
polár,-e *mb.* polar, **ylli polar:** pole-star.
polemík/ë,-a *f.* polemic; controversy.
poliambulánc/ë,-a *f.sh.* -a dispensary.
políc,-i *m.sh.* -ë constable, policeman, *fam.* cop, copper, bobby; *(i fshehtë)* detective; **qen policie:** bloodhound.
policí,-a *f.* 1. police; **rajoni i policisë;** police-station. 2. *(efektivi)* police force.
policór,-e *mb.* 1. police; **forca policore:** police forces. 2. **roman policor:** detective story.
poliglót,-e *mb.* polyglot.
poligón,-i *m.sh.* -e *usht.* shooting-gallery, shooting-range.
polikliník/ë,-a *f.sh.* -a central dispensary.
politeník,-e *mb.* polytechnic.
politeknikúm,-i *m.sh.* -e polytechnic school.
polités/ë,-a *f.* politeness, civility,

courtesy; **sillem me politesë:** to behave politely (courteously, in a proper manner.)

politík,-e *mb.* political.

politikán,-i *m.sh.* **-ë** politician.

politík/ë-a *f.* 1. policy; **politikë e jashtme:** foreign policy; **politikë parimore:** principled policy. 2. politics; **merrem me politikë:** to be engaged in politics.

politikísht *ndajf.* politically.

pólk/ë,-a *f.sh.* **-a** *muz.* polka.

polonísht *ndajf.* in Polish.

polonísht/e,-ja *f.* Polish.

poltrón/ë,-a *f.sh.* **-a** armchair.

pomád/ë,-a *f.sh.* **-a** pomade, ointment.

pómp/ë,-a *f.sh.* **-a** pump; **pompë ajri:** air-pump; **pompë dore:** hand pump; **pompë thithëse:** sucking pump; **pompë uji;** water-pump.

pompím,-i *m.* pumping.

pompíst,-i *m.sh.* **-ë** pumpist.

pompój *f.k.* to pump, to pump up. — **pompohet** *f.jv.* to be pumped.

pompóz,-e *mb.* pompous.

pompozitét,-i *m.* pomposity.

ponç,-i *m.* punch.

póp/ël,-la *f.sh.* **-la** boulder.

pópu/ll,-lli *m.sh.* **-j** 1. people; **popujt e Evropës:** the peoples of Europe. 2. people, the masses.

popullaritét,-i *m.* popularity

popullarizím,-i *m.* popularization.

popullarizój *f.k.* to popularize. — **popullarizohet** *f.jv.* to be popularized.

populllát/ë,-a *f.sh.* **-a** population.

popullím,-i *m. (i një vendi)* peopling

popullój *f.k. (një vend)* to people. — **popullohet** *f.jv.* to be populated.

popullór,-e *mb.* 1. popular. 2.

mass; **lëvizje popullore:** mass uprising.

popullsí,-a *f.sh.* — population; **popullsi qytetare:** the town (urban) population.

póqa *f.k.* (past tense of the v. **pjek**) 1. I met. 2. I roasted.

por *lidh.* but; **ha, por me masë:** eat your fill, but not in excess; **më kujtohet vendi, por jo data:** I remember the place but not the date.

por,-i *m.sh.* **-e** stove.

porcelán,-i *m.sh.* **-e** porcelain; china; **enë porcelani:** chinaware.

porción,-i *m.sh.* **-e** portion.

pórdh/ë,-a *f.sh.* **-a** fart.

pór/e,-ja *f.sh.* **-e** *anat.* pore.

pornografí,-a *f.* pornography.

porosí,-a *f.sh..* — 1. advise, instruction; **zbatoj porositë e dikujt;** to act upon someone's instructions; **porositë e Partisë:** the Party's instructions. 2. *treg.* errand, command, order; **kostum me porosi;** suit made to measure (to order).

porosís *f.k.* 1. to instruct, to recommend, to advise. 2. to order; **porosis një kostum:** to order a suit. — **porositem** *f.jv.* to be recommended, to be advised.

porosítur (i,e) *mb.* commended, recommended; **letër e porositur** registered letter.

poróz,-e *mb.* porous.

porsá *ndajf.* just as; just now; **porsa e pashë:** I have just seen him; **letra juaj porsa më ra në dorë:** I have just received your letter.

porsaárdhur (i,e) *mb.* new-comer.

porsalíndur (i,e) *mb.* new-born.

porsamartúar (i,e) *mb.* newly-married.

porsé *lidh.* but.

porsí *lidh.* as, like, likewise.

port,-i *m.sh.* -e port, harbour.
pórt/ë,-a *f.sh.* -a 1. door; *(e madhe me hekura në hyrjen e një oborri)* gate; *(portë e jashtme e një shtëpie)*; front door. door-way, street-door; **portë e prapme:** back-door; **portë me dy kanata:** folding door; *(e madhe)* portal. 2. *(futbolli)* goal.
portiér,-i *m.sh.* -ë 1. door-keeper, gate-keeper, usher, porter. 2. *sport.* goal-keeper.
portofól,-i *m.sh.* -ë *(për para)* wallet, *amer.* billfold.
portokáll,-i *m.sh.* -e *bot.* orange; *(druri i portokallit)* orange-tree; **reçel portokalli:** orange-jam; **ngjyrë portokalli:** orange colour.
portollámb/ë,-a *f.sh.* -a socket (of an electric lamp).
portrét,-i *m.sh.* -e portrait.
portugéz,-i *m.sh.* -ë Portuguese.
portugéz,-e *mb.* Portuguese.
posá l. *ndajf.* barely, scarcely; **mësuesi posa kishte ardhur:** the teacher had scarcely come. II *lidh.* as, as soon as; **posa ju pashë:** as soon as I saw you.
posáç/ëm (i),-me(e) *mb.* special; **botim i posaçëm;** special edition.
posaçërísht *ndajf.* especially, particularly.
posedím,-i *m.* possession.
posedój *f.k.* to possess. – **posedohet** *f.jv.* to be possessed.
posedúes-i *m.sh.* possessor.
posí *ndajf.* surely, just so.
posí *paraf.* as, like; **i zi posi katrani:** pitch-black.
post,-i *m.sh.* -e 1. post; **post i përparuar:** outpost. 2. position, appointment, duty, office.
postáf,-i *m.sh.* -ë sink.
postár,-e *mb.* postal; **shpenzime postare:** postage.

postát,-i *m.sh.* -e flower-bed.
postbllo/k,-ku *m.sh.* -qe postblock.
póst/ë,-a *f.* 1. *(zyra)* post-office. 2. *(shërbimi postar)* mail; **postë ajrore;** air-mail; **pullë poste:** postage stamp; **shpërndarës i postës:** postman; **dërgoj me postë:** to mail, to send by post.
postiér,-i *m.sh.* -ë postman, mail--man; **çantë postieri:** post-bag.
postój *f.k.* to mail, to post, to send by post, – **postohet** *f.jv.* to be mailed.
póshtë l. *ndajf.* down, down-ward; **zbres poshtë:** to get down, to go down, to come down; **hedh poshtë:** to throw down, to cast down; **lart e poshtë:** up and down; **atje poshtë:** down there; **si më poshtë:** as follows. – *Lok.* **hedh poshtë një kërkesë:** to reject a demand (a request); **hedh poshtë një argument:** to confute (to refute) an argument; **e vë poshtë dikë:** to knock someone down, to throw someone down. II. *paraf.* 1. under; **poshtë tavolinës:** under the table. 2. down; **poshtë bregores:** down the hill.
pósht/ëm (i),-me(e) *mb.* kati i poshtëm: downstairs, bottom flat.
póshtër (i,e) *mb.* mean, wicked, ignoble, ignominous, nefarious. vicious, infamous, vile; **njeri i poshtër:** wicked (vicious) person.
poshtërím,-i *m.sh.* -e humiliation, abasement, degradation, debasement.
poshtërój *f.k.* to humiliate, to humble, to abase, to debase, to degrade. – **poshtërohem,** *f.jv.*

to be humbled (debased, humiliated).

poshtërsí,-a *f.sh.* – meaness, vileness, baseness, infamy, ignobleness.

poshtërsísht *ndajf.* meanly, vilely, basely, ignobly, ignominously, infamously.

poshtërúes,-e *mb.* degrading, debasing, humiliating.

poshtëshëním,-i *m.sh.* -e postscript.

poshtëshënúar (i,e) *mb.* below-mentioned.

potás,-i *m. kim.* potassium.

potér/e,-ja *f.* din, bustle, roistering, uproar, jangle; **bëj potere:** to jangle.

poterexhí,-u *m.sh.* -nj pugnacious, boisterous person.

potk/úa.-oi *m.sh.* -nj horseshoe; **mbath kalin me potkonj:** to horseshoe.

potpurí,-a *f.sh.* – *muz.* pot-pourri (of songs).

pothúaj *ndajf.* almost, nearly, well-nigh, all but; hereabout; **pothuaj i vdekur;** all but dead; **pothuaj i gjithë qyteti:** practically the whole town; **pothuaj fare (hiç):** hardly anything.

pothúajse *ndajf.* shih **pothuaj.**

póz/ë,-a *f.sh.* -a pose; posture; attitude; **marr pozë:** to pose.

pozición,-i *m.sh.* -e position.

pozít/ë,-a *f.sh.* -a 1. position; **jam në pozitë të vështirë:** to be in an awkward position. 2. rank; **njeri me pozitë:** a man of high rank.

pozitív,-i *m.sh.* -a *fot.* positive.

pozitiv,-e *mb.* 1 positive: **përgjigje pozitive:** positive (favourable) answer. 2. *mat.* **numër pozitiv:** positive number.

pozitivísht *ndajf.* positively.

pra *lidh.* therefore, in consequence.

pra/g,-gu *m.sh.* -gje 1. *(dere)*

threshold, doorstep. 2. *(dritare-je)* sill, window.-sill. 3. *fig.* eve; **në pragun e Vitit të Ri:** on the eve of the New Year.

praktík,-e *mb.* practical: **metodë praktike:** practical method; **njeri praktik:** a practical man; **në mënyrë praktike:** in a practical manner.

praktikánt,-i *m.sh.* -ë practitioner.

praktík/ë,-a *f.* practice; **zbatoj në praktikë:** to put into practice; **mjek me praktikë:** a doctor with practice; **bëj çdo ditë dy orë praktikë:** to practise two hours every day.

praktikísht *ndajf.* practically; in practice.

praktikój *f.k.* to practise (a profession). – **praktikohem** *f.jv.* to be practised.

pramatár,-i *m.sh.* -ë peddler, hawker.

prandáj *lidh.* that is why, for that reason, therefore.

pránë I. *paraf.* near, by; **pranë zjarrit:** near the fire, by the fire: **ai u ul pranë tryezës:** he sat by the table; **rri pranë meje:** stand by me (near me); **ne banojmë pranë fshatit:** we live near the village; **eja më pranë meje:** come nearer, move up closer
II. *ndajf.* near, near by, close-by; **ai banon këtu pranë:** he dwells near by (close-by); **rri pranë! (mos u largo):** stand near, (near by, close by)! **dyqani është aty pranë:** the shop is near by (at a little distance).

pránga,-t *f.sh.* irons, fetters, shackles, handcuffs, manacles, bonds; **i vë prangat:** to shackle, to fetter, to chain up, to manacle, to put handcuffs upon; **i heq prangat:** to unshackle, to unchain.

pranÍ,-a f. presence; **në prani të:** in the presence of.

pranÍm,-i m.sh. -e 1. (në një parti) admission (to a party). 2. (i një propozimi) acceptation (of a proposal). 3. (i një gabimi) confession, avowal. 4. (nga të dy palët) mutual agreement. 5. (në një konkurs etj.) admission. **pranÍsh/ëm(i),-me(e)** mb. present.

pranój f.k. 1. to accept; **pranoj me kënaqësi:** to accept with pleasure; **pranoj një ftesë:** to accept an invitation. 2. (gabimin) to confess, to avow, to recognize (a fault). 3. (kërkesën e dikujt) to accede to the request of someone. 4. (në një konkurs) to admit (at a competition). 5. (mendimin e dikujt) to agree (with someone). 6. (miq, mysafirë) to receive (friends, guests). – **pranohem** f.jv. to be admitted. **pránuar (i,e)** mb. admitted; agreed; **mendim i pranuar nga të gjithë:** prevailing opinion. **pranuésh/ëm(i),-me(e)** mb. admissible; acceptable; **arsye e pranueshme:** plausible argument. **pranvér/ë,-a** f.sh. -a 1. spring, spring-time; **në pranverë fushat vishen me blerim;** in spring the fields are dressed in green. 2. fig. prime; **në pranverën e jetës:** in one's prime. **pranverór,-e** mb. vernal; **mbjellje pranverore:** spring sowing. **prapa** I. ndajf. back, behind; backwards; **muri prapa:** the wall behind; **lë dikë prapa:** to leave someone behind; **mbetem prapa:** to stay (to drop, to fall) behind; **pesëdhjetë vjet prapa:** fifty years back; **bëj një hap prapa:** to take a step backwards; **mbetem prapa në më-**

sime: to be behind the rest of the class; **nga prapa:** from behind; **i shtyrë nga prapa:** pushed on from behind; **ora ime mbetet prapa:** my watch is slow; **kthehem prapa:** to turn round. – Lok. **bjeri prapa kësaj pune:** attend to this work. II. paraf. behind; **prapa derës:** behind the door; **prapa kujt jam ulur?** behind whom am I sitting? **që prapa murit;** from behind the wall; fig. **prapa tij ka të tjerë:** he has supporters behind him. **prapambétj/e,-a** f. backwardness; **Pushteti Popullor e nxori vendin nga prapambetja:** the People's Power has lifted the country out of backwardness. **prapambétur (i,e)** mb. backward; **vend i prapambetur;** backward country. **prapaník,-e** mb. backward; **njeri prapanik:** backward person. **praparój/ë,-a** f.sh. -a rear-guard. **prapaskén/ë,-a** f.sh. -a teat. back-stage: fig. **veproj në prapaskenë:** to act behind the scenes. **prapashtés/ë,-a** f.sh. -a gram. suffix. **prapavájtj/e,-a** f. regress, regression. **prapaveprím,-i** m. 1. after – effect. 2. retroaction. **prapaveprúes,-e** mb. retroactive; **ligj me fuqi prapavepruese:** retroactive law. **prapavíj/ë,-a** f.sh. -a rear; **sulmoj prapavijën e armikut:** to attack the enemy in the rear. **prapë** ndajf. again, back, anew, afresh; **ai erdhi prapë:** he came again, he came back. **prápë (i,e)** mb. naughty, wayward; **fëmijë i prapë:** naughty (wayward) child.

prapëseprapë *lidh.* yet, neverthe-less; **prapëseprapë e dua:** I love him nevertheless.
prapësí,-a *f.sh.* — mishap, mis-chief, playful trick.
prapësím,-i *m.sh.* -e rejection.
prapësój *f.k.* 1. *(një kërkesë)* to reject, to refuse (a request). 2. *(armikun)* to repel, to force back (the enemy). 3. *(një urdhër, një porosi)* to rescind, to cancel. — **prapësohem** *f.jv.* to withdraw.
prápi (së) *lok. ndajf.* in reverse; **i marr fjalët së prapi:** to take someone's words amiss; **bëj një punë së prapi:** to put the cart before the horse; **eci së prapi:** to move back-ward, to go backwards.
prápm/ë (i,)-e(e) *mb.* rear, hinder, posterior; **ana e prapme e një stofi:** the back side of a cloth; **ana e prapme e medaljes:** the reverse side of a medal.
praps *f.k.* to repel, to force back, to drive back, to push back; **praps armikun:** to repel the enemy. — **prapsem** *f.jv.* to with-draw, to draw back.
praptas *ndajf.* backwards.
prarim,-i *m.* gilding.
prarój *f.k.* to gild, to plate, to wash, to overlay with gold.
prarúar (i,e) *mb.* gilt, gilt-over, gold-plated.
prarúes,-e *mb.* gilding.
pras,-i *m.sh.* **presh** *bot.* leek; *fig.* **kapem me presh në duar:** to be caught in the act (red-handed).
prashájk/ë,-a *f.sh.* -a *krah.* hoe.
prashís *f.k.* to hoe. — **prashitet** *f.jv.* to be hoed.
prashítj/e,-a *f.sh.* -e hoeing.
pre-ja *f.* prey; **bie pre:** to fall a prey to.
predikím,-i *m.sh.* -e preaching, preachment.

predikój *f.jk.* to preach. — **prediko-het** *f.jv.* to be preached.
predikúes,-i *m.sh.* — preacher.
predikùes,-e *mb.* preaching.
prédh/ë,-a *f.sh.* -a projectile, shot, missile.
prefékt,-i *m.sh.* -ë prefect.
prefektúr/ë,-a *f.sh.* -a prefecture.
preferénc/ë,-a *f.* preference.
preferím,-i *m.* shih **preferencë**
preferój *f.k.* to prefer. — **prefero-hem** *f.jv.* to be preferred.
preferúar (i,e) *mb.* preferred, fa-vourite.
preferúesh/ëm(i),-me(e) *mb.* preferable.
préfës/e,-ja *f.sh.* -e *(lapsash)* pencil-sharpener.
préhem *f.jv.* 1. to rest. 2. to lie, to lie down; **këtu prehet:** *(mbi-shkrimi i një varri):* here lies (inscription upon a tomb).
préh/ër,-ri *m.* lap; **në prehrin tim:** on my lap.
préhj/e,-a *f.* rest, repose.
prej *paraf.* 1. *(origjinë, burim)* from; **jam prej** *(një vendi):* to come from, to be a native of (a country); **hekuri nxirret prej tokës në gjendje të papastër:** iron is obtained from the ground in an impure state; **një britmë e fortë u dëgjua prej pullazit:** a violent scream was heard from the hen-roost; **djathi bëhet prej qumështi:** cheese is made from milk. 2. *(kohë)* from; **prej mëngjezit deri në mbrëmje:** from morning till night; **prej fillimit deri në mbarim:** from the beginning to the end; **prej një kohe që s'mbahet mend:** from time immemorial. 3. *(drejtim)* from; **vij prej Tirane:** I am coming from Tirana. 4. *(nu-mërim)* **numëroj prej një-shit deri te dhjeta:** to count from one to ten. 5. of; *(lëndë)*

lugë prej druri: spoon of wood; 6. *(sasi)* .of; një popull prej tre milionësh: a people of three millions. 7. *(kohë)* since; prej kohësh; of old; prej vitit 1900: since 1900. 8. of; dy prej nesh: two of us; qëndrim prej armiku: hostile attitude.

prejárdhj/e,-a *f.* origin, descent, derivation; *(e një populli)* origin, descent; prejardhje e një gjuhe: origin of a language; *gram. (e një fjale)* origin, derivation (of a word); me prejardhje Shqiptare: Albanian by origin.

prejárdhur (i,e) *mb. gram.* derived.

prek. *f.k.* 1. to touch; prek një send: to touch a thing. 2. to feel; prek pulsin: to feel the pulse. 3. to treat; prek një çështje një temë: to treat a subject. — prekem *f.jv.* 1. to take offence. 2. to be affected, to be moved (of joy, of sorrow, etc.).

prékës;-e *mb.* touching, affecting, moving, emotive.

prékj/e,-a *f.* 1. touch. 2. feeling, sensation.

préksh/ëm(i),-me(e) *mb.* 1. touchy. 2. palpable, tangible, 3. impressionable, sensitive. 4. vulnerable.

prekshmërí,-a *f.* sensibility; susceptibility, vulnerability.

prékur (i,e) *mb.* 1. *(nga sëmundja)* affected. 2. touched, moved, affected.

premiér/ë,-a *f.sh.* -a premiere.

prémt/e(e),-ja(e) *f.sh.* -e(të) Friday.

premtím,-i *m.sh.* -e promise; premtim me gojë: verbal promise; mbaj premtimin : to keep one's promise; ai nuk u mbajti

premtimin: he did not keep his promise.

premtimdhënës,-e *mb.* promising.

premtój *f.k.* 1. to promise. 2. to give hope for, to give cause for.

premtúes,-e *mb.* promising.

prénk/ë,-a *f.sh.* -a freckle; fytyrë me prenka: freckled face.

prérazi *ndajf.* categorically.

prerë (i,e) *mb.* 1. cut. 2. irrevocable, peremptory; vendim i prerë: peremptory verdict. 3. set; çmim i prerë: set price. 4. categorical; përgjigje e prerë: flat (categorical) reply; ton i prerë: categorical tone; refuzoj në mënyrë të prerë: to refuse flatly (categorically).

prérj/e,-a *f.* 1. cut, cutting. 2. *anat.* incision. 3. *(e kokës)* beheading, decapitation. 4. *(e një gjymtyre)* amputation (of a member of the body). 5. rupture; prerje e marrëdhënieve miqësore: rupture of friendly relations; *(e ndihmave dhe kredive)* cutting off (of aid and credits).

pres I. *f.k.* (p.t. preva, p.p. prerë). 1. to cut, to chop, to hew; pres me thikë: to cut with a knife, to chop; pres me sëpatë: to hew, to hack, to cut with an axe; pres flokët: to have the hair cut; pres një pemë: to cut down a tree. 2. *(kokën dikujt)* to behead, to cut off (the head of seomeone). 3. *(një palë rroba)* to cut (a suit). 4. pres në copa të vogla: to chop, to cut into pieces. 5. *(me gërshërë)* to shear, to clip, to cut (with shears). 6. *anat. (gjymtyrët)* to amputate, to cut off (a member of the body). 7. *(letrat e lojës)* to cut (the cards). 8. *(rrugën)* to bar (the way); I pres rrugën importit: to bar

the way to imports. – **pritem**
f.jv. 1. to cut oneself. 2. *gjeom.*
(vijat) to intersect (lines). 3.
(qumështi) : to turn sour (milk).
– *Lok.* **m'u pre fuqia:** my
strength is failing me.
II. *f.jk.* to cut; **thika ime nuk
pret:** my knife does not cut,
(it is blunt).
pres *f.k.* (p.t. **prita,** p.p. **pritur)**
1. to wait, to expect; *(dikë të
vijë)* to wait for, to expect
(someone to come). 2. to receive; **pres miq:** to receive
friends (guests, visitors); **pres
ftohtë dikë:** to receive someone
coldly: **pres me dashamirësi:**
to receive cordially. kindly; **pres
e përcjell miq për ditë:** to
keep open house. – **pritem**
f.jv. 1. to be received. 2. **s'më
pritet:** I'm itching for (to),
I'm dying for; **në kundërshtim
me sa pritej:** contrary to expectation.
prés/ë,-a *f.sh.* -a press, compre-
ssing machine.
presidént,-i *m.sh.* -e president.
presidiúm,-i *m.sh.* -e presidency.
presión,-i *m.sh.* -e 1. *fiz.* pressure.
2. constraint, compulsion.
présj/e,-a *f.sh.* -e *gram,* comma.
prestár,-i *m.sh.* -ë tailor.
prestarí,-a *f.* sewing-shop.
prestígj,-i *m.* prestige.
presh,-të *m.sh.* shih **pras.**
pretékst,-i *m.sh.* -e pretext, pretense; **nxjerr si pretekst:** to
put forward as pretext; **me pretekst të shëndetit të keq:**
on pretense of ill health.
pretendím,-i *m.sh.* -e pretention,
unfounded claim; **pa preten-
dime:** unassuming, unpreten-
ding, unpretentious; **me pre-
tendime:** pretentious.
pretendój *f.k.* to pretend, to claim,

– **pretendohet** *f.jv.* to be clai-
med.
pretendúes,-i *m.sh.* – pretender.
pretendúes,-e *mb.* pretentious.
prevedé,-ja *f.* jelly.
preventív,-i *m.sh.* –a estimate;
preventivi i një ndërtese: the
estimate of a building.
preventív,-e *mb.* preventive; **masa preventíve:** preventive measures.
prezantím,-i *m.sh.* -e introduction;
bëj prezantimin: to introduce
people to one another.
prezantój *f.k.* to introduce; **ju
prezantoj gruan time:** may
I introduce my wife? – **prezan-
tohem** *f.jv.* to introduce oneself.
prezénc/ë,-a *f.* presence.
prezént,-e *mb.* present.
prift,-i *m.sh.* -ërinj priest, clergyman.
priftërésh/ë,-a *f.sh.* -a priestess.
priftërí,-a *f.* clergy.
priftërór,-e *mb.* clerical, priestly.
prij *f.k.* (p.t. **priva,** p.p. **prirë)** to
lead, to guide; **Partia i prin
popullit tonë në ndërtimin e
socializmit:** the Party guides
our people in the socialist construction. – **prihem** *f.jv.* to be
led, to be guided.
prijës,-i *m.sh.* -a leader.
prík/ë,-a *f.sh.* -a dowry.
prill,-i *m.* April; **në prill:** In April.
primitív,-e *mb.* primitive; **në
gjendje primitive:** in a primitive state.
princ,-i *m.sh.* -a prince; **princi
trashëgimtar:** the heir prince.
princésh/ë,-a *f.sh.* -a princess.
principát/ë,-a *f.sh.* -a principality,
princedom.
prind,-i *m.sh.* -ër parent; **duhet t'u
bindemi prindërve:** we ought
to obey our parents.
prindërór,-e *mb.* parental; **da-**

shuri prindërore: parental affection.

prir/ë (i,e) *mb.* 1. led, guided. 2. inclined, disposed, prone.

prirj/e,-a *f.sh.* -**e** 1. inclination, propensity, bent, leaning. 8. calling, vocation.

prish *f.k.* 1. to destroy, to demolish; *(një mur, një shtëpi)* to destroy, to demolish (a wall, a house). 2. *(një vepër arti)* to destroy (an artistic work). 3. *(një makinë)* to damage (a machine). 4. *(një punë, për ta bërë përsëri)* to undo (a work). 5. *(një qytet nga themelet)* to ravage, to ruin, to raze to the ground (a town). 6. *(një fjalë)* to scratch (a word); to rub off (a word). 7. *(të holla)* to waste away, to spend (money); *(të holla me vend e pa vend)* to dissipate, to squander, to spend lavishly or wastefully, to throw away (money). 8. *(një marrëveshje)* to declare void (an agreement). 9. *(nervat)* to shatter (one's nerves). 10. **prish gojën:** to say bad words. 11. **prish dorën:** to cease doing good work. 12. *(ndërgjegjen, karakterin)* to corrupt (the consciousness, the character). 13. *(qetësinë)* to break (the silence). 14. *(zakonet)* to pervert (customs). 15. *(planet)* to thwart (the plans). 16. to rot; **të ngrohtit prish mishin dhe peshkun:** meat and fish go bad in hot weather. − **prishet** *f.jv.* 1. to be destroyed (demolished). 2. to be decayed, to get rotten (meat). − *Lok.* **prishem me dikë:** to break with someone, to end a friendship with someone. **prishës,-i** *m.sh.* − 1. *(i pasurisë)* waster (of fortune). 2. *(i moralit)* corruptor (of morals).

prishës,-e *mb. (të hollash)* wastful, prodigal, thriftless.

prishj/e,-a *f.* 1. *(godinë, muri)* demolition, destruction (of a building, of a wall). 2. *(e një vegle, e një makine)* damaging. 3. *(të hollash)* waste (of money). 4. *(e një kontrate)* breaking up, annulment, invalidation (of a contract). 5. *(e një shoqërie tregtare)* dissolution, breaking up (of a society, of a company). 6. *(e stomakut)* disorder (of stomach). 7. *(e ushqimeve)* rottenness, decay (of food). 8. *(e zakoneve)* perversion (of customs, of manners.)

prishur (i,e) *mb.* 1. *(ndërtesë)* demolished, destroyed. 2. *(mall)* damaged. 3. *(stomak)* disordered (stomach). 4. *(ushqime)* rotten (food). 5. *fig.* **i prishur nga mentë:** demented, crazy.

prishura (të),-t(të) *f.sh. (para)* small money, small change.

prit/ë,-a *f.sh.* -**a** ambush, ambuscade; **bie në pritë:** to fall into an ambush; **zë (rri në) pritë:** to lie in ambush (in wait).

pritj/e,-a *f.* 1. reception; **pritje e ftohtë:** cold reception; **pritje e ngrohtë, e përzemërt:** rousing welcome, cordial welcome, warm welcome; **pritje miqësore:** friendly reception. 2. waiting, expectation, expectancy; **në pritje të përgjigjes suaj:** in expectancy of your answer; **jam në pritje:** to be in expectancy (in waiting); **dhomë pritjeje:** parlour.

pritsh/ëm (i),-me(e) *mb.* hospitable.

pritshmëri,-a *f.* non-activity, expectancy; **në pritshmëri:** in expectancy, in abeyance.

privát,-im. *sh.* -**ë** private shopowner.

privát,-e *mb.* 1. private, personal;

shtëpi private: personal house, private house; **jetë private:** private life. 2. not official; **akt privat:** private act.

privatisht *ndajf.* privately, in private.

privilégj,-i *m.sh.* -e privilege.

privilegjój *f.k.* to privilege. — **privilegjohem** *f.jv.* to be privileged.

privím,-i *m.* privation; **privim lirie:** confinement, custody; **i dënuar me privim lirie:** condemned by confinement; **privim i të drejtave civile:** deprivation of civil rights.

privój *f.k.* to deprive; **privoj (dikë) nga një e drejtë:** to deprive (someone) of a right. — **privohet** *f.jv.* to be deprived.

príz/ë,-a *f.sh.* -a *el.* plug.

príz/ëm,-mi *m.sh.* -ma *gjeom.* prism.

pro *paraf.* pro, in favour; **jam pro:** to be pro, to be for, to stand for; **pro dhe kundër:** pro and con.

probabilitét,-i *m.* probability.

problém,-i *m.sh.* -e 1. *mat.* problem; **zgjidh një problem:** to solve a problem. 2. question, matter; **problem i ditës:** question of the hour; **problem kyç:** key (crucial) problem, main problem.

problematík,-e *mb.* problematical, problematic.

procedím,-i *m.* 1. *drejt.* lawsuit. 2. procedure.

procedój *f.k.* 1. *drejt.* to proceed; **procedoj dikë:** to proceed against someone. 2. to proceed, to go on, to continue. — **procedohet** *f.jv.* to be proceeded.

procedúr/ë,-a *f.* procedure.

procés,-i *m.sh.* -e 1. *drejt.* process; **proces gjyqësor:** juridical pro-

cess. 2. process; **proces mësimor:** teaching process.

procesverbál,-i *m.sh.* -e report.

próçk/ë.-a *f.sh.* -a blunder, faux pas.

pródukt,-i *m.sh.* e 1. product 2. *kim.* preparation; **produkte kimike:** chemicals.

produktív,-e *mb.* productive, fertile.

prodhím,-i *m.sh.* -e 1. production, yield, output; **prodhimi i përgjithshëm:** overall output; **prodhimi i drithrave:** production of cereals. 2. article, product, manufactured article; **prodhime ushqimore:** alimentary products, food-stuff.

prodhimtarí,-a *f.* productivity.

prodhój *f.k.* to produce, to yield, to manufacture; *(artikuj industrialë)* to manufacture. — **prodhohet** *f.jv.* to be produced.

prodhúar (i,e) *mb.* made; **prodhuar në Shqipëri:** made in Albania.

prodhúes,-i *m.sh.* — producer, manufacturer.

prodhúes,-e *mb.* productive; **forcat prodhuese:** productive forces.

prodhueshmërí,-a *f.* productiveness.

profecí,-a *f.sh.* — prophecy, prediction.

profesión,-i *m.sh.* -e profession; trade; **me profesion:** by profession.

profesionál,-e *mb.* professional; **bashkimet profesionale:** trade unions.

profesioníst,-i *m.sh.* -ë professionist.

profesioníst,-e *mb.* professionist.

p rofesór,-i *m.sh.* -ë professor

profét,-i *m.sh.* -ë prophet.

profetík,-e *mb.* prophetic, prophetical.
profetizím,-i *m.* prophecy.
profetizój *f.jk.* to prophesy, to predict, to foretell.
profíl,-i *m.sh.* -e profile.
profilaksí,-a *f. mjek.* prophylaxis.
profilaktík,-e *mb.* prophylactic.
prófk/ë,-a *f.sh.* -a nonsense, palaver.
prognóz/ë,-a *f.sh.* -a *mjek.* prognosis.
prográm,-i *m.sh.* -e 1. program; **program politik**: platform, political program. 2. *(i një shfaqjeje)* play-bill.
progrés,-i *m.* progress, advance.
progresión,-i *m.sh.* -e *mat.* progression; **progresion aritmetik, gjeometrik**: aritmetic, geometric progression.
progresív,-e *mb.* progressive.
projékt,-i *m.sh.* -e project, design.
projektím,-i *m.sh.* -e projection.
projektój *f.k.* 1. to project, to design. 2. to plan. − **projektohet** *f.jv.* 1. to be projected. 2. to be planed.
projektór,-i *m.sh.* -e projector.
projektplán,-i *m.sh.* -e draft-plan.
projektúes.-i *m.sh.* − projector, designer, planner.
proklamát/ë,-a *f.sh.* -a proclamation.
prokúr/ë,-a *f.sh.* -a proxy; **me prokurë**: by proxy.
prokurór,-i *m.sh.* -ë public prosecutor, attorney, *amer.* district attorney; **prokuror i përgjithshëm**: Attorney General.
prokurorí,-a *f.* attorney's office; **Prokurori e Përgjithshme**: Attorney General's Office.
proletár,-i *m.sh.* -ë proletarian.
proletár,-e *mb.* proletarian; **klasë proletare**: the proletarian class. the working class.
proletariát,-i *m.* proletariat; **dik-**

tatura e proletariatit: the dictatorship of the proletariat.
pronar,-i *m.sh.* -ë owner, proprietor; **pronar tokash**: landowner, landlord.
prón/ë,-a *f.sh.* -a property; **pronë private**: private property; **pronë shoqërore**: social property; **pronë e përbashkët**: common property.
pronësí,-a *f.* ownership; **e drejta e pronësisë**: ownership.
pronór,-e *mb. gram.* possessive; **përemër pronor**: possessive pronoun.
propagánd/ë,-a *f.* propaganda.
propagandím,-i *m.* propagation.
propagandíst,-i *m.sh.* -ë propagandist, propagator.
propagandistík,-e *mb.* propagative.
propagandój *f.k.* to propagandize, to propagate, − **propagandohet** *f.jv.* to be propagated.
propozím,-i *m.sh.* -e 1. proposal; **propozim martese**: offer, proposal (of marriage). 2. *(në mbledhje)* motion. 3. proposition; **bëj një propozim**: to make (to submit) a proposition, to forward a proposition.
propozój *f.k. (një zgjidhje)* to propose; to suggest (a solution; *(kandidaturën e dikujt)* to recommend. − **propozohem** *f.jv.* to be recommended,
prostát,-i *m. mjek.* prostatitis.
prostitución,-i *m.* prostitution.
prostitút/ë,-a *f.sh.* -a prostitute.
proshút/ë,-a *f.* ham, bacon.
protagoníst,-i *m.sh.* -ë protagonist.
protektorát,-i *m.* protectorate.
protestánt,-i *m.sh.* -ë *fet.* protestant.
protést/ë,-a *f.sh.* -a protest, protestation.

protestím,-i *m.* protestation.
protestój *f.jk.* to protest, to make (to lodge) a protest.
protestúes,-i *m.sh.* – protestant.
protéz/ë,-a *f.sh.* -a *mjek.* prosthesis.
protokóll,-i *m.sh.* -e protocol.
protokollój *f.k.* to protocol, to minute, to record.
protoplázm/ë,-a *f. anat.* protoplasm.
prototíp,-i *m.sh.* -a prototype.
provérb,-i *m.sh.* -a proverb.
próv/ë,-a *f.sh.* -a 1. *(fizike, kimike)* test, experiment. 2. *(fakte)* proof, testimony, evidence; **si provë:** by way of proof. 3. *(gjeometrie)* demonstration. 4. *(kostumi)* trying on, fitting (of a suit). 5. *(teatri)* rehearsal; **provë e përgjithshme** *(teatri)*; dress rehearsal; **bëj provat:** to rehearse. 6. *(miqësie)* proof (of friendship). – *Lok.* **vë në provë:** to put to trial, to put to the test; **i qëndroj provës, përballoj provën:** to stand the test.
próvëz,-a *f.sh.* -a *kim.* test-tube.
provím,-i *m.sh.* -e examination; **provim me gojë:** oral examination; **provim me shkrim:** written examination; *(në fund të vitit shkollor)* terminal examination; *(për pranimin në një institut)* entrance examination; **marr në provim:** to examine; **marr provimin:** to pass an examination; **nxënësi ose studenti që merret në provim:** examinee; **mësuesi ose profesori që pyet në provim:** examiner; **mbetem në provim:** to fail in an examination.
provizór,-e *mb.* provisory, temporary.
provój *f.k.* 1. *(me fakte)* to prove, to show by facts. 2. *(një teoremë)* to demonstrate, to prove

(a theorem). 3. *(kostumin)* to try on, to fit *(a costume).* 4. *(një nxënës)* to examine (a pupil). 5. *(dikë)* to put (someone) to the test. 6. *(të bëj diçka)* to try, to attempt (to do something). – **provohet** *f.jv.* to be proved.
provokación,-i *m.sh.* -e provocation.
provokatór,-i *m.sh.* -ë provocateur.
provokím,-i *m.sh.* -e provoking, provocation.
provokúes,-e *mb.* provoking, provocative.
provúes,-e *mb.* 1. probational, probationary. 2. examining.
provúesh/ëm(i),-me(e) *mb.* provable.
prozatór,-i *m.sh.* -ë prose-writer.
próz/ë,-a *f.* prose.
prózh/ëm,-mi *m.sh.* -ma shih **korie.**
prúra *f.k.* (past tense of the v. **bie, sjell)** I brought.
prúrës,-i *m.sh.* – bringer.
prúsh,-i *m.* livel-coal, embers.
psal *f.jk.* to psalm.
psalm,-i *m.sh.* -e psalm.
psalt,-i *m.sh.* -ë psalmodist.
pse *ndajf.* why; **pse jo?** why not? **pse kështu?** why so? **pse nuk erdhe?** why did you not come?
pse *lidh.* because, wherefore; **s'kam pse të qahem:** I have no reason to complain.
pse,-ja *f.sh,* – the reason, the cause, the whys and wherefores.
pseudoním,-i *m.sh.* -e pseudonym, pen-name.
psikiát/ër,-ri *m.sh.* -ër *mjek.* psychiatrist.
psikiatrí,-a *f. mjek.* psychiatry.
psikiatrík,-e *mb.* psychiatric; **klinikë psikiatrike:** mental home.
psikológ,-u *m.sh.* -ë psychologist.
psíkologjí,-a *f.* psychology.

psikologjik,-e *mb.* psychological.

psikopát,-i *m.sh.* -ë psychopath.

psikóz/ë,-a *f.sh.* -a psychosis.

psonís *f.k.* to shop, to purchase goods; **shkoj të psonis:** to go shopping.

psherëtíj *f.jk.* to sigh.

psherëtím/ë,-a *f.sh.* -a sigh; **lëshoj një psherëtimë:** to heave a sigh.

publicíst,-i *m.sh.* -ë publicist.

publicitét,-i *m.* publicity.

publík,-u *m.* public.

publík,-e *mb.* public.

publikísht *ndajf.* publicly.

púç/ërr,-rra *f.sh.* -rra *mjek.* pustule, pimple; **fytyrë me puçrra:** pustulous face.

púd/ër,-ra *f. (fytyrë)* face-powder; **kuti pudre:** puff-box.

pudíng,-u *m.* pudding; **puding me stafidhe:** plum-pudding.

pudrós *f.k.* to powder. — **pudrosem** *f.jv.* to powder one's face.

púfk/ë,-a *f.sh.* -a puff.

puhí,-a *f.* shih **fllad.**

pulastrén,-i *m.sh.* -ë *zool.* chicken.

pulénd/ër,-ra *f.* shih **mëmëligë.**

púl/ë,-a *f.sh.* -a *zool.* hen; **pulë klloçkë:** sitting hen; **zog pule (pulastren):** chicken; **kotec pulash:** hencoop, hen-house; *fig.* **pulë e lagur:** milksop, faint-hearted fellow. — *Prov.* **më mirë një vezë sot sesa një pulë mot:** a bird in the hand is worth two in the bush.

pulëbárdh/ë,-a *f.sh.* -a *zool.* sea-mew, sea-gull.

pulëdéti *f.sh.* -e *zool.* turkey-hen.

pulísht,-i *m.sh.* -e *zool.* shih **kërriç.**

pulís *f.k.* **pulis sytë:** to screw up one's eyes.

pulóv/ër,-ri *m.sh.* -ra sweater.

pulp/ë,-a *f.sh.* -a *anat.* calf (of the leg).

puls,-i *m. anat.* pulse; **rrahje e pulsit:** pulsation.

pulverizatór,-i *m.sh.* -ë sprayer, pulverizer, atomizer.

pulláz,-i *m.sh.* -a roof, roofing.

púll/ë,-a *f.sh.* -a 1. *(pullë këmishe)* button (of a shirt). 2. *(arnimi)* patch. 3. *(njollë)* speck, spot, stain. 4. *(lie)* mark (of pox). 5. *(poste)* postage-stamp; **letër me pullë:** prepaid letter; **letër pa pullë:** unpaid letter.

pún/ë,-a *f.sh.* -ë 1. labour, work, business, job, affair, task; **punë e detyruar:** forced labour; **punë fizike, punë krahu:** manual labour; **punë e keqe:** bad job, bungle; **bëj një punë shkel e shko:** to bungle a work; **punë e lehtë:** easy work, child's play; **punë mendore:** mental work, brain work; **kam punë të lehtë:** to have an easy job; **punë e ngutshme:** pressing, urgent work; **punë prodhuese (në prodhim):** productive labour; **rroba pune:** working clothes; **punë e rëndë:** drudgery, toil, toilsome work; **punët shtëpiake:** house-work; **punë vullnetare:** voluntary work; **aftësi për punë:** working capacity; **ditë pune:** work-day, working day; **krahë pune:** labour force, hand; **rendiment në punë:** labour productivity; **shok pune:** fellow worker; **zyra e punës:** register — office. 2. work, job, occupation; **pushoj nga puna:** to dismiss, to discharge; **gjej punë:** to find work; **hyj (pajtohem) në punë:** to be employed; **kërkoj punë:** to seek work, to look for work. — *Lok.* **i përvishem punës:** to get down to work; **s'prish punë:**

it doesn't matter, it is no matter; **shikoni punën tuaj**: mind your business; **mos u përzieni në punët e të tjerëve**: don't meddle in others affairs; **vajtl puna ime!** It's all up with me! **si është puna?** what is the matter with you? **kjo s'është puna juaj**: it is no business of yours; **i vë punët në vijë**: to put one's affairs in order; **jam shumë i zënë me punë**: to be up to the eyes in work, to be too busy; **kjo më mbaron punë**: it answers my purpose; **në punë!** at work!

punëdhënës,-i *m.sh.* — employer.

punëtór,-i *m.sh.* -ë worker, workman, workingman, labourer; **punëtor gërmimi**: digging worker, digger; **punëtor llaçi**: mortar worker; **punëtor me mëditje**: piece-worker, time-worker; **jam punëtor i madh**: to be a slogger, a hard worker, *amer.* to be a plugger; **punëtor ngarkim-shkarkimi (anijesh)**: docker.

punëtór,-e *mb.* 1. laborious, industrious, hard-working; **nxënës punëtor**: hard-working pupil. 2. working; labour; **klasa punëtore**: the working class.

punëtorí,-a *f.sh.* — 1. working class. 2. workroom, workshop.

puním,-i *m.sh.* -e 1. *(i drurit)* woodworking; *(i hekurit)* hammering (of iron); *(i tokës)* tillage (of the soil). 2. *sh. (të një kongresi)* proceedings. 3. *(artistik etj.)* work (of art).

punísht/e,-ja *f.sh.* -e workshop.

punój *l. f.jk.* 1. to work, to labour; **punoj pa pushim**: to work without rest; **punoj jashtë masës**: to overwork; **punoj për bukën e gojës**: to work for one's daily bread; **punoj shkel**

e shko: to bungle. 2. to function; **ora ime nuk punon**: my watch does not go. II. *f.k.* to elaborate; *(tokën)* to till (the ground), *(hekurin)* to forge, to hammer (the iron). — — *Lok.* **ia punoj dikujt**: to play a trick on someone.

punónjës,-i *m.sh.* — workman; **punonjës i hekurudhës**: railway worker.

punónjës,-e *mb.* working, labouring; **masat punonjëse**: the working (labouring) masses.

punúar (i,e) *mb.* 1. wrought; **material i punuar**: wrought material. 2. tilled; **tokë e punuar**: tilled land.

punúesh/ëm(i),-me(e) *mb.* 1. malleable, forgeable; **hekur i punueshëm**: forgeable iron. 2. arable; **tokë e punueshme**: arable land.

pùp/ël,-la *f.sh.* -la 1. feather; **dyshek me pupla**: feather-bed. 2. *sport.* **pesha pupël**: feather weight.

pupláj/ë,-a *f.* plumage (of birds), feathers.

puplín,-i *m.sh.* -e puplin.

puq *f.k.* to join, to connect.— **puqet** *f.jv.* to be joined; **na puqet karakteri**: to be in harmony with one another, to hit it off well with someone.

puq me *paraf.* next to, near, close to.

puré-ja *f.* mash; **pure patatesh**: mash of potatoes.

purgatív,-i *m.sh.* -ë *mjek* purgative.

púro,-ja *f.sh.* — cigar.

púro *mb.* pure, natural; unmixed.

púrpurt (i,e) *mb.* purple.

purték/ë,-a *f.sh.* -a 1. perch. 2. *(hekuri)* bar (of iron).

pus,-i *m.sh.* -e 1. well, pit. 2. *(minierë)* pit; **pus nafte**: oil

well. 3. *(i ujrave të zeza)* chesspool. – *Lok.* **qielli u bë pus:** the sky became overcast (cloudy).
Pusí,-a *f.sh.* – shih **pritë.**
Pusúll/ë,-a *f.sh.* -a note.
Push,-i *m.* flue, fluff, plush; **me push:** plushy, velvety.
Pushím,-i *m.sh.* -e 1. cessation; **pushim zjarri:** truce; **pa pushim:** without respite, unceasingly; **ra gjithë ditën shi pa pushim:** it rained all day long without interruption. 2. rest, repose; **bëj një pushim:** to take a rest. 3. *(i shkurtër gjatë punës)* break. 4. *(në shkollë)* break. 5. *(vjetor i paguar)* annual leave; vacation, holiday; **pushimet verore:** summer holidays; summer vacations; **ditë pushimi:** holiday. 6. *mjek.* **pushim zemre:** heart failure. 7. *muz.* **pushim i plotë:** whole rest. 8. **pushim nga puna:** discharge, dismissal from work.
pushkatár,-i *m.sh.* -ë shootman, rifleman, shooter.
pushkatím,-i *m.sh.* -e shooting.
pushkatój *f.k.* to shoot, to kill, to execute with a fire-arm. – **pushkatohem** *f.jv.* to be shot, to be killed (executed) with a fire-arm.
púshk/ë,-a *f.sh.* -ë gun, rifle, fire-arm; **qytë pushke:** gunstock; **shufër pushke:** gunstick; **shtie me pushkë:** to shot' with a rifle; **një e shtënë pushke:** shooting, discharge; **pushkë për fëmijë (me tapë):** pop-gun.
pushó! *pasth.* hush! silent! cease! quiet! keep quiet! keep silent! hold up your tongue!
pushój I. *f.jk.* 1. to cease, to stop; **pushoi era:** the wind died away (out); **pushoj së qari:** to stop crying; **pushoj së je-**

tuari: to die, to cease to live, to pass away. 2. to rest; *(pas punës)* to rest, to repose. II. *f.k.* 1. *(gjakun)* to stop (the blood). 2. *(nga puna)* to discharge, to dismiss (from work). – **pushohem** *f.jv.* to be dismissed, to be discharged.
pushtét,-i *m.* power; **pushtet i pakufizuar:** unlimited authority; **pushteti buron nga populli:** power emanates from the people.
pushtím,-i *m.sh.* -e conquest, invasion, occupation (of a country).
pushtój *f.k.* 1. to conquer, to invade, to occupy (a country). 2. *(dikë)* to embrace.
pushtúar (i,e) *mb.* 1. *(vend)* invaded, occupied, conquered (country). 2. seized; **i pushtuar nga frika:** seized by terror.
pushtúes,-i *m.sh.* – conqueror, invador.
pushtúes,-e *mb.* invading, occupying.
pushtúesh/ëm (i),- me (e) *mb.* conquerable.
pút/ër,-ra *f.sh.* -ra paw.
puth *f.k.* to kiss. – **puthem** *f.jv.* to kiss; **puthem me dikë:** to kiss one another.
púthj/e,-a *f.sh.* -e kiss, kissing.
puthís *f.k.* to close hermetically, to interlock. – **puthítet** *f.jv.* to fit, to tally; **rrobë që puthitet pas trupit:** form-fitting dress.
puthítj/e,-a *f.* interlocking.
púthur(e),-a(e) *f.sh.* -a(të) kiss; **më jep një të puthur:** give me a kiss.
pýes *f.k.* (p.t. **pyeta,** p.p. **pyetur**) 1. to ask, to demand; **pyes sa është ora:** to ask what time is it. 2. to question, to interrogate; **pyes një nxënës në provim:** to question a schoolboy in an examination. 3. to

query, to ask; **pyes për shëndetin e dikujt:** to ask after
someone, to ask after someone's
health. 4. *(një të pandehur)*
to interrogate (an accused). —
pyetem *f.jv.* 1. to be asked.
2. to be questioned. 3. to be
interrogated.
pýetës,-e *mb.* 1. interrogative.
2. *gram.* **përemër pyetës:** interrogative pronoun.
pýetj/e-a *f.sh.* -e 1. question;
bëj një pyetje: to put a question, to make a question. 2.
drejt. interrogation, examination. 3. *(në parlament)* interpe-
llation. 4. *(provimi)* examina-
nation question.

pyjór,-e *mb.* forest; **rrugë pyjore:**
forest road.
pýk/ë,-a *f.sh.* -a peg, wedge;
fus pykë: to wedge; **futem
si pyke:** to be an intruder.
pyll,-i *m.sh.* **pyje** forest, wood;
pyll i dendur; dense wood;
roje pylli: forester; **rrëzë pylli:** border of a forest; **shkenca
e pyjeve:** silviculture.
pyllëzím'-i *m.* afforestation, forest planting.
pyllëzój *f.k.* to forest, to afforest.
— **pyllëzohet** *f.jv.* to be afforested.
pyllëzúar (i,e) *mb.* afforested;
vend i pyllëzuar: woodland.
pylltarí,-a *f.* silviculture, forestry.

Q

q, Q (letter of the Albanian alphabet) q, Q.
qáf/ë,-a *f.sh.* -a 1. neck; **qafë e
shtrembër;** wry neck, stiff neck.
2. *(e këmishës)* collar, neck (of
a shirt). 3. *gjeog. (mali)* pass.
4. *(e shishes)* neck (of a bottle).
— *Lok.* **rrok për qafe:** to embrace;
thyej qafën: to break one's
neck; **thyej qafën!** get out
with you! **heq qafe:** to get
rid of, to make away with;
marr më qafë dikë: to drive
someone to ruin; **marr veten
më qafë:** to go to rack and
ruin, to fall (to go) to ruin;
i bie më qafë dikujt: to bother (to molest) someone.

qafëgjátë *mb.* long-necked.
qafështrémbër *mb.* wry-necked,
stiff-necked.
qafók,-e *mb.* short-necked.
qafúk,-u *m.sh.* -ë short-necked
person.
qafór/e,-ja *f.sh.* -e 1. collar;
qafore qeni: dog collar. 2. necklace.
qaj *f.jk.* 1. to cry, to weep, to shed
tears; *(me zë të ulët)* to whim-
per; **qaj me dënesë:** to sob;
mekem së qari: to sob someone's heart out; **ënjtem së qari:**
to cry one's eyes out, to cry
oneself out; **më qajnë sytë:**
my eyes water; **më qan syri**

për: to long for. – **qahem** *f.jv.* to repine, to complain.

qamét,-i *m.* calamity.

qar,-i *m.* shih **përfitim.**

qaramán,-e *mb.* peevish, plaintive, techy, tetchy.

qárë (të),-t(të) *as.* crying, weeping: *(me dënesë)* sobbing; *(me zë të ulët)* whimpering.

qárj/e,-a *f.* complaint.

qar/k,-ku *m.sh.* -qe 1. *gjeom.* circle. 2. *el.* circuit. 3. country, region, district.

qark *ndajf.* round, around; **qark e qark:** round and round.

qarkór,-i *m.sh.* -e regional committee.

qarkór,-e *mb.* regional.

qarkór/e,-ja *f.sh.* -e circular, circular letter.

qarkullím,-i *m.* 1. circulation; qarkullim i gjakut; circulation of blood. 2. *(i automjeteve, etj).* traffic; **leje qarkullimi:** pass (of circulation), permit (of circulation); **bllokim qarkullimi:** traffic jam. 3. *(i mallrave)* turnover, circulation (of goods, commodities). 4. *(i monedhës)* currency (of money); **vë në qarkullim monedhë të re:** to emit new money. 5. *(bujqësor)* rotation; **sistem i qarkullimit bujqësor:** crop rotation, rotation of crops.

qarkullój *f.jk.* to circulate, to rotate.

qarkullúes,-e *mb.* circulatory, circulating; **kapital qarkullues:** circulating, floating capital.

qártas *ndajf.* clearly, plainly, distinctly, obviously, explicitly, evidently, in a clear manner, intelligibly; **flas qartas;** to speak plainly.

qártë (i,e) *mb.* clear, plain, evident, explicit, obvious, lucid; **bëj të qartë:** to make clear; **fare**

e qartë: plain, flat; **kuptim i qartë:** distinct meaning.

qartësí,-a *f.* clearness, lucidity.

qartësísht *ndajf.* shih **qartas.**

qartësój *f.k.* to clarify, to make clearer, to clear up. – **qartësohem** *f.jv.* to become clear, to clear.

qas *f.k.* 1. to approach. 2. *(në shtëpi)* to receive (at home). – **qasem** *f.jv.* 1. to approach, to advance, to draw near. 2. *krah.* to withdraw, to go away; **qasu që këtej!** get away from here!

qatíp,-i *m.sh.* -ë *vjet.* scribe.

qe (third person sing. of the past tense of the verb **jam**) **ai (ajo) qe:** he (she) was.

qe,-të *(zool.* (plural of **ka**) oxen.

qebáp,-i *m.sh.* -ë 1. shish kebab. 2. *vjet.* coffee roaster.

qedér,-i *m. gj. bis.* 1. damage, 2. worry. 3. grieve; **s'kam qeder:** I don't care a bit.

qederósem *f.jv. gj, bis.* to worry about, to be anxious, to grieve.

qefíl,-i *m.sh.* -ë *vjet.* guarantor, guarantee.

qefín,-i *m.sh.* -ë shroud, cerecloth, cerement; **mbështjell me qefin:** to shroud.

qéfu/ll,-lli *m.sh.* -j *zool.* mullet.

qehajá,-i *m.sh.* -llarë *vjet.* bailiff.

qejf,-i *m.* 1. pleasure; **në qejfin tim:** at my pleasure; **i bëj qejfin:** to please someone, to comply someone's wishes; **me gjithë qejf:** with pleasure; **pranoj me gjithë qejf:** to accept with pleasure (willingly). 2. delight, delectation, amusement; **bëj qejf:** to enjoy oneself, to amuse oneself; **bëni qejf!** enjoy yourselves! amuse yourselves! **bëj kokrrën e qejfit:** to enjoy oneself to the utmost, to have the time of one's life. 3. humour, temper;

jam në qejf: to be in good humour, to be in high spirits; jam pa qejf: to be out of temper, to be in ill humour; to be unwell, to be under the weather, to be in a bad way. 4. desire; bëj një gjë me qejf: to do something with pleasure (willingly, with a cheerful heart); bëj një gjë pa qejf: to do something unwillingly; kam qejf të: to desire, to want to; sipas qejfit: as one wishes (pleases); i vij pas qejfit dikujt: to be compliant; më bëhet qejfi: to be pleased, to be glad. − Lok. vij në qejf: to be tipsy; më mbetet qejfi: to be offended; ai nuk e bën qejfin qeder: he does not care a straw, he does not care a bit, he does not give (care) a fig.

qejflí,-e mb. 1. liver; playful. 2. wooer.

qejfpapríshur mb. compliant, compliable.

qelb,-i m. pus; zë qelb (plaga): to pus, to fester, to suppurate.

qelb f.k. to stink. − qelbem f.jv. 1. to get dirty. 2. (mishi etj.) to get rotten; (djathi) to get stung. 3. to smell bad, to offend the nostrils.

qelbaník,-e mb. dirty.

qélbës,-i m.sh. -a zool. polecat, fitchew, ferret.

qelbësír/ë,-a f.sh. -a 1. dirtiness, fetidness, putridity, stench. 2. fig. dirty person, fetid person.

qelbëzím,-i m. suppuration, purulence, fester.

qelbëzóhet f.jv. to suppurate, to fester.

qelbëzúar (i,e) mb. purulent.

qélbur (i,e) mb. dirty, filthy, nasty; fetid, stinking, putrescent.

qelepír,-i m. sponge; ha e pi qelepir: to sponge on someone.

qelepirxhí,-u m.sh. -nj sponger.

qelésh/e,-ja f.sh. -e fez.

qelí,-a f.sh.− cell.

qelibár,-i m. amber.

qelíz/ë,-a f.sh. -a anat. cell.

qelizór,-e mb. cellular.

qelq,-i m. 1. glass; fabrikë qelqi: glassworks; qelq opak: opaque (vision proof) glass. 2. (për të pirë, gotë) drinking glass; një qelq me verë: a glass of wine. − Lok. koha u bë qelq: the weather cleared up.

qélqtë (i,e)mb. glass; tub i qelqtë: glass tube.

qelqurína,-t f.sh. glasswares.

qemán/e,-ja f.sh. -a vjet. violin. fam. fiddle.

qemér,-i m.sh. -e lintel; (ure) arch (of a bridge).

qen,-i m.sh.−zool. dog; qen gjahu: hound, grey-hound; qen policie: blood hound; qen roje: watch-dog; qen stani: collie, sheep-dog; qen -ujk: wolf-hound. − Lok. bëj jetë qeni: to lead a dog's life. − Prov. kujto qenin, rrëmbe shkopin: talk of the devil and he will appear.

qénd/ër,-ra f.sh. -ra 1. centre; qendër e gravitetit: centre of gravity; e qytetit: the centre of the town. 2. centre; qendër banimi: dwellling centre; qendër pune: work centre; qendër industriale: industrial centre. 3. centre; qendër e studimeve albanologjike: centre of Albanological studies.

qendrór,-e mb. 1. central; Komiteti Qendror: Central Committee. 2. essential, main, basic; ideja qendrore: the central idea (of).

qénë (të),-t(të) as. being, existence.

qénë (p.p. of the verb jam) been,

kam qenë: I have been; **duke qenë:** being.
qéng/ël,-la *f.sh.* **-la** girth (of a horse); **shtrëngoj me qengël:** to girth, to fasten with a girth.
qengj,-i *m.sh.* **-a** *zool.* lamb; **mish qengji:** lamb.
qéni/e,-a *f.sh.* **-e** 1. being. 2. *(e gjallë)* living being; **qenie njerëzore;** human being.
qep *f.k.* 1. to sew, to stitch; **qep një plagë:** to put stitches into a wound. 2. **qep një kostum:** to make a suit. — **qepem** *f.jv.* to sew one's clothes; **i qepem dikujt:** to cling to someone; to follow someone closely.
qepáll/ë,-a *f.sh.* **-a** *anat.* eyelid.
qepén,-i *m.sh.* **-a** shutter (of a shop).
qép/ë-a *f. sh.* **-ë** *bot.* onion; **qepë të njoma:** fresh onions.
qépës,-e *mb.* sewing; **makinë qepëse:** sewing-machine.
qépj/e'-a *f.sh.* **-e** sewing, stitch; **gjilpërë për qepje:** sewing needle.
qepújk/ë,-a *f.sh.* **-a** *bot.* small onion,
qeramídh/e,-ja *f.sh.* **-e** tile, roof-tile.
qeramík,-e *mb.* ceramic, keramic.
qeramík/ë,-a *f.* ceramics, keramics.
qerás *f.k.* to treat someone to something.
qerásj/e,-a *f.sh.* **-e** treat.
qér/e,-ja *f. mjek.* tinea, ringworm.
qeréç,-i *m.* mortar.
qeresté,-ja *f.* timber, lumber.
qerestexhí,-u *m.sh.* **-nj** lumberer, lumber man.
qerós,-i *m.sh.* **-ë** sufferer from ringworm.
qerpíç,-i *m.sh.* **-ë** adobe, sun--dried brick; **ndërtesë me qer-**

piçë: adobe building; **mur me qerpiçë:** mud-wall.
qerpík,-u *m.sh.* **-ë** *anat.* eyelash.
qershí,-a *f.sh.* - *bot.* cherry; *(druri)* cherry-tree; **qershi e egër:** wild-cherry; **bërthamë qershie:** cherry-stone.
qershór,-i *m.* June.
qérthu/ll,-lli *m.sh.* **-j** reel.
qerratá,-i *m.sh.* **qerratenj** crafty fellow, sly old fox.
qérr/e,-ja *f.sh.* **-e** cart; **bart me qerre:** to cart, to carry (to convey) with a cart.
qerrtár,-i *m.sh.* **-e** carter.
qése,-ja *f.sh.* **-e** bag; *(të hollash)* wallet, purse; **qese duhani:** tobacco-pouch.
qesëndí,-a *f.* raillery, mockery.
qesëndis *f.k.* to banter, to jeer, to mock.
qesk/ë,-a *f.sh.* **-a** 1. small bag. 2. *anat. (e ujit të hollë)* bladder.
qesh *f.jk.* 1. to laugh; **qesh nën hundë:** to snigger, to laugh up one's sleeve; **qesh si budalla:** to laugh in a foolish manner; **qesh me gjithë shpirt:** to laugh one's head off; **këtu s'ka gjë për të qeshur:** it's no laughing matter; **ç'më bëre për të qeshur!** don't make me laugh! **më vjen për të qeshur:** I can't help laughing. 2. to mock, to banter; **qesh me dikë:** to jest, to joke, to laugh at (to make fun of) someone. — *Prov.* **qesh mirë ai që qesh i fundit:** he laughs best who laughs last.
qesharák,-e *mb.* funny, droll, comical, farcical, ridiculous; **bëhem qesharak:** to become ridiculous, to make a fool of oneself; **njeri qesharak:** a ridiculous person.
qeshj/e,-a *f.* laugh, laughing, laughter; **qeshje nën hundë;** snig-

ger; **qeshje e marrë:** wild laughter.

qéshur (i,e) *mb.* smiling; **fytyrë e qeshur:** smiling face.

qéshur (e), -a(e) *f.sh.* **-a(të)** laughter; **të qeshura në sallë:** hilarities.

qéshur(të),-it(të) *as.* laugh; **shkulem së qeshuri:** to have a good laugh.

qétë (i,e) *mb.* calm, still, quiet, sedate, restful, tranquil, serene, placid; **njeri i qetë;** quiet man; **jetë e qetë;** still life; *(në pikture)* **natyrë e qetë:** still life; **rri i qetë;** to stand still; **më lёr të qetë:** let me alone.

qetë-qetë *ndajf.* tranquilly, peacefully.

qetësi,-a *f.* calm, calmness, tranquillity, stillness, sedateness, quietness, composure, quietude; **qetësi e përkohshme:** momentary calmness (stillness); **qetёsi shpirtёrore:** ease, quietude, tranquillity. serenity (of spirit); **mbaj qetёsinё:** to keep silent; **prish qetёsinё;** to break the silence; to disturb the peace; **vendos qetёsinё në klasё:** to reduce a class to silence; **qetёsi!** silence! keep quiet! be quiet!

qetёsisht *ndajf.* tranquilly, silently quietly.

qetёsój *f.k.* 1. *(një dhembje)* to appease, to calm, to allay, to assuage (a pain). 2. *(një fёmijё)* to tranquilise (a child); *(dikё)* to calm down, to tranquilise (someone). 3. *(ndёrgjegjen)* to clear one's consciousness. — **qetёsohem** *f.jv.* to recover one's serenity, to be appeased, to calm down.

qetёsúes,-e *mb.*1. calming, assuaging. 2. *mjek.* anodyne, sedative; **ilaç qetёsues:** anodyne (sedative) medicine.

qeth *f.k.* 1. to cut the hair. 2. *(bagёtinё)* to shear, to fleece. — **qethem** *f.jv.* to have one's hair cut.

qéthёs,-e *mb.* shearing, clipping; **makinë qethёse:** a) hair-clipper, clippers; b) *(për bagёtinё)* sheep-shearer.

qéthj/e,-a *f.sh.* **-e** 1. *(e flokёve)* hair cut. 2. *(e dhenve)* shearing, fleece (of sheep).

qéthur (i.e) *mb.* shorn, sheared. — *Lok.* **shkoj për lesh e kthehem i qethur:** go for wool and come back shorn.

qeverí,-a *f.sh.* — government.

qeverís *f.k.* 1. *(shtetin)* to govern (the state). 2. *(shtёpinё)* to keep house. 3. *(një ndёrmarrje)* to run, to manage (an enterprise). — **qeverisem** *f.jv.* to be governed.

qeverísj/e,-a *f.* 1. governing, ruling. 2. running, management.

qeveritár,-i *m.sh.* **-ё** governor.

qeveritár,-e *mb.* governmental.

qё I. *paraf.* 1. *(vendi)* from; **qё në burim:** from the source; **qё kёtu:** from here; **qё nga Shkodra:** from Shkodra. 2. *(kohe)* from, since; **qё atёhere:** since then, from that time; **ne e dimё qё nga ajo kohё:** we know it ever since that time; **qё mё parё:** beforehand, in advance; **qё tani:** from this moment; **qё pa gdhirё:** before dawn; **qё prej vitit 1900:** since 1900; **qё sot e tutja:** from this day forth, henceforth. II. *lidh* 1. that; **në mёnyrё qё, me qёllim qё:** in order that; **mё vjen keq qё nuk erdhe:** I'm sorry you didn't come; **dua qё tё mёsosh se:** I want you to learn that. 2. for; **tё falemnderit qё erdhe:** I thank you for coming. 3. that; **tani qё e kryet punёn mund tё luani:**

now (that) you have done your work you may play; **e di që ai mungon:** I know (that) he is absent. III .*pl.* 1. *(për njerëz)* that, who; **ai burrë që hyri:** the man who (that) came in; *(për sende, kafshë)* that, which; **sistemi që jep rezultatet më të mira:** the system that (which) gives the best results; **penicilina që u zbulua nga Flemingu:** penicillin, which was discovered by Fleming. 2. (accusative) that, who, whom; **vajza që sheh është ime motër:** the girl (that, whom) you see is my sister; **libri që po lexoj:** the book (that, which) I'm reading. 3. *(kohe)* that, when, in (on) which; **ditën që të takova:** the day (that) I met you; **atë kohë që ishe jashtë shtetit:** when you were abroad. 4. which, this; **më lavdëruan, gjë që më kënaqi shumë:** they praised me, which made me very pleased; **ty nuk të pëlqejnë librat, gjë që mua më habit:** you are not fond of books, which (and this) surprises me. IV. *fjalëz.* (particle); **erdhën që të dy:** they came both.

qëkúr *ndajf.* long ago; **ka qëkur që ka ndodhur:** that happened long ago.

qëkùri *ndajf.* long ago, a long time ago; **kam qëkuri që po ju pres:** I have been waiting for you for a long time.

qëkúrse *lidh.* since; **jam më mirë qëkurse erdha këtu:** I am better since I have been here.

qëllím,-i *m.sh.* -e intention, aim, goal, purpose, intent, design, object, end; **arrij qëllimin:** to attain one's aim; **uroj që t'ia arrini qëllimit!** may you attain

your aim! may you achieve your goal! **për këtë qëllim:** for that purpose; **kam për qëllim:** to intend; **me ç'qëllim?** for what purpose (end)? **me qëllim të keq:** evil-minded, ill intentioned, ill-advised; **me qëllim të mirë:** well-minded, well-intentioned; **pa qëllim:** unintentionally, aimlessly; **shetis pa ndonjë qëllim të caktuar:** to wander about without any definite object; **me qëllim që:** with the intention of, intending to with a view to, in order to.

qëllimísht *ndajf.* intentionally, purposely, on purpose, designedly.

qëllimór,-e *mb.* intentional, intentioned, purposeful.

qëllój I. *f.k.* 1. *(me grusht)* to strike, to hit (with the fist), to fist; **qëlloj me shpullë dikë:** to slap someone. 2. *(me pushkë)* to fire, to shoot (with a firearm). − **qëllohem** *f.jv.* to be hit to be struck. II. *f.jk.* to happen, to befall, to chance; **qëllova aty (qëlloi të ndodhesha aty):** I happened to be there; **qëllon shpesh:** it happens often.

qëmóç/ëm(i),-me(e) *mb.* primeval, ancient, of the earliest time, bygone, of the past time.

qëmóti *ndajf.* of yore, in ancient times, in olden times.

qëndís *f.k.*, *f.jk.* to embroider.

qëndísj/e,-a *f.* embroidery; **kuti për qëndisje:** work-box.

qëndistár,-i *m.sh.* -ë embroiderer.

qëndísm/ë,-a *f.sh.* -a fancy-work, needle-work, embroidery.

qëndrés/ë,-a *f.* resistance.

qëndrím,-i *m.sh.* -e 1. stop, halt; **vend qëndrim i autobuzave:** bus-stop; *(i trenave)* station. 2. *(i përkohshëm në një vend)* sojourn. 3. attitude, view;

mbaj qëndrim kritik: to take a critical view of; kush është qëndrimi juaj për këtë çështje? what is your attitude towards this question?

qëndrój *f.jk*. 1. to stop, to halt. 2. to stand; qëndroj i patundur: to stand one's ground, to stand firm; qëndroj më kёmbё: to stand on foot; qëndroj drejt: to stand straight; qëndroj galiç: to squat; *(mbi ujë)* to float. 3. *(përkohësisht në një vend)* to sojourn. to reside, to stay (for a time in a place). 4. *(zogu mbi degë)* to perch, to sit (upon a perch). 5. to consist; ku qëndron vështirësia? where does the difficulty consist in? 6. to resist; tulla shamot i qëndron nxehtësisë: the firebrick resists heat.

qëndrúesh/ëm (i),-me(e) *mb.* 1. resistant, resisting, resistible; material i qëndrueshëm: resistible material. 2. firm, steady, constant; karakter i qëndrueshëm: firm character. 3. durable, lasting; për një paqe të qëndrueshme: for a lasting peace. 4. solid.

qëndrueshmërí,-a *f.* 1. resistance; qëndrueshmëria e një materiali: resistance of a material. 2. firmness, steadiness; qëndrueshmëri karakteri: firmness of character. 3. stability; qëndrueshmëri e kohës: stability of the weather.

qëpárë *ndajf.* a moment before.

qërój *f.k.* 1. *(patate)* to peel (patatoes). 2. *(arra)* to shell (walnuts). 3. *(orizin)* to clean (the rice). 4. *(dhëmbët)* to pick one's teeth. 5. *(mishin nga kockat etj.)* to take out the bones. — *Lok.* qëroj hesapet me: to settle accounts with.

— qërohem *f.jv.* to go away; qërohu l get you gone! off you go!

qibár,-e *mb.* fastidious.

qíb/ër,-ra *f.* fastidiousness.

qíe/ll,-lli *m.sh.* -j sky; heaven; qielli i kthjellët: serene sky; qiell i vrenjtur: cloudy sky; bojë qielli: sky-blue, azure. — *Lok.* e ngre dikë në qiell: to loud, (to extol) someone to the skies.

qiellgërvishtёs,-i *m.sh.* — sky--scraper.

qiellór,-e *mb.* heavenly; kupa qiellore: firmament.

qíellz/ё,-a *f.sh.* -a *anat.* palate.

qiellzór,-e *mb. anat.* palatal.

qilár,-i *m.sh.* -e cellar; pantry, pantry-room, larder.

qilím,-i *m.sh.* -a carpet; shtroj dhomën me qilim; to carpet the room.

qilimpunúes,-i *f.sh.* — carpet maker.

qím/e,-ja *f.sh.* -e 1. hair; qime kali: horse hair; qime e ashpër: bristle, coarse hair; shkul një qime: to pull out a hair. 2. *(sahati)* hair-spring. 3. *mjek. pop.* gangrene. — *Lok.* ai shpëtoi për një qime: he escaped by the skin of his teeth, he escaped by a hair's breadth, he had a hair-breadth escape. — *Prov.* ujku qimen e ndërron, huqin s'e harron: can the leopard change its spots?

qimegështénjë *mb.* chestnut-haired.

qimegjátë *mb.* long-haired; qen qimegjatë: a long-haired (shaggy) dog.

qimekúq,-e *mb.* red-headed; kalë qimekuq: sorrel horse.

qimez/í,-ézë *mb.* black-haired; kalë qimezi: black-haired horse.

qimtón *f.jv.* it snows.

qind,-i *m.sh.* -ra hundred; **një për qind:** one per cent; **qind për qind:** hundred per cent; **me qindra:** by hundreds; **me qindra mijë:** hundreds of thousands.

qindárk/ë,-a *f.sh.* -a cent (the hundredth part of a standard money); **s'kam asnjë qindarkë:** I have not a farthing.

qíndësh/e,-ja *f.sh.* -e 1. hundred. 2. bank-note of 100 leks.

qindravjeçár,-e *mb.* age-old, centuries-old; **pemë qindravjeçare:** centuries-old tree.

qindvjeçár,-e *mb.* centenarian, hundred-year old.

qindvjetór,-i *m.* centenary, centennial.

qíng/ël,-la *f.sh.* -la grith (of a horse).

qiparís,-i *m.sh.* -ë *bot.* cypress.

qipí,-a *f.sh.* – stack; *(bari)* hayrick, hay-stack, hay - cock; *(kashte)* straw-stack.

qíq/ër,-ra *f.sh.* -ra *bot.* chick-pea.

qirá,-ja *f.sh.* – 1. lease; **jap me qira:** to lease; **marr me qira:** to hire; **marrje ose dhënie toke me qira:** leasehold; **karrocë me qira:** hackney carriage. 2. *(shuma e qirasë)* rent; **sa është qiraja?** what is the rent? **paguaj qiranë:** to pay the rent. – *Lok.* **nuk ia vlen barra qiranë:** it is not worth while.

qiradhënës,-i *m.sh.* – hirer.

qiramárrës,-i *m.sh.* – tenant; *(dhome)* lodger; *(me kontratë)* lessee; *(toke)* leaseholder.

qiraxhí,-u *m.sh.* -nj 1. hirer of horses. 2. tenant, lodger, *renter*

qirí,-ri *m.sh.* -nj candle, wax--candle; *(i hollë)* taper.

qiríç,-i *m.* glue, gum; *(prej mielli)* paste.

qiríthi *ndajf.* **ngrihet qirithi (kali):** to prance (a horse).

qit *f.k.* 1. to take out; **qiti duart nga xhepi:** take your hands out of your pockets. 2. *(një dhëmb)* to have a tooth extracted. 3. *(me pushkë)* to fire, to shoot. 4. **i qit gjumin dikujt:** to wake someone up. – **qitet** *f.jv.* to be pulled off.

qitës,-i *m.sh.* – shooter; *(i mirë)* sharp-shooter.

qitj/e,-a *f.sh.* -e 1. *(me pushkë)* firing. 2. *(artilerie)* gunnery, shooting; **vend për qitje me pushkë:** shooting-range, shooting-gallery.

qítro,-ja *f.sh.* – *bot.* lime.

qivúr,-i *m.sh.* -e coffin, bier.

qófsha (the optative mood of the v. jam) may I be!

qóft/e,-ja *f.sh.* -e croquette.

qóftë *lidh.* 1. **qoftë . . . qoftë...:** either... or; **qoftë ai, qoftë dikush tjetër, për mua s'ka rëndësi:** either him or someone else it doesn't matter to me. 2. both.... and; **qoftë unë qoftë gruaja do të vimë:** both my wife and I will come.

qóftë (third person sing. of the optative of the v. jam) be; **ashtu qoftë!** be it so! **çfarëdo qoftë:** whatever it is; **mallkuar qoftë!** curse it!

qoftëlárg,-u *m.* the Devil.

qortím,-i *m.sh.* -e 1. chiding, scolding, reproach, reproof. rebuke, reprimand, blame; **qortim i ashpër:** vituperation. 2. *(i gabimeve)* correction (of mistakes).

qortój *f.k.* 1. to chide, to scold, to reproach, to reprove, to rebuke, to reprimand, to blame, to censure, *fam.* to tell off; **qortoj dikë për diçka:** to reproach someone for something; *(ashpër)* to vituperate; **qortoj veten:** to blame oneself. 2. *(gabimet)* to correct (the mistakes). –**qor-tohem** *f.jv.* to be scolded, to be chid (chidden).

qortúes,-e *mb.* blameful, reproachful; **me ton qortues**: with a reproachful tone.

qortúesh/ëm (i),**-me(e)** *mb.* blamable reprehensible; **sjellje e qortueshme**: a blamable conduct.

qorr,-i *m.sh.* -**a** blindman; *(nga njëri sy)* one-eyed person.

qorr,-e *mb.* 1. blind; *(nga njëri sy)* one-eyed. 2. **groshë qorre**: small kidney-beans of a brown colour. 3. *anat.* **zorra qorre**: appendicitis, blind gut, **qórrazi** *ndajf.* blindly.

qorrfishék,-u *m.sh.* -**e** 1. firework. 2. blank cartridge.

qorrój *f.k.* to blind. – **qorrohem** *f.jv.* to be blinded; **u qorrua nga flakët**: he was blinded by the flames.

qorrsokák,-u *m.sh.* -**ë** blind-alley.

qós/e,-ja *f.sh.* -**e** bald man, beardless man.

qóse *mb.* bald, beardless, hairless.

qosték,-u *m.sh.* -**ë** *vjet.* watchchain, watch-guard.

qósh/e,-ja *f.sh.* -**e** 1. corner; **në qoshe**: at the corner; *(pranë zjarrit)* chimney-corner. 2. *(e fshehur)* nook.3. side; **qoshe më qoshe**: everywhere, throughout.

qoshk,-u *m.sh.* **qoshqe** stall, stand, kiosk; **qoshk gazetash**: newsstand.

qúaj *f.k.* 1. to call, to name; **si ju quajnë?** what is your name? 2. to consider, to judge, to regard; **unë e quaj të pafajshëm**: I consider him (to be) unguilty; **e quaj veten me fat**: I consider myself lucky. – **quhem** *f.jv.* 1. to be called; **si quhet kjo kafshë?** what is that animal called? **si quheni?** what is your name? **unë quhem**: my

name is; 2. to be considered (jugded, regarded); **ai quhet njeri i ndershëm**: they consider him an honest person.

qúajtur (i,e) *mb.* named; **ndryshe i quajtur**: alias, otherwise named.

quk *f.k.* to peck.

qukapík,-u *m.sh.* -**ë** *zool.* wood pecker.

qúk/ë,-a *f.sh.* -**a** pock.

qull *f.k.* to drench, to soak. – **qullem** *f.jv.* to be soaked, to get wet through (to the skin), to get drenched.

qull *ndajf.* **bëhem qull**: to get soaked to the skin.

qull,-i *m.* pap; *(për fämijë)* pap for infants; **qull me miell misri**: pap of maize; *(me miell thekre ose tërshëre)* porridge, gruel, oatmeal.

qullós *f.k.* *(një punë)* to bungle, to botch (a work).

qúllur (i,e) *mb.* drenched, wet, soaking.

qúmësht,-i *m.* milk; **qumësht pluhur;** powdered milk; **qumësht i kondensuar:** condensed milk; **qumësht i piksur:** clotted milk; **qumësht i prerë:** sour-milk; **një gotë qumësht:** a glass of milk; **me qumësht:** with milk, milky; **i jap qumësht fëmijës:** to feed (to nurse) the baby; **qumësht i paskremuar:** whole milk, full-cream milk; **qumësht i skremuar:** skimmed milk; **ajkë qumështi:** cream; **dyqan për shitjen e qumështit:** milk shop, dairy shop; **prodhime qumështi:** dairy produce. – *Lok.* **i kam buzët me qumësht:** to be green, to be still wet behind the ears.

qumështór,-i *m.* custard pie.

qumështór,-e *mb.* 1. milk; **lopë qumështore:** milk cow. 2. mil-

ky. 3. fig. green: je qumështor akoma; you are a greenhorn yet.
qumështshítës,-i m.sh.- milkman.
qúrra,-t f.sh. snot, mucus of the nose.
qurramán,-e mb. shih qurravec.
qurrásh,-e mb. shih qurravec.
qurravéc,-e mb. snotty.
qyfýr,-i f.sh. -e pleasantry.
qyl,-i m. sponging; njeri që l bie qylit: sponger; i bie qylit te dikush: to sponge on (upon) someone; rroj qyl në kurriz të shokëve: to sponge on one's friends.
qylxhí,-u m.sh. -nj sponger.
qyméz,-i m.sh. -ë chicken-coop, hen-coop, hen-house.
qymýr,-i m.sh. -e (druri) charcoal.
qymyrgúr,-i m. coal; pluhur qymyrguri: coal dust; shtresë qymyrguri: coal-bed; minierë qymyrguri: colliery, coal-mine; punëtor qymyrguri: collier, miner.
qymyrxhí,-u m.sh. -nj charcoal-burner.
qymyrshítës,-i m.sh. - charcoal seller.
qyn/g,-gu m.sh. -gje 1. pipe, tube; qyng nafte: pipe-line; qyng oxhaku; flue. 2. (në strehët e çative, ose ulluk) spout water-spout.
qyp,-i m.sh. -a jar, earthen pot.
qyqár,-i m.sh. -ë poor man; lonesome man.
qyqár,-e mb. lonesome, forsaken.
qýq/e,-ja f.sh. -e zool. cuckoo.

qýqja! pasth. alas!
qyrék,-u m.sh. -ë trowel.
qyr/k,-ku m.sh. -qe furcoat, furs.
qyrkpunúes,-i m.sh. - furrier.
qysqí,-a f.sh. - crowbar, lever.
qysh I. ndajf. how, what; qysh jeni? how are you? how do you do? qysh thatë? what did you say? qysh e quajnë atë? what is his name?
II. paraf. since, from; qysh nga viti 1900: since 1900; qysh atëherë: since then, ever since; qysh tani: from this moment.
qytét,-i m.sh. -e town; (i madh) city; lagje qyteti: ward, quarter, amer. borough; lagje e jashtme e një qyteti: suburb, outskirts; i qytetit: urban.
qytetár,-i m.sh. -ë cityman, citizen, townsman, town-dweller, city-dweller.
qytetár,-e mb. civil; të drejtat qytetare: civil rights.
qytetarí,-a f. citizenship.
qytetërím,-i m.sh. -e civilization.
qytetërój f.k. to civilize. - qytetërohem f.jv. to become civilized, to be civilized.
qytetërúar (i,e) mb. civilized.
qytetërúes,-e mb. civilizing.
qytétës,-e mb. of the town; shkollë qytetëse: town school.
qytét muzé m. muzeum town (city).
qytéz/ë,-a f.sh. -a 1. small town. 2. fortress.
qýt/ë,-a f.sh. -a (pushke) butt (of a rifle).

R

r, R (letter of the Albanian alphabet) r, R.
ra (third person of the past tense

of the v. bie) fell; ai ra në fushën e betejës: he fell in the battlefield; më ra ndërmend

diçka: an idea crossed my mind, it occurred to me.
rabéck/ë,-a *f.sh.* -a *zool.* sparrow.
rác/ë,-a *f.sh.* -a 1. *(kafshësh)* breed; **prej race jo të pastër:** of mixed breed; **race, l racës:** pedigree, thorough-bred; **kalë race:** thorough-bred horse. 2. *(për njerëz)* race.
raciál,-e *mb.* racial; **dallim racial;** racial discrimination.
ración,-i *m.sh.* -e ration, portion. share; **i vë racion:** to put on rations.
racionál,-e *mb.* rational.
racionalísht *ndajf.* rationally.
racionalizatór,-i *m.sh.* -ë rationalizator.
racionalíz/ëm,-mi *m.* rationalism.
racionalizím,-i *m.sh.* -e rationalization.
racionalizój *f.k.* to rationalize. — **racionalizohet** *f.jv.* to be rationalized.
racioním,-i *m.* rationing, apportionment.
racionój *f.k.* to ration, to ration out. — **racionohet** *f.jv.* to be rationed.
radiatór;-i *m.sh.* -e radiator.
radikál,-e *mb.* radical.
rádio,-ja *f.sh.* — 1. radio, wireless. 2. *(aparat radioje)* radio set, wireless; **ndez radion:** to turn, on the radio (wireless).
radiografí,-a *f.sh.-* — *mjek.* radiography, X-ray. 2. X-ray picture, radiograph.
radiográm,-i *m.sh.* — radiogram.
radiológ,-u *m.sh.* -ë *mjek* radiologist.
radiologjí,-a *f. mjek* radiology.
radiomárrës,-i *m.sh.* - radio (wireless) receiver, radio-receiving set.
radiopërhápj/e,-a *f.* broadcasting.
radioskopí,-a *f. mjek.* radioscopy.

radiostación,-i *m.sh.* -e radio station.
radiotransmetím,-i *m.* broadcast.
radiotransmetúes,-i *m.sh.* – transmitter.
radíst,-i *m.sh.* -ë wireless (radio) operator.
rádhazi *ndajf.* consecutively.
rádh/ë,-a *f.sh.* -ë 1. row, file, line, queue, rank; **rrimë në radhë:** to stand in a queue, to be sitting in a row; **vihemi në radhë:** to queue up, to line up, to get into line; **në radhë për një:** in single file; **një radhë e gjatë makinash:** a long line of cars; *fig.* **shtrëngojmë radhët:** to close the ranks. 2. queue; **mbaj (zë) radhën:** to queue up. 3. rank; **jam në radhën e parë:** to be in the first rank. 4. turn; **me radhë;** by turns. — *Lok.* **në radhë të parë:** first of all, before all; **e kështu me radhë:** and so on.
radhíq/e,-ja *f.sh.* -e *bot.* chicory.
radhít *f.k.* to rank, to range, to set in a row, to put into a row. — **radhitem** *f.jv.* to stand in row (in rank, in file).
radhítës,-i *m.sh.* — *tipog.* type-setter.
radhítj/e,-a *f.* type-setting, alinement, alignment.
radhór,-i *m.sh.* -ë register.
radh/ua,-oi *m.sh.* -nj copy-book.
rafinerí,-a *f.sh.* - refinery.
rafiním,-i *m.* refining.
rafinój *f.k.* to refine (by distillation). — **rafinohet** *f.jv.* to be refined.
rafinúar (i,e) *mb.* 1. refined; **vaj i rafinuar;** refined oil. 2. *fig.* sly, foxy, cunning; **njeri i rafinuar:** a cunning person.
raft,-i *m.sh.* -e 1. shelf; **raft librash:** book-case. 2. *(për pjata etj.)* side-board.

rajá,-ja *f.sh.* — *vjet.* rayah, raia.
rajón,-i *m.sh.* -e region.
rajonizím,-i *m. bujq.* streak, stripe.
rajonizój *f.k. bujq.* to streak, to stripe. — **rajonizohet** *f.jv.* to be streaked.
rakét/ë,-a *f.sh.* -a 1. *(tenisi)* racket (of tennis). 2. *(lufte)* rocket, missile.
rakí,-a *f.* raki, rakee.
rakitík,-e *mb. mjek.* rachitic.
rakitíz/ëm,-mi *m. mjek.* rachitis.
ran/g,-gu *m.sh.* -gje rank; **në rang ambasadorësh:** at ambassadorial level.
ranísht/e,-ja *f.sh.* -e sandbank, sandbar.
ranòr,-e *mb.* sandy.
rapórt,-i *m.sh.* -e 1. report, account. 2. *mat.* proportion, ratio; **në raport me:** in proportion to.
raportím,-i *m.sh.* -e report, information.
raportój *f.k.* to report.
raportór,-i *m.sh.* -ë *gjeom.* protractor.
raportúes,-i *m.sh.* — reporter.
rasát,-i *m.sh.* — *bujq.* selected seed.
rás/ë,-a *f.sh.* -a 1. *(prifti)* cassock; *(murgu)* frock, a monk's habit.
rás/ë,-a *f.sh.* -a *gram.* case; **rasa emërore:** nominative case; **rasa gjinjóre:** possessive case.
rast,-i *m.sh.* -e 1. occasion; opportunity; **me rastin e:** on the occasion of; **përfitoj nga rasti:** to take the occasion, to avail oneself of the opportunity; **ruaj rastin:** to watch the occasion. 2. circumstance; **në asnjë rast:** under no circumstances. 3. case; **në rast nevoje:** in case of need; **në çdo rast:** in any case, at all events; **në rast:** in case of, in the event of; **në këtë**

rast: in this case. — *Lok.* **në rast të kundërt:** otherwise, or else; **me rast:** on occasion.
rastësí,-a *f.* accident, chance.
rastësísh/ëm(i),-me(e) *mb.* occasional, casual, accidental, eventual, circumstancial.
rastësísht *ndajf.* by chance; **rastësisht e takova:** I chanced to meet him, I met him by chance.
rastís *f.jk.* to chance, to happen; **rastisa aty:** I happened to be there.
ráshë (past tense of the verb bie *f.jk.*). I fell; **rashë të flinja:** I went to bed.
rashqél,-i *m.sh.* -e rake; **pastroj me rashqel:** to rake.
ratifikím,-i *m.sh.* -e ratification.
ratifikój *f.k.* to ratify. — **ratifikohet** *f.jv.* to be ratified.
re,-ja *f.sh.* — cloud: *(e zezë)* black cloud; **kohë me re:** cloudy weather; **mbushur me re:** overcast.
re,-ja *f.muz.* re; **re bemol maxhor:** D flat major.
re(vë) *fj. palak.* to observe, to note, to remark, to state; **vini re!** attention! **vihet re:** to be observed; **pa vënë re:** unseen unperceived; **vini re! vini re.** *pasth.* attention! attention!
re(e),-ja(e) *f.sh.* -ja(të) I. daughter in law, bride. 2. news; **ç'të reja kemi?** what is the news?
re(e) *mb.* (feminine of i ri) new young; recent; **vajzë e re:** young girl; **gjë e re:** new thing; **ngjarje e re:** recent event; **lajme të reja:** fresh news.
reagím,-i *m.sh.* -e reaction.
reagój *f.jk.* to react.
reaksión,-i *m.sh.* -e 1. *mjek.* reaction. 2. *polit.* reaction. 3. *kim.*

reaction; **reaksion zinxhir:** chain reaction.
reaksionár,-i *m.sh.* -ë reactionary.
reaksionár,-e *mb.* reactionary.
reaktív,-i *m.sh.* -ë *kim.* reagent.
reaktív,-e *mb.* reactive.
reál,-e *mb.* real, true.
realíst,-i *m.sh.* -ë realist.
realíst,-e *mb.* realistic.
realísht *ndajf.* really.
realíz/ëm,-mi *m.* realism.
realitét,-i *m.* reality.
realizím,-i *m.sh.* -e realization, fulfilment; **realizim i planit;** fulfilment of the plan.
realizój *f.k.* to realize, to fulfil; **realizoj një dëshirë:** to fulfil one's wish. — **realizohet** *f.jv.* to be realized, to be fulfilled.
realizúesh/ëm(i),-me(e) *mb.* realizable.
rebél,-i *m.sh.* -ë rebel.
rebél,-e *mb.* rebellious.
rebelím,-i *m.* rebellion, riot.
rebelíz/ëm,-mi *m.* rebellion.
recensím,-i *m.sh.* -e review.
recensión,-i *m.sh.* -e shih **recensim.**
recensúes,-i *m.sh.* — reviewer.
recensój *f.k.* to review, to write a review of.
recét/ë,-a *f.sh.* -a *(mjekësore)* prescription; *(gatimi)* recipe.
reciprók,-e *mb.* reciprocal, mutual.
reciprokísht *ndajf.* reciprocally, mutually.
recitím,-i *m.sh.* -e recitation, reciting.
recitój *f.k.* to recite, to declaim. — **recitohet** *f.jv.* to be recited (declaimed).
recitúes,-i *m.sh.* — reciter.
reçél,-i *m.* jam; **vazo me reçel:** jam-pot.
redaksí,-a *f.sh.* — editorial office; editorial staff.

redaktím,-i *m.sh.* -e editing.
redakój *f.k.* to edit. — **redaktohet** *f.jv.* to be edited.
redaktór,-i *m.sh.* -ë editor.
redingót/ë,-a *f.sh.* -a frock-coat.
referát,-i *m.sh.* -e report.
referénc/ë,-a *f.sh.* -a reference.
referím,-i *m.* referring, reference.
referój *f.k.* to report, to give an account of. — **referohet** *f.jv.* to refer; **i referohem diçkaje:** to refer to something.
referúes,-i *m.sh.* — referrer.
refléks,-i *m.sh.* -e reflex.
reflektím,-i *m.sh.* -e reflection.
reflektój *f.k.* to reflect. — **reflektohet** *f.jv.* to be reflected.
reflektór,-i *m.sh.* -e reflector.
reflektúes,-e *mb.* reflecting, reflective.
reformatór,-i *m.sh.* -ë reformer.
refórm/ë,-a *f.sh.* -a reform, reformation; **reformë agrare:** agrarian reform; **reformë arsimore:** educational reform.
reformíst,-i *m.sh.* -ë reformist.
refrén,-i *m.sh.* -e refrain.
refugját,-i *m.sh.* -ë refugee.
refuzím,-i *m.sh.* -e refusal, rejection; **refuzim i prerë, kategorik;** flat refusal.
refuzój *f.k.* to refuse, to reject, to decline; **refuzoj një kërkesë:** to reject a request.
regj *f.k.* 1. *(lëkurë)* to tan (hides). 2. *fig.* to harden. — **regjem** *f.jv.* to become hard.
regjénc/ë,-a *f.* regency.
regjént,-i *m.sh.* -ë regent.
régjës,-i *m.sh.* — *(lëkurësh)* tanner (of hides, of skins).
regjím,-i *m.sh.* -e 1. regimen, diet. 2. *pol.* regime; **regjimi i vjetër:** the old regime. 3. *tek.* operation, running; **regjim pune:** working rate.
regjimént,-i *m.sh.* -e *usht.* regiment.

regjisór,-i *m.sh.* **-ë** producer, *amer.* director.
regjíst/ër,-ri *m.sh.* **-ra** 1. register, book. 2. *treg.* ledger. 3. *(i gjendjes civile)* record (of the civil state); *(i klasës)* class register.
regjistrím,-i *m.sh.* **-e** 1. registration: **regjistrim i popullsisë:** census. 2. entry. record. 3. *(radio)* recording, recorded programme. 4. *mek.* adjustment, setting, regulation: **regjistrim i frenave:** brake adjustment.
regjistrój *f.k.* 1. to register, to book, to record. 2. *(në shkollë)* to inscribe, to matriculate (in a school) 3. *(në radio etj.)* to register, to record. 4. *mek.* to adjust, to set, to regulate. **regjistróhem** *f.jv.* to inscribe.
regjistrúes, -e *mb.* recording.
régjj/e,-a *f.* *(lëkurësh)* tanning (of hides); **punishte për regjjen e lëkurëve:** tannery.
régjur (i,e) *mb.* 1. *(lëkurë)* tanned (skin, hide). 2. *(në tregti)* well-used (to business). 3. *(fizikisht)* hardened.
rehát *ndajf.* comfortably; **lëmë rehat:** leave me alone! let me alone!
rehát,-i *m.* calm, tranquility, ease.
rehatí,-a *f.* comfortableness, easiness.
rehatój *f.k.* to rest, to repose; to calm, to appease. − **rehatohem** *f.jv.* to be appeased.
rehátsh/ëm(i),-me(e) *mb.* 1. cosy, snug, comfortable; **kolltuk i rehatshëm:** comfortable armchair; **dhomë e rehatshme:** cosy room. 2. easy, smooth; **udhëtim i rehatshëm:** an easy journey.
rehén,-i *m.* pawn; **lë rehen (një gjë):** to pawn.
reklám/ë,-a *f.sh.* **-a** advertisement.

reklamím,-i *m.sh.* **-e** advertising.
reklamój *f.k.* *(diçka)* to advertise, to publicize. − **reklamohet** *f.jv.* to be advertised.
reklamúes,-i *m.sh.*- advertiser, advertizer, advertising man.
rekomandé *mb.* **letër rekomande:** registered letter.
rekomandím,-i *m.sh.* **-e** commendation, recommendation; **letër rekomandimi:** letter of recommendation.
rekomandój *f.k.* to commend, to recommend. − **rekomandohet** *f.jv.* to be recommended, to be advisable.
rekomandúesh/ëm(i),-me(e) *mb.* recommendatory.
rekórd,-i *m.sh.* **-e** *sport.* record; **mbaj rekordin:** to hold a record; **thyej rekordin:** to break (to beat) a record.
rekrút,-i *m.sh.* **-ë** *usht.* recruit.
rekrutím,-i *m.* *usht.* recruitment, enlistment; **zyra e rekrutimit:** recruiting office.
rekrutój *f.k.* to recruit, to enlist.
rektifikím,-i *m.sh.* **-e** requisition.
rekuizój *f.k.* to requisition. −**rekuizohem** *f.jv.* to be requisitioned.
relación,-i *m.sh.* **-e** report, account.
relatív,-e *mb.* relative.
relatívisht *ndajf.* relatively; **ai është relativisht i ri:** he is relatively young.
relatój *f.k.* to brief, to report. − **relatohet** *f.jv.* to be briefed.
reliév,-i *m.* relief.
relík/ë,-a *f.sh.* **-a** relic.
rem,-i *m.* brass, copper.
rém/ë,-a *f.sh.* **-a** mill race, mill run.
remtár,-i *m.sh.* **-ë** brass-worker, copper-smith.
rend,-i *m.sh.* **-e** 1. order; **sipas rendit alfabetik, kronologjik:** in alphabetical order, in chronological order. 2. **rendi i di-**

tës: order of the day, agenda.
3. **rendi publik:** the public
order. 4. **rendi shoqëror:** social order; **rendi i vjetër:** the
old order.

rend *f.jk.* to run; **mos rendl** don't
run l

rénd/e,-ja *f.sh.* -e rasp, gratter;
grij në rende *(karrota)*: to
rasp away, to grind, to grate
(carrots).

réndës,-i *m.sh.* – runner.

rendimént,-i *m.sh.* -e output,
productivity, yield; **rendiment i
punës:** labour productivity.

rendít *f.k.* to put in order, to
place in a proper order, to set
in a row. **-renditem** *f.jv.* to be
set in a row.

rendítj/e,-a *f.* ordering.

réndj/e,-a *f.* running.

rendór,-e *mb.* ordinal; **numër
rendor:** ordinal number.

renegát,-i *m.sh.* -ë renegade, turncoat.

rént/ë,-a *f.* rent.

repárt,-i *m.sh.* -e 1. division, ward;
(pune) workshop. 2. *(ushtarak)*
unit.

repertór,-i *m.sh.* -ë repertory, re-
pertoire.

reportér,-i *m.sh.* -ë *(gazete etj.)*
correspondent.

republikán,-i *m.sh.* -ë republican.

republikán,-e *mb.* republican.

republík/ë,-a *f.sh.* -a 1. republic;
**Republika Popullore Socialiste
e Shqipërisë:** the People's Socialist Republic of Albania.
2. *(kapelë republike)* bowler hat,
derby.

rés/ë,-a *f.* envy.

respékt,-i *m.* respect, regard, deference; *(i thellë)* veneration;

me respekt: with respect, res-
pectfully; **mungesë respekti:**
disrespectfulness.

respektím,-i *m.* respectability.

respektój *f.k.* 1. to respect, to
honour; **respektoj të moshua-
rit:** to respect the elders. 2.
(orarin, ligjin) to respect; **çdo
qytetar duhet të respektojë
ligjet:** all citizens must respect
the laws. – **respektohem** *f.jv.*
to be respected (honoured).

respektúesh/ëm(i), -me(e) *mb.*
respectable.

restaurím,-i *m.sh.* -e restoration.

restaurój *f.k.* to restore. – **restau-
rohet** *f.jv.* to be restored.

restaurúes,-i *m.sh.* – restorator.

restaurúes,-e *mb.* restorative.

restaurúesh/ëm(i),-me(e) *mb.*
restorable.

restoránt,-i *m.sh.* -e restaurant.

réshje,-t *f.sh.* precipitation.

resht *f.jk.* to cease, to stop.

réshtj/e,-a *f.* ceasing; cessation.

réshtur (pa) *ndajf.* without respite
(reprive), unceasingly.

retín/ë,-a *f.* anat. retina.

reumatíz/ëm,-mi *m.* mjek. rheu-
matism.

revan,-i trot; **eci revan:** to trot.

revaní,-a *f.* a kind of cake.

revíst/ë,-a *f.sh.* -a magazine, periodical; **revistë letrare:** literary review.

revizión,-i *m.sh.* -e revision.

revizioním,-i *m.sh.* -e revision.

revizioníst,-i *m.sh.* -ë revisionist.

revizioníz/ëm,-mi *m.* revisionism.

revizionój *f.k.* to revise.

revizór,-i *m.sh.* -ë *(finance)* auditor.

revólt/ë,-a *f.sh.* -a revolt.

revoltój *f.k.* to revolt; **hipokrizia
jote më revolton:** your hy-
pocrisy revolts me. – **revolto-
hem** *f.jv.* to revolt, to be indignant.

revoltúes,-e *mb.* revolting
revolución,-i *m.sh.* -e revolution;
**Revolucioni i Madh Socialist
i Tetorit:** The Great October
Socialist Revolution; **revolucioni tekniko-shkencor:** the technical-scientific revolution; **stuhi e revolucionit:** the storm
of revolution; **revolucioni proletar:** proletarian revolution; **revolucioni socialist:** socialist
revolution.
revolucionár,-i *m.sh.* -ë revolutionary, revolutionist.
revolucionár,-e *mb.* revolutionary; **mendime revolucionare:**
revolutionary ideas.
revolucionarizím,-i *m.* revolutionization.
revolucionarizój *f.k.* to revolutionize.
revolvér,-i *m.sh.* -ë revolver, pistol; **një e shtënë revolveri:**
a pistol shot; **këllëf revolveri:**
pistolholster.
réz/e,-ja *f.sh.* -e latch (of a door).
rezérv/ë,-a *f.sh.* -a 1. *(ushqimesh)*
reserve (of food); **po mbarohen
rezervat:** food reserves have
almost run out. 2. *usht.* reserve. 3. reservation, reserve;
i premtova ta ndihmoja pa rezervë: I promised to help
without reservation; **me rezervë:**
reservedly, with reserve; **pa rezerva:** without reserve, unreservedly. 4. *sport.* reserve.
rezervím,-i *m.* reservation.
rezervíst,-i *m.sh.* -ë *usht.* reservist; **oficer rezervist:** reserve officer.
rezervój *f.k.* 1. to save up, to put
by (aside), to reserve. 2. to
book, to reserve; **rezervoj një
tavolinë në restorant:** to reserve a table at a restaurant;
**rezervoj të drejtën për të
bërë diçka:** to reserve the

right to do something. – **rezervohem** *f.jv.* to be reserved (reticent).
rezervúar (i,e) *mb.* 1. reserved;
vend i rezervuar: reserved place. 2. reserved, reticent.
rezisténc/ë,-a *f.* 1. *(e personit)*
resistance, endurance. 2. *(e gjërave)* durability, wearability.
rezistój *f.jk.* to resist.
rezolút/ë,-a *f.sh.* -a resolution.
rezultát,-i *m.sh.* -e 1. result (edhe
mat.); **pa rezultat:** without
any result; unsuccesful, fruitless.
2. *sport.* score.
rezultón *f.jk.* to result, to ensue;
rezulton se: it results that,
it follows that.
rëndés/ë,-a *f. fiz.* gravity; **qendra e
rëndesës:** the centre of gravity.
rëndë *ndajf.* 1. gravely, badly;
plagosur rëndë: badly wounded; **i sëmurë rëndë:** gravely
sick. 2. harshly, rudely; **i foli
rëndë:** he spoke harshly to
him.
rëndë-rëndë *ndajf.* proudly; **eci
rëndë-rëndë:** to walk pridefully, proudly.
rëndë (i,e) *mb.* 1. heavy, weighty;
peshë e rëndë: heavy weight;
ngarkesë e rëndë: heavy load.
2. burdensome; **taksa të rënda:**
oppressive, burdensome taxes.
3. hard, difficult; **mësim i rëndë:**
hard (difficult) lesson. 4. grave;
gabim i rëndë: grave mistake.
5. bad; **plagë e rëndë:** bad
wound. 6. stuffy; **ajri është i
rëndë në këtë dhomë:** the
air is stuffy in this room.
rëndësí,-a *f.* importance, significance; **me rëndësi:** significant,
important; **me rëndësi të madhe:** very important, of a great
importance; **pa pikë rëndësie:**
unimportant, insignificant, of no

importance; **me pak rëndësi:** of little (slight) importance; **merr rëndësi:** to become important; **ka rëndësi:** to be important, to be significant; **fjala juaj ka rëndësi:** your word is of much importance; your word carries great weight; **i jap rëndësi diçkaje:** to attach importance to something; **s'ka rëndësi:** it doesn't matter; **pak rëndësi ka:** it matters little.

rëndësísh/ëm(i),-me(e) *mb.* important; **fjalim i rëndësishëm:** important speech; **e rëndësishme është të:** the important thing is.

rëndój I. *f.k.* 1. to make heavy. 2. to burden, to overload. 3. *fig. (situatën etj.)* to worsen, to make worse, to aggravate; **rëndoj fajin:** to aggravate the fault. 4. *(me taksa)* to burden (with taxes). **-rëndohem** *f.jv.* 1. to become heavy. 2. *(situata)* to become (to get, to grow) more grave (serious); *(gjendja e të sëmurit)* to get worse, to worsen. II. *f.jk. (mbi diçka)* to press upon (something).

rëndóm *ndajf.* frequently; **kjo fjalë përdoret rëndom:** this word is frequently used.

rëndómtë (i,e) *mb.* 1. common, ordinary; **njeri i rëndomtë:** common fellow; **veshje e rëndomtë:** ordinary dress.

rëndúes,-e *mb.* worsening, aggravating; **rrethana rënduese:** aggravating circumstances.

rëni/e,-a *f.sh.* -e falling, fall, downfall; **rënia e një perandorie:** the fall (the collapse) of an empire; **rënie e temperaturës:** a fall in the temperature; **rënie e çmimeve:** a fall in (of) prices; **rënie e flokëve:**

falling of hair; **rënie e fletëve, e gjetheve:** falling of leaves, of foliage; *el.* **rënie tensioni:** voltage drop.

rënkím,-i *m.sh.* -e moan, groan; **lëshoj një rënkim:** to utter a moan (a groan).

rënkój *f.jk.* to moan, to groan.

rër/ë,-a *f.sh.* -a sand; **gur rëre:** sandstone; **kodër rëre:** dune; *(e lëvizshme)* quick-sand; **vend me rërë:** sandy ground.

ri (i),-u(i) *m.sh.* -nj (të) young man, youngster, stripling, youth.

ri(të),-të (të) *as.* youth, youthfulness. – *Prov.* **kush nuk punon në të ri, vuan në pleqëri:** a young man idle, an old man needy.

ri(i),-re (e) *mb.* 1, young; **djalë i ri:** young fellow, boy; **grua e re:** young woman; **më i ri nga:** younger than; **më i riu nga të gjithë:** the youngest of all; **ai tregon i ri:** he looks younger for his age. 2. *fig. (axhami)* greenhorn; inexperienced; **është i ri në këtë zanat:** he is a novice, he is inexperienced in this craft. 3. new; **një libër i ri:** a new book; **lajmet më të reja:** the latest news; **lajme të reja:** new tidings; **Viti i Ri:** New Year.

riabilitím,-i *m.sh.* -e rehabilitation.

riabilitój *f.k.* to rehabilitate. – **riabilitohem** *f.jv.* to be rehabilitated.

riarmatím,-i *m.* rearmament, rearming.

riarmatós *f.k.* to rearm. – **riarmatosem** *f.jv.* to be rearmed.

riarmatósj/e,-a *f.* rearmament.

riatdhesím,-i *m.sh.* -e repatriation.

riatdhesój *f.k.* to repatriate. – **riatdhesohem** *f.jv.* to be repatriated.

ribëj *f.k.* to remake, to do over again, to make again.
riblej *f.k.* to buy again, to purchase again.
ribotím,-i *m.sh.* -e reprint, new edition.
ribotój *f.k.* to reprint, to republish. – **ribotohet** *f.jv.* to be reprinted, to be republished.
ricín,-i *m. bot.* castor-fean; **vaj ricini**: castor-oil.
riedukím,-i *m.* reeducation.
riedukój *f.k.* to re-educate. – **riedukohem** *f.jv.* to be re-educated.
rifillím,-i *m.* recommencement; *(i shkollave)* beginning (of classes, of the school-year); **rifillimi i punës**: resumption of work.
rifillój *f.k.* to recommence, to start afresh (anew), to begin again; *(punën e ndërprerë)* to resume work. – **rifillohet** *f.jv.* to be recommenced, to be resumed (work).
rifitím,-i *m.* regain; recovering.
rifitój *f.k.* 1. to regain, to gain back; **rifitoj kohën e humbur**: to regain the lost time, to make up for the lost time. 2. *(shëndetin)* to recover (one's health); *(dritën e syrit)* to recover (the eyesight).
rig/ë,-a *f.sh.* -a rule.
rigón,-i *m. bot.* marjoram.
rigoróz,-e *mb.* rigorous, strict, severe.
rigorozísht *ndajf.* rigorously.
rigorozitét,-i *m.* rigour, sternness, strictness.
riháp *f.k.* to re-open, to open again. – **rihapet** *f.jv.* to be re-opened.
rihápj/e,-a *f.* re-opening.
rikáp *f.k.* to catch again (back), to seize back; to overtake. – **rikapet** *f.jv.* to be caught again.
rík/ë,-a *f.sh.* -a *zool.* duckling.

rikopjím,-i *m.sh.* -e ricopying.
rikopjój *f.k.* to recopy. – **rikopjohet** *f.jv.* to be recopied.
rikrijím,-i *m.sh.* -e re-creation.
rikrijój *f.k.* to re-create, to create anew. – **rikrijohet** *f.jv.* to be recreated.
rikthéj *f.k. (një send)* to return (a thing).
rikujtím,-i *m.sh.* -e recall, recalling, remembrance, remembering.
rilevím,-i *m.sh.* -e *(i tokës)* surveying (of land).
rilevój *f.k. (tokën)* to survey (lands).
rilínd *f.jk.* to be rebornt, to come back to life.
rilíndas,-i *m.sh.* – representative of the Albanian Renaissance.
rilíndj/e,-a *f.* 1. Renaissance. 2. revival, rebirth.
rimartúar (i,e) *mb.* newly-married; **të rimartuarit**: the new couple.
rím/ë,-a *f.sh.* -a rhyme.
rimëkëmb *f.k.* to set on one's feet (legs). – **rimëkëmbem** *f.jv. (nga shëndeti)* to recover one's health.
rimëkëmbj/e,-a *f.* restoration, reestablishment; *(e shëndetit)* recovery (of health).
rimój *f.k.* to rhyme.
rimorkím,-i *m.* towing, tow.
rimórkio,-ja *f.sh.* – trailer.
rimorkiój *f.k.* to tow, to drag.
rindárj/e,-a *f.sh.* -e redivision.
rindërtím,-i *m.* rebuilding, reconstruction.
rindërtój *f.k.* to rebuild, to reconstruct. – **rindërtohet** *f.jv.* to be rebuilt, to be reconstructed.
ringjáll *f.k.* 1. to resuscitate, to reanimate, to restore to life, to revive, to revivify. – **ringjallem** *f.jv.* to resuscitate, to revive, to recover one's senses.
ringjállj/e,-a *f.* resurrection, reanimation, revival, reviving.
riní,-a *f.* 1. youth, the young folk.

2. youthfulness, juvenility, juvenescence; **në lulen e rinisë**: in the prime of youth.

rinoj *f.k.* to make young again, to make younger, to restore to youth, to rejuvenate, **-rinóhem** *f.jv.* to make oneself look younger.

rinoqerónt,-i *m.sh.* -ë *zool*. rhinoceros.

rinór,-e *mb*. youthful, juvenile.

rinxéh *f.k.*to heat again;to heatback.

riorganizím,-i *m*. reorganization.

riorganizój *f.k.* to reorganize. – **riorganizohet** *f.jv.* to be reorganized.

riparím,-i *m.sh.* -e repair; **në riparim**: under repair.

riparój *f.k.* to mend, to repair. – **riparohet** *f.jv.* to be repaired.

riparúesh/ëm (i),-me(e) *mb*. reparable.

ripërtýp *f.k.* to ruminate, to chew again.

ripërtýpës,-e *mb*. ruminative.

ripërtýpj/e,-a *f*. rumination.

ripohím,-i *m.sh.* -e re-affirmation.

ripohój *f.k.* to re-affirm.–**ripohohet** *f.jv.* to be avowed again,to be reaffirmed.

riprodhím,-i *m.sh.* -e reproduction.

riprodhój *f.k.* to reproduce. – **riprodhohet** *f.jv.* to be reproduced.

ripuním,-i *m.sh.* -e retouch, remaking, new elaboration.

ripunój *f.k.* to remake, to revise, to make again. – **ripunohet** *f.jv.* to be revised, to be remade, to be made again.

rishfáq *f.k.* *(një dramë)* to show again (a drama). -**rishfaqet** *f.jv.* 1. to be shown again (a performance). 2. to reappear.

rishfáqj/e,-a *f*. reappearance.

rishikím,-i *m.*review, reexamination.

rishikój *f.k.* to review, to reexamine. – **rishikohet** *f.jv.* to be reviewed (reexamined).

rishqyrtím,-i *m*. shih **rishikím**.

rishqyrtóhet *f.jv.* shih **rishikohet**.

rishqyrtój *f.k.* shih **rishikoj**.

rishtas *ndajf*. 1. newly, recently, lately; **i martuar rishtas**: newly married. 2. again, back.

rishtýp *f.k.* to reprint. – **rishtypet** *f.jv.* to be reprinted.

rishtýpj/e,-a *f*. reprint.

rit,-i *m.sh.* -e *fet*. rite.

rit/ëm,-mi *m.sh.* -me rhythm.

ritmík,-e *mb*. rhythmic.

ritmikísht *ndajf*. rhythmically.

rituál,-e *mb*. ritual.

rituál,-i *m.sh.* -ë ritual.

rivál,-i *m.sh.* -ë rival.

rivál,-e *mb*. rival.

rivalitét,-i *m*. rivalry.

rivalizój *f.k.* to vie, to rival. – **rivalizohet** *f.jv.* to be vied, to be rivaled, to rival.

rivendós *f.k.* 1. *(qetësinë)* to restore (the silence). 2. *(një send)* to put back, to replace (a thing). – **rivendosem** *f.jv.* *(në një vend)* to be reinstated.

rivendósj/e,-a *f*. *(e qetësisë)* re--establishment, restoration, reinstatement.

riviér/ë,-a *f*. riviera.

rivlerësój *f.k.* to re-estimate, to revalue, to re-evaluate.

rfz/ë,-a *f.sh.* -a towel.

rizgjédh *f.k.* to reelect. – **rizgjidhem** *f.jv.* to be re-elected.

rizgjédhj/e,-a *f*. re-election.

rob,-i *m.sh.* -ër 1. *vjet*. people, man. 2. *(lufte)* prisoner (of war). 3. *fig.* *(i parasë)* slave (of money).

robëdëshámb/ër,-ri *m.sh.* -re dressing-gown.

robëri-a *f*. servitude, bondage, slavery, yoke.

robërím,-i *m*. enslavement.

robërój *f.k.* to yoke, to enslave. – **robërohem** *f.jv.* to be enslaved.

robërúes,-e *mb.* enslaving.
robtóhem *f.jv.* to work oneself too hard, to work oneself to death.
rodhán,-i *m.sh.* -ë bobbin.
rodh/e,-ja *f.sh.* -e *bot.* bur; **tërë rodhe:** burry, full of burs.
roís *f.jk.* 1. *(bleta)* to swarm (bees), to hive off.
roítj/e,-a *f. (e bletës)* swarm.
rój/ë,-a *f.sh.* -a guardian, watchman, warden; **rojë pylli:** forester, ranger; *(bregdeti)* coast-guard; *(burgu)* goaler, turnkey, warden; *(fshati)* rural constable, (field) watchman; *(kufiri)* border guard; *(roje nate)* night-watcher; **roje personale:** body-guard; *usht.* sentry, sentinel, **oficer roje:** officer on duty; *bëj rojë:* to keep watch, to be on watch (on guard, on duty).
rojtár,-i *m.sh.* -ë forester.
rol,-i *m.sh.* -e role; **luaj një rol:** to play a role, to play the part; **s'luan rol:** it is of no importance; **ai ka luajtur një rol të madh në jetën time:** he has played an important part in my life.
román,-i *m.sh.* -e novel.
romantík,-e *mb.* romantic.
romb,-i *m.sh.* -e *gjeom.* rhomb, rhombus; **në trajtë rombi;** rhomboid.
rosák,-u *m.sh.* -ë *zool.* drake.
rós/ë,-a *f.sh.* -a *zool.* duck; **ro-së e egër:** wild duck; **zog rosse:** *(bibë)* duckling.
rósto,-ja *f.* roast.
rozmarín/ë,-a *f.sh.* -a *bot.* rosemary.
rúaj *f.k.* 1. to guard, to watch. 2. *(paqen)* to safeguard (the peace). 3. *(shëndetin)* to protect (one's health). 4. *(ushqimet që të mos prishen)*: to preserve (foods). 5. *(një vend)* to reserve

(a place). 6. *(rastin)* to watch (the occasion), to wait (the opportunity). — **ruhem** *f.jv.* to preserve oneself, to be on one's guard; to take heed; to pay attention; **ruhuni nga boja** !mind the paint!
rúajtës,-i *m.sh.* — 1. guardian. 2. **ruajtës dhish:** goat-herd.
rúajtës,-e *mb.* preservative.
rúajtj/e,-a *f.* preservation; *(e renditi)* preservation, keeping (of the public order); *(e traditave)* preservation (of traditions); *(e paqes)* safeguard (of the peace); *(e shëndetit)* perservation (of the health); *(e ushqimeve nga prishja)* conservation, preservation (of foods).
rúb/ë,-a *f.sh.* -a kerchief, mantilla.
rubín,-i *m.sh.* -ë ruby.
rubinét,-i *m.sh.* -a tap, cock, stopcock; **hap rubinetin:** to turn on the tap; **mbyll rubinetin:** to turn off the tap.
rubrík/ë,-a *f.sh.* -a column; rubric, heading.
rufís *f.k.* to sip.
rul,-i *m.sh.* -a roller.
rum,-i *m.* rum.
rumún,-i *m.sh.* -ë Romanian, Rumanian.
rumún,-e *mb.* Rumanian.
rumanísht *ndajf.* in Rumanian.
rumanisht/e,-ja *f.* Rumanian.
rus,-i *m.sh.* -ë Russian.
rus,-e *mb.* Russian.
rusísht *ndajf.* in Russian.
rusísht/e,-ja *f.* Russian.
rutín/ë,-a *f.* rotine.
ryshfét,-i *m.sh.* -e bribe; graft; **jap ryshfet:** to bribe, to grease *(fig.)*; **dhënie ryshfeti:** bribery; **marr ryshfet:** to take bribe.
ryshfetçí,-u *m.sh.* -nj grafter.

Rr

rr, Rr (letter of the Albanian alphabet).

rradák/e,-ja *f.sh. gj. bis.* 1. cranium, skull. 2. head.

rrafsh,-i *m.sh.* **-e** *gjeom.* plane.

rrafsh *ndajf.* 1. flatly, evenly. 2. to the brim, full; **i mbushur rrafsh:** brimful, filled to the brim.

rráfshët (i,e) *mb.* plane, flat, even, horizontal; **tokë e rrafshët:** even ground.

rrafshím,-i *m.*1. levelling flattening. 2. *(i një qyteti)* destruction, ruin.

rrafshín/ë,-a *f.sh.* **-a** *gjeog.* plain.

rrafshnált/ë,-a *f.sh.* **-a** *gjeog.* tableland, plateau, high plain.

rrafshój *f.k.* 1. to level, to even, to flatten. 2. *(me tokën)* to raze (to the ground). — **rrafshohet** *f.jv.* to be levelled.

rrah *f.k.* 1. to beat, to strike; **rrah me shkop:** to beat with a stick, to bastinado; *(me shkelma)* to kick, to beat with kicks; *(me grushte)* to fist, to hit, to strike with fists, with fisticuffs; *(me pëllëmbë)* to slap, to buffet; *(me rrip)* to strap; *(me kamzhik ose me fshikull)* to whip, to flog, to flagellate, to lash, to scourge. 2. *(qumështin)* to churn (the milk). 3. *fig. (një çështje)* to thrash out(a question, a problem). — *Lok.* **rrah ujë në havan:** to

beat the air. — *Prov.* **hekuri rrihet sa është i nxehtë:** strike while the iron is hot. — **rrihem** *f.jv.* to be beaten, to be struck.

rráhës,-i *m.sh.* — beater; *(gruri)* flail, swingle.

rráhës,-e *mb.* beating.

rráhj/e,-a *f.* 1. beating; *(me shkop)* beating with a stick; *(me shkelma)* kicking; *(me grushte)* fisticuffs *(me pëllëmbë)* buffet; *(me kamxhik)* flogging, whipping, scourging. 2. *(e pulsit)* beat, beating, throbbing; *(e zemrës)* throb, throbbing, palpitation. 3. *(e krahëve)* flutter; *(e shuplakave)* clapping. 4. *(e një çështjeje)* debate, discussion, deliberation, controversy (of a problem).

rráhur (i,e) *mb.* 1. beaten, struck. 2. *fig.* **i rrahur me punë:** well-used in labour, experienced in labour.

rraketák/e,-ja *f.sh.* **-e** rattle.

rrállas *ndajf.* rarely, scarcely, seldom.

rrallés/ë,-a *f.* scarcity, scarceness, rarity, rareness.

rrállë *ndajf.* rarely; **nga një herë më të rrallë:** once in a way, once in a while; **rrallë e shohim atë:** we see little of him.

rrallë (i,e) *mb.* 1. rare, scarce; **plaçkë e rrallë:** rare article; **i kam shokët të rrallë:** to be unmatched. 2. thin; **flokë të rrallë**: thin hair.

rrallë *ndajf.* rarely, scarcely, once in a way.

rrallim,-i *m.* rarefying, rarefaction.

rrallój *f.k.* to rarefy, to make less dense. — **rrallohet** *f.jv.* to be rarefied.

rrángulla,-t *f.sh.* rubbish.

rrangullina,-t *f.sh.* shih **rrangulla.**

rrap,-i *m.sh.* **rrepe** *bot.* plane-tree.

rrapisht/ë,-a *f.sh.* -a plane-tree grove.

rráqe,-t *f.sh.* frippery.

rras *f.k.* to squeeze together, to compress; **rras kapelën në kokë**: to put down one's hat over one's ears.

rrás/ë,-a *f.sh.* -a slate.

rraskapit *f.k.* to overtire, to weary, to exhaust, to overstrain. — **rraskapitem** *f.jv.* to tire oneself beyond measure, to overwork, to work oneself to death, to be tired to death.

rraskapítës,-e *mb.* fatiguing, exhausting.

rraskapítj/e,-a *f.* overworking, lassitude, prostration. exhaustion.

rraskapítur (i,e) *mb.* haggard, exhausted, fatigued, fagged, tired to death.

rráthë,-t *m.sh.* (plural of **rreth**) circles.

rrebésh,-i *m.sh.* -e shower, ~~pit~~ ~~ching~~ rain, pouring rain; **bie rrebesh**: it showers; **rrebesh i shkurtër**: April shower.

rrébull,-i *m. mjek.* seborrhea.

rréck/ë,-a *f.sh.* -a rag, tatter, trinket; **i veshur me rrecka**: dressed in rags (tatters, fripperies, trinkets, old clothes.)

rreckós *f.k.* to reduce to tatters, to rag, to tatter. — **rreckosem** *f.jv.* to become ragged (tattered).

rreckósur (i,e) *mb.* ragged, tattered, shabby.

rrégull,-i *m.* order; **pa rregull**: in disorder; **vë në rregull**: to put in order, to place in order; **çdo gjë është në rregull**: all is in order (in good order); **në rregull!** good! all right! shipshape!

rrégull,-a *f.sh.* -a rule; **shkel një rregull**: to break a rule; **si rregull i përgjithshëm**: as a rule; **rregull gramatikor**: grammatical rule.

rregullím,-i *m.* regulation, arrangement, adjustement; *(i një ore etj.)* regulation (of a clock, etc.).

rregullísht *ndajf.* regularly.

rregullój *f.k.* 1. to regulate, to arrange, to adjust; *(punët)* to put (one's affairs) in order. 2. *(një hesap)* to settle, to pay (an account). 3. *(një vegël, një makinë)* to adjust (a tool, a machine). 4. *(veshjen)* to arrange one's dress; *(flokët)* to arrange, to do (one's hair). 5. to arrange; **ai e rregulloi të shkojë në plazh**: he arranged to go to the sea-side. — **rregullohem** *f.jv.* 1. *(në një vend)* to settle down, to settle oneself. 2. to dress, to get oneself up. 3. *(me dikë)* to come to an agreement, to arrange (with someone). 4. to be adjusted, to come (to go) right; **kjo do të rregullohet**: that will turn out all right. 5. *(në punë)* to get settled (in work).

rregullór/e,-ja *f.sh.* -e regulation, order; *(e universitetit)* statute; *(e një shoqërie)* rule; *(e policisë)* by-law.

rregullshmërí,-a regularity.

rrégullt (i,e) *mb.* 1. *gram.* **folje e rregullt**: regular verb. 2. *(lëvizje)* uniform, steady. 3. *(tipare)* regular (features). 4. *(jetë)* regular (life). 5. *drejt. (pasaportë etj.)* valid; *(procedurë)* normal (procedure). 6. *mjek. (puls)* regular, steady. 7. *usht., mat., fiz.* regular. 8. *fam.* **ai është njeri i rregullt:** he is a regular fellow.

rregullúes,-i *m.sh.* – regulator.
rregullúes,-e *mb.* regulating.
rrej I. *f.k.* to dupe.
  II *f.jk.* to lie, to fib.
rrem,-i *m.sh.* -a oar (of a riverboat).
rremtar -i *msh..* -ë oarsman.
rréma (të),-t(të) *as.* fibs, falsehoods.
rrémë (i,e) *mb.* 1. false, fallacious; **dëshmitar i rremë:** false witness; **xhevahir i rremë:** false jewel. 2. illusory; **botë e rreme:** illusory world.
rrenacák,-u *m.sh.* -ë liar, fibber.
rrenacák,-e *mb.* lying, deceitful.
rrén/ë,-a *f.sh.* -a lie, fib.
rren/g,-gu *m.sh.* -gje ill turn, villainous trick; **i luaj dikujt një rreng:** to play a trick, to do an ill turn to someone.
rrép/ë,-a *f.sh.* -a *bot. (e bardhë)* turnip.
rréptë (i,e) *mb.* severe, stern, strict, rigorous.
rreptësí,-a *f.* severity, sternness strictness, rigour.
rreptësísht *ndajf.* severely, sternly, rigorously; **ndalohet rreptësisht:** it is strictly prohibited (forbidden).
rreshk *f.k. (bukën)* to toast, to brown (bread); *(mishin)* to toast (meat). – **rreshkem** *f.jv.* to wither, to become wizened, to become dry.
rresht,-i *m.sh* -a rank, line; **rreshti i fundit:** rear rank, rear line; **vihem në rresht:** to line up.
rresht *ndajf.* successively, con-

secutively, in succession, one after the other; **dy javë rresht:** two weeks running; **tri gota rresht:** three glasses in a row (one after the other).
rreshtér,-i *m.sh.* -ë *usht.* sergeant.
rreshtím,-i *m.sh.* -e 1. alignment. 2. *usht.* dressing.
rreshtój *f.k.* to align, to line up, to set in line. – **rreshtohem** *f.jv.* to dress, to fall into line.
rreshtór,-e *mb. gram.* ordinal; **numëror rreshtor:** ordinal numeral.
rreth,-i *m.sh.* **rrathë** 1. hoop; **rreth fuçie;** hoop of a barrel (of a cask); **shtrëngoj një fuçi me rrathë:** to hoop a barrel; *(që luajnë kalamajtë)* hoop; **luaj me rreth:** to trundle a hoop. 2. *mek.* coil. 3. *(unazë)* ring, ringlet. 4. *gjeom.* circle; **gjysmë rrethi:** semi-circle. 5. *(studimi)* study circle; **rreth letrar:** literary circle. 6. **rreth shpëtimi:** lifebuoy. 7. **rreth shoqëror:** social circle. 8. *(administrativ)* district, region, territorial administrative division.
rreth *ndajf.* around; about; round; **rreth e përqark:** all around, round about, round and round.
rreth *paraf.* 1. round, around; **rreth zjarrit partizan:** round the partisan fire; **rreth botës:** round the world; **të bashkuar rreth Partisë:** rallied (united) around the Party. 2. about; **rreth 2000 vjet më parë:** about 2000 years ago. 3. about, on; **flas rreth një çështjeje:** to speak about a subject.
rrethán/ë,-a *f.sh.* -a circumstance; **rrethana rënduese, lehtësuese:** aggravating, mitigating circumstances; **në këto rrethana:** under such circumstances, under existing circumstances; **përfitoj**

nga rrethanat: to take advantage of the occasion.
rrethanór,-i *m.sh.* -ë *gram.* complement.
rrethanór,-e *mb.* circumstantial.
rrethím,-i *m.sh.* -e 1. enclosure, encirclement; **rrethimi i një oborri:** enclosure of a yard. 2. *usht. (qyteti)* siege (of a town); **ngre rrethimin:** to raise a siege; **vendos rrethimin:** to lay a siege to. 3. *(i një ushtrie)* encirclement (of an army).
rrethín/ë,-a *f.sh.* -a environs.
rrethój *f.k.* 1. to surround, to enclose; *(me mur një oborr)* to wall, to enclose (a yard with a wall); *(me gardh)* to surround (with a fence or stockade), to fence. 2. *(një kala)* to bisiege, to beset, to beleaguer, to lay siege (to a fortress). 3. *(ushtrinë e armikut)* to encircle (the enemy army).
rrethój/ë,-a *f.sh.* -a palisade; **rrethojë me dërrasa:** paling.
rrethór,-e *mb. gjeom.* circular.
rrezatím,-i *m.sh.* -e irradiation, radiation, radiance.
rrezatój *f.k.* to irradiate, to radiate. — **rrezatohet** *f.jv.* to be irradiated (radiated).
rrezatúes,-e *mb.* radiant.
rréz/e,-ja *f.sh.* -e 1. *(dielli)* sunbeam, beam, ray. 2. *(gjeom.) (e një rrethi)* ray (of a circle). 3. *(e një rrote)* spoke (of a wheel). 4. **rreze veprimi:** ray of action.
rrézi/k,-ku *m.sh,* -qe risk, danger, peril, jeopardy; **jam në rrezik;** to be in danger; **jam jashtë rrezikut:** to be out of danger; **jeta juaj është në rrezik:** your life is at stake; **vë kokën në rrezik:** to risk one's neck.
rrezikój *f.k.* 1. *(jetën)* to risk, to endanger, to put in danger, to stake, to venture, to hazard,

to jeopardize. 2. *(famën, emrin, shëndetin)* to risk (one's reputation, one's health). — **rrezikohem** *f.jv.* to be in danger, to run the risk of; **rrezikohem kot së koti:** to run uselessly into danger.
rrézíksh/ëm(i),-me(e) *mb.* 1. dangerous, perilous, risky; **vend i rrezikshëm:** dangerous place. 2. redoutable, formidable.
rrezikshmërí,-a *f.* dangerousness, riskiness, perilousness.
rrëféj *f.k.* 1. to tell, to narrate; **rrëfej një përrallë:** to tell (to narrate) a story. 2. *(me gisht)* to point to. 3. to show, to indicate; **rrëfej udhën:** to show the way; **rrëfemë një libër:** show me a book. — **rrëfehem** *f.jv. fet* to confess one's sins.
rrëfénj/ë,-a *f.sh.* -a tale, story.
rrëfím,-i *m. fet.* confession.
rrëfýes,-i *m.sh.* — 1. teller, narrator. 2. *fet.* confessor.
rrëgjím,-i *m.* stuntedness, dwarfishness.
rrëgjój *f.k.* to dwarf, to stunt the growth (of something). — **rrëgjohem** *f.jv.* to become stunted (dwarfish); **sa vjen e po rrëgjohet:** he is becoming stunted more and more every day.
rrëké,-ja *f.sh.* -e stream, torrent, brook, valley-brook; *(mali)* mountain-stream; *(e vogël)* streamlet; trickle; *(e fuqishme)* gush; *(shiu)* rain torrent; **rrëke lotësh: a** torrent of tears.
rrëkëlléj *f.k.* 1. *(një fuçi)* to roll (a barrel). 2. *(kupën)* to drink at a stroke. — **rrëkëllehem** *f.jv.* to be rolled up.
rrëkëllím,-i *m.* rolling.
rrëmbéj *f.k.* 1. to carry away, to take away; to snatch, to grab. 2. *(dikë si peng)* to kidnap. 3. **rrëmbej armët:** to take up

arms. – **rrëmbehem** *f.jv.* to
act hastily (rashly); to get hot,
to be exalted.
rrëmbím,-i *m.sh.* -e 1. abduction,
rape, snatch, grab. 2. *(fëmijësh)*
kidnapping, rape (of children).
3. *(frymëzim)* rapture, exaltation, inspiration. 4. *(në punë)*
rashness; **me rrëmbim**: hastily,
impetuously.
rrëmbýer (i,e) *mb. (nga karakteri,
nga temperamenti)* rash, passio-
nate, vehement.
rrëmbýes,-i *m.sh.* – kidnapper.
rrëmbýesh/ëm (i), -me (e) *mb.
(shi)* torrential (rain).
rrëmét,-i *m.* crowd, multitude.
rrëmíh *f.k.* to dig, to excavate.
– **rrëmihet** *f.jv.* to be dug.
rrëmíhës,-i *m.sh.* – digger.
rrëmím,-i *m,* digging, excavation.
rrëmój *f.k.* 1. to dig up, to grub.
2. to rummage, to ransack, to
search carefully (minutely). –
rrëmohet *f.jv.* 1. to be dug.
2. to be rummaged.
rrëmujaxhí,-u *m.sh.* -nj trouble-
-maker.
rrëmúj/ë,-a *f.* confusion, disorder, disarray, hurlyburly, helter-
-skelter, topsy-turvy, upside
down; fuss, stir, tumult, riot; **bëj
rrëmujë**: to make a mess of, to
mess something up; **në rrëmujë**:
in disarray, in disorder, in a
mess.
rrëngjéth *f.k.* to shudder, to creep.
– **rrëngjethem** *f.jv.* to feel a
cold tremor.
rrëngjéthës,-e *mb.* shuddering,
creepy, trembling, horrible; **krim
rrëngjethës**: horrible crime,
blood curdling crime.
rrëngjéthj/e,-a *f.* 1. *(nga të ftohtit)* shiver. 2. *(nga frika)* shudder.
rrëním,-i *m.sh.* -e ruin, destruction, devastation.
rrënój *f.k.* 1. to ruin, to destroy,

to ravage, to demolish, to
lay in ruins. 2. to impoverish,
to ruin. – **rrënohem** *f.jv.* 1. to
be ruined (destroyed, ravaged),
to fall into ruin. 2. to ruin oneself.
rrënúes,-e *mb.* ruinous, destructive.
rrënxím,-i *m. mjek.* hernia, rupture.
rrënxóhem *f.jv.* to be ruptered.
rrënj/ë,-a *f.sh.* -ë 1. root; **rrënjë e një bime**: root of a plant;
zë rrënjë: to take root, to
strike root. 2. tree; **rrënjë hardhie**: vine. 3. *mat.* root; **rrënjë katrore**; square root; **nxjerr
rrënjën katrore**: to draw (to extract) the square root. 4. *gram.
(e një fjale)* root (of a word).
rrënjësísht *ndajf.* radically, funda-
mentally.
rrënjësór,-e *mb.* radical.
rrënjós *f.k.* 1. to root. 2. *fig. (në
mendje)* to inculcate (in the
mind). – **rrënjoset** *f.jv. fig.* to
be inculcated.
rrënjósj/e,-a *f.* 1. rooting. 2. *(za-
koni)* inveteracy. 3. *(në mendje)*
inculcation.
rrëpír/ë,-a *f.sh.* -a abyss, precipice, steepness.
rrëpírët (i,e) *mb.* steep; **shkëmb
i rrëpirët**: crag, steep rock.
rrëshinór,-e *mb.* resinous.
rrëshír/ë,-a *f.* resin.
rrëshqás *f.jk.* 1. to slip, to slide,
to glide; **rrëshqas në akull**:
to slide on the ice; **rrëshqas me
ski**: to ski; *(me slitë)* to sledge.
2. *(toka)* to slide, to subside.
3. *(iki tinës)* to steal out (away).
rrëshqítës,-e *mb.* slippery.
rrëshqítës/e,-ja *f.sh.* -e sleigh,
sledge.
rrëshqítj/e,-a *f.* sliding, slide.
rrëz/ë,-a *f.sh.* -a 1. *(lumi)* river-
side. 2. *(mali)* mountainside.
3. *(pylli)* border (of a forest).

rrëzîm,-i *m.sh.* -e falling, fall, tumble, overthrow.
rrëzój *f.k.* 1. *(një shtëpi, një mur)* to pull down, to throw down (a house, a wall). 2. *(përtokë një njeri)* to throw down, to bring down, to knock down (a person). 3. *(një pemë, një dru)* to cut down (a tree). 4. *(një aeroplan)* to shoot down (a plane). 5) *fig. (një nxënës në provim)* to flunk, to pluck, to plough (a pupil in examination). — **rrëzohem** *f.jv.* 1. to tumble, to tapple, to tumble down. 2. *(në provim)* to be flunked, to be ploughed, to be plucked.
rri *f.jk.* (p.t. **ndenja** or **ndejta,** pp. **ndenjur** or **ndejtur)** 1. to sit; **rri ulur:** to sit down; **rri pranë:** to sit near. 2. to stand; **rri më këmbë:** to stand up, to stand on foot; **rri pranë meje:** stand near me, stand by me (by my side); **rri mënjanë:** to stand aside; **rri i qetë:** to stand still. 3. **rri shtrirë:** to lie, to rest in a recumbent position; **rri në bisht:** to squat; **rri urtë!** keep quiet: be silent! 4. to stay; **rri në shtëpi:** to stay at home. — *Lok.* **rri duarkryq:** to lie idle.
rrík/ë,-a *f.sh.* -a *bot.* horse-radish.
rrip,-i *m.sh.* -a 1. *(pantallonash)* belt (of trousers), girdle; **shtrëngoj me rrip:** to fasten with a strap, to strap; **rrah me rrip:** to strap, to beat with a strap; **ngjesh rripin:** to tighten the belt; **zgjidh rripin:** to ungirdle, to take off the belt. 2. *(qeni)* leash. 3. *(transmisioni)* strap. 4. *(për mprehjen e briskut)* razorstrap, strap. 5. *(pushke)* bandoleer. 6. *(shpate)* sword-belt. 7. *(toke)* tract (of land), promontory. *[handwritten:] 8. strap, band (of watch)*

rrísk/ë,-a *f.sh.* -a slice, steak; **një rriskë buke:** a slice of bread.
rrit *f.k.* 1. *(moshën)* to augment, to increase (the age). 2. *(fëmijë)* to breed, to bring up (children). 3. *(bagëti)* to rear (cattle). 4. *(lule)* to grow (flowers). — **rritem** *f.jv.* 1. to increase. 2. to grow up, to become greater; **në pranverë bimët fillojnë të rriten:** in the spring plants begin to grow; **rritet jashtë masës:** to overgrow.
rrítës,-i *m.sh.* — grower, breeder.
rrítës,-e *mb.* increasing, crescent.
rrítj/e,-a *f.* 1. *(e moshës, e popullsisë etj.)* augmentation, increase (of the age, of the population etc.). 2. *(e fëmijëve)* breeding (of children). 3. *(e bagëtive)* rearing (of cattle). 4. *(e luleve)* growing (of flowers); **rritje e shpejtë:** rapid growth.
rrítur (i,e) *mb.* grown, grown up; **i rritur jashtë masës:** overgrown, **njeri i rritur:** adult.
rrjedh *f.jk.* (p.t. **rrodha,** p.p. **rrjedhur)** 1. *(lumi, rrëkeja)* to flow (a stream, a river). 2. *(ena)* to leak (a vessel); **rrjedh çurkë:** to trickle; **rrjedh me vrull:** to gush. 3. *(një fjalë)* to derive (a word). 4. *(si përfundim)* to result, to ensue 5. to come of, to issue, to be descended; to spring from; **ai rrjedh nga një familje e shquar:** he comes of an illustrious family.
rrjédh/ë,-a *f.* 1. *(e një lumi)* flow, course. 2. *(e ngjarjeve)* course, run (of events).
rrjédhës,-e *mb.* current; **llogari rrjedhëse:** current account.
rrjédhím,-i *m.sh.* -e 1. consequence; deduction; **si rrjedhim:** in consequence (of), hence; **vjen si rrjedhim i:** it follows as a

consequence of. 2. *mat.* corollary.

rrjédhj/e,-a *f.* 1. flowing. 2. leakage.

rrjedhór,-e *mb. gram.* ablative; rasa rrjedhore: ablative case.

rrjedhór/e,-ja *f. gram.* ablative case.

rrjédhshëm *ndajf.* fluently, freely; flas rrjedhshëm një gjuhë të huaj; to speak fluently a foreign language.

rrjédhsh/ëm (i,) -me(e) *mb.* 1. running, passing; ujë i rrjedhshëm: running water. 3. *(të folur)* fluent.

rrjedhshmërí,-a *f.* fluency; rrjedhshmëri në të folur: fluency of speech

rrjep *f.k.* (p.t. rropa, p.p. rrjepur). 1. *(një shtazë të therur)* to flay, to strip, to skin. to peel off. 2. *(një pulë)* to pluck (a hen). 3. *(fig.) (dikë)* to rob, to strip (someone) of something. – rripem *f.jv.* to be peeled off.

rrjepacák,-u *m.sh.* -ë ragamuffin, ragged man.

rrjépës,-i *m.sh.* – flayer.

rrjépj/e,-a *f.* stripping. flaying.

rrjet,- i *m.sh.* -e network; rrjeti hekurudhor: railway net - work.

rrjét/ë,-a *f.sh.* -a 1. *(peshkimi)* net, fishing net: *(për të kapur zogj)* net (for catching birds). 2. *(pazari për të psonisur)* shopping basket.

rrobalárës/e,-ja *f.sh.* -e laundress, washer-woman.

rrobaqépës,-i *m.sh.* – taylor, dressmaker; *(grash)* ladies' taylor.

rrobaqépës/e,-ja *f.sh.* -e seamstress, needle-woman, dress-maker woman.

rrobaqepësí,-a *f.* 1. sewing. 2. sewing shop.

rrobashítës,-i *m.sh.* – old clothesman.

rrób/ë,-a *f.sh.* -a dress; outfit; clothes; një palë rroba burrash, grash: a man's suit, a woman's suit; rroba zije: mourning; rroba dhëndërie: bride-groom's suit; rroba pune: working clothes; rroba të gatshme: ready-made clothes; rroba të grisura: ragged clothes; rrobë dhome: dressing gown; rrobë nate: night gown.

rróbu/ll,-lli *m.sh.* -j bot. mountain pine-wood.

rróg/ë.-a *f.sh.*-a wage, salary, pay; i jap rrogë; to give a salary to; rrogë shumë e vogël: pittance; marr rrogën: to draw one's pay.

rrogëtár,-i *m.sh.* -ë payee.

rrogóz,-i *m.sh.* -a straw-mat, matting.

rroj *f.jk.* 1. to live, to exist, to subsist; rroj i lumtur: to live happily; rroj me të keq: to live a miserable life, to live from hand to mouth, to live poorly; më rrofsh: thank you: ..rrofsh sa malet: may you live as long as the mountains! rroftë Një Maji! hurrah the First of May! rroftë marksizëm-leninizmi! long live Marxism-Leninism! 2. *(rroba)* to wear well, to last. – Lok. rroj me ëndrra: to feed on empty hopes, to daydream.

rrój/ë,-a *f.* shaving; brisk rrojet blade razor, safety razor; sapun rroje: shaving soap; furçe rroje: shaving brush.

rrójtj/e,-a *f.* living, livelihood.

rrojtór/e,-ja *f.sh.* -e shaving-shop.

rrok *f.k.* 1. to grab, to grip, to grasp; rrok për beli: to clutch, to seize strongly by the waist.

2. *(për qafe)* to embrace, to cuddle. 3. *fig. (me mend)* to grasp, to seize, to take in; **s'ma rrok mendja:** I don't grasp its meaning. – **rrokem** *f.jv. (për qafe me dikë)* to cuddle, to embrace closely (one another).

rrókj/e,-a *f.sh.* -e 1 - grasp; *(duarsh)* hand-shake; *(për qafe)* embrace. 2. *gram.* syllable.

rrokullím/ë,-a *f.* 1. precipice. 2. *fin.* downfall.

rrokullís *f.k.* to roll, to roll over. – **rrokullisem** *f.jv.* to roll up; to roll downhill.

rrokullísj/e,-a *f.* rolling.

rropát *f.k.* to tire out. – **rropatem** *f.jv.* to wear oneself out.

rropullí,-të *f.sh.* entrails, tripes, pluck (of animals).

rrotatív,-i *m.sh.* -a rotary printing-press.

rrót/ë,-a *f.sh.* -a 1. wheel; *(karroce)* wheel; *(hidraulike)* flutter-wheel; *(makinerie)* fly-wheel; *(mulliri)* mill-wheel. 2. *(automobili, biçiklete)* tire, pneumatic--tire. 3. *(me dhëmbëza)* pinion. 4. *fig. fam,* fool.

rrótk/ë,-a *f.sh.* -a *(peri)* bobbin, spool.

rrótull-,a *f.sh.* -a 1. *anat.* vertebra. 2. beater (of a churn). 3. *(djathi)* round block (of cheese).

rrótull I. *ndajf.* round, around; **vij rrotull:** to turn round. – *Lok.* **i vij rrotull dikujt:** to court, to woo someone; **më vjen mendja rrotull:** to feel dizzy; **to be all at sea, not to make head or tail of it; vij rrotull** *(për të vjedhur etj.):* to prowl. II. *paraf.* around; **rrotull zjarrit:** around the fire; **rrotull botës:** round the world; **aty rrotull:** round-about.

rrotullím,-i *m.sh.* -e revolving, rotation; **rrotullimi i Tokës rreth Diellit:** the revolving of the Earth round the Sun.

rrotullój *f.k.* to revolve, to rotate, to turn. – **rrotullohem** *f.jv..* to turn round, to rotate.

rrotullúes,-e *mb.* rotative, rotatory.

rrúaj *f.k.* to shave; **rruaj mjekrën:** to shave the beard; **rruaj dikë:** to give someone a shave. – **rruhem** *f.jv.* to shave; **duhet të rruhem:** I must have a shave.

rrúarj/e,-a *f.sh.* -a shave, shaving.

rruáz/ë,-a *f.sh.* -a 1. bead, beading; **stolisem me rruaza:** to bead, to ornament with beads. 2. *anat.* vertebra; **rruazat e qafës:** cervical vertebrae; **rruazat e gjakut:** globules of blood; **rruazat e kuqe:** red globules, red corpuscles: **rruazat e bardha:** white globules.

rrudh *f.k.* to wrinkle, to erumple; *fig.* **rrudh vetullat:** to pucker up one's brows, to knit one's brows; **rrudh hundën:** to make a wry face. – **rrudhem** *f.jv.* to become wrinkled (puckered), to shrivel.

rrúdh/ë,-a *f.sh,* -a crease, wrinkle, crumple, pucker; *(rrudhë fustani, pantallonash etj.)* frill, ruck (of a shirt, of trousers, etc.).

rrúdhur (i,e) *mb.* wrinkled, shrunk, puckered; **ballë i rrudhur:** puckered brow, wrinkled brow.

rrufé,-ja *f.sh.* – thunder-bolt. thunder-clap; **i goditur nga rrufeja:** thunder-struck.

rrufeprítës/e,-ja *f.sh.* -e lightning-conductor, lightning-rod.

rrufésh/ëm(i),-me(e) *mb.* fulminant; **goditje e rrufeshme:** fulminant knock.

rrúf/ë,-a *mjek.* catarrh; **jam me rrufë**: to have a running nose.
rrufít *f.k.* to sip. – **rrufitet** *f.jv.* to be sipped.
rrufítj/e,-a *f.* sipping.
rrufján,-i *m.sh.* .-ë rruffian.
rrúfkë *mb.* soft boiled; **vezë rrufkë**: soft boiled egg.
rrugáç,-i *m.sh.* -ë street-urchin, hooligan, *amer.* hoodlum.
rrúg/ë,-a *f.sh.* -ë 1. street; road; way; route; *(qyteti)* street; *(e gjerë qyteti me pemë anash ose midis)* avenue, broad street, boulevard; *(me kalldrëm)* paved street; **rrugë e rrahur**: beaten path; **rrugë pak e rrahur**: by-path, by-way; **rrugë pa krye**: dead-lock, cul-de-sac; **rrugë kopshti**: alley, passage (in a garden). 2. travel; **nisem për rrugë**: to start off; **jam për rrugë**: I'm going to set out for a journey. 3. way, alternative; **rrugë tjetër s'ka**: there is no other way, there is no choice (alternative). 4. solution; **i jap rrugë një çështjeje**: to solve a problem. – *Lok.* **me rrugë ajrore**: by air; **me rrugë detare**: by sea; **me rrugë tokësore**: by land, overland; **tregoj rrugën**: to show the way; to lead the way; **zë rrugën**: to bar the way; **çoj në rrugë të drejtë**: to lead on the right way; **jam në rrugë të drejtë, të gabuar**: to be on the right, wrong way; **çoj në rrugë të shtrembër**: to lead on the wrong way, to lead astray, to mislead; **gjatë rrugës**: along the way ; **rrugës**: on the way; **cilën rrugë të marrim?** which way shall we go? **marrim këtë rrugë**: let us go this way; **cila rrugë të çon në stacion?** which way leads to the station? **si e gjete rrugën?** how did you find the way? **jam në rrugë të madhe**: to be without lodging, to be homeless (houseless); **lë në mes të rrugës**: to leave something half-way.
rrugëdálj/e,-a *f.sh.* -e way out; **autori nuk tregon rrugë dalje**: the author does not give a way out; **gjej një rrugëdalje**: to find a way out.
rrugëkrýq,-i *m.sh.* -e cross-road.
rrugíc/ë,-a *f.sh.* -a lane, by-lane, narrow street.
rrugín/ë,-a *f.sh.* -a corridor.
rrugór,-e *mb.* road; **policia rrugore**: road inspection; **rrjeti rrugor**: road network.
rrumbullák,-e *mb.* 1. round, rotund, spherical. 2. *(nga trupi)* plump, dumpling, chubby.
rrumbullákët (i,e) *mb.* round, rotund, spherical.
rrumbullakím,-i *m.* roundness; rounding.
rrumbullakój *f.k.* to round, to make round. – **rrumbullakohet** *f.jv.* to become (to grow) round.
rrumbullój *f.k.* to eat greadily. – **rrumbullohem** *f.jv.* to satiate oneself.
rrush,-i *m.* 1. grape; **rrush i thatë (stafidhe)**: raisin, dried grapes; **lëng rrushi**: grape juice; **veshul rrushi**: a bunch of grapes; **vjel rrushin**: to vintage; **vjelja e rrushit**: vintage; **rrush mali**: myrtle.
rruzár/e,-ja *f.sh.* -e rosary.
rrúzu/ll,-lli *m.sh.* -j *gjeog.* globe, orb; **rruzull tokësor**: terrestrial globe.

rruzullim,-i *m.* universe.
rrým/ë,-a *f.sh.* **-a** 1. current;
rrymë ajri: draft, current of
air; **rrymë lumi:** flow, current
of a river. 2. *(elektrike)* electric current.
rrypín/ë,-a *f.sh.* **-a** *gjeog.* *(токе)*
isthmus, tract of land.

S

s,S (letter of the Albanian alphabet) s,S.
s' *ndajf.* no, not (the same as **nuk**):
s'kam kohë *(nuk kam kohë):*
I have not time, I haven't time.
sa I. *ndajf.* 1. how, how much,
how many; what; **sa vjeç jeni?**
how old are you? **sa para?**
how much money? **sa para
keni?** how much money do
you have? **sa e bleve këtë
libër?** how much have you
bought this book? what was
the price of the book?;
sa larg është që këtu?
how far is it from here? **sa
libra ka aty?** how many books
are there? 2. how! what! **sa
kënaqësi është të ulesh nën
hijen e këtyre pemëve të
bukura!** how delightful it is
to sit in the shade of these
fine trees! **sa e mirë je!** how
good you are! **sa i marrë!** what
a fool! **sa e bukur është natýra!** how beautiful is nature!
sa i madh është deti! how
large is the sea! **sa shpejt
ёcën ai!** how fast he goes! 3.
as; **ju nuk jeni aq i zgjuar sa
ai:** you are not so clever as he
is; **ju jeni po aq i zgjuar sa**
ai: you are as clever as he is;
e vogël sa një lajthi: small as
a hazelnut.
II. *paraf.* as; **sa më gjatë:** as long
as possible; **ikni sa më shpejt
që të mundeni:** run as quickly as you can; **sa më shpejt:**
as soon as possible; **sa për
mua:** as for me, as to me;
për sa i përket: as regards;
me sa di unë: as far as I
know, for all I know; **sa herë
që:** whenever.
III. *lidh.* that, as; **çeliku është
aq i fortë sa mund të
presë hekurin:** steel is so
hard that it can cut iron;
**disa njerëz flasin aq ulët
sa nuk dëgjohen:** some people
speak so low that one cannot
hear them; **ai thirri aq fort sa
u ngjir:** he shouted so loudly
that he got hoarse; **mund të jetë
njeriu aq budalla sa ta besojë
këtë?** can anyone be so silly as
to believe this?—*Prov.* **hekuri rrihet sa është i nxehtë;** strike
while ron is hot.
sabotatór,-i *m.sh.* **-ë** saboteur.
sabotím,-i *m.sh.* **-e** sabotage.
sabotój *f.k.* to sabotate. — **sabotohet** *f.jv.* to be sabotated.

saç,-i *m.sh.* **-e** metal baking cover.

sáçm/ë,-a *f.sh.* **-a** lead shot, pellet.

sáde *mb.* **mish sade:** meat without vegetables; **kafe sade:** coffee without sugar.

sadó *ndajf.* 1. enough. 2. however; **sado e keqe që të jetë gjendja· juaj:** however grave your situation may be; **sado i mençur që të jetë:** however wise he may be.

sadopák *ndajf.* ever so little.

sadóqë *lidh.* although.

safí *mb.* pure.

sahán,-i *m.sh.* **-ë** bowl.

sahàt,-i *m.sh.* **-ë** 1. clock; watch; *(muri)* wall-clock; *(dore)* watch, wristwatch; **sahat diellor:** sundial; **sahat me rërë:** hourglass; **fushë sahati:** clockdial, clock-face; **gur sahati:** ruby (of a clock); **mekanizëm sahati:** clock-work. 2. *(gazi, uji, elektriku)* counter. 3. hour; **sa është sahati?** what time is it? *fig.* **sahat i lig:** unearthly hour.

sahatçí,-u *m.sh.* **-nj** clockmaker, watchmaker.

saj **(i,e)** *p.pr.* her; (nominative case) **çanta e saj:** her handbag; **libri i saj:** her book; **djali i saj:** her son; **djemtë i saj,** her sons; (genitive case) **i, e djalit të saj:** of her son; **i, e djemve të saj:** of her sons; (dative case) **djalit të saj:** to her son; **djemve të saj:** to her sons; (accusative case) **djalin e saj:** her son; **djemtë e saj:** her sons.

saj/i(i),-a(e) *p.pr.* hers; **çanta është e saja:** the handbag is hers; **libri është i saji:** the book is hers, the book belongs to her; **këto nuk janë të sajat:** these are not hers.

sajdí,-a *f. gj. bis.* respect.

sajdís *f.k. gj. bis.* to respect.

sáje (në) *fj. plk.* **në saje të:** thanks to, owing to; **në saje të tij:** thanks to him; **në saje tuaj:** thanks to you.

sáj/ë,-a *f.sh.* **-a** sledge, sleigh; **rrëshqas me sajë:** to sledge.

sajím,-i *m.sh.* **-e** invention, fabrication, concoction.

sajój *f.k.* to invent.

sakáq *ndajf.* instantaneously, immediately, on the instant.

sakát,-i *m.sh.* **-ë** cripple, invalid.

sakát,-e *mb.* maimed, disabled, crippled.

sakatím,-i *m.sh.* **-e** mutilation.

sakatllëk,-u *m.* infirmity.

sakatój *f.k.* 1. to maim, to lame, to mutilate, to cripple. 2. *fig.* *(një tekst etj.)* to mangle, to murder. — **sakatohem** *f.jv.* to become crippled.

sakatúar(i,e) *mb.* crippled, mutilated, maimed.

sakrifíc/ë,-a *f.sh.* **-a** sacrifice.

sakrifikój *f.k.* to sacrifice. — **sakrifikohem** *f.jv.* to be sacrificed.

sakrilégj,-i *m.sh.* **-e** sacrilege.

saksí,-a *f.sh.* — flower-pot.

sákte (i,e) *mb.* 1. exact, precise, accurate; **punë e saktë:** accurate work. 2. normal, sound; **njeri i saktë:** a sound man.

saktësí,-a *f.* exactness, precision, accuracy, justness; **me saktësi:** accurately.

saktësísht *ndajf.* exactly, precisely.

sálc/ë,-a *f.sh.* **-a** sauce; **salcë domateje:** tomato sauce; **enë për salcë:** sauce-box.

saldatór,-i *m.sh.* **-ë** solderer, welder.

saldatríç/e,-ja *f.sh.* **-e** soldering-iron.

saldím,-i *m.* soldering, welding.

saldój *f.k.* to solder, to weld.

saldohet *f.jv.* to be soldered, to be welded.

salép,-i *m.* 1. *bot.* orchis. 2. a hot drink prepared with orchis.

salmón,-i *m.sh.* -**ë** *zool.* salmon.

salnít/ër,-ri *m.* shih **salpetër**.

salpét/ër,-ri *m. kim.* salpeter, nitrate of potash.

salsíç/e,-ja *m.sh.* -**e** sausage.

sallahán/ë,-a *f.sh.* -**a** slaughter-house, shamble.

sallaís *f.k.* to tack, to baste.

sallám,-i *m.sh.* -**e** salami, sausage.

sallamerí,-a *f.sh.* – pork-butcher's shop.

sallamúr,-i *m.* corned-meat, preserved meat.

sallát/ë,-a *f.* salad; **sallatë marule**: lettuce.

sallatór,-i *m.sh.* -**ë** cucumber.

sáll/ë,-a *f.sh.* -a hall; **sallë mbledhjesh**: meeting room, public room; **sallë pritjeje**: waiting-room, reception- room; **sallë vallëzimi**: ball-room, dancing-room.

sállo,-ja *f.* pig's fat; *(e shkrirë)* lard.

sallón,-i *m.sh.* -**e** saloon, drawing-room, large reception-room; *fig.* njeri i **salloneve**: a man of fashion, a man about town.

salltanét,-i *m.* luxury, luxuriance, ostentation, sumptuosity, pomposity; **plot salltanet**: sumptuous, luxurious.

samár,-i *m.sh.* -**ë** 1. saddle. 2. **samar breshke**: carapace.

samarbërës,-i *m.sh.* – saddler.

samarxhí,-u *m.sh.* -nj shih **samarbërës**.

samovár,-i *m.sh.* -**ë** samovar, tea-urn, tea-pot, tea-kettle.

sanatoriúm,-i *m.sh.* -**e** sanatorium.

sandál/e,-ja *f.sh.* -**e** sandals.

sandáll,-i *m.sh.* -**e** punt.

sanduíç,-i *m.sh.* -**ë** sandwich.

sán/ë,-a *f.* hay.

sanitár,-e *mb.* sanitary; **qendër sanitare**: sanitarium.

sapllák,-u *m.sh.* -**ë** mug, cup, goblet.

sapó *lidh.* 1. this moment, just now; **ai sapo u kthye nga shkolla**: he has just returned from school; **ai sapo doli**: he has just gone out; **ai sapo erdhi**: he has just come. 2. right away; **e njoha sapo e pashë**: I recognized him (her) right away (straight off, at the very first).

sapún,-i *m.sh.* -**ë** soap; **sapun pluhur**: powdered soap; **sapun rroje**: shaving soap; **flluskë sapuni**: soap bubble; **shkumbë sapuni**: soap-suds, lather of soap; **ujë sapuni**: suds, soapy water.

sapunís *f.k.* to soap, to wash with soap, to lather. – **sapunisem** *f.jv.* to soap oneself down, to wash oneself with soap.

saráç,-i *m.sh.* -**ë** saddler.

saraçinésk/ë,-a *f.sh.* -a *mek.* stop-cock.

saráf,-i *m.sh.* -**ë** 1. money-changer. 2. *fig.* miser.

sarahósh,-i *m.sh.* -**ë** drunkard, tippler, boozer.

saráj,-i *m.sh.* -**e** *vjet.* seraglio, palace (building).

sardél/e,-ja *f.sh.* -**e** *zool.* sardine, pilchard.

sárg/ël,-la *f.sh.* -la grafting-tool.

sarkastík,-e *mb.* sarcastic.

sarkáz/ëm,-mi *m.* sarcasm.

sárk/ë,-a *f.sh.* -a *anat.* constitution.

sasí,-a *f.* quantity; **sasi e madhe**: a large quantity, a great deal (of).

sasiór,-e *mb.* quantitative.

saták,-e *mb.* satanic.

satelít,-i *m.sh.* -**ë** *astron.* satellite.

satén,-i *m.* satin.

satër,-i *m.sh.* -e chopper, cleaver.
satír/ë,-a *f.* satire.
satirík,-e *mb.* satiric.
satráp,-i *m.sh.* -ë satrap.
savån,-i *m.* cere-cloth, shroud,
cerements, grave-cloth; **mbështjell me savan:** to shroud.
savån/ë,-a *f.* savana.
sáz/e,-ja *f.sh.* -e *muz.* harmonica,
mouth-organ.
sazexhí,-u *m.sh.* -nj musician of
popular orchestra.
se *lidh.* 1. that; **shpresoj se do
të kthehet së shpejti:** I hope
that he will return soon. 2. than;
më mirë vonë se kurrë: better late than never; **ai është më
i ri se unë:** he is younger
than me. 3. because, for; **nuk
erdha se isha i zënë:** I did
not come because I was busy.
4. (to express a doubt) **kam
frikë se vallë vjen:** I doubt
he will not come. 5. otherwise,
or else; **vrapo, se do të vonohesh:** run or else you will be
late; **eja, se do të pendohesh:**
come, otherwise you will be
sorry.
se *p.pk.* what; **me se shikoni ju?**
what do you see with? **prej se
është bërë tavolina?** what is
the table made of? **me se laheni ju?** what do you wash
yourself with? **për se duhen
pincat?** what are pincers for?
seánc/ë,-a *f.sh.* -a sitting, session;
seancë plenare: plenary session.
sebép,-i *m.sh.* -e *gj. bis.* 1. cause, motive. 2. pretext.
secíla *p.pk. (fem.)* each one; **ato
kushtojnë dhjetë lekë se-
cila:** each of them costs ten
leks.
secíli *p.pk. (mashk.)* each; **secili
sipas gustos së vet:** each
to his own taste.

sedéf,-i *m.* mother-of-pearl.
séd/ër,-ra *f.* self-respect, sense
of pride, self-pride.
sedërmádh,-e *mb.* self-respectful.
sefergjén,-i *m. bot.* shih **borzilok.**
segmént,-i *m.sh.* -e *gjeom.* seg-
ment.
sehír,-i *m. gj. bis.* **bëj sehir:** to
look on; to contemplate.
sehirxhí,-u *m.sh.* -nj *vjet.* looker-
on, spectator, bystander, beholder.
sejmén,-i *m.sh.* -ë *vjet.* body-
guard.
sekónd/ë,-a *f.sh.* -a second.
sekreción,-i *m.sh.* -e secretion.
sekrét,-i *m.sh.* -e secret.
sekretár,-i *m.sh.* -ë 1. secretary.
2. clerk, writer.
sekretarí,-a *f.sh.* — clerk's office;
secretary's office.
sekretariát,-i *m.* 1. secretary-
ship. 2. secretariat, secretariate.
seks,-i *m.sh.* -e sex; **seksi i
bukur:** the fair sex.
seksër,-i *m.sh.* -ë broker; *(sekser
burse)* stockbroker.
seksíon,-i *m.sh.* -e section.
seksuál,-e *mb.* sexual.
sekt,-i *m.sh.* -e sect.
sektár,-e *mb.* sectarian.
sektaríz/ëm,-mi *m.* sectarianism.
sektór,-i *m.sh.* -ë sector.
sekuestrím,-i *m.sh.* -e sleques-
tration.
sekuestròj *f.k.* to sequestrate. —
— **sekuestrohet** *f.jv.* to be
sequestrated.
sekuestrúes,-i *m.sh.* — seques-
trator.
sekúsh *p.pk.* krah. somebody;
sekush erdhi: somebody came.
seleksioním,-i *m.* selection.
seleksionòj *f.k.* to select, to choose.
— **seleksionohet** *f.jv.* to qe.
selected (chosen).
seleksionúes,-i *m.sh.* — selector.
selfián,-i *m. bot.* shih **borzilok.**

sell,-a *f.sh.* – *treg.* seat.
selinó,-ja *f.:bot.* celery.
selísht/ë,-a *f.sh.* -a courtyard.
selví,-a *f.sh.* *bot.* cypress-tree.
semést/ër,-ri *m.sh.* -ra semester.
seminár,-i *m.sh.* -e 1. seminary. 2. seminar.
senát,-i *m.sh.* -e senate.
senatór,-i *m.sh.* -ë senator.
send,-i *m.sh.* -e thing, article, object; commodity; **sende të vlefshme**: valuables; **sende ushqimore**: food-stuffs.
senét,-i *m.sh.* -e debenture.
sentimentál,-e *mb.* sentimental.
separatíst,-i *m.sh.* -ë separatist.
separatíz/ëm,-mi *m.* separatism.
sepét/e,-ja *f.sh.* -e basket; (me *kapak)* hamper.
sépj/e,-a *f.sh.* -e *zool.* sepia, cuttle-fish.
sepsé *lidh.* because, for; **lepuri fle me sy hapur, sepse është shumë frikacak**: the hare sleeps with its eyes open, because it is haunted with fear; **e shpërbleva, sepse punoi mirë**: I rewarded him for he worked hard.
serenát/ë,-a *f.sh.* -a serenade.
sér/ë,-a *f.* bitumen.
sér/ë,-a *f.sh.* -a glass-house, green--house.
sergjén,-i *m.sh.* -ë dresser, open cupboard.
serí,-a *f.sh.* – series; **në seri; serially, in series.
serióz,-e *mb.* 1. *(pamje)*; serious, grave (appearance); *(argument)* serious, weighty (argumentation); *(plagë, sëmundje)* serious, grave, dangerous (wound), illness); *(njeri)* serious, earnest, responsible (person).
seriozísht *ndajf.* seriously, earnestly, in earnest; **marr seriozisht**: to take in earnest.
seriozitét,-i *m.* seriousness, earnestness; **pa seriozitet**: light-

-heartedly; **me gjithë seriozitetin**: in all seriousness.
serm,-i *m. vjet.* silver.
serpentín/ë,-a *f.sh.* -a *tek.* serpentine.
sértë (i,e) *mb.* 1. restive; **kalë i sertë**: restive horse. 2. rigid, not pliant; **tel i sertë**: rigid wire. 3. *(karakter)* crabbed, bitter (character).
serúm,-i *m. mjek.* serum.
servíl,-i *m.sh.* -e servile, subservient person, groveller.
servíl,-e *mb.* servile, menial.
servilíz/ëm,-mi *m.* servility; **me servilízëm**: servilely, slavishly.
servís,-i *m.sh.* -e service.
sesá *ndajf.* than; **më shumë sesa duhej**: more than it was necessary. – *Prov.* **më mirë një vezë sot sesa një pulë mot**: a bird in the hand is better than two in the bush.
sesí *ndajf.* **s'ka sesi**: it is not possible; there is no reason; **s'kam sesi ta ndihmoj**: it is impossible for me to help him.
sesión,-i *m.sh.* -e session, sitting.
sét/ër,-ra *f.sh.* -ra coat, jacket.
seváp,-i *m. vjet.* alms, almsgiving; charity; **bëj sevap:** to give alms.
sevdá,-ja *f. vjet.* love, affection, amor.
së I. *nyjë e përparme* (former article, placed before a feminine noun or adjective of the genitive, dative and ablative case) of; **në oborrin e shkollës së Skënderit**: in the yard of the school of Skënder. II. *pjesëzë* it is used in a number of locutions, as for example: **së shpejti**: soon.
së áfërmi *ndajf.* soon.
së báshku *ndajf.* together, conointly.

së dýti *ndajf.* secondly.

së fúndi *ndajf.* lastly, finally, in the end.

së jáshtmi *ndajf.* externally.

së páku at least;

së pári first, first of all.

sëkëlldí,-a *f. gj. bis.* malaise; **jam në sëkëlldi**: to be at a loss.

sëkëlldís *f.k.* to make anxious, to trouble, to annoy. — **sëkëll-disem** *f.jv.* to be anxious, to trouble oneself, to trouble about, to be annoyed.

sëllój *f.k. krah.* to strike hard.

sëmbím,-i *m.* twinge, acute pain, sudden sharp pain.

sëmbón (më) *f.jv.* to have a twinge (a shooting, a darting pain).

sëmbònjës,-a *mb. mjek* shooting.

sëmúndj/e,-a *f.sh.* -e malady, disease, illness, sickness; **së-mundje e lehtë**: slight disease; **sëmundje e rëndë**: grave malady; **sëmundje e pashëruesh-me**: incurable malady; **sëmundje ngjitëse**: contagious disease; **sëmundja e detit**: sea-sickness; **sëmundja a sheqerit**: diabetes; **sëmundja e tokës**: epilepsy; **sëmundja e zemrës**: carditis, heart disease; **sëmundje pro-fesionale**: professional disea-se; **marr një sëmundje**: to catch a malady.

sëmúr *f.k.* 1. to render ill. 2. *fig.* to annoy; **ai më sëmur**: I am sick and tired of him. — **së-murem** *f.jv.* to fall ill (sick), to get sick, to become sick, to sicken.

sëmúr/ë(i),-i(i) *m.sh.* -ë(të) sick person; **kujdesem për të së-murët**: to take care of the sick.

sëmúrë (i,e) *mb.* ill, sick, sickly, unwell; **njeri i sëmurë**: sick person; **jam i sëmurë nga mël-**

çía: to have liver-trouble; **sy, vesh, i sëmurë**: a sore eye, a sore ear.

sëndís *f.k.* to grieve, to make sad. — **sëndisem** *f.jv.* to grow sad (grieved).

sëndísur (i,e) *mb.* sad.

sëndúk,-u *m.sh.* -ë chest, large box, trunk.

sëpát/ë,-a *f.sh.* -a axe; *(e vogël)* hatchet; **pres me sëpatë**: to axe.

sër/ë,-a *f.sh.* -ë rank.

sërísh *ndajf.* anew, again.

sëríshmi *ndajf.* anew. afresh.

sfér/ë,-a *f.sh.* -a sphere.

sferík,-e *mb.* spherical, rotund, globular.

sfilít *f.k.* 1. to beat someone black and blue. 2. to tire someone to death. — **sfilitem** *f.jv.* to get dog-tired, to get tired to death.

sfilítj/e,-a *f.* exhaustion, weariness, prostration.

sfond,-i *m.sh.* -e background.

sfrat,-i *m.sh.* -e dike, dam, weir.

sfungjér,-i *m.* sponge.

sfur/k,-ku *m.sh.* -qe pitch-fork.

si,-a *f. muz.* B, si.

si I. *ndajf.* 1. how; **si është babai?** how is your father? **si jeni?** how are you? how do you do? **si e kaluat kohën?** how did you spend your time? 2. what; **si ju quajnë?** what is your na-me? **si thatë?** what did you say? **si i thonë shqip?** what is the Albanian for?

II. *paraf. lidh.* 1. how; **të shohim si ju rri** *(një kostum)*; let us see how it fits you. 2. like, as; **ai luftoi si luan**: he fought like a lion; **si një nga aktivitetet kryesore**: as one of the main activities; **ai foli si gjykatës**: he spoke like a judge; **ju flas si shok**: I speak to you as a friend; **si të doni**: as you please, as you like; **si i ati dhe i biri**: like father, like son; **si gjithë mbiemrat e tjerë**: like any other adjectives; **duket si**: it looks like; **si kjo**: like this; **sillu si njeri**: behave like a man. 3. both; **si të trupit ashtu dhe të mendjes**: both of the body and the mind. 4. after; **si u kthye nga shkolla**: after returning from school. 5. somewhat; **m'u duk si i mërzitur**: he looked to me somewhat dispirited. − *Lok.* **ai përpiqet si e si t'ua kalojë shokëve**: he tries his best to overpass his comrades, he makes all efforts to overpass his fellows; **e gjeta si mos më keq**: I found him in a deplorable state; **si sot një javë**: this day week.

sič *lidh.* as; **siç e pamë**: as we have seen; **siç duhet**: in a proper manner, in a suitable manner.

sidokudó *ndajf.* in a rush, carelessly.

sidomós *ndajf.* especially, particularly.

sidóqë *lidh.* although; **sidoqë nuk e njoh**: although I don't know him.

sidoqóftë *lidh.* however, anyhow, in any case, at all events, after all.

sifilíz,-i *m. mjek.* syphilis.

sifilitík,-e *mb.* syphilitic.

sifón,-i *m.sh.* -ë siphon.

sigurés/ë,-a *f.sh.* -a cut-out.

sigurí,-a *f.* security; **me siguri**: surely, certainly, for certain.

sigurím,-i *m.* 1. security; **organet e sigurimit**: security forces. 2. insurance; **kontratë sigurimi**: insurance certificate; **sigurimet shoqërore**: social insurances; **sigurim kundër zjarrit**: fire insurance.

sigurísht *ndajf.* surely, certainly, for certain.

sigurój *f.k.* 1. *(nga një rrezik etj.)* to secure (against a danger, etc.). 2. to provide, to furnish, to supply oneself (with). − **sigurohem** *f.jv.* 1. *(nga një rrezik etj.)* to be secured. 2. to make sure; **sigurohu para se**: make sure before.

sígurt (i,e) *mb.* 1. sure, certain; **jam i sigurt**: I am sure. 2. secure; **në vend të sigurt**: in a secure place.

sigurúar (i,e) *mb.* insured; **person i siguruar**: insured person.

siharíq,-i *m.sh.* -e good tiding, good news.

sikërdís *f.k.* to send away.

siklét,-i *m.* anxiety, torment.

sikúndër *lidh.* as; **sikundër e dini**: as you know.

sikúr *lidh.* if, as if, as it were; **sikur të isha i ri**: if I was young; **ai bisedon sikur të ish**: he talks as if he were; **ai bën sikur s'di gjë**: he feigns to know nothing; **edhe sikur të ish e vërtetë**: even though it was true, even if it were true.

sikúrse *lidh.* as, like; **sikurse e shihni**: as you see.

sikúsh *p.pk.* anyone.

silázh,-i *m.sh.* -e fodder.

silazhím,-i *m.* ensilage.

silazhój *f.k.* to ensilage. − **silazhohet** *f.jv.* to be ensilaged.

silós,-i *m.sh.* -ë silo.

silúr,-i *m.sh.* -ë torpedo.

silurím,-i *m.* torpedoing.

silurój *f.k.* to torpedo. − **silurohet** *f.jv.* to be torpedoed.

síll/ë,-a *f.* breakfast.

simból,-i *m.sh.* -e symbol.

simbolík,-e *mb.* symbolic.

simbolizój *f.k.* to symbolize. − **simbolizohet** *f.jv.* to be symbolized.

për siguri   for safety's sake

síme (shih im) vajzës sime: to my daughter; e vajzës sime: of my daughter.

simetrí,-a *f.* symmetry.

simetrík,-e *mb.* symmetrical.

simfoní,-a *f.sh.* symphony.

simfoník,-e *mb.* symphonic; orkestër simfonike: symphonic orchestra.

slmít/e,-ja *f.sh.* -e bun (of bread), roll (of bread).

simót/ër,-ra *f.sh.* -ra *(gazeta)* contemporary (papers).

simpatí,-a *f.* sympathy.

simpatík,-e *mb.* sympathetic.

simpatizój *f.k.* to sympathize. – **simpatizohem** *f.jv.* to be sympathized.

simpatizúes,-i *m.sh.* – sympathiser.

simptomátík,-e *mb.* symptomatic.

simptóm/ë,-a *f.sh.* -a symptom.

sináp,-i *m. bot.* mustard; farë sinapi: grains of mustard.

slndikál,-e *mb.* syndicalistic.

sindikalíst,-i *m.sh.* -ë syndicalist.

sindikát/ë,-a *f.sh.* -a trade-union, syndicate.

siní,-a *f.sh.* – tray.

sinisí,-a *f.sh.* – gjeog. peninsula.

sinkópë,-a *m. mjek.* syncope.

sinoním,-i *m.sh.* -e synonym.

sinoptik,-e *mb.* synoptic.

sinór,-i *m.sh.* -ë vjet. limit, boundary.

sinqerísht *ndajf.* sincerely, frankly, openly, fairly, truthfully, truly, unfeignedly.

sinqeritét,-i *m.* sincerity, truthfulness, frankness, fairness, open-heartedness, openness; juaji me sinqeritet: yours truly.

sinqértë (i,e) *mb.* sincere, truthful, frank, candid, unaffected, open-hearted, open-minded, outspoken.

sintáks/ë,-a *f. gram.* syntax.

sintetík,-e *mb.* synthetic.

sintéz/ë,-a *f. kim.* synthesis.

sinús,-i *m. mat.* sine.

sinjál,-i *m.sh.* -e signal; jap sinjale: to make signals to.

sinjalizím,-i *m.* signalling.

sinjalizój *f.k.* to notify, to report. – **sinjalizohet** *f.jv.* to be notified (reported).

sinjalizúes,-i *m.sh.* – flagman, signalman.

slpás *paraf.* 1. according to, after; sipas të dhënave të: according to the data of; sipas një plani të caktuar: according to a definite plan; sipas autorit: according to the author; sipas rendit alfabetik: in alphabetical order; bëj diçka sipas një modeli: to do something after a model. 2. at; sipas dëshirës: at will. 3. in conformity to; sipas ligjit në fuqi: according to the law in force; sipas udhëzimeve të: in conformity with the instructions of.

sípër I. *ndajf.* above, on the top; on it, upon it, over it; vëri një letër sipër: put a paper over it; ngjitem sipër: to go upstairs; si më sipër: as above; në këtë e sipër: just then, meanwhile. II. *paraf.* on, upon, over, above; kapela është sipër tavolinës: the hat is on the table; ata banojnë sipër nesh: they dwell above us.

sipërfáq/e,-ja *f.sh.* -e 1. surface; në sipërfaqe: on the surface. 2. *mat.* surface.

sipërfaqësór,-e *mb.* superficial.

sipërfáqsh/ëm (i),-me (e) *mb.* superficial, shallow; ngjasim i sipërfaqshëm: a superficial resemblance.

sípërm(i),-e(e) *mb.* upper; kati i sipërm: the upper floor; në katin e sipërm: upstairs; pjesa e sipërme: the upper part.

sipërmárrës,-i *m.sh.* — undertaker, *(ndërtimi)* buildings contractor, masterbuilder.

sipërmárrj/e,-a *f.* undertaking.

sipërór,-e *mb. gram.* superlative; shkalla sipërore: superlative degree.

sipërpërméndur(i,e) *mb.* aforementioned, above-mentioned, afore-indicated, named before.

sipërthënë (i,e) *mb.* afore-said.

serén/ë,-a *f.sh.* -a 1. siren, 2. mermaid.

sirtár,-i *m.sh.* -e drawer (of a table, etc.).

sís/ë,-a *f.sh.* -a *anat.* breast, bosom; i jap sisë një foshnje: to suckle a child, to breast-feed a child, to give a child the breast.

foshnjë në sisë: suckling, a child at the breast.

sisór,-e *mb.* mammalian.

sisórë,-t *m.sh. zool.* mammalia, mammals.

sistém,-i *m.sh.* -e 1. system; pa sistem: without a system. 2. *pol.* system; sistemi feudal: feudal system. 3. *mjek., mat., astron.* system.

sistematík,-e *mb.* systematic, systematical.

sistematikísht *ndajf.* systematically.

sistemím,-i *m.* systematization.

sistemój *f.k.* to systematize. — sistemohet *f.jv.* to be systematized.

sit *f.k.* to sift; sit miell: to sift flour. — sitet *f.jv.* to be sifted.

sít/ë,-a *f.sh.* -a sieve.

sítj/e,-a *f.* sifting.

sitís *f.k.* to sift.

situát/ë,-a *f.sh.* -a situation.

siujdhés/ë,-a *f.sh.* -a *gjeog.* peninsula.

sivjét *ndajf.* this year.

sivjétsh/ëm (i), -me (e) *mb.* of this year.

sixhadé,-ja *f.sh.* — rug.

sizmík,-e *mb.* seismic.

sizmografí,-a *f.* seismography.

sizmologjí,-a *f.* seismology.

sjell *f.k.* (p.t. solla, p.p. sjellë) 1. to bring; ma sill atë lugë: bring me that spoon; sjell me vete: to bring with oneself; *(prej diku)* to fetch. 2. to cause, to bring about, to give; kjo më sjell kënaqësi: it gives me pleasure. 3. to turn. — *Lok.* sjell ndërmend: to remember, to call to one's mind; sjell në vete: to bring to life; sjell rrotull dikë: to delude someone, to beguile someone with promises. — sillem *f.jv.* 1. to behave, to bear oneself; sillem keq: to misbehave. 2. *(vërdallë)* to dawdle, to loaf, to loiter.

sjéllës,-i *m.sh.* — bringer, bearer, fetcher.

sjéllj/e,-a *f.* 1. behaviour, conduct; sjellje e mirë: good behaviour, well conduct; nxënës me sjellje të mira: a well-behaved pupil. 2. bringing, fetching.

sjéllsh/ëm(i), -me (e) *mb.* well-mannered, well-behaved.

skadím,-i *m. treg.* expiration, falling due (of a bill of exchange).

skadój *f.jk. treg.* to expire (a bill), to fall due.

skadúar(i,e) *mb.* 1. *(plaçkë)* worn out, spiled, damaged (clothes, things). 2. *fin.* due; kambial i skaduar: bill due.

skaj,-i *m.sh.* -e extremity, end.

skalít *f.k.* (p.t. skalita, p.p. skalitur) *(gurin)* to carve ; to cut (stone); *(drurin)* to engrave (on hard wood). — skalitet *f.jv.* to be carved (engraved, cut).

skalítës,-i *m.sh.* — carver, graver; *(guri)* carver, stone — cutter, engraver; *(druri)* carver on hard wood.

skalítj/e,-a *f,s.h.* **-e** engraving, carving; *(guri)* stone-cutting; *(druri)* carving on hard wood; *(metali)* chasing.

skámës,-i *m.sh.* – poor, poor man.

skámj/e,-a *f.* poverty; **rroj në skamje:** to live in poverty, to live from hand to mouth.

skandál,-i *m.sh.* **-e** scandal.

skandalizój *f.k.* to scandalize. – **skandalizohem** *f.jv.* to be scandalized.

skandalóz,-e *mb.* scandalous.

skárco,-ja *f.sh.* – discard, reject, throw-out; **mallra skarco:** rejects.

skár/ë,-a *f.sh.* **-a** 1. *(mishi etj)* gridiron; **pjek në skarë:** to broil upon a gridiron. 2. *(pori, stufe)* fire-grate. 3. *(për derdhjen e ujrave)* grate (for the leakage of waters).

skarlatín/ë,-a *f. mjek.* scarlet-fever.

skartím,-i *m.* throwing out, rejecting, discarding.

skartój *f.k.* to discard, to reject, to throw out.

skeç,-i *m.sh.* **-e** sketch.

skedár,-i *m.sh.* **-ë** 1. card-index, card-file. 2. card-index box.

skéd/ë,-a *f.sh.* **-a** filing-card, index-card, slip.

skelarí,-a *f.sh.* – scaffolding (of a building).

skelét,-i *m.sh.* **-ë** 1. *anat.* skeleton. 2. *(aeroplani, anijeje)* carcass (of an aircraft, of a ship); *(ndërtese)* carcass, frame-work (of a building).

skél/ë,-a *f.sh.* **-a** 1. *det.* wharf, quay, port; **zbres në skelë:** to land, to disembark. 2. *(ndërtimi)* scaffold (for building).

skematík,-e *mb.* schematic.

ském/ë,-a *f.sh.* **-a** scheme.

skén/ë,-a *f.sh.* **-a** 1. stage, scene; **vë në skenë:** to stage, to put on. 2. *fig.* scene, quarrel, row; **mos na bëj skena:** don't make a scene. – *Lok.* **dal nga skena:** to disappear from the scene; **dal në skenë:** to come on the scene.

sképt/ër,-ri *m.sh.* **-ra** scepter, sceptre.

skepticíz/ëm,-mi *m.* scepticism.

skeptík,-e *mb.* sceptic.

skërfít *f.k.* to scratch.

skërfítj/e,-a *f.* scratching.

skërfýell,-i *m.sh.* **-j** *anat.* windpipe, trachea.

skërk/ë,-a *f.sh.* **-a** abrupt land, crag, cliff.

skërmít *f.k. (dhëmbët)* to gnash (the teeth). – **skërmitem** *f.jv.* to gnash one's teeth.

skërmítj/e,-a *f.* gnashing of teeth.

skëtérr/ë,-a *f.* hell; **jetë skëterre:** hellish life, infernal life.

ski,-të *f.sh.* 1. ski; **një palë ski:** a pair of skis; **rrëshqas me ski:** to ski, to go skiing. 2. skiing; **ski mbi ujë:** water-skiing; **gara me ski:** skiing competition (contest).

skiatór,-i *m.sh.* **-ë** skier.

skíc/ë,-a *f.sh.* **-a** sketch, outline; **bëj skicën e një vizatimi:** to outline (to sketch) a picture.

skicój *f.k.* to outline, to delineate, to sketch.

skiftér,-i *m.sh.* **-ë** *zool.* hawk, falcon.

sklép/ë,-a *f.sh.* **-a** *mjek.* eye-rheum; **sy me sklepa:** bleary eyes.

skllav,-i *m.sh.* **skllevër** slave.

skllavërí,-a *f.* slavery.

skllavërím,-i *m.* enslavement.

skllavërój *f.k.* to enslave.– **skllavërohem:** to be enslaved.

skllavërúes,-e *mb.* enslaving.

skllotín/ë,-a *f.* sleet.

skocéz,-i *m.sh.* -e Scot, Scotsman, Scotchman.
skocéz,-e *mb.* Scottish, Scott, Scots, Scotch.
skocísht *ndajf.* in Scottish, in Scotch.
skolastík,-e *mb.* scholastic.
skorbút,-i *m. mjek.* scorvy.
skrófull,-a *f. mjek.* scrofula.
skuád/ër,-ra *f.sh.* -ra 1. *usht.* squad. 2. *sport.* team.
skúfj/e,-a *f.sh.* -e head-dress.
skulptór,-i *m.sh.* -ë sculptor.
skulptúr/ë,-a *f.* sculpture.
skumbrí,-a *f.sh.* – *zool.* mackerel.
skuq *f.k.* 1. to redden, to make red. 2. *(mishin)* to roast (meat). –
   skuqem *f.jv.* 1. *(nga turpi)* to blush, to flush 2. *(hekuri)* to become (to turn) red.
skúqj/e,-a *f.* 1. *(e lëkurës)* reddening (of the skin). 2. *(nga turpi)* blushing, blush. 3) *(e metalit)* reddening incandescence (of a metal). 4. *(e mishit)* roasting (of meat).
skurrjál/ë,-a *f.sh.* -a skeleton, bones of a dead body.
skút/ë,-a *f.sh.* -a 1. recess; **skutat e ndërgjegjes:** the recesses of the conscience. 2. nook.
skutín/ë,-a *f.sh.* -a *krah.* diaper.
slít/ë,-a *f.sh.* -a sleigh, sled; **rrëshqas me slitë:** to sledge.
sllav,-i *m.sh.* -ë Slav.
sllav,-e *mb.* Slavic, Slavonic, Slav.
smalt,-i *m.* 1. enamel. 2. *(në qeramikë)* glaze. 3. *(i dhëmbëve)* enamel.
smaltím,-i *m.* 1. enamelling. 2. glazing.
smaltój *f.k.* 1. to enamel. 2. to glaze.
smeráld,-i *m.sh.* -ë emerald.
smokíng,-u *m.sh.* -ë dinner-jacket.
snajpér,-i *m.sh.* -ë sharpshooter.
sobaxhí,-u *m.sh.* -nj stove-maker.
sób/ë,-a *f.sh.* -a stove, heater; **sobë me dru:** stove; *(elektrike*

e me gaz) heater.
sociál,-e *mb.* social.
socialíst,-e *mb.* socialist.
socializ/ëm,-mi *m.* socialism.
sociológ,-u *m.sh.* -ë sociologist.
sociologjí,-a *f.* sociology.
sód/ë,-a *f. kim.* soda, sodium carbonate; **sodë kaustike:** caustic soda.
sodit *f.k.* to gaze, to contemplate. –
sodítem *f.jv.* to be gazed (contemplated).
sodítës,-e *mb.* contemplative.
sodítj/e,-a *f.* gaze, contemplation.
sóf/ër,-ra *f.sh.* -ra 1. dining-table with short legs. 2. table; **shtroj sofrën:** to lay the table; **ngre sofrën:** to clear the table; **ulem në sofër:** to sit down to table; **sofër e pasur:** copious meal, copious repast.
sofrabéz,-i *m.sh.* -ë table-cloth.
soj,-i *m.sh.* -ë 1. kin, relative; **soj e sorollop:** the kith and kin. 2. kind, sort, species; **nga ai soj:** of that kind.
sojlí,-e *mb.* that descends of a good family, blue – blooded.
sojsëz,-e *mb.* knave, knavish.
sokák,-u *m.sh.* -ë *vjet.* street.
sokëllíj *f.jk.* to shriek, tp scream.
sokëllím/ë-a *f.sh.* -a shriek, scream, sharp and shrill outcry.
sokól,-i *m.sh.* -ë brave, valiant man.
solémn,-e *mb.* solemn.
solemnísht *ndajf.* solemnly.
solemnitét,-i *m.* solemnity.
solidár,-e *mb.* solidary.
solidarësí,-a *f.* solidarity.
solidaritét,-i *m.* shih **solidarësi.**
solidarizóhem *f.jv.* to solidarize
solíst,-i *m.sh.* -ë solist, solo singer.
sólo,-ja *f. muz.* solo.
solución,-i *m.sh.* -e solution.
somnambúl,-i *m.sh.* -ë sleepwalker, night-walker, somnambulist.

somnambulíz/ëm,-mi *m.* somna-
mbulism.
sondázh,-i *m.sh.* -e 1. sounding. 2.
fig. survey, poll, sampling test,
inquiry.
sónd/ë,-a *f.sh.* -a 1. *tek* grill. 2.
mjek. probe.
sondój *f.k.* to sound; to probe.
sónë *p.v.* our; e shkollës sonë:
of our school; e Partisë sonë:
of our Party (shih jonë, e).
sónte *ndajf.* tonight, this night.
sop,-i *m.sh.* -e 1. bung, plug of
cask. 2. low hill, rise, height.
sorkádh/e,-ja *f.sh.* -e *zool.* gazelle,
antelope.
sorrollát *f.k.* 1. *(një punë)* to hold
over, to lay over, to let (the
matter) stand, to procrastinate (a
work). 2. *(dikë)* to hold at bay,
to ward off (someone). — sorro-
llatem *f.jv.* to dally over, to
loiter, to gad about.
sorrollátj/e,-a *f.sh.* -e perambula-
tion; procrastination.
sos I. *f.k. vjet.* to finish, to achieve.
II. *f.jk.* to reach one's destination.
— sosem *f.jv.* to reach one's destination.
sósj/e,-a *f.* 1. arrival. 2. end, death;
po i vjen sosja: he is nearing his
end.
sot *ndajf.* today, this day; sot dy
javë: this day fortnight; sot
një javë: this day week; që sot
e tutje: from this day forth;
henceforth, henceforward.
sót/ëm(i),-me(e) *mb.* 1. of today,
of this day; që nga dita e sotme: from this day. 2. contemporary.
sótsh/ëm(i),-me(e) *mb.* shih i so-
tëm.
sovájk/ë,-a *f.sh.* -a shuttle (of a
sewing machine).
sovrán,-i *m.sh.* -ë sovereign.
sovrán,-e *mb.* sovereign.

sovranitét,-i *m.* sovereignty.
spalét/ë,-a *f.sh.* -a *usht.* shoulder
loop, shoulder board, epaulet(te).
spángo,-ja *f.* twine, string.
spanjísht *ndajf.* in Spanish.
spanjísht/e,-ja *f.* Spanish.
spanjóll,-i *m.sh.* -ë Spaniard.
spanjóll,-e *mb.* Spanish.
spastrím,-i *m.sh.* -e 1. cleansing,
purification; spastrim dherash:
cleansing of grounds. 2. *fig.*
purge.
spastrój *f.k.* 1. to cleanse, to scour,
to clean. 2. *fig.* to purge someone
off. — spastrohem *f.jv.* to
clean oneself.
spázm/ë,-a *f.sh.* -a *mjek.* spasm.
spec,-i *m.sh.* -a 1. *bot.* pepper; i
kuq spec: as red as a cherry,
as scarlet as fire. 2. *(pluhur)*
pepper.
specialíst,-i *m.sh.* -ë specialist.
speciál,-e *mb.* special.
specialitét,-i *m.sh.* -e speciality.
specializím,-i *m.* specialization.
specializój *f.k.* to specialize. —
specializohem *f.jv.* to be spe-
cialized.
specifík,-e *mb.* specific; pesha
specifike: specific weight.
specifikím,-i *m.* specification.
specifikój *f.k.* to specify. — specifi-
kohet *f.jv.* to be specified.
spektatór,-i *m.sh.* -ë by-stander,
looker-on, onlooker, beholder,
spectator.
spekulatór,-i *m.sh.* -ë speculator,
sponger.
spekulím,-i *m.sh.* -e speculation.
spekulój *f.k.* 1. to speculate. 2. to
take advantage of, to exploit (something). — spekulohet *f.jv.* to
be speculated; spekulohet me
paditurinë e njerëzve: to take
advantage of people's ignorance.
spérm/ë,-a *f. anat.* sperm.

spërëng/ë,-a *f.sh.* **-a** *bot.* asparagus.

spërkát *f.k.* 1. *(me baltë)* to splash, to spatter, to bespatter. 2. *(me ujë)* to sprinkle, to besprinkle. — **spërkatem** *f.jv.* 1. *(me baltë)* to splash oneself. 2. *(me ujë)* to sprinkle oneself.

spërkátj/e,-a *f.sh.* **-e** 1. *(me baltë)* spattering. 2. *(me ujë)* sprinkling.

spíc/ë,-a *f.sh.* **-a** 1. spill, splinter. 2. *fig.* intrigue; **fut spica:** to intrigue.

spíc *mb.* veshur spic *(krah.)*: elegantly dressed.

spikát *f.jk.* 1. to show up, to catch the eye, to be striking to be conspicuous. 2. to stand out (among, from), to tower (above); **ai spikat midis shokëve për zgjuarësinë që ka:** he towers above his companions in intelligence.

spikátës,-e *mb.* salient, prominent, conspicuous, noticeable.

spikátj/e,-a *f.* conspicuousness, prominence.

spináq,-i *m. bot.* spinach.

spirál/,e-ja *f.sh.* **-e** spiral.

spiránc/ë,-a *f.sh.* **-a** *det.* anchor; **hedh spirancën:** to cast the anchor, to let go the anchor, to drop the anchor.

spitál,-i *m.sh.* **-e** hospital; **spital fushor:** field-hospital; **spital psikiatrik:** madhouse, mental-home.

spiún,-i *m.sh.* **-ë** spy.

spiunázh,-i *m.* spying.

spiunòj *f.k.* to spy. — **spiunohem** *f. jv.* to be spied.

sport,-i *m.sh.* **-e** sport.

sportdáshës,-i *m.sh.* — sports lover, *faм ſīn general̲*

sportél,-i *m.sh.* **-a** ticket-window, box-office, booking — office.

sportelíst,-i *m.sh.* **-ë** cashier.

sportíst,-i *m.sh.* **-ë** sportsman.

sportív,-e *mb.* sportive; **gara sportive:** athletic contest.

spróv/ë,-a *f.sh.* **-a** test, proof; **vë në sprovë:** to test.

sprovój *f.k.* to test, to put to the poof. — **sprovohem** *f.jv.* to be put to the proof, to be tested.

spuntím,-i *m.* ticking.

spuntój *f.k.* to tick, to mark with a sign. — **spuntohet** *f.jv.* to be marked.

sqap,-i *m.sh.* **sqep.** *zool.* billy-goat.

sqarím,-i *m.sh.* **-e** explanation, elucidation, clarification.

sqarój *f.k.* to clarify, to explain, to elucidate, to clear up; to render intelligible (plain, evident). — **sqarohem** *f.jv.* 1. to explain oneself. 2. to be elucidated.

sqarúes,-e *mb.* explanatory; explicative explanatory notes.

sqarúesh/ëm(i),-me (e) *mb.* explainable.

sqep,-i *m.sh.* **-a** beak, bill (of birds).

sqepár,-i *m.sh.* **-ë** adze, adz.

sqótull,-a *f.sh.* **-a** *anat.* armpit, axilla.

sqím/ë,-a *f.* vanity, coquetry; **veshur me sqimë:** coquetly dressed.

sqoll,-i *m.sh.* **-e** sink.

sqúfur,-i *m. kim.* sulphur.

squfurór,-e *mb.* sulphureous.

squk/ë,-a *f.sh.* **-a** brood-hen, sitting-hen.

stabilimént,-i *m.sh.* **-e** establishment.

stabilitét,-i *m.* stability.

stabilizatór,-i *m.sh.* **-ë** stabilizer.

stabilizím,-i *m.* stabilization.

stabilizój *f.k.* to stabilize. — **stabilizohet** *f.jv.* to be stabilized.

stación,-i *m.sh.* **-e** station; **stacion hekurudhor;** railway station; **përgjegjës stacioni hekurudhor:** station-master; **stacion i fundit:** terminal station, terminus.

stadiúm,-i *m.sh.* -e stadium.
stafét/ë,-a *f.sh.* -a 1. *sport.* relay, relay race. 2. estafette.
stafídh/e,-ja *f.sh.* -e dried grape, currant raisin.
stáll/ë,-a *f.sh.* -a stable; **stallë lopësh:** ox-stable; **stallë kujash:** horse-stable; **stallë derrash:** pigsty; **pleh stalle:** stable dung.
stalliér,-i *m.sh.* -ë stable-man, stable-boy; *(kuajsh)* groom.
stan,-i *m.sh.* -e dairy-hut, shepherd's alpine summer hut.
stanár,-i *m.sh.* -ë stock-breeder, breeder of cattle; cheesemonger.
standárd,-i *m.sh.* -e standard.
standardizím,-i *m.* standardization.
standardizój *f.k.* to standardize. - **standardizohet** *f.jv.* to be standardized.
stap,-i *m.sh.* -ë *vjet.* stick.
statík/ë,-a *f.* statics.
statistík/ë,-a *f.* statistics.
statistikór,-e *mb.* statistic, statistical.
statúj/ë,-a *f.sh.* -a statue.
statút,-i *m.sh.* -e statute, charter.
stáv/ë,-a *f.sh.* -a heap, pile; **stavë me dru:** pile of wood.
stazh,-i *m.* probation.
stazhiér,-i *m.sh.* -ë probationer.
sték/ë,-a *f.sh.* -a cue (of billiard)
stél/ë,-a *f.sh.* -a kennel (for dogs).
stém/ë,-a *f.sh.* -a badge, blazon, emblem.
sténd/ë,-a *f.sh.* -a board.
stenográf,-i *m.sh.* -ë stenographer, shorthand writer.
stenografí,-a *f.* stenography, shorthand writing.
stenografój *f.k.* to stenograph, to write shorthand. — **stenografohet** *f.jv.* to be stenographed.
stépem *f.jv.* 1. to hesitate. 2. to abstain.
tép/ë -a *f.sh.* -a *gjeog.* steppe.

steré,-ja *f. vjet.* mainland.
sterlín/ë,-a *f.sh.* -a sterling, pound note.
stérn/ë,-a *f.sh.* -a tank, cistern.
stérrë *mb.* very black, pitch – black.
stetoskòp,-i *m,sh.* -ë *mjek.* stethoscope.
stërdhëmb,-i *m.sh.* -ë overtooth, irregular tooth.
stërgjýsh,-i *m.sh.* -ër ancestor, forefather; **stërgjyshërit tanë:** our ancestors, our progenitors, our forebears.
stërgjýsh/e,-ja *f.sh.* -e greatgrandmother, foremother, progenitress.
stërhóllë(i,e) *mb.* quibbling, hair splitting.
stërhollím,-i *m.* hair-splitting.
stërhollój *f.k.* to split hairs, to subtilize. – **stërhollohet** *f.jv.* to be subtilized.
stërmbés/ë,-a *f.sh.* -a greatgranddaughter.
stërníp,-i *m.sh.* -ër great-grandson, grand nephew, great-nephew; **stërnipërit tanë:** our descendants
stërqók,-u *m.sh.* -ë *zool.* male of jackdaw.
stërqók/ë,-a *f.sh.* -a *zool.* jackdaw.
stërvít *f.k.* to train, to drill, to practise. – **stërvitem** *f.jv.* to train oneself.
stërvítj/e,-a *f.* training, exercise; **stërvitje ushtarake:** drill, military training.
stil,-i *m.sh.* -e style.
stilistík,-e *mb.* stylistic.
stilistík'ë,-a *f.* stylistics.
stilográf,-i *m.sh.* -ë fountain pen.
stilokalém,-i *m.sh.* -a ball point pen.
stiloláps,-i *m.sh.* -a shih **stilokalem.**
stimu/l,-li *m.sh.* -j stimulus, incentive.

stimulój *f.jv.* to incite, to urge, to stir, to prod, to stimulate.

stín/ë,-a *f.* season; **stina e shirave**: the rainy season; **fruta të stinës**: fruits in season.

stív/ë,-a *f.sh.* -a heap, pile.

stivím,-i *m.* heaping.

stivój *f.k.* to heave, to pile up. – **stivohet** *f.jv.* to be heaped.

stof,-i *m.sh.* -ëra cloth, tissue, stuff, textile fabric; *(i hollë leshi)* crepon; **stof leshi me kutia**: plaid, checkered woolen cloth.

stoicíz/ëm,-mi *m.* stoicism.

stoík,-u *m.sh.* -ë stoic.

stoík,-e *mb.* stoic.

stok,-u *m.sh.* **stoqe** stock, stockpile; **stoqe mallrash**: stock of wares.

stol,-i *m.sh.* -a stool.

stolí,-a *f.sh.* – trimings, ornaments.

stolís *f.k.* to ornament, to adorn, to trim, to dress out, to deck, to bedeck, to set off, to decorate. – **stolisem** *f.jv.* to adorn (to deck) oneself.

stolísj/e,-a *f.* trimming, ornamentation.

stomák,-u *m.sh.* -ë *anat.* stomach; **inflamacion i stomakut**: gastritis; **mbush stomakun**: to have one's fill; **me stomakun bosh**: with an empty stomach.

stómn/ë,-a *f.sh.* -a jar pitcher. – *Lok.* **bie shi me stomna**: it rains cats and dogs.

stoním,-i *m.* dissonance, discord, discordance.

stonój *f.jk.* to be out of tune.

stonúes,-e *mb.* dissonant, discordant, out of tune.

stopán,-i *m.sh.* -ë cheesemonger.

strájc/ë,-a *f.sh.* -a bag, small sack

strall,-i *m.* flintstone.

stratég,-u *m.sh.* -ë strategist.

strategjí,-a *f.* strategy.

strategjík,-e *mb.* strategic.

streh/ë,-a *f.sh.* -ë 1. eaves. 2. edge; *(kapele)* visor (of a hat); *(kaskete)* peak (of a cap). 3. *(banesë)* shelter, shed; lodging; **gjej strehë**: to take shelter, to take refuge; **pa strehë**: unsheltered, bleak.

strehím,-i *m.* 1. accomodation. 2. refuge, shelter; **strehim politik**: political asylum.

strehój *f.k.* 1. to accomodate, to lodge, to harbour. – **strehoem** *f.jv.* to put up at; to take shelter (lodging).

strehúes,-e *mb.* accomodating.

stríng/ël-la *f.sh.* -la knick-knack, trinket.

stróf/ë.-a *f.sh.* -a strophe, stanza.

strófu/ll,-lli *m.sh.* -j lair (of wild beast), den; *(lepuri etj.)* burrow.

stróm/ë,-a *f.sh.* -a mattress.

struc,-i *m.sh.* -ë *zool.* ostrich.

strúkem *f.jv.* 1. to hide oneself. 2. to crouch, to creep into, to squat down.

struktúr/ë,-a *f.* structure.

strumbullár,-i *m. sh.* -ë pivot.

studént,-i *m.sh.* -ë student, collegian, undergraduate; **student i vitit të parë**: fresher, freshman, a first-year studroom.

studím,-i *m.sh.* -e study, learning; **dhomë studimi**: study-room.

stúdio,-ja *f.sh.* – studio; artist's work-room.

studiój *f.jk.* to study, to learn. – **studjohet** *f.jv.* to be studied.

studiúes,-i *m.sh.* – scholar.

studiúes,-e *mb.* studious.

stúf/ë-a *f.sh.* -a stove; **stufë ekonomike (kuzhine)**: kitchenrange, cooking-range, kitchener.

stuhi,-a *f.sh.* – storm, tempest, squall, gust, hurricane, thunderstorm; **stuhi dëbore**: snowstorm, blizzard; (e fortë në oqean) typhoon, tornado.

stuhish/ëm(i),-me (e) mb. stormy, squally, tempestous; **det i stuhishëm:** stormy sea.

stúko,-ja f. lute, putty; **zë me stuko:** to lute, to putty, to cement with putty.

stukój f.k. to lute, to putty.

súaj p.pr. your, of your; **oborri i shkollës suaj:** your schoolyard; **i thashë vajzës suaj:** I told your daughter.

suáz/ë,-a f. cadre, framework.

subjékt,-i m.sh. -e subject.

subjektív,-e mb. subjective; **arsye subjektive;** subjective reasons.

subvención,-i m.sh. -e subvention, subsidy.

subvencionój f.k. to subsidize, to give subvention (to).

suedéz,-i m.sh. -ë Swedish.

suedéz,-e mb. Swedish.

suedísht/e,-ja f. Swedish.

suferín/ë,-a f. vortex, gale, whirlwind.

suficít,-i m. surplus.

suflér,-i m.sh. -ë (teatri) prompter (of a theater).

sugjerím,-i m.sh. -e suggestion.

sugjerój f.k. to suggest. – **sugjerohet** f.jv. to be suggested.

suít/ë,-a f.sh. -a suite, attendants.

suksés,-i m.sh. -e success; **korr (kam, dal me) sukses:** to succeed, to be successful; **pa sukses:** without success; **nuk kam sukses:** to be unsuccessful; **arrij suksese:** to reach successes.

sukséssh/ëm(i),-me (e) mb. successful.

súlem f.jv. to rush, to dash, to dash forward; **sulem mbi armikun:** to rush at the enemy, to fall upon the enemy.

sulfát,-i m.sh. -e kim. sulphate.

sulín/ë,-a f.sh. -a krah. pipe, tube.

sulm,-i m.sh. -e 1. assail, assault, attack; (i befasishëm) sally; (i përgjakshëm) onslaught; **marr me sulm:** to take by attack (by assault, by storm); **hidhem, kaloj në sulm:** to take a offensive. 2. fig. sally, sudden outburst of work; **muaj sulmi:** a month of intensive work, the month of assault; **në sulm!** ahead!

sulmím,-i m. agression, assailing.

sulmój f.k. to attack; (në befasi) to sally. – **sulmohem** f.jv. to be assailed (attacked).

sulmúes,-i m.sh. – assailant, assaulter.

sulmúes,-e mb. assailant, assaulting, attacking; **brigadë sulmuese:** shock-brigade; **punëtor sulmues:** shock-worker.

súmbull,-a f.sh. -a button.

sundim,-i m.sh. -e rule, domination; **sundim i botës:** world hegemony.

sundimtár,-i m.sh. -ë ruler.

sundój f.k. to rule, to reign. – **sundohem** f.jv. to be dominated (subdued).

sundúes,-i m.sh. – ruler.

sundúes,-e mb. ruling; **klasat sunduese:** the ruling classes.

sup,-i m.sh. -e anat. shoulder; **mbledh supet:** to shrug one's shoulders; **sup më sup:** shoulder to shoulder.

superfuqí,-a f.sh. – superpower.

superprodhím,-i m. over-production.

supersticióz,-e mb. superstitious.

superstruktúr/ë,-a f. superstructure.

súp/ë,-a f.sh. -a soup, broth; **supë me barishte:** vegetable soup; **supë me lëng mishi:** beef-tea, meat-soup; **supë peshku:** fish-soup; **supë pule:** chicken-

broth; **pjatë supe**: soup-plate.
supiér/ë,-a *f.sh.* -a soup-tureen.
suplementár,-e *mb.* supplementary; **rrogë suplementare**: perquisite.
supór/e,-ja *f.sh.* -e shoulder-strap, epaulet.
supozím,-i *m.sh.* -e supposition, hypothesis.
supozój *f.k.* to suppose; **le të supozojmë**: let us suppose. — **supozohet** *f.jv.* to be supposed.
suprimój *f.k.* to abolish, to do away with; **suprimoj një post**: to do away with a post. — **suprimohet** *f.jv.* to be abolished, to be done away with.
súrbull *mb.* **vezë surbull**: halfboiled egg.
surpriz/ë-a *f.sh.* -a surprise.
surrát.-i *m.sh.* **surretër** *gj. bis.* face.
surrogát,-i *m.sh.* -e surrogate, substitute, replacement; **kafe surrogat**: coffee surrogate, ersatz coffee.
súst/ë,-a *f.sh.* -a 1. spring; **krevat me sustë**: spring bed; **sustë krevati**: spring mattress. 2. *el.* button; **shkel sustën**: to press the button.
sút/ë,-a *f.sh.* -a *zool.* doe, hind.
suvá,-ja *f.* plaster; **vë suva**: to plaster.
suvatím,-i *m.* plastering.
suvatój *f.k.* to plaster. — **suvatohet** *f.jv.* to be plastered.
suvatúes,-i *m.sh.* — plasterer.
suxhúk,-u *m.sh.* -ë sausage.
sy,-ri *m.sh.* — *anat.* 1. eye; **bebja e syrit**: the pupil of the eye, the apple of the eye; **gropa (zgavra) e syrit**: eyehole, socket of the eye, cavity of the eye, orbit; **kapaku i syrit**: eyelid; **dhëmbi i syrit**: eyetooth; **me një sy**: one-eyed; **pa sy**: blind, eyeless,

sightless; **më dhembin sytë**: I have an eye-ache; **më lotojnë sytë**: my eyes run; **sy çakërr**: squint eyes; **sy të skuqur**: bloodshot eyes; **sy të sëmurë**: sore eyes; **sy të përlotur**: eyes moistened with tears; **sy të zgurdulluar**: bulging eyes, goggle eyes; **zgurdulloj sytë**: to goggle, to stare, to strain the eyes, to look with fixed eyes wide upon; **kapsallit sytë**: to wink the eyes, to winkle the eyes; **i nxjerrin sytë njëri-tjetrit**: they tear away their eyes, they quarrel with one another. 2. sight; **drita e syrit**: eye sight; **ngelem pa sy**: to lose the sight. — *Lok.* **hap sytë!** look out! be on your guard! beware of! pay attention! take care! **mbyll sytë**: to close one's eyes; **laj sytë**: to wash one's face; **ngre sytë**: to look up; **ngul sytë**: to fix the eyes upon; **i shkel syrin dikujt**: to wink at someone; **ul sytë**: to look down; **shikoj me bishtin e syrit**: to look from the corner of the eye; **hedh sytë**: to look; **hedh një sy**: to cast a glance (a look); **i hedh një sy gazetës**: to cast (to take) a glance at the newspaper; **i hedh një sy të kaluarës**: to look back on; **i hedh hi syve dikujt**: to throw dust in a person's eyes; **në sy**: in the face; **sy ndër sy**: face to face; **në sy të të gjithëve**: in the face of all; **shikoj në sy dikë**: to look someone in the face; **ia them në sy**: to say in the face; **bie në sy**: to attract attention; **që bie në sy**: showy; **sa çel e mbyll sytë**: in the winking of an eye; **sa të ha syri**: within sight, as far as the eye can reach; **si e ke syrin?**

which is your intention? **më ra
në sy:** It caught my eye; **nuk
shikoj mirë nga sytë:** I don't
see well; **nuk kam mbyllur
sy gjithë natën:** I did not
have a wink all night, I did
not sleep a wink all night; **bëj
(marr) një sy gjumë:** to nap;
i bëj sytë katër: to be all eyes;
me sy hapur: open-eyed; **më
qan syri për të:** I have set my
heart upon it (him, her); **m'u
errën sytë:** my eyes were dazzled;
**më marrin me sy të mirë
(diku):** to be in someone's
good graces; **ha me sy:** to
gloat; **sy i lig:** bad look;
marr sytë e këmbët: to make
one's escape, to make away, to
go away, to withdraw; **bëj një
sy të verbër:** to close one's eyes
to. – *Prov.* **më mirë (të të dalë)
syri se nami:** better to lose
one's eye than one's good name.
sybárdhë *mb.* white-eyed.
syçákërr,-e *mb.* squint-eyed, goggle-eyed.
syhápur *mb.* open-eyed, vigilant,
wide-awake.
syjeshíl *mb.* green-eyed.
sykáltër *mb.* blue-eyed.
sylarúsh,-e *mb.* shih **sykaltër.**
sylésh,-e *mb.* ninny.

symbýllazi *ndajf.* blindly.
symbýllthi *ndajf.* shih **symbyllazi.**
symbýllur *mb.* close-eyed.
sympréhtë *mb.* lynx-eyed.
synét,-i *m.* circumcision; **bëj sy-
net:** to circumcise.
syním,-i *m.sh.* -e aim, purpose,
intention.
synój *f.jk.* to aim at, to attempt. –
synohet *f.jv.* to be aimed (at).
sypatrémbur *mb.* intrepid.
sypetrít *mb.* hawk-eyed.
sypíshë *mb.* watchful, vigilent.
syrgjýn,-i *m.* exile.
syrgjynós *f.k.* to banish, to deport.
– **syrgjynosem** *f.jv.* to be bani-
shed (deported).
syrgjynósj/e,-a *f.* banishment, deportation.
syrgjynósur (i,e) *mb.* outlandish,
deported.
syshqipónjë *mb.* eagle-eyed.
syshtrémbër *mb.* squint-eyed,
goggle-eyed.
sytliáç,-i *m.* rice-pudding.
syth,-i *m.sh.* -a 1. *bot.* bud. 2.
(çorapi, rrjetë) mesh (of a net,
of stockings).
sýze,-t *f.sh.* spectacles, eye-glasses,
glasses; **syze dielli:** sunglasses.
sýzë *mb.* vezë **syzë:** poached egg.
sýz/ë,-a *f.sh.* -a *(tavoline)* drawer
(of a table).
syz/i-ézë *mb.* black-eyed.

SH

sh, Sh (letter of the Albanian
alphabet) sh, Sh.
shabllón,-i *m.sh.* -e stencil.
shafrán,-i *m. bot.* saffron; **i hi-**

dhur shafran: as bitter as
saffron.
shah,-u *m.* chess, check; **gurë
shahu:** chessmen; **fushë shahu:**

chessboard; **luaj shah**: to play chess.
shah,-u *m.sh.* **-ë** shah.
shahíst,-i *m.sh.* **-ë** chess-player.
shahít,-i *m.sh.* **-ë** *vjet.* witness.
shaj *f.k.* 1. to. offend, to insult, to defame, to inveigh; *(prapa krahëve)* to backbite. 2. to scold, to chide, to reproach; **atë do ta shajnë për këtë sjellje**: he will be scolded for this conduct. — **shahem** *f.jv.* 1. to be offended (scolded). 2. *(me dikë)* to quarrel (with someone).
shaják,-u *m.* felt.
shajáktë (i,e) *mb.* felty; **rroba të shajakta**: felty clothes.
shájk/ë,-a *f.sh.* **-a** rivet; **ngul një shajkë**: to rivet.
shajní,-a *f.* hallucination, vision.
shaká,-ja *f.sh.* — joke, jest; **shaka me kripë**: witty joke; **bëj shaka**: to joke, to jest; **ai nuk di shaka**: he cannot see the joke; **për shaka**: for fun, for sport.
shakaxhí,-u *m.sh.* **-nj** joker, jester, punster.
sháku/ll,-lli *m.sh.* **-j** leather bottle; **shakull djathi**: cheese-skin.
shakullím/ë,-a *f.* whirlwind, vortex.
shál/ë,-a *f.sh.* **-ë** 1. *(kali)* saddle (of a horse); **kalë me shalë**: saddle-horse; **i vë shalë kalit**: to saddle a horse. 2. *anat.* thigh.
shalëgjátë *mb.* lanky, long-legged.
shalój *f.k.* to saddle. — **shalohet** *f.jv.* to be saddled.
shalqí,-ri *m.sh.* **-nj** *bot.* watermelon.
shall,-i *m.sh.* **-e** shawl; scarf; *(qafe)* neckerchief, scarf, neckcloth; *(i madh)* shawl.
shallváre,-t *f.sh.* slacks.
shamataxhí,-u *m.sh.* **-nj** boisterous person.
shamát/ë,-a *f. gj. bis.*din, bustle, jangle; **bëj shamatë**: to jangle.

shamí,-a *f.sh.* — handkerchie f; *(koke)* kerchief, mantilla; **sham i pionieri**: red tie; *(qafe)* scarf, neckerchief.
shamót,-i *m.* fire-clay.
shampánj/ë,-a *f.* champagne, *fam.* fizz.
shámpo,-ja *f.* shampoo; **laj flokët me shampo**: to shampoo one's hair.
shandán,-i *m.sh.* **-ë** candleholder, candelstick.
shantázh,-i *m.sh.* **-e** threat, menace.
shap,-i *m. kim.* alum.
shápk/ë,-a *f.sh.* **-a** 1. cap; *(ushtari me strehë)* kepi. 2. sliper. 3. *zool.* snipe, woodcock.
shaptilográf,-i *m.sh.* **-ë** mimeograph.
shaptilografój *f.k.* to mimeograf. — **shaptilografohet** *f.jv.* to be mimeographed.
shaptór/e,-ja *f.sh.* **-e** *zool.* woodcock.
sharapíqem *f.jv.* to writhe.
shár/ë/ë,-a(e) *f.sh.* **-a (të)** insult, offense; reproach; **s'ka të sharë**: it is unreproachable.
shárj/e,-a *f.sh.* **-e** insult, bad language.
sharlatán,-i *m.sh.* **-ë** charlatan, mountebank; **prej sharlatanësh**: quackish.
sharlataníz/ëm,-mi *m.* quackery, charlatanism.
shartím,-i *m.sh.* **-e** grafting; **thikë shartimi**: grafting-knife.
shartój *f.k.* to graft. — **shartohet** *f.jv.* to be grafted.
shárr/ë,-a *f.sh.* **.a** 1. saw; **sharrë dore**: handsaw. 2. *(pylli)* sawmill.
sharrëxhí,-u *m.sh.* **-nj** sawyer.
shárrëz,-a *f. mjek.* tetanus.
sharrím,-i *m.sh.* **-e** sawing.
sharrój l. *f.jk.* to saw. — **sharrohet** *f.jv.* to be sawed.

II. *f.jk. (për të ngrënë)* to be dying of hunger.
shasí,-a *f.sh.* — chassis.
shastís *f.k.* 1. to stun. 2. to astonish, to astound. — **shastisem** *f.jv.* 1. to be stunned. 2. to be astonished.
shastísj/e,-a *f.* 1. astonishment. 2. giddiness, dizziness.
shastísur (i,e) *mb.* 1. astonished. 2. absent-minded; **njeri i shastisur:** absent-minded person.
shát/ë,-a *f.sh.* -a hoe: **punoj me shatë:** to hoe.
shatërván,-i *m.sh.* -e fountain.
shavár,-i *m. bot.* sedge.
shebój/ë,-a *f.sh.* -a *bot.* gillyflower.
shef,-i *m.sh.* -a chief.
sheftelí,-a *f.sh.* — *bot.* peach; *(druri)* peach-tree.
shegért,-i *m.sh.* -ë apprentice.
shég/ë,-a *f.sh.* -ë *bot.* pomegranate.
shejtán,-i *m.sh.* -ë 1. devil, shaitan, sheitan. 2. *fig.* wayward child.
shejtanllë/k,-ku *m.sh.* -qe devilry, witchcraft.
shéku/ll,-lli *m.sh.* -j century.
shekullór,-e *mb.* secular, centennial; century-old.
shelég,-u *m.sh.* -ë *zool.* lamb above one year.
shelg,-u *m.sh.* -gje *bot.* willow; **shelg lotues:** weeping willow.
shelgjísht/ë,-a *f.sh.* -a willow grove, salicetum.
shelgjisht/ër,-ra *f.sh.* -ra *bot.* wicker.
shemb *f.k.* 1. to demolish, to pull down, to destroy. 2. *mjek. (një gjymtyrë të trupit)* to contuse *(a member of the body).* — **shembet** *f.jv.* 1. to be demolished, to fall down; **shembet nga pesha:** to be overthrown

under weight. 2. to be contused.
shémbj/e,-a *f.* 1. demolition, falling down. 2. *mjek.* contusion. 3. *(e një perandorie)* downfall *(of an empire).*
shémbu/ll,-lli *m.sh.* -j example, instance; **për shembull:** for instance; **bëhem shembull për:** to set an example for; **marr shembull:** to follow someone's example.
shembullór,-e *mb.* exemplary, model; **grua shembullore:** model wife; **sjellje shembullore:** exemplary behaviour (conduct).
shémbur (i,e) *mb.* 1. demolished. 2. contused.
shém/ër,-ra *f.sh.* -ra rival.
shemërí,-a *f.* rivalry.
shénj/ë,-a *f.sh.* -a 1. *(plage)* cicatrice, scar, mark. 2. *(gjurmë)* trace, track. 3. *(qitjeje)* target, aim. 4. *(dalluese)* mark, distinctive mark, sign. 5. *(dashurie, miqësie, kujtimi)* token; **në shenjë dashurie (miqësie):** as a token of love (of friendship). 6. **shenjë pikësimi:** punctuation mark. 7. omen; **shenjë e mirë:** good omen. 8. *(në fytyrë)* beauty-spot. 9. *(sëmundjeje)* symptom (of a malady). 10. *(sinjalizimi)* signal. — *Lok.* **marr shenjë:** to take aim; **qëlloj në shenjë:** to hit the bull's eye, to hit the mark; **nuk qëlloj në shenjë:** to shoot wide of the mark; **bëj shenjë me dorë:** to make signal with the hand, to beckon; **bëj shenjë me gisht:** to point; **bëj shenjë me kokë:** to nod; **bëj shenjë me sy:** to wink, to winkle; **jap shenjë:** to signal.
shenjt,-i *m.sh.* -ë saint.
shénjtë (i,e) *mb.* 1. *fet.* holy. 2. sacred; **kufijtë e shenjtë të**

atdheut tonë: the sacred borders of our Homeland.

shenjtërí,-a *f.* holiness, saintliness; **Shenjtëria Juaj:** Your Holiness, Your Worship.

shenjtërím,-i *m.* sanctification.

shenjtërój *f.k.* to sanctify; to hallow, to consecrate. — **shenjtërohet** *f.jv.* to be hallowed.

shenjtërúar (i,e) *mb.* sanctified.

shenjtór,-i *m.sh.* -ë saint.

sheqér,-i *m.* 1. sugar, **sheqer kokërr:** lump sugar; **sheqer pluhur:** granulated sugar; **fabrikë sheqeri:** sugar refinery; **kallam sheqeri:** sugar-cane; **panxhar sheqeri:** sugar-beet; **prodhime sheqeri:** sweetmeats. 2. *mjek.* **sëmundje e sheqerit:** diabetes.

sheqérk/ë,-a *f.sh.* -a candy, goody, sugar-candy, sweet-meat.

sheqerór,-e *mb.* sugary.

sheqerós *f.k.* to sugar, to sugar-coat. — **sheqeroset** *f.jv.* to be sweetened (candied), to become candied (sugary).

sheqerósj/e,-a *f.* sugariness.

sheqerósur (i,e) *mb.* sugared, sugar-coated.

sheqerxhí,-u *m.sh.* -nj confectioner.

sherbét,-i *m.* 1. syrup. 2. *(sherbet gëlqereje)* white-lime, whitewash; **lyej me sherbet gëlqereje:** to white-wash.

shermashék,-u *m.sh.* -ë *bot.* ivy.

sherménd,-i *m. bot.* vine-branch.

sherr,-i *m.sh.* -e quarrel, wrangle; **mollë sherri:** bone of discord; **e pushuan sherrin:** they made up their quarrel.

sherrxhí,-u *m.sh.* -nj pugnacious person.

sherrxh/í,-éshë *mb.* pugnacious, quarrelsome.

shes *f.k.* to sell; **shes me pakicë:** to retail; **shes me shumicë:** to sell wholesale; **shes me humbje:** to sell at loss; **shes në ankand:** to sell by auction, to auction; *(rrugëve ose fshat më fshat)* to hawk about. — **shitet** *f.jv.* to be sold. — *Lok.* **shes mend:** to give oneself airs.

shesh,-i *m.sh.* -e square, place (of a city); *(brenda pyllit)* glade (in a forest). — *Lok.* **gjej shesh e bëj përshesh:** to take advantage of to abuse (something).

shesh *ndajf.* horizontally.

sheshím,-i *m.* levelling.

shéshit *ndajf.* 1. on the surface. 2. plainly, clearly.

sheshój *f.k.* 1. to make even, to level; to smooth down. 2. *fig.* to smooth down, to smooth over. — **sheshohet** *f.jv.* to become smooth, to smooth down.

shëllír/ë,-a *f.* brine, pickle; **vë në shëllirë:** to cure, to put into brine.

shëmbëlléj *f.jk.* to resemble.

shëmbëllím,-i *m.sh.* -e 1. resemblance. 2. image.

shëmbëlltýr/ë,-a *f.sh.* -a image.

shëmták,-e *mb.* ugly, unsightly, deformed.

shëmtí,-a *f.* ugliness, deformity.

shëmtím,-i *m.* shih shëmti.

shëmtír/ë,-a *f.* shih shëmti.

shëmtój *f.k.* to make ugly, to disfigure, to deform, to deface. — **shëmtohem** *f.jv.* to grow ugly (unsightly), to be disfigured (deformed).

shëmtúar (i,e) *mb.* 1. ugly, unsightly. 2. hideous; **krim i shëmtuar:** hideous crime, horrible crime, horrid crime; **vepër e shëmtuar:** disgraceful act.

shëndét,-i *m.* health; **jam mirë me shëndet:** to enjoy good health, to be well; **shëndeti juaj!** your health! **për shëndetin e :** to the health of!..., here's to the health of!... **me shëndet!** all health! **shëndet paç!** health to you also! the same to you!

shëndetësí,-a f. public health, sanitation.

shëndetësór,-e mb. sanitary, medical, health; **në gjendje të mirë shëndetësore:** in good health; **shërbimi shëndetësor:** health service.

shëndetlíg,-ë mb. sickly, unhealthy.

shëndétsh/ëm(i),-me (e) mb. 1. healthy, healthful, hale, sound, wholesome, in good health; **klimë e shëndetshme:** healthy climate; **njeri i shëndetshëm:** healthy person. 2. salubrous; **klimë e shëndetshme:** salubrous climate; **vend i shëndetshëm:** salubrious place.

shëndósh f.k. 1. to heal, to cure. 2. to make stronger. 3. to fat, to fatten. − **shëndoshem** f.jv. to be healed. 2. to get stronger. 3. to grow fat.

shëndóshë ndajf. sound, hale; **jam shëndoshë e mirë:** I enjoy good health; **të vesh shëndoshë!** good trip!

shëndóshë (i,e) mb. 1. hale, sound; **mendje e shëndoshë në trup të shëndoshë:** a sound mind in a sound body. 2. strong, vigorous, stout. 3. fat, thick, plump, corpulent.

shëndóshj/e,-a f. fatness, stoutness, plumpness, obesity.

shëním,-i m.sh. **-e** annotation, note: **mbaj shënime:** to take down notes; **fletore shënimesh:** note-book.

shënój f.k. 1. (një fjalë) to put down, to note down (a word).

2. (me bojë) to mark. 3. (me pushkë) to take aim. 4. (një gol) to score (a goal). − **shënohet** f.jv. 1. to be noted. 2. to be marked. 3. to be scored.

shënúar(i,e) mb. 1. marked; noted. 2. memorable; **ngjarje e shënuar:** important event, memorable event.

shënjést/ër,-ra f.sh. **-ra** usht. sight.

shërbéj f.jk., f.k. 1. to serve, to wait on, to wait upon, to attend; **i shërbej vendit:** to serve one's country; **shërbej drekën:** to serve the dinner; **i shërbej një klienti:** to serve a customer, to wait on a client. 2. to be of use; **përse shërben kjo?** what is the use of it? **kjo shërben për:** it is used for; **kjo nuk shërben për asgjë:** it is of no use (of no avail, out of use). − **shërbehem** f.jv. to be waited on, to be served.

shërbëtór,-i m.sh. **-ë** vjet. servant.

shërbëtór/e,-ja f.sh. vjet. **-e** maid, housemaid, servant maid.

shërbím,-i m.sh. **-e** 1. service; **shërbim ushtarak:** military service; **thirrem në shërbim ushtarak:** to be called up. 2. duty, service; **jam me shërbim:** to be on duty; **jam në shërbimin tuaj:** I am at your service. 3. favour, service; **ju lutem më bëni një shërbim:** please, do me a service (a favour).

shërbýes,-i m.sh. − servant, valet.

shërbýes/e,-ja f.sh. **-e** servant-maid.

shërím,-i m. recovery; **pa shërim:** without remedy; **shkoj drejt shërimit:** to be well on the way to recovery.

shërój f.k. to heal, to cure, to restore to health. - **shërohem** f.jv. to be cured (healed), to recover one's health.

shërúes,-i *m.sh.* – healer; **koha është shërues i madh**: time is a great healer.
shërúes,-e *mb.* curative.
shërúesh/ëm(i),-me (e) *mb.* curable, remediable, healable.
shët! *pasth.* hush!
shëtít *f.jk.* to walk, to go for a walk, to stroll, to promenade; **shëtis me kalë**: to ride, to go for a ride (on horseback); **shëtis me makinë**: to take a drive; *(me varkë)* to boat.
shëtítës,-e *mb.* ambulant, ambulatory; **shitës shëtitës**: hawker, pedler.
shëtítj/e,-a *f.* walk, stroll, promenade; **bëj një shëtitje**: to take a walk, to go for a walk; *(me makinë)* drive; *(me kalë, me biçikletë)* ride (on bicycle, on horseback); *(me varkë)* cruise; *(e gjatë)* excursion, long promenade, long walk.
shëtitór/e,-ja *f.sh.* -e avenue, boulevard.
shfajësím,-i *m.sh.* -e justification.
shfajësój *f.k.* to justify. – shfajësohem *f.jv.* to justify oneself.
shfaq *f.k.* 1. to display, to show (a spectacle); to exhibit. 2. *(dashuri, gëzim, urrejtje)* to manifest (love, joy, hate). 3. *(mendime)* to give, to state, to voice (one's opinion). – shfaqem *f.jv.* to show up, to appear; **shfaqem befas**: to spring up.
shfáqj/e,-a *f. sh.* -e 1. performance, show, spectacle, play; **shkoj në shfaqje**: to go to a play. 2. *(dashurie, urrejtjeje, gëzimi)* display, manifestation (of love, of hate, of joy). 3. *(mendimi)* stating, voicing (of one's opinion).
shfarós *f.k.* to exterminate, to wipe out, to destroy completely. – shfarosem *f.jv.* to be exterminated (wiped out, destroyed).

shfarósës,-e *mb.* exterminating, destroying.
shfarósës,-i *m.sh.* exterminator, destroyer.
shfarósj/e,-a *f.* extermination, wiping out, whole destruction; **kampet naziste të shfarosjes**: Nazi extermination camps
shfletím,-i *m.* foliation, leafing (of a book).
shfletój *f.k. (një libër)* to turn over the leaves (of a book); to glance (to skim) through (a book). -shfletohet *f.jv. (një libër)* to be glanced through.
shfrej *f.jk.* to fly into a passion, to wreak; **shfrej dufin, inatin**: to wreak one's passion, one's anger.
shfrenój *f.k.* to unbridle. – shfrenohet *f.jv.* to be unbridled.
shfrenúar (i,e) *mb.* uncontrolled, unbridled.
shfronësím,-i *m.sh.* -e dethronement.
shfronësój *f.k.* to dethrone. – shfronësohem *f.jv.* to be dethroned.
shfryj I. *f.k.* 1. *(gomën)* to deflate. (a tire).2. *(hundët)* to blow (the nose). 3. **i shfryj një fëmije**: to scold (to chide) a child. – shfryhet *f.jv. (topi, goma)* to be deflated (a ball, a tire). II. *f.jk.* to snore; **shfryn kali**: the horse snores.
shfrýrj/e,-a *f.* 1. deflating, deflation; *(e topit, e gomës)* going flat. 2. *(ndaj një fëmije)* scolding, chiding. 3. *(e hundëve)* blowing (of the nose).
shfrytëzím,-i *m.* 1. exploitation, utilization: *(i një miniere)* exploitation; working (of a mine). 2. exploitation; **shfrytëzim i njeriut nga njeriu**: exploitation of man by man.
shfrytëzój *f.k.* 1. to exploit, to

make use of; **shfrytëzoj një mi-nierë:** to exploit a mine. 2. to exploit. − **shfrytëzohem** *f.jv.* to be exploited.

shfrytëzúes,-i *m.sh.* − exploiter.

shfrytëzúes,-e *mb.* exploiting.

shfrytëzúesh/ëm(i),-me(e) *mb.* utilizable, exploitable; **tokë e shfrytëzueshme:** exploitable (cultivable) ground.

shfuqizím,-i *m. (i një ligji etj.)* invalidity (of a law, etc.)

shfuqizòj *f.k. (një ligj)* to invalidate, to abrogate, to render invalid (a law). − **shfuqizohet** *f.jv.* to be abrogated.

shi,-u *m.sh.* **-ra** rain; **shi i imët:** misty rain, drizzling rain; **shi i rrëmbyer, rrebesh:** pitching rain, pelting rain; **kohë me shi:** rainy weather; **pikla shiu:** rain − drops; **ujë shiu:** rain-water; **bie shi:** it rains; **po bie shi:** it is raining; **bie shi me stomna:** it is raining cats and dogs; **duket se do të bjerë shi:** it looks like rain. − *Lok.* **bie nga shiu në breshër:** to go out of the frying-pan into the fire.

shiatík,-u *m. mjek.* sciatica.

shiatík,-e *mb. mjek* sciatic; **nervi shiatik:** sciatic nerve.

shif/ër,-ra *f.sh.* **-ra** cipher.

shifrár,-i *m.sh.* **-ë** register of correspondence.

shifrój *f.k.* to cipher.

shigjét/ë,-a *f.sh.* **-a** arrow.

shih (imperative mood of the v. **shoh**) see! behold! look! look here!

shij *f.k. (grurin etj.)* to thrash, to thresh (the wheat, etc.). − **shihet** *f.jv.* to be thrashed (threshed).

shíj/e,-a *f.* 1. taste, savour, smack, flavour; **shije e këndshme:** relish, flavour; **pa shije:** tasteless;

i jap shije një gjelle: to relish a stew. 2. enjoyment, relish; **ha me shije:** to eat with relish. 3. taste, liking; **vishem me shije:** to dress in taste; **është sipas shijes tënde kjo kravatë?** is this tie to your liking?

shijím,-i *m.* tasting; enjoying, relishing, savouring.

shijoj *f.k.* 1. to taste. 2. to enjoy, to relish, to savour. 3. *fig.* to enjoy, to appreciate; **e shijoj muzikën:** to appreciate music. − **shijohet** *f.jv.* to be tasted, to be enjoyed (relished).

shíjsh/ëm(i),-me (e)*mb.* tasty, tasteful, delicious, savoury.

shik *mb.* elegant.

shikím,-i *m sh.* **-e** 1. look; **shikim i ëmbël:** sweet look; **shikim i ngulët:** piercing look, glare; **shikim i shpejtë:** glance; **në shikim të parë:** at first sight. 2. eye; **gjer ku arrin shikimi:** as far as the eye can see.

shikój *f.k.* to see, to look; **shikoj me ëmbëlsi:** to look kindly, gently; **shikoj shtrembër:** to give a nasty look: **shikoj me bishtin e syrit:** to look sideways (at someone); **shikoj prapa:** to look back, to look behind; **shikoj nga:** to look out of; **shikoj vjedhurazi:** to peep; **shikoj me habi:** to stare; **shikoj me kujdes:** to observe, to look carefully; **shikoj rreth e rrotull:** to look about, around; **gëzohem që po ju shikoj!** I am glad to see you! − *Lok.* **shikoni punën tuaj!** mind your business. − **shikohem** *f.jv.* 1. *(në pasqyrë)* to look at oneself (in the mirror). 2. *(te doktori)* to be examined (by a doctor). 3. *(shtrembër, me sy të keq)* to be seen (with an evil eye) (shih edhe **shoh**).

shikúes,-i *m.sh.* – beholder, looker-on, onlooker, bystander, spectator.

shilárem *f.jv.* to swing, to rock.

shilárës,-i *m.sh.* -a see-saw, swing.

shilárth,-i *m.sh.* -e a piece of wood used as support to bear pails on shoulders.

shílt/e,-ja *f.sh.* -e sitting cushion.

shín/ë,-a *f.sh.* -a rail (of railway).

shiník,-u *m.sh.* -ë *vjet.* bushel.

shíra(të),-t(të) *f.sh.* thrashing. threshing (of cereals).

shírës,-e *mb.* thrashing; **makinë shirëse:** thrashing machine, thresher.

shiríng/ë,-a *f.sh.* -a *mjek.* syringe.

shirít,-i *m.sh.* -a 1. ribbon, tape, band, strap; **metër shirit:** tape metre; **shirit magnetofoni:** tape; **shirit për makinë shkrimi:** type-writer ribbon. 2. *zool.* tapeworm, tenia.

shírj/e,-a *f.* thrashing (of cereals).

shish,-i *m.sh.* -ë 1. spit. 2. dagger. poniard; **vras me shish:** to dagger, to poniard, to stab, to kill with a poniard.

shíshe,-ja *f.sh.* -e 1. bottle; *(vaji, uthulle për tavolinë)* cruet; **gryka e shishes:** the neck of a bottle: **fundi i shishes:** the bottom of a bottle. 2. *(boje)* inkpot, inkstand. 3. *(llambe)* lamp-chimney; *(e vogël)* phial.

shishqebáp,-i *m.* shish kebab.

shitblérj/e,-a *f.* bargain, dealing, transaction.

shítës,-i *m.sh.* – dealer, seller, salesman, vendor, vender, monger; **shitës mallrash me pakicë:** retail dealer, retailer; *(me shumicë)* wholesale dealer; **shitës shëtitës:** costermonger, peddler, hawker, ambulant seller; *(artikujsh ushqimore, ose bakall)* grocer; *(artikujsh optikë)* optician; *(gazetash)* newsboy;

(lëndësh ndërtimi) lumberer; *(mishi)* butcher; *(pemësh)* fruiter; *(perimesh)* green-grocer; *(pijesh alkoolike)* gin – seller; *(plaçkash të vjetra)* dealer in old clothes; *(vesh – mbathjesh)* clothes –dealer, clothes-man.

shítës/e,-ja *f.s.h* -e saleswoman, seller-woman, shop-girl; **shitëse lulesh:** flower-girl.

shítj/e,-a *f.sh.* -e sales, selling; *(me pakicë)* retail; *(me shumicë)* wholesale; **shitje në ankand:** sale by auction; **shitje me kredi:** selling on credit; **shitje me para në dorë:** selling on cash.

shítur (i,e) *mb.* 1. sold. 2. *(njeri)* corrupt, sold; mercenary.

shkáb/ë,-a *f.sh.* -a *zool.* eagle.

shka/k,-ku *m.sh.* -qe 1. cause, motive, reason; **për shkak të, nga shkaku i:** because of, on account of; **i vetmi shkak:** the sole cause of; **pa shkak:** without motive; **zemërohem pa ndonjë shkak:** to be offended without reason; **nga ky shkak:** for this reason. 2. pretext; **gjej një shkak:** to find a pretext.

shkakór,-e *mb.* causal.

shkaktár,-i *m.sh.* -ë person responsible; **jam shkaktari i diçkaje:** to be responsible for something, to answer for something.

shkaktój *f.k.* 1. to cause, to bring about, to give rise to, to lead to; **shkaktoj dëm:** to cause damage. 2. to inflict; **i shkaktoj humbje armikut:** to inflict losses upon the enemy. – **shkaktohet** *f.jv.* to be caused (brought about).

shkallár/e,-ja *f.sh.* -e stair, step (of a stair-case) stepping-stone.

shkáll/ë,-a *f.sh.* -ë 1. stair-case; **kreu i shkallës:** stair-head, the top of the staircase; **ngjit shka-**

llët: to mount the stairs, to ascend, to step up, to scale. 2. *(muratori, bojaxhiu)* ladder; *(lëvizëse)* escalator. 3. *(grafike)* (graphic, graphical) scale. 4. stair. step. 5. *gram.* degree; **shkalla krahasore, sipërore;** comparative, superlative **degree.** 6. *muz.* gamut, scale. – *Lok.* **në shkallë botërore:** on a world scale; **në shkallë të gjerë:** on a wide scale; **në shkallën më të lartë:** to the highest degree.

shkállë-shkállë *ndajf.* gradually, by degrees.

shkallëzím,-i *m.sh.* -e 1. gradation. 2. escalation.

shkallëzój *f.k.* 1. *(një instrument).* to graduate. 2. to grade, to scale – **shkallëzohet** *f.jv.* 1. to be graduated. 2. to be graded (scaled)

shkallëzúar (i,e) *mb.* 1. graded. 2. *(termometër etj.)* graduated.

shkallmím,-i *m.* break, breaking.

shkallmój *f.k.* to break, open. – **shkallmohet** *f.jv.* to be broken, to smash to pieces.

shkallój *f.jk.* to go mad (crazy) to loose one's wits.

shkallúar (i,e) *mb. gj. bis.* cracked, foolish, mad, crazy.

shkapërdérdh *f.k.* to scat er. – **shkapërderdhet** *f.jv.* to be scattered.

shkapërdérdhj/e,-a *f.* scattering

shkárazi *ndajf.* cursorily.

shkárj/e,-a *f.* slip, slide, sliding.

shkarkím,-i *m.*1. unloading. 2. *(nga puna, nga detyra)* dismissal, dismission, discharging (from office, from service).

shkarkój *f.k.* 1. to unload, to unlade, to unburden, to disburden; **shkarkoj mallra:** to unload wares, goods. 2. *(nga puna)* to dismiss, to discharge, to cashier

(from a post, duty, **office of** employment); **to recall, to revoke** (from service **an** envoy, an ambassador). — **shkarkohem** *f.jv.* 1. to disburden (to relieve) oneself. 2. *(nga puna)* to be dismissed (discharged). 3. *fig.* to be relieved of anything annoying or oppressive.

shkarkúar (i,e) *mb.* 1. unloaded, unburdened, disburdened. 2. *(nga puna)* dismissed, discharged (from a duty, an employment). 3. *(nga një borxh)* quit, discharged (of a debt).

shkárp/ë,-a *f. sh.* -a twig; **një krah shkarpa:** an armful of twigs; **një vandak me shkarpa:** fagot. a bundle of twigs.

shkarravín/ë,-a *f.sh.* -a scrawl, scribble, illegible writing.

shkarravít *f.k.* to scribble, to scrawl. – **shkarravitet** *f.jv.* to be scribbled (scrawled).

shkarravítës,-i *m.sh.* – scribbler.

shkarravítj/e,-a *f.* scribbling, scrawling.

shkas *f.jk.* to slip, to slide, to glide.

shkatërrím,-i *m.sh.* -e ruin, ravage, destruction; **shkatërrim i një shtëpie, i një ndërtese:** destruction (demolition) of a building. 3. *(i një perandorie)* decay (of an empire).

shkatërrimtár,-e *mb.* destructive; **luftë shkatërrimtare, shfarosëse:** disastrous war, exterminatory (exterminative) war; **pasoja shkatërrimtare:** disastrous effects.

shkatërrój *f.k.* 1. to ruin, to destroy; **shkatërroj një qytet:** to ruin (to destroy, to ravage) a town. 2. *(armikun)* to defeat, to rout (the enemy). 3. *(një mekanizëm)* to damage heavily (a mecanism). 4. *(shëndetin)* to ruin (the health). – **shkatërrohem** *f.jv.* to ruin oneself; to be ruined, to fall in ruin.

shkatërrúes,-e *mb.* ruinous, disastrous, destructive.

shkáthët (i,e) *mb.* skilful, deft, dexterous, handy, clever.

shkathtësí,-a *f.* skillness, deftness, dexterity, cleverness; **me shkathtësi:** deftly.

shkel *f.k.* 1. *(me këmbë)* to step on, to crush, to tread under the feet, to stamp, to trample on. 2. *(sumbullën etj.)* to press (the button). 3. *(ligjin)* to violate, to infringe, to transgress (the law). 4. *(betimin)* to break an oath, to forswear oneself. 5. *(një vend të panjohur)* to explore (an unknown land). – *Lok.* **bëj një punë shkel e shko:** to bungle (to botch, to muddle) a work.

shkélës,-i *m.sh.*- - *(i ligjit)* transgressor, breaker (of law).

shkélj/e,-a *f.* 1. *(me këmbë)* stamping, crushing (with feet). 2. *(ligji)* infringement, transgression, violation (of a law). 3.*(betimi)* breaking, breach (of an oath).

shkelm,-i *m.sh.* -a kick (of a horse, of a man); **i bie me shkelma:** to kick.

shkelmój *f.k.* to kick. – **shkelmohet** *f.jv.* to be kicked.

shkénc/ë,-a *f.sh.* -a science.

shkencërísht *ndajf.* scientifically.

shkencëtár,-i *m.sh.* -ë scientist.

shkencór,-e *mb.* scientific.

shkés,-i *m.sh.* -ë middleman, *fam.* go-between.

shkëlqéj I. *f.jk.* to brighten, to grow bright; **dielli shkëlqen:** the sun shines. II. *f.k.* to make bright.

shkëlqesí,-a *f.* excellency; **Shkëlqesia Juaj:** Your Excellency.

shkëlqím,-i *m.* 1. brightness, bri-

lliancy, lustre; **me shkëlqim:** brilliantly. 2. *fig.* splendour; **shkëlqim i rremë:** false splendour; **pa shkëlqim:** wan, tarnished; **humb shkëlqimin:** to lose lustre.

shkëlqýer (i,e) *mb.* bright, brilliant; **nxënës i shkëlqyer:** brilliant pupil, excellent pupil.

shkëlqýesh/ëm (i), --me(e) *mb.* shih **i shkëlqyer.**

shkëlqýesh/ëm *ndajf.* brilliantly.

shkëmb,-i *m.sh.* -inj rock; *(buzë detit)* cliff; *(i thepisur)* crag; **varg shkëmbinjsh në det:** reef.

shkëmbéj *f.k.* to exchange, to change, to swap: *(mall me mall)* to barter (goods). – **shkëmbehem** *f. jv.* to be exchanged.

shkëmbím,-i *m.sh.* -e 1. exchange, trade, swap, barter; **shkëmbim mendimesh:** exchange of views; **jap si shkëmbim:** to give in return; **shkëmbim i nxehtësisë:** heat exchange (transfer).

shkëmbór,-e *mb.* rocky, craggy; **tokë shkëmbore:** rocky ground.

shkëndíj/ë,-a *f.sh.* -a spark.

shkëpút *f.k.* to detach, to separate, to disjoin. – **shkëputem** *f.jv.* to be detached (separated).

shkëpútj/e,-a *f.sh.* -e detaching, detachment, separation; **shkollë pa shkëputje nga puna:** full-time school.

shkëpútur(i,e) *mb.* detached, separated, disjoined.

shkishërím,-i *m. fet.* excommunication.

shkishërój *f.k. fet.* to excommunicate. – **shkishërohem** *f.jv.* to be excommunicated.

shkishërúar(i,e) *mb.* excommunicated.

shkoj I. *f.k.* (p. t. **shkova,** p. p. **shkuar)** 1. to go; **shkoj të**

fle: to go to sleep, to go to bed; **shkoj jashtë shtetit:** to go abroad; **shkoj përmes:** to go across; **shkoj përpara:** to go ahead (forward); **shkoj prapa:** to go backward; **duhet të shkoj:** I must be off, I must go: **eja të shkojmë!** let us go! 2. to fit, to suit; **këpucët ju shkojnë shumë:** your shoes fit you well; **të shohim nëse ju shkon ky kostum:** let us see whether this suit fits you or not; **ky ju shkon për mrekulli:** it fits you admirably. − *Lok.* **si shkoni?** how do you do? **më shkoi mendja:** it crossed (came into) my mind; **ky shembull nuk shkon:** this example doesn't go; **puna shkon mirë:** business is brisk; **puna shkon keq:** business is slack; **po të shkojë gjithçka mirë:** if everything goes well; **shkoj mirë me dikë:** to be on good terms with someone, to get on well with someone, to hit it off with someone. II. *f.k.* 1. to pass; **shkoj kohën:** to pass the time. 2. **shkoj perin (në gjilpërë):** to thread. 3. **shkoj poshtë një kafshatë buke:** to swallow a mouthful of bread.

shkoklavít *f.k.* to unravel, to disentangle. − **shkoklavitet** *f.jv.* to be unraveled, to be disentangled.

shkoklavítj/e,-a *f.* unravelling, disentangling.

shkolít *f.k.* to unglue, to disjoin. − **shkolitet** *f.jv.* to be unglued (disjoined).

shkolítj/e,-a *f.* unglueness, disjoining.

shkollár,-i *m.sh.* -ë school-boy.

shkollár/e,-ja *f.sh.* -e school-girl.

shkóll/ë,-a *f.sh.* -a 1. school;

shkollë fillore: primary school, *amer.* grade-school; **shkollë e mesme:** secondary school, middle-school; **shkollë e lartë:** high school, college; **shkollë profesionale:** vocational school: **shkollë nate:** evening school, evening classes; **shkollë me shkëputje nga puna:** part-time school; **drejtor shkolle:** headmaster; **shok shkolle:** school-fellow; **vazhdoj shkollën:** to attend the school; **ndjek shkollën e natës:** to attend the evening school. 2. learning, erudition; **ai nuk kish shkollë të madhe:** he was not a man of much learning; **njeri me shkollë:** learned person; **njeri pa shkollë:** illiterate.

shkollòr,-e *mb.* school, of school; **reforma shkollore:** school reform; **viti shkollor:** school year; **fillimi i vitit shkollor:** the beginning of the school year.

shkombëtarizím,-i *m.* denationalization.

shkombëtarizój *f.k.* to denationalize. − **shkombëtarizohet** *f.jv.* to be denationalized.

shkop,-i *m.sh.* −inj stick, staff; *(udhëtimi)* walking cane, stick, walking staff.

shkopsít *f.k.* to unbutton. − **shkopsitem** *f.jv.* to unbutton (one's skirt, etc.)

shkoq *f.k. (misrin)* to hull, to husk (the corn from the cob).

shkóqës,-e *mb.* hulling; **makinë shkoqëse:** hulling machine.

shkoqít *f.k.* to explain, to elucidate, to clear up; **shkoqit një çështje të errët:** to explain an enigma. − **shkoqitet** *f.jv.* to be explained (elucidated, cleared up).

shkoqítj/e,-a *f.* explanation, elucidation.

shkóqur(i,e) *mb.* 1. hulled, husked. 2. *fig.* clear.

shkóqura(të),-t(të)*f.sh.* small money, small change; **s'kam të shkoqura:** I have not small money.

shkórs/ë,-a *f.sh.* -a rug.

shkorrét,-i *m.sh.* -e *bot.* brushwood, bush, shrub.

shkóz/ë,-a *f.sh.* -a *bot.* hornbeam.

shkreh *f.k.* (pushkën) to fire, to discharge (a gun)- – **shkrehet** *f.jv.* to be discharged.

shkréhj/e,-a *f.sh.* -e (pushke) firing, discharging (of firearms); detonation, explosion.

shkrep I. *f.k.* (armën) to fire, to shoot, to discharge. – **shkrepet** *f.jv.* to be fired (shot, discharged). – *Lok.* **ia shkrep gazit:** to burst out laughing; **s'ia shkrep fare:** to be dull-witted, to be dull-brained; **më shkrepet:** to come to one's mind, to get into one's head. II. *f.jk.* **shkrep dielli :**the sun rises; **më shkrepi një ide:** an idea came to my mind.

shkrépës/e,-ja *f.sh.* -e match, safety-match; **ndez një shkrepëse:** to strike a match.

shkrepëtím/ë,-a *f.sh.* -a lightning. **shkrepëtín** *f.jk.* (third person sing.) 1. it lightens; **po shkrepëtin:** it is lightening. 2. to brighten; **atij i shkrepëtinë sytë:** his eyes brightened.

shkrés/ë,-a *f.sh.* -a paper, offical document.

shkresurín/ë,-a *f.sh.* -a waste – – paper.

shkrétë(i,e) *mb.* 1. (njeri) lonesome, forsaken (person); **i shkretil** poor him! the unfortunate! **i shkretl djalë!** poor thing! poor boy! 2. (vend) deserted, desert (place).

shkretëtír/ë,-a *f.sh.* -a desert.

shkretím,-i *m.* destruction, devastation.

shkretój *f.k.* to raze to the ground, to desolate, to devastate. – – **shkretohet** *f. jv.* to become desert (desolate).

shkrif *f.k.* bujq. (tokën) to harrow (the land).

shkrifërím,-i *m.* bujq. (i tokës) harrowing (of land).

shkrifërój *f.k.* shih *shkrif.*

shkrífët (i,e) *mb.* friable, soft.

shkrij I. *f.k.* 1. to melt; to thaw; **shkrij dyllë:** to melt wax; **dielli e shkrin borën:** the sun melts the snow. 2. *met.* to melt to smelt, to fuse; **shkrij hekur:** to smelt iron. II. *f.jk.* 1. to melt, to fuse: **alumini shkrin në temperaturë të ulët:** aluminium melts at a low temperature. 2. to melt, to thaw. – **shkrihem** *f.jv.* 1. to melt, to fuse; **u shkri akulli:** the ice has melted. 2. *fig.* to unite, to merge. -Lok. **shkrihem së qeshuri:** to burst out laughing.

shkrim,-i *m. sh.* -e writing; **mënyrë shkrimi:** hand-writing, hand; **letër shkrimi:** writing paper; **bojë shkrimi:** ink; **makinë shkrimi:** type-writer, typewriting machine;**tavolinë shkri-, mi:** writing-table, writing-desk; **shkrim i bukur:** good hand, good writing; **shkrim i lexueshëm:** legible writing; **me shkrim:** in writing.

shkrimtár,-i *m.sh.* -ë writer author.

shkrírë (i,e) *mb.* melted; **dhjamë i shkrirë:** melted fat.

shkr̤ës.-i *m.sh.* – melter.

shkrírj/e,-a *f.* 1. (hekuri) melting, fusion; **uzinë e shkrirjes së metaleve:** iron and steel foundry; **pika e shkrirjes:** melting point. 2. *(e akullit)* **thaw** (of the ice).

shkríjsh/ëm(i),-me (e) *mb.* fusible.

shkrónj/ë,-a *f.sh.* -a letter (of alphabet), character; **shkronja kursive:** italic types (characters), italics; **shkronja gotike:** black letters; **shkronja kapitale:** capital letters.

shkrúaj *f.k.* 1. to write; **shkruaj një fjalë:** to write a word; **shkruaj bukur:** to have a good handwriting, to have a fine hand; **shkruaj keq:** to have a bad handwriting; **po shkruaj:** I am writing; **ai e shkroi me dorën e vet:** he wrote it with his own hand. 2. *(me makinë)* to typewrite. – **shkruhem** *f.jv.* 1. to be written. 2. *(në shkollë)* to register.

shkrúar(i,e) *mb.* 1. written. 2. **sy të shkruar:** sea-green (bluish-green) eyes.

shkrúes,-i *m.sh.* – clerk.

shkrumb,-i *m.* char, cinder; **bëj shkrumb:** to incinerate, to carbonise; **bëj shkrumb e hi:** to reduce to ashes, to reduce to dust.

shkrumbós *f.k.* to char, to carbonise, to incinerate. – **shkrumbosem** *f. jv.* to be reduced to ashes.

shkrumbósj/e,-a *f.* charring, incineration, cremation.

shkúar (i,e) *mb.* 1. gone, last; **vitin e shkuar:** last year. 2. *gram.* **koha e shkuar:** past tense. 3. **i shkuar nga mosha:** old, aged.

shkúar(e),-a(e) *f.* past; **si në të shkuarën:** as in the past time, as in the past.

shkúes,-i *m.sh.* – shih **shkes.**

shkuesí,-a *f.* intermediation.

shkúesh/ëm(i),-me(e) *mb.* 1. passable. 2. sociable.

shkujdésem *f. jv.* to get care-free (heedless, jaunty).

shkujdésj/e,-a *f.* carelessness, heedlessness, remissness, unconcern, disinterestedness, indifference.

shkujdésur(i,e) *mb.* care-free, heedless, jaunty, mindless.

shkul,-i *m.sh.* -e hank, skein.

shkul *f.k.* 1. to extirpate, to root out, to uproot, to extract, to pull off; **shkul dhëmbin:** to have a tooth extracted; **shkul veshin:** to twitch the ear; **shkul flokët:** to tear away the hair. 2. *fig. (armikun nga një vend i fortifikuar)* to dislodge (the enemy from a fortification). – **shkulem** *f. jv.* to be extirpated (unrooted, extracted). – *Lok.* **shkulem së qeshuri:** to burst out laughing, to split one's sides with laughter; to laugh heartily.

shkúlj/e,-a *f.* extirpation, uprooting, extraction.

shkullój *f.jk. (kupën)* to empty (the glass).

shkumák,-e *mb.* frothy, foamy.

shkúm/ë,-a *f.* froth, foam, spume; **me shkumë:** frothy, foamy, spumy; **shkumë sapuni:** lather, soap suds; *(birre)* yeast; **shkumë e dallgëve:** foam of waves; **verë me shkumë:** mossed wine.

shkúmës,-i *m.sh.* -a chalk; **shko më gjej një copë shkumës:** go and fetch me a piece of chalk.

shkúmëz,-a *f.sh.* -a *bot.* soapwort.

shkumëzój I. *f.k.* to froth, to foam, to spume. – **shkumëzohem** *f.jv.* to froth; to scum; *(kali)* to be in a foam.

✱ shlodhur (i,e) ml
relaxed

II. *f.jk. (birra)* to froth; to scum; **shkumëzoj nga inati:** to foam with rage.

shkund *f.k.* to shake up; *(nga pluhuri)* to dust; to shake off; *(një pemë)* to shake down (the fruits).

shkúndj/e,-a *f.* shake, shaking down.

shkurdís *f.k.* 1. *(orën etj.)* to unwind. 2. *(një vegël muzikore)* to untune (an instrument).

shkurdísj/e,-a *f.* 1, unwinding. 2. distune, discordance.

shkurorëzím,-i *m.sh.* -e 1. divorce. 2. *(i një mbreti)* dethronement.

shkurorëzòj *f.k. (një mbret)* to dethrone (a king). — **shkurorëzohem** *f.jv.* 1, to be divorced. 2. to be dethroned.

shkurt,-i *m.* February.

shkurt *ndajf.* briefly, shortly, curtly, in a few words, in short; **ia pres shkurt:** to cut someone short.

shkurtabíq,-i *m.sh.* -ë dwarf.

shkurtaláq,-e *mb.* undersized, puny.

shkúrtas *ndajf.* briefly, shortly.

shkúrt/ë,-a *f.sh.* -a *zool.* quail.

shkúrtër(i,e) *mb.* 1, short, curt, brief; **kohë e shkurtër:** short time; **rruga më e shkurtër:** the shortest way; **relacion i shkurtër:** brief exposure. 2. *(i shkurtër nga trupi)* undersized, dwarfish; **i shkurtër dhe i trashë:** dumpy.

shkurtím.-i *m.sh.* -e shortening; *(i një plaçke, i kohës , i rrugës)* shortening (of a cloth, of time, of way); *(i një libri)* abridgement; *(i një fjale): (i flokëve)* clipping of hair, curtailment of hair; *(i shpenzimeve)* reduction (of expenditures).

shkurtimísht *ndajf.* shortly, bri-

efly; *(për një mësim)* summarily; *(për një tregim)* briefly, shortly.

shkurtój *f.k. (kohën)* to shorten (the time); *(pantallonat)* to shorten, to make shorter (the trousers); **shkurtoj rrugën:** to take a short-cut (a ' cut-off); *(shpenzimet)* to reduce, to curtail (the expenditures); *(një libër)* to abridge (a book); *(një fjalë)* to abbreviate (a word).— **shkurtohem** *f.jv.* to grow shorter, to be shortened.

shkúrr/e,-ja *f.sh.* -e. *bot.* brushwood, bush, shrub.

shkurrnáj/ë,-a *f.sh.* -a brushwood, bush, shrub.

shlfv/ë,-a *f.* plum-brandy, plum-rakee

shlýej *f.k.* (p.t. shleva, p. p. shlyer). 1) *(një borxh)* to pay off (a debt). 2. *(një llogari)* to settle, to liquidate (an account). 3. *(një fjalë)* to efface, to erase, to rub out (a word). 4. *(mëkatet)* to expiate (one's sins). — **shlyhet** *f.jv.* 1. to be liquidated. 2. to be erased,

shlýerj/e,-a *f.* 1. *(e një borxhi)* payment (of a debt). 2. *(e një llogarie)* liquidation (of an account). 3. *(e një fjale etj.)* effacement (of a word, etc.)

shlýesh/ëm(i),-me (e) *mb.* 1 payable. 2. effaceable.

shllapurítem *f.jv.* to blunder into the mire.

shllíg/ë,-a *f. zool.* viper, adder.

shmang *f.k.* to shun, to avoid. — **shmangem** *f. jv.* to deviate: — **shmangem një goditjeje:** to shun (to avoid, to guard against) a blow; **i shmangem detyrës:** to neglect one's duty; **i shmangem rrugës së drejtë:** to deviate (to swerve) from the right path.

shmángj/e,-a *f.* shunning, avoidance; swerving, deviation; digression.

shmángsh/ëm (i),-me (e) *mb.* avoidable.
shndërrím,-i *m.sh.* -e transformation.
shndërrój *f.k.* to transform. — — **shndërrohem** *f.jv.* to be transformed.
shndërrúesh/ëm (i,)-me (e) *mb.* transformable.
shndrit *f.k.* to shine, to be bright; **shndrit dielli**: the sun shines; **i shndrit fytyra**: his face shines.
shndrítsh/ëm(i). -me (e) *mb.* shiny, bright, brilliant.
shofér,-i *m.sh.* -ë driver; *(tramvaji)* motor-man; *(kamioni)* lorry-driver, *amer.* truck driver.
shogán,-e *mb.* bald.
shógem *f.jv.* to grow bald.
shóg/ë,-a *f. anat. (e kokës)* pate, crown of the head.
shógët(i, e) *mb.* bald.
shoh I. *f.jk.* (p.t. **pashë,** p.p. **parë**) to see, to look at; **shoh me habi**: to stare, to look with one's eyes wide open; **a e sheh?** do you see? **nuk shoh mirë!** I don't see well.
II. *f.k.* to see; **shoh një fotografi**: to see a picture; *(së largu)* to see from afar; **gëzohem që po ju shoh**: I am glad to see you. — **shihem** *f.jv.* 1. to look at oneself; **shihem në pasqyrë**: to look at oneself in the mirror. 2. *(me dikë)* to meet someone; **kur do të shihemi?** when shall we meet? **do të shihemi nesër**: we shall meet tomorrow. 3. **shihem te mjeku**: to see (to consult) a doctor.
shok,-u *m.sh.* -ë fellow, mate, comrade, friend, *gj. bis.* chum, buddy; **shok dhome**: chum; room-mate; **shok fëmijërie**: playfellow; **shok loje**: partner, play-fellow; **shok lufte**: companion of arms, comrade-in-arms; ✳ *(esp. among Communists)*

shok i ngushtë: intimate (close) friend; **shok pune**: fellow-worker, colleague; **shok shkolle**: school-mate, school-fellow; **shoku-shokun**: one another.
shóll/ë,-a *f.* 1. *(këpuce)* sole (of boots). 2. *(e këmbës)* sole (of the foot).
shoq,-i *m.* 1. husband; **im shoq**: my husband; **i shoqi**: her husband. 2. comrade, fellow, mate; **ai s'e ka shoqin**: he is unmatched (unrivalled); **shoqi-shoqin**: one another.
shoqát/ë,-a *f.sh.* -a association.
shóq/e,-ja *f.sh.* -e 1. companion. 2. wife; **ime shoqe**: my wife; **e shoqja**: his wife.
shoqërí,-a *f.sh.* - 1. society, community; **detyrat ndaj shoqërisë**: duties towards society. 2. *treg.* company, firm, society; **shoqëri aksionare**: joint-stock company. 3. company, fellowship, companionship, partnership.
shoqërím,-i *m.* 1. accompaniment, attendance. 2. sociability.
shoqërísht *ndaf.* socially; amicably.
shoqërój *f.k.* to accompany, to escort; *(një shok)* to keep (to bear) a friend company. — **shoqërohem (me dikë)** *f.jv.* to keep company with someone, to bear someone company.
shoqërór,-e *mb.* social; **rend shoqëror**: social order; **gjendja shoqërore**: social state; **shkencat shoqërore**: social sciences; **në mënyrë shoqërore**: in a friendly manner, as a friend.
shoqërúes,-i *m.sh.* — attendant, escort.
shoqërúesh/ëm(i),-me (e) *mb.* sociable.
short,-i *m.* lot; **heqim short**: to draw (to cast) lots.
shosh *f.k.* 1. to screen, to seave.

to sift, to bolt; **shosh grurin:** to screen wheat; **shosh miellin:** to sift (to bolt) the flour − shoshet *f. jv.* to be screened (bolted).

shoshár,-i *m.sh.* **-ë** screen-maker.

shósh/ë,-a *f.sh.* **-a** sift, screen; pastroj me shoshë *(grurin etj.):* to screen, to pass through a screen (the wheat, etc.); *fig.* **i. bërë shoshë nga plumbat:** riddled with bullets. − *Lok.* mbaj ujë me shoshë: to carry coals to Newcastle.

shoshít *f.k.* to scan, to sift, to bolt, to scrutinize, to examine carefully. − **shoshitet** *f.jv.* to be scanned (sifted, bolted, examined) carefully.

shoshítj/e,-a *f.* scanning, bolting, sifting.

shóshj/e,-a *f.* screening, bolting.

shoshóne,-t *f.sh.* bootee.

shovinist,-i *m.sh.* **-ë** chauvinist.

shovinist,-e *mb.* chauvinist.

shoviníz/ëm,-mi *m.* chauvinism.

shpagím,-i *m.* avenge; revenge; retaliation, requital.

shpagúaj *f.k.* to pay someone back in his own coin. − **shpaguhem** *f.jv.* to be avenged (revenged), to have one's revenge.

shpagúes,-i *m.sh.* - avenger.

shpalós *f.k.* 1. to unfold; **shpalos flamurin:** to unfold (to spread) the flag. 2. *(velat)* to unfurl (the veils, the sails). 3. *(çarçafin)* to unwrap (the sheet). − shpaloset *f.jv.* to be unfolded (unfurled, unwraped).

shpalósj/e,-a *f.* unfolding; unfurling, unwraping.

shpall *f.k.* 1. to publish; **shpall në gazetë:** to publish in a newspaper. 2. *(vdekjen e një të afërmi etj.)* to announce (the death of a parent, etc.) 3. *(një ligj)* to promulgate (a law).

4. *(luftë)* to declare (war). 5. *(republikën)* to proclaim (the republic). 6. *(një konkurs)* to open a competition (a competitive examination). − **shpallem** *f.jv.* to be published (announced); to be declared, to be proclaimed; to be opened.

shpállj/e,-a *f.sh.* **-e** 1. *(në gazetë)* publication (in a newspaper). 2. *(vdekjeje)* announcement (of death). 3. *(ligji)* promulgation (of a law). 4. *(lufte)* declaration (of war). 5. *(e pavarësisë)* proclamation (of the independence). 6. *(konkursi)* advertisement (of a competition).

shpargu/ll,-lli *m.sh.* **-j** *bot.* asparagus.

shpartallím,-i *m. (i një ushtrie)* rout (of an army).

shpartallój *f.k. (një ushtri)* to defeat, to rout (an army). − − **shpartallohem** *f.jv.* to be defeated (routed).

shpat,-i *m.sh.* **-e** *(mali)* slope, descent (of a mount);*(kodre)* hillside.

shpatár,-i *m.sh.* **-ë** swordman.

shpát/ë,-a *f.sh.* **-a** sword, sabre; *(dueli)* rapier; **këllëf shpate:** sheath, scabbard; **rrip shpate:** sword-belt; **goditje me shpatë:** stroke with a sword; **nxjerr shpatën nga milli:** to draw the sword, to unsheath the sword; **ngjesh shpatën:** to sheath, to put the sword into the sheath (into the scabbard).

shpatúk,-e *mb.* flat.

shpátull,-a *f.sh.* **-a** *anat.* 1. scapula, shoulder-blade. 2. shoulder; **gjerësi e shpatullave:** breadth of shoulders; **me shpatulla të gjera:** broadshouldered. −*Lok.* mbaj mbi shpatulla: to bear upon one's shoulders, to assume the responsability; **vë dikë me shpatulla për**

muri: to put someone with his back to the wall.

shpatullgjérë *mb.* broad-shouldered.

shpejt *ndajf.* 1. soon, quickly, speedily, rapidly, hastily; **shpejt ose vonë:** sooner or later; **shpejt e shpejt:** quickly, hastily, rapidly; **tani shpejt:** recently; **së shpejti:** soon; **sa më shpejt që të jetë e mundur:** as soon as possible; **sa më shpejt më mirë:** the sooner the better; **shpejt!** quick! be quick! make haste! 2. soon, early; **çohem shpejt nga shtrati:** to get up early; **eja sa më-shpejt që të mundesh:** come as early as you can.

shpéjtë(i,e) *mb.* quick, rapid, swift, fast, speedy, hasty; **hap i shpejtë:** quick step; **iki me të shpejtë:** to hasten away, to go away quickly.

shpejtësí,-a *f.* speed, quickness, haste, rapidity, velocity, celerity; **me tërë shpejtësinë:** at full speed; **me një shpejtësi prej:** at a speed of; **lëviz me shpejtësi:** to move quickly.

shpejtim,-i *m.* acceleration.

shpejtój I. *f.k.* to speed up, to hasten; **shpejtoj hapin:** to hasten the step. — **shpejtohem** *f.jv.* to hurry, to hasten, to haste, to make haste.
II. *f.jk.* to hurry, to hasten, to make haste; **mos u shpejto!** don't hurry! take your time.

shpejtúes,-i *m.sh.* — accelerator.

shpéll/ë,-a *f.sh.* **-a** cave, grotto.

shpend,-i *m.sh.* **-ë** *zool.* fowl; **shpendë shtëpiakë:** poultry; **rritja e shpendëve:** aviculture.

shpénd/ër,-ra *f.sh.* **-ra** *bot.* anemone.

shpengím,-i *m.* disengagement.

shpengój *f.k.* to disengage. —

shpengohet *f.jv.* to be disengaged.

shpengúar (i,e) *mb.* disengaged.

shpenzím,-i *m.sh.* **-e** expenditure, expense, outlay, outgo; **shpenzimet:** expenditures, expenses, outgoings; **shpenzime transporti:** transport expenses; *(udhë-timi)* travelling expenses; **shpenzime pa vend:** useless expenditures; **pakësoj shpenzimet:** to reduce the expenses; **me shpenzimet tuaja:** at your own charge; **nuk pyes për shpenzimet:** not to mind the expenses.

shpenzój *f.k.* to spend, to expend; to disburse; *(pa vend)* to waste, to spend lavishly, to squander; **shpenzoj kohën:** to spend the time.

shpés/ë,-a *f.sh.* **-ë** bird.

shpesh *ndajf.* often, frequently, constantly.

shpeshhérë *ndajf.* often.

shpéshtë (i,e) *mb.* 1. frequent; **vizita të shpeshta:** frequent visits. 2. dense; **pyll i shpeshtë:** dense wood.

shpeshtí,-a *f.* frequency.

shpëláj *f.k.* to rinse; **shpëla enët, rrobat:** to rinse the dishes, the clothes. — **shpëlahem** *f.jv.* to give one's face, etc. a good rinse.

shpëlárë (i,e) *mb.* 1. rinsed; **shishe e shpëlarë:** cleansed bottle. 2. *fig.* një gjë e shpëlarë: a trite thing, a stale thing.

shpëlárj/e,-a *f.* rinse, rinsing.

shpërbléj *f.k.* to reward, to recompense, to requite, to remunerate; *(një punëtor, një nëpunës)* to remunerate (a worker, an employee for a work). — **shpërblehem** *f.jv.* to be rewarded; to be remunerated.

shpërblés/ë,-a *f.* ransom.

shpërblím,-i *m.* 1. reward, recompense, remuneration; payment; **shpërblim i merituar**: just reward. 2. *(i një mjeku)* fee; **ei shpërblim për**: in return of. **shpërdór** *f.k.* to misuse, to illuse. — **shpërdoret** *f.jv.* to be misused, ill-used.

shpërdorím,-i *m.sh.* -e 1. misuse, ill-usage, misusage. 2. abuse; **shpërdorim i besimit**: abuse of confidence.

shpërdorój *f.k. (besimin e dikujt)* to abuse (the confidence of someone); *(autoritetin)* to abuse (one's authority). — **shpërdorohet** *f.jv.* to be abused.

shpërdorúes,-i *m.sh.* - waster; abuser.

shpërdrédh *f.k.* to untwist, to untwine, to unravel; to disentangle. — **shpërdridhet** *f.jv.* to be untwisted.

shpërdrédhj/e,-a *f.* disentanglement.

shpërgënj,-të *m.sh.* diapers.

shpërgëtí,-a *f. mjek.* eczema.

shpërndáj *f.k.* 1. to disperse, to scatter; **shpërndaj turmën**: to disperse the crowd. 2. to dissipate, to drive in different directions; **era shpërndan retë**: the wind dissipates the clouds. 3. *(plehra, etj.)* to distribute (manure, etc.). 4. *(ushtrinë)* to disband (an army). 5. to spread; **kjo lule shpërndan erë të mirë**: this flower spreads (emits a good odour. — **shpërndahet** *f.jv.* to be dispersed (scattered); to be dissipated; to be spread, to be distributed.

shpërndárës,-i *m.sh.* - *(ushqimesh etj.)* distributer; **shpërndarës gazetash**: newsboy; **shpërndarës poste**: postboy, postman.

shpërndárj/e,-a *f.* 1. dispersion, dissipation; **shpërndarje e reve**:

dissipation of clouds. 2. *(ushqimesh etj.)* distribution (of provisions, etc.) 3. *(e parlamentit ose e një shoqërie)* dissolution (of the parliament, of a partnership).

shpërngúl *f.k.* 1. to transfer. 2. to expel, to deport, to banish. — **shpërngulem** *f.jv.* 1. to immigrate, to go to a new country. 2. to change residence.

shpërngúlj/e,-a *f.* 1. transfer of residence. 2. immigration; *(në masë)* transmigration.

shpërpjesëtím,-i *m.sh.* -e disproportion.

shpërpjesëtój *f.k.* to disproportionate.

shpërthéj I. *f.k.* 1. *(derën)* to break open. 2. *(frontin)* to break through. 3. *(një luftë, një sulm)* to unleash (a war), to launch (an attack).
II. *f.jk.* 1. to burst, to burst into; **shpërthej në vaj, në lot**: to burst into tears; **shpërthej në gaz**: to burst out laughing. 2. *(lufta)* to break out. 3. *(ujrat)* to overflow (waters). 4. *(bomba, dinamiti)* to explode, to detonate.

shpërthím,-i *m.sh.* -e 1. *(i një dere)* breaking (of a door). 2. *(i një bombe, i dinamiti)* explosion, detonation (of a bombshell, of dynamite). 3. *(i luftës)* outbreak (of war). 4. *(gazi)* burst (of joy, of laughing). 5. *(vullkani)* eruption (of a volcano).

shpërthýes,-e *mb.* eruptive, bursting forth.

shpëtím,-i *m.* 1. rescue, lifesaving; **mjet shpëtimi**: life preserver, life-saving device; **shkallë shpëtimi**: fire-escape. 2. *det.* salvage; **brez shpëtimi**:

life-belt; **varkë shpëtimi:** life-boat.

shpëtimtár,-i *m.sh.* **-ë** saver, rescuer, deliverer.

shpëtimtár,-e *mb.* saving, rescuing.

shpëtój I. *f.k. (dikë nga një rrezik)* to save, to rescue, to deliver someone from a danger; **shpëtoj nga vdekja:** to rescue from death; **i shpëtoj jetën dikujt:** to save someone's life. II. *f.jk.* to escape; *(nga duart),* to slip out, to slip away; *(nga burgu etj.)* to escape; **ai i shpëtoi dënimit:** he escaped the punishment; **shpëtoj për një qime:** to have a narrow escape.

shpëtúar(i),-i(i) *m.sh.* - **(të)** *(nga një mbytje anijeje, ose nga një fatkeqësi e natyrës)* rescued, survivor, survival.

shpíe *f.k.* (p.t. **shpura,** p. p. **shpënë)** 1. to carry, to bear, to convey; *(mallra nga një vend në një tjetër)* to carry, to convey (goods from one place to another). 2. *(një letër)* to send (a letter). 3. *(të holla)* to remit, to send (money). 4. to go, to lead; **cila rrugë të shpie në stacion?** which way leads to the station? – *Lok.* **shpie deri në fund një punë:** to carry a work through to the end.

shpif *f.k.* to calumniate, to slander, to defame, to asperse.

shpifarák,-u *m.sh.* **-ë** calumniator, slanderer, defamator.

shpífës,-i *m.sh.* - shih **shpifarak.**

shpífës,-e *mb.* defamatory, slanderous.

shpífj/e,-a *f.sh.* **-e** calumny, slander, defamation, aspersion.

shpik *f.k.* to invent, to contrive; *(fjalë të reja)* to coin (new words). – **shpiket** *f.jv.* to be invented (contrived).

shpíkës,-i *m.sh.* inventor.

shpíkj/e,-a *f.sh.* **-e** invention, contrivance.

shpim,-i *m.sh.* **-e** 1. *tek.* boring, perforation; *(i një pusi)* sinking (of a well); **makinë shpimi:** perforator, boring-machine. 2. *(i një gome)* puncture (of a pneumatic tire).

shpín/ë,-a *f.sh.* **-a** 1. *anat.* spine, back; **në shpinë:** on the back; **i kthej shpinën dikujt:** to turn one's back on someone. 2. back; **shpina e dorës:** the back of the hand; **shpina e një karrigeje:** the back of a chair.

shpirt,-i *m.* 1. soul; spirit; **heq shpirt:** to die, to expire; **pa shpirt:** soulless, lifeless, spiritless; merciless; **njeri pa shpirt:** pitiless (merciless) person; **me gjithë shpirt:** with all one's soul; **ai i shërbeu vendit të tij me gjithë shpirt:** he served his country with all his soul; **e kam shpirtin të vrarë:** to be brokenhearted. 2. human being; **sa shpirt bëheni?** how many persons are you?

shpirtbárdhë *mb.* generous, bountiful.

shpirtdëlírë *mb.* chaste, morally pure.

shpirtdëlirësí,-a *f.* chastity.

shpirtërísht *ndajf.* spiritually, morally; **vuaj shpirtërisht:** to suffer morally.

shpirtërór,-e *mb.* spiritual; **gjendje shpirtërore:** mood, frame of mind.

shpirtkázmë *mb.* pitiless, merciless, black-hearted.

shpirtkéq *mb.* malevolent, wicked.

shpirtlíg *mb.* shih **shpirtkeq.**

shpirtligësí,-a *f.* malevolence, malignity, ill-will.
shpirtmádh,-e *mb.* magnanimous, high-souled.
shpirtmadhësí,-a *f.* magnanimity.
shpirtmírë *mb.* indulgent, benevolent, good-hearted;njeri shpirtmirë: good-hearted person.
shpirtmirësí,-a *f.* benevolence, good-will.
shpírto,-ja *f.* 1, *krah.* alcohol. 2. safety-match.
shpirtplásur *mb.* broken-hearted.
shpirtvógël *mb.* mean, petty.
shpirtvogëlsí,-a *f.* meanness.
shpirráq,-i *m. mjek.* asthmatic person.
shpírr/ë,-a *f. mjek.* asthma.
shpjegím,-i *m.sh.* -e explanation.
shpjegój *f.k.* to explain; to expound. — shpjegohem *f.jv.* to explain oneself; to explain one's intentions. — *Lok.* si shpjegohet që...? how is it that...?
shpjegúes,-e *mb.* explicative, explicatory, explanatory.
shpjegúesh/ëm(i),-me (e) *mb.* explainable, explicable.
shpleks *f.k.* to unravel, to disentangle. — shplekset *f.jv.* to be unraveled (disentangled).
shpléksje,-a *f* unraveling, disentanglement.
shpluhurós *f.k.* to dust.
shpoj I. *f.k.* 1. to pierce; shpoj një vrimë: to pierce a hole. 2. *(një gomë)* to puncture (a pneumatic tire). 3. *(potkoj kuajsh)* to punch (horse-shoes). 4. *(me turjelë një dërrasë)* to bore, to drill, to pierce (a plank with a drill). 5. *(me gjilpërë)* to pick with a needle. 6. *(me heshtë)* to spear. 7. *(me thikë, me kamë)* to poniard, to stab, to pierce (with a pointed weapon); ai e shpoi tejpërtej me shpatë: he ran his sword through his body. 8.

(tokën për të hapur pus) to sink (a well). 9. *(veshin)* to pierce shpohem *f.jv.* to prick oneself; m'u shpua goma: I have got a puncture.
II. *f.jk.* më shpon veshi: to have a twitch of pain into the ear.
shpopullím,-i *m.* depopulation.
shpopullòj *f.k.* to dispeople, to depopulate. — shpopullohet *f.jv.* to be dispeopled (depopulated).
shporét,-i *m.sh.* -e cooking range, kitchener.
shportár,-i *m.sh.* -ë basket-maker.
shportarí,-a *f.* basketry.
shpórt/ë,-a *f.sh.* -a basket; *(pemësh)* fruit basket.
shporr *f.k.* to get rid of, to dispose of, to drive away. — shporrem *f.jv.* to be sent away; shporru I get you gone I be offI
shpreh *f.k.* to express, to utter. — shprehem *f.jv.* 1. to express oneself. 2. to be expressed (conveyed).
shpréhës,-e *mb.* expressive; significant.
shprehí,-a *f.* habit, custom, practice.
shprehimísht *ndajf.* expressively, expressly, tersely, in plain terms.
shpréhj/e,-a *f.* 1. expression, utterance, wording. 2. *gram.* expression, idiom, phrase.
shprés/ë,-a *f.sh.* -a hope, expectancy; humbas shpresën: to lose hope, to lose heart, to give up all hope; pa shpresë: hopeless, desperate; me shpresë: hopeful, full of hope; me shpresë se: hoping that.
shpresëdhënës,-e *mb.* promising, promisory.
shpresój *f.k.* to hope for, to be in hope that; shpresoj se do t'ju kënaqë: I hope it will please you; duke shpresuar: hoping.

— **shpresohet** *f.jv.* to be hoped
shprestár,-i *m.sh.* -ë hoper, one
who hopes.
shprétk/ë,-a *f.sh.* -a *anat.* spleen.
shprish *f.k.* 1. *(flokët)* to dishevel
(the hair). 2. *(leshin)* to unravel,
to comb (wool).
shpronësím,-i *m.sh.* -e expropriation, dispossession.
shpronësój *f.k.* to expropriate, to
dispossess. — **shpronësohet** *f.jv.*
to be expropriated (dispossessed).
shpronësúes,-i *m.sh.* - expropriator.
shpúarj/e,-a *f.* perforation: *(e një
gome)* puncture (of a pneumatic
tire).
shpúes,-i *m.sh.* - perforator.
shpúes,-e *mb.* 1. pearcing..2. *fig.*
dhembje shpuese: piercing
pain, keen pain, penetrating pain.
shpúll/ë,-a *f.sh.* -a smack, slap
in the face; **i jap një shpullë:**
to slap, to smack.
shpupurit *f.k.* 1. *(zjarrin)* to poke
(the fire). 2. *(flokët)* to dishevel,to
tousle, to put in disorder(the hair).
shpúra (past tense of the verb
shpie).
shpúr/ë,-a *f.sh.* -a attendants,
followers, suite.
shpút/ë,-a *f.sh.* -a 1. *(e këmbës)*
sole (of the foot). 2. *krah.* slap;
i jap një shputë: to slap, to
smack someone's face.
shpúz/ë,-a *f.* 1. ember. 2. *fig.*
smart fellow (girl).
shpyllëzím,-i *m.sh.* -e disafforestation, deforestation.
shpyllëzój *f.k.* to disafforest, to
deforest. — **shpyllëzohet** *f.jv.*
to be disafforested.
shpyllëzúar (i,e) *mb.* deforested.
shqarth,-i *m.sh.* -a *zool.* marten.
shqelm, -i *m.sh.* -a shih shkelm.
shqelmój *f.k.* shih **shkelmoj.**
shqém/e,-ja *f.sh.* -a *bot.* sumac,tan

shqep *f.k.* 1. to unsew, to unstitch. 2. shqep në dru dikë:
to beat up (to thrash soundly,
to beat black and blue) someone. — **shqepem** *f.jv.* to be
unsewed. — *Lok.* shqepem së
ngrëni: to eat sumptiously.
shqépj/e,-a *f.* unsewing.
shqérr/ë,-a *f.sh.* -a *zool.* lamb.
shqetësím,-i *m.sh.* -e 1. trouble,
disquietude, embarrassment;
shqetësim nervor: nervous trouble. 2. worry, alarm; gjithë
familja ishte në shqetësim:
all the family was full of worry. 3. *(fizik)* uneasiness, ailment; kam një shqetësim në
trup: to be uneasy.
shqetësój *f.k.* 1. *(dikë)* to trouble,
to perturb, to disturb (someone)
2. *(familjen)* to alarm (one's
family).— **shqetësohem** *f.jv.* to
trouble about, to worry about.
shqetësúar(i,e) *mb.* disturbed, anxious.
shqetësúes,-e *mb.* 1. alarming;
lajme shqetësuese: alarming
news. 2. grave, serious; gjendje
shqetësuese: grave situation.
shqéto *mb.* mish shqeto: meat
without vegetables.
shqip *ndajf.* in Albanian; flas
shqip: to speak Albanian.
shqip,-e *mb.* Albanian; gjuha shqipe: the Albanian language.
shqíp/e,-ja *f.* Albanian, the Albanian language.
shqipërím,-i *m.* rendering into
Albanian.
shqipërój *f.k.* to translate (to render) into Albanian. — shqipërohet *f.vj.* to be translated (to
be rendered) into Albanian.
shqipërúes,-i *m.sh.* - translator
into Albanian.
shqipónj/ë,-a *f.sh.* -a *zool.* eagle;
zog shqiponje: eaglet; fole
shqiponje: eagle nest; shqi-

[heraldic] (two-headed)

ponja dykrenare: bicephalous eagle.

shqiptár,-i *m.sh.* -ë Albanian.

shqiptarísht *ndajf.* after the Albanian fashion.

shqiptarizím,-i *m.* Albanization

shqiptarizój *f.k.* to Albanize. − − **shqiptarizohem** *f.jv.* to be Albanized.

shqiptím,-i *m.sh.* -e pronunciation.

shqiptój *f.k.* to utter, to pronounce, to articulate; **shqiptoj keq një fjalë:** to mispronounce a word. − **shqiptohet** *f.jv.* to be pronounced.

shqís/ë *f.sh.* -a sense; **shqisa e të nuhaturit:** smell; **shqisa e të dëgjuarit:** hearing.

shqit *f.k.* to detach, to disconnect, to disjoin, to separate, to unglue. − **shqitem** *f.jv.* to be detached (disjoined).

shqitj/e,-a *f.* detachement, disconnection, disjointure, separation.

shqóp/ë,-a *f. bot.* heath, heather.

shqopísht/ë,-a *f.sh.* -a *bot.* heath grove.

shqúaj *f.k.* 1. to distinguish, to discern. − **shquhem** *f.jv.* 1. to be distinguished (discerned.) 2. to distinguish oneself.

shqúar (i,e) *mb.* 1. renowned, famous, illustrious, remarkable, distinguished; **burrë i shquar:** outstanding (distinguished) man; **familje e shquar:** illustrious family. 2. *gram.* definite.

shqýej *f.k.* (p.t. **shqeva,** p.p. **shqyer)** to lacerate, to mangle; to rend, to rip, to tear up, to tear to pieces. − **shqyhem** *f.jv.* to be lacerated.

shqýerj/e,-a *f.* tearing, rending, laceration.

shqyrtím,-i *m.* 1. examination, examining, review; (i imët) close examination, scrutiny. 2. de-

bate, discussion. 3. analysis; **marr në shqyrtim një problem:** to analyse a problem, to debate an issue.

shqyrtój *f.k.* 1. to review, to examine; (imtësisht) to scrutinize, to examine minutely and thoroughly. 2. to debate, to discuss, to deliberate; **shqyrtoj një çështje:** to debate a question, to deliberate over a problem. − − **shqyrtohet** *f.jv.* 1. to be examined. 2. to be discussed.

shqyrtúes,-i *m.sh.* - reviewer, examiner.

shqýtk/ë,-a *f.sh.* -a *krah.* diaper.

shrapnél,-i *m.sh.* -ë shrapnel.

shrrégull,-a *f.sh.* -a sea-saw.

shtab,-i *m.sh.* -e. *usht.* staff. headquarters; **shtabi i përgjithshëm:** general staff, general headquarters.

shtág/ë,-a *f.sh.* -a shih **purtekë.**

shtámb/ë *f.sh.* -a. pitcher, jar.

shtámp/ë,-a *f.sh.* -a stamp.

shtampós *f.k.* to stamp. − **shtamposet** *f.jv.* to be stamped.

shtampósj/e,-a *f.* stamping.

shtang *f.k.* to astound, to amaze, to consternate, to take ones breath away, to dumbfound, to strike dumb. − **shtangem** *f.jv.* to be astounded (consternated, amazed).

shtángi/e,-a *f.* consternation, astoundment, amazement, bewilderment.

shtángës,-e *mb.* amazing, astounding.

shtángur (i,e) *mb.* thunderstruck, dumbfounded.

shtapós *f.k.* to uncork. − **shtaposet** *f.jv.* to be uncorked.

shtat,-i *m.* stature, height.

shtatənik,-e *mb.* prematurely born.

shtátë *num. them.* seven.

shtátë (i,e) *num.rresht.* seventh.

shtatëdhjétë *num. them.* seventy

shtatëdhjétë(i,e) *num. rresht.* seventieth.
shtatëfísh,-e *mb.* sevenfold, septuple.
shtatëmbëdhjétë *num. them.* seventeen.
shtatëmbëdhjétë (i,e)*num. rreshc.* seventeenth.
shtatëqind *num.them,* seven hundred.
shtatgjátë *mb.* tall, of high stature; njeri shtatgjatë: tall man.
shtathédhur *mb.* slim, slender.
shtathóllë *mb.* slim, thin.
shtatmadhorí,-a *f.sh.* - *usht.* general headquarters.
shtatór,-i *m.* September.
shtatzënë *mb.* pregnant, in the family way.
shtazarák,-e *mb.* bestial; në mënyrë shtazarake: beastly.
shtáz/ë,-a *f.sh.* -ë 1. beast, animal; shtazë e egër: wild beast. 2. *fig.* brute, brutal person.
shtazór,-e *mb.* 1. bestial, beastly, beastlike. 2. animal; bota shtazore: animal kingdom.
shteg,-u *m.sh.* shtigje 1. footway, foot-path. 2. *(dalje nga një situatë e vështirë)* loophole, vent, issue, outlet. − *Lok.* mos i lë shteg (të bëjë diçka): don't give him a chance (to do something).
shtegtár,-i *m.sh.* -ë 1. nomad. 2. migrator.
shtegtár,-e *mb.* 1. migrant, migratory; zog shtegtar: migratory bird, bird of passage. 2. migrant, nomadic; popull shtegtar: nomadic people, nomad people.
shtegtím,-i *m.sh.* -e migration.
shtegtój *f.jk.* to migrate.
shter *f.jk.* to dry up, to run dry; burimi ka (është) shteruar: the spring has dried up (is dry).

− shterem *f.jv.* to dry up, to run dry.
shterím,-i *m.* drying, desiccation.
shterój *f.jk.* shih shter.
shtérpë *mb.* 1. barren; bagëti shterpë: barren animal; lopë shterpë: barren cow, dry-cow; grua shterpë: barren woman. 2. sterile, arid; tokë shterpë: arid soil, improductive land.
shterpësí,-a *f.* barreness; sterility; improductivity.
shterúesh/ëm (i),-me (e) *mb.* exhaustible.
shtés/ë,-a *f.sh.* -a 1. *(libri)* appendix; *(flete në një revistë)* insertion, supplement. 2. *(rroge etj.)* augmentation, increase, rise; shtesë rroge: rise in wages (in pay).
shtet,-i *m.sh.* -e state; burrë shteti: statesman.
shtétas,-i *m.sh.* - citizen.
shtetërór,-e *mb.* of the state, state; national; hua shtetërore: national debt.
shtetësí,-a *f.* 1. nationality; me shtetësi shqiptare: of Albanian nationality. 2. naturalization; marr shtetësinë shqiptare: to be made an Albanian subject.
shtetëzím,-i *m.* nationalization.
shtetëzój *f.k.* to nationalize. − − shtetëzohet *f.jv.* to be nationalized.
shtetrrethím,-i *m.* curfew; shpall shtetrrethimin : to order a curfew.
shtëllúng/ë,-a *f.sh.* -a 1. flake; *(leshi)* hank. 2. *(tymi)* wreath. 3. *(pluhuri)* eddy.
shtëmbár,-i *m.sh.* -ë potter.
shtëmëng *f.k.* shih shmang.
shtën/ë(e),-a(e) *f.sh.* -a(të) *(pushke)* gunshot; me një të shtënë: at a single shot.
shtënë (i, e) *mb.* fond, impassio-

ned; **i shtënë pas muzikës:**
fond of music; **i shtënë shumë
pas së ëmës:** brought up at
his mother's apron-strings.
shtëng/ë,-a *f.sh.* **-a** perch.
shtëpí,-a *f.sh.* **-** **1.** house; **shtëpi njëkatëshe:** single-storied ho-
use; **shtëpi e vogël:** small
house, cottage; **shtëpi fshati:**
country house; **rri si në shtëpinë tënde:** make yourself at home
larg shtëpisë: abroad, away
from home (from the family);
2. lodging; **ku rrini me shtëpi?**
where do you dwell? **3.** family,
home; **në shtëpi:** at home; **pa
shtëpi:** homeless; **i zoti i
shtëpisë:** host, **e zonja e
shtëpisë:** hostess; **bukë shtëpie:** home-made bread.ˈ **4. shtëpi
botuese:** publshing house. **5.
shtëpi e fëmijës:** orphanage.
6. shtëpi pushimi: rest home;
shtëpi kulture: house of
culture. *−Lok.* **mbaj shtëpinë:**
to keep one's family; **mbaj
hapur shtëpinë:** to keep open
house.
shtëpiák,-e *mb.* **1.** domestic; house
hold; **grua shtëpiake:** house-
wife, house-keeper; **punë shtëpiake:** house-keeping. **2.** domestic; **kafshë shtëpiake:** domestic animal.
shtërg,-u *m.sh.* **shtërgje** *zool.*
stork.
shtërgát/ë,-a *f.sh.* **-a** storm, tempest, gale, hurricane.
shtíe *f.k.* **1.** to pour; **shtie ujë
në një gotë:** to pour water in a
glass. **2.** to inject; **shtie gjak:**
to inject blood. **3.** (i)**shtie
frikë dikujt:** to frighten (to
scare) someone. **4.** (i) **shtie
sytë:** to cast a glance (at). *−
Lok.* **shtie në dorë:** to lay
one's hands on; (ia) **shtie në
mendje (të bëjë diçka):** to

remind someone (to do something); **shtie dashuri më dikë**
to fall in love with; **shtie në
punë diçka:** to make use of
something. *−* **shtihem** *f.jv.* **1.**
(pas studimit etj.) to devote oneself of (study, etc.). **2.** to feign.
to simulate.
shtim,-i *m.* **1.** increase; augmentation, increment. **2.** accretion;
shtimi i popullsisë: rise of
the population.
shtíqem *f.jv.* to stretch oneself
out.
shtírem *f.jv.* to feign, to simulate;
shtirem (si) i sëmurë: to
malinger.
shtírj'/e,-a *f.* simulation, sham.
shtíz/ë,-a *f.sh.* **-a 1.** lance, spear.
2. *(çorapi, trikoje)* knitting-need-
le. **3.** *(flamuri)* flagstaff. **4.** *(peshkimi)* harpoon.
shtjellím,-i *m.sh.* **-e** development,
working out, broader treatment.
shtjellój *f.k.* to develop; **shtjelloj
një temë:** to develop a theme,
− **shtjellohet** *f.jv.* to be developed.
shtog,-u *m.* *bot.* elder.
shtoj *f.k.* to add; to increase, to
augment. *−***shtohet** *f.jv.* to increase, to augment.
shtójc/ë,-a *f.* **1.** *(në një libër)*
appendix (of a book). **2.** *(në
një gazetë ose revistë)* supplement (of a newspaper, magazine).
shtojzováll/e,-ja *f.sh.* **-e** nix.
shtrat,-i *m.sh.* **shtretër 1.** bed,
bedstead; **shtrat fëmijësh:** cot,
child-bed; **shtrat portativ:** portable bed, cot; **shtrati i vdekjes:** death bed; **në shtrat:** abed.
2 *(automobili)* chassis. **3.** *gjeog.*
shtrat lumi: river bed. **4.** *(bimësh)* hot-bed. **5.** *(topi)* gun-
carriage. **6.** *(i pushkës)* breech

(of a rifle). – *Lok.* zë shtratin: to fall ill.

shtratëzim,-i *m.* stratification.

shtratëzóhet *f.jv.* to stratify.

shtrembaník,-u *m.sh.* -ë deformed man.

shtrembaník,-e *mb.* deformed, misshapen.

shtrémbër *ndajf.* 1. awry, askew; lop-sidedly; **eci shtrembër:** to walk lop-sidedly; **shikoj shtrembër:** to look askew. 2. *fig.* iniquitously.

shtrémbër(i,e) *mb.* 1. not straight, bent, crooked; **mur i shtrembër:** biased wall; **vijë e shtrembër:** crooked line, banding line; **këmbë të shtrembëra:** crooked legs. 2. *fig.* wrong, unjust; **veprim i shtrembër:** unjust (wrong) act.

shtrembërím,-i *m.sh.* -e 1. warping, flexure; *(i një hekuri)* bending (of an iron bar). 2. *fig. (i fakteve)* distortion (of facts).

shtrembërój *f.k.* 1. *(hekurin)* to bend (an iron bar). 2. to deform, to crook. 3. *fig. (faktet)* to distort, to falsify (the facts). – *Lok.* shtrembëroj buzët: to make a wry face. –shtrembërohem *f.jv.* to be deformed, to grow crooked.

shtrenjt *ndajf.* dearly, at a high price; **e bleva shtrenjt:** I bought it at a high price; **kjo shitet shtrenjt:** that fetches a high price. -*Lok.* do të ma paguash shtrenjt: you will smart for this.

shtrénjtë (i,e) *mb.* 1. dear, costly, expensive; **shumë i shtrenjtë:** excessively dear, uncommonly dear. 2. *fig.* dear, cherished.

shtrenjtësí,-a *f.* costliness.

shtrenjtím,-i *m.* rising of prices.

shtrenjtój *f.k.* to raise (to rise)

the price of. – shtrenjtohet *f.jv.* to grow dear (costly).

shtrés/ë,-a *f.sh.* -a 1. mattress. 2. *(pluhuri etj.)* layer. 3. *gjeol.* stratum, layer, bed; **shtresë qymyrguri:** coalbed. 4. class, strata; **shtresat shoqërore:** social strate; **shtresa e lartë, e pasur, e mesme, e ulët shoqërore:** the upper class, the wealthy class, the middle class, the low class of the (capitalist) society.

shtresím,-i *m.* stratification.

shtresój *f.k.* to stratify. – shtresohet *f.jv.* to stratify.

shtrétër,-it pl.of shtrat.

shtrëngát/ë,-a *f.sh.* -a shih shtërgatë.

shtrëngés/ë-a *f.* constraint, compulsion, coercion.

shtrëngím,-i *m.* 1. *(i një vide)* tightening (of a screw). 2. *(shtrën-gim duarsh)* handshake, clasping of hands. 3. constraint, coercion; **masa shtrëngimi:** coercive measures; **me shtrëngim:** by force, by constraint.

shtrëngój *f.k.* 1. *(një vidë)* to tighten (a screw). 2. *(rripin)* to tighten (the belt). 3. *(dhëmbët)* to clench one's teeth. 4. to shake, to clasp; **i shtrëngoj dorën dikujt:** to shake someone's hand. 5. *(dikë në krahëror)* to grasp, to press (someone to the breast to the bosom). 6. **t'i shtrëngojmë radhët rreth Partisë:** to close the ranks around the Party. 7. to constrain, to force, to ccerce, to compel; **e shtrëngoj dikë:** to constrain, to force, to compel someone. – shtrëngohem *f.jv.* to close up, to stand (to sit) closer together; **shtrëngohemi rreth (përreth):** to press round.

shtrëngúar (i,e) *mb.* 1. tight-fisted; **njeri i shtrënguar:** co-

vetous person, tight-fisted person. 2. tight; **pantallona 'të shtrënguara:** tight trousers. 3. close, serried; **me dhëmbë të shtrënguar:** with clenched teeth. 4. forced, constrained; **jam i shtrënguar të:** to be constraine (forced) to.
shtrëngúes,-e *mb.* coercive; **masa shtrënguese:** coercive measures.
shtrig,-u *m.sh.* **-anë** wizzard.
shtríg/ë,-a *f.sh.* **-a** hag, witch; **shtrigë e vjetër:** old hag.
shtrij *f.k.* 1. to lay, to lay down; **shtrij përdhe:** to throw down. 2. *(këmbët)* to stretch (one's legs); **shtrij dorën:** to stretch one's hand. – **shtrihem** *f.jv.* 1. to stretch oneself out, to sprawl, to lie down. 2. *(fusha)* to spread.
shtrim,-i *m.* 1. *(në spital)* hospitalization. 2. *(dyshemeje)* flooring.
shtrírë *ndajf.* lying, in bed; **shtrirë përmbys:** in a prone position, with the face downwards; **rri shtrirë;** to lie down.
shtrírë (i,e) *mb.* lying; **pozicion i shtrirë:** recumbent position.
shtrírj/e,-a *f.* 1. extent, extension. 2. *(e një lëkure, stofi)* stretching. 3. *(e afatit)* prolongation. 4. *(e industrisë etj.)* extension, spreading.
shtrófk/ë,-a *f.sh.* **-a** *(egërsirash)* den (of wild beasts), lair; *(lepuri)* burrow.
shtrófull,-a *f.* shih **shtrofkë.**
shtroj *f.k.* (p.t. **shtrova,** p.p. **shtruar)** 1. to lay; *(tavolinën, sofrën)* to lay the table (the cloth). 2. *(dhomën me qilim)* to carpet, to cover (the floor with a carpet). 3. *(dyshemenë me pllaka)* to pave (the floor). 4. *(në spital dikë)* to hospitalize (someone). 5. *(për shqyrtim*

një çështje) to moot, to put forward (a question for discussion). – **shtrohem** *f.jv.* 1. *fig.* to sober down, to settle down. 2. *(rruga, dyshemeja)* to be paved. 3. **shtrohem në punë:** to get down to work. 4. **shtrohem të ha:** to sit down to table. 5. **shtrohem në spital:** to be hospitalized. 6. **i shtrohem fatit:** to resign oneself. 7. *(një pyetje)* to be asked, to be put (a question).
shtrúar *ndajf.* slowly; **merre shtruar:** take your time.
shtrúar (i,e) *mb.* 1. *(rrugë)* paved (street, road); **rrugë e shtruar me asfalt:** asphalted street (road). 2. **sofër e shtruar:** laid table. 3. *fig.* **njeri i shtruar:** dutiful (obedient) fellow.
shtrydh *f.k.* 1. to squash, to press, to squeeze; **shtrydh një limon:** to squash (to press, to squeeze) a lemon. 2. *(rrobat e lagura)* to wring out wet clothes. 3. *(një çiban)* to squeeze (a blain). – **shtrydhem** *f.jv.* to be squeezed, to be pressed.
shtrýdhës/e,-ja *f.sh.* **-e** mangle.
shtrýdhj/e,-a *f.* 1. *(e një limoni)* squeezing, pressing (of a lemon). 2. *(e rrobave të lagura)* wringing dry. 3. *(e një çibani)* squeezing (of a blain).
shtúesh/ëm(i),-me(e) *mb.* fertile, prolific.
shtuf,-i *m.* pumice stone.
shtún/ë(e),-a(e) *f.sh.* **-a (të)** Saturday; **të shtunën:** on Saturday.
shtúp/ë,-a *f.sh.* **-a** tow, plug.
shtupój *f.k.* to tow, to plug.
shtúr/ë,-a *f.sh.* **-a** *zool.* starling.
shtyj *f.k.* 1. to push; **shtyj tavolinën:** to push the table; **shtyj me bërryl:** to elbow; **shtyj dikë me duar:** to jostle, to

shove, to push along; *(lehtë)* to jog, to push slightly; **shtyjmë njëri-tjetrin**: to jostle one another; **shtyj përpara**: to drive on (fonward), to shove, to push forward, to propel; **shtyj prapa**: to drive back. 2. *(afatin)* go delay, to postpone; **shtyj afatin e një pagese**: to postpone a payment, to obtain a delay for a payment; *(për më vonë një punë)* to defer, to postpone, to procrastinate, to put off to a future time, to delay. 3. *(dikë për të bërë keq)* to impel, to urge, to incite, to instigate. — **shtyhem** *f.jv.* 1. to be pushed. 2. to be delayed (postponed. 3. to be incited.

shtýll/ë,-a *f.sh.* -a 1. *(ndërtese)* column, pillar (of a building). 2. *(telegrafi)* pillar. 3. *(feneri)* lamppost. 4. *(për tregimin e rrugës)* finger-post. 5. *(gazete, shifrash)* column (of a newspaper, of numbres). 6. *anat.* **shtyllë kurrizore**: back-bone. 7. *fig. (e shtëpisë)* pillar (of the family).

shtyp *f.k.* 1. to crush, to flatten out, to squash. 2. to crush, to quell, to repress, to put down; **shtyp një kryengritje**: to crush (të quell, to repress, to put down) a revolt (a riot). 3. *(me havan)* to pound. 4. *(sustën elektrike)* to press (the button). 5. *(rrush)* to crush (grapes). 6. *(një libër)* to print (a book); *(një shkresë në makinë shkrimi)* to typewrite (a letter on a typewriter). 7. *fig. (një popull)* to oppress (a people). — **shtypem** *f.jv.* 1. *(nga makina)* to be run over (by a motorcar). 2. *(midis turmës)* to be crushed, to crush; **njerëzit po shtypeshin për të hyrë**: there was a great crush to get in. 3. *(nga një armik)*

to be oppressed (by the enemy). **shtyp,-i** *m.* 1. press; newspapers. 2. printing press; **libër që ndodhet në shtyp**: book in press; **kopjet e shtypit**: press copies; **bojë shtypi**: printing ink; **makinë shtypi**: printing press. **shtýpës,-i** *m. sh.* - 1. *tek.* crusher. 2. *fig.* oppressor. **shtýpës,-e** *mb.* oppressive. **shtýpës/e,-ja** *f.sh.* -e rammer. **shtýpj/e,-a** *f.* 1, crushing. 2. *(e një kryengritjeje)* crushing, repression (of a revolt). 3. *(e popullit)* oppression. 4. **shtypje atmosferike**: pressure, atmospheric pressure. 5. *(gazetash, librash)* printing (of newspapers, of books). **shtypshkrím,-i** *m.* printing, impression. **shtypshkríme,-t** *f.sh.* printed papers. **shtypshkrónj/ë,-a** *f.sh.* -a typography, printing-office; **punëtor shtypshkronje**: printer, typographer; **korrektor shtypshkronje**: proof reader. **shtýrë (i,e)** *mb.* 1. pushed, shoved. 2. incited. **shtýrj/e,-a** *f.* 1. push, shove; *(e lehtë)* jog; *(përpara)* propulsion. 2. incitement, instigation. 3. *(afati)* delay, postponement, procrastination; *(e një pagese)* postponement, delay (of a payment). **shtýtës,-i** *m.sh.* - instigator. **shtýtës,-e** *mb.* 1. propulsive. 2. inciting. **shtýtj/e,-a** *f.sh.* -e push, shove. **shthurr** *f.k.* 1. *(një triko, çorape)* to undo (a sweater, socks). 2. *(një gërshet)* to unbraid, to unplait. 3. *(një gardh)* to destroy, to pull down (a fence). 4. *fig. (dikë)* to debauch, to corrupt. to deprave, to pervert (someone).

— **shthurrem** *f.jv.* to be co-rrupted.

shthúrrj|e,-a *f.* 1. *(e një trikoje)* undoing (of a sweater). 2. *(e gërshetit)* unbraiding. 3. *(e moralit)* perversion, corruption, debauchery, depravity, profligacy.

shthúrrur (i,e) *mb.* debauched profligate, dissolute; **njeri i shthurrur:** debauched person; **jetë e shthurrur:** intemperate life.

shúaj *f.k.* 1. *(dritën, zjarrin)* to put off, to put out, to extinguish; *(qiriun)* to blow out, to put out. 2. *(gëlqeren)* to slake (the limestone). 3. *(etjen)* to quench (the thirst). 4. *(një fjalë)* to erase, to efface, to scratch; to obliterate (a word). 5. *(një kryengritje)* to crush, to repress, to put down (a revolt). — **shuhem** *f.jv.* 1. *(zjarri)* to go out; *(qiriu)* to blow out. 2. *(një familje)* to die out. 3. *fig. (zhurma)* to die away; *(pasioni)* to die down. — *Lok.* **shuhem në punë:** to work for hours at a stretch.

shúa/ll,-lli *m.sh.* -j sole (of the foot).

shúar (i,e) *mb.* 1. extinct, extinguished 2. quenched.

shúarj|e,-a *f.* 1. *(e zjarrit, e dritave)* extinction, extinguishing. 2. *(e etjes)* quenching (of thirst). 3. *(e gëlqeres)* slaking (of limestone). 4. *(një fjale)* erasure, effacement; obliteration (of a word).

shúes,-i *m.sh.* - *(i flakës)* damper; *(i zjarrit)* extinguisher.

shúes,-e *mb.* extinctive.

shúf|ër,-ra *f.sh.* -ra rod; bar.

shuk *ndajf.* mblidhem shuk: to crouch, to squat; **mblidhet shuk (stofi):** to shrink (a tissue).

shúku/ll,-lli *m.sh.* -j *bot.* mignonette.

shul,-i *m.sh.* -a 1. ▼*(dere)* bolt,

bar (of a door). 2. *(i pushkës)* breech-block (of a gun).

shulák,-e *mb.* stout, corpulent.

shúllë,-ri *m.* sunny place.

shullëhem *f.jv.* to sit in the sun.

shumánsh/ëm(i),-me (e) *mb.* manysided, multifarius, manyfold.

shúm/ë,-a *f.sh.* -a 1. sum; **një shumë e madhe:** a large sum of money. 2. *mat.* amount; **gjej shumën e dy numrave:** to add up two numbers, to add two numbers together; **shuma e përgjithshme:** total amount.

shúmë *ndajf.* 1. very, much, very much, too much; a great deal of; **ju dua shumë:** I love you very much; **faleminderit shumë:** thank you very much; **shumë ujë:** much water; **shumë zhurmë për asgjë:** much ado about nothing; **kisha shumë dëshirë të flija:** I wanted very much to sleep; **e keni ·shumë gabim:** you are completely wrong. 2. *(para një emri shumës)* many; **ai ka shumë miq:** he has many friends; **në shumë raste:** in many cases; **shumë shkrimtarë përdorin:** most writers use; **shumë prej tyre:** a great number of them; **ata ishin shumë:** they were numerous. 3. *(para një ndajfoljeje)* very, too; **shumë pak:** very little, too little. 4. *(para një krahasoreje)* much; **varka e tij ishte shumë më e lehtë se e imja:** his boat was much lighter than mine. 5. *(para një mbiemri)* very; **shumë i zoti:** very capable; **shumë i trembur:** very much frightened.

shumëfish,-i *m.sh.* -ë *mat.* multiple.

shumëfishím,-i *m.* multiplication.

shumëfishój *f.k.* to manifold, to

multiply. – **shumëfishohet** *f.jv.* to be multiplied.
shumëfishtë (i,e) *mb.* manifold.
shumëkátësh,-e *mb.* many-storied.
shumëkëmbësh,-i *m.sh.* -a *zool.* myriapod.
shumëkëmbësh,-e *mb.* myriapod, myriapodan.
shumëkëndësh,-i *m.sh.* -a *gjeom.* polygon.
shumëkómbësh,-e *mb.* multinational.
shúmë-shúmë *ndajf.* at most.
shumëkúsh *p.pk.* anyone; several people.
shumëllójshëm (i,)-me (e) *mb.* varied, multifarious.
shumëllojshmërí,-a *f.* variety, diversity.
shumëngjýrësh,-e *mb.* multicolored.
shúmës,-i *m. gram.* plural.
shumëvjeçár,-e *mb.* perennial.
shumëvúajtur (i,e) *mb.* longsuffering.
shumëzím,-i *m.sh.* -e multiplication.
shumëzój *f.k.* to multiply. – **shumözohet** *f.jv.* to be multiplied.
shumëzúar(i),-i(i) *m.sh.* - (të) *mat.* multiplicand.
shumëzúes,-i *m.sh.* - *mat.* multiplier.
shumëzúesh/ëm(i),-me (e) *mb.* multiplicable, multipliable.
shumíc/ë,-a *f.* 1. multitude; **një shumicë njerëzish:** a multitude of men, a lot of men, a great many people; **shumica e njerëzve:** most of the people, the greatest number of the people. 2. abundance, plenty; **ka me shumicë nga ky lloj:** here are plenty of this kind. 3. *treg.* **tregti me shumicë:** wholesale trade; **tregtar me shumicë:** wholesale dealer. 4.

majority; **shumica dërrmuese:** the overwhelming majority; **me shumicë votash:** by a majority of votes; **në shumicën e rasteve:** in most cases.
shumój *f.k.* to increase, to multiply. – **shumohet** *f.jv.* to be multiplied, to be increased.
chúmta (e) *f.* most; **në më të shumtën e rasteve:** in most instances.
shúmtë (i,e) *mb.* numerous. – *Lok.* **ai shkoi me të shumtët:** he died, he joined the majority.
shungullím/ë,-a *f.* clatter.
shungullój *f.jk.* to clatter.
shuplák/ë,-a *f.sh.* -a slap, buffet; **i jap një shuplakë fytyrës dikujt:** to slap someone's face; to smack someone's face.
shur,-i *m.* shih rërë.
shurdhamán,-i *m.sh.* -ë deaf man; deaf.
shúrdhër (i,e) *mb.* deaf; **bëj veshin e shurdhër:** to turn a deaf ear to. – *Prov.* **s'ka njerí më të shurdhër se ai që nuk do të dëgjojë:** none is so deaf as he that won't hear.
shurdhím,-i *m.* deafness.
shurdhmeméc,-i *m.sh.* -ë deafmute, deaf and dumb person.
shurdhój *f.k.* 1. to deafen. 2. *fig.* to split someone's ears. – **shurdhohem** *f.jv.* to go deaf.
shurísht/ë,-a *f.sh.* -a sandbank.
shurúp,-i *m.sh.* -e syrup.
shurrák,-u *m.sh.* -ë pisser.
shurramán,-i *m.sh.* -ë shih shurrak.
shúrr/ë,-a *f.* urine, piss; *(e kafshëve),* stale (of animals).
shurrós *f.k.* to piss, to make water. – **shurrosem** *f.jv.* to piss oneself.
shurrós/e,-a *f.* pissing; *(e kafshëve)* staling, discharging of water.

shurrtór/e,-ja *f.sh.* -e public urinal.
shushát *f.k.* to dumbfound, to stun. – **shushatem** *f.jv.* to be dumbfounded, to be stunned.
shushátës,-e *mb.* stunning.
shushátj/e,-a *mb.* stunning.
shushúnj/ë,-a *f.sh.* -a 1. *zool.* leech, blood sucker; *(kali)* horse leech. 2. vampire.

shushurím/ë,-a *f.* rustle.
shushurít *f.jk.* to rustle.
shyqýr *fj. p.k. gj. bis.* what a blessing.
shyt,-ë *mb.* unhorned; hornless; **dhi shytë**: unhorned she-goat, hornless she-goat.
shýta,-t *f.sh. mjek.* mumps.

T

t' T (letter of the Albanian alphabet) t, T.
ta *p.v.* (united form of the pers. pron **të** + **e**, sing. for both genders) **ta dhashë**: I gave it to you.
tabák,-u *m.* *(letre)* sheet (of paper).
tabaká,-ja *f.sh.* - tray; **tabaka çaji**: tea-tray.
tabáko,-ja *f.* shih **burrnot**.
tabán,-i *m.sh.* -e 1. *anat. (i këmbës)* sole (of the foot). 2. *(i kokës)* pate, crown (of the head). 3. *(këpuce)* sole (of shoes, of boots).
tabél/ë,-a *f.sh.* -a 1. *(dyqani)* board (of a shop). 2. *mat.* **tabelë shumëzimi:** multiplication table. 3. **tabelë nderi:** stand of honour.
tablét/ë,-a *f.sh.* -a *mjek.* tablet, pill.
tabló,-ja *f.sh.* - 1. painting, picture. 2. **tablo muzikore:** muzical performance.

tabór,-i *m.sh.* -e *usht. vjet.* battalion.
tabút,-i *m.sh.* -e coffin.
táç/e,-ja *f.sh.* -e *bot.* bramble, blackberry bush.
tagár,-i *m.sh.* -ë 1. an ancient measure of cereals (about 12 kg). 2. fan, winnow; **hedh grurin me tagar:** to fan, to winnow wheat. 3. *(zjarri)* brazier, charcoal-pan.
tág/ër,-ri *m.sh.* -ra *vjet.* 1. right; **është tagri i tij:** it is his own right. 2. tax, duty.
tagrambládhës,-i *m.sh.* - tax-collector.
tagjí,-a *f.* 1. fodder. 2. *bot.* oat.
tahmín (me) *ndajf.* by guess.
táj/ë,-a *f.* 1. nurse. 2. *mek.* screw. 3. lathe.
tajís *f.k.* to suckle (a baby).
takát,-i *m. vjet.* force.
taketúk/e,-ja *f.sh.* -e ash-tray.
ták/ë,-a *f.sh.* -a heel (of boots).
takëm,-i *m.sh.* -e 1. service; **takëm çaji:** tea-service. 2. *(shtë-*

pie) movables, furniture. 3. **takëm shkrimi:** inkstand, pen and penholder. 4. *(kali)* trappings, harness. 5. **takëm tualeti:** dressing-case.
takíj/ë,-a *f.* shih **kësulë.**
takím,-i *m.sh.* -e meeting, appointment, encounter; **lë takim:** to make an appointment (a meeting); **kam takim:** to have an appointment; **nuk shkoj në takim:** to break an appointment; **vij me kohë në takim:** to keep an appointment; **vend takimi:** meeting place.
takój I. *f.k.* to come across, to meet, to encounter; **ai takoi anëtarët e delegacionit:** he met the mem - bers of the delegation. II. *f.jk.* 1. to happen; **takon shpesh:** it happens often. 2. to belong; **kjo i takon atij:** it belongs to him. – **takohem** *f.jv.* to meet, to encounter, to come across.
taks *f.k. gj.bis.* to mean (something for someone).
táks/ë,-a *f.sh.* -a tax, duty, impost; **taksë doganore:** custom duty; **taksë importi:** duties on imported goods; **taksë tregu:** market tax; **ngarkoj (rëndoj) me taksa të rënda:** to overtax, to levy heavy taxes (to someone).
taksí,-a *f.sh.* - taxy, cab, taxycab.
taksidár,-i *m.sh.* -ë tax-collector.
taksirát,-i *m.sh.* -e *vjet.* mishap; trouble.
taksój *f.k.* to tax, to assess, to fix (to set) a tax on something.
takt,-i *m.* tact; **me takt:** with tact; **pa takt:** tactless.
taktík/ë,-a *f.* tactics.
talént,-i *m.* talent, gift.
talentúar(i,e) *mb.* talented, gifted.
talík/ë,-a *f.sh.* -a four-wheeled carriage, waggon.

talk,-u *m.* talc; **pudër talk:** talc powder.
tall *f.k.* to make fun of, to banter, to scoff, to deride, to jeer. – – **tallem** *f.jv.* to mock, to jeer, to scoff, to laught at; to make sport of.
tallagán,-i *m.sh.* -ë mantle, a loose garment.
tallásh,-i *m.* saw dust, sawpowder.
talláz,-i *m.sh.* -e wave.
tállës,-e *mb.* mocking, jeering.
tállj/e,-a *f.* banter, mockery, pleasantry.
tallón,-i *m.sh.* -a voucher (of a check, etc.).
tahmaqár,-i *m.sh.* -ë glutton, insatiable person, greedy person.
tahmaqarllëk,-u *m.* gluttony, insatiability; **ha me tahmaqarllëk:** to eat gluttonously (greedily, ravenously, voraciously).
tamám *ndajf.* just, exactly, perfectly, just the same, precisely.
tamburá,-ja *f.sh.* - *muz.* threestringed guitar.
tánë *p. pr.* our; **shokët tanë:** our mates (companions, comrades); **stërgjyshërit tanë:** our ancestors; *fig.* **jemi tanët:** we are akin; we are friends.
tangjént,-e *mb. gjeom.* tangent.
tangjént/e,-ja *f.sh.* -e *gjeom.* tangent.
taní *ndajf.* now, at present, this moment; **tani për tani:** for the moment, actually, for the time being; **tani e tutje:** henceforth, henceforward, hereafter; **deri tani:** till now, up to now; **tani sapo u kthye:** he has just returned; **që tani:** this moment; now.
tanimë *ndajf.* already.
tanísh/ëm(i),me(e) *mb.* present, actual; *gram.* **koha e tanishme:** present tense.

tank,-u *m.sh.* **-e** *usht.* tank.
tankíst,-i *m.sh.* **-ë** *usht.* tanker.
tapánxh/ë,-a *f.sh.* **-a** 1. paw (of an animal). 2. *fig.* large hand.
táp/ë,-a *f.sh.* **-a** cork, stopper; *(prej druri)* bunghole; **heq tapën:** to draw the cork; **mbyll me tapë një shishe:** to cork (to stop) a bottle. – *Lok.* **bëhem tapë:** to be intoxicated.
tapí,-a *f.sh.* - land-patent.
tapicerí,-a *f.* tapestry, wall-paper, hangings.
tapiciér,-i *m.sh.* **-ë** upholsterer.
tapós *f.k.* to cork, to stop (a bottle). – **taposet** *f.jv.* to be corked.
taráf,-i *m.sh.* **-e** coterie.
tarafllëk,-u *m.* nepotism.
tarallák,-u *m.sh.* **-ë** idiot, buzzard, stupid, dull fellow, dull, simpleton.
taratór,-i *m.* a dish prepared with yogurt (yoghurt), olive oil and crushed garlics mixed together.
tár/ë,-a *f. treg.* tare.
tárg/ë,-a *f.sh.* **-a** *(makine)* number-plate, plate, *amer.* license plate, plate.
taríf/ë,-a *f.sh.* **-a** 1. tariff, pricelist, rate, scale of charges; **tarifa postare të brendshme:** inland postage.
tartabíq,-i *m.sh.* **-e** *zool. krah.* bug.
tarrác/ë,-a *f.sh.* **-a** terrace; **kodër me tarraca:** terraced hill.
tas,-i *m.sh.* **-a** bowl.
tásk/ë,-a *f.sh.* **-a** *krah. (duhani)* ash-tray.
tasqebáp,-i *m.* fricassee.
tastiér/ë,-a *f.sh.* **-a** *muz.* keyboard, key-frame.
tatëpjétë *ndajf.* 1. down, downward; **marr tatëpjetë:** to go downward.
tatëpjét/ë (e),-a(e) *f.sh.* **-a (të)** 1. slope, declivity, slant, descent. 2. *fig.* decline; **e tatëpje-**

ta e një perandorie: the decline of an empire.
tatëpjétë (i,e) *mb.* slant, abrupt.
tatím,-i *m.sh.* **-e** impost, tax, duty; **tatim mbi të ardhurat:** income-tax; **tatim fitimi:** revenue-tax.
tatój *f.k.* to tax. – **tatohem** *f.jv.* to be taxed.
tatuázh,-i *m.sh.* **-e** tattoo.
taván,-i *m.sh.* **-e** ceiling.
tavanxhí,-u *m.sh.* **-nj** carpenter.
tavérn/ë,-a *f.sh.* **-a** tavern.
táv/ë,-a *f.sh.* **-a** baking-pan, roaster; **tavë balte:** baking earthenware.
táv/ëll,-lla *f.sh.* **-lla** 1. *(duhani)* ash-tray. 2. *(lojë)* backgammon.
tavolín/ë,-a *f.sh.* **-a** table; desk; **tavolinë kuzhine:** kitchen table; *(mesi, e rrumbullakët)* round table; **tavolinë pune:** worktable; *(shkrimi, zyre)* desk, writing-table; **mbulesë tavoline** : table-cloth; **shtroj tavolinën:** to lay the table, to set the table; **ngrej tavolinën:** to clear the table; **ulem në tavolinë (për të ngrënë):** to sit down to a meal, to be at table.
táze *mb.* fresh, newly picked; **domate taze:** fresh tomatoes; **gjalpë taze:** fresh butter.
te (tek) *paraf.* at, to; **te dera:** at the door; **ai shkoi tek i ungji:** he went to his uncle's.
teát/ër,-ri *m.sh.* **-re** theater.
teatrál,-e *mb.* theatrical.
tebeshír,-i *m.* chalk.
tegél,-i *m.sh.* **-a** selvage, seam (of a cloth).
teh,-u *m.sh.* **-e** blade, edge; **teh thike:** knife-blade.
tej I. *ndajf.* 1. far; **atje tej:** far off, far younder; **më tej:** onward; **shko më tej:** go farther. **II.** *paraf.* 1. beyond; **tej masës:** beyond measure. 2. through;

tej e mbanë: from side to side, from end to end.
tejçój *f.k.* to transmit.
tejçúes,-i *m.sh.* - *el.* conductor.
tejdúksh/ëm(i),-me (e) *mb.* transparent.
téje (prej) *p.v.* of you (shih ti).
tejembánë *ndajf.* from side to side, from end to end.
tejkalím,-i *m.sh.* -e overfulfilment.
tejkalój *f.k.* 1. to surpass, to overfulfil; tejkaloj planin: to overfulfil the plan. 2. *(në numër)* to outnumber. 3. *(në rendje)* to outrun. 4. *(masën)* to exceed, to go beyond (the measure or limit). 5. *(dikë në zotësi)* to excel someone in capability. — tejkalohet *f.jv.* (plani) to be overfulfilled (of a plan).
tejpërtéj *ndajf.* through, from side to side.
tejqýr/ë,-a *f.sh.* -a spy-glass.
tejshikím,-i *m.* foresight.
tejshikój *f.k.* to foresee.
tejshikúes,-i *m.sh.* - clear-sighted person.
tejshkúar (i,e) *mb. gram.* anterior; koha e kryer e tejshkuar: past perfect tense.
téjz/ë,-a *f.sh.* -a *anat.* tendon.
tek *ndajf.* being (making up) an odd number.
tek,-e *mb.* odd, uneven; numër tek: odd number, uneven number.
tek *lidh.* while; tek isha duke shkuar: while I was going; ja tek është: there he is.
tek *paraf.* at, to; vajti tek i biri: he went to his son; tek oborri i shkollës: at the schoolyard.
tekanjóz,-e *mb.* whimsical, freakish, capricious, wayward; fëmijë tekanjoz: wayward child.
téket (më, të, i) *f. jv.* to have a fancy for, atij iu tek të shkonte në Berat: some whim induced him to go off to Berat.

ték/ë,-a *f.sh.* -a whim, freak, caprice, fancy.
teklíf(pa) *ndajf.* free and easy, unceremoniously, without ceremony; ha pa teklif! eat your fill free and easy!
teknefés,-e *mb. vjet.* asthmatic; kalë teknefes: asthmatic horse.
tekník,-u *m.sh.* -ë technician; teknik ndriçimi: light technician.
tekník,-e *mb.* technical; terma teknike: technical terms.
tekník/ë,-a *f.* 1. technics. 2. technique; teknika e të pikturuarit: painting technique.
teknikísht *ndajf.* technically.
teknikúm,-i *m.sh.* -e industrial school, *amer.* vocational school, training school.
teknológ,-u *m,sh.* -ë technologist.
teknologjí,-a *f.* technology.
teknologjík,-e technological.
tekst,-i *m.sh.* -e text.
tekstíl,-e *mb.* textile; kombinati i tekstilit: textile mill.
tekstilíst,-i *m.sh.* -ë weaver.
tekstualísht *ndajf.* textually.
tek-tuk *ndajf.* here and there; tek-tuk kishte ndonjë gabim: there were a few mistakes here and there.
tel,-i *m.sh.* -a 1. wire; tel telefoni: telegraphic wire; tel me gjemba: barbed wire; rrjetë teli: wire netting, lattice work; uzinë e telave: wire-mill; prej teli: wiry. 2. *muz.* chord, string; tel kitare: guitar string, etc.; vegla muzikore me tela: stringed instruments.
telásh,-i *m.sh.* -e embarrassment, scrape, predicament, plight; jam në telash: to be in a pretty pass, to be in a predicament, to be in a sorry plight; to be into a scrape; nxjerr telashe: to cause trouble, to give a great deal of trouble; shpëtoj nga

një telash: to get out of a scrape; **plot telashe**: full of scrape (of care); **pa telashe**: careless.
teleferík,-u *m.sh.* -ë cable-car, telpher.
telefón,-i *m.sh.* -a 1. phone, telephone;**numär telefoni**: telephone number; **kërkoj dikë në telefon**: to phone someone, to call (to ring) someone up; **i bëj një telefon dikujt**: to give someone a ring (a call), *amer.* to give someone a buzz. 2. public telephone.
telefoník,-e *mb.* telephonic; **centrali telephonik**: telephonic central; **kabinë telefonike**: telephone box (booth), call-box.
telefoníst,-i *m.sh.* -ë telephonist, telephone operator, switchboard operator.
telefonój *f. jk.* to phone, to telephone, to ring up, to call up; **nuk munda t'i telefonoja shokut tim**: I wasn't able to phone my friend.
telegráf,-i *m.* telegraph.
telegrafík,-e *mb.* telegraphic.
telegrafíst,-i *m.sh.* -ë telegrapher, telegraph operator, telegraphist.
telegrafój *f.jk.* to wire, to cable, to telegraph, to send a telegram (a wire).
telegrám,-i *m.sh.* -e wire, telegram, *amer.* cablegram; **telegram me përgjigje**: reply-paid telegram.
telendís *f.k.* 1. to indispose, to give a great deal of trouble. 2. to bring discredit upon someone. — **telendisem** *f.jv.* 1. to be indisposed; to be troubled, to be embarrassed. 2. to be discredited.
telendísj/e,-a *f.* 1. trouble, embarrassment. 2. discredit.

telepatí,-a *f.* telepathy.
teleskóp,-i *m.sh.* -ë telescope.
televizión,-i *m.* television.
televizív,-e *mb.* television; **program televiziv**: TV programme.
televizór,-i *m.sh.* -rë television set, televisor, *fam.* TV, telly.
telikós *f.k.* to wear out, to weaken. — **telikosem** *f.jv.* to wear out, to weaken.
telláll,-i *m.sh.* -ë bellman, herald, town-crier, public crier.
tematík,-e *mb.* thematic.
temená,-ja *f.sh.* — *vjet.* cringe, servile bow; **bëj temena**: to kowtow, to cringe.
tém/ë,-a *f.sh.* -a theme, topic, subject; **shumë libra janë shkruar mbi këtë temë**: many books have been written on this subject; **largim nga tema**: digression; **dal jashtë temës**: to digress.
temján,-i *m.* incense.
temjaníc/ë,-a *f.sh.* -a censer, thurible.
temperamént,-i *m.sh.* -e nature, temperament.
temperatúr/ë,-a *f.* 1. temperature; **rënie e temperaturës**: drop in temperature. 2. *mjek.* temperature, fever; **kam pak temperaturë**: to have a slight temperature.
temp,-i *m.* rhythm.
témpu/ll,-lli *m.sh.* -j temple.
tendénc/ë,-a *f.sh.* -a tendency.
tendencióz,-e *mb.* tendencious, tendentious.
ténd/ë,-a *f.sh.* -a tilt, canopy, awning, sun-blind.
tendós *f.k.* to stretch. — **tendoset** *f.jv.* to be stretched.
tendósj/e,-a *f.* stretching, stretch.
tendósur(i,e) *mb.* stretched, tense, drawn tightly, tight, taut; **me nerva të tendosura**: with tense nerves.

teneqé,-ja *f.sh.* – 1. tin; **punishte teneqeje:** tinwork; **artikuj prej teneqeje:** tin-wares. 2. *(plehrash)* bin (for filths). 3. *(uji)* tin vessel.
teneqepunúes,-i *m.sh.* – tinsmith, tinman.
teneqexhí,-u *m.sh.* -nj shih **teqepunues.**
tenís,-i *m.* tennis; **raketë tenisi:** tennis-raquet.
tenór,-i *m.sh.* -ë *muz.* tenor.
tensión,-i *m.* 1. *el.* tension. 2. *mjek. (tension i gjakut)* blood pressure. 3. *pol.* tension.
tentatív/ë,-a *f.sh.* -a attempt, try; **bëj një tentativë:** to make an attempt, to have a try.
tentój *f.k.* to attempt, to try.
tenxhér/e,-ja *f.sh.* -e pot, stewpan, stewpot; **vë tenxheren në zjarr:** to put on the pot; **tenxhere me presion:** pressure-cooker.
ténj/ë,-a *f.sh.* -a *zool.* woodworm.
teológ,-u *m.sh.* -ë theologian.
teologjí,-a *f.* theology.
teorém/ë,-a *f.sh.* -a *mat.* theorem.
teorí,-a *f.sh.* theory.
teorík,-e *mb.* theoretical.
teorikísht *ndajf.* theoretically.
tepelék,-u *m. gj.bis.* **tepeleku i kokës:** the top of the head, the crown of the head.
tép/ë,-a *f. bot.* wild wheat.
tépér *ndajf.* too, too much, overmuch, excessively; **tepër i shtrenjtë:** excessively costly. *–Lok.* **për më tepër:** moreover, furthermore.
tépërm(i),-e(e) *mb.* superfluous, excessive.
tépërmi (së) *ndajf.* excessively, at excess; **lodhem së tepërmi:** to overtire oneself.
tépërt (i;e) *mb.* shih **i tepërm.**
teprí,-a *f.* 1. excess, overplus; **pi me tepri (alkool):** to drink

at excess (spirits). 2. exageration.
tepríc/ë,-a *f.sh.* -a overplus, surplus; **ka me tepricë:** there are in abundance; **dorëzim i tepricave të drithrave:** delivery of the surplus of cereals.
teprój *l. f.k.* to exaggerate, to overstate; **ai po e tepron:** he exaggerates, he goes beyond bounds. ll. *f.jk.* to remain, to be left over; **po më teproi koha do të shkoj:** if there is any time left l shall go.
tepsí,-a *f.sh.* baking-pan, pie-pan.
teptís *f.jk. krah.* 1. *(gjaku)* to spout (blood). 2. *(uji)* to gush, to overrun, to overflow (water).
teptísj/e,-a *f.* 1. *(e gjakut)* spouting (of blood), hemorrhage. 2. *(e ujit)* gush, overflow, eruption (of water).
téqe,-ja *f.sh.* -e small mosque, masjid.
ter *f.k.* to dry up; **ter këmishët:** to dry up the shirts. – **terem** *f.jv.* to be dried up.
terezí,-a *f.sh.* – *vjet.* 1. balance. 2. plumb of mason. – *Lok.* **me terezi:** carefully, moderately.
term,-i *m.sh.* -a term, word; **terma shkencore:** scientific terms.
terminologjí,-a *f.* terminology.
termomèt/ër,-ri *m.sh.* -ra thermometer.
termosifón,-i *m.sh.* -a thermosiphon.
terpentín/ë,-a *f.* turpentine.
ters *ndajf.* amiss; **i marr fjalët ters:** to take the words amiss.
ters,-e *mb.* perverse, wayward, froward, impertinent, cross-grained; **fëmijë ters:** wayward child; **numër ters:** unlucky number.

tersllëk,-u *m.* mischance, bad luck.

tertíp,-i *m.sh.* -e order; **punoj me tertip**: to work regularly (systematically, according to a system).

terr,-i *m.* darkness.

terrén,-i *m.sh.* -e ground; land; **terren sportiv**: sports ground, playing-field; *fig.* **fitoj terren**: to gain ground.

terrín/ë,-a *f.* darkness; darkening.

territór,-i *m.sh.* -e territory.

terrór,-i *m.* terror.

terroríst,-i *m.sh.* -ë terrorist.

terroríst,-e *mb.* terrorising.

terroríz/ëm,-mi *m.* terrorism.

terrorizój *f.k.* to terrorize. — **terrorizohem** *f.jv.* to be terrorized.

téser/ë,-a *f.sh.* -a card; **teserë partie**: party-card.

tespíhe,-t *f.sh.* — beads, chaplet, rosaries.

testamént,-i *m.sh.* -e testament, will; **bëj testamentin**: to make one's will; **lë me testament**: to bequeath by will, to leave something to someone by will (in one's will).

tésha,-t *f.sh. krah.* 1. linen; **laj teshat**: to wash one's linen. 2. *(të sipërme)* clothes, clothing; **një palë tesha**: a complete suit of clothes. 3. *(udhëtimi)* baggage, luggage.

teshtíj *f.k.* to sneeze.

teshtím/ë,-a *f.sh.* -a sneeze, sneezing.

tetanós,-i *m. mjek.* tetanus.

tetár,-i *m.sh.* -ë *usht.* corporal.

tétë *num. them.* eight; **tetë Marsi është dita e gruas**: March 8 is the Woman's Day.

tétë (i,e) *num. rresht.* eight.

tetëdhjétë *num. them.* eighty.

tetëdhjétë (i,e) *num. rresht.* eightieth.

tetëdhjetëvjeçár,-e *mb.* octogenarian.

tetëfísh,-i *m.* eightfold.

tetëfísh,-e *mb.* eightfold, octuple.

tetëmbëdhjétë *num. them.* eighteen.

tetëmbëdhjétë (i,e) *num. rresht.* eighteenth.

tetëqínd *num. them.* eight hundred.

tetëqíndtë (i,e) *num. rresht.* eight hundredth.

tetëvjeçár,-e *mb.* octennial; **shkollë tetëvjeçare**:eight-year school, 8-grade (8-year) school.

této,-ja *f.sh.* — aunt.

tetór,-i *m.* October.

teveqél,-i *m.sh.* -ë simpleton, dolt, fool.

teveqél,-e *mb.* silly, foolish, dull, noodle.

téz/e,-ja *f.sh.* -e aunt, mother's sister.

téz/ë,-a *f.sh.* -a 1. thesis, dissertation; **mbroj tezën**: to defend one's dissertation (thesis). 2. idea, opinion; **mbështes (mbroj) një tezë**: to uphold an idea.

tézg/ë,-a *f.sh.* -a 1. litter, stretcher. 2. stoll, stand.

tezgjáh,-u *m.sh.* -e loom, handloom.

të I. *p.v.* 1. thou, you (used in a familiar way); **unë të shoh**: I see you. 2. contractive form of *atë*; **pa të (atë) nuk shkoj**: I don't go without him (or her); **e ruaj për të (atë)**: I keep it for him (or her).
II. *nyje e përparme* 1. (former) article of the genitive, dative and ablative cases); (genitive) **i shokut të tij**: of his comrade; (dative) **shokut të tij**: to his comrade; (ablative) **prej shokut të tij**: from his comrade. 2. (article having an atributive function) **i dua mollët të**

ёmbla: I like sweet apples; I like apples to be sweet. III. *pjesëz* 1. (particle placed before verbs in the past participle and infinitive) **bëj të ditur:** to make known, to inform; **për të folur mirë një gjuhë:** to speak well a language. 2. (particle placed before verbs of the subjunctive mood) **të jetojmë të punojmë dhe të mendojmë si revolucionarë:** we must live, work and think as revolutionaries; **duhet të shkoj:** I must go, I have to go. 3. (particle placed before verbs of the future tense) **do të shkoj:** I shall go. 4. (before verbs of the conditional mood) **do të shkoja:** I should go; (in conditional cases) **po të doni:** if you please, if you like. 5. (as particle it is used to form some indefinite pronouns) **të gjithë, të tërë:** all; **të gjithë për një, një për të gjithë:** all for one and one for all.

tëhárr *f.k.* 1. *(arën)* to weed, to clear from weeds (the ground). 2. *(vreshtin)* to prune (the vine). – **tëharret** *f.jv.* 1. to be weeded. 2. to be pruned.

tëhárrje-a *f.* 1. weeding. 2. pruning.

tëhú *ndajf.* that way; **tutje-tëhu:** here and there.

tëlýn,-i *m.* butter.

tëmb/ël,-li *m.sh.* **-la** *anat.* biliary vesicle.

tëmth,-i *m.sh.* **-a** *anat.* temple; **po thinjesh te tëmthat:** you are going grey at the temples.

tënd *p.pr.* thy, your; **shiko punën tënde:** mind your business; **shiko në librin tënd:** look at your book.

tëpkë *mb. vjet.* identic, identical;

ai është tëpkë i ati: he is the very image of his father.

tërbím,-i *m.* 1. rabies. 2. *fig.* fury, rage; **me tërbim:** furiously, in a rage.

tërbój *f.k.* to enrage, to make furious, to drive wild. – **tërbohem** *f. jv,* to grow rabid; to be enraged; **ai u tërbua nga inati:** he got furious with anger.

tërbúar (i,e) *mb.* 1. rabid; **qen i tërbuar:** rabid dog. 2. *fig.* furious, frantic.

tërë *ndajf.* all, full; **tërë gaz:** full of joy; **tërë natën:** all night long.

tërë (i, e) *p.pk.* all; **i tërë fshati:** all the village; **e tërë fusha:** all the field; **të tërë njёrёzit:** all the people.

tёr/ё(e),-a(e) *f.* whole; **pjesёt qё pёrbёjnё tё tёrёn:** the parts which make up the whole.

tёrёsí,-a *f.* integrity; **tёrёsia tokёsore:** territorial integrity; **nё tёrёsi:** on the whole.

tёrёsísht *ndajf.* wholly, entirely, completely, totally; **e lexova tёrёsisht:** I read it wholly.

tёrfíl,-i *m. bot.* clover, trefoil, shamrock.

tёrhéq *f.k.* 1. to attract; **magneti e tёrheq hekurin:** a magnet attracts iron. 2. *(karrocën)* to draw (a carriage); *(një anije)* to tow, to tug. 3. *(fjalën)* to retract, to take back (one's word). 4. *(vёmendjen)* to draw (to attract) the attention, to call attention to. 5. **tёrheq zvarrё:** to drag; to trail, to haul, to lug. – **tёrhiqem** *f.jv.* to draw back, to withdraw; *(nga jeta, nga puna)* to retire (from active life, from business).

tёrhéqёs,-e *mb.* attractive, inviting.

tёrhéqj/e,-a *f.* 1. *(me kafshё,*

me makinë) traction. 2. *fiz.* attraction. 3. *fig.* attraction, appeal. 4. *(e një ushtrie)* withdrawal, retreat. 5. *(nga shoqëria)* retirement.

tërkúz/ë,-a *f.sh.* -a rope.

tërmét,-i *m.sh.* -e earthquake; **tërmeti, i tërmetit**: seismic.

tërsëllëm (me) *ndajf.* impetuously, violently.

tërshër/ë,-a *f. bot.* oat; **qull tërshëre**: oatmeal.

tërthórazi *ndajf.* 1, indirectly, in a roundabout way. 2. transversally.

tërthórtë (i,e) *mb.* 1. indirect. 2. transversal; **vijë e tërthortë:** cross-line.

ti *p.v.* thou, you (used in a familiar way); **ti je:** you are.

tifo,-ja *f. mjek.* typhus; **tifo e zorrëve:** enteric typhus.

tifóz,-i *m.sh.* -ë fan, lover, enthusiast, fanatic; **tifoz futbolli:** a football fan.

tifóz,-e *mb.* enthusiastic, keen.

tigán,-i *m.sh.* -ë pan, frying-pan, sauce-pan.

tiganís *f.k.* to fry. − **tiganiset** *f.jv.* to be fried.

tiganísj/e,-a *f.* frying.

tiganísur (i,e) *mb.* fried; **patate të tiganisura:** fried potatoes.

tíg/ër,-ri *m.sh.* -ra *zool.* tiger.

tij (i,e) *p.pr.* his; **libri i tij:** his book; **nëna e tij:** his mother.

tíjat (të) *p.pr.* his own; **janë të tijat:** they belong to him.

tíllë (i,e) *mb.* such, like; **në një mënyrë të tillë:** in such a manner; **të tillë njerëz:** such people.

tim *p.pr.* my; to my; **tim vëlla e falënderuan:** they thanked my brother; **tim vëllai:** to my brother; **i shkrova tim vëllai:** I wrote to my brother.

tíme *p.pr.* (for feminine); **time**

motër, motrën time: my sister

timón,-i *m.sh.* -a *(anijeje)* helm rudder (of a ship); *(automobili)* steering-wheel; *(biçiklete)* handle-bar; *(karroce)* pole (of a coach); *(plugu)* beam (of a plough); **drejtimi i timonit:** streerage.

timoniér,-i *m.sh.* -ë helmsman, steersman, wheelsman.

tinár,-i *m.sh.* -ë. keg, vat.

tínës *ndajf.* stealthily, secretly; **iki tinës:** to sneak, to steal away.

tinëzísht *ndajf.* shih **tinës.**

tingëllím,-i *m.sh.* -e shih **tingëllimë.**

tingëllím/ë,-a *f.sh.* -a sounding, ringing; *(i një zileje)* ringing (of a bell); *(i kambanës)* tolling, chime (of a church-bell); *(i shkurtër dhe i mprehtë)* tinkling, clickling, clank, twang.

tingëllój *f.k.* to ring, to toll, to tingle; **një notë që tingëllon keq në vesh:** a jarring note.

tingëllúes,-e *mb.* sonorous, sounding.

tíngthi *ndajf.* hopping on one leg; **kërcej tingthi:** to hop on one leg; **lojë tingthi:** hopscotch.

tíngu/ll,-lli *m.sh.* -j sound, ring; **tingulli i bories:** honk of a cornet; *(i një teli mandoline etj.)* twang (of a string).

tíngullt (i,e) *mb.* sonourous.

tinzár,-i *m.sh.* -ë sly person, sneak, slyboots.

tinzár,-e *mb.* sly, sneaky, crafty, foxy.

tip,-i *m.sh.* -a type; **ai është tip më vete:** he is original.

tipár,-i *m.sh.* -e feature, character.

tipográf,-i *m.sh.* -ë typographer, printer.

tirán,-i *m.sh.* -ë tyrant, despot, oppressor.

tiraní,-a *f.* tyranny.

tiraník,-e *mb.* tyrannical.
tiranizój *f.k.* to tyrannize. - **tira-nizohem** *f.jv.* to be tyrannized.
tiránta,-t *f.sh. krah.* shih **bretele.**
tirázh,-i *m.sh.* -e run, edition; *(i gazetës)* circulation; **tirazh i madh:** long run; **tirazh i vogël:** short run.
tír/ë,-a *f.sh.* -a wine vat.
tirk,-u *m.sh.* **tirqe** a kind of close fitting trousers.
títu/ll,-lli *m.sh.* -j 1. title; **titulli i një libri:** title of a book; *(i një artikulli të një gazete):* head-line (of an article). 2. *(nderi)* honorary title. 3. *(shkencor)* qualification.
titullár,-i *m.sh.* -ë *(i një zyre)* official, office-holder.
titullój *f.k.* to entitle. - **titullohet** *f.jv.* to be entitled.
tjégull,-a *f.sh.* -a tile, roof-tile; **punishte tjegullash:** tile-works.
tjérë (të) *p.pk.* others; **e të tjera** *(etj.):* and others; and so on, and so forth (etc.)
tjerr *f.k. (lesh)* to spin (wool.) - **tirret** *f.jv.* to be spinned.
tjérrë (i,e) *mb.* spun; **lesh i tjerrë:** spun wool.
tjérrës,-i *m.sh.* - spinner.
tjérrës,-e *mb.* spinning; **makinë tjerrëse:** spinning jenny, spining machine, throstle.
tjérrj/e,-a *f.* spinning.
tjétër *p.pk.* 1. other, another; **tjetër gjë:** other thing; **doni gjë tjetër?** do you want anything else (something else)? **një tje-tër:** another; **të ndihmojmë njëri-tjetrin:** we must help one another (each other). 2. next; **vitin tjetër:** next year; **tjetri, tjetra:** the next (person), the other, the sequent. - *Lok.* **pa tjetër:** without fail.
tjetërkúsh *p.pk.* somebody else.

tjetërkúnd *ndajf.* elsewhere, somewhere else.
tjetërsój *f.k. drejt.* to alienate.
tjetërsój *ndajf.* otherwise, differently.
tkurr *f.k.* to contract, to shrink up. - **tkurrem** *f.jv.* to contract, to shrink.
tkúrrj/e,-a *f.* contraction, shrin-king; **tkurrja e muskulit:** the contraction of a muscle.
tmerr,-i *m.* terror, dismay, scare, dread, horror; **për tmerr:** horribly, terribly, dreadfully.
tmerrësísht *ndajf.* terribly, awfully, tremendously.
tmerrój *f.k.* to terrify, to dismay, to horrify, to appall. - **tmerro-hem** *f.jv.* to be terrified, to be dismayed (scared, dreaded).
tmérrsh/ëm(i),-me (e) *mb.* terrible, horrible, horrid, dreadful.
tmerrúes,-e *mb.* terrifying, horrific.
tog,-u *m.sh.* **togje** 1. heap, pile, mass; **një tog plehrash:** a mass of filths. 2. sheave; **një tog me kallinj gruri:** a sheave of wheat.
togér,-i *m.sh.* -ë *usht.* lieutenant.
tóg/ë,-a *f.sh.* -a *usht.* platoon.
tóg/ë,-a *f.sh.* -a robe; *(gjykatësi)* gown, magistrates'robe.
tój/ë,-a *f.sh.* -a *zool.* shih **ku-rrillë.**
tój/ë,-a *f.* fishing line.
tok *ndajf.* both, together; **të dy tok:** both; **të shkojmë të dy tok:** let us go together.
tok *f.k. (dorën)* to shake (hands).
tók/ë,-a *f.sh.* -a 1. earth; **rrotulli-mi i tokës rreth boshtit të vet:** rotation of the earth round its axis. 2. earth, land; **një rrip i ngushtë toke futet në det:** a narrow stretch of land extends into the sea; **në tokë:** on land, ashore, on shore; **zbres në tokë:** to land, to come on shore, to descend on shore, to disem-

bark. 3. land, earth, soil; **lëroj tokën**: to plough the land; **tokë pjellore**: fertile soil; **tokë e papunuar**: uncultivated ground, waste land, virgin land; **tokë e punuar**: cultivated (tilled) ground; **tokë shterpë**: sterile (fruitless) ground; **tokë e zezë**: black soil, humus; **ngastër toke**: a plot (a patch) of ground. 4. ground; floor; **hedh një send në tokë (për tokë)**: to throw an object to the ground; **ngre një laps nga toka**: to pick up a pencil from the ground. 5. land, property, estate; **shes një tokë**: to sell an estate. 6. country; **toka jonë**: our country. 7. *mjek.* **sëmundje e tokës**: epilepsy.

tokësór,-e *mb.* 1. territorial, terrestrial; **ndarje administrative tokësore**: territorial administrative division. 2. land; **forca ushtarake tokësore**: land forces. 3. overland; **transport tokësor**: overland transport.

tókëz,-a *f.s.h.* -a clasp, fastener; *(rripi)* buckle (of a belt); **mbërthej me tokëz**: to fasten with a clasp.

tokëzím,-i *m. el.* earthing, *amer.* grounding.

tokmák,-u *m.sh.* -ë ram.

toleránc/ë,-a *f.* toleration.

tolerój *f.k.* to tolerate. — **tolerohet** *f.jv.* to be tolerated.

tolloví,-a *f.* riot, revolt, rebellion, muting, tumult, agitation, perturbation, confusion.

tómbol,-a *f. (lojë)* tombola (game and lottery).

ton,-i *m. sh.* -e 1. tone, accent; **flas me një ton qortues**: to speak with a scolding tone. 2. *muz.* tone, pitch; **gjysmë toni**: fret, half tone.

ton,-i *m.sh.* -ë *zool.* tunny-fish, tuna.

ton,-i *m.sh.* -ë *treg.* ton.

tóna *p.pr. (fem.)* our, ours; **vajzat tona**: our girls; **ato janë tonat**: they are ours (shih **tonë**).

tonalitét,-i *m.sh.* -e *muz.* tonality.

tonázh,-i *m.sh.* -e *(i një anijeje etj.)* tonnage (of a ship, etc.).

tonelát/ë,-a *f.sh.* -a *treg.* ton (shih **ton**).

tónë *p.pr.* our; (dative) **i shkrojtëm shokut tonë**: we wrote to our comrade; (accusative) **shokun tonë e kritikuan**: they criticized our comrade.

toník,-e *mb.* 1. *gram.* tonic; **theks tonik**: tonic stress. 2. *mjek.* tonic, invigorating; **ilaç tonik**: tonic medicine. 3. *muz.* tonic.

top,-i *m.sh.* -a 1. *(lufte)* cannon, gun; **qitje me top**: cannon shot; **rrahje me top**: cannonade; **shtrati i topit**: gun-carriage. 2. ball; **top futbolli**: football, soccerball; **top tenisi**: tennis ball. 3. **top dëbore**: snowball.

topáll,-i *m.sh.* -ë cripple, lame person.

topáll,-e *mb.* lame.

topçí,-u *m.sh.* -nj gunner, cannoneer, artillery-man.

topít *f.k.* to disconcert, to benumb. — **topitem** *f.jv.* to be disconcerted, to grow torpid (numb, torpescent, bewildered).

topítj/e,-a *f.* torpidity, numbness, bewilderment.

topográf,-i *m.sh.* -ë topographer.

topolák,-e *mb.* plump, chubby, podgy, dumpy, short and thick fat and round, buxom.

toptán *ndajf. treg.* wholesale.

topúz,-i *m.sh.* -ë cudgel.

tórb/ë,-a *f.sh.* -a bag, small sack

holdall, hiking-sack; *(kali)* nose-bag (of horses).

tórf/ë,-a *f.* turf.

tórk/ë,-a *f.sh.* **-a** hank, skein.

torním,-i *m. mek.* turning, turnery.

tornitór,-i *m.sh.* **-ë** turner, lathe-hand.

tórno,-ja *f.sh.* – *mek.* lathe; **punoj në torno:** to lathe; **torno automatike:** automatic (self- acting) lathe; **torno druri:** wood-turning lathe; **repart tornosh:** lathe works.

tornój *f.k.* to turn (on a lathe). – **tornohet** *f.jv.* to be turned (on a lathe).

torollák,-e *mb.* foolish, stupid.

torollák,-u *m.sh.*-**ë** fool, simple-ton.

torpéd/ë,-a *f.sh.* **-a** *usht.* torpedo.

torpediniér/ë,-a *f.sh.* **-a** *det., usht.* torpedo-boat.

torpíl/ë,-a *f.sh.* **-a** shih **torpedë.**

torpilój *f.k.* to torpedo. – **torpilohet** *f.jv.* to be torpedoed.

tortúr/ë,-a *f.sh.* **-a** torture.

torturím,-i *m.* torturing.

turturój *f.k.* to torture. – **torturohem** *f.jv.* to be tortured.

tor/úa,-ói *m.* presence of mind; **ai nuk e humbi toruan për asnjë çast;** not for a moment he had lost his presence of mind; **humbas toruan:** to be at one's wit's end.

toskërísht *ndajf.* in the Southern dialect (of Albanian language).

toskërísht/e,-ja *f.* the Southern dialect of the Albanian langu-age.

toz,-i *m.* powder; **toz limoni:** citric acid.

tra,-u *m.sh.* **-rë** beam; *(trau i një dyshemeje)* girder, joist; *(çatie)* rafter (of a roof); *(i trashë)* balk, heavy timber.

tradicionál,-e *mb.* traditional.

tradít/ë,-a *f.sh.* **-a** tradition.

tradhtár,-i *m.sh.* **-ë** traitor, betra-yer.

tradhtár,-e *mb.* treacherous, trai-torous.

tradhtí,-a *f.* treason, treachery, betrayal; **tradhti e lartë:** high treason; **tradhti bashkëshortore:** perfidy.

tradhtísht *ndajf.* treacherouslv.

tradhtój *f.k.* to betray. – **tradhtohem** *f.jv.* to be betrayed.

trág/ë,-a *f.sh.* **-a** 1. trace, track (of a wheel). 2. hope; **s'ka tragë:** there is no hope.

tragjedí,-a *f.sh.* - tragedy.

tragjík,-e *mb.* tragic.

trajnér,-i *m.sh.* **-ë** *sport.* trainer, coach.

trájt/ë,-a *f.sh.* **-a** 1. shape; **merr. trajtë:** to take shape. 2. *gram* form; **trajta e shquar dhe e pashquar:** definite and inde-finite form.

trajtím,-i *m.* treatment; treating.

trajtój *f.k.* 1. to treat; **trajtoj mirë dikë:** to treat someone kindly; **ai nuk di t'i trajtojë njerëzit:** he does not know how to handle men; **trajtoj keq dikë:** to mal-treat someone, to treat someone badly. 2. *(shtjelloj)* to deal with, to treat; **trajtoj një çësh-tje gjerë e gjatë:** to treat a subject at length. – **trajtohem** *f.jv.* 1. to be treated; to be han-dled. 2. to be dealt with, to be treated.

trakt,-i *m.sh.* **-e** leaflet, tract; **ngjit trakte:** to stick leaflets.

traktát,-i *m.sh.* **-e** treaty; **traktat paqeje:** a peace treaty; **lidh një traktat:** to close a treaty.

traktór,-i *m.sh.* **-ë** tractor.

traktoríst,-i *m.s.h* **-ë** tractor driver.

trallís *f.jv.* shih **shastis.**

tram,-i *m.sh.* -e tramcar, tramway, *amer.* tram, street-car.

tram (tramba) *fj.plk.* bëj tramba një kalë: to barter a horse.

trampolín/ë,-a *f.sh.* -a springboard.

tramváj,-i *m.sh.* -e tramcar, tramway, *trolley, streetcar*

trángu/ll,-lli *m.sh.* -j *bot.* cucumber.

transferím,-i *m.sh.* -e 1, transfer; kërkoj transferim: to ask for a transfer. 2. removal, move.

transferój *f.k.* to transfer, to move, to remove. – transferohem *f.jv.* to be transferred; to move.

transformatór,-i *m.sh.* -ë *el.* transformer.

transformím,-i *m.sh.* -e transformation, change; pëson transformim: to undergo changes, to be changed.

transformój *f.k.* to transform, to change. – transformohem *f.jv.* to be transformed (changed).

transfuzión,-i *m.* transfusion; transfuzion gjaku: blood transfusion.

transkriptím,-i *m.* transcription.

transkriptój *f.k.* to transcribe. – transkriptohet *f.jv.* to be transcribed.

transmetím.-i *m.sh.* -e 1. *mek.* gearing, transmission. 2. *(me anë të radios)* broadcasting, broadcast; *(televiziv)* telecasting, telecast; transmetim direkt: direct (live) telecast.

transmetój *f.k.* 1. *mek.* to transmit. 2. *(me radio)* to broadcast.

transmetúes,-e *mb.* transmitting; aparat transmetues: transmitter.

transmetúesh/ëm (i),-, me (e) *mb.* transmissible, transmittible.

transmisión,-i *m.sh.* -e *mek.* transmission; rrip transmisioni: belt.

transpórt,-i *m.* transport, transportation, carriage; mjete transporti: means of transport, vehicles; shpenzime transporti: transport expenses; transport ajror: air transport; transport detar: water-borne transport, marine transport; transport hekurudhor: rail transport, transport mallrash: freight transport, transport (carriage) of goods.

transportím,-i *m.* transportation, conveyance, carriage.

transportój *f.k.* to transport, to convey; transportoj mallra: to transport goods; *(me lundër)* to ferry; *(me tërheqje)* to haul. – transportohet *f.jv.* to be transported (conveyed).

transportúes,-i *m.sh.* - transporter, carrier.

transversál,-e *mb.* transverse, transversal.

transversalísht *ndajf.* transversally.

tranzitív,-e *mb.* *gram.* transitive; folje tranzitive (kalimtare): transitive verb.

tranzitór,-e *mb.* transitory; flamur tranzitor: challenge banner; periudhë tranzitore: transitory period, period of transition.

trap,-i *m.sh.* -e 1. ferry-boat, ferry, raft; transportoj me trap: to ferry. 2. ditch. 3. snare; kap me trap: to snare, to catch with a snare.

trapán,-i *m.sh.* -ë *mek.* gimlet, borer, boring-machine.

trapéz,-i *m.sh.* -ë *gjeom.* trapezium.

trapéz/ë,-a *f.sh.* -a *vjet.* table.

trapezoíd,-i *m.sh.* -ë *gjeom.* trapezoid.

trapezoidál,-e *mb.* trapezoidal.

trasé,-ja *f.sh.* - track; *(hekurudhe)* rail-way track.

trást/ë,-a *f.sh.* -a bag.
trash *f.k.* 1. to thicken, to make thick; *fig.* **ata i trashën fjalët:** they began to quarrel. 2. *(një lëng):* to condense (a liquid). — **trashem** *f.jv.* to grow stout.
trashalúq,-i *m.sh.* -ë obese, corpulent person.
trashalúq,-e *mb.* obese, corpulent.
trashamán,-i *m.sh.* -ë shih **trashaluq**
tráshë (i,e) *mb.* 1. thick; **burrë i trashë:** corpulent man. 2. *fig. (nga mendja)* thick-headed, thick-witted, thick-skulled.
trashëgím,-i *m.* inheritance, legacy, heritage; **lë trashëgim:** to bequeath; **lë pa trashëgim:** to disinherit.
trashëgimí,-a *f.* inheritance, heirship, heredity.
trashëgimór,-e *mb.* hereditary.
trashëgimtár,-i *m.sh.* -ë heir; **trashëgimtar i ligjshëm:** rightful heir.
trashëgój *f.k.* to inherit. — **trashëgohet** *f.jv.* to be inherited; **që trashëgohet:** congenital, hereditary; **sëmundje që trashëgohet:** congenital malady. — *Lok.* **të trashëgoheni!** may you be happy in marriage and have a long conjugal life!
trashësí,-a *f.* thickness.
tráshj/e,-a *f.* 1. thickening. 2. *(e një lëngu)* clotting, condensation (of a liquid).
travérs/ë,-a *f.sh.* -a cross-bar, traverse.
trazír/ë,-a *f.sh.* -a riot, tumult.
trazój *f.k.* 1. *(një lëng)* to stir, to agitate, to mix. 2. *(zjarrin)* to poke (the fire). 3. *(dikë)* to tease (someone). — **trazohet** *f.jv.* to be agitated (mixed).
trazováç,-i *m.sh.* -ë busybody, shooper, meddler.

tre *num. them.* three.
tredh *f.k.* (p.t. **trodha,** p.p. **tredhur)** to geld, to castrate, to emasculate.· — **tridhet** *f.jv.* to be gelded, castrated.
tredhak,-u *m.sh.* -ë gelding.
tredhëmbësh,-e *mb.* tridentate, having three teeth or prongs.
trédhj/e,-a *f.* castration.
trédhur (i) *mb.* gelded, castrated; **kalë i tredhur:** gelded horse.
trefísh,-i *m.* the triple, the threefold, the treble.
trefísh,-e *mb.* triple, threefold, treble, triplicate.
trefishím,-i *m.* threefolding, trebling.
trefishój *f.k.* to triple, to multiply by three, to triplicate. — **trefishohet** *f.jv.* to be tripled.
tre/g,-gu *m.sh.* -gje market; *(vendi i tregut)* market place; *(i frutave)* fruit market; *(i peshkut)* fish market; *(i shpendëve)* poultry market.
tregím,-i *m.sh.* -e tale, story, narration.
tregimtár,-i *m.sh.* -ë teller, narrator.
tregój *f.k.* 1. to show, to indicate; **tregomë një libër:** show me a book. 2. *(me gisht)* to point at. 3. to tell, to narrate; **tregoj emrin:** to tell the name; **tregomë një përrallë:** tell me a tale. — **tregohem** *f.jv.* to show oneself to be, to prove to be; **u tregua shumë i zoti:** he showed himself to be very able.
tregtár,-i *m.sh.* -ë merchant, dealer, trader, businessman, tradesman; *(me shumicë)* wholesale dealer; *(me pakicë)* retailer.
tregtár,-e *mb.* commercial, mercantile, merchant, business; **marrëdhënie tregtare:** commer-

cial intercourse, transactions; **firmë tregtare**: commercial (business) house (firm); **flotë tregtare**: mercantile fleet, merchant-fleet.

tregtí,-a *f*. trade, business, trading, commerce; **tregti ambulante**: peddling, ambulant trade; **tregti e jashtme**: foreign trade; **tregti me shumicë**: wholesale trade; **tregti me pakicë**: retail trade; **bëj tregti**: to trade, to deal.

tregtím,-i *m*. dealing, business intercourse.

tregtój *f.jk*. to trade, to deal.

tregúes,-e *mb*. index; **numër tregues**: index number; **gishti tregues**: index finger, forefinger.

tregúes,-i *m.sh*. - *(i librit)* index, contents.

trekátësh,-e *mb*. three-storied; **shtëpi trekatëshe**: three-storied house.

trekëmbësh,-i *m.sh*. -a gallows.

trekëmbësh,-e *mb*. three-legged; **tavolinë trekëmbëshe**: three-legged table.

trekëndësh,-i *m.sh*. -a *gjeom*. triangle.

trekëndësh,-e *mb*. triangular.

tremb *f.k*. to frighten, to scare; **ajo zhurmë më trembi**: that noise frightened me. — **trembem** *f.jv*. to be frightened (scared), to take fright, to get a fright.

trembëdhjétë *num.them*. thirteen.

trémbj/e,-a *f*. fright

trémbur (i,e) *mb*. frightened, scared.

trém/ë,-a *f.sh*. -a vestibule.

tremúajsh,-e *mb*. three months old.

tremujór,-i *m.sh*. -ë quarter (of a year), trimester.

tremujór,-e *mb*. quarterly, trimestrial.

tren,-i *m.sh*. -a train; **me tren**: by rail; by train; **tren ekspres**: express-train; **tren mallrash**: goods (freight) train; **më lë (ikën) treni**: to miss one's train.

trengjýrësh,-e *mb*. tricolour; **flamur trengjyrësh**: tricolour flag.

treqínd *num.them*. three hundred.

trerrokësh,-e *mb*. trisyllabic.

tresh,-i *m.sh*. -a three.

tret *f.k*. 1. *(ushqimin)* to digest (the food). 2. to thaw, to dissolve, to melt; *(dhjamin)* to melt (fat); *(sheqerin)*; to dissolve (sugar). 3. to lose; **i treta paratë**: I lost my money. — **tretem** *f.jv*. 1. to be digested. 2. to melt, to thaw. 3. to get thin, to loose weight, to grow thinner.

trétë (i,e) *num.rresht*. third; **veta e tretë**: third person; **një i tretë**: a third person.

trétës,-i *m.sh*. - solvent.

trétës,-e *mb*. digestive; **aparati tretës**: digestive apparatus.

trétj/e,-a *f*. 1. *(e ushqimeve)* digestion, assimilation (of food). 2.*(e dhjamit)* melting, dissolution.

trétsh/ëm (i),-me (e) *mb*. 1. dissolvable, dissoluble. 2. digestible, assimilable.

tretshmërí,-a *f*. 1. solvability (of a substance). 2. digestibility (of food).

trétur (i,e) *mb*. 1. *(dhjamë)* melted (fat); **sheqer i tretur**: dissolved sugar. 2. *(kufomë)* decomposed (corpse). 3. *(nga fytyra, nga trupi)* thin, lean.

trevjeçár,-i *m.sh*. -ë three years, three-year period.

trevjeçár,-e *mb*. triennial.

trëndafíl,-i *m.sh*. -a *bot*. rose; *(bima)* rose-bush, rose-plant; *ngjyrë trëndafili*: pinky, rose colour; **trëndafil i egër**: eglantine, sweet briar, dog-rose.

tri *num.them*. three; **tri vajza dhe**

tre djem: three girls and three boys.

tribún/ë,-a *f.sh.* -a tribune.

triciík/ël,-li *m.sh.* -la tricycle.

tridhjétë *num. them.* thirty.

tridhjétë(i,e) *num. rresht.* thirtieth.

trigonometrí,-a *f.* trigonometry.

tríko,-ja *f.sh.* — 1. jersey; **thur triko:** to knit, to do knitting. 2 blouse, jersey.

trikotázh,-i *m.* knitwear, hosiery, **fabrikë trikotazhi:** hosiery mill, knitwear mill; **artikuj trikotazhi** *(trikotazhe):* hosiery, knitwear.

tríkul,-i *m.sh.* -a tridentate pitchfork.

trill,-i *m.sh.* -e 1. freak, caprice, whim. 2. vicissitudes.

trillím,-i *m.sh.* -e fib, flam, machination, artifice.

trillój *f.k. (një gënjeshtër)* to invent, to contrive, to devise. — **trillohet** *f.jv.* to be invented.

trillúar (i,e) *mb.* fictive, fictious; **argument i trilluar:** specious argument.

trim,-i *m.sh.* -a valorous man, valiant person, brave man.

trim,-e *mb.* brave, bold, courageous, intrepid, hardy, valiant, valorous, dauntless, heroic.

trimést/ër,-ri *m.sh.* -ra trimester, quarter (of a year); **trimestri i parë:** the first quarter.

trimërí,-a *f.* bravery, prowess, heroism, valour, intrepidity.

trimërísht *ndajf.* bravely, courageously, valiantly.

trín/ë,-a *f.* 1. harrow. 2. hurdle

tríng/ë,-a *f.sh.* -a *zool.* finch, bullfinch.

tringëllíj *f.jk.* shih **tringëllój.**

tringëllím/ë,-a *f.sh.* -a 1. clang, clank, jingle; **tringëllímë e zileve:** clangor (jingle) of small bells. 2. *(e gotave)* chink (of drinking glasses).

tringëllój *f.jk.* to trinkle, to jingle, to clink.

trinój *f.k.* to harrow. — **trinohet** *f.jv.* to be harrowed.

trinóm,-i *m.sh.* -e *mat.* trinom.

trío,-ja *f.sh.* — *muz.* trio.

trísk/ë,-a *f.sh.* -a 1. card. 2. *(ushqimi)* food-card, ration-card.

triskëtím,-i *m.* rationing; **sistem i triskëtimit:** ration-system.

triskëtój *f.k.* to apply the ration-system. — **triskëtohet** *f.jv.* to be distributed by the ration — system.

trishtíl,-i *m.sh.* -ë *zool.* tit, titmouse, tomtit.

trishtím,-i *m.* sadness, dejection. melancholy, sorrow.

trishtój *f.k.* to sadden, to make sad. — **trishtohem** *f.jv.* to become sad.

trishtúar (i,e) *mb.* sorrowful, rueful, sad.

trishtúesh/ëm (i), - **me(e)** *mb.* sadly, gloomy, moody.

triúmf,-i *m.sh.* -a triumph.

triumfój *f.jk.* to triumph.

triumfúes,-i *m.sh.* — triumphator.

triumfúes,-e *mb.* triumphant.

troç *ndajf.* openly, bluntly, outright; **i them gjërat troç:** to speak openly; **ai ta thotë troç:** he speaks openly, he does not mince his words; **thuaje troç:** say it outright (openly).

tróft/ë,-a *f.sh.* -a *zool.* trout.

trok,-u *m.* trot (of a horse); **ecën trok (kali):** to trot (the horse).

trokás *f.k. (në derë)* to knock (at the door).

trókë *ndajf.* 1. **jam trokë:** I am penniless, I am broke: 2. dirty; **u bëra trokë:** I became dirty.

trók/ë,-a *f.sh.* -a 1. *(e një zileje) ose kambane)* knocker (of a bell, of a church bell). 2. *(e një dere)* knob, doorknob.

trokëllím/ë,-a *f.* 1. *(në derë)* knock. 2. *(në kalldrëm)* footsteps (on a pavement).

trokítj/e,-a *f.sh.* -e 1. *(në derë)* knock. 2. *(e duarve)* clapping (of hands), applause. 3. *(e këmbëve)* stamping (of feet). 4. *(e zemrës)* beating (of heart).

trókthi *ndajf.* at a trot; **eci trokthi**: to trot.

trondít *f.k.* 1. to jolt, to shake up. 2. to upset, to perturb, to disturb, to unsettle. — **tronditem** *f.jv.* to be upset (perturbed); **tronditem së tepërmi**: to be greatly startled, to have a terrible upset.

trondítës,-e *mb.* upsetting, perturbing.

trondítj/e,-a *f.* 1. *(shpirtërore)* distemper; upset. 2. *(nga makina)* commotion, trepidation. 3. *(nga karroca)* jolt. 4. *(e trurit)* concussion (of the brain).

tropík,-u *m.sh.* -ë *gjeog.* tropic.

tropikál,-e *mb.* tropical.

troshít *f.k.* to jolt, to jerk, to toss up and down. — **troshitem** *f.jv.* to jolt, to jerk, to bump.

troshítj/e,-a *f.* jolt, jerk.

trotuár,-i *m.sh.* -e sidewalk, wayside, road-side.

tru-ri *m.sh.- anat.* brain; **truri i vogël**: cerebellum, the little brain; **me tru**: brainy; **i trurit**: cerebral. — *Lok.* **ia hedh trutë në erë**: to blow out someone's brains; **njeri me tru**: brainy person, sharp-witted person; **njeri pa tru**: brainless person, idiot. — *Prov.* **njerëzit pa tru flasin më shumë**: empty vessels make most sound.

trúall,-i *m.sh.* **troje** site; ground; soil.

trullós *f.k.* to stun, to daze, to stupefy; *(pijet alkoolike)* to befuddle. — **trullosem** *f.jv.* to lose

one's head, to be stunned, to get befuddled.

trullósj/e,-a *f.* stunning, dazing, stupefaction; *(nga pijet)* befuddling.

trumbetár,-i *m.sh.* -ë trumpeter.

trumbét/ë,-a *f.sh.* -a trumpet, cornet.

trumbetím,-i *m.* trumpeting.

trumbetój *f.k.* to trumpet; *(një sekret)* to divulge (a secret). — **trumbetohet** *f.jv.* to be trumpeted; to be divulged.

trumcák,-u *m.sh.* -ë *zool.* sparrow.

trúmz/ë,-a *f.sh.* -a *bot.* thyme.

trun/g,-gu *m.sh.* -gje 1. *(pemë)* bole, trunk, stock (of a tree). 2. tree; **trung gjenealogjik**: the genealogical tree. 3. *fig.* heavy dull person.

trup,-i *m.sh.* -a 1. body; **trupi i njeriut**: the human body. 2. physique, build, frame; **kam trup atleti**: to have an athletic physique. 3. *fiz.* body; **trupa qiellorë**: the heavenly bodies. 4. staff, personnel; **trupi mësimor**: the teaching staff. 5. *usht.* corps, force; *sh.* troops; **trupa ushtarake**: military troops.

trúpazi,-a *f. mjek.* common dropsy, hydropisy.

trupërísht *ndajf.* corporally.

trupgjátë *mb.* tall; **njeri trupgjatë**: a tall man.

truplídhur *mb.* square-built, strong, stout.

trupmádh,-e *mb.* burly, hefty, corpulent.

trupòr,-e *mb.* corporal, bodily, physical; **ushtrime trupore**: physical exercices.

trupvógël *mb.* short, puny.

truthár/ë,-a *m.sh.* -ë dull-headed, thick-headed.

tryéz/ë,-a *f.sh.* -a 1. table; **tryezë pune**: work-table. 2. **tryezë e lëndës**: table of contents.

tu (e) *p.pr.* your; **djemtë e tu:** your sons.

túa (e) *p.pr.* your; **vajzat e tua:** your daughters.

túaj *p.pr.* to your; **shokut tuaj:** to your comrade.

túajat *p.pr.* yours; **janë tuajat:** they are yours, they belong to you.

tualét,-i *m.* toilet; **takëm tualeti:** toilet-set; **bëj tualet:** to make one's toilet, to make oneself up.

túat (të) *p.pr.* yours; **janë të tuat:** they belong to you, they are yours.

tub,-i *m.sh.* -a pipe, tube; **tub qelqi:** glass tube; **tub kanalizimi:** drain pipe; **tub uji:** water pipe.

tuberkulóz,-i *m.* *mjek.* tuberculosis, pulmonary, consumption, phthisis.

tubét,-i *m.sh.* -a small tube.

tufán-i *m.sh.* -e storm, tempest; **tufan me dëborë:** snowstorm, blizzard.

túf/ë,-a *f.sh.* -a 1. *(me lule)* nosegay, bouquet (of flowers). 2. *(me presh)* bunch (of leeks). 3. *(njerëzish)* crowd (of people). 4. *(me bagëti)* flock (of cattle). 5. **tufë çelsash:** bunch of keys; **bëj tufë, lidh tufë:** to bundle, to gather into bunches, to put in bunches.

tuháf,-e *mb.* eccentric, odd, whimsical.

tuhafilëk,-u *m.* eccentricity.

tukéqur (i,e) *mb.* *krah.* weak, feeble.

tul,-i *m.* 1. *(i frutave)* pulp (of fruits). 2. *(buke)* crumb (of bread). 3. *(i trupit)* flesh; **tërë tul, plot tul:** fleshy, pulpy, crumby, full of flesh (of pulp, of crumb).

tulítem *f.jv.* to crouch.

túltë (i, e) *mb.* pulpy, fleshy, crumby.

tullác,-i *m.sh.* -ë bald man.

tullác,-e *mb.* bald; **me kokë tullace:** bald-headed.

túll/ë,-a *f.sh.* -a brick; **tullë shamot:** fire-brick; *fig.* **e ka kokën tullë:** he is bald-headed.

tuílúmb,-i *m.sh.* -a water-pump.

tumáne,-t shih **çitjane.**

tumór,-i *m.sh.* -ë *mjek.* tumor; **tumor në kokë:** tumor in the head.

tumullác,-i *m.sh.* -ë *anat.* bladder, blister, vesicle.

tund *f.k.* 1. to rock, to lull; *(foshnjen në djep)* to rock, to lull asleep, to lull to sleep (a child). 2. *(një lëng në shishe)* to agitate, to shake, to stir violently (a liquid in a bottle). 3. *(qumështin)* to churn (milk). 4. *(kokën)* to shake, to toss (the head). 5. *(kapelën)* to wave (the hat).— **tundem** *f.jv.* 1. *(nga vendi)* to budge, to move (from one's position). 2. *(duke ecur)* to strut along, to swagger. 3. *(toka)* to quake, to shake (the earth).

túndës,-i *m.sh.* -a churner.

tundím,-i *m.sh.* -e temptation.

túndj/e,-a *f.* 1. *(e një lëngu)* agitation, stirring (of a liquid). 2. *(e tokës)* quaking, shaking (of the earth). 3. *(e kokës)* shake, toss (of the head). 4. *(e qumështit)* churning (of milk).

túndsh/ëm (i),-me (e) *mb.* movable; **pasuri e tundshme:** movable estate.

tunél,-i *m.sh.* -e tunnel.

tungjatjéta! *pasth.* hello! how do you do?

tunxh,-i *m.* bronze, brass.

turbín/ë,-a *f.sh.* -a turbine.

túrbull *ndajf.* 1. vaguely, obscurely; **shoh turbull:** to see vaguely (obscurely, dimly). 2. confusedly; **shprehem turbull:** to express oneself confusedly.

turbullím,-i *m.* disturbance, disturbing.

turbullír/ë,-a *f.* 1. tumult, riot, agitation. 2. turbidity.

turbullój *f.k.* 1. to trouble, to confuse, to disconcert, to perturb, to disturb. 2. *(ujët)* to muddy, to puddle (the water). – **turbullohem:** to be troubled.

túrbullt (i,e) *mb.* 1. *(ujë)* turbid, muddy. 2. *(kohë)* agitated (time). 3. *(mendim)* obscure, vague. – *Lok.* **peshkoj në ujë të turbullt:** to fish in troubled waters.

turbullúes,-e *mb.* 1. troublous; troubling; **person turbullues:** troublesome person. 3. subversive.

turí,-ri *m.sh.* **-nj** 1. muzzle, snout (of a beast). 2. face (of a man), (used contemptuously).

turfullím,-i *m. (i një kali)* snorting (of a horse).

turfullón *f.jk. (kali)* to snort (the horse).

turisëz,-e *mb.* surly, sullen.

turíst,-i *m.sh.* **-ë** tourist.

turistík,-e *mb.* touristic.

turíz/ë,-a *f.sh.* **-a** muzzle.

turíz/ëm,-mi tourism.

turjél/ë,-a *f.sh.* **-a** auger, borer, gimlet, drill; **shpoj me turjelë:** to bore (to pierce) with a drill.

turk,-u *m.sh.* **-turq** Turk.

turk,-e *mb.* Turkish.

túrm/ë,-a *f.sh.* **-a** *(njerëzish)* crowd mob, multitude, throng; **mblidhen turmë (njerëzit):** to crowd.

turn,-i *m.sh.* **-e** shift, change; **ndërrim turni:** change of shifts.

turné,-u *m.sh.* – tour; **bëj një turne:** to make a tour; **bëj një turne në gjithë vendin:** to tour the country.

turp,-i *m.* shame, infamy, ignominy; **me turp:** shamefully, bashfully, blushfully; **kam turp:** to be ashamed; **për turp!** for shame! **turp të kini!** fie! fie upon you; shame on you!

turpërím,-i *m.* libel, defamation, dishonour.

turpërój *f.k.* 1. to shame, to put (someone) to shame, to disgrace. 2. *(familjen)* to dishonour (one's family). 3. *(një vajzë)* to dishonour (a girl). – **turpërohem** *f.jv.* 1. to be ashamed, to feel ashamed; to blush, to go red. 2. to be dishonoured.

túrpsh/ëm (i),-me (e) *mb.* 1. blushful, timid, coyish, shy; **fëmijë i turpshëm:** shy (timid, blushful) child. 2. shameful, obscene, indecent; **fjalë të turpshme:** foul words, obscene words; **sjellje e turpshme:** indecent (shameful) behaviour (conduct); **në mënyrë të turpshme:** shamefully.

turqísht *ndajf.* in Turkish.

turqísht/e,-ja *f,* Turkish.

turshí,-a *f.* pickle, pickles; **lakër turshi:** sour-crout; **vë turshi:** to pickle, to souse.

túrt/ë,-a *f.sh.* **-a** torte.

túrtu/ll,-lli *m.sh.* **-j** *zool.* turtle-dove, turtle.

túrrem *f.jv.* to rush, to set upon; **turrem mbi armikun:** to dash at the enemy.

túrr/ë,-a *f.sh.* **-a** pile; **turrë drush:** pile of firewood.

túta/,-t *f.sh.* flannels.

tutél/ë,-a *f.* tutelage, ward; **nën tutelë:** under the ward.

tútem *f.jv.* to be frightened (scared).

tút/ë,-a *f.* fright, scare.

tútje *ndajf.* far away, away from; **më tutje:** farther; onward; **bëj më tutje:** go farther; **që sot e tutje:** from this day forth, hereafter, henceforth.

tutkáll,-i *m.* carpenter's glue.

tutkún,-i *m.sh.* **-ë** nitwit, simpleton.

tutkún,-e *mb.* idiot, stupid, thick-
-witted.
tutór,-i *m.sh.* **-ë** *(i një fëmije)*
guardian.
tutórí,-a *f.* guardianship, tutelage.
tuxhár,-i *m.sh.* **-ë** *vjet.* dealer,
trader.
ty *p.v.* you; **ty të flas:** to you I
speak.
tyl,-i *m.* tulle.
tym,-i *m.* smoke. — *Lok.* **flas më
tym:** to talk without thinking,
to babble on. — *Prov.* **s'ka tym
pa zjarr:** there is no smoke
without fire.
tymós *f.k.* 1. to fill with smoke.
2. to smoke, to cure, to smoke-
-cure; **tymos peshkun:** to smoke
(to cure) fish; **peshk i tymosur:**
smokedried fish. 3. *(cigare)* to
smoke a cigarette. — **tymoset**
f.jv. 1. to be filled with smoke.
2. to be smoked.
tymósj/e,-a *f.* 1. fumigation. 2.
smoking, curing.
tymósur (i,e) *mb.* 1. filled with
smoke. 2. smoked, smoke-cured;
peshk i tymosur: smoke-cured
fish; **hareng i tymosur:** kipper.
týre (i,e) *p.pr.* their; **shoku i tyre:**
their comrade; **shoqja e tyre:**
their comrade.
týt/ë,-a *f.sh.* **-a** *(e pushkës)* barrel.

TH

th, Th. (letter of the Albanian
alphabet) th, Th.
tha *(ai, ajo)* (past tense of the v.
them, third pers. sing.) (he,
she) said.
thaj *f.k.* 1. to dry, to dry up; to
desiccate; **thaj mollë në diell:**
to dry apples in the sun. 2. to
drain, to dry up; **thaj një kënetë:**
to drain a swamp. — **thahem**
f.jv. 1. to dry; to dry up; to become dry. 2. *(përroi)* to run
dry, to go dry. 3. *(frutat etj.)* to
dry up, to be desiccated; *(pema)*
to drop, to fade. — *Lok.* **thahem
së ftohti:** to be frozen, to be
freezing.
thán/ë,-a *f.sh.* **-a** *bot.* cornel;
(druri) cornel-bush.

thárbët (i,e) *mb.* shih **i thartë.**
tháres,-i *m.sh.* - desiccator, dryer,
drier.
tháres,-e *mb.* desiccative.
thárj/e,-a *f.* 1. desiccation, drying
up; *(e barit)* drying (of the hay);
(e këmishave) drying (of linen).
2. draining; *(e një kënete)*
draining (of a swamp). 3. *(e
trupit)* emaciation (of the body).
thar/k,-ku *m.sh.* **-qe** 1. enclosure;
(dhensh) sheepfold. 2. marriage;
fëmijë e tharkut të parë:
child of the first wife.
thártë (i,e) *mb.* sour, sourish,
tart, acerb, acid; **verë e thartë:**
tart wine.
thartësí,-a *f.* acidity, tartness, sourness, acerbity.

thartím,-i *m.* acidification, acetification.

thartír/ë,-a *f.* 1. sourness, tartness. 2. *mjek. (e stomakut)* heartburn, gastritis.

thartój *f.k.* to sour, to make sour, to acetify; to acidulate, to render slightly acid. — **thartohet** *f.jv.* to become sour, to be acetified.

thartúar (i,e) *mb.* turned, sour; **qumësht i thartuar:** turned milk.

thashethéme,-t *f.sh.* - gossip, gossiping, tittle-tattle, hearsay; **merrem me thashetheme:** to gossip; **njeri që merret me thashetheme:** gossip.

tháshë (p. t. of the verb. them) I said, I told; **i thashë të vijë:** I told him to come; **tani sapo i thashë:** I have just told him.

thataník,-e *mb.* scrággy, scrawny, lanky, skinny.

thátë *ndajf.* **ha bukë thatë:** to eat bread only, to dine poorly. — *Lok.* **nuk e ha thatë:** he is clever (keen-witted).

thátë (i,e) *mb.* 1. dry, desiccated; **bukë e thatë:** dry bread. 2. *(tokë)* dry, arid (land). 3. emaciated, lank, bony, lean.

thátë,-t (të) *m. mjek.* furuncle, boil.

thatësír/ë,-a *f. (e tokës)* drought, dryness, barrenness, aridity; **kohë me thatësirë:** dry weather.

thek,-u *m.sh.* -ë 1. frazzle, fringe. 2. *bot.* stamen.

thek *f.k.* 1. *(bukën)* to toast (bread), to brown (the bread). 2. *(këmbët)* to warm one's feet (near the fire). — **thekem** *f.jv.* 1. *(buka)* to be toasted. 2. *(pranë zjarrit)* to warm oneself (by the fire).

thék/ër,-ra *f. bot.* rye; **kashtë thekre:** rye straw.

theks,-i *m.sh.* -e *gram.* stress, accent.

theksím,-i *m.* accentuation; emphasis.

theksój *f.k.* 1. to stress; **theksoj një fjalë:** to stress a word. 2. to underline; **theksoj diçka me shumë rëndësi:** to underline something of great importance. — **theksohet** *f.jv.* 1. to be stressed. 2. to be underlined.

thékur (i,e) *mb.* toasted; **bukë e thekur:** toasted bread.

thelb,-i *m.sh.* **thelpinj** 1. *bot.* kernel, core; **thelpinj hudhre:** cloves of garlic. 2. *fig. (i një çështjeje)* gist, substance, main point, essence (of a matter).

thelbësór,-e *mb.* essential.

thél/ë,-a *f.sh.* -a slice, steak; **thelë buke:** a slice of bread; **thelë mishi:** a steak of meat, beefsteak.

théllë *ndajf.* 1. deeply, profoundly; **gërmoj thellë tokën:** to dig deeply the ground. 2. thoroughly; **i hyj thellë një çështjeje:** to examine thoroughly a matter; **i prekur thellë:** deeply moved.

théllë (i,e) *mb.* 1. deep; **një hendek dhjetë metra i thellë:** a ditch ten metres deep; **lumë i thellë:** a deep river; **det i thellë:** a deep sea. 2. *fig.* deep, profound; **dashuri e thellë:** deep love; **njohuri të thella:** profound knowledge.

thellësí,-a *f.sh.* - 1. depth; **ka 100 metra thellësi:** to be a hundred meters in depth (deep); **në thellësi:** deeply, into the depth 2. *fig.* depth.

thellësísht *ndajf.* deeply; **i prekur thellësisht:** deeply touched (moved).

thellím,-i *m.* deepening; **thellimi i demokratizimit socialist të shkollës:** the deepening of socialist democratization of school.

thellój *f.k.* 1. to deepen, to make deeper; **thelloj një pus:** to deepen a well. 2. *(një studim etj.)* to probe, to investigate thoroughly. – **thellohem** *f.jv.* 1. to widen one's knowledge of. 2. *(diçka)* to be deepened, to become deeper.

them I. *f.k.* (p.t. **thashë**, p. p. **thënë**). 1. to say; **them një fjalë:** to say a word; **them diçka për shaka:** to say something as a joke. 2. to utter; **nuk tha asnjë fjalë:** he did not utter a word. 3. to say, to recite; **them një vjershë:** to recite a poem. 4. to tell; to express; **s'të them dot sa më gëzoi letra jote:** I cannot tell you how pleased I was by your letter. 5. to mean; **çdo të thotë kjo fjalë?** what does this word mean? II. *f.jk.* 1. to tell, to speak; **më thuaj a e njeh?** tell me, do you know him?. 2. to state, to declare, to say. 3. to tell, to order; **bëni siç ju thashë:** do as I told you. 4. to think (of). – *Lok.* **le të themi se:** let us suppose; **të them të drejtën:** properly speaking; – **thuhet** *f.jv.* they say, it is rumoured about. – *Prov.* **më thuaj me kë rri të të them se cili je:** you can tell a man by the company he keeps.

thémb/ër,-ra *f.sh.* -ra heel; *(e këpucës)* heel.

themél,-i *m.sh.* -e base, basis, groundwork, foundation; **hedh themelet e një ndërtese:** to lay the foundations of a building; **prish nga themelet:** to destroy completely.

themelí,-a *f.* foundation.

themelím,-i *m.* foundation, founding; **themelimi i Partisë Komuniste:** the founding of the Communist Party.

themelój *f.k.* 1. to found; to lay the foundations of. 2. to found; **themeloj një qytet:** to found a city. – **themelohet** *f.jv.* to be founded, to be built.

themelór,-e *mb.* fundamental, essential, basic. + *cardinal (number*

themelúes,-i *m.sh.* - *(i një qyteti, (numeral i një doktrine, i një shoqërie)* founder (of a city, of a doctrine, of a society).

thep,-i *m.sh.* -a 1. *(mali)* ridge (of a mountain). 2. *usht.* **thepi i pushkës:** muzzle (of a gun).

thepísur (i,e) *mb.* abrupt, rugged; **vend i thepisur:** abrupt place.

ther *f.k.* to cut (to slit) someone's throat, to butcher, to slaughter. – **therem** *f.jv.* 1. to be masacred (slain). 2. *(bagëtia)* to be slaughtered, to be butchered.

thérës,-e *mb.* 1. sharp; pungent, intense; **të ftohtë therës:** bitter cold; **dhembje therëse:** sharp pain. 2. *fig.* pungent, cutting; biting; **përgjigje therëse:** cutting reply.

thérj/e,-a *f.* slaughter, butchery, throat-cutting.

therór,-i *m.* martyr; **bie theror:** to die a martyr.

therorí,-a *f.* martyrdom.

thertóre,-ja *f.sh.* -e slaughter-house, butchery.

thérur (e),-a (e) *f.sh.* -a (të) *mjek.* shooting (of pain); **kam të therura në zemër:** to have shootings in the heart.

thes,-i *m.sh.* **thasë** 1. sack, bag. 2. sack (ful), bag (ful) **një thes qymyr:** a sack of coal. 3. *fig.* a great deal, a lot; **ai ka një thes me para:** he has a lot (heaps) of money; *fig.* **thes i shpuar:** a spendthrift person.

thesár,-i *m.sh.* -e treasure; *(i shtetit)* treasury.

théva (p. t. of the verb **thyej**) I broke.

thëllëz/ë,-a *f.sh.* **-a** *zool.* partridge, grouse.

thëllím,-i *m.* frosen wind, ice wind.

thënë (p. p. of the v. **them**) said; **me të thënë me të bërë**: no sooner said than done; **është e thënë**: it is said, it is written; **si me thënë**: so to say, so to speak.

thënë (e),-a (e) *f.* destiny.

thëngjí/ll,-lli *m.sh.* **-j** live-coal; *fig.* **thëngjill i mbuluar**: dissembler.

thëni/e,-a *f.sh.* **-e** saying.

thëríj/ë,-a *f.sh.* **-a** *zool.* egg of lice.

thërrés I. *f.k.* 1. to call; **thërres dikë**: to call someone; **detyra më thërret**: the duty calls me. 2. to send for, to call in, to summon; **thërres mjekun**: to call in the doctor. 3. *(në gjyq dikë)* to summon, to cite (someone to a law court). 4. *(një mbledhje)* to convoke (a meeting). 5. to call, to name; **atë e thërrisnin Luan**: they called him Luan. II. *f.jk.* 1. to shout, to cry out; to yell; to scream. 2. shout; **mos thërrit, se nuk jam i shurdhër**: don't shout, I'm not deaf. − **thërritem, thirrem** *f.jv.* to be called; **thërritem (thirrem) nën armë**: to be called up.

thërrím/e,-ja *f.sh.* **-e** 1. *(buke)* crumb (of bread). 2. driblet, smithereen(s); bit, scrap, grain; **bëj thërrime diçka**: to smash something to smithereens; to crumble, to break to bits; **asnjë thërrime**: not a bit; **s'ka mbetur asnjë thërrime ëmbëlsirë**: there is not a bit of cake left.

thërrítj/e,-a *f.* call, calling, roll-call.

thërrmíj/ë,-a *f.sh.* **-a** particle, granule.

thërrmím,-i *m.* crumbling.

thërrmój *f.k.* 1. *(bukën)* to crumble (the bread). 2. *(një gjë të fortë)* to crush, to smash. − **thërrmohet** *f.jv.* to be crumbled; to be crushed (smashed).

thëthíj *f.k.* shih **thith**.

thëthítj/e,-a *f.* shih **thithje**.

thi,-u *m. zool.* pig.

thík/ë,-a *f.sh.* **-a** knife, poniard; *(xhepi që hapet e mbyllet)* pocket-knife, clasp-knife; *(për prerjen e letrës)* paper-cutter, paper-knife; *(për mprehjen e pendëve që shërbenin për të shkruar)* penknife; *(këpucari)* shoemakers' knife; *(krasitjeje)* pruning-knife; *(shartimi)* grafting-knife; *(gdhendjeje)* carving-knife; *(e madhe)* jack-knife; *(plori)* plowblade; **thikë e pamprehur**: blunt-knife; **këllëf thike**: sheath, scabbard; **teh i thikës**: knife blade, knife-edge; **pres me thikë**: to cut with a knife; **shpoj me thikë**: to poniard, to stab with a poniard; **goditje me thikë**: stab.

thíkë *mb.* abrupt, steep.

thíkë *ndajf.* vertically, perpendicularly.

thilé,-ja *f.sh.* − button-hole.

thimjám,-i shih **temjan**.

thimth,-i *m.* sting (of an insect).

thinj *f.k.* to make hoar (grey, gray). − **thinjem** *f.jv.* to grow grey, to grow hoary.

thínj/ë,-a *f.sh.* **-a** grizzle.

thínjur (i,e) *mb.* hoar, grey, grizzled.

thírra (p.t. of the verb. **thërres**) I called, I have called.

thírrj/e,-a *f.* call, calling, appeal; **me thirrjen e Partisë**: at the Party's call; **thirrje nën armë:** draft, roll-call; *(në gjyq)* summon, citation (to appear before a court); **thirrje lufte:** battlecry; **bëj thirrje:** to call, to call upon, to appeal.

thirrm/ë,-a *f.sh.* -a exclamation.

thirrmór,-e *mb.* exclamative.

thirrór/e,-ja *f. gram.* vocative.

thith I. *f.k.* 1. *(me buzë)* to suck; *(fëmija qumështin nga gjiri i nënës)* to suckle. 2. *(me hundë)* to inhale, to aspire, to breath. 3. *(cigaren)* to smoke. 4. *(burrnot)* to take (snuff). 5. *(erën e një luleje)* to smell (a flower). II. *f.jk. (oxhaku):* to draw out smoke (a chimney). — **thithet** *f.jv.* 1. to be sucked, to be suckled. 2. to be inhaled.

thíth/ë,-a *f.sh.* -a *anat.* 1. *(e një femre)* nipple. 2. *(e lopës)* dug (of a cow) 3. *(qumështi për fëmijë)* soother.

thithëlóp/ë,-a *f. zool.* (paddock)

thíthës,-i *m.sh.* - *(i ajrit)* aspirator; *(i gjakut)* bloodsucker.

thíthës,-e *mb.* 1. absorbent; **letër thithëse:** absorbent paper, blotting paper. 2. aspiratory.

thíthj/e,-a *f.* 1. *(me buzë)* sucking; *(e qumështit nga gjiri i nënës)* suckling (of milk). 2. *(cigareje)* smoking. 3. *(me hundë)* inhalation. 4. *(burrnoti)* taking (of snuff), snuffing.

thíthk/ë,-a *f.sh.* -a soother.

thjérr/ë,-a *f.sh.* -a *bot.* lentil.

thjérrëz,-a *f.sh.* -a *fiz.* lens.

thjesht *ndajf.* 1. merely, purely; **thjesht ar:** purely gold. 2. simply, plainly, modestly; **jetoj thjesht:** to live simply.

thjéshtë (i, e) *mb.* 1. pure; not mingled. 2. simple, plain, modest; **njeri i thjeshtë:** simple man. 3. simple, easy; **problem i thjeshtë:** an easy problem.

4. simple; **metodë e thjeshtë:** a simple method. 5. natural, simple, unaffected; **flas në mënyrë të thjeshtë:** to talk in an unaffected way.

thjésht/ër,-ri *f.sh.* -ra step-son.

thjeshtësí,-a *f.* simplicity, modesty.

thjeshtësísht *ndajf.* simply.

thjeshtësój *f.k.* shih **thjeshtoj.**

thjeshtój *f.k.* to simplify. — **thjeshtohet** *f.jv.* to be simplified.

thjeshtúesh/ëm (i),-me(e) *mb.* reductible.

thnég/ël,-la *f.sh.* -la *zool.* ant, emmet.

thúa, thói *m.sh.* thonj 1. *anat.* nail; **furçë thonjsh:** nail brush. 2. *(i maces, i shqiponjës etj.)* claw (of a cat, of an eagle).

thúajse *ndajf.* high, nearly, almost.

thumb,-i *m.sh.* -a 1, dart, sting. 2. *(këpucari)* rivet, small nail; **këpucë me thumba:** spiked shoes. 3. *fig.* sarcastic remark, taunt, gibe.

thumbím,-i *m.* sting, bite.

thumbój *f.k.* to sting, to bite.

thumbúes,-e *mb.* biting, mordant, sarcastic.

thúnd/ër,-ra *f.sh.* -ra 1. *(këpucë)* heel (of boots). 2. *(kali)* hoof (of a horse). — Lok. **nën thundrën e:** under the heel of.

thundrór,-ët *m.sh. zool.* ungulate.

thúp/ër,-ra *f.sh.* -ra 1. wand, stick. 2. *(pushke)* cleaning-rod, *amer.* ram-rod.

thur *f.k.* 1. *(çorape, triko)* to knit (stockings, a woollen blouse). 2 *(një gardh)* to construct (a fence). 3. *(gërshet)* to braid (a tress). 4. *fig.* **thur lavde:** to cover with praises, to glorify; **thur komplote:** to plot, to hatch up plots. — **thuret** *f.jv.* to be knitted; to be plaited (braided).

thúrj/e,-a *f.* 1. *(çorapi)* knitting.
(of stockings). 2. *(gardhi)* fencing. 3. *(gërsheti)* braiding (of
a tress). 4. *(komploti)* plotting.
thúrur (i,e) *mb.* 1. knitted. 2.
braided, plaited.
thuthúq,-i *m.sh.* -ë lisper.
thýej *f.k.* (p. t. theva, p. p. thyer)
1. to break; thyej një gotë: to
break a glass; thyej copë-copë:
to break to pieces, to smash into
smithereens; thyej kokën:
to break one's head; thyej qafën: to break one's neck; 2. *fig.*
to go away. 3. to bend; thyej
gjurin: to bend the knee. 4.
fig. thyej rekordin: to beat
the record. 5. *fig. (normat, li-*
gjet) to break (the norms, the
laws). – thyhem *f.jv.* 1. to
break down, to be broken, to
give way. 2. *(personi)* to break up.
thýer (i.e) *mb.* 1. broken. 2. *(nga*
mosha) aged, old. 3. *fig.* zemër
e thyer: broken heart.
thýerj/e,-a *f.* 1. *(e një gote)*
breaking (of a glass). 2. *(e*
disiplinës) breach (of discipline).
thýes,-i *m.sh.* - *(i grevës)* scab.
thýes/e,-ja *f.sh.* -e *(arrash, laj-*
thish etj.) nut-cracker; (gurësh);
breaker-machine.
thýes/ë,-a *f.sh.* -a *mat.* fraction.
thyesór,-e *mb.* fractional.
thýesh/ëm(i),-me(e) *mb.* break-
able, fragile, brittle.

U

u, U (letter of Albanian alphabet)
u, U.
u. *p.v.* them; to them (pers. pronoun, third pers. pl. of the dative
case); u thashë të më presin:
I told them to wait me.
u *pjesëz që shërben për të formuar*
kohën e kryer të foljeve jovep-
rore (particle used to form
the past tense of the passive
verbs and reflexive verbs); u
tremba: I was frightened; u
vesha sa më shpejt që munda:
I dressed myself as fast as I
could.
u l *pasth.* alas!
ua l *pasth.* hum!
uá *p.v.* them, to them; (short form
of the personal pronoun, third
pers. pl. of the dative case).
ua dhashë librin: I gave the
book to them.
ububú! *pasth.* alas!
údh/ë,-a *f.sh.* -ë 1. road, track,
path, way, street; udhë fshati:
village road; *(e ngushtë ose*
shteg) path, foot path. 2. passage, route; çaj udhën: to
open the way, to push one's
way; gjatë udhës: along the
way; gaboj udhë: to stray,
to take the wrong way; humbas udhën: to lose one's way;
nisem për udhë: to start on
a journey, to set off on a journey; hap udhë përmes dë-

borës: to make a way through the snow; **pres udhën:** to bar the way; **udha e mbarë!** good trip to you! pleasent journey to you! **largohuni nga udhal** stand out of the way! – *Lok.* **bëj udhë:** to give ground, to give way; **çoj në udhë të drejtë:** to set (to put) someone on the right path; **çoj në udhë të shtrembër:** to mislead, to lead astray; vihem **në udhë të drejtë:** to take the right path, to go the right way; **i jap udhë një çështjeje:** to give a solution to a problem, to resolve a problem; **largohem nga udha e drejtë:** to deviate from the right path.

udhëhéq *f.k.* to lead, to guide; to show the way; **Partia jonë e udhëheq popullin nga fitorja në fitore:** our Party leads the people from victory to victory. – **udhëhiqem** *f.jv.* to be led (guided, conducted).

udhëhéqës,-i *m.sh.* - leader, guide, chief; **udhëheqësit e një partie:** the leaders of a party.

udhëhéqj/e,-a *f.* leadership, guidance; **nën udhëheqjen e:** under the leadership of.

udhëkrýq,-i *m.sh.* -e cross-road.

udhërrëfýes,-i *m.sh.* - guide.

udhëtár,-i *m.sh.* -ë traveller, passenger.

udhëtím,-i *m.sh.* -e travel, journey; voyage; *(në det)* voyage, cruise; *(i shkurtër)* trip, tour; *(me kalë)* ride; **dietë udhëtimi:** travelling pay, travelling allowance; **shpenzime udhëtimi:** travelling expenses.

udhëtój *f.jk.* to travel, to walk, to journey; *(më këmbë)* to walk on foot; *(kaluar, me biçikletë, me automobil, me karrocë)* to ride; *(me det)* to voyage.

udhëzím,-i *m.sh.* -e instruction, orientation.

udhëzój *f.k.* to give instructions. – **udhëzohem** *f.jv.* to be instructed, to be orientated.

udhëzúes,-i *m.sh.* - guide; **libër udhëzues:** guide-book.

udhëzúes,-e *mb.* guiding, guide; **tabelë udhëzuese:** guidepost.

ugár,-i *m.sh.* -e lea, fallow; **tokë ugar:** fallow land.

uíski *m.* wisky.

ujdí,-a *f.sh.*- 1. compromise, understanding, mutual agreement. 2. transaction, agreement; *(tregtare)* commercial transaction; **bie në ujdi:** to come to terms, to agree, to come to an understanding, to settle by mutual agreement.

ujdís I. *f.k. gj. bis.* to set, to adjust, to arrange, to regolate; **ujdis orën:** to adjust the watch; **ujdis një punë:** to regulate an affair. II. *f.jk.* to accommodate, to fit; **ujdisin që të dy:** they are both fit (adapt). – **ujdisem** *f.jv.* 1. to get oneself fixed up. 2. to be adjusted (arranged).

ujdísj/e,-a *f.* arrangement, adjustment, regulation.

ujdhés/ë,-a *f.sh.* -a *gjeog.* isle, island.

ujém,-i *m.* grist.

új/ë,-i *m.sh.* -ëra 1, water; **ujë i ndenjur:** standing water, stagnant water; **ujë burimi:** brook water, fountain water; **ujë mineral:** mineral water; **ujë i rrjedhshëm:** running water; **ujë shiu:** rain water; **ujë i kripur:** salt water, brine; **ujë i pijshëm:** drinkable (potable) water; **ujë i turbullt:** troubled (muddy) water; **bojëra uji:** water-colours; **kanë (poçe) uji:** water-jug, water-bottle, decanter; **kovë uji:** water-bucket; **mulli me ujë:** water-mill; **tub uji:** water-

pipe; **zambak uji**: water-lily;
mbush ujë: to fetch (draw) water; **dal mbi ujë**: to emerge;
qëndroj mbi ujë: to float. – *Lok.*
fjalët tuaja nuk pijnë ujë:
your words don't hold water;
bëj një vrimë në ujë: to drop
a bucket into an empty well;
to carry coals to New-castle;
to make a worthless work; **rrah
ujë në havan**: to beat the air,
to strike the air with a sword;
jam bërë ujë: to be all in
perspiration, to be drenched to
the skin.

ujës,-e *mb.* aquatic; **bimë ujëse**:
aquatic plant; **shpend ujës**:
aquatic fowl, water fowl.

ujëvár/ë,-a *f.sh.* **-a** waterfall, cascade, cataract.

ujít *f.k.* (p. t. **ujita.** p. p. **ujitur**) 1.
to water; **ujis lulet**: to water
the flowers. 2. *(tokën)* to irrigate (a ground). – **ujitet** *f.jv.*
to be watered, to be irrigated.

ujítës/e,-ja *f.sh.* **-e** water-pot,
watering-pot.

ujítj/e,-a *f.* 1. watering. 2. irrigation.

ujk,-u *m.sh.* **-ujq** *zool.* wolf;
këlysh ujku: whelp, the young
of a wolf. – *Prov.* **ujku qimen
ndërron por huqin s'e harron**:
the wolf casts its hair but not
its habitude; can the leopard
change its spots?

ujkónj/ë,-a *f.sh.* **-a** bitchwolf.

ujór,-e *mb.* watery.

újsh/ëm (i),-me(e) *mb.* liquid.

ukubét,-i *m vjet.* privation, poverty; **rroj me ukubet**: to
live poorly.

ul *f.k.* 1. to lower; **ul zërin**: to
lower the voice. 2. *(perdet)* to
pull down, to let down, to lower
(the blinds). 3. *(çmimin)* to
lower, to reduce (the price). 4.
(kokën, sytë) to lower, to drop

(the head, the eyes). 5. *fig.*
ul kurrizin: to bend one's back.

ulem *f.jv.* 1. *(në një vend)* to sit
down (on a seat, on a chair);
ulem në tavolinë për të ngrënë: to sit down to table; **uluni**
sit down! take a seat! take a
chair! 2. *(nga një lartësi)* to
descend, to come down.

ulëríj *f.jk.* (p.t. **ulërita,** p.p.
ulëritur) 1. to shriek, to bawl,
to vociferate. 2. *(qeni, ujku)*
to howl (the dog, the wolf).
3. *(era)* to howl (the wind),
(deti) to roar (the sea).

ulërím/ë,-a *f.sh.* **-a** 1. shriek,
bawl, vociferation. 2. *(e qenit,
ujkut)* howl. 3. *(e erës)* howl(of
the wind), (e detit) roar (of
the sea).

úlët (i,e) *mb.* 1. low; **karrigia
është e ulët**: the chair is low.
2. *(zë)* low; **flas me zë të
ulët**: to speak in a low voice.
3. lowly; **njerëz të shtresës së
ulët**: men of low birth; people
of lowly origin. 4. *gjeog.* low;
Vendet e Ulëta: Low countries.
5. *fig.* low, mean, vile, base,
chabby, despicable; **njeri i ulët**:
a vile person; **gjë e ulët**: meanness, shabbiness, baseness.

úlët *ndajf.* 1. low; **fluturoj ulët**:
to fly low. 2. in a low voice;
folë më ulët: speak in a lower.
voice.

úlj/e,-a *f.* 1. descent; **ulja zgjati
dy orë**: the descent took two
hours. 2. reduction, fall; **ulje
çmimesh**: fall in prices.

ulók,-u *m.sh.* **-ë** paralytic.

ulók,-e *mb.* paralytic, paralysed.

ultësír/ë,-a *f.sh.* **-a** *gjeog.* lowland.

ultimatúm,-i *m.sh.* **-e** ultimatum

úlur *ndajf.* sitting; **rri ulur**: to be
seated, to be sitting.

ullí,-ri *m.sh.* **-nj** olive; *(druri)*

olive-tree; **degë ulliri:** olive branch; **vaj ulliri:** olive-oil.

ullísht/ë,-a *f.sh.* -a *bot.* olive-grove.

ullú/k,-u *m.sh.* -qe spout, water-spout, gutter, chamfer.

unanimísht *ndajf.* unanimously.

unáz/ë,-a *f.sh.* -a 1. ring; **unazë martese:** wedding ring; **gishti i unazës:** ring finger. 2. *mek.* coil.

únë *p.v.* I; me; **kush është atje? unë:** who is there? I am; **jam unë, mos u tremb:** it is me, don't be afraid.

ungj,-i *m.sh.* -ër uncle; **i ungji:** his uncle; **im ungj:** my uncle.

ungjí/ll,-lli *m.sh.* -j gospel.

ungjillór,-e *mb.* evangelical.

unifórm/ë,-a *f.sh.* -a uniform; **uniformë parade:** full-dress.

uník,-e *mb.* unique, single.

unitét,-i *m.* unity, harmony.

universál,-e *mb.* universal.

universitár,-i *m.sh.* -ë university student.

universitár,-e *mb.* university; **kurs universitar:** university course.

universitét,-i *m.sh.* -e university, *amer.* college.

únsh/ëm (i,)-me(e) *mb.* *krah.* hungry.

uraniúm,-i *m.* *kim.* uranium.

urát/ë,-a *f.* 1. benediction, blessing; **paç uratën!** bless you! 2. priest.

urbán,-i *m.sh.* -ë urban bus.

urbán,-e *mb.* urban, city, town.

urbanistík/ë,-a *f.* town planning, *amer.* city planning.

úrdh/ër,-ri *m.sh.* -ra 1. order, command; **sipas urdhrit të:** by order of; **marr urdhër:** to take, to receive an order; **kam urdhër të:** I have order to; **jam nën urdhrin tuaj:** I am under your orders; **jap urdhër:** to give an order, to give a command; **deri në një urdhër të dytë:** till further order; **anulloj një ur-**

dhër: to countermand, to revoke an order; **urdhër i prerë:** peremptory order. 2. warrant; **urdhër arrestimi:** warrant for arrest; **urdhër kontrolli:** search warrant.

urdhërés/ë,-a *f.sh.* -a ordinance, order by-law.

urdhërój *f.k.* to order, to command. — **urdhërohem** *f.jv.* to be ordered, to take an order. — *Lok.* **na urdhëroni!** you are welcome! **urdhëroni?** please?

urdhërór/e,-ja *f.* *gram.* imperative, imperative mood.

urdhërúes,-e *mb.* commanding, imperative; **flas me një ton urdhërues:** to speak in a commanding tone.

úrdhj/e,-a *f.* *krah.*, *mjek.* shih **bythë-pule.**

úr/ë,-a *f.sh.* -a *(zjarri)* fire-brand, brand, burning piece of wood. *Lok.* **shtyj urët:** to pour oil on the flame (s).

úr/ë,-a *f.sh.* -a 1. bridge; *(e ngushtë për kalimtarë)* foot-bridge; **urë e varur:** suspensionbridge, flying-bridge; **këmbë ure:** abutment of a bridge; **qemer ure:** arch of a bridge; **kaloj urën:** to cross the bridge. 2. *(anijeje)* deck. 3. *(në dhëmbë)* bridge.

úrët (i,e) *mb.* hungry, starving.

urgús *f.k.* *mjek.* 1. to distend, to swell the stomach. 2. *fig. (dikë)* to bother (someone). — **urgusem** *f.jv.* to be swelled, to grow flatulent, to have a distended stomach.

urgúsj/e,-a *f.* *mjek.* 1. flatulence, distention, swelling of the stomach. 2. *fig.* bothering.

urgjénc/ë,-a *f.* urgency.

urgjént,-e *mb.* urgent, pressing. **punë urgjente:** pressing affair

urgjentísht *ndajf.* urgently.

urí,-a *f.* hunger; **kam uri:** to be

hungry; **me uri**: hungrily, greedily; **greva e urisë**: hunger strike; **vdes nga uria**: to starve.

urím,-i *m.sh.* -e 1. wish; **urimet e mia më të mira për Vitin e Ri**: my best wishes for the New-Year; **urime!** all the best! *(për ditëlindjen)* many happy returns (of the day)!

urín/ë,-a *f.* urine; *(e kafshëve)* stale (of animals); **bëj urinën**: to make water, to piss, to discharge urine.

urítur (i,e) *mb.* hungry; starving; **jam i uritur**: to be hungry; **jam shumë i uritur**: to be starving.

uríth,-i *m.sh.* -ë *zool.* mole; **fole urithi**: mole-hill.

urój *f.k.* 1. to wish; **të uroj shëndet**: I wish you good health; **ju uroj për shumë vjet ditëlindjen**: many happy returns of the birthday; **i uroj mirëseardhjen dikujt**: to bid someone welcome; **i uroj rrugë të mbarë dikujt**: to wish someone a good journey. 2. *(prindi fëmijët)* to bless (one's children). 3. *(uroj dikë për diçka)* to congratulate (someone on something). – **urohem** *f.jv.* to be congratulated (on).

uróv,-i *m. bot.* vetch.

úrtë (i,e) *mb.* 1. still, quiet, silent, noiseless; **fëmijë i urtë**: a quiet child. 2. sage, wise; **njeri i urtë**: a sage man, a wise man.

úrtë *ndajf.* wisely, softly, gently; **rrini urtë!** be quiet! keep quiet! keep silent! be silent! stand still!, silent! – *Lok.* **urtë e butë, me të butë**: softly, gently.

urtësí,-a *f.* 1. wisdom. 2. meekness, prudence; **me urtësi**: prudently, meekly, gently, softly.

urtësísht *ndajf.* 1. softly, gently,

meekly. 2. prudently; wisely.

urtësój *f.k.* to render sage (wise, prudent). – **urtësohem** *f.jv.* to become sage (prudent, meek, gentle).

urtí,-a *f.* wisdom.

urtój *f.k.* shih **urtësoj.**

urth,-i *m.* smut blight (a disease of the wheat); **i prekur nga urthi**: smutty.

urth,-i *m. bot.* ivy.

urúar (i,e) *mb.* blessed.

urréj *f.k.* to hate, to detest, to abhor, to execrate, to abominate, to dislike, to regard with aversion. – **urrehem** *f.jv.* to be hated (detested, abhoard).

urréjtj/e,-a *f.* hate, hatred, abomination, execration, detestation, aversion, repulsion, repugnance, abhorence, dislike.

urréjtsh/ëm(i),-me(e) *mb.* abominable, detestable, execrable, despicable.

urrýer (i,e) *mb.* hateful, odious, heinous, loathsome; horrid, horrible; **krim i urryer**: horrible crime.

ustá,-i *m.sh.* **-llarë** 1. stone-mason. 2. master.

ushkúr,-i *m.sh.* -ë lace, tie.

ushqéj *f.k.* 1. to feed, to nourish. 2. *(një fëmijë)* to nurse (a child). 3. *(një dëshirë)* to nourish (a desire). – **ushqehem** *f.jv.* to be nourished, to feed oneself; *fig.* **ushqehem me shpresa**: to cherish illusions, to cherish false hopes.

ushqím,-i *m.sh.* -e 1. food; nurture, nutriment, nutrition, grub, nourishment; **ushqim i keq**: malnutrition; **ushqim i përkorë**: spare diet; *(për bagëti)* fodder, provender. 2. *(ushqim që hahet në kohë të caktuara si mëngjes, drekë, darkë)* meal, repast. 3. *pl.* provisions, victuals, food, eatables; **furnizoj me ushqime**: to provide (to supply) with food.

ushqimór,-e *mb.* nutritive; **artikuj ushqimorë**: groceries, eatables.

ushqimór/e,-ja *f.sh.* -e grocer's shop.

ushqýerit (të) *as.* feeding.

ushqýes,-e *mb.* nourishing; *tek.* **aparat ushqyes**: feeder.

ushqýesh/ëm (i),-me (e) *mb.* nutritious, nutritive.

ushtár,-i *m.sh.* -ë soldier; **vishem ushtar**: to be conscripted into the army.

ushtarák,-u *m.sh.* -ë soldier, military man.

ushtarák,-e *mb.* military; **shërbim ushtarak i detyrueshëm**: compulsory military service.

ushtarakísht *ndajf.* militarily, soldierly; in military fashion; like a soldier; **nderoj ushtarakisht**: to salute in military fashion.

úsht/ë,-a *f.sh.* -a lance, spear, pike.

úshtër *mb.* unripe; **pemë ushtër**: unripe fruit.

ushtím/ë,-a *f.sh.* -a echo, resound, resounding.

ushtón *f.jk.* 1. to resound; **salla ushtonte nga duartrokitjet**: the public hall resounded with applauses. 2. *(topi)* to roar (the cannon).

ushtré,-ja *f.sh.* - unripe fruit.

ushtrí,-a *f.sh.* - 1. army, armed forces; **ushtri e përhershme**: standing army; **hyj në ushtri**: to join the army; **Ushtria Nacionalçlirimtare**: the National Liberation Army. 2. *fig.* host, crowd, army.

ushtrím,-i *m.sh.* -e 1. exercise, drill; **bëj ushtrime**: to make

(to practice) exercises; **ushtrime gjimnastikore**: bodily exertions, physical training, (gymnastic) exercises; **ushtrime me trup të lirë**: free-standing exercises. 2. *(shkolle)* exercises. 3. *(profesioni)* practice, practising (of a profession). 4. exercise, exertion, wielding; **ushtrim i pushtetit**: exercise (wielding) of power.

ushtrój *f.k.* 1. *(mendjen)* to exercise (the mind). 2. *(një zanat)* to practise (a profession); *(tregtinë)* to carry on (a trade). 3. *(pushtet etj.)* to exercise, to wield (power). – **ushtrohem** *f.jv.* to practise, to exercise oneself; **duhet të ushtrohesh në anglisht**: you must practise your English.

ushúj,-i *m.* lard saindoux.

utopí,-a *f.* utopy.

utopík,-e *mb.* utopic.

uturím/ë,-a *f.sh.* -a shih **oshëtimë**.

uth,-i *m.* *mjek.* heartburn; **kam uth**: to have heartburn in the stomach.

úthull,-a *f.* vinegar; **vë në uthull**: to season with vinegar.

uthullím,-i *m.* acidification.

uthullísht/e,-ja *f.sh.* -e *bot.* wild sorrel.

uthullník,-u *m.* vinegar can.

uthullóhet *f.jv.* to be acidulated.

uzdáj/ë,-a *f.* *krah.* hope.

uzín/ë,-a *f.sh.* -a factory, works, plant; **uzinë metalurgjike**: iron and steel works, metallurgical plant.

úzo,-ja *f.* anisette.

uzurpatór,-i *m.sh.* -ë usurper.

uzurpím,-i *m.* usurpation.

uzurpój *f.k.* to usurp. – **uzurpohet** *f.jv.* to be usurped.

V

v, V (letter of Albanian alphabet) v, V.

va,-u *m.sh.* -e ford; **kaloj lumin në va:** to ford.

váde,-ja *f. vjet.* shih **afat.**

vád/ë,-a *f.sh.* **-a** ditch, channel (for irrigation).

vadít *f.k.* to water; to irrigate. — **vaditet** *f.jv.* to be watered, to be irrigated.

vadítës,-e *mb.* watering; **kanal vadítës:** irrigation canal.

vadítës/e,-ja *f.sh.* -e wateringcan, watering-pot.

vadítj/e,-a *f.sh.* -e watering; irrigation; **sistemi i vaditjes:** the irrigation system.

vagabónd,-i *m.sh.* -ë vagabond, scamp, rascal, rogue; rover, wanderer, *fam.* rolling stone; **një bandë vagabondësh:** a pack of rogues.

vagabondázh,-i *m.* vagrancy; vagabondage, vagabondism.

vagëllój *f.jk. (sytë)* to dim.

vagëllùar (i, e) *mb.* 1. dim; **një dritë e vagëlluar:** a dim light. 2. *fig.* vague, dim.

vagón,-i *m.sh.* **-a** *(për njerëz)* railway carriage, railway coach, car, *amer.* steer-car; *(mallrash)* goods wagon, van, *amer.* freight car; **vagon udhëtarësh:** passenger car (coach); **vagon cisternë:** cistern, tank wagon (car).

vaj,-i *m.* oil; **vaj ulliri:** olive oil; **vaj liri:** linseed oil; **vaj luledielli:** sunflower oil; **vaj lubrifikant:** lubricant; **vaj peshku:** whale oil; **fabrikë vaji:** oil mill; **bojra vaji:** oil colours;

pikturë me bojra vaji: oil painting; **lyej me vaj:** to oil; to lubricate. — *Lok.* **çdo gjë shkoi si në vaj:** everything went off smoothly.

vaj,-i *m.sh.* -e lamentation, bewailing, whine; **këngë vaji:** funeral lament, dirge.

vaj l *pasth.* alas!

váj/ë,-a *f.sh.* -a nurse.

vajgúri *m.* petroleum, mineral oil, rock-oil: *(i rafinuar)* kerosene, refined petroleum; **furnelë me vajguri:** oil-burner.

ajgurór,-e *mb.* oil, petroliferous; **fushë vajgurore:** oil-field

vajgursjéllës,-i *m.sh.* - oil pipeline, petroleum pipeline.

vajník,-u *m.sh.* -ë oil-can.

vajór,-e *mb.* oleaginous, oily.

vajós *f.k.* to oil, to lubricate. — — **vajoset** *f.jv.* to be lubricated.

vajósj/e,-a *f.* oiling, lubrication.

vájta *(p.t.* of the verb **vete)** I went.

vajtím,-i *m.sh.* -e lament, lamentation, whine, bewailing.

vájtj/e,-a *f.* going; **biletë vajtje--ardhje:** return ticket.

vajtój *f.k., f.jk.* to lament, to wail.

vajtúesh/ëm **(i),-me(e)** *mb.* lamentable, deplorable.

vájtur (i,e) *mb.* 1. out of use; **është e vajtur:** it is out of use. 2. dead; **ai ishte i vajtur:** he was already dead.

vájz/ë,-a *f.sh.* **-a 1.** girl, lass; **vajzë çapkëne:** romp, boisterous girl. **vajzë shkolle:** school girl. 2' *(e madhe, e pamartuar)* spinster'

unmarried girl. 3. daughter; **vajzë e vetme**: only daughter.
vajzërí,-a *f*. maidenhood.
vajzërór,-e *mb*. maidenly.
vak *f.k.* to make tepid. — **vaket** *f.jv.* to grow tepid.
vakánt,-e *mb*. vacant; **vend va- kant**: vacant place.
vakëf,-i *m.sh.* -e *fet*. temple.
vákët (i,e) *mb*. tepid, lukewarm; **ujë i vakët**: tepid water, luke- warm water.
vákj/e,-a *f*. tepidity, tepidness.
vaksín/ë,-a *f.sh.* -a *mjek*. vaccine.
vaksiním,-i *m.sh.* -e vaccination.
vaksinój *f.k.* to vaccinate. — **vak- sinohet** *f.jv.* to be vaccinated.
vakt,-i *m.sh.* -e 1. time; **në vaktin e drekës**: at midday. 2. meal, repast. — *Lok.* **ai ia ka vaktin**: he is well-to-do.
valanídh,-i *m. bot*. sumac.
valénc/ë,-a *f.sh.* -a *kim*. valency.
vál/ë,-a *f.sh.* -ë 1. wave; **në më- shirën e valëve**: at the mercy of the waves; **det me valë**: wavy sea. 2. *fiz*. wave; **gjatësi vale**: wavelength.
válë (i,e) *mb*. hot, boiling; **ujë i valë**: hot water, boiling water.
valëprítës/e,-ja *f.sh.* -e break- water.
válë-válë *ndajf*. wave upon wave.
valëvítet *f.jv.* (third pers. sing.) to wave, to flutter; **valëvitet flamuri**: the flag flutters.
valëzím,-i *m*. waving, swaying, undulation, rippling; **valëzimi i terrenit**: undulation of the land.
valím,-i *m*. boiling, ebullition.
valíxh/ë,-a *f.sh.* -a suitcase, *fam*. case, trunk, *amer*. travelling-bag; *sh*. **valixhet**: suitcases, luggage *amer*. bags, baggage; **përgatis valixhet**: to pack a trunk with clothes, to pack clothes into a trunk.

valój I. *f.k.* to boil, to seethe; **valoj ujë**: to boil water. II. *f.jk.* to boil.
vals,-i *m.sh.* -e *muz*. waltz.
valút/ë,-a *f.sh.* -a foreign currency.
válvul,-a *f.sh.* -a *mek*. valve; **val- vul sigurimi**: safety valve.
váll/e,-ja *f.sh.* -e dance; dancing; **hedh valle**: to dance; **valle popullore**: folk-dance, popular- -dance.
vállë *pjes*. 1. perhaps, possibly; **mos vallë ka dëshirë të?** does he possibly want to. . .? *(shpesh nuk përkthehet)* **mos vallë kuj- ton se unë jam më mirë?** do you think I'm any better off? 2. (when we are in doubt); **kam frikë se vallë do të vijë**: I doubt he will not come.
vallëzím,-i *m.sh.* -e dancing; **mbrë- mje vallëzimi**: dancing party.
vallëzój *f.jk.* to dance.
vallëzùes,-i *m.sh.* - dancer.
valltár,-i *m.sh.* -ë dancer.
vandák,-u *m.sh.* -ë faggot, bundle; **një vendak me degë**: a fag- got of twigs.
vandalíz/ëm,-mi *m*. vandalism.
vangósh,-e *mb*. squint-eyed.
vanílj/e,-a *f. bot*. vanilla; *(druri)* vanilla-tree.
váp/ë,-a *f*. heat; **kam vapë**: to be hot; to feel hot; **është vapë**: it is hot; **vapë e madhe**: swel- tering hot, sultry hot; **plas nga vapa**: to swelter.
vapór,-i *m.sh.* -ë steamer, steam- boat, steam-ship, ship; **vapor udhëtarësh**: packet-boat, pas- senger boat.
var *f.k.* 1. to hook, to suspend, to hang up; **var një fotografi (në mur)**: to hang up a picture (on the wall). 2. *(një kriminel)* to hang (a criminal). — *Lok.* **var shpresat te dikush**: to pin one's hopes on someone;

var buzët: to pout; var kokën: to hang down one's head. − − varem *f.jv.* 1. to hang oneself. 2. to be depended (on), to be subordinate (to); **varet nga ju:** it depends on you; **planet e mia varen shpesh nga ato të. .** . : my plans are often subordinate to those of.` . .

várës/e,-ja *f.sh.* -e *(rrobash)* hanger, suspensor (of clothes); **varëse peshqirësh:** towel-horse; **varëse çadrash:** umbrella-stand; **kapela është në varëse:** the hat is on the peg.

varfanják,-u *m.sh.* -ë poor man, needy person.

varfanják,-e *mb.* poor, needy, destitute.

várfër **(i,e)** *mb.* poor, destitute, indigent; **shtresat e varfëra:** the poor strata.

varfërí,-a *f.* poverty, poorness; **varfëri e madhe:** indigence, ⊠ pauperism.

varfërím,-i *m.* impoverishment.

varfërisht *ndajf.* poorly.

varfërój *f.k.* to impoverish. − − **varfërohem** *f.jv.* to grow poor, to be impoverished

varfërúar **(i,e)** *mb.* impoverished.

var/g,-u *m.sh.* -gje 1. *(pemësh)* row, range (of trees). 2. *(njerëzish)* file, train (of persons); **në varg për një:** in Indian file. 3. *(malesh)* range, chain, ridge (of mountains). 4. *(vjershe)* verse (of a poetry); **përrallë në vargje:** fable (tale) in verse; **i shkruar në vargje:** written in verse.

varg *ndajf.* in file; **ecim varg:** to walk in file; **vihemi varg:** to stand in file.

vargán,-i *m.sh.* -ë 1. *(udhëtarësh)* caravan (of travellers). 2. *(anijesh)* convoy (of ships).

vargëzím,-i *m.* *(vjershe)* versification.

vargëzój *f.k.* to make verses, to versify.

vargím,-i *m.* lining up.

vargój *f.k.* to line up.

vargór,-e *mb.* ordinal; **numër vargor:** reference number.

varg/úa,-ói *m.sh.* -onj chain; *sh.* **vargonj:** chains, irons, fetters.

variación,-i *m.sh.* -e variation; change.

variánt,-i *m.sh.* -e variation, variant; **paraqitet në variante të ndryshme:** there are several variations of it.

varietét,-i *m.sh.* -e variety.

várj/e,-a *f.* hanging; **dënim me varje:** condemnation by hanging.

varkár,-i *m.sh.* -ë boatman, boat-keeper.

várk/ë,-a *f.sh.* -a boat, river-boat; *(me motor ose maunë)* barge; **varkë peshkimi:** fishing boat; **varkë shpëtimi:** life-boat; **lidh varkën me litar:** to moor; **lundroj me varkë:** to row.

vártës,-i *m.sh.* - subordinate.

vártës,-e *mb.* subordinate, subsidiary, subaltern.

vartësí,-a *f.* dependence; **jam nën vartësinë e dikujt:** to be under someone; **ka shumë njerëz në vartësi:** he has many men under him.

várur **(i,e)** *mb.* 1. suspended, pending, hanging, in suspense. 2. depending, dependent *(nga,* on).

várur *ndajf.* in suspense; **çështje e lënë varur:** matter in suspense, undecided matter, hanging matter.

varr,-i *m.sh.* -e grave, tomb, sepulchre; **gropë varri:** vault (of a grave); **gur varri:** grave-stone; **heshtje varri:** deathlike silence.

varréz/ë,-a *f.sh.* -a cemetery, burial ground, burial place, grave-yard, church-yard.

varrím,-i *m.sh.* **-e** burial; **shpenzime varrimi:** funeral expenses *ceremoni varrimi:* obsequies.

varrmíhës,-i *m.sh.* - gravedigger.

varrós *f.k.* to bury, to entomb, to inhume, to sepulchre. — **varrosem** *f.jv.* to be buried.

varrósj/e,-a *f.* burying, interment, entombment.

vasál,-i *m.sh.* **-ë** 1. vassal. 2. *fig.* dependent, servant.

vasál,-e *mb.* vassal.

vásk/ë,-a *f.sh.* **-a** 1. *(banje)* bath, bathtub, tub. 2. *tek.* tank, vat.

vásh/ë,-a *f.sh.* **-a** girl, maiden, lass.

vashërí,-a *f.* maidenhood.

vat,-i *m.sh. fiz.* watt.

vatán,-i *m. vjet.* fatherland, mother-land.

vát/ë,-a *f.* wad, pad; **mbush me vatë:** to wad, to pad.

vát/ër,-ra *f.sh.* **-ra** 1. hearth; fire-place. 2. *(kulture)* hearth (of culture). 3. *mjek.* *(e një sëmundjeje)* seat, focus, centre (of a sickness). 4. focus; **vatra e revolucionit:** the hotbed (the cradle, the centre, the heart, the soul) of revolution.

váth/ë,-a *f.sh.* **-a** fold, cote, sheep-fold, sheep-pen.

vazelín/ë,-a *f. mjek.* vaseline, petroleum jelly.

vázo,-ja *f.sh.* - 1. vase, pot, receptacle. 2. *(lulesh)* bowl, flower-vase, flower-pot.

vázhd/ë,-a *f.sh.* **-a** 1. *(parmende)* furrow, trench. 2. *(e një rrote)* rut, trail, track (of a wheel). 3. *fig.* trace, signs *pl.,* vertiges *pl.*

vazhdím,-i *m.* 1. continuation, continuance; **vazhdimi i punimeve:** the continuation of the works. 2. *(i një artikulli)* continuation (of on article); *(i një*

romani) sequel; **ky roman është vazhdimi i atij që ke lexuar:** this novel is the sequel to the one you have read. 3. course; **viti në vazhdim:** the current year, this year, the going on year.

vazhdimësí,-a *f.* continuity, continuance.

vazhdimísht *ndajf.* continually, continuously, non-stop, unceasingly, uninterruptedly, ceaselessly; **më kërkon vazhdimisht këshilla:** he is continually asking me advice.

vazhdój I. *f.k.* 1. to continue (with), to go on (with); **vazhdo punën!** go on with your work! **vazhdoj udhëtimin;** to continue one's trip; **vazhdoj leximin:** to go on reading, to go on with one's reading. 2. *(studimet)* to pursue (one's studies).

II. *f.jk.* 1. to go ahead, to go on, to continue, **puna vazhdon me vrull:** the work is going ahead briskly; **kështu s'vazhdojmë dot më:** we can't go on like this any more. 2. to keep on; **ai vazhdon të më ftojë:** he keeps on asking me round.

vazhdúar (i,e) *mb.* continuous, uninterrupted, unceasing; **rrymë e vazhduar:** direct (continuous) current.

vazhdúes,-e *mb.* going on; under way.

vazhdúesh/ëm (i),-me(e) *mb.* 1. continuous, unbroken, nonstop, uninterrupted. 2. continual, endless, incessant, constant; **shirë të vazhdueshme:** continual rain. 3. *(i shpeshtë)* continual, constant, frequent; **grindje të vazhdueshme:** constant qua-rrelling.

vdékj/e,-a *f.sh.* **-e** death; **vdekje nga pleqëria:** natural death; *(nga uria)* starvation; **çehre e**

vdekjes: deathlike paleness; **grahmat e vdekjes:** death-rattle; **kambana e vdekjes:** death-bell, passing-bell, toll, knell; **dënim me vdekje:** capital punishment; **dënoj me vdekje:** to sentence (to condemn) to death, to put to death; **një çështje për jetë a vdekje:** a matter of life or death; **plagë për vdekje:** murderous wound, mortal wound; **i lodhur për vdekje:** dead tired; **i plagosur për vdekje:** deadly (mortally) wounded; **shtrati i vdekjes:** death-bed; **gjer në vdekje:** until one dies; **e mërzis dikë për vdekje:** to bore someone to death; **vepra të botuara pas vdekjes** *(së autorit)*: posthumous works, postmortem works; **përqindja e vdekjeve:** death-rate. — *Lok.* **gjej vdekjen:** to meet one's death.

vdekjeprúrës,-e *mb.* mortal, lethal, deadly, murderous; fatal; **plagë vdekjeprurëse:** mortal wound.

vdéksh/ëm (i),-me(e) *mb.* mortal.

vdekshmërí,-a *f.* mortality.

vdékur (i),-i (i) *m.sh.* - **(të)** deceased, dead, dead person; **shtëpia ku pat banuar i vdekuri:** the house of the deceased; **i vdekur i pakallur:** person who is at death's door.

vdékur (i,e) *mb.* 1. dead; lifeless; **ai është i vdekur:** he is dead, he is lifeless; **fëmijë i lindur i vdekur:** still-born child. 2. *fig.* dead; **gjuhë e vdekur:** dead language.

vdes l. *f.jk.* to die, to expire, to die away, to pass away; *(për kafshët)* to burst; *(për bimët)* to wither; **vdes për vendin tim:** to die for one's country; **vdes me lavdi:** to die gloriously, to

die a glorious death; **vdes i ri:** to die young; **vdes nga hidhërimi:** to die of grief; **vdes nga pleqëria:** to die a natural death; **vdes nga uria:** to starve, to die of hunger; **vdes nga sëmundja:** to die of an illness (a disease); **vdes nga plagët:** to die from wounds. — *Lok.* **vdes së qeshuri:** to split one's sides with laughing; **vdes nga frika:** to almost die of fright, to be scared to death; **vdes nga dëshira për diçka:** to be longing (dying) for something; **vdes të të shoh edhe një herë:** I am longing to see you again. II. *f.k. (dikë)* to kill (someone); *fig.* **më vdiqe!** you'll be the death of me!

vdíqa *(p.t.* of the verb **vdes)** I died.

ve,-ja *f.sh.* - shih **vezë.**

ve (i,e) *mb.* widow, relict; **burrë i ve:** widower, widowman; **grua e ve:** a widow, a widow woman.

veç l. *ndajf.* 1. separately; **ata rrojnë veç:** they live separately; **veç e veç:** one by one. II. *lidh.* exept, besides; **veç kësaj:** besides, in addition moreover; unless; **veç në qoftë i marrë:** unless to be mad.

veçán *ndajf.* apart, separately; individually; **ai më tërhoqi veçan:** he took me apart.

veçanërísht *ndajf.* especially, particularly.

veçántë (i,e) *mb.* 1. special, particular; **shenja të veçanta:** special signs. 2. peculiar, odd, of one's own; uncommon; **kjo bukë ka një shije të veçantë:** this bread has a taste of its own.

veçantí,-a *f.* particularity; peculiarity; **në veçanti:** a) apart, in private; b) particularly, in particular.

véças *ndajf.* separately, apart.
veçím,-i *m.sh.* **-e** 1. separation; isolation. 2. *(nga shoqëria)* seclusion, withdrawal, retirement (from the society).
véçmas *ndajf.* shih **veças.**
veçój *f.k.* to isolate, to separate, to keep separate; to seclude. — **veçohem** *f.jv.* 1. to leave *(nga dikush,* someone), to part (from), to part company (with); **ata u veçuan nga grupi:** they left the group. 2. to be separated.
veçorí,-a *f.sh.* - peculiarity, characteristic, peculiar feature.
véçse *lidh.* 1. only, other, but; **ai s'bën gjë tjetër veçse qan:** he does nothing but cry. 2. but, and yet, still though, nevertheless; **këto lule janë të bukura, veçse s'kanë aromë:** these flowers are beautiful, but they have no scent
véd,-ër,-ra ra pail, bucket.
vég/ël,-la *f.sh.* **-la** 1. tool, implement; instrument; **vegla bujqësore:** farm instruments. 2. *(muzikore)* instrument; **vegla fryme:** wind instruments. 3. *fig.* instrument, tool; **revizionistët janë vegla të kapitalistëve:** revisionists are tools in the hands of the capitalists.
vegím,-i *m.sh.* **-e** vision; daydreaming.
vegullí,-a *f.* vision, hallucination.
végj/ë,-t *f.sh.* loom, hand-loom.
vegjëlí,-a *f.* 1. the poor, the common people, the disinherited class. 2. childhood; **në vegjëli:** in the childhood.
vejní,-a *f.* widowhood.
vejúsh/ë,-a *f.sh.* **-a** widow.
vel,-i *m.sh.* **-a** 1. *(anijeje)* sail (of a ship); **pëlhurë për vela:** sail-cloth; **anije me vela:** sailing vessel. 2. *(fytyre)* veil, cover (of face).

vel *f.k.* to satiate, to cloy, to surfeit. — **velem** *f.jv.* to surfeit, to cloy oneself.
velénx/ë,-a *f.sh.* **-a** woolen cover, woolen blanket.
vélj/e,-a *f.* surfeit, satiety.
vélët (i,e) *mb.* sated, satiated, surfeited, cloyed; fed up, sick.
vémj/e,-a *f.sh.* **-e** *zool.* caterpillar, grub.
vend,-i *m.sh.* **-e** 1. place; **libri nuk është në vendin e vet:** the book is not in its right place. 2. room, space; **nuk ka më vend në valixhe:** there is no more room in the suitcase. 3. seat; **është i lirë ky vend?** is this seat free? **ndërroj vend:** to change one's seat. 4. place, position; **zë vendin e parë (në klasifikim):** to get the first place. 5. job, post, position. 6. place, spot; **ç'vende të bukura!** what beautiful places! 7. country, land, region, territory; native land, nation; **vend bujqësor:** agricultural country; **vendi ynë:** our country; **në vend të huaj:** in a foreign country, abroad; **vend kolonial:** colonial country; **Vendet e Ulëta:** Low Countries. — *Lok.* **vdes në vend:** to fall dead on the spot; **fjalë me vend:** just word; **fjalë pa vend:** incongruous word; **flas me vend e pa vend:** to speak at a venture; **po të isha në vendin tuaj:** if I were you; if I were in your place.
vendbaním,-i *m.sh.* **-e** dwelling, residence, domicile, abode; **me vendbanim në:** dwelling in, residing in, with domicile in; *(i përkohshëm)* sojourn, temporary residence.
vendburím,-i *m.sh.* **-e** source, origin.
véndës,-i *m.sh.* - native, inborn,

autochthon, aborigine, indigene.
véndës,-e *mb.* native, aboriginal,
autochthonous; **popullsia ven-
dëse:** aborigines.
vendím,-i *m.sh.* -e 1. decision;
verdict, sentence; **marr vendim**
(të bëj diçka): to make (to take)
a decision, to decide, 2. *(gjyqi)*
decision, judgement, ruling, decree; verdict, sentence, award. 3.
resolution; **vendim qeverie:** governmental resolution.
vendimtár,-e *mb.* decisive, crucial; **betejë vendimtare:** decisive battle; **vit vendimtar:**
crucial year.
vendlíndj/e,-a *f.sh.* -e 1. birth-
place. 2. native-land.
vendós I. *f.k.* 1. to decide, to fix,
to arrange; **duhet të vendosim
ditën e nisjes:** we must fix the
day of departure. 2. *(diçka në
një vend)* to place, to put; **vendos me radhë:** to range, to
set in a row; **vendos me rregull:**
to put in order. 3. to establish;
**vendos marrëdhënie diplo-
matike:** 'to establish diplomatic
relations.
II. *f.jk.* 1. to decide; **të takon
ty të vendosësh:** it is up to
you to decide. 2. to make up
one's mind, to decide; **ai s'vendos kurrë:** he can never make
up his mind. – **vendosem** *f.jv.*
1. to settle, to establish oneself;
vendosem në punë: to get
settled in a work; **vendosem
në një dhomë:** to get settled in
a room. 2. to be decided; **u vendos që ai të nisej menjëherë:**
it was decided that he should
eave immediately.
vendósj/e,-a *f.* placing, putting,
establishing.
vendosmërí,-a *f.* determination,
resolution, resoluteness, decisi-
veness; *(e patundur)* firmness,

steadiness; **me vendosmëri:** resolutely, decidedly, firmly.
vendosmërísht *ndajf.* resolutely,
decidedly, firmly.
vendósur (i,e) *mb.* 1. decided,
resolute, firm; **njeri i vendosur:**
resolute man. 2. set, fixed, established.
vendqëndrím,-i *m.sh.* -e *(auto-
buzi)* (bus) stop; *(i trenave):*
halt (railway) station.
venerián,-e *mb.* venerial; **sëmundje veneriane:** venerial disease.
vén/ë,-a *f.sh.* -a *anat.* vein.
veníi *f.k.* to fade. – **venitem** *f.jv.*
to dwindle, to droop, to wane,
to fade away, to pine away.
venítj/e,-a *f.* fading, drooping. .
venítur (i,e) *mb.* faded, wan;
dritë e venitur: flickering light,
unsteady light.
ventíl,-i *m.sh.* -a *mek.* faucet.
ventilatór,-i *m.sh.* -ë ventilator,
fan.
vép/ër,-ra *f.sh.* -ra 1. deed; action,
act; **kryej një vepër të mirë:**
to perform a good action; **vepër heroike:** heroic act, heroic
deed. 2. work; **përparimi është
vepër e njeriut:** progress is the
work of man. 3. *(letrare, artistike)* work; **vepër arti:** work
of art; **vepra të plota:** complete works.
veprím,-i *m.sh.* -e 1. action, act,
deed; **veprime jo të mira:**
wrongdoings, evil deeds; **mënyrë veprimi:** procedure, manner
of proceeding; **njeri i veprimit:**
man of action. 2. *mek.* motion,
action, movement; **vë në veprim:** to set in motion, to set
going, to start. 3. *kim.* action;
**veprimi i acideve mbi meta-
let:** action of acids on metals.
4. *usht.* action, engagement;
veprime luftarake: military action. 5. *mat.* operation; **të katër**

veprimet themelore: the four
arithmetical operations.
veprimtarí,-a f. activity; veprimtari armiqësore: subversive (hos-
stile) activity.
veprój f.jk. 1. to act, to operate;
veproj në emër të kryetarit:
to act on behalf of the chairman;
veproj sipas ligjit: to act
according to the law. 2. to have
effect, to take effect; ilaçi qe-
tësues po vepron: the sedative is taking effect. 3. to behave;
veproj keq : to behave badly.
veprór,-e mb. gram. active; trajta veprore (e një foljeje):
active voice (of a verb).
veprúes,-e mb. acting.
verbál,-e mb. verbal, oral; deklaratë verbale: verbal statement; proces-verbal: minute.
vérbazi ndajf. blindly, groping,
eci verbazi: to grope, to feel
one's way with the hands.
vérbër (i,e) mb. blind, sightless,
eyeless; krejt i verbër: stone-
blind; njeri i verbër: blindman.
verbërí,-a f. blindness.
verbërísht ndajf. blindly.
verbím,-i m. blinding; dazzling.
verbój f.k. to blind; to dazzle;
dielli të verbon: the sun is
dazzling; fig. inati e verboi:
he was blinded by rage. − ver-
bohem f.jv. to be blinded, to
be dazzled.
verbúes,-e mb. dazzling, blinding;
dritë verbuese: dazzling light.
verdh f.k. to yellow, to make yellow. − verdhem f.jv. to become yellow, to grow pale, to
turn pale (wan, yellow).
verdhacák,-e mb. shih verdhacuk.
verdhacúk,-e mb. pallid, pale,
wan.
vérdhë,-t (të) as. 1. të verdhët
e vezës: yolk of egg. 2. mjek.
jaundice, icterus.

vérdhë (i,e) mb. yellow; pale'
livid; ngjyrë e verdhë: yellow
colour; që vjen si e verdhë:
yellowish, palish.
vérdhëz,-a f. mjek. jaundice, icterus.
verdhón f.jk. to look yellow.
verdhúshk/ë,-a f.sh. -a krah. gold
coin.
verém,-i m. mjek, vjet. tuberculosis, pulmonary tuberculosis,
phthisis.
veremósur (i,e) mb. vjet. tuber-
culous, phthisical.
veresíe ndajf. on credit, on tick;
blej e shes veresie: to buy
and sell on credit. − Lok. dëgjoj
veresie: to hear inattentively;
flas veresie: to speak at a
venture (at random).
vér/ë,-a f.sh. -a summer; pas
pranverës vjen vera: after spring
comes summer; mesi i verës:
midsummer; rroba vere: summer clothes. − Prov. nuk vjen
vera me një lule: one swallow
does not make a summer.
vér/ë,-a f.sh. -ëra wine; verë e
ëmbël: sweet wine; verë e
kuqe: claret, red wine; verë
e bardhë: white wine; gotë
vere: wine-glass; një gotë verë:
a glass of wine; shishe vere:
wine bottle.
vergjí,-a f. vjet. tax, duty; impost.
verí,-u m. 1. gjeog. north; drejt
veriut: northward; Poli i Veriut: the North Pole, erë veriu:
north (northerly) wind. 2. north
wind, ice wind, gale; fryn veriu:
it blows north wind.
verifikím,-i m.sh. -e verification.
verifikój f.k. to verify. − verifi-
kohet f.jv. to be verified.
veríg/ë,-a f.sh. -a 1. metal ring,
chain link. 2. sh. verigat: irons,
fetters. 3. bunch; një verigë
rrush: a bunch of grapes.

verilindj/e,-a f. gjeog. north-east.
verím,-i m. holiday, holidays, amer. vacations; **shkoj për verim:** to be away on holiday.
veriór,-e mb. gjeog. northern; **Oqeani i Ngrirë Verior:** Arctic Ocean; **Poli Verior:** the North Pole.
veriperëndím,-i m. gjeog. northwest.
verník,-u m. lacker, lacquer, varnish.
verój l. f.jk. to go on holiday, to pass the summer in the country. ll. f.k. *(bagëtinë)* to take the cattle to summer-pastures.
verór,-e mb. summer; **pushime verore:** summer holidays, summer vacations; **rroba verore:** summer clothes.
vertebrál,-e mb. vertebral.
vertikál,-e mb. gjeom. vertical.
vertikál/e,-ja f.sh. -e vertical line.
vertikalísht ndajf. vertically.
vérza,-t f.sh. anat. *(e peshkut)* fish-gills.
verzóm/ë,-a f.sh. -a 1. large net for fishing.
ves,-i m.sh. -e vice; **njeri me shumë vese:** vicious man; **shpëtoj nga një ves:** to free oneself from a vice.
vés/ë,-a dew; **vesa e natës:** nightdew; **vesë shiu:** drizzle, drizzling rain, fine misty rain, mizzle, dribble.
vesón f.jk. it drizzles, it dribbles.
vesh,-i m.sh. -ë 1. anat. ear; **bulë e veshit:** earlap, lob of the ear; **daullja e veshit:** ear-drum; **dylli i veshit:** ear-wax, cerumen; **dëgjoj me veshë** *(një të sëmurë)*: to sound (a sickman); **sëmundje veshi:** otitis; **dhembje veshi:** ear-ache; **buçitje e veshëve:** singing (humming) of the ears; **më buçasin veshët:** my ears are

singing. 2. *(i një filxhani, i një poçeje etj.)* handle (of a cup, of a pot, etc.); **veshët e qypit:** the ears of a jug. 3. **një vesh rrush:** a bunch of grapes. — *Lok.* **i rëndë nga veshët:** hard of hearing, deaf; **bëj veshin e shurdhër:** to turn a deaf ear; **heq veshin:** to pull the ear; to scold; **kam vesh për muzikë:** to have good ear for music; **marr vesh:** to understand; **s'marr vesh se ç'bëhet:** not to understand what is going on; **mbaj vesh:** to lend an ear, to hearken, to ear; **vë veshin:** to heed, to listen, to pay attention; **ngreh veshët:** to prick one's ears; **merremi vesh:** to come to terms, to make arrangements; to understand one another; **jam gjithë veshë:** to be all ears.
vesh f.k. 1. to dress, to clothe; **vesh fëmijën:** to dress a baby. 2. *(rrobat)* to put on, to wear one's clothes; **vesh pantallonat:** to put on one's pants. 3. *(me astar një xhaketë)* to line (a coat). 4. *(një mur me letër)* to paper (a wall), to tapestry. 5. *(me fuqi)* to invest (with power). 6. *(fajin)* to attribute, to ascribe, to impute (the fault). — **vishem** f.jv. to dress oneself, to get dressed; to dress, to wear; **vishem me shije:** to dress tastefully; **vishem trashë:** to put on heavy clothes, to dress in heavy clothes; **vishem si për festë:** to wear party clothes, to dress up one's Sunday best; **vishem me të zeza:** to dress in black, to wear black.
veshgját/ë,-i m.sh. -ë donkey, ass.
véshj/e,-a f.sh. -e 1. article of clothing, garment; clothes, clothing, wear; *(burrash)* suit;*(grash)*

dress; **veshje burrash:** men's wear, men's clothing. 2. *(e një faji):* attribution, ascription (of a fault). 3. *(e mureve me tapipiceri)* papering (of a wall).

véshk/ë,-a *f.sh.* **-a** *anat.* kidney; *(e bagëtive)* kidney.

veshllapúsh,-i *m.sh.* **-ë** long-eared person.

veshllapúsh,-e *mb.* long-eared.

veshmbáthj/e,-a *f.* clothes, dress.

veshník,-u *m.* earthen baking cover.

veshók/e,-ja *f.sh.* **-e** eye-flap, bliker (of horses).

véshtull,-i *m. bot.* mistletoe.

veshtullí,-a *f.* viscosity.

veshtullór,-e *mb.*viscous, adhesive.

veshúl,-i *m.sh.* **-ë** bunch; **një veshul rrush:** a bunch of grapes.

véshur (i,e) *mb.* 1. dressed, clothed, clad, worn; **i veshur elegant:** dressed elegantly; **i veshur hollë:** lightly dressed; **i veshur mirë:** well dressed. 2. used; **rroba të veshura:** used dresses, worn clothes.

vet (i,e) *p.pr.* 1. own; **ai e pa me sytë e vet:** he saw it with his own eyes. 2. his, her; **djali i vet:** his son; **vajza e vet:** her daughter. 3. its; **vlni çdo gjë në vendin e vet:** put everything in its place; **njeriu do preferonte të humbiste pasurinë e vet sesa namin e vet:** one had rather lose one's fortune than one's good name.

véta,-t *m.* persons; **dy veta:** two persons.

vèt/e,-ja *f.* oneself; **mbledh veten:** to collect oneself, to control oneself; **e ndjej veten:** to feel (oneself); **vij në vete:** to regain consciousness, to recover one's senses, to come to oneself; **vras veten:** to commit suicide; **zotëroj veten:** to con-

trol oneself; **zotërim i vetes:** self-control; **për veten time:** a) as for me; b) for myself; **e bleva për veten time:** I bought it for myself; **shtet më vete:** independent state; **marr me vete:** to carry with oneself. — *Lok.* **bëj për vete dikë:** to charm, to captivate, to enthral someone; **më duket vetja:** to think, to fancy, to suppose that; **ai s'është në vete sot:** he is not quite himself today.

véte *f.jk.* 1. to go; **vete në pazar:** to go to market. 2. to suit; **kjo nuk më vete** *(për një kapelë etj.):* this doesn't suit me.

veterán,-i *m.sh.* **-ë** veteran.

veterán,-e *mb.* veteran.

veterinár,-e *mb.* veterinary.

veterinér,-i *m.sh.* **-ë** veterinary, veterinarian.

veterinarí,-a *f.* veterinar ymedicine.

vétë *p.pr.* 1. oneself, myself, yourself, himself, herself, ourselves, yourselves, themselves; **do ta bëj vetë:** I will do it myself; **kjo nuk bëhet (nuk ndodh) vetë:** that won't happen (come about) of itself; **plaga u mbyll vetë:** the wound cicatrized by itself. 2. in person, personally; **t'i jepet vetë personit:** to be delivered to the addressee in person.

vét/ë,-a *f.sh.* **-a** *gram.* person; **veta e parë njëjës:** first person singular.

vétë *parashtesë* self (prefix).

vetëbesím,-i *m.* self-confidence, self-assurance; **njeri me vetëbesim:** self-assured person.

vetëbíndj/e,-a *f.* self-conviction.

vetëdáshës,-i *m.sh.* - volunteer.

vetëdáshës,-e *mb.* self-willed, voluntary.

vetëdáshj/e,-a *f.* free will; **me vetëdashje:** of one's own free will.

vetëdíj/e,-a *f.* consciousness; **vetëdija e klasës:** class conscousness; **me vetëdije:** with consciousness, knowingly.

vetëdíjsh/ëm(i),-me(e) *mb.* conscientious, conscious, self-conscious.

vetëflijím,-i *m.* self-sacrifice.

vetëkënáqem *f.jv.* to satisfy oneself.

vetëkënaqësí,-a *f.* self-satisfaction, complacence, complacency.

vetëkuptóhet *f.jv.* to be understood; **kjo vetëkuptohet:** it goes without saying.

vetëkurdísës,-e *mb.* self-winding.

vétëm *ndajf.* 1. alone; **jam vetëm:** to be alone; **mbetem vetëm:** to remain alone; **po ju lë vetëm:** I leave you alone. 2. only, alone, solely; **vetëm një fjalë:** only a word; **ia thuaj vetëm atij:** tell him alone, tell only to him. 3. simply, merely; **mos e fshi briskun e rrojes, vetëm shpëlaje:** don't wipe the blade, simply rinse it. 4. only, merely, just; **vetëm më lini të shpjegohem:** just let me explain myself. – *Lok.* **jo vetëm:** not only.

vét/ëm (i),-me (e) *mb.* single, sole, only; **djalë i vetëm:** only son, only child; **është i vetmi:** he is unique (unparalleled); **i vetmi shqetësim që kam:** my sole (only, one) care; **si një trup i vetëm:** like one man.

vetëmbrójtj/e,-a *f.* self-defence.

vetëmohím,-i *m.* self-denial, abnegation, self-sacrifice.

vetëmohúes,-e *mb.* self-denying.

vetëndézës,-e *mb. (motor)* self-starter (engine).

vetëqeverísj/e,-a *f.* self-government.

vetëqúajtur (i,e) *mb.* self-styled.

vetëshërbéhem *f.jv.* to serve oneself.

vetëshërbím,-i *m.* self-service.

vetëshkarkúes,-e *mb.* self-unloading; **makinë vetëshkarkuese:** unloading vehicle.

vetëtím/ë.-a *f.sh.* **-a** lightning; flash of lightning.

vetëtímthi *ndajf.* like a shot, like lightning.

vetëtín I. *f.jk.* 1. it lightens. 2. *fig.* to sparkle, to gleam; **sytë e tij vetëtinin nga gëzimi:** his eyes sparkled with joy. II. *f.k.* to brighten, to make bright.

vetëvendós *f.k.* to self-determine.

vetëvendósj/e,-a *f.* self-determination.

vetëveprím,-i *m.* self-action.

vetëveprúes,-e *mb.* self-acting.

vetëvrásës,-i *m.* suicide.

vetevrásj/e,-a *f.* suicide, self-murder, self-slaughter.

vetí,-a *f.sh.* characteristic, peculiarity, feature.

vetíu *ndajf.* by itself; **kjo kuptohet vetiu:** it goes without saying; **aty lulet rriten vetiu:** the flowers grow there by themselves.

vetják,-e *mb.* personal; **pronë vetjake:** personal property.

vetmí,-a *f.* seclusion, loneliness, solitude, retirement.

vetmój *f.k.* to seclude. – **vetmohet** *f.jv.* to be secluded.

vetmuár (i,e) *mb. (nga shoqëria)* secluded, retired (from society), lonely, lonesome.

véto,-ja *f.* veto.

vetór,-e *mb. gram.* personal; **përemër vetor:** personal pronoun.

vétull,-a *f.sh.* **-a** *anat.* eye-brow, brow; **vrër vetullat:** to knit one's brows, to frown.

vetullán,-e *mb.* beetle-browed.

vetullngrýsur *mb.* frowning· scowling.

vetullz/í,-ézë *mb.* black-browed.

vetúr/ë,-a *f.sh.* **-a** car; motor-car.

vetvét/e,-ja *f.* oneself, itself, në vetvete: in itself.

vetvetísh/ëm(i),-me(e) *mb.* spontaneous; në mënyrë të vetvetishme: spontaneously.

vetvetíu *ndajf.* by itself, spontaneously.

vetvetór,-e *mb. gram.* reflexive; folje vetvetore: reflexive verb.

vezák,-e *mb.* oval, egg-shaped, ovoidal, ovoid.

véz/ë,-a *f.sh.* -ë 1. egg; vezë pule: hen's egg; vezë rose: duck's egg; vezë e prishur (bajate): addle egg, putrid egg; vezë e freskët (taze): new-laid egg; vezë rrufkë (surbull): few-boiled egg; vezë e fërguar: vezë syzë poached egg fried egg, omelet; e verdha e vezës: yolk of egg; shitës vezësh: egg dealer; bën vezë (pula): to lay eggs; ngroh (pula) vezë: to hatch (eggs), to brood, to sit on eggs; vezë peshku: roe of fishes, ova of fishes. – *Prov.* më mirë një vezë sot sesa një pulë mot: one bird in the hand is better than two in the bush.

vezëshítës,-i *m.sh.* - egg-dealer.

vezír,-i *m.sh.* -ë vizier.

vézm/e,-ja *f.sh.* -e *usht.* pouch, cartridge-pouch, cartridge-box.

vezór,-e *mb.* oval.

vezór/e,-ja *f.sh.* -e ovary.

vezullím,-i *m.sh.* -e twinkle, scintillation, glimmer, gleam, glint, shimmer, sparkle.

vezullón *f.jk.* to twinkle, to scintillate, to gleam, to glimmer, to glint, to shimmer.

vezullúes,-e *mb.* twinkling, sparkling.

vë *f.k.* (p. t. vura, p. p. vënë) 1. to put, to place; vë çdo gjë në vendin e vet: to put everything in its place; vë mënjanë: to put aside, to lay aside; vë ka-

pelën në kokë: to put on the hat; vë në dukje: to point out; vë në dispozicionin tuaj: to place at your disposal. 2. to set; vë në radhë: to set in row, to range; vë në lëvizje: to set in motion, to set going; vë zjarr: to set fire. 3. to lay; vë bast: to make a bet, to bet, to stake. – *Lok.* vë në vijë një punë: to put a business in order. – vihem *f.jv.* 1. to place oneself. 2. to set about; i vihem një pune: to set down to work.

vëll/á,-ái *m.sh.* -ezër brother; vëllai i vogël: the younger brother; vëlla prej babe: step-brother; vëlla qumështi, vëlla prej nëne: foster-brother, half-brother.

vëllám,-i *m.sh.* -ë best man.

vëllavrásës,-i *m.sh.* - fratricide.

vëllavrásës,-e *mb.* fratricide; luftë vëllavrasëse: intestinal struggle, civil war.

vëllavrásj/e,-a *f.* fratricide.

vëllazërí,-a *f.* brotherhood, fraternity.

vëllazërím,-i *m.* fraternization.

vëllazërísht *ndajf.* fraternally.

vëllazërój *f.k.* to fraternize. – vëllazërohem *f.jv.* to be fraternized.

vëllazërór,-e *mb.* fraternal; miqësi vëllazërore: fraternal friendship.

vëllím,-i *m.sh.* -e 1. *gjeom. (i një trupi, i një ene)* volume (of a body, of a receptacle); me vëllim të madh: voluminous, bulky. 2. *(i një vepre)* volume (of a book); me dy vëllime: in two volumes.

vëméndj/e,-a *f.* attention, heed; vëmendje e madhe: close attention; i kushtoj vëmendje: to pay attention to, to pay heed to; lexoj me vëmendje: to read

attentively (heedfully); **i tërheq vëmendjen dikujt:** to draw
(to call) someone's attention to.
vëméndsh/ëm (i),-me(e) *mb.*
attentive, heedful, mindful.
vëngërt (i,e) *mb.* squint-eyed,
cross-eyed.
vëni/e,-a *f.* 1. putting, placing;
vënie në shitje: putting up for
sale. 2. setting, starting; **vënie
në lëvizje:** setting in motion,
starting; **vënie në skenë:**
staging, putting on.
vërdállë *ndajf.* up and down;
vij vërdallë: to walk up and
down, to go backwards and forwards, to saunter, to stroll about,
to hang about.
vëréj *f.k.* 1. to observe, 2. to remark, to notice. — **vërehet** *f.jv.*
to be observed, to be remarked.
vëréjtës,-i *m.sh.* - observer, onlooker.
vëréjtj/e,-a *f.sh.* -e 1. remark,
observation, comment; objection; **bëj vërejtje:** to make an
objection, to raise (to put forward) an objection. 2. attention; **shikoj me vërejtje, dëgjoj me vërejtje:** to look attentively, to listen attentively (heedfully); **tërheq vërejtjen:** to attract attention. 3. *fig.* observation;
custody; **mbaj nën vërejtje:**
to keep under observation, to
take into custody.
vër/ë,-a *f.sh.* -a hole. — *Lok.* **bëj
një vërë në ujë:** to carry coals
to Newcastle.
vërs/ë,-a *f. krah.* age.
vërsník,-u *m.sh.* -ë age-companion.
vërsník,-e *mb.* (of) the same
age; **jam vërsnik me dikë:**
to be of the same age with someone.
vërsúlem *f.jv.* 1. to rush on, to
dash on, to dash forward, to fall

upon; **vërsulem mbi armikun:**
to rush on the enemy. 2. to
swoop, to pounce; **vërsulem
mbi gjahun:** to pounce (to
swoop, to fall upon) a prey.
vërsúlj/e,-a *f.* rushing, dashing
forward.
vërshëlléj *f.k.* to whistle, to hiss,
to fizz.
vërshëllím/ë,-a *f.sh.* -a whistle;
hiss, hissing, fizz.
vërshëllór/e,-ja *f.sh.* -e *gram.*
sibilant.
vërshím,-i *m.sh.* -e overflow, gush;
vërshim uji: gush; **vërshim
gjaku:** hemorrhage.
vërshój *f.jk. (uji)* to overflow, to
overrun, to gush (water).
vërtét *ndajf.* indeed, verily, truly,
really; **ai është vërtet i sëmurë:** he is really sick, he is
sick indeed.
vërtétë (i,e) *mb.* true, real, genuine, right, actual; **është e
vërtetë:** it is true; **është më
se e vërtetë:** it is only too true;
s'është e vërtetë; it is untrue;
është plotësisht e vërtetë:
it is absolutely true; **është e
vërtetë se:** it's true that.
vërtétë (e),-a (e) *f.* verity, reality,
truth, truthfullness; **të them të
vërtetën:** to tell the truth, to be
quite honest; **në të vërtetë:** really, truly, in truth for sooth, indeed.
vërtetësí,-a *f.* truthfulness, vera-
city; **vërtetësia e një deklarate,
e një deponimi, e një dëshmie:**
the truthfulness of a statement,
of an affidavit, of a witness.
vërtetím,-i *m.sh.* -e 1. attestation,
verification. 2. certificate; **lëshoj një vërtetim:** to deliver
a certificate.
vërtetój *f.k.* 1. to verify, to attest,
to certify. 2. *(një lajm)* to confirm a piece of news. 3. *mat.*
to prove, to demonstrate; **vër-**

tetoj një teoremë: to demonstrate a theorem. – **vërtetohet** *f.jv.* 1. to be attested, to be verified. 2. to be certified. 3. to be confirmed. 4. to be demonstrated.

vërtetúes,-i *m.sh.* – attester, attestor, verifier; demonstrator.

vërtetúesh/ëm, (i),-me(e) *mb.* attestant, verifiable.

vërtít *f.k.* to revolve, to turn. – **vërtitem** *f.jv.* to turn round; **vërtitem rreth një boshti:** to turn round a pivot.

vërtítj/e,-a *f.* turning, revolving.

vërvít *f.k.* to throw, to launch, to hurl; **ia vërtit syve:** to fling, to throw violently. – **vërvitem** *f.jv.* to rush on, to dash on.

vërvítj/e,-a *f.* throw, hurl, casting.

vërrí,-a *f.* winter pasture.

vërrój *f.jk.* to winter, to hibernate.

vështírë *ndajf.* hard; **vështirë do të jetë:** it will be hard; **vështirë se vij nesër:** I am unlikely to be able to come tomorrow.

vështírë (i,e) *mb.* hard, difficult; **punë e vështirë:** hard work; **mësim i vështirë:** difficult lesson; **i vështirë për t'u kuptuar:** difficult to understand (to be understood); **e pata të vështirë ta bindja:** I had a hard time persuading him.

vështirësí,-a *f.sh.* - difficulty, hardness; **vështirësi financiare (ekonomike):** financial (economic) difficulties; **me vështirësi:** hardly, labouriously.

vështirësój *f.k.* to render more difficult. – **vështirësohet** *f.jv.* to grow difficult (hard).

vështrím,-i *m.sh.* -e look; *(i shpejtë)* glance; **hedh një vështrim:** to cast, to throw a glance.

vështrój *f.k.* to look, to see, to eye; **vështroj rreth e rrotull:** to look around; **vështrojmë njëri-**

-tjetrin: to look one another; **vështroj me bishtin e syrit:** to look from the corner of the eye. – **vështrohem** *f.jv.* 1. to look oneself; **vështrohem në pasqyrë:** to look at oneself in the mirror. 2. *(te mjeku)* to be examined (by a doctor).

vëth,-i *m.sh.* -ë ring, ear-ring, ear-drop.

vëzhgím,-i *m.sh.* -e close observation, watch.

vëzhgój *f.k.* to search closely, to observe, to watch. – **vëzhgohem** *f.jv.* to be searched, to be watched.

vëzhgúes,-i *m.sh.* - observer.

viç,-i *m.sh.* -a *zool.* 1. calf; **mish viçi:** veal; **bërxollë viçi:** veal chop. 2. *fig.* silly, ninny.

víd/ër,-ra *f.sh.* -ra *zool.* otter.

vidh,-i *m.sh.* -a *bot.* elm-tree.

vídh/ë,-a *f.sh.* -a *mek.* screw; **çelës për shtrëngimin e vidhave:** screw-jack; **vidhë pa mbarim:** worm-screw.

vidhós *f.k.* to screw. – **vidhoset** *f.jv.* to be screwed.

vidhósj/e,-a *f.* screwing.

vig,-u *m.sh.* -vigje 1. stretcher, litter. 2. coffin.

vigán,-i *m.sh.* -ë giant.

vigán,-e *mb.* gigantic, colossal.

vigjilénc/ë,-a *f.* watchfulness, vigilance.

vigjilént,-e *mb.* watchful, vigilant, wide-awake.

vigjílj/e,-a *f.* eve; **në vigjiljen (në pragun) e Vitit të Ri:** on the New Year's eve.

vigjilój *f.jk.* to be on the watch, to be on one's guard.

vigjilúes,-e *mb.* vigilant, watchful.

vij *f.jk.* *(p.t.* erdha, p.p. ardhur) to come; **vij në kohë:** to come just in time; **vij përsëri:** to come back, to return; **vij pas:** to come after; **ja ku po vijnë!**

here they come! – *Lok.* **vij në këtë botë:** to be born, to come into the world; **vij në vete:** to recover consciousness; **javën që vjen:** next week; **më vjen keq:** I am sorry; **më vjen në majë të hundës:** to be unable to stand it any longer, to have had enough (of it); **më vjen turp:** to be (to feel) ashamed (of).

vija-vija *mb.* streaked, striped.

vij/ë,-a *f.sh.* -a 1. *(uji)* ditch (for draining). 2. *gjeom.* line; **vijë e drejtë:** straight line; **vijë e përkulur:** curve; **në vijë të drejtë:** in a straight line; **heq një vijë:** to draw a line; **vijë hekurudhore:** railway line. 3. *(e rrotave)* rut, track (of wheels). 4. **vijë politike:** political line; **vija e partisë:** the party line.

vijëz,-a *f.sh.* -a *gram.* dash.

vijëzím,-i *m.* lineament.

vijëzój *f.k.* to line.

vijím,-i *m.* 1. following. 2. succession; **vijim i ngjarjeve:** succession of events.

vijimísht *ndajf.* continually.

vijój *f.jk.* to follow, to continue, to go on.

vijós *f.k.* to line, to draw lines.

vijúesh/ëm (i),-me (e) *mb.* continual.

vikát *f.jk. krah.* to shriek, to shrill, to scream.

vikátj/e,-a *f. krah.* shriek, shrill, scream.

viktím/ë,-a *f.sh.* -a victim; **bie viktimë:** to fall victim.

vilaní,-a *f. mjek.* faint, fainting, swoon.

víle,-ja *f.sh.* - bunch; **një vile rrush:** a bunch of grapes.

víl/ë,-a *f.sh.* -a villa.

vinç,-i *m.sh.* -a *mek.* crane; **vinç hidraulik;** water-crane; **ngre**

me vinç: to crane, to raise with a crane.

violénc/ë,-a *f.* violence; **me violencë:** by violence.

viól/ë,-a *f.sh.* -a *muz.* viola.

violín/ë,-a *f.sh.* -a *muz.* violin, fiddle; **hark violine:** fiddle bow, fiddle stick; **tel violine:** fiddle string; **luaj në violinë:** to fiddle, to play the fiddle.

violiníst,-i *m.sh.* -ë fiddler, violinist.

violíst,-i *m.sh.* -ë violist.

violonçél,-i *m.sh.* -ë *muz.* violoncello.

violonçelíst,-i *m.sh.* -ë *muz.* violoncellist.

virán,-i *m.sh.* -ë rascal, scoundrel.

vírgjër (i,e) *mb.* virgin, virginal; **vajzë e virgjër:** virgin; **tokë e virgjër:** virgin land.

virgjërésh/ë,-a *f.* virgin, maiden.

virgjërí,-a *f.* virginity, maidenhood.

virgjërór,-e *mb.* virginal.

virtuóz,-e *m.sh.* -ë *muz.* virtuoso.

virtuóz,-e *mb.* virtuoso.

virtýt,-i *m.sh.* -e virtue.

virtýtsh/ëm(i),-me(e) *mb.* virtuous, honest, upright.

virús,-i *m.sh.* -e *mjek.* virus.

vis,-i *m.sh.* -e land, country.

visár,-i *m.sh.* -e treasure.

visk,-u *m.sh.* - visq *zool.* young donkey.

víshnj/ë,-a *f.sh.* -a *bot. (fruti)* cherry; **druri i vishnjës:** cherrytree; **bojë vishnjë:** cherry colour, dark red, murrey.

víshtull,-a *f.sh.* -a *bot.* mistletoe

vit,-i *m.sh.* -e year; **Viti i Ri:** New Year; **dita e Vitit të Ri:** New Year's Day; **gëzuar Vitin e Ri!** A happy New Year! **vit i brishtë:** leap year; **vit shkollor:** school year; **çdo vit:** every year; **vit për vit:** year in year out; **një herë në vit:** once a year; **që prej vitit 1910:**

since 1910; **sa vjeç jeni?** how old are you?

vitál,-e *mb.* vital, essential.

vitalitét,-i *m.* vitality.

vitamín/ë,-a *f.sh.* -a *mjek.* vitamin.

vitór/e,-ja *f.* fairy.

vitrín/ë,-a *f.sh.* -a shop-window, glass-case, show-case.

víthe,-t *f.sh.* - 1. crupper, rump, croup (of a horse, etc.). 2. buttocks.

vithíset *f.jv. (toka)* to subside, to slip, to fall in (the ground).

vithísj/e,-a *f. (e tokës)* subsidence, landslip, landslide, earthslip, slipping, falling down (of the earth).

vizatím,-i *m.sh.* -e drawing; **vizatim teknik:** blueprint; *(skicë)* draft, drawing, sketch, outline; *(në trup)* tattoing (on the body).

vizatój *f.k.* to draw, to picture, to delineate; *(një rreth)* to describe, to circumscribe (a circle); *(një skicë)* to sketch, to outline (a sketch); *(në trup)* to tattoo. - − **vizatohet** *f.jv.* to be drawn, to be pictured.

vizatúes,-i *m.sh.* - drawer, designer.

víz/ë,-a *f.sh.* -a 1. *(pasaporte)* visa. 2. *fig.* visa, approval; **jap vizën për diçka:** to give something one's approval.

vizít/ë,-a *f.sh.* -a visit; **vizitë mjekësore:** medical visit; **bëj një vizitë:** to pay a visit; **kthej një vizitë:** to return a visit.

vizitój *f.k.* to visit, to pay a visit; *(një qytet)* to go sight-seeing. − **vizitohem** *f.jv.* to be visited; *(nga mjeku)* to have a medical examination (check-up).

vizitór,-i *m.sh.* -ë vizitor.

vizój *f.k.* to line.

vizor/e,-ja *f.sh.* -e ruler.

vízh/ë,-a *f.sh.* -a *zool.* cockchaffer, chaffer.

vjásk/ë,-a *f.sh.* -a *mek.* spiral groove.

vjédull,-a *f.sh.* -a *zool.* badger, brock.

vjedh *f.k.* to rob, to steal, to purloin, to pilfer, to thieve, to take away. − **vidhem** *f.jv.* 1. to be robbed. 2. to steal away, to slip away, to sneak away.

vjedharák,-u *m.sh.* -ë robber, thief.

vjedharák,-e *mb.* furtive, stealthy; **në mënyrë vjedharake:** furtively, stealthily.

vjédhës,-i *m.sh.* − thief, robber; *(dyqanesh, shtëpish)* burglar, house-breaker; *(i xhepave)* pickpocket.

vjédhj/e,-a *f.sh.* -a robbery, stealth, theft; *(dyqanesh, shtëpish)* burglary.

vjédhurazi *ndajf.* stealthily, furtively; **iki vjedhurazi:** to slip off, to sneak out.

vjéhërr,-i *m.sh.* -a father-in-law.

vjéhërr,-a *f.sh.* -a mother-in-law.

vjel *f.k.* 1. to pick, to pick up, to gather, to pluck, to cull; *(prodhimin)* to gather, to get in (cereals, grains, crops); **vjel pemët:** to pick up (to gather) fruits. 2. to collect; *(kuotat e antarësisë)* to collect (the quotas); *(taksat)* to collect (taxes). − **vilet** *f.jv.* to be gathered, to be picked up, to be yielded.

vjélës,-i *m.sh.* - 1. gatherer; *(i pemëve)* a fruit gatherer; *(i rrushit)* grape-gatherer, vintager. 2. collector; *(i taksave)* collector (of taxes).

vjélj/e,-a *f.* 1. *(e pemëve)* gathering (of fruits); *(e rrushit)* gathering (of grapes), vintage; **shportë për vjeljen e pemëve:** fruit-basket. 2. *(e kuotave, e taksave)* collection (of quotas, of taxes).

vjell *f.jk.* to vomit, to spew

më vjen për të vjellë: to feel like vomiting.

vjélla,-t (të) *f.sh.* vomits.

vjéllët (të) *as.* vomit, vomitting; që shkakton të vjellët: nauseous, emetic.

vjérsh /ë,-a *f.sh.* -a verse poetry.

vjershëtór,-i *m.sh.*-ë versifier, poet.

vjerr *f.k. krah.* to hang.

vjeshtàk,-e *mb.* autumnal.

vjésht /ë,-a *f.sh.* -a autumn, *amer.* fall.

vjet,-i *m.sh.* - *krah.* year; për shumë vjet ditëlindjen: many happy returns of the day.

vjet *ndajf.* last year.

vjetár,-i *m.sh.* -ë year-book; vjetar statistikor: statistical year-book.

vjétëm (i), -me(e) *mb.* of the last year.

vjétër (i, e) *mb.* old, ancient, antique; kohë e vjetër: ancient time, antique time, antiquity; rroba të vjetra: old (worn out, used) clothes; fjalë e vjetër: archaic word; e modës së vjetër: old-fashioned, gone, out of date.

vjetërsí,-a *f.* seniority, service, length of service; vjetërsi në punë: seniority, length of service.

vjetërsír /ë,-a *f.sh.* -a old clothes, old things; dyqan vjetërsirash: slop-shop.

vjetór,-e *mb.* annual, yearly; e ardhur vjetore: yearly income.

vjetrím,-i *m.* wear.

vjetrój *f.k.* to wear out, to wear down, - vjetrohet *f.jv.* to wear out, to wear down.

vjetrúar (i,e) *mb.* worn, worn out, worn down; old fashioned; shumë i vjetruar: thread-bare, shabby.

vjétsh / em(i), - me (e) *mb.* of the last year.

vjóllc /ë,-a *f.sh.* -a *bot.* violet;

ngjyrä vjollcë: violet colour.

vlág /ë,-a *f.* humidity, moisture.

vlágët (i, e) *mb.* humid, wet.

vléfsh /ëm (i),-me (e) *mb.* 1. valuable, precious. 2. valid.

vléft /ë,-a *f.* value, worth; pa vleftë: valueless, worthless.

vlej *f.jk.* 1. to be of value (of worth); që ia vlen: worthwhile; që nuk vlen: worthless. 2. to be valid, to be in effect; a vlen më kjo pasaportë? is this passport still valid? 3. to be of use, to avail, to serve; le të të vlejë si mësim: let it be a lesson to you. 4. to be worth; një dollar vlente gjashtëqind lireta: one dollar used to be worth six hundred liras. - *Lok.* nuk e vlen barra qiranë: it is not worth the trouble.

vlér /ë,-a *f.sh.* -a value, worth, valuour; pa vlerë: worthless; njeri pa vlerë: a worthless person; asgjë me vlerë: nothing good; pa ndonjë vlerë të madhe: of no great value.

vlerësím,-i *m.* valuation, estimation, appreciation, appraisement; vlerësim i vetvetes: self-estimation.

vlerësój *f.k.* 1. to esteem, to appreciate. 2. to appraise, to estimate; to assess, to evaluate, to value; tablonë e vlerësuan 1000 lekë: the painting has been appraised at one thousand leks. - vlerësohem *f.jv.* 1, to be esteemed (appreciated). 2. to be appraised (evaluated, valued).

vlerësúes,-i *m.sh.* - valuator, appraiser.

vlérsh /ëm(i),-me(e) *mb.* valuable, estimable.

vlés /ë,-a *f.* betrothal.

vlim,-i *m.* boil.

vobekësí,-a *f.* poverty.
vobekësój *f.k.* to impoverish, to render poor. − **vobekësohem** *f.jv.* to be impoverished, to grow poor.
vobékët (i,e) *mb.* poor, indigent.
vócërr (i,e) *mb.* wee, tiny, puny, petty, little.
vocërrák,-u *m.sh.* -ë little boy.
vocërrák,-e *mb.* shih **i vocërr.**
vocërrój *f.k.* to make tiny. − **vocërrohem** *f.jv.* to grow tiny.
vódk/ë,-a *f.* vodka.
vógël (i,e) *mb.* little, small; paltry; **vajzë e vogël:** little girl; **copë e vogël:** small piece; **pagë e vogël:** paltry pay, pittance; **para të vogla:** small change; **më i vogël:** smaller; **më i vogli nga të gjithë:** the smallest of all; **më i vogli i fëmijëve:** the youngest of the children.
vogëlí,-a *f.* childhood.
vogëlím,-i *m.* lessening, reduction, decrease, diminution.
vogëlím/ë,-a *f.sh.* -a trifle, triviality, bauble.
vogëlój *f.k.* to lessen, to diminish, to decrease, to reduce. − **vogëlohem** *f.jv.* to grow smaller, to diminish, to decrease.
vogëlsí,-a *f.* smallness, littleness; pettiness, meanness.
vogëlsír/ë,-a *f.sh.* -a shih **vogëlimë.**
vogëlúsh,-i *m.sh.* -ë little boy, small child, kid.
vokál,-e *mb.* vocal.
volánt,-i *m.sh.* -ë fly-wheel.
volejbóll,-i *m.* volley-ball.
volejbollíst,-i *m.sh.* -ë volley-ball player.
volfrám,-i *m. kim.* volfram.
volí,-a *f.* convenience.
volít (më) *f.jk.* to be convenient; **më volit më shumë të kap trenin e orës pesë:** it is con-venient for me to catch the five o'clock train.
volítsh/ëm(i),-me(e) *mb.* 1. handy; manageable; **vegël e volitshme:** manageable tool. 2. favourable, convenient, propitious; **në një kohë të volitshme:** in a favorable time, in a propitious time; **rast i volitshëm:** opportunity.
volt,-i *m.sh.* -ë *fiz.* volt.
voltázh,-i *m. fiz.* voltage.
vólt/ë,-a *f. (e vdekjes)* death rattle.
vóna,-t (të) *f.sh.* - late (slow-ripening) crops.
vonés/ë,-a *f.sh.* -a tardiness, delay, retardation, lateness; **erdha me vonesë:** I came late; **jam me vonesë:** to be late; **pa vonesë:** without further delay, immediately, at once; **më falni për vonesën:** sorry I'm late, excuse me for my being late.
vónë *ndajf.* late, tardily; **më vonë:** later on afterward's; **shumë vonë:** too late; **para se të jetë tepër vonë:** before it is too late; **herët a (ose) vonë:** sooner or later; **u bë vonë:** I am late; **ai erdhi vonë për drekë:** he came late for dinner; **tani vonë:** lately, recently, newly. − - *Lok.* **s'më bëhet vonë:** I am not troubled of it; I don't care a bit. − *Prov.* **nuk është kurrë vonë për të mësuar:** it is never too late to learn; **më mirë vonë se kurrë:** better late than never.
vónë (i,e) *mb.* 1. late, delayed, tardy; **në një orë të vonë:** late. 2. *(frutë)* late, slow-ripe-ning.
voním,-i *m.* delay, retardation.
vonój *f.k.* to delay, to hold up, to retard. − **vonohem** *f.jv.* to be late, to be in delay; **treni u**

vonua: the train was behind time; **vonohem në një takim:** to be late for an appointment.

vónsh/ëm(i),-me (e) *mb.* late, tardy.

vonúar (i, e) *mb.* delayed, tardy; **gjyle me plasje të vonuar:** bomb shell with delayed explosion.

vórb/ë,-a *f.sh.* -a whirlwind, whirlpool, wortex, swirl.

vót/ë,-a *f.sh.* -a vote, ballot; **kuti e votave:** ballot-box; **e jap votën time për dikë:** to give someone one's vote, to vote for someone; **e drejta e votës:** the right to vote; **me vota të fshehta:** by secret ballot; **zgjidhem me shumicë votash:** to be elected by a majority; **vë (hedh) në votë një propozim:** to put a proposal to the vote.

votëbesím,-i *m.* vote of confidence.

votím,-i *m.sh.* -e vote, voting, suffrage, ballot; **votim i fshehtë:** secret ballot; **fletë votimi:** ballot, voting-paper; **listë votimi:** poll; **qendër votim:** center of voting; **kabinë votimi:** polling booth; **e drejta e votimit:** right of voting, suffrage.

votój *f.jk.* to vote; **votoj për dikë:** to vote for someone; **shkoj për të votuar:** to go to vote, to go to the polls. – **votohet** *f.jv.* to be voted, to be put to the vote.

votúes,-i *m.sh.* - voter.

vozapunúes,-i *m.sh.* - cooper.

vóz/ë,-a *f.sh.* -a barrel, tun; *(e madhe)* hogshead; **punishte vozash:** cooperage, workshop of coopers.

vozít *f.jk. (me varkë)* to row.

vozítj/e,-a *f. (me varkë)* rowing.

vrah,-u *m.sh.* -e fan; ·hedh vrahun: to fan, to winnow.

vráj/ë,-a *f.sh.* -a scar, gash.

vrap,-i *m.* run, running, race; **me vrap:** with speed, speedily. – *Lok.* **një vrap pele:** within a stone's throw (of).

vrapím,-i *m.sh.* -e racing, race, running; **vrapime me kuaj:** horse racing, horse race; **vrapime me pengesa:** a hurdle race; **kalë vrapimi:** race-horse; **fitoj në vrapim:** to win the race.

vrápoj *f.jk.* to run, to race; to hurry, to be quick, to rush; **sapo morëm lajmin, vrapuam këtu:** as soon as we heard the news we rushed here.

vrapúes,-i *m.sh.* - runner, racer.

vrár/ë (i,e) *mb.* killed.

vrár/ë (i,)-i (i) *m.sh.* -ë (të) killed person.

vras I. *f.k.* 1. to kill, to murder, to slay; *(me pushkë)* to shoot, to kill (with a fire-arm); *(me thikë)* to poniard, to stab, to kill (with a pointed weapon); *(me gurë)* to stone to death; *(pa gjyq)* (especially the Negroes) to lynch; **vras veten:** to kill oneself, to commit suicide. 2. *(gishtin)* to hurt, to injure (the finger, etc.). 3. fig. *(mendjen)* to puzzle, to rack one's brains. – **vritem** *f.jv.* 1. to be killed; **shumë ushtarë u vranë në luftën e fundit:** many soldiers fell in the last war. 2. to hurt oneself.

vrásës,-i *m.sh.* - killer, assassin, assassinator, murderer.

vrásj/e,-a *f.* killing, murdering, assassination.

vrázhdë (i,e) *mb.* harsh, surly, sullen, murky, scurrilous, fretful, austere, morose, ill-natured, grave, stern, severe, bad-tempered.

vrenjt *f.k.* to frown; **vrenjt vetullat:** to frown (to knit) one's brows. – **vrenjtem** *f.jv.* 1. to

grow gloomy (dim, obscure);
u vrenjt koha: the weather is
getting cloudy (gloomy, dim).
2. to frown.
vrénjtj/e,-a f. 1. darkening, glooming. 2. (e vetullave) frowning.
vrénjtur (i,e) mb. gloomy, murky,
dark, obscure, sullen; fytyrë
e vrenjtur: gloomy face; kohë
e vrenjtur: nebulous (cloudy)
weather; dukem i vrenjtur:
to look sullen.
vrer,-i m. 1. anat. bile; qeska e
vrerit: the vesicle of the bile.
2. venom, poison; nxjerr vrer
nga goja: to vent one's spleen;
plot vrer: full of malice; jam
vrer: to be very sad.
vrerós f.k. to grieve, to sadden,
to afflict. – vrerosem f.jv. to
grow sad, to be afflicted.
vrerósj/e,-a f. affliction, sadness.
vrerósur (i,e) mb. grieved, afflicted,
sad.
vresht,-i m.sh. -a vineyard.
vreshtár,-i m.sh. -ë vine-grower,
vine-dresser.
vreshtarí,-a f. viticulture, vine-
growing.
vrër f.k. to darken, to obscure;
vrër vetullat: to frown (to knit)
one's brow.
vrërët (i, e) mb. gloomy, murky,
surly, austere, morose, dismal.
vrik ndajf. krah. quickly, soon.
vríma-vríma mb. full of holes·
vrím/ë,-a f.sh. -a hole; vent,
aperture; vrima e kyçit: key-
hole; vrimë kopse: button-hole;
vrimat e hundës: nostrils; vrimë e gjilpërës: eyelet, eye
(of a needle); zë vrimat e
dritares, të derës: to stuff
the holes of a window, of a
door; zë një vrimë me tapë:
to plug a hole. – Lok. bëj një
vrimë në ujë: to beat the air.

vringëllím/ë,-a f.sh. -a jingle,
clink, clank, clang.
vringëllój f.k. to jingle, to clink,
to clank, to clang; (armët) to
brandish (the weapons).
vrojtím,-i m.sh. -e observation.
vrug,-u m bot. blight, smut.
vrull,-i m. impetus, vigour; driving force; me vrull: impetuously, vigorously; në vrullin
më të madh: in full swing.
vrúllsh/ëm (i),-me (e) mb. impetuous, vigorous.
vrrág/ë,-a f.sh. -a rut; vrragë e
rrotave: rut of wheels.
vúaj f.jk. to suffer, to undergo
sufferings; vuaj së tepërmi:
to suffer extremely.
vúajtj/e,-a f.sh. -e suffering.
vúar (i,e) mb. hard-boiled, sea-
soned, experienced.
vúl/ë,-a f.sh. -a seal, stamp; vë
vulën: to affix the seal, to
seal. – Lok. i vë vulën diçkaje: to put (to set) the seal on
something; më shkon, më ecën
vula: to have ascendancy (over).
vulós f.k. to seal, to seal up, to
affix the seal, to stamp.
vulósj/e,-a f. sealing, stamping.
vullkán,-i m.sh. -e volcano.
vullkaník,-e mb. volcanic.
vullnét,-i m. 1. will; tregoj vullnet të mirë: to show one's
good will; kundër vullnetit:
against one's will. 2. perseverance; vullnet në punë: perseverance in work.
vullnetár,-i m.sh. -ë volunteer.
vullnetár,-e mb. voluntary; punë
vullnetare: voluntary work.
vullnetarísht ndajf. voluntarily, willingly.
vullnetmírë mb. good-willed.
vullnétsh/ëm (i),-me(e) mb. per-
severant, steady.
vurrát/ë,-a f.sh. -a scar, gash.
výer (i, e) mb. 1. precious: gur

i vyer: precious stone. 2. *fig.* precious, valuable; **kёshilla tё vyera:** valuable advice.
vyshk *f.k.* to shtrivel up, to wither. — **vyshkem** *f.jv.* to shrivel, to wither.

výshkёt (i,e) *mb.* withered, shrivelled.
výshkj /e,-a *f.* withering, shrivelling.

X

x, X (letter of the Albanian alphabet) x, X
xanxár,-e *mb.* untamed, wild; **mush kё xanxare:** untamed mule, kicker.
xánx /ё,-a *f.sh.* -a defect, vice.
xeh *f.k.* to anger, to irritate. — **xehem** *f.jv.* to get angry (shih nxeh).
xeherór,-i *m.sh.* -ё mineral, ore.
xeherór,-e *m.* mineral.
xing,-u *m. kim.* zinc.
xinxíf /e,-ja *f.sh.* -e *bot.* jujube; *(druri)* jujube-tree.
xíx /ё,-a *f.sh.* -a spark.

xixёllím,-i *m.sh.* -e sparkling, sparkle, scintillation.
xixёllón *f.jk.* to sparkle, to scintillate, to twinkle, to glitter, to flare; **yjtё xixёllojnё:** the stars are twinkling (glittering).
xixёllónj /ё,-a *f.sh.* -a *zool.* firefly.
xixёllúes,-e *mb.* sparkling.
xunkth,-i *m. bot.* rush.
xunkthёtár,-i *m.sh.* -ё basket maker.
xunkthtarí,-a *f.* basket-work.
xúrxull *ndajf.* drunk, intoxicated

xverk m. ache, pain

XH

xh, Xh letter of the Albanian alphabet.
xháde,-ja *f.sh.* -e highway, public road.
xhahíl,-i *m.sh.* -ё *vjet.* unlearned person.

xhahíl,-e *mb. vjet.* unlearned, ignorant.
xháj /ё,-a *m.sh.* -allarё uncle.
xhakét /ё,-a *f.sh.* -a jacket; *(e shkurtёr)* jerkin.
xham,-i *m.sh.* -a 1. glass; **xham me ngjyrё:** stained glass; **xham**

sahati: watch-glass. 2. sheet (plate) of glass, pane, glass; window; **mbyll xhamat**: to close the windows.

xhamadán,-i *m.sh.* **-ë** doublet.

xhamaprérës,-i *m.sh.* - glass-cutter, glazier.

xhambáz,-i *m.sh.* **-ë** horse-dealer.

xhamí,-a *f.sh.* - mosque.

xhamllëk,-u *m.* glass-partition; glass-roof.

xhámtë (i,e) *mb.* glassy.

xhan,-i *m. vjet.* 1. soul. 2. beloved.

xhanán,-e *mb. vjet.* gentleman (gentlewoman).

xhandár,-i *m.sh.* **-ë** gendarme.

xhandarmërí,-a *f. vjet.* 1. gendarmerie. 2. police station.

xhaxhá,-i *m.sh.* **-llárë** uncle.

xháxhi *m.* shih **xhaxha**.

xháxho,-ja *m.sh.* - shih **xhaxha**.

xhɛz -i *muz.* jazz.

xheç *fj. plk.* something; **xheç dua t'ju them**: I have something to tell you.

xhehném,-i *m. vjet.* hell, *fam.* Hades.

xhéku *ndajf.* somewhere; **xheku do vemi**: we shall go somewhere.

xhelá,-ja *f.* polish.

xhelát,-i *m.sh.* **-ë** executioner, hangman, headsman.

xhelatín/ë,-a *f.* 1. *kim.* gelatine, gelatin. 2. jelly.

xhelép,-i *m. vjet.* tax (on cattle, in former regimes).

xhelóz,-e *mb.* jealous.

xhelozì,-a *f.* jealousy; **me xhelozi**: jealously.

xhenét,-i *m. vjet, fet.* paradise·

xheniér,-i *m.sh.* **-ë** *usht.* sapper·

xhénio,-ja *usht.* the engineers, *amer.* Engineer Corps; **ushtar i xhenjos**: sapper.

xhentíl,-e *mb.* kind, polite, courteous; **ai është xhentil me**

të gjithë: he is polite to everyone.

xhentilés/ë,-a *f.* kindness, politeness, courtesy; **me xhentilesë**: kindly, courteously.

xhenxhefíl,-i *m. bot.* ginger; **kulaç me xhenxhefil**: ginger bread

xhep,-i *m.sh.* **-a** pocket; **xhep sahati**: watch-pocket, fob; *(prapa pantallonave)* hip-pocket; **të holla (pare) xhepi**: pocket-money; **fut në xhep**: to pocket, to put into pocket; **futi duart në xhep**: put your hands into your pockets! **hiqi duart nga xhepat**! take your hands out of your pockets!

xhepshpúar *mb.* spendthrift.

xheráh,-u *m.sh.* **-ë** *vjet.* bone-setter.

xhevahír,-i *m.sh.* **-ë** jewel, pearl.

xhézv/e,-ja *f.sh.* **-e** coffee-pot.

xhin,-i *m.* gin.

xhind,-i *m.sh.* **-e** *vjet.* jinn, jinnee, ghost.

xhindós *f.k.* to anger, to chafe, to irritate, to enrage. — **xhindosem** *f.jv.* to get angry (furious).

xhindósj/e,-a *f.* rage, fury, ire.

xhindósur (i,e) *mb.* frantic, furious.

xhíng/ël,-la *f.sh.* **-la** tinsel, knickknack, grimrack, trinket.

xhingëríma,-t *f.sh.* - ornamental trifles, trinkets.

xhins,-i *m.* race, blood, *(fig.)* breed; **xhins i keq**: bad race.

xhips,-i *m.sh.* **-e** jeep.

xhirím,-i *m.sh.* **-e** 1. *(filmi)* shooting. 2. *treg.* endorsement: **xhirim kambjali**: endorsement of a bill of exchange.

xhiro,-ja *f.sh.* - 1. walk, turn; **bëj një xhiro**: to make a turn, to go for a turn to take a stroll.

2. *(e helikës)* turn, rotation (of a wheel). **3.** *(sport) (rreth pistës)* lap; **vrapuesi i ka lënë kundërshtarët gjysmë xhiroje prapa:** the runner is a half-lap ahead of his opponents. **4.** *treg.* turnover.

xhirój *f.k.* **1.** *(një film)* to shoot (a film). **2.** *(treg) (një kambjal)* to endorse (a bill of exchange). — **xhirohet** *f.jv.* **1.** to be shot, to be taken. **2.** *treg.* to be endorsed.

xhirúes,-i *m.sh.* - **1.** *(filmi)* shooter. **2.** *treg.* endorser of a bill.

xhixhímës,-i *m.sh.* **-a** *zool.* titmouse, tit, tom-tit.

xhók/ë,-a *f.sh.* **-a** short woolen jacket.

xhúfk/ë,-a *f.sh.* **-a 1.** *(kapeleje)* tassel, crest (of a cap). **2.** *(xhufkat e misrit)* tuft of stamens (of the mais).

xhúng/ë,-a *f.sh.* **-a 1.** hump, hunch, protuberance; *(mbi kurriz)* hump, protuberance (on the back) **2.** *(nga goditja)* swelling (caused by a blow).

xhúng/ël,-la *f.sh.* **-la** jungle.

xhup,-i *m.sh.* **-a** pedded jacket.

xhurá,-ja *f.sh.* - fife, shepherd's pipe.

xhuxh,-i *m.sh.* **-ë** shih **xhuxhmaxhuxh.**

xhuxhmaxhúxh,-i *m.sh.* **-ë** dwarf, pigmy, shrimp man.

xhýbe,-ja *f.sh.* **-e** velvet coat, overcoat, gown.

xhymért,-e *mb.* *vjet.* generous, spendthrift.

y, Y (letter of the Albanian alphabet) y, Y.

yçk/ël,-la *f.sh.*-la **1.** trick, trickery. **2.** pretext.

yjór,-e *mb.* starry.

ylbér,-i *m.* rain-bow.

yll;-i *m.sh.* **yje, yj** l. star; aster; **ylli i mëngjesit (i karvanit):** morning-star, day-star; **ylli i mbrëmjes:** evening-star, Vesper; **ylli Polar:** North star, Pole-star; **yll me bisht:** comet; **yll që këputet (meteor):** falling-star, shooting-star, **qiell plot yje:** starry sky, star-spangled sky. **2.** *zool.* **yll deti:** starfish.

yndýr/ë,-a *f.* grease.

yndyrsh/ëm (i),-me(e) *mb.* greasy.

yndyrshmërí,-a *f.* greasiness.

yndýrtë (i,e) *mb.* greasy.

ynér,-i *m.sh.* **-e** *krah.* pride.

ýnë *p.pr.* our; a) **emërore (nominative):** sing. masc. **vendi ynë:** our country; sing. fem. **Partia jonë:** our Party; pl. masc. **stërgjyshërit tanë:** our ancestors; pl. fem. **shkollat tona:** our schools. b) **gjinore (genitive):** sing.masc. **i(e) vendit tonë:** of our country; sing. fem. **i(e) Partisë sonë:** of our Party;

pl.masc. **i(e) stërgjyshërve ta-në:** of our ancestors; pl. fem. **i(e) shkollave tona:** of our schools. c) **dhanore (dative):** sing. masc. **vendit tonë:** to our country; sing. fem. **Partisë sonë:** to our Party; pl.masc. **stërgjyshërve tanë:** to our ancestors; pl. fem. **shkollave tona:** to our schools.ç) **kallëzore (accusative)** sing. masc. **vendin tonë:** our country; sing. fem **Partinë tonë:** our Party; pl. masc. **stërgjyshërit tanë:** our ancestors; pl. fem. **shkollat tona:** our schools.

ýni *p.pr.* ours; sing.masc. **është yni:** it is ours, it belongs to us; pl.masc. **janë tanët:** they are ours, they belong to us; sing. fem. **është jona:** it is ours, it belongs to us; pl. fem. **janë tonat:** they are ours, they belong to us.

yrné/k,-ku *m.sh.* -qe *vjet.* pattern, model.

yrýsh,-i *m. gj.bis.* impetus; rush; me **yrysh:** impetuously; **yrysh!** forward! ahead!

yst,-i *m. vjet.* surplus.

yt *p.pr.* your; a) **emërore (nominative):** yt bir: your son; sing.masc. **djali yt:** your son; sing. fem. **vajza jote:** your daughter; pl. masc. **djemtë e tu:** your sons; pl. fem. **vajzat e tua:** your daughters. b) **gjinore (genitive):** sing. masc. **i(e) djalit tënd:** of your son. sing. fem. **i(e) vajzës sate:** of your daughter. pl. masc. **i(e) djemve të tu:** of your sons; pl. fem. **i(e) vajzave të tua:** of your daughters. c) **dhanore (dative):** sing.masc. **djalit tënd:** to your son; sing.fem. **vajzës sate:** to your daughter; pl. masc. **djemve të tu:** to your sons; pl. fem. **vajzave të tua:** to your daughters. ç) **kallëzore (accusative):** sing.masc. **djalin tënd:** your son; sing. fem. **vajzën tënde:** your daughter; pl. masc. **djemtë e tu:** your sons; pl.fem. **vajzat e tua:** your daughters.

ýti *p.pr.* yours; sing. masc. **është yti:** it is yours, it belongs to you; **i yti është ky djalë?** is it your son? pl.masc. **janë të tutë:** they are yours, they belong to you; sing. fem. **është jotja:** it is yours, it belongs to you; pl.fem. **janë të tuat:** they are yours, they belong to you.

yxhým *pasth. vjet.* ahead! forward!

yzengjí,-a *f.sh.* - stirrup; **rrip yzengjie:** stirrup strap.

Z

z, Z (letter of the Albanian alphabet) z, Z.

zabarí,-a *f. bot.* head of asparagus.

zabél,-i *m.sh.* -e thicket, grove, bocage.

zabërhán-i *m.sh.* -ë rascal, scoundrel.

zab/úa,-oi *m.sh.* -onj linchpin.

zagár,-i *m.sh.* -ë 1. *zool.* hunting dog, greyhound. 2. *fig.* scoundrel, rascal.

zagushí,-a *f.* sultryness, sultry weather; **sa zagushi që bën!** what a sultry weather!

zahiré,-ja *f. vjet.* store, stock of eatables, supply.

zahmét,-i *m. vjet.* hardness; **me zahmet:** hardly.

zaíf *mb. vjet.* unwell, indisposed; **jam zaif:** I am unwell, I am under the weather.

zaifllëk,-u *m. vjet.* indisposition, unconfortableness.

zakón,-i *m.sh.* -e 1. habit, practice; custom; **e kam zakon të bëj diçka:** to be accustomed to doing something. 2. pl. morals, manners.

zakonísht *ndajf.* usually, habitually, commonly, ordinarily.

zakónsh/ëm(i),-me(e) *mb.* usual, habitual, customary, ordinary, common, vulgar.

zalí,-a *f. mjek.* faint, fainting, swoon, swooning; **më vjen zali:** to feel faint.

zalísem *f.jv.* to faint, to faint away, to feel faint, to swoon.

zalísj/e,-a *f.* swoon, fainting.

zall,-i *m.sh.* -e grit, gravel.

zallísht/ë,-a *f.sh.* -a gritty earth,

gravely earth, sandy earth.

zam,-i *m.sh.* -e glue.

zamáre,-ja *f.sh.* -e fife.

zambák,-u *m.sh.* -ë *bot.* ly; **zambak uji:** water-lily.

zámk/ë,-a *f.* glue.

zanafíll/ë,-a *f.sh.* -a origin, beginning (of a thing); **e ka zanafillën në:** it originates in, it takes its rise from.

zanát,-i *m.sh.* -e craft, trade, profession; **mësoj një zanat:** to learn a craft (a profession); **ushtroj një zanat:** to carry on a trade; **mësim i një zanati:** apprenticeship.

zanatçí,-u *m.sh.* -nj handicraftsman, artisan, craftsman.

zán/ë,-a *f.sh.* -a fairy.

zanór,-e *mb.* vocal.

zanór/e,-ja *f.sh.* -e vowel.

zaptím,-i *m.* conquest, occupation, invasion.

zaptój *f.k.* to occupy, to invade, to conquer. - **zaptohem** *f.jv.* to be occupied.

zaptúes,-i *m.sh.* -ë conqueror, occupier, invader.

zar,-i *m.sh.* -e 1. sphere, ball; **kushinetë me zare:** ballbearing. 2. *(loje)* dice; **luaj me zare:** to play dice; **hedh zaret:** to throw (to cast) the dice; *fig.* **zaret u hodhën:** the dice is cast.

zarár,-i *m.* damage.

zarbaník,-u *m.sh.* -ë scoundrel, rascal.

zárb/ë,-a *m.sh.* -a shih zarbanik.

zarf -i *m.sh.* -e envelope; **mbyll në zarf:** to put into an envelope;

me **zarf të veçantë:** by special envelope.

zarzaváte,-t *f.sh.* - greens, vegetables; **shitës zarzavatesh;** greengrocer.

záten *ndajf.* precisely.

zbardh I. *f.k.* 1. to whiten, to make white; to bleach. 2. *(fig.)* **zbardh dhëmbët:** to grin, to sneer. II. *f.jk.* to peep, to dawn; **po zbardh dita:** it is dawning. – **zbardhem** *f.jv.* 1. to grow (to turn) white. 2. to go white, to turn grey; **është zbardhur para kohe:** he has gone prematurely grey.

zbardhëllén *f.jv. (dita)* to peep, to dawn; to break.

zbardhëllím,-i *m. (i ditës)* dawn, breaking (of the day).

zbardhëllón *f.jv.* shih **zbardhëllen.**

zbárdhj/e,-a *f.* bleaching.

zbardhój *f.k.* to whiten, to make white, to bleach.

zbarkím,-i *m.sh.* -e landing.

zbarkój I. *f.k.* to land, to put ashore, to disembark. II. *f.jk.* to land, to disembark.

zbatíc/ë,-a *f.sh.* -a ebb-tide, low-tide.

zbatím,-i *m.sh.* -e 1. application; **zbatim i një metode:** application of a method. 2. *(i një urdhri)* execution (of an order). 3. *(i një porosie mjekësore):* observance; **vë në zbatim:** to carry out, to execute, to carry into execution.

zbatój *f.k.* 1. to apply, to put into practice; **zbatoj një metodë:** to apply a method. 2. *(një urdhër)* to execute (an order, a command). 3. *(porosinë e mjekut)* to observe (a doctor's advice). – **zbatohet** *f.jv.* 1. to be applied. 2. to be executed. 3. to be observed.

zbatúes,-i *m.sh.* - applicant.

zbatúesh/ëm (i),-me(e) *mb.* applicable.

zbath *f.k.* 1. *(këpucët)* to take off (one's shoes); *(çorapet)* to pull off (stockings). – **zbathem** *f.jv.* to take off one's shoes; to pull off one's stockings.

zbáthur *ndajf.* barefoot.

zbavít *f.k.* to amuse, to divert. – **zbavitem** *f.jv.* to amuse oneself, to entertain oneself, to divert.

zbavítës,-e *mb.* amusing.

zbavítj/e,-a *f.* amusement, divertissement, entertainment.

zbeh *f.k.* to make pale (livid). – **zbehem** *f.jv.* to grow pale (livid), to turn pale, to become wan.

zbéhj/e,-a *f.* paleness, wanness, lividity.

zbéhtë (i,e) *mb.* pale, pallid, wan, livid, ghastly; **çehre e zbehtë:** pale face; **faqe të zbehta:** pale cheeks.

zbehtësí,-a *f.* paleness, pallor.

zbërthéj *f.k.* 1. *(një dërrasë)* to pull apart, to unnail (a plank). 2. *(rrobën)* to unbutton. 3. *(një makinë)* to dismount (a machine). 4. *(një lëndë kimike)* to decompose, to disintegrate (a chemical substance). 5. fig. *(një problem)* to resolve (a problem); *(një material, një studim)* to analyse (a material, a study). - **zbërthehem** *f.jv.* 1. to be unbuttoned. 2. to be dismounted. 3. to be decomposed. 4. to be resolved. 5. to be analysed.

zbërthím,-i *m.sh.* -e 1. *(i një dërrase)* pulling apart, unnailing (of a plank). 2. *(i rrobave)* unbuttoning. 3. *(i një makine)* dismounting (of a machine). 4. *(i një lënde kimike)* decomposition, disintegration (of a sub-

stance). 5. *fig. (i një problemi)*
solution (of a problem): *(i një
materiali, i një studimi)* analysis
(of a material, of a study).
zbërthýesh/ëm(i),-me(e) *mb.* de-
composable; resolvable.
zbokth,-i *m.* dandruff, scurf; **flokë
me zbokth**: scurfy hair.
zborák,-u *m.sh.* -ë *zool.* chaffinch.
zbraz *f.k.* 1. *(çajin)* to pour out
(tea). 2. *(një gotë)* to empty (a
glass). 3. *(një qytet)* to evacuate
(a town). 4. *fig.* **zbraz barkun**:
to pour out one's heart. − **zbra-
zem** *f.jv.* 1. to be emptied. 2.
to be evacuated. 3. *fig.* to pour
out one's heart.
zbrazësí,-a *f.* emptiness.
zbrázët (i,e) *mb.* empty, void,
vacant.
zbrazëtí,-a *f.* shih **zbrazësi.**
zbrázj/e,-a *f.* 1. emptying. 2. evacuation.
zbres I. *f.jk.* (p. t. **zbrita,** p.p.
zbritur) 1. to descend, to go
down, to get down, to come
down; **zbres nga mali**: to
descend (to come down) the
mountain. 2. *(nga kali)* to dismount (from a horse). 3. *(nga
anija)* to land.
II. *f.k.* 1. to come down, to go
down, to descend; **zbres shkallët**: to go downstairs. 2. *mat.
(një numër)* to substract (a number). 3. *(shpenzimet)* to reduce
(expenses).
zbrítj/e,-a *f.* 1. *(nga mali)* des-
cending, descent. 2. *(çmimesh)*
lowering (of prices). 3. *(shpen-
zimesh)* reduction (of expenses).
4. *mat.* substraction.
zbruj *f.k.* 1. *(biskotën)* to imbibe
(a biscuit). 2. *fig.* **zbruj dikë
në dru**: to beat someone black
and blue.
zbukurím,-i *m.sh.* -e 1. embellishment, ornamentation, beauti-

fying, adornment. 2. ornament.
zbukurój *f.k.* to beautify, to embellish, to ornament, to adorn. −
zbukurohem *f.jv.* to embellish
oneself, to be adorned, to grow
beautiful.
zbukurúes,-e *mb.* ornamental, bea-
utifying, embellishing.
zbulím,-i *m.sh.* -e 1. uncovering.
2. *(vendesh të panjohura)* dis-
covery, exploration (of unknown
lands). 3. *(shkencor)* invention.
4. *(gjeologjik)* prospection. 5.
(shërbimi i zbulimit) intelligence
service.
zbulój *f.k.* 1. to uncover. 2. to
find out, to discover. 3. *(fytyrën)*
to unveil (one's face). 4. *(të
vërtetën)* to reveal (the verity,
the truth). 5. to contrive, to
invent. 6. *(vende të panjohura)*
to explore, to discover (new
land). − **zbulohem** *f.jv.* 1. to
unveil (one's face). 2. to be
uncovered, to be discovered. 3.
to be invented. 4. to be explored.
zbulúar (i,e) *mb.* 1. overt; **fytyrë
e zbuluar**: unveiled face, bare
face. 2. discovered. 3. invented.
4. explored.
zbulúes,-i *m.sh.* - 1. contriver,
inventor. 2. *(tokash të reja)*
explorer. 3. *usht.* scout.
zbut *f.k.* 1. to soften. 2. *(një kafshë të egër)* to tame (a wild
beast); *(zbus një kalë)* to break
(a horse). 3. *(një dhimbje)*
to soothe (an ache, a pain);
(një brengë) to assuage, to
appease, to calm, to allay, to
relieve (a sorrow, a grief).
4. *(një dënim)* to mitigate, to
commute (a punishment, a condemnation). − **zbutem** *f.jv.* 1. to
become soft (mellow), to grow
milder. 2. *(egërsira)* to be tamed
(a wild beast). 3. *(dhimbja)*

to be soothed. 4. *(dënimi)* to be mitigated.

zbútës,-i *m.sh.* - *(i egërsirave)* tamer.

zbútës,-e *mb.* calming, assuaging.

zbútj/e,-a *f.* 1. softening. 2. *(e një dhimbjeje)* alleviation, appeasement; *(e një brenge)* relief (of a sorrow). 3. *(e një dënimi)* mitigation (of a punishment).

zbútsh/ëm (i),-me (e) *mb.* tamable.

zbyth *f.k.* to repel, to push back. − **zbythem** *f.jv.* to retreat.

zbýthj/e,-a *f.* retreat.

zdru/g,-gu *m.sh.* -gje plane; **zdrug qorr**: jack plane.

zdrugím,-i *m.* planing (of wood).

zdrugój *f.k.* to plane (wood). − **zdrugohet** *f.jv.* to be planed.

zdrugulína,-t *f.sh.* scraps of planed wood.   /

zdrukth,-i *m.sh.* -e shih **zdrug**.

zdrukthëtár,-i *m.sh.* -ë joiner.

zdrukthëtarí,-a *f.sh.* - 1. joinery; **punime zdrukthëtarie**: joinery works. 2. joiner's shop.

zdrukthój *f.k.* to plane (wood). − **zdrukthohet** *f.jv.* to be planed.

zdryp *f.jk. krah.* to descend.

zéb/ër,-ra *f.sh.* -ra *zool.* zebra.

zefír,-i *m.sh.* -ë zephir.

zég/ël,-li *m.sh.* -la *zool.* gadfly.

zehér,-i *m.* poison, venom.

zeherój *f.jk.* to embitter, to poison.

zéj/ë,-a *f.sh.* -e craft, handicraft, trade, profession.

zejtár,-i *m.sh.* -ë handicraftsman, artisan, craftsman.

zejtarí,-a *f.* craftsmanship, handicraft, craftwork.

zekth,-i *m.sh.* -a *zool.* gadfly.

zell,-i *m.* zeal, industry; **me zell të madh**: with great zeal; **punoj me zell**: to work zealously.

zéllsh/ëm (i),-me(e) *mb.* zealous, industrious; **nxënës i zellshëm**:

diligent (assiduous, hardworking) boy.

zelltár,-i *m.sh.* -ë zealot.

zemberèk,-u *m.sh.* -ë *(sahati)* spring, mainspring (of a watch).

zém/ër,-ra *f.sh.* -ra 1. heart; **dhimbje e zemrës**: heartache; **sëmundje zemre**: heart trouble (disease); **i sëmurë nga zemra**: sufferer from heart disease; **krizë zemre**: crisis of the heart; **pushim zemre**: heartfailure; **rrahjet e zemrës**: heartbeat; **sëmbim në zemër**: twinge in the heart. 2. *fig.* heart; **ai ka zemër të mirë**: he has a good heart; **s'kishte zemër ta rrihte**: he didn't have the heart to beat him; **njeri pa zemër**: heartless (merciless) person. − *Lok.* **me gjithë zemër**: with all one's heart, heartily, whole-heartedly; **e dua me gjithë zemër dikë**: to love someone with all one's heart; **uroj me gjithë zemër**: to wish with all one's heart; **uroj nga thelbi i zemrës**: to wish from the bottom of one's heart; **me zemër të hapur**: frankly, candidly; **bisedë me zemër të hapur**: heart-to-heart talk; **i hap zemrën dikujt**: to open (to pour out) one's heart to someone; **i jap zemër dikujt**: to encourage (to hearten, to cheer) someone; **marr zemër**: to take heart, to take courage; **i fitoj zemrën dikujt**: to win someone's heart; **më copëtohet zemra**: my heart is breaking; **ma theu zemrën**: he disappointed me; **më pikon në zemër**: it cuts me to the heart; **vë dorën në zemër**: to have mercy (pity) for; **sa t'ju dojë zemra**: as much as you want.

zemërák,-e *mb.* peevish, petulant, irascible, techy.
zemëráshpër *mb.* hard-hearted.
zemërát/ë,-a *f.* wrath, anger, ire.
zemërbárdhë *mb.* bountiful, generous, good-hearted.
zemërbútë *mb.* mild, softhearted, benignant.
zemërçélur *mb.* open-hearted, clean-hearted; unfeigned, sincere, fair, candid, ingenuous.
zemërdërrmúar *mb.* shih **zemërthyer.**
zemërdjégur *mb.* heart-broken, afflicted.
zemërdëlírë *mb.* clean-hearted.
zemërdëlirësí,-a *f.* heartiness, sincerity, candour, frankness.
zemërdhémbshur *mb.* compassionate, merciful, pitiful.
zemërgúr,-e *mb.* cruel, stony-hearted.
zemërgjérë *mb.* bountiful, generous, tolerant.
zemërgjerësí,-a *f.* bountifulness, generosity, tolerance.
zemërhápur *mb.* shih **zemërçelur.**
zemërím,-i *m.* anger, spite, wrath, indignation: *(i popullit)* effervescence, excitement (of the people); *(i papërmbajtur)* petulance.
zemërkatrán,-e *mb.* shih **zemërlig.**
zemërkëllírë *mb.* shih **zemërlig.**
zemërlèpur *mb.* cowardly, pusillanimous.
zemërlíg,-ë *mb.* evil, malevolent.
zemërligësí,-a *f.* malevolence, spitefulness.
zemërmírë *mb.* good-hearted, kindhearted; **njeri zemërmirë:** a good hearted person, a kind person; a gentle person.
zemërngrírë *mb.* apathetic, impassible.
zemërngúshtë *mb.* narrow, petty, mean, ungenerous.

zemërój *f.k.* to offend, to anger, to fret, to vex, to irritate. – **zemërohem** *f.jv.* to get angry, to be offended; **zemërohem për hiçgjë:** to get angry for nothing.
zemërpërvëlúar *mb.* shih **zemërthyer.**
zemërpísë *mb.* shih **zemërlig.**
zemërplásur *mb.* shih **zemërthyer.**
zemërpúlë *mb.* chicken-hearted, hen-hearted.
zemërqén,-e *mb.* shih **zemërlig.**
zemërshkrétë *mb.* shih **zemërlig.**
zemërthýer *mb.* heart-broken, heartsore, broken-hearted.
zengjín,-i *m.sh.* -ë *vjet.* rich man.
zengjín,-e *mb.* rich, wealthy.
zeníth,-i *m. astr.* Zenith.
zepelín,-i *m.sh.* -ë Zeppelin.
zerdelí,-a *f.sh.* - apricot.
zéro,-ja *f.sh.* - 1. zero, nought: **dhjetë gradë nën zero:** ten degrees below zero; **zero presje dy (0,2):** nought point two (0,2); *sport.* nil, zero; **rezultati ishte dy me zero** *(në një ndeshje)* the result of the game was 2-0 (two-nil).
zeshkán,-i *m.sh.* -ë dark-skinned person, swarthy person.
zeshkán,-e *mb.* brown, dark-skinned, swarthy.
zeshkán/e,-ja *f.sh.* -e brunette.
zéshkët(i,e) *mb.* brown, dark-skinned.
zevzék,-e *mb.* restless; **djalë zevzek:** restless boy.
zezák,-u *m.sh.* -ë negro; **tregti e zezakëve:** negro-trade; **tregtar zezakësh:** negro-dealer.
zezák,-e *mb.* negro.
zezák/e,-ja *f.sh.* -e negress.
zéz/ë (e),-a (e) *f.* black.
zézë (e) *mb.* shih **i zi.**
zë,-ri *m.sh.* -ra 1. voice; **zë i ashpër:** harsh (grating) voice; **zë i ngjirur:** hoarse voice; **zë i lartë:** loud voice; **me zë të**

lartë: in a loud voice, aloud, out loud; **zë i ulët:** low voice; **me zë të ulët:** in a low voice; **flas me zë të ulët:** to whisper. **2.** sound; **përhapja e zërit:** propagation of the sound; **humbja e zërit:** aphonia. **3. zëri i popullit:** the voice of the people. - *Lok.* **ngre zërin kundër një padrejtësie:** to raise one's voice against an injustice; **mos bëj zë!** don't speak! hush up! keep mum! **i bëj zë dikujt:** to call someone; **qarkullojnë zëra:** it is rumoured that. **zë** I. *f.k.* (p. t. **zura,** p. p. **zënë**) 1. to catch, to seize; **zë një zog:** to catch a bird; **zë në befasi:** to catch by surprise; **zë rob dikë:** to take (to make) someone prisoner. 2. *(një pikë që rrjedh)* to plug up (a leak) 3. *(burimin)* to knead (dough). 4. *(vendin e parë në një garë)* to get (the first place in a competition). 5. *(vendin e dikujt)* to take (the place of someone). 6. to find; **zë punë:** to get a job, to find work. - *Lok.* **le ta zëmë se:** let's suppose that. - **zihem** *f.jv.* 1. to be caught; **zihem në grackë:** to be caught into a snare. 2. **zihem me dikë:** to quarrel (with someone). II. *f.jk.* 1. to take; **zë rrënjë:** to take root. 2. to begin; **zuri (të bjerë) shiu:** it began to rain. **zëdhënës,-i** *m.sh.* - spokesman. **zëëmbël** *mb.* sweet-voiced. **zëm/ër,-ra** *f.* tea, a light meal in the late afternoon. **zëmërhér/ë,-a** *f.* afternoon; **në zemërherë:** in the afternoon. **zënë (i, e)** *mb.* 1. occupied; **vend i zënë:** occupied place. 2. *(i zënë me punë)* busy; **jam i zënë:**

I am busy. 3. caught; **i zënë rob:** to be caught prisoner. **zëni/e,-a** *f.sh.* -e quarrel, strife, wrangling, fight; *(fytafytas)* close fight, hand-to-hand fighting. **zënk/ë,-a** *f.sh.* -a quarrel. **zësh/ëm (i),-me(e)** *mb.* sonorous; vocal; **tingull i zëshëm:** vowel. **zët,-i** *m.* dislike; **e kam zët dikë:** to dislike (to detest) someone. **zëv.** abbreviation of **zëvendës. zëvéndës,-i** *m.sh.* - substitute, deputy. **zëvendësím,-i** *m.sh.* -e substitution, replacing. **zëvendëskryetár,-i** *m.sh.* -ë vice-chairman. **zëvendësminíst/ër,-ri** *m.sh.* -ra vice-minister. **zëvendësój** *f.k.* to replace, to substitute. - **zëvendësohem** *f.jv.* to be replaced, to be substituted (for). **zëvendësprokurór,-i** *m.sh.* -ë deputy attorney. **zëvendëssekretár,-i** *m.sh.* -ë vice-secretary. **zëvendësúesh/ëm(i),-me(e)** *mb.* replaceable. **zgalém,-i** *m.sh.* -ë *zool.* petrel. **zgárb/ë,-a** *f.sh.* -a hollow. **zgáv/ër,-ra** *f.sh.* -ra cavity, hollow; **zgavra e barkut:** abdomen. **zgávërt (i ,e)** *mb.* hollow; **dru i zgavërt:** hollow-tree. **zgërbónj/ë,-a** *f.sh.* -a shih **zgarbë. zgërdhéshj/e,-a** *f.sh.* -e giggle. **zgërdhíhem** *f.jv.* to snicker, to giggle. **zgrip,-i** *m.* edge; **në zgrip të greminës:** on the edge of the abyss. **zgurdullój** *f.jk. (sytë)* to goggle (the eyes). **zgjas** I. *f.k.* 1. to lengthen, to extend; **zgjas këmishën tre centimetra:** to lengthen (to let down) a shirt (by) three centimetres. 2. *(kohën)* to prolong, to extend; **zgjas pushimet:** to prolong one's holidays. 3. *(shtrij)* to stretch (out), to spread out; **zgjas këmbët:** to stretch one's legs; **zgjas dorën:** to extend one's hand to reach ˜out one's hand fcr. 4. *(rrugën)* to lengthen (the way). 5. *(afatin e një pagese)* to delay, to postpone (a payment). – **zgjatem** *f.jv.* 1. to grow taller. 2. *(në kohë)* to grow longer, to be prolonged (extended); **qëndrimi i tij u zgjat tetë muaj:** his stay was extended by eight months. II. *f.jk.* to last; **sa zgjat filmi?** how long does the film last? **zgjatím,-i** *m.sh.* -e extension. **zgjátj/e,-a** *f.sh.* - 1. prolongation, extension. 2. *(në kohë)* duration. **zgjatój** *f.k.* to make ꞏlonger, to extend. - **zgjatohet** *f.jv.* to be extended.

zgjebaník,-e *mb.* scabby, scurfy, mangy.

zgjebarák,-e *mb.* shih **zgjebanik.**

zgjéb/e,-ja *f. mjek.* scab, itch; *(qeni)* mange.

zgjébem *f.jv.* to become scabby (mangy).

zgjebósem *f.jv.* shih **zgjebem.**

zgjebósur (i, e) *mb.* scabby, mangy.

zgjedh *f.k.* 1. to choose, to select, to pick. 2. to elect; **zgjedh deputet:** to elect deputy. – **zgjidhem** *f.jv.* to be elected.

zgjédh/ë,-a *f.* yoke; **vë nën zgjedhë:** to yoke.

zgjédhës,-i *m.sh.* - elector; **lista e zgjedhësve:** poll.

zgjedhím,-i *m.sh.* -e *gram. (i një foljeje)* conjugation (of a verb).

zgjédhj/e,-a *f.* 1. choice, selection. 2. election; **fushata e zgjedhjeve:** election campaign.

zgjedhój *f.k. gram.* to conjugate.

– **zgjedhhohet** *f.jv.* to be conjugated.

zgjédhur (i,e) *mb.* 1. chosen selected; **vepra të zgjedhura:** selected works. 2. elected; **organet e zgjedhura:** elected organs.

zgjerím,-i *m.* widening, enlargement; *(në hapësirë)* extention.

zgjerój *f.k.* 1. to enlarge, to broaden, to extend. 2. *(një xhaketë)* to widen, tc let out (a coat). - **zgjerohet** *f.jv.* 1. to be enlarged (extended). 2. to be widened, to be let out.

zgjesh *f.k.* to ungird; **zgjesh shpatën:** to take off the sword, to unsheathe the sword.

zgjéshur *ndajf.* openly; **flas zgjeshur:** to speak openly.

zgjidh *f.k.* 1. to untie, to unfasten; **zgjidh një plagë:** to untie a wound. 2. *(qenin)* to unleash (a dog); *(nga prangat)* to unchain (from irons). 3. *(një problem)* to solve, to resolve (a problem). 4. *(një kontratë)* to annul, to cancel (a contract). – **zgjidhem** *f. jv* 1. to be untied. 2. to be resolved. 3. to be annulled (a contract).

zgjidhj/e,-a *f.sh.* -e 1. *(e një plage)* untying, unfastening (of a wound). 2. *(e një problemi)* solution (of a problem). 3. *(e një kontrate)* canceling, annulling (of a contract); **zgjidhje martese:** divorce.

zgjídhsh/ëm (i),-me(e) *mb.* resolvable; **problem i zgjidhshëm:** resolvable problem.

zgjim,-i 1. *(nga gjumi)* waking, rising. 2. *(i ndjenjës patriotike)* rousing, stirring up (of patriotic feelings).

zgjoj *f.k.* 1. *(nga gjumi)* to wake (up), to rouse; **më zgjo në, orën gjashtë:** wake me up at six. 2. *fig.* to‑ rouse, to arouse to stir; **zgjon interesim**: to rouse (to arouse) interest. — **zgjohem** *f.jv.* 1. *(nga gjumi)* to awake, to wake up, to get up (from sleep); **zgjohem vonë**: to wake up late. 2. *fig.* to rouse oneself.

zgjúa,-zgjói *m.sh.* zgjoj hive, bee-house, bee-hive, apiary.

zgjúar (i, e) *mb.* clever, intelligent, shrewd.

zgjúar *ndajf.* *(nga gjumi)* awake; **jam zgjuar**: to be awake.

zgjuarsí,-a *f.* cleverness, intelligence, shrewdness.

zgjýr/ë,-a *f.* rust, slag; **me zgjyrë**: rusty, slaggy.

zgjyrós *f.k.* to make rusty (slaggy). — **zgjyrosem** *f.jv.* to rust, to grow rusty.

zgjyrósur (i, e) *mb.* rusty.

zi,-a *f.* 1. mourn, mourning; **jam në zi**: to be in mourn; **mbaj zi**: to wear mourning; **rroba zie**: mourning dress, weeds; **zi kombëtare**: public mourning. 2. famine, dearth, starvation; **zi buke**: famine, extreme dearth, **vit zie**: crop failure.

zi (i),-zézë (e) *mb.* 1. black; **sterrë i zi, pisë i zi**: pitch-black. 2. unfortunate; **i ziu djalë**: the unfortunate boy. 3. **tregu i zi**: black market.

zi (të),-të (të) *as.* black, blackness. — *Lok.* **heq të zitë e ullirit**: to suffer extremely.

zibelín/ë,-a *f.sh.* -a *zool.* sable.

zíej I. *f.k.* to boil; **ziej qumështin**: to boil milk; **ziej mishin**: to boil meat; *(mengadalë)* to simmer.
II. *f.jk.* 1. to boil; **ujët po zien**: the water is boiling. 2. *fig.* **ziej nga inati**: to seethe. — *Lok.* **diçka zien këtu**: something is brewing; **më zien koka**: to be in a

maze; **më zien gjaku**: my blood is up.

zíer (i,e) *mb.* boiled; **mish i zier**: boiled meat.

zíerj/e,-a *f.* 1. boiling. 2. *(e rakisë)* distillation (of brandy).

zift,-i *m.* tar.

zigzág,-u *m.sh.* -e zigzag.

zigzág *ndajf.* zigzag. + *alarm (o clock)*

zíle,-ja *f.sh.* -e 1. bell; **zile biçiklete**: bicycle-bell; **zilja e shkollës**: bell (of school), handbell; **zile elektrike**: electric-bell; **tingëllimi i ziles**: ringing of the bell; **i bie ziles**: to ring the bell.

ziléps *f.k.* to make someone envious. — **zilepsem** *f.jv.* to envy, to feel envy of.

zilí,-a *f.* envy, grudge, covetousness; **kam zili**: to envy, to covet.

ziliqár,-i *m.sh.* -ë envious person.

ziliqár,-e *mb.* envious, covetous.

zink,-u *m.* *kim.* zinc.

zinxhír,-i *m.sh.* -ë 1. chain; **zinxhir sahati**: watch-guard, watch chain; **hallkë zinxhiri**: link of a chain; **lidh me zinxhir**: to chain, to fetter; **lëshoj nga zinxhiri** *(qenin)*: to unleash. 2. *(pranga)* fetters, shackles; **këpus zinxhirët**: to break the shackles.

zjarr,-i *m.sh.* -e 1. fire; **bëj një zjarr**: to make a fire; **rri pranë zjarrit**: to stand (to sit) by the fire; **ndez zjarrin**: to lighten the fire; **trazoj zjarrin**: to poke the fire; **shuaj (fik) zjarrin**: to put out the fire; **u shua zjarri**: the fire went out; **dru zjarri**: fire-wood; **gur zjarri**: flint, silex. 2. *usht.* **armë zjarri**: fire-arms; **zjarr!** fire! — *Lok.* **fus zjarr**: to intrigue; **i shtie zjarrit benzinë**: to pour oil on the flames; to blow the coals; **marr zjarr:** to get exited.

zjarrfíkës,-i *m.sh.* - fireman.

zjarrfíkës,-e *mb.* fire-extinguishing; **skuadër zjarrfikëse:** fire-brigade; **makinë zjarrfikëse:** fire-engine.

zjarrfíkës/e,-ja *f.sh.* -e fire-extinguisher, fire-engine.

zjarrmí,-a *f.* 1. glow, ardour, fervour. 2. *mjek.* fever, heat, temperature; **i sëmuri ka zjarrmi:** the sickman has fever.

zjárrtë (i,e) *mb.* ardent, fervent, fiery, ebullient; **rini e zjarrtë:** fiery youth.

zjarrvënës,-i *m.sh.* - firebug.

zjarrvënës,-e *mb.* incendiary.

zmadhím,-i *m.* enlargement; amplification, magnification.

zmadhój *f.k.* to enlarge, to amplify, to magnify. — **zmadhohet** *f.jv.* to be enlarged, to be amplified, to grow bigger.

zmadhúes,-i *m.sh.* - enlarger, magnifier.

zmadhúes,-e *mb.* enlarging, magnifying; **xham zmadhues:** magnifying glass.

zmadhúesh/ëm (i),-me(e) *mb.* expansional, extensional.

zmbraps *f.k.* to repel, to drive back, to force back, to push back; **zmbraps armikun:** to repel the enemy. — **zmbrapsem** *f.jv.* to retreat, to withdraw, to draw back; **zmbrapsem para një detyre:** to flinch from a duty.

zmbrápsj/e,-a *f.* retreat; *(e një ushtrie)* withdrawal, retreat (of an army).

zmeráld,-i *m.sh.* -e emerald.

zmeríl,-i *m.* emery.

zog,-u *m.sh.* **-zogj** *zool.* 1. bird; **zog grabitqar:** bird of prey.

rapacious bird; **zog këngëtar:** singing bird; **zog shtegtar:** migratory bird; **fole zogjsh:** nest, bird-nest; **një tufë zogjsh:** a flock of birds. 2. *(pule)* chick; **zog i porsadalë nga veza:** spring chicken; **çel zogj** *(pula);* to hatch.

zógëz,-a *f.sh.* -a *zool.* 1. young bird, nestling. 2. *(pule)* chicken.

zogorí,-a *f.* pack (of hounds).

zokth,-i *m.* little bird.

zón/ë,-a *f.sh.* -a *gjeog.* 1. zone; **zonë tropikale:** tropical zone; **zonë kufitare:** border-land. 2. *(elektorale)* electorate, electoral district.

zónja (e) *mb.* able, capable; **jam e zonja për:** I am able to (shih **i zoti).**

zónja (e) *f.sh.* -t (të) *(e shtëpisë)* hostess, patroness, mistress (of a house), house-keeper.

zónj/ë,-a *f.sh.* -a lady; *(shtëpie)* mistress.

zonjúsh/ë,-a *f.sh.* -a miss; young lady.

zoológ,-u *m.sh.* -ë zoologist.

zoologjí,-a *f.* zoology.

zoologjík,-e *mb.* zoological; **kopshti zoologjik:** zoological garden, zoo.

zootekní,-a *f.* veterinary.

zootekník,-u *m.sh.* -ë veterinarian.

zor,-i *m. gj. bis.* 1. difficulty. 2. constraint, compulsion; **më detyruan me zor që të ikja:** I was forced to leave. 3. embarrassment, uneasiness; **më vjen zor nga dikush:** to feel uneasy (embarrassed) in someone's presence.

zórsh/ëm (i),-me (e) *mb. gj. bis.* hard, difficult.

zórr/ë,-a *f.sh.* -ë 1. *anat.* intestine, gut, bowel; **zorrët e holla:** small intestines; **zorrë qorre (e**

verbër): appendicitis, blind gut, **zorrë e trashë:** large intestine, colon. 2. *(llastiku)* hose; *(zjarrfikësash)* hose, fire-hose; *(për ujitje)* hose (for watering). – *Lok.* **nxjerr zorrët:** to vomit.

zorrëthárë *mb.* hungry, starving.

zot,-i *m.sh.* **-ërinj** 1. mister; **zoti Kuk:** Mr. Cook. 2. **zot shtëpie:** host, house-keeper. 3. **zot malli:** owner. 4. God, Lord, Providence. – *Lok.pop.* **në dorë të zotit:** to the dispensations of Providence; **një zot e di! Godness** knows: **i dal për zot dikujt:** to put someone under one's protection, to protect someone.

zotërí,-a *m.sh.* **-nj** 1. mister, gentleman; *(i nderuar)* sir; **burrë zotëri** :gentleman, well-bred man; **i dashur zotëri** *(në krye të një letre)*: Dear Sir! (at the top of a letter). 2. Lord.

zotërím,-i *m.sh.* **-e** 1. possession, holding; *(malli)* ownership; **zotërim i vetes:** self-restraint, self-possession, self-control. 2. domination; **nën zotërimin e:** under the domination of. 3. assimilation. 4. pl. possessions.

zotërój *f.k.* to possess, to hold, to own; **zotëroj një gjuhë:** to have a good command of a language, to master a language. – **zotërohem** *f.jv.* to be dominated.

zotërúes,-i *m.sh.* - possessor, owner, proprietor.

zotësí,-a *f.* ability, capacity, aptitude; skill; **me zotësi të madhe:** with great skill.

zóti (i) *m.sh.* **-ët (të)** 1. *(i një fabrike etj.)* owner. 2. *(i shtëpisë)* host, house-keeper; owner (of the house).

zóti (i) *mb.* able, capable; **jam i zoti të bëj gjithçka:** to be able

to do everything, to be a Jack of all trades.

zotím,-i *m.sh.* **-e** engagement, pledge; **mbaj zotimin:** to keep one's engagement; **shkel zotimin:** to break one's engagement; **marr zotim** *(për të bërë diçka)*: to bind oneself (to do something).

zotní,-a *m.* shih **zotëri.**

zotóhem *f.jv.* to bind oneself, to promise, to pledge oneself.

zotróte (term of politeness used in a conversation between two persons as a token of respect) sir; **zotrote si je?** how are you, sir?

zukát *f.jk.* to buzz, to hum.

zukátj /e,-a *f.* buzz, humming.

zullúm,-i *m.sh.* **-e** damage.

zullumqár,-i *m.sh.* **-ë** rascal, scoundrel, nefarious man.

zullumqár,-e *mb.* nefarious, villainous.

zumpará,-ja *f.* sandpaper, emery paper.

zurkáj /ë,-a *f.sh.* **-a** cataract, water fall.

zús'ç /ë,-a *f.sh.* **-a** bitch; whore.

zuzár,-i *m.sh.* **-e** rascal.

zvarraník,-e *mb.* reptilian.

zvarraník,-u *m.sh.* **-ë** *zool.* reptile.

zvárrë *ndajf.* **hiqem zvarrë:** to crawl, to creep, to creep along; **heq zvarrë:** to drag; *fig.* **lë zvarrë një punë:** to procrastinate an affair.

zvarrít *f.k.* 1. to draw, to drag, to trail, to haul, to lug. 2. *(një punë)* to procrastinate (an affair). 3. *(fjalët)* to drawl (the words). –**zvarritem** *f.jv.* to creep along, to crawl along, to grovel.

zvarrítes,-e *mb.* dragging, trailing.

zvarrítj /e,-a *f.* 1. dragging, creeping, trailing, lugging. 2. *fig.* *(e një pune)* procrastination (of a work).

zverdh *f.k.* to make yellow, to turn yellow, to yellow. – zverdhem *f.jv.* 1. to yellow, to turn yellow. 2. to grow pale, to turn white, to turn yellow, to wan.

zverdhím,-i *m.* yellowing.

zvérdhj/e,-a *f. (e fytyrës)* paleness, wanness (of the face).

zverdhém/ë (i),-e (e) *mb.* yellowish.

zverdhón *f.jk.* to take a yellow colour.

zverk,-u *m.sh.* zverqe *anat.* nape.

zvetëním,-i *m.* degeneration.

zvjerdh *f.k.* to wean. – zvirdhem *f.jv.* to be weaned.

zvjérdhj/e,-a *f.* weaning, weaness, wean, ablactation.

zvicerán,-i *m.sh.* -ë Swiss.

zvicerán,-e *mb.* Swiss.

zvogëlím,-i *m.* lessening, diminution, reduction, decrease.

zvogëlój *f.k.* to make smaller, to decrease, to diminish, to lessen, to belittle, to reduce. – zvogëlohem *f.jv.* to become (to get) smaller, to decrease, to diminish.

zvogëlúes,-e *mb.* diminitive, reductive; decreasing; progresion zvogëlues: decreasing progression

zvogëlúesh/ëm(i),-me(e) *mb..*reducible.

zymbýl,-i *m.sh.* -a 1. basket. 2. *bot.* jacinth, hyacinth (flower).

zýmtë (i, e) *mb.* gloomy, sullen, sulky, dismal; ill-natured; pamje e zymtë: dismal sight.

zýr/ë,-a *f.sh.* -a office, bureau; zyra e postës: post office; zyra e punës: labour office; zyra e gjendjes civile: Registry office; punë zyre: office work.

zyrtár,-i *m.sh.* -ë employee.

zyrtár,-e *mb.* official; të dhëna zyrtare: official reports (data); lajme zyrtare: official news; vizitë zyrtare: official visit; bëj një vizitë zyrtare në një vend: to visit a country officially (in one's official capacity).

zyrtarísht *ndajf.* oficially; jo zyrtarisht: unofficially; fejohem zyrtarisht: to become officially engaged.

zyrtaríz/ëm,-mi *m.* officialism.

ZH

zh, Zh (letter of the Albanian alphabet).

zháb/ë,-a *f.sh.* -a *zool.* toad.

zhabín/ë,-a *f.sh.* -a bot. buttercup.

zhangëllím/ë,-a *f.* confused noise, dissonance.

zhangëllón *f.jk.* to discord.

zhangëllúes,-e *mb.* dissonant, discordant.

zhapí,-u *m.sh.* -nj *zool.* lizard.

zhapík,-u *m.sh.* -ë shih zhapí.

zhardhók,-u *m.sh.* -ë *bot.* tuber.

zharetér/ë,-a *f.sh.* -a garter.

zhargón,-i *m.sh.* -e slang, jargon; zhargon studentësh: school-boy slang.

zhavórr,-i *m.* grit, gravel; shtroj me zhavorr një rrugë: to macadamize a road.

zhbëj *f.k.* to undo. - zhbëhet *f.jv.* to be undone.

zhbllokím,-i *m.sh.* -e release, un-blocking, freeing.

zhbllokój *f.k.* to open up, to release; to free. - zhbllokohet *f.jv.* to be released.

zhburrním,-i *m.* emasculation.

zhburrnój *f.k.* to emasculate, to unman. - zhburrnohem *f.jv.* to be emasculated (unmanned).

zhdëmtím,-i *m.sh.* -e indemnity.

zhdëmtój *f.k.* to indemnify. - zhdë-mtohet *f.jv.* to be indemnified.

zhdëp *f.k. (në dru)* to belabour. - zhdëpem *f.jv. (së ngrëni)* to be satiated, to eat one's fill.

zhdërvjéll *f.k.* to unravel, to un-tangle. - zhdërvillem *f.jv.* to be unravelled.

zhdërvjéllët (i, e) *mb.* agile, nimble, supple, lissom.

zhdërvjéllj/e,-a *f.* unravelling.

zhdërvjelltësí,-a *f.* agility, lissom-ness.

zhdoganím,-i *m.* payment of cus-tom duties.

zhdoganój *f.k.* to get something after payment of custom duties.

zhdredh *f.k.* to untwist. - zhdri-dhet *f.jv.* to be untwisted.

zhdrédhj/e,-a *f.* untwisting.

zhdréjtë (i,e) *mb.* indirect; kun-drinor i zhdrejtë: indirect object.

zhduk *f.k.* 1. to hide, to conceal. 2. to steal, to rob. 3. to kill, to bump off. - zhdukem *f.jv.* to disappear, to vanish; to fade away, to go; shenjat e opera-

cionit janë zhdukur: the scars of the operation have gone (faded away); zhdukem pa rënë në sy, pa u vënë re: to slip off, to steal away.

zhdúkj/e,-a *f.* disappearance; abo-lishment; zhdukja e skllavërisë; abolishment of slavery.

zhdyllós *f.jk.* to unseal; zhdyllos një letër: to unseal a letter. - zhdylloset *f.jv.* to be unsealed.

zheg,-u *m.* dog days.

zhegulí,-a *f.* the kids.

zhél/e,-ja *f.sh.* -e rag, tatter, cast of clothes; me zhele: in tatters, ragged.

zhezhít *f.jk.* to putrefy, to rot, to decay. - zhezhitet *f.jv.* to be putrefied (decayed, rotten).

zhezhítj/e,-a *f.* putrefaction, rotten-ness, putridity.

zhgënjéj *f.k.* to disillusion; to delude, to disappoint, to balk. - zhgënjehem *f.jv.* to be de-ceived (deluded, disappointed).

zhgënjím,-i *m.sh.* -e disillusion-ment, disillusion, balk.

zhgënjýes,-e *mb.* deceptive, illu-sory, fallacious.

zhgërrýej *f.k.* to roll in the mire. - zhgërryhem *f.jv.* to wallow, to roll one's body in the mire.

zhgjakësím,-i *m.* vengeance, re-venge.

zhgjakësóhem *f.jv.* to avenge (to revenge) oneself, to take re-venge, to be revenged.

zhilé,-ja *f.sh.* - vest, waistcoat; zhile pambuku: flannel vest; zhile leshi: woolen vest.

zhiruét/ë,-a *f.sh.* -a weather-cock, vane.

zhív/ë,-a *f. kim.* quicksilver, mer-cury; barometër pa zhivë; aneroid barometer.

zhúb/ër,-ra *f.sh.* -ra 1. *(në fytyrë)* wrinkle, ridge (on the face). 2. *(në pantallona)* crease (on pants).

zhubrós *f.k.* to crumple, to rumple; *(një plaçkë)* to crease (a tissue). - zhubroset *f.jv.* to be crumpled; to be creased.

zhubrósur (i,e) *mb.* *(plaçkë)* creasy (tissue).

zhumbín/ë,-a *f.sh.* -a *anat.* gum of teeth.

zhupón,-i *m.sh.* -a short petticoat.

zhurí,-a *f.sh.* - jury; zhuri e gjyqit: jury of a tribunal; anëtar zhurie: juror, juryman; kryetar zhurie: head of a jury.

zhurít *f.k.* to char, to scorch. - - zhuritet *f.jv.* to be scorched (charred, burnt).

zhurítj/e,-a *f.* charring, scorching, burning.

zhurítur (i,e) *mb.* charred, scorched, burnt; *fig.* zemër e zhuritur: broken heart.

zhúrm/ë,-a *f.sh.* -a noise, ado; *(shurdhuese)* din; shumë zhurmë për asgjë: much ado about nothing; me zhurmë: noisy; pa zhurmë: noiseless; pa zhurmë! silent! mos bëni zhurmë! keep silent!

zhurmëmádh,-e *mb.* noisy, rowdy.

zhuzhák,-u *m.sh.* -ë 1. *zool.* scarab, cock-chafer. 2. *fig.* dwarf (a contemptuous term for a short man).

zhuzhíng/ë,-a *f.sh.* -a *zool.* scarab.

zhvar *f.jk.* to unhook.

zhvat *f.k.* 1. to spoil, to rob. 2. to devour. 3. *fig.* to obtain by trickery, to get out of; më zhvati 100 lekë: he got a hundred leks out of me. - zhvatem *f.jv.* to be robbed (of).

zhvátës,-e *mb.* spoliative.

zhvátj/e,-a *f.* spoliation.

zhvendós *f.k.* 1. to displace, to move, to shift. 2. *(trupa ushtarake)* to dislocate (troops). -

zhvendosem *f.jv.* to move over (up), to shift; theksi zhvendoset në rrokjen e fundit: the accent shifts to the final syllable.

zhvendósj/e,-a *f.* 1. moving, shifting; move, shift. 2. *el.* zhvendosje në fazë: phase shift. 3. *usht.* dislocation (of troops). 4. *(e shtresave gjeologjike)* upheaval.

zhvesh *f.k.* 1. to undress. 2. *fig.* to take away, to strip (someone) of. - zhvishem *f.jv.* 1. to undress oneself, to take off one's clothes, to get undressed; zhvishem lakuriq: to strip oneself. 2. *fig.* to divest oneself (of); zhvesh nga një funksion: to divest someone of a function.

zhvéshj/e,-a *f.* undressing.

zhvéshur (i, e) *mb.* undressed, nude, naked.

zhvidhós *f.k.* to unscrew. - zhvidhosem *f.jv.* to become unscrewed.

zhvillím,-i *m.* development; growth; në zhvillim: developing, in the course (process) of development, under development. 2. *(i një teze)* development, treatment. 3. *(i ngjarjeve)* development (of events).

zhvillój *f.k.* 1. to develop, to expand, to build up, to increase; zhvilloj tregti: to develop trade. 2. to strengthen, to develop; sporti t'i zhvillon gjymtyrët: sport strengthens the limbs. - zhvillohem *f.jv.* 1. to develop; to grow; to strengthen; mendja zhvillohet me të mësuar: the mind develops with study. 2. to expand, to increase, to grow. 3. *(ngjarjet)* to occur, to happen, to come about.

zhvillúar (i,e) *mb.* 1. developed; strong, sturdy; një djalë i zhvi-

lluar: a sturdy boy. 2. marked, strong.
zhvillúes,-i *m.sh.* - *kim.* developer.
zhvirgjërím,-i *m.* loss of virginity, defloration.
zhvirgjërój *f.k.* to deflower. - **zhvirgjërohem** *f.jv.* to lose one's virginity; to be deflowered.
zhvleftësím,-i *m.sh.* -e devaluation; **zhvleftësimi i një monedhe:** devaluation of a currency.
zhvleftësój *f.k.* to devalue, to devaluate; **zhvleftësoj një monedhë:** to devalue a currency. - **zhvleftësohet** *f.jv.* to be devaluated, to fall in value.
zhvleftësúar (i,e) *mb.* devalued, devaluated; **mallra të zhvleftësuara:** second-hand goods.
zhvlerësím,-i *m.* shih **zhvleftësim.**
zhvlerësój *f.k.* shih **zhvleftësoj.**
zhvoshk *f.k.* 1. *(lëkurën)* to skin lightly. 2. *(misrin)* to husk, to decorticate (corn). 3. *(drurin)* to take off the bark (of a tree).- **zhvoshket** *f.jv.* to be skinned.
zhvóshkj/e,-a *f.* 1. *(e misrit)* decortication, husking (of the corn). 2. *(e lëkurës)* skinning.
zhvulós *f.k.* to unseal. - **zhvuloset** *f.jv.* to be unsealed. l
zhvulósj/e,-a *f.* unsea lng.
zhyt *f.k.* to dip, to plunge, to dive, to sink, to immerse. - **zhytem** *f.jv.* 1. to sink, to plunge. 2. *(në mendime)* to be lost (in thoughts): **i zhytur në paragjykime:** plunged in prejudices.
zhýtës,-i *m.sh.* - plunger, diver, dipper, sinker.
zhýtj/e,-a *f.sh.* -e plunging, dipping, sinking, immersion.
zhýtur (i,e) *mb.* 1. plunged, dipped, sunk. 2. *(në mendime)* lost (in thought).

SHTOJCË - APPENDIX

Foljet   Verbs

A. Zgjedhimi i foljes ndihmëse *kam*
Conjugation of the auxiliary verb *to have*

I. Mënyra dëftore

II. Indicative mood

1. *E tashme*
. Unë kam
Ti ke
Ai (ajo) ka
Ne kemi
Ju keni
Ata (ato) kanë

1. *Present*
I have
You have
He (she) has
We have
You have
They have

2. *E pakryer*
Unë kisha
Ti kishe
Ai (ajo) kishte
Ne kishim
Ju kishit
Ata (ato) kishin

2. *Imperfect*
I had
You had
He (she) had
We had
You had
They had

3. *E kryer e thjeshtë*
Unë pata
Ti pate
Ai (ajo) pati
Ne patëm
Ju patët
Ata (ato) patën

3. *Simple past tense*
I had
You had
He (she) had
We had
You had
They had

4. *E kryer*
Unë kam pasur
Ti ke pasur

4. *Present perfect* or *past indefinite.*
I have had
You have had

Ai (ajo) ka pasur	He (she) has had
Ne kemi pasur	We have had
Ju keni pasur	You have had
Ata (ato) kanë pasur	They have had

5. *E kryer e plotë*

Unë kisha pasur
Ti kishe pasur
Ai (ajo) kishte pasur
Ne kishim pasur
Ju kishit pasur
Ata (ato) kishin pasur

5. *Pluperfect* or *past perfect*

I had had
You had had
He (she) had had
We had had
You had had
They had had

6. *E ardhme*

Unë do të kem
Ti do të kesh
Ai (ajo) do të ketë
Ne do të kemi
Ju do të keni
Ata (ato) do të kenë

6. *Future*

I shall have
You will have
He (she) will have
We shall have
You will have
They will have

7. *E ardhme e përparme*

Unë do të kem pasur
Ti do të kesh pasur
Ai (ajo) do të ketë pasur
Ne do të kemi pasur
Ju do të keni pasur
Ata (ato) do të kenë pasur

7. *Future perfect*

I shall have had
You will have had
He (she) will have had
We shall have had
You will have had
They will have had

I. Mënyra kushtore

1. *E tashme*

Unë do të kisha
Ti do të kishe
Ai (ajo) do të kishte
Ne do të kishim
Ju do të kishit
Ata (ato) do të kishin

II. Conditional mood

1. *Present*

I should have
You would have
He (she) would have
We should have
You would have
They would have

2. *E kryer*

Unë do të kisha pasur
Ti do të kishe pasur
Ai (ajo) do të kishte pasur
Ne do të kishim pasur
Ju do të kishit pasur
Ata (ato) do të kishin pasur

Past tense

I should have had
You would have had
He (she) would have had
We should have had
You would have had
They would have had

III. Mënyra lidhore	**III. Subjunctive mood**
1. *E tashme*	*Present* This mood is confounded
të kem etj.	have with the indicative mood:
2. *E pakryer*	*imperfect* *dëshiroj të*
të kisha etj.	had *kem një fjalor*
3. *E kryer*	: I wish I
	Present perfect had a dictionary.
të kem pasur etj.	have had
4. *E kryer e plotä*	*Past perfect*
të kisha pasur etj.	have had

V. Mënyra dëshirore	**IV. Optative mood**
E tashme	*Present*
paça	may I have
paç	may you have
pastë	may he (she) have
paçim	may we have
paçi	may you have
paçin	may they have

V. Mënyra urdhërore	**V. Imperative mood**
E tashme	*Present*
ki! kini!	have!

VI. Mënyra pjesore	**VI. Participle mood**
E tashme	*Present*
pasur	had
E kryer	*Past*
pasë pasur	had had

VII. Mënyra paskajore	**VII. Infinitive mocd**
E tashme	*Present*
për të pasur	to have

VIII. Mënyra përcjellore	**VIII. Gerund mood**
E tashme	*Present*
duke pasur	having
E kryer	*Past*
duke pasë pasur	having had

B. Zgjedhim i foljes ndihmëse *jam*
Conjugation of the auxiliary verb *to be*

Mënyra dëftore

1. *E tashme*

Unë jam
Ti je
Ai (ajo) është
Ne jemi
Ju jeni
Ata (ato) janë

2. *E pakryer*

Unë isha
Ti ishe
Ai (ajo) ishte
Ne ishim
Ju ishit
Ata (ato) ishin

3. *E kryer e thjeshtë*

Unë qeshë
Ti qe
Ai (ajo) qe
Ne qemë
Ju qetë
Ata (ato) qenë

4. *E kryer*

Unë kam qenë
Ti ke qenë
Ai (ajo) ka qenë
Ne kemi qenë
Ju keni qenë
Ata (ato) kanë qenë

5. *E kryer e plotë*
Unë kisha qenë
Ti kishe qenë
Ai (ajo) kishte qenë
Ne kishim qenë
Ju kishit qenë
Ata (ato) kishin qenë

I. Indicative mood

1. *Present*

I am
You are
He (she) is
We are
You are
They are

2. *Imperfect* or *preterite*

I was
You were
He (she) was
We were
You were
They were

3. *Simple past tense* or *past definite*

I was
You were
He (she) was
We were
You were
They were

4. *Present perfect* or *past indefinite*

I have been
You have been
He (she) has been
We have been
You have been
They have been

5. *Pluperfect* or *past perfect*
I had been
You had been
He (she) had been
We had been
You had been
They had been

6. E ardhme
Unë do të jem
Ti do të jesh
Ai (ajo) do të jetë
Ne do të jemi
Ju do të jeni
Ata (ato) do të jenë

6. Future
I shall be
You will be
He (she) will be
We shall be
You will be
They will be

7. E ardhme e përparme
Unë do të kem qenë
Ti do të kesh qenë
Ai (ajo) do të ketë qenë
Ne do të kemi qenë
Ju do të keni qenë
Ata (ato) do të kenë qenë

7. Future perfect
I shall have been
You will have been
He (she) will have been
We shall have been
You will have been
They will have been

II. Mënyra kushtore
1. E tashme
Unë do të isha
Ti do të ishe
Ai (ajo) do të ishte
Ne do të ishim
Ju do të ishit
Ata (ato) do të ishin

II Conditional mood
1. Present
I should be
You would be
He (she) would be
We should be
You would be
They would be

2. E kryer
Unë do të kisha qenë
Ti do të kishe qenë
Ai do të kishte qenë
Ne do të kishim qenë
Ju do të kishit qenë
Ata (ato) do të kishin qenë

2. Past tense
I should have been
You would have been
He (she) would have been
We should have been
You would have been
They would have been

III. Mënyra lidhore

III. Subjunctive mood

1. E tashme
të jem

Present
be

2. E pakryer
të isha

Imperfect
were

3. E kryer
të kem qenë

Present perfect
were

4. E kryer e plotë
të kisha qenë

Past perfect
had been

IV. Mënyra dëshirore	**IV. Optative mood**
E tashme	*Present*
qofsha	may I be
qofsh	may you be
qoftë	may he (she)be
qofshim	may we be
qofshi	may you be
qofshin	may they be

V. Mënyra urdhërore	**V. Imperative mood**
E tashme	*Present*
ji! jini!	be!

VI. Mënyra pjesore	**VI. Participle mood**
E tashme	*Present*
qenë	been
E kryer	*Past*
pasë qenë	had been

VII. Mënyra paskajore	**VII. Infinitive mood**
E tashme	*Present*
për të qenë	to be

VIII. Mënyra përcjellore	**VIII. Gerund mood**
E tashme	*Present*
duke qenë	being
E kryer	*Past*
duke pasë qenë	having been

C. Zgjedhimi i foljes vetvetore «lahem» Conjugation of the reflexive verb «to wash oneself» (in the present and in the past tense of the indicative).

Mënyra dëftore	Indicative mood .
1. *E tashme*	**1.** *Present*
Unë lahem	I wash myself
Ti lahesh	You wash yourself
Ai (ajo) lahet	He washes himself

Ne lahemi
Ju laheni
Ata (ato) lahen

She washes herself
We wash ourselves
You wash yourselves
They wash themselves

2. *E kryer e thjeshtë*

Unë u lava
Ti u lave
Ai (ajo) u la

Ne u lamë
Ju u latë
Ata (ato) u lanë

2. *Past tense*

I washed myself
You washed yourself
He washed himself
She washed herself
We washed ourselves
You washed yourselves
They washed themselves

Disa folje të parregullta
Some irregular verbs

Nr.	Shqip: In Albanian			Anglisht: in English		
	E tashme (dëftore)	E kryer e thjeshtë (dëftore)	Pjesore	Infinitive	Past tense	Past participle
1.	bëj	bëra	bërë	to make	made	made
				to do	did	done
2.	bërtas	bërtita	bërtitur	to shout	shouted	shouted
3.	bie	prura	prurë	to bring	brought	brought
4.	bie	rashë	rënë	to fall	fell	fallen
5.	blej	bleva	blerë	to buy	bought	bought
6.	bredh	brodha	bredhur	to wander	wandered	wandered
7.	dal	dola	dalë	to get out	went out	gone out
				to come out	came out	come out
8.	di	dita	ditur	to know	knew	known
9.	djeg	dogja	djegur	to burn	burnt	burned
10.	dua	desha	dashur	to want	wanted	wanted
				to love	loved	loved
11.	eci	eca	ecur	to walk	walked	walked
12.	flas	fola	folur	to speak	spoke	spoken
13.	fle	fjeta	fjetur	to sleep	slept	slept
14.	gjej	gjeta	gjetur	to find	found	found
15.	ha	hëngra	ngrënë	to eat	ate	eaten
16.	iki	ika	ikur	to go	went	gone
17.	jap	dhashë	dhënë	to give	gave	given
18.	kall	kalla	kallur	to drive in	drove in	driven

	Shqipi in Albanian			Anglishti in English		
Nr.	E tashme (dëftore)	E kryer e thjeshtë (dëftore)	Pjesore	Infinitive	Past tense	Past participle
19.	kërcas	kërcita, krisa	kërcitur, krisur	to crack	cracked	cracked
20.	lë	lashë	lënë	to leave	left	left
21.	luaj	luajta	luajtur	to play	played	played
22.	marr	mora	marrë	to take	took	taken
23.	mas	mata	matur	to measure	measured	measured
24.	mbaj	mbajta	mbajtur	to hold, to keep	held, kept	held, kept
25.	mërdhij	mërdhiva, mardha	mërdhirë, mardhur	to shiver, to feel cold	shivered, felt cold	shivered, felt cold
26.	ndjek	ndoqa	ndjekur	to pursue, to follow	pursued, followed	pursued, followed
27.	ngas	ngava	ngarë	to drive	drove	driven
28.	ngas	ngava	ngarë	to tease	teased	teased
29.	ngre	ngrita	ngritur	to raise, to lift up	raised, lifted up	raised, lifted up
30.	nxë	nxura	nxënë	to learn	learned	learned
31.	pëlcas	pëlcita, plasa	pëlcitur, plasur	to burst, to crack	burst, cracked	burst, cracked
32.	përkas	përkita	përkitur	to touch; to belong	touched; belonged	touched; belonged
33.	pi	piva	pirë	to drink	drank	drunk
34.	pres (dikë)	prita	pritur	to wait	waited	waited

	Shqip∣ In Albanian			Anglisht∣ In English		
Nr.	E tashme (dëftore)	E kryer e thjeshtë (dëftore)	Pjesore	Infinitive	Past tense	Past participle
35.	pres (diçka)	preva	prerë	to cut	cut	cut
36.	rri	ndejta	ndenjur	to stand, to sit	stood, sat	stood, sat
37.	rroj	rrojta	rrojtur	to live	lived	lived
38.	shes	shita	shitur	to sell	sold	sold
39.	shkas	shkava	shkarë	to slip, to slide	slipped, slid	slipped, slidden
40.	shoh	pashë	parë	to see	saw	seen
41.	shpie	shpura	shpënë	to carry,	carried	carried
42.	shtie	shtira	shtënë	to inject	injected	injected
43.	them	thashë	thënë	to say	said	said
44.	thërres	thërrita, thirra	thërritur, thirrur	to call, to shout	called, shouted	called, shouted
45.	vdes	vdiqa	vdekur	to die	died	died
46.	vete	vajta	vajtur	to go	went	gone
47.	vë	vura	vënë	to put, to place	put, placed	put, placed
48.	vij	erdha	ardhur	to come	came	come
49.	vras	vrava	vrarë	to kill	killed	killed
50.	vuaj	vuajta	vuajtur	to suffer, to undergo	suffered, underwent	suffered, undergone
51.	zbres	zbrita	zbritur	to descend, to go down	descended, went down	descended, gone down
52.	zë	zura	zënë	to catch, to seize	caught, seized	caught. seized

Zgjedhimi i foljes «Shoh» në pohore, mohore dhe pyetëse
Conjugation of the verb «to see» in the affirmative, negative and interrogative

	Pohore: Affirmative	Mohore: Negative	Pyetëse: Interrogative

A. *Mënyra dëftore:* Indicative mood

1. *E tashme* / Present

Unë shoh	I see	Unë nuk shoh	I don't see	Shoh unë? Do I see?
Ti sheh	You see	Ti nuk sheh	You don't see	Sheh ti? Do you see?
Ai (ajo) sheh	He (she) sees	Ai (ajo) nuk sheh	He (she) doesn't	Sheh ai(ajo)? Does he (she) see?
Ne shohim	We see	Ne nuk shohim		
Ju shihni	You see	Ju nuk shihni	We don't see	Shohim ne? Do we see?
Ata (ato) shohin	They see	Ata (ato) nuk shohin	You don't see	Shihni ju? Do you see?
			They don't see	Shohin (ata)(ato)? Do they see?